Communicating with the Gods

Prognostication in History

Edited by

Michael Lackner (*Friedrich-Alexander-University Erlangen-Nürnberg*)
Chia-Feng Chang (*Taiwan National University*)
Klaus Herbers (*Friedrich-Alexander-University Erlangen-Nürnberg*)
Alexander Fidora (*ICREA – Autonomous University of Barcelona*)

Series Coordinator

Fabrizio Pregadio

VOLUME 11

The titles published in this series are listed at *brill.com/prhi*

Communicating with the Gods

Spirit-Writing in Chinese History and Society

Edited by

Matthias Schumann
Elena Valussi

BRILL

LEIDEN | BOSTON

Cover illustration: *Mengying honglou: Lüshun bowuguan zang Sun Wenhui quanben Honglou meng* 夢影紅樓：旅順博物館藏孫溫繪全本紅樓夢. Shanghai: Shanghai guji chubanshe, 2017, 191.

The Library of Congress Cataloging-in-Publication Data is available online at https://catalog.loc.gov
LC record available at https://lccn.loc.gov/2023026763

Typeface for the Latin, Greek, and Cyrillic scripts: "Brill". See and download: brill.com/brill-typeface.

ISSN 2589-4404
ISBN 978-90-04-54904-3 (hardback)
ISBN 978-90-04-67790-6 (e-book)

Copyright 2024 by Matthias Schumann and Elena Valussi. Published by Koninklijke Brill NV, Leiden, The Netherlands.
Koninklijke Brill NV incorporates the imprints Brill, Brill Nijhoff, Brill Schöningh, Brill Fink, Brill mentis, Brill Wageningen Academic, Vandenhoeck & Ruprecht, Böhlau and V&R unipress.
Koninklijke Brill NV reserves the right to protect this publication against unauthorized use. Requests for re-use and/or translations must be addressed to Koninklijke Brill NV via brill.com or copyright.com.

This book is printed on acid-free paper and produced in a sustainable manner.

Contents

Acknowledgments IX
List of Figures and Tables X
Note on Formal Conventions XII
Dynastic Table XIII

1 Introduction to the Volume 1
   Matthias Schumann and Elena Valussi

PART 1
Overview Papers

2 Making the Gods Write: A Short History of Spirit-Written Revelations in China, 1000–1400 39
   Vincent Goossaert

3 Spirit-Writing Practices from the Song to Ming Periods and Their Relation to Politics and Religion 91
   Wang Chien-chuan 王見川

4 Women, Goddesses, and Gender Affinity in Spirit-Writing 133
   Elena Valussi

PART 2
Changing Techniques and Practices

5 Terminology and Typology of Spirit-Writing in Early Modern China: A Preliminary Study 171
   Hu Jiechen

6 The Transcendent of the Plate: The *Lingji zhimi* 靈乩指迷 (Instructions on the numinous stylus) and the Reform of Spirit-Writing Techniques during the First Half of the Twentieth Century 206
   Fan Chun-wu 范純武

PART 3
Spirit-Writing and the Literati Elites in Late Imperial China

7 Instantiating the Genealogy of the Way: Spirit-Writing in the Construction of Peng Dingqiu's Confucian Pantheon   255
Daniel Burton-Rose

8 A Credulous Skeptic: Ji Yun on the Mantic Arts and Spirit-Writing   291
Michael Lackner

9 The Liu-Han Altar: Between a Literati Spirit-Writing Altar and Popular Religion   311
Zhu Mingchuan 朱明川

PART 4
Spirit-Writing and Redemptive Societies

10 "Protecting the Dao and Transmitting the Classics": The New Religion to Save the World and the Confucian Dimension of Spirit-Writing in Republican China   355
Matthias Schumann

11 Spirit-Writing and the Daoyuan's Gendered Teachings   402
Xia Shi

12 The Phoenix Perches in the Land of the Kami: Spirit-Writing from Yiguandao to Tendō   444
Nikolas Broy

PART 5
Local Communities and Transregional Networks

13 The Nineteenth-Century Spirit-Writing Movement and the Transformation of Local Religion in Western Guangdong   487
Ichiko Shiga

14 The Rise of Spirit-Writing Cults in Chaozhou: Reassessing the Role of Charitable Halls   532
Li Guoping 李國平

15   Spirit-Writing Altars in Contemporary Hong Kong: A Case Study of Fei Ngan Tung Buddhism and Daoism Society   564
     Luo Dan 羅丹

16   A Motley Phoenix? On the Diversity of Spirit-Writing Temples and Their Practices in Puli, Taiwan   600
     Paul R. Katz

Index   635

Acknowledgments

This volume developed from a seminal conference on this topic held at the International Consortium for Research in the Humanities (IKGF) at the University of Erlangen-Nürnberg in June 2019, organized by the two co-editors, who were both fellows of the IKGF at that time, with the essential support of the IKGF's administrative coordinator, Petra Hahm. The conference brought together a number of international scholars on this field: Daniel Burton-Rose, Philip Clart, Fan Chun-wu 范純武, Vincent Goossaert, Janet Hoskins, Hu Jiechen 胡劼辰, Paul R. Katz, Michael Lackner, Li Guoping 李國平, Luo Dan 羅丹, Xia Shi, Shiga Ichiko 志賀市子, Matthias Schumann, Elena Valussi, Wang Chien-chuan 王見川, and Zhu Mingchuan 朱明川. All of the participants and their presentations were essential to the success of the conference. While not all of the papers were included in the final book, we wish to acknowledge everyone's contribution. We also wish to thank the conference attendees, especially Terry Kleeman, Barend ter Haar and Fabrizio Pregadio, for their valuable input. Moreover, we wish to thank the IKGF, particularly its director Michael Lackner (who originally proposed the idea of organizing such a conference to us), for the inspiration and continued support of this endeavor. We would also like to express our gratitude to our language-editor Dr. Sue Casson as well as the research assistants Dr. Li Gang and Carolin Tzschentke for their meticulous work, which saved us from numerous errors and oversights. Finally, we are grateful to Patricia Radder and Bart Nijsten for their efforts and swift work during the publication process.

Matthias Schumann & Elena Valussi
January 2023

Figures and Tables

1 Figures

4.1　Inviting Zigu (*xiying Zigu* 喜迎紫姑). *Dianshizhai huabao* 點石齋畫報, no. 213 (1889): 8–9. Bayerische Staatsbibliothek München, L.sin. K 175–14/22, p. 405. urn:nbn:de:bvb:12-bsb00075645-2.　137

5.1　"扶乱" instead of "扶乩," in *Suiyuan shihua* 隨園詩話 (Poetry talk from Suiyuan)　185

5.2　"扶乱" and "扶乩" on the same page, in *Zhi wen lu* 咫聞録 (Records of close hearsay)　185

6.1　The board of the Scientific Numinous Stylus; photo by the author of a board in his possession　215

6.2　The cover of the *Lingji zhimi* held at Shanghai Library　221

6.3　Advertisement by Jinwen tang in the *Shenbao*, April 30, 1934, 10　234

9.1　Members of the Liu-han Altar　316

9.2　Plaque stating the "Prime Minister in the Purple Cloud Palace" (Zixia neixiang 紫霞内相) at the Liu-han Altar, Hong Kong; photo by author, January 13, 2019　326

9.3　Plaque donated by Sizi 伺子 in the Marshal Temple, Fuzhou; photo by author, April 3, 2019　328

9.4　Spirit-written ordination certificate in Xiguan Lüzu Palace, Fuzhou; photo by author, April 4, 2019　330

9.5　Images of Deng Bingquan, Grannie Huang, and the Elder Sisters in Xiguan Lüzu Palace, Fuzhou; photos by author, April 4, 2019　332

9.6　Images of Xiafu Immortal Officials, who used to be loyalists or martyrs during the late Ming dynasty, and Perfected Wang Biqing at the Liu-han Altar, Hong Kong; photos by author, January 1, 2019　333

9.7　Stuffed foxes and Master Bai displayed together on the altar; photo by author, December 21, 2020　338

9.8　A painting scroll enshrined by residents at their private altar in contemporary Fuzhou; photo by author, July 2021　342

13.1　The spread and publication of the *Yuhuang zhenjing* 玉皇真經　499

15.1　Spirit-writing ritual in FNT, March 2011; photo by author　596

2 Tables

5.1   "*jibu* 箕卜" (Sieve divination)   189
7.1   Confucian Figures Who Descended to Dingqiu's Altar and the Inclusion of Historically-Attested Writings in *Rumen fa yu* by Ming Confucians Who Became Spirit-Altar Deities   284
14.1 Number of organizations destroyed and members arrested   553
14.2 Spirit-writing Altars and *shantang* in Xiashan Town   557
16.1 Puli's Phoenix Halls   623

Note on Formal Conventions

This volume generally uses a modified *Hanyu pinyin* 漢語拼音 system for the transliteration of Chinese names and terms. Exceptions are made for individuals that are better known under an alternative spelling (such as Sun Yatsen) or have their own preferred spelling. For Japanese the revised Hepburn system of romanization is used.

Characters are given in complex (traditional) form throughout.

The contributions in this volume make extensive use of premodern sources. To improve clarity, we have generally used "*juan* 卷" (lit. scroll) to refer to the sections within premodern works, whereas "volume" refers to individual volumes of modern reprint editions or *collectanea* (*congshu* 叢書). Different editions of specific collections, such as the Daoist Canon (Daozang 道藏), are specified in the bibliographies of the individual contributions.

This volume uses the Chicago Manual of Style (16th ed.) with slight variations.

Dynastic Table

Shang 商 Dynasty	ca. 1600–ca. 1045 BCE
Zhou 周 Dynasty	ca. 1045–256 BCE
Spring and Autumn 春秋 Period	770–481 BCE
Warring States 戰國 Period	481–221 BCE
Qin 秦 Dynasty	221–206 BCE
Han 漢 Dynasty	206 BCE–220 CE
Three Kingdoms 三國 Period	220–280 CE
Jin 晉 Period	265–420 CE
Northern and Southern Dynasties 南北朝 Period	317–589 CE
Sui 隋 Dynasty	581–618 CE
Tang 唐 Dynasty	618–907 CE
Five Dynasties 五代 Period	907–960 CE
Song 宋 Dynasty	960–1279
Northern Song 北宋	960–1127
Southern Song 南宋	1127–1279
Yuan 元 Dynasty	1279–1368
Ming 明 Dynasty	1368–1644
Qing 清 Dynasty	1644–1911
Republican 中華民國 Period	1912–1949
People's Republic of China 中華人民共和國	1949–present

CHAPTER 1

Introduction

Matthias Schumann and Elena Valussi

This volume marks the first attempt to produce a comprehensive study of spirit-writing in a Western language. It brings together scholars from different geographical areas and fields of research, to provide a summative collection which showcases the variety of forms that spirit-writing takes, while at the same time indicating longstanding and common themes and opening up possible new avenues for research.[1]

1 What Is Spirit-Writing and Why Does It Matter?

Chinese spirit-writing is a religious technique, attested since at least the Song dynasty, that connects a person, or more often a community, gathered around an altar, to a specific divinity, in an effort to achieve positive outcomes regarding personal requests, access healing, receive moral guidance on a personal or societal level, and in many cases seek self-divinization. The divinity responds to these requests by descending into the body of a medium, and dictating shorter responses or longer scriptures, using a variety of writing implements (a brush, wicker basket, or bifurcated wooden implement) to write on a sheet of paper or bed of sand or ashes. When writing on sand, the words are read aloud and written down by two attendants. At times, the divinity possesses the implement without the need for a human medium. The short responses or longer scriptures are then distributed to the individuals and/or the whole community. Printing the scriptures and distributing them among the community members was and remains part of the religious practice, gaining merit and authority for the community, and strengthening its bond with the divinity. Spirit-writing is not always connected to a specific religious tradition, but draws on a variety of ritual elements and divine figures. It is used by both

---

1 Fan Chun-wu's edited collection on spirit-writing culture, *Fuluan wenhua yu minzhong zongjiao*, was published in 2020. Vincent Goossaert's book on spirit-writing, *Making the Gods Speak* (2022), was in progress while this book was being edited. A new journal in Taiwan, *Shanshu, jingjuan yu wenxian* 善書經卷與文獻, regularly publishes articles related to texts received via spirit-writing.

clerics as well as lay communities, which sometimes employ religious specialists to perform the related rituals.

Seeking a personal connection with the divine world in the form of written communication is a long-standing Chinese religious practice. In the early Heavenly Master Daoism (Tianshidao 天師道, which emerged at the end of the Eastern Han), priests began to send written petitions (zhang 章) to the deities above.[2] The deities, in their turn, revealed scriptures to the humans below. The work of scholars of Daoism on the formation of the early Daoist scriptures are excellent examples that detail the history of "divine revelations."[3] Although the specific techniques varied, one might argue that spirit-writing forms part of this larger tradition of written revelations. The practice is commonly traced back to the cult of the female deity Zigu 紫姑, the Purple Maiden, who was invoked by female devotees since at least the fifth century to provide insights on silk production, an activity generally associated with females. During the Song period, spirit-writing became increasingly sophisticated and it is at this point that we see an increased use of this practice among the literati class, for amusement, to communicate with deceased ancestors and family members, and to learn examination results. At the same time, as Vincent Goossaert outlines in this volume, spirit-writing became closely connected to Daoist ritual practice. Daoist priests essentially claimed the practice as their purview, and used it to communicate with the divine bureaucracy, comparable to the earlier Heavenly Master petitions mentioned above.

Scholars are still struggling to bridge the gap between the twelfth-century emergence of the practice and its well-studied flourishing during later periods.[4] We thus have a number of studies which detail the increasing prominence of the practice in the religious lives of the literati and officials during the Ming-Qing transition, and the purposes for which it was used.[5] While the specific reasons for this are yet to be explored, we can state with confidence that, from the 1600s onward, the use of spirit-writing, the communities that adopted it, and the resulting scriptures, expanded considerably, becoming a central creative force within Chinese religions, inspiring the production of countless, diverse

---

2   Verellen, "The Heavenly Master Liturgical Agenda."
3   Many early Shangqing 上清 (Upper Clarity) revelations, such as the *Zhen'gao* 真誥 (Declarations of the perfected), consist of written transcriptions of oral announcements by the Perfected (*zhenren* 真人), which materialized before the medium. See Bokenkamp, *A Fourth-Century Daoist Family*.
4   Vincent Goossaert's book, *Making the Gods Speak*, sheds some light on this period.
5   See, for example, Zeitlin, "Spirit Writing and Performance"; Elman, *A Cultural History of Civil Examinations*, 319–22; Burton-Rose, "Establishing a Literati Spirit-Writing Altar."

religious texts and collections. Many of the scriptures presented eschatological worldviews, and the gods were summoned to provide moral guidance to humans who had lost their way and so avert the impending disaster of the end of the world. This creative force continued during the Republican period, when "redemptive societies" (*jiushi tuanti* 救世團體, see below) sometimes replaced and/or absorbed local spirit-writing communities and used this practice in order to receive spiritual guidance from the gods during uncertain times. In the contemporary period, spirit-writing continues to be a central element in the religious life of the Chinese, with very active communities in Taiwan 台灣, Hong Kong, Guangdong 廣東, and, increasingly, other parts of China as well as East and Southeast Asia.

With this in mind, it is becoming clear that spirit-writing was and is not a marginal religious activity in China. In fact, while we are only now starting to gain a clearer picture of the earlier period, we can safely say that spirit-writing lay at the very center of religious life and religious text production during the Qing dynasty and Republican period. Although it is impossible to quantify the number of small community altars in existence during the Qing period, and how many of them were used for spirit-writing, there is increasing evidence that they were ubiquitous. Historians are discovering countless examples in different regions of China, often linked via loose networks of influence and textual transmission, which were the real motor in the religious life during this period. These tended to be lay communities, congregating around altars to different divinities, like Lüzu 呂祖, Wenchang 文昌, Guandi 關帝, Doumu 斗母 and others, receiving and transmitting scriptures, and providing ritual support and charitable activities for the surrounding area.[6]

These altars had ties to local, often Daoist temples, but were also devoted to local divinities, or belonged to migrant communities (like guildhalls, *huiguan* 會館); they connected with their local community by providing essential services like *xizi* 惜字 (the proper disposal of paper containing writing), free burials, support for widows, education for orphans, and food for the indigent.[7]

Alongside this growing knowledge about local altars, scholars are also coming to terms with the increasing amount of published and unpublished archival material that resulted from the widespread use of spirit-writing. Particular attention has been paid to collections like the *Daozang jiyao* 道藏輯要 (Essentials of the Daoist Canon), the most important collection of Qing dynasty

---

6 Works by Lai, "Qingdai sizhong *Lüzu quanshu*," Hu, "*Wendi quanshu*," and Valussi, "The Transmission of the Cult of Lü Dongbin," all highlight the lay nature of some of these communities.

7 Valussi discusses this in her work on a Sichuanese community in "The Transmission of the Cult of Lü Dongbin."

Daoist texts, whose core texts were produced via spirit-writing. Detailed research on the origins and printing history of the *Daozang jiyao* has highlighted the essential importance of spirit-writing to Chinese religions, especially Daoism, and inspired new research, which has helped us to understand the development and growth of spirit-writing within lay communities in the late Ming and throughout the Qing periods.[8] This research has underscored the essential role played by lay communities in the panorama of religious life during the late Ming and Qing periods, in terms of both textual production and innovation as well as community-based activities. Long-term research on the above mentioned *Daozang jiyao*, but also the *Lüzu quanshu* 呂祖全書 (Complete collection of Patriarch Lü), *Wendi quanshu* 文帝全書 (Complete collection of Thearch Wen), *Zhang Sanfeng quanji* 張三丰全集 (Complete collection of Zhang Sanfeng) and other Qing compendia, is just beginning and will probably yield further valuable insights.[9] What appears from the growing amount of textual evidence is the variety of textual genres, which often seem to be linked to specific communication modes and contexts. Shorter personal communications about deceased relatives are collected in the form of personal essays, and late imperial poetry collections often include communications between humans and gods, transmitted via spirit-writing; extensive Daoist collections, like the *Daozang jiyao*, include longer religious texts with ritual instructions, meditation practices, and moral guidelines received from the gods. During the Ming and Qing periods, books received via spirit-writing (*luanshu* 鸞書) were also published as "morality books" (*shanshu* 善書), for the moral advancement of the general population.[10] Each community tailored its relationship with the divine according to its needs. The directness and immediacy of the responses meant, on the one hand, ritual and practical innovations and, on the other, a copious amount of textual production.

  This textual production also raises important questions for scholars regarding the authorship of spirit-written texts. This is an issue that touches on the relationship between the divinity who transmits the text, the medium

---

8 Esposito, "The Invention of a Quanzhen Canon," and *Facets of Qing Daoism*; Lai, "Qingdai sizhong *Lüzu quanshu*." Prof. Lai Chi-tim at Chinese University on Hong Kong organized a major conference on the subject in December 2014: "International Conference on Lay Groups and Religious Innovations in Qing Daoism: Lüzu and Other Cults"; this resulted in a 2015 special issue of the journal *Daoism: Religion, History, and Society* dedicated to spirit-writing and the cult of Lüzu. More recently, Prof. Lai edited the *Daozang jiyao tiyao* 道藏輯要提要 (Companion to the *Essentials of the Daoist Canon*).

9 See the work done in the Chinese Religious Text Authority project https://crta.info/wiki/Main_Page.

10 On this topic, see Goossaert, *Livres de morale révélés par les dieux*.

INTRODUCTION

who utters it, the assistant who writes it down, and the community which receives and disseminates it. Questions arise specifically about the relationship between the God and the medium. Who is ultimately in charge of the tool and the transmission? Does the stylus move by itself? Does the deity descend into the stylus? Do humans participate in the creation of the scripture? Sources and emic descriptions of the practice fail to yield a unitary picture. Sometimes, the passive nature of the medium is stressed, although moral self-cultivation is always required, while, at other times, the movements are described as resulting from a merging of the "numinous energies" (*ling* 靈) of humans and deities. The terminology also provides hints regarding the agency of the actors involved, as Philip Clart and Vincent Goossaert aptly note. A term such as *jiang* 降 ("to descend," "to make descend," or "to take possession of") describes the acts of the deity, while *fu* 扶 ("to wield," or "to support"; note here as well the different emphases of the translations) points to the medium.[11] While no conclusive answers to these questions can be given, it is important to consider them, and also to analyze the power relationships between all of the actors involved in this complex process. These relationships may differ for each case and community, and we hope that the variety of examples provided in this volume will help to untangle the complexity underlying the production of religious texts.

The textual transmission went hand in hand with the diffusion of religious cults throughout China during the late Ming and Qing periods, more specifically those of gods like Guandi, Wenchang, and Lüzu, mentioned above.[12] Thus, the communities behind these compilations were often tied into extensive networks of devotion and textual transmission. Today, through a close analysis of the paratextual materials, we can begin to follow these Qing dynasty networks all across China.[13]

The prominence of spirit-writing in the religious life of the Republican period can be more easily traced. Due to the fragmentation of the Chinese state, particularly during the period 1916–1927, but also due to the flourishing publishing market, spirit-written texts, both reprinted and newly-produced, could be widely sold and distributed. The early Republican period can be considered the heyday of spirit-writing, also due to the rise of many new religious movements, which are commonly termed "redemptive societies."[14] It has been

---

11   Clart and Goossaert, "Spirit-Writing."
12   Goossaert, "Spirit Writing, Canonization and the Rise of Divine Saviours."
13   Hu Jiechen researched the Wenchang cult for his dissertation: Hu, "*Wendi quanshu*." Lai Chi-tim researched the worship of Lüzu in: Lai, "Qingdai sizhong *Lüzu quanshu*."
14   First coined by Prasenjit Duara. See Duara, "The Discourse of Civilization and Pan-Asianism."

argued that redemptive societies were the most influential, active, and growing part of Chinese religions during that period,[15] mainly due to their ability to refashion much of their religious repertoire, in order to avoid (largely) the state's persecution of "superstitious" activities.[16] Their religious activities, first openly and then more covertly following the takeover by the Nationalist Party in 1927, also involved the production of religious texts through spirit-writing.[17] Despite the crackdown on redemptive societies and spirit-writing that followed the founding of the People's Republic in 1949, the practice has survived until the present day, and research on contemporary spirit-writing communities in Taiwan, Hong Kong, and Guangdong has appeared during the past decade.[18] However, to date, very few works have touched upon its development in other parts of mainland China.

A persistent theme throughout this volume, and one that is increasingly reflected in this area of research, is diversity. During the past few years, the research on spirit-writing has expanded geographically as well as chronologically, and uncovered stylistic and thematic diversity. This is also illustrated in many of the contributions to this volume, encompassing a wide chronological span, a variety of different geographic locations, and various religious traditions, communities and textual genres. Below are some important areas that highlight this variety, starting with the terminology.

2   Terms and Definitions

This volume seeks to be specific, accurate, and detailed with regard to the terminology and definitions related to spirit-writing, distinguishing insider and outsider perspectives, emic and etic points of view, and practitioners' versus scholarly language and definitions. The most commonly used etic term in English for the various Chinese practices that are studied in this volume is "spirit-writing." The term originated at a time when spiritualism was still

---

15   Cf. Goossaert and Palmer, *The Religious Question in Modern China*, 121.
16   For overviews of redemptive societies, see Ownby, "Redemptive Societies in the Twentieth Century," 685–727, and Schumann, "Redemptive Societies." For a critical theoretical assessment of the concept, see Palmer, "Chinese Redemptive Societies and Salvationist Religion," and Broy, "Syncretic Sects and Redemptive Societies."
17   On the textual production of redemptive societies, see Clart, Ownby, and Wang, *Text and Context in the Modern History of Chinese Religions*.
18   For Taiwan, Katz in this volume provides a good starting point. For Hong Kong, see Lai, You, and Wu, *Xianggang Daojiao*. For both Hong Kong and Guangdong, see Shiga, *Xianggang Daojiao yu fuji xinyang*, "Difang Daojiao zhi xingcheng."

INTRODUCTION 7

gripping the Western imagination and served as a convenient frame of reference for mediumistic practices around the world. When Western observers familiar with spiritualism became aware of the Chinese practices of spirit-writing, they were quick to make the connection. This was helped by the use of comparable techniques in Europe. French spiritualists in the mid-nineteenth century employed a piece of wood supported by two wheels, referred to as a "planchette" (a "small board" in French), to transmit messages from the dead.[19] The similarities to Chinese practices were not lost on the Western writers who, during the second half of the nineteenth century, began to compare them to the French planchette.[20] Accordingly, "planchette-writing" became the standard designation for Chinese spirit-writing among observers both within and outside China. Even the Chinese practitioners themselves made the connection once the spiritualist discourses reached China during the early twentieth century. At that time, the term was complemented by the designation "spirit-writing," which similarly originated within an European spiritualist context, where it served as a relatively loose designation for messages transmitted by spirits, either directly through a medium, not unlike what some presume happened with regard to the Shangqing 上清 (Upper Clarity) revelations, or written on a slate. Other synonyms were therefore "slate writing" or "automatic writing."[21] In the Chinese context, both "planchette-writing" and "spirit-writing" were used interchangeably to refer to phenomena witnessed at spirit-writing altars.[22] Subsequently, as spiritualism slowly faded from the collective consciousness in both Europe and the United States, the generic term "spirit-writing" increasingly replaced references to the planchette in the Western scholarship.[23] It now became the dominant etic term, although specific definitions can vary among different scholars. While we note a few core

---

19 Enns, "The Undead Author," 64.
20 An early reference to Chinese spirit-writing as making use of a "planchette" appears in Sargent, *Planchette*, 397–98. The first article in an English-language newspaper published in China to mention the term "planchette" is Dudgeon, "Chinese Arts of Healing." An early eyewitness account by the diplomat Herbert A. Giles (1845–1935), which mentions the planchette as a means of divination, was published in 1879. See Katz, "Spirit-writing and the Dynamics of Elite Religious Life," 283, and Giles, *Religions of Ancient China*, 34.
21 Oppenheim, *The Other World*, 22–23. The term "automatic writing" was also used to refer to Chinese spirit-writing, notably by Alan J.A. Elliott, in his study of mediumistic practices in Singapore. See Elliott, *Chinese Spirit-Medium Cults in Singapore*, 141–42.
22 See "Spiritualism in the Chinese City" for an account from 1924 which uses the term, apparently referring to the activities of the Lingxue hui 靈學會 (Spiritualist Society) in Shanghai.
23 The term is still employed by a number of scholars. See, for example, Tan, *Chinese Religion in Malaysia*.

aspects, such as the use of writing instruments, we will refrain from offering a specific definition ourselves. The techniques, instruments, and terminology evolved together, wherefore a rich vocabulary related to spirit-writing developed over the several centuries under investigation.

The complexity underlying the terminological changes related to spirit-writing practices has been emphasized by several scholars, and is the topic of Hu Jiechen's chapter in this volume. In a recent publication, Clart and Goossaert introduce the varying terminology related to this practice, detailing its historical changes and the different contexts in which it emerged: the term *fuji* 扶箕 (wielding the sieve) evolved from the cult of Zigu, the Purple Maiden, otherwise also known as the Goddess of the Privy, associated with women's religious practices, and was common from the eleventh century onward; the "sieve" was the first term for an implement to appear in the extant texts; *jiangbi* 降筆 (causing gods to descend into a brush) is commonly used from the Song dynasty by Daoist priests to describe their communication with the gods within a ritual context, and clearly involved a brush as the main implement; *zhaoxian* 召仙 (inviting immortals) and *pijiang* 批降 (obtaining a god-written response on a document submitted to him) were also used in a similar Daoist ritual context; *feiluan* 飛鸞 (flying phoenix), and later *fuluan* 扶鸞 (wielding the phoenix), developed in Sichuan 四川 at the beginning of the twelfth century within a network of lay devotees of the god Wenchang. According to contemporary sources, the "phoenix" referred to here was a five-colored bird hanging from the ceiling of a ritual space, which was said to transmit divine messages by wielding a brush affixed to its beak.[24] In modern Taiwan, it instead refers to the Y-shaped wooden Phoenix-stylus (*luanbi* 鸞筆), the exact origin of which remains unclear. The term *feiluan*, and the texts received within the context of this practice, have been the most well studied so far.[25] According to Fan Chun-wu in this volume, it has several recorded forms: *taiji luan* 太極鸞 (taiji phoenix), *bijia luan* 筆架鸞 (brush-stand phoenix), *xuanluan* 懸鸞 (suspended phoenix), and *fengxia luan* 封匣鸞 (phoenix in a sealed box). Two of these, the "sealed box" and "brush-stand," survived into the modern period.[26] Another term involving a bird is *fuhe* 扶鶴 (supporting the crane). In the sixteenth century, there further emerged the term *fuji* 扶乩 (supporting the stylus), which remains widely used today and is the closest Chinese equivalent of a generic

---

24 See Kleeman, *A God's Own Tale*, 17, and Wang, "Song-Ming shiqi de fuji," 66–75. See also Wang's contribution to this volume.
25 Clart and Goossaert, "Spirit-Writing."
26 See the contribution by Fan Chun-wu in this volume. Hu Jiechen in this volume also mentions these categories.

term for spirit-writing. Hu Jiechen in this volume further discusses the term *bilu* 筆籙 (brush register), used specifically from the late Ming period onward in relation to the imperial examination; at first employed for the composition of eight-legged essays, it involved the use of a pen-brush and paper, without a basket or stylus.[27] Ethnographic research still attests terminological varieties. Zhu Mingchuan in this volume thus documents the use of "sailing the raft," *kaifa* 開筏, as a designation for spirit-writing in Fuzhou. This, as well as the association between the phoenix and Sichuan, also seems to highlight the importance of regional traditions, but the regional differentiation between the spirit-writing traditions and its impact on the terminology and specific technology require further study. *Kaisha* 開沙, or "opening the sand," is another term used in contemporary communities, especially those connected to redemptive societies.[28]

Spirit-writing practices usually took place within communities, which differed in terms of their names, structures, and activities. The authors in the volume use a variety of terms to indicate these communities as well as their practices and the locations where they took place. Terms like *jitan* 乩壇, short for *fuji daotan* 扶乩道壇, and *luantan* 鸞壇 (both translated as spirit-writing altars), thus indicate both the place and the communities gathered around the altars,[29] as well as the implement used during the spirit-writing session.[30]

A difference in terminology often indicates differences in the community structure and different emphases on the activities surrounding spirit-writing. The terms *Daotan* 道壇 (Daoist altar), or *Daotang* 道堂 (Daoist halls), and *Rutan* 儒壇 (Confucian altar), for example, indicate a more specific religious affiliation, whereas *shantan* 善壇 and *shantang* 善堂 (charitable altar/hall) refer more to the charitable activities that took place alongside spirit-writing. The latter are discussed in more detail by Li Guoping in this volume. Spirit-writing is also often practiced at vegetarian halls, or *zhaitang* 齋堂, thus emphasizing a different devotional aspect. Spirit-writing thus takes place within highly diverse communities and the role and importance attached to spirit-writing within them may vary as well. Likewise, when discussing spirit-writing, it is essential also to identify other activities taking place at the same time, such as meditation, charity, healing, divination, scripture chanting, the pronouncing of sermons promulgating morality (*xuanhua* 宣化, *xuanjiang* 宣講), and

---

27 See the contribution by Hu Jiechen in this volume.
28 See "Di yi ci Dongying budao riji," 5, for an example from a 1930s source associated with the Daoyuan 道院.
29 Goossaert, *Making the Gods Speak*.
30 In more modern times, scholars also refer to these communities as *fuji tuanti* 扶乩團體 (spirit-writing groups).

their relation to spirit-writing. These activities might be part and parcel of the spirit-writing practice (rituals, meditation, divination), a result of the connection between gods and humans (healing, sermons, charity), or might happen in the same space but not be directly connected (reading and chanting scriptures).

Further, the terms that are used for both spirit-writing and its communities can be interchangeable, and are not static; they change over time, as the communities and their needs and activities also change. As the contributions of both Luo Dan and Li Guoping in this volume show, changes in nomenclature were also linked to changes in the general and political context. Spirit-writing communities, at times, consciously chose specific designations to avoid scrutiny by the authorities or elevate their public standing, particularly from the late nineteenth century onward, when sentiments against "superstition" grew more prominent. In such a context, a designation such as "charitable hall" may prove less problematic than "spirit-writing altar." The names of specific communities should not, therefore, be taken at face value but related to their activities and structures.

3   Regional Variety and Transregional Networks

According to Wang Chien-chuan's contribution to this volume, the earliest regional religious centers associated with repeated and continuous spirit-writing practice are the Wudang Mountains 武當山 of Hubei 湖北 and certain areas of Sichuan, during the period from the Southern Song until the Ming. In his chapter, Wang clearly defines the importance of the cult of Zhenwu 真武 on Mount Wudang and how Daoist monasteries there received and disseminated spirit-written scriptures attributed to him. Similarly, Sichuan during the Southern Song period saw the appearance of the Imperial Ruler Zitong 梓潼, later associated with the god Wenchang, and several scriptures associated with him were composed through spirit-writing in the Sichuan area from the Southern Song to the Ming periods.[31] Sichuan would continue to be an important center for the history of spirit-writing. Together with the larger Southwest region, the area has recently garnered much attention in other publications, and is a prime example of the richness and variety of spirit-writing activities that occurred during the Qing dynasty. Sichuan was an important area for the flourishing of lay communities who used spirit-writing to transmit scrip-

---

31   See Wang in this volume. See also Kleeman, *A God's Own Tale*.

tures in a millenarian religious context.[32] Specifically, the Longnü si 龍女寺 (Temple of the Dragon Maiden) in Dingyuan 定遠 began producing books through spirit-writing from at least 1840. The main divinity who descended to the altar was Guandi, who, "in a series of increasingly eschatological revelations, attempted to prevent an apocalypse by exhorting people to repent and reform themselves morally."[33] The scriptures revealed at the Longnü si were widely disseminated regionally and influenced the emergence of other local altars, which continued to receive and disseminate similar scriptures in subsequent decades. Sichuan, in connection to nearby areas, was and continued to be a hub for the production and transmission of scriptures related to the worship of both Wenchang and Guandi.[34] The communities receiving these scriptures comprised Confucian literati and the aim of the scriptures was to restore morality and promote a Confucian ethos. Sichuan was, therefore, central regarding the production and dissemination of Confucian-inspired scriptures at this time.[35] The impetus to restore morality also included the promotion of physical self-cultivation, so part of these scriptures contained instructions on inner alchemical practice (*neidan* 內丹) for both men and women.[36] Finally Sichuan, and Chengdu 成都 in particular, was the site of the republication and expansion of the *Chongkan Daozang jiyao* 重刊道藏輯要 (Reprint of the *Essentials of the Daoist Canon*), which preserves several scriptures tied to local spirit-writing groups.[37] In our volume, both Shiga and Luo Dan discuss the community and textual transmission connections between the southern coastal areas and Sichuan. Outside this volume, scholars have also investigated the Western regions, especially the intersection between Sichuan, Yunnan 雲南, and Guizhou 貴州.[38]

The Jiangnan region, and the literati's use of spirit-writing for amusement, to ask questions regarding the examination system, or to communicate with deceased family members (often women), was the focus of much of the earlier

---

32 For this, and specifically the Longnü temple, see the extensive studies by Wang, "Cong xin ziliao kan jindai Zhongguo de 'fuji yundong,'" and Takeuchi, "Qingmo Sichuan de zongjiao yundong."
33 Wang, "Popular Groups," 92.
34 On these networks, see Hu, "Qingdai liuzhong Wendi lei quanshu."
35 Wang, "Spirit-writing Groups in Modern China," "Popular Groups," "Cong xinziliao kan jindai Zhongguo de 'fuji yundong.'" Also see Zhu, "'Gengzi Chuandong shenjiao chu.'"
36 Valussi, "Printing and Religion," "The Transmission of the Cult of Lü Dongbin," and "Li Xiyue and the Western School."
37 Yuria, "Being Local through Ritual," and Hu, "Qingmo Chuanqian diqu."
38 Discussed in Hu, "*Wendi quanshu*" and "Qingmo Chuanqian diqu"; and Wang, "Popular Groups."

research, and has continued to be central in the field.[39] In the present volume, this region and its literati's involvement with spirit-writing is addressed by both Daniel Burton-Rose, who focuses on the important Peng 彭 lineage from Suzhou 蘇州 in his research,[40] and Michael Lackner.

While the majority of the ethnographic research on spirit-writing communities continues to concentrate on Taiwan and Hong Kong, the research interest is expanding to coastal China and southern China, which have recently been the focus for both historians and anthropologists. In this volume, contributions cover Guangxi 廣西, Hong Kong, the Chaozhou 潮州 area of Guangdong, but also North China (Ji'nan 濟南 and Tianjin 天津), which is generally a neglected geographical area.

In this volume, we are also careful to identify possible textual and community-based networks across the provinces. Work in this direction has progressed steadily and, inside our volume and beyond, increasing attention is being paid to both the specificity of localized cases, and the networks that connect them. The contributions of Li Guoping and Shiga Ichiko on the Guangdong and Guangxi areas, respectively, reveal how different spirit-writing altars and halls were connected through networks sustained by trade routes or religious affiliations.

Recently, furthermore, much work has been done on tracing the transmission of spirit-writing activities outside China. Vietnam, and the redemptive society Caodai in particular, has been the focus of recent scholarship, and a paper on this topic was presented at our conference, introducing the transmission of spirit-writing to communities in Vietnam, the expansion of the pantheon, and how spirit-writing communications influenced the political sphere there.[41] Exciting research in this direction, which shows how Chinese religious textual traditions feature within Caodai and how they were "occulted" through the use of French spiritualist language, has been conducted by Jeremy Jammes and David Palmer.[42] Luo Dan's chapter in our volume examines this process in reverse, discussing how a Vietnamese refugee was involved in the development of a spirit-writing cult in Hong Kong. Initial work has also been undertaken

---

39　Zeitlin, "Spirit Writing and Performance"; Wang, "You Tong yu wan Ming Qing chu Suzhou"; Liu, "Of Poems, Gods and Spirit-Writing Altars"; Wang, "Gendering the Planchette."

40　See, especially, his PhD dissertation: Burton-Rose, "Terrestrial Rewards as Divine Recompense."

41　At the conference, Janet Hoskins presented a paper entitled "Reveal and Conceal: Spirit-Writing as a Clandestine Practice in Vietnam and its Diaspora." For Caodai and spirit-writing in Vietnam more generally, see her *The Divine Eye and the Diaspora*, as well as Jammes and Palmer, "The *Bible of the Great Cycle*," and Jammes, *Les Oracles du Cao Đài*.

42　Jammes and Palmer, "Occulting the Dao."

regarding the ties between China and Korea, showing how spirit-writing spread to Korea as part of a transregional Guandi cult, sounding a familiar eschatological message that eventually resulted in the production of spirit-written texts by high-ranking Chosŏn officials during the late nineteenth century. Significantly, due to an inability to produce a wooden stylus, Korean spirit-written messages were written directly onto paper using a regular writing brush.[43] While Korean Guandi worship was promoted by officials, during the late imperial period, these transregional ties were often the product of the trade and merchant networks, which spread religious practices such as spirit-writing among the Chinese-speaking communities within Southeast Asia, where they could be adapted and appropriated by local actors.

Recent research has also started to highlight how spirit-writing, at least since the early twentieth century, became embedded within an increasingly globalized religious sphere. While Western observers were analyzing Chinese spirit-writing against the background of global spiritualism, Chinese practitioners were busy appropriating European spiritualist practices. Fan Chun-wu in this volume thus provides an example of a 1930s technique that appears to have been inspired by the Ouija board. Redemptive societies extended this global approach further. Reflecting the religious universalism that some of them embraced (see below), they established branch societies overseas and embraced numerous foreign members.[44] This globalization was not limited to practices and institutions. During the Republican period, international figures and deities from Jesus, Mohammed, the Apostle John, to Aristotle and Karl Marx began to transmit spirit-written messages at numerous altars nationwide. These globalization processes, which we can see affecting Chinese religions more generally, continue unabated. The Yiguandao 一貫道 (Way of Pervading Unity) in particular has been able to globalize its religious message,[45] a process illustrated by Nikolas Broy in this volume, showing its spread to Japan. Research on spirit-writing within a global context seems to be another fruitful future research avenue, taking into account both the international networks of individual communities as well as spirit-writing as a particular technique within a global plethora of "automatic writing."

---

43   Kim, "Enlightenment on the Spirit-Altar," and "Expansion of Spirit-writing."
44   The redemptive society Daoyuan 道院 thus forged an alliance with the Ōmoto-kyō 大本教, a new religious movement from Japan, and boasted of the latter's branch societies as its own. Sun, "Jishin no shūkyōgaku."
45   See Yang, "Between Cultural Reproduction and Cultural Translation," and Broy, "Global Dao." See also Broy, "Maitreya's Garden in the Township."

4 Social Diversity

Spirit-writing was used by a wide variety of communities and permeated all levels of society. It was relevant, therefore, not only as a strictly religious practice, but also as a social one. Contributors capture these differences by discussing the different social backgrounds of practitioners, the gender differences that emerge, the different roles that exist within these communities, and how these differences affected devotion and practice.

Spirit-writing was never part of the officially-endorsed religious practices, but was nevertheless promoted by large swathes of the literati and state officials. As mentioned above, it was practiced by the literati as early as the Song dynasty, when officials and scholars engaged in and wrote about it. These literati and officials were also vital for the proliferation of spirit-writing during the late imperial period. They promoted textual projects, such as the *quanshu*-canons mentioned above, as well as the state canonization of important deities, such as Guandi, Lüzu, and Wenchang.[46] Indeed, spirit-writing was an important part of the religious lives of many members of the elite, who forged an emotional bond with deities with whom they exchanged poems and conversed on moral values, religious doctrines, and practices of self-cultivation. Even literati defenders of Confucian orthodoxy, who were otherwise somewhat skeptical of many religious practices, considered spirit-writing valuable with regard to the moral lessons it imparted and the accuracy of its divinatory predictions.[47] The involvement of literati and officials expanded further with the emergence of eschatological discourses from the early seventeenth century onward; as Goossaert notes, we have several comprehensive corpuses with detailed records about the groups who produced and circulated them.[48] These discourses were particularly visible in the eschatological revelations at the Longnü si in Sichuan in 1840. In this context, the practice provided them with an outlet for expressing their religious and moral sentiments in light of the increasing social and political instability.[49]

Spirit-writing could even be found at the imperial court. The best-known example is probably Ming Emperor Jiajing 嘉靖 (r. 1522–1566), who was known for his enthusiastic participation in spirit-writing sessions for which an altar

---

46 Goossaert, "Spirit-Writing, Canonization and the Rise of Divine Saviors."
47 For the examples of Ji Yun 紀昀 (1724–1805) and Zeng Guofan 曾國藩 (1811–1872), see the contribution by Michael Lackner in this volume, and Wang, "Qing mo guanshen yu fuji," 36.
48 Goossaert, "Modern Daoist eschatology."
49 Wang, "Popular Groups."

was set up in the inner court.[50] The engagement of emperors and scholar-officials in spirit-writing questions the depiction of "Chinese popular religion," long influential in academia and beyond, as separate and distinguishable from the "elite religion."[51] Rather, as we move forward, it will be important to study more extensively the different social groups involved in spirit-writing and the resulting differences in devotional practice, but also their interactions and the tensions that arise from the joint use of this practice. As an example of this important research direction, Zhu Mingchuan, in his contribution to the volume discussing a spirit-writing altar in the late nineteenth century highlights the at times conflicting understandings of the practices and deities among the elites and non-elites. In a similar way, Michael Lackner's contribution shows how scholar-officials such as Ji Yun 紀昀 (1724–1805, also known as Ji Xiaolan 紀曉嵐) engaged with spirit-writing. While he "maintained a prudent distance" from such "popular" practices, he at the same time tested the boundaries of what was "acceptable." Contributions to this volume thus show how men and women from different backgrounds used spirit-writing in many ways, utilizing processes of legitimation,[52] negotiation, appropriation, and transformation. These processes allowed communities to both test and to re-affirm boundaries between elite culture and popular practices in complex ways that produced both collaboration and tensions, and that do not easily fit into the pre-existing dichotomies we as scholars have long assigned them.

With the fall of the dynasty in 1911, scholars have been able to pinpoint a growing diversification of spirit-writing communities, certainly also reflecting the greater availability of sources. The Confucian elite remained vital for the promotion of spirit-writing and the establishment and leadership of spe-

---

50　The Emperor surrounded himself with Daoist ritual specialists, who, through spirit-writing and inner alchemy, were to help him to achieve longevity. See the contribution by Wang Chien-chuan to this volume.
51　Here, see the still influential article by Catherine Bell who describes how the academic study of Chinese religion moved beyond the "elite" vs. "popular" religion dichotomy, and also beyond the dichotomy of unity vs. diversity of Chinese religious beliefs and practices, towards a more holistic approach, focused on how men and women actually generated both unity and diversity in their beliefs and practices. Bell saw ritual as a key in this respect. Bell, "Religion and Chinese Culture."
52　Processes of legitimation are particularly visible in the contributions by Daniel Burton-Rose and Matthias Schumann in this volume, which both show how spirit-writing practitioners, who were at the same time officials, tried to legitimize spirit-writing as an "orthodox" means of transmitting Confucian discourse. Such processes illustrate both the implicit and explicit boundaries that existed between accepted and potentially transgressive forms of religious practices as well as the means through which such boundaries could be negotiated.

cific communities. They were joined by military and political officials, reaching the highest echelons of the new republican state. Many became members and disciples of specific deities, while others even started practicing spirit-writing themselves. Indeed, recent research has emphasized the shared moral and religious outlook between many spirit-writing communities and the political establishment of the Beiyang 北洋 period (1916–1927) more broadly.[53]

Constituting a trend that started during the late imperial period and continued and accelerated during the Republican era, scholars have also pointed to the involvement of merchant and business communities in spirit-writing groups. Shiga Ichiko, in her contribution to this volume, shows how eschatological scriptures spread from Yunnan to Guangdong during the late nineteenth century through the trade routes of Cantonese merchants.[54] For the Republican era urban elite, spirit-writing provided a venue for discussing and encouraging various forms of social activism, but also a means of coping with life crises.[55] This tallies with the research by Paul R. Katz in this volume, who mentions, in relation to the case of Puli 埔里 in Taiwan, the importance of the local elite, many members of which are rice merchants, in sustaining "phoenix halls."

In line with the thrust of this volume, however, Katz also emphasizes the diversity of the members who came together in Taiwanese phoenix-halls in terms of their social, economic, and ethnic background. Looking at spirit-writing communities in general, this assessment seems equally valid. Both now and in the past, they appealed to a wide spectrum of the population, depending also on the focus of their activities, the emphasis of their teachings, or the amount of membership fees they solicited. While some were dominated by elite networks, others welcomed the participation and sometimes even leadership of less socially advantaged groups.

The Republican period also saw the increasingly prominent involvement of women. Due to their role in the Zigu cult, female worship lies at the basis of spirit-writing's history but, as Elena Valussi shows in her contribution, women were increasingly marginalized once the male literati stepped in. During the imperial period, we therefore have very few cases of women serving as medi-

---

53 See Goossaert and Palmer, *The Religious Question in Modern China*, chap. 4; Ownby, "Sainthood, Science, and Politics." See also Schumann, "Redemptive Societies," 188–89, and his contribution in this volume.

54 See Shiga Ichiko's contribution to this volume. See, also, Shiga, "Manifestations of Lüzu in Modern Guangdong." Valussi, "The Transmission of the Cult of Lü Dongbin" also reveals the importance of communities of migrant merchants in establishing a spirit-writing altar in Sichuan.

55 Katz, "Spirit-writing and the Dynamics of Elite Religious Life." See also Wang, "Lufei Kui yu 'Shengde tan,' 'Lingxue hui.'"

ums or of female spirit-writing communities.[56] In line with the general changes in gender relations, we also see a more prominent role for women in the early twentieth century. Many redemptive societies set up gender-segregated sub-organizations and while these, as Xia Shi shows in this volume, were usually subordinated to their male counterparts, they also provided women with an outlet to engage in social activism, mostly charity, and subtly transformed the traditional Confucian gender perspectives. Nevertheless, in most societies women were in the minority and mostly joined when their husbands or fathers became members.[57] To shed light on the roles of women in spirit-writing, whose involvement is rarely prominent in the written sources, ethnographic research is especially valuable. Paul R. Katz, for example, in his chapter on the present-day Taiwanese "phoenix halls," shows how many women do not engage in spirit-writing directly but, rather, focus on scripture chanting or liturgy.[58] Citing the research by Huang Pingying 黃萍瑛, Katz also laments that women have, therefore, often been neglected in the research on spirit-writing although their scripture chanting activities can be a major source of prestige and income. This volume made efforts to investigate the reflections of gender in spirit-writing's history, but the role of women in spirit-writing, and how this diverged from the male practices, is an important avenue for future research.

5   Religious Affiliations and Networks

This volume also aims to explore the question of the religious affiliation of the communities practicing spirit-writing. As mentioned above, and discussed in detail by Valussi in this volume, early examples of spirit-writing practices during the Song period emerged from the worship of the popular female deity Zigu, and therefore not within a specific religious community. At the same time, Goossaert in this volume makes a strong case for the concomitant emer-

---

56   A prominent exception are the female communities devoted to inner alchemy that Elena Valussi explores in her research: Valussi, "Men and Women," "Female Alchemy and Paratext," and her contribution to this volume. See also Gao, "Jin'gaishan wangluo" for a discussion of the growing involvement of women in the spirit-writing network on Mount Jin'gai 金蓋.

57   The Yiguandao is an exception in this respect, as it included many female members, who could also aspire to leadership positions. Clart, "Yīguàn Dào."

58   At the 2019 conference, Philip Clart's paper discussed the gender ratios in contemporary spirit-writing communities in Taiwan, and highlighted the different queries that men and women posed to the descending divinity.

gence of spirit-written communications as part of the ritual practices of Daoist priests. Goossaert challenges in part the assumption about the centrality of the lay community in the initial formation and development of spirit-writing. He convincingly argues that this technique, at its inception, was closely tied to the Daoist milieu, and employed by Daoist clerics in order to process Daoist rituals, and even create ritual compendia. Yet, spirit-writing, as pointed out above, was practiced in different contexts for different purposes. It was, therefore, not the purview of any one specific group, at least not permanently. This is also shown by research outside this volume. Lai Chi-tim 黎志添 has argued how, during the Ming dynasty, it was lay Daoist rather than clerical communities who were most active in the innovative creation of religious texts. These communities sought a non-mediated connection to divinities, thereby effectively side-stepping the authority of the Daoist clerics and directly accessing the divinity and their messages, as well as working on their own self-divinization.[59] Paul Katz's research in this volume confirms the importance of lay Daoists for present-day Taiwanese spirit-writing communities, but it was not only Daoist communities, whether lay or clerical, that practiced spirit-writing.

Recent research outside this volume has unearthed the strong Confucian component of many of the spirit-writing communities during the Qing and Republican periods. Sichuan, and the South West area in general, were the areas where these groups were active.[60] The Qing Confucian elite supported and practiced spirit-writing, while popular religious groups resorted to the moralizing power of the sermons sent down by powerful gods and goddesses who protected them from annihilation. In this volume, the paper by Burton-Rose traces the centrality of the Confucian messages and lineages back to the Ming-Qing transition, showing how the literati made use of spirit-writing in order to validate and add authority to their position within the Confucian lineages and intellectual world that they proudly inhabited. Also in this volume, Schumann adds a Republican perspective to the Confucian development of spirit-writing, by providing an in-depth analysis of the Confucian texts utilized by redemptive societies to bolster their authority in what was a rapidly-changing, hazardous situation for religious groups. Recent fieldwork undertaken by Zhu Mingchuan reveals that the Confucian altars, widespread in Sichuan during the mid-Qing period and continuously active until the 1950s, are now experiencing

---

59 Lai, "The Cult of Spirit-Writing in the Qing."
60 Wang, "Popular Groups"; Valussi, "The Transmission of the Cult of Lü Dongbin"; Zhu, "Rutan jingdian ji qi yingyong."

a resurgence,[61] while scholars have also researched the connection between spirit-writing and Confucian elites in Taiwan.[62]

Less clear, and definitely an avenue that is debated by scholars and requires further exploration, is the Buddhist dimension of spirit-writing. Buddhist elements can be detected in early spirit-written texts. Wang Chien-chuan, for instance, identified the *Wudangshan Xuandi chuixun* 武當山玄帝垂訓 (Instructions handed down by the Dark Emperor on Mount Wudang), which was transmitted via spirit-writing in 1301 to a Daoist monastery on Wudang mountain, which adds Buddhist characteristics to the earlier biographies of the Daoist deity Zhenwu, such as a vegetarian diet, alms-giving, and other Buddhist values. The text also recalls descriptions present in Buddhist apocalyptic scriptures, thus using a Daoist voice to spread Buddhist as well as Confucian and popular religious values.[63] Generally, several Buddhist gods and goddesses (Guanyin, Maitreya, Jigong 濟公 ...) were invoked at spirit-writing altars, especially from the mid-nineteenth century onward. The resulting texts were sometimes completely Buddhist in nature.[64] We also know of a long-standing engagement with spirit-writing on the part of lay Buddhist intellectuals such as Peng Shaosheng 彭紹升 (1740–1796).[65] This interest continued into the Republican period, when prominent lay Buddhists, such as Wang Yiting 王一亭 (1867–1938) and Ding Fubao 丁福保 (1874–1952), participated in the religious and philanthropic activities of spirit-writing organizations.[66] Buddhist clerics, on the other hand, were generally less enthusiastic about spirit-writing. Even though they conceded the moral nature of the teachings transmitted to the spirit-writing altars, they denied that actual Buddhist deities would stoop so low as to attend such rites, thereby criticizing the involvement of Buddhist

---

61   Zhu Mingchuan, personal communication on recent fieldwork for the Sichuan Religions project (https://sichuanreligions.com), January 15, 2022.

62   See Katz's contribution to this volume.

63   See Wang's contribution to this volume.

64   Valussi, "Li Xiyue and the Western School," discusses the inclusion of the collection *Ruyi baozhu* 如意寶珠 (*Cintamani* wish-fulfilling jewel), which includes esoteric Buddhist scriptures, in the *Zhang Sanfeng quanji*, a compilation of Daoist scriptures. For the revelation of apocalyptic scriptures revolving around Maitreya, see the contribution by Broy in this volume.

65   See the case of Peng Shaosheng, who, in the *Yixing juji* 一行居集 (Writings of the layman Yixing), discusses the spirit-writing activities of his circle in the mid-Qing Jiangnan period. See Wang, "Jindai Zhongguo fuji tuanti de cishan yu zhushu," 91–92.

66   Katz discusses the overlap between Buddhism and spirit-writing in the late imperial and modern era in his contribution to this volume; see also Katz, "Spirit-writing and the Dynamics of Elite Religious Life," 275–350; Schumann, "Science and Spirit-Writing"; Fan, "'Zhanxin Pusa yi jinshi'."

believers.[67] Famous Republican era Buddhist cleric Yinguang 印光 (1862–1940) discussed in somewhat negative terms the commentary on the Diamond sutra, allegedly transmitted via spirit-writing by Lü Dongbin in 1921 (*Jingangjing zhijie* 金剛經直解).[68]

Generally, however, the spirit-writing communities adopted elements from various religious traditions and were and remain, therefore, hybrid creatures that defy easy categorization. In our volume, Luo Dan thus discusses the interaction between Buddhist and Daoist rituals at spirit-writing halls in Hong Kong. This mixing of texts and religious symbols is a trait of many spirit-writing altars and reflects the popular discourse of the "unity of the three teachings" (*sanjiao heyi* 三教合一) more generally.[69] A number of Republican era communities further complemented the three teachings with Christianity and Islam and it was not uncommon to have representatives of all of these different religious traditions descending to the same altar. An affiliation with the "world religions" promised legitimacy at a time when the concept of religion itself had only recently been introduced into China.[70] However, such discourses, in reality, rarely translated into religious pluralism, and one teaching was often considered superior or more essential than others. Often, one deity would serve as the principal divinity but this did not prevent other deities descending. Sometimes, a division of labor and responsibility could even emerge, where certain deities were responsible for answering queries on specific topics by the members (e.g., Lüzu answered questions on meditation). What is clear is that, when practicing spirit-writing, often more important than the religious affiliation was a direct connection to a divinity and the possibility of self-divinization among the practitioners.

6   Political and Legal Challenges

Part of the reason why spirit-writing has so long been a neglected research topic is the opposition that it often encountered from officialdom. Despite the wide and increasing popularity of spirit-writing, its legal and social status always remained ambivalent, which, in turn, also affected the scholarship on the practice over the last century. Indeed, from its very earliest stages during the Song

---

67   Fan, "Jinxiandai Zhongguo Fojiao yu fuji."
68   See Wang, "Jindai Zhongguo fuji tuanti de cishan yu zhushu," 90–91.
69   On the doctrine of *sanjiao heyi*, see, for example, Gentz, "Religious Diversity in Three Teachings Discourses."
70   Schumann, "Redemptive Societies," 194–95.

INTRODUCTION   21

era until the end of the imperial period, spirit-writing was prohibited.[71] This prohibition was not necessarily effective and there were very few prosecutions of those engaged in spirit-writing.[72] Nevertheless, it gave spirit-writing a dubious air and moved it dangerously close to the category of "heterodox techniques" (*xieshu* 邪術). This was reinforced by a general aversion to mediumistic practices and their practitioners among parts of officialdom and the Confucian elite.[73] Consequently, even emperors could be criticized for engaging in this "sinister method" (*zuodao* 左道; lit. "way of the left," i.e., improper).[74]

The fall of the Qing dynasty led to the emergence of heterogeneous, widely differing views on spirit-writing and made it something of a paradox. While many religious practices continued to be viewed negatively by the state authorities, spirit-writing was no longer prohibited. This, together with the newly-declared freedom of religious belief, which also facilitated the founding of numerous redemptive societies, created a favorable environment for the advocates of spirit-writing. The practice was also embraced by members of the modern educated elite, who strove to emphasize the rational, scientific nature of the practice, as Fan Chun-wu shows in his contribution to our volume. In parallel to the imperial period, moreover, many political and military officials joined spirit-writing groups and some even learned the craft themselves. The involvement of these political figures also helps to explain why spirit-writing was usually not seen as a political concern, at least at the political center in Beijing.[75]

On the other hand, the Republican period also heralded the first concerted attack on spirit-writing, which aimed to end the practice in general. In 1918, a number of intellectuals associated with the radical journal *Xin qingnian* 新青年 (New youth) used arguments drawn from evolutionary theory, materialist science, psychology, and simple polemics to label spirit-writing "superstition" (*mixin* 迷信).[76] This was, to our knowledge, the first time that spirit-writing

---

71 In 1116, the Northern Song court ordered the spirit-writing halls in the capital city of Kaifeng to be destroyed. Wang, "Song-Ming shiqi de fuji," 59–60. A similar prohibition was issued during the reign of Ming Emperor Taizu 太祖 (r. 1368–1398) and eventually found its way into the Ming and later the Qing Code. Ibid., 76.
72 Clart and Goossaert, "Spirit-Writing"; Jiang, *The Mandate of Heaven*, 91–99.
73 Sutton, "From Credulity to Scorn."
74 See Wan, "Building an Immortal Land," 95, and Wang Chien-chuan's contribution to this volume.
75 See Schumann, "Redemptive Societies," 188–89, and his contribution to this volume.
76 The attack was largely directed against the Shanghai Lingxue hui 靈學會 (Spiritualist Society), a local spirit-writing altar run by a few figures from the burgeoning publishing industry, which sought to legitimize spirit-writing by linking it to practices and ideas

has been systematically attacked as superstition and set a paradigm for labeling and assessing the practice among academics, as well as successive secular elites and regimes, that persists today. Indeed, from the beginning, the scientific superstition discourse and scholarship on spirit-writing have been intimately intertwined. Xu Dishan 許地山 (1893–1941), a pioneer of the study of spirit-writing, in his oft-cited and otherwise immensely useful book from 1941, revealingly titled *Fuji mixin di yanjiu* 扶乩迷信底研究 (An investigation of the superstition of spirit-writing), thus attributes belief in religious phenomena such as spirit-writing to a lack of scientific knowledge.[77]

The Nationalist government inherited and continued this discourse. After the Guomindang 國民黨 (Nationalist Party of China) came to power in 1927, spirit-writing was defined as superstition and as lying beyond the confines of the legally-sanctioned religious freedom. A number of spirit-writing organizations were, therefore, prohibited. This approach not only chimed with the modernizing project of the Guomindang but also allowed the government to weaken the societal influence of the former Beiyang elite, who were active within these organizations.[78] It was also wary of the appeal that practices such as spirit-writing could wield over some members of the Guomindang, many of whom belonged to religious communities that engaged in such practices.[79]

In 1949, the Guomindang transferred its modernizing policies to Taiwan. Freedom of religious belief was enshrined in the constitution, but the corporatist approach of the Nationalist government, meaning that all religious organizations had to register with specific umbrella institutions, did not suit the hybrid nature of many of the spirit-writing communities. Even though some phoenix hall leaders in Taiwan have had prominent public lives, and some even became prominent politicians,[80] spirit-writing itself continued to be considered superstition and some communities, most notably the Yiguandao, were seen as subversive and so subjected to government repression.[81] Since 1987, however, when martial law was lifted and all religious organizations were permitted, the situation changed radically. Spirit-writing communities, both large

---

associated with spiritualism (*lingxue* 靈學). On the Lingxue hui and the critique that it attracted, see Huang, "Lingxue yu jindai Zhongguo de zhishi zhuanxing," and Wang, "Lufei Kui yu 'Shengde tan,' 'Lingxue hui.'"

77 Xu, *Fuji mixin di yanjiu*.
78 Nedostup, *Superstitious Regimes*, chap. 2; Ownby, "Redemptive Societies in the Twentieth Century," 700–6.
79 Ownby, "Li Yujie."
80 See Paul R. Katz's contribution in this volume.
81 See Katz, "Religion and the State"; Laliberté, "The Regulation of Religious Affairs"; Lu, *The Transformation of Yiguan Dao*; Jordan and Overmyer, *The Flying Phoenix*.

INTRODUCTION 23

and small, have greatly flourished and Taiwan has become a center for the research on spirit-writing, due both to leading historical and ethnographic studies as well as major compilations of spirit-written texts.

Following the founding of the People's Republic in 1949, spirit-writing became swept up in the campaign against "reactionary religious sects" (*fandong huidaomen* 反動會道門), in which it appeared as one among many superstitious practices used by redemptive societies to trick guileless believers.[82] As a consequence, scholarship on spirit-writing and redemptive societies in mainland China was largely impossible until 1978, when it continued to be dominated by the critical political framework.[83] During the 2000s, however, more neutral and sometimes even positive assessments began to appear in the mainland scholarship, particularly emphasizing spirit-writing's role in fostering morality and promoting charity. This was helped by the visible role of religious organizations in disaster relief following the 2008 Wenchuan 汶川 earthquake.[84] In recent years, as reflected in a number of contributions to this volume, the research on spirit-writing in the PRC has greatly increased, both in quantity and in terms of its interpretive frames.

Obstacles remain, however, and the ambivalent status of spirit-writing continues to impact research even today. The texts and collections resulting from spirit-writing mentioned throughout this volume are often labeled as non-canonical within the field of classical and religious studies, and until recently have been deemed marginal, understood as lying outside both the Buddhist and Daoist Canons as well as the Confucian classics. For this reason, they were and continue to be overlooked and, as a result, are less easily accessed. Some of them have recently been gathered into *ad hoc* collections, but many are not collected at all but scattered across personal collections or in libraries.[85] Because of the superstitious label discussed above, scholars were and are not

---

82 For a recent study of redemptive societies under the CCP, see Smith, "Redemptive Religious Societies."
83 Despite its overly critical approach, the scholarship pursued under the framework of "secret societies" (*mimi shehui* 秘密社會) and "religious sects" (*huidaomen*) produced extremely valuable research. A book which follows the fate of numerous religious organizations up until the PRC and details many of their religious activities, including spirit-writing, is Shao, *Zhongguo huidaomen*.
84 A pioneer in the study of redemptive societies and spirit-writing is Guo Dasong 郭大松. See Guo, "Ji'nan Daoyuan." For a positive view, see Liu Ping's assessment of the modern nature and social value of the Hongwanzi hui 紅卍字會 (Red Swastika Society) and its charitable activities, which marks a clear departure from the former scholarship. Liu, "E zhi hua?"
85 For example, Hu et al., *Zangwai daoshu*.

now encouraged to focus on such practices, and libraries often do not preserve and correctly catalog these texts and collections. Further, archives are difficult to access, and the local archives, in which many of the relevant sources are preserved, have only slowly been reopened to the public, and more recently closed again. Moreover, the government sources, regardless of whether they are the imperial state, Nationalist government or PRC, come with their own ideological assumptions and biases. The contributions in this volume are, therefore, careful to balance the archival sources with materials produced from individual altars or collected during fieldwork. Contributors are also careful to distinguish between emic and etic views and avoid using pejorative terminology that might hinder a balanced assessment of these groups.

7 Overview of the Volume

This volume attempts to provide a comprehensive history of spirit-writing by including both broader overviews as well as more focused research articles. It begins with three overview chapters that cover specific periods and aspects of the history of spirit-writing from a broader perspective.

In the first overview chapter, Vincent Goossaert explores the relation to Daoism in early spirit-writing. He argues—against a palpable tendency in research to stress the lay character of spirit-writing—that, from the eleventh to the fifteenth centuries, spirit-writing was considered the preserve of Daoist ritual masters (*fashi* 法師) and practiced within the emerging exorcistic ritual traditions (*daofa* 道法). Spirit-writing, in this context, served as a means of communication between the Daoist priests and the high gods, allowing the latter to be present during rituals. In light of this evidence, Goossaert calls for a re-evaluation of the role of the Daoist priest within the early history of spirit-writing. Goossaert's chapter tallies with the second overview chapter by Wang Chien-chuan, which details the emergence of different spirit-writing techniques from the Song to Ming periods and their relation to different sites, regions, and communities. He particularly focuses on the emerging spirit-writing communities on Mount Wudang in Hubei province as well as in Sichuan province, which centered around Daoist temples and monasteries. Using a wide variety of sources, he demonstrates the breadth of spirit-writing, which included lay literati participants and even emperors, but was also strongly linked to religious communities, which were not only Daoist but, since the late Ming period, also included Buddhist believers. The third overview chapter by Elena Valussi focuses on the role of women within the history of spirit-writing, a group which has hitherto been neglected in research.

While, historically, spirit-writing was tightly connected to women and female deities, it soon became dominated by male practitioners, especially literati and Daoist priests, who controlled the "gendered relations" at the altars wherefore both women and female deities became sidelined. Valussi explores this gender dimension of spirit-writing and particularly focuses on the few cases in which women did serve as mediums or participated in spirit-writing communities, uncovering the specificities of female worship and devotion and the relations between female believers and divinities.

The second section of the volume explores the technical and typological diversity that we find within the history of spirit-writing. Hu Jiechen delineates how spirit-writing evolved from the use of a straw figurine to transmit simple yes-or-no answers to a figurine with chopsticks attached that gained the ability to write during the Song dynasty. He shows how this step resulted in an increase in the variety of deities that descended as well as the variety of textual genres produced. While Hu's article complements the chapter by Goossaert and Wang by emphasizing the importance of the lay literati's practice, he also shows the importance of Daoist practitioners in introducing new techniques for revealing religious scriptures. Spirit-writing, in terms of its content as well as technique, continued to develop in close connection with the general social and intellectual context. In his article, Fan Chun-wu introduces the case of the "Transcendent of the Plate" (*diexian* 碟仙), a simplified form of spirit-writing that emerged during the Republican period and made use of a plate similar to a Ouija-board. The technique was marketed as a "Scientific Numinous Stylus" (*kexue lingji* 科學靈乩) and raises important questions about the technical development of spirit-writing, its boundaries as well as its links to discourses on science and spiritualism, which were extremely popular concepts at the time.

The third section explores the role of spirit-writing in the lives of the literati elite in late imperial China. Daniel Burton-Rose examines the attempts of a prominent early Qing literatus to legitimize the unorthodox practice of spirit-writing and to fashion his own Neo-Confucian orthodoxy through spirit-written communications with apotheosized Confucian figures such as Zhou Dunyi 周敦頤 (1017–1073) and Cheng Yi 程頤 (1033–1107). He thereby extends our knowledge about the self-identified Confucian spirit-writing altars, which has so far focused on the late imperial period. Yet, Burton-Rose also questions a narrow focus on Confucian identity, pointing to the broad literary and devotional interests of many literati. Michael Lackner focuses on another member of the literati elite, namely Ji Yun, compiler of the *Siku quanshu* 四庫全書 (Complete books from the four treasuries), a project of state orthodoxy. In his writings, Ji frequently touched upon spirit-writing, subsuming the practice under the category of the mantic arts, or *shushu* 術數 (arts and codes). Ji held that these practices could yield important predictions and insights, but also emphasized the importance of human agency in making them "efficacious" (*ling* 靈). This allowed him to question individual messages and retain a critical distance. Ji's case shows how individual scholars attempted to come to terms with a practice that was widespread among the literati yet not state-sanctioned and which did not always produce writings that were intellectually convincing. In the last article of this section, Zhu Mingchuan introduces the history of the Liu-han Altar 了閑壇, which was originally founded by members of the influential Guo 郭 family in Fuzhou during the late Qing Dynasty. With more than 120 years of uninterrupted practice, the altar presents a remarkable example, showing how its members sought to navigate the changing social and political contexts in which they lived. Through spirit-written communications, the Guo family attempted to come to terms with their fate as loyalists to the Qing dynasty during the Republican period, and as exiles from mainland China under British colonial rule. Zhu also explores the differences in the beliefs and devotional practices that emerged at the altar once it spread transregionally and included participants from a broader social spectrum.

During the early twentieth century, many spirit-writing altars became integrated into new religious movements or redemptive societies, which lie at the heart of the third section of this volume. Xia Shi's contribution introduces the case of the Daoyuan 道院, which was founded in 1921 and evolved into a national religious and charitable organization. Xia Shi focuses particularly on the Daoyuan's views on women and gender, as articulated in spirit-written publications. The Daoyuan encompassed several all-female organizations that practiced spirit-writing. Xia demonstrates how the Daoyuan sought to reconstruct a "gendered morality" to provide stability in a period of change. While generally subordinating women to men and emphasizing the former's domestic duties, it also promoted virtues such as charity as a contribution to the larger social good, thereby opening up space for women to assume new roles in public life. In his article, Matthias Schumann focuses on the role of Confucian texts and Confucianism more generally within redemptive societies by examining the case of the Jiushi xinjiao 救世新教 (New Religion to Save the World). Schumann shows how members of the redemptive societies, many of whom were trained under the traditional education system, strove to come to terms with the complicated Confucian legacy at a time when many reformers considered it obsolete. From the mid-1920s onward, a number of prominent members of the political and military elite began to transmit commentaries on Confucian classics, claiming to have finally restored the true interpretation of these important texts. Through their commentaries, they integrated the Confucian classics into their own religious program of self-cultivation and moral reform, stressing the role of the deities as the agents of retribution but also emphasizing the classics' cultural value for the Chinese nation. In the third contribution of this section, Nikolas Broy charts the changing forms, functions, and meanings of spirit-writing within the Yiguandao from the late nineteenth century to the present. He shows how spirit-writing was used to legitimize institutional and doctrinal decisions, make predictions about political developments and, through the revelation of scriptures, enable groups such as Yiguandao to claim their own religious identity. Spirit-writing served as a creative force that contributed to the many schisms in Yiguandao history, but also allowed the group to spread worldwide. Broy explores the fate of Yiguandao-related groups in Japan, which were set up by Taiwanese missionaries in the 1940s, showing how Japanese practitioners have adapted the practice in both linguistic terms as well as with regard to content.

The focus of the last section of this volume is the communities and networks that shaped the history of spirit-writing both locally and regionally and from which many of the abovementioned redemptive societies emerged. In her contribution, Shiga Ichiko investigates the nineteenth century spirit-writing movement, which grew to a national scale after 1840, from the perspective of Western Guangdong. In particular, she shows how eschatological spirit-written scriptures (*jiujie jing* 救劫經; scriptures to save humanity from the apocalypse) spread from Sichuan to Guangdong and further through networks of merchants and morality book publishers. These scriptures voice similar eschatological themes and struck a note with local people who suffered due to the Bubonic Plague of the 1890s. Shiga also shows, however, that, while spirit-writing in Guangdong was integrated into a larger transregional movement, the local religious traditions and practices (such as specific deities germane to the place) persisted as well. Adopting a similar perspective, Li Guoping in his article contextualizes spirit-writing in the Chaozhou area of Guangdong within both the larger spirit-writing movements as well as the local religious milieu. Li particularly focuses on local "charitable halls" (*shantang*) to show their close link to spirit-writing practice, but also to offer a more precise understanding of their nature and characteristics. He develops a typology of charitable halls that is attentive to the local traditions and characteristics, yet also considers their heterogeneity and transregional links.

In her contribution, Luo Dan focuses on the Fei Ngan Tung Buddhism and Daoism Society 飛雁洞佛道社, a Lüzu cult from Hong Kong. Through her ethnographic work, she shows how the society adapted not only to the changing urban setting of the city but also to the challenges and opportunities emerging from mainland China. The society increasingly adopted Daoist rituals in an attempt to gain legitimacy as an "orthodox" religious community, while setting out on a journey to find their mainland roots in Sichuan province. Luo shows how spirit-writing, through its continuous rapport with Lüzu, provided assurance and guided the members during the process. In the last chapter of the volume, Paul R. Katz introduces the variety of spirit-writing traditions, or phoenix halls, in present-day Puli, Taiwan, in terms of their membership, activities, as well as time period and region. He emphasizes the importance of elite networks, many of which are Hakka, in guiding and maintaining the phoenix halls, but also points to the important role of women, who have often been neglected due to the fact that their devotional activities tend to differ from those of their male counterparts. While the phoenix halls are diverse in nature, Katz also points to several common aspects which might account for their popularity and clarify their position within Puli's religious landscape. Many of them thus place emphasis on individual self-cultivation and social activism, that are less prominent activities in the larger public temple cults. Following a number of previous studies,[86] the works in this section also show how it is possible to trace the contemporary practices back through the historical records, handwritten manuscripts, and local memories, and provide highly specific, localized trajectories for them. Conversely, they also indicate that, by starting from the historical records, it is still possible to find contemporary remnants, or revivals, of past communities.

Bibliography

Bell, Catherine. "Religion and Chinese Culture: Toward an Assessment of 'Popular Religion.'" *History of Religions* 29, no. 1 (1989): 35–57.

Bokenkamp, Stephen. *A Fourth-Century Daoist Family: The Zhen'gao, or Declarations of the Perfected*. Vol. 1. Berkeley: University of California Press, 2020.

Broy, Nikolas. "Syncretic Sects and Redemptive Societies: Toward a New Understanding of 'Sectarianism' in the Study of Chinese Religions." *Review of Religion and Chinese Society* 2, no. 2 (2015): 145–85.

---

86 Examples of attempts to combine historical and ethnographic research include the pioneering work by Jordan and Overmyer, *The Flying Phoenix*; Clart, "Confucius and the Mediums," and "Moral Mediums"; and Katz, "Spirit-writing Halls and the Development of Local Communities." See also the recent introduction by Philip Clart on the challenges associated with connecting philology with ethnography: "Text and Context in the Study of Spirit Writing Cults."

Broy, Nikolas. "Maitreya's Garden in the Township: Transnational Religious Spaces of Yiguandao Activists in Urban South Africa." *China Perspectives*, no. 4 (2019): 27–36.

Broy, Nikolas. "Global Dao: The Making of Transnational Yiguandao." In *Chinese Religions Going Global*, edited by Nanlai Cao, Giuseppe Giordan, and Fenggang Yang, 174–93. Leiden: Brill, 2020.

Burton-Rose, Daniel. "Terrestrial Rewards as Divine Recompense: The Self-Fashioned Piety of the Peng Lineage of Suzhou, 1650s–1870s." PhD diss., Princeton University, 2016.

Burton-Rose, Daniel. "Establishing a Literati Spirit-Writing Altar in Early Qing Suzhou: The *Optimus* Prophecy of Peng Dingqiu (1645–1719)." *T'oung Pao* 106, no. 2 (2020): 358–400.

Clart, Philip. "Confucius and the Mediums: Is There a 'Popular Confucianism'?" *T'oung Pao* 89, no. 1–3 (2003): 1–38.

Clart, Philip. "Moral Mediums: Spirit-Writing and the Cultural Construction of Chinese Spirit-Mediumship." *Ethnologies* 25, no. 1 (2003): 153–90.

Clart, Philip. "Yīguàn Dào." In *Handbook of East Asian New Religious Movements*, edited by Lukas Pokorny and Franz Winter, 429–50. Leiden: Brill, 2018.

Clart, Philip. "Text and Context in the Study of Spirit Writing Cults: A Methodological Reflection on the Relationship between Philology and Ethnography." In Clart, Ownby, and Wang, *Text and Context in the Modern History of Chinese Religions*, 309–22.

Clart, Philip, David Ownby, and Chien-chuan Wang, eds. *Text and Context in the Modern History of Chinese Religions: Redemptive Societies and Their Sacred Texts*. Leiden: Brill, 2020.

Clart, Philip, and Vincent Goossaert. "Spirit-Writing." In *Techniques of Chinese Prognostication*, edited by Stephan Kory. Leiden: Brill, forthcoming.

"Di yi ci Dongying budao riji 第一次東瀛佈道日記." In *Dongying budao riji* 東瀛佈道日記. Reprint, Taipei: Shijie hongwanzi hui Taiwan shengfenhui, 1977.

Dudgeon, John. "Chinese Arts of Healing." *Chinese Recorder and Missionary Journal*, July 1, 1870.

Duara, Prasenjit. "The Discourse of Civilization and Pan-Asianism." *Journal of World History* 12, no. 1 (2001): 99–130.

Elliott, Alan J. *Chinese Spirit-Medium Cults in Singapore*. London: Department of Anthropology, London School of Economics and Political Science, 1955.

Elman, Benjamin A. *A Cultural History of Civil Examinations in Late Imperial China*. Berkeley: University of California Press, 2000.

Enns, Anthony. "The Undead Author: Spiritualism, Technology and Authorship." In *The Ashgate Research Companion to Nineteenth-Century Spiritualism and the Occult*, edited by Tatiana Kontou and Sarah Wilburn, 55–78. Farnham: Ashgate, 2012.

Esposito, Monica. "The Invention of a Quanzhen Canon: The Wondrous Fate of the *Daozang jiyao*." In *Quanzhen Daoists in Chinese Society and Culture, 1500–2010*, edited by Xun Liu and Vincent Goossaert, 44–77. Berkeley: University of California Press, 2013.

Esposito, Monica. *Facets of Qing Daoism*. Paris: UniversityMedia, 2014.

Fan Chun-wu 范純武. "Jinxiandai Zhongguo Fojiao yu fuji 近現代中國佛教與扶乩." *Yuanguang Foxue xuebao* 圓光佛學學報, no. 3 (Feb. 1999): 261–91.

Fan Chun-wu 范純武. "'Zhanxin Pusa yi jinshi, kexue Ou wen dou liaoxiao': Shilun 1930, 40 niandai Shanghai Fojiao jushi fuji tuanti 'Laisu she' 「嶄新菩薩宜今世、科學歐文都了曉」：試論 1930、40 年代上海佛教居士扶乩團體「來蘇社」." *Minsu quyi* 民俗曲藝, no. 162 (2008): 171–215.

Fan Chun-wu 范純武, ed. *Fuluan wenhua yu minzhong zongjiao guoji xueshu yantaohui lunwenji* 扶鸞文化與民眾宗教國際學術研討會論文集. Taipei: Boyang wenhua, 2020.

Gao Wansang 高萬桑 [Vincent Goossaert]. "Jin'gaishan wangluo: Jinxiandai Jiangnan de Quanzhen jushi zuzhi 金蓋山網絡：近現代江南的全真居士組織." In *Quanzhendao yanjiu* 全真道研究, edited by Zhao Weidong 趙衛東, vol. 1, 319–39. Jinan: Qilu shushe, 2011.

Gentz, Joachim. "Religious Diversity in Three Teachings Discourses." In *Religious Diversity in Chinese Thought*, edited by Perry Schmidt-Leukel and Joachim Gentz, 123–40. New York: Palgrave MacMillan, 2013.

Guo Dasong 郭大松. "Ji'nan Daoyuan ji Hongwanzi hui zhi diaocha 濟南道院及紅卍字會之調查." *Shandong wenxian* 山東文獻 19, no. 2 (1993): 52–71.

Giles, Herbert A. *Religions of Ancient China*. London: Archibald Constable & Co, 1905.

Goossaert, Vincent, and David A. Palmer. *The Religious Question in Modern China*. Chicago and London: The University of Chicago Press, 2011.

Goossaert, Vincent. *Livres de morale révélés par les dieux*. Paris: Les Belles Lettres, 2012.

Goossaert, Vincent. "Modern Daoist Eschatology: Spirit-writing and the Rise of Elite Eschatology in Late Imperial China." *Daoism. Religion, History & Society*, no. 6 (2014): 219–46.

Goossaert, Vincent. "Spirit Writing, Canonization and the Rise of Divine Saviours: Wenchang, Lüzu and Guandi, 1700–1858." *Late Imperial China* 36, no. 2 (2015): 88–125.

Goossaert, Vincent. *Making the Gods Speak: The Ritual Production of Revelation in Chinese Religious History*. Cambridge, MA: Harvard University Press, 2022.

Hoskins, Janet. *The Divine Eye and the Diaspora: Vietnamese Syncretism Becomes Transpacific Caodaism*. Honolulu: University of Hawai'i Press, 2015.

Hu Daojing 胡道靜, Chen Yaoting 陳耀庭, Duan Wengui 段文桂, Ling Wanqing 林萬清 et al., eds. *Zangwai daoshu* 藏外道書. Chengdu: Bashu shushe, 1992–1994.

Hu Jiechen 胡劼辰. "*Wendi quanshu* yanjiu: Qingdai Wenchang dijun xinyang de wenxian shi《文帝全書》研究：清代文昌帝君信仰的文獻史." PhD diss., Chinese University of Hong Kong, 2017.

Hu Jiechen 胡劼辰. "Qingdai liuzhong Wendi lei quanshu de chubanshi yanjiu 清代六種文帝類全書的出版史研究." *Zhongyang yanjiuyuan lishi yuyan yanjiusuo jikan* 中央研究院歷史語言研究所集刊 91, no. 2 (2020): 227–92.

Hu Jiechen 胡劼辰. "Qingmo Chuanqian diqu keyi wenben de jiaoshe 清末川黔地區科儀文本的交涉." Talk given at the International Conference on the *Daozang jiyao* and Daoism in the Ming and Qing Dynasty, May 1–2, 2021, Chinese University of Hong Kong.

Huang Ko-wu 黃克武 [Max K.W. Huang]. "Lingxue yu jindai Zhongguo de zhishi zhuanxing: Min chu zhishi fenzi dui kexue, zongjiao yu mixin de zai sikao 靈學與近代中國的知識轉型：民初知識分子對科學、宗教與迷信的再思考." *Sixiangshi* 思想史, no. 2 (2014): 121–96.

Jammes, Jérémy. *Les Oracles du Cao Đài: Étude d'un mouvement religieux vietnamien et de ses réseaux*. Paris: Les Indes savants, 2014.

Jammes, Jeremy, and David A. Palmer. "Occulting the Dao: Daoist Inner Alchemy, French Spiritism, and Vietnamese Colonial Modernity in Caodai Translingual Practice." *Journal of Asian Studies* 77, no. 2 (2018): 405–28.

Jammes, Jeremy, and David A. Palmer. "The *Bible of the Great Cycle of Esotericism*: From the Xiantiandao Tradition to a Cao Đài Scripture in Colonial Vietnam." In Clart, Ownby, and Huang, *Text and Context in the Modern History of Chinese Religions*, 258–308.

Jiang, Yonglin. *The Mandate of Heaven and* The Great Ming Code. Seattle and London: University of Washington Press, 2011.

Jordan, David, and Daniel Overmyer. *The Flying Phoenix: Aspects of Chinese Sectarianism in Taiwan*. Princeton: Princeton University Press, 1986.

Katz, Paul R. "Religion and the State in Post-war Taiwan." *The China Quarterly* 174 (2003): 395–412.

Katz, Paul R. "Spirit-writing Halls and the Development of Local Communities: A Case Study of Puli 埔里 (Nantou 南投 County)." *Minsu quyi* 民俗曲藝, no. 174 (2011): 103–84.

Katz, Paul R. "Spirit-writing and the Dynamics of Elite Religious Life in Republican Era Shanghai." In *Jindai Zhongguo zongjiao de fazhan lunwenji* 近代中國的宗教發展論文集, 275–350. Taipei: Guoshiguan, 2015.

Kim, Jihyun. "Enlightenment on the Spirit-Altar: Eschatology and Restoration of Morality at the King Kwan Shrine in *Fin de siècle* Seoul." *Religions* 11, no. 6 (2020): 1–33.

Kim, Jihyun. "Expansion of Spirit-writing in the Late Chosŏn Korea." Paper presented at the conference *Daozang jiyao* yu Ming Qing Daojiao guoji xueshu yantaohui《道藏輯要》與明清道教國際學術研討會, Chinese University of Hong Kong, May 2, 2021.

Kleeman, Terry. *A God's Own Tale: The Book of Transformations of Wenchang, the Divine Lord of Zitong*. Albany: State University of New York Press, 1994.

Lai Chi-Tim 黎志添. "Qingdai sizhong *Lüzu quanshu* yu Lüzu fuji daotan de guanxi 清代四種《呂祖全書》與呂祖扶乩道壇的關係." *Zhongguo wenzhe yanjiu jikan* 中國文哲研究集刊 42 (2013): 183–230.

Lai Chi-Tim 黎志添. *Daozang jiyao tiyao* 道藏輯要提要. Hong Kong: Chinese University of Hong Kong Press, 2021.

Lai, Chi-Tim. "The Cult of Spirit-Writing in the Qing: The Daoist Dimension." *Journal of Daoist Studies* 8 (2015): 112–33.

Lai Chi-Tim 黎志添, You Zi'an 游子安 and Wu Zhenhe 吳真合. *Xianggang Daojiao: Lishi yuanliu ji qi xiandai zhuanxin* 香港道教：歷史源流及其現代轉型. Hong Kong: Zhonghua shuju, 2010.

Laliberté, André. "The Regulation of Religious Affairs in Taiwan: From State Control to Laisser-faire?" *Journal of Current Chinese Affairs* 38, no. 2 (2009): 53–83.

Liu Ping 劉平. "E zhi hua? Shan zhi guo? Hongwanzi hui toushi 惡之花？善之果？—紅卍字會透視." *Shijie zongjiao wenhua* 世界宗教文化, no. 4 (2012): 39–44.

Liu, Xun. "Of Poems, Gods and Spirit-Writing Altars: The Daoist Beliefs and Practices of Wang Duan, 1793–1839." *Late Imperial China* 36, no. 2 (2015): 23–81.

Lu, Yunfeng. *The Transformation of Yiguan Dao in Taiwan: Adapting to a Changing Religious Economy*. Lanham, MD: Lexington Books, 2008.

Nedostup, Rebecca. *Superstitious Regimes: Religion and the Politics of Chinese Modernity*. Cambridge, MA and London: Harvard University Asia Center, 2009.

Oppenheim, Janet. *The Other World: Spiritualism and Psychical Research in England, 1850–1914*. Cambridge: Cambridge University Press, 1985.

Ownby, David. "Redemptive Societies in the Twentieth Century." In *Modern Chinese Religion*, part II: *1850–2015*, edited by Vincent Goossaert, Jan Kiely, and John Lagerwey, vol. 2, 685–727. Leiden and Boston: Brill, 2016.

Ownby, David. "Li Yujie and the Rebranding of the White Lotus Tradition." *Cross-Currents: East Asian History and Culture Review* 6, no. 2 (2017): 505–29.

Ownby, David. "Sainthood, Science, and Politics: The Life of Li Yujie, Founder of the Tiandijiao." In *Making Saints in Modern China*, edited by David Ownby, Vincent Goossaert, and Ji Zhe, 241–71. New York: Oxford University Press, 2017.

Palmer, David A. "Chinese Redemptive Societies and Salvationist Religion: Historical Phenomenon or Sociological Category?" *Minsu quyi* 民俗曲藝 172 (2011): 21–72

Peng Shaosheng 彭紹升. *Yixing juji* 一行居集. 1825. Unpaginated facsimile reproduction. Reprint, Taipei: Xinwenfeng, 1973.

Shao Yong 邵雍. *Zhongguo huidaomen* 中國會道門. Shanghai: Shanghai renmin chubanshe, 1997.

Sargent, Epes. *Planchette, or, the Despair of Science, Being a Full Account of Modern*

Spiritualism, Its Phenomena, and the Various Theories Regarding It; With a Survey of French Spiritism. Boston: Roberts Brothers, 1869.

Schumann, Matthias. "Redemptive Societies." In *Handbook on Religion in China*, edited by Stephan Feuchtwang, 184–212. Cheltenham: Edward Elgar Publishing, 2020.

Schumann, Matthias. "Science and Spirit-Writing: The Shanghai Lingxuehui 靈學會 and the Changing Fate of Spiritualism in Republican China." In Clart, Ownby, and Wang, *Text and Context in the Modern History of Chinese Religions*, 126–72.

Shiga, Ichiko. "Manifestations of Lüzu in Modern Guangdong and Hong Kong: The Rise and Growth of Spirit-Writing Cults." In *Daoist Identity: History, Lineage, and Ritual*, edited by Livia Kohn and Harold D. Roth, 185–209. Honolulu: University of Hawai'i Press, 2002.

Shiga Ichiko 志賀市子. "Difang Daojiao zhi xingcheng: Guangdong diqu fuluan jieshe yundong zhi xingqi yu yanbian 地方道教之形成：廣東地區扶鸞結社運動之興起與演變 (1838–1953)." *Daoism: Religion, History and Society* 道教研究學報：宗教、歷史與社會, no. 2 (2010): 231–67.

Shiga Ichiko 志賀市子. *Xianggang Daojiao yu fuji xinyang: Lishi yu rentong* 香港道教與扶乩信仰：歷史與認同. Translated by Song Jun 宋軍. Hong Kong: Chinese University Press, 2013.

Smith, Stephen Anthony. "Redemptive Religious Societies and the Communist State, 1949 to the 1980s." In *Maoism at the Grassroots: Everyday Life in China's Era of High Socialism*, edited by Jeremy Brown and Matthew D. Johnson, 340–64. Cambridge, MA and London: Harvard University Press, 2015.

"Spiritualism in the Chinese City, Art by Unseen Hands: Conversations with Confucius and Shakespeare." *The North-China Herald and Supreme Court & Consular Gazette*, June 28, 1924.

Sun Jiang 孫江. "Jishin no shūkyōgaku: Jūku nijūsan nen Kōmanji-kai daihyō-dan no shinsai imon to Ōmoto-kyō 地震の宗教学―――九二三年紅卍字会代表団の震災慰問と大本教." In *Ekkyō suru higashi Ajia no minshū shūkyō: Chūgoku, Taiwan, Honkon, Betonamu soshite Nihon* 越境する近代東アジアの民衆宗教：中国・台湾・香港・ベトナム、そして日本, edited by Takeuchi Fusaji 武內房司, 83–100. Tokyo: Akashi Shoten, 2011.

Sutton, Donald S. "From Credulity to Scorn: Confucians Confront the Spirit Mediums in Late Imperial China." *Late Imperial China* 21, no. 2 (Dec. 2000): 1–39.

Tan, Chee-Beng. *Chinese Religion in Malaysia: Temples and Communities*. Leiden and Boston: Brill, 2018.

Takeuchi Fusaji 武內房司. "Qingmo Sichuan de zongjiao yundong: Fuluan, xuanjiangxing zongjiao jieshe de dansheng 清末四川的宗教運動－扶鸞, 宣講型宗教結社的誕生." In *Ming Qing yilai minjian zongjiao de tansuo* 明清以來民間宗教的探索, edited by Wang Chien-chuan 王見川 and Jiang Zhushan 蔣竹山, 240–65. Taipei: Shangding wenhua chubanshe, 1996.

Valussi, Elena. "Female Alchemy and Paratext: How to Read *nüdan* in a Historical Context." *Asia Major* 21, no. 2 (2008): 153–93.

Valussi, Elena. "Men and Women in He Longxiang's *Nüdan hebian*." *Nan Nü* 10 (2008): 242–78.

Valussi, Elena. "Printing and Religion in the Life of Qing Dynasty Alchemical Author Fu Jinquan." *Daoism: Religion, History, and Society* 道教研究學報：宗教、歷史與社會, no. 4 (2012): 1–52.

Valussi, Elena. "The Transmission of the Cult of Lü Dongbin to Sichuan in the Nineteenth Century, and the Transformation of the Local Religious Milieu." *Daoism: Religion, History, and Society* 道教研究學報：宗教、歷史與社會, no. 7 (2015): 117–69.

Valussi, Elena. "Li Xiyue and the Western School of Daoist Alchemy." Forthcoming.

Verellen, Franciscus. "The Heavenly Master Liturgical Agenda according to Chisong Zi's Petition Manual." *Cahiers d'Extrême-Asie* 14 (2004): 291–343.

Wan, Maggie C.K. "Building an Immortal Land: The Ming Jiajing Emperor's West Park." *Asia Major*, 3rd ser., 22, no. 2 (2009): 65–99.

Wang, Anning. "Gendering the Planchette: Female Writer Qian Xi's (1872–1930) Spiritual World." *The Journal of Chinese Literature and Culture* 4, no. 1 (April 2017): 160–79.

Wang Chien-chuan 王見川. "Qing mo guanshen yu fuji: Jian tan qishi liushi de chenyan 清末官紳與扶乩：兼談其時流行的讖言." In *Mazu yu minjian xinyang: Yanjiu tongxun* 媽祖與民間信仰：研究通訊 (2), edited by Xingang fengtian gong Mazu wenhua yanjiu ji wenxian zhongxin 新港奉天宮媽祖文化研究暨文獻中心, 34–47. Taipei: Boyoung wenhua, 2012.

Wang Chien-chuan 王見川. "Lufei Kui yu 'Shengde tan,' 'Lingxue hui': Jian tan Minchu Shanghai de lingxue fengchao 陸費逵與'盛德壇'、'靈學會'：兼談民初上海的靈學風潮." In *Lishi, yishu yu Taiwan renwen luncong (3): "Renwu" zhuanji* 歷史、藝術與臺灣人文論叢 (3):「人物」專輯, edited by Liu Wenxing 劉文星, Xiao Baifang 蕭百方, and Wang Chien-chuan 王見川, 65–86. Taipei: Boyang wenhua, 2013.

Wang Chien-chuan 王見川. "Cong xinziliao kan jindai Zhongguo de 'fuji yundong' 從新資料看近代中國的「扶乩運動」." *Taipei chengshi keji daxue tongshi xuebao* 臺北城市科技大學通識學報, no. 5 (2016): 151–69.

Wang Chien-chuan 王見川. "You Tong yu wan Ming Qing chu Suzhou de fuji: Jiantan Jin Shengtan fuji de xingzhi 尤侗與晚明清初蘇州的扶乩：兼談金聖叹扶乩的性質." In *Lishi, yishu yu Taiwan renwen luncong* 歷史、藝術 與台灣人文論叢 11, edited by Li Shiwei 李世偉, 233–53. Taipei: Boyang wenhua, 2016.

Wang Chien-chuan 王見川. "Jindai Zhongguo fuji tuanti de cishan yu zhushu: Cong *Yinguang fashi wenchao* tanqi 近代中國扶乩團體的慈善與著書：從《印光法師文鈔》談起." In *Jibian Rujiao: Jinshi Zhongguo de zongjiao rentong* 激辯儒教：近世中國的宗教認同, edited by Cao Xinyu 曹新宇. Special issue *Xin shixue* 新史學 10 (2019): 89–124.

Wang Chien-chuan 王見川. "Song-Ming shiqi de fuji, fuluan yu qing xian: Jian tan 'fuji,' 'enzhu' deng ci de qiyuan 宋—明時期的扶箕、扶鸞與請仙：兼談「扶乩」、「恩主」等詞的起源." In *Fuluan wenhua yu minzhong zongjiao guoji xueshu yantaohui lunwenji* 扶鸞文化與民眾宗教國際學術研討會論文集, edited by Fan Chun-wu 范純武, 53–88. Taipei: Boyang wenhua, 2020.

Wang, Chien-chuan. "Spirit-writing Groups in Modern China (1840–1937): Textual Production, Public Teachings, and Charity." In *Modern Chinese Religion*, part II: *1850–2015*, edited by Vincent Goossaert, Jan Kiely, and John Lagerwey, vol. 2, 651–84. Brill: Leiden, 2016.

Wang, Chien-chuan. "Popular Groups Promoting 'The Religion of Confucius' in the Chinese Southwest and Their Activities since the Nineteenth Century (1840–2013): An Observation Centered on Yunnan's Eryuan County and Environs." In *The Varieties of Confucian Experience: Documenting a Grassroots Revival of Tradition*, edited by Sébastien Billioud, 90–121. Leiden: Brill, 2018.

Xu Dishan 許地山. *Fuji mixin di yanjiu* 扶乩迷信底研究. Changsha: Shangwu yinshuguan, 1941.

Yang, Hung-Jen. "Between Cultural Reproduction and Cultural Translation: A Case Study of Yiguandao in London and Manchester." In *Chinese Religions Going Global*, edited by Nanlai Cao, Giuseppe Giordan, and Fenggang Yang, 157–73. Leiden: Brill, 2020.

Yuria, Mori. "Being Local through Ritual: Quanzhen Appropriation of Zhengyi Liturgy in the *Chongkan Daozang jiyao*." In *Quanzhen Daoists in Chinese Society and Culture, 1500–2010*, edited by Xun Liu and Vincent Goossaert, 171–207. Berkeley: University of California Press, 2013.

Zeitlin, Judith T. "Spirit Writing and Performance in the Work of You Tong 尤侗 (1618–1704)." *T'oung Pao*, 2nd ser., 84, fasc. 1/3 (1998): 102–35.

Zhu Mingchuan 朱明川. "Rutan jingdian ji qi yingyong: Yi Sichuan Jianyou diqu de 'Zixia tan' wei li 儒壇經典及其應用—以四川江油地區的「紫霞壇」為例." *Shanshu jingjuan yu wenxian* 善書、經卷與文獻 1 (2019): 139–165.

Zhu Mingchuan 朱明川. "'Gengzi Chuandong shenjiao chu': Jindai Zhongguo qishi jingdian shengchan moshi de xingcheng 「庚子川東神教出」：近代中國啟示經典生產模式的形成." *Shanshu, jingjuan yu wenxian* 善書、經卷與文獻 3 (2020): 53–74.

PART 1

Overview Papers

CHAPTER 2

Making the Gods Write: A Short History of Spirit-Written Revelations in China, 1000–1400

Vincent Goossaert

In the *jiashen* year of the Jiading reign (1224), our patriarch the transcendent lord Xu manifested himself in Jinling (present-day Nanjing), exposed the teaching of loyalty and filial piety, and converted crowds of people who all joined the correct way.

嘉定甲申之歲，祖師許真君降于金陵，示陳忠孝之教，溥化眾生，咸歸正道。[1]

∴

This sort of record is found in overwhelming numbers in Chinese religious history, particularly as here in a Daoist context but by no means exclusively so. Gods, ancestors, Buddhas, and immortals keep manifesting themselves in the world, events that are described by terms such as *jiang* 降 (lit. descend *or* make descend, but which also translate as "manifesting a divine presence" for reasons explained below), *lin* 臨 (approach), *xia* 下 (come down) ...

What happens when a god manifests itself? How are we to understand statements such as the one translated above? What happened? Did Xu appear in the flesh, did a medium channel him, or did a statue move? How did he expose his teachings? Did he talk, write, or hand out some sort of document? The text fails to reveal this, although we will see that, in this particular case, we can discover this from other sources—what happened was spirit-writing, but highly similar language is used to describe other ways of making gods instruct humanity. This chapter will explore how spirit-writing, considered as one of several modes of the ritual creation of divine presence, came to play a central role in the Chinese production of revelations.[2]

---

[1] *Xishan Xu zhenjun bashiwu hua lu*, preface 跋.
[2] This chapter is a shortened version of chapters 3 and 4 of Goossaert, *Making the Gods Speak*.

1 Introduction

1.1 The Question and the Sources

From a religious perspective, revelations simply happen but, from a scholarly one, they are produced. China has developed, over time, different techniques for producing revelations; even as new techniques emerged, earlier ones continued to be practiced; they thus coexisted in a revelatory ecology. These different techniques served different purposes and allowed for different types of contents. In this ecology, spirit-writing like other ritual techniques, thrived in niches whence it made specific contributions to the religious discourse and practice.

Three main types of sources shed light on revelations: narrative accounts, revealed texts, and ritual documents that prescribe the acts of making gods talk or write; in other words, context, contents, and technique. The narratives of the events are crucial not only to our understanding of what happens during a revelation but also of how Chinese people, not necessarily party to or even sympathetic toward the revelation, received it. Some narratives are attached to the revelations, in the form of prefaces, glosses, or commentaries, but we also have a large number of stories about revelatory events of which nothing else survives. The rich Chinese hagiographical tradition can be endlessly mined for stories about revelations. At a more critical distance, we also possess the equally rich genre of stories and anecdotes (*biji* 筆記). Second, the revelations themselves and their contents offer a very different perspective, focusing less on social dynamics and more on the contents. In ideal circumstances, historians have both the revealed texts themselves and narratives of the revelation, but this is far from being the case in many, if not most, cases. Accordingly, some of the historiography on spirit-writing—which is expertly analyzed in Hu Jiechen's contribution to this volume and so not discussed here—leans in one direction, and some in another. Third, and so far largely neglected by the scholars of spirit-writing, are the liturgical prescriptions: how precisely does one perform it to produce spirit-written texts? My interest in spirit-writing as a ritual technique, and therefore in this last type of source, informs this chapter's analytical framework, which is significantly different from the existing literature.

Much of the scholarship on spirit-writing focuses on the late imperial period, even if at times referring to Song-period Imperial Lord Wenchang 文昌帝君 (henceforth Wenchang) texts and Purple Maiden (Zigu 紫姑) divination. By contrast, I attempt to provide as comprehensive a survey as possible of the first stage of spirit-writing's development, between ca. 1000 and 1400, in order to demonstrate how the specific niche of spirit-writing developed and matured within the larger economy of Chinese religious texts. A second stage developed from the late sixteenth century onward, but this lies outside the scope of the present chapter. Also, I aim to place the production of revelations within the larger array of uses of spirit-writing, but my focus is on revealed texts; it is less a social history of the practice than a religious history of revelations.

1.2 *The Thesis*

What I hope to demonstrate in this chapter is that spirit-writing is one particular ritual technique of creating divine presence that is usually deployed by religious specialists with the same aims as other techniques: requesting blessings, obtaining cures and salvation, asking questions about the future and destiny of the deceased, and learning the intentions of the gods. In a minority of cases, it led to revelations, which I define as discursive teachings of a general nature (concerning the order of the universe and ways to salvation) presented as given by a spirit to one or several living humans. Historically, it was often practiced in conjunction with other ritual techniques, and therefore cannot be studied entirely separately from these since, combined they formed a ritual repertoire. All such techniques required training and initiation. In the case of spirit-writing, I will argue that, during the first phase (the early modern period), the variegated spirit-writing techniques were codified and routinely used by Daoists (primarily the *fashi* 法師 exorcists) and largely associated with them, based on earlier sources (notably spirit-mediums and Tantric techniques).

It is important to keep in mind that this category of Daoists include monastic and temple-dwelling clerics but also at-home married priests, fully embedded in their local society, as well as a large number of people who had been initiated into a Daoist ritual tradition but pursued other professions (officials, merchants, soldiers, teachers, farmers, etc.); the term "Daoist" is not the opposite of "lay" but of "non-initiated." Also, it is unlikely that all of the Daoists in that period used spirit-writing; it was clearly listed as one possible way, among others, to obtain a divine response to one's questions, so some Daoists presumably chose other techniques; the hundreds of references to it in the early modern texts in the Daoist Canon, however, strongly suggest that it was not marginal.

While various kinds of people (such as literati) attempted to exploit the technique for their own purposes, doubtless with varying degrees of success, all of the spirit-written revelations that we possess from the early modern period come from a clear Daoist context. At the same time, these revelations, although substantial and varied, are less abundant than the flood of new spirit-written texts that appeared from the late Ming onward. For this reason, my argument here is *not* that there is a "Daoist aspect" of spirit-writing, as opposed to other aspects, but that the Daoists codified and routinely used it, being widely considered experts in that particular set of techniques and producers of substantial revelations through it. This did not, of course, prevent other people from trying their hand at spirit-writing for various purposes, some of them purely ephemeral.

1.3 *Definitions*

For the purposes of the present paper, I define **revelation** as discursive content that is presented as given by a divine entity (a god, saint, Buddha, immortal, ancestor, etc.) to one or more living humans, that was of general interest as opposed to answering a specific issue raised by one person. Revelations often provide explanations about the origins and functioning of the cosmos, the identity, history, and roles of the gods, the laws that govern human destiny, and how humans may obtain salvation. The standard modern Chinese term for revelation is *qishi* 啟示, but both terms—revelation and *qishi*—are etic categories that encompass many different emic concepts.

Because it distinguishes between contents of general interest as opposed to answers to specific issues, this definition is intimately linked to that of **divination** and, more precisely, inspired divination (as opposed to natural divination, where gods do not intervene), which I define here as an exchange between a human asking a question and a deity providing an answer. For my present purposes, I consider that certain divinatory exchanges can qualify as a revelation (e.g. a person asking how to obtain salvation and a god detailing a program of self-cultivation) while others do not (e.g. a patient asking for the outcome of an illness and a god telling him it will be favorable). The former tend to be destined for publication and dissemination while the latter do not, yet the boundary can be relatively moot. In other words, some revelations are the result of divination, while others are not; conversely, divination can lead to revelation but usually does not.

The same qualification (contents of general interest) explains why not all pronouncements by supernatural entities are revelations. The spirit of a deceased person can manifest itself, through a medium or other means, typically to request sacrifices or help from the living. This is not a revelation. By contrast, when higher gods express themselves, their words typically carry weight and qualify as revelations.

One further category, that lies at the core of the comparative study of revelation, is **prophecy**. I use this term here as a sub-category of revelations—all prophecies are revelations but not all revelations are prophecies. A prophecy predicts future events of concern to the whole empire (including the births, deaths, and successions of emperors, changes of dynasties) or the whole of humanity (major disasters and eschatological events). Typically, prophecies are spontaneous rather than answers to human questions.

Spirit-writing is a Western etic term that encompasses a broad range of Chinese techniques. Various scholars have used various definitions; the broadest ones naturally span a longer time period and include early cases of divinely-inspired writing that the stricter definitions exclude. Notably, written revelations granted by high gods during the late fourth century CE that resulted in the Shangqing 上清 scriptures are sometimes described as early examples of spirit-writing, while other scholars (including myself) insist that they resulted from a different mode of revelation, based on visualization: there was no witness (a single medium received texts, alone in his meditation room, that he then showed to his patrons) and no mention of rituals to induce possession.

Here, I define spirit-writing as any technique where spirits (from high gods to recently deceased humans) are invited through prescribed ritual means (typically involving incantations, *zhou* 咒, and/or talismans, *fu* 符) to possess ("descend," *jiang* 降) either a writing implement (a brush or piece of wood) and/or the person(s) wielding this implement in order to write characters, often in response to questions. An important aspect of the practice is that it is usually collective, with people observing the process and thus serving as witnesses to its reliability. There are instances of solitary practice, however, such as the practice of *bilu* 筆籙 (register with the brush) used by late imperial literati, including during examinations.

Defined in this way, spirit-writing seems to appear in the eleventh and twelfth centuries and thus constitutes one aspect of the religious transformations of early modern China. From there, the practice diffused to other parts of the sinophone world (notably Vietnam, Korea, and Japan), where it interacted with the local traditions of spirit-possession and inspired writing.[3]

2 Revelations through Controlled Possession

There were medieval (third to sixth centuries) modes for creating divine presence, including revelations, that continued to be widely practiced during the

---

3 For an example of how spirit-writing was locally appropriated in Japan, see the contribution by Nikolas Broy in this volume.

early modern period down to the present day, including visualizations, secret encounters with gods, discoveries of texts in caves, and spirit-mediums chanelling the voices of gods. New techniques emerged from the tenth century onward, however, that enlarged the array of possibilities and opened up the way for new types of revelations: the priestly-controlled and -initiated possession, which I do not see in pre-Song sources.

Controlled possession is produced during an event of divine presence (*jiang* 降) made perceptible to an audience by ritual means performed by an initiated, literate person, and typically described and precisely situated in space and time, often with the names of the humans who created the event (such as the priests or, less frequently, the mediums); this type notably includes spirit-writing. It involves possession but is brought under firm control by ordained priests, although gods also maintain their agency alongside that of priests, and can be described as taking the initiative; priests can be relied upon to make a revelation happen. They can be relied upon because they use specific techniques for summoning gods, primarily talismans and invocations.

In modern times, the main ritual specialists for producing controlled-possession revelations are the Daoists, but they hold no monopoly. The techniques for summoning gods to ask them questions through a priest controlling a medium are, to a very significant extent of Tantric (that is, Indian and central Asian) origin. Tantric rites were introduced into China during the Tang period and proved highly successful; among them was the ritual manipulation of mediums (Skt. *āveśa*, Ch. *aweishe* 阿尾奢). Several Tang-period manuals (from around 700 onward) provide detailed instructions and claim that, through these techniques, one could enquire about the future or enlist the gods' assistance; these techniques were still practiced by Buddhist *fashi* traditions during the Song period, and were similar to and in competition with the Daoist equivalents. The *āveśa* techniques obviously inspired the *daofa* 道法 (Ritual techniques of the Dao), who developed them further; Tantric rites seem to be entirely oral or visual in nature, whereas the *daofa* rites entailed mediums writing as well as speaking.[4] Techniques for divining using a bowl of water or mirror, found in the Tang Tantric texts, are also later closely associated with spirit-writing in the *daofa* texts. Both demonstrate close attention to strict priestly control over the medium (this accounts for the vast majority of the liturgical instructions), notably through talismans and incantations; these two ritual techniques for summoning spirits were continuously developed in

---

4 Davis, *Society and the Supernatural*, 123–25; Strickmann, *Chinese Magical Medicine*; Orzech, Sørensen, and Payne, *Esoteric Buddhism and the Tantras in East Asia*.

an interchange between Buddhist and Daoist specialists. Yet, I am unaware of any revelation produced by such Buddhist ritual specialists based on these techniques (by contrast to what many *daofa* did), possibly simply because this topic has never been researched. For this reason, I will not discuss Tantric techniques for producing divine presence any further here.

These techniques, called *fa* 法, or *daofa*, are essentially exorcistic and apotropaic in nature, and involved, in some cases, spirit-possession and the cult of meat-eating; violent, impure deities (some of whom were local gods of demonic origin) who, once they had submitted to the Daoist law, could act as powerful enforcers of this law against malevolent spirits. Some of these traditions developed at the margins of institutional Daoism, in a zone shared with some vernacular Buddhist specialists. Their practitioners were called *fashi* 法師, and at least some *fashi* were not ordained *daoshi* 道士 (ordained Daoists), and were considered as ranking below them.[5] The most important element in the practice of a *daofa* was the knowledge and mastery of talismans (*fu*) used to summon martial gods who exorcise, heal, and generally undertake the work of the *fashi*. The manipulation of violent martial spirits was already part of the early Heavenly Master church (Tianshidao 天師道, founded second century) liturgy, but the *daofa* developed an intense personal bond between the priest and his allied divine warrior.

By explicit contrast to the art of spirit-mediums, early modern *fashi* priests developed a whole array of techniques for producing a perceptible divine presence within a bureaucratic framework using methods that guaranteed authenticity. This they did by several means, the most important of which was triangulation: instead of a dual relationship between god and medium (Possession) or god and Daoist (Visualization), these techniques introduce a triangle: priest 法師—medium (*tongzi* 童子)—god (*shen* 神). The priest validates the revelation (he is qualified to summon gods in the heavenly bureaucracy, and confirm the identity of the god made present and the validity of his revelations) while the medium makes it objective; that is, perceptible to others.

The Daoists have, for two millennia, criticized (in some cases, struggled against) the mediums, developed cooperation with them, and appropriated/reformulated their techniques. In the early modern and contemporary periods, Daoist priests often train and assist mediums. The new *daofa* ritual techniques of the early modern period explicitly employ mediums for controlled possession for exorcistic and therapeutic purposes, as well as to make the dead speak

---

5 Davis, *Society and the Supernatural*; Meulenbeld, *Demonic Warfare*; Sakai Norifumi, "Sōdai dōkyō ni okeru dōhō no kenkyū."

during funerary rituals. These spectacular manifestations of divine presence contributed to the success of the new Daoist ritual traditions.

These techniques revolve around the key term *jiang* 降, here, in a causative sense: to make gods manifest their presence. Whereas *jiang* is employed very frequently in pre-Song texts to describe both the willful manifestation of a god and the act of inviting gods to a sacrifice or offering, it is with the new *daofa* that the priests are said to *jiang* gods in the sense of making them manifest. I call these techniques "perceptible presence" because they affect the senses (hearing, sight, other bodily sensations) rather than only the mind. Being able to create a divine presence that people can witness defines a priest. Indeed, a Yuan-period commentator on the extremely widespread *Beidoujing* 北斗經 (Northern Dipper scripture), revealed in the early Song period, states: "when you have mastered this teaching, you become a master of creating divine presence, and all the spirits will fear you" (得此道後，乃為降靈之師，萬鬼自怖也).[6] The techniques are codified and written down, even though they form priestly knowledge subject to initiation and were not thus readily available to laypersons in the way that the manuals in the Canon are now accessible to us.

Contrary to secret encounters (*ganyu* 感遇) based on the adept's merit, where the immortal takes a human as a disciple, techniques for creating a perceptible presence are based on a more reciprocal bond. *Fashi* priests contract an alliance with martial gods to work together; they swear an oath of alliance (*shizhang* 誓章) that spells out their respective duties.[7] The alliance between the priest and the god is made visible to third parties. In certain spirit-writing traditions, the human practitioners become the disciples (*dizi* 弟子) of the god, but with an equally strong personal and emotional bond.

Last but not least, controlled-possession revelations (including spirit-writing) are entirely open to, and indeed geared toward, witnesses. *Fashi* priests, and modern Daoists in general, regularly practiced visualizations and were perfectly able to produce revelations through this means; if they engaged in controlled-possession rites, it was to create something that visualizations could not: an experience for others.

2.1   *Modes of Perceptible Presence*

The generic terms for referring to the priestly production of a perceptible divine presence are *jiangshen* 降神 and *jiangling* 降靈, that basically work as syn-

---

[6] *Taishang xuanling beidou benming changsheng miaojing*, 3.13b.
[7] Mozina, "Oaths and Curses in Divine Empyrean Practice."

onyms. These terms are often used in a rather Pythic sense, without making the precise mode of presence explicit, but not always. When authors wish to be explicit, they typically use expressions that combine the word *jiang* with the mode of the perceptible presence: sound, readable text, or vision. Frequently, the early modern narratives of revelation show that different modes were used by the same priests to produce the presence of the same gods, sometimes in the same context; that is why we cannot isolate spirit-writing from the other modes.

The first mode is producing divine talk, *jiangyu* 降語 and *jiangyan* 降言. While these may be interchangeable in certain contexts, they tend to refer to different situations: *jiangyu* is usually used to describe the deceased speaking through mediums, while *jiangyan* is usually reserved for pronouncements by higher gods. The term *jiangyan* first appears systematically within a particularly important text in the history of Chinese revelations, the *Yisheng baode zhuan* 翊聖保德傳 (Hagiography of [the Transcendent Lord] Who Assists the Saint and Protects Virtue), dated 1016: this is the earliest (as far as I am aware) systematic record of the oral revelations of a god (in our case, the fierce *daofa* general Black Killer [Heisha 黑殺]), a genre that would later become very popular in the form of the "recorded sayings" (*yulu* 語錄). The text recounts how a Daoist priest, Zhang Shouzhen 張守真 (930–996), could make his divine ally speak and answer questions, and produce teachings on liturgy, self-cultivation, and morality; such teachings would go on to be widely quoted (included in morality books) in later times.

The second mode is divinely-inspired dreams, a very significant vector of religious innovation in early modern times.[8] These would seem at first sight to lie outside the field of the ritually-induced modes of divine presence. However, Daoists could ask the gods questions and expect a response in a dream, which shows that this was considered a procedure that was under some sort of control. Such techniques were also opened up to ordinary people: dreaming temples have been active since the early modern period, where the vision of gods in dreams is arranged through ritual preparations.[9] In Song and Yuan-period liturgies, we find instructions on how to induce such dreams. Dreams and spirit-writing are frequently closely associated. One important early morality book, that later spurred the development of spirit-written texts, and which is closely connected to the new exorcistic liturgies, was revealed in 1171 through

---

8 On dream divination, see Drège and Drettas, "Oniromancie." See also Campany, *The Chinese Dreamscape, 300 BCE–800 CE*.
9 Baptandier, "Entrer en montagne pour y rêver."

a dream: the *Taiwei xianjun gongguoge* 太微仙君功過格 (Ledger of merits and demerits of the Stellar Lord Taiwei).

The third mode is spirit-writing, to which we will shortly turn. Before that, however, we should consider what purpose was served by the *fashi* priests' use of such techniques to produce divine presence.

2.2   *The Need for a Divine Response,* baoying 報應

Because rituals consist of summoning gods, there has to be a way to verify, prove, and sense that gods are present. At the least, a divine presence is verified by divination: priests routinely throw blocks (if the result is negative, then the invitation is performed anew). People expect signs of a presence: typically, it should rain following a Daoist offering ritual. In some cases, however, people expect more obvious proofs and a more immediate experience: in this context, the miracles (*lingyan* 靈驗, including lights, smells, and sounds) are actually expected proofs that the invitation of the gods was properly and effectively performed.

The divine presence must, in some cases, be more specific than signs. Daoist rituals hinge on written communication between priests and gods and no communication can work only one way; indeed, Daoists ceaselessly write in their documents "I have received an edict from the Jade Emperor" (*wu feng Di chi* 吾奉帝敕) or similar phrases. What does this mean exactly? The documents that priests write, present, and send (by burning them) to the gods, the models for which fill thousands of pages in the Daoist canon, are of various kinds. In some, the priest simply makes a request to the gods, normally on behalf of an individual or community, but he also promulgates (*ban* 頒, *gao* 告) divine orders, such as the act of absolving a deceased person's sins (*sheshu* 赦書). In this case, he writes that he "proclaims (the document) having received an order (from the gods mandating him to do so)" (*chenggao fengxing* 承誥奉行). Here, we have a divine document that is physically written and issued by an authorized living person, i.e. a Daoist priest. These are not revelations; they always follow a standard form (nothing new is ever said), yet they show how the Daoist priests are authorized to make the gods write.

There is more: when priests submit their requests to the gods, they often explicitly request a formal response from them; it is based on this formal response that the Daoist may continue with the ritual, including issuing documents in the name of the gods. This act of requesting a formal divine response is expressed in different terms, the most frequent of which are "obtaining a response" (*qu baoying* 取報應) and "obtaining a [divine] edict" (*quzhi* 取旨). Many *daofa* ritual manuals show that this procedure was taken very seriously and the response from the god not taken for granted. Because a formal nomination to a position in the divine bureaucracy constitutes the core of any Daoist ordination or salvation rite and is therefore crucial, the whole process of securing a heavenly edict is sacralized.

How was this achieved? One description of how "obtaining a (divine) edict" happens in practice is entirely based on visualization techniques.[10] In another document about requesting a nomination edict during an ordination, the priest writes that he and his disciple have already received an initial positive response in a dream, and now request a formal document.[11] Some of the *daofa* traditions needed some form of divine response to the priestly request, including written instructions, that were more compelling than visualizations. A fascinating case is the ash-table (*huitan* 灰壇) techniques, which are mentioned in a number of *daofa* manuals belonging to different traditions, showing that they were relatively widespread. We have one explicit description of the procedure, entitled *Huitan xianji baoying mifa* 灰壇現跡報應祕法 (Secret liturgy for obtaining a response through manifested traces on the ash-table).[12] The text is undated but included in a late Yuan compendium. It describes how the priest sets a table covered with ash before the stove with a seat for the Big Dipper, then goes outside, invites the stars of the Big Dipper as well as Black Killer, visualizes them as they descend (*jiang*), chants incantations, utters his questions, and then goes to examine the traces left in the ash. These traces follow various patterns which the manual provides and deciphers. One tantalizing aspect of this method is that it uses an ash-table which also later became (along with the sand-table) an essential implement for spirit-writing.

In the same context, there also existed a ritual technique that fully fits our definition of spirit-writing, used to obtain divine answers to ritual petitions, called *pijiang* 批降 (obtaining a god-written response on a document submitted to him) or its synonyms *pibao* 批報 and *pishi* 批示. These terms appear frequently in Song-Yuan-Ming ritual texts as well as narrative sources, and we also have a full-fledged liturgy for performing the technique.[13] In this description, a medium (*tongzi*) is manipulated by the priest who summons a divine general to descend into the medium's hand and write. The term *pi* is also found in narrative sources to qualify the action of the god answering a question through spirit-writing.[14] Further cases include *fengbi* 封臂, *jiebi* 借臂 or *fubi*

---

10   *Shangqing Lingbao dafa*, 44.1a–2b.
11   "Zou quzhi baoying," in *Gaoshang shenxiao yuqing zhenwang zishu dafa*, 12.9b–10a.
12   *Fahai yizhu*, 42.18a–23a.
13   Ibid., 37.4b–5a.
14   See, for example, a twelfth-century story from northern China: "Huang zhenren 黃真人," in *Xu Yijian zhi*, 34.

附臂 (consecrating/borrowing/possessing the arm [of a medium]): the *fashi* priest causes the arm of the medium to be possessed by a god who can then write down his orders and responses.[15]

Another similar ritual method is simply called *jiangbi* (the most common term for spirit-writing) or "moving the brush," *yunbi* 運筆; this makes it possible to obtain the response of a thunder general (the fierce gods at the core of the thunder rites, a major category of *daofa*) in the process of healing people through inducing possession.[16] When the medium's hand grows hot, then the god is present and can write. The term *yunbi* is very telling; in the Daoist canonical sources, this usually refers to writing talismans (*fu*). This is not the only term that, in different contexts, can mean either "writing a talisman" or spirit-writing: this is also the case for *huabi* 化筆 or *shenbi* 神筆. Indeed, these two ritual techniques share important aspects in common: the consecration of the writing implement and the descent of the god into it.[17] It is likely that the experience of writing talismans inspired the Daoists who developed spirit-writing techniques.

As a result, priests in need of a divine response had a large array of techniques at their disposal that, in addition to visualization, covered most of the gamut of the controlled-possession techniques. Daoists who codified the liturgies of the *daofa* saw them as complementary, rather than exclusive. Consider, for instance, the following passage from the same manual that describes the ash-table technique:

> If you want to practice that ritual, you have three ways of obtaining a divine response: obtaining a god-written response on a document submitted to him (*pibao*), obtaining a response in a dream, and obtaining a response on the ash table.
>
> 凡行持此法，報應有三，批報、附夢報、灰壇報。[18]

The intimate connection between spirit-writing, obtaining a divine response during the ritual (*baoying*), and the *daofa* exorcistic traditions is further docu-

---

15   See, notably, descriptions in *Daofa huiyuan*, 151.6a and 255.12b–13a; and *Fahai yizhu*, 37.8b–9a.
16   "Taiyi huoxi leifu Zhu jiangjun kaofu dafa 太一火犀雷府朱將軍考附大法," in *Daofa huiyuan*, 227.25b–26a.
17   *Lingbao yujian*, 16.19a describes how the priest causes the divine *qi* to descend into the brush (*jiang bi zhong* 降筆中).
18   *Fahai yizhu*, 42.14b.

mented by yet another liturgical manual in the canon: *Deng tianjun xuanling bamen baoying neizhi* 鄧天君玄靈八門報應內旨 (Inner instructions on obtaining a divine response through the eight gates of the dark spirits, [revealed by] Heavenly Lord Deng). This undated document was probably composed during the late Song or Yuan periods. It describes itself in the first sentence as having been revealed by the heavenly lord through spirit-writing (*jiangbi*)[19] before detailing a rather complex set of divinatory methods for priests that includes visualizations and computations of times and directions. The priest actualizes Deng (a fierce thunder god) and ascends to heaven with him to question the gods and obtain a response, in the context of curing patients; the responses take the form of various signs and visions to be interpreted.

3   The Variety of Spirit-Writing in the Early Modern Period (Tenth–Fourteenth Centuries)

We have seen how, by the early modern period, the Daoist priests, especially practitioners of the new *daofa*, were using spirit-writing as one of the ritual techniques at their disposal to produce divine presence, particularly a divine response to their requests made during the course of rituals. I now wish to place this practice within the larger field of spirit-written practices during that period. In this section, we will examine all of the evidence on the various forms of spirit-writing dating from the Song and Yuan periods, in order to determine its contours and logic; some of these sources are poorly dated, so we will proceed analytically before attempting to sketch a historical development in the conclusion. This section will examine the practice of spirit-writing (who, where, why, how?) while the next will focus on the revelations themselves and their contents.

The first factor to note is the considerable variety of terms and techniques. Terms that can be translated by spirit-writing, according to our definition, include: "making a god present in a brush" (*jiangbi* 降筆); "wielding the sieve" (*fuji* 扶箕), "sieve-brush" (*jibi* 箕筆); "wielding the phoenix" (*fuluan* 扶鸞); "making the phoenix fly" (*feiluan* 飛鸞); "the phoenix brush" (*luanbi* 鸞筆); "summoning immortals" (*zhaoxian* 召仙): "inviting immortals" (*qingxian* 請仙); "welcoming the Purple Maiden" (*ying Zigu* 迎紫姑); "making immortals manifest themselves" (*jiangxian* 降仙); "consecrating an arm" (*fengbi* 封臂); "obtaining a god-written response on a document submitted to him" (*pijiang*

---

19   *Deng tianjun xuanling bamen baoying neizhi*, 1a.

批降); "a phoenix-sieve" (*luanji* 鸞箕); "a brush register" (*bilu* 筆籙); and further combinations of these terms. The most common word in modern usage, *fuji* 扶乩, only appears in the late Ming period and is characteristic of the second stage of the historical development of spirit-writing. I will, therefore, exclude it here.

The abundant vocabulary describing spirit-writing clearly shows that it was not a monolithic tradition, but something that was constantly adopted, adapted, and elaborated by various parties to fulfil various aims. Some of these terms refer to the specific implement employed: the sieve or winnow basket, *ji*; the phoenix, *luan*, a wooden iconic instrument; or simply the brush. Others refer to the divine entities being made present, while yet others refer to the human action, such as inviting the gods, or writing. Many of these terms refer to specific traditions of spirit-writing, but are often not water-tight; in many instances, different terms are used in a single source and thus appear interchangeable. *Jiangbi* seems, until the Ming period, to be the most general, encompassing term as well as the most common.

To what extent these various spirit-writing practices interacted or were independent traditions is unclear under the present state of research. They seem to have served different functions, even though there may have existed important overlaps. The flying phoenix produced scriptures, while the *fengbi*, *pijiang*, and similar techniques largely served the need for judicial paperwork in the course of conducting exorcistic judgments and ordinations, and the Purple Maiden technique was apparently closest to divination, i.e. asking the gods specific questions about one's life.

Hsieh Tsung-hui 謝聰輝 has argued for a strict distinction between the *feiluan* (focusing on revelations by Wenchang) and the *fuji* (wielding the sieve) traditions: he proposes that the latter is popular and essentially aimed at divination, while the former is elite and entirely integrated into the cult of the Jade Emperor; *feiluan* practitioners see themselves as ministers of the Heavenly bureaucracy and transmitters, through *feiluan* revelations, of the edicts and orders of the Jade Emperor.[20] While his analysis has radically refreshed our understanding of spirit-writing, I wish to refine and nuance it further; other high gods apart from Wenchang also revealed scriptures yet without using the *luan* vocabulary. Terms were often recombined by authors; a late-Yuan story discusses "suspended sieve, wielding the phoenix, and summoning immortals" (懸箕扶鸞召仙) apparently not as different practices but as a single one.[21]

---

20   Hsieh, *Xin tiandi zhi ming*, 105–12.
21   "Jixian yongshi 箕仙詠史," in *Nancun chuogenglu*, *juan* 20, 245–46; this provides the full text of a long spirit-written poem recounting the whole history of China.

My own approach is to view the various forms of spirit-writing as part of the even more varied array of *daofa* priests' techniques to invite gods to intervene in human affairs; these priests are all, by definition, heavenly officials and evince a strong bureaucratic ethos. From that perspective, *feiluan* is merely one of the forms of a larger phenomenon in continuity with divination and ritual paperwork.

3.1   *Contexts and Purposes*
3.1.1   The Zigu Cult

Most scholars who have discussed the origins of spirit-writing trace it to the cult of the Purple Maiden, Zigu, or Goddess of the Privy.[22] As this issue is discussed in Hu Jiechen's chapter, I will not dwell on it here. In short, the Zigu cult was originally a divination technique implying possession. By the eleventh century, it has been developed into a way of writing more developed texts, using a sieve manipulated by children or mediums (*tongzi* meaning either). These are among the earliest references to spirit-written texts, but we only have a few poems of this nature included in stories and notes written by literati. Scholars, starting from Xu Dishan 許地山, have relied on the few existing records of this particular practice to argue that spirit-writing was, from its origins, largely a lay practice that people usually engaged in playfully, to exchange poetry with the deceased or imaginary friends, such as young, talented female ghosts. While such a practice existed, it concerns only a very small proportion of the evidence about early modern spirit-writing, which is largely about divining serious business issues or instructing humans in religious techniques. Su Shi 蘇軾 (Dongpo 東坡, 1037–1101) recounts a séance with the sieve that took place in 1094 in the room of a Daoist master with a lofty title—suggesting that this was a technique used by the Daoists: "a divine being descended into his room, saying she was a female transcendent" (有神仙降於其室, 自言女仙也); she wrote highbrow mystical poetry which Su judged to be incomparable with Zigu's vulgar utterances.[23] Indeed, many records about spirit-writing, and indeed producing a divine presence in general, take pains to caution against playfulness lest it be interpreted as disrespect to the gods, as well as the dangers of inviting gods and spirits into unclean spaces or circumstances.[24] The Daoist literature is replete with cautionary stories about how easy it is to summon gods (includ-

---

22   Xu, *Fuji mixin de yanjiu*; Boltz, "On the Legacy of Zigu"; Wang, "Song-Ming shiqi."
23   *Dongpo zhilin*, 3/96.
24   "Xi'an Zigu 西安紫姑," in *Yijian zhi, zhijing* 支景, *juan* 6, 928–29 where a participant during a spirit-writing session is punished by the god for having brought in a prostitute.

ing for spirit-writing) but that doing so without good reason may anger them, and an angry thunder god is a very scary prospect.

There can be little doubt, as some anecdotal stories show and Hu Jiechen argues in his chapter, that spirit-writing was engaged in playfully by persons who were not qualified, ordained specialists. The fact that stories and essays denounce such playfulness proves its existence. I find, however, that the early modern references to spirit-writing in a ritual context under the control of a priest are far more numerous than stories about literati engaging with spirits out of curiosity. More importantly, as I focus on revelations in this essay, I should point out that all of the spirit-written texts that we possess for the early modern period emanate from a very explicit Daoist priestly context.

3.1.2   Divination

Most of the records mentioning Zigu (either the deity herself or the practice of "inviting Zigu") concern divination, and we have many more instances of spirit-writing using either a sieve or other implements to question gods and spirits about future events and the fate of the dead. Anecdotal records document how spirit-writing was, at an early stage, used as an *ad hoc* technique for divination purposes; the literati anguished about their personal fate or examinations results, or generals and officers seeking to divine the outcome of battles, resorted to spirit-writing experts—apparently some officials had such an expert on their staff. A very telling example is provided by a story included in a late Song compilation about the cult of the god of Lushan 廬山 (northern Jiangxi 江西). The story tells of a revolt that was staged in 1206 by a military officer in Sichuan 四川. The Song general fighting him had among his retinue a man who was "good at making all sorts of gods manifest their presence" (*shan jiang zhushen* 善降諸神); he performed spirit-writing (*jibi* 箕筆) and received a message from the god of Lushan stating that Shangdi would execute the rebel, but that this divine decision should be kept secret for three months.[25] The secret nature of divine revelations concerning state affairs echoes similar remarks found in the oral revelations of Black Killer as well as stories about Zhenwu 真武, such as that concerning a travelling official who first sees Zhenwu appear and then talk (*jiangyan* 降言), then enjoins him to keep the information secret and for the emperor's ear only.[26] This sets us in a very different world from the playful poetry exchanged through the sieve between literati and their deceased friends.

---

25   "Kaixi zhu ni Xi shi 開禧誅逆曦事," in *Lushan Taiping xingguogong Caifang zhenjun shishi*, 7.12b–14a; also 3.15a.
26   "Zhenhe xingfu 鎮河興福," in *Xuantian shangdi qishenglu*, 6.6b–7b.

However, spirit-writing also developed into more permanent, institutionalized ways of asking the gods questions. We have seen how priests deployed spirit-writing along with other techniques as a way of routinely communicating with the gods during rituals. They also devised ways to provide such access to laypeople. From the Song period onward, people could question their favorite personal god through oracles (*lingqian* 靈籤).[27] The connection between oracles and spirit-writing is extremely intimate. Of the eight sets of oracles within the Daoist Canon, all dated from the Southern Song, Yuan, or early Ming periods, almost all are from deities known to practice spirit-writing: Zhenwu, Wenchang, and the Xu brothers. Furthermore (as is frequently the case in later times), at least one set presents itself as having been explicitly revealed through spirit-writing: the undated *Sisheng zhenjun lingqian* 四聖真君靈籤 (Oracles of the Four Saints Transcendent Lords) begins with "sagely words to admonish the world [revealed by] manifested divine presence" (降靈勸世格言), a spirit-written moral tract that provides a framework for the contents of the 49 oracles. Wenchang's oracles are preceded by a preface that was spirit-written by himself, in which he explains that he used to answer questions from his devotees through dreams but, because of the demand at his temples, he has composed this set of oracles.[28] A southern Song scholar also speaks approvingly of another set of oracles revealed through *jibi* 箕筆.[29]

3.1.3   Ritual Contexts

Like all ritual services, spirit-writing could be offered at temples, in the home of patrons who requested the service from a specialist as part of a private or family ritual, or during communal rituals in public spaces; we possess early modern narrative accounts for all three contexts. The third case is important because it shows how spirit-writing was articulated with other ritual techniques for producing divine presence. We have already seen that the techniques were largely employed, among other ways of creating divine presence, by priests in the course of their communications with the gods. Such communications were not necessarily public and performed for audiences. There were, however, other occasions, notably toward the end of a communal celebration, especially *jiao* 醮 offerings, when all of the gods were invited.

Revelations during a *jiao* are not limited to explicit spirit-writing cases; oral revelations were also frequent, such as the several cases in the *Yisheng baode zhuan*. We also have the fascinating case of a short scripture revealed

---

27   Kalinowski, "La littérature divinatoire dans le Daozang."
28   *Xuanzhen lingying baoqian.*
29   Liu Kezhuang 劉克莊 (1187–1269), "Ba Cijiqian 跋慈濟籤," in *Quan Songwen*, 330.61.

in northern China in 1143, the *Taishang yuhua dongzhang bawang dushi shengxian miaojing* 太上玉華洞章拔亡度世昇仙妙經 (Marvelous scripture of the cavern-stanzas of the jade flower of the Supreme [Lord] for saving souls from hell, saving the world, and ascension to heaven), a scripture for saving humans through morality and alchemy. Appended to the scripture is a detailed narrative of the revelations: a young shepherd boy became a medium and healer; the Daoists of the local monastery invited him to reveal the scripture at three successive *jiao*, during which they received the document written on silk, which they then had printed and disseminated. Here, we have a controlled-possession revelation and it is likely that the Daoists acted as *fashi*, controlling the young medium, even though it remains unclear whether the medium boy was writing or speaking.[30]

One late Yuan description of a ritual performed in a Hangzhou temple in 1356, praying for rain, relates how the god, once present, started to spirit-write (*jiangbi*) about himself.[31] Another Mongol-period story relates how a man who had grown rich during the early years of the Yuan met the Zhang Heavenly Master in Nanjing and asked him to perform a *jiao* offering and practice spirit-writing (*zhao shen jiangbi* 召神降筆) during the ritual in order to enquire about his destiny. The pontiff obliged and set up a suspended phoenix (*xuan luanbi* 縣鸞筆), which then writes a message predicting imminent disaster for the patron.[32]

3.1.4 Divinization and Self-Divinization

Revelation techniques have been used to process divinization and promote living and deceased adepts since medieval times: dialogues between Yang Xi 楊羲 (330–386) or other Shangqing practitioners and the transcendents during visualization séances often dealt with such issues. In the early modern period, both visualizations and controlled-possession techniques were used to produce divine appointments, often with a formal nomination edict issued by the heavenly authorities. Confirming the divine status of their deceased masters and predecessors was a key concern of all of the *daofa* traditions. Self-divinization was also a central goal of all of the spirit-writing groups, and continues to be so to the present day.[33] Naturally, *fashi* and *daoshi* were already living gods, having through ordination obtained a rank in the divine bureau-

---

30 "Xu chuanshou jing shi 敘傳授經事," appendix to *Taishang yuhua dongzhang bawang dushi shengxian miaojing*.
31 "Lidi 厲狄," in *Nancun chuogenglu*, juan 27, 342.
32 *Yinju tongyi*, 30.13a. *Xian* 縣 is a common substitute for *xuan* 懸, "suspended."
33 On self-divinization, see Goossaert, *Bureaucratie et salut*.

cracy. The leaders of the spirit-writing altars (which were like all altars, *tan*, the institution in the name of which a *fashi* priest performed rituals, and could affiliate acolytes and sometimes lay disciples) were referred to in texts by such divine titles: for instance, Liu Ansheng 劉安勝 (late twelfth century) produced many early Wenchang revelations and is called, for instance, the Transcendent assistant of the immortals in the Phoenix bureau (鸞府侍仙眞人).[34]

Through spirit-writing, high gods could confirm the canonization in the Thunder ministries of apotheosized *fashi*, and the latter could also communicate directly with their disciples and continuators. An early example of such a phenomenon is provided by the figure of Ning Benli 寧本立 (1101–1181), a major codifier of the Lingbao dafa 靈寶大法 tradition (one of the most influential *daofa* traditions); at one point punished by the gods for having disrespected ritual procedures (he goes blind), he nonetheless undergoes posthumous apotheosis, as confirmed by spirit-writing.[35]

Another case is Lei Shizhong 雷時中 (Mo'an 默庵, 1221–1295), a central figure in another *daofa* ritual tradition, the Hunyuan teachings 混元教. Lei's personal Thunder deity was Lord Xin 辛天君.[36] His hagiography concludes:

> After his death, the Thunderclap god (Xin) produced several spirit-written revelations, saying "Shangdi (Heaven) has promoted Transcendent (Lei) to the function of Minister of the Arcane Capital, and to the title of Transcendent Lord saving the whole of humanity, from the Hunyuan mystic tradition, and Heavenly Worthy spreading the teaching of the Noisy Thunder."

> 後雷霆累降筆云：上帝已陛真人為玄都上相、混元妙道普濟真君、雷聲演教天尊。[37]

These spirit-written teachings from Lord Xin are documented. Lei's commentary on the *Durenjing* 度人經 (Scripture of the salvation of humanity) includes a spirit-written exhortation, dated 1290, in which Xin admonishes the priests under his authority to be morally upright and serve humanity, promiseing them

---

34   *Gaoshang dadong Wenchang silu ziyang baolu*, 1.2b.
35   "Zanhua xiansheng Ning zhenren shishi 贊化先生寧真人事實," in *Daofa huiyuan*, 244.3a–8a.
36   On Lei Mo'an's hagiography, see Goossaert, *Vies des saints exorcistes*, 189–85.
37   *Lishi zhenxian tidao tongjian xubian*, 5.11b–14a.

a career in the divine bureaucracy.[38] This revelation shows how a discourse on morality and divinization formed part of the spirit-written exhortations from Thunder gods to their priests, as well as lay devotees: Xin's exhortation addresses first his descendants in the *daofa* (lineage), *fazi* 法子, then the lay adepts, *xinshi* 信士.[39] It is characterized by the god speaking in the first person ("I adjure you ...") and directly addressing his adepts, describing his own divine career as an example to follow, and promising help and eventual divinization. This text ends with a question raised by a priest (regarding the ordination ranks) and Lord Xin's response (*pi* 批) to it.

One of Lei's disciples, Xue Jizhao 薛季昭 (fl. 1303), relates, in his own commentary on the *Durenjing*, how he himself received revelations from both Lord Xin and the divinized Lei Mo'an, some through spirit-writing and some in dreams, also confirming their divine apotheosis.[40] Another member of Lei's lineage and ritual tradition, named Zhang Tianquan 張天全 (1275–?), is described in a late Yuan anecdote as extraordinarily adept at causing gods to manifest themselves in this world, either through spoken words or phrases written in ink (託諸言語筆墨以顯於世). He caused a Heavenly lord (a thunder marshal) to write in the house of a Mongol official in such sublime calligraphy that they had it printed.[41]

Besides confirming the divine apotheosis of priests, spirit-writing also played, from its earliest stages, an important role in the invention and identification of new local gods. Spirit-written revelations frequently involve the god introducing him or herself and providing an autobiography—the *Zitong dijun huashu* 梓潼帝君化書 (Book of transformations of the Imperial Lord of Zitong) is the most exalted form of this type of revelation, which was already proliferating in more modest forms throughout the Song empire. In his great geographical encyclopedia, Wang Xiangzhi 王象之 (*jinshi* 1196) provides a telling example when discussing a local cult (a hero who lived in the tenth century) located in modern-day Sichuan. Wang found a stele inscription, where the god told of his own life through *jiangbi*; he comments: "In general, vernacular ritual specialists in Sichuan often make up stories through spirit-writing or dreams so as to give divine authority to their inventions" (大抵蜀之巫師多假降筆及

---

38 On the revelations of Lord Xin and his various *daofa* traditions, see Xu, "Xin tianjun fa yu Hunyuan daofa de gouzao."
39 *Duren shangpin miaojing tongyi*, 4.28a–30b.
40 *Yuanshi wuliang duren shangpin miaojing zhujie*, "houxu 後序."
41 "Ti Zhang Tianquan suoke tianjun jiangbi hou 題張天全所刻天君降筆後," in *Yunyangji*, 10.5a–b.

夢想以神其事耳).[42] Spirit-written confirmations of gods' integration within the divine bureaucracy were particularly useful and welcome when these gods had contentious identities; for instance, in the story of the Wuxian 五顯 (the orthodox titles of the notorious Wutong 五通) related in a local gazetteer and followed by the note: "spirit-written" (降筆之文也).[43] The spirit-written nomination edicts for a living adept or a spirit were brief, relatively formulaic texts, certainly, but they were frequently produced (this happened everytime someone living or dead received an ordination in the *daofa* traditions, an extremely common situation); in some cases, they could be the occasion for a longer, more substantial revelation, such as a god offering his biography or a divinized master providing instructions to his living disciples.

The revelation of divine titles for gods granted by the Jade Emperor (*yufeng* 玉封) and revealed through spirit-writing (sometimes with a full edict) became extremely common in late imperial times. We will see it already being criticized by the Daoist codifier, Lü Yuansu 呂元素, in the thirteenth century (see below).

One story in Hong Mai 洪邁's (1123–1202) *Yijian zhi* 夷堅志 (Record of the listener) encapsulates nicely these different facets of spirit-writing. It relates how Chen Wenshu 陳文叔, a young scholar who was studying for the examinations, learned the spirit-writing technique (*ying zhi jishen* 迎致箕神) from someone in his home county (the one date given in the story is 1178).[44] He proved extraordinarily gifted, producing remarkable poems. The god who was writing through him revealed his identity as a transcendent, Penglai zixia zhenren 蓬萊紫霞真人, and performed miracles, so that people started to organize *jiao* offerings in his honor. He excelled at exorcisms and cures, and wrote petitions to the higher gods on special paper. Then, one day, he possessed (*ping* 憑) someone who said (thus through oral possession, not spirit-writing) that he had manifested himself among humans as an exiled immortal but had now completed his time, was returning to Heaven and would no longer manifest himself. So here we have a spirit-writing performer who starts providing divination services; as the cult expanded, the god became integrated into the Daoist pantheons and the performer came to serve as an exorcist.

3.2   *The Performers*

Contrary to the idea sometimes found in the secondary literature that this was a "popular" practice engaged in, more or less playfully, by pretty much anyone

---

42   *Yudi jisheng*, 175.9b.
43   *Shuzhong guangji*, 79.11b. On the history of the Wutong cult, including its more or less sanitized forms, see von Glahn, *The Sinister Way*, chap. 4–5.
44   "Penglai zixia zhenren 蓬萊紫霞真人," in *Yijian zhi*, *sanzhi* 三志, xin 辛, *juan* 10, 1463.

who cared to, the vast majority of narrative accounts mention that it was done by an expert (*fangshi* 方士, *shushi* 術士). Even Xu Dishan, who ignored the Daoist material in his survey of spirit-writing, noticed the role of ritual specialists.[45]

In many narrative accounts, the performer is not mentioned, only the host (typically, the family in which the performance is taking place or the organizer of the communal ritual). This does not necessarily mean that there was no specialized performer involved—indeed, *biji* accounts, for reasons of narrative efficacy, often fail to mention ritual roles and foreground the god and the human hero of the story (who may be a passive participant in the ritual/performance). Narratives of possession rarely mention that the spirit or god is speaking through a medium but this is obvious to the readers. Some narratives of spirit-writing explicitly state that the hand doing the writing belonged to someone who was unprepared for this—and, even then, we do not know whether there was a priest staging the performance or not. Some stories about literati engaging in the practice to request poems or divine examination results tend to suggest they were wielding the sieve themselves; Zhou Mi 周密 (1232–1308) collected several, which he introduced by saying that people think that those who wield the sieve are simply frauds, or merely remember poems, but he insists that the technique is real.[46] The fact that certain scholars could perform it, however, does not necessarily mean that anyone could and that it was a ritual technique for which one did not require training.

Many stories reveal that both Daoist priests and mediums were involved; I disagree on this point with Hsieh Tsung-hui's otherwise remarkable study of the Wenchang spirit-writing cults when he claims that most mediums were not (identified as) Daoists.[47] In a story set in 1157, a court official who had received a high-level Daoist ordination visited Huagai mountain 華蓋山 (central Jiangxi) to pray to the local saints. The temple's medium was suddenly possessed by them; he first spoke strangely then requested paper and ink and wrote a poem and a postface stating that immortals would come and visit him. The official proposed to build a Yuanguang ting 圓光亭, that is, a pavilion to practice "perfect light" mediumistic divination;[48] he has a Daoist priest from the temple ask

---

45   Xu, *Fuji mixin de yanjiu*, 29.
46   "Jiangxian 降仙," in *Qidong yeyu*, 16. 14b–17a. Zhou describes relatives and other scholars wielding the sieve (*pengji* 捧箕).
47   Hsieh, *Xin tiandi zhi ming*, 124–32.
48   This divination method is well-documented as early as medieval times: it involves a mirror or water basin, on which the priest makes incantations, and a boy medium who then looks at it and sees things.

the immortal whether he agrees and requests a response (*baoying*); they obtain a "decree from the immortal" (*xianzhi* 仙旨), which is a spirit-written answer, asking him also to build a pavilion for talismanic healing. When both pavilions had been built, the medium was again possessed in order to provide the immortal's answer (*baoying*).[49]

We possess stories of literati who wish to engage in spirit-writing and seek a qualified Daoist priest for this purpose.[50] Other stories focus on these priests. One Yuan story tells of a Hangzhou priest, Ying Zhongfu 應中甫, who had mastered the spirit-writing ritual (請仙降筆法). He could not afford to buy sacrificial offerings for his divine generals, but managed to borrow some from the immortals who made themselves present to him through spirit-writing (*jiangbi, jiangxian*).[51]

The performer need not be a professional, full-time priest, but he certainly needs an initiation, often resulting in a Daoist identity. This initiation is necessary in order to master the summoning ritual techniques (talismans, incantations, etc.); I have not seen any indication of an initiation for spirit-writing specifically, showing that it was learned alongside other rites. Moreover, regular intimate co-presence with gods requires one to become a god oneself. This is clearly explained in an anecdote related by Hong Mai. The story, set in 1135, concerns a local official and his friend, who "knows how to psalmody and performs the instructions to invite the great immortals" (能誦訣邀大仙) using a sieve. The official engages in an intense relationship with the spirit (a recently deceased literatus) through his friend. The spirit then tells him that he has Daoist bones and will become an immortal; he instructs him to set up a clean, sealed off room for practicing and to create a sieve with a brush that should be suspended from the rafter, promising that he will come and write answers to all questions. The official does as instructed but, once he is ready, his friend has gone, he has not memorized the ritual instructions for inviting the spirits (*qingjue* 請訣), and the latter never returns.[52] What we read about here is an official who invites an initiated specialist to perform spirit-writing for his family and friends and becomes engrossed in the experience, fancies himself a Daoist, and wishes to practice himself but fails.

Therefore, the most common situation for spirit-writing in Song and Yuan China was for an initiated Daoist to take charge of the process; in some cases,

---

49 "Zhenxian jiangfu tongzi 真仙降附童子," in *Huagaishan Fuqiu Wang Guo san zhenjun shishi*, 5.13a–14a.
50 "Jixian youyan 箕仙有驗," in *Nancun chuogenglu, juan* 26, 328.
51 *Shanju xinhua*, 1.8a.
52 "Xu Nanling qing daxian 徐南陵請大仙," in *Yijian zhi*, zhiyi 支乙, *juan* 8, 855–56.

the priest caused the possession of a medium who wrote (and/or spoke), and in others he wrote himself. In all cases, I call this controlled possession: the control is effected by the status of the priest and the very detailed ritual procedures he follows. The modalities of control evolved in later times (it became more commonly group control in the post-Ming period), but the principle remained. Interpretations of spirit-writing as a secularized way of communicating with gods and dispensing with clerical mediation are quite off the mark.

3.3 The Gods

The spirits who were invited through spirit-writing can be broadly divided into two categories; the deceased and the high gods. The former are questioned about the fate of deceased family members or future events, and write poetry. No substantial text of this type has been preserved. The latter account for revelations, properly speaking. Let us now examine these high gods who communicated on a regular basis with living humans.

3.3.1 Zhenwu and Other Exorcists

We cannot but note how a large part of the gods associated with spirit-writing during the early modern period are those of the *daofa* traditions, notably their fierce thunder generals. We have already encountered two of them, Deng and Xin, and will meet the Transcendent Lord Xu below. Tianyou 天猷, the tantric deity closely associated with Black Killer and Zhenwu, is also present in the spirit-written revelations.[53] Probably the most frequently mentioned and most prominent of these martial gods bent on manifesting their divine presence in words is Zhenwu (aka Xuantian Shangdi 玄天上帝), one of the highest-ranking deities of the *daofa* traditions beginning with Tianxin zhengfa 天心正法.[54]

The corpus of texts related to Zhenwu in the Daoist canon is the largest of all the deities; it includes a large number of scriptures, liturgies, and hagiographies. References to manifestations of his divine presence abound and are particularly detailed in two important works: the commentary by Chen Zhong 陳 伀 (fl. 1236) on one of his scriptures (*Taishang shuo Xuantian dasheng Zhenwu benzhuan shenzhou miaojing* 太上說玄天大聖真武本傳神呪妙經, "Marvelous

---

[53] Tianyou is the author of prefaces to the spirit-written *Yuhuangjing*, on which more below: Hsieh, *Xin tiandi zhi ming*, 127.

[54] On the emergence of the Zhenwu cult, see Chao, *Daoist Ritual*; De Bruyn, *Le Wudang shan*; and Wang, "Zhenwu xinyang." On Zhenwu revelations, see Wang and Pi, *Zhongguo jinshi minjian xinyang*, 214–24.

scripture of the divine incantations and hagiography of Zhenwu, Great Saint of Dark Heavens, preached by the Supreme [Lord]") and the large compendium of his miracles, the *Xuantian shangdi qishenglu* 玄天上帝啟聖錄 (Record of the saintly manifestations of the Supreme Emperor of Dark Heaven). Furthermore, an important moral tract, revealed by Zhenwu in 1302, is not included in the canon but was widely disseminated in the later period, and I will return to this document below.

What is possibly the record of the earliest spirit-writing revelations of texts concerns a group of devotees of Zhenwu who were active in early Song Sichuan, especially the Chengdu region. The dating for this is, as so often, rather delicate: the account is found in a large liturgical compendium, the *Daomen kefan daquanji* 道門科範大全集 (Great compendium of the liturgical norms of Daoism), which was edited with many additions in the early fifteenth century. One passage devoted to Zhenwu tells of two people who received his revelations, a certain Ash Li 燼灰李 (a possible reference to writing on an ash table?) and a Du Ming 杜明—neither is documented anywhere else.[55] Zhenwu manifested himself at their home altar on a number of occasions; sometimes he spoke (*jiangyu* 降語), sometimes he appeared in dreams, and sometimes he transmitted scriptures, presumably through spirit-writing; he is said to have transmitted the Five bushel scriptures to Li (真君降於其家，傳以五斗經，行於世).[56] This is intriguing because these extremely popular scriptures, especially the Northern Dipper one (*Taishang xuanling beidou benming changsheng miaojing* 太上玄靈北斗本命長生妙經, "Marvelous scripture on long life and fundamental destiny [based in the] big dipper, of the Most High Mysterious Spirit"), present themselves as having been revealed to Zhang Daoling by Taishang laojun in 155 CE, but do not appear before the Song period; it is entirely possible that they were spirit-written in the early Song period, which would make them the earliest known spirit-written scriptures. Our text narrates in more detail the career of Du Ming, which resembles that of his near-contemporary, Zhang Shouzhen. He begins to offer ritual services from home during the Xianping 咸平 era (998–1004); his revelations play a role in quashing a military rebellion and he becomes successful, settling in a major Daoist temple where he runs the Zhenwu cult and delivers further oral revelations. Zhenwu also announces through him that he will visually appear to the emperor.

---

55   *Daomen kefan daquanji*, 63.3a–5b.
56   *Daomen kefan daquanji*, 63.4a.

Stories related by Chen Zhong and the *Qishenglu* similarly show Zhenwu manifesting himself by a wide variety of means. He occasionally appears visible, especially during battles when he scares the enemy, or in the presence of the emperor. He can possess mediums and talk,[57] but is equally bent on spirit-writing. Chen Zhong repeatedly quotes his spirit-written sayings, and even mentions ten times his *Jiangbi shilu* 降筆實錄 (Records of spirit-written words), which is unfortunately lost; the quotes concern Zhenwu's own history and place in the pantheon.[58] Chen describes the revelation in some detail; it happened in 1184 at a Zixu altar 紫虛壇 in Xiangyang 襄陽; the head of the altar was a Daoist named Zhang Mingdao (降授道士張明道).[59] It was edited and revealed by a thunder deity on the order of Zhenwu, named the Transcendent lord Dong 董真君; Wenchang and other deities also wrote prefaces and other revelations which Chen quotes. The terms used include *jiangbi* and *pijiang* (which, as we have seen, refer primarily to written communication between priest and god during a ritual), but there is no mention of the phoenix.

3.3.2 Wenchang

The best-studied early spirit-writing cult is that of Imperial Lord Wenchang, certainly because it represents the earliest well-documented stage in the history of the production of spirit-written books (as opposed to short poems): I rely here on the pioneering work of Terry Kleeman and Hsieh Tsung-hui.[60] The cult originated in Zitong, northern Sichuan. It did not rely solely on spirit-writing, and the god manifested himself in visible human form several times before starting to write. He also conveyed prognostications through the weather (wind and storms) and in dreams; there was a hall for requesting dreams (*yingmeng tai* 應夢臺) at the god's temple at Zitong from the Song period onward.[61]

The Wenchang spirit-written revelations developed in Sichuan from the late twelfth century, when a network of devotees produced various texts in various locations. The earliest was the *Taishang wuji zongzhen Wenchang dadong xianjing* 太上無極總真文昌大洞仙經 (Great cavern immortal scripture, by Wenchang, [head of] all transcendents, of the supreme Ultimate), a revised

---

57 In "Fuyu qiqing 附語祈晴," in *Xuantian shangdi qishenglu*, 4.17b–19a, the medium is clearly described as unconscious when Zhenwu possesses him (*jiangyu, jiangling*).
58 *Taishang shuo Xuantian dasheng zhenwu benzhuan shenzhou miaojing*, 6.5b.
59 Ibid., 1.4b; 6.27b; see also Hsieh, *Xin tiandi zhi ming*, 119–21.
60 Kleeman, *A God's Own Tale*; Hsieh, *Xin tiandi zhi ming*.
61 Kleeman, *A God's Own Tale*, 13–15.

version of the fourth-century Shangqing scripture, revealed in 1168. The same group, led by Liu Ansheng, revealed, between 1168–1177, a short divine autobiography entitled *Qinghe neizhuan* 清河內傳 (Esoteric biography of Qinghe).[62] Next came an ordination register, the *Gaoshang dadong Wenchang silu ziyang baolu* 高上大洞文昌司祿紫陽寶籙 (Precious purple *yang* register of the Wenchang Office for Official Careers, of the Most High Great Cavern). This allowed the members of the spirit-writing group and devotees to become gods in Wenchang's heavenly administration—thus fulfilling the self-divinization purpose of spirit-writing in a standardized Daoist manner. That same year, and to the same group, Wenchang revealed the long version of his hagiography, the *Zitong dijun huashu* in 73 "transformations"; that is, successive lives—additional lives were revealed in subsequent sessions from 1194 to 1316 by various other groups in Sichuan, Guizhou 貴州, and Guangxi 廣西. Furthermore, according to Hsieh Tsung-hui, a Wenchang altar, closely connected to those who had produced the above revelations, also revealed the *Gaoshang Yuhuang benxing jijing* 高上玉皇本行集經 (Collected scripture of the fundamental acts of the Venerable Jade Emperor, henceforth *Yuhuangjing*), spirit-written in 1218 and again, with corrections, in 1220. This scripture was to become the most commonly chanted text in modern Daoism; it describes the career and salvific role of the Jade Emperor.[63] Wang Chien-chuan, for his part, argues that the Wenchang revelation consisted of the commentary, preface, and editing of the *Yuhuangjing*, but not the scripture itself, although they were close in terms of theological content.[64]

The Wenchang revelations share a lot in common with those of Zhenwu and other deities in terms of their social context and content. One of its most original features is the term *feiluan*, referring to the name of the wooden writing implement sculpted in the shape of the legendary bird; it was apparently wielded by a single person. Furthermore, within the Wenchang cult communities, there also existed a specific technique of revelation (apparently) without a medium: the phoenix was suspended from the rafters by a rope moved by itself in a locked room called a Jiangbiting 降筆亭 and, when it had finished, a bell rang, and the devotees, led by the local official, opened the door to find sheets of paper covered in the revealed texts, which they took "to read the god's response"

---

62 This revelation is found in the first part (1a–3a) of the expanded book of that name in the Daoist canon.
63 Hsieh, *Xin tiandi zhi ming*, chap. 4 retraces in great detail all of the various altars that contributed to these successive revelations. Wang, "Song-Ming shiqi" provides several further modifications.
64 Wang, "Song-Ming shiqi."

(*guan baoying* 觀報應).⁶⁵ This is a special case within the realm of spirit-writing techniques; we are not apprised of any ritual procedures, and the witnesses are made to see the *a posteriori* results of the divine presence rather than feel the presence itself. However, as we will see, this automatic spirit-writing technique was listed alongside *jiangbi* and other terms among the various *daofa* rites for making gods write. It was not unique to the Wenchang cult, and is mentioned in other contexts. For instance, a twelfth-century story in northern China relates how a local administration employee, who was "good at praying to immortals" (*hao qi xian* 好祈仙), set up a cult to Immortal Huang, with a suspended brush in front of his portrait (*xuan bi hua qian* 懸筆畫前).⁶⁶ Such references continue to appear in later, Ming and Qing sources.

Wenchang's revelations were (with the exception of the ordination register and lost liturgical manuals) in open circulation and widely distributed. A proclamation in which he speaks in the first person and expounds his mission of transforming (*hua* 化) the populations of Sichuan was carved on a stele in 1207, which constitutes one of the earliest spirit-written texts made into a public monument.⁶⁷

3.3.3 Transcendent Lord Xu

Equally important within the larger picture of Chinese religious history are the revelations from Transcendent Lord Xu 許真君 (Xu Xun 許遜) and his ritual tradition, the Pure and Bright, loyal and filial liturgy (Jingming zhongxiao fa 淨明忠孝法—henceforth Jingmingfa). Xu is a local saint from northern Jiangxi, who reputedly lived in the fourth century and had already been adopted by the Daoists during the Tang; the pilgrimage remains vibrant to this day.⁶⁸ During the Song period, his cult developed its own set of exorcistic and healing *daofa* rituals that form part of the larger family of Lingbao liturgy. The well-documented codification, which has continued uninterrupted until the present (unlike many of the *daofa* traditions), includes moral rules and self-divinization procedures for adepts, as well as prophecies. Spirit-writing has been closely associated with them from their origin and through the ages. As in other traditions, spirit-writing did not exclude other revelation techniques, as its moral code, a ledger of merits and demerits, was revealed through a dream in 1171.

---

65 This description is first found in Wenchang's entry in the late Yuan hagiography, *Xinbian lianxiang Soushen guangji*, 33, and again in Ming sources: Hsieh, *Xin tiandi zhi ming*, 111.
66 "Huang zhenren," *Xu Yijian zhi*, 34.
67 "Zifu Feixiadong ji 紫府飛霞洞記," in Long and Huang, *Ba-Shu Daojiao beiwen jicheng*, 154–55.
68 Xu, *Duanlie yu jiangou*.

MAKING THE GODS WRITE   67

The most explicit description of early Jingmingfa spirit-writing is the narrative of events in 1131 that led to a canonical manual, *Lingbao jingming xinxiu Jiulao shenyin fumo mifa* 靈寶淨明新修九老神印伏魔秘法 (Lingbao Jingming secret method for subduing demons with the divine seal newly-created by the Nine Elders). The preface to this work does not employ any technical term for spirit-writing, but is entirely unambiguous. In that year, "the six transcendents manifested their divine presence in Yushui and revealed the secret liturgy of Lingbao jingming" (六真降神於渝水，出示靈寶淨明秘法). The following year, Lord Xu suddenly descended (*shanchua lin* 覢欻臨) to his main temple (the Yulong wanshougong 玉隆萬壽宮). He gathered his adepts at an "altar" called Yizhentan 翼真壇, and there, when they had doubts or problems regarding the scriptures, they could always consult the god (凡經典疑難，悉聽扣問). As a result, the present liturgy was compiled. Once completed, it was presented to the Lord for inspection, who approved it (書成，以呈真鑒，賜可).[69] Indeed, three gods are listed as the authors of this book. Even though there is no specific, technical term employed for spirit-writing here, this entirely fits my definition of it because we have a ritual set-up (an altar) which implies ritual procedures for inviting the gods; written questions to the gods; and written answers by them, which were then published as instructions issued by the gods in the first person to named disciples.

Two further Jingming texts document the spirit-written exchanges between living adepts and their divine mentors, about ritual procedures but also doctrine and inner alchemy (*neidan* 內丹) self-cultivation; these two aspects were closely linked since the thunder rites entirely hinged on inner-alchemical procedures. Both record the questions posed by a certain Zhou Fangwen 周方文 to his transcendent master, Xu. Zhou is not known elsewhere but provides a short account of his pursuit of inner alchemy with various (living masters) and mentions that he was a local official.[70] In these texts, the *Lingbao jingming huangsu shu shiyi mijue* 靈寶淨明黃素書釋義秘訣 (Secret formulas and glosses of the yellow and white book of the Lingbao Jingming lineage), and the *Lingbao jingmingyuan jiaoshi Zhou zhengong qiqing huayi* 靈寶淨明院教師周真公起請畫一 (Questions for unification by the instructor from the Jingming court transcendent master Zhou), Zhou formulates his question and then provides the Xu's answer. The language used by Zhou is unmistakably that of spirit-writing: "I await your jade edict" (*fuwang yuzhi* 伏望玉旨); "I humbly beg you to reveal

---

69   *Lingbao jingming xinxiu Jiulao shenyin fumo mifa*, preface.
70   However, recent scholars have shown he was the main priest behind the 1131 revelations and his two texts form part of the same effort. Wang, "Nansong Jingmingdao de fa, zhi, lu," building on the seminal work of Xu Wei.

your clear explanation" (伏乞分明指示); "I hope you will grant me oral instructions" (*yuan ci koujue* 願賜口訣), "I humbly beg my transcendent master to reveal a transcendent book in order to teach the members of the altar" (伏乞真師頒示真本，以教在壇之士), and "I beg you to respond to my request (*baoying*) and explain in detail" (乞報應詳示). Although some of the instructions are described by both Zhou and Xu as "oral secrets," Zhou uses the language for submitting written requests (*chengfu* 呈覆, *bingwen* 稟問) and asks for Xu's written response, *pishi* or *pihui* 批誨 (a standard term for responding to a letter from a student). Xu's answers are relatively straight-forward, he uses "I" and "you," and recounts his own initiation and training. The questions range from technical aspects of ritual practice to advice on his moral life. They resemble the "recorded sayings" (*yulu*) of living masters, and thus constitute the earliest case of a *yulu* between living adepts and divine masters produced by spirit-writing; we have seen that medieval adepts could question their divine master during visualizations, and that the early Song *Yisheng baode zhuan* already contained a proto-*yulu* record of the oral responses by the god to personal questions on self-cultivation and morality. Here, for the first time, these two books are entirely devoted to a spirit-written pedagogical dialogue.

One question concerns the initiation of Jingmingfa Daoists. Zhou, quoting liturgical documents, states that the ordinand must pray to Lord Xu who will then answer (*baoying*), in a dream, or through a "decree from the immortals" (*xianzhi* 仙旨); that is, he will offer spirit-written approval.[71] We thus have here the first and only early systematic description of the use of spirit-writing for initiating adepts, accepted individually by the immortal master, which continues to be practiced in modern and contemporary times.

Other Jingming texts bear traces of similar activities and events. We saw in the introduction to this paper how the preface to a Jingming hagiography relates how Lord Xu revealed his teachings in Nanjing in 1224.[72] More importantly, the 1131 revelation is also discussed in the compendium of Jingmingfa teachings compiled by Liu Yu 劉玉 (1257–1308) and his disciple Huang Yuanji 黃元吉 (1271–1326) and placed in an eschatological context (the wars between the Song and Jin).[73] In Liu's hagiography within that compendium, we read that the 1131 revelation was the foundation of this tradition that Liu Yu wished to renew: he had visions of immortals who predicted that Lord Xu would make himself present in his home (*xiajiang zi jia* 下降子家) in 1297, just as he had done back in 1131. He did indeed, and bestowed various scriptures which are

---

71　*Lingbao jingmingyuan jiaoshi Zhou zhengong qiqing huayi*, 7b.
72　*Xishan Xu zhenjun bashiwu hua lu*, preface 跋, 1a.
73　Hsieh, *Xin tiandi zhi ming*, 124–25; *Jingming zhongxiao quanshu*, 1.19b.

included in the same compendium.[74] This rich biography essentially comprises accounts of successive revelations of different types, showing how virtuosi such as Liu Yu could relatively freely use the vast repertoire of revelatory techniques and deploy them at their altar (*tan*) in order to recruit disciples: in some cases, he is explicitly engaging in visualizations and ascending to Heaven or other otherworldly realms to meet gods; in others, the latter descend for spectacular encounters, with visions, smells, and divine objects conferred on him, and other sensory experiences; his disciple, Huang Yuanji, is also instructed in dreams, and given texts, mostly by Lord Xu's subordinate gods. These texts are instructions signed by the gods, spoken in the first person and addressing Liu and other initiates as "descendants in my ritual lineage" (*fazi*), exactly as in Lord Xin's 1290 spirit-written revelations. It thus appears that, even if no technical word such as *jiangbi* is used in the Jingmingfa corpus, *jiang* here refers to spirit-writing.

The Jingming practices are far better documented in the Daoist Canon than those associated with Wenchang or Zhenwu. Whereas, for Wenchang, we have only the open-circulation texts (scriptures and hagiography), for Jingming we have, in addition to these, internal, restricted-circulation documents including liturgy and "secret" instructions. This is clearly due to the fact that the Jingming groups have existed continuously from the early twelfth century until the present.

3.3.4 Altars as Venues for Spirit-Writing

The 1131 description of Jingming revelations is, to my knowledge, the earliest record of adepts grouped at an altar (*tan*), and taken as disciples (*dizi*) by a god who instructs them through spirit-writing. This model was also, a few years later, developed by the Wenchang groups who established various *tan*.[75] By 1184, we also have records of Zhenwu spirit-writing at a Zixu altar 紫虛壇. By the Qing period, this vocabulary of altars and discipleship becomes a very common way to refer to the members of a spirit-writing group, and descriptions of the operation and rules of such an altar begin to appear, which we do not have for the Song, Yuan, or Ming periods.

I have not found any evidence of people claiming to be the disciples of gods and permanent members of an altar outside a spirit-writing context. Expressions such as "disciples of the altar" (*tan dizi* 壇弟子), or the "community of the altar" (*tanzhong* 壇眾), refer, in Buddhist and (less commonly) Daoist

---

74 *Jingming zhongxiao quanshu*, 1.20a.
75 A very convenient list in Hsieh, *Xin tiandi zhi ming*, 135–36.

contexts, to ordinands, but they are only called this during the ordination ritual, not permanently, and are the disciple of the living ordination master, not a god. In Song-period liturgical texts, these expressions can also refer to the Daoist troupe, that is, the main priest (*gaogong* 高功, *shi* 師, *fashi* 法師) and his acolytes; the latter are also called *fazi* 法子 (or *fazhong* 法眾). Only in a few modern liturgical manuals for lamp or penance rituals (where they are all allowed to stand next to the priest, unlike in the *jiao*) are the lay participants called *tanzhong*, but, again, only for the duration of the ritual.

With the twelfth-century emergence of spirit-writing altars, we thus see the rise of a new idea: through the practice of spirit-writing, laypeople (not only ascetics engaged in advanced self-cultivation) become the disciples of a god or an immortal as well as permanent members of a divine community. Why were these spirit-writing communities called altars? I think it was because they are established by an initiated *fashi* priest; a group of priests working together is called a *tan*, and *daofa* practitioners in particular are organized around their *leitan* 雷壇. Individual *tan*, as durable entities with their own names, is an innovation of the Song-period *daofa* and do not seem to have existed beforehand.

Unlike the typical *tan* of exorcistic priests that only counted as members a few ritualists performing as a troupe, some *tan* initiated and ordained lay disciples to perform (or assist with) spirit-writing and other rituals and spread the teachings of the exorcistic gods revealed through spirit-writing. The Lord Xin revelation is addressed to both priests (*fazi*) and lay adepts (*xinshi*), suggesting that some of these altars observed two degrees of ordination. All of the spirit-writing deities we have met have their own ritual tradition (*fa*), even if, in the case of Wenchang, this is less prominent than for Lord Xu, Lord Xin, or Zhenwu. Yet, even in the case of Wenchang, one of the revelations was an ordination register (*Gaoshang dadong Wenchang silu ziyang baolu*), full of exorcistic language, that empowered adepts to perform certain rites, and which explicitly mentions a companion Dadongfa 大洞法, that was revealed at the same time but apparently lost. In his spirit-written auto-hagiography, Wenchang himself recounts how he became an exorcistic priest.[76]

Furthermore, several sources show that these spirit-writing altars performed rituals for the laity; the later supplements to the *Huashu* itself discuss how devotees visited the spirit-writing altars in times of disaster to offer a memorial prayer to Heaven.[77] Chen Zhong, the Zhenwu devotee writing around 1236, relates a Wenchang spirit-writing (*jiangbi*) revelation in 1197 which transmitted

---

[76]   *Zitong dijun huashu*, transformation no. 12.
[77]   Hsieh, *Xin tiandi zhi ming*, 119.

MAKING THE GODS WRITE   71

an order from the Jade Emperor that all people should collect funds to organize a massive *jiao* offering ritual, during which they should register in order to escape the coming apocalypse 度末劫, and that Wenchang was in charge of the written communication between them and himself.[78] Chen Zhong goes on to mention other cases where spirit-writing (*jiangbi, pijiang*) is used to process communications between the Jade Emperor, Wenchang, lower-level gods (City gods, Earth gods), and Daoist priests, in a ritual context, to administer salvation. Besides such rituals that aimed at universal salvation, the spirit-writing altars also provided more mundane ritual services; these were, and remain today, institutions providing ritual services where people could come and request healing, advice, and other forms of divine help. Cults like Zhenwu, Wenchang, Transcendent Lord Xu, and others, are both universal and local.[79]

3.4   Spirit-Writing as Part of the daofa Exorcistic Liturgy

We have seen how the gods and practitioners of spirit-writing were frequently part of the *daofa* traditions, and that the *fashi* priests used the techniques to communicate with their martial gods. We can now go further and explore how spirit-writing was codified as part of the *daofa* traditions. Of course, priests never held an effective monopoly over spirit-writing at any point in history—the Song-period anecdotal evidence (see Hu Jiechen's chapter) proves the opposite—but the point is that they felt they should.

There are several sources documenting claims by Song-Yuan period *fashi* priests that spirit-writing was their preserve. First, the *Tianhuang zhidao taiqing yuce* 天皇至道太清玉冊 (Most pure and precious books on the supreme Dao of August Heaven; a comprehensive encyclopedic description of Daoism compiled in 1444 by Zhu Quan 朱權 [1378–1448]),[80] lists various techniques for spirit-writing within its enumeration of the *daofa* traditions, showing that they were considered at that time as knowledge that was monopolized by the *fashi* priests (all *daofa* placed great stress on the need to avoid showing liturgical documents and manuals to the unnitiated).[81] The end of this list reads: summoning cranes (*zhaohe* 召鶴), perfect light mediumistic divination (*yuanguang*), spirit-possession (*futi* 附體), dancing immortal lads (*wu xiantong* 舞仙

---

78 *Taishang shuo Xuantian dasheng zhenwu benzhuan shenzhou miaojing*, 5.11b–12a.
79 Wang, "Song-Ming shiqi" shows that the group around Liu Ansheng provided healing services.
80 On this encyclopedia and its author, see Schachter, "Nanji Chongxu Miaodao Zhenjun." On pp. 516–18, Schachter comments on this list and wonders whether Zhu Quan may have practiced spirit-writing, or revealed texts through spirit-writing once divinized.
81 *Tianhuang zhidao taiqing yuce*, 3.3.31b.

童), visiting the world of the dead (*guoyin* 過陰), catching (the spirits, *zhuishe* 追攝), spirit-writing (*jiangbi*), the phoenix of the Great ultimate (*taiji luan* 太極鸞), the phoenix with a brush affixed to a frame (*bijia luan* 筆架鸞), the phoenix suspended from a silk thread (*xuansi luan* 懸絲鸞), and the phoenix inside a sealed box (*fengxia luan* 封匣鸞).

This remarkable list combines various spirit-writing techniques with other divination methods, all of which allow one to obtain divine answers to questions and most of which involve a priest manipulating a medium. I have not found any other reference to the latter four, but their names evoke the Wenchang automatic revelations, mentioned above. We also have a story that evokes the last name; a Song scholar wrote that "the methods of spirit-writing are very diverse; the one called 'spirit-writing within a closed book' is the most mysterious" (降筆之法甚多，封書降筆者最異) and went on to criticize it as a fraud.[82]

The clearest proof that spirit-writing was overseen by *fashi* priests is that the only liturgies—actual instructions for performers as opposed to factual descriptions by witnesses—we have for the early modern period are all to be found in two main compendia of ritual manuals for the exorcistic traditions: the *Daofa huiyuan* and the *Fahai yizhu*. We have already seen some of them in the context of instructions to priests on how to obtain divine responses (*baoying*) during rituals. The most detailed, and the one with the clearest connections to modern practice, is found in the latter collection and entitled *Zhao Zigu xian fa* 召紫姑仙法 (Liturgy for summoning Zigu immortals). It can be no later than the compendium itself, which was probably compiled in the late Yuan period.[83] We owe to Judith Boltz a translation and analysis of this text, which provides a comprehensive script of the process, including talismans and spells for conjuring the gods. She argues that this liturgy was clearly intended for *fashi* priests, and involves visualizations and ritual offerings.[84] The text analyzed by Judith Boltz is not the only one among the vast corpus of *daofa* liturgies to describe spirit-writing; we have also seen above the liturgy for *pijiang* and *fengbi* in the same compendium.

The relationship between spirit-writing and *daofa* rituals went beyond the fact that priests used the former to process the rituals; they also sometimes used it actually to create the whole ritual tradition: indeed, some of the *daofa* liturgies were revealed through spirit-writing. We have already encountered an example in the short manual *Deng tianjun xuanling bamen baoying neizhi* and,

---

82 "Qing fengshu xian 請封書僊," in *Quyi shuo*, 10b–11a.
83 *Zhao Zigu xian fa*, *Fahai yizhu*, 20.1a–4b.
84 Boltz, "On the Legacy of Zigu."

MAKING THE GODS WRITE 73

more importantly, the Jingming manual. Two particularly important examples contain records of revelations during the early twelfth century. The first is the Great Rites of the Jade Hall (Yutang dafa 玉堂大法). This tradition was created by Lu Shizhong 路時中 (fl. 1120–1130) in the Maoshan and Nanjing area. It is based on the earlier Tianxin zhengfa, adding meditation practices and *liandu* rituals to save the dead; this tradition presents itself as characterized by recruitment among literati (including officials) and disdain for "vulgar Daoists (i.e. vernacular priests without an elite education)."[85]

In a colophon within his liturgical compendium, Lu recounts:

> All the instructions on the seven levels [of ordination] given above are oral instructions given by secret manifestations of the Heavenly Lord, master of the Teachings, repeatedly between the 15th day of the 1st month and the 7th day of the 7th month of 1107. After that and until 1119, the *Book of Ordination Levels* and the *Book of Exorcisms* were revealed through spirit-writing (*jiangbi*). ... When the Heavenly Lord manifested himself in the meditation room, he spoke in a voice like that of a small child; only myself and my disciple, Zhai Ruwen, were able to hear and record it.
>
> 已上七品格言，並大觀元年正月十五日至七月初七日，累受大教主天君密降口訣。自後至宣和元年，《品書》、《禁書》並降筆。... 天君降靖中，如嬰兒聲，惟時中與弟子翟汝文親聞筆記也。[86]

Thus, the Jade Hall liturgy is the result of several types of revelatory techniques; the most sacred texts (the talismans) are produced via the time-honored method of cave discovery, but the far more abundant discursive material that makes them usable is revealed through first oral and then written methods, using mediums. The note on the god speaking in the voice of a child, very similar to what was noted about Zhang Shouzhen, clearly hints at the presence of a child acting as the medium.

4 Revealed Texts, 1000–1400

Divine discourses appearing in the early modern period (1000–1400) include forms of revelations already current in earlier times as well as new types,

---

85 *Wushang xuanyuan santian yutang dafa*, 26.1a–3a.
86 *Wushang xuanyuan santian yutang dafa*, 28.7b–8a.

characterized by controlled possession, including spirit-writing. The dynamics between the different types of revelations is not fruitfully analyzed as a result of the competition between different religious groups which stuck to their own established ways of making their own gods talk and write—indeed, we have seen several cases of traditions that simultaneously made use of different types. Rather, it allows for the production of different sorts of revealed texts from different categories of gods. Spirit-written texts are revealed by gods that answer summons from the ritual specialists and are, therefore, not the highest gods—even though Zhenwu and Wenchang were granted exalted positions. The tianzun, the Buddhas, who preach sutras, were not subjected to spirit-writing or other *jiang* procedures. I will briefly analyze here the genres of early modern spirit-written texts and their place within a larger ecology of revealed texts.[87]

4.1 *A Textual Ecology of Revelations*

There is a clear connection between the mode of revelation and the discursive contents; for expounding general principles, sutras are the most appropriate; for intervening in the course of human affairs, spirit-written instructions are more appropriate. For this reason, these two genres have coexisted in a sort of textual ecology since the emergence of spirit-writing. Indeed, although ritual techniques for producing controlled-possession texts were available, sutras continued to be produced in large numbers during the Song and Yuan periods, and ever since. Even in the *daofa* milieu, key texts produced during the Song and Yuan periods, and later, still present themselves as preached in heaven, without giving any indication whatsoever regarding how they reached humans.

This becomes particularly clear when we examine the textual legacy of the most important revealing gods of the early modern period: Zhenwu, Wenchang, and Transcendent Lord Xu. In all three cases, we see, from the twelfth century onward, the formation of corpora of texts by and about these deities that comprise both sutra-style *jing* 經, without any indication of time and space, and spirit-written (as well, in the case of Zhenwu, oral) revelations that do not carry the word *jing* in their title, but rather provide hagiographic accounts, tracts and anthologies (*lu* 錄). Consider Zhenwu, from whom we have five different scriptures; one of them, the *Taishang shuo Xuantian dasheng zhenwu benzhuan shenzhou miaojing*, was commented on by Chen Zhong who abundantly quotes spirit-written contents, but the scripture itself is a sutra

---

87 This analysis is developed with detailed discussions of specific texts in Goossaert, *Making the Gods Speak*, chap. 5.

preached in Heaven and simply ends with the indication that "these words were secretly recorded in a jade box, waiting for a later time when an exiled immortal would transmit it to humans" (祕籙琅函，後有謫仙，傳於人世). Indeed, during the early modern period, spirit-writing is more frequently associated with oral instructions as well as commentaries on the scriptures than with the scriptures themselves.[88]

One cannot exclude the possibility that these *jing* were actually produced by spirit-writing, but I have not seen any hint to that effect. There are three exceptions: first, the *Taishang xiuzhen tiyuan miaodaojing* 太上修真體元妙道經 (Scripture on the Marvelous Dao of cultivating transcendence and embodying the origin, by the Lord on High). This relatively long scripture on cosmology and self-cultivation appears rather similar in language and contents to other sutra-style Daoist scriptures, except that it fails to offer an initial scene of dispensation in the heavens. Nevertheless, a colophon tells us that it was revealed through spirit-writing in 1261 in the house of a certain Liu Yuanrui 劉元瑞, a Daoist devotee who is not known otherwise. Liu could not understand the "transcendent book from the divine presence" (*jiangling zhenben* 降靈真本) and hid it but, after his death, it was published by another adept. The revealing deity has a title from a thunder ministry and seems to be Zhang Daoling. Second, the *Taishang wuji zongzhen Wenchang dadong xianjing* was spirit-written in 1168 and, most importantly, the *Yuhuangjing*. Such cases would become very numerous in the next phase of the history of spirit-writing, from the late Ming onward. For the early modern period, however, the general rule remains that whoever composed *jing* felt that he should not mention himself, possibly because *jing* are given by the high gods to exceptional humans (Zhang Daoling and the like), not to present-day people.

Among the new revelations of early modern times, there is another type of texts in which spirit-writing did not play a major role: inner alchemy. The vast majority of alchemical teachings by immortals during that period cannot be ascribed to spirit-writing and instead seem to be the result of other types of revelation. The most important divine author, Lü Dongbin, produced a large amount of revelations, such as poems left on walls, but no clear mention to spirit-writing exists before the late Ming period, when we begin to see entirely new types of spirit-written scriptures giving Patriarch Lü a new role and personality.[89] The only piece identified as spirit-written in the late Yuan

---

88   In *Making the Gods Speak*, chap. 5, I discuss more cases, such as the scriptural commentaries edited by Xu Daoling 徐道齡 (fl. 1330s).
89   Lai, "Ming Qing Daojiao Lüzu jiangji xinyang de fazhan."

anthology *Minghe yuyin* 鳴鶴餘音 (Echoes of the cranes' songs), a large collection of Daoist self-cultivation poetry with many pieces by immortals and gods, is revealed by a Thunder god, Lord Xin.[90]

4.2 Spirit-Written Revelations: Contents and Innovations

By contrast to these few early modern spirit-written scriptures and alchemical instructions, we have a larger amount of other types of revelations. The most important types of texts produced through spirit-writing fall into three main genres: prophecy, moral tracts, and poetry.

4.2.1 Prophecy and Eschatology

The prophetic nature of controlled-possession revelations was already obvious in the *Yisheng baode zhuan*; not only did the revelations of Black Killer play a decisive role in the succession of the suspiciously deceased Taizu, but the divine messages are informed throughout by messianic prophecies of an imminent age of Great peace, Taiping; the god admonishes the emperor and his officials to make this happen and promises them eternal life. The most famous spirit-written political prophecies, however, were the words of Zhenwu. During the wars between the Jin and the Song, and the subsequent Mongol invasion of southern China, Zhenwu revealed various texts about the invasions and regime change through *jiangbi*, with specific revelations dated 1217 and 1233, which have been thoroughly gathered and analyzed by Pierre-Henry De Bruyn.[91]

Even more importantly, a late Yuan source spells out the anti-Mongol nature of the Zhenwu prophecies:

> In 1276, when Jiangnan had just been submitted [to Yuan rule], a poem to the tune of Xijiangyue spirit-written by Zhenwu at Wudangshan was widely circulating among the people. It was carved onto wood blocks, printed on yellow paper and pasted onto walls. It went:
> The nine and nine of heaven and earth have been fixed
> Flowers blossom after the Qingming festival
> Mi and Tian (*Fan* 番, barbarians) have turned the world into chaos
>   like [scattered grains of] hemp
> We are waiting for the dragon and snake (Chinese) to follow after the
>   horses (Mongols).
> Then, like of old, China will [again] be a blessed land,

---

90 *Minghe yuyin*, 3.11a. This poem is simply entitled "Spirit-written at Wudang(shan)" (*Wudang jiangbi* 武當降筆).

91 De Bruyn, *Le Wudang shan*, 121–33.

And the Gu-Yue (*Hu* 胡, barbarians) will return home.
But, for now, if you are hoping for a good life,
You will die under the moon at East river.

至元十三年，江南初內附，民間盛傳武當山真武降筆書長短句曰西江月者，鋟刻于梓，黃紙模印，貼壁間。其詞云：九九乾坤已定，清明節候開花。米田天下亂如麻，直待龍蛇繼馬。依舊中華福地，古月一陣還家。當初指望作生涯，死在西江月下。[92]

The same source contains another spirit-written demonological prophecy, this time with the term *fuji*, and without any identified divine author.[93]

The eschatological message in the Wenchang revelations is somewhat different. All of the texts spirit-written by Wenchang during the southern Song period as well as the two early scriptures of the Wenchang cult expounding Wenchang's mission and cosmic role, *Yuanshi tianzun shuo Zitong dijun benyuanjing* 元始天尊說梓潼帝君本願經 (Scripture of the original vow of the Imperial Lord of Zitong, preached by the Heavenly Worthy of Primordial Beginning) and *Yuanshi tianzun shuo Zitong dijun yingyanjing* 元始天尊說梓潼帝君應驗經 (Scripture of the miraculous responses of the Imperial Lord of Zitong, preached by the Heavenly Worthy of Primordial Beginning), develop a discourse in which the gods are about to unleash apocalyptic disasters onto humanity and Wenchang is sent on a mission, using spirit-writing, to save as many as possible. This narrative was accepted beyond the circles of the Wenchang cult in Sichuan. In his commentary on a Zhenwu scripture, Chen Zhong also offers a long, detailed account of the process through which the Jade Emperor announced the end of the kalpa in 1197 and the brutal punishment of sinful humanity, tasked Wenchang to practice spirit-writing in order to warn people, and himself spirit-wrote an edict.[94]

4.2.2 Moral Tracts

Moral teachings were an important component of *jiang* revelations from the start, as all of the gods who are made present through ritual means are committed to moral reform and the enforcement of the divine codes.[95] The *Yisheng baode zhuan* is replete with injunctions to morality, notably for officials to be

---

92 "Wudangshan jiangbi 武當山降筆," in *Nancun chuogenglu*, *juan*, 26, 328.
93 "Fuji shi 扶箕詩," in *Nancun chuogenglu*, *juan* 27, 343. I follow the translation in ter Haar, "Rumours and Prophecies," 391.
94 *Taishang shuo Xuantian dasheng zhenwu benzhuan shenzhou miaojing*, 5.12a–15a.
95 Goossaert, "Divine Codes."

fair, loyal, and disinterested. Wenchang's autobiography, the *Huashu*, shows him performing all of the standard acts of morality—filial piety, loyalty, compassion, sexual restraint—and his mission, as appointed by the Jade Emperor, is to "rectify people's hearts" (*zheng renxin* 正人心). Zhenwu's revealed teachings, in both written and oral form, are equally informed by the god's desire to change humans' perverse way of life.

The corpus of Wenchang revelations contains two short tracts that are the direct antecedents of a genre (short admonitions, *xunwen* 訓文) that would strongly flourish from the late Ming period onward. The first is *Quan jing zizhi wen* 勸敬字紙文 (Exhortation to respect papers with characters written on them), calling people to respect written characters. The moral injunction not to sully any written character dates back to the early medieval Daoist precepts (*jie* 戒) and would become a major theme in modern morality books.[96] The second is the *Jie shizi wen* 戒士子文 (Admonishment to scholars), revealed by Yan Hui 顏回, Confucius's favorite disciple who, by Song times, had carved out a career within Wenchang's divine administration.[97]

Arguably the most influential of all moral tracts revealed through spirit-writing during the early modern period is the *Wudangshan Xuantian shangdi chuixunwen* 武當山玄天上帝垂訓文 (Instructions revealed by Supreme Emperor of the Dark Heavens from Wudang Mountains), dated 1302.[98] This text was largely circulated during the Ming and Qing periods and was frequently included in anthologies as one of the four "classics" of morality books.[99] This short, powerful exhortation, deeply tinged with apocalyptic overtones, repeatedly evokes the final cataclysm, when hordes of murderous demons will usher in the end of this world (*mojie* 末劫); it calls on humans to follow Zhenwu and his moral teachings in order to be spared. Like the revelations of Lord Xin, Zhenwu speaks in the first person, recalls his own divine career and exhorts his adepts to act morally, quoting the *Taishang ganyingpian* 太上感應篇 (The Supreme Lord's tract on action and retribution); unlike them, he does not explicitly mention priests as the recipients of the revelations, but the text still presents itself as revealed in the most important temple of the most important exorcistic god.

---

96   "Hua shi shayu 華氏殺魚," in *Xuantian shangdi qishenglu*, 8.5a–6b.
97   *Qinghe neizhuan*, 13b–14b and 14b–18b respectively. Yan Hui is also mentioned with the same divine title in Chen Zhong's *Taishang shuo Xuantian dasheng Zhenwu benzhuan shenzhou miaojing*, 5.14a.
98   Goossaert, *Livres de morale révélés par les dieux*, 53–67; Wang, "Zhenwu xinyang," 106–10.
99   The "four classics" are *Taishang ganyingpian*, *Wenchang dijun yinzhiwen* 文昌帝君陰騭文, *Guansheng dijun jueshi zhenjing* 關聖帝君覺世真經, and the *Wudangshan Xuantian shangdi chuixunwen*.

4.2.3 Poetry

Anecdotal sources have shown that the exchange of poetry between the living and spirits was a significant aspect of early modern spirit-writing. A significant part of the known revelations, including the moral tract introduced above, is in poetic format. One spirit-writing cult, however, made its mark as a locus for conjoining spirituality, Daoist ritual, and *belles-lettres*: the Hong'en lingji zhenjun 洪恩靈濟真君 cult, devoted to the two Xu Brothers (Xu Zhizheng 徐知證 and Xu Zhi'e 徐知諤), historical figures who lived in the tenth century—they were adoptive brothers of the founder of the southern Tang dynasty—and quickly became the object of a thriving cult in and around the city of Fuzhou (Fujian 福建).[100] The Daoist canon contains an abundant, varied amount of documents about the cult, including liturgies, historical records, and official proclamations—notably linked to the patronage of the cult at the Ming court.

The spirit-writing activities of the Xu brothers and their devotees are documented in two ways. First, several historical records mention them, although with few details, using various terms, such as *luanji* or *jibi*. One document claims that the practice started in 955: that year, "the princes (their then title) started to use spirit-writing to allocate talismans and drugs to heal people" (後周顯德二年乙卯王始降筆判符藥以濟人).[101] This may be the earliest known record, but it is not very reliable. What is certain is that the cult was based on temples offering ritual services from the resident Daoist priests, among which spirit-writing (for healing, divination, and exorcism) was central: this model continued to thrive during the Ming and Qing periods.

Second, we have a whole anthology of their spirit-writing production, the *Xuxian hancao* 徐仙翰藻 (*Belles-lettres* of the Immortal Xus). This fourteen-*juan* book looks like a standard literary anthology of a scholar, with all major genres represented: lyrical prose (*fu* 賦), stele inscriptions, essays, and poetry of various genres and meters. The collection was apparently completed in 1305, the date of the colophon, but few of the pieces are dated. This cult produced, among other texts, one short scripture, in which a high-ranking Daoist deity reveals that he has sent the Xu brothers to Earth to teach morality and save humanity, which is on the brink of collapse under the weight of its own sins.[102] This is the longest spirit-written collection before the Qing period.

---

100 Davis, "Arms and the Tao, 1"; and Davis, "Arms and the Tao, 2."
101 *Xuxian zhenlu*, 1.13a.
102 *Lingbao tianzun shuo Hong'en lingji zhenjun miaojing*.

In conclusion, the above survey of early-modern spirit-written revelations shows that, by the early Ming period, this type of divine text had become varied, and influential. However, a wider view of the divine texts shows that, by that time, spirit-writing still occupied a specific, relatively small niche within the larger economy of revelations. Concerning their quantity, there were only around twenty fully-fledged book-length revelations. Second, all of the revelations that we have surveyed were produced in clearly Daoist contexts and are now preserved in the Daoist canon—the 1302 Zhenwu revelation is only superficially an exception (it was not included in the Canon but is very closely related to canonical material); some of them were not in open circulation. Other religious groups and traditions adopted the controlled-possession modes of revelations only very gradually and at a later stage, beginning from the late Ming period onward.

5 Spirit-Writing's Discontents

As with any practice involving interactions between humans and supernatural entities, spirit-writing generated a fair amount of criticism. There is an uninterrupted string of comments by literati from the Song period to the present criticizing or ridiculing this practice as a fraud, although such material is not particularly abundant and there exist no grounds for suggesting that the majority of scholars entirely rejected it—the opposite is considerably more likely. More informative are two types of critique; those from the very milieu that practiced it, the Daoists, and those from the state that attempted to ban it.

5.1 *Internal Critique: Daoists*

The Daoists themselves developed critiques of spirit-writing at an early stage; these critiques form part of a larger field of vibrant debates that animated the Daoist milieus through the Song, Yuan, and early Ming periods concerning the new ritual techniques introduced by the *daofa*. These critiques were the other side of the coin in the process of adopting the gods, languages, and techniques of these traditions within the classical liturgy: while such adoption went very deep and transformed the whole of Daoist practice, each practitioner and codifier drew his own red lines and identified what was judged unacceptable. Spirit-writing was as contentious as other practices involving possession and direct interventions by gods of questionable origins. An important example is provided by Lü Yuansu in his *Daomen dingzhi* 道門定制 (Fixed institutions for Daoism, preface 1188). When discussing the names of the celestial officers that can be addressed in ritual requests and memorials, Lü warns against adding those not warranted by the classical liturgical sources.

Lü insists that gods known through spirit-writing are not trustworthy (若降筆所傳，皆未可信)[103] and that "spirit-writing is a demoniac (perversion) of our teaching (Daoism) and the Daoist novices who 'sell words' know nothing about liturgy" (降筆爲教門之魔而鬻字道童不曉科教).[104] One of the most powerful voices in these debates is the towering figure of Bai Yuchan 白玉蟾 (1194–1229?), one of the most influential authors on the *daofa* traditions, who did not shy away from polemics. In a dialogue with his disciples, Bai states:

> Some mix the oral techniques of the "shamans" with the proper liturgy; others call "secret transmission" the words obtained from spirits and immortals through spirit-writing. When asked, they say that conforms to the liturgy; when shown that they are wrong, they cling to their revelations, saying it is true transmission. Alas! The errors of these perverse masters are not the fault of the masses but the result is that the blind lead the many and that delusion produces more delusion. What a pity!
>
> 或以師巫之訣而雜正法，或以鬼仙降筆而謂祕傳，問之則答為依科，別之則執為真授，嘻！邪師過謬，非眾生咎，一盲引眾，迷以傳迷。哀哉！[105]

This sort of judgement, and the fear of allowing spirit-writing practitioners to introduce uncontrolled innovations, found their way into the codifications and ritual documents—including the hugely influential *Tiantan yuge* 天壇玉格 (Jade rules for the Heavenly altar), the manual for codifying ordinations compiled (probably during the Yuan period) and used at Longhu shan.[106]

In its important summary of Daoist history, doctrine, and practice, *Daomen shigui* 道門十規 (The Ten principles of Daoism), the 43rd Heavenly Master Zhang Yuchu 張宇初 (1361–1410) very explicitly rejects it along with other divination techniques, in a list quite similar to that of Zhu Quan:

> Perfect light [divination], spirit-possession, making divine generals manifest their presence, sieve-possession, wielding the phoenix, water contemplation [divination]: all of these perverse ideas and practices are not things that practitioners of the correct rituals should mention.

---

103   *Daomen dingzhi*, 3.49a.
104   Ibid., 7.36b.
105   *Haiqiong Bai zhenren yulu*, 2.15b.
106   "Baoguan zhuang shi 保官狀式," in *Tiantan yuge*, *Daofa huiyuan*, 249.15a.

又等圓光、附體、降將、附箕、扶鸞、照水諸項邪說行持，正法之士所不宜道.¹⁰⁷

We also possess a pronouncement by an unnamed master of the Qingwei tradition that restates the same idea in a more nuanced way. This passage discusses how the thunder gods can arrive immediately and should not be summoned (made present) lightly:

> Spirit-possession, opening the light,¹⁰⁸ making divine generals manifest their presence, obtaining a [divine] response in one's fingers, water contemplation, consecrating the arm [of a medium], seizing the dead, causing the banners to fall:¹⁰⁹ in all cases, the spirits of the dead [thus summoned] are not divine, and the rituals performed for them do not produce [divine] responses. They are mere techniques. One could use them to teach people based on the gods, but people who really know the Dao do not engage in them.

> 附體、開光、降將、報指、照水、封臂、攝亡、墜幡。其鬼不神，其事不應，皆術法也。可以神道設教，知道者不為也。¹¹⁰

In other words, our codifier recognizes that priests use spirit-writing (here *fengbi*), among other techniques, to makes spirits present, but this is a lower technique.

One cannot fail to notice that it is the very same Daoist milieus that both use spirit-writing with abandon and criticize it. Indeed, Lü Yuansu has no qualms about quoting approvingly a theological statement from an oral revelation by Zhenwu.¹¹¹ Zhang Yuchu included many spirit-written texts in the Daoist canon whose compilation he oversaw—even Lord Xin's spirit-written revelation discussed above in a text he edited himself. This is not a case of two forms of Daoism ("popular" and "elite," if you will), which differ with regard to orthodoxy and heterodoxy. Rather, we see a moment of extremely intense ritual and

---

107   *Daomen shigui*, 12a.
108   This certainly refers here to a divination technique similar to *yuanguang* rather than the more common meaning of consecrating an icon.
109   I have found only one other mention of this technique in the Daoist canon, which does not provide any explanation.
110   *Qingwei yuanjiang dafa*, 25.7b. This passage, with some variants, is also included in *Daofa huiyuan*, 1.6a, which adds: "these are not *daofa*" (*fei daofa ye* 非道法也).
111   *Daomen dingzhi*, 2.1b.

textual creativity with a number of persons in authority who both use the spirit-written texts and practices they approve of, and are wary of what others may do if left to spirit-write with their own devices. This tension, already plainly evident during the early stages of spirit-writing history, would always remain.

5.2 *State Interventions*

The Daoists critiqued spirit-writing for theological reasons; the attacks by officials were very different, as they were concerned about the popularity of spirit-writing halls. Writing in the early thirteenth century, Yue Ke 岳珂 (1183–1234, scholar-official and grandson of Yue Fei) denounces two popular religious activities in the capital (Hangzhou) that he finds abhorrent; while Buddhists engage in public shows of self-mutilation, Daoists set up "shops" along the streets to practice spirit-writing (列肆通衢爲箕筆之妖). While he reports people assuming that there is nothing the state can do about this, he invokes an 1116 imperial edict (which indeed features in the official records) that successfully wiped out similar practices in the then-capital Kaifeng: he quotes this edict as saying "[ruffians] use spirit-writing to build temples and gather crowds, and give [their gods] titles such as Heavenly worthy or Great immortal; the words they write are useless and their spoken words are nonsense" (以箕筆聚衆立堂，號曰天尊大仙之名。書字無取，語言不經).[112] This edict points to how the practice was organized, public, and popular as well as controversial, from an early stage. It also makes the important point that oral and written revelations were practiced in the same place and by the same specialists. In continuity with the Song precedents, in a famed 1370 edict against a broad range of religious practices, the first Ming emperor banned "all techniques including mediums, wielding the phoenix, praying to the saints, writing talismans, and incanted water" (巫覡、扶鸞、禱聖、書符、咒水諸術).[113]

6 A Synthesis

The abundant data discussed above was arranged analytically in order to make sense of the various types of sources and contexts regarding the practice of spirit-writing in general and revealing texts in particular; as a conclusion, it will be useful to place these on a timeline in order to attempt to identify a developmental logic.

---

112 "Xianshi yijiao zhi jin 仙釋異教之禁," *Kuitanlu*, 6.15b–16b; for the 1116 edict, see *Song huiyao jigao*, 65.
113 *Jin yinci zhi* 禁淫祠制, *Ming Taizu shilu*, 53.1037.

In all likelihood, the earliest forms of spirit-writing were possession practices, where mediums wrote instead of or, more likely, in addition to speaking. They caused the deceased, known or unknown, to write down brief information, advice, and prognostication. At some point, during the tenth century at the latest, Daoists started to work with such mediums and develop new rites (the *daofa*) for integrating these mediums and their gods into a Daoist bureaucratic framework and deploying them for their own purposes. As a result, they developed controlled-possession rites, that make gods perceptible by the audience who can hear them talk or see them write, within a framework dense with control procedures: liturgies for precisely staging the manifestation of divine presence, procedures for nominating gods and humans to occupy divine positions, and moral codes for ensuring that no priest or god becomes unruly. Many spirit-writing and other controlled-possession rites during this period involved a *fashi* controlling a medium, but not all, as *fashi* also practiced controlled self-possession (such as in the Wenchang tradition); in any case, it is the control framework that distinguishes the controlled-possession production of a divine presence and revelations from simple possession.

While the controlled-possession rites (notably spirit-writing) of the *fashi* thrived from the tenth century onward, the tradition of the mediums naturally continued but, by the Song period, the Daoist *fashi* were the most respected, most sought after, and possibly most common performers of spirit-writing. They included many educated laypeople, even officials, who had been initiated as *fashi* but not living as professional priests,[114] hence the common but flawed impression that spirit-writing was a lay technique providing ordinary people with unmediated communication with the divine. These *fashi* often used spirit-writing during communal rituals or at the request of patrons; it formed part of the Daoist liturgical toolkit and therefore served different purposes in different contexts.

Because manifestations of a divine presence, as practiced by the *fashi*, took place within a moral bureaucratic framework, it could—indeed, should—have been used to manifest spirits of a higher level than simply the dead. The *fashi* priests, first and foremost, performed rites to produce the divine presence of their divine allies, to whom they were sworn brothers, disciples, or subordinate officials, not the unknown dead or distant deities. These divine allies mainly comprised the ambiguous and powerful gods of the *daofa*: the thunder gods and other martial exorcists. such as Black Killer and Zhenwu, as well as, in a more civilian (but still eschatological and exorcist) mode, Wenchang and Tran-

---

114 Boltz, "Not by the Seal of Office Alone."

scendent Lord Xu. The *fashi* made their allied gods write down divine edicts and judgments, notably when nominating humans in the heavenly bureaucracy (the living when ordained, the dead when receiving posthumous salvation). This was routine practice. In some cases (not routine), they requested advice on ritual and self-cultivation practices, and the advice came, as recorded question-and-answer sessions, tracts and exhortations, moral narratives (the gods relating their own lives as a model for living humans to emulate), technical instructions, commentaries and explanations on scriptures, and, in a few cases, as scriptures themselves. All of these constitute spirit-written revelations, a discursive product of the wider use of spirit-writing by *fashi* priests.[115]

A few tenth- and eleventh-century cases of such revelations are mentioned in later sources, but not firmly confirmed. They become a solid fact from the twelfth century onward. From the early years of the southern Song period, we see complex texts produced by groups dedicated to the worship of savior gods: 1107 for Zhao Sheng, 1131 for Xu Xun, 1168 for Wenchang, and 1184 for Zhenwu. These are regional variations (Zhao Sheng in Jiangnan, Wenchang in Sichuan, Xu in Jiangnan and Jiangxi, Zhenwu in Hubei 湖北) of the same model. The groups that produced these texts, often called altars, *tan* (that is, a troupe under the orders of an ordained *fashi*), are characterized by three elements that would later become constant features of the late imperial, modern, and contemporary spirit-writing groups. The first element is the affiliation of adepts to the god producing the revelations as disciples within an altar that is directed by a *fashi* priest and provides ritual services to the population; in modern times, the presence of the *fashi* priest is no longer standard. The second element is the representation of the revealing god as both a fully-fledged member of the Heavenly bureaucracy, and a personal savior playing a unique role in the salvation of humanity and caring individually for each of his devotees. The revealing gods promise personal attention and salvation but also threaten their disciples with a horrible death should they disregard his teachings.

The third element is an eschatological inspiration: early Wenchang texts present him as sent by the Jade Emperor to help humans avoid the apocalypse—a basic theme that has been elaborated on by subsequent groups ever since.[116] The preface to the *Huashu* explains that the *feiluan* spirit-writing tech-

---

115   I concede that none of the manuals describing the use of spirit-writing to expedite ritual procedures can be dated earlier than the twelfth-century revelations, suggesting that my developmental scheme (first, the routine use of spirit-writing by *fashi* for their ritual needs, then some groups expanding the practice into the production of revelation) is not based on a bullet-proof textual chronology.
116   Hsieh, *Xin tiandi zhi ming*, 113–15; Goossaert, "Modern Daoist eschatology."

nique was devised in Heaven precisely to save humans in a time of eschatological urgency (作飛鸞闡化之法，筆降人間，為幽明通貫之理，仰蒙帝意，仁愛下民).[117] The same message is found in the Jingming and Zhenwu revelations; the 1131 Jingming texts are set in the context of the disastrous Jurchen invasions and clearly discuss the salvation of the Chinese; the Zhenwu texts are apocalyptical through and through.

What innovations did spirit-writing bring to the repertoire of techniques to make the gods talk and write? It combined the advantages of two pre-existing types of revelation: like possession, it was public and could offer the sensory experience of divine presence to audiences, and therefore convince and involve them in the works of the gods; yet, like visualization, it allowed advanced adepts to secure divinization and advancement in the divine bureaucracy. Its personal instructions, although tied to specific humans, were deemed of general use and value, and published. Yet, the niche occupied by spirit-writing in the larger ecology of Chinese revelations was rather specific by the early and mid-Ming period. The situation changed rapidly from the 1560s onward, with the rise of a new, probably simpler, technique, called *fuji* 扶乩, that practitioners often learned from Daoist priests but then transmitted among themselves, and a new type of altar, called *jitan* 乩壇, that was more open to interested members and actively engaged in charity. The *jitan* are the bedrock of modern and contemporary spirit-writing; they both continue their Song and Yuan period predecessors and introduce innovations by producing morality books as well as scriptures in far greater numbers than the early modern corpus. This lies outside our scope here, but it is hoped that this chapter has demonstrated its roots within the early modern ritual techniques.

References

Abbreviations

DZ: *Daozang* 道藏, numbers following Kristofer Schipper and Franciscus Verellen, eds. *The Taoist Canon: A Historical Companion to the Daozang* (*Daozang Tongkao* 道藏通考). Chicago: University of Chicago Press, 2004, 3 vols.

Primary Sources

Daofa huiyuan 道法會元. Early fourteenth c. DZ 1220.
Daomen dingzhi 道門定制. DZ 1244.

---

117   *Zitong dijun huashu*, preface, 4a.

Daomen kefan daquanji 道門科範大全集. DZ 1225.
Daomen shigui 道門十規. DZ 1232.
Deng tianjun xuanling bamen baoying neizhi 鄧天君玄靈八門報應內旨. DZ1266.
Dongpo zhilin 東坡志林. *Siku quanshu* 四庫全書 edition.
Duren shangpin miaojing tongyi 度人上品妙經通義. DZ 89.
Fahai yizhu 法海遺珠. Late Yuan? DZ 1166.
Gaoshang dadong Wenchang silu ziyang baolu 高上大洞文昌司祿紫陽寶籙. DZ 1214.
Gaoshang shenxiao yuqing zhenwang zishu dafa 高上神霄玉清真王紫書大法. DZ 1219.
Haiqiong Bai zhenren yulu 海瓊白真人語錄. DZ 1307.
Huagaishan Fuqiu Wang Guo san zhenjun shishi 華蓋山浮丘王郭三真君事實. DZ 778.
Jingming zhongxiao quanshu 淨明忠孝全書. DZ 1110.
Kuitanlu 愧郯錄. Yue Ke 岳珂 (1183–1234). *Sibu congkan* 四部叢刊 edition.
Lingbao jingming xinxiu Jiulao shenyin fumo mifa 靈寶淨明新修九老神印伏魔秘法. Preface 1131. DZ 562.
Lingbao jingmingyuan jiaoshi Zhou zhengong qiqing huayi 靈寶淨明院教師周真公起請畫一. DZ 554.
Lingbao tianzun shuo Hong'en lingji zhenjun miaojing 靈寶天尊說洪恩靈濟真君妙經. DZ 317.
Lingbao yujian 靈寶玉鑑. DZ 547.
Lishi zhenxian tidao tongjian xubian 歷世真仙體道通鑑續編. DZ 297.
Long Xianzhao 龍顯昭 and Huang Haide 黃海德, comp. *Ba-Shu Daojiao beiwen jicheng* 巴蜀道教碑文集成. Chengdu: Sichuan daxue chubanshe, 1997.
Lushan Taiping xingguogong Caifang zhenjun shishi 廬山太平興國宮採訪真君事實. DZ 1286.
Ming Taizu shilu 明太祖實錄. Taipei: Academia Sinica, 1962.
Minghe yuyin 鳴鶴餘音. DZ 1100.
Nancun chuogenglu 南村輟耕錄. Tao Zongyi 陶宗儀 (fl. 1360–1368). Beijing: Zhonghua shuju, 1959.
Qidong yeyu 齊東野語. Zhou Mi 周密 (1232–1308). *Siku quanshu* 四庫全書 edition.
Qinghe neizhuan 清河內傳. DZ 169.
Qingwei yuanjiang dafa 清微元降大法. DZ 223.
Quan Songwen 全宋文. Edited by Liu Lin 劉琳 and Zeng Zhaozhuang 曾棗莊. Shanghai: Shanghai cishu chubanshe, Anhui jiaoyu chubanshe, 2006.
Quyi shuo 祛疑說. Chu Yong 儲泳 (Song). *Siku quanshu* 四庫全書 edition.
Shangqing Lingbao dafa 上清靈寶大法. Transmitted by Ning Quanzhen (Benli) 寧全真 (1101–1181). DZ 1221.
Shanju xinhua 山居新話. Yang Yu 楊瑀 (1285–1361). *Siku quanshu* 四庫全書 edition.
Shuzhong guangji 蜀中廣記. Cao Xuequan 曹學佺 (1574–1647). *Siku quanshu* 四庫全書 edition.
Song huiyao jigao 宋會要輯稿. Beijing: Zhonghua shuju, 1957.

Taishang shuo Xuantian dasheng zhenwu benzhuan shenzhou miaojing 太上說玄天大聖真武本傳神呪妙經, With a commentary by Chen Zhong 陳伀. DZ 754.

Taishang xuanling beidou benming changsheng miaojing 太上玄靈北斗本命長生妙經. DZ 623.

Taishang yuhua dongzhang bawang dushi shengxian miaojing 太上玉華洞章拔亡度世昇仙妙經. DZ 77.

Tianhuang zhidao taiqing yuce 天皇至道太清玉冊. Zhu Quan 朱權 (1378–1448). DZ 1483.

Wushang xuanyuan santian yutang dafa 無上玄元三天玉堂大法. DZ 220.

Xinbian lianxiang Soushen guangji 新編連相搜神廣記. Qin Zijin 秦子晉. Late Yuan. Vol. 2 of the *Zhongguo minjian xinyang ziliao huibian* 中國民間信仰資料彙編, edited by Wang Qiugui 王秋桂 and Li Fengmao 李豐楙. 30 vols. Taibei: Taiwan xuesheng shuju, 1989.

Xishan Xu zhenjun bashiwu hua lu 西山許真君八十五化錄. DZ 448.

Xu Yijian zhi 續夷堅志. Yuan Haowen 元好問 (1190–1257). Beijing: Zhonghua shuju, 2006.

Xuantian shangdi qishenglu 玄天上帝啟聖錄. DZ 958.

Xuanzhen lingying baoqian 玄真靈應寶籤. DZ 1299.

Xuxian hanzao 徐仙翰藻. DZ 1468.

Xuxian zhenlu 徐仙真錄. DZ 1470.

Yijian zhi 夷堅志. Hong Mai 洪邁 (1123–1202). Beijing: Zhonghua shuju, 1981.

Yinju tongyi 隱居通議. Liu Xun 劉壎 (1240–1319). *Siku quanshu* 四庫全書 edition.

Yisheng baode zhuan 翊聖保德傳. 1016. DZ 1285.

Yuanshi tianzun shuo Zitong dijun benyuanjing 元始天尊說梓潼帝君本願經. DZ 29.

Yuanshi tianzun shuo Zitong dijun yingyanjing 元始天尊說梓潼帝君應驗經. DZ 28.

Yuanshi wuliang duren shangpin miaojing zhujie 元始無量度人上品妙經註解. Xue Jizhao 薛季昭 (fl. 1303). DZ 92.

Yudi jisheng 輿地紀勝. Wang Xiangzhi 王象之 (*jinshi* 1196). *Xuxiu Siku quanshu* 續修四庫全書, vol. 585.

Yunyangji 雲陽集. Li Qi 李祁 (*jinshi* 1333). *Siku quanshu* 四庫全書 edition.

Zitong dijun huashu 梓潼帝君化書. DZ 170.

Secondary Literature

Baptandier, Brigitte. "Entrer en montagne pour y rêver: Le mont des Pierres et des Bambous." *Terrains*, no. 26 (1996): 83–98.

Boltz, Judith Magee. "Not by the Seal of Office Alone: New Weapons in Battles with the Supernatural." In *Religion and Society in T'ang and Sung China*, edited by Patricia Buckley Ebrey and Peter N. Gregory, 241–305. Honolulu: University of Hawai'i Press, 1993.

Boltz, Judith Magee. "On the Legacy of Zigu and a Manual on Spirit-writing in her

Name." In *The People and the Dao: New Studies in Chinese Religions in Honour of Daniel L. Overmyer*, edited by Philip Clart and Paul Crowe, 349–88. Sankt Augustin: Monumenta Serica, 2009.

Chao, Shin-yi. *Daoist Ritual, State Religion, and Popular Practices: Zhenwu Worship from Song to Ming (960–1644)*. London: Routledge, 2011.

Campany, Robert Ford. *The Chinese Dreamscape, 300 BCE–800 CE*. Cambridge: Harvard University Asia Center, 2020.

Davis, Edward L. "Arms and the Tao, 1: Hero Cult and Empire in Traditional China." In *Sōdai no shakai to shūkyō* 宋代の社会と宗教, edited by Sōdai kenkyū-kai 宋代史研究会, 1–56. Tokyo: Kyūko shoin, 1985.

Davis, Edward L. "Arms and the Tao, 2: The Xu Brothers in Tea Country." In *Daoist Identity: History, Lineage and Ritual*, edited by Livia Kohn and Harold D. Roth, 149–64. Honolulu: University of Hawai'i Press, 2002.

Davis, Edward L. *Society and the Supernatural in Song China*. Honolulu: University of Hawai'i Press, 2001.

De Bruyn, Pierre-Henry. *Le Wudang shan: Histoire des récits fondateurs*. Paris: Les Indes savantes, 2010.

Drège, Jean-Pierre, and Dimitri Drettas. "Oniromancie." In *Divination et société dans la Chine médiévale—Étude des manuscrits de Dunhuang de la Bibliothèque nationale de France et de la British Library*, edited by Marc Kalinowski, 369–404. Paris: Bibliothèque nationale de France, 2003.

Goossaert, Vincent, ed., transl. *Livres de morale révélés par les dieux*. Paris: Belles-Lettres, 2012.

Goossaert, Vincent. "Modern Daoist Eschatology: Spirit-writing and Elite Soteriology in Late Imperial China." *Daoism. Religion, History & Society* / 道教研究學報：宗教、歷史與社會, no. 6 (2014): 219–46.

Goossaert, Vincent. *Bureaucratie et salut: Devenir un dieu en Chine*. Genève: Labor & Fides, 2017.

Goossaert, Vincent. "Divine Codes, Spirit-writing, and the Ritual Foundations of Morality Books." *Asia Major* 33, no. 1 (2020): 1–31.

Goossaert, Vincent. *Vies des saints exorcistes: Hagiographies taoïstes, 11ᵉ–16ᵉ siècles*. Paris: Les Belles Lettres, 2021.

Goossaert, Vincent. *Making the Gods Speak: The Ritual Production of Revelations in Chinese Religious History*. Cambridge, MA: Harvard University Press, 2022.

Hsieh Tsung-hui 謝聰輝. *Xin tiandi zhi ming: Yuhuang, Zitong yu feiluan* 新天帝之命：玉皇、梓潼與飛鸞. Taipei: Shangwu yinshuguan, 2013.

Kalinowski, Marc. "La littérature divinatoire dans le Daozang." *Cahiers d'Extrême-Asie* 5 (1989): 85–114.

Kleeman, Terry F. *A God's Own Tale: The Book of Transformations of Wenchang, the Divine Lord of Zitong*. Albany: State University of New York Press, 1994.

Lai Chi Tim 黎志添. "Ming Qing Daojiao Lüzu jiangji xinyang de fazhan ji xiangguan wenren jitan yanjiu 明清道教呂祖降乩信仰的發展及相關文人乩壇研究." *Journal of Chinese Studies* 中國文化研究所學報, no. 65 (2017): 139–79.

Meulenbeld, Mark R.E. *Demonic Warfare: Daoism, Territorial Networks, and the History of a Ming Novel.* Honolulu: University of Hawai'i Press, 2015.

Mozina, David. "Oaths and Curses in Divine Empyrean Practice." *Journal of Chinese Religions* 48, no. 1 (2020): 31–58.

Orzech, Charles, Henrik Sørensen, and Richard Payne, eds. *Esoteric Buddhism and the Tantras in East Asia.* Leiden: Brill, 2010.

Sakai Norifumi 酒井規史. "Sōdai dōkyō ni okeru dōhō no kenkyū 宋代道教における道法の研究." PhD diss., Waseda University, 2011.

Schachter, Bony Braga. "Nanji Chongxu Miaodao Zhenjun: The *Tianhuang zhidao taiqing yuce* and Zhu Quan's (1378–1448) Apotheosis as a Daoist God." PhD diss., Chinese University of Hong Kong, 2018.

Strickmann, Michel. *Chinese Magical Medicine.* Edited by Bernard Faure. Stanford: Stanford University Press, 2002.

ter Haar, Barend. "Rumours and Prophecies: The Religious Background of the Late Yuan Rebellions." *Studies in Chinese Religions* 4, no. 4 (2019): 382–418.

von Glahn, Richard. *The Sinister Way: The Divine and the Demonic in Chinese Religious Culture.* Berkeley: University of California Press, 2004.

Wang Chien-chuan 王見川. "Zhenwu xinyang zai jinshi Zhongguo de chuanbo 真武信仰在近世中國的傳播." *Minsu yanjiu* 民俗研究, no. 3 (2010): 90–117.

Wang Chien-chuan 王見川. "Song-Ming shiqi de fuji, fuluan yu qingxian: Jiantan fuji, enzhu deng ci de qiyuan 宋—明時期的扶箕、扶鸞與請仙：兼談扶乩、恩主等詞的起源." In *Fuluan wenhua yu minzhong zongjiao guoji xueshu yantaohui lunwenji* 扶鸞文化與民眾宗教國際學術研討會論文集, edited by Fan Chun-wu 范純武, 53–88. Taipei: Boyang wenhua, 2020.

Wang Chien-chuan 王見川 and Pi Qingsheng 皮慶生, *Zhongguo jinshi minjian xinyang: Song Yuan Ming Qing* 中國近世民間信仰—宋元明清. Shanghai: Shanghai renmin chubanshe, 2010.

Wang Ya 王亞. "Nansong Jingmingdao de fa, zhi, lu yu Dongshenbu lujie de chedi fuhaohua 南宋淨明道的法、職、籙與洞神部籙階的徹底符號化." *Hongdao* 弘道, no. 2 (2016): 96–104.

Xu Dishan 許地山. *Fuji mixin de yanjiu* 扶乩迷信的研究. Changsha: Shangwu yinshuguan, 1941.

Xu Wei 許蔚. *Duanlie yu jiangou: Jingmingdao de lishi yu wenxian* 斷裂與建構：淨明道的歷史與文獻. Shanghai: Shanghai shudian chubanshe, 2014.

Xu Wei 許蔚. "Xin tianjun fa yu Hunyuan daofa de gouzao 辛天君法與混元道法的構造." *Daoism Religion, History & Society* / 道教研究學報：宗教、歷史與社會, no. 9 (2017): 141–159.

CHAPTER 3

Spirit-Writing Practices from the Song to Ming Periods and Their Relation to Politics and Religion

Wang Chien-chuan 王見川

During the past few years, the amount of research on Chinese spirit-writing[1] has gradually increased and produced significant results, specifically for the period between the end of the Ming and beginning of the Qing and the modern era.[2] The spirit-writing activities that took place between the Song and the Ming periods, however, are far less well-understood and many gaps remain. Three years ago, I published a paper in which I discussed this topic, and made initial attempts to clarify the circumstances of the spirit-writing associations from the Song to the Ming periods,[3] particularly the approximate time during which the term "supporting the stylus" (*fuji* 扶乩) appeared. I was able to show that this happened during the Wanli 萬曆 reign (1573–1620).[4] However, due to the discovery of new sources,[5] this field of study still has much potential. Accordingly, based on my previous paper, this article attempts to describe and analyze the circumstances and characteristics of specific forms of spirit-writing, such as "supporting the sieve" (*fuji* 扶箕), "supporting the phoenix" (*fuluan* 扶鸞),

---

1 Please note that the term "spirit-writing" is used in this article as an etic and generic designation for a variety of different techniques and not a direct translation from the sources. When highlighting differences between the various techniques, more specific translations will be used. For a more thorough discussion of the emic and etic terminology of spirit-writing, see the introduction to this volume.
2 For the previous research on spirit-writing during the late Ming and early Qing periods, see Wang, "Song-Ming shiqi de fuji," 53–54. On spirit-writing in modern China, see Wang, "Spirit-writing Groups in Modern China," 651–84; and Wang, "Popular Groups Promoting 'The Religion of Confucius,'" 90–121.
3 Wang, "Song-Ming shiqi de fuji."
4 Ibid., 85–87.
5 Vernacular novels from the Song and Yuan periods, such as the *Xinke wanfa guizong* 新刻萬法歸宗 (Newly carved edition of the *Ten Thousand Methods to Return to the Origin*) and the *Yang xunjian Meiling shiqi ji* 楊巡檢梅嶺失妻記 (A record of Military Inspector Yang losing his wife in Meiling), as well as brush notes from the Song, such as the *Zhiya tang zachao* 志雅堂雜鈔 (Miscellaneous writings from the Hall of the Pursuit of Elegance), the *Yinju yongyi* 隱居通議 (Exchanging arguments while living in seclusion) and others, all reflect the appearance of this new phenomenon of spirit-writing by the sieve.

"supporting the stylus" (*fuji* 扶乩), "descending into the brush" (*jiangbi* 降筆) and "calling on transcendents" (*qingxian* 請仙) during this period by drawing on brush notes (*biji* 筆記), spirit-written religious scriptures and other documents. Moreover, it will also discuss the relation between spirit-writing, politics, and religion—focusing on Buddhism and Daoism—during the mid-Ming period.

1 Spirit-Writing Practices from the Song to Ming Periods[6]

As is well known, divination is an ancient technique that was traditionally employed in China to learn about the future and solve practical problems. As far as we know, during the Song Dynasty at the latest, there evolved two types of techniques of spirit-mediumship used in divination, one featuring a human medium and the other an instrument. The former was spirit-possession (referred to as *fushen* 附身, "taking possession of the body," or *jiang tong* 降童, "descending into a child"),[7] while the technique that relied on an instrument was variously referred to as "supporting the sieve" (*fuji*), "descending into the brush" (*jiangbi*) or "supporting the phoenix" (*fuluan*); techniques that are commonly referred to as "spirit-writing" in the English language. This section will discuss the circumstances and characteristics of spirit-writing from the Song to the Ming periods. First, I will examine the technique of "supporting the sieve," while the following section will consider the practices related to the designations "descending into the brush" and "supporting the phoenix."

1.1 *"Supporting the Sieve" and "Calling on Transcendents" during the Song Dynasty*[8]

From Xu Xuan's 徐鉉 (916–991) *Jishen lu* 稽神錄 (Records of investigating the divine), we know that, as early as the Five Dynasties period, there existed a practice called "supporting the sieve." At that time, a rice winnowing sieve, into which chopsticks had been inserted, was used to divine by writing on a tray filled with rice flour, a practice that occurred only on the fifteenth day of the first lunar month.[9]

---

6 Xu Dishan 許地山 touched on these topics at a relatively early stage. See Xu, *Fuji mixin di yanjiu*. See also Shiga, *Chūgoku no kokkurisan*. This section is based on Wang, "Song-Ming shiqi de fuji."
7 See Hong, *Yijian zhi*, vol. 2, 855–56.
8 Many important materials for the study of spirit-writing during the Song period are quoted in Xu, *Fuji mixin di yanjiu*.
9 Xu, *Jishen lu*, juan 6, 108. See also, "Fuji 扶箕," in Yu, *Chaxiang shi congchao*, juan 14, 322–23.

At the beginning of the Song Dynasty, so only slightly later, this kind of practice had already become relatively popular and was called "inviting [the deity] Zigu" (*ying Zigu* 迎紫姑).[10] According to the account in Shen Kuo's 沈括 (1031–1095) *Mengxi bitan* 夢溪筆談 (Brush talks from the dream brook) from the Jingyou 景祐 reign of Emperor Renzong 仁宗 (1034–1038), the practice had the following characteristics at that time:

1. Unlike earlier practices that involved the sieve, the practice of "Inviting Zigu" was no longer restricted to the fifteenth day of the first lunar month, but the deity could be summoned whenever necessary.
2. It was regarded as an entertaining pastime, frequently participated in by children.
3. There were already a few literati who engaged in the practice in their homes.
4. The *Nü xian ji* 女仙集 (Collection of writings by female transcendents), a collection of poems (transmitted by the deity Zigu), was already in circulation.
5. The deity Zigu not only divined the future, but also transmitted medical prescriptions.[11]

This indicates that the dates, character, and functions of the practice of "inviting Zigu" continuously shifted and broadened over time. Only slightly later, Su Shi 蘇軾 (1037–1101), an official at the court of Emperor Shenzong 神宗 (r. 1067–1085), published two relevant articles: "Zigu shen ji 子姑神記" (An account of the deity Zigu)[12] and "Tianzhuan ji 天篆記" (An account of heavenly writings),[13] detailing his experiences regarding the practice of "supporting the sieve" and reflecting on the shape of the practice during the mid-Northern Song period. He reports that, at that time, "supporting the sieve" was sometimes practiced in private homes. The divine intentions were transmitted through chopsticks or a brush made of straw and wood that was placed in the hands of a woman so that she might write down the characters or draw images. The practice was used to compose poetry or answer questions on religion and other matters.

By 1117, at the end of the Northern Song period, the practice of "supporting the sieve" had developed further. In the capital city of Kaifeng 開封, there even

---

10 On this practice, see also the contributions by Hu Jiechen and Elena Valussi in this volume.
11 Shen, *Xin jiaozheng mengxi bitan, juan* 21, 213–14. See also chapter three in Hsieh, *Liuchao zhiguai xiaoshuo*, 82–83.
12 See vol. 2 of Su, *Su Shi wenji, juan* 12, 406–7. See also chapter three in Hsieh, *Liuchao zhiguai xiaoshuo*, 80–81.
13 See vol. 2 of Su, *Su Shi wenji, juan* 12, 407–8.

appeared associations that centered on the practice and instructed the broader public through spirit-written messages attributed to deities that were referred to as "heavenly worthy" (*tianzun* 天尊) and "great transcendent" (*daxian* 大仙).[14] As a consequence of this growing institutionalization, the authorities issued a prohibition and demolished those halls in Kaifeng and other regions where it was practiced.[15] This swift action on the part of the government at that time in fact reflected the threat to the political and public order as perceived by the authorities when messages transmitted through the sieve gradually led to the establishment of religious teachings. This particular government measure was not only directed at associations which engaged in "sieve-writing," however, but formed part of a whole range of measures that the Song Emperor Huizong implemented from the Chongning 崇寧 reign (1102–1106) onward to reform religious activities ("demonic teachings" [*yaojiao* 妖教], "licentious shrines" [*yinci* 淫祠], and "spirit-mediums" (*shiwu* 師巫), as well as illegal vegetarian halls [*zhaitang* 齋堂] were all banned).[16] According to the *Pingzhou ketan* 萍州可談 ([Matters] from Pingzhou worthy of discussion), this ban put an end to the transmission of spirit-written messages by Zigu.[17] In reality, however, this assessment exaggerates the reach and efficacy of the authorities. Associations that engaged in the practice of "supporting the sieve" outside the capital prefecture of Kaifeng probably merely went into hiding and lowered their profile. Moreover, only a few years later, the Northern Song period descended into unrest, with widespread banditry and rebellions, wherefore it was soon vanquished by the Jin 金 Dynasty (1115–1234). Under these circumstances, one imagines that the effect of prohibiting the practice of "supporting the sieve" must have been very limited!

This is also indicated by the fact that this practice continued to flourish during the Southern Song period. During that time, several brush notes, such as *Youhuan jiwen* 游宦紀聞 (Records of a traveling official),[18] *Kenqing lu* 肯綮錄 (Records of scraps of important [matters]),[19] and *Yijian zhi* 夷堅志 (Records of the listener), contain accounts of the practice.[20] These records demonstrate that the practices of "inviting Zigu" and "supporting the sieve" during the Southern Song period were similar to the practices during the Northern

---

14 Hsieh, *Xin tiandi zhi ming*, 107.
15 Ibid.
16 Yin, *Song Huizong*, 134–35.
17 Zhu, *Pingzhou ketan*, juan 3, 161.
18 Zhang, *Youhuan jiwen*, juan 3, 22.
19 Zhao, *Kenqing lu*, 143.
20 Hong, *Yijian zhi*, vol. 1, 328–29, vol. 2, 855–56, vol. 4, 1486–87, 1668.

Song period: they were used to compose poetry and predict the future. However, the Southern Song brush notes provide more details about the practice; for example, the methods became more heterogenous. A stylus made of a winnowing basket could be used, but also a wooden hand that would clutch the brush, or the medium him/herself could hold the brush directly. The sites at which it was practiced became more heterogeneous as well, including private homes, Buddhist temples, and Daoist monasteries. Characters were written either upon ash or sand, and oral incantations were recited to invite the gods to descend.[21] To ask a question, people had to pay a fee. Lastly, "supporting the sieve" was sometimes referred to as "calling on the great transcendent" (*qing daxian* 請大仙) or "inviting the great transcendent" (*ying daxian* 迎大仙).

Because of a lack of sources, it is difficult to trace how these changes came about. The fact that spirit-writing deities were sometimes referred to as "great transcendents" (*daxian*), however, indicates that it was no longer necessarily Zigu who descended, and a host of deities started to be involved. If the deity was well-known or powerful, he/she was called "a great transcendent." If a regular or unknown deity descended, he/she was merely called "a transcendent." Ye Shaoweng 葉紹翁 (1194?–?) of the Southern Song period thus mentions, in his *Sichao wenjian lu* 四朝聞見錄 (A record of hearsay from the reigns of four emperors), that a deity who descended into the brush to predict that Emperor Guangzong 光宗 (r. 1189–1194) would ascend the throne was merely called Little Chen (Xiao Chen 小陳).[22]

The increasing diversity of divinities involved in spirit-writing is even more obvious for the North. Yuan Haowen's 元好問 (1190–1257) *Xu Yijian zhi* 續夷堅志 (Supplement to *Records of the Listener*) from the late Jin period mentions an episode involving a transcendent called Huang 黃 and a certain Mister Yang Zheng 楊徵.[23] Relaying this episode, Yuan refers to this kind of spirit-writing practice as "praying to the transcendents" (*qixian* 祈仙). Within the vernacular novel *Yang xunjian Meiling shiqi ji* 楊巡檢梅嶺失妻記 (A record of Military Inspector Yang losing his wife in Meiling) from the Song-Yuan period, moreover, an advertizement in a country inn near Meiling in Guangdong 廣東 is men-

---

21   On page 18, Xu Dishan in his *Fuji mixin di yanjiu* quotes the *Zhiya tang zachao*, which mentions that one has to "recite incantations" to call on transcendents. Other documents indicate that one must also burn talismans.
22   Cai, *Lishi de yanzhuang*, 466.
23   Yuan, *Xu yijian zhi, juan* 2, 34, 59. This episode occurred around the Taihe 泰和 reign (1201–1205) of the Jin Dynasty and Jiatai 嘉泰 reign (1201–1204) of Emperor Ningzong 寧宗 of the Southern Song.

tioned, which reads: "Yang Diangan can call on the transcendents to descend into the brush so that they [may provide] a norm for good and bad luck and [predict] fortune and misfortune without making any mistakes" (楊殿幹請仙下筆，吉凶有準，禍福無差).[24] This indicates how the practice of "calling on the great transcendent" spread in South China at that time. Zhou Mi's 周密 (1232–1298) *Zhiya tang zachao* 志雅堂雜鈔 (Miscellaneous writings from the Hall of the Pursuit of Elegance), from the same period, moreover, mentions Hu Tianfang 胡天放 (no dates), who was famous for calling on transcendents to descend into the sieve. His method roughly went like this:

1. Recite the *Jing tiandi zhou* 淨天地咒 (Incantation to cleanse heaven and earth).
2. Recite the *Beidou zhou* 北斗咒 (Incantation of the Northern Dipper).
3. Recite the *Jiedi zhou* 揭地咒 (Incantation to uncover the earth) seven times.
4. Recite the *Jiedi zhou* 揭諦咒 (Incantation to uncover the true meaning) seven times.
5. Write a talisman.
6. Write *sha* 煞 (evil spirit) and other characters.
7. Recite a secret incantation.
8. Recite the four incantations: "I now call on the great transcendent. I wish him to descend from his palace in Penglai, riding a crane to descend from the clouds to recite verses ceaselessly about the bright moon." (我今請大仙，願降蓬萊闕。騎鶴下雲端，談風詠明月不絕。)[25]

I have not seen any other records that discuss this method. Moreover, the descriptions of similar methods in the popular encyclopedia *Wanfa guizong* 萬法歸宗 (Ten thousand methods to return to the origin) also differ (see below). Hence, this method may be unique.

This diversification of spirit-writing continued beyond the Song period. Tao Zongyi 陶宗儀's *Nancun chuogeng lu* 南村輟耕錄 (Nancun's records from resting from ploughing) from the Zhizheng 至正 (1341–1370) reign of the late Yuan period thus mentions another synonym for "calling on the transcendents"; namely "summoning transcendents" (*zhao xian* 召仙). The passage in question reads:

> Hanging the sieve, supporting the phoenix, summoning the transcendents: these all refer to the arrival of eminent persons of old. Among the poems that were thus produced, many were excellent.

---

24 Hong, *Qingping shantang huaben jiaozhu*, juan 3, 214.
25 Zhou, *Zhiya tang zachao*, 109.

懸箕扶鸞召仙，往往皆古名人高士來格，所作詩文，間有絕佳者。[26]

Other Yuan period sources also use the designation "the transcendents of the sieve" (*jixian* 箕仙) to refer to the deities concerned.[27]

1.2   The Practices of "Descending into the Brush" and "Supporting the Phoenix" from the Southern Song to the Ming Periods

Having discussed the secular lay-practices, let us now turn our focus to spirit-writing techniques as they were practiced within Daoist circles during that period. Daoists, however, did not refer to the sieve, but called spirit-writing "descending into the brush" (*jiangbi*) or "supporting the phoenix" (*fuluan*). Based on our current sources and research, we know that there were centers of Daoist spirit-writing in both Sichuan 四川 and on Mount Wudang 武當.[28]

1.2.1   The Practice of "Descending into the Brush" on Mount Wudang from the Southern Song until the Ming Periods[29]

As far as we are aware, during the Northern Song period, Mount Wudang was a prominent site for both Daoists and Buddhists. It hosted Daoist monasteries as well as Buddhist temples. According to tradition, Wulong monastery 五龍宮 had already been established at that point.[30] During the Shaoding 紹定 reign of the Southern Song (1228–1233), there was even a temple in Tingzhou 汀洲 in Fujian 福建, that was linked to Mount Wudang through incense division (*fenxiang* 分香),[31] although we do not know currently whether any spirit-writing took place there. Our most important source on spirit-writing on Mount Wudang is the *Xuandi shilu* 玄帝實錄, or *Authentic Records of the Dark Emperor*. The original book, which had been revealed by Dong Suhuang 董素皇, was compiled in 1184 and given to Jiang Renyu 蔣人玉 (no dates) to have it printed and published by Zhang Mingdao 張明道 (no dates), the group leader (*banzhang* 班長) of the Zixu altar 紫虛壇 (Altar of Purple Vacuity) from Xiangyang 襄陽. Previous scholars have keenly noticed that the *Xuandi shilu* was produced through spirit-writing. Its aim was to propagate

---

26   Tao, *Nancun chuogeng lu*, juan 20, 245.
27   Ye, *Caomuzi*, juan 4, 59.
28   Hsieh, *Xin tiandi zhi ming*, 135–36.
29   This section is largely based on Wang and Pi, *Zhongguo jinshi minjian xinyang*, 214–24.
30   Chao, *Daoist Ritual*, 79–81.
31   Wang and Pi, *Zhongguo jinshi minjian xinyang*, 211–12. TN: During the ritual of incense division, coal is taken from the incense burner of one temple and given to another, which is thereby marked as a subsidiary of the donor temple. Through this ritual, extensive networks among temples can be created.

the deeds of Xuandi and make known the close connection between the deity and Mount Wudang. As such, it received much attention from the Daoists who resided on Mount Wudang during the Song and Yuan periods. Xuandi, the Dark Emperor, is one of the designations of the deity Zhenwu 真武, whose cult is closely associated with Mount Wudang. On the basis of this still extant source, we can ascertain that the mountain was occupied by Daoists, who venerated Zhenwu, from the Southern Song until the Yuan period. Moreover, the source also shows that spirit-writing activities were taking place in other locations, such as Xiangyang, which is located around 150 km to the East of Mount Wudang.

The *Xuandi shilu*, which was originally also called *Jiangbi shilu* 降筆實錄 (Authentic records [obtained through the practice of] descending into the brush),[32] confirms that it was in fact transmitted through spirit-writing which was, in this Daoist context, usually referred to as "descending into the brush" (*jiangbi*). Given the popular belief in Zhenwu at the time, believers—eager to gain a clearer understanding of the object of their faith—began to explore the life of Zhenwu and the reason why he was born, for which they used the sacred method of "descending into the brush." The fact that this book was also called *Dong zhenjun jiangbi shilu* 董真君降筆實錄 (Authentic records of the Transcendent Master Dong descending into the brush) reveals that the main deity of the altar at which the book was transmitted was the Transcendent Master Dong. This means that Dong Suhuang was a deity when this book was revealed rather than a human. The spirit-writing altar was located at Xiangyang. It was called Zixu tan and the main spirit-writing medium (*luanshou* 鸞手) was Zhang Mingdao. The fact that he called himself the group leader indicates that he was head of the spirit-writing community of that altar and possibly even a Daoist priest.[33]

---

[32] Wang and Yang, *Wudang Daojiao*, 77. Previous scholars have argued that the content of *juan* 卷 one of the *Xuantian Shangdi qisheng lu* 玄天上帝啟聖錄 (Record of epiphanies by the Supreme Emperor of the Dark Heaven), which was edited during the Yuan dynasty, was identical to the *Xuandi shilu*, revealed by Dong Suhuang, a work which is also called *Jiangbi shilu*. See Chou, *Daojiao lingyan ji*, 173–75. In fact, however, the original name of the *Xuandi shilu* associated with Dong Suhuang should be *Dong zhenjun jiangbi shilu* 董真君降筆實錄 (Authentic records of the Transcendent Master Dong descending into the brush), *Jiangbi shilu* or *Yuxu xuxiang Zhenwu shilu* 玉虛虛相真武實錄 (Authentic records of Zhenwu of Jade Vacuity and Empty Form). As the divine title Xuantian shangdi 玄天上帝 (Emperor of the Dark Heaven; also referred to as Xuandi) only appeared during the Yuan dynasty, we know that the title *Xuandi shilu* can have only been added during the Yuan period or later, rather than when Dong Suhuang's *Jiangbi shilu* was originally transmitted.

[33] For a comprehensive discussion of the link between Daoism and early spirit-writing, see the contribution by Vincent Goossaert in this volume.

Our sources indicate that the Zixu tan again practiced spirit-writing in 1185, pleading with the believers to kneel and enthusiastically chant the recently transmitted *Xuandi shilu*. In 1184–1185 another deity by the name of Zhang Ya 張亞 appeared. In the *Xuandi shilu*, this deity is referred to as Shangyuan jiutian zhangji yutang xueshi ... shangxian zhi huangjun 上元九天掌籍玉堂學士 ... 上仙之皇君 (The Scholar from the Jade Hall and Librarian of the Upper Prime of the Ninefold Heaven ... Who is the Imperial Lord of all Transcendents in the High Heavens) as well as Jinque haotian jianjiao dong shangxian yuanhuang chunyi Zhang zhenren 金闕昊天檢校洞上仙元皇純一張真人 (Highest Transcendent and Primordial Emperor, the Pure Perfected Zhang from the Proofreader's Grotto of the Golden Gate in the Vast Heavens). The name "Zhang Ya" and the divine title "Original Emperor" are all very similar to the title of a deity named Zhang Ya, which is mentioned in the *Wudang fudi zongzhen ji* 武當福地總真集 (A collection of all of the transcendents from the monasteries on [Mount] Wudang), which circulated during the Yuan dynasty. The said title is Jiutian zhangji shangxian yuanhuang dijun 九天掌籍上仙元皇帝君 (Librarian of the Ninefold Heaven, Highest Transcendent, Original Emperor and Divine Lord).[34] We can infer from this that the Original Emperor Zhang Ya is no other than the deity Zhang Ezi 張惡子 from Zitong 梓潼, who later came to be revered as Wenchang dijun 文昌帝君 (Divine Lord Wenchang).[35] This shows that, around the year 1184, this deity from Zitong appeared as a spirit-writing deity in Daoist spirit-writing associations. That the deity descended to spirit-writing altars at Xiangyang at that time was no coincidence, but reflects a more general tendency of this deity to participate in spirit-writing.[36]

Generally speaking, the *Xuandi shilu* had a significant influence on the Daoists on Mount Wudang. This book was not only included in the *Xuantian Shangdi qisheng lu* 玄天上帝啟聖錄 (Record of epiphanies by the Supreme Emperor of the Dark Heaven) from the Yuan period in a revised and adapted form, but also practically influenced the belief in Xuandi a.k.a. Zhenwu. The clearest example is the fact that the Daoists on Mount Wudang established the Tianyi zhenqing gong 天一真慶宮 (Palace of Heavenly Unity and Perfected Fortune) at Nanyan 南岩 during the early Yuan period. There is a clear record

---

34 Liu, *Wudang fudi zongzhen ji*, juan 3, 439.
35 TN: Zitong is the name of a region in Sichuan, which had been associated with the cult of a zoomorphic viper deity (*ezi* 蠶子/惡子) since at least the fourth century. Through many transformations, this deity eventually turned into the famous god Wenchang 文昌, who remains associated with Zitong to date. See Kleeman, *A God's Own Tale*.
36 Wang and Pi, *Zhongguo jinshi minjian xinyang*, 218–20.

of this project in the *Xuandi shilu*, which mentions that an abode designed as a residence for Zhenwu was to be set up in the Tianyi zhenqing gong.[37]

Naturally, the appearance of the *Xuandi shilu* indicates that, at that time, Mount Wudang was already a sacred place, associated with Zhenwu. The imperial title that was conferred on to him by the Emperor in 1257, during the Southern Song period, also substantiates this view.[38] We can therefore conclude that spirit-writing also penetrated the Xiangyang region at around the same time. At the close of the Southern Song period, it then seemingly also spread to Mount Wudang, which was then perceived as a safe haven. Many deities instructed people to go there to seek shelter from disasters.[39] It is, therefore, unsurprising that some of the monasteries on the mountain at the time also disseminated a few spirit-written instructions, attributed to Zhenwu, which advised people to seek refuge there.[40]

On this point, the book *Gui'er ji* 貴耳集 (A collection [of writings] for noble ears) by Zhang Duanyi 張端義 (fl. late twelfth to mid-thirteenth centuries), from the end of the Southern Song period, provides supporting evidence:

> Mount Wudang in Junzhou is the place where Zhenwu rose to heaven. Here, he responds efficaciously, like an echo. When Junzhou had not yet fallen, the Tartars (i.e., the Mongols) came, and the sage descended into the brush to say: "The black killer of the North has risen. I should abdicate in his favor." Afterwards, he appeared for three days at the top of a pine. All the people saw him.
>
> 均州武當山，真武上昇之地，其地靈應如響。均州未變之前，韃至，聖降筆曰："北方黑煞來，吾當避之"。繼而真武在大松頂現三日，民皆見之。[41]

---

37   It is worth noting that, in addition to the palace for Zhenwu, in the Lingying monastery 靈應觀, a Guiji Palace 桂籍殿 was established at that time, which offered sacrifices to the Original Emperor Zhang Ya. Liu, *Wudang fudi zongzhen ji*, juan 2, 431.

38   Liu, *Wudang fudi zongzhen ji*, juan 3, 438, states that "... [Previously, the deity] had been offered [the titles] Supporting Sageliness and Fortune and Virtue. Now, it is only proper that I should take the opportunity to add the title 'Enduring Auspiciousness.' How excellent and bright! This will also serve to spread the praise of Junyang [i.e., Junzhou 均州, where Mount Wudang is located]." (奉佑聖而崇福德，迨予眇沖固當增衍慶之封，嘉爾聰明，亦既述均陽之讚 ...).

39   "Renshi men 人事門," in *Huhai xinwen yijian xu zhi, qianji* 前集, juan 1, 50, and "Daojiao men 道教門," "Yuzhi guozuo 預知國祚," in *Huhai xinwen yijian xu zhi, houji* 後集, juan 1, 170.

40   "Renlun men 人倫門," in *Huhai xinwen yijian xu zhi, qianji* 前集, juan 1, 29–30.

41   Zhang, *Gui'er ji*, juan 3, 4315–16.

Zhang Duanyi was in no sense a follower of Daoism. The reason why he recounts this episode is that this spirit-written revelation was corroborated by later events.[42] Adding a dimension of religious warfare, Zhang's account details how the leaders of the Yuan army at that time spread the rumor that Dahei tianshen 大黑天神 (Great God of the Black Heaven), which refers to the deity Mahākāla whom the Mongols venerated, would attack Junzhou and certainly prevail, in order to motivate their soldiers. Such rumors seemingly reached the Daoists on Mount Wudang, who, as mentioned above, used spirit-writing to declare in Zhenwu's name that the deity would abdicate in favor of the Black Killer from the North, which, in turn, undermined the people's will to resist. Several scholars in fact believe that this was a rumor spread by enemy forces as a form of psychological warfare.

The same method was later used to placate the people in the regions which had recently come under the authority of the Yuan. Tao Zongyi's *Nancun chuogeng lu* from the Yuan states that, in 1276, people living in those areas of Jiangnan 江南 that had only recently come under the control of the Yuan, proclaimed that Zhenwu from Mount Wudang descended into the brush to transmit writings that should be stamped on yellow paper and hung on the walls.[43] These writings, the text continues, were composed according to the *Xijiang yue* 西江月, which is the name of a *ci* 詞 tune that was popular during the Song dynasty.[44] Apparently, these writings used a pattern that was popular at the time, and relied on the name of Zhenwu from Mount Wudang to instruct the people and legitimize the rule of the Yuan. The believers at that time considered these instructions to be equivalent to an imperial edict and posted them everywhere to notify the people. Such instructions continued to circuluate widely during the Ming Dynasty,[45] by which time, however, their content had already changed. They no longer foretold that the Yuan would replace the Song, but rather predicted the demise of the Yuan, serving as a *post-factum* confirmation and legitimation of the rise of the Ming.[46]

---

42   Ibid. TN: Zhang's story relates to the military campaign of the Mongol Army against the Song during the 1230s, when Junzhou fell and many Daoists on Mount Wudang were killed. See Ma, "Meng Yuan shidai Zhenwu," 85–98, and Chao, *Daoist Ritual*, 82–83.
43   Tao, *Nancun chuogeng lu*, juan 26, 328.
44   The name can be traced back to a poem by Li Bai 李白 (701–762). Each line contains six characters, and a poem has eight lines, with specified tonal patterns (*pingze* 平仄). Xijiang alludes to the Yangtze.
45   See "Xijiang yueci 西江月詞," in Lang, *Qixiu leigao*, juan 27, 287.
46   One such *Xijiang yue*, which dates to the mid-Ming period and was not spirit-written, featured Liu Bingzhong 劉秉忠 (1216–1274) as its author. It was printed by literati who

In the monasteries on Mount Wudang, the Daoist priests consistently maintained the practice of letting Xuandi instruct the people through spirit-writing. In 1301, during the Yuan period, the Lingying guan 靈應觀 (Monastery of the Numinous Response) produced the *Wudangshan Xuandi chuixun* 武當山玄帝垂訓 (Instructions handed down by the Dark Emperor on Mount Wudang) via spirit-writing.[47] This text clarified Xuandi's background: "I am called the God of Fortune who brings order to the world, the Great General Who Guards the Northern Heavens, in Buddhism [I am called] Amitabha (Chin. Wuliangshou 無量壽), in Daoism [I am] the reincarnation of the Golden Gate (i.e., the Jade Emperor)" (吾號治世福神，鎮北天大將軍，佛中即無量壽，道乃金闕化身). His duty was "to patrol all of heaven and earth, master the world's *qian* and *kun*, support the heavenly way at the end of the kalpa, and protect the grand ministers of the king, [as he was] unable to bear this evil world of five impurities and how the sentient beings suffer hardships and endure disasters of droughts and floods, hunger and starvation as well as diseases and epidemics" (巡遊諸天諸地，掌握世界乾坤。扶助末劫天道，護祐國王大臣，不忍五濁惡世，眾生受苦遭辛。旱澇饑饉疾疫). On the "three primes" (*san yuan* 三元; fifteenth day of the first, seventh, and tenth lunar months), eight solar nodes (*ba jie* 八節), three annual assemblies (*san hui* 三會),[48] five *la* days (*wu la* 五臘),[49] seven fast days (*qi zhai* 七齋) and three fast days of each month (*san qi* 三七; i.e., the seventh, seventeenth, and twenty-seventh day), the day that corresponds to one's natal horoscope,[50] as well as the *jiazi* 甲子 and *gengshen* 庚申 days, he would descend into the human realm to prosecute, distinguishing between the crimes and blessings, good and evil of the common people, handing out beneficial retribution or punishments accordingly. The believers were to be saved from the end of the kalpa, while the non-believers were to perish. Setting himself up as an example, the deity instructed the people of the world to be respectful and

---

attributed it to Liu, a mythical figure who helped Kublai Khan (Emperor Shizu 世祖, r. 1271–1294) to unite China.

47 TN: On this text, see also Goossaert, "Divine Codes, Spirit-Writing, and the Ritual Foundations," 27–29.

48 This refers to the annual assemblies of Tianshidao 天師道 (Heavenly Master) communities, during which the merits and faults of all parishioners are to be examined. They take place on the seventh day of the first, the seventh day of the seventh as well as the fifteenth day of the tenth lunar months.

49 According to the lunar calendar, these are the first day of the first, the fifth day of the fifth, the seventh day of the seventh, the first day of the tenth, and the eight day of the twelfth months.

50 i.e., the day on which the heavenly stems and earthly branches (*tiangan dizhi* 天干地支) correspond to those of one's birthday.

trustworthy, heed the instructions, and observe the ten good deeds (such as respecting heaven and earth, being filial and obedient to one's parents, etc.). If they were able to continue on this path, the wind and rain would be timely and favourable and there would be great peace among all under heaven. The text also emphasizes the effects of copying the scripture: with utmost effort, one would obtain glory and longevity; with average effort, one would be able to preserve one's body and one's family's safety; and with the least effort, one would be able to save one's ancestors and descendants. Finally, the text explains the nature of these instructions: coming from Xuandi, the text was to be considered a sacred, immutable code, referred to as "The Golden Law and Jade Code" (*Jinke yulü* 金科玉律). Its function was to admonish people in the lower realm, so it can be considered a "text for admonishing the world" (*quanshi jiewen* 勸世戒文).[51]

As shown above, the *Wudangshan Xuandi chuixun* contains several striking elements:

1. The text compares Zhenwu to Amitabha Buddha and stresses the equality of the three teachings.
2. It emphasizes that Xuandi will bring order to the world at the end of the kalpa, and that his role is to assist with saving people. If the believers are able to save themselves from the end of the kalpa, they will experience many years of great peace. The non-believers, on the other hand, will die and become ghosts.
3. It advocates vegetarianism, conversion to Buddhism and "the practice of abstinence" (*xiu zhai* 修齋), as well as alms-giving.[52]

In terms of its content, the *Wudangshan Xuandi chuixun* thus makes several additions to the biography of Zhenwu as it had been told during the Song and Yuan periods, such as observing a vegetarian diet, alms-giving, and other Buddhist values. Of particular interest is its apocalyptic thought and depiction of the apocalypse, which is close to the descriptions in Buddhist apocalyptic scriptures, such as the *Wugong jing* 五公經 (Sutra of the Five Lords) and the *Foshuo mojie jing* 佛說末劫經 (Sutra on the end of the kalpa as spoken by the Buddha).[53] One can say that, by using a Daoist voice to spread Buddhist, Confucian and popular religious values, it is a classical "admonitory text" (*xunjie wen* 訓戒文), which instructs people on how to behave in the world. From that perspective, the *Wudangshan Xuandi chuixun* can be called a "morality book" (*shanshu* 善書).

51　Wang and Pi, *Zhongguo jinshi minjian xinyang*, 224.
52　Ibid.
53　See Wang, "*Tuibei tu, Wugong jing*," 318–24. TN: On the *Wugong jing*, see also ter Haar, "Sutra of the Five Lords," 172–97.

Judging from our current sources, the *Wudangshan Xuandi chuixun* quickly became influential, as its effect can already be seen on Yuan drama.[54] Moreover, the *Wudangshan Xuandi chuixun* is also quoted with the title *Xuandi chuixun* in the morality book *Mingxin baojian* 明心寶鑑 (Precious mirror for enlightening the mind), from the beginning of the Ming period, which contains a wide variety of aphorisms and sayings to instruct the young.[55] Indeed, the renown of the *Xuandi chuixun* spread, together with the *Mingxin baojian* and other morality books. Moreover, a number of popular novels from the Ming period, such as the *Xiyou ji* 西遊記 (Journey to the West), contain quotes from the work.[56] Because of the reverence for Zhenwu that existed during the early Ming period, the *Wudangshan Xuandi chuixun* was continuously republished from newly-carved woodblock editions. As far as we are aware, woodblock editions from 1429, 1452, 1458, and 1596 are all extant.[57] In light of these many editions, the text certainly spread to an extent. Among those who came into contact with it are two particularly eminent figures: Jiang Zonglu 蔣宗魯 (1521–1588) and Chen Yongbin 陳用賓 (1550–1617), Grand Coordinator (Xunfu 巡撫) of Yunnan 雲南 in 1561 and 1604, respectively.[58] Jiang Zonglu argued that this text "simply urges people to be loyal, filial, friendly and respectful to one's elders, to transform oneself and others. It is really no deviant teaching" (無非要人忠孝友悌，化己化民，實非異教).[59] Chen Yongbin, moreover, argued that the *Wudang chuixin* was just like the legal code of the Great Ming, or the *Dagao* 大誥 (Great pronouncements) of Ming Emperor Taizu 太祖

---

54 The phrases "if one [does] remorseful [things] in secret, the eyes of the deities will strike like lightning" (暗室虧心、神目如電), for example, appears in the *Cui fujun duan yuanqin zhaizhu* 崔府君斷冤親債主 (Magistrate Cui judges the creditors of a wronged relative) and "The private talk of people is heard like thunder in the heavens. If one [does] remorseful [things] in secret, the eyes of the deities will strike like lightning" (人間私語、天聞若雷、暗室虧心、神目如電) in the Yuan drama *Wang Yueying yuanye liuxie ji* 王月英元夜留鞋記 (A record of Wang Yueying preserving her shoes on the night of the 15th of the first lunar month) and the encyclopedia for daily use *Zuantu zenglei shilin guangji* 纂圖增類事林廣記 (Comprehensive records from the forest of things, with compiled images and added categories). See Wang, *Yuanqu xuan jiaozhu*, bk. 3, juan 2, 2879, for the *Cui fujun duan yuanqin zhaizhu* and for the *Wang Yueying yuanye liuxie ji*, see Wang, *Yuanqu xuan jiaozhu*, bk. 3, juan 2, 3204. See also, *Zuantu zenglei shilin guangji*, pt. 2, juan 1, 38.
55 Wang, "*Mingxin baojiao yu Shuihu zhuan*," 195–98.
56 Ibid., 198–99.
57 Wang and Pi, *Zhongguo jinshi minjian xinyang*, 224–25.
58 This aspect has been studied by Chao Shin-yi 趙昕毅. See Chao, "Zhenwu xinyang zai Ming dai," 157–60; Chao, "Fuluan yu Zhenwu xinyang," 33–34, 47–48.
59 Xiao, *Yunnan Daojiao beike*, 74.

(r. 1368–1398),[60] since it shows how the human realm and netherworld work together to address wrongdoing.[61] The above indicates not only that the *Wudangshan Xuandi chuixun* circulated among a broad range of social strata but also that it circulated in many different shapes.

1.2.2 Religious Scriptures Composed through Spirit-Writing and Attributed to the Imperial Lord of Zitong in Sichuan during the Southern Song Period[62]

While Xuandi was engaging in spirit-writing activities on Mount Wudang, Sichuan, during the Southern Song period, saw the appearance of the Imperial Lord of Zitong, who was later venerated as the God Wenchang. Due to a dearth of sources, the circumstances of those spirit-writing activities remain difficult to clarify, but materials contained in the Daoist Canon reveal that at least the *Yuanshi tianzun shuo Zitong dijun yingyan jing* 元始天尊說梓潼帝君應驗經 (Scripture on the responses and proofs of the Divine Lord of Zitong as expounded by the Heavenly Worthy of Original Commencement) and the *Yuanshi tianzun shuo Zitong benyuan jing* 元始天尊說梓潼本願經 (Scripture on the original vow of Zitong as expounded by the Heavenly Worthy of Original Commencement) were composed through spirit-writing in the Sichuan area around that time. The aim of the former was to promote the Divine Lord Zitong from Mount Fenghuang 鳳凰 in Zitong. The inclusion in the text of the phrase "94 transformations" (*jiushisi hua* 九十四化) indicates that it was composed during the reign of Emperor Lizong 理宗 (r. 1224–1264) of the Southern Song.[63] Together with the *Yuanshi tianzun shuo Zitong benyuan jing*, it was included as one *juan* 卷 within the Daoist Canon. The emphasis of the latter text lies in explaining that the Jade Emperor (Yudi 玉帝) has fixed the date for the end of the kalpa (*ding jieshu* 定劫數) as humanity had fallen into degradation, and was prepared to send demon kings and other beings to wipe out all humans. However, as the text explains, the Transcendent Ciji 慈濟真人 and other divinities sorrowfully requested him to provide an escape route to preserve a glimmer of

---

60 TN: The *Dagao* was a provisional code, produced by Emperor Zhu Yuanzhang between 1385 to 1387. See Tam, *Justice in Print*, 5.
61 Xiao, *Yunnan Daojiao beike*, 124. The *Zhao shi Baowen tang shumu* 晁氏寶文堂書目 (Mister Zhao's book catalogue from the Hall of Precious Literature) from the Jiajing 嘉靖 reign (1522–1566) also contains an entry on the *Xuandi chuixun bing jinke yulü* 玄帝垂訓並金科玉律 (Instructions handed down by the Dark Emperor as well as the Golden law and jade code). Chao, *Chao shi bao wen tang shumu*, 226.
62 This section is based on Wang and Pi, *Zhongguo jinshi minjian xinyang*, 236–50.
63 Epigraphic records from this period mention that the transformations of the deity increased from 73 to 94. See Wang and Pi, *Zhongguo jinshi minjian xinyang*, 241.

hope for humanity. Thereupon, the deity Yuanshi tianzun 元始天尊 ordered the Imperial Lord of Zitong to descend to the realm of the mortals and save the world.[64]

At the end of the scripture, the Imperial Lord of Zitong is praised as the Compassionate Venerable of Qiqu (Qiqu cizun 七曲慈尊), with "only having a mindset of loyalty, filial piety, and compassion" (惟忠、惟孝、惟慈心) being the gist of his teaching. Only if one displayed penitence and sincerely "took refuge in the great compassionate light of Qiqu" (皈依七曲大慈光) would one be able "to seek progeny, prosperity, and a path for survival" (求嗣求祿求生方). Moreover, the text calls the God of Zitong "Teacher Wenchang from Qiqu" (Wenchang Qiqu shi 文昌七曲師) and "the Benevolent Ruler of Great Compassion from the Hall of Laurel Fragrance" (Guixiang dian Shangci beizhu 桂香殿上慈悲主). This suggests that the scripture intends to promote the Imperial Lord Zitong as a deity who stems from Mount Qiqu in Zitong.

The occurrence of the phrase "more than ninety transformations" (*jiushi yu hua* 九十餘化), which appears in the *Yuanshi tianzun shuo Zitong benyuan jing*, further indicates that this scripture was produced after the *Jiushisi hua shu* 九十四化書 (The book of 94 transformations)[65] and composed in the latter part of the Southern Song period. Moreover, in the book, the phrase "entrusted to practice the flying phoenix" (*weixing feiluan* 委行飛鸞) appears, which makes it clear that it was transmitted through spirit-writing.[66] Through my own research, I found that the transmission of the widely-circulated *Jiushisi hua shu* during the reign of Emperor Lizong, which records the transformations that the God of Zitong experienced during his lifetime, was also connected to the spirit-writing activities taking place on Mount Fenghuang in Zitong.[67]

The *Wenchang dijun qishisan hua shu* 文昌帝君七十三化書 (The book of the 73 transformations of the Divine Lord Wenchang), on the other hand, which was likewise transmitted by the God of Zitong, is believed to be connected to Liu Ansheng 劉安勝 (no dates). Terry Kleeman, a specialist in the study of Wenchang, has long drawn attention to Liu Ansheng and the members of his organization.[68] Due to a dearth of sources, however, scholars have managed to establish very little regarding the background and activities of this community. We can only rely on the records about Liu contained in the extant

---

64 Ibid., 242.
65 TN: On this book, its history and different editions, see Kleeman, *A God's Own Tale*.
66 Wang and Pi, *Zhongguo jinshi minjian xinyang*, 242.
67 Ibid., 240–42.
68 See Kleeman, *A God's Own Tale*, esp. 16–19.

scriptures of the Imperial Lord Wenchang.[69] From the preface to the *Wenchang dijun qishisan hua shu*, we learn, for example, that the core members of the spirit-writing community of Liu Ansheng were Liu himself, his sons Liu Dangcheng 劉當程 and Liu Yunqia 劉允洽, as well as his older brother or cousin Liu Jianshan 劉兼善. In other words, this spirit-writing community was based on family ties.[70]

Previous scholars have argued that the preface was composed at the spirit-writing altar of Liu Ansheng in the Chengying lou 誠應樓 (Tower of Sincere Response) on Mount Baoping 寶屏 in Sichuan in 1181.[71] This suggests that this community did not practice spirit-writing in a monastery but, rather, in a tower that was named after the beautiful environment in which it was located. This differs markedly from the context in which spirit-writing was practiced on Mount Wudang. Another difference is of a terminological nature. Practitioners on Mount Wudang or at the spirit-writing altar at Xiangyang referred to spirit-writing as "descending into the brush" (*jiangbi*), whereas Liu Ansheng's community called it "holding the brush" (*pengbi* 捧筆). Despite this difference, however, both communities referred to their activities as effecting "moral transformation" (*hua* 化).

In fact, the character "*hua*," meaning "moral transformation," or also "transformation" in the sense of "reincarnation," lies at the heart of the activities of Liu's community. According to the *Zitong dijun huashu* or the *Wenchang dijun huashu*, Liu Ansheng produced the *Qinghe neizhuan* 清河內傳 (Esoteric biography of Qinghe) through spirit-writing, and elaborated on the origins of the 73 transformations of the God of Zitong. Some thus assume that Liu, through spirit-writing, modified the phrase "having been scholars and officials for 73 generations" (七十三代為士大人), which was contained in the already circulating *Qinghe neizhuan*, by changing *dai* 代, meaning generations, to *hua* 化, meaning transformation. The implications of this change were huge, as it gave a completely new twist to the belief in the God of Zitong. The appearance of the original *Qinghe neizhuan* signals that the followers of the God of Zitong at that point already used spirit-writing to expound the background and character of the deity and legitimized and rationalized this deity by giving him a human biography.[72] In other words, the book presents a rationalized account

---

69 Hsieh, *Xin tiandi zhi ming*, 112.
70 Wang and Pi, *Zhongguo jinshi minjian xinyang*, 245.
71 Hsieh, *Xin tiandi zhi ming*, 112.
72 TN: The book links the God of Zitong, i.e., Wenchang, to a specific place and lineage, as Qinghe is a choronym of one of the most prominent Zhang 張 clans in the Wu 吳 region in Sichuan. The God of Zitong had long been associated with the surname Zhang, but

of the deity Zitong from the end of the Northern Song period, who had already begun to play a role in the civil-state examinations and literary production.[73] By changing "generation" to "transformation," Liu Ansheng further increased the significance of the feats that were ascribed to the God of Zitong and corroborated the circumstances surrounding the God of Zitong's reincarnations over a period of 73 generations. This is what the *Zitong huashu* refers to as "revealing the original beginning of the 73 transformations" (發揚七十三化之本始). Moreover, he thereby opened up the possibility that the God of Zitong would, in later ages, continuously be reincarnated in the human realm through spirit-writing. The *Jiushisi huashu* 九十四化書 (Book of the 94 transformations [of the God of Zitong]), *Jiushiqi huashu* 九十七化書 (Book of the 97 transformations), and *Jiushijiu huashu* 九十九化書 (Book of the 99 transformations) all adopted this line of thought.[74]

According to the findings of Hsieh Tsung-Hui 謝聰輝, the location of Liu Ansheng's spirit-writing activities was Mount Baoping in Pengxi 蓬溪 district in Sichuan province.[75] At that time, the God of Zitong, apart from revealing texts, also transmitted medical prescriptions.[76] There were other places, moreover, where the deity engaged in spirit-writing. According to the account of transformation 94 "Zhaoming hua 昭明化" (Transformation brightness) in *juan* four of the *Wenchang huashu* from 1645, the God of Zitong also descended to "prosperous Longyin, flourishing Wansong, refined Baizhang, and subsequently tranquil Pengxi" (昌之龍因，普之萬松、雅之百丈，遂寧之蓬谿), which all boasted spirit-writing altars.[77] At that time, "in Pengxi they explained and prefaced the *Yu jing* (Jade scripture), while in Wansong a title bestowed [on the deity] was transmitted" (蓬溪則解序玉經、在萬松則書降寵號). "Yang Si, a person from Yunsheng village in Baling, sponsored a ritual assembly for Wenchang" (巴陵運騰里人楊思作文昌星席) and further set up the Zhaoming yinghua tan 昭明應化壇 (Bright Altar Responding to the Transfor-

---

        the work makes this association explicit. In his biography in the *Zitong dijun huashu*, it is therefore stated that the God of Zitong had served as the prefect of Qinghe. See Kleeman, *A God's Own Tale*.

73 TN: Many candidates used to pray at Zitong and Wenchang temples before sitting the examinations.
74 Wang and Pi, *Zhongguo jinshi minjian xinyang*, 245.
75 Hsieh, "Yuhuang benxing ji jing," 187–89.
76 *Zitong dijun huashu*, juan 4, 96.
77 "Zhaoming hua 昭明化," in *Wenchang huashu*, juan 4, 354. The *Xiuxiang Wenchang huashu quanji* 繡像文昌化書全集 (Complete collection of *Wenchang's Book of Transformations*, with a portratit) records Pengxi 蓬溪 as Penglai 蓬萊. See "Zhaoming hua 昭明化," in *Xiuxiang Wenchang huashu quanji*, juan 4.

mation [of the God Zitong]).[78] Moreover, in 1207, during the rebellion of Wu Xi 吳曦 (1162–1207), who had been Vice Pacification Commissioner (*Xuanfu fushi* 宣撫副使) before defecting and declaring himself king, and the troubles in 1231, when the Mongol army raided Sichuan, Yang transmitted writings through spirit-writing which were designed to warn people and save them from the apocalypse.[79]

What needs clarification is the meaning of the sentence "in Pengxi they explained and prefaced the *Yu jing*." Hsieh Tsung-Hui argues that this phrase indicates that those who followed and identified with Liu Ansheng's spirit-writing community composed the *Yuhuang jing* 玉皇經 (Scripture of the Jade Emperor).[80] However, the context of the sentence clearly indicates that they only explained the scripture and wrote a preface, but did not compose the scripture itself. In other words, at that time, the *Yuhuang jing* had already been transmitted, and those following and identifying with Liu Ansheng's community merely explained and prefaced it through spirit-writing. This also becomes clear when we look at the postface to the scripture written by Cheng Gongxu 程公許 (?–1251): "When Sichuan suffered from the hardships caused by enemy forces, [people] in Qiqu relied on the phoenix [to compose] great books and induced [the people] constantly to recite these scriptures." (蜀罹敵難，七曲托鸞大書，以此經勸誘課誦。)[81] In light of the above, it is clear that this reference to "relying on the phoenix [to compose] long books" refers to the spirit-written explanation and preface to the *Yuhuang jing* which emphasized that one should recite this scripture in order to avoid disasters. Liu Ansheng's community thus did not compose new spirit-written scriptures to save the world from the apocalypse but, instead, invoked the will of the deities through spirit-writing to inform people that they could save themselves by reciting existing scriptures.

1.2.3 Spirit-Writing on Mount Fenghuang and Mount Qiqu during the Song and Yuan Periods

In the past, the majority of scholars who worked on the early history of spirit-writing in Sichuan focused on Liu Ansheng and his community, while very few considered the spirit-writing activities at the ancestral temples of the God of

---

78 "Zhaoming hua," in *Wenchang huashu*, juan 4, 354–55.
79 See transformation 95, "Hengtun hua 亨屯化," in *Wenchang huashu*, juan 4, 355. The punctuation of the corresponding sentence in the *Xiuxiang Wenchang huashu quanji* is problematic.
80 Hsieh, *Xin tiandi zhi ming*, 165–67.
81 Ibid., 213.

Zitong on Mount Qiqu and Mount Fenghuang. Accordingly, below, we will discuss the temples on these two mountains in Zitong district.

According to the "Zifu feixia dongji 紫府飛霞洞記" (Records from Feixia Grotto in the Purple Prefecture) from 1207, the temple of the God of Zitong near that grotto was built in 1146.[82] An anonymous stele inscription with the title "Wenchang ci 文昌祠" (Ancestral temple of Wenchang) from the Ming period further explains that the Zifu feixia grotto is on a terrace on the Eastern Thousand Buddha Cliff 東千佛岩臺 on Mount Fenghuang.[83] According to related sources, it was a father and son called Gou Zhu 苟洙 who completed the site in 1207 and began practicing spirit-writing there.[84] In other words, by 1207 at the latest, spirit-writing was taking place at the temple to the God of Zitong on Mount Fenghuang.

When did people at the ancestral temple on Mount Qiqu start to engage in spirit-writing? Based on the related records and research regarding the *Xinbian lianxiang soushen guangji* 新編連相搜神廣記 (Extensive records of the search for the divine, newly-compiled and combined) from the Yuan Dynasty, we know that *juan* one of the *Wenchang huashu*, "Lingying dadi huashu shishi 靈應大帝化書事實" (Circumstances of the book of transformations of the Great Emperor of Numinous Response) was written at the end of the Song period, possibly during the reign of Emperor Duzong 度宗 (r. 1264–1274).[85] If we compare this with other related accounts, we realize that one section of that book, which narrates the circumstances surrounding the Jiangbi ting 降筆亭 (Pavilion for Descending into the Brush) at the temple for the God of Zitong, is a revised version of the "Lingying dadi huashu shishi."[86] In other words, the passages in both the "Lingying dadi huashu shishi" and the *Xinbian lianxiang soushen guangji* illustrate the circumstances surrounding the practice of spirit-writing at the temple of the God of Zitong on Mount Qiqu at the end of the Southern Song period. Even though we do not know who participated in these activities due to a dearth of sources, we can ascertain that the spirit-writing practices at that time had the following characteristics:

1. The divinity wrote characters on paper using a brush fixed to the beak of a five-colored phoenix.
2. The site at which spirit-writing was practiced was hermetically-sealed.

---

82 Long and Huang, *Bashu Daojiao beiwen*, 154–55.
83 Ibid., 211.
84 See "Zifu feixia dongji 紫府飛霞洞記," in *Xiuxiang Wenchang huashu quanji, juan* 1.
85 Wang, "Song-Ming shiqi de fuji."
86 Ibid.

3. After the practice was completed, the tolling of a bell, apparently without human intervention, notified the temple staff that it was time to fetch the message for inspection.
4. The majority of these messages encouraged people to be loyal and filial. Sometimes texts were produced and, at other times, talismans.

Clearly, the spirit-writing practice at the temple of the God of Zitong on Qiqu Mountain was intended to emphasize that the divine will was being transmitted objectively, without human interference. Its unique writing instrument is striking here: a five-colored flying phoenix, holding a brush in its beak, as well as the fact that characters were written on paper rather than ash or sand. Based on this, it is possible that the use of "the flying phoenix" (*feiluan*) and "supporting the phoenix" (*fuluan*) as designations for spirit-writing originated with this particular practice.

One should bear in mind, however, that, at that time, "the flying phoenix" was a noun and designated the instrument used for spirit-writing. This is why the scripture *Yuanshi tianzun shuo Zitong benyuan jing*, mentioned above, describes spirit-writing as being "entrusted to practice the flying phoenix." It also contains the designations "hanging phoenix" (*chui luan* 垂鸞) and "dwelling in the phoenix" (*yu luan* 寓鸞). By the late Song at the latest, however, the phrase "letting the phoenix fly to inspire [moral] transformation" (*feiluan kaihua* 飛鸞開化) appeared in the *Jiushiqi huashu*.[87] Moreover, *juan* 13 of the roughly contemporaneous *Gaoshang dadong Wenchang silu ziyang baolu* 高上大洞文昌司祿紫陽寶籙 (Precious register of purple yang of Wenchang, Master of Emoluments from the Most High) also proclaims that "one can spread moral transformation through the flying phoenix and [thereby] relieve the world and bring peace to people" (可以飛鸞演化，濟世安民). At that point, thus, *feiluan* was already a verb, similar in use to *fuluan*, "supporting the phoenix."

In addition to the spirit-writing activities in the temples for the God of Zitong on Mount Qiqu and Fenghuang, records in the *Zhengtong daozang* 正統道藏 (Daoist canon of the Zhengtong reign) edition of the *Zitong dijun huashu* 梓潼帝君化書 (Book of the transformations of the Divine Lord of Zitong) indicate that there were also other spirit-writing altars dedicated to the God of Zitong in Lechang 樂昌 in Fuling 涪陵 prefecture during the Southern Song period; namely, the Zhaoming yinghua luantai 昭明應化鸞台 (Bright Phoenix Terrace Responding to the Transformation [of the God of Zitong]), Yueluan tan 月鸞壇 (Moon Phoenix Altar) in Yuexia 月峽, and Yingji zhentan 英集真壇 (Perfected Altar Where the Heroes Gather) in the Xia region.[88]

---

87 *Wenchang huashu, juan* 4, 354–55.
88 *Zitong dijun huashu, juan* 4, 97–99.

According to the record in Zhao Yanzhi's 趙延之 (no dates) "Xingci ji 行祠記" (A record of temple visits) from the Yuan period, the temple of the God of Zitong on Mount Qiqu was given the title "Temple Assisting Culture and Accomplishing Moral Transformation" (Youwen chenghua zhi ci 佑文成化之祠) in 1316. Local officials among the temple staff, such as the *shisheng* 侍生, or main phoenix-medium, Yang Shiren 楊世仁, the temple workers Wang Shouyong 王壽永 and Wang Jun 王鈞 (all no dates) as well as others, had donated money to construct the temple of the God of Zitong.[89] Moreover, the "Xingci ji" also reveals that, at that time, several high officials believed in spirit-writing, and some even left their carriage to ask questions via spirit-writing. This indicates the prestige that the practice must have enjoyed in Sichuan at that time.

This reputation gradually spread and influenced several religions and religious beliefs. The famous spirit-writing temple in the ancestral temple of Xu Zhizheng 徐知證 and his brother in Fuzhou 福州 during the Yuan dynasty is an example of this. *Juan* nine of the *Xu xian hanzao* 徐仙翰藻 (Literary writings of the Xu transcendents) reads:

> Zitong once descended into the brush on the peak of [Mount] Min, where they have been greatly praying for the blessing of the Primordial Emperor (i.e, Wenchang, the Divine Lord of Zitong). …

> 梓槿（typo for 潼）嘗降筆於岷峨，侈拜元皇之賀 …[90]

The *Xu xian hanzao* is a collection of the finest spirit-written texts by the Xu transcendents. They were even referred to as "serving in the position of Managers of the Registers of Wenchang" (任文昌司祿之職), indicating their close connection with the God of Zitong.[91] By the Ming dynasty, this temple was also transmitting medical prescriptions via spirit-writing. Tradition has it that the Ming Emperor Chengzu 成祖 (r. 1402–1424) fell ill and was treated with his transcendent prescriptions, in return for which the temple received a grand ceremony as a token of his gratitude.[92]

---

89   Zhao, "Xingci ji," 45.
90   *Xu xian hanzao, juan* 9, 225.
91   Ibid., *juan* 11, 242.
92   Wang, *Mingdai lingji daopai*, 176–78.

2 Spirit-Writing under the Prohibitions of the Yuan and Ming Periods and Its Relation to Politics, Buddhism, and Daoism

2.1 Official Prohibitions against "Supporting the Phoenix" during the Yuan and Ming Periods

Even though it gradually became commonplace among Daoist believers since the Southern Song period to engage in spirit-writing in the monasteries and temples on Mount Wudang, and on Mount Qiqu and Fenghuang in Sichuan, there were also opposing views in Daoist circles. Bai Yuchan 白玉蟾 (1134–1229), for example, criticized those studying Daoist practices (*fa* 法) individually who became fascinated by experiences of spirit-mediumship connected to the ritual of "opening the light" (*kai guang* 開光),[93] or engaged in spirit-written communication with spirits and deities. Bai refers here to people engaging in this kind of esoteric transmission and considers this a transmission from "heterodox teachers" (*xieshi* 邪師).[94] In *juan* 7 of the *Daomen dingzhi* 道門定制 (Prescribed rules for the Daoist community) by Lü Yuansu 呂元素 (no dates), written in 1201, we thus find the phrase "spirit-writing is a demonic [perversion] of Daoism" (降筆為教門之魔).[95]

However, the Daoist leader at the time, the Heavenly Master Zhang (Zhang tianshi 張天師) from the Longhu 龍虎 Mountain, nevertheless condoned spirit-writing. Liu Xun's 劉壎 (1240–1319) *Yinju tongyi* 隱居通議 (Exchanging arguments while living in seclusion) from the end of the Southern Song or early Yuan period records that, when asked to hold a *jiao* 醮 ritual[96] in Jinling 金陵 during the early Duanzong 端宗 reign of the Southern Song (1275–76), he summoned the deities to divine fortune and misfortune through spirit-writing. At that time, Heavenly Master Zhang ordered a suspended phoenix brush to be set up within a curtain made of yellow cloth.[97]

On the state level, we can discern a critical attitude toward spirit-writing. The legal text *Tongzhi tiaoge* 通制條格 (Articles from the comprehensive regulations) from the early Yuan period, for example, mentions that, from 1274, officials began to prohibit "praying to the gods, community festivals and processions, supporting the phoenix, and praying to sages" (祈神、賽社、扶鸞、

---

93 TN: This is a ritual performed to call down the spirits and deities and make them reside in an image of a deity or an effigy of the deceased. See Asano, "Kaiguang 開光," 596.
94 Bai, *Bai Yuchan zhenren quanji*, juan 9, 1321–22.
95 Lü, *Daomen dingzhi*, juan 7, 78.
96 TN: A *jiao*, meaning "offering," is a community ritual, lasting several days, that aimed to reconfirm relations with a group's tutelary deity and fend off harm. See Andersen, "Jiao."
97 Liu, *Yinju tongyi*, juan 30, 316.

禱聖) as well as other practices.[98] After Emperor Taizu of the Ming established his dynasty, he revised the Yuan laws concerning religion and religious beliefs. During the sixth lunar month of 1370, for example, he gave orders that certain popular religious practices were to be prohibited: "… practices such as supporting the phoenix, praying to sages, writing talismans, and charm water are prohibited. [Everyone] is ordered to comply with this." (… 扶鸞、禱聖、書符、咒水諸術並加禁止 … ，詔從之。)[99] This order by Emperor Taizu continued the prohibitions that had been issued by officials since the early Yuan period. As it was later included in the *Daming lü* 大明律 (Code of the Great Ming), we can say that "spirit-writing," or more specifically, "supporting the phoenix," was illegal during the Ming dynasty. Although the Daoist book *Tianhuang zhidao yuce* 天皇至道玉冊 (Jade books on the highest way of the Heavenly Emperor) from 1444 mentions all sorts of spirit-writing techniques, such as "the phoenix of the highest ultimate" (*taiji luan* 太極鸞), "brush rack phoenix" (*bijia luan* 筆架鸞), "phoenix suspended on a thread" (*xuansi luan* 懸絲鸞), and "phoenix in a box" (*fengxia luan* 封匣鸞),[100] which illustrates that Daoists continued to view the phoenix as an instrument for communicating with the deities, the majority acknowledged that this was to be practiced only internally and not in public.

Indeed, due to the prohibition contained in the Ming legal code, there are very few records of the public practice of "supporting the phoenix" from that time. Accounts of "supporting the sieve" or "calling on transcendents," on the other hand, are relatively common. Zhou Qifeng 周岐鳳 (no dates), for example, who had mastered numerous scholarly disciplines and skills and was a skilled poet, after his death in the capital during the Tianshun 天順 reign (1457–1464), often "attached himself to the phoenix *ji*" (*fu luanji* 附鸞乩) in places where he had formerly resided, in order to transmit poetry.[101] It is clear from the account that the practice described was identical to "supporting the phoenix" as it was practiced at the time. That the section is nevertheless entitled "Zhou Qifeng descends into the brush" (*Zhou Qifeng jiangbi* 周岐鳳降筆) clearly reflects the author's intention to avoid mentioning the designation of the illegal practice of "supporting the phoenix." The account contains another curious aspect, namely its reference to the character *ji* 乩. Some may be tempted to think that the phrase "Zhou Qifeng attached himself to the phoenix *ji*" indicates that the character *ji* was already used in the sense of a "stylus" at the time,

---

98   See "Qisai deng shi 祈賽等事," in Tongzhi tiaoge *jiaozhu*, juan 28, 673.
99   Quoted in Wang, *Cong Monijiao dao Mingjiao*, 347.
100 Shiga, *Chūgoku no kokkurisan*, 112–13.
101 Wang, *Yupu zaji*, juan 9, 129.

SPIRIT-WRITING PRACTICES FROM THE SONG TO THE MING   115

as it came to be used later. This, however, is in appearance only, because the said spirit-written text contains a description of the practice, which specifies that "the sieve was moving as if it were flying" (*ji yun ru fei* 箕運如飛).[102] This indicates that, at that time, it was still a sieve that was used for the practice of "supporting the phoenix."

Other accounts similarly specify how spirit-writing was practiced under the official prohibition. During the Hongzhi 弘治 (1488–1505) reign of the Ming Emperor Xiaozong 孝宗 (r. 1487–1505) and the Zhengde 正德 reign of Emperor Wuzong 武宗 (1506–1521), the famous official Du Mu 都穆 (1458–1525) respectfully stated that "at times, it happens that spirits and deities descend into the brush. Recently, I saw it [in the home] of one Mister Zou. It was truly marvelous" (鬼仙降筆時有之。近余在鄒氏所見頗奇).[103] The *Gengsi bian* 庚巳編 (A compilation from the year *gengsi*) of Lu Can 陸粲 (1494–1552) from the mid-Zhengde reign (1510–1519), moreover, states that, in 1499, there were people in the capital praying to transcendents. A scholar called Cheng Huangdun 程篁墩 arrived "and said by descending into the brush: I was traveling through the night together with [Su] Dongpo and heard that some were calling on transcendents" (降筆云：夜偕東坡遊，聞有請仙者).[104] The real name of this scholar was Cheng Minzheng 程敏 (1446–1499), who had been sent to prison because the head examiner had found some problems with his metropolitan examination. After being released from prison, he died indignant. When he reappeared in spirit-form, he had not been dead for long and his appearance caused a stir among the spirit-writing circles of the time. Later, he again descended in the capital to tell of his lofty ambitions and wasted talent.[105] Shen Zhou's 沈周 (1427–1509) *Shitian weng kezuo xinwen* 石田翁客座新聞 (News from the guests of old Shitian), on the other hand, mentions an incident in which "a transcendent of the sieve descended into the brush to seek out the corpse of a dead person" (仙箕降筆尋屍).[106] This episode took place in 1502 and indicates that spirit-writing activities involving a sieve remained widespread at that time. All of the above examples illustrate that the prohibition against spirit-writing, or more specifically "supporting the phoenix," proved futile. As long as one avoided using the specific designation "supporting the phoenix" (*fuluan*) and rather referred to "supporting the sieve," "descending into the brush," or "calling on the transcendents," there was still room for these medi-

---

102 Ibid.
103 Du, *Dugong tanzuan*, juan 2, 186.
104 Lu, *Gengsi bian*, 28.
105 Chen, *Zhishi yuwen*, 16.
106 Shen, *Shitian weng kezuo xinwen*, juan 10, 392–93.

umistic practices to take place. Of course, when discussing the practice in their brush notes, scholars would care little about the illegal nature of spirit-writing anyway. What mattered to them was the function of spirit-writing: not only was it a literary pastime, but it also allowed people to address their life problems, satisfy the literati's interests, provide information about their career prospects, and help with the production of literary texts. In other words, its utility, as well as mystical and marvelous nature of spirit-writing, incentivized the literati to forget that they were breaking the law when participating in this practice.

There are two other aspects, aside from the traditional functions of spirit-writing such as poetry,[107] story-telling and painting,[108] as well as divination[109] that deserve mention when discussing the practice at that time: firstly, the use of spirit-writing to hint at the fate of the country; and, secondly, the use of spirit-writing to influence politics. Let me mention a few examples.

In 1486, a spirit-medium from Jiaxing 嘉興 summoned transcendents for spirit-writing. He asked about current events and received a poem that was structured according to the twelve two-hour periods of the day (*shi'er chen* 十二辰). The poem mentioned that the divine dragon (*shenlong* 神龍), although it had not yet encountered difficulties, was in shallow waters. Since the dragon was a symbol of the emperor, the poem suggested that the monarch would face trouble. True enough, in the following year, it so happened that the Emperor Xianzong 憲宗 (r. 1464–1487) died. Hence, this was interpreted by the people of the time as meaning that the prediction of this spirit-medium had been accurate.[110] Similar accounts, relating to political events, are common at the end of the Ming period. For example, both the *Zaolin zazu* 棗林雜俎 (Miscellaneous offerings from the forest of jujubes)[111] and the *Mingji beilüe* 明季北略 (Northern campaigns during the Ming period),[112] mention that the deity Xuandi indicated, through spirit-writing, that the Ming dynasty had come to an end and would shortly be replaced by a new dynasty. The deity predicted that people were also facing hard times due to disasters and wars. During the mid- and late Ming period, using spirit-writing to assess the fate of the country had already become a means for people to cope with crises.

---

107 Lang, *Qixiu leigao*, juan 32, 353; juan 37, 403.
108 Ibid., juan 45, 479–80.
109 Ibid., juan 49, 518. See also "Linshui furen ji 臨水夫人記" (Records of lady Linshui) by a Ming author, Gao Cheng 高澄, in Jiang, *Mazu wenxian*, 85.
110 *Jiuchao tanzuan*, vol. 3, 1019.
111 Tan, *Zaolin zazu*, 91.
112 Ji, *Mingji beilüe*, juan 14, 235.

In addition, some came to use spirit-writing to influence the emperor and meddle in politics. There were two prominent examples at the time: Li Zisheng 李孜省 (?–1487) during the Chenghua 成化 reign (1465–1487) and Lan Daoxing 藍道行 (no dates) during the Jiajing reign (1522–1566). While the latter case has been touched upon by previous scholars, Li's case is less well-known. In reality, Li was the first to use spirit-writing to influence court politics. According to Yang Yi's 楊儀 (no dates) *Gaopo yizuan* 高坡異纂 (A compilation of strange [phenomena] from Gaopo), Li was from Nanchang 南昌 in Jiangxi 江西, and initially served as a low-ranking official. After arriving in Beijing, however, he displayed his skills in Daoist thunder rites (*leifa* 雷法) and attracted the attention of the Ming Emperor Xianzong, who was deeply fond of Daoist ritual techniques.[113] The *Huang Ming lichao zizhi tongji* 皇明歷朝資治通紀 (The Imperial Ming's comprehensive records from previous dynasties to aid administration) from the Jiajing period states that Li was accused of graft. He was arrested and interrogated by Inspector-General and Imperial Censor Yang Shousui 楊守隨 (1435–1519), before subsequently being punished by banishment and compulsory military service. He escaped to the capital, however, and, due to his social connections, was able to enter the imperial palace. Through the use of talismanic water, he secured the trust and favor of emperor Xianzong. He was subsequently appointed Assistant to the Court of Imperial Sacrifices in the Board of Rites (Libu taichang sicheng 禮部太常寺丞). Due to the intervention of Imperial Censor Yang Shousi, his position was changed and he was put in charge of the hunting grounds within the imperial mausoleum park. However, shortly afterward, he was again promoted to the post of Vice-Minister of the Board of Rites. At that point, Li received a secret order from the Emperor to serve as his eyes and ears and monitor other officials. He wrote short notes which were inserted in documents to be presented to the emperor who, in return, held Li in high esteem.[114]

The *Yecheng kelu* 冶城客論 (Talk among guests from Yecheng), which is quoted in the *Jiuchao tanzuan* 九朝談纂 (A compilation from nine courts [of the Ming]), on the other hand, gives a different account. The text states that Li rose up through the ranks due to an incident that occurred in 1471. At that time, the son of the highest-ranking imperial concubine (who was named Zheng 鄭), whom Emperor Xianzong loved dearly, died. The Emperor missed him very much, and his mother fell ill due to grief. At that point, they were told

---

113 Yang, *Gaopo yizuan*, 405.
114 The *Huang Ming lichao zizhi tongji* is also known as *Huang Ming tongji*. See Chen, *Huang Ming tongji*, juan 24, 918–19.

that Li Zisheng was able to summon the souls of the dead. Hence, the concubine Zheng recommended that the emperor summon Li Zisheng and ask him to use his skills so that they could both meet the soul of their dead son. As a consequence of this service, Li eventually received a large reward and was given an official position. After that initial episode, the Emperor again asked Li Zisheng to call on the deities, which brought him into contact with the Eight Transcendents (baxian 八仙). This further strengthened the Emperor's belief in Li's skills.[115] Afterwards, the decisions regarding the appointment of top-level officials were mostly based on Li's recommendations.[116] One person, therefore, accused him of wreaking havoc on politics by using his heterodox techniques, and thereby rocking the base of the country.[117] In the third month of 1487, Li was nevertheless promoted to Minister of the Board of Works, which put him in charge of the clerks in the Office of Transmissions (Tongzheng sishi 通政司事) that controlled all memorials to be presented to the emperor. Five months later, however, Emperor Xianzong died, whereupon the crown prince replaced him and sentenced Li to death. All of the officials who had been affiliated with the former Emperor were dismissed.[118]

While this put an end to Li's activities at court, the above suggests that, during the 17-year period from 1471 to 1487, political affairs were heavily influenced by spirit-writing. There is no other case like this before or since. It was mainly due to Emperor Xianzong's trust in him that Li Zisheng was able to gain such influence. This trust is also reflected in another episode recorded in the *Yecheng kelun*. Here, we learn that Li Zisheng competed with the Heavenly Master Zhang, who had come to court for an audience, regarding their ability to summon transcendents. It states: "The Heavenly Master memorialized the Emperor, demanding that Zisheng should be punished for misleading the emperor." (天師奏孜省惑亂天聽，當誅。) The Emperor laughingly replied: "If someone's able to trick the emperor, his skills can't be that bad. [Hence, I] will continue to treat him favorably, like before" (能欺人主，其術亦不淺。寵待如故).[119] This shows that the Emperor was certain that Li possessed magical skills and trusted that he would use them to help the court rather than advance his own agenda. He therefore gave him preferential treatment until he died.

The case involving Lan Daoxing at the court of the Jiajing Emperor followed a different pattern. As is generally known, the Jiajing Emperor was a fervent

---

115   *Jiuchao tanzuan*, vol. 3, 1126–28.
116   Chen, *Huang Ming tongji, juan* 24, 922–29.
117   Ibid., 921.
118   Ibid., 929–30.
119   *Jiuchao tanzuan*, vol. 3, 1128–29.

believer in Daoism and deeply interested in all sorts of Daoist rituals and practices. According to the *Mingshi shiji benmo* 明史記事本末 (Historical events from the Ming period in their entirety) by Gu Yingtai 谷應泰 (1620–1690) from the late Ming or early Qing periods, the Jiajing Emperor's increasing belief in the existence of deities and spirits was due to two incidents: first, a murder plot staged by a female palace servant Yang Jinying 楊金英 and others in 1543, and, second, the seizure of the traitor Wang San 王三 (no dates) by border soldiers in Datong 大同 in winter 1544. In addition to profusely rewarding the Transcendent Tao Zhongwen 陶仲文, the Emperor gradually started to believe in the practice of spirit-writing. In autumn 1545, because of a message received through spirit-writing, he gave an order to bury the bones of abandoned corpses and issued a general pardon to all officials. He was admonished by a minister at the time, who pleaded with him not to believe in spirit-writing. The minister was demoted to commoner status as a result,[120] indicating the intensity of the Emperor's belief in spirit-writing.

During the fourth lunar month of 1561, having held power for a long time, the Grand Secretary Yan Song 嚴嵩 (1480–1567) was removed from office. This was an important incident which is conventionally thought to have been connected to Lan Daoxing, who is described as a "master of techniques" (*fangshi* 方士). It is thought that it was Lan who used spirit-writing to advise the removal of Yan Song and his son. The *Mingshi* 明史 (History of the Ming), compiled during the Kangxi 康熙 (1661–1722) reign, reads:

> The Daoist master Lan Daoxing used [the technique of] "supporting the stylus" to win the favor of the throne, and the Emperor secretly inquired [of him] whether officials were virtuous or not. Daoxing fabricated spirit-written messages, which all stated that Song and his son had abused their power. This was why the emperor grew distant from Song and appointed Xu Jie [instead].
>
> 方士藍道行以扶乩得幸，帝密問輔臣賢否。道行詐為乩語，具言嵩父子弄權狀，帝由是疏嵩而任徐階。[121]

The text continues:

> Lan Daoxing found favor with the throne by using the technique of "supporting the phoenix." Whenever [the Emperor] had a question, it would

---

120   Gu, *Mingshi jishi benmo, juan* 52, 551.
121   "Liezhuan 列傳 98," in *Mingshi*.

be sealed in a box and a eunuch would be dispatched to burn it at the altar. The responses tended to diverge from what [the emperor] had intended. The emperor blamed the eunuch for being indecent and he became fearful.[122] He approached Daoxing, who began to look [at the messages] before burning them, which is when they started to accord with the intentions of the emperor. The emperor was delighted, and asked: "Where in all under heaven is there anything that is not properly governed?"

藍道行以扶鸞術得幸，有所問，輒密封遣中官詣壇焚之，所答多不如旨。帝咎中官穢褻，中官懼，交通道行，啟視而後焚，答始稱旨。帝大喜，問：「今天下何以不治？」[123]

Daoxing thus deliberately wronged Yan Song by faking a divine message that accused him of treason. To that, the Emperor replied: "If it were really the case (that he had committed treason), why did the transcendents above not kill him?" (果爾，上仙何不殛之？) The answer was: "They waited for the Emperor to kill him himself." (留待皇帝自殛。) The Jiajing Emperor was moved by this and wondered whether to remove Yan Song from office. Just at that moment, the Imperial Censor Zou Yinglong 鄒應龍 (presented scholar of 1556) submitted a memorial, impeaching Yan Song. As a consequence, the Jiajing Emperor dismissed Song and sent him back to his native place. Shortly after this event, the son of Yan Song learned that this had been Lan Daoxing's doing and initially wanted to change the official stance on his father by paying 120,000 cash, which offer was refused.[124] Thereupon, he bribed people near the Emperor to reveal that Lan Daoxing had become arrogant after gaining the favor of the throne, abused his power and done other unlawful things. As a consequence, Lan Daoxing was arrested, thrown into prison and executed.[125]

The reason why the *Mingshi*, which was finished much later, refers to the technique of "supporting the phoenix" as a designation for spirit-writing is because it throws a negative light on the episode as the practice had long been proscribed under that name. The fact that it also uses the expression "supporting the stylus," on the other hand, reflects the spread of the new term

---

122   TN: Moral uprightness, often expressed by the term "sincerity" (*cheng* 誠), is usually assumed to be a prerequisite for successful communication with deities and transcendents. This is possibly what the Emperor was hinting at when he blamed the content of the messages on the indecency of the eunuch.
123   TN: This passage is also translated, slightly differently, in Wan, "Building an Immortal Land," 95.
124   Huang, *Guoshi weiyi, juan* 7, 207.
125   "Liezhuan 列傳 195," in *Mingshi*.

ji for a stylus at the beginning of the Qing period. Gu Yingtai's *Mingshi jishi benmo*, which was a contemporaneous source, instead uses the phrase "supporting the sieve" to describe Lan's activities.[126] The *Guankui xiaozhi* 管窺小識 (A small record from a restricted view) from the Wanli reign also mentions that he used the technique of "supporting the sieve" to gain the trust of the Jiajing Emperor.[127] The contemporary Zhang Xuan 張萱 (no dates), in his *Yi yao* 疑耀 (Doubting brilliance), likewise reports that the Jiajing Emperor Shizong 世宗 (1507–1567) dismissed a high-level minister in 1545 due to messages transmitted through the sieve.[128] Shortly afterwards, the emperor again had officials arrested based on messages received via a platform for the transcendents of the sieve (*jixian tai* 箕仙台) that had been erected by a minister.[129] The above accounts and analysis reveal one thing: namely, the Jiajing Emperor believed in spirit-writing but could not tolerate anyone using it to express his/her personal views and meddle with court politics. Lan Daoxing, when he abused his powers as a medium, violated this taboo and was therefore executed.

2.2 *The Influence of Spirit-Writing on Daoism and Buddhism: Spirit-Written Messages by Lüzu, Guandi, and Bodhisattvas*

Our current sources demonstrate that there appeared a new phenomenon in spirit-writing circles during the period from the Jiajing to the Wanli reigns; namely, the descent of the deities Lüzu 呂祖 and Guandi 關帝. Qian Xiyan's 錢希言 (no dates) *Kuai yuan* 獪園 (Garden of mischief) mentions that, at this time, the *Wanshou jinshu* 萬壽金書 (Golden book presented on the emperor's birthday), which was transmitted by Lüzu through spirit-writing, was presented to the Jiajing Emperor.[130] This suggests that, by the Jiajing period at the latest, Lüzu was already participating in spirit-writing activities. In 1589, the Daoist disciple Li Yingyang 李應楊 (no dates) and others also transmitted the *Bapin xianjing* 八品仙經 (Transcendent scripture in eight chapters) via spirit-writing.[131]

---

126   Gu, *Mingshi jishi benmo*, juan 52, 554.
127   *Guankui xiaozhi*, 12. On page 31, the *Guankui xiaozhi* also states: "The two Ministers of Personnel Xiong Beiyuan and Li Zhizhai were both from Jiangxi. However, one of them had remonastrated about the transcendents of the sieve ... [and] they were both dismissed." (熊北原厲治齋二冢宰，皆江西人也。然一已諫箕仙...俱去。)
128   Zhang, *Yi yao*, 162.
129   Ibid., 162.
130   Qian, *Kuai yuan*, 62.
131   *Lüzu quanshu*, juan 9, 7. TN: The *Bapin xianjing* originally consisted of several texts, transmitted to different altars, that were later compiled and included in the *Lüzu quanshu* 呂祖全書 (Complete canon of Patriarch Lü). See Lai, "Qingdai sizhong *Lüzu quanshu*," 190–91.

With regard to Guandi's appearance in spirit-writing, the *Guandi lidai xiansheng zhizhuan* 關帝歷代顯聖誌傳 (A record of the sagely manifestations of Emperor Guan through the ages), a hagiography of Guandi from the end of the Ming period, provides an example from 1432.[132] Moreover, the *Liuqing rizha* 留青日札 (Daily jottings of Liuqing), from the Wanli reign, also mentions that people called on King Guan 關王 (i.e., Guandi) to descend into the sieve to answer questions.[133] In addition, the Governor-General of Fujian also communicated with Guandi via spirit-writing about how to defend China against Japan.[134] Lastly, the *Jiyi xinchao* 集異新鈔 (A new collection of strange phenomena) from the late Ming period states how Guandi descended into the stylus to answer the questions of a certain *juren* 舉人 (recommended man) by the name of Cai 蔡 regarding his career prospects.[135]

At the same time that these Daoist deities began to descend, Buddhist divinities also started to participate in spirit-writing. Feng Mengzhen's 馮夢禎 (1548–1606) *Kuaixue tang riji* 快雪堂日記 (A diary of the Hall of Swift Snow) states: "During the fourth lunar month of the year 1600 … on day fifteen … we invited a Buddha and the Buddha descended. Three people supported the tray. The tray moved in a way comparable to [the practice of] supporting the stylus." (四月 … 十五日 … 請佛，佛降，三人持盤，盤轉動如扶乩之狀 …)[136] Unfortunately, this is all we know about this early instance of a Buddhist deity participating in spirit-writing, but the above examples nevertheless illustrate two points: first, the descent of Daoist and Buddhist deities gradually became more widespread during the late Ming period; and, second, a new designation for spirit-writing appeared, namely "supporting the stylus."

2.3   The Spread and Influence of the Term "Supporting the Stylus" (fuji 扶乩)

"Supporting the stylus" (*fuji*) is today an ubiquitous, generic term for spirit-writing, which merits a closer look at its origins. Generally speaking, there were various different designations in use during the end of the Ming period. Lang Ying's 郎瑛 (1487–1566) *Qi xiu lei gao* 七修類稿 (Manuscript arranged in seven categories), which stems from the period from the Jiajing to the early Wanli reigns, thus uses the expression "supporting the sieve" to desig-

---

132   Mu, *Guandi lidai xiansheng zhizhuan*, 67–68.
133   Tian, *Liuqing rizha, juan* 28, 421.
134   Lu, *Guansheng dijun shengji tuzhi quanji*, 235.
135   *Jiyi xinchao, juan* 7, 216.
136   Feng, *Kuaixue tang riji, juan* 12, 153.

nate spirit-writing activities. In this book, Lang Ying mentions several spirit-written poems, which were produced when people at that time "summoned the transcendents" (*zhaoxian*).[137] Concurrently, books began to appear that specifically taught people how to practice the technique of "sieve-writing." The *Wanfa guizong*, for example, includes in its first *juan* a method for calling on the transcendents to descend into the sieve. Likewise, the *Wu che ba jin* 五車拔錦 (Five carts of selected marvels), an encyclopedia for daily-use from the Wanli reign, also contains "a technique for writing by descending into the sieve" (*jiangji bifa* 降箕筆法), in the section on Daoism (Xuanjiao 玄教). From this text, we also learn that the ritual of "supporting the sieve" was relatively complex and unlike its depictions in some of the brush notes, which seem to indicate that one could simply chant a few incantations and burn some talismans, then the transcendents would descend. The above-mentioned books also show that the practice of spirit-writing was widespread during the mid-Ming period, when manuals even appeared through which people could learn how to practice spirit-writing themselves. They also indicate that the phrases "descending into the sieve" and "supporting the sieve" remained the most widespread designations for spirit-writing at the time.

However, at that exact time, we see a change taking shape. During the Hongzhi reign, the expression "descending into the stylus" (*jiangji* 降乩) was already in use as a designation for spirit-writing.[138] During the mid-Zhengde reign (1510–1519), the *Gengsi bian* refers to a spirit-medium being engaged, "who took possession of the stylus" (*fuji* 附乩) to summon a divine general to decide on matters. The surge in the use of the term "stylus"[139] indicates that, by the mid-Ming period, some people were apparently already using a new instrument to summon transcendents; namely, the stylus. Expressions such as "supporting the stylus" or "descending into the stylus" also successively appear in the brush notes of the Wanli reign.[140] Wang Shizhen 王世貞 (1526–1590), for example, mentions, in his *Yanzhou shanren xugao* 弇州山人續稿 (Supplemented drafts by the hermit from Yanzhou), that, in 1581, a scholar called Wan Yuanyu 王元馭 was taught the following method for inviting the transcendent Zigu into the stylus by an old Confucian scholar from the Guanxi 關西 region:

1. First, spread sand on the floor or the desk of the altar.
2. If the stylus moves, it will write down traces of characters.

---

137 Lang, *Qixiu leigao*, 403.
138 Shen, *Kezuo xinwen*, 493.
139 Lu, *Gengsi bian*, 36.
140 Mo, *Bichen*, 203; Feng, *Kuaixue tang riji*, juan 11, 133–34; and Qian, *Kuai yuan*, 106, 252.

3. Someone should identify the characters and write them down.[141]
The divinities who descended at that time included Lü Chunyang 呂純陽 (Lüzu), Zhang Guo 張果, and others from among the Eight Transcendents. If one compares this method with the accounts in other sources of the time, such as the *Yanzhou shanren xugao*,[142] it clearly has little resemblance to the practice of "inviting Zigu" from the Song period. One important difference was that the instrument employed was the stylus, and no longer the sieve. We find a description of the stylus in the *Songchuang mengyu* 松窗夢語 (Dream talk from the pine window), a book from 1593: "Wu Zhongyi, a student at the imperial academy, held an instrument made of peach wood. He was good at summoning all sorts of transcendents by using talismanic water, which predicted fortune and misfortune in the human realm" (吳中一監生，執桃木機，善以符水召致諸仙，言人間禍福).[143] Apparently, the stylus was made of peach wood and was thus very similar to the one used in modern-day spirit-writing. The *Kuai yuan*, from the late Wanli reign, also mentions a few cases of literati using the stylus.[144] This book also has a special entry on "transcendents of the stylus" (*jixian* 乩仙), which includes twelve cases of spirit-writing from all sorts of regions.[145] *Juan* eight of the *Meihua caotang bitan* 梅花草堂筆談 (Brush talks from the plum flower cottage) by Zhang Dafu 張大復 (1554–1630), which was published around the same time, recounts how a frail lay Buddhist printed a book entitled *Ling hui* 靈薈 (Numinous collection), which had been written by numerous transcendents who had descended into the stylus.[146] Moreover, there is an entry in the section on Daoism in the *Xu shi hong yu lou shumu* 徐氏紅雨樓書目 (Mister Xu's book catalogue from the Red Rain Tower) from 1602, which mentions the book *Qunxian jiangji shi* 群仙降乩詩 (Poems [transmitted] by numerous transcendents descending into the stylus).[147] Lastly, the *Lu*

---

141 Wang, *Yanzhou shanren xugao*, juan 156, 7152.
142 In Wang, *Yanzhou shanren xugao*, juan 74, 3637, it is stated that, "The deity Zigu attached herself to the stylus to transmit [writings], mostly using the names of high transcendents. ... The deity also attached herself to the stylus and argued that Daoists should achive transcendence ... so that when they die they will be set free. And eight days after their passing, they would attach themselves to the stylus. [The deity also] stated: I have been [dispatched] by the Supreme Emperor Master Lü ..." (紫姑神附於乩以傳，所托多上真名稱。... 神亦附乩言道人當得仙 ... 脫然而逝。逝之又八日而托於乩，言：我從呂師之上帝所 ... 。)
143 Zhang, *Songchuang mengyu*, 118.
144 Qian, *Kuai yuan*, 106, 252.
145 Ibid., 101–9.
146 Zhang, *Meihua caotang bitan*, juan 8, 528.
147 Xu, *Xu shi hong yu lou shumu*, 356.

shu 露書 (Book of dew), from the beginning of the Tianqi 天啟 reign (1621–1627), also makes numerous references to the practice of "supporting the stylus."[148]

Thereafter, an increasing number of sources mention the expressions "supporting the stylus" or "descending into the stylus" and describe the circumstances of the practice. The term "stylus" seems to have appeared in the mid-Ming period while, by the Wanli period, the expression "supporting the stylus" gradually began to spread. Until the Ming-Qing transition, "supporting the stylus" had become virtually synonymous with spirit-writing more generally.[149] As a consequence, the spread of the expression "supporting the stylus" also influenced the names of some of the more traditional religious practices; for example, when deities take possession of children (*tongzi* 童子), this came to be called *tongji* 童乩 or *jitong* 乩童.

3   Conclusion

Based on the above, we can glean important insights into the early history of spirit-writing. We learn that, during the mid-Northern Song period, spirit-writing was already popular among the literati. By 1116 at the latest, religious associations began to emerge in Kaifeng, the capital of the Northern Song, which practiced spirit-writing. These spirit-writing activities grew even more prominent during the early Southern Song period, when we can distinguish two distinct forms. On the one hand, spirit-writing was practiced by literati and commoners, which became a widespread and public phenomenon. On the other hand, spirit-writing was practiced in a less open manner within the Daoist temples and monasteries, where it was referred to as "holding the brush" (*pengbi*) or "supporting the phoenix" (*fuluan*). The functions of these two forms also varied: popular-literati spirit-writing produced collections of poetry and responsive poems (*changhe* 唱和), while Daoist spirit-writing transmitted or commented on scriptures. Among such Daoist spirit-written texts, the *Wudangshan Xuandi chuiwen*, which urged people to practice virtue, as well as prophetic texts on the fate of the country, proved particularly influential on the later history of spirit-writing.

Spirit-writing activities attracted the attention of the state authorities from an early stage. During the Northern Song period, prohibitions appear that tar-

---

148 Yao, *Lu shu*, juan 13, 311, 323.
149 For a preliminary study of spirit-writing during the Ming period, see Kou, *Mingdai Daojiao wenhua*, 543–51. However, my opinion differs. See Wang, "Song-Ming shiqi de fuji."

geted halls in Kaifeng where "supporting the sieve" was practiced. For political reasons, the early Yuan government further prohibited the discussion of astronomy, spirit-mediumship and other related activities, including spirit-writing, which was designated as "supporting the phoenix." As a consequence, "supporting the phoenix" became illegal. This policy was continued by later rulers.

These prohibitions, however, failed to prevent spirit-writing from both continuing to spread in general and also playing a political role. During the mid-Ming period, spirit-writing thus entered the realm of politics. As seen above, Li Zisheng was able to convince Ming Emperor Xianzong of his mediumistic skills by summoning deceased relatives and transcendents, leading the emperor to trust and condone his spirit-writing activities and even evaluate other officials on the basis of the transmitted messages. The Jiajing Emperor believed strongly in spirit-writing, which likewise came to feature in court politics, yet he retained a more rational attitude and punished practitioners who attempted to use spirit-writing to meddle in politics.

During the late Ming period, we see a few other trends that came to prove decisive for the history of spirit-writing. The deities Lüzu and Guandi begin to appear in spirit-writing activities, leading to the transmission of scriptures. Likewise, spirit-writing entered Buddhist circles and some spirit-written Buddhist scriptures began to be transmitted. At the same time, during the mid-Wanli reign, the stylus (*ji*) appeared. According to contemporary sources, it was made from peach wood and thus was probably the forerunner of the peach stylus used by Chinese phoenix halls and spirit-writing altars today.

During the Ming-Qing transition, a time of great social and political turmoil, spirit-writing entered a new phase, in which it flourished. Apart from the above-mentioned activities, which were all continued, this period saw the emergence of a few new phenomena that I will briefly mention here. One was a cross-fertilization between spirit-writing and Confucianism. Famous deceased Confucian scholars began to descend into the stylus, while the literati began to expound Confucian classics and Song Neo-Confucianism through spirit-writing.[150] At the same time, spirit-writing associations began to spread widely, some even transregionally. However, at this early stage, these associations did not yet attempt to effect a moral transformation of the country (which later revolved around the "eight virtues," *ba de* 八德) and politics (in the form of "public lectures," *xuanjiang* 宣講). Likewise, they did not yet talk about saving

---

150 On the role of Confucianism at spirit-writing altars, see also the contributions by Daniel Burton-Rose and Matthias Schumann in this volume.

the world (*jiushi* 救世) or saving people from the end of the kalpa (*jiujie* 救劫), nor had they yet entered the realm of popular religion. The latter are important developments that began during the mid-Qing period. Whether and how these are related to the spirit-writing tradition and associations of earlier periods is a question worthy of further exploration!

(*Translated by Matthias Schumann*)

Bibliography

Andersen, Poul. "Jiao." In *Encyclopedia of Taoism*, edited by Fabrizio Pregadio, vol. 1, 539–44. London: Routledge, 2008.

Asano, Haruji. "Kaiguang 開光, Opening the Light." In *Encyclopedia of Taoism*, edited by Fabrizio Pregadio, vol. 1, 596. London: Routledge, 2008.

Bai Yuchan 白玉蟾. *Bai Yuchan zhenren quanji* 白玉蟾真人全集. Compiled by Peng Helin 彭鶴林, edited by Xiao Tianshi 蕭天石. Taipei: Ziyou chubanshe, 1993.

Cai Hanmo 蔡涵墨. *Lishi de yanzhuang: Jiedu daoxue yinying xia de Nansong shixue* 歷史的嚴妝：解讀道學陰影下的南宋史學. Beijing: Zhonghua shuju, 2016.

Chao Li 晁瑮. *Chao shi bao wen tang shumu* 晁氏寶文堂書目. In *Chao shi bao wen tang shumu, Xu shi hong yu lou shumu* 晁氏寶文堂書目、徐氏紅雨樓書目. Shanghai: Shanghai guji chubanshe, 2005.

Chao Shin-Yi 趙昕毅. "Zhenwu xinyang zai Mingdai Yunnan 真武信仰在明代雲南." In *Daofa ziran, dehua tianxia: Zhongguo Yunnan Daojiao wenhua guoji xueshu yantaohui lunwenji* 道法自然、德化天下：中國雲南道教文化國際學術研討會論文集, edited by Liao Dongming 廖東明, 168–74. Beijing: Zongjiao wenhua chubanshe, 2018.

Chao Shin-Yi 趙昕毅. "Fuluan yu Zhenwu xinyang: Cong *Xuandi chuixun* tanqi 扶鸞與真武信仰：從《玄帝垂訓》談起." In *Fuluan wenhua yu minzhong zongjiao guoji xueshu yantaohui lunwen ji* 扶鸞文化與民眾宗教國際學術研討會論文集, edited by Fan Chun-wu 范純武, 33–52. Taipei: Boyang wenhua, 2020.

Chao, Shin-Yi. *Daoist Ritual, State Religion, and Popular Practices? Zhenwu Worship from Song to Ming, 960–1644*. London: Routledge, 2011.

Chen Hongmo 陳洪謨. *Zhishi yuwen* 治世餘聞. In *Zhishi yuwen, Jishi jiwen, Songchuang mengyu* 治世餘聞、繼世紀聞、松窗夢語, punctuated and collated by Sheng Dongling 盛冬鈴. Beijing: Zhonghua shuju, 1997.

Chen Jian 陳建. *Huang Ming tongji* 皇明通紀. Punctuated and collated by Qian Maowei 錢茂偉. 2 vols. Beijing: Zhonghua shuju, 2008.

Chou Hsi-po 周西波. *Daojiao lingyan ji kaocha: Jingfa yanzheng yu xuanyang* 道教靈驗記考察：經法驗證與宣揚. Taipei: Wenjin chubanshe, 2009.

Du Mu 都穆. *Dugong tanzuan* 都公談纂. 2 vols. In *Caomuzi wai sanzhong* 草木子外三種. Shanghai: Shanghai guji chubanshe, 2012.

Feng Mengzhen 馮夢禎. *Kuaixue tang riji* 快雪堂日記. Punctuated and collated by Ding Xiaoming 丁小明. Shanghai: Fenghuang chubanshe, 2010.

Goossaert, Vincent. "Divine Codes, Spirit-Writing, and the Ritual Foundations of Early-Modern Chinese Morality Books." *Asia Major*, 3rd ser., 33, no. 1 (2020): 1–31.

Gu Yingtai 谷應泰. *Mingshi jishi benmo* 明史記事本末. Taipei: Sanmin shuju, 1969.

Guankui xiaozhi 管窺小識. In *Xiangtai ji, Guankui xiaozhi* 香臺集、管窺小識. Taipei: Weiwen tushu chubanshe, 1977.

Hong Mai 洪邁. *Yijian zhi* 夷堅志. 4 vols. Punctuated and collated by He Zhuo 何卓. Beijing: Zhonghua shuju, 2006.

Hong Pian 洪楩. *Qingping shantang huaben jiaozhu* 清平山堂話本校注. Collated and annotated by Cheng Yizhong 程毅中. Beijing: Zhonghua shuju, 2012.

Hsieh Ming-Hsiun 謝明勳. *Liuchao zhiguai xiaoshuo gushi kaolun: Chuancheng xushi wenti zhi kaocha yu xilun* 六朝志怪小說故事考論：傳承虛實問題之考察與析論. Taipei: Liren shuju, 1999.

Hsieh Tsung-Hui 謝聰輝. "*Yuhuang benxing jijing* chushi de beijing yu yinyuan yanjiu 《玉皇本行集經》出世的背景與因緣研究." *Daojiao yanjiu xuebao: Zongjiao, lishi yu shehui* 道教研究學報：宗教、歷史與社會, no. 1 (2009): 155–99.

Hsieh Tsung-Hui 謝聰輝. *Xin tiandi zhi ming: Yuhuang, Zitong yu feiluan* 新天帝之命：玉皇、梓潼與飛鸞. Taipei: Shangwu yinshuguan, 2013.

Huang Jingfang 黃景昉 (1596–1662). *Guoshi weiyi* 國史唯疑. Shanghai: Shanghai guji chubanshe, 2002.

Huhai xinwen yijian xu zhi 湖海新聞夷堅續志. Punctuated and collated by Jin Xin 金心. In *Xu yijian zhi, Huhai xinwen yijian xu zhi* 續夷堅志 湖海新聞夷堅續志. Beijing: Zhonghua shuju, 1998.

Ji Liuqi 計六奇. *Mingji beilüe* 明季北略. 2 vols. Punctuated and collated by Wei Deliang 魏得良 and Ren Daobin 任道斌. Beijing: Zhonghua shuju, 2006.

Jiang Weitan 蔣維錟, ed. *Mazu wenxian ziliao* 媽祖文獻資料. Fuzhou: Fujian renmin chubanshe, 1990.

Jiuchao tanzuan 九朝談纂. 3 vols. Taipei: Weiwen tushu chubanshe, 1977.

Jiyi xinchao 集異新鈔. Transcribed by Li Zhenqing 李振清. In *Jiyi xinchao, Gaoxin yanzhai zazhu* 集異新鈔、高辛硯齋雜著, punctuated and collated by Luan Baoqun 欒保群. Beijing: Wenwu chubanshe, 2017.

Kleeman, F. Terry. *A God's Own Tale: The Book of Transformations of Wenchang, the Divine Lord of Zitong*. Albany, State University of New York Press, 1994.

Kou Fengkai 寇鳳凱. *Mingdai Daojiao wenhua yu shehui shenghuo* 明代道教文化與社會生活. Chengdu: Bashu shushe, 2016.

Lai Chi-tim 黎志添. "Qingdai sizhong *Lüzu quanshu* yu Lüzu fuji daotan de guanxi 清代四種《呂祖全書》與呂祖扶乩道壇的關係." *Zhongguo zhexue yanjiu jikan* 中國文哲研究集刊 42 (2013): 183–230.

Lang Ying 郎瑛. *Qixiu leigao* 七修類稿. Shanghai: Shanghai shudian chubanshe, 2001.
Liu Daoming 劉道明. *Wudang fudi zongzhen ji* 武當福地總真集. 3 *juan* 卷. In *Daozang yaoji xuankan* 道藏要籍選刊, edited by Hu Daojing 胡道靜, Chen Liansheng 陳蓮笙, and Chen Yaoting 陳耀庭, vol. 7. 3rd ed. Shanghai: Shanghai guji chubanshe, 1995.
Liu Xun 劉壎. *Yinju tongyi* 隱居通議. Taipei: Xinwenfeng chuban gongsi, 1984.
Long Xianzhao 龍顯昭 and Huang Haide 黃海德, eds. *Bashu Daojiao beiwen jicheng* 巴蜀道教碑文集成. Chengdu: Sichuan daxue chubanshe, 1997.
Lu Can 陸粲. *Gengsi bian* 庚巳編. In *Gengsi bian, Kezuo zhuiyu* 庚巳編、客座贅語, punctuated and collated by Tan Dihua 譚棣華 and Chen Jiahe 陳稼禾. Beijing: Zhonghua shuju, 1997.
Lu Zhan 盧湛. *Guansheng dijun shengji tuzhi quanji* 關聖帝君聖蹟圖誌全集. In vol. 2 of *Zhencang guji daoshu shizhong* 珍藏古籍道書十種. Taipei: Xinwenfeng chuban gongsi, 2001.
Lü Yuansu 呂元素. *Daomen dingzhi* 道門定制. In vol. 8 of *Daozang yaoji xuankan* 道藏要籍選刊, edited by Hu Daojing 胡道靜, Chen Liansheng 陳蓮笙, and Chen Yaoting 陳耀庭. Shanghai: Shanghai guji chubanshe, 1995.
Lüzu quanshu 呂祖全書. Compiled by Liu Tishu 劉體恕 and Huang Chengshu 黃誠恕. Taipei: Taipei guangwen shuju, 1980.
Ma Xiaolin 馬曉林. "Meng Yuan shidai Zhenwu da heitian gushi wenben liuchuan kao 蒙元時代真武大黑天故事文本流傳考." *Zangxue xuekan* 藏學學刊 10 (2014): 85–98.
Mingshi 明史. Compiled by Zhang Tingyu 張廷玉 (1672–1755). *Siku quanshu* edition.
Mo Shilong 莫是龍. *Bichen* 筆塵. In *Congshu jicheng xinbian* 叢書集成新編, edited by the Xinwenfeng chuban gongsi 新文豐出版公司, vol. 88. Taipei: Xinwenfeng chuban gongsi, 1985.
Mu Shi 穆氏, ed. *Guandi lidai xiansheng zhizhuan* 關帝歷代顯聖誌傳. Shanghai: Shanghai guji chubanshe, 2003.
Qian Xiyan 錢希言. *Kuai yuan* 獪園. Punctuated and collated by Luan Baoqun 欒保群. Beijing: Wenwu chubanshe, 2014.
Shen Kuo 沈括. *Xin jiaozheng mengxi bitan* 新校正夢溪筆談. Collated and annotated by Hu Daojing 胡道靜. Hong Kong: Zhonghua shuju, 1987.
Shen Zhou 沈周. *Kezuo xinwen* 客座新聞. *Biji xiaoshuo daguan* 筆記小說大觀, vol. 40, bk. 10. Taipei: Xinxing shuju, 1985.
Shen Zhou 沈周. *Shitian weng kezuo xinwen* 石田翁客座新聞. *Xuxiu siku quanshu* 續修四庫全書, vol. 1167.
Shiga Ichiko 志賀市子. *Chūgoku no kokkurisan: Furan shinkō to Kajin shakai* 中國のこっくりさん：扶鸞信仰と華人社會. Tokyo: Taishūkan, 2003.
Su Shi 蘇軾. *Su Shi wenji* 蘇軾文集. Punctuated and collated by Kong Fanli 孔凡禮. Beijing: Zhonghua shuju, 1999.
Tam, Ka-Chai. *Justice in Print: Discovering Prefectural Judges and Their Judicial Consistency in Late-Ming Casebooks*. Leiden: Brill, 2020.

Tan Qian 談遷. *Zaolin zazu* 棗林雜俎. Punctuated and collated by Luo Zhonghui 羅仲輝 and Hu Mingxiao 胡明校. Beijing: Zhonghua shuju, 2009.

Tao Zongyi 陶宗儀. *Nancun chuogeng lu* 南村輟耕錄. 3rd ed. Beijing: Zhonghua shuju, 1997.

Tongzhi tiaoge *jiaozhu* 《通制條格》校注. Collated and annotated by Fang Linggui 方齡. Beijing: Zhonghua shuju, 2011.

ter Haar, Barend J. "The *Sutra of the Five Lords*: Manuscript and Oral Tradition." *Studies in Chinese Religion* 1, no. 2 (2015): 172–97.

Tian Yiheng 田藝衡. *Liuqing rizha* 留青日札. Hangzhou: Zhejiang guji chubanshe, 2012.

Wan, Maggie C.K. "Building an Immmortal Land: The Ming Jiajing Emperor's West Park." *Asia Major*, 3rd ser., 22, no. 2 (2009): 65–99.

Wang Chien-chuan 王見川. *Cong Monijiao dao Mingjiao* 從摩尼教到明教. Taipei: Xinwenfeng chuban gongsi, 1992.

Wang Chien-chuan 王見川. "*Tuibei tu, Wugong jing, Shaobing ge* ji qita 《推背圖》、《五公經》、《燒餅歌》及其他." In *Hanren zongjiao, minjian xinyang yu yuyanshu de tansuo* 漢人宗教、民間信仰與預言書的探索, 311–36. Taipei: Boyang wenhua, 2008.

Wang Chien-chuan 王見川. "*Mingxin baojian* yu *Shuihu zhuan, Xiyouji* guanxi chutan 《明心寶鑑》與《水滸傳》、《西遊記》關係初探." In *Xiyouji xinlun ji qita: Laizi Fojiao yishi, xisu yu wenben de shijiao* 《西遊記》新論及其他：來自佛教儀式、習俗與文本的視角, edited by Hou Chong 侯沖 and Wang Chien-chuan 王見川, 177–200. Taipei: Boyang wenhua, 2020.

Wang Chien-chuan 王見川. "Song-Ming shiqi de fuji, fuluan yu qingxian: Jiantan 'fuji,' 'enzhu' deng ci de qiyuan 宋—明時期的扶箕、扶鸞與請仙：兼談「扶乩」、「恩主」等詞的起源." In *Fuluan wenhua yu minzhong zongjiao guoji xueshu yantao hui lunwen ji* 扶鸞文化與民眾宗教國際學術研討會論文集, edited by Fan Chun-Wu 范純武, 53–88. Xinbei: Boyang wenhua, 2020.

Wang, Chien-ch'uan [Chien-chuan]. "Spirit-writing Groups in Modern China, 1840–1937: Textual Production, Public Teachings, and Charity." Translated by Vincent Goossaert. In *Modern Chinese Religion, Part 2: 1850–2015*, edited by Vincent Goossaert, Jan Kiely, and John Lagerwey, vol. 1, 649–84. Leiden: Brill, 2015.

Wang, Chien-Chuan. "Popular Groups Promoting 'The Religion of Confucius' in the Chinese Southwest and Their Activities since the Nineteenth Century, 1840–2013: An Observation Centered on Yunnan's Eryuan County and Environs." Translated by Stacy Mosher. In *The Varieties of Confucian Experience. Documenting a Grassroots Revival of Tradition*, edited by Sébastien Billioud, 90–121. Leiden: Brill, 2018.

Wang Chien-chuan 王見川 and Pi Qingsheng 皮慶生. *Zhongguo jinshi minjian xinyang: Song Yuan Ming Qing* 中國近世民間信仰：宋元明清. Shanghai: Renmin chubanshe, 2010.

Wang Fuhai 王福海. *Mingdai lingji daopai yanjiu* 明代靈濟道派研究. Chengdu: Bashu shushe, 2013.

Wang Guangde 王光德 and Yang Lizhi 楊立志. *Wudang Daojiao shilüe* 武當道教史略. Beijing: Zhongguo ditu chubanshe, 2006.

Wang Qi 王錡. *Yupu zaji* 寓圃雜記. Punctuated and collated by Li Jianxiong 李劍雄. In *Caomuzi wai sanzhong* 草木子外三種. Shanghai: Shanghai guji chubanshe, 2012.

Wang Shizhen 王世貞. *Yanzhou shanren xugao* 弇州山人續稿. Taipei: Wenhai chubanshe, 1970.

Wang Xueqi 王學奇. *Yuanqu xuan jiaozhu* 元曲選校注. Shijiazhuang: Hebei jiaoyu chubanshe, 1994.

Wenchang huashu 文昌化書. N.p., 1645 (first year of the Longwu 隆武 reign).

Xiao Jihong 蕭霽虹, ed. *Yunnan Daojiao beike jilu* 雲南道教碑刻輯錄. Beijing: Zhongguo shehui kexue chubanshe, 2013.

Xiuxiang wenchang huashu quanji 繡像文昌化書全集. Blocks cut by Zhou Changnian 周長年 from Jinling 金陵. N.p., n.d.

Xu Bo 徐燉. *Xu shi hong yu lou shumu* 徐氏紅雨樓書目. In *Chao shi bao wen tang shumu, Xu shi hong yu lou shumu* 晁氏寶文堂書目、徐氏紅雨樓書目. Shanghai: Shanghai guji chubanshe, 2005.

Xu Dishan 許地山. *Fuji mixin di yanjiu* 扶箕迷信底研究. Reprint, Changsha: Shangwu yinshuguan, 1941.

Xu xian hanzao 徐仙翰藻. In *Zhengtong daozang* 正統道藏, vol. 59. Taipei: Xinwenfeng chuban gongsi, 1995.

Xu Xuan 徐鉉. *Jishen lu* 稽神錄. Punctuated and collated by Bai Huawen 白化文. In *Jishen lu, Kuoyi zhi* 稽神錄、括異志. 3rd ed. Beijing: Zhonghua shuju, 2012.

Yang Yi 楊儀. *Gaopo yizuan* 高坡異纂. In *Mingdai biji xiaoshuo* 明代筆記小說, edited by Zhou Guangpei 周光培, vol. 18. Shijiazhuang: Hebei jiaoyu chubanshe, 1995.

Yao Lü 姚旅. *Lu shu* 露書. Punctuated and collated by Liu Yaojie 劉彥捷. Fuzhou: Fujian renmin chubanshe, 2008.

Ye Ziqi 葉子奇. *Caomuzi* 草木子. Punctuated and collated by Wu Dongkun 吳東昆. In *Caomuzi wai sanzhong* 草木子外三種. Shanghai: Shanghai guji chubanshe, 2012.

Yin Peixia 尹佩霞 [Patricia Ebrey]. *Song Huizong* 宋徽宗. Translated by Han Hua 韓華. 5th ed. Guilin: Guangxi shifan daxue chubanshe, 2019.

Yu Yue 俞樾. *Chaxiang shi congchao* 茶香室叢鈔. Punctuated and collated by Zhen Fan 貞凡, Gu Xin 顧馨, and Xu Minxia 徐敏霞. 4 vols. 2nd ed. Beijing: Zhonghua shuju, 2006.

Yuan Haowen 元好問. *Xu yijian zhi* 續夷堅志. Punctuated and collated by Chang Zhenguo 常振國. In *Xu yijian zhi, Huhai xinwen yijian zhi* 續夷堅志、湖海新聞夷堅志. Beijing: Zhonghua shuju, 2006.

Zhang Dafu 張大復. *Meihua caotang bitan* 梅花草堂筆談. Shanghai: Shanghai guji chubanshe, 1986.

Zhang Duanyi 張端義. *Gui'er ji* 貴耳集. 3 *juan* 卷. In *Song Yuan biji xiaoshuo daguan* 宋元筆記小說大觀, edited by Shanghai guji chubanshe 上海古籍出版社, vol. 4. Shanghai: Shanghai guji chubanshe, 2001.

Zhang Han 張瀚. *Songchuang mengyu* 松窗夢語. In *Zhishi yuwen, Jishi jiwen, Songchuang mengyu* 治世餘聞、繼世紀聞、松窗夢語, punctuated and collated by Sheng Dongling 盛冬鈴. Beijing: Zhonghua shuju, 1997.

Zhang Shinan 張世南. *Youhuan jiwen* 游宦紀聞. Punctuated and collated by Zhang Maopeng 張茂鵬. In *Youhuan jiwen, Jiuwen zhengwu* 游宦紀聞、舊聞證誤. Tang Beijing: Zhonghua shuju, 1997.

Zhang Xuan 張萱. *Yi yao* 疑耀. Punctuated and collated by Luan Baoqun 欒保群. Beijing: Wenwu chubanshe, 2019.

Zhao Shuwen 趙叔問. *Kenqing lu* 肯綮錄. In *Quan Song biji* 全宋筆記, edited by Zhu Yi'an 朱易安, Fu Xuancong 傅璇琮, and Zhou Changlin 周常林, vol. 3, bk. 6. Kaifeng: Daxiang chubanshe, 2008.

Zhao Yanzhi 趙延之. "Xingci ji 行祠記." In *Zhengtong daozang* 正統道藏, vol. 5. Taipei: Xinwenfeng chuban gongsi, 1995.

Zhou Mi 周密. *Zhiya tang zachao* 志雅堂雜鈔. In *Zhiya tang zachao, Yunyan guoyan lu, Chenghuai lu* 志雅堂雜鈔、雲煙過眼錄、澄懷錄, punctuated and collated by Deng Zimian 鄧子勉. Beijing: Zhonghua shuju, 2018.

Zhu Yu 朱彧. *Pingzhou ketan* 萍州可談. In *Houshan tancong, Pingzhou ketan* 後山談叢 萍州可談, punctuated and collated by Li Weiguo 李偉國. Beijing: Zhonghua shuju, 2007.

Zitong dijun huashu 梓潼帝君化書. In *Zhengtong daozang* 正統道藏, vol. 5. Taipei: Xinwenfeng chuban gongsi, 1995.

Zuantu zenglei shilin guangji 纂圖增類事林廣記. In *Shilin guangji* 事林廣記, by Chen Yuanliang 陳元靚. Beijing: Zhonghua shuju, 1999.

CHAPTER 4

Women, Goddesses, and Gender Affinity in Spirit-Writing

Elena Valussi

1   Introduction to the Gendering of the Religious Subject

> Examining how male-female differences are conceptualized in particular cultures; interrogating constructions, representations, and performances of masculinity and femininity in religious traditions; detecting the underlying, often hidden, gender patterns that represent the deep structures of religious life; critically analyzing the gender lenses through which Ultimate Reality is perceived.[1]

In this paper, I wish to continue the work spearheaded in other religious traditions aimed at "filling the gaps" in a knowledge base that largely excluded or was indifferent to women.[2] I am less interested in conducting a single case study here, but will attempt to present an overview of the presence of women and goddesses in spirit-writing circles from the earliest materials available to us, in an effort to make women more visible and their activities more acknowledged. I wish to explore the role of actual women within spirit-writing circles, the role of goddesses as communicators and transmitters of texts, and the gender-specific connection established between women and goddesses during this transmission. I also wish to render the implicit gender roles of male and female divinities more explicit in the context of spirit-writing transmission. The history of spirit-writing, and especially of women's presence within it, is far from complete so, in this paper, I will shift between periods, regions, types of literature, and social contexts, in order to provide an initial introduction to this topic.

While the jury remains undecided about the details regarding the emergence of spirit-writing, as the detailed discussions by Goossaert, Hu and Wang in this volume show, it is becoming increasingly clear that spirit-writing has a strong connection with the Daoist ritual context, from as early as the eleventh

---

1   Calef, "Charting New Territory," 2.
2   Ibid.

century. In this context, the communication and relationship between gods and receivers were entirely male conduits: the early gods are male, "fierce thunder generals," as are the ritual masters, or *fashi* 法師. Little is known about the lay community of believers, which may be composed by both genders. At the same time, and even prior to the development of spirit-writing within the Daoist ritual tradition, we also have the well-documented presence and development of a tradition involving a female divinity, Zigu 紫姑, communicating with and transmitting messages to groups of women in intimate family settings.

Later, during the Ming and Qing periods, we see a momentous transition in the practice of spirit-writing, whereby small, lay, spirit-writing altars emerge all over China. In these spirit-writing circles, Zigu becomes less central, and the divinities in charge of the majority of the transmission are Lüzu 呂祖, Wenchang 文昌, and Guandi 關帝, who are all male. Vincent Goossaert has written about the powerful rise of these three divine saviors and their elevation in status by the Jiaqing 嘉慶 emperor (r. 1796–1820) in the early nineteenth century.[3] When scholars have investigated those responsible for the reception and consequent printing of spirit-written materials, they have also concentrated on male figures, mostly because the most visible figures in the process, those recording and recorded in the prefaces, are male. On the other hand, little is yet known about the role of women in these communities. It may be claimed, as in other contexts, that the activities of women are less recorded than those of men. It is also possible that roles with ritual importance were generally inaccessible to women. Finally, women had less access to the education needed to write, read, and interpret the words sent by the gods. Accordingly, the questions I wish to explore are related to the involvement of women in this tradition. Specifically, my focus is on the following questions:

1. Women

    How present and relevant are women in spirit-writing communities? Are there female-only communities at the receiving end of transmission? When women are involved, do we see similar goals to what we observe in the general context of spirit-writing: self-divinization, healing, salvation from impending disaster?

2. Goddesses

    Are there powerful female divine saviors in spirit-writing? How important are female divinities in spirit-written texts? When and where do they appear? How are they represented?

---

3 Goossaert, "Spirit Writing, Canonization, and the Rise of Divine Saviors," 82–125.

3. Their relationship
   During the intimate connections and conversations between goddesses and female audiences, which themes tend to arise most, and is there a gendered dimension to these? Are any messages passed between goddesses and female believers that are less present or obvious in all-male contexts? Which language is used? Do these conversations reveal a gendered relationship?

In other words, is it important to look through/for a gender lens? What will we learn by doing so? The research in this area remains in its early stage, but we can possibly draw some initial conclusion. Finding a female perspective requires more effort, because the presence of women and goddesses within the textual history of spirit-writing is less evident.

I will start this survey by retelling the oft-told origin story of spirit-writing: that of the cult of the female divinity Zigu. What I find particularly significant in this story is how the shift from oral to written divinatory practices also coincides with the transition from a female to a male group of practitioners and audience. I will mention women involved in spirit-writing activities in elite communities in the Jiangnan region, who have been studied by various scholars. Here, I wish to understand which roles women and goddesses played in small, elite, lay communities. I will then focus briefly on one kind of text that was transmitted through spirit-writing, starting in the late Ming and Qing dynasties, concerning the self-cultivation of women, or female alchemy. This case study will demonstrate the direct connection between the women in the audience, the goddesses in charge of the transmission, and the topic of the texts transmitted.

2 Zigu and the Beginning of Spirit-Writing

As several scholars have discussed, Zigu is the female divinity who appears to lie at the origins of the tradition of spirit-writing.[4] Scholars describe in detail how the cult of Zigu started among a group of women. According to the legend, Zigu was a concubine who was harassed by a jealous first wife to such an extent that Zigu died in the latrines on the fifteenth day of the first month. For

---

4 On Zigu and the origins of spirit writing, see Chao, "The Origins and Growth of the Fu Chi"; Xu, *Fuji mixin de yanjiu*, chap. 1, 8–28; Boltz, "On the Legacy of Zigu"; Goyama, *Min Shin jidai*, 324–63; Kleeman, *A God's Own Tale*, introduction; Jordan and Overmeyer, *Flying Phoenix*, chapter 3, 36–90; Zeitlin, "Spirit Writing and Performance." In his chapter in this book, Goossaert indicates the importance of Daoist ritual and Daoist religious specialists in the early development of spirit writing in the period from 1000–1400.

this reason, she is celebrated on that day every year, and is also alternatively called Cegu 廁姑 (Goddess of the latrines). In written sources, the first reference to this divination practice, also called the invitation of Zigu (*qing Zigu* 請紫姑 or *ying Zigu* 迎紫姑), or Zigu divination (*Zigu bu* 紫姑卜), is recorded in the fifth century, in the *Yiyuan* 異苑 (A garden of marvels) by Liu Jingshu 劉敬叔 (dated ca. 468),[5] although the cult may be far older. In her study of texts relating to this cult, Judith Boltz refers to a "long standing oral tradition" prior to the first written description in the fifth century.[6] A later but still early written source for this cult is the *Jing Chu suishi ji* 荆楚歲時記 (Annual customs and festivals in Jing and Chu) by Zong Lin 宗懍 (ca. 500–560).

Although we have few textual details in relation to this, the early recorded story of Zigu is described as happening completely within the confines of the inner quarters, and developing in relation and reaction to another woman (Lady Cao 曹, the first wife). The practice that emerges is also initially confined to the inner quarters, so the divination is seen as generally conducted by women for women through a female figure; the goddess descends into a likeness of herself, which is generally understood to be constructed of straw (in later illustrations of this practice we see women holding a straw basket with chopsticks – fig. 4.1). If the goddess has descended, the straw likeness is heavy. The audience asks simple questions. If the answer is positive, the likeness will dance; if negative, it will remain still. The questions asked of Zigu are also generally understood to be the purview of women, mainly the silkworm and mulberry leaves for the coming year, related to the production of silk, a process that pertained completely to women. The timing of the yearly divination also matches the kind of questions asked, about the mulberry leaves and the silkworms: the 15th day of the first lunar month coincides with the time when the white mulberry leaves, the best for feeding silkworms, start to grow, in the very early spring.

In the early descriptions, men are not part of the practice: Zigu is remembered, worshipped, and questioned by women, in the inner quarters. As an example of Zigu's power, a woman tries to hold the image still but she is bounced off of it.[7] This indicates that it was women who surrounded and interacted with the divinity. It seems, therefore, that this worship of a female deity arose in a female environment, and the practice continued to pertain to women over a long period of time. At this point, there is no evidence that this early prac-

---

5 See Chao, "The Origins and Growth of the Fu Chi," 12, and Boltz, "On the Legacy of Zigu," 353.
6 Boltz, "On the Legacy of Zigu," 353.
7 This process is detailed in two early descriptions, in the *Yiyuan* and *Jing Chu suishi ji*. See Chao, "The Origins and Growth of the Fu Chi," 12.

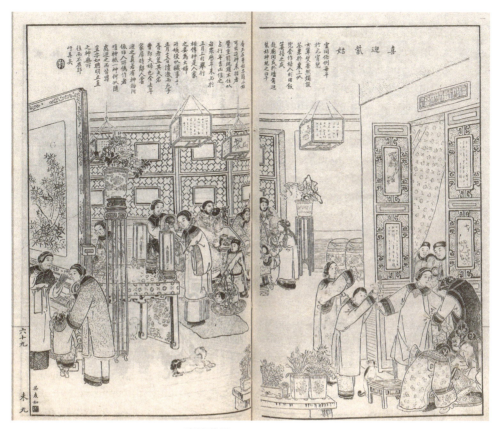

FIGURE 4.1 Inviting Zigu (*xiying Zigu* 喜迎紫姑)

tice involved recording the goddess's words in writing, as the women involved in it were unlikely to be fully literate, and possibly not from an elite background. To prove this point, during the Tang period, this practice is identified negatively as a popular practice: "I am ashamed to follow the country people to play the invitation of Tzu-Ku (Zigu)."[8] However, as Boltz also points out, while the early accounts of this practice are sparse and vague, they become increasingly specific when it is adopted by elite literati during the Song period. While there are several examples of the emergence of writing as a central element of the practice, the account of this practice by Su Shi 蘇軾 (1036–1101) is the most extensive, and highly instructive as it describes the transition from nonliterary to literary.[9] Here, the setting is described quite differently, at the house of a Metropolitan graduate, with the likeness of the goddess being lifted by two

---

8 Li Shangyin 李商隱 (813–858), quoted in Chao, "The Origins and Growth of the Fu Chi," 12–13.
9 See Chao, "The Origins and Growth of the Fu Chi" for shorter quotations, 13, and for a full translation of Su Shi's account, 14. See also Boltz, "On the Legacy of Zigu," 354, for a summary.

young boys. This account contains further details about Zigu's life, her marriage, and, interestingly, the fact that, during her life on earth, she had studied and so could read and write, which was quite unusual for a woman in any period, and especially this early. This is an important detail because, critically, at this point, the goddess herself also acquires the ability to write and paint, in her divine communication with her audience. She responds to queries no longer simply by movement (dancing or stillness), as described in the *Yiyuan*, but she writes, using two chopsticks tied to her straw likeness. Thus, in this shift from a female to a male audience/milieu, and from a more popular to a more elite practice, writing replaces, or is added to, dancing. It is easy to see how writing is more the purview of male literati, who felt more comfortable with this form of communication than women, especially during this early period. From the Song period onward, descriptions of Zigu's ability to write poems and prose, and of her style and wit, are common, and here is where the "writing" of "spirit-writing" enters the scene. Interestingly, in Su Shi's account, Zigu still retains the ability to dance, but also acquires the ability to write ("I will remain a while and shall compose poems and dance for your amusement" 公少留而爲賦詩，且舞以娛公). In Su Shi's account, Zigu also discusses the fact that "there are many kinds of so-called Zigu deities nowadays, but none possessed my distinction" (蓋世所謂子姑神者，其類甚眾，然未有如妾之卓然者也), indicating that, at this point, this practice is so widespread that there exist several "fake" Zigus.[10] Also, she acquires virtues that could be seen as common male literati virtues: she is not only well-educated and can write literary compositions and poems (自幼知讀書屬文), but also "well-bred," "likes literature" and is "ashamed to be unknown" (知好文字而恥無聞於世). Fame was generally understood to be a feature of male literati wishing to perpetuate their name through the generations.[11] Hu Jiechen, in his contribution to this volume, translates the poem "Jibu 箕卜" (Sieve divination), by Lu You 陸遊 (1125–1209), which describes a similar situation, whereby a bamboo sieve dressed in women's clothes, held by two people, writes answers to questions about examinations, but is also used as a form of entertainment at gatherings of friends.[12]

This important transition from a non-written to a written practice has received insufficient attention from scholars who have discussed the emergence of spirit-writing, often reading the early accounts of Zigu through the lens of the

---

10   Hu, in this volume, provides several examples in which the process of "inviting Zigu" was used to summon other divinities.
11   All quotations are translated in Chao, "The Origins and Growth of the Fu Chi," 14. Original in *Dongpo quanji*.
12   See the contribution by Hu Jiechen in this volume.

literati culture that made this practice widespread among the elites. "Although we have no direct evidence for this, it seems safe to assume that the Purple Lady began to communicate through **the more expressive means of spirit-writing** sometime during the Tang. It would have been easy to see in the goddess's ecstatic dancing the outlines of a character, then conclude that the goddess was trying to communicate."[13] This suggests that Zigu's dancing was always an attempt to create characters in the air. In fact, it seems that, for several centuries, the communication through movement, dancing, and bouncing were considered adequate by the female audience, and that writing became required only after the transition to a male audience. Overmyer, in his description of the history of spirit-writing, is the first to point out clearly the transition from a non-literate to a literate tradition, and from a female to a male milieu, during the Song period.[14] As he suggests, this transition also involved the emergence of other gods, many of whom were male, and the distancing from a specific date (the fifteenth day of the first lunar month) for this practice. This also catered to the new needs of the literati class, at a time when the civil service examination was revived and anxiety about the questions and results propelled the development of spirit-writing and the freedom to consult Zigu at any time.[15]

Boltz also highlights the presence of the Zigu cult and of spirit-writing in a Daoist ritual context, controlled by Daoist ritual specialists. She analyses a text in the *Daoist Canon* where the Zigu ritual is firmly controlled by a Daoist ritual specialist, and uses all of the elements of a Daoist ritual.[16] Goossaert, in this volume, deepens and widens the research on spirit-writing's early development as being closely connected to Daoist rituals, a practice led by Daoist ritual masters, who channel the messages of "fierce thunder gods" like Zhenwu and Wenchang. In his analysis, however, Zigu does not play a central role. According to Hsieh Tsung-hui, the more popular practice of inviting Zigu (often associated with the term *fuji* 扶箕) was well-known among, but often criticized by, the Daoist ritual masters, and seen as very different from the practice of *feiluan* 飛鸞, through which ritual masters received messages from gods like Wenchang. This, according to Hsie, indicates the existence of tension between what the ritual masters saw as belonging to the inferior realm of divinatory practices (*fuji*), and their higher realm of connection to fierce ritual gods through *feiluan*. It also indi-

---

13   Kleeman, *A God's Own Tale*, 10. Emphasis added by the author.
14   Jordan and Overmyer, *Flying Phoenix*, 39.
15   This transition from non-literary to literary is also discussed in Shiga, *Xianggang Daojiao yu fuji xinyang*, 42.
16   Boltz, "On the Legacy of Zigu," 365.

cates that these categories may have been less clear, and the boundaries may have often been crossed; hence the repeated warnings against *fuji*.[17]

There is, then, during the Song period, a definite repudiation of practices that are closer to divination and possession in favor of ones more focused on ritual and writing, in both a Daoist ritual context and, later, a lay one. As Kleeman explains, even though by the Song period, there were still several low-level female transcendents (he suggests that this is possibly because the mediums themselves were female), the descent of female transcendent was increasingly seen as negative and aroused suspicion. In one account, the self-identification of the transcendent as Zigu is doubted on the ground that the words produced are too exalted, indicating that Zigu could not have possessed literary skills.[18] Kleeman goes on to describe the rise of the powerful Zitong 梓潼 as a spirit-writing divinity, his power mostly tied to his ability to divine the results of the civil service examinations, which was a central concern among male literati for centuries.[19]

Even though spirit-writing changed and morphed from the Song to the Ming periods, from the Ming to the Qing periods and all the way up until today, in fact, the worship of Zigu, now divorced from spirit-writing, does not disappear but continues to be practiced consistently and continually. We have many examples of this in gazetteers, from the Yuan dynasty all the way up to the Republican period, relating in different ways the story of Zigu and its practice.[20] While both Susan Naquin and Susan Mann mention this cult in their work, it would be worth studying it and exploring how it developed independently from spirit-writing in later centuries.[21] There are very lively images in the *Dianshizhai huabao* 點石齋畫報 (Illustrated news of the lithographic studio), a collection dating to the late nineteenth century, that repeat the story of Zigu *verbatim*, and still describe it as a practice pertaining specifically to women, practiced inside the inner quarters, and relating to a straw image.[22] Thus, this practice continued alongside spirit-writing, but no longer intersected with it, especially with the spirit-written production of lengthy treatises that was typi-

---

17 Hsie, *Xin tiandi zhi ming*, 105–10.
18 Kleeman, *A God's Own Tale*, 10.
19 Ibid.
20 A search of gazetteers accessed via the Airusheng 愛如生 database reveals hundreds of references to the compounds "Zigu 紫姑," "qing Zigu 請紫姑," "Zigu bu 紫姑卜," "ying Zigu 迎紫姑."
21 Mann, *Precious Records*, 178–200; Naquin, "The Peking Pilgrimage to Miaofengshan."
22 See "Xiying zigu 喜迎紫姑," *Dianshizhai huabao*, no. 213 (1889): 8–9; "Zigu lingyi 紫姑靈異," *Dianshizhai huabao*, no. 440 (1896): 2; "Zigu wei sui 紫姑為祟," *Dianshizhai huabao*, no. 289 (1892): 13–14.

cal of the mid-Qing period. In fact, during the period in which spirit-writing was most common (the mid- to late Qing and beyond), Zigu rarely features in the list of main divinities. Even within the tradition of female alchemy, directed at women, whose texts were also transmitted by spirit-writing, and whose transmitting divinities tended to be female, Zigu is merely a minor presence, being mentioned only once in the lineage of female alchemy transmitting goddesses. This may be due to the fact that Zigu, with her humble beginning and persistent link to popular female religious practices, is not seen as a divinity who is capable of transmitting universal moral messages.

Women, and goddesses, then, played a role in the early development of this technique, and its diffusion; however, it seems that, by the Song period, and certainly the Ming dynasty, the techniques had changed in terms of its practitioners, means, and targets. No longer were women largely in charge of the ritual, but men were; no longer was only a basket used, but a stylus was attached to it; no longer was dancing involved, but writing; and no longer was the goal to hear about the mulberry leaves and silk harvest, but mostly examination results (an eminently male domain) and the connection with deceased family members. The divinities also changed, from one female divinity to a variety of male ones; including, among others, Wenchang, Zhenwu and, later, Guandi and Lüzu.

The milieu changed too, from an intimate practice among female family members and friends, to a more public space, groups of literati, still within a family but a far more public, large, and prestigious endeavor, or to Daoist ritual spaces in which gods are asked about the future of humanity.

3 Women's Involvement in Spirit-Writing in Late Imperial China

In the Ming and Qing periods, a major avenue for the development of spirit-writing techniques was within literati groups, especially in the Jiangnan region. In these communities, women were, in different ways, active participants.

Previous scholars have provided a good basis for understanding the world of the literati and their use of spirit-writing during the late Ming period, especially regarding anxiety about their future and examination results, and to connect to deceased family members.[23] Even though the results of spirit-writing sessions were often collected and distributed by males, the literati's use of spirit-writing

---

23   Burton-Rose, "Prolific Spirit"; Zeitlin, "Spirit Writing and Performance"; Xu, *Fuji mixin de yanjiu*; Goyama, *Min Shin jidai no josei to bungaku*; Wang, "Peng Dingqiu yu Qingchu Suzhou Daojiao."

to divine the future and connect with the past was not solely a male endeavor, and it is possible to find traces of women's involvement in this process.

The Confucian norms of gender difference are seen to divide men and women into *nei* and *wai* spheres; however, as Francesca Bray and Dorothy Ko argue, these spheres are best seen as interconnected, with boundaries that shift according to the circumstances.[24] In this section, we will see how the boundaries not only between the male and female realms but also between the world of the dead and the world of the living intersect, overlap, and shift. We will see how women, through spirit-writing, take up, in this world, roles that might traditionally be reserved for men, or fantasize about the different possibilities afforded to them in the other, less restrictive world. On the other hand, we see men maintaining gender roles in this world while, at the same time, fantasizing about romantic encounters with extraordinary women in the other world. For both men and women, contact with the other world revealed a larger array of possibilities that transcended what was allowed under the stricter reality of real life. This aspect of spirit-writing has not been widely explored in the secondary literature. However, the literature on spiritualism in the West has revealed how this highly similar practice disrupted the social binaries, revealed their inherent instability and, especially for female mediums, allowed a reconfiguration of their subjectivities.[25] Female mediums were preferred to male ones during the Victorian era, because of a belief in their inherent fragility and proneness to illness, which features were thought to make them more introspective and attuned to the spiritual world than men.[26] Lying at the center of this religious practice, that took women beyond their physical body, allowed the kind of release from the social boundaries that would have been impossible otherwise, thereby also setting an example beyond the séance room for other women in society. In China, the presence and activity of mediums are not discussed at length in the sources, and were not perceived as central, as mediums were rarely female, according to our sources. This makes it more difficult for female mediums to exemplify changes on a larger scale. However, the women who were the medium's clients were nonetheless able to use spirit-writing activities in order to enlarge their own spheres of activity and power beyond this world.

As discussed by Lai and others, during the Ming and Qing periods, spirit-writing altars were often erected in people's homes and held together by family

---

24   Bray, *Technology and Gender*; Ko, *Teachers of the Inner Chambers*.
25   Tromp, "Spirited Sexuality," 78.
26   Owen, *The Darkened Room*, 206.

WOMEN, GODDESSES, AND GENDER AFFINITY   143

and close friendship ties.[27] This development indicates that, to a certain extent, "the domestic domain eclipsed the monastic order as the site of religious practice for men and women."[28] The examples provided below also suggest intimate relationships within the community as well as between the community and the divinities. Frequently, husband and wife/concubine, sons and daughters all participated in these activities in different roles. Does this focus on the domestic realm indicate that it was easier for women to participate in an active, meaningful way, or was the process still driven mainly by men?

Within the context of the male literati culture, especially in the wealthier coastal and southern regions, it was not uncommon to receive and exchange poems with divinities through spirit-writing. Xu Dishan 許地山 (1894–1941)'s classic study of spirit-writing is based mostly on the *Jiangbibu jishi* 降筆部紀事 (Chronicle of the section on spirit-written materials) section of the *Gujin tushu jicheng* 古今圖書集成 (Complete collection of illustrations and writings from the earliest to current times), an imperially-dictated encyclopedia, which would not have included sources related to popular religion or ones including eschatological discourses.[29] This source, on the other hand, reflects the activities and interests of the literati, as reported in Xu Dishan's study.[30] Despite these limitations, Xu Dishan's work remains an excellent source of information on the religious practices of the elites, and lists dozens of cases of literati families and circles engaging in this practice. One outstanding example described is the Beishantan 北山壇 (Altar of the Northern Mountain), located at Xiaomei Peak 小梅領, north of Zhangzhou 漳州, in Fujian 福建. This altar was related to the cult of a young Ming dynasty woman who died prematurely, Liangshi xiaocainü 梁氏小才女, later also named Jinxianzi 金仙子 (Golden transcendent). During the Qing period, her cult developed into a large-scale operation whereby literati would meet to relax and exchange poems with several divinities. This is the model for many other literati groups, and these exchanges were later collated into poetry collections.[31]

The cult of Tanyangzi 曇陽子, a young woman born into a high-ranking literati family, also started in the late Ming period; the support she received during both her life and her afterlife as a divinity from several members of

---

27 Hu, "*Wendi quanshu* yanjiu"; Lai "Qingdai sizhong 'Lüzu quanshu'"; Burton-Rose, "Prolific Spirit."
28 Ko, *Teachers of the Inner Chambers*, 199.
29 *Jiangbibu jishi*.
30 For a more detailed discussion of Xu Dishan's sources, see Fan, *Qingmo Minchu cishan shiye*, 14–15.
31 Xu, *Fuji mixin de yanjiu*, 69–72.

the literati community combined the practice of self-cultivation and the cult of female chastity, and also grew in intensity during the Qing period.[32] Even though Tanyangzi and her mentor Wang Shizhen 王世貞 (1526–1590) did not openly support spirit-writing, communities such as these often communicated with female immortals or deceased female family members who were thought to have become immortals.

3.1 Literati Circles in Suzhou

A group of late Ming/early Qing period literati in the Suzhou area provides a good case study for the gendered relations between the literati, their female family members, and the male and female divinities, in the context of spirit-writing.[33] You Tong 尤侗 (1618–1704), Qian Qianyi 錢謙益 (1582–1664), Ye Shaoyuan 葉紹袁 (1589–1648), Peng Dingqiu 彭定求 (1645–1719), and Jin Shengtan 金聖嘆 (1608–1661), who were prominent literati in the Suzhou area during the late Ming/early Qing period, all practiced spirit-writing in one form or another. With the exception of Peng Dingqiu, all of them, at some point in their life, also came into contact with the worship of Le'an Dashi 泐庵大師, or Legong 泐宫, a female divinity whose altar was set up by Jin Shengtan, the medium through whom she communicated. Moreover, many of them were able to communicate with deceased female family members through her.[34] The story of Le'an is described in the *Tiantai Le fashi lingyi ji* 天台泐法師靈異記 (Record of the strange and mysterious [story] about Master Le from Tiantai), written by the well-known literatus Qian Qianyi.[35] According to Qian, Le'an related her life story during a spirit-writing session, revealing that, in a previous life, she had been a male Buddhist disciple called Lang Zhi 郎智, before being reborn in a woman's body, as the daughter of a certain Mister Chen 陳. One day, while out with her mother, on a bridge, she saw a man wearing a purple shirt and an official's cap, brandishing a Ruyi 如意 scepter (a symbol of religious power and good fortune) and summoning her to him. On returning home, she fell ill and died, after which she was transported to a celestial place called Ciyue gong 慈月宫, which looked like a traditional village. There, people fell ill but were given medicine which cured them; there were also demons, but these were

---

32 He, "Tanyang ciguan de yanbian"; Waltner, "T'an-yang-tzu and Wang Shih-chen."
33 Studied in Zeitlin, "Spirit Writing and Performance"; Wang, "You Tong yu wan Ming Qing chu de fuji"; Lu, *Jinshengtan shishi yanjiu*, 96–129; Goyama, *Min Shin jidai no josei to bungaku*; Burton-Rose, "Prolific Spirit."
34 On Jin Shengtan, his altar and his relationship with Master Le'an, see Lu, "Jin Shengtan zaoqi fuji."
35 *Muzhai chu xue ji*, juan 43, 6b–9a.

suppressed by talismans. In 1627, Le'an descended for the first time onto Jin Shengtan's altar, the only medium to whom she ever appeared. Jin was trusted by several local scholars and connected them all with Le'an. Jin Shengtan asked Qian Qianyi to write about Le'an, presenting her as a Buddhist divinity, to make her worship more acceptable. Qian therefore wrote the *Tiantai Le fashi lingyi ji*, in which he described her descent as a goddess. He also collected ten poems attributed to her, the *Xiantan changheshi shishou* 仙壇唱和詩十首 (Ten call and response poems [received] at the Immortal's Altar).[36]

You Tong started practicing spirit-writing while in his twenties, with a friend, both for fun and also as a way to connect with famous men from the past, in times of illness or death. He also connected with the female immortal Zigu. Later in life, following the suicide of the last Ming Emperor and the death of his wife, You Tong returned to spirit-writing to assist his mourning process. He attended Jin Shengtan's altar and connected with his wife through Le'an. Through this connection, he learned that, after her death, she had reached a safe place in the Heavens, and had entered the Place of the Celestial Concubine (Tianfei gong 天妃宮), where she was waiting for him to join her. While reaching out to his wife, he also connected with several female immortals, and received their poems, seeking a wider spiritual, but also emotional and romantic, connection to the spiritual world, "recording ephemerous words by female immortals and deceased women through the exchange of poetry."[37] Zeitlin interprets this desire as a way to empower the male subject as protector and savior, reclaiming the female's poetry from death, while at the same time acting on the anxiety that his own poetry will not last.

A similar situation is found with Ye Shaoyuan who, together with his family, was fond of spirit-writing and practiced Buddhism and Daoism. After the premature death of his favorite daughter Ye Xiaoluan 葉小鸞 (1617–1632), followed by that of her sister Ye Xiaowan 葉小紈 and, three years later, of his wife Shen Yixiu 沈宜修 (both no dates), Ye Shaoyuan attempted to find out about their fate through attending spirit-writing séances with Le'an, carried out between 1636 and 1642 in his home. He became convinced that his female family members had become immortals, which conviction was confirmed by Le'an: his daughters and wife were residing in a realm reserved for female immortals, and served by female attendants.[38] Ye Shaoyuan recorded the séances and the

---

36 Ibid., *juan* 10, 13b–16b.
37 Zeitlin, "Spirit Writing and Performance," 116.
38 On Ye Xiaoluan and his family members, see Gerritsen, "The Many Guises of Xiaoluan." On the spirit-writing séances connecting Ye with his daughters and his wife, see Zeitlin, "Spirit Writing and Performance."

poems transmitted by Xiaoluan through spirit-writing in his *Wumen tang ji* 午夢堂集 (Collection from the Noon Dream Hall).[39] At times, Ye connected to Le'an and, at other times, directly to Xiaoluan: within an intimate question and answer format, we hear of Xiaoluan's whereabouts, her current condition in the afterlife, and the reasons for her death. Her early death is attributed to the bad deeds of a female immortal who, having indulged in illicit relations with another immortal, was sent to the mortal realm to live in a morally upright family, in order to atone for her sins. Once she had atoned and repented, she was sent back to her immortal realm, and so had to die in the mortal world. She was Xiaoluan.[40] Ye Xiaoluan's status, as an immortal who could transmit poetry from her Heavenly abode, continued unabated, and her posthumous poems continued to be reprinted. She repeatedly re-appeared as a female immortal: in August 1837, for example, the literatus Lu Changchun 陸長春 (no dates) from Wuxing 吳興 in Zhejiang 浙江 (near Wujiang 吳江, where Ye Xiaoluan had lived), recorded the descent of a "female scholar (*guixiu* 閨秀) Ye Xiaoluan from Wujiang" onto his ancestral altar during a spirit-writing séance. She transmitted three poems, which he recorded and then published.[41]

Gerritsen points out that Ye Shaoyuan's efforts to create immortal personae for his deceased family members definitely grew out of his genuine despair and grief about their departure. However, this process of divinization was led by his attempt to create a legacy not only for them, but also for himself. Ye saw to it that Xiaoluan's poems were collected, published, and distributed widely, and they became part of the canon of poetry by women. Chen Wenshu 陳文述 (1774–1845), a generation later, prominently included them in his collection of poetry from the inner chamber *Xiling guiyong* 西泠閨詠 (Poems from within the inner chambers at West Lake). Therefore, the divinization of his female family members, and especially of the highly talented Ye Xiaoluan, served also to enhance his own legacy.[42]

In all of the above cases, the divinized Le'an was the *trait d'union* of all of these male literati to their deceased female family members. We see the close, intense involvement of male literati in creating and supporting her worship. As we will see later, it is not unusual for a female intermediary to be used in order to connect to deceased female family members, who might reside in all-female spaces. There are also ways in which these literati support their own diviniza-

---

39 *Wumen tang ji*, "Xu Yaowen 續窈聞," 1–6.
40 Gerritsen, "The Many Guises of Xiaoluan."
41 Ref. in Xu, *Fuji mixin de yanjiu*, 36–38. Ko also lists a series of instances of Ye Xiaoluan being invoked as an immortal. Ko, *Teachers of the Inner Chambers*, 202, and fn. 78.
42 Gerritsen, "The Many Guises of Xiaoluan."

tion, through the words of the female divinities that they record, print, and disseminate. Further, for men, publishing women's poetry relating to the death of a family member not only enhanced their own legacy through a public display of the talents and virtues of these women but was also a way to make public feelings of intense sorrow in a way that men could not express, by attributing them to women.[43]

It is harder to find information, for this period, about the women who engaged in the spirit-writing process, not as immortals or divinized humans, but as mediums, altar managers, and, in general, active members of the spirit-writing community. However, as more primary materials surface and more scholars become interested in the gender dynamics within spirit-writing, further traces of women are emerging.

Xun Liu discusses in detail the life of Wang Duan 汪端 (1793–1839), the daughter-in-law of Chen Wenshu, a famous scholar in the Suzhou area, who supported elite women's cultural endeavors and published the afore-mentioned collection of female poetry *Xiling guiyong*, which includes spirit-written poems by Ye Xiaoluan. Wang Duan, who had been brought up following the Confucian tenets and eschewing a belief in Daoism or Buddhism, joined a family that was deeply devoted to Daoism, with an established spirit-writing practice. She embraced her new family and their religious practices and formed a bond with her female family members. Following the premature death of first her husband and then her son, Wang Duan became even more interested and immersed in religious practices, and started to communicate with her husband through spirit-writing, much like You Tong and Ye Shaoyuan had done with their wives and children a century earlier. Several women in Chen Wenshu's family circle (his cousin and Daoist nun Chen Lanyun 陳蘭雲 (no dates), his concubine Lady Guan Yun 管筠, and other female family members and friends) participated actively in spirit-writing activities, erected spirit-writing altars, and worshipped specific divinities such as Doumu 斗姆 and Magu 麻姑, as well as the local male poet Chen Qiaoyun 陳樵雲 (1730–1785). Wang Duan became an active member of their circle of spirit-writing altars between Hangzhou, Yangzhou, and Suzhou at the end of the eighteenth century. This group of elite lay and monastic women were inspired by the Longmen patriarch Min Yide 閔一得 (1758–1836), who also regularly received texts via spirit-writing from the immortal Lüzu. These women not only identified with Daoist teachings but also interacted with other religious beliefs and practices, both Buddhist and Confucian. Liu argues that Wang Duan and her female commu-

---

43 Fong and Widmer, *The Inner Quarters and Beyond*, 52–53.

nity of elite lay believers, built upon family ties and mentorship, constituted a powerful constituency in the religious landscape of late imperial Jiangnan, as they were active leaders and innovators. Wang Duan herself demonstrated "her agency in reshaping the beliefs and practices of local cults and the spirit-writing communities based in Suzhou, Hangzhou and Yangzhou."[44] Apart from sponsoring spirit-writing altars and cults, they were also interested in female self-cultivation and participated in the transmission and printing of one such text, the *Xiwangmu nüxiu zhengtu shize* 西王母女修正途十則 (Xiwangmu's ten precepts on the proper female path), which had previously also been revealed to Min Yide.[45]

Another example of a woman who was actively interested and involved in spirit-writing is Qian Xi 錢希 (1872–1930), a female poet from an elite family who lived in the area of Changzhou, close to the Suzhou/Hangzhou/Yangzhou area discussed in the examples above. Her family was already well-versed in the practice of spirit-writing, since her brother had learned how to perform the ritual. Following the deaths of her husband and young son, Qian Xi became more personally involved in it, exchanging poems with the deceased and maintaining an emotional bond with her deceased family members. Again, this example reminds us of the afore-mentioned cases of You Tong and Ye Shaoyuan and their efforts to contact their deceased female family members. However, in this case, as in the above case of Wang Duan, a woman was at the center of the exchange. During this process, she connects not only with her husband and son but, similarly to Wang Duan, also with the wider community, consisting of close female family members, with whom she shares a passion for spirit-writing. Together with her sister and several cousins, through a female immortal called He Ziyun 何紫雲, Qian discovers that they were all, in a previous life, part of a community of female immortals. Through this revelation, based on a subsequent poetic exchange with female immortals, Qian is able to move beyond the constrictions and frustrations of being a woman and a widow, and be recognized for both her immortal self and her poetic genius.[46] Qian Xi used spirit-writing for literary inspiration but also emotional connection. She sought a connection with female immortals, attempting to build a female community across the divide between the worlds of the living and the dead.

---

44   Liu, "Of Poems, Gods and Spirit Writing Altars," especially 67. On Chen Wenshu, see also Gao, "Jin'gaishan wangluo."
45   Contained in the *Daozang xubian* 道藏續編 (Sequel to the *Daoist Canon*), a collection of late imperial Daoist texts, collated by Min Yide.
46   Wang, "Gendering the Planchette," 170.

Above, I surveyed cases of literati communities in the Jiangnan area using spirit-writing to connect to female immortals and deceased female family members both emotionally and also as a way to perpetuate their own literary immortality. I also surveyed women who used spirit-writing to create a real-life community as well as a connection with immortals, usually females, with whom they felt a special affinity. It is striking that, in many cases, the deceased women or the women communicating with the afterlife through spirit-writing have female communities to connect to in the afterlife. The female community and connection with immortals gives them agency in the mortal world while also allowing them to move beyond its frustrations and restrictions, imagining themselves in a less constricted world. We will see that the theme of female communities is relevant also when we discuss female alchemy below.

It is thus possible to observe traces of women's involvement in spirit-writing through the copious collections of poetry collected by late Ming and Qing male literati, and the above examples relate to elite literati families living in the wealthy Jiangnan region and entail the use of spirit-writing, largely but not solely, to communicate with deceased family members. However, it is harder to discover information about females' involvement in more overtly religious communities, where the theme of the emotional bond between this world and that of the immortals, so important in poetic production, is not central. This is the context to which we will now turn our attention.

4 Women and Goddesses in Religious Groups

The cases above are better-known because of a bias toward the study of literary sources. However, it has become increasingly clear during the last two decades of research on late imperial religious texts that the majority of "popular religious" texts are, in fact, emerging from a spirit-written milieu. Therefore, for scholars interested in religion and gender in the late imperial period, it is essential to explore this exciting trove of materials in greater depth.

In the early to mid-Qing period, spirit-writing practices were widely adopted by overtly religious and even sectarian groups.[47] This reveals a different milieu for these practices; moving from the close elite literati circles enquiring about examination results or attempting to communicate with deceased family members to the larger, less deeply-explored milieu of the popular religious move-

---

47   Jordan and Overmyer, *Flying Phoenix*, chap. 3; Shiga, "Difang Daojiao de xingcheng"; Fan, *Qingmo Minchu cishan shiye*; Wang, "Cong xin ziliao kan jindai Zhongguo de 'fuji huodong.'"

ments, which sometimes assume eschatological dimensions. As Goossaert notes, discourses on the end of the world dominated the majority of the texts that were transmitted by these circles. Often, the context for the transmission of these texts is a perception of impending disaster or seeking a resolution to a disaster that has already occurred. The impending end of the world was perceived to have been initiated by the bad behavior of humans, which angered the gods who, in turn, meted out punishment in the form of disasters (fires, floods, wars, epidemics). The apocalypse was conceived as the end of a *kalpa* (or cosmic cycle), *jie* 劫, and this term had a large continuum "ranging from individual to collective, and from specific disasters (in which some may die) to all-round apocalypse in which all humanity (bar the elect) will perish."[48] The contents of the texts included descriptions of how individuals might improve their fate, through engaging in good actions or self-cultivation.

4.1   *Women*

Women were present and active in religious groups during the Qing period. Let us take the Taiping 太平 rebellion as an example. The ideology of the Taiping leaders, at least in theory, strongly supported gender equality, banned foot-binding and concubinage, allowed women to sit examinations and gain prominent roles in the public sphere, and organized female military units. This was aided by the fact that, in Hakka society, the largest ethnic group within the Taiping, women already enjoyed far greater freedom than did Han women.[49] Women were also present in a variety of other religious groups, which often segregated their followers by their gender. The Red Lanterns movement in Sichuan 四川, thought to be a companion rebel group to the Boxers (both active between 1890 and 1901), was mainly constituted by very young women, who trained in martial arts and participated in anti-foreign attacks. Some of the leaders of this group were elevated to the status of goddesses, like Huanglian shengmu 黃蓮聖母 and Cuiyun jie 翠雲姐. There was also a large female membership within the White Lotus movement, who took prominent leading roles in it, and may, at times, have constituted the majority of the sect's members.[50]

There is also evidence that women were very active in the smaller lay communities involved in spirit-writing. Goossaert reports that women frequently attended spirit-writing altars in the Jiangnan region. At the Jueyun tan 覺雲壇, an altar in Shanghai that served a large community, it is recorded that

---

48   Goossaert, "Modern Daoist Eschatology," 1.
49   Michael and Chang, *The Taiping Rebellion*, 445–46, and Pan, "The Position of Women in T'ai-p'ing T'ian-kuo."
50   Prazniak, *Of Camel Kings and Other Things*, 158–63.

almost half of the 1,000 members were female, mainly married women who attended the altar's activities because their husband or other family members were members too.[51] Fan Chun-wu also discusses the female members of another spirit-writing altar, the Qingyun tan 青雲壇 in Beijing. According to his research, women held prominent leadership positions at this altar and took charge of accepting, training, and organizing all the female adepts, keeping them separate from the male ones.[52] While women were very active as believers and held leadership roles in these communities, there is less evidence of women acting as mediums, and also a lack of female divinities said to be directly transmitting texts through spirit-writing.

4.2   Goddesses

Richard Von Glahn has described the rise of goddesses in the Chinese religious landscape as beginning during the Song period but continuing and intensifying through the Ming and Qing periods. Speaking specifically of Guanyin 觀音, but including other goddesses as well, he termed this process "the feminization of compassion": female deities who accept all newcomers, their mercy in sharp contrast to the sterner, more bureaucratic male deities.[53] He sees this process as reflecting an effort to build a "more personal relationship with the divine."[54] In his study of the goddess Bixia yuanjun 碧霞元君, Kenneth Pomeranz highlights the fact that women (the majority of the believers in Bixia) approached her for assistance with personal family matters: "to deal with ... [the] lonely life of a widow serving a father-in-law, to protect their reputation, to escape a lustful official," to pray for "children, long life for in-laws ..."[55] Bixia was also increasingly disparaged by elite men, who saw her worship as a manifestation of the "ignorant" practices of their women.[56] What they found objectionable was "the ways in which she allows the initiative of young women and a broader set of roles than orthodoxy allowed."[57] Bixia's ritual authority directly linked two females, without any male or textual intermediaries. Goddesses are frequently seen as mothers, just as women's expected role in society is to be a mother, and their central qualities are those of mercy and compassion. The most ubiquitous female deity of this period was Wusheng Laomu 無生老母,

---

51   Gao, "Jin'gaishan wangluo," 325–27. For a later discussion of the Jueyun altar, see Katz, "Spirit-writing and the Dynamics of Elite Religious Life."
52   Fan, *Qingmo Minchu cishan shiye*, 151–53.
53   Von Glahn, *The Sinister Way*, 151.
54   Ibid., 179.
55   Pomeranz, "Orthopraxy, Orthodoxy and the Goddess(es) of Taishan," 27, 38.
56   Ibid., 34.
57   Ibid., 38.

a goddess who appears first in the late Ming period, within the Luo religious movement (Luojiao 羅教), as the originator of all beings, equated with the emptiness that lies at the origin of the whole universe, the personification of an impersonal creation principle.[58] This deity is present widely in a vast array of religious movements throughout the Qing dynasty and her role is seen in different ways within different traditions: she is "a compassionate deity sorrowfully watching her children who are immersed in the sea of suffering ... she wants to rescue and deliver them to their native place in heaven" or also described simply as "what existed before Heaven and Earth ... the source of all beings, which produces everything, but is not produced" and the "primordial state of the cosmos."[59] Often, these two meanings—the merciful mother and the originator of the cosmos—co-existed in the minds of the believers.

Sangren discusses the case of Miaoshan 妙善, a reincarnation of the Buddhist goddess of mercy Guanyin, and analyzes the reasons for the strong connection between goddesses and mercy. He suggests that, despite the amount of informal power women yield within the family as mothers, in fact, Chinese patrilineality "obviates women as subjects ... symbolically repressing full recognition of women's productive agency."[60] The constant representation of women as outsiders in Chinese familial relations adds to their suffering. The repression of women's agency, both in their natal families and in the families into which they marry, forms a deep understanding of suffering and a deep empathy for those who suffer; this is the quality of mercy that is often associated with female deities. Several *baojuan* 寶卷 (precious scrolls) recount the story of Miaoshan and Guanyin, and lay bare the strong contradiction between a religious path to personal salvation that women wish to follow and achieve, and filial piety, the duty to produce children as well as take care of parents and in-laws. Women and goddesses equally struggle due to this contradiction.[61]

The rise of female deities and their characteristic of all-encompassing mercy does not seem to make them central to the transmission of texts, however; textual transmission is clearly more of a male domain, as it is connected to bureaucracy, literacy, and power. Wusheng Laomu communicated with her flock through intermediary agents like Laojun 老君, but not directly; Guanyin often played a role in requesting texts from the Jade Emperor, but the act of transmission was often enacted by the three saints (*sansheng* 三聖), Lü Dong-

---

58   Seiwert, *Popular Religious Movements*, chapter 5 and specifically 220 and 229. Nikolas Broy in this volume discusses her role at length.
59   Seiwert, *Popular Religious Movements*, 302–3.
60   Sangren, *Filial Obsessions*, 283.
61   Idema, *Personal Salvation and Filial Piety*, 2–3.

bin, Wenchang and Guandi.[62] Thus, the gods in charge of textual transmission for many of the spirit-writing groups in Qing China tend to be male. Even though these female deities do not appear widely within spirit-writing transmission in general, their mercy, close connection, and affinity with women are displayed in more intimate settings, such as during the communications with deceased family members described above, or in the specifically female context of female alchemy texts. Interestingly, in this new popular religious milieu, Zigu, who also presided over séances which brought women together in intimate settings, does not feature among these major female divinities, but does continue to be worshipped in the original context in which her cult emerged, as attested by her presence in popular literature, gazetteers, etc.

5 Female Divinities and Female Alchemy

A different perspective emerges for one specific kind of spirit-written textual transmission: that of self-cultivation for women. Self-cultivation texts feature prominently in the textual production of spirit-writing altars from the late Ming and early Qing periods and are especially prominent around the mid-Qing period. They are often seen as part of a general, much needed behavioral correction that will steer humanity away from disaster toward a harmonious, morally upright future. Some of these texts have a more eschatological nature while others focus most on Confucian virtues and are less insistent on end-of-the world narratives and salvation from destruction. The transmitting gods in this context remain predominantly Lüzu, Wenchang, and Guandi, or other divinized local notables. A large number of texts received through spirit-writing pertain to inner alchemical practices, many of which are again transmitted by the Daoist divinity Lüzu. This is attested by, for example, the *Lüzu quanshu* 呂祖全書 (Complete works of Patriarch Lü), a large collection of texts received through spirit-writing from Lüzu, mostly at an altar in Hunan 湖南, the Hansan gong 涵三宮, and published in 1744,[63] which includes several sections on self-cultivation.[64]

---

62 See Wang, "Spirit Writing Groups in Modern China."
63 The *Lüzu quanshu*'s first complete edition in 32 chapters was published in 1744, but it includes several texts preceding this date. The textual history of the *Lüzu quanshu* and the Hansan gong is described in detail in Lai, "Qingdai sizhong 'Lüzu quanshu'"; and Li, "Lüzu quanshu yanjiu," 65–69. See also Esposito, *Creative Daoism*, especially parts 3–4; Wang, "Qingdai de Lüzu xinyang yu fuji."
64 On Daoist self-cultivation within collections of texts received from Lü Dongbin, see Esposito, *Facets of Qing Daoism*, and Lai, "Qingdai sizhong 'Lüzu quanshu.'"

The self-cultivation found in spirit-written materials, especially those transmitted by Lüzu, forms part of the Daoist tradition of *neidan* 內丹, or inner alchemy. The corpus of Lüzu-related scriptures, notably the *Lüzu quanshu*, and the *Daozang jiyao* 道藏輯要 (Essentials of the *Daoist Canon*), contains a large amount of *neidan* materials. Other compilations, like the *Zhang Sanfeng quanji* 張三豐全集 (Complete works of Zhang Sanfeng), also received through spirit-writing, indicate how to practice Daoist self-cultivation.[65]

In the context of the transmission of self-cultivation texts in relation to the cult of Lüzu, at some point within the early to mid-Qing period, we witness the emergence of female alchemy, or *nüdan* 女丹, a self-cultivation technique that was directly targeted at female practitioners.[66] Apart from specific physiological instructions regarding this practice, manuals on female alchemy often contain a large component of moral injunctions regarding women's behavior. Within this tradition, although the afore-mentioned male divinities remain present, there exists a large number of female divinities who transmit texts, in poetry and prose, directly to female audiences and address women directly in their prefaces, including Xiwangmu 西王母, Sun Bu'er 孫不二, and He Xiangu 何仙姑. In many cases, these female divinities are seen as forming a lineage of transmission through which specific instructions for women are sent. The importance of the female lineage of divinities is manifested by the very act of creating and discussing it explicitly and prominently in the prefaces. I will investigate all the above issues to understand whether it is important to highlight the female identity within these relationships.

I will briefly discuss the importance of body specificity and gender differences in self-cultivation practice for women. However, for the purpose of this paper, because the core element of a spirit-written text is a close, intimate connection and dialogue between a divinity and a community of receivers, or a single receiver, I particularly wish to examine the interaction between goddesses and female audiences as expressed in prefaces and poetry. Several of the texts in female alchemy collections are transmitted by goddesses and received by women, and it is within this act of transmission from woman to woman that I wish to investigate the specificity of the gendered dimension. What are the topics, exhortations, goals, experiences, and concerns that emerge during this interaction? Why is it important to have female divinities like Xiwangmu, Sun Bu'er, He Xiangu, and others speak to women? How are these goddesses represented in their hagiographies, which also form part of the collections?

---

65 *Lüzu quanshu*; *Zhang Sanfeng quanji*.
66 For a comprehensive history of female alchemy, see Valussi, "Beheading the Red Dragon"; and Valussi, "Female Alchemy and Paratext."

5.1 Hagiographies of Female Immortals

Collections of female alchemy also include hagiographies of female immortals and collect their poems. The *Qunzhen shijue* 群真詩決 (Poetic formulae by all the perfected), also included in the *Nüjindan fayao* 女金丹法要 (Essential methods for the female golden elixir), includes the hagiographies and poems of six female immortals: Wucailuan xiangu 吳采鸞仙姑 (Female Immortal Wu, Colored Phoenix), Fanyunqiao xiangu 樊雲翹仙姑 (Female Immortal Fan of the Cloudy Feathers), Yuehuajun Cui shaoxuan 月華君崔少玄 (Small Mystery Cui, the Lady of the Moon Brightness), Tang Guangzhen zhenren 唐廣真真人 (the Perfected Tang of Wide Perfection), Xuanjing sanren Zhou yuanjun 玄靜散人周元君 (Original lady Zhou, the Ubiquitous Woman of Mystery and Calm), and Qingjing sanren Sun Bu'er yuanjun 清靜散人孫不二元君 (Original lady Sun the non-second, Serene Lady of Purity and Calm). The fact that their hagiographies are included in the *Nüjindan fayao* indicates that their lives are taken as exemplary, as a guideline for mortal women to follow.[67] It is again relevant that all of the hagiographies here are of women. If we compare the *Nüjindan fayao* with the *Lüzu quanshu*, for example, *juan* 卷 2 of the *Lüzu quanshu* contains dozens of biographies of immortals, but only two relate to women: He Xiangu and Tang Guangzhen. In comparison, in the *Nujindan fayao*, the sections on hagiographies (*Nüdan shiji qianbian* 女丹詩集前編) and *Nüdan shiji houbian* 女丹詩集後編, (Collection of poems on female alchemy—first and second sections, respectively) are composed solely of hagiographies of women. Which elements of their life stories might appeal to women? To what events can common women relate? The topics that frequently emerge are often linked to women's lives, and the constraints they face regarding the religious path. Issues related to family duties (the clash between family duties and the desire to practice self-cultivation) often come to the fore in these biographies. There follows an example from Tang Guangzhen:

> Tang Guangzhen was from Yanzhou; **she served her mother with extreme filiality.** After marrying, she contracted a disease of the blood. Having dreamed of a Daoist with a medicine, she recovered. From then on, she devoted herself to the Dao and revered He Xiangu. ... An immortal asked her: "Do you desire to transcend the mortal world and enter sagehood? To stay in your body and live in the world? Or to abandon your bones and become immortal?" She responded: **"My mother's still alive.**

---

67 Some of their stories are included in other anthologies of famous Daoist immortals. Wu Cailuan's life story is included in *juan* 5 of the *Lishi zhenxian tidao tongjian houji* and the *Youxiang liexian quanzhuan, juan* 4, 12a–b. Fan Yunqiao's life story is included in the *Lishi zhenxian tidao tongjian houji, juan* 4 and *Yongcheng jixian lu, juan* 6, 16.

I wish to have the honor of nurturing her until the end. [If you] award me one grain of elixir, I'll swallow it and continue not to eat grains." Afterward, she was summoned to enter the Palace of Virtue and Long Life, and given the name of Quiet and Serene Perfected who congeals the spirit.[68]

唐廣眞嚴州人，事母至孝。旣嫁得血疾，夢道人與藥而愈，自是好道
虔奉何仙姑 … 仙問曰：汝欲超凡入聖耶？留形住世耶？棄骨成仙耶？
對曰: 有母在。願奉終養。賜丹一粒吞之遂不穀食。後召入德壽宮，封
寂靜凝神眞人。

There are other similar examples revealing that, within female alchemy, female self-cultivation needs to be achieved through strict Confucian moral norms, and these norms are guided by female divinities who model and encourage this path. These biographies echo those of other female religious figures like, for example, Miaoshan, whose story combines utmost compassion for her parents with an utmost commitment to her religious calling. Miaoshan refuses to marry, in defiance of her father's wishes, to commit herself fully to a life of religious observance. Her father kills her and, from beyond the grave, she saves him from a mortal illness by donating her eyes and arms to him.

This story, and the conflict between religious salvation and filiality for women, has been extensively discussed by several scholars, especially in the Buddhist context. Their work has revealed how it is far more difficult for women to abandon the family than it is for men, and how circuitous the justification for entering a religious path needs to be for women, who must justify their own individual salvation by combining it with that of their parents and the whole world.[69] The gender affinity I discuss in this paper also arises from the deep understanding, by goddesses, of the plight of common women.

5.2   *Gender Affinity*
Apart from the qualities of mercy and empathy, developed by goddesses for all believers but especially women, in female alchemy, we have a more specifically physiological aspect of affinity. As the female self-cultivation process itself

---

68   In *Nüdan shiji qianbian*, 5a–b. This is followed by several poems by her. A biography of Tang Guangzhen that contains an illustration features in *Youxiang liexian quanzhuan*, *juan* 8, 8a–b. The illustration is in *juan* 8, 27b. These biographies are extremely similar in content.

69   Grant, "Patterns of female religious experience"; Grant and Idema, *Escape from Blood Pond Hell*; Levering, "Stories of Enlightened Women in Ch'an"; Idema, *Personal Salvation and Filial Piety*.

is gender-specific, and entails progressing from pollution to purity by refining the most polluting agent in the female body, menstrual blood, it makes sense that the divinities who can directly discuss this and guide women through it should be women. Further, as discussed above, women and goddesses alike have a keen awareness of their duties surrounding the family, so it seems "natural" that indications of proper behavior for women should come from the same gender.

Several examples are found in morality books from the same period, in which the goddess He Xiangu features prominently. A good example is the *He Xiangu xunnei wen* 何仙姑訓內文 (He Xiangu instructs the inner chambers), received through spirit-writing from He Xiangu, with a preface dating to 1858.[70] In the preface, similarly to the female alchemy prefaces, He identifies closely with the women whom she is instructing: "When I started to manifest and transform myself, I took pity on the common folk, and wrote many things in the manner of exhortations. In general, most were exhorting people of the inner [chambers] (women); since I was originally an inner person myself (a woman), I use the inner to exhort the inner" (余始顯化。悲憫世人。數著為訓。大抵訓內者居多。蓋余本內人。與內訓內).[71] As will be discussed for the *Kunning miaojing* 坤寧妙經 (Wondrous scripture on Kun's peace) below, He Xiangu focuses on the gender affinity between herself and her female audience. In the last chapter of the book, He also fiercely criticizes ordained nuns for abandoning their parents and being unfilial, thus angering the gods. In another spirit-written morality book, the *Xunnü baozhen* 訓女寶箴 (Precious admonitions for the instruction of women), received in Yunnan in 1921, several female divinities descend in order to admonish women to be filial, chaste, and follow the Confucian virtues and gender relations, especially obedience to their husbands.[72] There are chapters clearly criticizing freedom of marriage (*jie ziyou jiehun ge* 戒自由結婚歌) and disobedience to husbands (*xun nüzi zaijia congfu zhang* 訓女子在家從父章).[73] As exemplified in Chung Yun-ying's research, this text appears to reveal a tension between the traditional, strict social hierarchy, and the novel ideas of gender equality, introduced at the beginning of the twentieth century, which opened up new opportunities for women to enter the public sphere, work, and even divorce their husband. Xia Shi, in this volume, also discusses the reconfiguration of

---

70   *Zhenben shanshu*, vol. 85.
71   Ibid., 2b.
72   This text has been studied in Chung, "Xianzhi wo ziwo shixian?"; and Clart, "Chinese Tradition and Taiwanese Modernity."
73   *Xunnü baozhen, juan* 2.

the gender norms within the Republican religious organization Daoyuan 道院, and how the spirit-written messages received by the women in this organization both maintained and reformulated the essential Confucian concepts of "inner and outer" (*neiwai* 內外), "talent and virtue" (*cai yu de* 才與德), and "three followings and four virtues" (*sancong side* 三從四德). For example, she mentions how talent in women is no longer seen negatively if paired with virtue, and there is less emphasis on obedience to one's father, husband, and son.[74] In the examples provided above, it is goddesses who instruct women to maintain Confucian virtues and not to follow practices that might disrupt the social order. Clart indicates that this kind of book was supposed to be read aloud to women by their husband or male relatives, who were more literate, so there was a male intermediary even in this female-to-female transmission.[75]

5.3   *Building a Lineage of Female Immortals*

The recurrence of women as transmitters of the texts of *nüdan* is also highly significant. As described above, prior to the emergence of female alchemy, we see few female immortals transmitting and explaining texts to women. Several texts on female alchemy mention the presence of various female divinities at the time of the transmission of the texts, while others are more specific, actually providing a detailed lineage through which the transmission of female alchemy texts reached the human world. Most of these lineages feature only female immortals.

These female divinities can share common concerns, duties, and behaviors with the female audience to build affinity. Many of the goddesses involved in the transmission have life stories that have been widely recounted, which often include the need to combine their duties as women with their aspirations as religious practitioners. Goddesses exhort the women in the audience to be filial and morally upright, channeling the instruction that was common in the *baojuan* and *shanshu* 善書 (morality books) literature for women which was widespread at the time, and often share their own personal experiences in that regard. This is a way of creating a closeness and a direct conduit between the goddess and the audience which might be more difficult to create between a male divinity and a female audience. A large proportion of the transmitted texts on female alchemy, in fact, comprises of specific behavioral instructions for women.

---

74   See the contribution by Xia Shi in this volume.
75   Clart, "Chinese Tradition and Taiwanese Modernity."

Some of the female immortals in these lineages are the same as those in the poems exchanged in literary circles described above: Magu, Tianfei, Doumu. Some belong more to the strictly Daoist tradition, like Wei Huacun 魏華存, Xiwangmu and Sun Bu'er, but had not participated in the spirit-written transmission of texts up to this point. Finally, we have He Xiangu, an extremely popular female divinity who appeared in both the *baojuan* and Daoist literature of this period. Of these goddesses, Xiwangmu is the most remote, residing in her immortal abode at the Yao pond (Yaochi 瑤池), and is often mentioned as the one whom women reach at the end of their journey, or as being situated at the very origin of the transmission; on the other hand, Sun Bu'er and He Xiangu are more frequently charged with the actual transmission of the texts to women. Interestingly, Wusheng Laomu, a divinity who was very popular among religious groups during this period, does not appear here. As mentioned above, she does not appear to be involved in the direct transmission of texts and is often associated with an origin principle rather than with female characteristics.

Why is it necessary to specify this, at times lengthy and complex, line of transmission, and why are the divinities mostly female? The answer to the first question is, of course, legitimacy. If the text is bestowed by a long line of illustrious divinities, it will be considered truthful and powerful. This is especially important for a text transmitted by female divinities, who were not traditionally always as powerful as male divinities. The second question is explained in some of the prefaces to the texts themselves. For example, the case of Lin Chunxiu 林淳修 (no dates), the first attested female medium who received a self-cultivation text for women, provides insights into the need for gendered affinity in the transmission of the *Kunning miaojing*, one of the first texts of female alchemy. The text was transmitted as part of the wider process of the transmission of several texts which eventually formed the *Wendi quanshu* 文帝全書 (Complete works of the Divine Lord Wenchang),[76] and was later included in the *Nüjindan fayao*.[77] In one of the prefaces to this text, Wenchang himself, who is the transmitting divinity, recognizes the importance of finding a female

---

[76] This transmission has a complex history which happens mainly between 1733 and 1743. Hu, "*Wendi quanshu* yanjiu," describes in detail the transmission of these texts between Chongqing and Guizhou.

[77] This text is included in the *Jiyizi zhengdao mishu shiqizhong* 濟一子證道秘書十七種 (Jiyizi's seventeen secret books on the verification of the Dao), collected by Fu Jinquan 傅金銓 (fl. 1800), with a preface dated 1813. Fu attributed several of the texts included in this collection to Lüzu. For more on Fu, see Valussi, "Printing and Religion."

medium to receive instructions for women. This medium needed to possess a strong affinity with the community: "In order to transmit scriptures for women, it is necessary to find someone with an affinity" (以女經之傳，須覓有緣).[78]

Lin herself, speaking to an audience of female immortals and of ordinary women, refers to this gender affinity in her own words: "For this reason, I manifested in a female form, I borrowed a woman's hand, I discussed women's methods, I transmitted instructions for women." (以余現女人身，借女人手，說女人法，垂女人教。)[79] Another example is the case of Sun Bu'er and the transmission of the *Xiwangmu nüxiu zhengtu shize*; in this case the god Lüzu specifically sought a goddess to continue the interrupted transmission of a text on female alchemy. Hence, Lü "**commanded** the Immortal Sun Bu'er to abridge and edit it meticulously, to collect it and transmit it to the world, in order to continue the lineage (channel, *mai*) of women perfected" (吾甚憫之，愛命不二仙子，息心刪訂，輯述授世，以續女真一脈).[80] Thus, there is an acknowledgement, by male divinities, of the necessity for gender affinity between the goddess transmitting, the medium as a conduit of the transmission, and the audience receiving it.

6   Conclusions

Do gender patterns exist? Certainly. Going back to Zigu and the shift from non-written to written communication, from a female to a male milieu, it seems that the very act of the transmission of writing, especially salvific writing, needs to be performed by males, thus linking literacy and the power of writing with men.

The environment and the actors involved in the emergence of spirit-writing within the Daoist ritual tradition, as described by Goossaert in this volume, involved communications between fierce exorcistic male deities and male Daoist ritual masters, *daoshi* and *fashi*, excluding women from both the transmission, control, and manipulation of important salvific messages.

Turning to a later period, during the interactions of male literati with female immortals and deceased family members, we see how spirit-writing provides a method for male literati not only to connect emotionally with the deceased but also to perpetuate their own literary immortality. For the women within these circles, on the other hand, spirit-writing is used to create a real-life com-

---

78   *Kunning miaojing xu*, in *Nüjindan fayao* 6a.
79   *Kunning miaojing*, preface, in *Nüjindan fayao*, 6b.
80   *Xiwangmu nüxiu zhengtu shize*, 1a–b, preface. This passage only appears in the preface reprinted in the *Zangwai daoshu*.

munity as well as a connection with female immortals, with whom they have a special affinity, who can provide solace and agency beyond the constrictions and frustrations of being a woman in this world and be recognized both for their immortal self and poetic genius. In late imperial period religious groups, women are present, active, and sometimes in leadership positions; however, and outside the female alchemy tradition, they are not seen as mediums at spirit-writing altars and are not in charge of directly connecting with and receiving the words of the divinity. Further, despite the presence of a variety of female divinities in the late imperial period, these deities are generally associated with mercy, succor, hearing and listening to suffering. Steven Sangren, in his analysis of the cults of Guanyin, Mazu 馬祖, and Wusheng Laomu, highlights the fact that all of these goddesses had to prove their purity by circumventing the polluting event of marriage (thus pregnancy and childbirth) by sidestepping it and directly embodying the role of mother, at the same time performing in the most filial manner.[81] This avoidance is not required of male deities, who ascend to divinity through other, bureaucratic means, and have other concerns, associated with ideas of hierarchy, authority, and legitimacy. It is mostly male divinities who have the power to transmit salvific spirit-written messages. Female divinities are preferred when the audience is mainly female and the topic is related to women, as clearly exemplified in the female alchemical tradition and the morality book tradition mentioned above. Conversely, as in the example of the Jade Princess discussed by Shiga Ichiko in this volume, it is often the efforts of groups of women that keep alive the worship of and the connection with female divinities.[82] I explain this in terms of "affinity," because female divinities and immortals, having gone through life as a woman, are believed to be better able to connect personally with women and advise them on matters of physical self-cultivation, moral development, and pitfall avoidance. However, the roles of male and female deities still follow specific gender patterns: gods have the power to originate texts, and goddesses transmit them to women with whom they have a close affinity.

As for the gender relation between gods and goddesses in the process of transmission, in female alchemy texts, both male guidance and a female conduit are necessary. At the same time, as far as we are aware, there are no non-specifically gendered texts that were transmitted by goddesses. Lüzu, Wenchang, and Guandi were all sanctioned as state cults by the Jiaqing emperor and, as Vincent Goossaert has discussed, their role as divine saviors is firmly

---

81 Sangren, "Female Gender in Chinese Religious Symbols," 12–13.
82 See the contribution by Shiga in this volume.

embedded within the spirit-writing tradition. There are no equivalent female divine saviors with the same power, efficaciousness (*ling* 靈), and place in the hierarchical structure within the spirit-writing circles. As mentioned above, Wusheng Laomu, a widely revered goddess, did not generally directly transmit texts through spirit-writing, and nor did Guanyin or Bixia yuanjun. The religious efficacy of the goddesses within spirit-writing circles, if it happens at all, is in the context of female instruction and in the presence or with the permission of male divinities.

Further, not only gods but also men see themselves as enablers in the process of forming a direct connection between women, goddesses, and textual transmission.

He Longxiang, 賀龍驤 (ca. 1900) in the preface to his collection of female alchemy, the *Nüdan hebian* 女丹合編 (Collection of female alchemy), published in Chengdu in 1906, clearly sees his efforts in this light, when he describes women's self-cultivation practice and goals. He sees himself as the champion of the women in his family, because he painstakingly collected the female alchemy texts in the *Nüdan hebian*. In his preface to this, he describes how his instructions will allow more female immortals to stand by the side of Xiwangmu on the day of her festival:

> I, in turn, instruct women, all of those who receive this text, that they should cut the seven feelings and get rid of the six desires … push forward, despite all the frustrations, not retreat even when they meet demons, refine blood into *qi*, *qi* into spirit, spirit into vacuity, vacuity into nothingness, and the result will be Golden Immortality that the hundred million disasters cannot destroy. Above, they will have an audience with the Queen Mother of the West, and below they will save all sentient beings. I think that, during the festival in honor of the Queen Mother of the West, it is necessary not to allow male immortals alone to stand on her right. Women should strive in that direction [too].

> 再囑女流凡有奉此編者務須絕七情除六欲 … 百折不回，遇魔不退，煉血化炁，煉氣化神，煉神還虛，煉虛還無，果證金仙，億刧不壞。上朝王母，下度眾生，吾想蟠桃會上當不讓男仙獨出其右，女流勉之。[83]

---

[83] *Nüdan hebian*, preface, 7a–b.

Bibliography

Abbreviations

DZ *Daozang* 道藏, numbers in the bibliography are following Kristofer Schipper and Franciscus Verellen, eds. *The Taoist Canon: A Historical Companion to the Daozang (Daozang Tongkao* 道藏通考). 3 vols. Chicago: University of Chicago Press, 2004.

Databases

Beijing Airusheng shuzihua jishu yanjiu zhongxin 北京愛如生數字化技術研究中心.
Dongpo quanji 東坡全集: https://zh.m.wikisource.org/zh-hant/子姑神記. Accessed June 5, 2020.

Primary Sources

Daozang jiyao 道藏輯要. Chengdu: Bashu shushe, 1995.

Daozang jinghua 道藏精華. Compiled by Xiao Tianshi 蕭天石 (1908–1986). Taipei: Ziyou chubanshe, 1956–1983.

Daozang xubian 道藏續編. Compiled by Min Yide 閔一得 (1758–1836), on Mount Jin'gai, Jiangsu, 1834. Reprint, Beijing: Haiyang chubanshe, 1989, and Beijing: Shumu wenxian chubanshe, 1993.

Dianshizhai huabao 點石齋畫報. Shanghai: Shenbaoguan, 1884–1898. Reprint, Guangzhou: Guangdong renmin chubanshe, 1984.

Gongxing xinchan 躬行心懺. In *Wendi quanshu*, appendix *Qunzhen zhushu* 群真著述.

Gujin tushu jicheng 古今圖書集成. Edited by Jiang Tingxi 蔣廷錫 (1669–1732). Reprint, Shanghai: Tushu jicheng yinshuju, 1884.

He Xiangu xunnei wen 何仙姑訓內文. Attributed to He Xiangu, preface dated 1858. In *Zhenben shanshu*, vol. 85.

Jiangbibu jishi 降筆部紀事. In *Gujin tushu jicheng*, juan 310.

Jing Chu suishi ji 荊楚歲時記. Zong Lin 宗懍 (ca. 500–560). Lost, reconstructed, republished, Wuhan: Hubei renmin chubanshe, 1982.

Jiyizi zhengdao mishu shiqi zhong 濟一子證道秘書十七種. Compiled by Fu Jinquan 傅金銓 (fl. 1820). Sichuan: Shudong shanchengtang, 1813–1844. Reprinted in *Zangwai daoshu*, vol. 11, 1–720.

Kunning miaojing 坤寧妙經. Qingzhen nüguan xingxing miaohua zhenren 清真女冠興行妙化真人. Preface dated 1743. In *Nüjindan fayao*, 6a–31a.

Lishi zhenxian tidao tongjian houji 歷世真仙體道通鑑後集. Zhao Daoyi 趙道一 (fl. 1294–1307). DZ 296. Reprint, Shanghai: Shangwu yinshuguan, 1923–26.

Lüzu quanshu 呂祖全書. 32 chapters. First complete edition 1744. Reprinted in *Zangwai daoshu*, vol. 7, 51–530.

Lüzu wupian zhu 呂祖五篇注. Attributed to Lü Dongbin 呂洞賓. Collected by Fu

Jinquan 傅金銓 (fl. 1820), preface dated 1823. In *Jiyizi zhengdao mishu shiqizhong*. Reprinted in *Zangwai daoshu*, vol. 11, 720–43.

Muzhai chu xue ji 牧齋初學集. Edited by Qian Qianyi 錢謙益 (1582–1664). Shanghai: Suihanzhai, 1910.

Nüdan hebian 女丹合編. Collected and published by He Longxiang 賀龍驤 (fl. 1906) at the Erxian An 二仙庵. Chengdu: 1906.

Nüdan shiji qianbian 女丹詩集前編. In *Nüdan hebian*, n.p.

Nüdan shiji houbian 女丹詩集後編. In *Nüdan hebian*, n.p.

Nüjindan fayao 女金丹法要. Compiled by Fu Jinquan 傅金銓 (fl. 1820) in 1813. Reprinted in *Zangwai daoshu*, vol. 11, 512–41.

Qingjing yuanjun Kunyuanjing 清靜元君坤元經. Ca. 1657. In *Nüjindan fayao*. Reprinted in *Zangwai daoshu*, vol. 7, 357–59.

Tiantai Le fashi lingyi ji 天台泐法師靈異記. 1910 edition. In *Muzhai chuxue ji*, juan 43.

Wang tianjun yulu 王天君語錄. In *Guanxinzhai jiwen*, n.p.

Wenchang dijun yulu 文昌帝君語錄. In *Guanxinzhai jiwen*, n.p.

Wendi quanshu 文帝全書. Compiled by Liu Qiao 劉樵 (fl. 1727–1749). 1794 edition, housed in Shanghai Library.

Woyun yuanjun yulu 斡運元君語錄. In *Guanxinzhai jiwen*, n.p.

Wumen tang ji 午夢堂集. Edited by Ye Shaoyuan 葉紹袁 (1589–1648), 1636. Reprint, Shanghai: Ningjian tang chongkan, 1916.

Wuzhen pian sanzhu 悟真篇三注. Xue Shi 薛式 (d. 1191) and Lu Shu 陸墅, 1169. In DZ 142. Reprint, Shanghai: Shangwu yinshuguan, 1923–26.

Xiantan changheshi shishou 仙壇唱和詩十首. *Muzhai chuxue ji*, juan 10, 13b–16b.

Xiling guiyong 西泠閨詠. Edited by Chen Wenshu 陳文述, 1827. Reprint, *Congshu jicheng xubian* 叢書集成續編, vol. 64. Shanghai: Shanghai shudian, 1994.

Xiwangmu nüxiu zhengtu shize 西王母女修正途十則. Attributed to Xiwangmu. Reprinted in *Zangwai daoshu*, vol. 10, 533–40.

Xunnü baozhen 訓女寶箴. 1921. in *Zhenben shanshu*, vol. 91.

Yiyuan 異苑. Compiled by Liu Jingshu 劉敬叔 (fl. fourth to fifth century). *Siku quanshu* edition.

Yongcheng jixian lu 墉城集仙錄. Compiled by Du Guangting 杜光庭 (850–933). In DZ 783. Reprint, Shanghai: Shangwu yinshuguan, 1923–26.

Youxiang liexian quanzhuan 有象列仙全傳. N.d. Reprinted in *Zangwai daoshu*, vol. 31, 576–735.

Zangwai daoshu 藏外道書. Compiled by Hu Daojing 胡道靜 et al. 36 vols. Chengdu: Bashu shushe, 1992–1994.

Zhang Sanfeng quanji 張三豐全集. In *Daozang jiyao*, vol. 7, 292–405.

Zhenben shanshu 珍本善書. Shanghai: Leshanshe, Dazhong shuju, 194?

Secondary Sources

Boltz, Judith. "On the Legacy of Zigu and a Manual on Spirit Writing in Her Name." In *The People and the Dao: New Studies in Chinese Religions in Honour of Daniel L. Overmyer,* edited by Philip Clart and Paul Crowe, 349–88. Sankt Augustin: Institut Monumenta Serica, 2009.

Bray, Francesca. *Technology and Gender: Fabrics of Power in Late Imperial China.* Berkeley: University of California Press, 1997.

Burton-Rose, Daniel. "A Prolific Spirit: Peng Dingqiu's Posthumous Career on the Spirit Altar, 1720–1906." *Daoism: Religion, History and Society* / 道教研究學報：宗教、歷史與社會, no. 7 (2015): 7–63.

Calef, Susan. "Charting New Territory: Religion and 'the Gender-Critical Turn.'" In "Women, Gender and Religion," supplement 5, *Journal of Religion and Society,* edited by Susan Calef and Ronald A. Simkins (2009): 1–6.

Chao, Wei-pang. "The Origins and Growth of the Fu Chi." *Folklore Studies* 1 (1942): 9–27.

Clart, Philip. "Chinese Tradition and Taiwanese Modernity: Morality Books as Social Commentary and Critique." In *Religion in Modern Taiwan: Tradition and Innovation in a Changing Society,* edited by Philip Clart and Charles Jones, 84–97. Honolulu: University of Hawai'i Press, 2003.

Chung Yun-Ying 鍾雲鶯. "Xianzhi huo ziwo shixian? Minchu luanshu *Xunnü baozhen* dui nüxing ziyou pingdengguan de liangzhong taidu 限制或自我實現？——民初鸞書《訓女寶箴》對女性自由平等觀的兩重態度." Unpublished manuscript.

Esposito, Monica. *Creative Daoism.* Wil and Paris: UniversityMedia, 2013.

Esposito, Monica. *Facets of Qing Daoism.* Wil and Paris: UniversityMedia, 2014.

Fan Chunwu 范純武. *Qingmo Minchu cishan shiye yu luantang yundong* 清末民初慈善事業與鸞堂運動. Boyang publishing, 2015.

Fong, Grace S., and Ellen Widmer. *The Inner Quarters and Beyond: Women Writers from Ming through Qing.* Leiden and Boston: Brill, 2010.

Gao Wansang 高萬桑 [Vincent Goossaert]. "Jin'gaishan wangluo: Jinxiandai Jiangnan de Quanzhen jushi zuzhi 金蓋山網絡—近現代江南的全真居士組織." *Quanzhendao yanjiu* 全真道研究 1, (2011): 319–39.

Gerritsen, Anne. "The Many Guises of Xiaoluan: The Legacy of a Girl Poet in Late Imperial China." *Journal of Women's History* 17, no. 2 (2005): 38–61.

Goossaert, Vincent. "Modern Daoist Eschatology: Spirit-Writing and Elite Soteriology in Late Imperial China." *Daoism: Religion, History and Society* / 道教研究學報：宗教、歷史與社會, no. 6 (2014): 219–46.

Goossaert, Vincent. "Spirit Writing, Canonization, and the Rise of Divine Saviors: Wenchang, Lüzu, and Guandi, 1700–1858." *Late Imperial China* 36, no. 2 (December 2015): 82–125.

Goyama Kiwamu 合山究. *Min Shin jidai no josei to bungaku* 明清時代の女性と文学. Tōkyō: Kyūko Shoin, 2006.

Grant, Beata. "Patterns of Female Religious Experience in Qing Dynasty Popular Literature." *Journal of Chinese Religions* 23, no. 1 (1995): 29–58.

Grant, Beata, and Wilt L. Idema, trans. *Escape from Blood Pond Hell: The Tales of Mulian and Woman Huang*. Seattle: University of Washington Press, 2011.

He Yanran 賀晏然. "Tanyang ciguan de yanbian yu wanming yijiang de jibai huodong 曇陽祠觀的演變與晚明以降的祭拜活動." *Aomen ligong xuebao* 澳門理工學報, 2018.4:68–76.

Hsieh Tsung-hui 謝聰輝. *Xin tiandi zhi ming: Yuhuang, Zitong yu feiluan* 新天帝之命：玉皇, 梓潼與飛鸞. Taipei: Taiwan Shangshu yinshuguan, 2003.

Hu Jiechen 胡劼辰. "*Wendi quanshu* yanjiu: Qingdai Wenchang dijun xinyang de wenxian shi 文帝全書研究：清代文昌帝君信仰的文獻史." Ph.D. diss., Chinese University of Hong Kong, 2017.

Idema, Wilt, trans. *Personal Salvation and Filial Piety: Two Precious Scroll Narratives of Guanyin and Her Acolytes*. Honolulu: University of Hawai'i Press, 2008.

Jordan, David, and Daniel Overmeyer. *Flying Phoenix: Aspects of Chinese Sectarianism in Taiwan*. Princeton University Press, 1986.

Katz, Paul. "Spirit-writing and the Dynamics of Elite Religious Life in Republican Era Shanghai." In *Jindai Zhongguo de zongjiao fazhan lunwenji* 近代中國的宗教發展論文集, edited by Ting Jen-Chieh 丁仁傑 et al., 275–350. Taipei: Guoshiguan, 2015.

King, Ursula, and Tina Beattie, eds. *Gender, Religion and Diversity: Cross Cultural Perspectives*. London: Continuum, 2005.

Kleeman, Terry F. *A God's Own Tale: The Book of Transformations of Wenchang, the Divine Lord of Zitong*. New York: SUNY Press, 1994.

Ko, Dorothy. *Teachers of the Inner Chambers: Women and Culture in Seventeenth-Century China*. Stanford: Stanford University Press, 1994.

Lai Chi-tim 黎志添. "Qingdai sizhong 'Lüzu quanshu' yu Lüzu fuji daotan de guanxi 清代四種「呂祖全書」與呂祖扶乩道壇的關係." *Zhongguo wenzhe yanjiu jikan* 中國文哲研究集刊, no. 42 (2013): 183–230.

Levering, Miriam. "Stories of Enlightened Women in Ch'an and the Chinese Buddhist Female Bodhisattva/Goddess Tradition." In *Women and Goddess Traditions in Antiquity and Today*, edited by Karen L. King, 137–76. Minneapolis: Fortress Press, 1997.

Li Jiajun 李家駿. "Lüzu quanshu yanjiu 呂祖全書研究." PhD diss., Chinese University of Hong Kong, 2012.

Liu, Xun. "Of Poems, Gods and Spirit Writing Altars: The Daoist Beliefs and Practices of Wang Duan, 1793–1839." *Late Imperial China* 36, no. 2 (2015): 23–81.

Loewe, Michael. *Ways to Paradise: The Chinese Quest for Immortality*. London: George Allen & Unwin, 1979.

Lu Lin 陸林. "Jin Shengtan zaoqi fuji jiangshen huodong kaolun 金聖歎早期扶乩降神活動考論." *Zhonghua wenshi luncong* 中華文史論叢 77 (2004): 247–74.

Lu Lin 陸林. *Jin Shengtan shishi yanjiu* 金聖歎史實研究. Beijing: Beijing renmin wenxue chubanshe, 2015.

Mann, Susan. *Precious Records: Women in China's Long Eighteenth Century*. Stanford: Stanford University Press, 1997.

Michael, Franz H., and Chung-li Chang. *The Taiping Rebellion: History and Documents*. Vol. 1, *History*. Seattle: University of Washington Press, 1966.

Naquin, Susan. "The Peking Pilgrimage to Miaofengshan: Religious Organization and Sacred Site." In *Pilgrims and Sacred Sites in China*, edited by Susan Naquin and Chun Fang-yü. Berkeley, University of California Press, 1992.

Owen, Alex. *The Darkened Room: Women, Power and Spiritualism in Late Victorian England*. Chicago: University of Chicago Press, 2004.

Pan, Yuh-C'heng. "The Position of Women in T'ai-p'ing T'ian-kuo." MA thesis, University of British Columbia, 1971.

Pomeranz, Kenneth. "Orthopraxy, Orthodoxy and the Goddess(es) of Taishan." *Modern China* 33, no. 1 (2007): 22–46.

Prazniak, Roxann. *Of Camel Kings and Other Things: Rural Rebels against Modernity in Late Imperial China*. Lanham: Rowman and Littlefield, 1999.

Sangren, Steven. "Female Gender in Chinese Religious Symbols: Kuan Yin, Ma Tsu, and the 'Eternal Mother.'" *Signs* 9, no. 1 (1983): 5–25.

Sangren, Steven. *Filial Obsessions: Chinese Patriliny and Its Discontents*. Palgrave Macmillan, 2017.

Seiwert, Hubert. *Popular Religious Movements and Heterodox Sects in Chinese History*. Leiden and Boston: Brill, 2003.

Shiga, Ichiko. "Difang Daojiao de xingcheng: Guangdong diqu fuluan jieshe yundong xingqi yu yanbian 地方道教的形成：廣東地區扶鸞結社運動支興起與演變 (1838–1953)." *Daoism: Religion, History, and Society* 道教研究學報：宗教、歷史與社會, no. 2 (2010): 231–67.

Shiga Ichiko 志賀市子. *Xianggang Daojiao yu fuji xinyang: Lishi yu rentong* 香港道教與扶乩 信仰：歷史與認同. Translated by Song Jun 宋軍. Hong Kong: Chinese University Press, 2013.

Tromp, Marlene. "Spirited Sexuality: Sex, Marriage, and Victorian Spiritualism." *Victorian Literature and Culture* 31, no. 1 (2003): 67–81.

Valussi, Elena. "Beheading the Red Dragon: A History of Female Inner Alchemy in China." Ph.D. diss., University of London, School of Oriental and African Studies, 2003.

Valussi, Elena. "Female Alchemy and Paratext: How to Read *nüdan* in a Historical Context." *Asia Major* 21, no. 2 (2008): 153–93.

Valussi, Elena. "Printing and Religion in the Life of Fu Jinquan: Alchemical Writer, Religious Leader and Publisher in Sichuan." *Daoism: Religion, History and Society* 道教研究學報：宗教、歷史與社會, no. 4 (2012): 1–52.

Valussi, Elena. "The Transmission of the Cult of Lü Dongbin to Sichuan in the Nineteenth Century, and the Transformation of the Local Religious Milieu." *Daoism: Religion, History, and Society* 道教研究學報：宗教、歷史與社會, no. 7 (2015): 117–169.

Von Glahn, Richard. *The Sinister Way: The Divine and the Demonic in Chinese Religious Culture*. Berkeley: University of California Press, 2004.

Waltner, Ann. "T'an-yang-tzu and Wang Shih-chen: Visionary and Bureaucrat in the Late Ming." *Late Imperial China* 8, no. 1 (1987): 105–23.

Wang, Anning. "Gendering the Planchette: Female Writer Qian Xi's (1872–1930) Spiritual World." *The Journal of Chinese Literature and Culture* 4, no. 1 (April 2017): 160–79.

Wang Chien-chuan 王見川. "Qingdai de Lüzu xinyang yu fuji: Yi Jiaqing huangdi cifeng wei kaocha zhongxin 清代的呂祖信仰與扶乩：以嘉慶皇帝賜封為考察中心." *Mazu yu minjian xinyang: yanjiu tongxun* 馬祖與民間信仰：研究通訊 4 (2013): 28–39.

Wang Chien-Chuan 王見川. "Cong xin ziliao kan jindai Zhongguo de 'fuji huodong' 從新資料看近代中國的'扶乩活動.'" *Taipei chengshi keji daxue tongshi xuebao* 臺北城市科技大學通識學報, no. 5 (2015): 151–69.

Wang Chien-Chuan 王見川. "Peng Dingqiu yu Qingchu Suzhou Daojiao: fuluan, lidou yu zhushu 彭定求 (1645–1719) 與清初蘇州道教：扶鸞，禮斗與著書." In *Lishi yishu yu Taiwan renwen luncong* 歷史藝、術與台灣人文論叢 10, edited by Wang Chien-Ch'uan, 85–105. Taipei: Boyang wenhua, 2016.

Wang Chien-Chuan 王見川. "You Tong yu wan Ming Qing chu Suzhou de fuji: jiantan Jin Shengtan fuji de xingzhi 尤侗與晚明清初蘇州的扶乩：兼談金聖叹扶乩的性質." In *Lishi, yishu yu Taiwan renwen luncong* 歷史、藝術 與台灣人文論叢 11, edited by Li Shiwei 李世偉, 233–53. Taipei: Boyang wenhua, 2016.

Wang, Chien-Chuan, "Spirit Writing Groups in Modern China, 1840–937: Textual Production, Public Teachings, and Charity." In *Modern Chinese Religion II: 1850–2015*, edited by Jan Kiely, Vincent Goossaert and John Lagerwey, vol. 1, 651–84. Leiden: Brill, 2015.

Wang, Chien-chuan. "Popular Groups Promoting the 'Religion of Confucius' in the Chinese Southwest and Their Activities since the Nineteenth Century, 1840–2013." In *The Varieties of Confucian Experience: Documenting a Grassroots Revival of a Tradition*, edited by Sebastien Billioud, 90–121. Leiden: Brill, 2018.

Xu Dishan 許地山. *Fuji mixin de yanjiu* 扶箕迷信底研究. Shanghai: Shangwu yinshuguan, 1941. Reprint, Taipei: Commercial Press, 1966.

Zeitlin, Judith T. "Spirit Writing and Performance in the Work of You Tong 尤侗, 1618–1704." *T'oung Pao* 84, fasc. 1/3 (1998): 102–35.

PART 2

Changing Techniques and Practices

CHAPTER 5

Terminology and Typology of Spirit-Writing in Early Modern China: A Preliminary Study

Hu Jiechen

1   Introduction

Fuji 扶乩, usually translated into English as spirit-writing, is a form of communication with the spiritual world, through which the practitioners write down the information revealed using the appropriate implement, which also makes it a means of textual production. It is an important phenomenon in Chinese history, playing germane roles in religion, literature, and popular customs. It originated in medieval China and became prevalent in the late imperial period. During the Republican era, despite the anti-superstition trends, local communities frequently performed spirit-writing as part of religious and/or charity associations. After 1949, the newly-established Communist government suppressed the practice, but it survived in contemporary Hong Kong, Taiwan, and Chinese diasporas worldwide. In the twentieth century, it attracted increasing attention from historians of religions and anthropologists. Recently, the investigation of spirit-writing has become a new scholarly field. In the last decade, three international conferences have been held, bearing fruitful outcomes on the interdisciplinary study of spirit-writing.[1]

In the last century, historians like Kōda Rohan 幸田露伴 (1867–1947), Xu Dishan 許地山 (1893–1941), and Chao Wei-pang 趙衛邦 (1908–1986) conducted general studies on the history of spirit-writing. Their evidence included exter-

---

1   In 2014, an international conference on "Lüzu Cult, Lay Groups and Religious Innovations in Qing Daoism" was hosted by the Chinese University of Hong Kong. Most of the presented studies were included in the special issue of *Daoism: Religion, History and Society* 7 (2015). Three papers presented in that conference have been published elsewhere. See Goossaert, "Spirit-Writing, Canonization, and the Rise of Divine Saviors"; Liu, "Of Poems, Gods, and Spirit-Writing Altars"; Lai, "*Lüzu quanshu zhengzong*." In 2018, an international conference on "Fuluan wenhua yu minzhong zongjiao 扶鸞文化與民眾宗教" (Spirit-Writing Culture and Folk Religion) was held at Foguang University, Taiwan. The conference proceedings were published in 2020 (Fan, *Fuluan wenhua yu minzhong zongjiao*). In 2019, an international conference on "Spirit-Writing in Chinese History" was held at the IKGF, Erlangen, which resulted in the present volume.

nal documents such as "brush notes and small talks" (*biji xiaoshuo* 筆記小說) and "accounts of the strange" (*zhiguai* 志怪), or other commonly transmitted literature.[2] Simultaneously, anthropologists and ethnologists conducted several preliminary field studies on Southern China and its religious practices.[3] Shiga Ichiko 志賀市子 offers a schematic review of this academic field.[4] Recent research reflects both historical and anthropological approaches, with the former focusing on spirit-writing groups and their textual production. As a consequence, scholars now have access to a plentitude of internal evidence and archives, that has helped to broaden and deepen our understanding of this topic.

It is important to emphasise, therefore, that the discovery of new materials rescued spirit-writing from its marginal scholarly status. At the same time, spirit-writing tends to become a self-explanatory and coherent category. Scholars sometimes take at face value terms such as *fuji* 扶乩, *fuji* 扶箕, and *fuluan* 扶鸞, as if they were different names for the same practice. For example, in the *Encyclopedia of Taoism*, the entry on *fuji* 扶乩 claims that "Planchette writing is called *fuji* (lit., 'support of the planchette stick'), *fuluan* 扶鸞 ('support of the phoenix'), or *jiangluan* 降鸞 ('descent of the phoenix')."[5] This definition may reflect the newly-discovered materials of late imperial China, in which these terms are interchangeable. The same *Encyclopedia* describes *fuji* in the following terms: "two persons hold a stylet (*jijia* 乩架) above a planchette whose surface is covered with sand (*shapan* 沙盤). One of them, possessed by a deity, moves the stylet and draws characters on the sand, which a third person interprets and transcribes on paper."[6] This description is coherent with how the practice is usually conducted in contemporary Taiwan. However, it is not uncommon in Hong Kong today for a single medium to perform spirit-writing.[7] The description mentioned above is only one kind of practice within the broad spectrum of spirit-writing.

---

2 See Kōda, "Furan no jutsu"; Xu, *Fuji mixin di yanjiu*; Chao, "Origin and Growth of the Fu Chi."
3 Kani, "Furan zakki"; Jordan and Overmyer, *Flying Phoenix*. It is also noteworthy that J.J.M. de Groot investigated the spirit-writing practice of Southern China in the late nineteenth century. See de Groot, *Religious System of China*, vol. VI, bk. II, 1295–323.
4 Shiga, *Chugoku no kokkurisan*, 107–08; Shiga, *Xianggang Daojiao yu fuji xinyang*, 38–39.
5 Catherine Despeux, "*fuji* 扶乩," in *EOT*, 428–29.
6 Ibid.
7 For the study of spirit-writing in contemporary Taiwan, see Jordan and Overmyer, *Flying Phoenix*; Clart, "Birth of a New Scripture"; Clart, "Phoenix and the Mother"; Clart, "Moral Mediums"; Wang, *Taiwan de zhaijiao yu luantang*; Katz, "Spirit-writing Halls." For Hong Kong, see Shiga, *Xianggang daojiao yu fuji xinyang*.

TERMINOLOGY AND TYPOLOGY OF SPIRIT-WRITING 173

By contrast, scholars of the early twentieth century consulted a vast amount of pre-Ming materials in order to deal with the differences existing between the aforementioned terms. For example, Kōda Rohan, one of the earliest students of spirit-writing, discussed in one of his articles the origins of the character *ji* 乩 in *fuji* 扶乩 and *luan* 鸞 in *fuluan* 扶鸞. He also investigated the relationship between spirit-writing and the "invitation of the Purple Maiden" (*qing Zigu* 請紫姑), which was a séance ritual of the latrine deity designed for amusement and/or divination.[8] Xu Dishan also discussed the typology of spirit-writing.[9] Shortly after the publication of Xu's book, *Fuji mixin di yanjiu* 扶箕迷信底研究 (A study of the superstition of supporting the sieve), Chao Wei-pang wrote a review of it and other independent articles, in which he discussed the relationship between divination, the invitation of the Purple Maiden (*qing Zigu*), and the practice of *fuji* 扶箕 in its early stages.[10] This early research offers much valuable information, especially regarding the historical study of spirit-writing and the typology of the practice.

It is also noteworthy that the recent scholarship has increasingly focused on the unstudied materials and communities of the late imperial period. Building on this growing field, several scholars have sought to advance the discussion on the typology of spirit-writing. For example, Goyama Kiwamu 合山究 attempted to highlight the different dimensions of late Ming spirit-writing as practiced by the literati.[11] In reviewing the history of spirit-writing, Shiga Ichiko discussed the different types of spirit-writing and their relationship with the various religious traditions.[12] Hsieh Tsung-hui 謝聰輝, in his discussion of the scriptures of the Jade Sovereign (Yuhuang 玉皇) and of Wenchang 文昌, approached different types of revelation from the early to the medieval periods.[13] Lastly, Wang Chien-chuan 王見川 investigated a series of pre-Ming materials and discussed the various forms and terminology of spirit-writing from the Song to the Ming.[14]

---

8 Kōda, "Furan no jutsu."
9 Xu, *Fuji mixin di yanjiu*.
10 Chao, "Review of *A Study of the Fu-chi Superstition*"; Chao, "Origin and Growth of the Fu Chi"; Chao, "Games at the Mid-Autumn Festival in Kuangtung."
11 Goyama, *Minshin jidai no josei to bungaku*, 324–64.
12 Shiga, *Chugoku no kokkurisan*, 106–47.
13 Hsieh, *Xin tiandi zhi ming*, 97–136. For the scripture of Jade Sovereign, see Schachter, "Gaoshang yuhuang benxing jijing"; Schachter, "Beyond the Kingly Metaphor." For the Wenchang cult in medieval China, see Kleeman, "Expansion of the Wench'ang Cult"; for the Wenchang cult and literature in late imperial China, see Hu, "Qingdai liuzhong wendi lei quanshu."
14 Wang, "Song-Ming shiqi de fuji." The details will be discussed below.

Considering the different terms used in history and by different scholars, it is essential to clarify the terminology adopted in this article. The term "spirit-writing" will be used as an etic category and defined here following Vincent Goossaert's definition as "any technique where spirits (from high gods to recently deceased humans) are invited through prescribed ritual means (typically involving incantations, *zhou* 咒, and/or talismans, *fu* 符) to possess ('descend,' *jiang* 降) either a writing implement (a brush or a piece of wood) and/or the person(s) wielding this implement in order to write characters, often in response to questions."[15] It covers, therefore, all of the practices described by emic terms such as *fuji* 扶箕, *feiluan* 飛鸞, *fuluan* 扶鸞, *fuji* 扶乩, *bilu* 筆籙, etc.[16] Two core components of this category are "spirit" and "writing," so other oral and/or martial traditions like *tâng-ki* 童乩 will not be discussed here. As for emic categories, I will use the literal translation in descriptions and citations, which means "supporting the sieve" for *fuji* 扶箕, "supporting the Phoenix" for *fuluan* 扶鸞, and "supporting the divination-stylus" for *fuji* 扶乩. The advantage of this strategy is that it clarifies the difference between emic and etic terms.

Furthermore, I argue that different categories, including *qing Zigu* 請紫姑, *fuji* 扶箕, *fuluan* 扶鸞 and *fuji* 扶乩 reflect the same development process: from a narrow perspective, each of them referred to a specific tool or method for communicating with the spiritual world, especially when it was originally invented and employed; it later developed into a broader category, referring to all practices related to spirit-writing. In the late imperial period, most authors refer to both the narrow and broader definitions at the same time.

Specifically, the terms *fuji* 扶箕, *fuluan* 扶鸞, and *fuji* 扶乩 are phrases with the structure Verb + Noun, in which *fu* is the verb "to support" while the second character is a noun denoting an instrument. The "sieve" was the first term to appear in the extant texts. It is connected to the ritual of the "invitation of the Purple Maiden," in which the figurine of the Purple Maiden was usually made of straw, a sieve or a broom. The term "Phoenix" appeared later, and might refer to an automatic device[17] used by some Wenchang cults in the Sichuan 四川 area during the Southern Song. It is unknown whether this Southern Song device was connected in any way with the Y-shape Phoenix-stylus (*luanbi* 鸞

---

15 See Vincent Goossaert's contribution to this volume.
16 According to Goossaert's definition, the term "spirit-writing" does not include earlier revelatory traditions, such as *Zhen'gao* 真誥 (Declarations of the Perfected) and other Shangqing 上清 scriptures, because there was no witness to the revelation of those texts, and the ritual and specific instruments for inducing possession were not mentioned either. See Vincent Goossaert's contribution to this volume.
17 "Automatic" here means that the specific spirit-writing device allegedly functioned automatically without requiring any human medium.

筆) used by spirit-writing halls in contemporary Taiwan. I have not identified any hard evidence in the medieval literature concerning the origins of the latter. The character *ji* 乩 was initially completely unconnected to spirit-writing, but later became synonymous with *ji* 箕 and *luan* 鸞. These three terms originally referred to the instrument used during the séance. From the Ming dynasty onward, terms such as "the invitation of the Purple Maiden," "supporting the sieve," "supporting the Phoenix," and "supporting the divination-stylus" started to be used as general categories for all kinds of spirit-writing. Therefore, the terms themselves acquired new meanings. Different kinds of instruments and methods were still applied so that, by the late imperial period, spirit-writing had achieved a far broader spectrum compared with the earlier stage. The detailed evidence will be discussed below.

In his contribution to this volume, Vincent Goossaert regards spirit-writing "as part of the *daofa* priests' techniques to make gods intervene in human affairs" and expertly scrutinises a considerable amount of materials related to this phenomenon in the Daoist canon. Therefore, here, I will merely focus on the extracanonical materials and discuss how spirit-writing was practiced, witnessed, recorded, and understood, especially at the periphery of the Daoist ecology. Building on recent research, as well as newly-discovered materials, this article provides a general introduction to the spirit-writing terminology in its synchronic and diachronic dimensions. The first part introduces the prehistory of spirit-writing which follows Xu Dishan and Chao Wei-pang by arguing that "supporting the sieve" originated from the "invitation of the Purple Maiden" in the pre-Song era. In the second part, I investigate the different instruments applied to various forms of spirit-writing. In the third part, I discuss the spirit-writing methods, as well as the relationship between the deities and practitioners.

2   The Prehistory of Spirit-Writing

Kōda Rohan was one of the earliest scholars to discuss the relationship between the "invitation of the Purple Maiden" and spirit-writing (Kōda adopted the term *fuluan* 扶鸞 to refer to all kinds of spirit-writing practices). He attempted to connect these two kinds of practices and assumed the Purple Maiden to be a frequently-summoned divinity in spirit-writing activities so that her cult led to the creation of an independent practice called "the invitation of the Purple Maiden."[18] In other words, Kōda implied that spirit-writing predated the

---

18   Kōda, "Furan no jutsu."

"invitation of the Purple Maiden." To some extent, this view reflects Kōda's categorization of all of the written traditions following from a séance, including the *Zhen gao*, as some kind of spirit-writing or, to use his category, "supporting the Phoenix."[19] In fact, however, we have no evidence indicating that the terms "supporting the sieve" or "supporting the Phoenix" predate the "invitation of the Purple Maiden." In his famous book *Fuji mixin di yanjiu*, Xu Dishan argued, contrarily to Kōda, that spirit-writing or, more specifically, "supporting the sieve" derived from the "invitation of the Purple Maiden." He regarded "supporting the sieve," rather than "supporting the Phoenix" as in Koda's case, as a general category of spirit-writing, but found it confusing because it was difficult to explain why the sieve was rarely used in the sources that he examined.[20]

Chao Wei-pang was the first scholar to clarify the relationship between "supporting the sieve" and the "invitation of the Purple Maiden." He explicitly interpreted the term *fuji* 扶箕 according to its literal meaning, as "supporting the sieve," rather than considering it as an etic and general term for spirit-writing. He further noted that, in the Song sources, "the invitation of the Purple Maiden" was closely related to the practice of "supporting the sieve" while the former could even be found in earlier materials. Therefore, Chao pointed out that the practice of "supporting the sieve" derived from the "invitation of the Purple Maiden" but neither replaced nor eliminated the latter. On the contrary, the "invitation of the Purple Maiden" can still be found in different areas of the realm as late as the end of the Qing dynasty.[21]

Based on the research outlined above, it is fair to say that the custom of the "invitation of the Purple Maiden" emerged no later than the Tang dynasty. In Liu Jingshu's 劉敬叔 (fl. fourth to fifth century) *Yiyuan* 異苑 (A garden of marvels), there is already a record of such a practice:

> In the world, there is a divinity called the Purple Maiden. According to ancient legend, she was a concubine within a certain family. The main consort envied her, so she was often given the dirtiest jobs to do. On the fifteenth day of the first month [of a given year], she died of grief. Therefore, the people created a figurine of her on that day and invited her in the latrine or beside the pigsty at night, praying: "Zixu isn't at home; '[Zixu is] the name of her husband'; Caogu has gone, too; 'Cao is the surname of his main consort.' Young lady, you may come out to play." When the practi-

---

19   Other scholars, such as Goyama Kiwamu and John Lagerwey, share the same point of view. Goyama, *Minshin jidai no josei to bungaku*, 332; Lagerwey, *Paradigm Shifts*, 239.
20   Xu, *Fuji mixin di yanjiu*.
21   Chao, "Games at the Mid-Autumn Festival in Kuangtung."

tioners felt that the figurine grew heavy, this was a sign that the divinity had arrived. Wine and fruit were offered to her, after which the figurine seemed to become vivid and start to jump unceasingly. The people asked about the prospects for silkworm and mulberry leaves in the coming year, and the divinity was also good at guessing the location of hidden objects. If the divination result were auspicious, [the figurine] would dance frenetically; if inauspicious, the figurine would lie asleep.

世有紫姑神，古來相傳云是人家妾，為大婦所嫉，每以穢事相次役。正月十五日，感激而死。故世人以其日作其形，夜於廁間或豬欄邊迎之，祝曰：「子胥不在」，是其婿名也；「曹姑亦歸」，曹即其大婦也；「小姑可出」。戲投者覺重，便是神來，奠設酒果，亦覺貌輝輝有色，即跳躑不住，能占眾事，卜未來蠶桑，又善射鉤。好則大儛，惡便仰眠。22

In addition, Zong Lin 宗懍 (fl. sixth century) also quoted this excerpt in his book *Jingchu suishiji* 荊楚歲時記 (Records of the seasonal festival [customs] in the Jingchu region). People who engaged in this custom treated the Purple Maiden as a specific figure, and her ritual itself was closely combined with the concrete festival.

From the Song dynasty onward, a given record in the *Mengxi bitan* 夢溪筆談 (Brush talks from the dream brook) by Shen Kuo 沈括 (1029–1093) shows that the "invitation of the Purple Maiden" could be practiced at any time of the year:

> According to the ancient custom, the latrine goddess, named the Purple Maiden, should be summoned on the fifteenth day of the first month. [Now] it is no longer necessary [that this activity takes place] in the first month, so that one may summon her at any time during the year.

舊俗正月望夜迎廁神，謂之紫姑。亦不必正月，常時皆可召。23

In addition, the term "the Purple Maiden" no longer referred to one specific figure only, but rather to a variety of divinities that could be invited for amusement. For example, Chen Shidao 陳師道 (1053–1101) stated in his *Houshan shi zhu* 后山詩註 (Commentary on Houshan's poetry):

---

22   *Yiyuan, juan* 5.
23   *Mengxi bitan, juan* 21.

Every new year, the youngsters in my hometown use a hairpin to decorate the sieve and broom and invite the Purple Maiden for fun. One year, a divinity descended and said: "I am the Transcendent Xu from Penglai." He loved poems and drawing, could answer all of the questions, and could keep writing without rest. People suspected that Lord Xu was a spirit from the same category as the Purple Maiden and so they should not necessarily treat him as a transcendent official.

吾里中少年，每歲首簪飾箕帚，召紫姑以戲，一歲有神下焉，曰：『吾蓬萊仙伯徐君也』。喜句畫，有求必答，下筆不休云云。世人或疑徐君乃紫姑之類，未必以仙官待之。[24]

The text mentions explicitly "a spirit from the same category as the Purple Maiden." Another example occurs in *Kuiche zhi* 睽車志 (Records of the cart full of ghosts) by Guo Tuan 郭彖 (fl. 1186–1187):

Following the death of Yue Fei, the generals and soldiers of the Xixi Fortress in Hangzhou invited the Purple Maiden, but Yue Fei descended and wrote down his name in an aggressive manner. All present grew surprised and frightened. They said that the signature was just like Yue's own.

岳侯死後，臨安西溪寨軍將子弟因請紫姑神，而岳侯降之，大書其名。眾皆驚愕，謂其花押則宛然平日真迹也。[25]

This story shows that other figures could make their presence felt during the "invitation of the Purple Maiden." Stronger evidence may be found in *Youhuan jiwen* 遊宦紀聞 (Records of official travel) by Zhang Shinan 張世南 (fl. 1233):

When I was young, I saw my relatives and friends inviting the transcendent Purple Maiden. They inserted a chopstick into a sieve and wrote on a table covered with ashes. [Among the descending figures] were those who were good at writing poems. They all wrote down their names first, and we found them to be the literati of recent times, such as Yuhu (i.e. Zhang Xiaoxiang 張孝祥 1132–c. 1169), Shihu (i.e. Fan Chengda 范成大 1126–1193), and Zhizhai (i.e. Chen Fuliang 陳傅良 1137–1203). There were also those who were able to write poems and rhapsodies, examination

---

24 *Houshan shi zhu*, juan 10.
25 *Kuiche zhi*, juan 1.

essays, prefaces and postscripts, and so on; most of these are written in a quick, elegant way; they make predictions about misfortune and good fortune, but are not effective.

世南少小時嘗見親朋間有請紫姑仙，以筯插筲箕，布灰棹上畫之。有能作詩詞者。初間必先書姓名，皆近世文人，如于湖、石湖、止齋者。亦有能作詩賦、時論、記跋之類，往往敏而工，言禍福卻多不驗。26

In this example, the goal of the mentioned practice is to invite, not the Purple Maiden, but random figures. These Song materials also suggest that the main elements informing the practice of "supporting the sieve" had already become a common custom. These included the act of supporting, the use of the sieve as the instrument, and the resulting written product. This process is very unlike that of the dancing figurine of the earlier stage. Shiga Ichiko argued that this transformation occurred due to the increasing male literati's participation in such customs during the Song dynasty.[27] Xu Dishan, Chao Wei-pang, and other scholars also noticed that, in Su Shi's 蘇軾 (1036–1101) anthology, there was an essay describing the "invitation of the Purple Maiden," in which he mentioned a similar practice and praised the descending divinity for her erudition.[28]

3 Terminology and Instruments

In the contemporary Hong Kong, Taiwan and Chinese diasporas, the practice of spirit-writing practice persists and is usually named "supporting the divination-stylus" (*fuji* 扶乩) or "supporting the Phoenix" (*fuluan* 扶鸞). The instrument and method used are similar but not identical. As I discuss below, however, our historical sources reflect a more diverse situation. Practitioners developed different instruments and methods throughout the history of spirit-writing.

---

26 *Youhuan jiwen*, juan 2.
27 Shiga, *Xianggang Daojiao yu fuji xinyang*, 42. It is worth mentioning that, in late imperial China, female literati also participated in spirit-wirting. For gender and spirit-writing, see Elena Valussi's contribution to this volume.
28 *Su Wenzhong gong quanji*, juan 12. It is also worth mentioning that the spirit-writing instrument described in the text was a dressed figurine holding a chopstick, supported by two children (衣草木爲婦人，而置箸手中，二小童子扶焉) rather than a sieve with a chopstick or brush, but the difference between Su's story and the early tradition of the "invitation of the Purple Maiden" was that this figurine could write with its chopstick (*yi zhu huazi* 以箸畫字).

The evidence above shows that the "invitation of the Purple Maiden" underwent a series of changes from the pre-Tang to the Song dynasties. The instrument changed from figurines to sieves, and the dancing changed to writing. Therefore, the practice of "supporting the sieve" probably derived from the "invitation of the Purple Maiden." Among the strongest pieces of evidence for this is the poem written by Lu You 陸遊 (1125–1209), which includes the phrase: "Supporting the sieve to invite the Purple Maiden" (扶箕迎紫姑).[29] In other words, originally, the term *fuji* 扶箕 undoubtedly referred to "supporting the sieve" literally but, according to anthropological investigations of the last century, even in de Groot's records, a T- or Y-shaped wooden divination-stylus is far more common than a sieve.[30] However, the sieve has never been totally excluded from the practice of spirit-writing. For example, it was still in use by the Kamlan Koon 金蘭觀 in contemporary Hong Kong.[31]

I argue that the appearance of terms such as "supporting the Phoenix" or "supporting the divination-stylus" was, to some extent, related to the development and diversification of the spirit-writing instruments. More specifically, I argue that *luan* 鸞 in *fuluan* refers to a device named the "Phoenix," while the *ji* 乩 was also related to a new kind of spirit-writing instrument (probably similar to the contemporary one) that replaced the sieve in many cases during the late imperial period.

3.1   Fuluan *and the Phoenix*

It is noteworthy that no such phrases as "supporting the Phoenix" or "supporting the divination-stylus" can be found in the textual materials of the Song dynasty. The earliest extant document where the term "supporting the Phoenix" is recorded is the *Dayuan Zhiyuan bianwei lu* 大元至元辨偽錄 (Notes on the distinction between falsity and truth in the Zhiyuan reign of the Great Yuan Dynasty), produced during the Yuan dynasty.[32] However, terms related to spirit-writing such as "flying Phoenix" (*feiluan* 飛鸞) and "to serve the Phoenix" (*shiluan* 侍鸞) were mentioned in the Wenchang scriptures included in the Ming Daoist Canon (*Daozang* 道藏). Some of the scriptures, such as the first 73 chapters of the *Huashu* 化書 (Book of transformations),[33] were suppos-

---

29   *Jiannan shigao, juan* 65.
30   De Groot, *Religious System of China*, vol. VI, bk. II, 1296, fig. 26; Kani, "Furan zakki," 70, fig. 1; Shiga, *Xianggang Daojiao yu fuji xinyang*, 34, photo 6.
31   Kamlan Koon is a Daoist temple dedicated to the immortal Patriarch Lü (*Lüzu* 呂祖). It originated from a spirit-writing altar established in Chaozhou 潮州 in 1831. See https://www.kamlankoon.com.hk/ (accessed May 30, 2020).
32   *Dayuan zhiyuan bianwei lu, juan* 2.
33   For a study on the 73-chapter *Huashu*, see Kleeman, *God's Own Tale*.

edly produced by a local Wenchang community, led by the ritual master Liu Ansheng 劉安勝 (fl. 1168–1181), while others were produced by later communities under the South Song and Yuan dynasties.[34]

Hsieh Tsung-hui argues that the connotations of both the character *luan* 鸞 (Phoenix) and the word *feiluan* 飛鸞 (flying Phoenix) are key to understand the emergence of the phrase "supporting the Phoenix," which was invented to differentiate this practice from the traditional expression, "supporting the sieve." Traditionally, a "Phoenix" connotes both transcendence (*shenxian* 神仙) and monarchy (*diwang* 帝王), while a "flying Phoenix" might refer to articles written by scholars of the Imperial Academy (*hanlin* 翰林) and/or the "cursive script" (*caoshu* 草書). Therefore, Hsieh claims that the Wenchang community of Liu Ansheng used the compound "flying Phoenix" intentionally, for at least three reasons: 1) to differentiate it from the popular practice of "supporting the sieve," which at least theoretically was prohibited by the Song court; 2) to show that the intellectual elite who received the sacred texts from the celestial Thearch were similar to the Imperial Academy officials who received the mandate from the emperor; and 3) to exhort and illuminate followers and save the world from the end of days.[35]

Hsieh's interpretation provides an inspiring insight, and also matches the historical context of these Wenchang texts, but he neglected the material dimension of this new term. In contrast to Hsieh's perspective, Wang Chien-chuan argues that the "Phoenix" might be an automatic device under the control of the Liu Ansheng community.[36] Evidence supporting this claim can be found in the "Lingying Dadi huashu shishi 靈應大帝化書事實" (Veritable account of the *Book of Transformations* of the Great Emperor of Numinous Response), included in an extracanonical edition of the *Huashu*:

> The Palace has a Jiangbi ting (Pavilion for the Descending Stylus.)[37] In the pavilion is a five-coloured flying phoenix, hung by golden ropes. It holds a pen-brush in its beak, and hundreds of pieces of paper decorated with golden flowers are left under the pen. The gate of the pavilion is

---

34 For the Wenchang scriptures included in the Daoist Canon, see the entries contributed by Terry Kleeman, Isabelle Robinet, and Kristofer Schipper in Schipper and Verellen, *Taoist Canon*, 1203–10.
35 Hsieh, *Xin tiandi zhi ming*, 97–124.
36 Wang, "Song-Ming shiqi de fuji."
37 *Jiangbi* 降筆 is another important emic term for spirit-writing. The term *jiang* 降 (descend or, in a causative sence, to force the deity to manifest its presence) was expertly scrutinised in Vincent Goossaert's contribution to this volume, so I will not discuss it here.

sealed extremely tightly by the local officials to prevent cheating. Once the descending of the words has been accomplished, the copper bell in the pavilion will ring spontaneously.

其殿有降筆亭，亭中以金索懸一五色飛鸞，鸞口嗬筆，用金花牋數百幅常留筆下。亭門本府差官封鎖甚嚴，以防欺偽之弊。降筆訖，其亭內銅鐘自鳴。[38]

Hsieh's interpretation is very important because it sheds light on why the symbol of the Phoenix was used to upgrade the spirit-writing instruments and theology. In the case of the historical practice of those Wenchang communities according to the Daoist Canon, however, I tend to agree with Wang that the term "Phoenix," sporadically seen in certain scriptures, refers to a specific device, which replaced the sieve in spirit-writing séances. This is supported by the later term *fuluan*, in which the character *luan* works as a noun, the object of the verb *fu*. Therefore, Liu Ansheng's Wenchang cult and its mode of scriptural revelation, i.e. the flying Phoenix, might differ significantly from what we found in most cases in the late imperial period. It is possible that Liu Ansheng and his followers claimed that their texts had been automatically produced by the divine device described above, rather than by the hands of mediums. This hypothesis can also be supported by Zhu Mingchuan's 朱明川 recent anthropological research. Zhu visited a certain Zixia tan 紫霞壇 (Purple Cloud Altar) in Sichuan in 2019, where the ritual master claimed that "flying Phoenix" differed from "supporting the divination-stylus": the former was a method for writing down characters automatically and rapidly without any human medium, while the latter was performed by hand and slowly. This kind of description can also be found in various local historical materials (*wenshi ziliao* 文史資料).[39] In addition, some Qing materials mention a kind of pavilion for the practice of the "flying Phoenix." For example, *Qingbai leichao* 清稗類鈔 (Classified anecdotes of the Qing Dynasty), a collection of anecdotal stories, has an entry named Phoenix Tower (*luanlou* 鸞樓):

> In the summer of the Jiachen year (1904) during the Guangxu reign, people from a certain county set up a flying Phoenix altar at a certain guildhall and built a Phoenix tower. At that time, around two or three thousand people from Hunan, Hubei, Henan, and Sichuan were among those who

---

38 *Wenchang huashu*, vol. 3.
39 Zhu, "Rutan jingdian ji qi yingyong," 140.

came. They all followed a vegetarian diet in order to recite the scriptures and focused on praying for the descent of deities. One day, the deity suddenly revealed the date (when the flying Phoenix was supposed to take place); all of the altar members started to prepare incense and paper money for the sacrifice and sets of hanging scrolls and couplets [for the writing]. There were also some nonmembers who presented paper for divine writings. At the appropriate time, [people] prepared about one *hu* (≈50L) of thick ink, a bunch of first rice crop, and a paper Phoenix. [They] arrayed those things in the tower and surrounded them with red braids and white sheets of paper. Candles were lit on the altar, and the light and fire were splendid. After setting everything up, they closed the tower gate. Soon, the music of *Sheng* and *Xiao* (like a flute and pipe) was heard in the skies; everyone held the incense and groveled on the blankets, holding their breath in awe. Then, people heard some sort of footsteps in the tower. After a long silence, they finally opened the gate and entered the tower. All of the white sheets of paper set on the red braids had very vivid black characters written on them. All of the characters were written in an unknown style. Those who received them honored them as the Jade Rules of the Golden Liturgy.

光緒甲辰夏，某邑設飛鸞壇於某會館，建鸞樓。時湘、楚、豫、蜀來者二三千人。均茹素誦經，壹志祝神之降臨。一日，神忽示以期，壇員遂各備香楮及屏幅聯對，然非壇員，亦有進紙索神筆者。及期，磨濃墨斛許，具新穎一束，製紙鸞一頭，排列樓上，四圍以紅縧架素紙，燒燭焚檀，光焰奪人。佈置畢，遂閉樓門。亡何而聞空際有笙簫聲，於是僉持香伏氍毹，震恐屏息。微聞樓上履聲橐橐，久之悄然，始啟關入。則前所架素紙，墨瀋塗鴉，綠痕欲滴。字體皆無骨格，而得之者乃皆奉為金科玉律也。[40]

In brief, there is no solid evidence showing the idea that the "flying Phoenix" in the early Wenchang texts corresponds to the "supporting the Phoenix" of late imperial China. Conversely, the extant materials indicate that the "flying Phoenix" could be a different spirit-writing technique, which was claimed to be automatic and rapid. This development could be attributed to a demand for longer scriptures, rather than poems and short prose.

---

40   *Qingbai leichao*, 4558–59.

3.2 Fuji *and the Divination-Stylus*

There are at least three reasons for the appearance of the emic term "supporting the divination-stylus" with the special Chinese character *ji* 乩. The first is philological, the second relates to the evolution of the instruments, while the third is connected to the law.

The character *ji* 乩 was originally a variant character (*yiti zi* 異體字) of *ji* 稽, which is why we find terms such as *kuaiji* 會乩 (= 會稽) and *yueruo jigu* 粵若乩古 (= 粵若稽古) in many medieval sources. During the Qing dynasty, however, this character was almost always related to spirit-writing. Kōda Rohan, following Hong Ruogao's 洪若皋 (fl. 1670) explanation, believed that *ji* 乩 is a variant character of *ji* 卟, and pronounced as *ji* 稽.[41] The *Yuchu xinzhi* 虞初新志 ([Anecdote teller] Yuchu's new records) records one entry by Hong:

> The character *ji* 乩 could also be written as *ji* 卟, which is identical to *ji* 稽; it means "to consult in order to ask about a doubt." Later, people referred to the descent of transcendents as a "comment on the divination-stylus," also calling it "stylus-transcendents," "sieve transcendents" or "supporting the Phoenix."
>
> "乩"或作"卟",與"稽"同,卜以問疑也。後人以仙降爲"批乩",名之曰"乩仙",亦謂"箕仙",又謂之"扶鸞"云。[42]

Later scholars also accepted this interpretation. From a philological perspective, it is no coincidence that phrases related to spirit-writing adopt the term *ji* 乩. First, the character *ji* 乩 has the component *zhan* 占, which means prognostication. Its pronunciation is like *ji* 稽, which is also identical to *ji* 箕, so it is a perfect replacement for the latter. Secondly, *ji* 乩 looks very similar to *luan* 亂, while the latter term's pronunciation is similar to the pronunciation of *luan* 鸞 in both the medieval and modern phonetic systems. More importantly, in some cases, *ji* 乩 is written as "乱," which makes it more similar to the character *luan* 乱. In fact, the term *fuluan* 扶乱 is also found in some late imperial materials, which links the two characters, *ji* 乩 and *luan* 鸞. In certain cases, *fuji* 扶乩 and *fuluan* 扶乱 even appear in the same text. (See figures 5.1 and 5.2)

Additionally, both the Xu Kai 徐鍇 (920–974) and Xu Xuan 徐鉉 (917–992) editions of the famous *Shuowen jiezi* 說文解字 (Explaining single-component

---

41 Kōda, "Furan no jutsu," 400.
42 *Yuchu xinzhi, juan* 15.

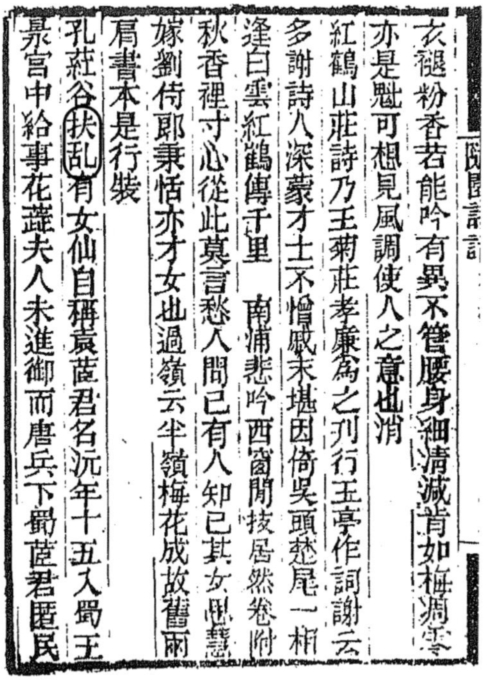
隨園詩話
衣裾粉香若能吟有興不管腰身細清減背如梅凋零
亦是魁可想見風調使人之意也消
紅鶴山莊詩乃王菊莊孝廉爲之刊行王亭作詞謝云
多謝詩人深蒙才士不憎威末堪因倚吳頭楚尾一枏
逢白雲紅鶴傳千里　南浦悲吟西窗閒拔居然卷附
秋香裡寸心從此莫言愁人問已有人知已其女甥慧
嫁劉侍郎秉恬亦才女也過嶺云半嶺梅花成故舊兩
肩書本是行裝
孔莊谷扶乱有女仙自稱袁茝君名沅年十五入蜀王
府宮中給事花蕊夫人未進御而唐兵下蜀茝君匿民

FIGURE 5.1
"扶乱" instead of "扶乩," in *Suiyuan shihua* 隨園詩話 (Poetry talk from Suiyuan)

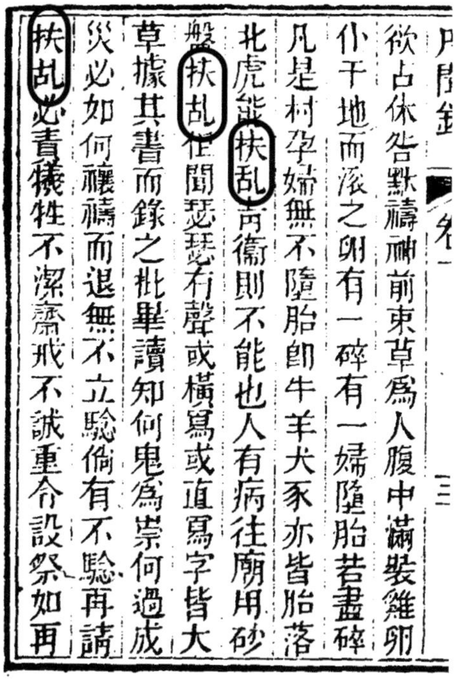
欲占休咎默禱神前東草爲人腹中滿裝雞卵
仆于地而滚之卵有一碎有一婦墮胎若盡碎
凡是村孕婦無不墮胎即牛羊犬豕亦皆胎落
北虎能扶乱夷衛則不能也人有病往廟用砂
盤扶乩在閒瑟瑟有聲或橫寫或直寫字皆大
草據其書而錄之批畢讀知何鬼爲祟何過成
災必如何禳禱而退無不立驗倘有不驗再請
扶乩必責犧牲不潔齋戒不誠重令設祭如再

FIGURE 5.2
"扶乱" and "扶乩" on the same page, in *Zhi wen lu* 咫聞録 (Records of close hearsay)

graphs and analysing compound characters) omitted the character *ji* 乩 but did include the character *ji* 卟:

> The character *ji* 卟 means "to consult in order to ask about a doubt." It has "mouth" (*kou* 口) and "to consult" (*bu* 卜) as its semantic constituents; it is read in the same way as the character *ji* 稽.
>
> "卟"，卜以問疑也，從"口"、"卜"，讀與"稽"同。[43]

Apparently, Kōda Rohan's remarks, which followed Hong Ruogao's explanation, actually derive from the *Shuowen jiezi*. Furthermore, Duan Yucai 段玉裁 (1735–1815) added a comment that less literate audiences could write the character *ji* 卟 as *ji* 乩 (*suzuo ji* 俗作"乩").[44] Therefore, the character *ji* 乩 might be

43 *Shuowen jiezi, juan* 3. For the format and style of *Shuowen jiezi*, see Yong and Peng, *Chinese Lexicography*, 102–8; Bottéro and Harbsmeier, "*Shuowen Jiezi* Dictionary".

44 *Shuowen jiezi zhu, juan* 3.

quite late, first as the variant character of *ji* 稽, but later as the popular character (*suzi* 俗字) for *ji* 卟, which connoted prognostication.

The change of instruments could also explain the appearance of the expression "supporting the divination-stylus." Although the materials mentioned above describe spirit-writing instruments (with the exception of the sieve) in an extremely vague manner, the Ming evidence shows that a wooden stylus came into use in the context of spirit-writing séances. For example, Shen Changqing 沈長卿 (fl. 1612) mentions such an instrument in his *Shenshi yishuo* 沈氏弋説 (Rediscovered talks of Mister Shen):

> Recently, those who summon the transcendents will use peach-wood to make the Phoenix-stylus and ask the children to support it. The transcendents will descend following the talisman.
>
> 近世召神仙者，以桃木爲鸞乩，命童子扶之，隨符而降。[45]

This excerpt indirectly supports my former point of view, according to which the terms *luan* 鸞 and *ji* 乩 refer to concrete instruments.

Wang Chien-chuan also pointed out that the character *ji* 乩 became prevalent partially because, at least theoretically, it was illegal to "support the Phoenix."[46] We find evidence supporting this claim both in the *Daming huidian* 大明會典 (Collected statutes of the Great Ming) and in the *Daqing lüli* 大清律例 (Codes and cases of the Great Qing). Furthermore, I recently found evidence that "supporting the sieve" became illegal as early as the Song. This claim is supported by Yue Ke's 岳珂 (1183–?) *Kuitan Lu* 愧郯錄 (Records of decrees and regulations).[47] It is probable that the expression "supporting the divination-stylus" was created in order to avoid the prohibition.

Although the original meaning of the terms "sieve" and "Phoenix" as concrete instruments are quite explicit, matters became complicated from the late Ming onward. The boundaries between the expressions "supporting the sieve," "supporting the Phoenix," and "supporting the divination-stylus" became vague. For example, in the *Nancun chuogeng lu* 南村輟耕錄 (Records of rest from plowing in the South Village), Tao Zongyi 陶宗儀 (c. 1329–c. 1412) states: "you hang the sieve, support the phoenix, and summon the transcendents, and those who come, in most cases, are the famous literati of yore" (懸箕扶鸞召

---

45 *Shenshi yishuo*, juan 5.
46 Wang, "Song-Ming shiqi de fuji."
47 *Kuitan lu*, juan 6.

TERMINOLOGY AND TYPOLOGY OF SPIRIT-WRITING

仙，往往皆古名人高士來格).[48] As we saw above, the *Yuchu xinzhi* by Zhang Chao 張潮 (fl. 1697) lists different terms for the descent of transcendents, such as "comment on the divination-stylus," "stylus-transcendents," "sieve transcendents," and "supporting the Phoenix," as synonymous.[49] Therefore, on some occasions, different terms were used to refer to the practice of spirit-writing in general; on other occasions, the same terms could refer to the spirit-writing instruments.

3.3   Bilu *and the Brush*

Another late Ming spirit-writing development relates to its close connection with the civil service examinations. In earlier periods, candidates relied on spirit-writing in order to ask the gods about the questions or results of the civil service examinations. However, the late Ming period witnessed the appearance of a new spirit-writing practice called the "brush register" (*bilu* 筆籙).[50] This practice was first used in the composition of eight-legged essays (*bagu wen* 八股文). In the *Xin Qixie* 新齊諧 (New tales of Qixie), Yuan Mei 袁枚 (1716–1797) shares a story about his comtemporary, Li Yuhong 李玉鋐 (1661–?):

> Li from Tongzhou, the Provincial Surveillance Commissioner; his name was Yuhong, and he achieved his *jinshi* degree in Bingxu year (1706). When young, he became fond of the brush register. ... Later, when participating in literati associations, once there was a topic [to write about], he would listen to whatever his brush wished to do. ... Li achieved *xiaolian* and then became a *jinshi*; [his success] was mostly due to the powers of the pen-brush-spirit.
>
> 通州李臬司，諱玉鋐，丙戌進士。少時好煉筆籙 ... 後文社之事，題下則聽筆之所爲。... 李舉孝廉，成進士，筆神之力居多。[51]

Another famous practitioner was Peng Dingqiu 彭定求 (1645–1719).[52] Peng's contemporary, Niu Xiu 鈕琇 (1644–1704), records the following remarks in his book *Gusheng xubian* 觚賸續編 (Supplemental volumes of leftovers in the goblet):

---

48   *Nancun chuogeng lu, juan* 20.
49   *Yuchu xinzhi, juan* 15.
50   For the brush register, see Hu, "'Bilu' gouchen."
51   *Xin qixie, juan* 13.
52   For Peng Dingqiu's spirit-writing practice, see Burton-Rose, "Terrestrial Reward as Divine Recompense"; Wang, "Peng Dingqiu yu Qingchu Suzhou Daojiao."

The Senior Compiler, Peng Dingqiu, from Suzhou, is the son of Master Yunke. When young, he worshipped the spirit-writing transcendents with the utmost respect. Yunke sternly prohibited him from doing so, but in the end, no one could stop him. After long practice of the [brush] register, he became capable of communicating with the deities. He discarded the divination-stylus and relied on his own wrist movements, requiring little thought. At first, he could write down poems and prose, and later even eight-legged essays. He let the pen-brush write the essays very rapidly, and all of them displayed an excellent compositional structure. In order to achieve the *Zhuangyuan* title in the civil examination, he used this technique.

吳門彭修撰定求，為雲客先生之子。幼奉乩仙甚謹，雲客嚴禁之，終莫能奪。籙鍊既久，遂能通神，廢乩運腕，不假思索。始為詩文，繼為制藝，隨筆疾書，悉為佳構。棘闈獲雋，用此技也。[53]

The historicity of these stories is not the focus of this paper but we still find some basic elements of the brush register practice in these records. Apparently, on account of its close connection with the civil examination, this practice was based exclusively on the usage of pen-brush and paper. The latter story even mentioned that Peng Dingqiu "discarded the divination-stylus and relied on his own wrist movements" (*feiji yunwan* 廢乩運腕). Without a doubt, the brush register was considered a form of spirit-writing practice.

It is also noteworthy that the community behind the very first Wenchang canon, the *Wendi quanshu* 文帝全書 (Complete Works of the Divine Lord Wenchang), also practiced the brush register, not only to help with the civil service examination but also to receive sacred texts from Wenchang and other deities.[54] In fact, one of the practitioners was a woman named Lin Ying 林瑩 (fl. 1745–1749), the concubine of the community leader, Liu Qiao 劉樵 (fl. 1727–1749). The text she received through the practice of the brush register (rather than ordinary spirit-writing) was the *Kunning miaojing* 坤寧妙經 (Wondrous scripture on Kun's peace), one of the early female alchemy texts in the Qing dynasty.[55]

---

53 *Gusheng xubian*, juan 3.
54 For the *Wendi quanshu*, see Hu, "Qingdai liuzhong wendi lei quanshu."
55 For the *Kunning miaojing*, see Valussi, "Female Alchemy and Paratext" and her contribution to this volume; for Liu Qiao and Lin Ying, see Hu, "Liu Qiao xiaokao."

4   Medium, Method, and Deities

The spirit-writing methods constitute another noteworthy dimension. Lu You wrote a poem titled "*jibu* 箕卜" (Sieve divination),[56] which vividly described Song dynasty séances:

TABLE 5.1   "*jibu* 箕卜" (Sieve divination)

①	In the first month, hundreds of kinds of herbs are effective; according to the old custom, we invite the Purple Maiden.	孟春百艸靈，古俗迎紫姑。
②	We take the bamboo sieve from the kitchen and dress it in a woman's skirt and coat.	厨中取竹箕，冒以婦帬襦。
③	[Two] children support it on both sides. Then they insert a pen into it and pray for writing.	豎子夾扶持，挿筆祝其書。
④	Shortly afterwards, it seems to become possessed; it can answer questions very quickly.	俄若有物憑，對答不須臾。
⑤	We ask about the results of the examination and the answer is not necessarily "yes"; we get the answers just for fun.	豈必考中否，一笑聊相娛。
⑥	Sometimes, it writes poems and chapters; wine and food are offered as demanded.	詩章亦間作，酒食隨所須。
⑦	It suddenly leaves upon being satisfied; [however,] who could hold its sleeve [to keep it from leaving]?	興闌忽辭去，誰能執其祛。
⑧	We give the sieve to the kitchen maid and throw the pen into the corner of the room.	持箕畀竈婢，棄筆臥牆隅。
⑨	The feast is over, and only scraps of food are left.	几席亦已徹，狼籍果與蔬。
⑩	What is the benefit of all of this chaos? Both humans and ghosts are just stupid.	紛紛竟何益，人鬼均一愚。

A lot of details are provided in this poem: ② The instrument needs female clothing. It is not a figurine but a sieve. ③ The character *jia* 夾 (press from both sides) shows that it needs two people to support it; this might explain why spirit-writing usually needs two mediums even when the instruments could be easily handled by a single individual. ⑤⑥ It could divine about examinations and write poems, but was mostly for entertainment. ⑧⑨⑩ The whole atmosphere is amusing rather than sacred since the instruments could simply be thrown away and the participants are just "stupid human beings and ghosts."

---

56   *Jiannan shigao, juan* 49.

Generally, most of the features of the later spirit-writing practices can already be found in this poem. More importantly, it also sheds light on vital elements of the practice, such as the role of the medium and the instruments, the relationship between them, and the method for inviting a deity.

4.1   The Relationship between the Medium and His/Her Instruments

In Lu You's poem, the mediums were children[57] while the instrument could be thrown away after the feast. This fully reflects the entertainment dimension of certain early spirit-writing practices. Once it became more solemn and related to the production of revealed texts, especially when it was combined with the *daofa* 道法 (Daoist rites) tradition (see the contribution by Goossaert in this volume), the instruments and/or a human medium became increasingly vital.

As mentioned before, however, the human medium is not always the core element of a spirit-writing ritual. Especially in the "flying Phoenix" rituals, spirit-writing instruments revealed texts automatically, without the participation of a human medium.[58] In other words, the human medium was absent from these rituals to guarantee the sacredness and mysterious aura of the revealed texts as well as the ritual producing them. Therefore, the Liu Ansheng community's claim to have received the Wenchang scriptures through the automatic Phoenix could be interpreted as endorsing their sacred nature.

Further corroborating the non-essential role of the human medium, Shiga Ichiko found that, in the Ming dynasty text *Tianhuang zhidao taiqing yuce* 天皇至道太清玉冊 (Jade slips of great clarity on the supreme path of the Celestial Sovereigns), the five highest stages in the so-called "Tongtian baolu dafa sanshisan jie 通天寶籙大法三十三階" (The 33 stages of the great method of the precious register for penetrating heaven) are related to spirit-writing; they are *jiangbi* 降筆 (descending words), *taiji luan* 太極鸞 (Phoenix

---

57   It is an open question whether the children here are child-mediums or not, but the word *shuzi* 豎子 could be derogatory so they might simply be ordinary children. For child-mediums in the Song dynasty, see Davis, *Society and the Supernatural*, 87–170.

58   In this article, I define the "human medium" in a spirit-writing séance as the person who holds the instrument and/or who becomes possessed during the procedure, which usually refers to the "spirit-writing-stylus hand" (*jishou* 乩手) or "Phoenix hand" (*luanshou* 鸞手) in contemporary practices. Therefore, the human medium is not necessarily the ritual specialist. In some cases, it is the human medium who leads the séance and performs as a ritual specialist while, in other cases, it is the client(s) who holds the instrument and the ritual specialist who performs the rites, without touching the instrument.

of the supreme ultimate), *bijia luan* 筆架鸞 (Phoenix of the propped stylus), *xuansi luan* 懸絲鸞 (Phoenix hung on a thread), and *fengxia luan* 封匣鸞 (Phoenix in the Sealed Box).[59] The text fails to provide any details about this "great method," but the name *fengxia luan* seems to refer to a kind of automatic technique similar to the five-colored Phoenix of the Wenchang cult.

Moreover, a similar but more detailed story was included in the *Lüzu quanshu* 呂祖全書 (Complete works of the Patriarch Lü) in the Qing dynasty:

> One day, [Shi Tianji] took a trip to the further peak of Hu Qiu (Tiger Hill). There stood a splendid temple with a quiet chamber immediately beside it, in which a statue (or portrait) of Lüzu was worshipped. In the center of its beam hung a wooden pen on a thread. Below it was a plate of sand and a square table. An old man was sitting next to it. [Shi Tianji] therefore asked him what these items were set for. The old man answered: "if anyone's any question to ask, they can pray silently and piously and use talismans to invite Lüzu to descend to the stylus, and they can decided for themselves what the answer is." Therefore, [Shi Tianji] burned incense and prayed silently. ... Soon, the wooden pen hanging in the air moved spontaneously and wrote down these words: ...

> （石天基）一日遊虎邱後山絕頂，殿宇輝煌，傍有靜室，供呂祖像。梁中以絲線挂木筆一枝，其下承有沙盤方几。傍坐老翁。因問設此何為。翁曰："凡有疑事啟問，即虔誠默禱，用符咒代請呂祖降乩，自臨判斷。"因焚香默叩。... 少頃，見懸空木筆，即自運動，遂判云：...[60]

This passage, as well as the "Phoenix in the Sealed Box" mentioned above, shows that, in certain cases, the spirit-writing activities in late imperial China did not require the participation of a spirit-medium. For the production of long scriptures or even big collections, this sort of spontaneous ritual was perceived as the most economic form of textual production, since it was unnecessary to write things down, character by character, as people did during the poem assembly; it also supported later claims about spirit-writing as the origin of texts.

Apart from the aforementioned forms of spirit-writing, there was another form of practice in the broad spectrum of Ming-Qing spirit-writing rituals. On

---

59 On the *Taiqing yuce* and its editions, see Schachter, "Printing the Dao."
60 *Lüzu quanshu, juan* 2.

certain occasions, the ritual master would lead the ritual while their clients played the role of the human medium. A related passage can be found in the famous novel *Rulin waishi* 儒林外史 (Unofficial history of the Confucian scholars):

> [Chen Li] asked the retainer to go to his residence to fetch the plate of sand and divination-stylus. Chen Li said: "Dear sirs, please pray silently by yourself." After the two noblemen prayed, they set up the divination-stylus. Chen Li himself made obeisances and burnt a talisman to force the deities to descend to the altar. Then he invited the two noblemen to support the stylus on both sides. He chanted a spell again and burned a talisman to invite the deities. People found that the stylus began to move. Chen Li asked the retainer to pour out a cup of tea, kneel down and offer it with both hands. The stylus drew a few circles and ceased. Chen Li burned another talisman and asked those present to be quiet. The retainer and his family (therefore) left the room. After a while, the supported stylus began to move and wrote four big characters: "Prepare for the verdict, Sir Wang." Supernumerary Wang threw the stylus in a rush, came down to kowtow four times, and asked: "May I know your precious name, dear Lord?" Afterwards, he resumed supporting the stylus. The stylus whirled rapidly and wrote a sentence: "I am Saint Guan, Thearch Lord who Subdues Demons." … [The stylus] did not move anymore. Chen Li said: "I guess his majesty's already returned to heaven; please don't bother him anymore." He burned another talisman for sending away, withdrew the stylus, incense burner, and plate of sand, and sat back again. The two noblemen paid him five *qian* of silver and wrote a recommendation letter for him.

> （陳禮）叫長班到他下處，把沙盤乩筆都取了來擺下。陳禮道：「二位老爺自己默祝。」二位祝罷，將乩筆安好，陳禮又自己拜了，燒了一道降壇的符，便請二位老爺兩邊扶著乩筆。又念了一遍咒語，燒了一道啓請的符，只見那乩漸漸動起來了。那陳禮叫長班斟了一杯茶，雙手捧著，跪獻上去。那乩筆先畫了幾個圈子，便不動了。陳禮又焚了一道符，叫眾人都息靜。長班家人站在外邊去了。又過了一頓飯時，那乩扶得動了，寫出四個大字：「王公聽判。」王員外慌忙丟了乩筆，下來拜了四拜，問道：「不知大仙尊姓大名。」問罷，又去扶乩。那乩旋轉如飛，寫下一行道：「吾乃伏魔大帝關聖帝君是也。」…再不動了。陳禮道：「想是夫子龍駕已經回天，不可再褻瀆了。」又焚了一道退送的符，將乩筆香爐沙盤撤去，重新坐下。二位官府封了五錢銀子，又寫了一封薦書。[61]

---

61 *Rulin waishi*, chapter 10.

One of the most interesting aspects of this description is that the two noblemen who support the divination-stylus are not professional mediums, but "clients," who requested the divination service. The ritual experts perform the rituals of praying, chanting, and burning talismans. In this context, those who support the stylus do not need ritual qualification, while the ritual expert does not touch the instrument at all. Moreover, the clients had to pay for the ritual afterward, which made the ritual master a "service provider" of spirit-writing.[62] This is quite different from what we see in other contemporary materials. A comparison of the two cases above with other early materials suggests that the instruments, rather than human mediums, are the objects of the possession.

In general, the original practice of the "invitation of the Purple Maiden" was carried out by children and women. The amusement element was a priority. Therefore, ritual experts were not necessary at all. In most of the anecdotal records of the Song dynasty, the ritual experts are usually absent. Even the human medium was not important in most cases. In the *Rulin waishi* scene, a ritual expert is important, but he is not a type of spirit-medium.

The human medium is, however, crucial in contemporary spirit-writing altars. Some communities have to cease their activities simply because they have lost the human medium (e.g. the spirit-writing activities of Singkung Chotong 省躬草堂 in Hong Kong ceased for years after the last human medium died.) It is easy to imagine that, even in late imperial China, techniques such as the Phoenix Tower, which did not require human participation, were regarded as overly mysterious and less credible as spirit-writing grew increasingly popular and, more importantly, increasingly public, but there was no audience to confirm the whole procedure of textual production. This is why the most important and influential spirit-writing collections, such as the *Lüzu quanshu* and the *Wendi quanshu*, were produced by human mediums, who on most occasions recorded their names and the precise dates when their rituals took place. From the late Ming onward, the human medium became increasingly important (at least in the extant narratives), for receiving long scriptures or revelations became the most vital issue within the spirit-writing communities.

Human mediums became even more fundamental when the elite literati commenced participating in, and tried to understand and even explain, the

---

62 Very similar scenes occur elsewhere, such as *Pinhua baojian* 品花寶鑒 (Precious mirror for appreciating flowers) (chapter 45) and, in a certain scene in *Hong lou meng* 紅樓夢 (Dream of the red chamber) (chapter 95), it was the medium and client together who held the stylus.

spirit-writing rituals. As argued by Michael Lackner, the elite literati, including figures such as Ji Yun 紀昀 (1724–1805), were attempting to explain a non-rational phenomenon in a rational manner. "The ghosts are not efficacious by themselves; they become efficacious by virtue of their contact with human beings" (鬼不自靈，待人而靈).[63] This kind of understanding was inherited not only by several redemptive societies but also by some scholars in the Republican period.[64] Chao Wei-pang, when explaining the spirit-writing practices of the redemptive societies during the Republican period, articulated his thoughts as follows: "human beings borrow the deity's power to be efficacious, and the deities borrow the human's power to be efficacious" (人假神靈，神假人靈).[65] It seems fair to say that these kinds of participants attributed spirit-writing phenomena to neither cheating nor mystery, but someplace in between.

4.2 Inviting Deities to Descend

The question "what role does a human medium play in a spirit-writing ritual?" can also be reformulated as "how does the human medium practice a spirit-writing ritual?" The aforementioned materials have already provided some clues. On one side of the spectrum, all the practitioner needed was a set of mysterious techniques, and sometimes the right talisman was enough. On the other side of the spectrum, a deity might require the altar members' devotion and morality.

For example, the first volume of the famous *Wanfa guizong* 萬法歸宗 (Ten thousand methods to return to the origin), a Ming dynasty collection of rites, spells, and talismans, focused on the rite of spirit-writing; namely the "rite of inviting the transcendent sieve" (*qing xianji fa* 請仙箕法).[66] It preserves spells and talismans to "command" (*chiling* 敕令) and "hurry" (*cui* 催) the deities to descend. In other sources, we find statements that are even more radical than the *Wanfa guizong* in their approach to the deities:

> Many people practice the art of summoning spirit-writing deities; there are many practitioners, so there are differences in transmission. I was fond of it when young. A Daoist master from Maoshan once gave me a book, the basic content of which was about writing a talisman with the seven stars,

---

63 Lackner, *Xiaodao youli*, 70–77.
64 For a case study of remptive society and spirit-writing, see Matthias Schumann's contribution to this volume.
65 Chao, "The Origin and Growth of the Fu Chi," 11.
66 *Wanfa guizong, juan* 1.

including *Kui, Zhuo*, etc. The transcendents would descend as soon as I burned the talisman in the [incense] burner; if they did not come, I could write another talisman to hurry them; this talisman was to be burned on the ground, and stamped on. Then, none [of the deities would dare] not to descend.

召乩之術，作者甚多，然其傳授亦各不同。余少時亦深好之，茅道人曾授一書，大率用魁魃等七星作符，焚之爐中，仙即隨運而至，不至則書催符一紙，焚於地上以足蹋之，無不立降。[67]

In this case, the spirit-writing deities were actually summoned rather than invited, not to mention worshipped, by the practitioners. This may either be a reverberation of the early practices of inviting the Purple Maiden or may be influenced by the tradition of Daoist rites. Similar situations could have also arisen when the literati assembled for poem games, where some descending deities were appreciated and others mocked.

On the other hand, the spirit-writing communities who produced the most important religious collections, such as the Lüzu canons, Wenchang canons, and even the famous *Daozang jiyao* 道藏輯要 (Essentials of the Daoist Canon), could be located on the other side of the spectrum. They abided by highly specific forms of self-identification and invented exclusive transmission lineages. They regarded themselves as the chosen disciples of Lüzu or Wenchang; therefore, they could receive sacred revelations through spirit-writing.[68] In these cases, the methods for learning or mastering the technique of spirit-writing were not recorded in the texts they produced. Instead, they felt the responsibility and, more importantly, were qualified to disseminate the sacred information revealed by spirit-writing to save as many people as possible.[69]

These two types of spirit-writing can also be compared with the two Daoist concepts of "Thunder Rites" (*leifa* 雷法) and "sending up a statement" (*shangshu* 上疏). In the Daoist tradition, the ritual masters who practiced Thunder Rites were dealing not only with the higher deities but also the marshal deities (*yuanshuai shen* 元帥神), who were always divinized demons.[70] Therefore,

---

67 *Huadang ge congtan*, juan 5.
68 For these Lüzu or Wenchang spirit-writing cults in the Qing dynasty, see Mori, "Shō Yobu no Ryoso fukei shinkō"; Mori, "Identity and Lineage"; Lai, "Qingdai sizhong *Lüzu quanshu*"; Lai, "*Lüzu quanshu zhengzong*"; Lai, "Mingqing daojiao Lüzu"; Goossaert, "Spirit-Writing, Canonization, and the Rise of Divine Saviors"; Hu, "Qingdai liuzhong wendi lei quanshu."
69 For eschatology and spirit-writing, see Goossaert, "Modern Daoist Eschatology."
70 For Thunder Rites, see Lowell Skar, "*leifa* 雷法," in *EOT*, 627–29; Meulenbeld, *Demonic Warfare*, 98–131.

they needed proper rites and talismans to control these fierce deities. However, the Statement tradition was to send up petitions (*shangzhang* 上章) or memorials (*shangbiao* 上表) to the celestial officials or supreme deities, which made the Daoist master a humble servant in the ritual.[71]

4.3 The Relationship between Practitioners and Deities

The different methods used by spirit-writing practitioners also reflect the diversification of their relationship with the descending deities. In a few cases, stories exhorting people to stay away from spirit-writing describe demonic beings descending to the stylus or even taking possession of the medium. More commonly, however, the spirit-writing pantheon of the late imperial period may be divided roughly into three categories: (1) female Transcendents or talented ghosts (*caigui* 才鬼); (2) deceased sages or mentors; and (3) higher deities, but these form only a spectrum rather than exclusive categories since some cases should be located in the intermediate areas.

The divinities descending in a poem game within the context of spirit-writing séances were talented ghosts or female transcendents. The latter were usually talented girls who died young. Although their titles recorded the label of transcendent (*xian* 仙), they were more often treated as something between real transcendents and ghosts. On the one hand, this may relate to the early stories about the Purple Maiden. On the other hand, the late Ming spirit-writing activities were, to some extent, influenced by the Tanyangzi 曇陽子 cult[72] and the Ye Xiaoluan 葉小鸞 (1616–1632) stories, especially in the Jiangnan area.[73] This process led to a pattern of poem games and even affectionate communication with female transcendents who died young.

In the late imperial period, it was common practice to transform deceased sages or recently deceased mentors into the deities or patrons of a given literatus' spirit-writing altar. For example, the two patron deities of Peng Dingqiu's

---

71 For the Statements, see Poul Andersen, "*baibiao* 拜表," in *EOT*, 206–7; Maruyama Hiroshi, "*shu* 疏," in *EOT*, 904–6.

72 The historical Tanyangzi (1558–1580) was the daughter of Wang Xijue 王錫爵 (1534–1610). She was already worshiped by contemporary high-ranking officials, including her father and Wang Shizhen 王世貞 (1526–1590), during her lifetime, and also believed to levitate to heaven when she died. For the Tanyangzi cult in the Ming dynasty, see He, "Tanyangzi xinyang de jianli."

73 Ye Xiaoluan was the daughter of the official Ye Shaoyuan 葉紹袁 (1589–1648). After she died young, her father started to communicate with her through spirit-writing. For the spirit-writing related to Tangyangzi and Ye Xiaoluan, see the contribution by Elena Valussi in this volume.

altar were Du Changchun 杜長春 (fl. 1616) and Huang Daozhou 黃道周 (1585–1646), both well-educated late Ming literati. Other deities who descended to the altars included famed Neo-Confucians, like Zhou Dunyi 周敦頤 (1017–1073), and famed poets, like Li Bai 李白 (701–762). In these cases, the deceased sages were regarded as celestial officials in the Jade Bureau under the charge of the Divine Lord Wenchang. In the example given above, the "pen-brush-spirit" that descended to Li Yuhong was Qian Xi 錢禧 (fl. 1631), another member of the Revival Society (Fu she 復社) during the late Ming.

The third type of spirit-writing deity was, arguably, the most common during the Qing dynasty. In earlier times, there were very few records of higher deities, including the Jade Emperor and the Divine Lords, descending to spirit-writing séances outside the Daoist scriptures and rituals. Since almost all of these séances, practiced by literati, contained some element of entertainment, the atmosphere was not completely appropriate for the appearance of higher deities. During the Qing dynasty, however, individuals and communities increasingly practiced spirit-writing to obtain sacred revelations. They went as far as dedicating themselves to one specific god, usually Lüzu or Wenchang. In many cases, the communities were unconnected with clerical Daoism or Buddhism; some were lay communities, while others developed a distinct identity. Several communities reinterpreted the Daoist and Buddhist pantheons from a Confucian standpoint, while others claimed to have transcended the framework of the three teachings.

In earlier times, including the Song dynasty, human participants and the descending beings enjoyed some degree of equality for, as Lu You commented, "both humans and ghosts are just stupid." During the Ming, this would apply to a few cases. The talented ghosts or female transcendents who died young could be regarded as a metaphor for the literati participants. This metaphor reflected the participants' self-pity with regard to their undervalued talents. Therefore, in extreme cases, including those of You Tong 尤侗 (1618–1704) and the female transcendent Flower Scribe of the Jasper Palace (Yaogong Huashi 瑤宮花史), the metaphor could develop into a romantic relationship.[74] In some cases, as the ritual manual *Wanfa guizong* recorded, practitioners or ritual experts could use talismans and chanting to command the spirit-writing divinities.[75]

The high deities could be regarded as a source of sacred authority in a Weberian sense. The descent of a recently deceased mentor or predecessor, how-

---

74 For You Tong's spirit-writing practice, see Zeitlin, "Spirit Writing and Performance."
75 *Wanfa guizong*, juan 5. For the relationship between exorcistic ritual traditions (*daofa* 道法) and spirit-writing, see Goossaert, *Making the Gods Speak*.

ever, is not about gaining authority, but about endorsing deification. If modern scholars gained access to these semi-private spirit-writing communities, and to all of the records revealed by patrons such as Huang Daozhou, it was because this information was published and disseminated. The *de facto* content of their revelation, however, does not deviate from the traditional teachings, and most of those revelations share highly similar themes. Therefore, the combination of spirit-writing and publication is intended to produce not only textual authority but also new deities through textual means. The publication and dissemination of books were linked not only to the value behind the information, but also to who was qualified and had the power to bear, transmit, and reveal the information.

5   Conclusion

In general terms, in this article, I have demonstrated that the occurrence of different terminology, such as "supporting the sieve," "supporting the Phoenix," and "supporting the divination-stylus," was closely related to the creation of new instruments. From the late imperial period onward, the boundaries between these emic terms became blurred and, in most cases, they all referred to spirit-writing in a broad sense, as do modern scholars. In addition, a close look at different materials could also reconstruct a wide spectrum of spirit-writing practices: some were deemed to take place in a spontaneous manner and with no human intervention, while others required a human medium; some required the correct technical apparatus while others required only devotion; some were entertainment-oriented while others were solemn.

In a study on the relationship between popular worship and the Daoist tradition, Kristofer Schipper found that "although we may look at Taoism as being something more powerful and impressive than popular religion, in fact, the situation is different: in modern China, in local society, the strength and scope of popular beliefs and practices surpass Taoism."[76] This observation might apply not only to Daoism but also to the "three teachings" in general. Spirit-writing, as a neutral practice that does not necessarily belong to any religious tradition, evolved from the "invitation of the Purple Maiden" into a very broad spectrum throughout the early modern period, thus penetrating into multiple aspects of Chinese society: agriculture, art, the military, bureaucracy, the media, and, of course, religion.

---

76   Schipper, "Sources of Modern Popular Worship," 19.

The Song and late Ming dynasties are two phases of the utmost importance for understanding how spirit-writing evolved from a diachronic perspective. The historian of Daoism may argue that, during the Song dynasty, Daoism began to absorb elements of popular religion because of urbanization and the development of local societies. On the other hand, however, because of the participation of well-educated literati, popular practices such as the "invitation of the Purple Maiden" or the early stage of the practice of "supporting the sieve" became far more comprehensive and capable of absorbing all kinds of elements originally connected to Daoism or even Confucianism and Buddhism. This fermentation process became explosive when, during the late Ming, spirit-writing became the business of the private and commercial publishing houses. The pantheon, liturgy, and theology of all three teachings were merged into spirit-writing practices, which led to the appearance of highly-diversified communities and the upsurge of new textual production.

How to approach spirit-writing and how to locate it within the spectrum of Chinese religions are still open questions for modern scholars. Xu Dishan tried to rationalize the phenomenon by reducing it to psychology and parapsychology on the one hand, while labelling it as "superstition" on the other. The contradiction informing such attempts obstructs our understanding of the religious and social meaning underlying the practice, which is far more valuable than the issue of authenticity itself. Michael Lackner rightly warned scholars of the danger of approaching Ji Yun's understanding of spirit-writing through the dichotomy of the "rational" versus the "superstitious."[77] This suggestion might also apply to our own understanding of spirit-writing.

Another open question is "how was the technique of spirit-writing transmitted and disseminated during the whole of history?" Vincent Goossaert's research shows that the *daofa* tradition played a vital role in the development of spirit-writing, especially in medieval China, so it is easy to imagine that these techniques could be preserved and transmitted by priests. From the late Ming onward, however, we can also identify printing materials related to spirit-writing rituals, such as the *Wanfa guizong*, which means that the technique of spirit-writing might have been circulating in a public or semi-public manner. Focusing on the diverse methods of the transmission and dissemination of these practices could provide an approach that is equally important to the spectrum of the practices themselves, which aspect awaits further scholarly research.

---

77 Lackner, *Xiaodao youli*, 76–77.

Acknowledgements

A previous version of this paper was presented at the conference on "Spirit-Writing in Chinese History," International Consortium for Research in the Humanities (IKGF), Erlangen, June 25, 2019. I am very grateful to the discussants at the conference for their comments and also to Bony Schachter, Elena Valussi, and Matthias Schumann for their in-depth reading of the draft. I must also thank my friend and colleague, Bony Schachter, for helping with the language editing. This research was financially supported by "The Fundamental Research Funds for the Central Universities 中央高校基本科研業務費," Hunan University.

Bibliography

Abbreviations

EOT   see Pregadio, Fabrizio, ed. *The Encyclopedia of Taoism*. London: Routledge, 2008.

CCAB see Chinese Classic Ancient Books (via ERUDITION).

Primary Sources

Daming huidian 大明會典. Compiled by Li Dongyang 李東陽 (1447–1516). Ming edition, CCAB.

Daqing lüli 大清律例. *Siku quanshu* 四庫全書 edition, CCAB.

Dayuan zhiyuan bianwei lu 大元至元辨偽錄. Compiled by Shi Xiangmai 釋祥邁 (fl. 1281). Yuan edition, CCAB.

Gusheng subian 觚賸續編. Compiled by Niu Xiu 鈕琇 (1644–1704). Qing edition, housed in the Tianjin Library.

Houshan shi zhu 后山詩註. Compiled by Chen Shidao 陳師道 (1053–1101). *Sibu congkan* 四部叢刊 edition, CCAB.

Huadang ge congtan 花當閣叢談. Compiled by Xu Fuzuo 徐復祚 (1560–?). Qing edition, CCAB.

Jiannan shigao 劍南詩稿. Compiled by Lu You 陸遊 (1125–1209). *Siku quanshu* edition, CCAB.

Jingchu suishiji 荊楚歲時記. Compiled by Zong Lin 宗懍 (fl. sixth century). Republican facsimile of a Ming edition, CCAB.

Kuiche zhi 睽車志. Compiled by Guo Tuan 郭彖 (fl. 1186–1187). *Siku quanshu* edition, CCAB.

Kuitan lu 愧郯錄. Compiled by Yue Ke 岳珂 (1183–?). *Sibu congkan* facsimile of a Song edition, CCAB.

Lüzu quanshu 呂祖全書. Compiled by Liu Qiao 劉樵 (fl. 1727–1749). Qing edition, housed in Staatbibliothek zu Berlin, call number: Libri sin. 688/690.

Mengxi bitan 夢溪筆談. Compiled by Shen Kuo 沈括 (1029–1093). *Sibu congkan* facsimile of a Ming edition, CCAB.

Nancun chuogeng lu 南村輟耕錄. Compiled by Tao Zongyi 陶宗儀 (c. 1329–c. 1412). *Sibu congkan* facsimile of a Yuan edition, CCAB.

Qingbai leichao 清稗類鈔. Compiled by Xu Ke 徐珂 (1869–1928). Reprint. Beijing: Zhonghua Shuju, 1984.

Rulin waishi 儒林外史. Compiled by Wu Jingzi 吳敬梓 (1701–1754). Qing edition, CCAB.

Shenshi yishuo 沈氏弋説. Compiled by Shen Changqing 沈長卿 (fl. 1612). Ming edition, CCAB.

Shuowen jiezi zhu 說文解字註. Compiled by Duan Xucai 段玉裁 (1735–1815). Reprint, Beijing: Zhonghua shuju, 2018.

Shuowen jiezi 說文解字. Compiled by Xu Shen 許慎 (c. 30–c. 124). Ming edition based on a North Song edition, housed in Waseda University, call number: ホ 04 00023.

Suiyuan shihua 隨園詩話. Compiled by Yuan Mei 袁枚 (1716–1797). 1749 edition, CCAB.

Su Wenzhong gong quanji 蘇文忠公全集. Compiled by Su Shi 蘇軾 (1037–1101). Ming edition, CCAB.

Tianhuang zhidao taiqing yuce 天皇至道太清玉冊. *Daozang* DZ no. 1483.

Wanfa guizong 萬法歸宗. Ming edition, CCAB.

Wenchang huashu 文昌化書. 1601 edition, housed in Shanghai Library, call number: 線善 T01181–83.

Wendi quanshu 文帝全書. Compiled by Liu Qiao 劉樵 (fl. 1727–1749). 1794 edition, housed in Shanghai Library, call number: 線普 494696–715.

Xin qixie 新齊諧. Compiled by Yuan Mei 袁枚 (1716–1797). Qing edition, CCAB.

Yiyuan 異苑. Compiled by Liu Jingshu 劉敬叔 (fl. fourth to fifth century). *Siku quanshu* edition, CCAB.

Youhuan jiwen 遊宦紀聞. Compiled by Zhang Shinan 張世南 (fl. 1233). Qing edition, CCAB.

Yuchu xinzhi 虞初新志. Compiled by Zhang Chao 張潮 (fl. 1697). 1700 edition, CCAB.

Zhen gao 真誥. *Daozang* DZ no. 1016.

Zhi wen lu 咫聞錄. Compiled by Yongne Jushi 慵訥居士 (fl. nineteenth century). 1843 edition, CCAB.

Zitong dijun huashu 梓潼帝君化書. *Daozang* DZ no. 170.

6.3 Secondary Sources

Bottéro, Françoise and Christoph Harbsmeier. "The *Shuowen Jiezi* Dictionary and the Human Sciences in China." *Asia Major* 21, no. 2 (2008): 249–71.

Burton-Rose, Daniel. "Terrestrial Reward as Divine Recompense: The Self-fashioned Piety of the Peng Lineage of Suzhou, 1650–1870." PhD diss., Princeton University, 2016.

Chao, Wei-pang. "Games at the Mid-Autumn Festival in Kuangtung." *Folklore Studies* 3, no. 1 (1944): 1–16.

Chao, Wei-pang. "The Origin and Growth of the Fu Chi." *Folklore Studies* 1 (1942): 9–27.

Chao, Wei-pang. "Review of *A Study of the Fu-chi Superstition* 扶箕迷信底研究 by Hsü Ti-Shan." *Folklore Studies* 3, no. 2 (1944): 144–49.

Clart, Philip. "Moral Mediums: Spirit-Writing and the Cultural Construction of Chinese Spirit-Mediumship." *Ethnologies* 25, no. 1 (2003): 153–90.

Clart, Philip. "The Birth of a New Scripture: Revelation and Merit Accumulation in a Taiwanese Spirit-Writing Cult." *British Columbia Asian Review* 8 (1994–1995): 174–203.

Clart, Philip. "The Phoenix and the Mother: The Interaction of Spirit-Writing Cults and Popular Sects in Taiwan." *Journal of Chinese Religions* 25 (1997): 1–32.

Davis, Edward. *Society and the Supernatural in Song China*. Honolulu: University of Hawai'i Press, 2001.

de Groot, J.J.M. *The Religious System of China*. Leiden: Brill, 1892–1910. Reprint, Taibei: Jingwen shuju, 1964.

Fan Chun-wu 范純武, ed. *Fuluan wenhua yu minzhong zongjiao guoji xueshu yantaohui lunwenji* 扶鸞文化與民眾宗教國際學術研討會論文集. Taipei: Boyang wenhua, 2020.

Goossaert, Vincent. *Making the Gods Speak: The Ritual Production of Revelation in Chinese Religious History*. Cambridge, Massachusetts: Harvard University Asia Center, 2022.

Goossaert, Vincent. "Modern Daoist Eschatology: Spirit-Writing and Elite Soteriology in Late Imperial China." *Daoism: Religion, History and Society* 6 (2014): 219–46.

Goossaert, Vincent. "Spirit-Writing, Canonization, and the Rise of Divine Saviors: Wenchang, Lüzu, and Guandi, 1700–1858." *Late Imperial China* 36, no. 2 (2015): 82–125.

Goyama, Kiwamu 合山究. *Minshin jidai no josei to bungaku* 明清時代の女性と文学. Tokyo: Kyuko shoin, 2006.

He Yanran 賀晏然. "Tanyangzi xinyang de jianli: jian lun wanming wenren zongjiao de tedian 曇陽子信仰的建立：兼論晚明文人宗教的特點." PhD diss., National University of Singapore, 2015.

Hsieh Tsung-hui 謝聰輝. *Xin tiandi zhi ming: Yuhuang, Zitong yu feiluan* 新天帝之命：玉皇、梓潼與飛鸞. Taiwan: Commercial Press, 2013.

Hu Jiechen 胡劼辰. "'Bilu' gouchen: Mingqing fuji de yige zi leixing '筆籙'鉤沉: 明清扶乩的一個子類型." Forthcoming in *Min-su ch'ü-i* 民俗曲藝.

Hu Jiechen 胡劼辰. "*Lüzu quanshu* yu *Wendi quanshu* bianzuan zhe Liu Qiao xiaokao 《呂祖全書》與《文帝全書》編纂者劉樵小考." *Daojiao xuekan* 道教學刊 5 (2020): 66–80.

Hu Jiechen 胡劼辰. "Qingdai liuzhong wendi lei quanshu de chuban shi yanjiu 清代六種文帝類全書的出版史研究." *Zhongyang yanjiu yuan lishi yuyan yanjiu suo jikan* 中央研究院歷史語言所集刊 91, no. 2 (2020): 227–92.

Jordan, David K., and Daniel L. Overmyer. *The Flying Phoenix: Aspects of Chinese Sectarianism in Taiwan.* Princeton: Princeton University Press, 1986. Reprint, Princeton: Princeton University Press, 2014.

Kani, Hiroaki 可兒弘明. "Furan zakki: minshu dōkyō no shuhen (sono ichi) 扶鸞雜記：民衆道教の周辺(その一)." *Shigaku* 史學 45, no. 1 (1972): 57–88.

Katz, Paul. "Spirit-writing Halls and the Development of Local Communities: A Case Study of Puli (Nantou County)." *Journal of Chinese Ritual, Theatre and Folklore* (民俗曲藝) 174 (2011): 103–84.

Kleeman, Terry. "The Expansion of the Wench'ang Cult." In *Religion and Society in T'ang and Sung China*, edited by Patricia B. Ebrey and Peter N. Gregory, 45–73. Honolulu: University of Hawai'i Press, 1993.

Kleeman, Terry. *A God's Own Tale: The Book of Transformations of Wenchang, the Divine Lord of Zitong.* New York: State University of New York Press, 1994.

Kōda, Rohan 幸田露伴. "Furan no jutsu 扶鸞之術." In *Rohan zenshū* 露伴全書, Vol. 16, 400–23. Tokyo: Iwanami Shoten, 1978.

Lackner, Michael [Lang Mixie 朗宓榭]. *Xiaodao youli: Zhongxi bijiao xin shiyu* 小道有理：中西比較新視域. Translated by Jin Wen 金雯 et al. Beijing: Sanlian Shudian, 2018.

Lagerwey, John. *Paradigm Shifts in Early and Modern Chinese Religion: A History.* Leiden: Brill, 2019.

Lai Chi-tim 黎志添. "Mingqing daojiao Lüzu jiangji Xinyang de fazhan ji xiangguan wenren jitan yanjiu 明清道教呂祖降乩信仰的發展及相關文人乩壇研究." *Zhongguo wenhua yanjiu suo xuebao* 中國文化研究所學報 65 (2017): 139–79.

Lai Chi-tim 黎志添. "Qingdai sizhong *Lüzu quanshu* yu Lüzu fuji daotan de guanxi 清代四種《呂祖全書》與呂祖扶乩道壇的關係." *Zhongguo wenzhe yanjiu jikan* 中國文哲研究集刊 42 (2013): 183–230.

Lai Chi-tim 黎志添. "*Lüzu quanshu zhengzong*: Qingdai Beijing Jueyuan tan de lishi ji qi Lüzu Tianxian pai xinyang. 《呂祖全書正宗》：清代北京覺源壇的歷史及其呂祖天仙派信仰." *Zhongguo wenzhe yanjiu jikan* 中國文哲研究集刊 46 (2015): 101–49.

Liu, Xun. "Of Poems, Gods, and Spirit-Writing Altars: The Daoist Beliefs and Practice of Wang Duan." *Late Imperial China* 36, no. 2 (2015): 23–81.

Meulenbeld, Mark. *Demonic Warfare: Daoism, Territorial Networks, and the History of a Ming Novel.* Honolulu: University of Hawai'i Press, 2015.

Mori, Yuria. "Dōzō shūyō to shō yobu no ryoso fukei shinkō 道藏輯要と蔣予蒲の呂祖扶乩信仰." *Tōhō shūkyō* 東方宗教 98 (2001): 33–52.

Mori, Yuria. "Identity and Lineage: The *Taiyi jinhua zongzhi* and the Spirit-Writing Cult to Patriarch Lü in Qing China." In *Daoist Identity: History, Lineage and Ritual*, edited by Livia Kohn and Harold D. Roth, 165–84. Honolulu: University of Hawai'i Press, 2002.

Schachter, Bony. "Beyond the Kingly Metaphor: A Sociological Reading of the Scripture of the Jade Sovereign." *Journal of Chinese Studies* 60 (2015): 95–158.

Schachter, Bony. "*Gaoshang Yuhuang benxing jijing* (Combined Scriptures of the Original Acts of the Exalted and Superior Jade Sovereign): An Annotated Translation and Study of Its First Chapter." *Monumenta Serica* 62 (2014): 153–212.

Schachter, Bony. "Printing the Dao: Zhou Xuanzhen, the Editorial History of the Jade Slips of Great Clarity and Ming Quanzhen Identity." *Daoism: Religion, History and Society* 10 (2018): 1–86.

Shiga Ichigo 志賀市子. *Chugoku no kokkurisan: furan shinkou to kajin shakai* 中国のこっくりさん：扶鸞信仰と華人社會. Tokyo: Taishukan Shoten, 2003.

Shiga, Ichigo 志賀市子. *Xianggang Daojiao yu fuji xinyang: lishi yu rentong* 香港道教與扶乩信仰: 歷史與認同. Translated by Song Jun 宋軍. Hongkong: The Chinese University Press, 2013.

Schipper, Kristofer. "Sources of Modern Popular Worship in the Taoist Canon: A Critical Appraisal." In *Minjian xinyang yu Zhongguo wenhua guoji yantaohui lunwen ji* 民間信仰與中國文化國際研討會論文集, edited by Lin Ru 林如, 1–23. Taipei: Hanxue yanjiu zhongxin, 1994.

Schipper, Kristofer and Franciscus Verellen ed. *The Taoist Canon: A Historical Companion to the Daozang*. Chicago and London: The University of Chicago Press, 2004.

Valussi, Elena. "Female Alchemy and Paratext: How to Read *nüdan* in a Historical Context." *Asia Major* 21, no. 2 (2008): 153–93.

Wang Chien-chuan 王見川. *Taiwan de zhaijiao yu luantang* 臺灣的齋教與鸞堂. Taibei: Nantian shuju, 1996.

Wang Chien-chuan 王見川. "Peng Dingqiu yu Qingchu Suzhou Daojiao: fuluan, lidou yu zhushu 彭定求與清初蘇州道教：扶鸞、禮斗與著書." *Lishi, yishu yu Taiwan renwen luncong* 歷史、藝術與臺灣人文論叢 10 (2016): 85–106.

Wang Chien-chuan 王見川. "Song-Ming shiqi de fuji, fuluan yu qingxian 宋明時期的扶乩、扶鸞與請仙." In *Fuluan wenhua yu minzhong zongjiao guoji xueshu yantaohui lunwenji* 扶鸞文化與民眾宗教國際學術研討會論文集, edited by Fan Chun-wu 范純武, 53–88. Taipei: Boyang wenhua, 2020.

Xu Dishan 許地山. *Fuji mixin di yanjiu* 扶箕迷信底研究. Changsha: Commercial Press, 1941.

Yong, Heming, and Jing Peng. *Chinese Lexicography: A History from 1046 BC to AD 1911*. New York: Oxford University Press, 2008.

Zeitlin, Judith. "Spirit Writing and Performance in the Work of You Tong (1618–1704)." *T'oung Pao* 84, nos. 1–3 (1998): 102–35.

Zhu Mingchuan 朱明川. "Rutan jingdian ji qi yingyong: yi Sichuan Jiangyou diqu de 'Zixia tan' wei li 儒壇經典及其應用：以四川江油地區的'紫霞壇'為例." *Shanshu, jingjuan yu wenxian* 善書、經卷與文獻 1 (2019): 135–61.

CHAPTER 6

The Transcendent of the Plate: The *Lingji zhimi* 靈乩指迷 (Instructions on the numinous stylus) and the Reform of Spirit-Writing Techniques during the First Half of the Twentieth Century

Fan Chun-wu 范純武

1 Introduction: A New Research Perspective on the Technical Evolution of Spirit-Writing

Spirit-writing, which is most commonly referred to in Chinese as *fuji* 扶箕 (supporting the sieve) or *fuji* 扶乩 (supporting the stylus), comprises a variety of historic designations, such as *fuluan* 扶鸞 (supporting the phoenix), *feiluan* 飛鸞 (flying phoenix), *fuhe* 扶鶴 (supporting the crane), *jiangbi* 降筆 (descending into the brush). Research has gradually expanded to examine this form of communication with the world of the spirits from various perspectives. Recent studies, however, mainly focus on the role of spirit-writing in the context of religious movements and in the cultural realm of modern China. By comparison, the evolution of the techniques used in actual practice received little attention.[1]

Xu Dishan's 許地山 (1893–1941) work and the contributions by Hu Jiechen 胡劼辰 and Wang Chien-chuan 王見川 in this volume examine the history of spirit-writing, together with its social functions and influences. Of specific relevance for this article is Xu Dishan's view that spirit-writing evolved from ancient divination methods, in which the diviner prognosticated from patterns forming under a winnowing sieve and which later evolved into forms that use writing. He describes the sieve's movements as a manifestation of "psychic power" (*xinling nengli* 心靈能力), a responsive awareness of the human senses and muscles (*ganzhi* 感知) or a manifestation of the power of ideas (*guannianli* 觀念力) and of psychic activity (*linggan huodong* 靈感活動). The sieve thus manifests a form of bodily response to spiritual or psychic transmission (*ganying* 感應) and the characters written by the sieve are the participants' subconscious ideas (*guannian* 觀念). Xu writes that spirit-writing is: "purely an expression of the

---

[1] For the terms and their connotations, see Xu, *Fuji mixin*; Wang, "Song Ming shiqi de fuji." For the historic origins of spirit-writing, see Hsieh, *Xin tiandi zhi ming*, 126–36. For a first exploration of scientific spirit-writing, see Fan, "Kexue lingji."

functions of the psyche that should be studied as a form of knowledge" (不過是心靈作用底一種表現，當一種知識去研究它). The author regarded his work as a survey for future specialist research rather than a study of spirit-writing in its own right.[2]

The question whether spirit-writing should be regarded as a form of prognostication or as part of psychical research leads to reconsidering the basic characteristics of spirit-mediumship. Anthropologists usually regard spirit-possession as a response to a personal or collective crisis, with the medium communicating between ordinary humans and spirits or deities to cure disease, drive out evil spirits, prognosticate, settle conflicts, or cure the inability of women to conceive, etc. Through practice and by presenting gifts, certain mediums come to be regarded as protectors of the local community, capable of warding off evil.[3] The central aspect is the communication between the human and the spiritual worlds and spirit-mediumship is commonly regarded as a specialist religious skill; creating, explaining, and displaying the oracle often involves complex religious and social abilities. The medium or the participants in spirit-mediumship may receive messages to forward or transmit to the public, such as "the descents of the perfected" (*jiangzhen* 降真) in Daoism. The *Zhen'gao* 真誥 (Declarations of the perfected), for instance, is an early, representative example of spirit-mediumship from the Jin period. The text is believed to have been transmitted orally through Yang Xi 楊羲 (330–c. 386) over an extended period of time. The practice required special knowledge and training in order to master ritual practices, such as "actualizing and visualizing an internal object" (*cunsi* 存思), "summoning [ghosts and spirits]" (*kaozhao* 考召), "applying secret instructions" (*chijue* 持訣), and "writing incantations" (*shufu* 書符).

Spirit-writing as well requires specialist religious skills. Xu Dishan and later scholars show that spirit-writing was popular with a significant proportion of the educated elite during the late imperial period, with literati actively participating in séances. The necessary precondition for this popularity is familiarity with the "techniques" involved. Ming and Qing sources show that these techniques were no longer the exclusive knowledge of Daoist or other religious groups. This poses the question how this technical knowledge was disseminated. Focussing on the specific techniques and their transmission may provide us with an answer to this question.

---

2   Xu, *Fuji mixin*, 91–92, 107.
3   For a discussion of spirit-mediumship within a local community, in this case in Northern Shaanxi 陝西, see Chau, *Miraculous Response*, chap. 3.

The reason why the Chinese designations for "spirit-writing" are derived from the techniques used rather than the ritual itself is due to the reliance on instruments in this form of spirit-mediumship. Whereas an oracle is spoken by the medium in a state of possession, in spirit-writing the transcendent manifests him- or herself through writing, making fraudulent manipulation relatively difficult. Both aspects are due to the nature of the instrument that is used.

According to dictionaries, a "technique" or "technology" (*jishu* 技術) is defined as the use of instruments, together with the related process, organizational structures, methods, and skills. Technology is both subject to knowledge evolution but also shapes social developments. This is exemplified in the considerable number of names used to designate spirit-writing that result from the different instruments employed. Xu Dishan, for instance, refers to *ji* 箕 (sieve) rather than *ji* 乩 (stylus) throughout, on the grounds that the *Shilin guangji* 事林廣記 (Comprehensive records from the forest of matters), a work of the late Song to early Yuan, and other sources on the origins of spirit-writing record the winnowing sieve as an instrument of prognostication.[4] Kani Hiroaki 可兒弘明 noticed a growing differentiation between the sieve and a wooden stylus that began in the Southern Song, with the wooden stylus gradually replacing the sieve. Wang Chien-chuan found both *ji* 箕 (sieve) and *ji* 乩 (stylus) in sources of the middle Ming and concluded that both instruments were still in use by that time.[5] Hsieh Tsung-hui 謝聰輝 suggested that the later designation *feiluan* 飛鸞 (flying phoenix) came into use to differentiate between spirit-writing in Daoist temples and by lay commoners.[6] These examples not only show that spirit-writing is an "umbrella term" that covers considerable diversity, they also indicate the different social functions behind these designations. *Feiluan*, for example, could imply differentiation between religious and lay practices.

Feiluan designates a writing instrument, which is either a brush or a wooden stylus, but the method itself is not always identical or standardized. There are four recorded forms, which are the *taiji luan* 太極鸞 (phoenix of the highest ultimate), the *bijia luan* 筆架鸞 (brush-stand phoenix), the *xuanluan* 懸鸞 (suspended phoenix) and the *fengjia luan* 封匣鸞 (phoenix in the sealed box). Two of these, the "sealed box" and the "brush-stand," survived into the modern

---

4   Chen, *Shilin guangji, jiji* 己集, *juan* 2, 165. Also, Liu, *Songdai minjian wushu yanjiu*, 69–78.
5   Kani, "Furan zakki"; Shiga, *Chūgoku no kokkurisan*, 42; Wang, "Song Ming shiqi de fuji," 211–43; Hsieh, *Xin tiandi zhi ming*, 126–36.
6   Hsieh, *Xin tiandi zhi ming*, 113 and chapter 4.

period.[7] Whether the stylus was held by a single person or by two participants is uncertain. Whether regional differentiation in traditions of spirit-writing also had an impact on specific techniques similarly awaits the discovery of new sources.

The focus on the technical dimension helps recognizing that spirit-writing made the descent of the deities much easier and thereby reduced the sacredness that was ascribed to divine oracles. Xu Dishan's comprehensive survey includes examples showing literati using spirit-writing in leisurely meetings to guess examination results or compose poetry. Occasional mention reveals that some of these literati had contacts with religious practitioners through teacher-pupil or family relations. In other cases, however, no religious specialists were involved, raising the question how the literati learned the skills necessary to communicate with deities through spirit-writing. The first possibility that comes to mind is knowledge transmission through printed books. With regards to the rituals involved in spirit-writing, we have a hand-written Republican period copy of the *Qingxian jifa* 請仙箕法 (Methods for requesting transcendent [messages] through the sieve). The manuscript describes the complete process in specific, practical detail, covering situations that might occur as well as the incantations and talismans involved. We find, for instance, an incantation that induces the departure of a spirit to be used in the event that a transcendent spirit had been successfully invited but showed no inclination to leave. The instructions are illustrated and sufficiently specific for putting them into practice. No earlier work of this type is known. The numerous "phoenix books" (*luanshu* 鸞書) of the Ming and Qing period, which were published as "morality books" (*shanshu* 善書) or by "phoenix transformation halls" (*hualuan tang* 化鸞堂), rarely mention specific practical aspects. The scarcity of evidence in extant published sources therefore suggests other channels of knowledge transmission.

In the late Ming, encyclopaedias for everyday use appeared in the book market in considerable variety and numerous editions. These provided general knowledge, moral education, and entertainment for ordinary people, covering agriculture, trade, law, medicine, moral and religious cultivation, prognostication, food, housing, routes of travel and transport, calendars, measures, and other fields of knowledge. Publishers categorized and introduced the topics, and also produced integrated compilations.[8] Looking though them, one finds

---

7 Wang and Pi, *Zhongguo jinshi minjian xinyang*, 105.
8 Well-known encyclopaedias are *Santai wanyong zhenzong* 三台萬用正宗 (The Santai authoritative guidance for ten-thousand uses), *Wenlin huijin wanshu yuanhai* 文林彙錦萬書淵海 (The forest of scholarship's compiled sources from ten-thousand books), *Wenlin miao-*

that quite a number include a section entitled "Jiang jibi fa 降箕筆法" (Methods for making [deities] descend into sieve and brush), with similar but not identical contents.⁹ The texts in printed encyclopaedia are evidence that spirit-writing was no longer "secret" knowledge of the initiated only. Moreover, as encyclopaedias were printed by commercial publishers, their content reflects market demand. We can therefore deduce that the practice was widely known by the late Ming and that these encyclopaedias served as one channel for the distribution of knowledge on spirit-writing techniques.¹⁰

In the Republican period, Western science and spiritualism impacted the evolution of spirit-writing. In an intellectual climate that embraced scientism and propagated the eradication of superstition, spirit-writing became a target of intense criticism. At the same time, however, spiritualism enjoyed growing popularity and religious groups, such as the Shanghai Lingxue hui 上海靈學會 (Shanghai Spiritualist Society) and the Beijing-based Wushan she 悟善社 (Society for Awakening to Goodness), used the technique of spirit-writing in their spiritualist activities. In this context, they also used the modern technology of spirit photography.¹¹

The May Fourth reverence for science directly impacted the development of spirit-writing, leading to the creation of the "Scientific Numinous Stylus" (*kexue lingji* 科學靈乩) that became popular in the 1930s and is still known as the "transcendent of the plate" (*diexian* 碟仙).¹² This technique makes use of a small, white porcelain plate that was inscribed with an arrow pointing to the rim and placed facing down on a board on which characters were inscribed in concentric circles. In a séance, usually three persons lightly placed a fin-

       jin wanbao quanshu 文林妙錦萬寶全書 (The forest of scholarship's compiled wonderous complete book of ten-thousand treasures), and *Wuku hebing wanbao quanshu* 五車合併萬寶全書 (Combined complete book of ten-thousand treasures from the Five Libraries).

9   Over a hundred popular encyclopaedias from the late Ming survived. Most were printed in Jianyang 建陽 in Fujian and are held in Japanese libraries. An accessible reprint is Zhongguo shehui kexueyuan lishi yanjiusuo wenhuashi, *Mingdai tongsu riyong leishu jikan*. An exhaustive collection is Sakade, Ogawa, and Sakai, *Chūgoku nichiyō ruisho shūsei*.

10   See Fan, "Ming Qing riyong leishu," 2–6.

11   This topic has been aptly explored by Matthias Schumann and Wang Hongchao 王宏超. Schumann, "Science and Spirit-Writing"; Wang, "Shenjie lingguang."

12   The name of this new form highlighted its scientific nature, while also differentiating itself from ordinary forms of "supporting the stylus" or spirit-writing (*fuji* 扶乩) as particularly "spiritually efficacious" (*ling* 靈). The term *ling*, which is prominently included in the name of this new technique, is notoriously difficult to translate. It is therefore sometimes translated as "numinous" and sometimes as "efficacious" in this article depending on the specific context in which it is used.

ger on the plate and silently prayed for the transcendent to descend. With the arrival of the transcendent, the plate began swirling on its own accord, and the participants could now ask their questions. The answers were obtained from the characters that the arrow pointed at. The contemporary Chen Weiyu 陳韋聿 assumes that the Transcendent of the Plate originated from the Western Ouija board and sees it as an "overseas toy" or board game.[13] Initial research by Republican scholars such as Chen Daqi 陳大齊 (1886–1983), Huang Yi 黃翼 (1903–1944), and Xu Dishan, on the other hand, employed the perspective of psychology.[14] In his *Diexian: yu xianglei xianxiang zhi xinli de jieshi* 碟仙：與相類現象之心理的解釋 (The Transcendent of the Plate: Psychological explanations of this and related phenomena) of 1937, for example, Huang Yi pointed to the similarity with the Ouija board that was popular in America and Europe during the same period, specifically the requirement of three participants, thus allowing movement by "ideo-motor action" or through subconscious communication.[15]

Records concerning the origin of the plate as a spirit-writing instrument are contradictory. Chen Weiyu attributes the invention to a certain Xu Tong 徐桐, referring to an advertisement in the daily Shanghai newspaper *Shenbao* 申報, which however mentions the name Bai Tong 白同.[16] One article in the Shenbao that did mention a Xu Tong was published on April 29, 1934. It states: "It is to be noted that the Transcendent of the Plate was invented by Mr. Xu Tong, a scholar who studied in Germany, and that it is entirely scientific and has nothing to do with strange phenomena" (注意：碟乩係中國留德科學界徐桐先生所發明，無神怪意味，全憑科學新法施乩).[17] The identity of this Mr. Xu remains unknown.[18] Other contemporary notes in periodicals more generally attribute the invention to a person who obtained a doctoral degree in Germany, and some even trace it to the Soviet Union. The sources agree, however, in linking the invention to leading international circles of spiritualism.[19]

---

13   Chen, "Lu Xun, Puyi, kexue lingji," 256–300.
14   Hou, "Minguo xuezhe de fuji yanjiu," 113–20.
15   Huang, "Diexian yu xianglei xianxiang," 181.
16   Chen, "Lu Xun, Puyi, kexue lingji," 295. Huang, "Diexian yu xianglei xianxiang," 179–81.
17   "Shenjun tuqi kexue lingji tu."
18   A high-ranking late Qing official of the same name is known, but is certainly a different person, as he was conservative and anti-foreign.
19   According to Xu Jian 徐健, Chinese students in Germany in the period 1876–1911 mainly came from Hubei, Jiangsu, and Zhejiang, and mostly studied military subjects and mining, later gradually shifting to law and other disciplines. Xu, "Wan Qing guanpai liude xuesheng yanjiu," 72–79, 112. In the absence of new sources, the issue of whether the scientist who held a German degree and developed an interest in spiritism is fact or fiction cannot be finally resolved.

Not only the origins of the "Scientific Numinous Stylus" remain insufficiently understood, also the motivation for developing a new technique as well as its connection to other spirit-writing techniques are still unclear. To answer these questions, this article explores the *Lingji zhimi* 靈乩指迷 (Instructions on the numinous stylus), a slender monograph dating to 1934 and held by the Shanghai Library. The title is not listed in contemporary catalogues of published works, appearing only in the list of books sold by the Shanghai publishing house Jinwen tang (Shanghai Jinwen tang 上海錦文堂).[20] It consists of six parts: (1) the origins of the Scientific Numinous Stylus, (2) practical operation, (3) theory, with special emphasis on spiritualist terms, (4) the interpretation of messages, (5) conditions for successful séances, (6) and accounts by users submitted in response to a call advertised in newspapers. The account on the origins names Wang Yishu 汪以恕 (no dates) as the inventor who developed the Transcendent of the Plate as a "scientific" (*kexue* 科學) form of spiritual communication. With regards to the inventor's biography, it records that he hailed from Shaoguan 韶關 in Guangdong 廣東 and studied psychology and philosophy in Germany. Originally a disbeliever, he changed his attitude during a trip to Chenzhou 辰州 in Hunan that he took at the age of 27 *sui* 歲, i.e. 25–27 years in Western age. Upon witnessing local practitioners using incantations to observable effect, he recognized the existence of phenomena that science could not explain. A couple of years later, he travelled to Germany to study. In Berlin, he met a scholar transliterated as Dr. Xindunbu'er 新頓不爾 who was interested in communications with the souls of the dead. Now believing in the existence of a spiritual world, he joined the German Spiritualist Society and studied the topic.[21] After returning to China at the age of 39, he founded the Huaxia zheyi chanwei she 華夏哲義闡微社 (Chinese Society for Occult Philosophy) with like-

---

[20] The book cover provides information on the publisher and the book contains no imprint. Appendix Three, "Gejie laihan zheng xin lu 各界來函徵信錄" (Letters from readers of all walks of life), contains a letter by Zhu Guangfu 朱光孚 addressed to "the honourable manager of Jinwen tang" ("Jinwen tang shuju zhishi xiansheng tai jian 錦文堂書局執事先生台鑒"), documenting Jinwen tang's involvement. The search in catalogues of the period produced a "Jinwen tang shuju da lianjia tushu huibao 錦文堂書局大廉價圖書彙報" (List of titles announced by Jinwen tang) of 1934, that records *Lingji zhimi* under "Xingxiang dili shulei 星相地理書類" (Astrology and geography) at the discount of 0.32 Yuan of the original price of 0.8 Yuan. The record identifies Jinwen tang as the publisher. Jinwen tang published an announcement with the call for reader's letters to be submitted by May 6 in the *Shenbao*, suggesting that the book's publication date was not long after May 6. For the advertisement, see Figure 3. For a discussion of these letters, see below.

[21] The society recorded in the sources as Deguo lingxue hui 德國靈學會 is relatively safely identified as the Deutsche Spiritistische Vereinigung. Dr. Xindunbu'er could not be identified.

minded friends, which was presumably located at Guangzhou or Hong Kong, as members are apparently associated with these cities. Four society members who are mentioned by name are Jiang Yuecun 江月邨, Zhang Weide 張未德, Jiang Dazhang 江大章, and Jiang Qi 姜齊 (all dates unknown). Activities were apparently limited due to the hostile social climate of the time. Wang invented the Scientific Numinous Stylus around 1916, and his friend Jiang Yuecun later popularized it beyond the group's circle. Though the *Lingji zhimi* confidently ascribes the invention of the Numinous Stylus Wang Yishu, it is the only source on him. Without new sources, a definite identification of the inventor's identity is therefore impossible.

Lingji zhimi was compiled by members of the society and editors of the publishing house, as we can infer from the text. The self-advertisement as "scientific" refers to its claim to fulfil standards of evidential science, implying experiments that would be verifiable under standardised conditions. Spirit-writing by plate thus established itself as qualitatively different from "traditional" forms of spirit-writing by stylus, which modern minds rejected as superstitious.[22]

Examining the technical "revolution" of spirit-writing, this article pays attention to three different aspects. First, the technical changes were a gradual process rather than a rupture. New "instruments" involve new practices, causing changes that have their own ramifications. As outlined above, as the sieve evolved into the stylus and the latter into the flying phoenix, these transformations were accompanied by changes in the social groups involved, from peasant women to literati to Daoists and other religious practitioners. The purposes for which the instruments were used also diversified. Thus, the same technique is suitable for moral guidance and the production of poetry or essays. With the shift to the plate, the instrument and the degree of sacredness changed again, reducing a sacred ritual conducted in a phoenix hall to a leisure activity at private gatherings. Second, changes in the medium through which this technical knowledge is transmitted and disseminated also have an effect. Thus, during the late imperial period, the encyclopaedias for daily use facilitated transmission, but the techniques remained difficult to master which limited their use to literati or religious specialists. The plate, by contrast, through the promotion of the new urban culture and the print media, became accessible to ordinary urbanites. Third, the intellectual significance of the technique can change together with the instrument's use. Thus, under the influence of a scientific worldview, the Shanghai Spiritualist Society and other groups began to explore the actual conditions in the world of spirits and deities to devise moral norms

---

22 For the anti-superstitious sentiments of the time, see Nedostup, *Superstitious Regimes*.

and standards. The Scientific Numinous Stylus, on the other hand, directly tied itself to the label of science to escape suspicion of superstition, while its application shifted to afterlife communications with deceased family members and friends.

In light of their different instruments, it may appear that spirit-writing by stylus and by plate can be perceived as two completely separate techniques of communication with deities and spirits. However, looking at the *Lingji zhimi*, it becomes clear that the two are actually closely associated.

2 The Emergence of a "Scientific" Form of Spirit-Mediumship: The Scientific Numinous Stylus in the *Lingji zhimi*

2.1 *The Invention of the "Scientific Numinous Stylus"* (Kexue lingji)

The name "Scientific Numinous Stylus" evidently identifies a method of spirit-writing distinguishable for being scientific. The Shanghai daily *Shenbao* of May 14, 1934 carried an article by an author who used the pen-name Mengruo 夢若 on a spirit-writing board printed by the Hong Kong publisher Kexue youyi she 科學遊藝社 (Society for Scientific Entertainment). Mengruo reported that the inventor held a German doctorate degree and that the board was made from coarse yellow paper, with a face in the centre and small characters written in concentric circles (he wonders whether the face might be that of a ghost). In addition, the set consisted of another sheet of paper with the instructions and a small porcelain plate with a similar ghostlike face. For a séance, the plate was placed in the centre of the board and three persons each placed a finger of their right hands on it while silently chanting "Transcendent of the Plate, please let us talk to …" (煩碟仙請某某到來談話) for some ten minutes, whereupon the plate would start rotating and moving. (This was the sign that the transcendent had descended into the plate.) When the plate stopped, the participants would look at which character it pointed to, and thus string words and sentences together that "explain what the soul wishes to say" (來解釋陰魂所說的是什麼話). The report continues by saying that the inventor invested much thought over many years in working out the board design, and that what he finally created followed purely scientific principles, without a trace of superstition, and hence was radically different from spirit-writing as it was known. Mengruo specifically points out that, if the participants were truly sincere, the method "will prove effective 100 times out of 100 attempts" (無不百試百驗).[23]

---

23 Mengruo, "Kexue lingji tu."

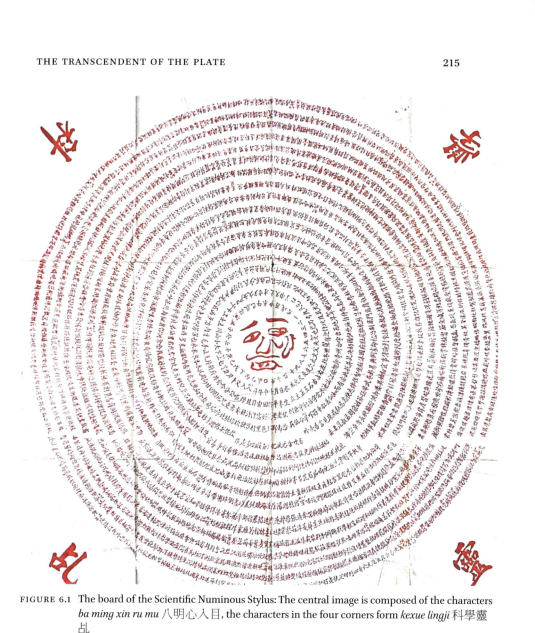

FIGURE 6.1 The board of the Scientific Numinous Stylus: The central image is composed of the characters *ba ming xin ru mu* 八明心入目, the characters in the four corners form *kexue lingji* 科學靈乩

PHOTOGRAPH BY THE AUTHOR OF A BOARD IN HIS POSSESSION

The *Shenbao* article is largely congruent with the account in *Lingji zhimi* paraphrased above, albeit identifying the inventor only as a scholar who held a German doctorate. Further material on Wang Yishu could not be located.[24] According to the *Lingji zhimi*, Wang was a child prodigy, studied abroad and

---

24 The biographical dictionary *Guangdong difang mingren lu* 廣東地方名人錄 (Personalities of the Guangdong area) of 1942, for example, contains no record.

became a scientist and spiritualist. He aspired to develop an easier and more effective form of communication with souls and spirits. As Shiga Ichiko pointed out, the method itself is reminiscent of Western forms of spirit-communication such as the planchette. This device, a heart-shaped wooden board fitted with two wheels for automatic writing, was very popular during the Victorian period. The Ouija board is a simplified adaptation of the planchette, which no longer produces writing but uses a small, roughly heart-shaped plate to identify letters on the board. Believers in paranormal phenomena were convinced that movement was caused by the soul or some other power, while scientists explained them as caused by the mind. Similarities also extend to the practice of *kokkurisan* (狐狗狸さん or コックリさん) that was popular in Japan at the end of the nineteenth century. This technique used a coin and a sheet carrying the words "yes," "no," a symbol to mark the centre, and the fifty hiragana syllables. Inoue Enryō 井上圓了 (1858–1919) suggested that this board was influenced by a planchette that the Western crew of the shipwreck at Izu 伊豆 in 1884 brought with them.[25]

The *Lingji zhimi* details that Wang Yishu encountered insurmountable difficulties in designing the board. The account relates that he overcame the bottleneck only by engaging in spirit-writing by stylus:

> Our teacher [Wang Yishu] was a scientist as well as a spiritualist but not a practitioner of spirit-writing by stylus. Uninitiated to incantations and talismans, his invention was evidently ordained by fate. When he was new to the art of communicating with spirits and souls, our teacher was not always successful. He therefore wished to find an easier method, yet found none. (At this time, he had no intention of transmitting his knowledge.) At the age of 43, he and several like-minded friends introduced a gentleman into their society who did not believe [in our teacher's] technique, and asked them to call for a deceased relative for proof. This relative had been dead for a decade and when our teacher called on him to descend, his incantations had no effect. The newcomer laughed and our teacher could offer no explanation. Upon this, he locked himself in his study to focus his mind entirely on finding an infallible method. At the time, Li Yunzhang (no dates), who excelled in spirit-writing by stylus and

---

25   Many thanks to Shiga Ichiko 志賀市子 for pointing this out to me. See also her book, *Chūgoku no kokkurisan*; and Foster, "Strange Games and Enchanted Science." Foster mentions that the practice was not unitary. In many places, it closely resembled the Oujia board or the Western practice of "table-turning."

a friend who had not met our teacher for some years, came in person to ask for the reason of our teacher's seclusion. Our teacher told him of the incident, and his friend laughed, saying that this was an easy matter, he could summon the soul. Thereupon they cleansed the room and set up the stylus and the board to invite the spirit. Our teacher asked the stylus to explain the reason why spirits at times responded and at others not. The stylus wrote in large characters: There are requirements for summoning souls. The requirements have to be met with when inviting deities with their perceptive wisdom, what would you expect with souls! He asked what the requirements were, and the stylus wrote: There are eight, if all are met, all deities, transcendents, spirits or sages will come when summoned, not only human souls. If not, nothing will happen. First: recite with true sincerity; second: have no other thought; third: no impurities in the room; fourth, no noise; fifth: patience and endurance; sixth: be reverent and wait for the right opportunity; seventh: (omitted because neither the author nor Jiang Yuecun could momentarily remember it); eighth: "clear the heart and focus the gaze" (*ming xin ru mu*). Of these eight, the eighth is the most important; without this requirement even in ten-thousand attempts, not a single one may be effective. If all are met, even without incantations and rites, inviting transcendent beings will be successful, and good results will be obtained, even beyond communicating with spirits.

Our teacher asked: The first seven requirements are immediately understandable, but what is meant by "clear the heart and focus the gaze"? The stylus replied: "clear the heart" means the absence of any other thought, concentration of the whole spirit, so that the heart is transparent, clear as a crystal. "Focus the gaze" means keeping all thoughts focussed on the invited deity or soul, as if it was standing in front of your very eyes. Maintaining this state for a quarter of an hour to half an hour, the deity, following the heart, solidifies, and the spirit, following the heart, is thus produced, and immediately both become present. Therefore, once the "heart is clear and the gaze focussed" the first, second, sixth, and seventh requirements are already met. Of the eight requirements the eighth is as important as the other seven taken together and, once fulfilled, efficacy becomes easy.

Our teacher asked: When inviting souls of the deceased, why is it often difficult to invite them? The stylus answered: As for transcendents, Buddhas, deities and spirits, people have an image in their minds, even if not real, they can think of it in their hearts as if it had real shape and thus reach the state of the "clear heart and focussed gaze." With the souls of the deceased, these are usually people that they have not known, and hence the difficulty of asking a specific soul to wield the stylus. The second reason is that with Daoist and Buddhist divinities, whom everyone reveres, sincerity comes naturally. Dead souls, however, are often treated with ridicule, and thus the requirements are not met. The third reason is that spirit-writing needs something to rely on. One only has to focus one's thought and the stylus will move as soon as the image [of a deity] takes shape in our [mind]. Yet souls belong to the realm of emptiness and thus there is nothing to rely on. These are three reasons why summoning the souls of deceased persons is so difficult.

先生為一科學家，又為靈魂學者，初非扶乩之術士，不知符籙為何事。其發明此科學靈乩，蓋有天數存焉。初，先生以與靈魂接談之術，不能每試有效，頗欲得一較為容易之法而無從。（蓋先生此時實無意於傳世）四十三歲時，與數同志欲介紹某公入會，某公不信其術，請召其戚某以試之，其戚蓋死已十餘年，先生依術召請，不驗。其公笑之。先生亦無以答。於是遂閉門不出，殫精竭慮，以研究百試百驗之法。時先生有友李雲章，善扶乩。因多年不見先生，遂親自過訪，問其閉門不出之原因。先生即以某公之事告之，李笑曰，此有何難，我當試為召之。乃於淨室中置乩盤，為之請神。先生即於乩前叩以召靈魂有驗有不驗之原因。乩大書曰：召靈魂有條件，夫以神之聰明，尚未備有條件不行。況靈魂乎？又問條件如何？乩又書曰：條件有八。具此則神仙靈聖，無不可召，不但人類之靈魂而已。不備具，則必不驗。其一、為起念真誠。其二、為不雜邪念。其三、為地不污穢。其四、為座無雜響。其五、為忍耐刻苦。其六、為敬以待機。其七為□□□□（著者適忘其第七條。月邨亦不能盡述，故暫從缺。）其八、為明心入目。此八項尤以第八項為最重要。若此項不具，則萬請無一驗。若能具此，則請乩時，雖不知符籙者，亦可有驗。非但召靈魂必有良效已也。

先生又問曰：以前七項，皆可在字面求解，所謂明心入目者何也？乩曰：明心者，心無雜念，全神貫注，此心洞明，有如水晶。入目者存想所欲召請之神靈或亡魂，仿彿已經在目前。如此過一刻乃至半時之久，神隨心結。靈隨心生，自然立驗。蓋明心入目則一二六七各項，已當然辦到。八條件中，七佔其五，自然易於有驗矣。

先生又問：召請靈魂，常比扶乩請神為尤難何也？乩曰：仙佛神靈，人心中先有印象，即使其像並不一定實在，但只須此像印在心頭，想像其容，亦可辦到明心入目之地步。召請亡魂，則往往為術者所不知，乩多請神，故召靈魂乃難於乩者一也。神仙佛道，人人多知敬禮，自然真誠。對亡魂則往往視為戲笑，條件往往不備。此其二也。扶乩有所憑藉，只須冥想乩筆將動，即形像全備，召亡魂則純屬虛空。無可憑藉，此其三也。有此三種原因。召亡魂安得不難於扶乩？²⁶

The quote shows that Wang Yishu, with Li Yunzhang's help, was able to clarify crucial questions through spirit-writing by stylus. He thus learnt about the eight requirements, of which the eighth "clear the heart and focus the gaze" was most crucial. The exchange also explains why summoning souls was harder than summoning deities: whereas in inviting transcendents and Buddhas, the participants had an image in mind and their attitude was reverent, this was impossible in most cases of summoning souls.

Having received these instructions, Wang asked the transcendent being to give him the eight requirements transmitted by a transcendent in written form for further study. The stylus thereupon wrote the five characters *ba ming xing ru mu* 八明心入目, or "Eight: clear the heart and focus the gaze," in the shape of a human face and this came to be the "transcendent of the plate," the character-image shown on the board sheet. The identity of the deity who gave the instructions is not entirely clear, but is thought to have either been Patriarch Lü (Lüzu 呂祖) or Lord Ji (Jigong 濟公). Following this revelation, Wang Yishu began working on improving the method of communication. Since he had been told that incantations and talismans were not essential for success, he began considering a change in instruments. Coincidentally, a small saucer was on his desk, and he wrote the five characters on it, together with an arrow. On a sheet of paper, he wrote several thousand frequently used characters. He waited for the saucer to move, expecting it to point out characters.[27] In this experiment, he had two persons holding the plate, following common practice in spirit-writing by stylus. When the plate remained still, he tried with three persons, still to no avail. The participants finally agreed to invite the earth [god] as their master, and over thirty minutes later, the plate moved violently. Upon asking which deity had descended, the arrow pointed to the characters *benzhai tudi* 本宅土地 (the earth [god] of this house). They asked why their séance had been effective and received the answer "*cheng ze ling* 誠則靈" (sincerity elicits spiritual efficacy).

Wang Yishu asked whether there was any method that would produce spiritual manifestations under all circumstances. The plate again moved violently and explained why the stylus could be replaced with the plate:

---

26 *Lingji zhimi*, 3–5.
27 There is no indication in the sources that Wang's time among European spiritualists played a role in his invention of the new technique.

"There are three reasons why this method is effective: First, your design has been perfected through long studies. It is not to be mentioned in the same breath with mere entertainment and still less to be called a baseless fabrication. Second, the five characters *ba mingxin rumu* are sacred words. Third, the Numinous Stylus is indeed in accordance with the wonders of the Dao, and this third point is most important, far above the others." With this, the instruction ended. The plate returned to the centre and responded no more.

「此法之驗,有三大原因:第一、為公設想之巧,蓋公研究已久,故有此成就,安得與造次戲作者相提並論,更不得謂為無異杜撰。第二、為有『八明心入目』五字為聖迹。第三、為靈乩之法,實合道妙,其中尤以第三項為最有關係,決不可以等閒視之也。」訓畢。碟遂回歸中心,再叩之,則寂然不動矣。[28]

The account shows that replacing the stylus with the plate was initially coincidental, and that procedures were adjusted through practical experiments. In this process, Wang developed the characteristics of the "Scientific Numinous Stylus," such as the three participants, the arrow on the round plate, the inscription of the five characters on the sheet board and on the plate, and the function of the plate to point out characters.

Wang Yishu intended to keep his invention secret, for use only among his friends. He left two boards, the original and a somewhat simplified copy that was easier to use. It was the simplified board that his friend Jiang Yuecun took to Beijing, and because results in spirit communications were convincing, numerous copies were taken and it gradually began to circulate.[29]

The introduction of the board for the Scientific Numinous Stylus to the general public in Beijing involves an intriguing story concerning an unnamed politician. This member of the Beijing government was immediately convinced that spirit-writing would make people believe in retribution and thus induce them to better their ways. In addition, spirit-writing would answer questions that caused confusion to many, and thus be doubly beneficial. When Jiang Yuecun and others voiced the concern that this might popularize superstitious beliefs, the politician reportedly answered: "Anyone who thinks this is superstition only has to try and see for himself, his doubts will soon dissolve, so why worry?" (若有以為迷信者,只須令他親自試之,則其惑自解,何足為病?)

---

28   *Lingji zhimi*, 8.
29   Ibid., 9–10.

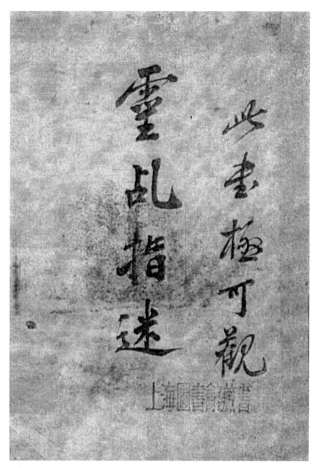

FIGURE 6.2 The cover of the *Lingji zhimi* held at Shanghai Library

He went ahead and had the board printed and distributed.[30] Though the name of the politician remains unknown, this anecdote indicates the interest that members of the political elite took in spirit-writing and which social functions they ascribed to it.[31]

According to the *Lingji zhimi*, copies of the board reached Shanghai, among other places. Reprints soon circulated, presumably based on the distributed copies. When some of these failed in séances, the Chinese Society for Occult

---

30   Ibid., 10.
31   On the engagement of the political elites in spirit-writing at the time, see also the article by Matthias Schumann in this volume.

Philosophy decided to print its own board. Since numerous imprints were on the market by this time, the accompanying publication appears to have been an effort to assert the "orthodoxy" of the society's board.

2.2   Science and Spirit-Writing

The *Lingji zhimi* contains detailed information for holding séances, as well as on theoretical principles and important aspects to be observed. The guide explains, for instance, that since the plate points at single characters, messages tend to be short, providing numerous examples as guidance in interpreting their hidden meaning. The book exemplifies a scientific, evidence-based approach to its subject that is characteristic of the period. By the early twentieth century, the term *shiyan* 實驗 in the sense of "experiment" as well as in the sense of evidence as a factually demonstrable basis for an argument had become established among the educated classes in China. At the same time, the term also referred to practical applicability and manifest proof. The experiments recorded in *Lingji zhimi* are not results of tests that employ scientific apparatus, but explanations of effects obtained in actual operations.

The explanation for the movement of the plate is an example for the practical detail of the instructions and of the "scientific" standards of the period. The sheet board was a square with an edge length of about 60 cm and, as described above, consisted of the face of the transcendent in the centre surrounded by two-thousand characters. The small plate was placed on the board to identify the characters. The operation is described as follows:

> When starting a séance, burning incense and lighting candles, bowing and showing obeisance is all unnecessary. It is sufficient to be reverent at heart; empty rites may be discarded. The notion that the transcendent will not descend without lighting incense candles is mere superstition. Inviting deities relies on sincerity, not on incense. When starting a séance, the participants may be seated. When the plate begins to move, however, they have to stand to show their respect. Besides, because the plate whirls around, a seated participant may find himself unable to follow its movement, which is highly inconvenient. All supporters of the plate have to keep the middle finger of their right hand on the plate, while the other four fingers are folded, and their wrists must be unsupported. Except for their middle finger lightly touching the plate, their hands and arms must be kept in the air, not touching any object, for this might hinder effectivity. Pressure on the plate must not be too great, yet the finger must also not leave it. The finger must follow all movements of the plate, without releasing it or pressing it down. Women can be plate holders,

THE TRANSCENDENT OF THE PLATE 223

but children under the age of fifteen cannot under any circumstances, as children generally lack earnest sincerity, and the séance may therefore be ineffective. Pregnant women are also disadvised from participating.

Before beginning, all that needs to be done is evenly spreading the board sheet on the table. A small white porcelain plate (a Western saucer is also possible) is needed, and the spirit face is to be drawn on it with an inked brush (as on the board). Following this, an arrow is to be drawn on the reverse of the plate towards the rim, to point out the characters. When the ink is dry, the turned-over plate is placed on the spirit face in the centre of the board sheet, so that the characters are face to face (i.e. the character 八 opposite its counterpart and the same for the four other characters). If they are mismatched, the séance will usually be ineffective. From the beginning, chatting and laughing are forbidden. Participants may observe the plate or close their eyes, sitting upright and reverently. Spectators similarly should not voice their guesses, chat, laugh or move around. The quieter and more earnest they are the better. The number of people is best kept small, for otherwise stillness might be impossible. All must enter a mental state of reverent concentration, awaiting the invited to descend. When bystanders chat and laugh, the holders' concentration may be broken, reducing will and sincerity and making it impossible to reach the state of "clear heart and focussed gaze."

開乩時，切勿燃香點燭，亦不必磕頭禮拜，蓋恭敬在一心，不在此種無謂之虛套也。或謂不燃香燭，神即不降，此實迷信之談，蓋請神在誠，決不在香燭也。開乩之初，扶乩者可坐。但碟動以後，則必須起立，以示敬意。其次則因碟往往旋轉不已，若坐定則不能隨碟旋轉，甚為不便。扶乩者均須用右手中指，其餘四指皆縮，手腕須懸空；除中指輕輕按住碟底外，其餘手腕肘臂，均須懸空，不得着物，否則有時不驗。按碟時不可太重，亦不可離開。碟動以後，即須隨碟移動，勿鬆亦勿重按。婦人亦可作乩手，但在十五六歲以下之男女，則決不可作乩手。因年幼者往往缺乏誠心，恐不驗也。惟婦人有孕者，亦以不作乩手為佳。

開乩之前，只須將靈乩圖平舖於枱子上。另取白色磁碟（洋磁亦可）一隻，用墨筆在正面畫一靈像。（即圖中所繪者）再於碟之背後一邊，畫一箭頭。為扶乩時指字之用，俟墨乾後，即覆於圖中央之靈像上，必須字字相對。（即八字與八字相對，明字心字人字目字，均各自相對。）若顛倒擺或橫擺，往往不驗。開乩時，切勿閒談說笑。如不注視碟背，則宜合目危坐，即在旁觀者，亦不宜作猜疑談笑等無意味之動作，總以愈肅靜愈妙。即人數亦最好勿過多，以免有喧嘩離嘈無法禁止之事。各人均須敬神如在，以靜待所召請者之降臨，蓋旁人說笑猜疑，亦能分乩手之心，使其減少志誠。不能實行『明心入目』四字之精神也。[32]

The section quoted above gives simple yet detailed instructions that explain the manifestation in bodily rather than religious terms. At the same time, setting and outlook nevertheless strongly resemble those in a "phoenix hall," the only specific difference being the exclusion of persons under fifteen years of age. Besides, as the plate points out characters, the participants are expected to be literate.[33] Apart from these practical considerations, scientific terminology is invoked—very much in tune with the scientific fashion of the time—to explain the efficaciousness of the practice. The following quote thus uses acoustic, chemical, optical, and electric theories in reasoning why exactly three participants were most efficient:

> Thunder arises from the discharge of electric energy. If a negative current has the value two, and a positive current has the same value, the two attract and neutralize each other, hence the electricity cannot be released. If the positive current is 3 and the negative 2, a third of the positive current cannot be neutralized, causing its discharge which releases light and thunder. This excess positive current is moreover easily attracted by any nearby negative current, although this attraction is usually not strong. In a round magnet, attraction is minimal, but in a U-shaped magnet that is covered except for its two ends, the attraction is concentrated here, and magnetism manifests itself. The first explanation tells us that when two persons support the stylus, their attraction might neutralize each other, leading to no pull on the object. But if three persons participate, neutralization is no longer possible, and the attraction of the third person is enough to summon the spirit. Just like the excess electricity, this force is particularly powerful. The second explanation shows that if two persons possess equal attraction, the third is like the covered magnet of which only the ends are exposed.

> 放雷，即由電氣激盪而起。如陰電之數量為二，陽電之數量亦為二，則互相吸引而中和，即不能放電。如陽電之數量為三，而陰電之數量為二，則陰陽兩電中和時，陽電有三分之一過剩而被排斥，於是即發

---

32 *Lingji zhimi*, 10–13.
33 Ibid., 14–16.

生放射作用而起雷，又此過剩之一分陽電，最易與他處之陰電互相吸引，若在平時，則其吸引力無如此之強。磁石為圓形時，其吸力甚微，若作U形，而塗其全體，僅露兩端則其吸力皆集中於兩端，而磁性甚顯。由第一說觀之，可知用兩人扶乩，則兩人之吸力適相中和，而不能吸物，惟有三人，則兩人之吸力相中和，而過剩之一人，其吸力方足以感召鬼神，而其力量亦如過剩之電，格外強盛也。由第二說觀之，則以三人扶乩，以兩人之吸力相當，而餘其一人，正如磁石之塗其全體而露其兩端也。[34]

The explanation used the likeness of spirit-writing to electricity and magnetism for a seemingly scientific explanation of why efficacy is highest for three plate holders.

A more systematic effort consisted in the association with Western spiritualism and psychical research, both considered scientific in the standards of the time. An example is the Shanghai Lingxue hui that Yang Xuan 楊璿 (no dates), Lufei Kui 陸費逵 (1886–1941), Ding Fubao 丁福保 (1874–1952), and others founded in 1917. Between 1918 and 1920, their magazine *Lingxue congzhi* 靈學要誌 (Spiritualist magazine) paid much attention to Western spiritualism and presented the new discipline as a serious science.

From the 1860s, the British Society for Psychical Research became known in Japan, and research on hypnosis (*cuimianshu* 催眠術), mesmerism (*chuanqishu* 傳氣術), spiritualism (*lingxue* 靈學), and psychical research (*xinlingxue* 心靈學) began.[35] Chinese students in Japan acquired the Japanese terminology of psychical studies and introduced the topic to China.[36] By the early twentieth century, psychical research had become a global fashion, and hypnosis and psychical research were regarded as advanced scientific disciplines.

In science textbooks of the period, the close connection between psychical research or spiritualism and science is most evident. In the four-volume compendium *The Outline of Science*, which was edited by the Scottish naturalist John Arthur Thomson (1861–1933), chapter 16 in volume 2 was devoted to "Psychic Science."[37] The popular work was immediately translated under chiefeditor Wang Yunwu 王雲五 (1888–1979) and published in 1923 as *Hanyi kexue*

34　Ibid., 18.
35　For the history of spiritualism, psychical research, and mesmerism in Britain, see Oppenheim, *The Other World*; and Winter, *Mesmerized*. For the United States, see, for example, the recent study by Ogden, *Credulity*.
36　Huang, *Wei shi zhi an*, 166. For the Japanese context, see Hardacre, "Asano Wasaburō and Japanese Spiritualism."
37　*The Outline of Science* was a best-selling multi-volume work, which was directed at a popular audience.

dagang 漢譯科學大綱 (Chinese translation of *The Outline of Science*).[38] Sir Oliver Lodge (1851–1940), the author of chapter 16, was a renowned physicist best known as one of the inventors of wireless electrics. He was also a leading member of the British Society for Psychical Research. His involvement was a response to the tragic loss of his son Raymond, who lost his life on the war front on September 14, 1914. In 1916, Lodge published *Raymond or Life and Death*, an account of his communications with his dead son through various mediums. The book became a representative work of experimental psychical research. Chapter 16 of *The Outline of Science* discusses various psychic phenomena, including automatic writing, providing specific examples as well as theoretical explanations. The chapter's translator Lu Zhiwei 陸志韋 (1894–1970) was a psychologist at Dongnan University. He acknowledged his initial reservations concerning the subject, and especially Lodge's use of spiritualist concepts, but concludes: "This chapter is nothing like our spirit-writing altars and their assorted products, and even further from charlatans who pretend the invocation of ghosts and transcendents" (本文內容猶非國內設壇斂貨，假託鬼仙者所可同日語也。).[39] Lu's attitude exemplifies the complex entwinedness of psychic studies with scientific concepts, as well as contemporary attitudes of academic psychology.

With regards to spiritualism and its research in China, two schools may be differentiated, one focussed on hypnosis and evolved to cover clairvoyance (*tianyantong* 天眼通), telepathy (*chuanxinshu* 傳心術), and psychic communication (*xinling tonggan* 心靈感通), and another centred on spirit-mediumship, i.e., communication with ghosts and spirits in the form of language and through the human soul. Proponents of the hypnosis approach were Bao Fangzhou 鮑芳洲 (no dates) and the Zhongguo jingshen yanjiuhui 中國精神研究會 (Chinese Mental Research Society) that he founded, as well as Yu Pingke 余萍客 (no dates) and his Zhongguo xinling yanjiuhui 中國心靈研究會 (Chinese Institute of Mentalism). The leading institution of spirit communication, on the other hand, was the Shengde Altar (Shengde tan 盛德壇) of the Shanghai Lingxue hui. Organizations such as the Institute of Mentalism usually referred to their activities as "psychical research" (*xinlingxue* 心靈學/*xinling yanjiu* 心靈研究) rather than spiritualism, but boundaries were blurry. Propelled by psychic research and spiritualism, spirit-writing by stylus acquired new functions beyond the traditional questions regarding personal fortune, cures against disease, and religious salvation as a central technique to explore phenomena of

---

38 For the Chinese translation, see Tangmusheng, *Hanyi kexue dagang*.
39 Tangmusheng, *Hanyi kexue dagang*, 1–6.

souls and spirits, of life and death, deities and ghosts. Trends in the new field are recorded in periodicals, such as *Lingxue yaozhi* 靈學要誌 (Essentials of spiritualism) and the *Lingxue congzhi*, the magazines published by the Wushan she and the Shanghai Lingxue hui, respectively.[40] Numerous well-known figures showed their interest in the field. An example is Yin Shuixin 印水心 (1883–1968), a native of Yancheng 鹽城 who studied and later taught at the Imperial University of Peking (Jingshi daxuetang 京師大學堂; the fore-runner of Bejing Normal University) and was among the early scholars in contact with Western scientific and technological knowledge. During a visit to Shanghai in 1909, he met Lufei Kui, who at the time worked at Shangwu yinshuguan 商務印書館 (The Commercial Press), and Yu Fu 俞復 (1856–1943), and the three founded the Shanghai Spiritualist Society in 1917. The group held weekly meetings with spirit-writing séances and discussions, actively publishing for several years.

As Chang Pang-yen 張邦彥 has pointed out, the two camps differed in their attitudes towards and knowledge of science and religion, tradition and modernity. Thus, proponents of hypnotism had reservations towards religion, and understood their field as "mental science" (*jingshen kexue* 精神科學) and considered it one way to explore psychic phenomena.[41] Members of the Shanghai Spiritualist Society, on the other hand, advocated the use of spirit-writing to request guidance from Buddhas or transcendents to study spiritualism, in order to make people turn back to traditional ethical values, and thus to offset the erosion of moral foundations caused by the suppression of superstition and the primacy of materialism. Regardless of their attitude towards religion or modernity, however, both camps were subject to criticism by the authors of the journal *New Youth* (*Xin qingnian* 新青年).

Both approaches employed Western scientific practices and vocabulary. The *Lingxue congzhi*, the magazine published by the Lingxue hui, provides an example of how people of the time employed potentially scientific explanations obtained through spirit-writing to highlight the scientific value of the practice as well as to demonstrate their knowledge in the field. One article entitled "Yunwei xianzi 'guang' shuo 雲蔚仙子「光」說" (An examination of light as explained by the Transcendent of the Cloud Rim) entails an elucidation offered by a transcendent on the relationship between visible light and *lingguang* 靈光 (spiritual light), a force associated with supernatural beings in religious lore, which is then interpreted by the recorders of the séance in terms

---

40 Huang, *Wei shi zhi an*, 163. Shiga, *Chūgoku no kokkurisan*, 176–94. Huang, "Minguo chunian Shanghai." For the links between spiritualism (*lingxue*) and China Bookstore, see Wang, "Lufei Kui."

41 Chang, *Jingshen de fudiao*, 50–53.

of nineteenth century optics. The recorded message explains the production and transmission of light as vibrations in a medium or substance identified by a special character that consists of *qi* 气 (breath, energy) in its upper part and *tai* 太 (ultimate) in the lower. The article's author or authors jumped to the conclusion that this referred to ether (*yitai* 以太 or *yitai* 乙太), the then assumed medium of light waves, suggesting that such concepts could be employed to explain spiritual phenomena.[42] Similar added interpretations are frequently met within the magazine.

The *Lingji zhimi* similarly reflects the influence of science when it tries to address objections commonly raised against practices of spirit-mediumship and trying to explain the principles behind spirit-writing by plate. Thus, the authors addressed the objection against literate persons holding the plate, as these would simply pick out the characters. They countered the objection by the difficulty of finding one in 3000 characters and the impossibility of controlling the sudden stop of the whirling plate by a human practitioner. The *Lingji zhimi* discussed a number of approaches popular at the time, such as electricity, psychology, and paralysis in spirit-mediumship, or the question of electric power in human hands; the belief that the plate was particularly easy to move, the issue of whether a paralysed finger would move without discernible pattern, etc. In discussing the question how a plate could move, the writers argued in practical terms that if it was completely ascribed to spirits or ghosts taking possession of it, the process would be too similar to superstition, yet there was no conclusive evidence for attributing the phenomenon entirely to the human spirit either. With regards to the question of how to bring together theories about the human mind, matter, and ghosts and deities, Wang Yishu hoped to explore the world beyond the known with a scientific attitude.[43] His attitude is documented in the following quote in which he explains of the movement of the Numinous Stylus:

> Talking about ghosts and spirits in this scientific age may encourage derision as mere superstition. However, the efficaciousness of the Numinous Stylus cannot be denied, it has been proven effective, as its evidence is placed in front of our very eyes. Just feeling amazed yet not searching for the reason behind it, is being gullible, and unworthy of a person living in the twentieth century. I believe that all matters that can be methodically explained, irrespective of whether their theory is correct or not, can be

---

42 "Yunwei xianzi 'guang' shuo."
43 *Lingji zhimi*, 21.

taken up in research and will ultimately contribute to true understanding. For this reason, I considered it my duty to provide my understanding of the principles of spirit-writing, whether correct or wrong.

在此科學昌明時代，我們還要來談鬼神，這似乎不能免於迷信之譏。但靈乩的靈驗，又是一件很顯明的，擺在眼前的事實，無從否認。現在在事實方面，只覺得他的神奇，而不研究他一個原因，這種囫圇吞棗的方法，也決非二十世紀的人物所應幹。我以為無論什麼事，不管他的理論，是否正當，只要能有條理的說出來，可供大家的研究，則真理終有明白之一日，所以我對於靈乩自動的原理，無論對不對，都應該負責地解釋一下。[44]

Another section asks whether the human body is made of cells only, that in turn consist of protein, iron and other components, or whether another, non-material power exists that commands nerves and cells. Reasoning that "cognition" (*shi* 識) exists independently from matter, the author concludes that the human being's cognizant spirit survives death. Possessing transcendent materiality, the cognizant spirit perceives and feels, yet it has no visible form or audible voice, nor does it rely on a material body. For this reason, the souls of deceased persons can be summoned through spirit-writing. Furthermore, the souls of the recently deceased are easier to summon because their cognizant spirits are comparatively active.[45]

Lingji zhimi is a practical handbook that also covers possible problems in séances. In case the plate fails to move, for example, the guide recommends checking nine aspects: (1) whether the plate holders were truly sincere; (2) whether they were fully focussed; (3) whether they regarded communication with spirits as a mere game; (4) whether the five-character faces on the board and on the plate were fully matching; (5) whether the plate was clean; (6) whether anybody used the index finger of their left hand; (7) whether all wrists were suspended; (8) whether the surroundings were quiet; (9) whether participants were in too much of a hurry. Additional possibilities were that the board was a faulty imitation, or that the participants were not as pure as required. When all factors that could lead to immobility of the plate were excluded, the séance would naturally succeed.[46]

Much of the book's second half is a guide for interpreting the messages, using examples from actual séances. For example, someone who brought a diamond

---

44   Ibid., 21.
45   Ibid., 28–32.
46   Ibid., 34.

and asked whether it was real received in answer the character *tong* 仝 (variant of *tong* 同, together). The participants were bewildered, and only later found the solution by dividing the character into two, i.e. *rengong* 人工 (man-made). Further examples illustrate other approaches, such as the use of a character of similar pronunciation if the intended character was not on the board or if the transcendent being did not know it, reading of one character as several and re-combining several characters into a single character. Examples are *ying* 影 (reflection) used to mean unsubstantial, or *zhong* 仲 (middle brother) for *zhongren* 中人, i.e. a middleman or -woman, to name but a few.[47]

The appendix of the book further contains a writing entitled "Ganying lu 感應錄" (Records of spiritual transmissions) which stemmed from the Chinese Society for Occult Philosophy, and exemplifies the experimental approach adopted in developing the Numinous Stylus. This writing shows that the group invested considerable efforts in proving the effectivity of their method and to exclude aspects that might lead to failure. Thus, in order to establish whether or not pregnant women could participate, they found 29 pregnant women willing to participate in séances. In their experiments, fourteen women suffered from sudden, violent headaches when holding the plate, while nine others developed other complaints. They concluded that pregnant women had better not participate. Another examination focussed on correlations between the year and month of birth and the effectivity of holders of the plate, in which they found that persons born in the year of the tiger frequently were unable to move the plate, and the same applied to persons born in the first month of the year. Moreover, persons for whom the pattern of the eight characters (*bazi geju* 八字格局) used for prognostication included the character *yin* 寅 were also less effective.[48]

Finally, the *Lingji zhimi* contains an appendix of a dozen reader's letters on practical experiences mailed to the publisher Jinwen tang. These indicate that various printed versions of the board were sold on the market before the publication of the book. Thus, one Zhou Decheng 周德澄 (no dates) wrote to express his satisfaction with his original board, advising others to make sure not to buy imitations by making their purchase directly at the Baixin bookstore (Baixin

---

47　Ibid., 35–40.
48　Ibid., 48–51. *Yin* 寅 is one of the Earthly Branches, which, together with the Heavenly Stems, are part of a complex system of calculating time in traditional China. A pair of stem and branch is known as a pillar, and the eight characters system consist of pairs of characters relating to year, month, day, and hour of birth. People who were either born during a year that contained the character *yin* or during a time of day that included *yin*, were considered unlucky.

shuju 百新書局) in Qipanjie 棋盤街, the outlet of the Jinwen tang. A couple of letters were mailed from outside Shanghai, for example from Yangzhou 揚州 in Jiangsu 江蘇, and from Haimen 海門 in Taizhou 台州, Zhejiang 浙江 province, reflecting the regional reach of the Shanghai press and market networks. The letters also show that customers bought the paper board without a plate. A shop owner at the Wanju matou jie 萬聚碼頭街 (Wanju Pier) near the Bund had so many customers buying small plates that he eventually acquired a copy of the paper board to try it out himself.[49]

With its records of experiments and specific technical detail, *Lingji zhimi* can be regarded as a response to May Fourth scientism. Whether it truly accorded to scientific standards is not the issue. As Chang Pang-yen's observations on hypnosis and psychical research have shown, being "scientific" in modern China was a claim to advanced status established by using the appropriate expressions, and closely connected to modernist and nationalist discourse. In the West as in East Asia, disciplines such as spiritualism and psychical research caused a debate, demonstrating the complexity and diversity of "science," depending on the perspective of the respective historical actors. The core aspect that requires attention here is how actors overcame their passive role as recipients of knowledge and constructed a scientific framework that provided room for flexibility and creativity.[50]

This creative process through which science was constructed at the time becomes visible, for example, in the different explanations that scholars of different disciplines provided for the principles underlying the movement of the stylus or plate. An anonymous article reflecting on the Scientific Numinous Stylus exemplifies this diversity of modernist, comparative discourse as well as the fluid borders between psychology and para-psychology:

> The Scientific Numinous Stylus is a toy of bored scholarly types, just as women entertain themselves by inviting the Purple Maiden.[51] It is also similar to the "Magic Pendulum"—to mention one of many comparable forms formerly popular in the West. Everybody knows about spirit-writing, and all have stories about characters written in the sand, of essays composed, of questions answered. Explained by modern psychology, these phenomena result from "Automatic Action." Irrespective of our conscious thoughts, the unconscious expresses itself in bodily move-

---

49 Ibid., 62–70.
50 Chang, *Jingshen de fudiao*, 47–51.
51 On the deity Purple Maiden and its link to spirit-writing, see the contributions by Hu Jiechen and Elena Valussi in this volume.

ments and hence leads to so-called automatic action. If this action is transmitted to the stylus, the pendulum or the plate, the objects will move, commonly following the person's innermost intentions. Thus, the objects are nevertheless moved by a human hand. Without relying on the human hand, ideas cannot be transmitted, and no object can possibly be set in motion.

科學靈乩」是和我國無聊文人所玩的扶乩，閨閣中所玩的請紫姑，是一樣的把戲。與古代西洋人所謂的「魔擺」(Magic Pendulum) 尤其相像。(其他同類的花樣還很多。) 扶乩是大家都知道的，有時很能在沙盤上寫幾個字，做幾名文章答人所問 ... 其實照現在心理學上的話解釋起來，這個現象卻完全出由於「自動作用」(Automatic Action)。原來我們心中不論懷了什麼思想，總不免於不知不覺之中，在身體上表露出來，發為動作，這名為自動作用。其動力傳於乩棒，魔擺，或靈乩之碟，於是那棒，擺或碟，亦便自起動作。且往往和心中的思想相符合。所以乩棒魔擺靈乩之碟，其所以能動，仍然是由於人手之自動。假使不藉人手，人的思想便無從傳達，那棒擺或碟是決不會動的。[52]

To this writer, psychology with its differentiation between conscious and subconscious levels in the human mind provides a rational explanation for techniques of spirit-mediumship. The persons holding stylus, pendulum, or plate were not consciously moving them, yet subconsciously wished to answer the question asked and thus produced an answer without being aware of what they were doing. The subconscious can be highly perspicacious, even more so than conscious thought and thus possess knowledge that the person is unaware of. Psychology provides examples for this phenomenon. Thus, the texts written by the stylus may be well above the stylus holder's conscious knowledge level. Similarly, while onlookers find it difficult to locate characters on the board used for the Numinous Stylus, those who hold the plate might be able to spot them instantly. Huang Yi, a renowned psychologist who held a professorship at Zhejiang University from 1930 to his death in 1944, explained spirit-writing in a similar fashion as a psychological phenomenon.[53]

Placing spirit-writing and the Numinous Stylus within the context of early twentieth century spiritualism and psychical research thus also invites reflection on the differing fate of two closely connected scholarly disciplines. In the early twentieth century, psychical research was devoted to the study of

---

52 "'Kexue lingji,'" *Shenbao*, May 1. The article was published anonymously.
53 Huang, "Diexian yu xianglei xianxiang zhi xinli de jieshi," 181.

the paranormal, whereas psychology researched common physiological experiences and activities. While the formation of the two fields dates to approximately the same period, their trajectories differed. Experimental psychology became an established academic discipline, whereas psychical research withered. Behaviourist psychology established through animal experiments fully fulfils the evidential standard of repeatable experiments, whereas the same is not achievable in psychic studies, which led to the gradual decline in this discipline's recognition.[54]

3 The Craze for the Transcendent of the Plate and the Shanghai Publishing Market

The Shanghai media coverage of the Scientific Numinous Stylus in 1934 demonstrates the great attraction of a technology that promised answering all questions. The Transcendent of the Plate, considerably easier to use than regular spirit-writing, became part of daily life. Sales of the board were remunerative, and numerous printers, publishers, bookstores, and other retailers entered this market. In addition to Jinwen tang, advertisements identify Xinguang shuju 新光書局 on North Sichuan Road (Bei Sichuan lu 北四川路), which advertised "Shenjun tuqi, kexue ling jj tu 神軍突起，科學靈乩圖" (The board of the Scientific Numinous Stylus—a rising spirit army), sold through eight outlets in Shanghai.[55] The connection between the publishing market—especially the publisher Jinwen tang—and the Transcendent of the Plate is therefore worth further examination.

Jinwen tang was a general publishing house that printed everything from the traditional four subjects of classics, history, ethics, and literary collections as well as public and private publications, religious and morality books, textbooks, and books in Western languages. It employed woodblock print, typo, and photo-lithography for printing. Its stores also sold stationary goods, calligraphy, fiction, magazines, prognostication materials and more. The company moreover collected old manuscripts, ancient books, and historic woodblocks for reprinting. It offered almost everything, at fair quality and at "quite modest wholesale prices" (批發亦較從廉). A list of titles distributed at the outlet store on Sima 四馬 Road in Shanghai confirms the broad range and considerable number of titles as well as the cheap pricing. The proclaimed aim was "a dedi-

---

54   Jinisi, *Xinlingxue*, 401–8.
55   "Shenjun tuqi kexue lingji tu."

FIGURE 6.3
Advertisment by Jinwen tang in the *Shenbao*, April 30, 1934, 10

cation to our task as cultural mediators and thus to advance the sharp tools of new knowledge, to minimise the economic burden of book buyers, and to contribute to general education and culture" (以盡介紹文化之職責,藉為輸送新智識之利器,減輕讀者購書負擔,普遍民眾文化教育). In fact, the company used low pricing to enlarge its market share. In a discount catalogue that Jinwen tang distributed to its readers in 1934—with the professed goal of reaching 50,000 of them, *Lingji zhimi* and the board for the Scientific Numinous Stylus were among the titles listed.[56]

The above-quoted advertisement of Xinguang shuju on the "rising spirit army" appeared on April 29, 1934. The very next day, Jinwen tang placed its own announcement. It stated that the Chinese Society of Occult Philosophy of Guangzhou offered the only original boards for the Scientific Numinous Stylus, which the publisher guaranteed to be efficacious with the right of return. It further provided four outlet addresses and warned against fakes that would leave customers with a loss. The "true original board" (*shichuang zhen tu* 始創真圖) was offered at 0.24 *yuan* or 0.33 *yuan* for mailing orders inclusive of postal

---

56   The book is included in Liu, *Minguo shiqi chuban shumu huibian*, vol. 16, 158–66.

THE TRANSCENDENT OF THE PLATE 235

fees. Users were invited to share their experience, with remuneration offered for submissions received by May 6.[57] We may safely assume that the letters printed in the appendix of *Lingji zhimi* are the responses to this announcement. In fact, it appears possible that the book was compiled to prove the originality of the board. An analysis of other advertisements of the period shows that Jinwentang's board was 0.04 yuan above the competition. Apart from Xinguang, other vendors existed in Shanghai, such as the Qishu yanjiuhui 奇術研究會 (Shanghai Research Society for Paranormal Arts), which advertised "With a single finger, automatic spirit-writing can answer all your questions and allows you to talk to the souls of the deceased" (神指一枚，能自動扶乩指示各事，可召亡魂談話), all for 0.2 *yuan*.[58] Relative to other commodity prices of the 1930s, the price was modest, as a daily newspaper cost 0.03 *yuan*, and 0.24 *yuan* would buy a good pound of pork. Competition soon led to a price war. A group that called itself the Xinling she 心靈社 (Mentalist Society) also sold a board, claiming that it was 100% effective and sold for only 0.16 *yuan* in stamps. Considering the low production costs of a printed sheet of coarse paper, the margins were high and the sliding price an inevitable trend, once businessmen got wind of the opportunity and joined the race.

By early May, boards for the Scientific Numinous Stylus appear as promotional gifts. As a conversational topic and a low-cost product, they were well suited to induce customers' interest and encourage other purchases. Sanxing 三星 Books, another Shanghai publisher, announced the distribution of 10,000 copies of the board for all purchases of over 0.5 *yuan* in celebration of its tenth anniversary.[59] Chunming 春明 Bookstore gave a free copy for all purchases upwards of 1 *yuan*. This publisher also claimed that its board was the original and permitted "conversing as if talking to a living person" (談話對答一如活人). To encourage loyalty, customers who possessed a board could exchange the promotional gift for a reading mark in the shape of a girl that was "preciously rare, wavy, and attractive" (萬金難覓、浪態動人).[60] The Minghua 明華 bookstore offered *Mingyun guwen* 命運顧問 (Consultations on fate), a book on the prognostication of professional success, together with a Numinous Stylus board for the package price of 0.6 *yuan*.[61] In and beyond Shanghai, the marketing campaign from late April to mid-May 1934 fanned a major craze for the

---

57 "Kexue lingji tu renqing."
58 See the advertisement "Kexue lingji," published in *Shenbao* on May 1 and again on May 9, 1934, on page 15.
59 See "Sanxing shuju chuangye shizhou jinian."
60 "Zengsong kexue lingji tu yi zhang."
61 "Shanghai Minghua shuju."

Transcendent of the Plate. The religious aspects and the mystery in inviting deities and communicating with transcended beings gave way to urban entertainment.

The phenomenon invited contemporary reflection, especially by journalists of the Shanghai press. A journalist writing under the pen-name Jiaxiang 嘉湘 commented that as curiosity had always been a Shanghai characteristic, possibly because of its large idle class, when the Scientific Numinous Stylus became fashionable "Shanghainese curiosity turned into a craze. ... Perceptive businesspeople cater to this Shanghainese disposition by coming up with new toys by the day, thus to expand their business" (好奇的上海人簡直要為此而瘋狂了 … 商人們識穿了上海人的心理，於是日日在想著變換新的玩意兒，來推廣他們的營業).[62] In the urban atmosphere permeated with business, money, and foreign flair, the Transcendent of the Plate, sailing under the flag of Western science, became yet another new toy.[63]

There were also voices of open mockery. On May 15, *Shenbao* carried a satire, entitled "Kexue lingji ji qita 科學靈乩及其他" (The Scientific Numinous Stylus and other matters) by an author using the pen-name Xizhen 席珍. The tone is set by presenting spirit-writing as the "divine yellow wind blowing over Shanghai" (神聖的黃色的風吹到了上海). The article depicts the "numinous" (*ling* 靈) mixing with coal fumes, rubbish, and cheap cosmetics, and stacks of yellow paper crammed on each newspaper stand, bookstall, and peddling tray. It describes the board as half of a learner's dictionary arranged in a circle, with a face in the centre that appears to be 30% human and 70% ghost, the whole claiming to be one of the great modern inventions, and completed by slogans, such as "the perfect scientific method" (完全科學方法), "eradicate superstition" (*pochu mixin* 破除迷信), "A single try proves its efficacy" (靈不靈一試便知), "communication with ghosts in three minutes" (三分鐘人鬼通話), or "the Scientific Numinous Stylus for 0.2 yuan" (科學靈乩每份祇售大洋二角). The author ridiculed the craze for the Transcendent of the Plate by implying Shanghainese thoughts, hopes, and dreams were "yellow" (*huang se* 黃色), which also denotes sex, throughout, hence the great attraction of a yellow sheet of paper that claimed to be a product of Western science. He added that sales surpassed those of *Ziye* 子夜 (Midnight), the most famous novel of the period, some five to six times, and that among the buyers were students, young ladies, grandmothers, aunties, and rickshaw men. By this evidence, the Scientific Numinous Stylus was indeed the greatest of scientific achievements.[64]

---

62 Jiaxiang, "Tiaodou."
63 Ye, *Shanghai shehui*, 418–19.
64 Xizhen, "Kexue lingji."

Xizhen's sarcasm and sometimes coarse humour was widespread in Chinese media of the period, entwining laughter and hardship. The background to the phenomenon was the need for brisk expansion in the highly competitive publishing market. In the 1930s, the *Shenbao* reached a circulation of 150,000, while in 1935 the publishing trade centred on Fuzhou Road comprised over 400 publishers and bookstores. Readers liked captivating stories, and the paranormal communication between humans and ghosts evidently made for a good topic of daily conversation.[65]

The records from séances in *Lingji zhimi* also contain questions concerning business investments, ship passages, lottery results, and even one asking the name of a spouse's lover. The Transcendent of the Plate was apparently willing to answer any question. A case in point is the movie star Ai Xia 艾霞 (1912–1934), who had suffered from unrequited love and ended her live on February 12, 1934. Many questions were asked to find out more about her suicide, making the transcendent into a tool for haunting ghosts in the afterlife.[66]

Reports from mid-May 1934 furthermore reflect the troubling effects of the craze. Women who gambled requested guidance from the Transcendent of the Plate, and set large sums on the indicated characters. Major losses in some cases shattered lives.

An article by Hu Tiandao 胡天道 (no dates) in *Chongminbao* 崇民報 of May 27 gives further information on dissemination and pricing. It relates that the Transcendent of the Plate became popular in Guangzhou in spring 1933, reaching Shantou 汕頭 in northern Guangdong by summer. The local price was 0.4 *yuan*, but soon began sliding. Hu denounced the board as an attempt to cheat people of poor judgement under the "guise of science" (藉著科學的美名) and expressed his conviction that it would soon be forgotten. He expressly warned traders in Shanghai to leave their hands off this product to avoid painful losses.[67]

Contrary to Hu's prediction, the excitement in Shanghai showed no sign of abating. In early June, the editor of the readers' corner in the *Shenbao* found himself inundated with letters on the Transcendent of the Plate. Within a couple of weeks, these had increased to half of all submissions. He announced that all letters on the topic would be discarded, adding that anyone with general knowledge knew that ghosts and superstition under the guise of science were

---

65 Lei, *Da bujing de niandai*, 37–38.
66 *Lingji zhimi*, pt. 6.
67 Hu, "Kexue lingji."

no more than opium for the people.[68] The fears expressed in *Lingji zhimi* that the technique would be misunderstood had come true.

Over the summer, criticism intensified. Newspaper journalists showed themselves particularly infuriated by the claim of this technique being scientific. Some years earlier, Lu Xun 魯迅 (1881–1936) had expressed his dejection that new systems, disciplines, or concepts upon arriving in China were dropped into black dye; they all came out stained, and science was no different.[69] An article entitled "Kexue huo 科學禍" (A scientific calamity) in the *Shenbao* denounced spirit-writing as a game under scientific pretence:

> Let us look at the facts: We still pray for rain, we chant incantations, we like fortune telling and spirit-writing. These practices are popular everywhere, showing that the brains of our nation are still in a state of confusion, lacking the desire for understanding as well as lacking basic scientific analytical abilities. If you tell someone that he is unscientific, he turns his magic device and immediately finds a scientific hat for it to wear, hence we have scientific fortune telling and the Scientific Numinous Stylus.

> 試把事實看看：我們國裡還是祈雨、打醮、算命、扶乩一類事件，到處風行，我們民族的頭腦，還停滯在一種模糊影響，不求甚解的形而上學的憧憬中，而沒有一般水平以上的明晰的科學頭腦。你說他不科學，他靈機一轉，立刻將科學帽子，戴在各種舊把戲上，便有科學算命，科學靈乩等出現。[70]

The background to the above critique were the multiple and deepening crises of the period. Japanese expansion put China under pressure, with the Manchukuo regime set up as thinly veiled colonial regime in northeastern China. Politics directly affected Shanghai in the January 28, 1932 incident, that led to over a month of military confrontation in and near Shanghai. Moreover, the Yangtze area experienced the worst drought in sixty years that caused serious famine in 1934. Prayers for rain were held in many places and organised by people from all walks of life. A famous example of the phenomena that Lu Xun criticized was the foundation of the Kālacakra Dharma Society (Shilun jingang fahui 時輪金剛法會) in Shanghai on March 11, 1934. Leading politicians, such as Dai Jitao 戴季陶 (1891–1949), Chu Minyi 褚民誼 (1884–1946), Ju Zheng 居正 (1876–1951), and others invited the Panchen Lama to Hangzhou 杭州 to inaugurate

---

68   A'ping, "Ziyoutan."
69   Lu, "Huabian wenxue, ougan." 479–80.
70   Zhaozhao, "Kexue huo."

the society. Huang Fu 黃郛 (1880–1936), Zhang Qun 張群 (1889–1990), and Zhang Xueliang 張學良 (1901–2001) supported the initiative and Chiang Kai-shek 蔣介石 (1887–1975) himself sent a cable to the Hangzhou city government. On April 28, the Ninth Panchen Lama held the altar opening ceremony at the Lingyin Temple (Lingyin si 靈隱寺), chanting sutras to pray for an end of the natural disaster and for peace on earth. The scale of the event caused considerable excitement as well as intense criticism. Journalists criticised both the Kālacakra Dharma Society and the Numinous Stylus as superstitious activities that were intolerable in the present age of science.[71]

Cenlou 岑樓, another author using a pen-name, reflects on the tragedies of his period by ridiculing the Scientific Numinous Stylus as well as the turn to tantric Buddhism. He begins bitterly: if three persons can make a plate move and point out characters, this miraculously easy method of requesting divine help should "amply equip us to beat back Japanese dumdum bullets and 500-pound airplane bombs" (我們就足以打倒日本達姆達姆彈以及五百磅飛機炸彈而有餘). Following the reference to the bombing of Shanghai in 1932, the author continues by outlining the ruin of rural and urban productive industries and the helplessness of the country in the face of imperialist aggression. He explains the popularity of the Scientific Numinous Stylus by pointing to the situation of ordinary urbanites who are left with no perspective for the future, and therefore turn to illusion for comfort and self-anesthetization as a path of escape. As the powerful have their Kalachakra Society, the ordinary citizens have their Scientific Numinous Stylus; two seemingly different, yet closely related trends. The article provides a perceptive dissection of salvation seeking among different social strata living under the shadow of war.[72]

The craze for the Scientific Numinous Stylus was not confined to Shanghai, but occurred in other places where conditions appeared profitable. Records of the Guomindang 國民黨 (Chinese Nationalist Party) government document the phenomenon for Nanjing 南京. The party ideology used superstition as a label of damnation, and the party leadership of Jiangsu province soon noticed the boards in the print market. A report stated that "in fact these promote the superstition of spirit-writing under the guise of science and should be classed as spirit-possession instead" (實為藉名科學，提倡扶乩迷信，已類巫祝方士所為), yet found the accompanying booklet even more deviant. Insisting that the human mind could be fully explained by natural sciences and that the

---

71   "Kexue zaoyu yu shetan zaoyu 科學造語與設壇造語—答朱明君." *Shenbao*, July 26, 1934, 15. See also Goossaert, "1898," and Goossaert and Palmer, "Introduction," for a thorough discussion of how the concept of "superstition" unfolded its influence in China.

72   Cenlou, "Kexue lingji."

soul did not exist, and as part of advancing scientific knowledge as well as the New Life Movement (Xin shenghuo yundong 新生活運動), the party ordered provincial and local authorities to strictly ban distribution through bookstores and -stalls in order to halt the spread of this superstition poison.[73]

According to the *Zhongyang ribao* 中央日報 (Central daily) of May 30, 1934, the Department of Social Affairs (Shehui ju 社會局) collected 177 boards when implementing the ban in Nanjing. The department, which attached considerable importance to matters concerning superstition, sent out inspectors to ensure that business was not resumed, while announcing that any infringement would be punished.[74] In February, Chiang Kai-shek had launched the New Life Movement, an attempt to rally the population for the coming war with Japan, and at the same time to reorganize daily life with the goal of creating "new citizens" (*xin guomin* 新國民). An author writing under the pen-name Zhengren 征人 published "Xin shenghuo yundong zhong de guai xianxiang 新生活運動中的怪現象" (Strange phenomena in the New Life Movement) that conceded that "you could call the toy really seductive, yet if you allow free reign to this evil omen for our nation, the Scientific Numinous Stylus could indeed become a fateful demon" (說這玩意，真玩的迷人，興許是國家的不祥之兆，科學靈乩沒准是妖孽).[75]

Lei Hsiang-lin 雷祥麟 has noted that while the May Fourth movement elevated "Mister Science" (Sai xiansheng 賽先生) on a pedestal, effects were greatest on the "invisible" level, namely in the rejection of metaphysics (*xuanxue* 玄學) and superstition.[76] Hu Shi 胡適 (1891–1962) and others called for the building of a "scientific outlook on human life" (*kexue de renshengguan* 科學的人生觀) that would be built on "scientific knowledge" (*kexue zhishi* 科學知識) and "known facts" (*yizhi de shishi* 已知的事實). Contributions by Zhang Junmai 張君勱 (1887–1969), Ding Wenjiang 丁文江 (1887–1936), and Hu Shi in the debate between science and metaphysics that began in 1923 show the two positions too far apart to engage at any point. With science regarded as either useless to real life or omnipotent, the debate could not reach any meaningful conclusion. At the same time, however, the force of science manifested itself in the process through which knowledge penetrated into real life.

In the dissemination of the Transcendent of the Plate in the Shanghai media, we can observe a gradual prevalence of scientific psychological knowledge. Psychology came to concede the reality of the movement of the plate, but only as

---

73 "Chajin kexue lingji tu."
74 "Kexue lingji tu Shehui ju jinzhi chushou."
75 Zhengren, "Cong kexue lingji shuoqi."
76 Lei, "Yinxing de Sai xiansheng."

a result of the subconscious. This interpretation reduced the Transcendent of the Plate to entertainment. Five years after the craze, students brought up the topic in a class taught by the renowned psychologist Zhang Huixiang 張耀翔 (1893–1964). Zhang flew into a rage so impressive that it made it into the news.[77]

From June 1932, the Scientific Numinous Stylus was banned in Jiangsu and Zhejiang. However, small-time traders in the foreign concessions of Shanghai still did brisk business and continued advertising the method of communication with souls, even of persons who had been dead for many years.[78] Towards the end of the year, newspapers reported that the designers of the board had made thirty to forty thousand *yuan*.[79]

From 1935, newspaper coverage dwindled, either because the craze had passed or suppression showed results. The remaining undeterred users were usually persons who grieved for family members or friends. The most famous of these was Gao Chuiwan 高吹萬 (1879–1958) of the Southern Society (Nanshe 南社), who had to bury his daughter Yunfen 韻芬 at a young age. Around 1937, he began a conversation using the Transcendent of the Plate that he carried on for over a year and recorded in his edited diaries. Wu Lingyuan 吳靈園 (no dates), the editor of the daily paper *Shibao* 時報 (Eastern Times), had Gao's impressions of the world after death serialized in his paper, with considerable success. He expressed the hope that "in this scientific age" (*kexue de shidai* 科學的時代) the issue of ghosts and spirits might be one day resolved by scientific means.[80] Another, less known case is Liu Danming's 劉瞻明 (no dates) *Xinling tonggan lu* 心靈感通錄 (Records of spiritual communication).

4 The *Xinling tonggan lu* 心靈感通錄 (Record of Spiritual Communication) as a Source on Technological Differences between Spirit-Writing by Stylus and Plate

Regarding the technologies of spirit-writing by stylus and plate, the examination of the accounts in the *Lingji zhimi* has shown the connectedness of the two forms in that Wang Yishu received instructions through spirit-writing by stylus. Although newspaper articles occasionally touch on differences between the two techniques, insider material by religious practitioners can offer more

---

77   Qingfeng, "Xinli xuejia Zhang Yaoxiang."
78   Shiyu, "Kexue lingji."
79   Folang, "Tan mixin."
80   Gao, *Chuiwan lou riji jiechao*, 1.

precise information. In fact, the suppression by the Guomindang government did not mark the end for the Transcendent of the Plate. Gao Chuiwan and other believers continued to practice and investigate the practice, also paying attention to technical differences between the stylus and the plate. Liu Danming's work is representative of these efforts.

The book of 107 pages was published in September 1943 by the Buddhist Dafalun shuju 大法輪書局 (Great Wheel of the Dharma Publishing House). The author records exchanges with transcendent beings, messengers of the nether world, and the souls of dead persons.[81] Liu Danming hailed from Hefei 合肥 and was the grandson of Liu Mingchuan 劉銘傳 (1836–1896), the first provincial governor of Taiwan. He was a lay Buddhist who studied with Yinguang 印光 (1862–1940), Xuyun 虛雲 (?–1959), and other masters, as reflected in exchanges with Yinguang in *Yinguang wenchao* 印光文鈔 (Yinguang's collected manuscripts). Liu fled to Shanghai in 1940, where his son Wenting 文頲 (no dates) suddenly fell ill and died. Together with Li Boqi 李伯琦 (1887–1958), who was the great-grandson of the late Qing statesman Li Hongzhang 李鴻章 (1823–1901) and had also recently lost his son, he turned to the Transcendent of the Plate. At first, however, the plate stayed immobile. As Wang Yishu before him, Liu Danming turned to an acquaintance, Li Angheng 李仰衡 (no dates), a lay Buddhist well versed in spirit-writing. Advised to prepare by cleansing his mind and quieting his thought, Liu gradually succeeded at making the plate move. At first, it indicated only single characters, the meaning of which were hardly decipherable. Subsequently, séances proceeded more smoothly. Liu's skilfully written account provides a vivid and detailed, almost visual image of the experience of over one hundred held séances, 77 of which are recorded in the book.

When the transcendent descended into the plate, he introduced himself as Tao Langting 陶朗庭, a late Ming official who gave his life in defending his dynasty and after death became an immortal food envoy, a spirit of food and drink, as he explained. When Liu Danming and the other participants expressed their surprise that an immortalised historic person had descended to their plate, whereas this was not known from other séances, Tao explained that the reason was that Liu Danming was half-believing, half-sceptical. Asked about Wu Dingyun 吳鼎雲 (no dates), Liu's master who had passed away, the food envoy answered that Wu had already been reborn to a family in Shili 十里 village west of Xuzhou 徐州, that his father was Jun Juhou 金鞠侯 and he was now five years old. Liu Danming and his friends used this specific address to

---

81   Liu, *Xinling gantong lu*, 95–301.

ask an acquaintance to make inquiries about the Jin family, concealing the origin of the information. When they received a letter confirming the facts, they regarded this as iron proof of reincarnation.

Through the food envoy, Liu Danming began inquiring about his son Wenting, who was in his thoughts day and night. Initially, his questions were similar to those of Gao Chuiwan, covering obvious topics, such as his well-being in the nether world, whether he had received the spirit-money burnt for him, or where to best place food offerings. Answers gradually provide an outline of Wenting's situation in the nether world. When Wenting was appointed to an official position, the participants began asking broader questions, such as what the body was like in the nether world, what deities actually were,[82] whether Master Yinguang had already departed for the Pure Land in the West, and even whether science would one day succeed in making human flesh. The transcendent answered all questions, providing quite rational, insightful answers. *Xinling gantong lu* can be regarded as an attempt at convincing readers of the existence of the transcendent world. As other works of this kind, it aimed at extolling belief in the unfathomable mysteries of the Dharma, and thus at awakening its readers' Buddhist faith and lead them to a moral life. While it was not fully compatible with the more orthodox views of the Buddhist publishing house, Chen Wuwo 陳無我 (1884–1967) proposed that for the Dharma to prevail, it would be necessary to first "prove the existence of the human, the heavenly, and the nether world" (徵實人天幽明之故) to awaken the masses from their state of confusion and enable them to enter the path of enlightenment. He therefore serialized Liu Danming's account in the semi-monthly magazine *Jueyouqing banyuekan* 覺有情半月刊 (Awakening all living creatures biweekly) that he edited.[83] If *Lingji zhimi* may be called the operation manual of spirit-writing by plate, *Xinling gantonglu* is the result report.

If we come back to the question in how far spirit-writing by stylus and plate differed, we already learned that the plate emerged from the stylus. The specific differences, however, require further analysis. Looking at contemporary sources from the 1930s provides further clues. An article in the *Shenbao*, for example, discusses both techniques:

---

82   They specifically mention two deities, the Venerable Patriarch (Laozu 老祖), the main deity of the Daoyuan 道院, a redemptive society, and the Wusheng Laomu 無生老母 (Venerable Eternal Mother). For more information on these deities, see the contributions by Xia Shi and Nikolas Broy in this volume.
83   Chen Wuwo 陳無我, "Ba 跋," in Liu, *Xinling gantong lu*, 299.

The so-called "Scientific Numinous Stylus" is admirable for precisely its scientific character, yet I also see reasons for considering it more progressed than old-style spirit-writing. In the old form, "characters" had to be written and it could not be "efficacious" (*ling*) without a degree of fraudulence, while the new form needs none of this. Furthermore, as two persons sitting opposite each other wield the stylus, their force is equal, and unless one of them intentionally uses greater force, movement is difficult, whereas the new form only requires participants to keep a finger on the plate, which is easy on the hands and for movement. For both reasons, the new form is far more frequently "efficacious."

所謂"科學靈乩"之玄妙即在於此，但我說它較舊式扶乩進化者亦有理由。舊式必書出"字"，不作偽即不"靈"，而此則無須；舊式用二人對立握乩桿，力易平均，若一方不故意用力，甚難運動，而此則之指按底，易於手痠和運動。所以"靈"的部份要比舊式多得了。[84]

With regard to the instruments, the author recognizes clear improvement. Believers such as Liu Danming, however, had a different view on the matter, especially on fraudulence. As a student of Yinguang, Liu would obviously have been aware that his teacher rejected spirit-writing. Yinguang regarded it as a technique that gave any spirit or ghost the opportunity to pretend they were divine beings, and through which they would use their spiritual knowledge of what people wished, and would show them exactly that, thereby misleading them.[85] Proving the veracity of the Transcendent of the Plate thus was crucial in asserting its superiority. Liu Danming wrote:

> In recent times, European and American scholars used mediums in their spiritual research, as the English author Yuesefen advocates in *On the Edge of the Etheric* states.[86] Unfortunately, his method has not been introduced to China yet. Apart from the latter, all [Western] methods that use writing to communicate with ghosts and deities are far inferior to spirit-writing. With regards to spirit-writing, two forms exist, the stylus

---

84 Bianzhe, "Kexue lingji."
85 *Yinguang fashi wenchao*, vol. 1, 268–69. As for Yinguang's view on spirit-writing, see Wang, "Jindai Zhongguo de fuji." 533–59.
86 It seems that Liu misattributed this work. A book under that title was published by James Arthur Findlay in Chinese as Yueqin Fentelai 約瑟·芬特萊, *Renling jiaotong ji* 人靈交通記 (Communication between humans and souls) in 1933 by the Xinshijie xinwenshe 世界新聞社. The original English publication dates to 1931.

and the Transcendent of the Plate. The former is in the tradition of the flying phoenix, requiring incantations and the setting up of an altar; making it unsuitable for spontaneous séances. The Transcendent of the Plate originated in the West and was introduced to China. It consists of an extra-large sheet of mulberry paper with a face in the centre and several thousand characters written in small regular script in circles around it, called the stylus board. In addition, a small plate, about two inches across, is needed, upon which the face is drawn just like on the board. The plate is turned upside down and placed on the board and three or two persons lightly place the middle fingers on it. After a long time, the plate starts whirling about, which shows the arrival of the ghosts and deities. Using this technique is easier than the stylus on sand, and fraud is more difficult.

近世歐美人士，研求靈學，有所謂靈媒者，英吉利人約瑟芬，為《人靈交通記》以張之，惜其術未至我國，捨此三者，假文字因緣，通鬼神情狀，莫尚乎乩矣，乩有二，一曰沙盤，二曰碟仙，沙盤為飛鸞遺法，憑符籙，建壇場，非隨時隨地可以為之，碟仙創自歐西，流傳中土，其法以巨楮寫靈像於中，細楷數千，周匝圍繞，成圓形，謂之乩圖，更取徑二寸碟，繪像如圖形，覆其上，扶著三人或二人，出中指輕按碟底，久之碟自旋轉，則所召之鬼神至矣，行法簡易於沙乩，而難於作偽。[87]

The above quote juxtaposes the relative inflexibility of spirit-writing by stylus against the simple operation of the plate, while emphasizing that the latter was also safer from fraudulence. Liu Danming is known to have discussed the different techniques of spirit-writing with friends. One of these was Ding Guijiao 丁桂樵 (1886–1952), who hailed from Changsha 長沙 in Hunan, had studied in Japan and become an educator after returning to China. Ding entered politics during the founding years of the Republic, but became disillusioned. Aged thirty, he moved to Shanghai and lived a hermit life dedicated to Pure Land Buddhism. He frequently used spirit-writing by stylus to explore the world of ghosts and deities.[88] According to Ding's opinion, fraudulent use of the plate was indeed more difficult than of the stylus. The reason was that manipulation in spirit-writing by stylus could simply be achieved by preparing an answer in advance and then simply recording it silently. The same was far more difficult with the plate because it moved at great speed:

---

87 Liu, *Xinling gantong lu*, 107.
88 Ibid., 170.

Now the plate points out characters while whirling around, it stops dead when the spiritual power breaks off, and jumps when it reconnects. Someone wanting to manipulate it for fun, would have to prepare an answer, and find the characters on the board. His head would swim after scanning a few circles. Fraud cannot be entirely excluded, but the situation is very different from the stylus on sand. Because the signalling of the arrival of the spirit and the formation of the characters all take place through the hands of the practitioners and are therefore linked to their minds. If the practitioners are able to empty their mind from all worldly concerns, leaving the plate to move on its own, characters will appear in the sand, forming sentences, as if a dike is breached and water flows forth. In this case all messages will be true, yet the quality of the writing and the depth of the meaning are a different matter.

蓋碟乩指字，左右盤旋，靈之塞者其乩滯，靈之通者其乩軼，有心作偽以嬉者，預置篇章，按圖尋繹，不待數匝，已目眩而頭岑岑矣。遑論乎無心之偽，而沙盤則不然，降神者憑於乩，應於手，形於文字，無不與扶者心靈相貫攝，果能萬綠空寂，一念不生，任其木筆知自動，畫沙為字，綴字成文，若決江河，沛然莫禦，是皆純真無偽，而文之工拙，義之淺深，皆不之計也。[89]

Xinling gantong lu contains a chapter entitled "Diexian yu shapan butong 碟仙與沙盤不同" (Where the Transcendent of the Plate and the stylus on sand differ) that discusses the qualitative differences between the two techniques. Liu Danming considered fraud to be relatively common in séances using the stylus, but differentiated between conscious and unconscious manipulations, the latter being worked by the soul rather than the one supporting the stylus, and being a consequence of the fact that even souls can be malevolent and immoral. In séances using the plate, messages result from the connection of several minds, due to the involvement of several plate holders. As positive examples of whole works obtained through spirit-writing by plate, he names *Dongming baoji* 洞冥寶記 (Precious records from the nether world) and *Pantao mingji* 蟠桃宴記 (Records from the nether world on the peach of immortality), two publications printed by the Shaoshan 紹善 Altar in Eryuan 洱源 in Western Yunnan 雲南. In his opinion, these writings matched the marvels of *Xiyou ji* 西遊記 (The journey to the West), yet he concedes that non-believers in retribu-

---

89   Ibid., 173.

THE TRANSCENDENT OF THE PLATE 247

tion might find them ridiculous and draw the opposite conclusion.[90] It may be added that Gao Chuiwan held similar views on the two forms of spirit-writing.[91]

A further core issue was the fact that spirit-writing by stylus usually invited Immortals and Buddhas, whereas the Transcendent of the Plate was commonly used for communication with the souls of the dead. For this reason, it might appear that deities would come only to the stylus. As contemporaries had no answer to this question, Liu Danming asked his son in the afterlife, who explained that high-ranking deities in fact do not personally come to altars practicing spirit-writing on sand but "as the living pray so earnestly, they look at them from afar and send a few words" (世人誠意祈禱之，仙神遙之，即示某某文言). The words would be sent down, much like a telegraph. In spirit-writing by plate, however, control from afar was impossible, the transcendent being had to be present and moreover he or she had to have some connection with the summoning person.[92] Hence, neither technique could attract the immediate presence of deities, but spirit-writing by stylus could at least receive their messages.

5 Conclusion: The Two Technical Reforms in Spirit-Writing

In his book *Mixin* 迷信 (Superstition), Fei Hongnian 費鴻年 (1900–1993) stated boldly: "Of all superstitions related to deities and ghosts, spirit-writing caused the most poisonous harm to Chinese society" (出於神鬼的觀念，而在中國社會上中毒最深的迷信，就是扶乩).[93] Within a matter of years after he uttered this statement, the Scientific Numinous Stylus became fashionable in spiritualist circles and among urban consumers. Scientific methodology involves repeatable experiments, a foundation in evidence and generalizable rules. The *Lingji zhimi* makes use of the experimental approach to argue for its easy technique of spirit-mediumship. Michael Lackner has pointed out that fortune-telling and prognostication, like many other traditional disciplines of science and technology, were regarded as part of the "minor ways" (*xiaodao* 小道). Although not highly appreciated by the literati, they were nevertheless considered indispensable in human life.[94] Seen in this light, the

---

90 Liu, *Xinling gantong lu*, 172.
91 Gao, *Chuiwan lou riji jiechao*, 10, 60, 108.
92 Ibid., 171.
93 Fei, *Mixin*, 48–49. The work first appeared in 1931 in the Wanyou wenku 萬有文庫 series. It was reprinted as an independent title in 1933.
94 Lang, *Xiaodao youli*, 82–83.

Transcendent of the Plate may not accord with our understanding of science today, yet operated as one discipline within a "pluralistic science" of its time.

If we consider the Transcendent of the Plate as a stage in the evolution of spirit-writing, we can see how techniques of spirit-mediumship changed in response to the necessities of the times and external challenges. In a different way from traditional spirit-writing by stylus, the Scientific Numinous Stylus made use of paper and plate. It was characterized by low cost and a simple set-up, the preconditions for the craze in Shanghai and the Lower Yangzi area that resulted from the promotion in the print media market. As a result, the technique spread beyond the circles of classically educated gentry to ordinary urban dwellers.

Another development of the early Republican period was the merging of spirit-writing with spiritualism and psychical research. Facing nationalism and calls for eradicating superstition, scientism was the unifying discourse. The Shanghai Lingxue hui and redemptive societies took spirit-writing into a new direction, moving it from the personal area of finding cures for illnesses, prognosticating fortune and finding religious salvation to a means for exploring spirits and souls, life and death. The Numinous Stylus achieved widespread popularity in urban entertainment culture, for which reason critics called it a "new toy" (*xin wanju* 新玩具) for adults. The engine that drove both transformations was the print media and book market. The production and burgeoning market for encyclopaedias for daily use, active from the late Ming onward, and the Shanghai publishers of 1934 directly and indirectly created the conditions for spreading the new technology through promotion and distribution channels. Business considerations provided the motivation in both cases. The demand on the part of the readers in both periods reflects a thirst for the unknown, for communication with beloved dead. These are needs that we all harbour while we live on this earth. The development of the Numinous Stylus shows that this applied even under the hegemony of science during the May Fourth period.

(*Translated by Nanny Kim*)

Bibliography

A'ping 阿蘋. "Ziyoutan 自由談." *Shenbao* 申報, June 2, 1934, 24.
Bianzhe 編者 [Editor]. "Kexue lingji 科學靈乩." *Shenbao benbu zengkan* 申報本埠增刊. May 5, 1934, 2.

Cenlou 岑樓. "Kexue lingji 科學靈乩." *Shenbao benbu zengkan* 申報本埠增刊, May 26, 1934, 2.

"Chajin kexue lingji tu 查禁科學靈乩圖." *Shenbao* 申報, May 18, 1934, 8.

Chang Pang-yen 張邦彥. *Jingshen de fudiao: Jindai Zhongguo de cuimianshu yu dazhong kexue* 精神的複調: 近代中國的催眠術與大眾科學. Taipei: Lianjing chubanshe, 2020.

Chau, Adam Yuet. *Miraculous Response: Doing Popular Religion in Contemporary China*. Stanford, CA: Stanford University Press, 2006.

Chen Weiyu 陳韋聿 [Emery]. "Lu Xun, Puyi, kexue lingji: Jindai Zhongguo de diexian gushi 魯迅、溥儀、科學靈乩：近代中國的碟仙故事." In *Gui de lishi: buguan shi shenme gui, dou gei wo lai yi dian* 鬼的歷史：不管是什麼鬼，都給我來一點, edited by Xie Jinyu 謝金魚, Chen Weiyu 陳韋聿, Shenqi Haishi 神奇海獅, and Haizhou Mao 海州貓, 256–300. Taipei: Lianhe wenxue, 2017.

Chen Yuanjing 陳元靚. *Shilin guangji* 事林廣記. Beijing: Zhonghua shuju, 1999.

Fan Chun-wu 范純武. "Kexue lingji: Diexian yu Min chu lingxue sichao xia fuji de xin neihan 科學靈乩：碟仙與民初靈學思潮下扶乩的新內涵." Paper presented at the International Conference on *Wenhua yu kexue de bianzou: jindai Zhongguo jiushi tuanti, xinyang wenhua de fazhan yu weilei* 文化與科學的變奏：近代中國救世團體、信仰文化的發展與未來, Foguang University, Taiwan, October 9–10, 2012.

Fan Chun-wu 范純武. "Ming Qing riyong leishu zhong de fuji fa 明清日用類書中的扶乩法." Forthcoming.

Fei Hongnian 費鴻年. *Mixin* 迷信. Taipei: Shangwu yinshuguan, 1961.

Findlay, James Arthur. *On the Edge of the Etheric: Being an Investigation of Psychic Phenomena, Based on a Series of Sittings with Mr. John C. Sloan, the Glasgow Trance and Direct Voice Medium*. London: Rider & Co., 1931.

Folang 佛朗. "Tan mixin 談迷信." *Shenbao* 申報, November 9, 1934, 16.

Foster, Michael Dylan. "Strange Games and Enchanted Science: The Mystery of Kokkuri." *Journal of Asian Studies* 65, no. 2 (2006): 251–75.

Gao Chuiwan 高吹萬. *Chuiwan lou riji jiechao* 吹萬樓日記節鈔. Shanghai Library. First published 1940 by Qinshan Chuiwan lou.

Goossaert, Vincent. "1898: The Beginning of the End for Chinese Religion?" *Journal of Asian Studies* 65, no. 2 (2006): 307–35.

Goossaert, Vincent, and David A. Palmer. Introduction to *The Religious Question in Modern China*, edited by Vincent Goossaert and David A. Palmer, 1–16. Chicago: University of Chicago Press, 2011.

Hardacre, Helen. "Asano Wasaburō and Japanese Spiritualism in Early Twentieth-Century Japan." In *Japan's Competing Modernities: Issues in Culture and Democracy, 1900–1930*, edited by Sharon A. Minichiello, 133–53. Honolulu: University of Haiwai'i Press, 1998.

Hou Yawei 侯亞偉. "Minguo xuezhe de fuji yanjiu 民國學者的扶乩研究." *Shijie zongjiao yanjiu* 世界宗教研究, no. 5 (2017): 113–20.

Hsieh Tsung-hui 謝聰輝. *Xin tiandi zhi ming: Yuhuang, Zitong yu feiluan* 新天帝之命：玉皇、梓潼與飛鸞. Taipei: Shangwu yinshuguan, 2013.

Hu Tiandao 胡天道. "Kexue lingji zai Shantou 科學靈乩在汕頭." *Chongmin bao* 崇民報, May 27, 1934, 4.

Huang Ko-wu 黃克武. "Minguo chunian Shanghai de lingxue yanjiu: Yi 'Shanghai Lingxue hui' weili 民國初年上海的靈學研究：以「上海靈學會」為例." *Zhongyang yanjiuyuan jindaishi yanjiu jikan* 中央研究院近代史研究集刊, no. 55 (2007): 99–136.

Huang Ko-wu 黃克武. *Wei shi zhi an: Yan Fu yu jindai Zhongguo de wenhua zhuanxing* 惟適之安：嚴復與近代中國的文化轉型. Taipei: Lianjing chuban gongsi, 2010.

Huang Yi 黃翼. "Diexian yu xianglei xianxiang zhi xinli de jieshi 碟仙與相類現象之心理的解釋." *Jiaoyu zazhi* 教育雜誌 27, no. 4 (1937): 179–181.

Jiaxiang 嘉湘. "Tiaodou 跳荳." *Shenbao* 申報, November 21, 1934, 12.

Jinisi 吉尼斯 [Ivor Grattan Guinness]. *Xinlingxue: xiandai Xifang chaoxinlixue* 心靈學：現代西方超心理學. Translated by Zhang Yanyun 張燕云. Shenyang: Liaoning renmin chubanshe, 1988.

Kani Hiroaki 可兒弘明. "Furan zakki: Minshū dōkyō no shūhen 扶鸞雜記：民眾道教の周邊." *Shigaku* 史學 45, no. 1 (1972): 57–88.

"Kexue lingji 科學靈乩." *Shenbao* 申報, May 1, 1934, 17.

"'Kexue lingji 科學靈乩.'" *Shenbao* 申報, May 22, 1934, 17.

"Kexue lingji tu renqing 科學靈乩圖認清." *Shenbao* 申報, April 30, 1934, 10.

"Kexue lingji tu Shehui ju jinzhi chushou 科學靈乩圖社會局禁止出售." *Zhongyang ribao* 中央日報, May 30, 1934, 10.

"Kexue zaoyu yu shetan zaoyu 科學造語與設壇造語—答朱明君." *Shenbao*, July 26, 1934, 15.

Lang Mixie 朗密榭 [Michael Lackner]. *Xiaodao youli: Zhong-Xi bijiao xin shiyu* 小道有理：中西比較新視閾. Translated by Jin Wen 金雯 and Wang Hongyan 王紅妍. Beijing: Sanlian shuju, 2018.

Lei Hsiang-lin 雷祥麟. "Yinxing de Sai xiansheng: Yi 'xing shishi' de lishi wei li 隱形的賽先生：以「性事實」的歷史為例." In *Wu si @ 100: Wenhua. Sixiang. Lishi* 《五四@100：文化・思想・歷史》, edited by Wang Dewei 王德威 and Song Mingwei 宋明煒, 90–97. Shanghai: Shanghai wenyi chuban, 2018.

Lei Qinfeng 雷勤風 [Christopher Rea]. *Da bujing de niandai: Jindai Zhongguo xin xiaoshi* 大不敬的年代：近代中國新笑史. Translated by Hsu Hui-lin 許暉林. Taipei: Maitian chuban, 2018.

Lingji zhimi 靈乩指迷. Edited by Huaxia zheyi chanwei she 華夏哲義闡微社. 1934. Shanghai Library.

Liu Hongquan 劉洪權, ed. *Minguo shiqi chuban shumu huibian* 民國時期出版書目彙編. Vol. 16. Beijing: Guojia tushuguan chubanshe, 2010.

Liu Liming 劉黎明. *Songdai minjian wushu yanjiu* 宋代民間巫術研究. Sichuan: Bashu shushe, 2004.

Liu Zhanming 劉瞻明. *Xinling gantong lu* 心靈感通錄. In *Zhongguo minjian xinyang, minjian wenhua ziliao huibian* 中國民間信仰、民間文化資料彙編, edited by Wang Chien-chuan 王見川, Hou Chong 侯沖, Fan Chun-wu 范純武, and Li Shih-Wei 李世偉, ser. 3, vol. 17, 95–301. Taipei: Boyang wenhua, 2017. First published 1943 by Da falun chunbanshe. Page references are to the 2017 edition.

Lu Xun 魯迅. "Huabian wenxue, ougan 花邊文學、偶感." In *Lu Xun quanji* 魯迅全集, vol. 5, 479–80. Beijing: Remin wenxue chubanshe, 1996.

Mengruo 夢若. "Kexue lingji tu 科學靈乩圖." *Shenbao* 申報, May 14, 1934, 22.

Nedostup, Rebecca. *Superstitious Regimes: Religion and the Politics of Chinese Modernity*. Cambridge, MA: Harvard University Press, 2009.

Ogden, Emily. *Credulity: A Cultural History of US Mesmerism*. Chicago: University of Chicago Press, 2018.

Oppenheim, Janet. *The Other World: Spiritualism and Psychical Research in England, 1850–1914*. Cambridge: Cambridge University Press, 1985.

Qingfeng 清鳳. "Xinli xuejia Zhang Yaoxiang yu kexue lingji 心理學家張燿翔與科學靈乩." *Xunbao* 迅報, no. 354 (September 21, 1939): 1.

Qingxian jifa 請仙箕法. Private collection by the author, publication details unclear.

Sakade Yoshinobu 坂出祥伸, Ogawa Yōichi 小川陽一, and Sakai Tadao 酒井忠夫, eds. *Chūgoku nichiyō ruisho shūsei* 中國日用類書集成. Tokyo: Kyūkoshoin, 2003.

"Sanxing shuju chuangye shizhou jinian 三星書局創業十週紀念." *Shenbao* 申報, May 12, 1934, 21.

Schumann, Matthias. "Science and Spirit-Writing: The Shanghai Lingxuehui (靈學會) and the Changing Fate of Spiritualism in Republican China." In *Text and Context in the Modern History of Chinese Religions: Redemptive Societies and Their Sacred Texts*, edited by Philip Clart, David Ownby, and Wang Chien-chuan, 126–72. Leiden: Brill, 2020.

"Shanghai Minghua shuju 上海明華書局." *Shenbao* 申報, May 11, 1934, 11.

"Shenjun tuqi kexue lingji tu 神軍突起科學靈乩圖." *Shenbao* 申報, April 29, 1934, 8.

Shiga Ichiko 志賀市子. *Chūgoku no kokkurisan: Furan shinkō to kajin shakai* 中國のっくりさん：扶鸞信仰と華人社會. Tokyo: Taishūkan shoten, 2003.

Shiyu 時雨. "Kexue lingji tu yiran liuxing 科學靈乩圖依然流行." *Jingang zuan* 金鋼鑽, June 5, 1934, 1.

Tangmusheng 湯姆生 [J. Arthur Thomson]. *Hanyi kexue dagang* 漢譯科學大綱, vol. 3, edited by Wang Yunwu 王雲五. Translated by Hu Mingfu 胡明復, Chen Zhen 陳楨, Hu Gangfu 胡剛復, et al. Shanghai: Shangwu yinshuguan, 1923.

Wang Chien-chuan 王見川. "Lufei Kui yu 'Shengde tan,' 'Lingxue hui': Jiantan Min chu Shanghai de lingxue fengchao 陸費逵與「盛德壇」、「靈學會」：兼談民初上海的靈學風潮." Paper presented at the International Conference on *Wenhua yu kexue de bianzou: jindai Zhongguo jiushi tuanti, xinyang wenhua de fazhan yu weilei* 文化與科學的變奏：近代中國救世團體、信仰文化的發展與未來, Foguang University, Taiwan, October 9–10, 2012.

Wang Chien-chuan 王見川. "Jindai Zhongguo de fuji, cishan yu mixin: Yi *Yinguang wenchao* wei kaocha xiansuo 近代中國的扶乩、慈善與迷信：以印光文鈔為考查線索." In *Xinyang, shijian yu wenhua tiaoshi: Disi jie guoji Hanxue huiyi lunwenji xiace* 信仰、實踐與文化調適：第四屆國際漢學會議論文集, edited by Kang Bao 康豹 [Paul R. Katz] and Liu Shu-fen 劉淑芬, vol. 2, 533–59. Taipei: Zhongyang yanjiu yuan, 2013.

Wang Chien-chuan 王見川. "Song Ming shiqi de fuji, fuluan yu qingxian: jiantan 'fuji,' 'enzhu' deng ci de qiyuan 宋明時期的扶箕、扶鸞與請仙：兼談「扶乩」、「恩主」等詞的起源." In *Fuluan wenhua yu minzhong zongjiao guoji xueshu yantaohui lunwenji* 扶鸞文化與民眾宗教國際學術研討會論文集, edited by Fan Chun-wu 范純武. Taipei: Boyang wenhua, 2020.

Wang Chien-chuan 王見川 and Pi Qingsheng 皮慶生. *Zhongguo jinshi minjian xinyang* 中國近世民間信仰. Shanghai: Shanghai renmin chubanshe, 2010.

Wang Hongchao 王宏超. "Shenjie lingguang: Shanghai Shengde tan zhi linghun zhaoxiang huodong 神界靈光：上海盛德壇之靈魂照相活動." *Shanghai wenhua* 上海文化, no. 6 (2016): 67–76.

Winter, Alison. *Mesmerized: Powers of Mind in Victorian Britain*. Chicago: Chicago University Press, 2000.

Xizhen 席珍. "Kexue lingji ji qita 科學靈乩及其他." *Shenbao* 申報, May 15, 1934, 19.

Xu Dishan 許地山. *Fuji mixin de yanjiu* 扶箕迷信底研究. Taipei: Shangwu yinshuguan, 1980.

Xu Jian 徐健. "Wan Qing guanpai liude xuesheng yanjiu 晚清官派留德學生研究." *Shixue jikan* 史學集刊, no. 1 (2010): 72–79, 112.

Ye Zhongqiang 葉中強. *Shanghai shehui yu wenren shenghuo* 上海社會與文人生活. Shanghai: Shanghai cishu chubanshe, 2010.

Yinguang fashi wenchao 印光法師文鈔. Vol. 1. Taipei: Daqian chubanshe, 2003.

"Yunwei xianzi 'guang' shuo 雲蔚仙子「光」說." *Lingxue congzhi* 靈學要誌 1, no. 7 (1918): 7–9.

"Zengsong kexue lingji tu yi zhang 贈送科學靈乩圖一張." *Shenbao* 申報, May 14, 1934, 14.

Zhaozhao 昭昭. "Kexue huo 科學禍." *Shenbao benbu zengkan* 申報本埠增刊, August 25, 1934, 1.

Zhengren 征人. "Cong kexue lingji shuoqi 從科學靈乩說起." *Chongmin bao* 崇民報, May 12, 1934, 4.

Zhongguo shehui kexueyuan lishi yanjiusuo wenhuashi 中國社會科學院歷史研究所文化室, ed. *Mingdai tongsu riyong leishu jikan* 明代通俗日用類書集刊. 16 vols. Chongqing: Xinan shifan daxue chubanshe, 2011.

PART 3

*Spirit-Writing and the
Literati Elites in Late Imperial China*

∴

CHAPTER 7

Instantiating the Genealogy of the Way: Spirit-Writing in the Construction of Peng Dingqiu's Confucian Pantheon

Daniel Burton-Rose

Scholarship on spirit-writing has been increasing dramatically over the last several decades, with close case studies of individual altars and spirit-altar scriptures and canons opening a new vista on the broad contours of the tradition and many of the pools and eddies along its course. One of the most striking elements of this big picture is the immense collective creativity channeled through spirit-altar production. Within the vast corpus of texts produced by spirit-writing, poetic literary production, new scriptures, and—to a lesser extent—commentaries and liturgies have received the greatest attention.[1] A small but growing subset of this scholarly literature examines self-consciously Confucian spirit-writing altars (*jitan* 乩壇). The groups analyzed were active in the Republican period (1912–49), with some originating in the mid-nineteenth century.[2] Promotion of Confucian values through spirit-writing remains relevant today in the form of redemptive societies.

Confucian spirit-writing altars prompted the same initial question from their contemporaries as they do from present day scholars: How Confucian can spirit-writing be? This skepticism stems from inherent elements of the rituals employed to call down deities and the combinatory discourse that was standard on late imperial and Republican altars.[3] As Vincent Goossaert has

---

1 For a detailed overview see the contribution by Goossaert in this volume.
2 The earliest self-identified Confucian spirit-writing altars that have received attention from scholars were active in Sichuan in the mid-nineteenth century. A critic used the term "Confucian spirit-altar" (*rutan* 儒壇) to describe them in 1901 or 1902. See the discussion in Wang, "Spirit Writing Groups in Modern China (1840–1937)," 664–68, and Zhu, "Rutan jingdian ji qi yingyong." See also Clart, "Confucius and the Mediums."
3 With the term "combinatory discourse" I refer to polemical assertions regarding the commonalities between two or all three of the "teachings" (*jiao* 教) of Buddhism, Confucianism, and Daoism. For case studies involving Peng Dingqiu 彭定求 (1645–1719) and his ancestors and descendants, see Chapter 5 of Burton-Rose, "Terrestrial Reward as Divine Recompense." To this earlier discussion I would add that these same figures used the grammatical and rhetorical conventions of (two or) three teachings discourse to discuss compatibility of schools

documented, the methods for summoning deities to communicate with mortals emerged in Song dynasty altars overseen by Daoists in which "spirit-writing was one of the ritual techniques they used to create a divine presence in ritual contexts in order to exorcise, heal, confirm divine appointments, and, occasionally, obtain doctrinal and practical instructions from the gods." This "intimate connection" between a corpus of Song dynasty Daoist rituals and spirit-writing continued into the late imperial period.[4] As for combinatory discourse, a Republican period account of a "Confucian spirit-altar" (*rutan* 儒壇) active in southern and western Sichuan 四川 stated: "In this area, what is called 'Confucianism' really is flying phoenix teachings that Confucianism, Buddhism, and Daoism are 'The Three Teaching with One Pervading Unity'." (此處所謂儒教, 係指儒釋道三教一貫之飛鸞教而言。)[5] New Religion to Save the World (Jiushi xinjiao 救世新教), the Confucian spirit-writing altar examined by Matthias Schumann in this volume, expanded the imperial Three Teachings rubric to a Five Teachings framework that hosted Christian and Islamic figures as well.

Clearly neither the form nor the content of spirit-writing approximated the norms of state-sanctioned orthodox Confucianism, which can be defined for our present purposes as the contested product of intellectual trends among the educated elite (both in and out of office) and the imperial will as expressed through the (ever-changing) civil service examination curriculum.[6] Qing dynasty spirit-writing groups, however, used a language of orthodoxy in a context that was not directly tied to state sanction. For example, the "Litan zongzhi 立壇宗旨" (Ancestral protocols for establishing the altar) that opens *Yuquan* 玉詮 (Jade expositions), a compendium of early and mid-Qing Suzhou spirit-altar transcripts, offers the following definition: "'Orthodoxy': that which should be done; [that which causes] awakening and unification." (正者：該乎；覺而統

---

within a single teaching: e.g., arguing that Wang Shouren's 王守仁 (1472–1529) teachings accorded with those of Mengzi 孟子 (Peng Dingqiu) and that there were no internal contradictions between the practice of Pure Land and Chan Buddhism (Dingqiu's great-grandson Peng Shaosheng 彭紹升). It is thus a broader phenomenon than Three Teachings discourse.

4 Goossaert, "Spirit-writing Altars and Daoist Rituals in Qing Jiangnan," 385. For an example of a product of Peng Dingqiu's spirit-altar invoking exorcistic thunder deities, see YJXC, 34b–35b.

5 *Xikang jiyao* 西康紀要, quoted in Wang, "Spirit Writing Groups in Modern China (1840–1937)," 666–67. "Flying phoenix" is a synonym for spirit-writing that dates to the Song dynasty. The "one pervading unity" in the slogan of combinatory discourse is an allusion to *Lunyu* 15.3. The groups criticized by the author of *Xikang jiyao* were associated with the Perfect Completion Society (Shiquan hui 十全會) of Thearch Guan (Guandi 關帝) devotees. For more on this group, see Wang, "Popular Groups Promoting 'The Religion of Confucius'," esp. 94–98.

6 See the discussion of "state orthodoxy" and of the relationship between "official orthodoxy" and "unofficial orthodoxies" in Wilson, *Genealogy of the Way*, 12, 24.

乎。)[7] This is very loose criteria that left wide latitude for individual actors to attempt to impose on others their personal sense of how things should be. Yet spirit-altar groups that foregrounded the promotion of Confucian ethics, solicited the descent of apotheosized Confucian figures, and discussed key concepts in the Confucian tradition invited scrutiny from fellow self-identified Confucians who regarded textual precedent as a limiting factor. No matter how much they employed key terms from the Five Classics (*Wujing* 五經) and Four Books (*Si shu* 四書),[8] the claims to orthodoxy of Confucian spirit-altars were always under the strain of the lack of clear sanction for this practice within the classics.

What, then, did practitioners seek to achieve by using such language? The short answer is: the benefits of affiliation with state power that was unique to Confucianism among the Three Teachings during the Qing dynasty. A longer answer includes modulating the strains between a narrow ideal of what a proper Confucian *should* do and the complexity and diversity of the devotional practices through which collective priorities were debated and enacted at local and regional levels.

The present article reframes existing scholarship on self-identified Confucian spirit-writing altars by moving their origin from the mid-nineteenth to the late seventeenth century. It does so by examining Confucian discourse in the spirit-writing corpus of Peng Dingqiu 彭定求 (1645–1719; *hao* Nanyun laoren 南昀老人; Fuchu xueren 復初學人). Dingqiu was a trained Daoist ritualist who used his expertise to facilitate successful communications with several high deities and a range of apotheosized spirits. Among the latter, past Confucian luminaries who expounded upon the importance of abiding by the Cheng-Zhu Learning program produced a significant portion of the surviving transcripts of Dingqiu's spirit-writing communications.

1 Cheng-Zhu Learning on the Spirit-Altar: An Inherent Contradiction?

Cheng-Zhu Learning is so named for the teachings of Cheng Yi 程頤 (1033–1107) and Zhu Xi 朱熹 (1130–1200), as systematized by Zhu. Zhu distilled the

---

7 *Yuquan* 1.2a. Peng Shaosheng stated that he edited this work. See his "Yu tan ji 玉壇記," in *Yixing juji*, 15.17b (723). Studies of *Yuquan* include Ding and Yang, "Suzhou Yutan fuji" and Lin, "Qing chu Suzhou Yutan."

8 On these two overlapping canons, see Nylan, *The Five "Confucian" Classics* and Gardner, *The Four Books*.

Confucian canon by shifting emphasis from the lengthy, complex, and demanding Five Classics to his own formulation of the Four Books. The Four Books consisted of two chapters from the *Liji* 禮記 (Book of rites)—the *Daxue* 大學 (Greater learning) and *Zhongyong* 中庸 (Application of equilibrium)—sandwiching the oral records of Confucius and Mencius compiled by their disciples (the *Lunyu* 論語 and *Mengzi* 孟子). Condemned as "false learning" (*weixue* 偽學) in Zhu's own day, his synthesis was implemented as the civil service examination curriculum under the Mongol Yuan dynasty (1271–1368).[9] In a reprise endorsement by a non-Han dynasty, Cheng-Zhu Learning was also promulgated by the early Qing emperors Shunzhi 順治 (r. 1644–61) and Kangxi 康熙 (r. 1661–1722). Doing so demonstrated their command over the textual corpus of their Chinese subjects while simultaneously serving as a barbed critique of the moral relativism that had come to prominence in the mid-Ming and developed into extreme positions in the late Ming.

Dingqiu's own inclinations within the Confucian patriline were more complex, and decidedly out of step with the orthodoxy implemented by the Kangxi emperor and several of his ethnic Han officials in the late 1670s and '80s.[10] This is clearest in Dingqiu's commitment to Daoist ritual, the teachings initiated by Wang Shouren 王守仁 (1472–1529; *hao* Yangming 陽明; *jinshi* 1499), and spirit-writing. Yet Dingqiu was very careful to insist on his own compliance with the broader imperial program, and the deities that descended to his altar frequently declared their adherence to Cheng-Zhu Learning. Thus Wenchang 文昌, in a preface to the *Yuju xinchan* 玉局心懺 (Jade bureau heart penance liturgy; dated 1680), offered the following summary: "These words of perfected officials: differentiate principle and desire, distinguish fortune and misfortune, and illuminate life and death. The books of the Four Masters, the quintessence of the Five Classics; all are included in this." (真官此言：別理欲也；辨吉凶也；明生死也。四子之書，五經之蘊，括於此矣。)[11] Dingqiu's great-grandson Peng Shaosheng 彭紹升 (1740–96; *jinshi* 1761; dharma name Jiqing 際清) used similar rhetoric as he consolidated Dingqiu's spirit-altar legacy in the 1770s. In his preface to his 1773 collection of Dingqiu's divine communications, Shaosheng termed *Yuju xinchan* and "Jiangxi lu 講習錄" ("Record of discussion and study"; introduced below) "a great elucidation of the lineages of Zhu and

---

9   On these developments, see the classic studies Schirokauer, "Neo-Confucians Under Attack," and Liu, "How Did a Neo-Confucian School Become the State Orthodoxy?"
10   Li Guangdi 李光地 (1642–1718) was arguably the foremost ethnic Han official in the implementation of Cheng-Zhu Learning during the Kangxi reign. For a defensive philosophical study of Li's career and commentaries, see Ng, *Cheng-Zhu Confucianism in the early Qing*.
11   "Wendi xu 文帝序," YJXC, 2.a.

Si [Rivers] and Lian and Luo [regions]" (*Dachan Zhu Si Lian Luo zhi zong* 大闡洙泗濂洛之宗), topographic metonyms for Confucius, Zhou Dunyi 周敦頤 (1017–1073), and his nephew Cheng Yi.[12]

It would be a mistake to view the insistence on the communications of Dingqiu's altar as distillations of Cheng-Zhu Learning as insincerity or a ruse. Rather, what Dingqiu sought to do through spirit-altar communications in the late 1670s and early '80s was entirely consistent with the goal of the Kangxi emperor at that time: to knit together the northern Manchu regime and its disproportionately northern ethnic Han officials with disaffected ethnic Han southerners. In order to please the former, Dingqiu used his altar communications to urge the men of his father's generation to turn from vain literary pursuits and dedicate themselves to ethical transformation. To entice the latter, he hosted Six Dynasties and Tang poets, and engaged in the Daoist rituals integral to local society. In this way we can acknowledge the obvious—that the deities hosted by Dingqiu and their human advocates "doth protest too much" in continually re-iterating their Cheng-Zhu commitments—while also recognizing that, in the circumstances in which they were produced, the concession represented by these statements was a significant one.

As with any thinking person, Dingqiu's own intellectual commitments were a work in progress. Spirit-altar discussions with deceased Confucian paragons played a major role in enabling Dingqiu to develop a distinctive synthesis. In the years following his establishment of himself as a spirit-altar supervisor in the capital (from the fall of 1678 to the spring of 1680), Dingqiu created an amalgam of two distinct but interpenetrated traditions of praxis. One was the teachings of Lu Jiuyuan 陸九淵 (1139–1193; *zi* Zijing 子靜, commonly called Xiangshan 象山) and Wang Shouren, as incorporated into the Confucian tradition articulated by Sun Qifeng 孫奇逢 (1585–1675) during the Ming-Qing transition.[13] The other was the positions of the Donglin Academy co-founders by Gu Xiancheng 顧憲誠 (1550–1612) and Gao Panlong 高攀龍 (1562–1626). These were generally sympathetic to Yangming Learning (as I will term the positions of Wang and his disciples), but reigned in the ontological "beyond good and evil" position available in Wang's own work and further developed by his student Wang Ji 王畿 (1498–1583). To combat the perceived lack of ethical mooring in Wang's teachings, the Donglin partisans insisted on a moral core to Confucian conduct.

Put simply, Dingqiu combined ethnic Han north and south: the newly assertive Henan Learning—what Dingqiu's teacher Tang Bin 湯斌 (1627–1687)

---

12   "Peng xu 彭序," ZSL, 2a.
13   See Sun's magnum opus *Lixue zong zhuan*.

termed "Learning from Luoyang" (Luoxue 洛學)—with the Donglin movement that originated with the eponymous academy founded by Gu and Gao in Wuxi 無錫, directly northwest of Suzhou 蘇州. Dingqiu developed Lu-Wang commitments within a framework of previous thinkers—Sun Qifeng foremost among them—that insisted on viewing Lu-Wang and Cheng-Zhu as part of the same shared inheritance of Confucianism. Dingqiu then promulgated this synthesis through his anthology *Rumen fa yu* 儒門法語 (Model words of the Confucian school, preface 1697), and continued to develop it through spirit-altar communications.

Dingqiu himself and many of those who participated in his altar were aware of the inherent tension between commitment to Cheng-Zhu Learning and service to Wenchang as a quintessentially Daoist deity, but it was a *productive tension* that fueled the creation of spirit-altar texts. The present article examines the spirit-altar transmissions of deities who held rank in Wenchang's divine administration in light of Dingqiu's non-spirit altar Confucian textual production. I argue that these works form a coherent project, despite being separated by divergent reception histories.

2   Overview of Dingqiu's Altar

Dingqiu oversaw his own altar for nearly forty-five years, dating from the autumn of 1674, when he received a prophecy of his immanent success at the highest level of the civil service examinations, and enduring until the winter of 1718–1719, only months before his death.[14] Within a year of his death Dingqiu returned to the altar to report that he was serving in Wenchang's celestial administration. This was the culmination of his initial receipt, in 1671, of the "Wenchang precious register" (Wenchang baolu 文昌寶籙) from the prominent Daoist ritualist Shi Daoyuan 施道淵 (1616–1678),[15] whom Dingqiu acknowledged as his teacher.[16] This register was clearly intended for literati who did

---

14   On Dingqiu's earliest independent communication, see my "Establishing a Literati Spirit-Writing Altar," 373–95. The last spirit-writing session at which Dingqiu was present is dated Kangxi 57.12 (Jan. 20–Feb. 18, 1719): ZSL, 47.39b–41b. Dingqiu passed away on Kangxi 58.4.9 (May 27, 1719).

15   For an excellent overview of the available primary and secondary sources on Shi, see Zhou, "Shi Daoyuan."

16   Dingqiu wrote in a poem: "I pledged myself in sincerity to the Great Salvation Master Shi, reverently receiving the Wenchang precious register" (余素飯依施大度師，敬受文昌寶籙). This poem is not included in Dingqiu's literary anthology, *Nanyun shi gao*, which only begins in 1695, but I accept it as authentic. It is included in the *Yuanmiao*

not need to practice Daoist ritual for their livelihood: for Dingqiu, receiving it was the first step in setting his sights on posthumous service in Wenchang's bureaucracy. By becoming a spirit-altar deity, he objectively obtained that goal. He remained active as a spirit-altar deity in the Yangzi Delta region into the early twentieth century.[17]

While Dingqiu was alive his altar included both disciples (*dizi* 弟子) who took an oath to serve Wenchang in life and posthumously[18] and more casual observers.[19] Altogether Dingqiu had documented spirit-altar congress with twenty deities, all of whom—with the exception of the Dipper Mother (Doumu 斗姆)—were male, and fifteen of whom were apotheosized historical figures.[20]

---

guan zhi 元妙觀志 (Gazetteer of the Abbey of Primordial Mystery) of Gu Yuan 顧沅 (1799–1851): 7.2b–3a (rpt. 696). According to Gu's "Introductory Remarks" (*liyan* 例言), he completed the *Yuanmiao guan zhi* in 1831 (*liyan* 1b; rpt. 670); it was not printed until 1927. Gu was friends with Dingqiu's descendants and had access to the Peng patriline archive, as evinced in his other works. The *Yuanmiao guan zhi* was also proofread by a disciple of Dingqiu's grandson Peng Qifeng 彭啟豐 (1701–1784).

17   On Dingqiu's posthumous career, see my "A Prolific Spirit."

18   The oath occurred on the Establishing Spring (Lichun 立春) day of Kangxi 18 (Feb. 5, 1679). In addition to Dingqiu, those who took the oath were Peng Sunyu, You Tong, and Peng Ningqiu (ZSL 46.10a–11a), on whom see below.

19   These two categories—divided by level of commitment—are referred to throughout YJXC as "disciples and other participants" (*dizi dengzhong* 弟子等眾): e.g., YJXC, 3a.

20   The deities who descended to Dingqiu's spirit-altar can be classified into three categories: 1) gods whose biographies do not clearly correlate to a single historical personage; 2) apotheosized historical figures; and 3) figures regarded as mythical by present-day scholars but whom Dingqiu regarded as historical.

The first category consists of Wenchang and the Dipper Mother, both of whose divine *curriculum vitae* included stints as mortals (for details, see Kleeman, *A God's Own Tale*, and Kohn, "Doumu," 163–64). It also includes three obscure figures: Celestial Lord Wei (Wei Tianjun 韋天君), the Ambassador of the Dipper Palace (Dougong shi zhe 斗宮使者), and Master Jade Void (Yuxu zi 玉虛子). The Jade Void Palace is associated with Zhenwu 真武, but there is insufficient information in this passage to make an identification. The passage attributed to Master Jade Void is included verbatim in *Yuquan yulu*, with the difference that editors have made Thearch Lü (Lüdi 呂帝) the transmitter of Master Jade Void's command (*ming* 命). See ZSL, 47.37a–b and *Yuquan yulu*, 77b–78a.

The second category is as follows, listed in chronological order of the births of the historical figures: Ge Hong 葛洪 (283–343), Tao Qian 陶潛 (365?–427), Li Bai 李白 (701–762), Li Bi 李泌 (722–789), Han Yu 韓愈 (768–824), Zhou Dunyi 周敦頤 (1017–1073), Cheng Yi 程頤 (1033–1107), Su Shi 蘇軾 (1037–1101), Xue Xuan 薛瑄 (1389–1464), Shang Lu 商輅 (1414–1486), Luo Hongxian 羅洪先 (1504–1564), Du Qiaolin (1571–1638), and Huang Daozhou (1585–1646).

The third category consists of Master Yellow Stone (Huangshi gong 黃石公; circa third century BCE) and Lü Yan 呂巖 (*zi* Dongbin 洞賓). In the biographical note on Lü in *Quan Tang shi* 全唐詩 (Complete poetry of the Tang), he is introduced as the grandson of an

Of this latter category, those most relevant to the present focus on spirit-altar engagement with Cheng-Zhu Learning were Zhou Dunyi and Cheng Yi—the two most prominent of the five Northern Song masters codified by Zhu Xi—and the Ming Confucians Xue Xuan 薛瑄 (1389–1464), Luo Hongxian 羅洪先 (1504–1564; *zhuangyuan* 1529), and Huang Daozhou 黃道周 (1585–1646; *hao* Shizhai 石齋; *jinshi* 1622).

Three of the apotheosized Ming Confucians who descended to Dingqiu's altar possessed titles in the celestial administration governed by Wenchang. This body was the Jade Bureau (*Yuju* 玉局). The name was inspired by the "Jade Throne" (*yuju*; a synonym of *yuzuo* 玉座) upon which the deified Laozi descended to the founder of the Celestial Masters church in the second century.[21] One group of Wenchang devotees in the late nineteenth century did explain *yuju* as a literal throne for Wenchang along the lines of that employed by Laozi,[22] but what was depicted in Dingqiu's divine communications was a division in the celestial bureaucracy overseen by the Jade Emperor. Apotheosized worthies could be transferred to the Jade Bureau from other duties of divine administration and they could be terminated if their service was unsatisfactory. The existence of the Jade Bureau was first revealed to Dingqiu in 1674. The first spirit with whom Dingqiu made contact introduced himself as "Celestial Official Du of Wenchang's Jade Bureau" (Wenchang Yuju tianguan Du 文昌玉局天官杜). The "speaker" was the posthumous form of Du Qiaolin 杜喬林 (1571–1638; *jinshi* 1616) of Huating 華亭 county in Songjiang 松江 prefecture, a late Ming official primarily known for suppressing a rebellion in Huzhou 湖州 prefecture, at the south of Lake Tai 太湖, and combating pirates in coastal Fujian 福建.[23] In 1679 in the capital the divine service of Huang Daozhou was revealed to the altar members who took an oath together. Huang was a Ming

---

official in the Board of Rites who unsuccessfully sat for the metropolitan examination during the Xiantong 咸通 reign (860–874): *Quan Tang shi*, 856.1a (24: 9675).

With the exception of the Dipper Mother, all of the above names come from ZSL. For dates of descent and page numbers in ZSL, see my "Terrestrial Reward as Divine Recompense," 322–25 (Appendix 3.1). For a discussion of the extant Dipper Mother transmission to Dingqiu, see my "Establishing a Literati Spirit-Writing Altar," 370–72.

21   On the history of the term Yuju, see my "Establishing a Literati Spirit-Writing Altar," 394. On the perpetuation of the term by later spirit-altar practitioners, see my "A Prolific Spirit," 28 and 34–37.

22   "Yuju jie 玉局解," in YJXC, reproduced in Liu, *Wendi quanshu*, 1876 edition, *fu* 附, 2a–b. I am not aware of a jade throne in Wenchang devotion prior to the need to explain Dingqiu's use of the term *yuju* and its subsequent adoption by other spirit-writing practitioners inspired by him.

23   SJGNP, 14b.

loyalist from Zhangpu 漳浦, Fujian, who had been executed by the Qing military after his service to the first two southern Ming emperors; reverencing him under the nose of the Kangxi emperor was a delicate matter.[24] For this reason on his first descent to the altar he spoke in the voice of a mythical recluse from the third century BCE, Master Yellow Stone (Huangshi gong 黃石公), and was only explicitly identified by Wenchang as Huang Daozhou after the altar members had sworn an oath. The Ming three-fold *optimus* Shang Lu 商輅 (1414–1486), for his part, began his posthumous service in 1706. The present article concentrates on texts produced by posthumous Du and Huang.

The participants in Dingqiu's altars met conventional sociological definitions of Confucians (*ru* 儒), such as engagement with the civil service examination curriculum, performance of government service, and self-conscious affiliation to scholarly patrilines. However, the intellectual historian Chen Lai's observation about Huang Daozhou holds equally true for Dingqiu and men of his father's generation, such as Peng Sunyu 彭孫遹 (1631–1700) and You Tong 尤侗 (1618–1704): "In reality, in his youth Huang Daozhou's personal aspirations were not as a Confucian, but as a talented literatus" (事實上，黃道周青少年時代的人格理想並不是儒者，而是才士).[25] These men had much greater commitments to literary pursuits than they did to textual scholarship or self-cultivation. The disjuncture between preparing for examinations and one's personal pursuits meant that one could achieve the highest degrees possible without a personal commitment to Cheng-Zhu Learning. A major sociocultural intervention of Dingqiu's altar was to exhort Yangzi Delta literati to turn away from literary pursuits and devote themselves to self-cultivation along Confucian—rather than Buddhist and Daoist—lines. Such exhortations were necessary precisely because Buddhist and Daoist (including alchemical) practices and discourse were so familiar to elite southern men of the conquest generation. On Dingqiu's altar the authority of the descending spirits was employed in a manner akin to the way in which many patients use the authority of physicians: to be told to do something they already know they should be doing, in the hope that they will at least do it a little more than they would if left entirely to their own devices.

Analysis of Dingqiu's altar enhances our knowledge of Confucian spirit-altar groups chronologically, spatially, demographically, and doctrinally. Chronologically, it moves the timeline back over a century and a half earlier than other

---

24   On the changing status of Huang from the early to mid-Qing, see Chan, "The Qianlong Emperor's New Strategy."
25   Chen, "Huang Daozhou de shengping," 88.

such groups that have received scholarly attention. Spatially, it is concentrated in the cultural, economic, and political centers of the empire—Suzhou and the capital (present day Beijing). This is a stark contrast to the Confucian spirit-altars associated with Thearch Guan devotees that were active in majority non-Han regions of southern and western Sichuan and quite similar to the New Religion to Save the World in the cities of the northeast.[26]

Demographically, Dingqiu and a number of the participants he attracted to his altar obtained some of the highest distinction possible in civil service examinations: it is not an accident that all three rank-holding members of the Jade Bureau had achieved presented scholar degrees (*jinshi* 進士) while alive. Dingqiu himself was a two-fold *optimus* (*eryuan* 二元), meaning that he took first place on both the metropolitan and palace examinations. Dingqiu's father Peng Long 彭瓏 (1613–1689) was a presented scholar of 1659. Peng Sunyu was both a presented scholar and the top candidate in the special examination of 1679. Sunyu was not from the Changzhou county branch of the Pengs, but his connection with Dingqiu's branch went back generations and Dingqiu addressed him as "uncle." You Tong was among the fifty successful candidates of the same special examination that Peng Sunyu topped. And Dingqiu's cousin Peng Ningqiu 彭寧求 (1649–1700) was the *tertius* (*tanhua* 探花; third-place candidate in the palace examination) of 1682. Given the centrality of imperial sanction in the definition of orthodoxy, these credentials provide an objective measure of the extent to which the men who participated in Dingqiu's altar adhered to early Qing standards of orthodoxy. However, as discussed below, these engagements with the examination system and office-holding fueled self-doubt regarding the permissibility of a range of cultural and devotional activities, including spirit-writing.

3   *Rumen fa yu* in Spirit-Altar Context

Doctrinally, Dingqiu's spirit-altar discussions with apotheosized Confucian luminaries prefigured and paralleled his non-spirit-writing compositions and editorial projects. Foremost among the latter was Dingqiu's own iteration of what Thomas Wilson dubbed the "genealogy of the Way": the anthology *Rumen fa yu*.[27] *Rumen fa yu* chronologically arranged one or more historically attested

---

26   Explored by Schumann in this volume.
27   Wilson did not specifically discuss Dingqiu's *Rumen fa yu* in his consideration of over sixty Confucian anthologies, but Dingqiu's work fits well within the broader phenomena of personalized and nuanced retroactive lineage construction examined by Wilson in *Genealogy*

pieces by up to twenty-one[28] celebrated Confucians from the Southern Song through the late Ming (with Yuan figures omitted completely). In doing so Dingqiu concretized his distinctive amalgam of Lu-Wang teachings and the Donglin founders discussed above.

Dingqiu completed *Rumen fa yu* after over two decades of supervising his spirit-writing altar. *Rumen fa yu* was thus the partial product of extensive conversations with Confucian luminaries with whom he engaged as descending spirit-altar deities before he editorially propagated writings by the spirit-altar deities' historical predecessors. *Rumen fa yu* did not contain any spirit-altar communications, but the ideas with which it was concerned and historical figures who articulated them figured prominently in the communications of Dingqiu's altar. Due to the way in which it adheres to the genre of Confucian anthology initiated by *Jinsi lu* 近思錄 (Reflections on things at hand) of Zhu Xi and Lü Zuqian 呂祖謙 (1137–1181),[29] the way in which *Rumen fa yu* resonates with Dingqiu's spirit-altar pantheon has not previously been noted. Seen in the light of *Rumen fa yu*, Dingqiu's spirit-altar pantheon was a living anthology that helped him directly relate the teachings of past Confucian paragons to the immediate issues that concerned him. Given the way in which Zhu Xi's vision of a Confucian transmission was inherently sacralized, we can perceive that Dingqiu constructed one unitary pantheon that was only fragmented by the expectations of readers of different types of material: i.e., readers of the lectures of historical figures recorded by their disciples and lectures by the apotheosized forms of those same historical figures recorded by spirit-altar participants.

---

    of the Way. The present article demonstrates that spirit-altar communication could invigorate retroactive lineage construction in Confucian circles.

28   A careful edition history of *Rumen fa yu* is necessary in order to: 1) confirm that Dingqiu himself initially included all the works that appear in later editions; and 2) track the way in which selective exclusions of anthologized individuals reflected the adaptation of Dingqiu's program by later editors and publishers. In their abstract of *Rumen fa yu* the editors of the *Siku quanshu* named twenty-one anthologized figures, but the two editions I have examined from prior to the *Siku* project in the 1770s had eighteen and nine anthologized subjects, respectively (these are the two earliest entries listed in the Appendix below). The number of subjects in post-*Siku* editions continued to vary widely. The pagination I provide below is to the 1922 Chengye tang edition, which includes nineteen figures. No editions of *Rumen fayu* are available in compendiums of facsimile reproductions. The 1922 edition has the advantage of being relatively complete and widely available in rare book collections. The only secondary study of *Rumen fa yu*—Peng Guoxiang's "Qingdai Kangxi chao Lixue de yijun"—also used the 1922 edition.

29   Wing-tsit Chan's 1967 annotated translation of this work was a monumental achievement, but his interpretive strategies merit revisiting.

Rumen fa yu was Dingqiu's most popular work.[30] Indeed, its popularity should call into question easy assumptions about the marginalization of the Lu-Wang school in the Qing dynasty.[31] It was reprinted in at least a dozen editions throughout the Qing, including four published by official schools and other government offices, and at least two Republican editions. Two abbreviated versions were also produced: *Rumen fa yu jiyao* 儒門法語輯要 (Essentials of the model words of the Confucian school) prepared by Tang Jinzhao 湯金釗 (preface 1814) and *Ru men fa yu ji* 儒門法語集 (Anthology of the model words of the Confucian school; undated) (see Appendix). As attested by an exemplar currently held by the National Archive of Japan that was formerly owned by Shōheizaka Gakumonjo 昌平坂学問所 (1790–1868), Dingqiu's formulation of the Confucian pantheon exerted an influence in early modern East Asia beyond the borders Qing dynasty—as did his spirit-altar communications.[32] Despite the widespread diffusion of *Rumen fa yu*, none of the printed editions are available in compendia of facsimile reproductions.

Historically-attested works by Xue Xuan, Luo Hongxian, and Huang Daozhou were all anthologized in *Rumen fa yu* after the posthumous forms of these figures had descended as spirit-altar deities to Dingqiu's altar: the spirit-altar cart before the biographical horse.[33] Such overlaps demonstrate how Dingqiu integrated spirit-altar communication into his broader intellectual program and help us perceive how the deities who descended to Dingqiu's altar were part of a pantheon that he diligently constructed and promoted in his non-spirit-writing activities. For example, in his subscript note on Xue Xuan's "Shendu zhai ji 慎獨齋記" (Record of the Caution-in-Solitude Studio) in *Rumen fa yu*, Dingqiu succinctly stated his sense of Xue's import. Dingqiu praised Xue for focusing on two key phrases from the classics (*Lunyu* and *Yijing* 易經 [Book of changes], respectively) which Zhu Xi had promoted as the essence of the scholarly path.[34] Dingqiu wrote: "Learning of the Principle in the Ming began

---

30   For an intriguing study of the publication of *Rumen fa yu* outside of the Yangzi Delta area, see Tang, "Rujia xiushen zhi zuo."

31   On Li Fu 李紱 (1673–1750), one of the highest profile advocates of Lu-Wang teachings in the early Qing, see Huang, *Philosophy, Philology, and Politics*.

32   As I have noted elsewhere, the composition claiming to be Dingqiu's first communication from Wenchang in 1674 was reprinted in Vietnam. In late nineteenth century Seoul Dingqiu was known as an exemplary Wenchang devotee among politically-connected spirit-writing practitioners: in a spirit-altar communication Wenchang praised the spirit medium of the Formless Altar (Musang dan 無相壇) Jong Hakku 丁鶴九 by comparing him to Dingqiu. See Kim, "Enlightenment on the Spirit-Altar," 19n31.

33   For Xue and Luo's spirit-altar visits and the works of theirs included in *Rumen fa yu*, see Table 7.1.

34   Zhu Xi, *Zhuzi yulu*, "Xue san 學三."

with Master [Xue] Jingxuan. He was the first to use 'residing in reverence' and 'exhausting the principle' as his central teachings." (有明理學始自敬軒先生。一以居敬窮理為宗。)³⁵

Readers were provided no such guidance as to why Xue mattered in the transcript of Xue's descent to Dingqiu's altar. However, viewed in light of Dingqiu's remarks in *Rumen fa yu*, we can understand why Dingqiu considered posthumous Xue to have been a qualified authority when he declaimed on the character traits necessary for a proper Confucian in the Song Learning mold: "As for Learning of the Principle scholars, he must harden his Qi and set his will." (理學之士，氣須剛，志須定。)³⁶ Dingqiu closed his note on Xue in *Rumen fa yu* by quoting from one of Xue's poems. Posthumous Xue on Dingqiu's altar also declaimed poetry, a parallelism of the form in which the Xue persona—inclusive of historical and posthumous modes—was qualified to communicate.

4 The Imperially Sanctioned Confucian Pantheon in the *Jade Bureau Heart Penance Liturgy*

The products of Dingqiu's altar repeatedly identified themselves as promoting Cheng-Zhu Learning. He worked out questions within the Confucian tradition through his conversations with apotheosized Confucian luminaries that then informed his non-spirit altar Confucian textual production. In this article I will move along the continuum from adherence to imperially mandated orthodoxy to Dingqiu's finer calibrations of a sacralized Confucian patriline on and beyond the spirit-altar.

Dingqiu's adherence to and simultaneous subtle modification of the imperially-mandated Cheng-Zhu lineage is evident in one of the most widely-circulated products of his altar: *Wenchang Yuju zhengzhen xuanhua jiujie chouen xinchan* 文昌玉局證真宣化救刼酬恩心懺 (The heart penance liturgy of Wenchang, evincing perfection, promulgating transformation, providing salvation from the turning of the Kalpa, and recompensing compassion; hereafter *Yuju xinchan*).³⁷ Dingqiu received this liturgy in the capital over the course of seven

---

35 Peng Dingqiu, *Rumen fa yu*, 10b.
36 ZSL, 46.4a.
37 *Wenchang Yuju zhengzhen xuanhua jiujie chouen xinchan* is the full name of the work given by Dingqiu when he described its reception in his autobiography (SJGNP 20b). The editors of the earliest printed edition dropped the "Yuju" from the full title, but then referred to it by the abbreviated title *Yuju xinchan*.

days in the second month of 1680. He returned to Suzhou soon afterwards, and was able to perform the penance liturgy at the Cultural Star Pavilion (Wenxing ge 文星閣) complex in Suzhou, along with his father and his father's students.[38]

The Cultural Star Pavilion was (and is) halfway between the Peng clan's residence, which is just inside the southeastern gate of Suzhou, and the Changzhou 長洲 county school in the northeastern corner of the walled city. The Cultural Star Pavilion was loosely affiliated with the Changzhou county school and was frequented by men—such as Dingqiu and his father Peng Long—who had passed through the Changzhou county school on their ascent of the civil service examination ladder, as well as those who still fervently aspired to do so. However, unlike the Changzhou county school, the Cultural Star Pavilion was not under official supervision. It thus offered more possibilities for a creative program of enshrinement, lecturing, and ritual performance; opportunities of which Peng Long, Dingqiu, and many of his descendants took ample advantage.

Dingqiu discussed the reception of the *Yuju xinchan* in his manuscript autobiography and it is listed in the table of contents of the original 1745 Liu Qiao 劉樵 Dexin tang 德馨堂 edition of the *Wendi quanshu* 文帝全書 (Complete works of the Cultural Thearch) as being included in the appended "Works by Assembled Perfecteds" (Qunzhen zhushu 羣真著述), a common mid-Qing catchall term for early Qing spirit-altar transcripts. However, the 1745 edition survives in only one incomplete exemplar—that held by Peking University—and the appendix did not survive.[39] In his 1773 preface to *Zhishen lu* 質神錄 (Record of soliciting confirmation from the spirits), Dingqiu's great-grandson Peng Shaosheng asserted that *Yuju xinchan* had long circulated independently. As with *Zhishen lu*, the earliest extant edition is in the 1775 edition of the *Wendi quanshu* prepared by Guan Huai 關槐 and Wang Lüjie 王履階. Preceded by spirit-altar prefaces by Wenchang, Lü Dongbin, and Jade Bureau emissary Huang Daozhou,[40] the ritual manual itself consists of three sections. The first is ten short mantras (*zhenyan* 真言; literally "true words"). These are a Buddho-Daoist hybrid that do not engage with Cheng-Zhu discourse. The second section is a Confucian pantheon that the mortal participants are instructed to propitiate. I translate this passage and discuss it in detail below.

---

38 SJGNP, 20b–21a.
39 Hu, "*Wendi quanshu* yanjiu," 136.
40 YJXC 2a–5a (prefatory material preceding the first page of the liturgy itself, with the *banxin* 版心 indicating each respective preface author while employing continuous pagination). As indicated by the table of contents immediately preceding YJXC, these prefaces were not part of the performance itself: *mulu* 目錄, 1a.

Neither of the first two sections of the printed *Yuju xinchan*—the mantras and the Confucian pantheon—was integral to the performance of the penance ritual. This is indicated by the instruction immediately following the list of Confucian figures: "When the prostrations are complete immediately open the penance liturgy" (*bai bi fang ru chan* 拜畢方入懺). The injunction to *ru chan* directed the presiding ritualist to open the physical copy of the ritual text; the analogous phrase common in other forms of Daoist ritual is "open the ritual text" (*ru ke* 入科).

The third section is the liturgy itself. The liturgy consists of ten sections, each of them culminating with reverencing a Daoist pantheon. At least four deities in that pantheon were higher than Wenchang: the Three Purities the Celestial Esteemed the Way and Its Potency, Numinous Treasure, and Primordial Commencement (Sanqing yuanshi lingbao daode tianzun 三清元始靈寶道德天尊) and the Exalted and Supreme Thearch of the Profound Heights, Celestial Esteemed Jade August of the Golden Parapets of Vast Heaven (Haotian jinque yuhuang da tianzun xuanqiong gao shangdi 昊天金闕玉皇大天尊玄穹高上帝: i.e., the Jade Emperor). Yet it was Wenchang who was singled out at the end of each iteration of Daoist deities to be propitiated. It is specified that he receive three prostrations rather than the single bow directed to the other deities.

Yuju xinchan thus contains two pantheons that initially appear to be entirely distinct: one Confucian and one Daoist. Given that the Daoist one is repeated ten times, the relationship between the two pantheons is hardly equal. Certain nineteenth century Wenchang devotees clearly viewed the Confucian pantheon as superfluous: in the 1876 edition of the *Wendi quanshu* the Confucian pantheon was moved from immediately preceding the penance liturgy to following it, thereby reducing it to an appendix. This editorial intervention misunderstood Dingqiu's intention and his Confucio-Daoist praxis.

The Confucian pantheon immediately preceding the *Yuju xinchan* emulated the enshrinement of Confucius and his disciples at the county school with which the Cultural Star Pavilion was affiliated. Dingqiu participated in the spring and autumn sacrifices to Confucius and his disciples at both the Changzhou county school and the Suzhou prefectural school. Including the same pantheon for a spirit-altar ritual at the Cultural Star Pavilion asserted the ritual's adherence to imperial orthodoxy, while at the same time Dingqiu could not conceivably have performed such a ritual at the Changzhou county school itself. At the Cultural Star Pavilion, however, he could perform the ritual with past and present students of the county school.

In the *Yuju xinchan* it was not Dingqiu but Wenchang's celestial officials who ordered the mortals to perform the obeisance to the Confucian pantheon. The command reads: "The perfected officials of Wenchang's Jade Bureau [command] their disciples and other participants to concentrate their heart-minds in reverent prostrations before. ..." (文昌玉局真官為弟子等眾志心敬禮。) The two figures with rank in Wenchang's Jade Bureau at this time were the above-mentioned Du Qiaolin—the credited author of the *Yuju xinchan*—and Huang Daozhou. The figures from the Confucian pantheon whom Dingqiu had hosted as spirit-altar deities prior to the delivery of the *Yuju xinchan* were Zhou Dunyi and Cheng Yi.

The Confucian pantheon is as follows:

> The First Teacher of Great Completion, The Ultimate Sage Master Kong 先師大成至聖孔子
> Restorer of the Sage Master Yan 復聖顏子
> Reverer of the Sage Master Zeng 宗聖曾子
> Recorder of the Sage Master Zisi[41] 述聖子思子
> Second Sage Master Meng 亞聖孟子
> All the Confucians [*Kong men*] enshrined as correlates 孔門從祀諸子
> Master Zhou Lianxi 濂溪周子
> Master Cheng Mingdao 明道程子
> Master Cheng Yichuan 伊川程子
> Master Shao Kangjie 康節邵子
> Master Zhang Hengqu 橫渠張子
> Master Zhu Ziyang 紫陽朱子
> The Perfected Confucians of the Learning of the Principle Through the Ages 歷代理學真儒[42]

This pantheon corresponds to the spirit tablets housed in special halls at the Confucian temples (*wenmiao* 文廟) and county and prefectural schools throughout the empire. It begins with Confucius and his four disciples, who bear the titles granted to them by the Yuan emperor Mingzong 明宗 (r. 1329)—the Khutughtu Khan Kuśala (1300–29)—and confirmed—but not raised—by the Jiajing 嘉靖 emperor (r. 1521–1567).[43] The phrase "All the Confucians enshrined as correlates" succinctly captures the gist of adherence to orthodoxy: this was a dynamic category, with the individual men so honored changing along with the trends in imperial favor of particular schools within the Con-

---

41   The translations of the titles of Yan Hui, Zeng Shen, and Kong Ji are from Wilson, *Genealogy of the Way*, 254.
42   YJXC, 3a–b.
43   See the discussion in Huang, *Confucianism and Sacred Space*, 156.

fucian tradition.[44] Reverencing them as a group deferred to imperial authority the selection of the actual men. What follows is Zhu Xi's formulation of the "Transmission of the Way" (Daotong 道統), picking up with Zhou Dunyi and Cheng Yi directly from Mengzi after nearly a millennium and a half interruption.

"The Perfected Confucians of the Learning of the Principle Through the Ages" refers to figures concurrent with or post-dating Zhu Xi. Unlike the previous placeholder "All the Confucians enshrined as correlates," this phrase was not deferential towards Cheng-Zhu orthodoxy. In the early Qing, Learning of the Principle (Lixue 理學) was a category that provoked dispute over the contributions of Lu Jiuyuan, Wang Shouren, and those inspired by them. Indeed, Peng Sunyu—one of the oath-bound members of Dingqiu's altar—went on to serve on the *Ming shi* 明史 (Ming history) commission that debated whether or not to have a separate "Learning of the Way" biographical section (*Daoxue zhuan* 道學傳) for such figures as opposed to other Confucians, as the *Song shi* 宋史 (Song history) had done. Peng Sunyu argued—ultimately unsuccessfully—for the separate Learning of the Way biographies. His opponents included Zhang Lie 張烈 (1622–1685; *jinshi* 1670), the author of an anti-Wang treatise *Wang xue zhiyi* 王學質疑 (Interrogating Yangming learning), and Lu Longqi 陸隴其 (1630–1692), the early Qing's most vocal detractor of Yangming Learning.[45] Lu did not serve on the *Ming shi* commission, but made his presence felt through his close collaboration with Zhang. In 1703, decades after the *Ming shi* controversy, Dingqiu authored "Yaojiang shi hui lu 姚江釋毀錄" (Record of explicating attempts to destroy the Yaojiang school), which quoted passages by Lu Longqi and refuted them one by one.[46] As with *Rumen fa yu*, Dingqiu's essay defending Yangming Learning incorporated arguments first made on his spirit-altar and mentioned Confucian figures who descended to his altar posthumously.

It is in this group of "The Perfected Confucians of the Learning of the Principle Through the Ages" that Dingqiu elaborated his own distinctive Confucian pantheon. The way in which this unitary pantheon overlapped between

---

44 For a comprehensive survey of the figures enshrined during the late Qing, see Watters, *A Guide to the Tablets*.

45 On Lu's campaign to elevate Zhu at the expense of Wang, see Geng, "Lu Longqi Lixue," Liu, "Zhang Lie zun Zhu chi Wang," Zhang "Lu Longqi de *Sishu* xue," and Zhang and Xiao, "Cong Zhang Lüxiang, Lü Liuliang dao Lu Longqi."

46 "Yaojiang shi hui lu" was not published until 1881, after which time it became part of Dingqiu's posthumous persona as a defender of Yangming Learning, as evinced in the anecdote "Peng Qinzhi jiangxue 彭勤止講學" (Learning-through-Discussion of Peng Qinzhi [Dingqiu]) preserved in Xu Ke, *Qingbai lei chao*, v. 10: 4548–49.

historically-attested compositions included in *Rumen fa yu* and spirit-altar communications by the posthumous forms of the same figures is demonstrated in Table 7.1.

Viewed from the perspective of Daoist ritual, the Confucian pantheon immediately preceding the *Yuju xinchan* corresponds to the section in Daoist liturgies called "opening the [lineage of] teachers" (*qi shi* 啟師). The section proceeds hierarchically from the highest deities down to the individual ritualist's own lineage, culminating in the ritualist's own teacher.[47] By using this section to honor a Confucian patriline, Dingqiu was being consistent with the sacralized nature of Zhu Xi's Transmission of the Way. In contrast to the filiation a conventional Daoist priest would have provided, Dingqiu asserted that his own lineage was an exclusively Confucian one. This despite the obviously non-Confucian origin of the ritual itself and Dingqiu's acknowledgement elsewhere of Shi Daoyuan as his master.

Within the archive of Dingqiu's spirit-altar communications, those who served in Wenchang's divine administration were referred to by a range of terms, including "celestial officials" (*tian guan* 天官), "perfected officials" (*zhen guan* 真官), and "perfecteds" (*zhenren* 真人). The term *tian guan* has classical precedent, as the name of chapters in both the *Zhouli* 周禮 (Comprehensive offices/Rites of Zhou) and in Sima Qian's 司馬遷 *Shiji* 史記 (Records of the Grand Historian).[48] *Zhenren* is a concept discussed in the "Dazong shi 大宗師" (Great ancestral teacher) chapter of the *Zhuangzi* 莊子 that became an indicator of celestial rank as Daoist movements fleshed out a celestial bureaucracy beginning in the second century of the common era.[49] In the list of unnamed Learning of the Principle figures, Dingqiu made the subtle change "perfected Confucians" (*zhen ru* 真儒) where the language of Confucian canonization employed "former Confucians" (*xian ru* 先儒; including in the spirit-altar production of Jade Bureau emissary Huang, on which see below).

Another significant change within the *Yuju xinchan* from that performed by non-literati ordained Daoist priests is that the ritualist referred to himself as a "post-holder" (*zhi* 職) rather than "minister" (*chen* 臣).[50] This was to

---

47　Two of the four exemplars of the Dipper Mother ritual analyzed by Tao Jin include Shi Daoyuan in their pantheon of teachers. See his "Suzhou Shanghai *Gao Dou keyi* zhong 'qishi' jieci chutan," 37.

48　The chapters are titled "Tianguan 天官" and "Tianguan shu 天官書," respectively. The former is translated in Biot, *Le Tcheou-li*, vol. 1, 120–70; the latter in Pankenier, *Astrology and Cosmology in Early China*, 458–511.

49　On the system of ranks for Daoist immortals, see Li, "Shenxian sanpin de yuanshi ji qi yanbian." I am grateful to Fabrizio Pregadio for bringing this article to my attention.

50　I am grateful to Tao Jin for this insight.

avoid confusion because, unlike ordained Daoist priests, so many of the Yangzi Delta elites engaged in spirit-altar ritual *were* actual officials who customarily referred to themselves as "ministers" (*chen*) when composing memorials to the (terrestrial) emperor.

As with *Rumen fa yu*, the *Yuju xinchan* was enormously popular: it was performed consistently in Suzhou from 1680 through the reign of the Qianlong 乾隆 emperor (r. 1735–1796).[51]

5 Learning-Through-Discussion on the Spirit-Altar: Posthumous Huang Daozhou's Spirit-Altar Lectures

The orthodox Confucian pantheon did not remain outside the *Yuju xinchan*. For example, in the praises of Wenchang that form the first section of the liturgy, among his qualities are: "Positioning Cheng [Yi] and Zhou [Dunyi] to be regarded as the cauldron and teaching that Kong[zi] and Meng[zi] are the limits of the enclosure." (位視伊周鼎鉉。教為孔孟藩籬。)[52] This language was characteristic of much of the Confucian-centered spirit-altar discourse on Dingqiu's altar, particularly that of emissary Huang Daozhou. It was not only the content but the form of Confucian material on Dingqiu's altar that promulgated his iteration of the learning of the sages. Most importantly, Confucian deities on Dingqiu's altar practiced learning-through-discussion (*jiangxue* 講學), a popular style of lecturing integral to the praxis of Yangming Learning.[53]

In the mid-Ming Wang Shouren developed his teaching into an actual social movement, with huge numbers of men attending his lectures and those of his followers.[54] As Lu Miaw-fen has shown, learning-through-discussion assumed many forms, from a presentation centered on a visiting celebrity on the lecture circuit to periodic discussion groups of local friends.[55] For both the historical Huang and Dingqiu we have concrete examples of what it meant to them: a selection of Huang's lectures survives as *Rong tan wenye* 榕檀問業 (Questions

---

51 Goossaert, "Spirit-writing Altars and Daoist Rituals in Qing Jiangnan," 394.
52 YJXC, 4b.
53 On the semantic range of *jiangxue*, see the discussion in Deng, "Like Tea and Rice at Home," esp. 161–66, and Huang, "Male Friendship and *Jiangxue*." I use a literal translation in order to convey the orality and the presence of interlocutors in the original term.
54 For an excellent integration of Wang's career and ideas, see Israel, *Doing Good and Ridding Evil in Ming China*.
55 Lu, *Yangming xueshiren shequn*, 73–110, is devoted to defining lecture meetings (*jianghui* 講會), the gatherings that centered on *jiangxue*.

on the [Confucian] vocation from [under the] banyans and sandalwoods),[56] while Dingqiu included his father's introduction to his own lecture curriculum in *Wenxing ge xiao zhi* 文星閣小志 (Modest gazetteer of the Cultural Star Pavilion).[57]

One common form of learning-through-discussion lectures was the speaker identifying a passage from a classic and riffing on it. This was what occurred in the first of posthumous Huang's lectures on the spirit-altar, which he delivered in the seventh month of 1679.[58] Two subsequent lectures were both given titles and complimented by paratexts. These were the "Fuchu lu 復初錄" (Record of returning to the fundamentals), which was delivered at the Wenchang Palace 文昌宮 in the capital in the twelfth lunar month of 1679—just two months before emissary Du transmitted the *Yuju xinchan*[59]—and "Jiangxi lu," transmitted in Suzhou in the second lunar month of 1698.[60] Unlike other products of Dingqiu's altar, there is no evidence that any of emissary Huang's three learning-through-discussion lectures circulated independently.

In the first of emissary Huang's lectures he cited phrases from Confucius' discussions with his disciples and offered his glosses. He began with the opening passage of the *Lunyu*. The words of Confucius that emissary Huang chose to address provide a window into Dingqiu's concerns at the time while serving in the capital. For example, *Lunyu* 1.3—"The Master said: 'Clever talk and affected manners are seldom signs of goodness.'"[61]—addresses the lack of correspondence between people's outer appearances and their inner states. Posthumous Huang's choice of discussion topics implied two parallels: that the Yangmingist style discussion engaged in by emissary Huang was a continuation of Confucius' original dialogues with his students, and that Dingqiu was a disciple of emissary Huang analogous to the disciples of Confucius named in the passages.[62]

Five months later emissary Huang descended again to give a lengthier communication on Dingqiu's altar; its title inspired Dingqiu to adopt the moniker

---

56　Huang, Rong tan wenye.
57　Peng Long, "Wenxing ge keye xu 文星閣課業序," in Peng Dingqiu, *Wenxing ge xiao zhi*, *juan* 2, 1a–2b (47–50). The preface is dated Kangxi 20.7 (Aug. 14–Sept. 11, 1681). There are no known exemplars of the work which it prefaced.
58　ZSL, 46.17b–20b.
59　Ibid., 46.21a–27a.
60　Ibid., *juan* 47, 1a–16b.
61　Ibid., 46.18b. Confucius, *The Analects*, 3.
62　The named disciples are Yan Hui 顏回 (521–481; *zi* Ziyuan 子淵), Bu Shang 卜商 (507 BCE–?; *zi* Zixia 子夏), Duanmu Ci 端木賜 (520–446 BCE; *zi* Zigong 子貢), Yan Yan 言偃 (506–443 BCE; *zi* Ziyou 子游), and Zhong You 仲由 (542–480 BCE; *zi* Zilu 子路).

"The Scholar Who Returns to the Fundamentals" (Fuchu xueren), with which he signed his preface to *Rumen fa yu*. "Fundamentals" is structured around three key concepts: "Making learning orthodox" (*zheng xue* 正學), "Managing one's household" (*qi jia* 齊家),[63] and "Conducting oneself properly" (*chu shi* 處世).[64] Emissary Huang's preface sheds light on his authoritative voice and his unique role among the deities who descended to Dingqiu's altar.

> My descent via the planchette is not to demonstrate [my] "grasp of oneself." I have come in order to illuminate-through-discussion the scholarly conundrums, to provide guidance as to how to proceed. I will comment on the aphorisms of previous personages, admonishing the flowing stream [of humanity] in the mortal realm. The *Application of Equilibrium* (*Zhongyong*) states: "They are substantial things and cannot be neglected."[65] Sincerity reaches to the ghosts and spirits. For this reason [if you display] "utmost sincerity" [you too can be like a deity].

> 吾來降乩,亦不得已[66]之心也。降以講明學問,提撕心術,述前人之格言,警斯世之流波。《中庸》言:「體物而不可遺」。誠既鬼神也。故「至誠」如神。[67]

The aphorisms (*ge yan* 格言) mentioned in the above passage were an important genre incorporated into spirit-altar production. Emissary Huang's repeated allusions to the *Zhongyong* are consistent with the disproportionate reliance on that text by Qing spirit-writing enthusiasts eager to assert a pre-Song dynasty origin for their manner of communicating with spirits.[68] *Zhongy-*

---

63 ZSL, 46.23b. The *locus classicus* of the phrase *qi jia* is as the third of the eight steps that the noble man must complete to cultivate his virtue in the *Daxue*. See Johnston and Wang, Daxue *and* Zhongyong, 46–47.
64 ZSL, 46.25a.
65 The translation is that of Johnston and Wang following Zhu Xi's commentary: Johnston and Wang, Daxue *and* Zhongyong, 437.
66 *De ji* appears to be an allusion to *Mengzi* 7A.9. Lau renders the relevant term "delight in himself": *Mencius*, 146. In this context I understand it to mean something closer to self-control, or even personal autonomy as opposed to being ordered to do something by a superior.
67 *Zhi cheng* 至誠 is a concept lauded repeatedly in the *Zhongyong*.
68 This work is best known in English as the Doctrine of the Mean, a translation that—among other problems—elides *yong*. For a brief discussion of problems this character posed for exegetes, see Plaks, Ta Hsüeh *and* Chung Yung, xvi–xvii, and Ames and Hall, *Focusing the Familiar*, 150–52. Here I adopt the translation of Paul Goldin in "The Consciousness of

ong was particularly well-suited to that role because of its elaboration of the way in which the individual cultivation can be extended to a matter of cosmic import.[69] Indeed, in 1773, when Peng Shaosheng compiled the spirit-altar communications from Dingqiu's altar, he titled it with an allusion to a passage that occurs twice in quick succession in chapter 31 of *Zhongyong*. The passage asserts that the ruler or noble man (*junzi* 君子) "solicits confirmation from the ghosts and spirits then [having received it] is without doubts" (質諸鬼神而無疑).[70] Shaosheng's collection of Dingqiu's spirit-altar transcripts was thus titled *Record of Soliciting Confirmation from the Spirits*. This framing was part of the classicizing strategy spirit-altar enthusiasts in the Peng lineage employed in order to be able to assert that the practices in which they engaged were the same in spirit as those testified to in canonical texts (in the case of the *Zhongyong*, both a chapter in one of the Five Classics and independently the culmination of Zhu Xi's sequence of the Four Books). Dingqiu provided the lead that Shaosheng followed in occasionally referring to the descent (*jiang* 降) of spirits as *ge si* 格思. This archaism invoked a passage from the poem "Yi 抑" in the *Shijing* 詩經 (Book of poetry) that was also quoted in the *Zhongyong*. It reads: "The arrival of the spirits cannot be fathomed. How much less can they be disparaged?" (神之格思，不可度思，矧可射思。)[71]

Emissary Huang continued:

---

the Dead," 86. For an overview of translations of the title into European languages from Dingqiu's day (the first was into Latin in 1687) to the present, see Johnston and Wang, Daxue *and* Zhongyong, 514.

69 See the discussion in Ames and Hall, *Focusing the Familiar*, 27.

70 *Zhongyong*, chap. 31. The passage is quoted and discussed in ZSL, 46.35a. Previous translations of this passage translate *zhi* in a manner that emphasizes either human action towards the spirits or divine action towards humans. Legge is an example of the former: "His presenting himself *with his institutions* before spiritual beings, without any doubts arising about them, shows that he knows Heaven." (Legge, *Chinese Classics*, vol. 1, 426; emphasis in original.) Johnston and Wang is an example of the latter: "The Way of the noble man (ruler) … is rectified by the ghosts and spirits, and is without doubt." In place of "rectified by" they also use "verified by." (Johnston and Wang, Daxue *and* Zhongyong, 361, 367.) My translation is intended to emphasize the cooperative nature of the endeavor between humans and spirits. I am grateful to Lai Guolong for engaging in extensive discussions of this issue.

71 "Yi" is poem number 256 in the Mao 毛 recension of the *Shijing*. My translation is adapted from Goldin, "The Consciousness of the Dead," 86. For the full poem and a literal translation, see Karlgren, *The Book of Odes*, 216–19. Dingqiu's grandson Peng Qifeng recalled Dingqiu quoting the full passage in the context of spirit-writing: Peng Qifeng, "Huang Shizhai xiansheng shoushu Zhou Zhongjie gong shendaobei ba 黃石齋先生手書周忠介公神道碑跋," *Zhiting xiansheng ji*, 18.12a.

As for the matter of my descent, there are none who do not criticize and mock it, regarding these as empty words without evidence. Alas! And what is the result? Suppose that these days orthodox learning was flourishing, with teachers and students mutually driving one another on, each day mutually exhorting one another to practice loyalty, filiality, benevolence, and righteousness, and mutually developing the patrilineal distillation of innate nature and lifespan, as with the regulations of the White Deer Grotto [Academy], as with the instructions on the Celestial Spring Bridge, then heterodoxy could be vanquished and sincerity preserved, doubts resolved and the true differentiated from the false. [If all this were the case,] then sincerity would not rely on the planchette in order to be enacted.

乃吾之來降，無不誚且笑之，以為是浮言無據。嗚呼！其果然乎？假使今日者，正學昌明，師友砥礪，日以忠孝仁義相勸，性命宗旨相發，如白鹿洞之規，如天泉橋之訓，可以閑邪存誠，析疑辯偽，則誠無籍於乩為矣。[72]

This passage reveals a defensiveness regarding the appropriateness of spirit-writing by self-identified Confucians. Emissary Huang's response is that such communications would not be necessary if the ethical caliber of scholars and officials was higher.[73] Dingqiu's conversations with the spirit-altar deities compensate for the poor quality of the men around him: i.e., those that staffed the metropolitan government. In terms of advocacy of Yangming Learning, it is also notable that emissary Huang placed a seminal discussion Wang had in Shaoxing in 1528 with his students Wang Ji and Qian Dehong 錢德洪 (1496–1574) on the same level as Zhu Xi's guidelines for his White Deer Grotto, which became the model for academies not only for the remainder of imperial Chinese history but elsewhere in East Asia as well.[74]

"Discussion and Study" was the first transmission after a seventeen-year break in the preserved spirit-altar transcripts. It is three times the length of "Fundamentals" and is more complex organizationally, with twenty-four items (*ze* 則) laid out in four schema of consistently increasing number. As emissary

---

72　ZSL, 46.21a–b.
73　For comparison, see the discussion of practitioners' justification of spirit-writing in Schumann's contribution to this volume.
74　Dingqiu opened *Rumen fa yu* with Zhu's influential regulations: "Bailudong shuyuan jieshi 白鹿洞書院揭示", *Rumen fa yu*, 1a–b. Wang, in contrast, left no similar programmatic statement for institutional development.

Huang put it in his preface: "It begins with Three Refusals, continues with Five Prohibitions, expands with Seven Differentiations, and investigates with Nine Proofs." (始以三闢，次以五禁，申以七辯，究以九證。)[75] Despite pushing the length-limit of coherency in a spirit-altar transmission, "Jiangxi lu" is essentially identical to "Fuchu lu" in using keywords as discussion points with which to hold forth on the problems of the day, as well as in expounding upon the proper means of conducting oneself to counter them. He employed canonical quotations to bolster his arguments.

In identifying a major preoccupation of Dingqiu's altar as learning-through-discussion, the clearest criteria is that the descending spirits themselves often explicitly used the term *jiangxue* to describe what they were doing. This is clear in emissary Huang's introduction to "Jiangxi lu." He stated:

> Sages regard not [engaging] in learning-through-discussion as a source of grief. Our contemporaries regard learning-through-discussion as a source of grief. Those who lament learning-through-discussion are little different from those who do not engage in learning at all. There are also those who speak of discussion but do not speak of studying. They do not know that which they are discussing. These types increase misunderstanding, resulting in sinning against the Former Sages. I wish to save [you] from these two wrongs. For this reason [I] regard discussion as study and study as discussion.
>
> 聖人以不講學為憂。時人以講學為憂。憂其講學，而大不便於不學之徒也。亦有言講而不言習者。不知所講何事。徒滋口舌。獲罪先哲。吾欲救此二弊。則以講為習，以習為講。[76]

Emissary Huang provided introductions and conclusions for both "Fuchu lu" and "Jiangxi lu."[77] As part of the collegial relationship of the Jade Bureau emissaries, "Jiangxi lu" includes a postface by emissary Du. In it he addressed the topic of Yangming Learning, immediately differentiating the practices with which Yangming Learning had become associated from Wang's own teachings.

---

75   ZSL, 46.1b.
76   ZSL, 47.1a.
77   In ZSL the former are termed prefaces but emissary Huang's conclusions are not termed postfaces. The openings of the prefaces are explicitly stated but not their closings; the distinction is clear due to the commencement of the itemized lecture format. Neither conclusion is identified as a postface; in "Fuchu lu" the conclusion is identified as a separate descent to the altar.

Emissary Du stated: "The Learning of Yaojiang has been caused by latter persons to sink-in-confusion into Chan; in doing so it greatly violates the original teachings of innate knowledge." (姚江之學，被後人謬墮入禪，大違致良知本教。)[78] Both of these points were concessions to early Qing critics of Yangming Learning such as Lu Longqi and Zhang Lie, who asserted that Yangming Learning was nothing more than Chan, and that Wang's teachings on "innate knowledge" were a perversion of the original meaning of the term, the *locus classicus* of which is in *Mengzi*.

Surprisingly, some editions of *Rumen fa yu* include a piece by Wang Ji, a first-generation disciple of Wang Shouren who was fiercely criticized in the late Ming and early Qing for emphasizing subjectivity to the extent that objective moral criteria no longer applied.[79] Dingqiu's inclusion of Wang Ji indicates that, in this case at least, he chose not to defend Wang by accusing Wang's students of distorting his teachings. The reference to "original teachings of innate knowledge" is also canny: the phrase appears in *Mengzi*. In Lu Longqi's critique, Wang Shouren had distorted this phrase, but on Dingqiu's altar, the "original teachings" were those of Wang himself.

Emissary Du then claimed the historical Huang Daozhou as a Yangmingist, which he was not.[80] Emissary Du asserted that it was precisely Huang's grasp of Wang's teachings that had enabled him to conduct himself in such as manner to become what Zhang Ying has termed "a *zhongxiao* celebrity": i.e., to embody the two most important qualities of the Confucian paragons of his age, loyalty (*zhong* 忠) and filiality (*xiao* 孝).[81] "In those days Master Huang made assiduous efforts, truly obtaining the heritage[82] of Yaojiang; it is for this reason that he took a 'principled stand against surrender'[83] and 'manifest[ed] his loyalty on his own.'" (黃先生當年下刻苦功夫，真得姚江骨血，以故抗節孤忠。)[84]

---

78   ZSL, 47.17a.
79   Wang Ji, "Penglai hui shen yue hou yu 蓬萊會申約後語," *Rumen fa yu*, 36a–39b.
80   In his influential intellectual filiation, Huang Zongxi placed Huang Daozhou in the "various Confucians" (*zhu ru* 諸儒) category. See his *Ming Ru Xue'an*, juan 56. In his "life and thought" study of Huang Daozhou, Chen Lai characterized him as "neither [a proponent] of Yangming Learning, nor a Learning of the Principle figure in the strict sense, but rather an independent thinker who was inclined towards Zhu [Xi] Learning's doctrine of the investigation of things." (黃道周不是王學，也不是嚴格意義的理學家，而是比較傾向於朱子學格物論的獨立思想家。) Chen, "Huang Daozhou de shengping yu sixiang," 87.
81   Zhang, *Confucian Image Politics*, 102–28.
82   Literally "bones and blood" (*gu xue* 骨血).
83   The *locus classicus* for this phrase is in the *Zhi an ce* 治安策 of Jia Yi 賈誼 (200–168 BCE).
84   ZSL, 47.17a.

Emissary Huang took a position that bolstered Dingqiu's minority stance advocating Yangming Learning against the onus of associations with excessive introspection (the Chan school). Dingqiu's "Yaojiang School" essay also identified Huang as an unambiguous proponent of Yangming Learning.[85] This was not the prevailing understanding of Huang either in Dingqiu's own day or since. In this 1698 spirit-altar production, emissary Huang first articulated a position that Dingqiu did not commit to paper until 1703, and even then declined to circulate in print.

Because of their length, "Fuchu lu" and "Jiangxi lu" had sufficient space to quote and discuss the major authorities. In this pantheon inside a pantheon, Dingqiu's iteration of the "Transmission of the Way" clearly emerges. It follows closely that of Zhu Xi, including Confucius, his top disciples Yan Hui 顏回 and Zeng Shen 曾參 (505–435 BCE), then moves from Mengzi and on to the Northern Song masters. Dingqiu's significant modifications were: 1) the omission of Shao Yong 邵雍 (1011–1077);[86] 2) the integration of Wang Shouren; and 3) the inclusion of Gao Panlong, a figure about whom Dingqiu was so enthusiastic that in his commentary on Gao's inclusion in *Rumen fa yu* he blurted out: "My teacher!" (*wu shi hu* 吾師乎).[87]

6   Conclusion

Dingqiu's spirit-altar communications used Cheng-Zhu Learning as an apotropaic mantra to ward off imperial prosecution. This was objectively a successful strategy: from 1678–1680 Dingqiu engaged in an activity prohibited by Qing law prior to and during his tenure as an official in the capital. But it was also one he could not sustain: Dingqiu did not engage in spirit-writing during his second term of service in the capital, from 1682–1689, nor for almost a decade more after his retirement.[88] Perhaps he feared what later happened to the Altar of the Source of Awakening (Jueyuan tan 覺源壇) under the Jiaqing emperor: spirit-

---

85   Peng Dingqiu, "Yaojiang shi hui lu," 1b.
86   Shao was the most tenuous inclusion in Zhu Xi's schema. See Wyatt, "Chu Hsi's Critique of Shao Yung." Ironically, Shao was the only one of the Northern Song figures for whom the historical Huang Daozhou had nothing but praise: see Chen, "Huang Daozhou de shengping yu sixiang," 12.
87   Rumen fa yu, 42a.
88   For a non-spirit-altar focused overview of Dingqiu's terms in office and activities after retirement, see Huang, "Kangxi shiwu nian zhuangyuan Peng Dingqiu" and "Peng Dingqiu wannian."

altar activity became part of the indictment against participants caught up in court intrigues.[89]

In his comprehensive survey of the Wenchang compendiums produced from 1645 to 1883, Hu Jiechen has drawn attention to the way in which they foreground the language of Confucian orthodoxy while their contents ranged quite far from the civil service examination curriculum.[90] This was a form of orthodoxy remote from the emerging standards of evidential learning (*kaozheng xue* 考證學); one that subscribed to a shared moral ideal without fretting over textual integrity. In her prosopography of the 1761 class of presented scholars—which included Peng Shaosheng—Iona Man-Cheong called for moving away from a concept of orthodoxy exclusively defined by state-backing: "In place of rigidly differentiated orthodoxies, we might consider orthodoxies more dynamically as categories defined by different authoritative interpretations imposed by groups who stand in different power relationships with each other."[91] She concluded that "the state … increasingly could no longer define so closely what constituted the elite or its ideology. … [S]tate-sponsored Confucianism was increasingly in competition with other intellectual trends that, with support from the scholar-elite, could now decenter imperially sponsored interpretations."[92] Wenchang devotion using the language of Confucian orthodoxy was an important part of the diffusion of Confucian identity and de-centering of state control.

Dingqiu became such a powerful symbol among Wenchang devotees and in the broader mid- and late Qing philanthropic milieu precisely because the biographical facts of his life validated the promises of a Wenchang devotee. Foremost among these was office for oneself and one's descendants through success on the civil examination system conceived of as a reward for virtuous conduct. In this sense Dingqiu's Cheng-Zhu Learning spirit-writing altar should be placed in a broad tradition of popular Confucianism which honored the ethical values promoted by the creed while formulating ideas and practices that spoke to the concerns of daily life. As a matter of policy, the strictly controlled spaces of the Confucian temples and their imperially-designated objects of worship could not fulfill such a function. Popular Confucianism attained new proportions in the Song dynasty (960–1279); Wenchang devotion was a key element,

---

89   On the Jueyuan tan, see Lai, "*Lüzu quanshu zhengzong*."
90   Hu, "*Wendi quanshu* yanjiu" and "Qingdai liuzhong Wendi lei quanshu de chubanshi yanjiu."
91   Man-Cheong, *The Class of 1761*, 13.
92   Ibid., 205–6.

alongside the twenty-four filial exemplars and cheap portraits of Confucius. When late Qing elites such as Kang Youwei 康有為 (1858–1927) attempted to create a Confucian religion from scratch, they were acutely aware that Wenchang devotion occupied the ground that they wished to secure for their own ideas and practices.[93]

One of the clearest takeaways from this study of Confucian discourse on Dingqiu's spirit-altar is the challenge of getting audiences to accept material that diverged significantly from their expectations. The communications on Dingqiu's altar most concerned with the Confucian tradition were not enthusiastically embraced and promulgated, while those that took the form of revealed morality book and penance liturgy circulated widely. Peng Shaosheng included emissary Huang's "Fuchu lu" and "Jiangxi lu" in *Zhishen lu* precisely because they had not been distributed by others, and were thus at risk of being lost. In stark contrast, the short compositions claiming to be Dingqiu's communications from Wenchang and the Dipper Mother in the fall of 1674 and the *Yuju xinchan*—none of which Shaosheng included in *Zhishen lu*— circulated as early as 1745, and continued to be frequently reprinted throughout the nineteenth century. As we have seen *Rumen fa yu*, too, was frequently reprinted in this period, but Wenchang-centered textual products did not mention it any more than *Rumen fa yu* engaged with Wenchang devotion. The readership of both works demonstrably overlapped in Dingqiu's descendants through the late eighteenth century, and presumably a wide range of examination takers shared an interest in the Wenchang canons of the eighteenth and nineteenth century alongside Confucian anthologies such as *Rumen fa yu*. However, generic conventions and the reader expectations that enforced them prevented the integration of the two realms that had been necessary to produce Dingqiu's spirit-altar *oeuvre* and his distinctive Confucian anthology.

Acknowledgments

I wish to thank Matthias Schumann and Elena Valussi for organizing the seminal conference that has culminated in the present volume and for providing timely and insightful editorial guidance. I am indebted to Tao Jin for sharing his insights with me regarding the structure of and pantheons in the *Yuju xinchan*. I wrote this article during the spring of 2021 while a Visiting Fellow at

---

93 Huang, *Confucianism and Sacred Space*, 180–81.

the "Fate, Freedom and Prognostication: Strategies for Coping with the Future in East Asia and Europe" Project of the International Consortium for Research in the Humanities at Friedrich-Alexander-Universität Erlangen-Nürnberg. I am grateful to staff and concurrent fellows for creating a stimulating research environment despite pandemic restrictions. In particular, I wish to express my gratitude to Lai Guolong 來國龍 for his perpetual willingness to discuss *xuewen* 學問. I also wish to express my thanks to Vincent Goossaert, Hu Jiechen, and Zhu Mingchuan for sharing their work and ideas. Thomas Wilson and Larry Israel provided valuable comments as well.

Appendix

Editions of Peng Dingqiu's Confucian Anthology *Rumen fa yu*
All exemplars listed have been personally examined by the author. This is not an exhaustive list of extant editions or holding libraries.
- 1697 (Kangxi 36). Dated by preface by Peng Dingqiu. Shanghai Library (線普 531940–41).
- 1752 (QL 17). Dated by postface by Peng Qifeng. Shanghai Library (線普 436850); National Archive of Japan (299–0126; formerly owned by Shōheizaka Gakumonjo 昌平坂学問所).
- 1822 (DG 2). Shanghai Library (線普長 634194).
- 1846 (DG 26). Additional printing history by Peng Yunce 蘊策 (*houxu* 後序 2a–b). Shanghai Library (線普 436851).
- 1852 (XF 2). Woodblocks held by Cunxing shuwu 存星書屋. Shanghai Library (線普 346413).
- 1865 (TZ 4). Woodblocks held by Yiyan tang 衣言堂 (Changzhou county Peng clan publisher). Shanghai Library (5 exemplars: 線普長 250517; 線普長 634195; 線普長 006440; 線普長 007935; 線普長 006435).
- 1875 (GX 1). Jiangsu xuezheng shu 江蘇學政署. Shanghai Library (2 exemplars: 線普長 016880; 線普長 108573).
- GX 23. Yangzhou Prefectural School (Yangzhou fuxue 揚州府學). Suzhou Library.
- Undated (Qing) manuscript. Shanghai Library (線普長 010077).
- 1922. Published by Chengye tang 承業堂. New Asia College Ch'ien Mu Library of the Chinese University of Hong Kong; Suzhou Library (2 exemplars); University of Chicago, Regenstein (1042 4235).
- 1926. Saoye shanfang 掃葉山房 lithographic edition, included in *Deyu congshu* 德育叢書. Shanghai Library (2 exemplars: 線普 530751; 線普 530822).

(Explicitly) Abbreviated Editions

Ru men fa yu ji 儒門法語集.

- Manuscript with postface dated 1821. Shanghai Library (線善 771739–40). Facsimile reproduction in *Siku quanshu cunmu congshu zi* 四庫全書存目叢書子 23: 284–323.

Rumen fayu jiyao 儒門法語輯要. Edited by Tang Jinzhao 湯金釗. Preface dated 1814 (JQ 19).

- 1881 (GX 7). Woodblocks held by E'yuan fushu 鄂垣撫署. In Peng Zuxian 彭祖賢 (1819–1885) collectanea *Changzhou Peng shi jia ji* 長洲彭氏家集 (Familial anthology of the Peng clan of Changzhou [County]); also titled *Peng shi suo zhu shu* 彭氏所著書 (Books written by [patriarchs of] the Peng clan). Many holding libraries: e.g., Shanghai Library (2 exemplars: 線普長 454773, 線普 436852).
- 1890 (GX 16). Tōbunken.

TABLE 7.1 Confucian figures who descended to Dingqiu's altar and the inclusion of historically-attested writings in *Rumen fa yu* by Ming Confucians who became spirit-altar deities

Names	Dates of descent	Source	Historically-attested writings included in *Rumen fa yu*; pagination according to 1922 Chengye tang edition
Zhou Dunyi (1017–1073)	Winter of Kangxi 17 (Nov. 14, 1678–Feb. 10, 1679); sixth month of Kangxi 18 (July 8–Aug. 5, 1679); eighth month of Kangxi 18 (Sept. 5–Oct. 4, 1679)	ZSL 46.7b–8b; 15b; 21a	Zhu Xi and Lu Jiuyuan are the only two Song figures whose compositions are included in *Rumen fa yu*
Cheng Yi (1033–1107)	Winter of Kangxi 17 (Nov. 14, 1678–Feb. 10, 1679)	ZSL 46.4a	
Xue Xuan (1389–1464)	Winter of Kangxi 17 (Nov. 14, 1678–Feb. 10, 1679)	ZSL 46.4a–b	"Shendu zhai ji" (Record of the Caution-in-Solitude Studio) 10a–b; "Jie zi shu 戒子書" (Admonitions to sons), 11a–b
Luo Hongxian (1504–1564)	Winter of Kangxi 17 (Nov. 14, 1678–Feb. 10, 1679)	ZSL 46.4b	"Da Guo Pingchuan zhiliangzhi shu 答郭平川致良知書" (Letter responding to Guo Pingchuan on extending innate knowledge to the utmost), 32a–b; "Da Menren wenxue shu 答門人問學書" (Letter in response to a disciple inquiring into learning), 33a; "Longchang Yangming ci ji 龍場陽明詞記" (Record of the shrine to [Wang] Yangming at Longchang), 34a–35a

TABLE 7.1 (cont.)

Names	Dates of descent	Source	Historically-attested writings included in *Rumen fa yu*; pagination according to 1922 Chengye tang edition
Huang Daozhou (1585–1646)	Winter of Kangxi 17 (Nov. 14, 1678–Feb. 10, 1679) [twice]; Kangxi 18.1–3 (May 10–Aug. 5, 1679); day after preceding session; shortly after preceding session; seventh month of Kangxi 18 (Aug. 6–Sept. 4, 1679); twelfth month of Kangxi 18 (Jan. 2–30, 1680); Kangxi 20.6.8 (July 22, 1681); Kangxi 20.6.9 (July 23, 1681); Kangxi 20.6.16 (July 30, 1681); second month of Kangxi 37 (March 12–April 10, 1698); on or shortly after Kangxi 45.2.9 (March 23, 1706)	ZSL 46.6b–7b; 9a–b; 12a–b; 12b–14a; 14a–15b; 17b–20b; 21a–27a; 34b–35b; 35b–39a; 39a–40b; 47.1a–16b; 30b–31a	"Lun Zhu Lu yitong 論朱陸異同" (On the similarities and differences of Zhu [Xi] and Lu [Jiuyuan]), 74a–75a

Works Cited

Abbreviations

SJGNP   Peng Dingqiu. *Shijiang gong nianpu* 侍講公年譜. Suzhou Museum manuscript, circa 1719.

YJXC   *Wenchang Yuju zhengzhen xuanhua jiujie chouen xinchan* 文昌玉局證真宣化救刼酬恩心懺. In 1775 *Wendi quanshu*, edited by Guan Huai. Waseda University exemplar.

ZSL   Peng Shaosheng 彭紹升, ed. *Zhishen lu* 質神錄. Preface 1773. Edition of 1775 included in Guan ed., *Wendi quanshu*.

Electronic Resources

Kanseki Repository
https://www.kanripo.org/

Primary Sources

Gu Yuan 顧沅 (1799–1851). *Chongyin Yuanmiao guan zhi* 重印元妙觀志. 13 *juan*. 1927. Reproduced in *Sandong shiyi* 三洞拾遺, vol. 15, 664–725, in *Zhongguo zongjiao lishi wenxian jicheng* 中國宗教歷史文獻集成, edited by Zhongguo zongjiao lishi wenxian jicheng bianzuan weiyuanhui 中國宗教歷史文獻集成編纂委員會. Hefei: Huang shan shushe, 2005.

Guan Huai 關槐 (js. 1780), corrector (*jiaoding* 校訂), and Wang Lüjie 王履階, expanding carver (*zengjuan* 增鐫). *Wendi quanshu* 文帝全書. 1775. Waseda University exemplar.

Huang Daozhou 黃道周 (1585–1646). *Rong tan wenye* 榕檀問業. 18 *juan*. Facsimile reproduction in *Siku quanshu*, vol. 717 (*Zi bu* 23).

Huang Zongxi 黃宗羲 (1610–1695). *Ming ru xue'an* 明儒學案. Beijing: Zhonghua shuju, 2008.

Liu Qiao 劉樵 (fl. 1743–49), ed. *Wendi quanshu* 文帝全書. 1876 edition, Tianjin Library exemplar. 32 *juan* plus two supplementary *juan*. Changjun 常郡: Yang yi miao Wenchang ge 陽邑廟文昌閣.

Peng Dingqiu 彭定求 (1645–1719). *Nanyun shi gao* 南畇詩稾. 27 *juan*. Preface 1709. Reproduced in vol. 167 of the *Qingdai shiwenji huibian* 清代詩文集彙編, 1–249. Shanghai: Shanghai guji chubanshe, 2010–12.

Peng Dingqiu 彭定求. *Peng Dingqiu shiwen ji* 彭定求詩文集. Punctuated by Huang Aming 黃阿明. 2 vols. Shanghai: Shanghai guji chubanshe, 2016.

Peng Dingqiu 彭定求, ed. *Wenchang ge xiao zhi* 文星閣小志. Facsimile of exemplar held by the Shanghai Library (線善 T368681) in *Zhongguo yuanlin mingsheng zhi congkan* 中國園林名勝志叢刊, edited by Zheng Xiaoxia 鄭曉霞 and Zhang Zhi 張智, vol. 31, 1–67. Yangzhou: Guangling shushe, 2006.

Peng Dingqiu 彭定求. "Yaojiang shi hui lu 姚江釋毀錄." Authored 1703; first published in *Changzhou Peng shi jia ji* 長洲彭氏家集; alternate title *Peng shi suo zhu shu* 彭氏所著書, compiled by Peng Zuxian 彭祖賢. 1881.

Peng Qifeng (1701–1784). *Zhiting xiansheng ji* 芝庭先生集. 1785. Facsimile reproduction in *Siku weishoushu jikan* 四庫未收書輯刊, edited by Siku weishoushu jikan bianzuan weiyuanhui 四庫未收書輯刊編纂委員會, series 9, vol. 23, 435–752. Beijing: Beijing chubanshe, 2000.

Peng Shaosheng 彭紹升 (1740–1796). *Yixing juji* 一行居集. Printed 1825. Reproduced in *Qingdai shiwenji huibian* 清代诗文集汇编, vol. 397, 661–764. Shanghai: Shanghai guji chubanshe, 2010–12.

Quan Tang shi 全唐詩. 1706. 25 vols. Beijing: Zhonghua shuju, 1980.

Sun Qifeng 孫奇逢 (1585–1675). *Lixue zong zhuan* 理學宗傳. Prefaces 1666. 26 *juan*. Beijing Library exemplar reproduced in *Xuxiu siku quanshu* 續修四庫全書, Masters division (*shi bu* 史部) vol. 514, 195–722.

Xu Ke 徐珂 (1869–1928). *Qingbai lei chao* 清稗類鈔. 13 vols. Beijing: Zhonghua shuju, 2010.

Yuquan 玉詮. 9 *juan*. Included in *Daozang jiyao* 道藏輯要, printed 1806. Collated Kanripō edition.

Yuquan yulu 玉詮語錄. In *Yulu daguan* 語錄大觀, 1.77a–88a. Included in *Daozang jiyao* 道藏輯要. Kanseki Repository collated edition (KR5i0053).

Zhang Lie 張烈 (1622–1685). *Wang xue zhiyi* 王學質疑. Facsimile reproduction in *Siku quanshu cunmu congshu zi* 四庫全書存目叢書子 23: 80–109.

Zhu Xi 朱熹 (1130–1200), ed. *Jinsi lu* 近思錄. Wenyuange exemplar of the *Siku quanshu* 四庫全書 edition in the Kanseki Repository.

Zhu Xi 朱熹. *Zhuzi yulu* 朱子語錄. 2 vols. Shanghai: Shanghai guji chubanshe, 2016.

Secondary Sources and Translations

Ames, Roger T., and David L. Hall. *Focusing the Familiar: A Translation and Philosophical Interpretation of the* Zhongyong. Honolulu: University of Hawai'i Press, 2001.

Biot, Édouard. *Le Tcheou-li; Ou, Rites des Tcheou*. 3 vols. Paris: Imprimerie Nationale, 1851.

Burton-Rose, Daniel. "A Prolific Spirit: Peng Dingqiu's Posthumous Career on the Spirit Altar, 1720–1906." *Daoism: Religion, History and Society* 道教研究學報：宗教、歷史與社會, no. 7 (2015): 7–63.

Burton-Rose, Daniel. "Terrestrial Reward as Divine Recompense: The Self-Fashioned Piety of the Peng Lineage of Suzhou, 1650s–1870s." PhD diss., Princeton University, 2016.

Burton-Rose, Daniel. "Establishing a Literati Spirit-Writing Altar in Early Qing Suzhou: The *Optimus* Prophecy of Peng Dingqiu (1645–1719)." *T'oung Pao* 106, nos. 3–4 (2020): 358–400.

Chan, Wing-Ming. "The Qianlong Emperor's New Strategy in 1775 to Commend Late-Ming Loyalists." *Asia Major* 13, no. 1 (2000): 109–37.

Chan, Wing-tsit 陳榮捷, trans. *Reflections on Things at Hand: The Neo-Confucian Anthology Compiled by Chu Hsi and Lü Tsu-ch'ien*. New York: Columbia University Press, 1967.

Chen Lai 陳來. "Huang Daozhou de shengping yu sixiang 黃道周的生平与思想." In *Guoxue yanjiu: di shiyi juan* 國學研究：第十一卷, primary editor Yuan Xingpei 袁行霈, 87–121. Beijing: Beijing daxue chubanshe, 2003.

Clart, Philip. "Confucius and the Mediums: Is There a 'Popular Confucianism'?" *T'oung Pao* 89, nos. 1/3 (2003): 1–38.

Confucius. *The Analects*. Translated by Simon Leys. Edited by Michael Nylan. New York: W.W. Norton and Company, 2014.

Deng, Hongbo. "Like Tea and Rice at Home: Lecture Gatherings and Academies during the Ming Dynasty." In *Confucian Academies in East Asia*, edited by Vladimír Glomb, Eun-Jeung Lee, and Martin Gehlmann, 159–96. Leiden: Brill, 2020.

Ding Peiren 丁培仁 and Yang Lu 楊璐. "Suzhou Yutan fuji zhong de Xifang jingtu xinyang 蘇州玉壇扶乩中的西方淨土信仰." *Xueshu luntan* 學術論壇 7 (2011): 26–30.

Gardner, Daniel K. *The Four Books: The Basic Teachings of the Later Confucian Tradition*. Indianapolis: Hackett Publishing Company, 2007.

Geng Fangchao 耿芳朝. "Lu Longqi Lixue 'Zun Zhu pi Wang' de nuli yu kaixin" 陸隴

其理學「尊朱辟王」的努力與開新. *Ezhou daxue xuebao* 鄂州大學學報 21, no. 8 (2014): 21–23.

Goldin, Paul. "The Consciousness of the Dead as a Philosophical Problem in Ancient China." In *The Good Life and Conceptions of Life in Early China and Graeco-Roman Antiquity*, edited by R.A.H. King, 59–92. Berlin: De Gruyter, 2015.

Goossaert, Vincent. "Spirit-writing Altars and Daoist Rituals in Qing Jiangnan." *Studies in Chinese Religions* 8, no. 3 (2022): 385–406.

Hu Jiechen 胡劼辰. "*Wendi quanshu* yanjiu: Qingdai Wenchang Dijun xinyang de wenxian shi 《文帝全書》研究：清代文昌帝君信仰的文獻史." PhD diss., Chinese University of Hong Kong, 2017.

Hu Jiechen 胡劼辰. "Qingdai liuzhong Wendi lei quanshu de chubanshi yanjiu 清代六種文帝類全書的出版史研究." *Zhongyang yanjiuyuan Lishi yuyan yanjiusuo jikan* 中央研究院歷史語言研究所集刊 91, no. 22 (2020): 227–92.

Huang Aming 黃阿明. "Kangxi shiwu nian zhuangyuan Peng Dingqiu shengping shishi shulüe 康熙十五年狀元彭定求生平史実述略." *Lishi dang'an* 歷史檔案, no. 4 (2013): 80–86.

Huang Aming 黃阿明. "Peng Dingqiu wannian de xianju shenghuo 彭定求晚年的閑居生活." *Suzhou keji xueyuan xuebao (shehui kexue ban)* 蘇州科技學院學報（社會科學版） 32, no. 5 (2015): 67–75.

Huang, Chin-shing. *Philosophy, Philology, and Politics in Eighteenth-century China: Li Fu and the Lu-Wang School Under the Ch'ing*. Cambridge: Cambridge University Press, 1995.

Huang, Chin-shing. *Confucianism and Sacred Space: The Confucius Temple from Imperial China to Today*. Translated by Jonathan Chin with Chin-shing Huang. New York: Columbia University Press, 2021.

Huang, Martin W. "Male Friendship and *Jiangxue* (Philosophical Debates) in Sixteenth-Century China." *Nan Nü* 9 (2007): 146–78.

Israel, George L. *Doing Good and Ridding Evil in Ming China: The Political Career of Wang Yangming*. Leiden: Brill, 2014.

Johnston, Ian, and Ping Wang 王平, trans. and annot. *Daxue* and *Zhongyong*. Bilingual Edition. Hong Kong: The Chinese University Press, 2012.

Karlgren, Bernhard. *The Book of Odes*. Stockholm: Museum of Far Eastern Antiquities, 1974.

Kim, Jihyun. "Enlightenment on the Spirit-Altar: Eschatology and Restoration of Morality at the King Kwan Shrine in *Fin de siècle* Seoul." *Religions* 11, no. 6 (2020): 1–33.

Kleeman, Terry F. *A God's Own Tale: The* Book of Transformations *of Wenchang, The Divine Lord of Zitong*. Albany: State University of New York Press, 1994.

Kohn, Livia. "Doumu: The Mother of the Dipper." *Ming Qing yanjiu* 9 (2000): 149–95.

Lai Chi-tim 黎志添. "*Lüzu quanshu zhengzong*: Qingdai Beijing Jueyuan tan de lishi ji qi Lüzu Tianxianpai xinyang 《呂祖全書正宗》—清代北京覺源壇的歷史及其呂祖天仙派信仰." *Zhongguo wenzhe yanjiu jikan* 中國文哲研究季刊 46 (2015): 101–49.

Legge, James. *The Chinese Classics*. Vol. 1, *Confucian Analects, the Great Learning, and the Doctrine of the Mean*. Hong Kong: 1861.

Li Fengmao 李豐楙. "Shenxian sanpin shuo de yuanshi ji qi yanbian: yi Liuchao Daojiao wei zhongxin de kaocha 神仙三品說的原始及其衍變：以六朝道教為中心的考察." In *Wuru yu zhejiang: Liuchao Sui-Tang Daojiao wenxue conglun* 誤入與謫降—六朝隋唐道教文學論叢, 33–91. Taipei: Taiwan xuesheng shuju, 1996.

Lin I. Luan 林一鑾 [Shi Huidou 釋慧鐸]. "Qing chu Suzhou Yutan de Jiangluan yinghua: yi Yuquan wei Zhongxin 清初蘇州玉壇的降鸞應化：以《玉詮》為中心." Unpublished paper.

Liu, James T.C. "How Did a Neo-Confucian School Become the State Orthodoxy?" *Philosophy East and West* 23, no. 4 (1973): 483–506.

Liu Zhonghua 劉仲華. "Zhang Lie zun Zhu chi Wang ji qi zai Qing chu xueshu chongjian zhong de jingyu 張烈尊朱斥王及其在清初學術重建中的境遇." *Shijiazhuang xueyuan xuebao* 石家莊學院學報 14, no. 1 (2012): 32–37.

Lu Miaw-fen 呂妙芬. *Yangming xueshiren shequn: lishi, sixiang yu shijian* 陽明學士人社群: 歷史思想與實踐. Second edition. Taipei: Zhongyang yanjiuyuan jindaishi yanjiusuo, 2010.

Man-Cheong, Iona. *The Class of 1761: Examinations, State and Elites in Eighteenth-Century China*. Stanford, CA: Stanford University Press, 2004.

Mencius. Translated with an Introduction and Notes by D.C. Lau. Revised edition. New York: Penguin Books, 2003.

Ng, On-Cho. *Cheng-Zhu Confucianism in the Early Qing: Li Guangdi (1642–1718) and Qing Learning*. Albany: State University of New York Press, 2001.

Nylan, Michael. *The Five "Confucian" Classics*. New Haven, CT: Yale University Press, 2001.

Pankenier, David W. *Astrology and Cosmology in Early China: Conforming Earth to Heaven*. Cambridge: Cambridge University Press, 2015.

Peng Guoxiang 彭國翔. "Qingdai Kangxi chao Lixue de yijun: Peng Dingqiu de *Rumen fayu* chutan 清代康熙朝理學的異軍：彭定求的《儒門法語》初探." In *Jinshi ruxue shi de bianzheng yu gouchen* 近世儒學史的辨正與鉤沉, 588–612. Taipei: Yunchen wenhua, 2013.

Plaks, Andrew. *Ta Hsüeh and Chung Yung: The Highest Order of Cultivation and On the Practice of the Mean*. New York: Penguin Books, 2003.

Schirokauer, Conrad. "Neo-Confucians Under Attack: The Condemnation of Wei-hsueh." In *Crisis and Prosperity in Sung China*, edited by John Winthrop Haeger, 163–98. Tucson: University of Arizona Press, 1975.

Tang Guiyan 唐桂艳. "Rujia xiushen zhi zuo *Rumen fayu* zai Shandong 儒家修身之作《儒門法語》在山東." *Renwen tianxia* 人文天下 152 (2019): 28–31.

Tao Jin 陶金. "Suzhou Shanghai *Gao Dou keyi* zhong 'qishi' jieci chutan: Daojiao yu Mijiao, Jiangnan yu Beijing 蘇州上海《誥斗科儀》中「啟師」節次初探：道教與密教，江南與北京." *Zhongguo Daojiao* 中國道教 2 (2012): 34–41.

Wang, Chien-ch'uan [Chien-chuan]. "Spirit Writing Groups in Modern China (1840–1937): Textual Production, Public Teachings, and Charity." In *Modern Chinese Religion II, 1850–2015*, edited by Vincent Goossaert, Jan Kiely, and John Lagerwey. Vol. II: 651–84. Leiden: Brill, 2016.

Wang, Chien-Chuan. "Popular Groups Promoting 'The Religion of Confucius' in the Chinese Southwest and Their Activities since the Nineteenth Century (1840–2013): An Observation Centered on Yunnan's Eryuan County and Environs." Translated by Stacy Mosher. In *Confucian Experience: Documenting a Grassroots Revival of Tradition*, edited by Sébastien Billioud, 90–121. Leiden: Brill, 2018.

Watters, Thomas. *A Guide to the Tablets in a Temple of Confucius*. Shanghai: America Presbyterian Mission Press, 1879.

Wilson, Thomas A. *Genealogy of the Way: The Construction and Uses of the Confucian Tradition in Late Imperial China*. Stanford, CA: Stanford University Press, 1995.

Wyatt, Don J. "Chu Hsi's Critique of Shao Yung: One Instance of the Stand Against Fatalism." *Harvard Journal of Asiatic Studies* 45, no. 2 (1985): 649–66.

Zhang Tianjie 張天傑. "Lu Longqi de *Sishu* xue yu Qing chu de 'You Wang fan Zhu' sichao 陸隴其的《四書》學與清初的「由王返朱」思潮." *Zhejiang shehui kexue* 浙江社會科學 10 (2016): 131–59.

Zhang Tianjie 張天傑 and Xiao Yongming 肖永明. "Cong Zhang Lüxiang, Lü Liuliang dao Lu Longqi: Qing chu 'Zun Zhu pi Wang' sichao zhong yitiao zhuxian 從張履祥、呂留良到陸隴其——清初「尊朱辟王」思潮中一條主線." *Zhongguo zhexue shi* 中國哲學史 no. 2 (2010): 116–23.

Zhang, Ying. *Confucian Image Politics: Masculine Morality in Seventeenth-Century China*. Seattle: University of Washington Press, 2017.

Zhou Ye 周冶. "Shi Daoyuan Qionglong shan fapai kaoshu 施道淵穹窿山法派考述." *Zongjiao xue yanjiu* 宗教學研究 4 (2018): 67–77.

Zhu Mingchuan 朱明川. "Rutan jingdian ji qi yingyong: yi Sichuan Jiangyou diqu de Zixiatan wei li 儒壇經典及其應用：以四川江油地區的「紫霞壇」為例." *Shanshu, jingjuan, yu wenxian* 善書、經卷與文獻 1 (2019): 135–63.

CHAPTER 8

A Credulous Skeptic: Ji Yun on the Mantic Arts and Spirit-Writing

Michael Lackner

For a volume on spirit-writing in the Chinese-speaking world, it may be appropriate to give a voice to an influential leading scholar of the eighteenth century. This voice represents an attitude that gives fundamental credit to techniques which are laden with the modern verdict of "superstition"; however, a close scrutiny of its utterings shows that our scholar was engaged in a theoretical endeavor to understand the mechanisms underlying predictive techniques—notwithstanding whether they are based on calculation or rely on inspiration. His thoughts are all the more precious because practitioners are rarely in the habit of cogitating over the principles of their activity. This remark is not intended to make a case for the long-obsolete idea of a division between popular and élite culture with regard to divinatory practices; our scholar was but a keen observer, who actively and even enthusiastically participated in procedures and rituals that were once labelled "popular." However, in the case of Ji Yun, the boundaries between élite and popular culture remain ambiguous and the social distance is never really overcome by his fascination with mantic arts.

1   Ji Yun and His Works

Ji Yun 紀昀 (1724–1805, also known as Ji Xiaolan 紀曉嵐) came from a family that had migrated to Hebei 河北 province in the early fifteenth century. For centuries, they had been landowners, enjoying a good reputation locally, but it was only Ji Yun's father Ji Rongshu 紀容舒 (1685–1764; called Yao'an gong 姚安公 "Lord Yao'an" in Ji Yun's writings because he served as a prefect in Yao'an, Yunnan 雲南 province,) who, in 1713, obtained a degree at the provincial level of the civil service examination. More than forty years later (in 1754), Ji Yun passed the top-level metropolitan examination and embarked on an illustrious career.[1]

---

[1] For a truly magisterial biographical sketch, see David Pollard's "Introduction" to his translation *Real Life in China*, xi–xxxii.

His posthumous fame is due to his three significantly different levels of activities and their respective perception. First and foremost, Ji is known as the editor-in-chief of the largest anthology in Chinese history, the *Siku quanshu* 四庫全書 (Complete library in four branches of literature) and its annotated catalog, to which he devoted more than twenty years of his life. The second level is to be found in popular anecdotes, where he "bests others with his wit," particularly during his confrontation with the Qianlong emperor's favorite Heshen 和珅 (1750–1799), an officer in the Manchu guard. This aspect of Ji Yun's popularity culminated in the 173 episodes of the Chinese TV series *Tiechi tongya Ji Xiaolan* 鐵齒銅牙紀曉嵐 (The eloquent Ji Xiaolan, 2002–2010). Lastly, Ji Yun left five collections of informal brush notes (*biji* 筆記), the *Yuewei caotang biji* 閱微草堂筆記 (see below for translations), with 1200-odd entries, written between 1789 and 1798. These notes, of varying lengths, offer an almost unexhaustible repository of annecdotes, situations, examples of good or bad conduct, and curiosities, populated by people from all strata of society and encompassing protagonists ranging from officials to bandits.

Numerous jottings are devoted to a particular type of curious phenomena; namely ghosts, spirits, demons, and mantic techniques. It is true that the bibliographies of the dynastic histories do not list spirit-writing as part of the mantic arts *shushu* 術數 (even Ji Yun's own introduction to this chapter in the *Siku* anthology does not mention the practice), but it seems that, for the author of the brush notes, this distinction was negligible. In one entry (see below), he even lists spirit-writing among the other arts of fortune-telling. As an *homme de lettres*, his interest in poetry is unsurprising: many entries deal with poems and some of them have been revealed either in dreams or by means of spirit-writing.

With the exception of Pu Songling 蒲松齡 (1640–1715) and his *Liaozhai zhiyi* 聊齋誌異 (Strange tales from the Liaozhai studio), no other Chinese writer of the Qing dynasty has attracted so much attention among western translators as Ji Yun. The editions of his brush notes *Yuewei caotang biji* are countless, but there is a considerable number of translations into various western languages. In a recent review, Vincent Durand-Dastès listed some of the most important ones:

> In 1983, Konrad Herrmann chose around three hundred pieces from all five books of the collection and published them under the title *Pinselnotizen aus der Strohhütte des Grossen im Kleinen* in what was then East Germany (Leipzig, Weimar: Kiepenheuer Verlag).
>
> Most of the later translations came out in the 1990s: *Note scritte nello studio Yuewei*, Edi Bozza, with forty-six tales (Torino: Bollati Boringhieri,

1992); *Notes de la chaumière des observations subtiles,* Jacques Pimpaneau, with 125 tales (Paris: Kwok-on, 1995); *Passe-temps d'un été à Luanyang,* Jacques Dars, with 297 tales (Paris: Gallimard, 1998); *Fantastic Tales by Ji Xiaolan,* Sun Hai-Chen, with 140 tales (Beijing: New World Press, 1998); and eventually *Shadows in a Chinese Landscape: The Notes of a Confucian Scholar,* David L. Keenan, with 112 tales (Armonk, NY: M.E. Sharpe, 1999).[2]

It is interesting to see to what extent these renderings reflect the individual predilections of each translator: Edi Bozza is predominantly interested in Ji Yun's depictions of social injustice; like many Chinese commentators and editors, Sun Haichen is convinced of the purely fictional character of the brush notes and therefore focuses on the "supernatural" appearance of ghosts and demons—as both his English and Chinese titles (*A Selection of Tales of the Miraculous by Ji Xiaolan, Ji Xiaolan zhiguai gushi xuan* 紀曉嵐志怪故事選) indicate, thus placing Ji Yun in the tradition of the "strange writing genre," *zhiguai*; however, when Ji Yun situated himself in this tradition, *zhiguai* by no means included disbelief in the "strange": according to another translator, Leo Tak-hung Chan,[3] the *Yuewei caotang biji* is "a *zhiguai* collection couched very clearly in the evidential mode ... the intellectual environment of evidential scholarship is evinced in Ji Yun's attempts to verify the truth of his tales and the scrutinizing investigations he made upon his collected data."[4]

David Keenan provides the reader with a detailed arrangement of the respective provenance of the "jottings" (e.g. "Tales about Chi Yün's Household," "Tales from members of Chi Yün's Household," and so on, with chapters on "Colleagues" and "Neighbors"). Keenan does justice to Ji Yun's conviction of the veracity of his accounts, because he "draws his material from his own experience and from a broad cross-section of his acquaintances."[5] In line with his Russian predecessor Olga Lasarevna Fischman, who also translated 300 pieces,[6] Konrad Herrmann opines that "the enlightener Ji Yun did not want to merely entertain by telling gruesome ghost stories, but he rather used the figures of ghosts and deities, deeply rooted in popular belief to reach a large audience and to set a moral standard."[7] Most of the translators agree that the tales of

---

2 Durand-Dastès, review of *Real Life in China at the Height of Empire,* 60.
3 Chan, *Discourse on Foxes and Ghosts.*
4 Both quotations follow Lin, "Two Translations of Ji Yun's *Close Scrutiny,*" 103–16. This article is an instructive account of a conversation between Chan and Pollard that took place in Hong Kong in December 2015.
5 Keenan, *Shadows in a Chinese Landscape,* XII.
6 Фишман, *Цзи Юнь.*
7 Herrmann, *Pinselnotizen,* 448. The translation is mine.

the brush notes contain a vivid picture of its author's times ("real life," in David E. Pollard's words), but there is considerable disagreement on how to judge Ji Yun's "belief" in his stories, especially those dealing with ghosts, demons, and mantic arts, which are often qualified as "supernatural," although that western epithet may be questionable. In his introduction, David E. Pollard offers a valuable compromise, stating "Needless to say, the viewpoint behind these stories varied greatly, from awe and trembling stemming from belief to deliberate exploitation as parables for comment on society."[8] There can be no doubt that, apart from his own experiences with the "supernatural," Ji Yun would not have quoted his father's numerous accounts had he not sincerely trusted their authenticity. So, the attempts to explain away the fact that "the Chinese people in Ji's time regarded the unseen world as part of, not separate from, the natural world"[9] must be ascribed to either a strong bias toward purely literary criticism (hence the emphasis on the "fictional" character) or to an ideological and anachronistic prejudice that gratuitously ennobles Ji Yun as an "enlightened" scholar, devoid of any kind of "superstition."[10] In the words of David Pollard: "So we cannot go along with Ji Xiaolan's modern celebrators who are eager to think of him as an enlightened thinker; on the contrary, he was a man of his times."[11]

However, Ji Yun's views and attitudes regarding the "supernatural," the mantic techniques, and spirit-writing are not easy to grasp.

2 The "Minor Ways" and Fate

In Chinese bibliographic history, Ji Yun is first and foremost known for being the co-compiler of the *Siku quanshu*, an enterprise that started in 1782. In the introduction section on mantic arts (*shushu*, "arts and codes"), Ji Yun states:

> Regardless of their benefit, the teachings of the techniques of the various schools have been present for a long time and their principles are difficult to dismiss entirely. Therefore, we group them under the heading of *shushu* (arts and codes). … "Arts of enjoyment" (*youyi*) are also studies of secondary importance, but if any one of the techniques enters a spiritual

---

[8] Pollard, *Real Life in China*, xiv.
[9] Pollard, *Real Life in China*, xiv.
[10] A representative example is Wu, Yuewei caotang biji *yanjiu*. According to ibid., 55, Ji Yun's "ideological concepts despised fantastic gods and spirits" (蔑視妖妄神異的思想觀念).
[11] Pollard, *Real Life in China*, xxvi.

realm, it becomes a vehicle of the *Dao*. Therefore, the "arts of enjoyment" are grouped under the general category of art. Both can be considered as minor ways.

百家方技，或有益或無益，而其說久行，理難竟廢，故次以術數。... 遊藝亦學問之余事，一技入神，器或寓道，故次以藝術 ... 以上二家，皆小道之可觀者。[12]

This statement shows the conscientious official at work. He maintains a prudent distance from *shushu*, but is reluctant to completely discard them. "Minor ways" is an allusion to *Lunyu* 論語 (The analects) 19:4, where Confucius' disciple Zixia 子夏 says: "Even in minor ways there is something worth being looked at; but if one delves too deeply into them, there is a danger of becoming bogged down. Therefore, the superior man does not practice them." (子夏曰：雖小道，必有可觀者焉，致遠恐泥，是以君子不為也。) Using the ambivalent judgment of the *Lunyu* ("something worth being looked at" vs. "the superior man does not practice them"), Ji Yun here reiterates the age-old literati suspicion with regard to the mantic arts; to some extent, they may be reliable, but it is their proximity to charlatanerie and profiteering that makes them questionable. Among the people of the "rivers and lakes" (*jianghu* 江湖, by Ji Yun's time already a deprecatory epithet), i.e. the inhabitants of a Sherwood Forest-like counter-universe, were many diviners. Commenting on this seemingly paradoxical attitude toward the "minor ways," I have mentioned that:

> The ambiguous attitude towards the "smaller paths" (i.e., minor ways) pervades Chinese history; senior officials were drawn to experts in interpreting the future, and liked to surround themselves with them, while at the same time publicly distancing themselves from such practices. The earliest records of Imperial prohibitions against certain divinatory practices date from the early years of the Song Dynasty, but one of the most prominent examples is the Yongzheng Emperor's *Amplified Instructions on the Sacred Edict* (*Shengyu guangxun* 聖諭廣訓) of 1724, intended to clarify a decree issued by his father: "The achievements of the saints and the principles of rule are all based on the orthodox teaching. As for writings that do not come from the saints, and those mediocre books which

---

12 See the general introduction to the part of Masters and Philosophers, *Zibu zongxu* 子部總敘, in *juan* 91 of the *Siku quanshu*.

only excite and disconcert the common people by sowing disorder and confusion, gnawing at the people and their prosperity like insects—all these are heterodox and must be forbidden.... The law cannot excuse the deception of the people, and the Empire has permanent punishments in store for the heterodox practices of such priests and leaders.... Belief in the lies of necromancers and geomancers ... will be punished by death." In further reference to the preceding decree, the text continues: "All they (wandering spirit-mediums) do is feign salvation and misfortune, good and bad luck in order to peddle their unproven ghost stories. In this pernicious way of making a living, they swindle people out of making their own." The Qing Dynasty Code of Law of 1805 further notes: "All persons who stand convicted of having written or published books on witchcraft and magic, or of using spells and incantations to foment and influence the spirit of the people, shall be beheaded after the usual period of imprisonment."

The self-same Yongzheng Emperor, however, displayed not the slightest antipathy towards horoscopy: on 6 June 1728, at the emperor's request, the governor of Shaanxi 陝西 province presented the horoscopes (that is the Eight Characters [*bazi* 八字]) of various individuals, including Wang Gang, Feng Yunzhong, and Yuan Jiyin, for his majesty's judgement. These bear notes written in the red ink reserved solely for the emperor's use, including the following: "The *bazi* of Wang Gang appear good to me, those of Feng Yunzhong not at all suitable, he has apparently already passed his peak and is barely maintaining his status quo." After requesting the "discreet proffering" (*mizou* 密奏) of further horoscopes, another Imperial rescript followed on 28 June, in which the emperor again confirms that he has studied the excellent *bazi* of Wang Gang, only it must "be feared that his lifespan will not be a long one". He writes: "We have no proficiency in the lore of fate, but his situation seemed to be well disposed, and the result is in keeping with our statements.... The foundations of the lore of fate are difficult and profound, and one must not dismiss them altogether."[13]

Given this double-edged and incongruous—but probably incongruous only to modern readers—attitude, it is little wonder that there is a certain difference between Ji Yun the official and Ji Yun the author of brush notes. His statement on a diviner is a clear avowal of his conviction that horoscopy is reliable: "Sec-

---

13   Lackner, "In the Empire of Signs," 56–57.

retary Yang Hu's ... physiognomic methods and his (fate) calculations on the basis of the Eight Characters and the Five Stars all proved right." (楊主事護 ... 相法及推算八字五星，皆有驗。)[14] (RS 8/2, 552)

A further passage corroborates this confidence:

> I once asked him who was right: those professional practitioners of horoscopes (school of Xu Ziping) who say that fate is determined, or those professional geomancers (i.e., practitioners of *fengshui* 風水) who say that fate is alterable. And he replied: To obtain an auspicious place [for the burial] is fate, and an inauspicious burial place chosen by mistake is also fate, the principle is but one. One can say this word has really got at the pervasive truth.
>
> 余嘗問以子平家謂命有定，堪輿家謂命可移，究誰為是？對曰：「能得吉地即是命，誤葬凶地亦是命，其理一也。」斯言可謂得其通矣。 RS 8/2, 553

From this sentence, we can observe that, for Ji Yun and many other scholars, the acceptance of one technique did not necessarily include the approval of other arts. Horoscopy, here, prevails over *fengshui* but even this judgment is far from being univocal. Having described an accurate prediction by a *fengshui* master, he adds:

> However, in the studies of the geomancers, there must be something unrefined and, moreover, there are some who make illicit profit and their words are unreliable, one should not indulge in credibility. But when there are irrefutable verifications, no false accusations should be made.
>
> 但地師所學必不精，又或緣以為奸利，所言尤不足據，不宜溺信之耳。若其鑿然有驗者，固未可誣也。 HX 12/2, 887

But the secret of an authentic dealing with the art of *fengshui*—as for many other mantic arts—lies in the past, when the Sages still mastered them:

---

14 The *Yuewei caotang biji* is divided into five parts: *Luanyang xiaoxia lu* 灤陽消夏錄 (henceforth LY) of 1789, the *Rushi wo wen* 如是我聞 (henceforth RS) of 1791, the *Huaixi zazhi* 槐西雜誌 (henceforth HX) of 1792, the *Guwang ting zhi* 姑妄聽之 (henceforth GW) of 1793, and the *Luanyang xulu* 灤陽續錄 (henceforth LYX) of 1798. My quotations give first the parts, then the respective *juan* of the entire collection and the chapter of the parts, followed by the page numbers in the Zhonghua shuju edition of the text.

Sir Liu Wenzheng said: "For choosing a place, one refers to the *Book of Documents*, for choosing a day, one refers to the *Rituals*. If there were not [the categories of] auspicious and inauspicious, how could the Sage divine? However, I am afraid that this is simply not something the professional practitioners of our time understand." This is really a balanced theory.

劉文正公曰:「卜地見書,卜日見禮,苟無吉凶,聖人何卜?但恐非今術士所知耳。」斯持平之論矣。 LY 1/1, 71

Ji Yun's lament is by no means original. Praising the glorious days of old, when the sages divined according to the Classics, may probably be traced back to Jia Yi's 賈誼 invectives against the diviner Sima Jizhu 司馬季主 in the second century BCE.[15]

However, when it comes to the intricate question of destiny, even more flagrant contradictions appear. On the one hand, Ji Yun firmly states: "All events are predestined, how could this not be true?" (事皆前定,豈不信然). On the other hand, he relates a story reported by his grandfather about a man who met with an official from the netherworld:

He asked: "A fixed code, can that be modified?" (i.e., what the fixed code—fate—predicts, can one do anything about it?).

"Yes, one can. In case an issue is something that is highly desirable, it can be modified; in case an issue is highly undesirable, it can be modified (i.e., one may do something about it.)"

Question: Who does the fixing? And who does the modifying?

He replied: "The persons concerned fix [what Heaven and Earth have produced] and modify it themselves. The ghosts and spirits have no handle on it."

問:「定數可移乎?」曰:「可。大善則移,大惡則移。」問:「孰定之孰移之?」曰:「其人自定自移,鬼神無權也。」 LY 2/2, 136–37.

Apparently, it is possible to negotiate with fate. The controversy around determinism (for instance, in the guise of "soft determinism," where only the life span and the place in society are preordained) and free will (albeit never addressed in these terms) has taken place in China, too; like in the West, it has

---

15   Sima, *Shiji*, 127:3215 ff. Cf. Watson, *Records of the Grand Historian*, 468–75.

never come to an end nor a satisfactory solution, and Ji Yun's seemingly contradictory statements precisely reflect this conundrum.

3   "Ghosts" and "Spirits"

Nevertheless, there is also the possibility of communicating with the world of "spirits" or "ghosts." We should bear in mind that the very use of the term "ghost" (as, for instance, in Sun Haichen's—see above—collection to make it more sensational) may be misleading for a modern or western reader. As Vincent Goossaert has shown,

> The term *gui* 鬼, often translated as "ghost," does not correspond to the Christian/Western concept of ghost. In Chinese culture, all human beings, after they die, are separated into distinct entities: the corpse and the more spiritual elements (souls) are called *gui* as long as they have not reached an ontological status (reincarnation, divinization, etc.). All humans thus become *gui*, as a rule temporarily. This distinction is key to understanding any discourse on *gui*.[16]

Like the painter Luo Ping 羅平 (1733–1799), with his "Ghost Amusements," *Guiqutu* 鬼趣圖 (who, on one page, plagiarized Andreas Vesalius' *De humani corporis fabrica* from 1543), his contemporary Ji Yun must have been deeply convinced of the potentiality of consorting with *gui*.

After a jocular story about robbers who broke into a house, pretending that they were "returning ghosts," Ji Yun adds:

> On the basis of this episode, the teaching of "returning ghosts" would seem erroneous. However, I have frequently seen with my own eyes the physical traces of returning ghosts. The ghosts and spirits are fuzzy and obscure, and when you really think about it, you don't understand what they are.

> 據此一事，回煞之說當妄矣。然回煞形跡，余實屢目睹之。鬼神茫昧，究不知其如何也。 LY 5/5, 312

The relationship of living humans with "ghosts," but also with the category of "spirits/gods/deities" (*shen* 神) is an essentially horizontal one, without any

---

16   Goosseart, "Une théologie chinoise de l'au-delà," 31.

similarity to the Christian trade with God. Paragraph sixteen of the *Zhongyong* 中庸 (Doctrine of the mean) already alludes to their omnipresence:

> How abundantly do spiritual beings display the powers that belong to them! We look for them, but do not see them; we listen to, but do not hear them; yet they enter into all things, and there is nothing without them. They cause all the people in the kingdom to fast and purify themselves, and array themselves in their richest dresses, in order to attend at their sacrifices. Then, like overflowing water, they seem to be over the heads, and on the right and left *of their worshippers.*

> 鬼神之為德,其盛矣乎!視之而弗見,聽之而弗聞,體物而不可遺。使天下之人齊明盛服,以承祭祀,洋洋乎如在其上,如在其左右。[17]

Ji Yun has no doubts about the presence of *gui* and *shen* and would probably disagree with the idea of "not seeing nor hearing them"; but, in any case, their powers must be activated by us: in a moment of doubt about a marriage, someone went to ask a spirit:

> He was dubious about the resolution and cast a lot at a spirit's [temple/statue]. He shook the basket [with the lots], but no lot fell out. He violently shook the basket a second time, but then all the lots dropped out: this was because the spirit was no more able to solve the problem than he was.

> 疑不能決,乞簽於神。舉筒屢搖,簽不出;奮力再搖,簽乃全出,是神亦不能決也。 GW 16/2, 1222

The connection between "supernatural" powers (and one must acknowledge how difficult it is to call them this in a traditional Chinese context) and living human beings is reciprocal; however, it is we who stimulate and set them in motion:

> It would appear that the spirits communicate with what the mind arouses, and images form portents of what the mechanisms of the *qi* have sprouted form into existence. These matters follow the same principle as dividing the yarrow stalks and heating the tortoise shell: it seems to be a miracle, but [in fact] it is not.

---

17   Translated by Legge in *The Chinese Classics*, 261. Parenthesis in original.

蓋精神所動，鬼神通之。氣機所萌，形象兆之。與揲蓍灼龜，事同一理，似神異而非神異也。RS 7/1, 420

A response by the spirits must not be called a miracle, because it relies on the principle of reaction:

> Now, the sprouts of disaster and blessing are first moved by the mechanisms of *qi*, and extraordinary portents do by principle not occur for nothing; but whether they are acceptable or blameworthy can simply not be predicted. My elder brother Qinghu used to say for these cases: People have the understanding that portents arise from spirits and that human affairs respond to them; but they don't understand that in point of fact portents arise from human affairs and the spirits respond to them, but they are by no means unpredictable.

蓋禍福將萌，氣機先動，非常之兆，理不虛來，第為休為咎，不能預測耳。先兄晴湖則曰：「人知兆發於鬼神，而人事應之；不知實兆發於人事，而鬼神應之。亦未始不可預測也」。LY 6/6, 359

There is a far echo of Wang Chong's 王充 (27–ca. 97) reflections on divining by the tortoise and the yarrow stalks, but Ji Yun's conclusions (which are embedded in the theory of "stimulus and response," *ganying* 感應, except that he replaces *gan* by *zhao fa* 兆發, "portents arise") do not extend as far as Wang Chong's radical skepticism:

> As a matter of fact, diviners do not ask Heaven and Earth, nor have weeds or tortoises spiritual qualities. That they have, and that Heaven and Earth are being interrogated, is an idea of common scholars. How can we prove that? *Tse Lu* asked *Confucius* saying, "A pig's shoulder and a sheep's leg can serve as omens, and from creepers, rushes, straws, and duckweed we can foreknow destiny. What need is there then for milfoil and tortoises?" "That is not correct," said *Confucius*, "for their names are essential. The milfoil's name means old, and the tortoise's, aged. In order to elucidate doubtful things, one must ask the old and the aged." According to this reply, milfoil is not spiritual, and the tortoise is not divine. From the fact that importance is attached to their names, it does not follow that they really possess such qualities. Since they do not possess those qualities, we know that they are not gifted with supernatural powers, and, as they do not possess these, it is plain that Heaven and Earth cannot be asked

through their medium. Moreover, where are the mouths and the ears of Heaven and Earth, that they may be questioned?[18]

4 Mantic Arts and Spirit-Writing

Marc Kalinowski has pointed to the fact that spirit-writing does not figure in either ancient or modern classifications of *shushu*. "The bibliographies of traditional China did not include divinatory statements produced by inspiration. The bibliographical classifications of 'mantic arts' (*shushu* 術數, always based on some kind of computation) have gradually expelled magical and exorcistic practices, but prophecies do not figure anywhere in these catalogs."[19]

Unlike his confrère Zhu Gui 朱珪 (1731–1807), who also worked on the *Siku quanshu* and "was simultaneously involved in canonizing Lüzu and Wenchang scriptures,"[20] Ji Yun appears to have been uninterested in the production of the often eschatologically inspired "morality books" (*shanshu* 善書), that are so closely connected with spirit-writing both in the eighteenth century and nowadays. Rather, his focus was on prediction and poetry. Whereas prediction was a vital part of his interest in *shushu*, the *homme de lettres* he embodied was naturally fascinated by both the magical style of the production within spirit-writing and its outcome, which was frequently in poetic form. Albeit being a skeptical observer of the séances he attended, Ji Yun principally trusted the oracle:

> When my father, the lord Yao'an, had not yet passed his examination, he met with a spirit-writing medium and asked whether he would have success and be famous. The judgment was: "Career [still] a way of 10.000 miles ahead of you." And he asked again in which year he would graduate. Answer: "Ah, but for graduation you'll have to wait 10.000 years." [My father's] understanding was that he had perhaps to advance on another path. But in the year 1713 when he passed the examination called "10.000 years" [held to celebrate the Kangxi emperor's sixtieth birthday], he realized the meaning of that word of "10.000 years."

---

18 Wang, *Lun-hêng*, 182, chap. XIV, "On Divination."
19 Kalinowski, "Typology and Classification."
20 "Best known to historiography as a top-ranking official, and as the preceptor of the future emperor Jiaqing, Zhu was also a devoted adept of self-cultivation and spirit-writing cults to Wenchang and Lüzu." See Goossaert, "Spirit-writing, Canonization, and the Rise of Divine Saviors," 101.

姚安公未第時，遇扶乩者，問有無功名，判曰：「前程萬里。」又問登第當在何年，判曰：「登第卻須候一萬年。」意謂或當由別途進身。及癸巳萬壽科登第，方悟萬年之說。 LY 4/4, 210[21]

There is a detour in this prediction, something that needs to be decrypted, even if only *a posteriori*, but a linear univocal oracle can never be really called an oracle.

This passage does not yet imply any theoretical reflection on the process of spirit-writing. However, one of the most serious ponderings with regard to this art can be found immediately following the passage quoted above:

> By and large, the illusionary arts involve lots of legerdemain and clever manipulation, only spirit-writing has definitely some reliability; but what counts in all cases is only the literacy of the acting spirit. If [the medium] names a precise spirit or a precise medium, this certainly is a false attribution. When he calls himself a certain person of a certain epoch and you inquire about a poem in this person's collection, he will often say that it was long ago and he has forgotten, so he cannot answer. If the medium runs into someone who is good at calligraphy, he will perform well crafted calligraphy, if the medium runs into someone good at poetry, he will perform well-crafted poetry, if they are not apt for either of them, a piece of writing will be achieved but it will be a stupid one. What we call spirits are not *ling* of themselves, but they depend on humans. The yarrow stalks [used for *Yijing* divination] and the tortoise shells are basically dried wood and rotten bones, but the ability to know the auspicious and the inauspicious relies on humans to make them *ling*.

> 大抵幻術多手法捷巧，惟扶乩一事，則確有所憑附，然皆靈鬼之能文者耳。所稱某神某仙，固屬假托，即自稱某代某人者，叩以本集中詩文，亦多云年遠忘記，不能答也。其扶乩之人，遇能書者則書工，遇能詩者則詩工，遇全不能詩能書者，則雖成篇而遲鈍。所謂鬼不自靈，待人而靈也。蓍龜本枯草朽甲，而能知吉凶，亦待人而靈耳。 LY 4/4, 211[22]

Three of Ji Yun's intertwined observations deserve special attention. Firstly, in his view spirit-writing prevails over the other methods of knowing the future.

---

21   Translated Pollard, *Real Life*, 73.
22   Translated Pollard, *Real Life*, 73–74, modified.

Secondly, for spirit-writing, he applies the same category he already used for the entire phenomenon of *shushu*. With his view on spirit-writing, he leaves the trodden paths of erudite classifications as contained in the traditional catalogs. The medium's messages depend on the questioner, as does their intrinsic quality (calligraphy, poetry). And, lastly, the *ling* 靈 (the numinous efficacy of the medium as well as that of the tortoise and the yarrow stalks, which are "dried wood" and "rotten bones"[23]) can be identified as a reaction to human inquiry. This is not to deny the existence of a "spiritual" realm, the spirits do exist, but they are in need of a human quester in order to respond.

Like the "dissecting of characters" (*cezi* 測字),[24] in Ji Yun's times, spirit-writing served as a pastime, enabling scholars to enjoy joyful company. Some of them, like Zhu Gui, took it so seriously that they compiled the messages of various deities by turning them into a kind of alternative to the *Siku* anthology. As we can see from the quotation above, Ji Yun also enjoyed attending *fuji* 扶乩 séances, but his view emphasized the literary character of the procedure, while still paying attention to the mysteries of the messages' transmission. However, even he was not unaware of the potential impact of spirit-writing on an individual's fate:

> Therefore, as for the art of genius spirit-writing, literati may arbitrarily divert themselves matching verses, as if they were watching a theater play, and then they are fine. However, in case of divining for the auspicious and inauspicious, the superior man has to fear the outcome.
>
> 故乩仙之術，士大夫偶然遊戲，倡和詩詞，等諸觀劇則可；若借卜吉凶，君子當怖其卒也。HX 11/1, 771[25]

The *Yuewei caotang biji* contains twenty-nine entries where the term *fuji* occurs. It is important to note that all of them relate a dialogue between a person who asks a question and the genius *xian* 仙, who responds by either delivering a "judgment" (*pan* 判) or "descends on the altar" (*jiang tan* 降壇, *xia tan* 下壇); in many cases, the response consists of one or several poems. In six entries, the

---

23   Once again, an allusion to Wang Chong: "When King *Wu of Chou* destroyed *Chou*, the interpreters put a bad construction upon the omens, and spoke of a great calamity. *T'ai Kung* flung the stalks away, and trampled upon the tortoise saying, 'How can dried bones and dead herbs know fate?'" See Wang, *Lun-hêng*, 187, chap. XIV, "On Divination."
24   For character manipulation with a divinatory and literary background, see Schmiedl, *Chinese Character Manipulation*.
25   Translated Pollard, *Real Life*, 76.

answer is given in "big characters" (*dashu* 大書), frequently as a "sudden" or "prompt" (*hu* 忽) response (LY 5/5, 295; RS 7/1, 402–3; RS 7/1, 439; HX 11/1, 753; HX 12/2, 905; HX 14/4, 18).

No mention whatsoever is made of messages in the form of "morality books," and the genius' utterings always point to a precise issue. Questions can concern a person's life span:

> A gentleman who had served as a Remonstrant under the Ming dynasty, once asked a *fuji* about his life span, and the genius judged year, month, and day when he was bound to die, a date that was not far away. He was in constant fear and terror, but, when the moment came, he stayed in good health. Afterwards, he entered the service of the present dynasty and was promoted to the ninth rank. It happened that he attended a *fuji* [session] with another official's family and the previous genius descended again, whereupon our gentleman asked why the judgment had not come true. Again, the judgment said: "That you haven't died, what can I do about it?" The gentleman fell into deep thought and all of a sudden he ordered a carriage and left the place. For the judgment had precisely indicated the nineteenth day of the third month of a *jiashen* year.

> 某公在明為諫官，嘗扶乩問壽數，仙判某年某月某日當死。計期不遠，恆悒悒。屆期乃無恙。後入本朝，至九列。適同僚家扶乩，前仙又降，某公叩以所無驗。又判曰'君不死，我奈何？'某公俯仰沈思，忽命駕去。蓋所判正甲申三月十九日也。 LY 2/2, 86–87

In their translation into modern Chinese, Shao Haiqing et al. comment that, on the predicted day the last Ming ruler, the Chongzhen 崇禎 emperor (r. 1627–1644) committed suicide, therefore the allusion reflects on the loyalty of the former Ming official, who should have died on the same day as his emperor, but did not—a carefully crafted reproach.[26] Two similar cases are dealt with in LXY 22/4, 1632, where a judgment about "two autumns" is mistaken for an age of sixty-two but, in fact, the person dies two years later. "This is because at times, the spirits do have a knowledge of the future" (蓋靈鬼時亦能前知也). On another occasion, the genius denies a response to the question concerning life span, on the grounds that it depends on a person's moral conduct, therefore "concerning the years of life, you ought to ask yourself and must not ask me" (然則年命之事，公當自問，不必問吾也, ibidem). The verification

---

26　Ji Yun, *Yuewei caotang biji* (Shao et al. edition), 27.

of a prediction is the rule, not the exception: an official named Fan consulted a spirit-writing place and the genius who descended was Lord Guan (Guandi 關帝), who scolded him for not repenting for his wrongdoings and predicted an awful end for him. The man died a few months later, but until his very last breath did not know the reason why he was admonished to repent (LY 5/5, 295).

In three jottings, explicit mention is made of the fact that the genius "made no words about" (buyan 不言) or "did not discuss" (butan 不談) good and bad fortune, xiujiu 休咎, but rather expressed himself or herself through poems. However, the quantity of the poems (shi 詩) or songs (ge 歌) is much higher: we find them in LY 3/3, 183; LY 4/4, 209; LY 6/6, 363; RS 7/1, 402–3; RS 7/1, 439; RS 10/4, 706; GW 15/1, 1148; GW 17/3, 1368; GW 18/4, 1411–12; GW, 18/4, 1425; LYX 19/1, 1504; LYX 21/3, 1582 and as an "inscription" (ti 題) in HX 14/4, 18. A characteristic feature of the description of this kind of poetic spirit-writing consists of the search for the provenance, i.e. the authenticity of the poem in question. In RS 7/1, 439 a medium asks a scholar for an inscription, and the scholar fulfils his request. Much later, another medium delivers the same poem during a séance. When Ji Yun calls the audience's attention to the identity of both poems, the medium's pen "suddenly did not move" (ji hu bu dong 乩忽不動) and the medium "left in discomposure" (fujizhe langbei qu 扶乩者狼狽去). Moreover, someone in the audience remarks with a sigh, "a genius can also steal sentences" (xian yi dao ju 仙亦盜句).[27] In LY 2/2, 102–3, Ji Yun has purchased a book containing strange inscriptions that must come from a medium. However, Ji Yun opines that "this is a ghost's poem, not a poem of a genius" (余謂此鬼詩，非仙詩也). This distinction definitely does not doubt the authenticity of the poem, but it attributes its provenance to another authority. Ji Yun's father, on hearing a story about a medium who expressed himself in both verse and prose, states: "When I saw his verses, I took [their author] for a spirit; but when I looked at this extensive discussion, he finally seemed to me a genius" (吾見其詩詞，謂是靈鬼；觀此議論，似竟是仙。LY 3/3, 183).

However, there is much evidence for the authenticity of a poem's genius authorship, too. In GW 15/1, 1148, the author of the verses delivered by the medium is clearly identified as the famous courtesan Li Wuchen 李無塵 of the late Ming dynasty. In many cases, the authentification process is highly sophisticated; when the topic and imagery of a poem markedly points to the courtesan and poetess Su Xiaoxiao 蘇小小 (479–502), someone in the audience remarks that the poem follows the rules of the seven-character, eight-line, regulated verse (qilü 七律) which cannot have existed in Su's lifetime; the judg-

---

27   Ju 句 could also be translated as "verses" or "couplets."

ment argues that "the Buddha did not understand Chinese—how come the texts appear in parallel style? Therefore we realize that the power of perception of people of thousand years ago is still present until today, they are able to fathom and understand present-day language and texts." (釋迦不解華言，疏文何行以駢體？是知千載前人，其性識至今猶在，即能解今之語，通今之文。GW 18/4, 1411–12). In this passage, the deceased embodied in the genius are not perceived as stagnant beings, but rather as constantly refreshing themselves and adapting to their contemporary environment.

A genius can also give precious advice for a lifetime: "In times of pleasure, don't be too satisfied; in times of frustration, don't complain too hastily—this is how to preserve good fortune for your lifetime" (得意時毋太快意，失意時毋太快口，則永保終吉。RS 10/4, 658). The person who had received this answer "recited it his whole life through" (*zhongshen song zhi* 終身誦之).

Not every genius reveals his or her identity: the genius of a medium from the Jiangnan 江南 area (who called himself "the man from the Crouching Tiger Mountain") was asked the family and personal name, whereupon he or she responded that "a person outside of this world need not leave a name" (世外之人，何必留名？LY 3/3, 183). In RS 8/2, 514–15, a physician genius offers excellent advice, whose "doctrine and principles all the doctors would not be willing to utter" (其說其理，皆醫家所不肯言), so "can we really trust in spirits?" (真有靈鬼憑歟?). Yes, we can: there was a medium, who "did not discuss good and bad fortune, but just delivered paintings, and there were doubts about his authenticity. However, having seen a colored scroll of landscape painting in the style of Cao Mutang (painter, 1709–1787) with the image of the drunk (Immortal) Zhong Kui 鍾馗, the workmanship of brush and ink was extraordinary" (不談休咎，惟作書畫，頗疑其偽托。然見其為曹慕堂作色山水長卷，及醉鍾馗象，筆墨皆不俗。LY 5/5, 313). Doubts are justified, but can be overcome by a realistic perception. Moreover, the authenticity of the medium is also corroborated by the fact that a poem he bestows on Dong Qujiang 董曲江 (a poet and politician, *jinshi* 進士 of 1752) "resembled very closely the kind of man Qujiang was" (亦酷肖曲江之為人).

A judgment uttered by a genius claiming to be Qiu Changchun 邱長春 (the famous Daoist master invited by Genghis Khan, 1148–1227) is so convincing that a member of the audience remarks that "in general, all these geniuses arrogate false names, but the language of which this genius is capable—couldn't that really be Qiu Changchun?" (乩仙大抵皆托名，此仙能作此語，或真是邱長春歟? RS 9/3, 609).

A genius, however, is not endowed with limitless power. One genius is able to "heal illness, but not fix fate" (*wu neng zhibing, bu neng zhi ming* 吾能治病，不能治命。RS 8/2, 514–15); another accepts a go game *yi* 弈 competition, but loses and confesses that he has underestimated his adversary, which leads to Ju Yun's jocular remark that "this defeat reveals the truth, there are dull ghosts even on the august streets of Chang'an" (一敗即吐實，猶是長安道上鈍鬼。HX 11/1, 753); yet another genius is identified as the Song dynasty author of a work on the go game but, although accepting the challenge, he gives himself up before the beginning. "The only thing where posterity has made progress is the go game, in all other matters they cannot touch the people of old, but in go, they all defeat the older" (後人事事不及古，惟推步與弈棋，則皆勝古。). His only remedy consists of "not possessing a method to win, but a method not to lose. If I don't play go, I will never lose" (無常勝法，而有常不負法。不弈，則常不負矣。GW 15/1, 1176–77). In Yili 伊犁, there was an excellent medium (*shan fujizhe* 善扶乩者), but he was an alcoholic. Accordingly, each time the genius descended, paper money was burnt and liquor was offered (LY 6/6, 363, a note that must have been recorded during Ji Yun's exile in Xinjiang between 1768 and 1771). When reprimanded for presenting an oblique metaphor, a genius grows angry and accuses the questioner of impoliteness, *xiaoer wuli* 小兒無禮 (HX 12/2, 905). A lengthy disquisition on a poem serving as a response to a precise question (*yi shi* 以事) ends with the conclusion that "all in all this was a ghost familiar with essays {for examination}, who unduly claimed to be a person from the Tang dynasty" (蓋略涉文翰之鬼，偽託唐人也。RS 10/4, 706).

Both the genius and medium may have their shortcomings, but real fraud is rarely observed, except perhaps in RS 7/1, 439 (see above). Ji Yun's doubts rather bear on a world where the "supernatural" proves to be utterly natural. There is surprise and sometimes amusement in the realm of the spirits, ghosts, geniuses and mediums but, in the end, they are of our kind.

Abbreviations

LY   *Luanyang xiaoxia lu* 灤陽消夏錄, 1789
RS   *Rushi wo wen* 如是我聞, 1791
HX   *Huaixi zazhi* 槐西雜誌, 1792
GW   *Guwang ting zhi* 姑妄聽之, 1793
LYX *Luanyang xulu* 灤陽續錄, 1798

All the above texts are part of the *Yuewei caotang biji*

Bibliography

Chan, Leo Tak-hung. *The Discourse on Foxes and Ghosts: Ji Yun and Eighteenth-Century Literati Storytelling*. Hong Kong: Chinese University Press, 1998.

Durand-Dastès, Vincent. Review of *Real Life in China at the Height of Empire: Revealed by the Ghosts of Ji Xiaolan*, by David E. Pollard. *China Review International* 22, no. 1 (2015): 59–62.

Фишман, Ольга Лазаревна. *Цзи ЮнЬ. Заметки из хижины "Великое в Малом"*. Москва: Наука, 1974. (Fischman, Olga Lasarevna. Zametki iz khizhiny "Velikoe v malom." Moscow: Nauka, 1974.)

Goossaert, Vincent. "Spirit-writing, Canonization, and the Rise of Divine Saviors: Wenchang, Lüzu and Guandi, 1700–1858." *Late Imperial China* 36, no. 2 (December 2015): 82–125.

Goosseart, Vincent. "Une théologie chinoise de l'au-delà: Visions des morts dans le *Yuli baochao* (XIXe siècle)." In *Fantômes dans l'Extrême-Orient d'hier et d'aujourd'hui, tome 1*, edited by Marie Laureillard and Vincent Durand-Dastès, 29–39. Paris: Presses de l'Inalco, 2017.

Herrmann, Konrad. *Pinselnotizen aus der Strohhütte der Betrachtung des Grossen im Kleinen: Kurzgeschichten und Anekdoten*. Leipzig, Weimar: Kiepenheuer Verlag, 1983.

Ji Yun 紀昀. *Yuewei caotang biji* 閱微草堂筆記. Translated by Shao Haiqing 邵海清 et al. Shanghai: Shanghai guji chubanshe, 2012.

Ji Yun 紀昀. *Yuewei caotang biji* 閱微草堂筆記. Translated and annotated by Han Ximing 韓希明. 3 vols. Beijing: Zhonghua shuju, 2014.

Kalinowski, Marc. "Typology and Classification of the Mantic Arts in China." In *Handbook of Prognostication and Prediction in China, Part 1: Introduction to the Field of Chinese Prognostication*, edited by Michael Lackner and Lu Zhao. Leiden: Brill, forthcoming.

Keenan, David L. *Shadows in a Chinese Landscape: The Notes of a Confucian Scholar*. Armonk, NY: M.E. Sharp, 1999.

Lackner, Michael. "In the Empire of Signs: Predicting the Future in the Chinese-Speaking Cultural Realm." In *Zeichen der Zukunft: Wahrsagen in Ostasien und Europa/ Signs of the Future: Divination in East Asia and Europe*, edited by Marie-Therese Feist, Michael Lackner, and Ulrike Ludwig, 52–59. Nuremberg: Verlag des Germanischen Nationalimuseums, 2021.

Legge, James. *The Chinese Classics: With a Translation, Critical and Exegetical Notes, Prolegomena, and Copius Indexes*, Vol. 1: Confucian Analects, The Great Learning, *and* The Doctrine of the Mean. Hong Kong: At the Authors; London: trübner & Co, 1861.

Lin, Lynn Qingyang. "Two Translations of Ji Yun's *Close Scrutiny*: The Translator, the Reader and the Settings of Translation." *Fudan Journal of the Humanities and Social Sciences* 10 (2017): 103–16.

Pollard, David E., ed. *Real Life in China at the Height of Empire: Revealed by the Ghosts of Ji Xiaolan*. Hong Kong: The Chinese University Press, 2014.

Schmiedl, Anne. *Chinese Character Manipulation in Literature and Divination: The Zichu by Zhou Lianggong, 1612–1672*. Leiden: Brill, 2020.

Sima Qian 司馬遷. *Shiji* 史記. Beijing: Zhonghua shuju, 1959.

Sima Qian. *Records of the Grand Historian of China*. Translated by Burton Watson. Vol. 2. New York: Columbia University Press, 1961.

The Confucian Analects, the Great Learning and the Doctrine of the Mean. Translated by James Legge. New York: Cosimo Classics, 2009.

Wang Chong. *Lun-hêng*, Part 1: *Philosophical Essays of Wang Ch'ung*. Translated by Alfred Forke, Alfred. New York: Paragon Book Gallery, 1962.

Wenyuange Siku quanshu 文淵閣四庫全書. Reprint, Taipei: Taiwan Shangwu, 1983–85.

Wu Bo 吳波. Yuewei caotang biji *yanjiu* 閱微草堂筆記研究. Shanghai: Shanghai guji chubanshe, 2005.

CHAPTER 9

The Liu-Han Altar: Between a Literati Spirit-Writing Altar and Popular Religion

Zhu Mingchuan 朱明川

In 1961, Tang Junyi 唐君毅 (1909–1978), a distinguished Chinese philosopher, twice noted in his diary that, "In the afternoon, I went to Wang Biqing's house to observe a spirit-writing ceremony" (下午至王弼卿处看扶乩).[1] Wang Biqing 王弼卿 (1895–1968), a brilliant engineer of the Republican period, fled from the chaos of the Chinese Civil War (1945–1950) before moving to Hong Kong, as did Tang in 1949. In Hong Kong, Wang became an educator. He taught at Chung Chi College, United College, and other universities, whereas Tang joined the New Asia College as a professor of Philosophy.[2] On weekdays, Wang Biqing mainly engaged in academic affairs; in his spare time, however, he devoted himself to religious activities. He studied numerology (*shushu* 數術) and practiced spirit-writing techniques.[3] Many Chinese scholars who were in exile in Hong Kong, like Tang, were invited by Wang Biqing to participate in spirit-writing ceremonies at his home.

The spirit-writing altar over which Wang Biqing presided is called "Liu-han Altar" 了閒壇, and is mainly dedicated to the Southern Ming (1644–1662) loyalist Master Lou (Lou zhenren 婁真人). In fact, this spirit-writing altar was not created by Wang. It was first established by the Guo 郭 family in Fuzhou during the late Qing dynasty and has a history of more than 120 years. During the Qing dynasty, many family members, who served as government officials, helped to establish the family's power in local society. The early participants in the Liu-han Altar were literati in Fuzhou, led by the Guo family. During the late Qing dynasty, Guo Zengxin 郭曾炘 (1855–1928) served as a high-ranking official in the central government of the empire. As a consequence of his service, the altar, and the cult of Master Lou, were brought to Beijing and Tianjin 天津, and then became popular among a group of scholar-officials (*shidafu* 士大夫) in the capital. During the Republican period, Guo Zeshou 郭則壽 (1883–1943), a banker

---

1 *Tang Junyi riji*, vol. 1, 244.
2 In 1963, New Asia College, Chung Chi College, and United College united to establish the Chinese University of Hong Kong.
3 On his interest in numerology, see Wang, *Zhouyi yu xiandai shuxue*.

who used to study abroad in Belgium, built a temple in downtown Fuzhou for Master Lou which was open to the public, and the public were exposed to this cult for the first time. In 1926, the cult spread to other places outside Fuzhou, and branch altars were established in Xiamen 廈門 and Zhangzhou 漳州. The altar in Xiamen was located in a villa on Gulangyu Island 鼓浪嶼. It attracted elites from various walks of life to visit the island and attend the spirit-writing ceremony, including Wang Biqing, who finally decided to become the Chief Spirit-writing Medium (*you siluan* 右司鸞) at his branch altar.[4] After 1949, the branch altars moved to Hong Kong and Taiwan, and the former remains active to date.[5] Furthermore, a large proportion of the cult members in Hong Kong are faculty members of the Chinese University of Hong Kong and other prestigious academic institutions.

Throughout its 120-year history of expansion, the Liu-han Altar was a literati spirit-writing altar; that is, an elite religious group. In previous studies of Chinese popular religion, scholars have mainly paid attention to the impact of the elites on popular culture. The local gentry were usually regarded as one of the most significant factors affecting the evolution of local deities; the question of whether or not the popular cults should exist depended strongly on the attitude of the Confucian intellectuals and officials.[6] Specifically, in the case of the literati spirit-writing groups, the scriptures produced and compiled by the elite intellectuals have greatly enriched the popular religious canon;[7] their participation in the scripture publishing industry allowed them to promote the development of sects that spread eschatological discourses.[8] Several aspects of this process have not yet been clarified, however. How did popular culture affect the elite's religious practice? How did the elite come into contact with popular religious culture? How did the common people view elite religious groups such as the literati spirit-writing altars? This paper, therefore, does not limit itself to the study of the unidirectional influence of the elites on popular culture, but rather attempts to examine the interaction between the two sides within the context of a spirit-writing cult. On the one hand, the Liu-han Altar is a perfect case-study because of its consistency. This altar was unaffiliated with

---

4 Normally, during spirit-writing ceremonies in Fuzhou, two mediums hold the stylus together. The one standing on the right of the stylus is the main medium, and the other the assistant.
5 As indicated above, the Liu-han Altar in Hong Kong was originally set up in private homes such as that of Wang Biqing. After Wang passed away, the altar moved to Tung Hing Building 東興大廈 in Mong Kok for a while, and finally relocated to Man Wah Building 文華樓 in Ferry Point in 1983. Since then, spirit-writing ceremonies have been held there each Sunday.
6 Hansen, *Changing Gods in Medieval China*.
7 Goossaert, "Spirit Writing, Canonization, and the Rise of Divine Saviors."
8 Wang, "Morality Book Publishing and Popular Religion in Modern China."

Buddhism, Daoism, or any specific sects, but continuously run and managed by social elites, including Confucian scholar-officials, technocrats, and university professors. On the other hand, during the Republican period, the Liu-han Altar opened up to the public and provided divination services. As a result, the worship of Master Lou and this elite-led group gradually came to be accepted by the local people, creating multiple records about this cult from various points of view which we may subject to analysis.

This paper will examine the local cultural background of the establishment of the Liu-han Altar as well as its development using historical materials and ethnographic data collected during fieldwork. These materials can be divided into three categories. The first is religious documents, mainly spirit-written books. All of the core members of the Liu-han Altar were intellectuals and social elites, who had a strong sense of the need to record history and preserve documents, so they edited and printed the spirit-written books every year since the establishment of the altar. These voluminous documents are rich in content and help us to understand the altar's main activities during different historical periods. The second category is the records of the participants. Since the late Qing dynasty, the literati who joined the altar have left numerous literary collections. Through their poems, diaries, and biographies, we can discover the participants' own feelings and emotions. Guo Zengxin, and especially his son Guo Zeyun 郭則澐 (1882–1947), were undoubtedly prominent figures in the literary field of the late Qing dynasty and Republic of China. Zeyun occupied an essential position in the literary history of republican China, and has attracted the attention of many scholars.[9] It is also noteworthy that Zeyun was keen to observe and record stories about the supernatural. His *Dongling xiaozhi* 洞靈小志 (Anecdotes of observing anomalies) was a famous *zhiguai* 志怪 (Records of the strange) novel, which recorded his family and friends' religious practices and miraculous experiences. The third type of material used in this paper is the outsiders' records of the altar, including local chronicles, newspapers, and literary sketches, all of which can demonstrate the public's cognition of and attitude toward this cult.

1   The Loyalist Mindset at the Literati Spirit-Writing Altar

The Guo Family 侯官郭氏 was famous for their success in the civil service examinations during the Qing dynasty. They lived in the core of downtown

---

9 See Lin, *Canghai yiyin*, 276–317; Zan, *Guo Zeyun cixue zhengli yu yanjiu*.

Fuzhou, now called "Three Lanes and Seven Alleys" (*san fang qi xiang* 三坊七巷). The Guo family set up a mansion in Guanglu Lane 光祿坊, one of the "Three Lanes," where the Liu-han Altar was established. The glorious history of the Guo family can be traced back to the mid-Qing dynasty. In 1816, Guo Jiesan 郭階三 (1778–1856) became a *juren* 舉人 (person who had passed the provincial examination in Imperial China), which meant that he was able to enter officialdom. After him, all of his five sons also successfully passed the Imperial Civil Examinations. Among them, his second son, Guo Baiyin 郭柏蔭 (1807–1884), passed the highest-level examination and became a *jinshi* 進士 (presented scholar); he eventually served as the governor of Hunan 湖南 and Hubei 湖北 province. His fourth son, Guo Baicang 郭柏蒼 (1815–1890), was a famous scholar, hydraulic engineer, and bibliophile. The Guo family's offspring continued to pass the imperial civil examinations, and five of them obtained the title of *jinshi*. By the end of the Qing dynasty, many members of the Guo family had been appointed as officials outside Fuzhou, and some of them even occupied important positions within the central government. Since the mid-nineteenth century, to reward the Guo family for their great contribution to the empire's rule, the emperors continuously honored them as a model family.[10] In other words, the reputation of the Guo family was closely related to the fate of the Qing dynasty. The following paragraphs will tell the story of Guo Zengxin, Guo Baiyin's grandson, who witnessed the fall of the Qing dynasty. He was also the key figure in the early history of Liu-han Altar.

In 1880, Guo Zengxin passed the final civil examination and obtained the title of *jinshi*. He then moved to the capital to work as a royal scholar at the Hanlin Academy (Hanlin yuan 翰林院, an academic and administrative institution within the central government, membership of which was preserved for the most knowledgeable scholars, who performed secretarial and literary tasks for the court). Prior to the demise of the empire in 1911, he had been promoted to the post of deputy minister of the Ministry of Rites (Libu youshilang 禮部右侍郎). Guo Zeyun, the eldest son of Zengxin, also became a *jinshi* in 1903, before going to study in Japan. On returning to China, Zeyun served as a magistrate in Zhejiang 浙江 Province. Influenced by the local religious culture (see details below), while the father and son were away, the other Guo family members started to practice spirit-writing techniques in the mansion on Guanglu Lane in Fuzhou (Chart 1). In 1898, they received an oracle from Master Lou, which commanded them to establish the Liu-han Altar in the mansion. No one had

---

10   On how the Guo Family was honored by Qing emperors, see "Huang En 皇恩," in Guo, *Fuzhou Guoshi* zhipu, 1.1a–15b; see also "Qing gu guanglu dafu houguan Guo Wenan gong muzhiming."

ever heard anything about Master Lou before. Based on the spirit-written self-introduction of the deity, it became known that the surname of the present deity was Lou. He had been born in Jiangyin 江陰, Jiangsu 江蘇 province, during the late Ming dynasty. After the Manchus conquered northern China and established their empire, he chose to remain loyal to the Ming dynasty and served as a scholar-official at the Southern Ming court. When the Southern Ming army was defeated, he refused to surrender to the Qing regime and died a martyr. After his death, it was said that he became a deity who held the position of "Thunder Master and Prime Minister in the Purple Cloud Palace" (Zixia neixiang leiyin puhua zhenren 紫霞內相雷音溥化真人).[11]

When Master Lou first descended in 1898, it was Guo Fuzhong 郭輔衷 (1872–?), Zengxin's cousin, who acted as the Chief Medium of the spirit-writing rites. In 1910, Fuzhong also became an official in the capital, serving in the national post office. Because of this, he was able to bring the cult and the legends of Master Lou from Fuzhou to Beijing. As a senior official and prominent figure in the literary field, Guo Zengxin often held poetry gatherings in his residence in Fangsheng Garden 芳盛園 in Beijing. Apart from family members, most of the guests were scholar-officials who came from Fuzhou and worked in the capital. After Guo Fuzhong moved the Liu-han Altar to Fangsheng Garden, spirit-writing became a regular activity at these literary gatherings. Guo Zeyun recalled:

> My father used to be an official in Beijing and rented houses south of Xuanwu Gate. He had to move many times, because the residences were always too dilapidated. Only the residence named Fangsheng Garden in Jiajia Hutong was newly-built. It was located on a dry, slightly elevated field. In the west part of the garden stood a small pavilion surrounded by bamboo groves and rocks. My uncle, Fuzhong, used to be an official of the National Post Bureau. Every time he came here, he would hold a spirit-writing ceremony in the pavilion, inviting Master Lou to write poems with other guests for entertainment. The name of the pavilion was "Bright Green" (Lüjing), a name given by the deity. My father created two pieces of literature entitled *Lüjing ting yezuo* (Night in the Bright Green Pavilion) and *He Moyuan zhang Lüjing ting wu gu sishi yun* (Forty verses from rhyming exchanges in five character poems[12] produced with my father-

---

11 "Lou dazhenren jiangtan ji."
12 *He yun* 和韻 poetry is always composed at poets' salons. The participants take turns to write verses. The successor should respond with the same rhyme as the predecessor, which requires great literary skill.

316 ZHU

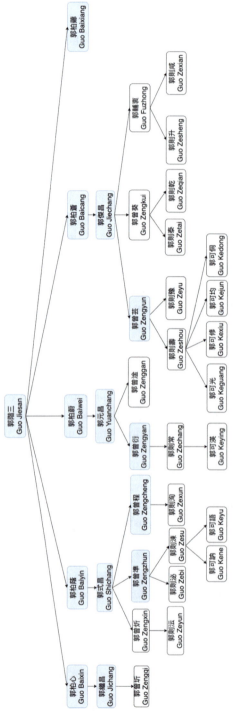

FIGURE 9.1 Members of the Liu-han Altar (names shown against a white background indicate those members of the Guo family who joined the Liu-han Altar in Fuzhou)

in-law Moyuan at the Bright Green Pavilion), both of which were written during a spirit-writing ritual.

曩從宦。宣南賃宅而居故，屢徙，多因簡陋。惟賈家衚衕芳盛園宅新構，稍爽塏。西院小亭，在竹石間。時仲起（郭輔衷）叔官郵曹，每來與群從扶乩為戲 ... 亭名「綠淨」，亦乩仙所賜。公有《綠淨亭夜座》及《和默園丈綠淨亭五古四十韻》，皆是時作 ...[13]

The latter work was included in Guo Zengxin's personal anthology, and before a poem he recorded the following:

> Leaving my hometown and living in another city made me feel very bored. Moyuan visited me every few days. He, my cousin and nephews always wrote poems through spirit-writing for entertainment. They used the same rhythm to write the verses in turn, as a way of killing time.

旅居無聊，默園間日一來，與弟侄兒輩為扶乩之戲。韻語酬答，頗足破悶 ...[14]

Moyuan refers to Huang Maoqian 黃懋謙 (1876–1950), Guo Zeyun's father-in-law. He also came from Fuzhou and was an official in Beijing during the late Qing dynasty.[15] Additionally, at the end of the Qing period, the participants at the Liu-han Altar in Fuzhou and Beijing also included other Guo family members, such as Guo Zesu 郭則涑 (1886–?), Guo Zebi 郭則泌 (1880–?), Guo Zeshou, and some of the central government officials from Fuzhou, such as Wang Hongshen 王鴻烒 (no dates) and Zhou Denghao 周登皞 (?–1940). What mainly attracted these well-educated people to participate in the Liu-han altar was the long tradition during the Ming and Qing Dynasties of literati creating literary works through the assistance of spirit-writing. According to Master Lou's self-introduction, he had been a scholar-official with a talent for writing poems, just like all who convened at the Liu-han Altar. It is for this reason that the scholar-officials at the end of the Qing dynasty were happy to communicate with him through writing poems. As Guo Zengxin recorded, at that time, they regarded spirit-writing as a recreational activity for literati.

After the Revolution of 1911, the Qing regime was overthrown. The Guo family and a group of Fuzhou-born Beijing officials decided to maintain their loy-

---

13　Guo, *Jiu de shu wen* 舊德述聞, vol. 24, 641–42.
14　Guo, *Paolu shicun*, 751.
15　For more details about their lives, see Lin, *Jielou shicihua*, 100.

alty to the Qing court. Guo Zengxin and others refused to serve in the new government, but chose to stay in Beijing in order to maintain their contact with the former emperor, Puyi 溥儀 (1906–1967). When Puyi was ousted from the Forbidden City in 1924, they followed him to Tianjin. During the Republic of China, these Qing loyalists no longer held political power, and so devoted more energy to literary creation. During this period, Guo Zengxin and his sons, as representatives of the former Imperial officials and literary leaders, actively joined and formed a series of literary societies, including the Bing she 冰社 (Ice Club) and Xu she 須社 (Stay Club). Guo Zeyun recorded a typical event at these societies:

> In spring 1926, I invited my teacher, Wang Ximin, to the Xu Building as a guest to accompany my father. Later, because the war broke out and traffic was blocked, he was trapped in Tianjin for more than three months. During this period, we held literary gatherings every day. Sometimes, we created poems through spirit-writing at night. Casually, I would write one verse rhyming with *jia* and *sha* and present it to Ximin. He would match it, just like my father. One after another we each [produced] twenty to thirty poems with the same rhyme. Slowly, two spirits, named Jingming and Chuzhen, corresponded with us by matching our rhyme. After that, companions who were fond of poetry in Beijing and Tianjin also participated in this activity. [This activity] produced a total of more than 200 poems, which was unprecedented. Therefore, we edited and published the *Xulou chouchang ji* (Anthology of corresponsive poems from the Xu Building).

> （1926年春）… 熙民師以山人之招來栩樓下榻，為文安公遊伴，會兵事道阻，留滯沽上三閱月。其間，文酒之會無日無之，夜闌或為扶鸞之戲。偶以加沙韻賦一律呈熙師，師和之，文安公復和之，先後疊韻各二三十首，漸而乩仙淨名、俶真更唱迭和，京津吟侶亦用是韻酬和，積至二百餘首，向來未有之盛也。因編《栩樓酬唱集》。[16]

After Guo Zengxin and his son moved from Beijing to Tianjin, the Xu Building in which they lived once again became a popular gathering place for literati. We do not have any details about the two spirits mentioned above, but we do know that Zengxin and his son were not only the leaders of the literary circle,

---

16   *Guo Zeyun ziding nianpu*, 62. See also Guo Zengxin, "Xulou yeyin shu jixian shi hou 栩樓夜飲書乩仙詩後," in *Paolu shicun*, 1102.

THE LIU-HAN ALTAR

but also the leaders of the spirit-writing groups among the Beijing and Tianjin loyalists. By organizing spirit-writing rituals, they fueled literary production. It is worth noting that, during this period, Zengxin and his son's attitude toward Master Lou changed. For them, writing poems with Master Lou was not only a recreation, but also held a deeper spiritual meaning. When the Qing regime was overthrown, the commonalities between Master Lou and every member of the Liu-han Altar increased: they were not only scholar-officials, but also loyalists to the former regime, who refused to surrender to the usurpers. The status of Master Lou changed, therefore, from an otherworldly pen pal into a deity of high moral standing, which made him more worthy of worship.

Although Guo Zengxin had already participated in the spirit-writing activities at the Liu-han Altar during the late Qing dynasty, he did not regard Master Lou as a holy deity worthy of worship. It was only after the Republic of China had been established that he decided to take refuge in Master Lou. He stated that "I was admitted to serve Master Lou at the altar in 1912" (壬子歲得侍仙壇),[17] which means that he was no longer a pen pal of the deity but a disciple. Guo Zeyun also recorded this change when he visited his father in Beijing:

> In spring 1912, I went to Beijing and lived in Fangsheng Garden for a few months. ... I accompanied my father, my uncle Guo Fuzhong, and my cousin Guo Zebi to participate in spirit-writing. Master Lou, a loyalist of the Ming dynasty, descended to the altar. The main topics he discussed with us were morality and righteousness.

> 是春（1912），北上省親，居住芳盛園數月 ... 又侍文安公與仲起（郭輔衷）叔、石琴（郭則泌）兄為扶鸞之戲。降乩者婁真人，為有明遺逸，所言皆道義之談。[18]

After the fall of the Qing dynasty, Master Lou not only wrote poems, but also moral sermons. Simultaneously, Guo Zeyun began to refer to him as a "loyalist" (*yiyi* 遺逸) rather than a spirit-writing immortal (*jixian* 乩仙). Guo Zengxin, moreover, decided to take refuge in him after the previous dynasty was replaced. Such a decision might be attributed to his deeply-held personal political beliefs, and also the fact that he had served as an official of the previous dynasty. At the end of the Qing dynasty, the Guos and Master Lou were all scholar-officials, and could communicate about poetry and prose but, in the

---

17   Guo Zengxin, "Lou dazhenren zhuan ba," 5a.
18   *Guo Zeyun ziding nianpu*, 37.

Republic of China, the Guos also faced the same situation that Master Lou had suffered previously. They all chose to remain loyal to the former dynasty. From this perspective, the Guos could regard Master Lou as a role model.

From then on, the amount of biographical information available about Master Lou gradually increased. The legend that had been revealed about him during the Qing dynasty was too brief. Consequently, in 1923, a new spirit-written biography was transmitted in Fuzhou, detailing the life of Master Lou. Thus, it was discovered that Master Lou's full name was Lou Dexian 婁德先 (1592–1645). Although we cannot find any information about Lou Dexian in the historical records, the new biography explained that his grandfather had been Yang Jisheng 楊繼盛 (1516–1555), a famous moral exemplar, who had been widely admired as a sage since the Ming dynasty.[19] Lou Dexian studied Neo-Confucianism in his youth, especially the theories of Zhou Dunyi 周敦頤 (1017–1073), Cheng Yi 程頤 (1033–1107), and Cheng Hao 程顥 (1032–1085) (於濂洛之學，悉心研究). He was also proficient in traditional Chinese medicine (於岐黃之術，涉獵尤精). Moreover, according to his biography, he had followed the well-known Confucian official Yang Lian 楊漣 (1572–1625) in impeaching Wei Zhongxian 魏忠賢 (1568–1627), who is commonly considered the archetype of the evil eunuch.[20] When the Manchus conquered northern China, Lou attempted to follow the famous anti-Qing general Shi Kefa 史可法 (1602–1645), one of the best-known loyal martyrs during the late imperial period.[21] After the Southern Ming regime was established in Fuzhou, he was ordered to guard Jian'ou County 建甌 in Fujian 福建 province. Finally, Lou was betrayed by a traitor, defeated, and killed by the conquering Manchus. The new biography and a painting of the deity were sent to Beijing from Guo's hometown in Fuzhou, from which Guo Zengxin was able to learn more about Master

---

19   Yang Jisheng was a Chinese court official during the reign of the Jiajing 嘉靖 Emperor (r. 1521–1567). He is remembered as a political opponent of the minister Yan Song 嚴嵩 (1480–1567), a traitor who was notorious for being corrupt and for dominating the Ming government for two decades. Although Yang Jisheng was arrested and eventually executed by Yan Song, the unjust manner of his death led to him being revered as a martyr for Confucian values. For more details, see *Mingshi* 明史, vol. 209.

20   For more details about the conflicts between Yang Lian and Wei Zhongxian, see *Mingshi*, vol. 244. Lou Dexian does not appear in this record, however (see below).

21   He is best remembered for his defense of Yangzhou 揚州. In 1645, Qing forces surrounded Yangzhou, a strategic spot, but lacked reinforcements. The Qing regent Dorgon 多爾袞 (1612–1650) wrote to the defender Shi Kefa to ask him to surrender. Although there was no chance of winning the war, Shi Kefa declined and was killed when Yangzhou fell. After his death, both the Southern Ming and Qing dynasties granted him the posthumous title of being "loyal" (*zhong* 忠).

Lou's life, which made him admire and respect the deity even more. The poem that Guo Zengxin wrote on the painting of Master Lou read:

> I have witnessed people in this world suffering from countless disasters.
> I saw no treasures in my room but just a scent of loyalty and piety.
> I heard that most deities used to be ordinary people. They remained loyal and dutiful when they were alive, and became deities after their death.
> I stroked my white hair and felt remorseful: why did I realize this principle too late?
> Now I cannot be martyred like you, and can only humbly drag out an ignoble existence.

> 擾擾群生方寸地，茫茫浩劫百千場。申徽寢室無余物，只有關西一瓣香。
> 神仙自在人間世，忠孝寧爭死後名。垂白自憐聞道晚，沉吟偷活愧先生。[22]

In his poem, he complained that the time he faced was very similar to that experienced by Master Lou. Although he admired the personality of Master Lou, he could not sacrifice himself and become a martyr. He felt ashamed, and had to do his best to maintain his loyalty to the Qing dynasty. In his later years, he recalled his life, when addressing Master Lou:

> In recent years, my age has advanced, but my knowledge has not increased. Nevertheless, a little comfort is that my behavior is consistent with the standards of loyal officials in history. I am gradually realizing my intention. I control my desires and endure poverty. I have not violated the teachings of the sages about loyalty, and still rank among those of moral accomplishment. This can mainly be attributed to your teaching.

> 比年以來，馬齒徒增，學不加進。差幸首自汗青，稍完素願。飲水茹蘖，不改清貧。未墜先人教忠之訓，猶在名流齒數之列。未始非得力先生之教益也。[23]

Notably, no one knew anything about the life of Lou Dexian before this spirit-written biography appeared. It is doubtful that Lou Dexian was a historical

---

22 Guo Zengxin, "Ti lou zhenren huaxiang 題婁真人畫像," in *Paolu shicun*, 11r1.
23 Guo Zengxin, *Lou dazhenren zhuan ba*, 5b.

figure. I have failed to discover any historical records about him to date. Around the time when his biography was being compiled, many other loyalists and martyrs of the Ming dynasty descended to the Liu-han Altar. Like Master Lou, they also became immortals in the Purple Cloud Palace, but were all historical figures recorded in the *Mingshi* 明史 (History of the Ming), such as Qi Xun 戚勳 (?–1644)[24] and He Hongren 何弘仁 (no dates).[25]

Even so, Guo Zengxin believed that he had insisted on being a loyalist for the rest of his life because he followed the instructions of Master Lou. Guo Zengxin died in 1928, but the loyalist mentality had become one of the characteristics of the Liu-han Altar. Most of the altar members who had joined afterwards suffered the same dilemma arising from having served as officials of the former dynasty but now facing new rulers so they deeply understood Lou's experience and regarded him as a model. One of the branches of the Liu-han Altar was, for example, located on Gulangyu Island in Xiamen, which was a foreign concession at that time. This altar had been established in 1926. Under the rule of the foreign colonial authorities, the altar members often felt oppressed, a feeling that was reflected in the poems produced through spirit-writing during this period. According to the local gazetteer:

> Zhou Xingnan was a follower of the Liu-han Altar, who wrote poems through spirit-writing. Every time he thought of good sentences, he would write them down. One day, he transmitted three poems about Koxinga (Zheng Chenggong 鄭成功, 1624–1662).[26] Two of them ran as follows:

> I hear the roar of the sea, and I see dark clouds covering my hometown.
> The reality is worse than three hundred years before (i.e., during the
>   Southern Ming dynasty).
> I would be too ashamed to face the grave of Tianheng.[27]

---

24 Qi Xun was an official during the late Ming dynasty. He guarded his hometown of Jiangyin county against the Manchu army. When the city fell, he refused to surrender and committed suicide. During the mid-Qing dynasty, he was enshrined by local people in Jiangyin. See *Jiangyin xianzhi*, vol. 16, 18b–19a. In 1923, it was he descended in the Liu-han Altar and wrote the biography of Master Lou.
25 He Hongren was a former county magistrate. After the fall of the Ming dynasty, he tried to commit suicide but failed, then became a monk and finally died, full of guilt. For more details, see Ho, *Sheng yu si*, 123.
26 After the Ming dynasty had fallen to the Manchus, Koxinga refused to serve the new dynasty and launched a military campaign against the Qing regime, summoning up a large force from his base in Fujian. In 1662, he even took Taiwan from the Dutch colonists.
27 Tian Heng (?–202 BCE) was a famous loyalist. After the establishment of the Han dynasty, he chose to commit suicide rather than serve the new government.

Weeds conquered the old palace.
Where are my lofty ambitions of old?
I hold my spear, only to find that I could not fight for you.
So I will stay here and wait for news of your victory.

Spirit-writing is certainly not credible. Yet, the tragic and desolation of the poem is not something that can be faked.

周醒南，了閒社信徒也，扶乩遇佳什，輒錄示。一日，示鄭延平詩三絕，錄二云：「大海狂濤入耳哀，故園翹首亂雲堆。傷心三百年前事，愧與田橫話夜台。」「荒煙蔓草舊樓台，昔日雄心安在哉。橫槊有慚吾計左，枕戈空盼好音來。」乩事固未可信，而此詩悲壯蒼涼，非社中人能假借。[28]

Zhou Xingnan 周醒南 (1885–1963) was an urban planner and a former director of the Xiamen Engineering Bureau. At the Liu-han Altar in Xiamen, he and Wang Biqing (see above) acted as the chief spirit-writing mediums. Unlike the Guo family, the members of the Xiamen altar were not loyal to the previous Qing dynasty, and served in the Nationalist Government. The change of regime in the early twentieth century had little impact on them. Because they were Chinese people living in a foreign concession, facing the potential menace of foreign enemies before the Sino-Japanese War, however, they felt distressed, and so worshiped the loyalists of the Southern Ming dynasty, such as Lou Dexian and Koxinga. By engaging with these cultural symbols, they displayed their political attitude through their religious practice. Moreover, during the same period, the focus of the loyalist mindset at the Liu-han Altar changed. With the fall of the imperial regime and frequent outbreak of national conflicts during the early twentieth century, the emphasis shifted toward loyalty to the nation instead of a particular regime, government, or party. During the Chinese Civil War of the late 1940s, some members of the Liu-han Altar fled the fighting in mainland China. When Wang Biqing, together with Zhou Xingnan, transferred the altar to Hong Kong in 1949, it became a place where newly-migrated Chinese intellectuals could come to terms with their national identities. Under British colonial rule in Hong Kong, these elites once again became another kind of loyalist, in this case to mainland China, the place from which they had escaped. Although mainland China had been controlled by another regime, they still hoped to return to their motherland and endeavor to do their best

---

28   *Xiamen shizhi*, 466.

for it one day. This is indicated by a spirit-written poem that was transmitted at the Liu-han Altar in the 1960s, when mainland China was suffering due to the Cultural Revolution: "Looking at the clouds in the sky, worrying about my motherland, but sitting in my small room, there is nothing I can do to help" (翹首雲天故國思，小軒靜坐賦秋詞).[29] At midnight on 1 July 1997, when the sovereignty over Hong Kong was transferred from the United Kingdom to the People's Republic of China, the Liu-han Altar held a grand celebration. The deceased loyalists descended and expressed their joy at the handover of Hong Kong.[30]

By understanding the social and religious background of the Guo family, we discover that the sacred narrative about Master Lou contained multiple layers. At the end of the Qing dynasty, Master Lou's main image was that of a scholar-official who could write poetry. During the Republic of China, he gradually became a model of loyalty and righteousness. His life began to be associated with many other loyal officials in history, and he became a martyr who refused to surrender to the new regime. In his new, spirit-written biography, he was constructed as a model representing those who remained loyal to the previous dynasty. That is why he came to be respected and worshipped by his disciples. This shift was similar to the fate of many former scholar-officials of the Qing dynasty. In this way, the Liu-han Altar changed from a literary society into a spiritual haven, where the frustrated elites could mutually provide comfort and encouragement to each other. They repeatedly experienced Master Lou's presence and conversed with him about morality and loyalty. By using their religious practice, they reiterated their political attitudes and expressed their emotions.

2   The Liu-Han Altar and Local Popular Religion

Among the early participants in the Liu-han Altar, some were members of the Guo family, and others were scholar-officials who maintained a close relationship with the Guos. Thus, the altar was initially a private elite religious group. One might ask how these literati, who had received a traditional Confucian education only, were able to use techniques such as spirit-writing, which were illegal at the time? It is necessary, therefore, to place the Liu-han Altar within the local religious-cultural environment of Fuzhou. Based on my fieldwork on

---

29   See the entry for October 27, 1968 in the *Gangtan luanzhang*, a compilation of the spirit-written texts transmitted to the Liu-han Altar in Hong Kong.

30   See the entry for June 1, 1997 in the *Gangtan luanzhang*.

the popular religious traditions in Fuzhou, as well as the Guo family's records, this section will present the evolution of the legend of Master Lou and the interaction between the elites and popular culture.

2.1 The Cult of the Purple Cloud Palace (Xiafu 霞府) in Downtown Fuzhou

We know that Lou Dexian received his celestial post in the "Purple Cloud Palace" after his death. Nowadays, we can still find a plaque stating "Prime Minister in the Purple Cloud Palace" (Zixia neixiang 紫霞內相) hanging on the wall behind the altar in Hong Kong (Figure 9.2). The "Purple Cloud Palace" was not a new notion, created by the Guo family, but related to the local religious tradition in downtown Fuzhou. This section will mainly discuss the relationship between the Fuzhou religious tradition, namely the Xiafu 霞府 (the Purple Cloud Palace) tradition, and the Guo family's spirit-writing altar. Some researchers have noticed that a local Daoist society called Doutang 斗堂 (Dipper Shrine) in Fuzhou enshrined the deities in the Xiafu,[31] but there is less information about the Xiafu itself.

The old residents of Fuzhou recalled that, in the past, the local deities were thought to belong to one of three different lineages: the Purple Cloud Palace, the Osmanthus Palace (Guigong 桂宮), or Mount Lü (Lüshan 閭山).[32] The Lüshan tradition relates to the goddess Chen Jinggu 陳靖姑, who has long been worshipped by exorcists in southeastern China.[33] Guigong designates a bureaucracy in heaven surrounding the god Wenchang 文昌, who played a vital role in the religious practice of intellectuals in late Imperial China.[34] It should be noted that the deities of the Lüshan and Guigong systems also had many adherents outside Fuzhou. The Xiafu is an indigenous religious tradition, however that exists only in Fuzhou and centers on spirit-writing (in the Fuzhou dialect, spirit-writing/*fuji* is also called "sailing the wooden raft," *kaifa* 開筏). Scholars who investigated the Daoist group Doutang from Fuzhou have also paid attention to the canonical scriptures of the Xiafu. They discovered that the priests of the Doutang chanted the *Zixia dujie zhimi jiubu zhenjing* 紫霞度劫指迷九部真經 (True scripture in nine chapters for crossing over the turning of the kalpa and pointing out the way in the Purple Cloud Palace), which was produced through spirit-writing and published during the late Qing dynasty. The

---

31　Ye, "Fuzhou Yuanshuai miao yueshen xinyang yu Doutang guanxi tankao," 53.
32　Guo Meiying 郭美英 (born 1936), interviewed by Zhu Mingchuan, April 3, 2019.
33　For more information about Chen Jinggu and the Lüshan tradition, see Baptandier, *The Lady of Linshui*.
34　Hu, "*Wendi quanshu* yanjiu," 5–6.

FIGURE 9.2 Plaque stating the "Prime Minister in the Purple Cloud Palace" (Zixia neixiang 紫霞內相) at the Liu-han Altar, Hong Kong
PHOTO BY AUTHOR, JANUARY 13, 2019

contents of this scripture were spirit-written by the Five Lineage Masters of the Purple Cloud Palace (*Xiafu wu zongshi* 霞府五宗師); namely, Kuang Fu 匡阜, Lüzu 呂祖, Master Bao 包宗師, Bai Yuchan 白玉蟾, and Marshal Tian 田公元帥.[35] Most of the members of the Doutang were from the elite class. These intellectuals and merchants were not professional Daoist priests who were hired by the community to conduct rituals, but still wanted to learn the Daoist rituals, such as "Worshipping Dipper" (Lidou 禮斗). For this purpose, they formed a special religious society to practice Daoist rituals. All of the Xiafu deities whom they venerated were able to descend through spirit-writing. The first character of the initiation names (*faming* 法名) of the members of the Doutang were assigned based on a generation poem (*zibeishi* 字輩詩) which had been revealed through spirit-writing by the Lineage Master. The awarding of the high priests' ordination grade (*fazhi* 法職) was also conducted through spirit writing.[36]

35 *Zixia dujie zhimi jiubu zhenjing*, 2.
36 Chen, "Lingbao shuiguan keyi zhi yanjiu," 17–21.

Among the five Lineage Masters of the Xiafu, Lüzu and Bai Yuchan are well-known nationwide; Kuang Fu is a Daoist plague deity; while Master Bao and Marshal Tian are mainly worshiped in Fuzhou. According to the Xiafu tradition, these deities, who transmit scriptures through spirit-writing, are collectively called "Masters" (shi 師). In addition, there is another typology of deities called "Immortal Masters" (xianshi 仙師), who can answer the questions of believers through spirit-writing to solve their life difficulties. We know that, in most popular Chinese cults, the relationship between believers and deities mimics that between servants and lords. With regard to the literati spirit-writing altars, Vincent Goossaert mentions that the adepts are considered the disciples (dizi 弟子) of the gods who produce the revelations.[37] As for the participants in the spirit-writing groups at Xiafu temples, their identities are more like a combination of both. In Fuzhou, dizi refers to those who enshrine and worship the deities but play no part in the spirit-writing activities. Adepts of the Xiafu deities instead call themselves "servant-disciples" (sizi 伺(嗣)子) in order to separate themselves from other believers (Figure 9.3). On the one hand, after taking refuge in the deities, they had a responsibility to worship the deities regularly, including participating in the celebrations for the deities' birthdays and temple festivals, as well as editing and publishing spirit-written texts. On the other hand, the deities still play the role of tutors, answering questions and granting them initiation names; for example, a reprinted edition of the Zixia dujie zhimi jiubu zhenjing was published by "Luo Kaicheng, the servant-disciple at the Orchids and Osmanthus Fragrance Club" (桂蘭聯社伺子羅開乘) in 1926. Another scripture, the Lüzu qingwei sanpin zhenjing 呂祖清微三品真經 (Lüzu's Qingwei veritable scripture in three chapters), was edited and printed by "the servant-disciple of the Purple Cloud Palace" (Xiamen sizi 霞門嗣子) at the Erxiang she 二香社 (Double Incense Club) in 1877.[38] The Liu-han Altar also adopted the special designation sizi, which is still used by its members today. Even in the poem that Guo Zengxin produced for Master Lou, he writes "It is destiny to meet the deity. I am sincerely following the Master's guidance" (邂逅驂鸞亦夙緣，服膺師訓每拳拳). He refers to Lou as "Master" (shi 師), and acknowledges that he had always been taught by the deity.

Due to the lack of historical sources, we cannot ascertain the details of the Xiafu in Fuzhou during the late Qing and Republican periods. Fortunately, this religious tradition has not disappeared. Conducting fieldwork at the existing

---

37　Goossaert, "Spirit Writing, Canonization, and the Rise of Divine Saviors."
38　"適霞門嗣子，有志為善，鋟刻斯經."

FIGURE 9.3 Plaque donated by Sizi 伺子 in the Marshal Temple, Fuzhou
PHOTO BY AUTHOR, APRIL 3, 2019

Xiafu Temples in Fuzhou can provide insights into how this unique religious tradition works. The most famous Xiafu temples in Fuzhou City today are Yushan Lüzu Temple 于山呂祖廟, the Marshal Temple 元帥廟 (Marshal Tian), and Peixian Palace 裴仙宮 (Immortal Master Pei 裴仙師). Nowadays, members of the Doutang still hold ceremonies to celebrate the Immortal's anniversary at Peixian Palace. During the birthday celebration at the Marshal Temple, believers will chant the *Zixia dujie zhimi jiubu zhenjing*. No spirit-writing activities take place in the aforementioned temples, however, which are relatively well-known. Due to the government's religious policies, spirit-writing is only carried out underground, in small temples and private houses. Xiguan Lüzu Palace 西關呂祖宮, now located near the West Lake in Fuzhou, provides us with a convenient opportunity to observe the religious activities of a modern Xiafu temple.

Xiguan Lüzu Palace was rebuilt on the first floor of a private apartment. This temple was established in 1983, and continues to host monthly spirit-writing activities. Deng Bingquan 鄧秉佺 (1924–1999), who founded this temple, converted to Lüzu's worship at an early age. His parents died when he was a child, and he was forced to earn his living as an apprentice in a bookstore. Once, when he fell ill, he was unable to afford any medical treatment, so went to a Lüzu Temple and obtained prescriptions transmitted through spirit-writing (*jifang* 乩方). As a consequence, his illness was cured, which he regarded as a blessing by Lüzu. Accordingly, he became a pious *sizi* of Master Lü. On reaching adulthood, Bingquan opened a herbal medicine shop. In 1964, he enshrined a photo of Lüzu in his house and worshipped it secretly every day. After the Cultural Revolution, he began to place wooden idols in his home, including those of Lüzu and Master Tian, then gradually added other Xiafu deities. Lüzu often revealed himself in his house. In 1980, he decided to build a temple to attract more believers. At that time, few temples were in operation in Fuzhou. Many believers, who used to belong to other Xiafu temples, thus came and made donations to support the construction of the new temple. During this period, Deng Bingquan began to practice spirit-writing techniques. On the first and fifteenth days of the lunar month and anniversary celebrations, Xiafu deities descended to the altar, and people could attend for divination or to obtain prescriptions. Moreover, the deities would grant black ink talismans (*fu* 符) to counteract evil forces and vermillion talismans to treat diseases. If the worshipper were sufficiently pious, after becoming a *sizi*, he could participate in more of the rites performed in the temple, such as scripture chanting or litanies. During the process of conversion and ordination, a permit (*pizhun* 批准) was needed, which required approval by the "Great Lineage Master Lü of Xiafu" (Xiafu Lü da zongshi 霞府呂大宗師) through spirit-writing (Figure 9.4). In 1999, Deng Bingquan died, and his daughter Deng Zhenwen 鄧貞文 (born 1961) took over his religious duties.[39]

In Lüzu Palace in Fuzhou, in addition to the five Lineage Masters mentioned above, are the Immortal Official Liu 柳仙官, the Immortal Official Bai 白仙卿, the Immortal Official He 何仙卿, and other deities who also belong to the Xiafu tradition. Unlike the "Lineage Masters" and "Immortal Masters," the "Immortal officials" are subordinate bureaucrats of the Xiafu system. Based on the "precious invocations" (*baogao* 寶誥, a type of short text for inviting deities), we can create a biographical sketch of these Immortal Officials:

> "Immortal Official Bai's invocation": He lived in Zhicheng [in his previous life]. After receiving instructions from the Perfected Ruler Hongjiao

---

[39] Deng Zhenwen, interviewed by Zhu Mingchuan, April 6, 2019.

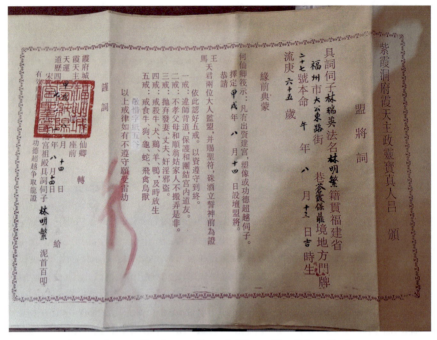

FIGURE 9.4 Spirit-written ordination certificate in Xiguan Lüzu Palace, Fuzhou
PHOTO BY AUTHOR, APRIL 4, 2019

(Hongjiao zhenjun)[40] after his death, he was able to return to perfection in the Purple Cloud Palace.

"Immortal Official Liu's invocation": He is a guard of heaven, serving in Xiafu. … He lived in Pingtan during his lifetime and left many miraculous legends there. … After his death, grateful that he was saved by Master Tian, he followed Master Tian [to descend] through spirit-writing rites to enlighten people. …

《白仙卿誥》：芝城托跡，紫府歸真 … 隨宏教真君之指引 …
　《柳仙官誥》：九天侍衛，霞府供差 … 平潭勝邑，留聖跡於当年 … 渥蒙田恩師之拔度，启化隨鸞 …[41]

40　Liu Shouyuan 柳守元, also known as Hongjiao zhenjun 宏教真君, has been an important deity at Lüzu altars since the early Qing dynasty. For more details, see Lai, "*Lüzu quanshu zhengzong*," 106.

41　See the *Xiafu shenggao* 霞府聖誥, which was published by the Xiguan Lüzu Palace in the 2010s.

Pingtan is an island near Fuzhou, whereas Zhicheng refers to Jian'ou, where Lou Dexian died. The text relates how both Immortal Officials lived in the area surrounding Fuzhou during their lifetime. After their death, they descended to downtown Fuzhou through spirit-writing rites, and were enshrined as Xiafu deities. Their experiences and process of divinization are very similar to those of Master Lou.

Additionally, a statue of Deng Bingquan stands in Xiguan Lüzu Palace, bearing the title "Deng, Law Enforcement Official of the Purple Cloud Palace" (Xiafu zhifa Deng shizhe 霞府執法鄧使者). This title was granted by the Xiafu Lineage Masters to Deng as a reward for founding the Palace, which indicates that Bingquan had become a new deity in the Xiafu tradition after his death. Another believer who was portrayed as a deity is Grannie Huang. Her title is "Secretary of the Purple Cloud Palace" (Xiafu shoushu Huang poguan 霞府收疏黃婆官). She was a *sizi* who generously donated to the palace during her lifetime. After her death, she was also commended and recognized as a new goddess. In the backyard of Lüzu Palace, several portraits of the "Elder Sisters" (*sanjie* 三姐) were enshrined. They were vital supporters during the early stage of the palace's reconstruction (Figure 9.5). As new deities of the Xiafu, the deceased mentioned above would also descend to the altar during spirit-writing ceremonies.

Although the present situation may not be exactly the same as it was a hundred years ago, by conducting fieldwork at the Xiafu temples in Fuzhou, we can roughly summarize several characteristics of this regional religious tradition:

1. The Xiafu cult originated in downtown Fuzhou and can be traced back to the mid-Qing dynasty. Spirit-writing is one of the most important elements of this cult.
2. The interaction between believers and deities mainly relies on spirit-writing rites. *Sizi* receive the teaching from the Masters through spirit-writing. The deities, in turn, support their believers with medical treatment and divination through spirit-writing.
3. Whether a person becomes a convert when alive or a deity after death must be confirmed through spirit-writing.

Scholars have noted that spirit-writing is a fast channel for divinization. The dead can directly obtain their sacred identity, without being certified by the central government or the Daoist Heavenly Masters.[42] It is this characteristic of spirit-writing that appealed to the intellectual groups, especially in late imperial China. Why did these elites, who had received a Confucian educa-

---

42   Goossaert, "Divine Codes," 26.

FIGURE 9.5 Images of Deng Bingquan, Grannie Huang, and the Elder Sisters in Xiguan Lüzu Palace, Fuzhou
PHOTOS BY AUTHOR, APRIL 4, 2019

tion, believe that spirit-writing could grant personal divinization? The case of the Guo family in Fuzhou shows that the "Xiafu," the local religious tradition, provided the technical knowledge about spirit-writing, divinization, and other rituals for these elites. Based on this kind of local knowledge, the Guo family set up an altar and turned Lou Dexian into a deity through spirit-writing. Many details can demonstrate the relationship between the Liu-han Altar and the Xiafu tradition in Fuzhou; for example, the early spirit-written books of the Liu-han Altar contain many records of revelations from the Xiafu Masters.[43] After the altar was established, an increasing number of people gradually descended and announced that they had become Xiafu deities through spirit-writing. Some of them were historical figures; scholar-officials who had been loyalists or martyrs during the late Ming dynasty, such as Qi Xun and He Hongren, mentioned above. Others were members of the Liu-han Altar who had made significant contributions; for example, Guo Zengxin became an Immortal Official,[44] and Wang Biqing was named "Perfected" (*zhenren* 真人) after his death (Figure 9.6). Today, there are no longer any Fuzhou people among the Liu-han Altar members in Hong Kong and they no longer understand the meaning of the Xiafu: however, many other traditions related to the Fuzhou local religion have survived. The current members of the Liu-han Altar in Hong Kong still use the long, Y-shaped wooden stylus, which is the typical Fuzhou style of spirit-writing. Although their native language is Cantonese, they still call spirit-writing *kaifa*, and converts call themselves *sizi*, which is consistent

---

43 "Xinhai qi yue chuba ri Bai dazhenren xiaguang."
44 "Guo Wumen xianqing zhuan lüe."

THE LIU-HAN ALTAR   333

FIGURE 9.6 Images of Xiafu Immortal Officials, who used to be loyalists or martyrs during the late Ming dynasty, and Perfected Wang Biqing at the Liu-han Altar, Hong Kong
PHOTOS BY AUTHOR, JANUARY 1, 2019

with the Fuzhou dialect. They also obtained an initiation name through spirit-writing that is in accordance with the generation name poem in other Xiafu temples in Fuzhou.[45] These details confirm that the Liu-han Altar was not created accidentally by the Guo intellectual family, but originated from the local popular religious culture in Fuzhou.

2.2   *The Liu-Han Altar and Master Lou from the Perspective of the Common People*

The above summary is based mainly on an investigation of religious texts, temples, Xiafu's believers, and ritual experts, but it may be assumed that the broader populace would care little about why the number of deities in the nearby temples increased or how the network of altars and temples was formed. When attending Xiafu altars or temples, they rather hope to solve their life problems through revelations from the deities. Therefore, the deities' origin is of little interest; what is more important is whether they possess sufficient

---

45   The generation poem of the Liu-han Altar is "守、理、崇、性." Only the top believers were entitled to include "性" in their given names. "性" is also the most elevated given name in the generation poem of the Xiafu tradition in Fuzhou.

spiritual power (*ling* 靈). Thus, the Xiafu deities, who can descend through spirit-writing, become a symbol of spiritual efficacy.

According to memoirs from the 1960s, there were many spirit-writing altars in downtown Fuzhou during the Republican period. Looking at their names, we can tell that there were various Masters belonging to the Xiafu tradition, far more than simply Master Lou of the Guo family:

> On Miao Lane stood the Shengsheng Shrine (Shengsheng chantang) founded by Lu Dao, which set up a spirit-writing altar for Master Kuang. The stylus of Master Cai was located in Zhenhai Tower on Mount Ping. The Protection Society (Hu she) on Gong Lane managed an altar and the stylus for Master Yan. The Liu-han Altar was located on Gudong Road. People could go to these places for divination or to obtain medical prescriptions through spirit-writing at any time. Some of these places also provided divination slips (*wenshi qian*) and medicinal slips (*yaoqian*). All of these services were free of charge. … The Master Lou Palace (Loushi gong) was located nearby the Office Square (*busi cheng*) and was established by Guo Zeshou of the Bank of China. Politicians often came here.

> 妙巷陸道即陸四所創的生生懺堂，設匡師筏；屏山鎮海樓的蔡師筏、宮巷護社的顏師筏、鼓東路了閒壇木筏等，隨時都有問事問病，或且設置有藥簽、問事簽，中間不取分文者有之 … 婁師宮設在布司埕，為中國銀行郭則壽倡辦，常有政治人物來往其間。[46]

For the local residents, the main functions of both Master Lou as well as the other masters were divination and medical treatment. The only subtle difference was that the participants in Master Lou's cult also included elites such as politicians. The visitors who sought out these practical services, however, usually did not choose to convert, but only sought help when they encountered difficulties.[47] Answering various questions is one of the main functions of every spirit-writing altar, but it was only the second most important one for the Liu-han altar.[48] The primary feature of the Liu-han Altar was its func-

---

46 Ye, "Fuzhou mixin huodong yipie," 246.
47 Xu, "Fujian shendao mixin," 194–196; "Liaoxian shiju"; See also *Xiamen shizhi*, vol. 35, 466; Su, *Woyunlou biji*, vol. 2, 117; Guo, *Dongling xiaozhi, xuzhi, buzhi*, 347.
48 This does not mean that the elite members did not rely on spirit-writing rites to solve practical problems, however. When Guo Zengxin and Zeyun fell ill, they used medical prescriptions and talismans written by Master Lou. See Guo, *Binglu riji*, 338–72. Another example is that, when Guos had to make a vital decision, they also divined through spirit-

tion as a literary club. The Liu-han Altar did not refuse outside requests for divination and medical treatment; for instance, nowadays, the spirit-writing ceremonies at the Liu-han Altar are separated into two sections. During the first part, the deities descend and write down poems in order to comment on current world events. The other part is a Q&A, in which visitors can ask the deities questions, mainly concerning their personal life, such as their career, investments, marriage, etc.[49] We can imagine that the procedures during the late Qing period would have been similar. Like other Xiafu temples or altars, these practical services were free. The difference is that the Liu-han Altar had no intention of expanding its scale or increasing its influence through these public services. A plaque made in 1968 stating "Only freedom from vanity can help to achieve something really lasting" (惟淡乃永) is displayed on the Liu-han Altar in Hong Kong. Master Lou once descended and wrote this sentence to warn managers not to be eager to become famous or attract too many visitors. This is precisely the long-term strategy that the Liu-han Altar adopted. Since its establishment, the Liu-han Altar has edited and printed spirit-writing records annually. According to these texts, the proportion of divination and medical prescriptions in the records, compared with other activities, is relatively low, accounting for only one-third of the Xiamen branch records.[50] In the early records of Fuzhou, the proportion is even lower. The majority of records consist of corresponsive poems and essays on the *Zhouyi* 周易 (Zhou changes) and Buddhist philosophy, written by Master Lou when he descended and communicated with the *sizi*, which clearly suits the preferences of literati and scholars

---

writing. In 1924, the warlord Feng Yuxiang 馮玉祥 (1882–1948) launched a military coup in Beijing. When Feng's army surrounded the Office of the President, people wondered if he would support the restoration of the monarchy. Guo Zeyun received a revelation from spirit-writing deities, which helped him to predict accurately that the abdicant emperor Puyi would be driven from the Forbidden City, where he had been allowed to remain after the founding of the Republic, according to the "Qing Di tuiwei youdai tiaojian 清帝退位優待條件" (Articles of favorable treatment of the Great Qing Emperor after his abdication). After the coup, Feng imprisoned the president Cao Kun 曹錕 (1862–1938) and took control of the Beijing government. The government initiated several reforms on Feng's behalf, including the expulsion of Titular Emperor Puyi. See *Guo Zeyun ziding nianpu*, 59.

49 Generally speaking, such Q&A sessions are relatively common at spirit-writing altars and most people who participate in spirit-writing rites pose similar questions. Philip Clart, in his presentation at the conference from which this volume originated, discussed several examples from a present-day Taiwanese spirit-writing altar. In the Liu-han Altar's collections of spirit-written texts during the early period, however, records of participants requesting divination were rare. Only since the 1930s, have there been more relevant records, especially at the branch altars in Xiamen and Hong Kong.

50 See *Lou Chengjiang xiansheng shiji*.

more closely.[51] Such writings not only appeared in the early records, but remain common in recent ones, suggesting that the Liu-han altar catered to an elite audience and did not try to attract supporters from the broader population.

Why, then, did many Fuzhou locals continue to venerate Master Lou, even though the Liu-han Altar did not promote this cult to the public? This mainly results from the local popular understanding of the Xiafu deities. In the folklore of Fuzhou, Master Lou has an entirely different image. For the common people of Fuzhou, he is not a loyal minister, scholar-official, or martyr, but a fox spirit. Indeed, in his work, Xu Dishan 許地山 (1893–1941) speculated that the prototype of the early spirit-writing goddess Zigu was a fox spirit.[52] In Fuzhou's popular religion, the fox spirit is also closely related to spirit-writing deities. It was said that, among the various fox spirits in the Fuzhou area during the Republic of China, the most famous four were Master Lou, Master Cai, Master Bai, and Master Pei. Judging from their titles, all of them are Xiafu deities. In the popular imagination of Fuzhou people since the Qing dynasty, it was believed that fox spirits could be promoted into Xiafu "Masters" after gaining immortality through long cultivation on earth, which required them to receive offerings from people continuously.[53] In her research on fox deities, Kang Xiaofei mentions that, during the late imperial period, there were folk legends presenting fox deities as "immortal guardians of the official seals" (*shouyin daxian* 守印大仙) who resided on the upper floor of government offices. She quotes early sinologists' records from Fuzhou during the late Qing dynasty which show that officials would store the official seals in an elevated place within the residence of the fox spirit and worship them to recruit their help with maintaining social order. In the governor-general's *yamen* in Fuzhou, for example, there was at least one clay image of a fox deity, represented as "a venerable old man seated in a chair."[54] This clay image may, at that time, have referred to Master Pei, who was also known as "Perfected Pei the Governor" (Dushu Pei zhenren 督署裴真人) and reverenced within the *yamen* of the governor-general of Fujian and Zhejiang. There are also sources that indicate that, during the Republican period, the governor of Fujian province, when he lost his official seal, had no

---

51   In the 1930s, to fulfill the members' interests in Buddhist philosophy, the Liu-han Altar in Xiamen invited famous monks, such as Master Yuanying 圓瑛 (1878–1953) and Master Hongyi 弘一 (1880–1942), to deliver lectures. For more details, see, e.g., Shi Yuanying, "He louzhenren yuan yun 和婁真人原韻," in *Yuanying dashi wenhui*, 240.

52   Xu, *Fuji mixin di yanjiu*, 16. For more on Xu Dishan's work on spirit-writing, see also the contribution by Fan Chun-wu in this volume.

53   Xu, "Fujian shendao mixin," 194–96.

54   Kang, *The Cult of the Fox*, 165–69.

choice but to donate money to the building of a temple dedicated to the fox deity, Master Pei. In today's Fuzhou, this temple is the largest Xiafu temple.[55] The notion that the immortal masters in the Xiafu are equivalent to fox spirits remains widespread in contemporary Fuzhou. Most believers avoid discussing this topic publicly. In a temple that enshrined Master Bai, however, I saw stuffed toy foxes placed in front of the statue (Figure 9.7), indicating that some believers may be aware of the subtle connection between the Xiafu deities and fox spirits.

These legends may be sufficient to prove that, in the popular imagination, there was some relationship between the Xiafu deities and fox spirits. As for the Xiafu deity at the Guos' altar, this is also corroborated by other sources. The Guo family succeeded in the imperial examinations and many family members served as officials; a good example is Guo Zengxin's father, who served as the governor of Hunan and Hubei province. By the end of the Qing dynasty, five members of the Guo family had received the title of *jinshi*. As a response, the rumor spread in the community that a fox spirit had blessed the family and helped them succeed in the exams. Guo Zeyun recalled that,

> The old house on Immortal Tower Street was built during the Ming dynasty. On the west side of the building, on the first floor, was a study room in which you could also enjoy a view of the flowers and trees in the courtyard. My father, Grandpa Chuanchang, Uncle Zengzhun, Uncle Zengcheng, and Uncle Chen Chunying all studied here. One after another, they all successfully passed the civil examinations and became *jinshi*. "Five *jinshi* in one house" (*yi zhai wu jinshi*) is what the neighbors called them. According to our neighbors' gossip, there was a fox spirit living in the old house. There were some witnesses who claimed that the fox spirit was an old man with a white beard. It was said that, if a teenager had a mild illness, you should just pray to him, and then they would recover.

> 仙塔街老屋，尚是明代結構。宅西有樓，樓下為書室。庭間花木蔚然。文安公（郭曾炘）嘗與子冶（郭傳昌）叔祖、少萊（郭曾準）、南陽（郭曾程）兩叔及陳幼海（陳春瀛）姑丈同讀書於此。先後俱登甲科，一齋五進士，里人稱之。相傳樓有狐仙，有見之者為一白須叟。兒女輩小恙禱之輒愈，不為患也。[56]

---

55   Xu, "Fujian shendao mixin," 194.
56   Guo, *Jiu de shu wen*, 594.

FIGURE 9.7 Stuffed foxes and Master Bai displayed together on the altar
PHOTO BY AUTHOR, DECEMBER 21, 2020

The residents nearby thus attributed the success of the Guo family in the examinations to the blessing of the fox spirit. Since the deities of the Guo's Liu-han altar resided in the Xiafu, it seemed natural to consider them as fox spirits. Although this kind of popular understanding did not accord with the primary intention of the Guo family, the accomplishments of the family members were enough to prove that their deity was efficacious, attracting more local people to come to request divination or medical prescriptions.

The Guo family may have noticed that the locals equated the Xiafu deity with a fox spirit. At least, they tried to address such rumors when the Liu-han Altar was first established. Before the appearance of Master Lou, another deity named the Immortal Lin had descended to the Guo family spirit-writing altar:

> Our family had a house on Huangpu Lane. From 1901 to 1902, there was an altar in the house dedicated to the Immortal Lin. It was said that his [mortal name] was Lin Hejing.[57] During spirit-writing ceremonies, he granted each disciple an initiation name and taught them ritual techniques (*fashu*). [His spiritual powers] could be used to conjure objects from distant places and make flowers bloom out of season. They were also able to cure diseases, and exorcize evil [spirits]. When a woman in the neighborhood was possessed by a demon, a priest was asked to visit her house with a wooden stylus. The priest pasted talismans on the door and windows, then set up an altar in the room. After he walked around the woman's body a few times carrying the wooden stylus, a fox suddenly appeared. The priest grabbed the fox, put it in a jar, and sealed the lid with talismans. The lid was smaller than the fox and no one knew how the priest had managed to put it in the jar. The fox trembled in the jar, and the priest used the wooden stylus to kill it through Five Thunder Magic (*wuleifa*).[58] After the jar was broken, there was only a piece of ore left in it. Then, a craftsman was ordered to break up the ore and found a piece of jade with a blood-red texture inside. We carved this jade into a seal with Master Lin's title: "Magnificent Immortal Master and Prime Minister in the Purple Cloud Palace" (Zixia neixiang tonghua xianshi). Since then,

---

57 Lin Hejing (967–1028) was a loyalist of the Kingdom of Wuyue 吳越 (907–978). After Wuyue pledged allegiance to the Northern Song, Lin was reluctant to serve the Song dynasty so he became an errant hermit around the West Lake. He rejected secular vanity and rejoiced in nature. He remained single throughout his life, declaring that the plum blossom was his wife and the cranes his children.

58 For more details about *wuleifa*, see Reiter, *Basic Conditions of Taoist Thunder Magic*, 81–84.

we would affix this seal to talismans. I saw this seal when I returned to Fuzhou to take the exam in autumn 1902.[59]

吾家黃璞里宅，辛丑（1901）、壬寅（1902）間奉有乩壇，主壇林仙，相傳為和靖。凡侍壇弟子，各錫法名，頗授以法術，能致遠道物產或非時卉果，亦為人療疾捉邪。里中某姓婦，為妖據，請乩往，乩書符遍粘門窗訖，即室中設壇，舉木筏繞婦身數匝，倏現一狐。法官捉置於壇，加符封其口，口小於狐，不知其何自入。既而壇中狐奔騰不已，乩殛以五雷法立斃，碎壇出之，乃一巨璞。命工剖之，得白玉，其紋有血絲，因琢為印，文曰「紫霞內相通化仙師」，蓋林仙位號也。自後書符即鈐用是印。余壬寅歸里應秋試，猶及見之。

According to this account, the Immortal Lin of the Guo family had been a Xiafu deity, and wiped out the fox spirit. This statement shows the Guo family's hostile attitude toward fox spirits, which is clearly at odds with the perception of the local religious believers. When Guo Fuzhong described how the Liu-han Altar was established, he also emphasized that the spirit-writing altar of the Guo family was unrelated to fox spirits:

> In 1898, I lived in a house on Guanglu Lane. ... At that time, Master Lin descended to the Tongyuan Altar (Tongyuan tan) to provide relief to the local community, and even [write about] wondrous phenomena and recount anecdotes. [These things] greatly fascinated us. In my leisure time, I started to practice spirit-writing for entertainment. After a little practice, I began to transmit more and more [messages]. Finally, Master Lou descended to the altar and asked us, "Why do you practice spirit-writing day and night? What is the purpose? People shouldn't practice it too often because, once you start spirit-writing, your essence and *qi* (*jing qi*) will be constantly connected [to supernatural powers]. If you encounter a malicious mountain spirit, forest demon (*shanxiao mumei*), or fox spirit residing in a vermillion mansion,[60] it will not only prove detrimental to your body and your mind, but will also decrease your essence and your *qi*." That night, in addition to myself, there were Guo Zengqi, who served as the Assistant Wielder, Huang Maoqian and his brother Huang Chengchao, as well as Guo Zeshou participating in the spirit-writing session. After receiving this revelation, our hair stood on end. Subsequently,

---

59 *Dongling xiaozhi, xuzhi, buzhi*, 347.
60 A "Vermillion mansion" refers to the houses of officials or the wealthy. As mentioned above, fox spirits were thought to live in officials' houses.

we abandoned the practice and asked Master Lou to gift us a talisman to consecrate our home [for protection].

歲戊戌（1898），堅（郭輔衷）寓居光祿吟台...其時通元壇林大真人開壇濟世，甚著靈異，談及軼事，輒令人傾倒。課余之暇，偶習扶鸞，以慰岑寂。花晨月夕，多有所傳。最後蒙妻大真人下光，諭云：「諸君連夕煉筏，是何宗旨？此事不宜屢行，因人生精氣，一經扶鸞，即有息息相通之感召。倘遇深山木魅、朱屋老狐，不特無益身心，且妨有損精氣。」是夕堅、勤(郭曾圻) 司左右，嘿（黃懋謙）、忍(黃承潮)、彬（郭則壽）侍壇。拜聆之余，毛髮俱竦。遂罷煉筏，而特請大真人頒賜信符，以備供奉家中...[61]

When Master Lou first descended to the altar, he thus warned the participants that fox spirits are dangerous and harmful to human beings, and suggested that the participants in the Guo family should keep away from them. It is notable that such narratives appeared repeatedly from the Guo family. Their private religious practice did not have to be explained to others but, when the cult formed at the literati altar began to attract wider attention among local residents, it became necessary to clear up any misunderstandings.

The case of the Liu-han Altar in Fuzhou shows that the Guos, as a family of officials' in late imperial China, acquired religious knowledge and techniques from the local popular religion in order to create their cult. The local religious Xiafu tradition provided a sophisticated model, ranging from specific rites, the methods of divinization, and the creation of scriptures to normal daily religious activities. As a consequence, however, Master Lou, as a Xiafu deity, was also identified in the local religious tradition and related popular imagination with a fox spirit, similar to other Immortal Masters. Although this interpretation increased the influence of Master Lou on the public, it also conflicted with the Guo family's original intention. Accordingly, the Guo family tried to dissociate themselves from this local interpretation and emphasized that the Liu-han Altar, as a literati altar, was unlike the popular spirit-writing altars, that would congregate with harmful, heterodox spirits such as foxes.

Nowadays, neither the Liu-han Altar nor the Palace of Master Lou, which had been built by Guo Zeshou, exist in Fuzhou. The cult of Master Lou, however, has not disappeared. There are still some residents in the Fuzhou area who venerate Master Lou in their homes (Figure 9.8). This shows that, despite everything, the cult of Master Lou had persisted in local society as part of the

---

61   "Lou dazhenren jiangtan ji."

FIGURE 9.8 A painting scroll enshrined by residents at their private altar in contemporary Fuzhou
Note: According to the spirit-written biography of Lou Dexian, he was proficient in traditional Chinese medicine. On this painting scroll, he holds a bunch of herbs in his left hand, with a gourd containing pills at his side.
PHOTO BY AUTHOR, JULY 2021

Xiafu tradition. Master Lou was no longer simply the "deity of the Guo family" or the "deity of the Liu-han Altar," but a deity for everyone.

3   Conclusion

According to the above analysis, different people held varying views about the Liu-han Altar and Master Lou. This article does not intend to emphasize the contradictions between the elite and popular religious practices. Rather, it uses the case of the Liu-han Altar to emphasize the connections and cross-fertilization between the two. Still, we must also acknowledge the tension between the two sides.

For the elites, such as the Guo family and Wang Biqing, what did literati hope to express through these religious practices? In his early research, Xu Dishan listed five of the most important contents transmitted through spirit-writing. One of them is the self-narration of the deities.[62] Upon first descending to the altar, spirits customarily announce their presence by identifying themselves through an introductory poem. Why do immortals relate their life experience to ordinary people? What does such a narrative mean? To answer these questions, it is worth analyzing the early history of the Liu-han Altar. The autobiography of Master Lou was multi-layered and grew in complexity. When the believers were still focused on literary creation, Master Lou was introduced as a traditional scholar-official. Later, when the participants experienced anxiety due to the ending of the Qing dynasty, Master Lou came to be worshiped as a moral model and spiritual leader who had been loyal to the dynasty he served. Past scholars have paid little attention to this phenomenon of spirit-writing and loyalism, but the Liu-han Altar is not an isolated case. In the history of spirit-writing during and after the Qing dynasty, a considerable proportion of the descending deities were loyal martyrs to the former dynasty; for example, during the Republican period, Jing Qing 景清 (?–1402), a scholar-official from the early Ming dynasty who was loyal to Emperor Zhu Yunwen 朱允炆 (1377–?, r. 1398–1402) and refused to serve the usurper Emperor Zhu Di 朱棣 (1360–1424, r. 1402–1424), descended to the altar of Chen Danran 陳澹然 (1859–1930) in Nanjing.[63] It should be noted that Chen Danran was a *juren* during the Qing dynasty who, during the Republic of China, joined the Kongjiao hui 孔教會 (Confucian Religion Association) and attempted to restore the monarchy.

---

62   Xu, *Fuji mixin di yanji*, 21–73.
63   *Weiyun xinyu*, vol. 2, 4a–7b.

Belonging to the overthrown dynasty, he communicated with loyalists to a former dynasty through spirit-writing at his altars to express his thoughts. Huang Daozhou 黃道周 (1585–1646) was the Minister of Rites of the Southern Ming dynasty, who fought against the Qing regime and became a martyr. After his death, he descended once to the altar of Peng Dingqiu. Peng was a well-known scholar-official during the early Qing dynasty. Although spirit-writing activities were prohibited by Qing law, he was never sanctioned on this account, possibly because the image of Huang Daozhou as a martyr and loyalist conformed to Confucian values, which made the content of Peng's altar appear to approximate the norms of "orthodox Confucianism" affiliated with the government.[64] The Guos did not need to consider the issue of legitimacy. In tandem with the tortuous destiny of these scholar-officials during the late Qing dynasty, the divine identity of Master Lou gradually grew more complex, and he eventually came to be worshipped as a model loyalist of the former Ming dynasty. At particular times and on specific occasions, by continuously holding spirit-writing sessions, the believers internalized the symbolic meaning of Master Lou and empathized with his fate. Such veiled intentions within the religious practices of literati deserve more attention, and the case of the Liu-han Altar may provide a fruitful avenue for further research.

When discussing traditional Chinese literati's religious life, scholars usually focus on the intersection between intellectuals and eminent monks or famous Daoists. As for the elite's participation in popular religious practices, the typical narrative is that they served as apologists for Confucian orthodoxy, governors, or local elites, who tried to suppress or reform "lascivious cults" (*yinsi* 淫祀). During this process, no matter whether these literati standardized or reformed the cults in accordance with orthodox practice, the public would give feedback on these actions, so that the local interpretations of deities and beliefs would also change.[65] Unlike these conventional narratives, cases of spirit-writing altars could be deemed a new category of literati's participation in local religious life. At the spirit-writing altars, instead of being attached to monks or Daoists for the ritual service, literati became ritual experts and arranged their religious life by themselves. For this purpose, they could not despise the local cult but drew inspiration from it.

Much research on spirit-writing is concerned with case studies of literati altars and elites' religious practices, and few studies focus on how literati, the

---

64   Burton-Rose, "Terrestrial Reward as Divine Recompense," 323. See also his contribution in this volume.
65   See Szonyi, "Making Claims about Standardization and Orthopraxy in Late Imperial China."

Confucian scholars, learned the technique of spirit-writing and established an altar as part of the local religious environment. Compared to other literati spirit-writing altars, which disappeared in the 1950s in mainland China, the uninterrupted history of the Liu-han Altar provides us with a unique opportunity to observe the development of a literati altar. It was impossible for Confucian scholar-officials to create a spirit-writing altar without a knowledge of the associated rituals and sufficient experience of running such a religious institution, and I believe that such knowledge could not be transmitted through books. We know that, at least since the Ming dynasty, there existed manuals on spirit-writing, published by various bookstores, which literati could obtain relatively easily. What these books offered was simply practical and technical guidance on spirit-writing. However, if spirit-writing as a technique could be learned by reading manuals, then the spirit-writing traditions of each region would be similar, which conflicts with our sources. Instead, as a local elite family from Fuzhou, the Guo family acquired knowledge and techniques from local popular religion to create a model for their religious practice. The local religious Xiafu tradition provided a sophisticated model, ranging from specific rites, the methods of divinization, and the creation of scriptures to normal daily religious activities, which the Guos selectively adopted. In this way, they created their own deity, Master Lou, through spirit-writing, while simultaneously adopting specific techniques and terminology from within the local religious milieu.

The relationship between the Liu-han Altar and local religious tradition was not uni-directional in nature, however. Within the local religious culture, Master Lou and the Guos' religious practice was also appropriated by locals to become part of the local popular religion, in the context of which spirit-writing deities who descended to this private altar of scholar-officials were interpreted quite differently. Rather than the moral model that the literati conceived, Master Lou was perceived as a fox spirit, like other local spirit-writing deities, who could solve the problems of daily life. The success of the Guo family in the secular world led the locals to believe that the deity that originated from the Guo family would be more effective than other deities of the same type, which attract more locals to venerate Master Lou and participate in the Liu-han Altar's rites. When Master Lou descended to the Guos' altar, therefore, the audience, including the believers from elite families and the other participants from the local community, may have had completely different understandings of his role and identity.

Speaking of the interaction between the Guos' altar and the local popular religion and popular imagination, Master Lou, as a Xiafu deity, was identified as a fox spirit. Although this interpretation increased the influence of Master Lou among the public, it also conflicted with the Guo family's original intention as it could be seen as implying that the flourishing of the Guo family was the result of worshipping an animal spirit rather than of good education and virtue. The Guo family, therefore, attempted to dissociate themselves from this local interpretation and even emphasized that the Liu-han Altar, as a literati altar, was unlike the popular spirit-writing altars that would congregate with harmful, heterodox spirits, such as foxes. This shows that the Guos, possibly due to their identity as scholar-officials, had reservations about certain aspects of the local popular religion, even as they adopted many aspects from it. They never directly denied or tried to reform the Xiafu or any other cults in Fuzhou, however. Indeed, they were reluctant to mention the Xiafu tradition at all. As local elites, Guo Zeyun and his other family members were keen to record various religious phenomena and legends in Fuzhou in their literary works, but little mention is made of the Xiafu. This may be due to the fact that there was still a stereotype that deemed Xiafu deities to be fox spirits. The more significant reason might be that the Guo family did not want their private beliefs to be associated with the religious traditions of the wider public.

Previous research has already studied the relationship between elite spirit-writing groups and the common people. Generally speaking, elite groups possess a high level of social capital, which allows them to mobilize people through organizing spirit-writing ceremonies; for instance, Paul R. Katz's research demonstrates the role of local elites (including intellectuals and merchants) during these processes. In the case of Taiwan, the Phoenix Hall (*luantang* 鸞堂) refers to a spirit-writing temple, managed by powerful families which constantly offered a platform for elites to impact local activities and the residents' communal life,[66] which is similar to the charitable halls (*shantang* 善堂) in late imperial China.[67] There has been a long tradition of spirit-writing groups playing important roles in their local communities. Moreover, at the time when the Liu-han Altar was forming, some spirit-writing groups turned into "redemptive societies," such as the Daoyuan 道院 (Society of the Way), or Wushan she 悟善社 (Society for Awakening to Goodness).[68] They were created by elites, but also attracted people across the social classes, exerting a significant influence

---

66 Katz, "Taiwan de Lü Dongbin xinyang," 40; Katz, "Spirit-writing Halls and the Development of Local Communities," 103. See also his contribution in this volume. For more information on the Daoyuan and Wushan she, see the articles by Xia Shi and Matthias Schumann in this volume.

67 On *shantang*, see the contribution by Li Guoping in this volume.

68 On this development, see David Ownby's overview, "Redemptive Societies in the Twentieth Century." On the Daoyuan and Wushan she, see also the contributions by Xia Shi and Matthias Schumann in this volume.

on both religions and charity during the Republican period.[69] A remarkable characteristic of this time was that various religious groups engaged actively in public life. Viewed from the macro-level, however, these groups, which were open to the public, do not represent the whole picture of modern Chinese spirit-writing. There were also a number of altars that were dominated by the elite and unwilling to participate in public life. Perhaps because of this, they are rarely included in the mainstream historical narrative. The Liu-han Altar, rather, belongs to the latter category. It originated within a scholar-official family and evolved into a literature club for intellectuals. Guo Zengxin and his son built their leadership of the literary circle by organizing spirit-writing activities, but did not wish to become religious leaders or manage a religious group with strong social capital. Since the altar's establishment, the records of its spirit-writing sessions were published annually, but the altar's leaders never tried to create new religious scriptures to disseminate their doctrines.[70] Although the Guo family was influential in Fuzhou, and the reputation of Master Lou spread within local popular religion, the Liu-han Altar failed to become a religious organization with extensive social influence.

As a comparison, the famous spirit-writing altar in Shanghai, the Shengde tan 盛德壇 (Altar of Flourishing Virtue) of the Lingxue hui 靈學會 (Spiritualist Society), a spiritualist spirit-writing group, was also established by elites during the early Republican period. In the popular understanding, the primary function of a spirit-writing altar is divination, allowing people to ask personal questions related to their daily life. Some core members of these altars, who were literati, however, were unwilling to provide such practical services in order to preserve their own intentions and sense of identity. To maintain the academic credentials of the Lingxuehui, in 1918, the Shengde Altar thus prohibited inquiries about personal welfare and medical issues by visitors.[71] The Liu-han altar likewise had reservations about the practical demands of the wider public, but chose a different approach to them. To fulfill the expectations of the public, the Liu-han Altar founded the Master Lou Palace as a public spirit-writing temple in 1933, to distinguish it from their literati altar. Yet, both the Liu-han Altar and Shengde Altar were reluctant to expand their organizations by attracting

---

69 Palmer, "Chinese Redemptive Societies and Salvationist Religion."
70 In the past hundred years, the Liu-han Altar has only produced one scripture, named *Wenchang dadong xianjing zhushi* 文昌大洞仙經注釋 (Annotation for *Wenchang's Transcendent Scripture of the Great Cavern*, 1936). This is an annotated version of the *Wenchang dadong xianjing*, an early Qing dynasty scripture, which was produced when Master Lou descended to the Liu-han Altar in Xiamen from 1929 to 1936, to answer believers' questions about the cult of Wenchang.
71 Schumann, "Science and Spirit-Writing," 159–63.

common people. The cult of loyalists in the case of the Liu-han Altar and the engagement with spiritualism in the case of the Shengde Altar had become focal points of self-identity and filters through which to select potential members.

The case study of the Liu-han Altar indicates the process of how a literati altar was established based on the local religious tradition and how the elite religious group distinguished themselves from the cult of spirit-writing in the public view. Through this comparative analysis, we can learn about the diversity among the literati and their attitudes toward spirit-writing.

Acknowledgements

I would like to express my deepest appreciation to Elena Valussi and Matthias Schumann, who were tolerant of my awkward English and proofread as well as commented on the manuscript. I am grateful to my supervisor Benjamin Penny and the anonymous reviewer for their careful reading and insightful suggestions. I would also like to express my special thanks to my friends in Fuzhou and Hong Kong, notably Zhang Jizhou, Zeng Junhan, Zheng Kui, Yu Lunlun, Qi Shao, Tsui Chee Yee, So Kim Wah, Lie Nga Sze, and Lau Yuet Fan, who have been highly supportive during my field trips in 2019 and 2020.

Bibliography

Primary Sources

Chen Danran 陳澹然. *Weiyun xinyu* 蔚雲新語. Nanjing: Jinggong ci 景公祠, 1923.

Gangtan luanzhang 港壇鸞章. Hong Kong, Liu-han Altar 1968.

"Guo Wumen xianqing zhuan lüe 郭無悶仙卿傳略." In *Liaoxian fentan luanzhang quanji* 了閒分壇鸞章全集, vol. 1, 41b. Xiamen: Gulangyu liaoxian bieshu 鼓浪嶼了閒別墅, 1931.

Guo Zengxin 郭曾炘. *Binglu riji* 邴廬日記. In *Lidai riji congchao* 歷代日記叢鈔, edited by Li Delong 李德龍 and Yu Bing 俞冰, vol. 183. Beijing: Xueyuan chubanshe, 2006.

Guo Zengxin 郭曾炘. *Paolu shicun* 匏廬詩存. Preface 1934. Reprinted in *Jindai Zhongguo shiliao congkan zhengbian* 近代中國史料叢刊·正編, edited by Shen Yunlong 沈雲龍, vol. 299. Taipei: Wenhai chubanshe, 1968.

Guo Zengxin 郭曾炘. "Lou dazhenren zhuan ba 婁大真人傳跋." In *Liaoxian zongtan luanzhang quanji* 了閒總壇鸞章全集 vol. 1, 5a–5b. N.p., 1933.

Guo Zeyun 郭則澐. *Dongling xiaozhi, xuzhi, buzhi* 洞靈小志·續志·補志. Beijing: Dongfang chubanshe, 2010.

Guo Zeyun 郭則澐. *Jiu de shu wen* 舊德述聞. Preface 1936. Reprinted in *Beijing tushuguan cang jiapu congkan, Min-Yue juan* 北京圖書館藏家譜叢刊·閩粵卷, edited by Zhang Zhiqing 張志清 and Xu shu 徐蜀, vol. 24, 641–642. Beijing: Beijing tushuguan chubanshe, 2000.

Guo Zeyun ziding nianpu 郭則澐自訂年譜. Nanjing: Fenghuang chubanshe, 2018.

Guo Zhaochang 郭兆昌, ed. *Fuzhou Guoshi zhipu* 福州郭氏支譜. N.p., 1920.

Jiangyin Xianzhi 江陰縣志. N.p., 1840.

"Liaoxian shiju 了閒詩句." *Changyan* 昌言, April 17, 1934.

Lin Gengbai 林庚白. *Jielou shicihua* 孑樓詩詞話. In *Minguo shihua congbian* 民國詩話叢編, edited by Zhang Yinpeng 張寅彭, vol. 6. Shanghai: Shanghai shudian chubanshe, 2002.

Lou Chengjiang xiansheng shij 婁澄江先生詩集. 3 vols. N.p., 1947.

"Lou dazhenren jiangtan ji 婁大真人降壇記." In *Liaoxian zongtan luanzhang quanji* 了閒總壇鸞章全集, vol. 1, 4a–4b. N.p., 1933.

Lüzu qingwei sanpin zhenjing 呂祖清微三品真經. Guilin: Tang wenguang tang 唐文光堂, 1877. Reprinted in *Zhonghua xu Daozang* 中華續道藏, edited by Kung Pengcheng 龔鵬程 and Chen Liao-an 陳廖安, vol. 18. Taipei: Xinwenfeng chuban gongsi, 1999.

Shi Yuanying 釋圓瑛. *Yuanying dashi wenhui* 圓瑛大師文匯. Beijing: Huaxia chubanshe, 2012.

Su Yiyun 蘇逸雲. *Woyunlou biji* 臥雲樓筆記. Xiamen: Xiamen daxue chubanshe, 2017.

Tang Junyi riji 唐君毅日記. 2 vols. Changchun: Jilin chuban jituan, 2014.

Wang Biqing 王弼卿. *Zhouyi yu xiandai shuxue* 周易與現代數學. Hong Kong: Rensheng chubanshe, 1960.

Wenchang dadongxianjing zhushi 文昌大洞仙經注釋. 1936. Reprinted in *Zangwai daoshu* 藏外道書, edited by Hu Daojing 胡道靜 et al., vol. 4, 345–413. Chengdu: Ba-Shu shushe, 1992–94.

Minguo Xiamen shizhi 民國廈門市志. 1948. Reprint, Beijing: Fangzhi chubanshe, 1999.

"Xinhai qi yue chuba ri Bai dazhenren xiaguang 辛亥七月初八白大真人下光." In *Liaoxian zongtan luanzhang quanji* 了閒總壇鸞章全集, vol. 1., 7a. N.p., 1933.

"Qing gu guanglu dafu houguan Guo wenan gong muzhiming 清故光祿大夫侯官郭文安公墓誌銘" In *Jindaishi suo cang li jingming dang'an* 近代史所藏李景銘檔案, edited by Ma Zhongwen 馬忠文, 35.217–224. Beijing: Guojia tushuguan chubanshe, 2021.

Zixia dujie zhimi jiubu zhenjing 紫霞度劫指迷九部真經. 1890. Reprinted in *Zhencang guji daoshu shizhong* 珍藏古籍道書十種, edited by Chen Liao-an 陳廖安. Taipei: Xinwenfeng chuban gongsi, 2001.

Secondary Sources

Baptandier, Brigitte. *The Lady of Linshui: A Chinese Female Cult*. Stanford, CA: Stanford University Press, 2008.

Burton-Rose, Daniel. "Terrestrial Reward as Divine Recompense: The Self-fashioned Piety of the Peng Lineage of Suzhou, 1650–1870." PhD diss., Princeton University, 2016.

Chen Yu-ming 陳郁明. "Lingbao shuiguan keyi zhi yanjiu: Yi Fuzhou Zhengyipai weili 靈寶水罐科儀之研究：以福州正一派為例," MA thesis, Fu Jen Catholic University, 2012.

Goossaert, Vincent. "Spirit Writing, Canonization, and the Rise of Divine Saviors: Wenchang, Lüzu, and Guandi, 1700–1858." *Late Imperial China*, no. 2 (2015): 82–125.

Goossaert, Vincent. "Divine Codes, Spirit-writing, and the Ritual Foundations of Early-Modern Chinese Morality Books." *Asia Major*, 3rd ser., 33, no. 1 (2020): 1–31.

Hansen, Valerie. *Changing Gods in Medieval China, 1127–1276*. Princeton, NJ: Princeton University Press, 2014.

Ho Koon Piu 何冠彪. *Sheng yu si: Mingji shidafu de jueze* 生與死: 明季士大夫的抉擇. Taipei: Lianjing chubanshe, 1997.

Hu Jiechen 胡劼辰. "*Wendi quanshu* yanjiu 《文帝全書》研究." PhD diss., Chinese University of Hong Kong, 2017.

Kang, Xiaofei. *The Cult of the Fox: Power, Gender, and Popular Religion in Late Imperial and Modern China*. New York: Columbia University Press, 2005.

Katz, Paul R. "Taiwan de Lü Dongbin xinyang: Yi Zhinan gong weili 台灣的呂洞賓信仰——以指南宮為例." *Xin shixue* 新史學, no. 4 (1995): 21–43.

Katz, Paul R. "Spirit-writing Halls and the Development of Local Communities: A Case Study of Puli (Nantou County)." *Minsu quyi* 民俗曲藝, no. 174 (Dec., 2011): 103–84.

Lai Chi-Tim 黎志添. "*Lüzu quanshu zhengzong*: Qingdai Beijing Jueyuan tan de lishi jiqi Lüzu tianxianpai xinyang 《呂祖全書正宗》：清代北京覺源壇的歷史及其呂祖天仙派信仰." *Zhongguo wenzhe yanjiu jikan* 中國文哲研究輯刊, no. 46 (Mar., 2015): 104–49.

Lin Li 林立. *Canghai yiyin: Minguo shiqi Qing yimin ci yanjiu* 滄海遺音：民國時期清遺民詞研究. Hong Kong: The Chinese University of Hong Kong Press, 2012.

Ownby, David. "Redemptive Societies in the Twentieth Century." In *Modern Chinese Religion*, Part II: *1850–2015*. Edited by Vincent Goossaert, Jan Kiely and John Lagerwey, vol. 2, 685–727. Leiden and Boston: Brill, 2016.

Palmer, David. "Chinese Redemptive Societies and Salvationist Religion: Historical Phenomenon or Sociological Category?" *Minsu quyi* 民俗曲藝. no. 172 (Jun., 2011): 21–72.

Reiter, Florian. *Basic Conditions of Taoist Thunder Magic*. Wiesbaden: Harrassowitz Verlag, 2007.

Schumann, Matthias. "Science and Spirit-Writing: The Shanghai Lingxuehui 靈學會 and the Changing Fate of Spiritualism in Republican China." In *Text and Context in the Modern History of Chinese Religions: Redemptive Societies and Their Sacred Texts*, edited by Philip Clart, David Ownby, and Wang Chien-chuan, 126–72. Leiden: Brill, 2020.

Szonyi, Michael. "Making Claims about Standardization and Orthopraxy in Late Imperial China: Rituals and Cults in the Fuzhou Region in Light of Watson's Theories." *Modern China*, 33, no. 1 (Jan., 2007): 47–71.

Wang, Chien-chuan. "Morality Book Publishing and Popular Religion in Modern China: A Discussion Centered on Morality Book Publishers in Shanghai," in *Religious Publishing and Print Culture in Modern China, 1800–2012*, edited by Philip Clart and Gregory Adam Scott, 233–64. Boston: de Gruyter, 2015.

Xu Dishan 許地山. *Fuji mixin di yanjiu* 扶箕迷信底研究. Changsha: Shangwu yinshuguan, 1941.

Xu Tiantai 徐天胎. "Fujian shendao mixin 福建神道迷信." In *Fujian wenshi ziliao xuanbian* 福建文史資料選編, vol. 2, 177–96. Fuzhou: Fujian renmin chubanshe, 2001.

Ye Chengqian 葉承謙. "Fuzhou mixin huodong yipie 福州迷信活動一瞥." In *Fujian wenshi ziliao xuanbian* 福建文史資料選編, vol. 2, 245–50. Fuzhou: Fujian renmin chubanshe, 2001.

Ye Mingsheng 葉明生. "Fuzhou Yuanshuai miao yueshen xinyang yu Doutang guanxi tankao 福州元帥廟樂神信仰與斗堂關係探考." *Wenhua yichan* 文化遺產, no. 2 (Mar., 2011): 45–59.

Zan Shengqian 昝聖騫. *Guo Zeyun cixue zhengli yu yanjiu* 郭則澐詞學整理與研究. Zhengzhou: Henan wenyi chubanshe, 2016.

PART 4

Spirit-Writing and Redemptive Societies

CHAPTER 10

"Protecting the Dao and Transmitting the Classics": The New Religion to Save the World and the Confucian Dimension of Spirit-Writing in Republican China

Matthias Schumann

1   Introduction

Toward the end of the Qing period, the Confucian classics lost their exalted political status due to the abolition of the civil service examinations in 1905 and the reorganization of the traditional academies (*shuyuan* 書院) into modern schools.[1] Yet, as the politicians and intellectuals were scrambling to find the cultural clay from which to build a Republican China, many turned their sight toward Confucianism and its textual canon. In late 1912, Chen Huanzhang 陳煥章 (1880–1933), under the spiritual leadership of Kang Youwei 康有爲 (1858–1927), founded the Kongjiao hui 孔教會 (Confucian Religion Association), which aimed to transform Confucianism into a religion comparable to Christianity, with its own scriptures, distinct doctrines, and liturgy.[2] Reformed in such a way, Confucianism was supposed to serve as the Chinese state religion and Chen, therefore, lobbied—unsuccessfully—for its incorporation into the new Republican constitution.[3] In addition, a wave of interest in the new discipline of "national learning" (*guoxue* 國學) gripped the country. From a political search for China's "national essence" (*guocui* 國粹), advocated by Zhang Binglin 章炳麟 (1869–1936) during the 1900s, "national learning" evolved into a heterogeneous enterprise that comprised the pursuit of "classical learning" (*jingxue* 經學) at special institutes, often situated within the newly-founded universities.[4] These institutes were complemented by other institutions that emerged at that time as locations for a renewed engagement with and inter-

---

1   Yuan, "The Status of Confucianism in Modern Chinese Education."
2   Goossaert and Palmer, *The Religious Question in Modern China*, 86–87; Chen, "Confucianism Encounters Religion," chap. 3.
3   See Chen, "Confucianism Encounters Religion," chap. 4.
4   The proponents of "national learning" held widely differing views of the Confucian classics, however. See Hon, "National Essence, National Learning, and Culture," and Sang, *Wan Qing Minguo de guoxue yanjiu*, for an overview of the field of "national learning."

pretation of the Confucian classics. Notable among these were the redemptive societies (*jiushi tuanti* 救世團體).

Prasenjit Duara coined the term "redemptive societies" in an influential article published in 2001, to describe the new religious organizations of the Republican period that embraced a global redemptive mission and moral self-transformation, combined with social service and relief work.[5] These societies generally held a socially conservative outlook and were closely aligned with prominent figures within the political establishment of the Beiyang 北洋 regimes.[6] Their members bemoaned the moral decline of society and perceived religion as a necessary counterweight to this. This also placed them in opposition to many of the leading figures of the New Culture Movement.[7] While some societies chose to adopt a decidedly universalistic stance, embracing all five religions[8] as part of their religious repertoire, others promoted Confucianism's moral values and emphasized its preeminent status.[9] The latter held a particular appeal for the "displaced scholarly elites," who had been educated under the former examination system but had lost their social status with the downfall of the dynasty.[10] Due to the prominent role of Confucianism among many of the redemptive societies, several scholars even consider them to be a form of "Confucian NRMs" (New Religious Movements).[11] Indeed, redemptive societies can be understood as one of the main forces driving the emergence of a "popular Confucianism," that sparked a renewed engagement with Confucian texts outside the traditional institutions.[12] Hence, many of them

---

5   Duara, "The Discourse of Civilization and Pan-Asianism." See also the introduction to this volume.
6   Called thus because many military leaders had previously served in the Beiyang Army of Yuan Shikai 袁世凱 (1859–1916).
7   Schumann, "Redemptive Societies." For an introduction to redemptive societies, see also the excellent overview by David Ownby, "Redemptive Societies in the Twentieth Century."
8   i.e., Confucianism, Buddhism, Daoism, Christianity, and Islam, usually in that sequence.
9   The Daode xueshe 道德學社 (Morality Society) is a prominent example. See Fan, "Confucian 'Religion' in the Early Republican Period," 144–50.
10 DuBois, "The Salvation of Religion?" 121; Palmer, Katz and Wang, "Introduction," 7.
11 See Palmer, Katz and Wang, "Introduction."
12 The term "popular Confucianism" (*minjian Rujiao* 民間儒教) is employed by a number of scholars, albeit with differing definitions, to confront the resurgence and revival of Confucian learning since the early twentieth century. Most relevant to the discussion here, Philip Clart used the term to describe the creative engagement with Confucian rituals and texts as well as the practice of Confucian moral virtues among spirit-writing groups in Taiwan that define themselves as Confucians. See Clart, "Confucius and the Mediums." For a useful conceptualization and application of the term, see also Yong Chen, "Conceptualizing 'Popular Confucianism'."

were intimately related to the wave of "national learning" mentioned above, promoting the study of the Confucian canon and its associated moral teachings.¹³ Some of these societies, however, were not content with gleaning the meaning of the classics from dusty pages and, rather, looked to spirit-writing as a means of securing the exegetical support of the Confucian sages themselves.

Spirit-writing was a prominent practice among the redemptive societies and some, such as the Daoyuan 道院 (Institution of the Dao) or the Zhongguo jisheng hui 中國濟生會 (China Life Saving Society), even emerged from local spirit-writing altars. The Confucian-leaning societies were not unanimous in their attitude toward the practice. Duan Zhengyuan 段正元 (1864–1940), the founder of the Daode xueshe 道德學社 (Morality Society), rejected it on the grounds that it was susceptible to fakery and preferred unmediated spiritual communion with the sages.¹⁴ Other societies, however, began to promote the practice, in an attempt to recover and promote the presumed essence of Confucianism. Spirit-writing thereby became a method for conversing with the Confucian sages and restoring the "correct transmission of the Dao" (*daotong* 道統). Using spirit-writing to reestablish Confucian orthodoxy produced fresh insights into the Confucian classics and bestowed legitimacy on the respective society. Such attempts were not without precedent, as Daniel Burton-Rose's contribution to this volume shows, but the frequent descent of Confucius himself to various spirit-writing altars, a novel phenomenon at the time, indicates that redemptive societies, freed from the fetters of imperial authority, took these activities to new heights.

This article examines the Confucian dimension of spirit-writing by exploring the case of the Jiushi xinjiao 救世新教 (New Religion to Save the World). The New Religion was founded in 1924 as a sub-organization of the Wushan she 悟善社 (Society for Awakening to Goodness), a redemptive society that was established in Beijing in 1920. Formed around a "spirit-writing altar" (*fuji tan* 扶乩

---

13   Wang Chien-chuan has shown that the Tongshan she 同善社 (Fellowship United in Goodness), a redemptive society that originated in Sichuan, established a wave of institutes for national learning (Guoxue zhuanxiu guan 國學專修館) in 1918–19 and even had close links with the Wuxi guoxue zhuanxiu guan 無錫國學專修館, a highly regarded institution of National Learning that was founded in 1920. Wang, "Tongshan she zaoqi de tedian," 153–56.

14   Fan, "Minchu Ruxue de zongjiaohua," 174–78. Moreover, as de Korne tells us, the Tongshan she, at least publicly, rejected the use of spirit-writing. See de Korne, *The Fellowship of Goodness*, 71. There is evidence, however, to indicate that at least individual members and branches of the Daode xueshe engaged in spirit-writing, possibly after Duan died. See Fan, "Minchu Ruxue de zongjiaohua," 177n31.

壇) dedicated to the deity Lü Dongbin 呂洞賓, the members of the Wushan she initially primarily engaged in charity and self-cultivation. Four years later, however, they founded the New Religion to Save the World, in an attempt to elevate public morality through the unification of the world religions.[15] Subsequently, the New Religion grew in importance and prominence, and eventually served as the public figurehead of the Wushan she.

From the mid-1920s, the New Religion's center of activity shifted to Tianjin 天津, where an illustrious circle of members, many connected with the changing Beiyang regimes, began to transmit commentaries on the Confucian classics through spirit-writing that were attributed to Confucius, Mengzi 孟子 (372?–289? BCE), and other Confucian sages. Through the composition of these new commentaries, the society positioned itself within a prominent field of exegetical literature, but their use of spirit-writing allowed them to access the sages directly and thereby imbue the classics with a new meaning. These activities were accompanied by a growing emphasis on Confucianism within the organization, as the primary religious tradition and "national essence" (*guocui*) of China. The members attempted to revive Confucian classical learning in order to restore morality and provide a cultural and religious foundation for the Chinese nation. The case of the New Religion thereby indicates the changing status of Confucianism during the Republican period and the attempts by differing actors to embrace this development.

In what follows, I will explicate the New Religion's view on Confucianism and the Confucian tradition, as well as its attempt to utilize Confucian writings for the reform of society and the state. To do so, I will employ a variety of sources, including the society's journals, archival materials as well as the commentarial literature that the society published. I will particularly focus on their commentaries on the *Daxue* 大學 (Great learning) and the *Zhongyong* 中庸 (Doctrine of the mean), two works that the New Religion regarded as closely intertwined and as containing the essence of Confucianism. The discussion will mainly be limited to the 1920s, the period during which the New Reli-

---

15 To date, the Wushan she and the New Religion have been rarely studied in detail. Besides shorter accounts scattered across the numerous books on "secret societies" (*mimi shehui* 秘密社會) and "popular religious sects" (*huidaomen* 會道門), we have Yoshitoyo Yoshioka's 吉岡義豐 early but unsystematic study in his *Zhongguo minjian zongjiao gaishuo*, 189–226. More recently, Mi Sumin wrote her Master's thesis on the Wushan she and later also published an article, which specifically targets the New Religion to Save the World. See Mi, "Minguo Wushan she yanjiu," and "Cong dang'an ziliao kan Minguo shiqi de Jiushi xinjiao." Moreover, in the last few years, additional research has been published. See Shi, "Minguo shiqi jiujie sixiang" and Li, "Minchu Wushan she."

gion was most active. From 1928, the Guomindang 國民黨 (Nationalist Party of China) initiated an attack on spirit-writing, which forced organizations such as the New Religion to lower their profile and prevented them from voicing their views as freely as previously.

2   From a Lü Dongbin Altar to a Confucianized World Religion

The New Religion to Save the World was founded as a sub-organization of the Wushan she. The latter had emerged from a small spirit-writing altar in Henan 河南 that was called the Altar for Spreading Goodness (*Guangshan tan* 廣善壇).[16] Here, a number of devotees assembled to receive the spirit-written instructions of the Imperial Lord Fuyou (Fuyou Dijun 孚佑帝君),[17] who is none other than the famous deity Lü Dongbin, who featured prominently in the eschatological spirit-writing movement that emerged after 1840.[18] A few years after the altar had been founded, the Imperial Lord ordered his devotees through spirit-writing to move to Beijing to establish a new altar and attract more supporters. This decision certainly reflected the status of Beijing as the political center of the time and set the stage for the establishment of a formal organization.[19] Those devotees who assembled regularly for the practice of spirit-writing came to be marked as disciples of Lü Dongbin (usually referred to as Imperial Teacher, Dishi 帝師) through receiving an initiation name (*daohao* 道號)[20] and, on July 3, 1920, after they were able to relocate to new premises, the Wushan she was officially founded as a "philanthropic society" (*shanshe* 善社).[21]

---

16   Beijing Jiushi xinjiao zonghui, *Jiushi xinjiao*, 2.
17   Wushan she, *"Lingxue yaozhi* yuanqi," 1.
18   See the contribution by Shiga Ichiko in this volume.
19   The changing governments in Beijing enjoyed international recognition and dominated the political agenda but, due to the political divisions of the time, were largely unable to project their policies beyond the capital area. For an overview of the political situation at the time, see Kuhn, *Die Republik China von 1912 bis 1937*. However, our view of the political and military actors of this period remains hampered by their sweeping inclusion in the category of "warlords" (*junfa* 軍閥). For an insightful historical treatment of the latter term, see Waldron, "Warlord."
20   The tradition of initiation names dates back to the Buddhist custom of accepting a religious name after officially joining the monastic order. It has been connected with spirit-writing at least since the twelfth century. See Goossaert, "Modern Daoist Eschatology," 225. Similar customs existed within other spirit-writing organizations, such as the Daoyuan.
21   "Wushan she chengli ji," 1–2.

The Wushan she initially focused on the practice of self-cultivation and philanthropy in an attempt to alleviate disasters and revert the alleged moral decay of the time.[22] A shared commitment to philanthropy was also the prime reason why prominent members of the Beiyang establishment initially joined the society. The most important leader, up until his death in 1943, was Jiang Chaozong 江朝宗 (1861–1943), a former military commander who was involved in various philanthropic and religious activities during the 1920s and 30s and collaborated with the Japanese after 1937.[23] In addition, the society boasted former Minister of Internal Affairs and twice Prime Minister Qian Nengxun 錢能訓 (1869–1924), Duan Qirui 段祺瑞 (1865–1936), leader of the so-called Anhui faction (Wan-xi 皖系), and the high officials Zhong Shiming 鍾世銘 (1879–1965) and Lu Zongyu 陸宗輿 (1876–1941) as members. In 1932, after the founding of the New Religion, even Wu Peifu 吳佩孚 (1874–1939) joined the organization after returning from exile in Sichuan 四川.[24]

These prominent members provided financial support and contributed to the legitimacy of the emerging organization while finding in the society a platform for their various social activities and interests. Both Jiang Chaozong and Qian Nengxun joined the society in 1920, when the North China Famine unfolded in the area around Beijing and united well-known philanthropists who were seeking an institutional outlet through which to distribute relief aid.[25] Lu Zongyu had already joined the emerging society in 1919 to initiate philanthropic projects and promote classical learning. These influential figures all received initiation names. Profiting from the financial and organizational resources of their new leaders, the Wushan she was able to conduct philanthropic activities on an increasing scale. Initially, these mainly focused on "emergency relief" (*jizhen* 急賑) during the North China Famine but were later institutionalized.[26] After the society was registered with the government

---

22   Ibid., 7.
23   He was a well-known Daoist authority in Beijing, supporting the White Cloud Monastery and involved in the publication of the Daoist canon in the mid-1920s by Commercial Press. Goossaert, *The Taoists of Peking*, 350–51. On his philanthropic activities, see Fuller, "Struggling with Famine in Warlord China."
24   Wu was urged to participate by Jiang, who had formerly served under him. Li, "Wu Peifu yu chuantong wenhua," 250.
25   As Mi Sumin has shown, it was the member Wang Zhonggao 汪仲高 (no dates), who had mentioned the Wushan she and its spirit-writing activities during a conversation with Jiang. See Mi, "Minguo Wushan she yanjiu," 11. See also "Yao Jichuan Zhenren zeng Jiang Huiji xu," 10. Here, it is mentioned that Jiang was introduced to the Society by Wang. For the first appearance of Qian in the sources of the Wushan she, see "Jishi" (1921), 38–45.
26   Beijing Jiushi xinjiao zonghui, *Jiushi xinjiao*, 2–3.

in 1920,[27] the Wushan she established a "general society" (*zongshe* 總社) in Beijing and branch societies in various Chinese cities and provinces.[28]

In 1924, however, when the Wushan she had been in existence for four years, it underwent a substantial reorganization. Within the confines of the society, the members established a religious sub-organization, the New Religion to Save the World. Disappointed at their inability to put an end to the frequent disasters of that period, contemporary sources explain,[29] the society turned to religion as a force able to strengthen morality and unite the people. The shift toward religion was spurred by spirit-written messages and the transmission of a new scripture.[30] The specific reasons for this religious turn are difficult to ascertain, but early sources of the Wushan she bemoan a lack of members and financial support. The members may have felt that establishing a religious organization would broaden their appeal and allow them to spread to a national scale. It seems likely, moreover, that this religious turn was, at least partially, inspired by the example of the Daoyuan, a redemptive society that aimed to unify the gist of the five world religions and with which the Wushan she had established close links.[31] The New Religion features certain institutional similarities with

---

27   Beijing Municipal Archives, J002–002–00055, 55. Please note that this document contains no printed page numbers, so reference here is to the numbers added to the file by hand.
28   In different sources, a total of 23 branch societies are mentioned, including Jingzhao 京兆, Tianjin 天津, Ha'erbin 哈爾濱, Ji'nan 濟南, Longkou 龍口, Nanjing 南京, Changzhou 常洲, Shanghai 上海, Wuhu 蕪湖, Nanchang 南昌, Pingjiang 平江, Fuzhou 福州, Putian 莆田, Ningnan 寧南, Baoshan 保山, Ningjin 寧晉, Lanzhou 蘭州, Kunming 昆明 and Qiaojia 巧家. See Beijing Jiushi xinjiao zonghui, *Jiushi xinjiao*, 3–4, and "*Lingxue yaozhi fenxiaochu*." Branches of the New Religion were usually established within these existing branch societies of the Wushan she.
29   Beijing Jiushi xinjiao zonghui, *Jiushi xinjiao*, 2–3.
30   The scripture is entitled *Xiantian hunyuan xuanxuan milu jiushi zhenjing* 先天渾元玄玄秘籙救世真經 (The secret registers of the true scriptures to save the world from the pre-celestial chaotic origin and darkest mystery) and contains cosmological theories and diagrams centering on familiar Daoist themes intended to save the whole of humankind. See "Xiantian hunyuan xuanxuan milu jiushi zhenjing." Unlike what many sources of the New Religion imply, this "religious turn" was already foreshadowed in 1921, when the spirit-written messages demanded that more attention be paid to religion as a force able to unite the people. Therefore, the deities descending at the spirit-writing altar made their view known about the need to establish a new, "true religion" (*zhenzheng zongjiao* 真正宗教) which was supposed to serve as the "state religion" (*guojiao* 國教). "Jishi" (1922), 3, 8.
31   Spirit-written messages instructed the members to link up with the Daoyuan. See "Zhisheng Xiantian Laozu yu Wushan zongshe ji Ji'nan Jining Tianjin Jingzhao ge yuan wen," 2. Thereafter, both organizations remained closely linked, and prominent members of the Wushan she, such as Qian Nengxun and Jiang Chaozong, assumed high leadership roles within the Daoyuan. See Mi, "Minguo Wushan she yanjiu," 29–30. While the Imperial Lord Fuyou continued to descend to the altar frequently, he was eclipsed by the Highest Sage

the Daoyuan and many of its leaders occupied positions in both organizations. This cooperation was potentially beneficial for both sides. The Wushan she could profit from the institutional model and vitality of the Daoyuan, which was rapidly expanding at the time and, unlike the Wushan she, was able to establish a nationwide organization. The Wushan she, on the other hand, was well-connected to the Beiyang governments and thus able to confer political legitimacy on the Daoyuan.

Once the New Religion had been founded, the philanthropic activities continued unabated, but gave way to a stronger emphasis on a universalist religious worldview that had previously been more of an undercurrent in the Wushan she. According to the sources of the New Religion, the five world religions of Confucianism, Buddhism, Daoism, Christianity, and Islam were considered as identical in terms of their moral teachings. They were all "teachings based on the divine way" (*shendao shejiao* 神道設教) and taught the moral precepts of their founders.[32] If everyone followed these precepts and practiced self-cultivation, they argued, peace in the world was attainable, while the individual could hope for an elevated existence after death. The New Religion aimed to coalesce the essential doctrines and "original meaning" (*yuanyou zhi yi* 原有之義) of these five religions. Their religion was, therefore, considered new not in a theological sense, so the members claimed, but only insofar as it provided a universalistic religious creed to counter warfare and usher in "great unity" (*datong* 大同).[33] After the fashion of the time, divine and human members jointly produced an "outline" (*jiaogang* 教綱) for the New Religion, and stipulated its "precepts" (*jiaofa* 教法) and "doctrines" (*jiaoyi* 教義), which were published as three separate books, thereby giving it a clear identity and institutional shape.[34]

---

and Pre-celestial Venerable Patriarch (Zhisheng Xiantian Laozu 至聖先天老祖), the highest deity of the Daoyuan, who also became the supreme deity within the Wushan she. He eventually even decreed the name of the New Religion. Cf. "Nanping Ji Fo cishan zi jie." For more information on the Daoyuan, see the article by Xia Shi in this volume.

32 The "divine way" served as a powerful conceptual tool to negotiate the novel concept of religion (*zongjiao* 宗教) and differences between the various religious traditions during the late nineteenth and early twentieth century. In official discourse of the late imperial period, the "divine way" was sometimes associated with Buddhism and Daoism (and Christianity) and negatively contrasted with Confucianism. See Tay, "Secularization as Sacralization," 51. The New Religion, however, similar to many other redemptive societies of the time, considered all world religions as "divine ways" (see also below).

33 Beijing Jiushi xinjiao zonghui, *Jiushi xinjiao*.

34 These three books were newly-composed but thought to encompass the main elements of the five religions.

In what may appear to be a slightly ironic twist, however, the founding of this universalistic New Religion was accompanied by a growing emphasis on the pre-eminence of Confucianism. While promoting the basic identity of all five religions, many sources began to portray Confucianism as the ideal creed and archetypal religion.[35] With reference to late imperial China, Joachim Gentz has pointed out that advocates of "the unity of the three teachings" (*sanjiao heyi* 三教合一) did not tend to assume true equality among the teachings. Instead, they considered one teaching as preeminent and regarded the scriptures of the others as mere commentaries, attesting to the validity of their beliefs.[36] One might argue that Confucianism inhabited a similar place within the New Religion. The members argued that Confucius had united the doctrines of all of the former sages, wherefore the meaning of all religions was already contained in the Confucian classics.[37] This was the reason "why the New Religion primarily revers Confucianism" (新教所以崇儒主) and why they "consider Confucianism the warp and the other four teachings [merely] as the weft" (以儒教為經諸教為緯).[38] One should note here that such an unequal relation between the different religions was not reflected in the sources published by the Wushan she during the early 1920s, but there was a general trend within the New Religion, which grew more pronounced in later years, to highlight the preeminence of Confucianism while never shedding the cloak of religious universalism.[39]

---

35   Beyond the reasons specified below, the prominence of Confucianism and the Confucian sages was also legitimized in reference to practical concerns. Thus, in the "guide to the reader" (*fanli* 凡例) of a joint edition of the "outline" and the "precepts" of the New Religion, it is explained that, while the content of the publication was jointly decided, it was revealed by Confucius rather than by the founders of all religions. This was testimony to the many philosophical masters of the Confucian tradition and the easy understandability of the Confucian writings, the text explained. For similar reasons, the deities decided that the teachings should be transmitted in Chinese. The "foreign" religious founders, who usually transmitted their messages in their own tongue (although Jesus used English), were therefore also barred from transmitting content. Cf. Jiushi xinjiao zonghui, *Jiushi xinjiao jiaogang jiaofa huibian*, 442. This may have reflected a lack of foreign language capability among the members, and one may assume that such practical concerns alone may have contributed to a greater reliance on Confucian voices and texts. The question of why Laozi, as a properly "Chinese" religious founder, was found unfit to undertake the editing remains unclear.
36   Gentz, "Religious Diversity in Three Teachings Discourses," 129.
37   Chen, "Gezhong zongjiao jiaoyi jie bu chu Rujiao fanwei," 2.
38   Beijing Jiushi xinjiao zonghui, *Jiushi xinjiao*, 2, 5.
39   Vividly reflected by the fact that Lü Dongbin was revered as the principal deity (*zongzhu* 宗主) within the Wushan she and the New Religion, and remained the deity who descended most frequently to their altars.

This development was most prominently reflected within the Tianjin branch society of the New Religion, which was founded during the seventh lunar month of 1926.[40] At the Altar of the Sages (Sheng tan 聖壇) in Tianjin, prominent members, such as Lu Zongyu, Jiang Chaozong, and Zhong Shiming, gathered to receive commentaries on the classics via spirit-writing.[41] Lu, who adopted the initiation name Huiyi 慧依, played a key role in this endeavor. He had graduated from Waseda University, before being awarded a new-style imperial degree in 1905. Publishing widely-read articles on constitutional government, he soon found his way into the Ministry of the Interior, where he worked to gather knowledge on the local conditions in the Chinese provinces in order to initiate political reform.[42] He remained a high official during the Beiyang period, but was widely vilified by May Fourth protesters for negotiating the 21 demands when he was dispatched to Japan as minister plenipotentiary.[43] Lu joined the Wushan she in 1919, the same year that he was forced to resign from office, after May Fourth movement protestors demanded his dismissal.[44] In the Wushan she and New Religion, he found a suitable outlet for pursuing his scholarly interests and put to use his considerable financial means. Lu was interested in classical learning (*jingxue*) and viewed spirit-writing as a way to converse with the deities on scholarly topics.

His interest in spirit-writing soon took a more practical turn and he began to learn it himself, eventually, from 1923, receiving messages by Confucius, who lectured on the meaning of the classics.[45] At this point, the divine Confucius urged Lu "temporarily to leave all human affairs behind and take up the task of protecting the Dao and transmitting the classics" (暫舍人事。以成衛道傳經之業).[46] While, initially, this seems to have involved relatively general explanations of the classics, Lu and his associates soon began to transmit more sophisticated commentaries that they received at the Tianjin altar. Lu personally wielded the *ji* (referred to as *shibi* 侍筆, lit. "serving the brush"), together with

---

40   Zhong Shiming, "Xu 序," in *Daxue zhengshi*, 51.
41   Confucius first descended in Tianjin in 1923, still at the local branch society of the Wushan she. This was probably also the time when the Altar of the Sages was founded. In 1926, Zhong Shiming decided to reopen the altar, apparently following a hiatus, for the purpose of continuing earlier lectures by Confucius. Cf. Zhong, "Xu," in *Daxue zhengshi*, 50–51.
42   See Thompson, *China's Local Councils*, 72–73.
43   Su, "'Shandong wenti' zhong de tielu wenti yu Wusi yundong."
44   Chen, "The May Fourth Movement," 158.
45   Lu Zongyu, "Yuanqi 緣起," in *Daxue zhengshi*, 3.
46   Lu, "Yuanqi," in *Daxue zhengshi*, 4.

another practitioner by the name of Dai Yifen 戴翊棻 (no dates).⁴⁷ The instructions were then noted down and "edited" (*jiaokan* 校勘) by, among others, Jiang Chaozong and Zhong Shiming.⁴⁸ This eventually resulted in the production of numerous volumes. I will focus here on the *Daxue zhengshi* 大學證釋 (*The Great Learning*, verified and explicated), published in 1926, and the *Zhongyong zhengshi* 中庸證釋 (*The Doctrine of the Mean*, verified and explicated), published in 1929, as both were regarded as closely intertwined.⁴⁹ These were interlinear commentaries, an established genre of exegesis that had emerged during the Han period at the latest. For the *Daxue* and *Zhongyong*, the main commentary was provided by divine Confucius while Lü Dongbin composed a sub-commentary. Other sages chimed in if necessary, while also composing longer paratexts. The composition of commentaries was not unique to the New Religion, as other spirit-writing organizations published similar works.⁵⁰ The above commentaries were remarkable, however, in terms of their sophistica-

---

47   I have not yet been able to trace the identity of this practitioner, but the fact that both Dai and Lu are listed as *shibi* seems to indicate that both wielded the stylus together, probably using a t-shaped instrument. Three other members were "attending to the records" (*shilu* 侍錄), thus putting the transmitted messages into writing. All of this betrays the typical set-up of a spirit-writing session.
48   See the *Zhongyong zhengshi* for a list of those involved in the production of these texts.
49   The New Religion published a similar commentary to the *Classic of Filial Piety* (*Xiaojing qianshi* 孝經淺釋, A short commentary on the *Classic of Filial Piety*), which is not currently at my disposal. It is mentioned at a source from 1927, so was transmitted before that point. The New Religion also published a tract on the *Yijing* 易經 (Book of changes) that was attributed to Lü Dongbin, entitled *Fuyou dijun Yi shuo muban* 孚佑帝君易說木板 (Wood print of Fuyou dijun's commentary on the *Changes*). This work was also produced prior to 1927. See "Beijing Jiushi xinjiao zonghui fashou gezhong shuji jiamubiao." At a later date, they further composed the *Yijing zhengshi* 易經證釋 (*The Classic of Changes*, verified and explicated), a 12-volume commentary on the *Book of Changes*. While the exact date of the latter's transmission remains unclear, it must have been published before 1938, as it is mentioned in a source dating from that year. See Beijing Jiushi xinjiao zonghui, *Jiushi xinjiao*, 4. For a partial study of the work, see Lin, "Jiushi xinjiao *Yijing zhengshi*." Lastly, in 1932, they published the *Jiushi xinjiao jiaojing* 救世新教教經 (Religious scriptures of the New Religion to Save the World), which was a distillation of the main ideas of all of the religious traditions on questions such as self-cultivation and morality, based on the reading of their sacred scriptures. This text, as well as parts of the commentary, were transmitted via spirit-writing and ascribed to the founders of the five religions and other important deities. It was published by the Study Society of the New Religion to Save the World (Jiushi xinjiao xuehui 救世新教學會), based in Tianjin. Jiushi xinjiao xuehui, *Jiushi xinjiao jiaojing*.
50   Philip Clart, for example, mentions a commentary on the *Zhongyong* that was recorded in Sichuan between 1907 and 1921 and first published by the Yunnan branch of the Tongshan she. Clart, "Confucius and the Mediums," 14.

tion and length (the commentary to the *Zhongyong* comprises four volumes). Through producing these works, the New Religion situated itself within the Confucian commentarial tradition and staked a claim to the transmission of the Dao.

3   The Confucian Classics and the Transmission of the Dao

Spirit-writing organizations in Republican China usually situated their teachings within the context of the moral decline and growing chaos they perceived in society. Some of them, such as the Yiguandao 一貫道 (Way of Pervading Unity), advanced a messianic cosmology that linked human depravity and recurring disasters to an approaching end of times. Unaware of their true nature, and increasingly attached to worldly desires and the phenomenal realm, humans could only place their hopes in the Eternal Venerable Mother (Wusheng Laomu 無生老母), the highest deity of the Yiguandao, who was the only deity capable of rescuing the believing elect from the end of the kalpa.[51] Such cosmological theories were closely linked to the mythology found in the "precious scrolls" (*baojuan* 寶卷) literature of the late imperial period and carried connotations of "heterodoxy" over into the Republican period.[52]

Similar in intention but more closely tied to Confucian discourses were theories about a loss of the correct knowledge of the Dao of the sages contained in the ancient classics. The idea that the true meaning of the classics had been lost, sparking a decline in morality and social order, was first voiced by Han Yu 韓愈 (768–824), who invoked this notion to propose a new interpretation of Confucian writings. He was also the first to claim that the "correct transmission of the Dao" (*daotong*), which had been initiated by Confucius, who had synthesized the way of the sages and transmitted it to his disciples, had been interrupted after Mengzi.[53]

---

51 Clart, "Yīguàn Dào," 439–40. For a succinct summary of Yiguandao's cosmology and history, see Billioud, *Reclaiming the Wilderness*, 5–21. See also Nikolas Broy's contribution to this volume.
52 For an introduction to this genre, see Overmyer, *Precious Volumes*. For a more recent book that includes fascinating ethnographic data, see Berezkin, *The Many Faces of Mulian*.
53 The claim that the true meaning of the Dao had been lost gained currency far earlier, but was linked to the concept of *daotong*, with its connotations of lineage and genealogy, only by Han Yu, probably inspired by the Buddhist notion of the "transmission of the Dharma." Cf. Hartman, *Han Yü and the T'ang Search for Unity*, esp. 159–66.

During the Song period, Zhu Xi 朱熹 (1130–1200) and his followers continued the discourse on the transmission of the Dao and constructed a specific lineage through which it had been transmitted.[54] Unsurprisingly, they claimed that the legitimate successors of Mengzi were the proponents of "Dao Learning" (Daoxue 道學, or Neo-Confucianism), i.e., the masters of their own school; namely, Zhou Dunyi 周敦頤 (1017–1073), Cheng Hao 程顥 (1032–1085), and Cheng Yi 程頤 (1033–1107).[55] Zhu Xi substantiated his claim through undertaking extensive exegetical work, which received political legitimation when his interpretation of the Confucian classics was posthumously accepted—albeit hesitatingly—by the Yuan Dynasty as the basis for the civil service examinations in 1313. The promotion of Dao Learning not only resulted in the enshrinement of the masters of this school (who eventually included Zhu Xi) in the Confucius temples but also had immediate consequences for the canonization of the Confucian textual heritage, which now focused on the Four Books (sishu 四書). Zhu Xi was the first to group the Daxue, Lunyu 論語 (Analects), Mengzi, and Zhongyong together and provided them with commentaries that located the essence of Confucianism within these texts.[56]

Claims about the lineage through which the Dao had been transmitted—or not—were the means for both the construction of orthodoxy and the legitimation of specific readings of the classics. As such, they were voiced repeatedly over the centuries following the emergence of Dao Learning.[57] To promote his interpretation of the mind (xin 心) and human nature, Wang Yangming 王陽明 (Wang Shouren 王守仁, 1472–1529) thus included Lu Xiangshan 陸象山 (Liu Jiuyuan 陸九淵, 1139–1193), a critic of Zhu Xi and evidently an inspiration to Wang, among the sages who had received the Dao from Mengzi.[58] During the late Qing period, Kang Youwei radically reinterpreted and reclassified the Confucian textual canon, criticizing the emphasis on the Four Books at the expense of the Six Classics, in order to promote political reform. Unlike his more modest predecessors, Kang Youwei unabashedly held that he was the one who had been elected to restore the true meaning of the Confucian teaching.[59] Similar claims over the importance of specific texts and the identity of the

---

54 On the Confucian lineages and their ideological functions, see Wilson, *Genealogy of the Way*.
55 Chan, "Chu Hsi's Completion of Neo-Confucianism."
56 Wilson, *Genealogy of the Way*.
57 The specific date to which the dissociation from the Dao was ascribed by various thinkers varied from the beginning of the Eastern Zhou (722 BCE) to the early Han periods. Wagner, "The *Zhouli* as the Late Qing Path to the Future," 362.
58 Wilson, *Genealogy of the Way*, 94–97.
59 Wagner, "The Philologist as Messiah."

correct proponents of the Dao continued to be voiced by "New Confucians" throughout the twentieth century.[60]

The New Religion situated its exegetical activities and textual production within this genealogical discourse. In his preface to the *Daxue zhengshi*, Lu Zongyu explained that the transmission had been interrupted after Mengzi and Xunzi 荀子 (third century BCE) due to mistakes in the bamboo manuscripts and the book-burning that occurred under the Qin dynasty. Not even the Confucians during the Song Dynasty, he pointed out, had been able to restore the true meaning of the Dao.[61] In his spirit-written postface to the *Daxue zhengshi*, the divine Zhu Xi shared this verdict, acknowledging his "restricted view" (*guankui* 管窺) and inconsolable shame.[62] The New Religion, however, did not form part of the anti-Dao Learning sentiment that arose alongside Han Learning (Hanxue 漢學) in the eighteenth century and continued into the Republican era. Rather, they lauded Song Confucians for their sincere efforts, even if these fell short.[63] Indeed, in the *Zhongyong zhengshi*, Cheng Yi was specifically praised for being "the purest scholar" (*zui chun zhi xueshi* 最醇之學士) among later Confucians and lauded for his achievements in the field of "practical learning" (*shixue* 實學).[64] Moreover, even while they denied the proponents of Dao Learning the status as the successors of the Confucian sages, they nevertheless adopted many of their genealogical and canonical assumptions.

The line in which the New Religion thought the Dao of the sages had been transmitted in antiquity was identical to that propagated by Zhu Xi and other Confucians. According to the spirit-written commentary to the *Zhongyong*, there was a golden age in antiquity, in which the Dao had been attained and virtue put into practice.[65] The Dao was first grasped by Yao 堯 and Shun 舜 and then transmitted to Yu the Great 大禹, Tang 湯, Kings Wen 文 and Wu 武, and

---

60 Makeham, "The New *Daotong*."
61 Lu, "Yuanqi," in *Daxue zhengshi*, 1–2.
62 Zhu Xi, "Ba yi 跋一," in *Daxue zhengshi*, 363. In his postface to the *Daxue zhengshi*, Zhu Xi, however, also pointed to some of his own merits, mentioning, for example, that he was the first to recognize the inaccuracy in the order of specific sentences and chapters in the received text. Ibid., 363.
63 Duan Qirui, "Xu 序," in *Daxue zhengshi*, 38.
64 See the sub-commentary by the deity Hongjiao zhenren 宏教真人 ("Hongjiao fu zhu 宏教附注"), attached to an interpretation of the *Zhongyong*, attributed to the divine Cheng Yi. "Cheng Mingdao xiansheng shushu 程明道先生疏述," in *Zhongyong zhengshi*, vol. 4. Please note that the four-volume edition of the *Zhongyong zhengshi* that I am using does not include page numbers. I will therefore provide a reference to individual sections in the respective volumes or indicate the chapters of the *Daxue* that are commented upon.
65 "Zhongyong Xuansheng jiangyi 中庸宣聖講義," in *Zhongyong zhengshi*, vol. 1.

the Duke of Zhou 周公.[66] Confucius then collected the writings of these sages. Moreover, by using the *Yijing* 易經 (Book of changes) to complement them, he even traced the vestiges of the Dao back to Fuxi 伏羲, Shennong 神農, and the Yellow Emperor 黃帝, two mythical figures with whom the work is usually associated.[67] Later, Confucius transmitted the Dao to his disciples, whence it came down to Mengzi and Xunzi. This lineage varies from that constructed by the followers of Dao Learning only with regard to Xunzi,[68] who, generally regarded as an important representative of the Confucian tradition until the Tang, was excluded from it by Han Yu, who considered him insufficiently thorough.[69] During the Song period, Zhu Xi even made Xunzi indirectly responsible for the disasters of the Qin dynasty.[70] His work only regained its prominence during the late Qing period, as part of a decided critique of Confucian orthodoxy and the rise of "national learning."[71]

The New Religion likewise considered Xunzi an important representative of the Confucian tradition and thus its members included him within their lineage. However, rather than sharing the iconoclastic tendencies of certain advocates of "national learning," the lineage of the New Religion reflects the search for a more inclusive vision of the Confucian tradition. The New Religion bemoaned the restrictive influence of an increasing factionalism on the development of Confucianism over the course of history, a trend that they dated back to the Warring States Period but to which they also attributed the limitations of the Song-Confucians.[72] Instead, they wanted to highlight the commonalities between various Confucian scholars, in order to impose unity on the different schools, such as Dao Learning and the "School of the Mind" (Xinxue 心學), which was associated with Lu Xiangshan and Wang Yangming.[73] Their aim was not to exclude Confucian scholars, but rather to paint

---

66   Commentary to chap. 1, section 1 (天命之謂性 …), in *Zhongyong zhengshi*, vol. 1.
67   See Lü Yan 呂喦 [Dongbin], "Xu 序," in *Zhongyong zhengshi*, vol. 1.
68   For the standard Neo-Confucian genealogies, cf. Wilson, *Genealogy of the Way*, 260–64.
69   Hartman, *Han Yü and the T'ang Search for Unity*, 159.
70   Goldin, "Xunzi."
71   Early proponents of "national learning," such as Zhang Binglin, attempted to look beyond Confucius and Neo-Confucianism when searching for the "national essence" of China. This brought into the fold philosophers such as Xunzi, who had been previously marginalized. Makeham, "The Revival of Guoxue." See also Kurtz, *The Discovery of Chinese Logic*, 292–93.
72   Lü Yan 呂喦 [Dongbin], "Xu 序," in *Daxue zhengshi*, 55–56.
73   Accordingly, they lauded the theories of Lu Xiangshan and Wang Yangming on "knowledge and action" (*zhixing* 知行) as emphasizing deeds over "empty words" and thus as beneficial for the Confucian teaching. Lü, "Xu," in *Daxue zhengshi*, 56. For the influence of Wang's ideas on the New Religion's interpretation of the *Daxue*, see Chung, "Minchu Jiushi

an inclusive picture of the Confucian teaching; a vision vividly illustrated by the descent of numerous Confucian—and even non-Confucian—sages at their spirit-writing altars. On a theoretical level, this was explained in reference to the all-encompassing nature of the Dao, to which everyone had access through self-cultivation; a position that also informed the New Religion's emphasis on the fundamental equivalence of all religious teachings.[74] From a practical perspective, this inclusive approach certainly also reflected the diminished status of Confucianism during the Republican era, which called for a united effort.

Their choice of texts deemed worthy of commentary followed the established orthodoxy. By emphasizing the *Daxue* and *Zhongyong*, they firmly followed in the footsteps of Dao Learning.[75] Zhu Xi chose the Four Books because they dealt with human morality and self-cultivation in a more straightforward manner than did the challenging classics of old. Their order, however, was also important. The *Daxue*, according to Zhu Xi, was linguistically the least challenging and contained straightforward prescriptions regarding the process of self-cultivation. The *Zhongyong*, on the other hand, discussed in a more abstract, subtle fashion human nature and morality. It was the philosophically most profound but also the most difficult to comprehend.[76] To a certain degree, the *Daxue* and the *Zhongyong* summed up the essence of the Confucian teaching even more concisely than the Four Books in total; a claim that was echoed by the New Religion and explains their selection of these two texts for commentary. One preface to the *Zhongyong zhengshi* by Lü Dongbin thus argues that the text discusses the cultivation of the Dao, while the *Daxue* explains virtue and benevolent government. "[Y]ou can see how the two books mutually constitute one single teaching and how they form the

---

xinjiao zhi *Daxue zhengshi* yanjiu," 113–14. Referring to the *Daxue*, Chung argues that the New Religion sought to combine the views of Dao Learning and the School of the Mind to interpret key aspects of the text. See Chung, "Minchu Jiushi xinjiao zhi *Daxue zhengshi* yanjiu," 116.

74 One preface by Lü Dongbin to the *Daxue zhengshi* makes explicit that their approach to the different Confucian schools is no different from their views on the various religions more generally. See his "Zongzhu xu li er 宗主序例二," in *Daxue zhengshi*, 79.

75 Moreover, by attributing the *Daxue* to Zengzi 曾子 (505?–436? BCE), a disciple of Confucius, and the *Zhongyong* to Zisi 子思 (Kong Ji 孔伋, 483?–402? BCE), an alleged grandson of Confucius, they continued a traditional claim about the authorship of the two works that became a consensus at least during the Han Dynasty before being formalized by Zhu Xi. Cf. Lü, "Xu," in *Zhongyong zhengshi*, vol. 1. Johnston and Wang, Daxue *and* Zhongyong, 2. For Kang Youwei's negative view of Zengzi's role in shaping the Confucian teaching, see Wagner, "The Philologist as Messiah," 154–57.

76 Gardner, *Zhu Xi's Reading of the* Analects, 21; Gardner, "Principle and Pedagogy," 70–74.

complete body of the Confucian teaching" (可見二書之互相為教，即儒教之全體也).[77] A preface attributed to the divine Confucius makes the same point:

> The root of the *Daxue* is illuminating virtue, while the root of the *Zhongyong* is illuminating the Dao. In reality, [however], they are identical. The ultimate of illuminating virtue is to understand the Dao. And at the heart (*zhong*) of illuminating the Dao is nothing other than illuminating virtue.
>
> 大學以明德爲本。中庸以明道為本。其實一也。明德之極。即明道。明道之中。不外明德。[78]

By explicating the Dao and virtue, the two works illustrated the source of human morality as well as its application in social and political life. They thus seemed to provide a comprehensive treatment of the individual and his/her place in society.

The Dao was a central concept for the New Religion, which interpreted it as a unifying principle in the world that was guiding their program of religious and moral reform. This also explains their focus on these two texts, as the *Zhongyong* in particular was supposed to contain the true understanding of that concept.[79] The New Religion explained the Dao and its presence in human life in reference to the opening lines of the text: "What heaven decrees is called 'nature.' Complying with nature is called the 'Way.' Properly practicing the Way is called 'teaching.'" (天命之謂性，率性之謂道，修道之謂教。)[80] This passage brings together the three crucial concepts, "heaven," "human nature" (*xing* 性), and the "Dao," which all feature prominently in the writings of the New Religion and were regarded as being closely intertwined. In his commentary to the *Zhongyong*, the divine Confucius pointed out that, while "[human] nature is bestowed by heaven" (*xing wei tian ming* 性為天命), "the beginning of heaven is created through the Dao" (天之始也。以道而成). Human nature was, therefore, also rooted in the Dao, consisting of "the *qi* of highest emptiness and primordial chaos" (*taixu hunyuan zhi qi* 太虛渾

---

77   Lü, "Xu," in *Zhongyong zhengshi*, vol. 1.
78   "Xuansheng xu li 宣聖序例," in *Zhongyong zhengshi*, vol. 1.
79   However, the society never denied the value of classical writings from other religious traditions such as the *Laozi* or the *Zhuangzi*. One of the central claims of the New Religion was that the Dao was the same within all religious teachings. It was only that the Confucian teaching had most clearly explained its practical application in human life.
80   Johnston and Wang, Zhongyong *and* Daxue, 214–15.

元之氣).[81] It constituted an incorruptible element of the Dao within the individual. As a postface by Lü Dongbin clarified: "After one has received [one's human nature] from heaven and earth, it will never change again. ... This is why it is called the essence of the Dao" (受之天地。無復變化 ... 故曰道體).[82] Human nature, in turn, comprised inherent virtues, such as benevolence (*ren* 仁) and righteousness (*yi* 義), which were natural expressions of the Dao. "Exhausting" (*jin* 盡) these virtues meant cultivating the Dao and following the teaching (*jiao* 教).[83] The main purpose of the commentaries published by the New Religion was to clarify the relation between human nature and the Dao, and demonstrate how the two could be realigned through the practice of the correct moral teachings (*jiao*). This understanding of the Dao and human nature immediately raises a question, however: given its incorruptible presence in human nature, how could the Dao have been lost and how could it be restored?

4 Spirit-Writing and the Restoration of the Dao

The deeper reasons behind the loss of the Dao—beyond mere editorial mistakes—were explained with reference to a human nature that was inherently good but susceptible to external stimuli, necessitating constant efforts regarding its cultivation and restoration. The idea that human nature merely needed to be restored to its pristine state originally had Daoist connotations, but was integrated into Confucian discourse by Li Ao 李翱 (772–841) in his *Fuxing shu* 復性書 (A book for returning to [one's true] nature), which contains a section on the *Zhongyong*. In the text, Li claims that one's true nature, which is bestowed by heaven, may become obfuscated by the emotions. Consequently, it must be restored to "brightness" through the practice of "sincerity" (*cheng* 誠) and the muting of emotional influences.[84] This momentous interplay between human nature and (excessive) emotions has remained a staple of Confucian discourse ever since and was taken up by Zhu Xi, who argued that the heavenly principle (*li* 理) inherent in human nature could be lost due to excessive emotions and desires caused by external stimuli. This principle had

---

81 Commentary to chap. 1, section 1 (天命之謂性 ...), "Xuansheng jiangyi 宣聖講義," in *Zhongyong zhengshi*, vol. 1.
82 Lü Yan 呂喦 [Dongbin], "Ba 跋," in *Zhongyong zhengshi*, vol. 4.
83 Commentary to chap. 1, section 1 (天命之謂性 ...), "Xuansheng jiangyi," in *Zhongyong zhengshi*, vol. 1.
84 See Barrett, *Li Ao*.

to be reinstituted through a restorative process of self-cultivation that involved the regulation of the desires and emotions in order to attain "balance" (*he* 和) and "sincerity."[85]

In the sources of the New Religion, we see many parallels to the above views. Human nature, they claimed, was originally good, as it was linked to the Dao and the state of "perfection" (*zhen* 真), with which the latter was associated.[86] The possibility of human corruption, in turn, was explained in reference to a general distinction between a "pre-celestial" (*xiantian* 先天) and a "post-celestial" (*houtian* 後天) state, that could be applied to every phenomenon in the world. This distinction, which describes the cosmogonic stages prior to and after the generation of heaven and earth, constituted a shared idea of Chinese cosmology.[87] The post-celestial period describes the physical world that we inhabit—with all of its material and emotional seductions—, while the pre-celestial period was imagined as a time when everything was in a gas-like state and heaven and earth, as well as yin and yang, had not yet been separated. It was imagined as a time of primordial chaos but also of simplicity and unity with the Dao. This twofold distinction shines through in divine Confucius' commentary to the *Zhongyong*:

> People only know that, when they are born, they possess a body that was completed through the nurturing from their parents. However, they do not know the body they had before they were born and where they were before they entered the womb of their mother. This principle is certainly not known to regular men and was only understood once the sages appeared.
>
> 人祇知生而有身。父母所育而成。而不知未生之身。及未入母胎之前之何在也。斯理固非常人所知。必待聖人而後明。[88]

In antiquity, on the other hand, humans were still aware of this distinction and of the ultimate realm that lay beyond humans' physical existence. Hence,

---

85 Shun, "Zhu Xi's Moral Psychology."
86 Jiushi xinjiao zonghui, *Jiushi xinjiao jiaogang jiaofa jiaoyi*, 22.
87 I adopt both terms from Fabrizio Pregadio, who himself may have taken them over from de Groot. See the latter's *Sectarianism and Religious Persecution*, vol. 1, 177. For a brief discussion of the pre- and post-celestial stages in reference to a well-known Daoist master, see Liu, *Cultivating the Tao*, 3–4. For a more general view, see also Pregadio, "Xiantian and houtian."
88 Commentary to chap. 1, section 1 (天命之謂性 ...), "Xuansheng jiangyi," in *Zhongyong zhengshi*, vol. 1.

they were still connected to the heavenly Dao, as they were pure and unadulterated.[89] This, of course, held true for the early sages as well. Later, however, humans indulged in desires and thereby distanced themselves from the Dao, leading to negative social consequences. As one spirit-written message from 1926 puts it:

> If one seeks the cause [of the negative development of the human sphere], then the reason lies in the valuing of desires and the distancing from the Dao. It is not the Dao that has distanced itself from humanity, [but] humans who have distanced themselves from the Dao.
>
> 追源其始。實為重欲遠道之故。道非遠人。人自遠道。[90]

Confucius' spirit-written commentary to the *Zhongyong* similarly argued that, when humans engage with the material world without regulating themselves, they will confuse their spirit through emotions, disperse their *qi* 氣, and become disconnected from the Dao.[91] The New Religion thus echoed the Neo-Confucian critique of excessive desires. However, rather than the abstract concept of "principle" used by Zhu Xi, they linked this process of human decline more concretely to the corruption of both human nature and spiritual capability.[92]

Spirit-writing, together with the theories explaining the practice, were integrated into this narrative about the transmission and corruption of the Dao. For this purpose, they added a longer, two-part essay, entitled "Shi ji li 釋乩理" (Explaining the principles of the stylus), to the *Daxue zhengshi*.[93] Principally, the members of the New Religion argued, humans were connected to the Dao and to the deities in high heaven through their nature and a shared ontological entity called "spiritual or numinous energy" (*ling* 靈).[94] This energy could be strengthened through self-cultivation and diminished through indulgence in desires. The sheer existence of spirit-writing, however, indicated that something was amiss regarding the flow of energy between the heavenly and earthly spheres. In principle, if one's spiritual energy were sufficient, direct

---

89 Chen, *Jiushi xinjiao wenda*, 37.
90 "Taiyi Laozu lun Dao," 1.
91 "Zhongyong Xuansheng jiangyi," in *Zhongyong zhengshi*, vol. 1.
92 "He Xian shuo gui," 8.
93 Cf. "Shi ji li 釋乩理," in *Daxue zhengshi*, 13–35.
94 For a brief discussion of this term and its reconfiguration during the Republican period, see Schumann, "Science and Spirit-Writing," 140–43.

contact between the human and the divine could be established. The essay, therefore, pointed out: "In high antiquity, all humans practiced the Dao and people were always connected to the deities. ... Therefore, no one had to use the stylus (*ji*)" (自上古時。人皆習道。皆與神通 ... 故無藉夫乩。).[95] Due to the decline in morality and humans' distance from the Dao, however, this ceased to be possible. Human nature, spiritual energy, and human *qi* had become contaminated by desires, so people were dissociated from the deities. Only the "sages and worthies" (*shengxian* 聖賢) were still able to connect with the divine.

In response, spirit-writing developed out of divine pity at the state of human affairs. It was essentially a short-cut to the divine that was adapted to the "end times" of the Dao, as it depended less on human perfection. In times when people were "blinded by desires" and unable to reach the divine, spirit-writing was the best way to guide humanity.[96] Qian Nengxun put this very succinctly:

> [Once the Dao had become obscured,] all of the transcendents, deities and Buddhas had no alternative but to descend and [effect a moral] transformation (*hua*) through the flying phoenix (i.e., spirit-writing), in the hope of at least slightly rescuing the human heart. Alas, this is because they cannot bear [to witness] the extermination of the human way. Therefore, they did not hesitate to exhaust their voices to preserve a glimmer [of hope] for morality.
>
> 不得已諸仙神佛乃飛鸞降化。以冀挽救人心於萬一。嗚呼。是蓋不忍人道之滅絕。故不惜嘵音瘏口。為道德留一線光曙也。[97]

While only sages such as Confucius had been able to transmit their teachings directly, the members of the New Religion saw themselves as worthies (*xian*) who use spirit-writing to make visible the spiritual energy of the deities and the Dao known to the world.[98] This also means that, fundamentally, the Chinese classics were considered identical to modern spirit-writing messages, differing only with regard to their technique of transmission.[99]

---

95   "Shi ji li," in *Daxue zhengshi*, 13.
96   Ibid., 14.
97   Qian, "*Lingxue yaozhi* xu," 1.
98   "Shi ji li," in *Daxue zhengshi*, 17.
99   Therefore, the ancient writings of Confucius, but also of Shakyamuni Buddha and Jesus, were explicitly likened to the writings transmitted through the stylus, as they all teach the way of the deities (*shendao*). Ibid., 13.

The use of spirit-writing to make a claim to the correct interpretation of the classics and the transmission of the Dao sets the New Religion apart from earlier exegetes, such as Zhu Xi or Kang Youwei. This approach was significantly assisted by the increasing divinization of the Confucian sages over the course of history. Many representatives of the Confucian tradition had gained divine rank, which made them prestigious sources of authority and enabled their appearance at spirit-writing altars. In his contribution to this volume, Vincent Goossaert thus details how Yan Hui 顏回 (Yanzi 顏子), Confucius's favorite disciple, was elevated in the god Wenchang's 文昌 divine administration during the Song period and so able to reveal scriptures through spirit-writing.[100] He features among the deities commenting on the *Daxue* and the *Zhongyong* at the altar of the New Religion. It is conspicuous, however, that Confucius was not a common presence at spirit-writing altars during the imperial period. So far, I have not come across any instance of Confucius featuring in spirit-writing sessions prior to the late Qing period.[101] Possibly, his status appeared too exalted for such an exchange.[102] This changed, however, around the turn of the century, when Confucius began to descend to various altars throughout the state.[103] This process intensified during the Republican period, when redemptive societies such as the Daoyuan, a universalist religious organization, mentioned above, enshrined Confucius as one of the founders of the five world religions and thus as principally of the same status as Jesus and Mohammed (to whom spirit-writing messages were ascribed as well). In that capacity, he descended to various altars of the Daoyuan to transmit messages of moral exhortation.[104] The case of the Daoyuan may also offer clues as to the reasons for this develop-

---

100   Yanzi even became one of the principal deities of spirit-altars in Yunnan, in the region west of Kunming, during the early twentieth century. Wang, "Tongshan she zaoqi de tedian," 147. For the appearance of other Confucian figures at a spirit-writing altar, see also the contribution by Daniel Burton-Rose in this volume.

101   Sebastien Billioud and Vincent Goossaert imply, in one of their articles, that Confucius sometimes appeared during spirit-writing sessions in imperial times without, however, indicating specific examples. Billioud and Goossaert, "Confucius and his Texts," 231.

102   Notably, Yao, Shun, and other "ancient sages" remained beyond the reach of spirit-writing practitioners.

103   Wang Chien-chuan has found that Confucius became a common deity among spirit-writing altars in Yunnan during the late Qing period. Wang, "Popular Groups Promoting 'The Religion of Confucius,'" 118. Philip Clart further mentions that Confucius contributed a preface to a commentary on the *Zhongyong*, that was transmitted in Sichuan in the early twentieth century. Notably, in this context, he had to defend his descent to a spirit-writing altar in light of his transmitted instruction to maintain a distance from spirits and deities. Clart, "Confucius and the Mediums," 15–16.

104   See "Fu wu jiao jiaozhu xunci," for a case in which the divine Confucius descends alongside

ment. During the late Qing era and the Republican period, Confucianism was transformed from the principal teaching (*jiao*) into one religion (*zongjiao* 宗教) among many (though often considered of exalted status). The redemptive societies were at the forefront of this development,[105] which may have helped them to conceive and legitimize new roles for Confucius.

For the New Religion, Confucius became part of a broad pantheon of sages who were concerned about the moral state of humankind and used spirit-writing to effect change. The phrase "descending [to effect] moral transformation through the flying phoenix" (*feiluan jianghua*), which appears in the quote by Qian Nengxun mentioned above and is echoed elsewhere,[106] clearly frames the activities of the New Religion as an extension of the post-1840 eschatological spirit-writing movement.[107] At a time of moral decline and distance from the Dao, the sages and deities were compelled to rely on spirit-writing to spread their teaching. Indeed, the essay "Shi ji li," mentioned above, was clearly intended to legitimize spirit-writing, which still carried notions of heterodoxy, as a means of transmitting "orthodox" Confucian thought.[108] Justifying the use of spirit-writing for "orthodox" purposes was an issue with which earlier spirit-writing practitioners had to grapple as well, as Daniel Burton-Rose shows in his contribution to this volume. Similar to Peng Dingqiu 彭定求 (1645–1719), a Ming scholar investigated by Burton-Rose, the New Religion legitimized spirit-writing and the descent of the Confucian sages in reference to an increasing moral decline and dissociation from the Dao. Such allusions to the extraordinary times could also be used to legitimate the unprecedented descent of Confucius. In the preface to a commentary on the *Zhongyong*, studied by Philip Clart, the spirit-writing Confucius points to the extraordinary times that impel orthodox deities to spread the "divine way" (*shendao*).[109] This was echoed by Duan Qirui in his preface to the *Daxue zhengshi*, where he argues

---

Laozi, Shakyamuni Buddha, Jesus, and Mohammed and explicitly mentions the *Zhongyong*.
105   Schumann, "Redemptive Societies," 193–96.
106   Cf, for example, Lü, "Xu," in *Daxue zhengshi*, 59. Here, it is explained that the founders of the various teachings, pitying the chaotic state of the world and disappearance of the "way of the sages" (*shengdao* 聖道), had little choice but "to let their divinity descend to earth and make their spiritual energy visible to humans" (降神於地。顯靈於人). This, the text continues, ushered in the founding of the New Religion.
107   See the chapter by Shiga Ichiko in this volume.
108   For that purpose, the text describes the stylus as an instrument for the transmission of the "sagely teaching" (*shengjiao* 聖教), comparable to the Yellow River Chart (Hetu 河圖) and the Luo Writ (Luoshu 洛書). Ibid., 28–29.
109   Clart, "Confucius and the Mediums," 16.

that "upheavals" had reached crisis point, prompting Confucius to descend into the stylus.[110] Spirit-writing was thus framed as something of a last resort to restore the Dao and "to save the world" (*jiushi* 救世).[111]

5 Making Known the "Divine Way" (*shendao*)

To restore the Dao, the New Religion approached the Confucian classics from two perspectives. On the one hand, they attempted to restore what they saw as the original structure of the texts. The editions of the *Daxue* and the *Zhongyong* that they published are thus markedly different from the versions compiled by Zhu Xi.[112] They hailed this as an achievement in itself. Only now, with the descent of Confucius to the altar, as the divine Zhu Xi pointed out in his spirit-written postface to the *Daxue zhengshi*, "had the meaning of the text been greatly illuminated and its order greatly improved, so that not one phrase or doctrine remains obscured" (文義已大明。字句已大順。更無一語之晦。一義之澀).[113] On the other hand, the commentaries transmitted by the New Religion linked the interpretation of the classics to the role of spirit-writing in effecting moral change. Specifically, the deities and sages were presented as divine guardians of the Dao, who would guide and supervise the cultivation and restoration of the Dao within human society. This offered a powerful, innovative perspective from which to interpret the classical texts and aligned their exegetical activities with their attempt to restoring the moral fiber of society.

Spirit-writing's value in "saving the world" (*jiushi*) was attributed to its ability to make known the way of the deities (*shendao*) in the human world. The descent of the deities and sages to the altar—and particularly their messages—indicated to everyone the existence of a higher force to which all were accountable. This role of the deities was closely related to the principle of "retribution" (*baoying* 報應) for good and bad deeds, which played a prominent role within the teachings of the New Religion.[114] The concept of retribution, which was

---

110   Lü, "Xu," in *Daxue zhengshi*, 56–57.
111   Lu, "Yuanqi," in *Daxue zhengshi*, 10.
112   These differences relate to changes in individual characters as well as the rearrangement of specific sections. For a discussion of the New Religion's edition of the *Daxue*, including the full text, see Chung, "Minchu Jiushi xinjiao zhi *Daxue zhengshi* yanjiu," 91–106.
113   Zhu Xi, "Ba yi," in *Daxue zhengshi*, 364.
114   Indeed, the journal *Lingxue yaozhi* 靈學要誌 (Essential magazine of spiritualism) that the mother organization of the New Religion, the Wushan she, had founded, was also established to indicate punishment for misdeeds based on retribution. "Hongjiao Zhenren Liu xu," 4.

popularized through "morality books" (*shanshu* 善書) and broadly accepted by the different social strata in late imperial China,[115] entailed that all human deeds had consequences depending on their moral nature. Deities were perceived as agents who would mete out these consequences. Accordingly, Jiang Chaozong, long-serving president of the New Religion, pointed out that people need to be taught:

> that because of the ever revolving [mechanism] of cause and effect (*yinguo*), if you enter life, you will certainly [face] retribution (*bao*). You may hope to escape [punishment in] the world of humans, but you may never hope to escape [punishment in] the netherworld (*mingming*). Other humans may not know what [happens] in a dark room or what [one harbors] in one's heart, but the deities and spirits, with their bright perceptiveness, will certainly investigate it. There may be places where [worldly] punishments do not reach, but the retribution of cause and effect is carried out without leaving anything uncovered. Wealth and power cannot be employed against this and the evil and wicked have nowhere to retreat. It is like the shining of the sun and moon, where there exists no darkness which it does not illuminate. It is like a shadow that chases the body, and there is no direction that it will not follow.

> 以循環之因果。經有生而必報。可以倖脫夫人世者。必不能倖逃夫冥冥也。暗室之內。方寸之中。人所不知。而鬼神之昭鑒必察。刑所不及。而因果之報施無虛。貴勢無所施焉。奸黠無所遁焉。如日月之照臨。無幽不燭。如形影之隨體。無往不從。[116]

Knowledge about the existence of divine beings and divine punishment, Jiang argued, could effect a change in human behavior, "so that the ignorant and the wise, the noble and the lowly, will all be cautious and fearful (*jingshen jieju*)" (愚智貴賤。莫不敬慎戒懼), "so that they will be filled with awe and no one will dare to do evil" (惟日懍懍。莫敢為惡).[117] It was exactly this role of admonishing people that spirit-writing was supposed to play due to the immediate experience of the divine which it afforded.

The New Religion's exegetical strategy was closely related to this moralistic approach and the role of the deities and sages in indicating the "divine way." Indeed, the assumed divine presence in human life was one vantage point from

---

115 Brokaw, *The Ledgers of Merit and Demerit*, chap. 2.
116 Jiang, "*Lingxue yaozhi* xu," 1–2.
117 Ibid.

which to explain the classics and bolstered a "religionized" understanding of Confucianism, as indicated above. In their commentary on the *Zhongyong*, for example, they interpret a well-known passage in light of divine supervision. The passage occurs at the beginning of the work and reads as follows:

> The Way cannot be departed from even for an instant; if it could be departed from, it would not be the Way. This is why the noble man is on guard and cautious where he is not seen; this is why he is fearful and apprehensive where he is not heard. There is nothing more apparent than what is hidden; there is nothing more manifest than what is obscure. Therefore, the noble man is cautious when he is alone.
>
> 道也者，不可須臾離也，可離非道也。是故君子戒慎乎其所不睹，恐懼乎其所不聞。莫見乎隱，莫顯乎微，故君子慎其獨也。[118]

This passage posed particular challenges for the commentators due to its relatively cryptic play with visibility and hiddenness and a lack of clarity concerning the dangers of solitude. Pre-Song commentators interpreted this section more or less literally, as expressing the superior moral stature of the "noble man" (*junzi*), who is cautious even when no one is around to watch him.[119] Zhu Xi, on the other hand, adopted a different approach. For him, *du* 睹 and *wen* 聞 were active verbs that refer to the things that one cannot see or hear. *Du* 獨, in turn, referred to a place that only oneself can assess while the "hidden" (*yin*) and the "obscure" (*wei*) invoke the subtle workings of the inner self about which the noble man must be careful, lest they give rise to negative desires.[120]

The commentary of the divine Confucius, transmitted by the New Religion, provides a multi-layered interpretation of this passage. It follows Zhu Xi by linking an attitude of fearfulness to the possible emergence of "human emotions and desires" due to humans' interaction with external things. In that context, the passage is seen as describing the inner workings of the self, the things that

---

118 Johnston and Wang, Daxue *and* Zhongyong, 215.
119 Zheng Xuan 鄭玄 (127–200 CE) explained that the "noble man" (*junzi*), unlike the petty man (*xiaoren* 小人), is "naturally well-ordered and correct" even when no one is around to see or hear him. Ibid., 215. Kong Yingda 孔穎達 (574–648) understood watchfulness in solitude as expressing the diligent, comprehensive approach to cultivating the Dao that the noble man displays. He is fearful and cautious, not behaving badly even when in seclusion, much less in full view of others. Ibid., 221–23. However, his point that people may observe the circumstances of hidden transgressions is less straightforward. Cf. ibid., 221. For a discussion of the commentators' views on this issue, see also ibid., 196–97.
120 Ibid., 407–11.

only oneself (*ji* 己), one alone (*du* 獨), can observe.[121] In a literal sense, *du* 獨 is also interpreted as referring to solitude, to a state when one is not being watched, as if "under the shadow of a blanket, in a secret chamber" (衾影之中。屋漏之下).[122] Under these circumstances, the noble man will remain cautious and "not be sluggish even for a little bit" (*bu gan shao dai* 不敢稍怠) in cultivating the Dao. The petty man (*xiaoren* 小人), on the contrary, puts on an act in public, but behaves carelessly when alone. In this way, the radical conclusion goes, he is more beast than human.[123]

There was hope, however, even for the petty man. This hope originated from the watchful presence of the deities and sages in human life, that would force him back onto the right track. It is from this vantage point that the commentary provides the most powerful and innovative interpretation of the passage "There is nothing more apparent than what is hidden; there is nothing more manifest than what is obscure."

> In general, humans are born and receive what is bestowed by heaven. When their body is filled with spiritual energy, they are connected to heaven. And when the heavenly deities shine brilliantly, [their shine] is reflected among humans. The heavenly deities observe and hear even that which cannot be observed or heard [by humans]. The spiritual energy of the heavenly deities is connected with the human heart. Not only what they do can be observed and heard by them, but every thought that arises, every move that they intend, can all be observed and heard [by them]. This is why their strict instructions[124] and the teaching about the arrival [of the deities] all indicate the inspection and presence of the deities. At no time may one be even the least bit complacent. This is why the hidden is [really] not hidden and why the obscure is [really] not obscure. What the deities are able to watch, humans believe to be hidden, without realizing that it is visible to upright deities. [What the deities are able to hear], humans believe to be obscure, without realizing that it is apparent to upright deities.
>
> 夫人受天命以生。含靈之體。時通于天。天神昭昭。時鑒于人。不聞不睹之閒。而天神實睹之聞之。天神之靈。通于人心。不徒行爲之能

---

121 Chap. 1, section 2 (道也者。不可須臾離 ...), "Xuansheng jiangyi," in *Zhongyong zhengshi*, vol. 1.
122 Ibid.
123 Ibid.
124 This might be an allusion to spirit-writing.

睹聞。即一念之生。一意之動。舉能睹之聞之。故其嚴之訓。格思之教。皆所以明神之鑒臨。無時或爽者也。故隱者非隱。微者非微。隱微之中。神明所矚。人以爲隱。而不知正神之所見也。人以爲微。而不知正神之所顯也。[125]

The commentary avoids the seeming paradox of the above passage—namely, why and to whom anything should be visible in a state of solitude—by invoking the constant supervision of divine forces, which serve as the guardians of the Dao. This might not seem entirely convincing in light of the commented passage only, as deities are not mentioned. However, by referring to "the arrival [of the deities]" (*gesi* 格思) the passage invokes a phrase from another section of the *Zhongyong* to corroborate their argument. In that passage, the historical Confucius quotes a song from the *Shijing* 詩經 (Book of odes), whence the phrase *gesi* stems, to discuss the characteristics of "spirits and deities" (*guishen* 鬼神). He argues that they appear to surround us, even if we cannot see or hear them, thus demanding an attitude of reverence.[126] This understanding gave credence to the New Religion's interpretation that one was always being investigated by the deities and thus had to be "on guard and cautious," even when alone.[127] Hence, not for an instant may one be careless—or leave the Dao—, lest the divine guardians of the Dao observe this. This means, of course, that any wrongdoing will also be seen and punished accordingly. For the believers assembling at the altar in Tianjin such a reading seemed only logical of course, given that their practice of spirit-writing provided a regular reminder of the divine presence in human life.

The above passage, which is not an isolated case,[128] may serve as an illustration of how the exegetical work of the New Religion was integrated with their

---

125   Chap. 1, section 2 (道也者。不可須臾離 …), "Xuansheng jiangyi," in *Zhongyong zhengshi*, vol. 1.

126   "The *Odes* says: 'The coming of deities cannot be determined. Still less can they be disrespected.'" (《詩》曰：神之格思，不可度思！矧可射思！) Translation slightly adapted from Johnston and Wang, Daxue *and* Zhongyong, 437.

127   I am extremely grateful to Daniel Burton-Rose for alerting me to the significance of the phrase *gesi*. Indeed, he argues that the term was used by Peng Dingqiu to designate spirit-writing itself, intending to obscure the more recent history of the practice and to conflate it with the orthodox methods for interacting with the ancestral spirits. Scholars of Dao Learning during the early Qing, moreover, emphasized the ethical dangers of being alone in a fashion similar to the New Religion. See the discussion in Burton-Rose's forthcoming book, *Celestial Officials of the Jade Bureau: Prophecy and Spirit-Writing in Qing Conquest China*.

128   In the "Shi ji li," in *Daxue zhenghsi*, 19, the state of caution mentioned in the *Zhongyong* is similarly linked to the supervision of the deities.

spirit-writing activities and other practices and beliefs. They approached the passage based on their understanding of the interaction between the divine and human spheres. As such, their commentaries formed part of an attempt to prove the viability of "the divine way" and foster its implementation in the human realm. Their spirit-written publications (including their commentaries, but also other writings, which were published chiefly in their journals) were supposed to convince people of the existence of deities, retribution, and life after death in a manner similar to "morality books." Such a realization was supposed to lead the morally negligent to refrain from committing evil acts and encourage the "noble man" (*junzi*) to engage in self-cultivation (*xiuxing* 修行 / *xiuyang* 修養). Similar to many other redemptive societies of the time, self-cultivation consisted of two components for the New Religion: ethical practice[129] and bodily cultivation (usually referred to as "techniques of seated [meditation]," *zuogong* 坐功, or *jingzuo* 靜坐, "quiet sitting"), aiming to remove desires, as well as social service in the form of philanthropic practice (*cishan shiye* 慈善事業). For the New Religion, these activities were all part of the "cultivation of the Dao" (*xiudao* 修道), which, if practiced, would enable the individual member to aspire to a divine existence after death while also contributing to the moral reform of society.[130]

This understanding of cultivating the Dao as comprising of a broad program of moral cultivation and social service, dictated by divine example and supervision, further explains the importance that the New Religion attached to the *Daxue* and *Zhongyong*. The former describes vividly the individual and social dimensions of self-cultivation, for which the latter provides the metaphysical framework. In its opening statements, the *Zhongyong* features maybe the most concise and forceful explication of the way, its link to human nature, and its application in human life.[131] All they needed to do was to integrate their interpretation of the texts with their moralistic approach and the role of the deities as guardians and transmitters of the Dao. Passages such as that quoted above offered a venue in which to do so. Indeed, it was also quoted almost verbatim by Jiang Chaozong above, referring to "the bright perceptiveness of spirits and deities" (*guishen zhi zhaojian* 鬼神之昭鑒) that is able to examine even a dark room and leaves one "cautious and fearful." In this way, the two texts, and

---

129   This was equated with the observation of ethical precepts, such as "benevolence" or "righteousness," which are prominently discussed in the *Daxue* and *Zhongyong*.
130   Schumann, "Between Science and Superstition," 106–20, chap. 7.
131   As early as 1921, Duan Qirui had quoted the opening passage, which indicates that the members had valued the text long before they began their commentarial work. See Duan, "*Lingxue yaozhi* xu."

the *Zhongyong* in particular, could be linked to spirit-writing and the divine way, which, one may assume, was another reason why they were chosen for commentary. This echoes the exegetical strategies of other spirit-writing organizations. In a study of a spirit-written commentary on the *Zhongyong* and *Daxue*, Chung Yun-Ying 鍾雲鶯 shows how the Yiguandao interpreted concepts such as the Dao, human nature, and filial piety in light of their eschatological theories and thereby gave the texts a more "religionized" meaning.[132] This ability to reinterpret creatively and refashion (or even create anew) texts of cultural value certainly contributes to the continued popularity of spirit-writing.

6   The Political Implications of Confucianism and Confucian Learning

Another aspect that shines through in the *Daxue zhengshi* and *Zhongyong zhengshi* is the political value that the New Religion attached to Confucianism and its textual canon. Indeed, by integrating their commentaries into a religious program that aimed to realize the moral reform of society, the activities of the New Religion always had political connotations. More concretely, promoting the Confucian classics and reestablishing the correct knowledge of the Dao was supposed to solve China's political problems against the background of a national crisis that the members of the New Religion saw as having intensified after the revolution of 1911.

Examining the Republican period from a broader perspective, it was not only the loss of the Dao to which the members of the New Religion ascribed China's current social and political malaise—after all the Dao had long been lost—but more general political developments were also at play. One factor that served to exacerbate China's crisis, the members of the New Religion argued, was the rise of political radicalism during recent decades. Duan Qirui, in his preface to the *Daxue zhengshi*, thus bemoaned the rise of political parties (*dang* 黨), which he found unbefitting for a Confucian scholar and argued were responsible for a rise in factionalism and egotism in the political field. He particularly singled out socialist parties, which he called "red parties" (*hongdang* 紅黨), as a negative global influence. Citing the case of Russia, he criticized the Communist forces for their oppressive influence on society, scholarship, and economic development. He saw the rise of Communism in Russia as resulting in the waste of human talent and the "creation of a nation of sluggards" (成一國之惰民), a

---

132   Chung, "Lun Yiguandao *Xue yong qianyan xinzhu*."

fate he similarly feared for China.[133] This critical attitude toward socialism and communism reflects the general political outlook of the Beiyang elites, who strove to counter "radical factions" in an attempt to preserve the social order, but it also echoes the positions voiced in other publications, both spirit-written and otherwise, of the New Religion and its parent organization, the Wushan she, during the 1920s. In their journals and publications, they bemoaned the influence of political concepts, such as "freedom" (*ziyou* 自由), "equality" (*pingdeng* 平等) and "rights" (*quanli* 權利), which they associated with communism and socialism and to which they attributed a corrosive influence on a social order they saw as heavenly-ordained.[134] Sources such as the commentaries by the New Religion thereby also provide insights into the social and political outlook of important power brokers, such as Duan Qirui, and the shared values between redemptive societies and the Beiyang elites, which have been attested by research.[135]

The critical attitude toward socialism and communism, moreover, is representative of a more general wariness regarding iconoclastic thought in the sources of the New Religion. While they were in no sense reluctant to engage with new concepts, practices, and institutions, as the creation of their religious organization itself vividly illustrates, the members of the New Religion were generally critical of demands for a more comprehensive cultural and social change. This, one article in a journal published by the New Religion argued, would lead to a disregard for China's inherent teachings with detrimental consequences for the morality of the people.[136] Given the eminence they ascribed to it, the members were especially concerned about attacks on Confucianism. Duan Qirui thus lamented an increasing rejection of Confucian learning since the founding of the Republic, quoting accounts that everywhere "reading the sagely classics is prohibited and that the Confucius temples are being destroyed" (禁讀聖經毀滅聖廟).[137] Such statements also indicate that the New Religion saw itself as a counterforce to the May Fourth modernization program, with which the criticism of Confucianism during that time is so closely associated. The confluence of these factors led the New Religion to make a damning assessment of the Republican period, considering the current chaos worse than

---

133   Duan, "Xu," in *Daxue zhengshi*, 39–40. A similarly negative view of socialism, communism, and anarchism is offered in the postface by Yao Zhen 姚震 (1885–1935). See Yao, "Ba san 跋三," in *Daxue zhengshi*, 378.
134   Schumann, "Between Science and Superstition," chap. 8.
135   Ownby, "Redemptive Societies in the Twentieth Century," 692–700; Schumann, "Redemptive Societies," 188–89.
136   Xiong, "Gonghe guomin," 3.
137   Duan, "Xu," in *Daxue zhengshi*, 41.

even that during the Five Dynasties, when "worthy literati" were still able to protect the Confucian teaching.[138] This explains the urgency with which the members promoted Confucianism.

The New Religion's attempt to promote Confucianism in order to save the Chinese nation from the chaos of the time comprised different levels, straddling the divide between the scholarly, religious, and cultural realms. With regard to their exegetical endeavors, the New Religion approached the classics from a more pragmatic perspective and thereby joined the voices that repeatedly criticized, during the late Qing, an overly metaphysical and/or philological interpretation of the Four Books.[139] This becomes visible when we look at their interpretation of the *Daxue*. As Chung Yun-Ying has highlighted in her insightful study, the New Religion conceded the importance of the text for individual self-cultivation in the fashion of Zhu Xi, but departed from the theories of the Song and Ming eras by stressing its political connotations. For them, the *Daxue* explicated the virtues of an ideal ruler.[140] As Chung argues, the New Religion emphasized the value of the *Daxue* for both the cultivation of "inner sagehood" (*neisheng* 内聖) as well as good governance. To aspire to ideal rulership, the "moral teachings" (*jiao*) and actual "policies" (*zheng* 政) had to be unified.[141] They thereby attempted to combine the views of different exegetes, exem-

---

138   Lü, "Xu," in *Daxue zhengshi*, 62–63. Such statements also seem to amount to an only slightly veiled criticism of the general political conditions existing during the Republic, although we do not find clear calls for a return to monarchy.
139   Rowe, *Saving the World*, 117–23.
140   This change in perspective becomes apparent in their reinterpretation of the key phrase "illuminating bright virtue" (*ming ming de* 明明德). As Chung Yun-Ying argues, Zhu Xi understood the phrase in reference to Buddhist thought (particularly Chan Buddhism) as referring to a process of recovering human inherent virtues that were originally "bright" (*ming*) but later became concealed by worldly desires. Chung, "Minchu Jiushi xinjiao zhi *Daxue zhengshi* yanjiu," 111–13. See also Jorgensen, "The Radiant Mind." The New Religion understood "illuminating bright virtue" as referring to virtuous political actions, such as "governing the state and bringing peace to the world" (*zhi guo ping tianxia* 治國平天下). Through actions worthy of a virtuous ruler, virtue would be "illuminated." As Chung points out, the New Religion thereby adopted the perspective of the commentators of the *Liji* 禮記 (Book of rites) prior to the Song era, which had similarly interpreted "bright virtue" as the external actions of a virtuous ruler. Chung, "Minchu Jiushi xinjiao zhi *Daxue zhengshi* yanjiu," 112. Zhu Xi, as mentioned above, eventually conceded defeat, acknowledging that his interpretations differed from those of the Master. The same emphasis on the practical application of virtue shines through the New Religion's interpretation of the *Zhongyong*. See, for example "Zongzhu xu zheng 宗主序證," in *Zhongyong zhengshi*, vol. 1, in which Lü Dongbin argues that "the Dao of the *Zhongyong* emphasizes practice" (中庸之道。重在實踐。) and prioritizes the "establishment of virtue" (*lide* 立德).
141   Chung, "Minchu Jiushi xinjiao zhi *Daxue zhengshi* yanjiu," 106–10.

plifying their inclusive view of the Confucian tradition. The ruler first had to begin by cultivating himself, in the manner in which the *Daxue* instructs. Only then would he be able to "transform" (*hua* 化) others by the power of example, instead of merely "commanding them" (*ling* 令) through the force of his position. Such a sage ruler would be able to ensure peace and benevolent government. Such an interpretation struck a chord with members such as Duan Qirui, for whom the *Daxue*, with its emphasis on self-cultivation and bringing order to the family and state at large, epitomized the social and political value of Confucianism.[142] Only a ruler who followed the "way of the sages," he argued, would be able to solve China's political problems.[143]

The New Religion's understanding of the *Daxue* and their call to unite moral teachings and politics, *jiao* and *zheng*, also raises important questions about the place of religion within the political sphere. As I have shown elsewhere,[144] the New Religion generally considered all religions as moral teachings (*jiao*) that were identical in the lessons they imparted. Confucian works such as the *Daxue* had merely formulated these moral virtues in the most straightforward manner.[145] For the members of the New Religion, however, Confucianism was not a humanist or even secular teaching, as some reformers came to argue.[146]

---

142 Duan, "Xu," in *Daxue zhengshi*, 37.

143 In his personal writings, Duan reflected on the sagely "heroes" (*yingxiong* 英雄) of the past who embodied such qualities. This also amounted to a critique of the political elites of his time (of which he was, of course, an important member), who seemed to lack such qualities. Chan, "Duan Qirui," 217.

144 Schumann, "Between Science and Superstition," chap. 6.

145 The views of individual members varied, of course. Duan Qirui became a devout Buddhist in the 1920s, which certainly influenced his evaluation of the different religious teachings. He viewed Confucianism and Buddhism as complementary. While Buddhism's ability to change people's behavior was unmatched due to its consideration of retribution and transmigration, Confucianism's key virtue lies in "morally transforming" (*jiaohua* 教化) people through its moral teachings. Chan, "Duan Qirui," 225–27.

146 The introduction of the neologism *zongjiao* at the turn of the century forced Chinese intellectuals to reassess Confucianism in light of the new category of "religion." Some, such as Kang Youwei, argued that Confucianism differed from Christianity since it was based on the "human way" (*rendao* 人道) rather than the "divine way." Cf. Meyer, "Der moderne chinesische 'Religionsbegriff.'" Even though the New Religion did not directly address Kang's position in their sources, their theories must also be seen in the context of the ensuing debate over the "religious" nature of Confucianism. One should note, however, that the New Religion read the novel term *zongjiao* through the lens of the familiar component *jiao*, which is, after all, the term used in the Confucian classics. Their understanding of *zongjiao*, therefore, differed from the contemporary European understanding of religion and included aspects of "education" (*jiaoyu* 教育) and "moral transformation" (*jiaohua*). Cf. Schumann, "Between Science and Superstition," chap. 6.

As shown in the previous section, they held that Confucianism, like all other religions, was based on the "divine way" and, at least in the end times of the Dao, its moral teachings gained force from divine supervision; it depended on a shared belief in the existence of divine forces. It was in this sense that religion in general, and Confucianism in particular, was thought to exert a stabilizing influence on society and the state; an influence that was threatened by radical ideas.[147] This understanding of religion made the members of the New Religion fiercely critical of secularization and certainly contributed to their critique of communism. When the Wushan she, the parent organization of the New Religion, applied for registration with the Beiyang government in 1921, its leaders used the opportunity to discuss the role of religion in society and politics more generally. They lamented the gradual separation of politics and religion that they witnessed in history. "All the states of Europe and the West have possessed a religion (*zongjiao*) [but] since the decay of the power of the Roman [Empire], politics and religion (*zheng yu jiao*) have become separated and subsequently corrupt practices have increased." (歐西諸國。咸有宗教。自羅馬勢力衰。政與教分。逐滋流弊。)[148] This was due to the fact that morality without religion was impossible. Religious teachings promote self-cultivation and altruistic behavior, thereby reducing conflict within society. Hence, if one wishes to counter China's social and political crisis, one needed religion.[149] Consequently, the New Religion called for the reintegration of religion into the political sphere and a revival of the ideology of "establishing teachings based on the divine way" (*shendao shejiao*), as outlined above. Such positions indicate the variety of views at the time concerning the best way to reform China. They also explain the time and effort that prominent political figures invested in redemptive societies. Many of them professed a belief in concepts such as retribution and considered religion an important part of their personal life.[150] Redemptive societies, such as the New Religion, with their emphasis on divine guidance, moral cultivation and social service, appeared to epitomize the particular form of "religious modernity" that these individuals regarded as China's political future.

---

147   Yu, "Shuo zhi luan yu jiao zhi guanxi."
148   Beijing Municipal Archives, J002–002–00055, 55–56.
149   Beijing Municipal Archives, J002–002–00055, 55.
150   Individuals' personal views are, of course, difficult to assess, but both Jiang Chaozong and Lu Zongyu attested in writing to their belief in retribution and spirit-writing's ability to provide proof of it. See Mi, "Minguo Wushan she yanjiu," 11–12, and Schumann, "Between Science and Superstition," 67–68. As mentioned above, Duan Qirui became a devout Buddhist in the 1920s, valuing the transformative force of ideas such as retribution. Chan, "Duan Qirui," 217.

Compared to other religious teachings, however, Confucianism had an additional political significance due to its cultural prestige and assumed connection to the Chinese nation. As Zhong Shiming pointed out:

> Generally speaking, classical learning (*jingxue*) has been China's special national essence (*guocui*) for thousands of years. Moreover, it is the most supreme cultural [essence] which the East (*dongfang*) possesses and which is unique in its history. Only if we preserve it and support it, will the customs of the world and the human heart remain unharmed and will the proper [Confucian views of] social relations and the social virtues (*gangchang lunji*) not decline.
>
> 夫經學為吾國數千年來特殊之國粹。且為東方自有歷史以來唯一無二最高上之文化。舉凡世道人心不弊。綱常倫紀之不墜。胥賴是維持而輔翼之。[151]

The term "national essence" is revealing in this context. During the late Qing period, a number of political reformers linked to the emergence of "national learning," such as Zhang Binglin, used the term to promote a Meiji-style modernization based on a reconfiguration of "native cultural traditions."[152] For Zhong Shiming, the Confucian classics and the moral values they promoted constituted such a "nativist tradition."[153] Confucianism's political value was

---

151   Zhong, "Xu," in *Daxue zhengshi*, 45.
152   Theorists of "national learning" tried to link the "essence" of Chinese culture, which was no longer confined to imperial Confucianism, more closely to a Chinese nation, which was defined as being in opposition to the ruling Manchus. In that context, attention was directed toward philosophical traditions beyond the Confucian mainstream, which could be refigured as part of the "native" traditions, but also to the alleged "racial roots" of the Chinese. See Furth, "Intellectual Change," 45–52; and Fung, *The Intellectual Foundations of Chinese Modernity*, 62–63.
153   The New Religion, while sharing the search for China's "essence," radically differed regarding their assessment of Confucianism. Zhang Binglin had approached the classics from a philological and linguistic perspective, seeing Confucius as a transmitter rather than a sage. He therefore rejected the canonical status of the classics, emphasizing instead the value of pre-Han philosophical writings, such as the *Hanfeizi* 韓非子. See Furth, "The Sage as Rebel." The New Religion neither tried to historicize the classics nor questioned their status as the preeminent element of "Chinese culture." On the contrary, they attributed the value of the classics to their close association with the divine figures of the sages. Pivoting away from that privileged heritage was seen as dangerous, and indeed this had caused China's malaise in the first place. In his postface to the *Daxue zhengshi*, the divine Zhu Xi criticized Confucians who emphasized philological inquiry, looked toward other schools such as the Mohists, parroted "the trite knowledge of foreigners" (*wairen yahui* 外人牙

therefore also attributed to its privileged connection to the Chinese nation. This is also reflected by the reference to "the East" (*dongfang*), a buzzword in the political and cultural discourses of that time. In the 1920s, "Eastern culture" (*dongfang wenhua* 東西文化) in particular became a term of political and cultural empowerment, which was invoked to challenge the notion of Western supremacy and argue for the continued value of Chinese civilization.[154] This civilization, for Zhong, was represented by Confucianism and should not be discarded in favor of introducing new knowledge. Ironically, Zhong emphasized the importance of Confucian learning for the Chinese nation by pointing to the fact that European universities were busy setting up institutes for the study of the Chinese classics, hoping thereby to improve morality and correct their previous overemphasis on science and physical education.[155] Even foreigners, that is to say, had realized the value of the Confucian classics and were spreading Chinese culture while many Chinese reformers wished to discard it. In that sense, the Confucian classics were not only the repositories of the true Dao but also important cultural symbols that had to be preserved against the onslaught of iconoclastic forces for the sake of the Chinese nation.

By presenting Confucianism as the moral, religious, and cultural essence of China, the New Religion could claim a political importance that added to its appeal and contributed to its ability to navigate the changing political context. Here, it is also worth pointing out that the New Religion, combined with its parent organization the Wushan she, did not uphold one persistent, consistent view of Confucianism's value for the nation and its relation to other religious teachings; rather, its positions and emphases shifted over time.[156] The New Reli-

---

慧), and relied on a superficial knowledge of science. Zhu Xi, "Ba yi," in *Daxue zhengshi*, 365. Apart from the critical view of foreign knowledge that shines through in this statement, it can be interpreted as a thinly-veiled attack on "national learning" and the philological inquiries of figures such as Zhang Binglin. Zhang's iconoclastic legacy may also explain why Duan Qirui criticized him as well. Duan, "Xu," in *Daxue zhengshi*, 41.

154 The emphasis on Eastern culture can be attributed to Liang Shuming 梁漱溟 (1893–1988) and his book *Dong-Xi wenhua jiqi zhexue* 東西文化及其哲學 (Eastern and western cultures and their philosophies), which was published in 1921. As material development had reached an apex, he claimed, only Eastern (for which read "Chinese") culture could calm the emerging "spiritual unrest" due to its emphasis on harmony and benevolence, manifested in the essence of Confucianism (as he understood it). See Alitto, *The Last Confucian*, 82–125.

155 Zhong, "Xu," in *Daxue zhengshi*, 48–49.

156 There may have also been differing emphases between different institutions associated with the New Religion or even between different branch societies. The Altar of the Sages in Tianjin seems to be the only altar at which commentaries on the classics were transmitted.

gion was generally able to adapt its views to the social and political context. In the 1920s, when the political division of China seemed to be the most pressing problem, they foregrounded a religious universalism that centered on Confucianism but generally stressed the compatibility and comparability of all five of the world religions. This religious universalism reflected the search for "great unity" (*datong*) after World War I, a concept influential both domestically as well as internationally before Japan's invasion in 1937, and matched the strategies employed by other redemptive societies. These strategies changed over time, however, together with the general political context.

The takeover of the Guomindang in 1927 significantly limited the redemptive societies' room for maneuver, but turned the New Religion's promotion of Confucianism into an important bargaining chip. In 1928, together with the Daoyuan and Tongshan she 同善社 (Fellowship United in Goodness), the Wushan she was banned by the new Nationalist government as a superstitious organization.[157] Spirit-writing was severely criticized in the same document, making it practically illegal. In the following years, the members of the New Religion tried to keep a low profile and await better times. They dropped the name Wushan she (which was linked to the ban) altogether, publicly distanced themselves from spirit-writing and instead foregrounded their philanthropic activities while biding their time. Eventually, in 1934, the New Religion applied for re-registration with the authorities. In that context, they adopted a two-pronged strategy: on the one hand, they emphasized their religious universalism, that could be used to foster national unity in light of China's religious diversity. On the other hand, they emphasized the national value of Confucianism, which was compatible with what Edmund Fung calls "a wave of neo-traditionalism [that] swept across the territory under Nationalist control" in the mid-1930s.[158] In February 1934, Chiang Kai-shek 蔣介石 (1887–1975) inaugurated the New Life Movement (Xin shenghuo yundong 新生活運動) that sought to reconstruct Confucianism in the service of modernization and to establish a modern civilized nation, based on Confucian values.[159] As such, the movement was accompanied by activities such as the Respect Confucius and Study the Classics (*zun Kong du jing* 尊孔讀經) movement, initiated by the pro-Nationalist strongmen He Jian 何鍵 (1887–1956) and Chen Jitang 陳濟棠 (1890–1954) in Guangdong.[160]

---

157   Xue, "Guomin Zhengfu Neizhengbu xunling." The New Religion was not mentioned in the document.
158   Fung, "Nationalism and Modernity," 799.
159   Dirlik, "The Ideological Foundations of the New Life Movement," 972–73.
160   Fung, "Nationalism and Modernity," 799.

After the movement began, the New Religion quickly realized that this presented a valuable opportunity to highlight its dedication to Confucian learning and thereby curry favor with the authorities. In August 1934, the then President of the New Religion Wu Peifu and Vice-president Jiang Chaozong wrote a letter to Chiang Kai-shek,[161] in which they stressed that the New Religion had been established to reverse China's moral decline.[162] In the context of the New Life Movement, they argued, the moralistic beliefs of the New Religion could contribute to the establishment of a civilized nation. To make the potential utility for the Nationalist government even more explicit, they added that the New Religion:

> exactly tallies with the current New Life Movement and suitably conforms to its emphasis on filial piety, brotherly love, loyalty, ritual propriety, righteousness, honesty, and sense of shame [which are perceived] as the root of human [life]. Hence, this religion is also fit to provide valuable assistance with expanding the New Life Movement.
>
> 正與現時之新生活運動，首以孝弟忠信禮義廉恥為人之本者適相符合，是本教亦足為擴大新生活運動一有力之援助。[163]

While the leaders of the New Religion mentioned the religious universalism advocated by the New Religion, they particularly highlighted the eminence of Confucianism to facilitate the re-registration with the government. Thus, the application for the re-registration of the New Religion stated that they had "founded a new religion that considers the Confucian teaching as its guiding principle and the other four religions as complementary evidence" (以儒教為綱領，其餘四教為參証，而創一新教).[164] This strategy found fertile ground and Chiang Kai-shek concluded that "[t]he work of this society is truly in accord with the intentions of the New Life Movement" (該會工作實與新生活運動意義符合).[165] The changed ideological context of the 1930s thus opened up a legitimate space for the New Religion, and the registration of its general society was consequently granted.

---

161 The letter was delivered by Zhong Shiming.
162 Gao, *Jiang Zhongzheng dang'an*, 27, 330–32. Note that the use of the name "Wushan she" is completely avoided.
163 Ibid., 330.
164 Beijing Municipal Archives, J002-002-00055, 68.
165 Gao, *Jiang Zhongzheng dang'an*, 27, 334.

The case of the New Religion thereby also provides an insight into the broader fate of redemptive societies during that time. An almost identical strategy was adopted by the Daoyuan, which similarly applied for re-registration in 1935. The organization emphasized its achievements in the field of charity while highlighting its new-found dedication to Confucian culture.[166] As a result, its society in Ji'nan 濟南 was similarly re-registered by the government. During that time, Confucianism was actively promoted by the government and served as a potential source of legitimacy. Even a decidedly universalist group, such as the Daoyuan, therefore came to emphasize the preeminence of Confucianism. At the same time, the limits of Confucianism were also far more clearly delineated during the 1930s. Spirit-writing was considered "superstitious" and there was thus less room for a "religionized" reading of the classics.

7   Conclusion

The New Religion to Save the World was part of a wave of newly-established redemptive societies that delved into various fields of social activism. From the promotion of philanthropic work and the establishment of its new universalist religion, it eventually shifted to an emphasis on Confucianism and its textual heritage. The New Religion's engagement with Confucianism led its followers into the field of "classical learning" (*jingxue*), which was experiencing a revival at the time within new institutional settings outside the previous examination system. Redemptive societies constituted an important driver of this revival and sought to prove the continued relevance of the Confucian classics. The New Religion united Confucian exegesis with its religious practice by using spirit-writing to compose commentaries that were attributed to the Confucian sages. These sages comprised Confucius himself, whose descent to the altar was legitimized in light of the unprecedented social and political crisis of the time. This development also reflected the changed status of Confucius, who was reconfigured as a "savior deity" alongside Lü Dongbin and other divine figures, who had driven the eschatological spirit-writing movement after 1840. By securing the help of the Confucian sages, the New Religion was able to stake a claim to the restoration of the transmission of the Dao (*daotong*). This was certainly appealing to its followers, many of whom had been educated in traditional Confucian institutions and for whom the prospect of communicating with Confucius must have seemed particularly exciting.

---

166   Schumann, "Between Science and Superstition," 405–10.

The New Religion's spirit-written commentaries offered novel interpretations as they were integrated with the organization's broader moral and religious beliefs. As the example of the above-quoted commentary on the *Zhongyong* showed, this allowed a fresh look at passages that might have otherwise remained cryptic. Freed from any fetters of imperial authority, the New Religion was unconcerned about issues of "heterodoxy" or the construction of schools and factions that had dominated Confucian debate after the Song period. Consequently, they felt little hesitation about bringing together Confucius, Mengzi, Zhu Xi, and Lü Dongbin in one and the same commentary. Although such a disregard for orthodoxy was shared by many modern Confucian scholars, their exegetical methods set the New Religion apart. Due to their association with spirit-writing, the commentaries of the New Religion were generally ignored by both representatives and scholars of the "New Confucianism" that arose in the early twentieth century.[167] Confucian "modernizers," however, were never their primary target in the first place. The New Religion, rather, preached to those segments of the population which still deemed the Confucian canon sacred and the existence of Confucian deities conceivable. In this realm of "popular Confucianism," which straddles the divide between the elites and the less-educated classes, the exegetical work of the New Religion had a definite impact. To date, the *Daxue zhengshi* and *Zhongyong zhengshi* (as well as their commentary on the *Book of Changes*) circulate in various editions and reprints, primarily in Taiwan.[168] Probably most significant, in the Chongde College 崇德學院 of the Yiguandao, it is the verified editions of the classics produced by the New Religion that are used, rather than the editions transmitted by Zhu Xi.[169] This attests to the value ascribed to their spirit-written commentaries, at least outside the academic study of Confucianism, and indicates the popularity of a Confucianism that combines a this-worldly emphasis on self-cultivation with "the way of the deities."

By presenting Confucianism as the best way to save the nation, the New Religion's Confucian program also gained a political appeal. Much of this appeal resulted from an emphasis on religion as a moral force that could be invoked to reverse China's ongoing crisis. This emphasis was shared by large swathes of the political elites, which explains the active membership of many politi-

---

167   Although New Confucianism was only in hindsight identified as a distinctive movement. See Makeham, "The Retrospective Creation of New Confucianism."
168   A title search of the catalogue of the National Central Library (Guojia tushuguan 國家圖書館) in Taipei alone yields nine reprints or editions of the *Daxue zhengshi* that were published during the last twenty years.
169   Lin, "Jiushi xinjiao *Yijing zhengshi*," 26–27.

cians and military leaders. While the New Religion never institutionalized their efforts toward classical learning, for example by founding an institute of national learning, their view of Confucianism as an essential cultural asset for the Chinese state provided them with crucial legitimacy during these politically volatile times. The critical views about socialism, communism, and iconoclasm in general, voiced in the publications of the New Religion, indicate that its activities should also be regarded as the formulation of an alternative path of national reform and modernization, apart from the ideas associated with the May Fourth and New Culture Movements. As such, the Confucian program of the New Religion particularly resonated during the 1920s, when the experience of World War I led many Chinese intellectuals to engage in soul-searching and question "Western material modernity."[170] The ability creatively to reinterpret the Confucian classics and highlight their importance for solving the pressing social and political issues of the day, however, made the New Religion's activities appealing beyond the context of its founding and secured its legacy even to date, as the example of the Yiguandao shows. Organizations such as the New Religion, therefore, must be taken seriously as an innovative extension of the Confucian commentarial tradition and an important expression of the reconfiguration of Confucianism post-1911.

Bibliography

Primary Sources

Beijing Jiushi xinjiao zonghui 北京救世新教總會, ed. *Jiushi xinjiao* 救世新教. Beijing: n.p., 1938.

"Beijing Jiushi xinjiao zonghui fashou gezhong shuji jiamubiao 北京救世新教總會發售各種書籍價目表." *Lingxue yaozhi* 靈學要誌 3, no. 11 (1927): n.p.

Beijing Municipal Archives, J002–002–00055.

Chen Wuxi 陳悟息 [Chenglie 丞烈], ed. *Jiushi Xinjiao wenda* 救世新教問答. Beiping [Beijing]: Jiushi xinjiao xuehui, 1932.

Chen Lianji 陳謙紀. "Gezhong zongjiao jiaoyi jie bu chu Rujiao fanwei wei yi shijie qushu bu neng bu lianhe ge jiaoshuo 各種宗教教義皆不出儒教範圍惟以世界趨勢不能不聯合各教說." *Jiushi xunkan* 救世旬刊, no. 13 (1928): 2–4.

Daxue zhengshi 大學證釋. Taizhong: Wentingge tushu youxian gongsi, 2008 [1927].

Duan Huiben 段慧本 [Qirui 祺瑞]. "*Lingxue Yaozhi* xu 靈學要誌叙." *Lingxue yaozhi* 靈學要誌 1, no. 9 (1921): 1–3.

---

170 Schumann, "Protecting the Weak or Weeding out the Unfit?"

"Fu wu jiao jiaozhu xunci 附五教教主訓詞." *Daode zazhi* 道德雜誌 4, no. 4 (1924): 10–11.

Jiushi xinjiao zonghui 救世新教總會, ed. *Jiushi xinjiao jiaogang jiaofa jiaoyi* 救世新教教綱教法教義. Beijing: Wenlanyi yinshuju, 1927.

Jiushi xinjiao zonghui 救世新教總會, ed. *Jiushi xinjiao jiaogang jiaofa huibian* 救世新教教綱教法彙編 [1926]. In *Meiguo Hafo daxue Hafo Yanjing tushuguan cang Minguo wenxian congkan* 美國哈佛大學哈佛燕京圖書館藏民國文獻叢刊, edited by Long Xiangyang 龍向洋, vol. 5, 415–579. Guilin: Guangxi shifan daxue chubanshe, 2011.

"Jishi 記事." *Lingxue yaozhi* 靈學要誌 1, no. 7 (1921): 1–48.

"Jishi 記事." *Lingxue yaozhi* 靈學要誌 2, no. 1 (1922): 1–20.

Gao Sulan 高素蘭, ed. *Jiang Zhongzheng dang'an, 27: Shilüe gaoben, Minguo 23 nian 7 yue (xia) zhi 9 yue (shang)* 蔣中正總統檔案（27）：事略稿本，民國23年7月（下）至9月（上）. Taipei: Guoshiguan, 2007.

"He Xian shuo gui 何仙說鬼." *Lingxue yaozhi* 靈學要誌 2, no. 2 (1922): 7–10.

"Hongjiao Zhenren Liu xu 宏教眞人柳序." *Lingxue yaozhi* 靈學要誌 1, no. 1 (1920): 3–5.

Jiang Huiji 江慧濟 [Chaozong 朝宗]. "*Lingxue yaozhi* xu 靈學要誌叙." *Lingxue yaozhi* 靈學要誌 1, no. 10 (1921): 1–3.

Jiushi xinjiao xuehui 救世新教學會, ed. *Jiushi xinjiao jiaojing* 救世新教教經. 2 vols. n.p.: Jiushi xinjiao xuehui, 1932.

"*Lingxue yaozhi* fenxiaochu 靈學要誌分銷處." *Lingxue yaozhi* 靈學要誌 3, no. 11 (Oct., 1927): n.p.

"Nanping Ji Fo cishan zi jie 南屏濟佛慈善字解." *Lingxue yaozhi* 靈學要誌 2, no. 10 (1924): 20–21.

Qian Xuanji 錢玄機 [Nengxun 能訓]. "*Lingxue yaozhi* xu 靈學要誌叙." *Lingxue yaozhi* 靈學要誌 1, no. 6 (1921): 1–4.

"Taiyi Laozu lun Dao 太乙老祖論道." *Lingxue yaozhi* 靈學要誌 3, no. 8 (1926): 1–2.

Wushan she 悟善社. "*Lingxue yaozhi* yuanqi 靈學要誌緣起." *Lingxue yaozhi* 靈學要誌 1, no. 1 (1920): 1–2.

"Wushan she chengli ji 悟善社成立記." *Lingxue yaozhi* 靈學要誌 1, no. 5 (1921): 1–12.

"Xiantian hunyuan xuanxuan milu jiushi zhenjing 先天渾元玄玄秘籙救世真經." In *Zangwai daoshu* 藏外道書, edited by Hu Daojing 胡道靜 et al., vol. 23, 849–970. Chengdu: Ba-Shu shushe, 1992–94.

Xiong Huixiu 熊悔修. "Gonghe guomin yi zunchong zongjiao shuo 共和國民宜尊崇宗教說." *Jiushi xunkan* 救世旬刊, no. 4 (1927): 1–4.

Xue Dubi 薛篤弼. "Guomin Zhengfu Neizhengbu xunling 國民政府內政部訓令." *Neizheng gongbao* 內政公報 1, no. 7 (1928): 15–16.

"Yao Jichuan zhenren zeng Jiang Huiji xu 姚姬傳眞人贈江慧濟序." *Lingxue yaozhi* 靈學要誌 2, no. 12 (1924): 9–11.

Yu Juechun 于覺純 [Changzao 長藻]. "Shuo zhi luan yu jiao zhi guanxi 說治亂與教之關係." *Jiushi xunkan* 救世旬刊, no. 4 (1927): 4–6.

"Zhisheng Xiantian Laozu yu Wushan zongshe ji Ji'nan Jining Tianjin Jingzhao ge yuan wen 至聖先天老祖諭悟善總社及濟南濟甯天津京兆各院文." *Lingxue yaozhi* 靈學要誌 2, no. 1 (1922): 1–3.

Zhongyong zhengshi 中庸證釋. 4 vols. Tianjin: Jiushi xinjiao hui, 1929.

Secondary Sources

Alitto, Guy S. *The Last Confucian: Liang Shu-ming and the Chinese Dilemma of Modernity.* Berkeley: University of California Press, 1979.

Barrett, T.H. *Li Ao: Buddhist, Taoist, Or Neo-Confucian?* New York: Oxford University Press, 1992.

Berezkin, Rotislav. *The Many Faces of Mulian: The Precious Scrolls of Late Imperial China.* Seattle and London: University of Washington Press, 2017.

Billioud, Sébastien, and Vincent Goossaert. "Confucius and His Texts: A Century of Crisis and Reinventions." In Confucius, *The Analects*, translated by Simon Leys, edited by Michael Nylan, 230–43. New York: W.W. Norton & Company, 2014.

Billioud, Sébastien. *Reclaiming the Wilderness: Contemporary Dynamics of the Yiguandao.* New York: Oxford University Press, 2020.

Brokaw, Cynthia J. *The Ledgers of Merit and Demerit: Social Change and Moral Order in Late Imperial China.* Princeton, NJ: Princeton University Press, 1991.

Chan Nicholas L. 陳煒舜. "Duan Qirui *Zhengdaoju ji* zhi ganshi zongzhi tanlun 段祺瑞《正道居集》之感世宗旨探論." *Zhongguo wenhua yanjiusuo xuebao* 中國文化研究所學報, no. 64 (Jan. 2017): 209–32.

Chan, Wing-tsit. "Chu Hsi's Completion of Neo-Confucianism." In *Chu Hsi: Life and Thought*, 103–38. Hong Kong: Chinese University Press, 1987.

Chen, Hsi-yuan. "Confucianism Encounters Religion: The Formation of Religious Discourse and the Confucian Movement in Modern China." PhD diss., Harvard University, 1999.

Chen, Yong. "Conceptualizing 'Popular Confucianism': The Cases of Ruzong Shenjiao, Yiguan Dao, and De Jiao." *Journal of Chinese Religions* 45, no. 1 (2017): 63–83.

Chen, Zhongping. "The May Fourth Movement and Provincial Warlords: A Reexamination." *Modern China* 37, no. 2 (Mar. 2011): 135–69.

Chung Yun-Ying 鍾雲鶯. "Lun Yiguandao *Xue yong qianyan xinzhu* de zhushu yiyi 論一貫道《學庸淺言新註》的注疏意義." *Taiwan Dongya wenming yanjiu xuekan* 臺灣東亞文明研究學刊 3, no. 1 (Jun. 2006): 163–87.

Chung Yun-Ying 鍾雲鶯. "Minchu Jiushi xinjiao zhi *Daxue zhengshi* yanjiu 民初救世新教之《大學證釋》研究." *Zhongyang daxue renwen xuebao* 中央大學人文學報, no. 35 (Jul. 2008): 83–123.

Clart, Philip. "Confucius and the Mediums: Is There a 'Popular Confucianism'?" *T'oung Pao*, 2nd ser., 89, fasc. 1/3 (2003): 1–38.

Clart, Philip. "Yīguàn Dào." In *Handbook of East Asian New Religious Movements*, edited by Lukas Pokorny and Franz Winter, 429–50. Leiden: Brill, 2018.

de Groot, J.J.M. *Sectarianism and Religious Persecution in China: A Page in the History of Religions*. 2 vols. Amsterdam: Johannes Müller, 1903.

de Korne, John Cornelius. *The Fellowship of Goodness (T'ung shan she): A Study in Contemporary Chinese Religion*. Grand Rapids, MI: self-published manuscript, 1941.

Dirlik, Arif. "The Ideological Foundations of the New Life Movement: A Study in Counterrevolution." *Journal of Asian Studies* 23, no. 4 (Aug. 1975): 945–80.

Duara, Prasenjit. "The Discourse of Civilization and Pan-Asianism." *Journal of World History* 12, no. 1 (Spr. 2001): 99–130.

DuBois, Thomas. "The Salvation of Religion? Public Charity and the New Religions of the Early Republic." In *Charities in the Non-Western World: The Development and Regulation of Indigenous and Islamic Charities*. Edited by Rajeswary A. Brown and Justin Pierce, 115–46. London and New York: Routledge, 2013.

Fan Chun-wu 范純武. "Minchu Ruxue de zongjiaohua: Duan Zhengyuan yu Daode xueshe de ge'an yanjiu 民初入學的宗教化：段正元與道德學社的個案研究." *Minsu quyi* 民俗曲藝, no. 172 (2011): 161–203.

Fan, C[h]unwu. "Confucian 'Religion' in the Early Republican Period: Historical Questions Concerning Duan Zhengyuan and the Morality Society." *Chinese Studies in History* 44, nos. 1–2 (2010–2011): 132–55.

Fuller, Pierre Emery. "Struggling with Famine in Warlord China: Social Networks, Achievements, and Limitations, 1920–21." PhD diss., University of California, Irvine, 2011.

Fung, Edmund S. "Nationalism and Modernity: The Politics of Cultural Conservatism in Republican China." *Modern Asian Studies* 43, no. 3 (May 2009): 777–813.

Fung, Edmund S. *The Intellectual Foundations of Chinese Modernity: Cultural and Political Thought in the Republican Era*. Cambridge, UK: Cambridge University Press, 2010.

Furth, Charlotte. "The Sage as Rebel: The Inner World of Chang Ping-lin." In *The Limits of Change: Essays on Conservative Alternatives in Republican China*, edited by Charlotte Furth, 90–112. Cambridge, MA: Harvard University Press, 1976.

Furth, Charlotte. "Intellectual Change from the Reform Movement to the May Fourth Movement, 1895–1929." In *An Intellectual History of Modern China*, edited by Merle Goldman and Leo Ou-Fan Lee, 13–96. Cambridge UK: Cambridge University Press, 2002.

Gardner, Daniel K. "Principle and Pedagogy: Chu Hsi and the Four Books." *Harvard Journal of Asiatic Studies* 44, no. 1 (Jun. 1984): 57–81.

Gardner, Daniel K. *Zhu Xi's Reading of the* Analects: *Canon, Commentary, and the Classical Tradition*. New York: Columbia University Press, 2003.

Gentz, Joachim. "Religious Diversity in Three Teachings Discourses." In *Religious Diversity in Chinese Thought*, edited by Perry Schmidt-Leukel and Joachim Gentz, 123–40. New York: Palgrave MacMillan, 2013.

Goldin, Paul R. "Xunzi." *Stanford Encyclopedia of Philosophy*, first published July 6, 2018. https://plato.stanford.edu/entries/xunzi/.

Goossaert, Vincent. *The Taoists of Peking, 1800–1949: A Social History of Urban Clerics*. Cambridge, MA and London: Harvard University Press, 2007.

Goossaert, Vincent. "Modern Daoist Eschatology: Spirit-Writing and Elite Soteriology in Late Imperial China." *Daoism: Religion, History and Society* / 道教研究學報：宗教、歷史與社會, no. 6 (2014): 219–46

Goossaert, Vincent, and David A. Palmer. *The Religious Question in Modern China*. Chicago: University of Chicago Press, 2011.

Hartman, Charles. *Han Yü and the T'ang Search for Unity*. Princeton NJ: Princeton University Press, 1986.

Hon, Tze-ki. "National Essence, National Learning, and Culture: Historical Writings in *Guocui xuebao*, *Xueheng*, and *Guoxue jikan*." *Historiography East & West* 1, no. 2 (2003): 242–86.

Johnston, Ian, and Wang Ping. Daxue *and* Zhongyong: *Bilingual Edition*. Hong Kong: Chinese University Press, 2012.

Jorgensen, John. "The Radiant Mind: Zhu Xi and the Chan Doctrine of *Tathāgatagarbha*." In *The Buddhist Roots of Zhu Xi's Philosophical Thought*, edited by John Makeham, 36–121. New York: Oxford University Press, 2018.

Kuhn, Dieter. *Die Republik China von 1912 bis 1937: Entwurf für eine politische Ereignisgeschichte*. 3rd revised and expanded edition. Heidelberg: Ed. Forum, 2007.

Kurtz, Joachim. *The Discovery of Chinese Logic*. Leiden and Boston: Brill, 2011.

Li Ping-i 黎秉一. "Minchu Wushan she *Lingxue yaozhi* jiqi lingxue lunshu yu shijian 民初悟善社《靈學要誌》及其靈學論述與實踐." *Taiwan Dongya wenming yanjiu xuekan* 臺灣東亞文明研究學刊 19, no. 2 (2022): 115–56.

Li Junling 李俊領. "Wu Peifu yu chuantong wenhua 吳佩孚與傳統文化." In *Wu Peifu yanjiu wenji* 吳佩孚研究文集, edited by Tang Xitong 唐錫彤, 248–60. Changchun: Jilin wenshi chubanshe, 2004.

Lin Yen-Ting 林彥廷. "Jiushi xinjiao *Yijing zhengshi* zhi Hetu Louoshu guan 救世新教《易經證釋》之河圖洛書觀." *Fuying tongshi jiaoyu xuekan* 輔英通識教育學刊, no. 3 (Mar. 2016): 25–49.

Liu, Yiming. *Cultivating the Tao: Taoism and Internal Alchemy; The Xiuzhen houbian (ca. 1798)*. Translated by Fabrizio Pregadio. Mountain View, CA: Golden Elixir Press, 2013.

Makeham, John. "The Retrospective Creation of New Confucianism." In *New Confucianism: A Critical Examination*, edited by John Makeham, 25–53. New York: Palgrave Macmillan, 2003.

Makeham, John. "The New *Daotong*." In *New Confucianism: A Critical Examination*, edited by John Makeham, 55–78. New York: Palgrave Macmillan, 2003.

Makeham, John. "The Revival of Guoxue: Historical Antecedents and Contemporary Aspirations." *China Perspectives*, no. 1 (2011): 14–21.

Meyer, Christian. "Der moderne chinesische 'Religionsbegriff' *zongjiao* als Beispiel translingualer Praxis: Rezeption westlicher Religionsbegriffe und -vorstellungen im China des frühen 20. Jahrhunderts." In *Religion in Asien? Studien zur Anwendbarkeit des Religionsbegriffs*, edited by Peter Schalk, 351–92. Uppsala: Uppsala Universitet, 2013.

Mi Sumin 密素敏. "Minguo Wushan she yanjiu 民國悟善社研究." MA thesis, Renmin daxue, 2009.

Mi Sumin 密素敏. "Cong dang'an ziliao kan Minguo shiqi de Jiushi xinjiao 從檔案資料看民國時期的救世新教." *Shijie zongjiao yanjiu* 世界宗教研究, no. 5 (2011): 18–25.

Pregadio, Fabrizio. "*Xiantian* and *houtian*." In *Encyclopedia of Taoism*, edited by Fabrizio Pregadio, vol. 2, 1094–95. Abingdon: Routledge, 2008.

Overmyer, Daniel L. *Precious Volumes: An Introduction to Chinese Sectarian Scriptures from the Sixteenth and Seventeenth Centuries*. Cambridge, MA and London: Harvard University Press, 1999.

Ownby, David. "Redemptive Societies in the Twentieth Century." In *Modern Chinese Religion*, Part II: *1850–2015*. Edited by Vincent Goossaert, Jan Kiely and John Lagerwey, vol. 2, 685–727. Leiden and Boston: Brill, 2016.

Palmer, David A., Paul R. Katz and Chien-chuan Wang. "Introduction: Redemptive Societies in Cultural and Historical Contexts." *Minsu quyi* 民俗曲藝, no. 172 (Jun. 2011): 1–12.

Rowe, William T. *Saving the World: Chen Hongmou and Elite Consciousness in Eighteenth-Century China*. Stanford, CA: Stanford University Press, 2001.

Sang Bing 桑兵. *Wan Qing Minguo de guoxue yanjiu* 晚清民國的國學研究. Shanghai: Shanghai guji chubanshe, 2001.

Schumann, Matthias. "Between Science and Superstition: Spirit-Writing Organizations in Early Republican China and Their Quest for Legitimacy." Unpublished PhD diss., Heidelberg University, 2017.

Schumann, Matthias. "Protecting the Weak or Weeding Out the Unfit? Disaster Relief, Animal Protection, and the Changing Evaluation of Social Darwinism in Japan and China." In *Protecting the Weak in East Asia: Framing Mobilisation and Institutionalisation*, edited by Iwo Amelung, Moritz Bälz, Heike Holbig, Matthias Schumann, and Cornelia Storz, 21–51. London: Routledge, 2018.

Schumann, Matthias. "Redemptive Societies." In *Handbook on Religion in China*. Edited by Stephan Feuchtwang, 184–212. Cheltenham: Edward Elgar Publishing, 2020.

Schumann, Matthias. "Science and Spirit-Writing: The Shanghai Lingxuehui 靈學會 and the Changing Fate of Spiritualism in Republican China." In *Text and Context in the Modern History of Chinese Religions: Redemptive Societies and Their Sacred Texts*, edited by Philip Clart, David Ownby, and Chien-chuan Wang, 126–72. Leiden: Brill, 2020.

Shi Lu 施 陸 [Erik Schicketanz]. "Minguo shiqi jiujie sixiang yu zhengzhi lunshu: yi

Wushan she yu Jiushi xinjiao wei zhongxin 民國時期救劫思想與政治論述—以悟善社與救世新教為中心." In *Fuluan wenhua yu minzhong zongjiao guoji xueshu yantaohui lunwenji* 扶鸞文化與民眾宗教國際學術研討會論文集, edited by Fan Chun-wu 范純武, 369–92. Taipei: Boyang wenhua, 2020.

Shun, Kwong-loi. "Zhu Xi's Moral Psychology." In *Dao Companion to Neo-Confucian Philosophy*, edited by John Makeham, 177–95. Heidelberg: Springer, 2010.

Su Shengwen 蘇生文. "'Shandong wenti' zhong de tielu wenti yu Wusi yundong 《山東問題》中的鐵路問題與五四運動." *Sanxia daxue xuebao* 三峽大學學報 32, no. 1 (2010): 87–91.

Tay, Wei Leong. "Secularization as Sacralization: Religion and the Formation of Modern Chinese Nationalism and Nation-State, 1840–1939." PhD diss., University of Oxford, 2019.

Thompson, Roger R., *China's Local Councils in the Age of Constitutional Reform, 1898–1911*. Cambridge, MA & London: Harvard University Press, 1995.

Wagner, Rudolf G. "The Philologist as Messiah: Kang Youwei's 1902 *Commentary on the Confucian Analects*." In *Disciplining the Classics: Altertumswissenschaft als Beruf*, edited by Glenn W. Most, 143–68. Göttingen: Vandenhoeck & Ruprecht, 2002.

Wagner, Rudolf G. "The *Zhouli* as the Late Qing Path to the Future." In *The Rituals of Zhou in East Asian History: Statecraft and Classical Learning*, edited by Benjamin A. Elman and Martin Kern, 359–87. Leiden and Boston: Brill, 2010.

Waldron, Arthur. "Warlord: Twentieth-Century Chinese Understandings of Violence, Militarism, and Imperialism." *American Historical Review* 96, no. 4 (1991): 1073–1100.

Wang Chien-chuan 王見川. "Tongshan she zaoqi de tedian ji zai Yunnan de fazhan, 1912–1937: jian tan qi yu 'luantan,' 'Rujiao' de guanxi 同善社早期的特點及在雲南的發展：兼談其與「鸞壇」、「儒教」的關係." *Minsu quyi* 民俗曲藝, no. 172 (2011): 127–59.

Wang, Chien-chuan 王見川. "Popular Groups Promoting 'The Religion of Confucius' in the Chinese Southwest and Their Activities since the Nineteenth Century (1840–2013): An Observation Centered on Yunnan's Eryuan County and Environs." In *The Varieties of Confucian Experience: Documenting a Grassroots Revival of Tradition*, edited by Sébastien Billioud, 90–121. Leiden: Brill, 2018.

Wilson, Thomas A. *Genealogy of the Way: The Construction and Uses of the Confucian Tradition in Late Imperial China*. Stanford, CA: Stanford University Press, 1995.

Yoshitoyo Yoshioka 吉岡義豐. *Zhongguo minjian zongjiao gaishuo* 中國民間宗教概說. Translated by Yu Wanju 余萬居. Taipei: Huayu chubanshe, 1986.

Yuan, Zheng. "The Status of Confucianism in Modern Chinese Education, 1901–49, A Curricular Study." In *Education, Culture, and Identity in Twentieth-Century China*, edited by Glen Peterson, Ruth Hayhof and Yongling Lu, 193–216. Ann Arbor: University of Michigan Press, 2004 [2001].

CHAPTER 11

Spirit-Writing and the Daoyuan's Gendered Teachings

Xia Shi

1 Introduction

1.1 *The Daoyuan*

Originating around 1916 in a northeastern Shandong 山東 town as an informal group of spirit-writing enthusiasts, most of whom were county military commanders and magistrates, the Daoyuan (School of the Way) would later become a major indigenous religious and charitable organization in Republican China (1912–49). In 1921, following the organizational model of Tongshan she 同善社 (Fellowship of Goodness), another of what historian Prasenjit Duara calls "redemptive societies,"[1] and adopting their meditation technique, a group of forty eight disciples formally established the Daoyuan in Ji'nan 濟南, the provincial capital, which became the "mother society" (*mushe* 母社, the founding branch).[2] As a religious organization, it drew upon China's sectarian and syncretic popular religious traditions while explicitly promoting a universalist vision by incorporating the Five Teachings of Laozi, Confucius, Buddha, Jesus, and Muhammad, although their members mainly practiced a combination of Confucianism, Buddhism, and Daoism.[3] Their presence was especially prevalent in Shandong, Hebei 河北, Anhui 安徽, Jiangsu 江蘇 provinces, and Northeast China.[4] Later, their leaders established a separate charitable wing, the Shijie Hongwanzi hui 世界紅卍字會 (Red Swastika Society, hereafter RSS),

---

1 Duara, "Of Authenticity and Woman," 343. Duara's use of the term "redemptive societies" is not without drawbacks. Paul Katz points out that this term "runs the risk of creating a false distinction between different religious groups that shared similar values and practices." See Katz, *Religion in China and Its Modern Fate*, 184, fn 72.
2 Goossaert and Palmer, *The Religious Question*, 101.
3 There were some Christians in the Daoyuan. For example, the American missionary Gilbert Reid (1857–1927) was an important member, and also an honorary president of the Worldwide Morality Society (Wanguo daode hui 萬國道德會). In addition, Wang Zhengting 王正廷 (1882–1961), a prominent Christian and also ambassador to the U.S and Foreign Minister of the Nationalist Government from 1928–31, was also a member.
4 Sung, "Minguo chunian Zhongguo zongjiao tuanti," 249.

based on the belief that spiritual cultivation alone was incomplete and inadequate. In addition to sitting meditation, charity should also be an inseparable part of self-cultivation and the *Dao*'s outer manifestation. Practically speaking, RSS was also established to meet the urgent social demands for relief work in an era with unusually frequent natural disasters and wars, and to fight against the expansion of Christianity in China, whose relief work in disaster-stricken areas often resulted in mass conversions, thus expanding foreigners' spheres of influence.[5] The RSS soon became the public face of the Daoyuan and their involvement in charity far exceeded that of other redemptive societies, such as Tongshan she and Zailijiao 在理教 (Teaching of the Abiding Principle). Moreover, compared to the Wanguo daode hui 萬國道德會 (Worldwide Morality Society), which focused primarily on building charity schools for the poor, RSS's charitable engagement was more comprehensive and of broad coverage, ranging from disaster, war, and poverty relief (including burying corpses), to setting up schools, orphanages, and hospitals.

Labeled as mere "superstition" by Chinese nationalist regimes, and largely overlooked by scholars until the late 1990s, the Daoyuan commanded a large following in cities before it was severely attacked and finally eradicated after CCP took over mainland China in 1949. It had attracted about 30,000 members nationwide by 1927, and seven to ten million followers a decade later.[6] During the Sino-Japanese war, it was China's largest charity.[7] Scholars have generally agreed that merchants, local officials, and the gentry tended to be the top three Daoyuan constituencies, with merchants on average occupying half of all memberships.[8] These men probably became members in their pursuit of religious merit and individual salvation rather than from a desire for personal fame.[9] Due to their political power and social connections, government officials and military men were crucial to the organization but were only allowed to hold honorable positions when the RSS adopted strict regulations in 1927 forbidding incumbent political officials from serving as leaders, in order to maintain an apolitical position as a charitable organization. The Daoyuan's powerful membership rolls enabled the organization to carry out relief work with little interference from local society. Their high government connections, together with their charitable reputation, helped them survive waves of anti-superstition campaigns during the Nationalist period, despite it being tem-

---

5 Sung, "Shishen shangren yu cishan," 141–79.
6 Duara, "Of Authenticity and Woman," 344.
7 Goossaert and Palmer, *The Religious Question*, 79.
8 Li, "Minguo Daoyuan ji Shijie Hongwanzihui," 108.
9 Sung, "Cishan yu gongde," 1.

porarily banned in 1928 as a "superstitious organization" (*mixin jiguan* 迷信機關) by the Nationalist Government.

The existing research on the Daoyuan has focused on the organization's nature and their male leadership or their concrete disaster relief activities.[10] However, few scholars have examined the female members of the Daoyuan, who often joined their husbands in order to practice spiritual cultivation and engage in public charity work. We also know little about the Daoyuan's gendered teachings and how these fit into the organization's overall vision of religion and charity.[11] Therefore, in this article, I chose to investigate the women's branches of the Daoyuan and their gendered teachings for women through spirit-writing. Most of the sources come from Shandong province, since this was not only where the Daoyuan originated, but also where it had the most women's branches as well as the most active and thus best-documented branches.

As this article will show, most Daoyuan women were domestic-focused, middle-aged or older married women, without a modern education. Many of them were the wives and concubines of merchants, from non-illustrious family backgrounds, and barely literate. As devout members, they regularly received exhortations from various deities through the Daoyuan's ritual of spirit-writing (*fuji* 扶乩) and were supposed to follow these instructions in their everyday life to guide their self-cultivation. Through a textual analysis of these spirit-writing texts, I will demonstrate how this powerful medium was used to give authoritative instructions to the female members on three major realms: gender doctrines, the value of charity, and admonitions against superstition. Furthermore, it situates these deities' exhortations in the context of the social and cultural changes of early twentieth century China to investigate their broad implications.

1.2   *Spirit-Writing*

The Daoyuan, as an organization, placed a high value on communication between humans and deities. It often issued exhortations that were acquired through the important ritual practice of spirit-writing at their different branches, and all members were supposed to obey these. Spirit-writing was an important method of divination for worshippers seeking practical aid and

---

10   For example, see Li, *Shijie Hongwanzi hui jiqi cishan shiye yanjiu*; Sung, "Minguo chunian Zhongguo zongjiao tuanti"; and Sung, "Shishen shangren yu cishan."

11   An exception would be Li and Guo, "Minguo Nüdaode she," 74–75. However, this article mostly unearths some basic historical information of the women's branches of the Daoyuan, based on the limited sources they have accessed.

advice from the deities through the planchette in ancient times. Lay Daoists in China had long used it to seek advice from the Immortals on alchemical cultivation, and it later became popular even among the gentry during the Ming and Qing period.[12] Their continued popularity in modern China constituted a striking example of how some Chinese elites made the Chinese tradition more respectable by appropriating the category of "science." By the early twentieth century, spirit-writing had unexpectedly gained a new layer of scientific authority, after Chinese overseas students noticed their connection with some contemporary Western (mostly French and British) methods of spirit communication, such as the Western academic field of "psychical research" on paranormal phenomena. These students imported the field of *lingxue* 靈學 (Spiritualism) to China by way of Japan, setting up dozens of associations in Shanghai and other large cities.[13] Several redemptive societies, such as the Daoyuan, realized that *lingxue* provided a scientific discourse that could be applied to Chinese spirit-writing and eagerly adopted it.[14] In this way, they could claim either that their practices were aligned with modern scientific standards, or that the Chinese tradition was already compatible with, or even superior to, Western science.

To date, we still know little about the gendered dimension of spirit-writing in Chinese history, even though the origin of spirit-writing was crucially tied to a divination cult devoted to *Zigu* 紫姑, the goddess of the latrine.[15] We know that, during the pre-literate phase of this tradition, there was far greater involvement on the part of women and girls than male literati.[16] However, in later centuries, women's participation was rarely seen in the existing records. According to Richard Smith, in Qing times, women did not normally engage in spirit-writing.[17] Daniel Overmyer notes that, by the nineteenth century, some *baojuan* 寶卷 (Precious scrolls) texts were produced specifically with women in mind, and women had a role in their preaching and distribution.[18] In this vol-

12   Goossaert and Palmer, *The Religious Question*, 95.
13   Ibid., 103. About *lingxue*, see Schumann, "Science and Spirit-Writing."
14   For the Daoyuan's connection to *lingxue*, see Chen, "Minguo xin zongjiao de zhiduhua chengzhang," 42.
15   It seems that, by the Song period, Zigu was considered a talented writer and artist. During the Qing period, however, she seems to have reverted to her Tang role as "a pre-literate oracle." See Smith, *Fortune-Tellers and Philosophers*, 230. For a focused study on Zigu and spirit writing, see Boltz, "On the Legacy of Zigu." See also the contributions by Hu Jiechen and Elena Valussi in this volume.
16   Jordan and Overmyer, *The Flying Phoenix*, 38–39.
17   Smith, *Fortune-Tellers and Philosophers*, 230.
18   Overmyer, "Values in Chinese Sectarian Literature."

ume, Daniel Burton-Rose examines the lack of female immortals on the early Qing literati altar of Peng Dingqiu in contrast to their prominence on late Ming literati spirit-writing altars. We also see that Elena Valussi's article explores the intimate interaction between a female divinity and a female audience by analyzing the spirit-written texts of female alchemy during the Qing period. Both studies provide rare, important perspectives that enrich our understanding of the gendered dimension of spirit-writing in the late imperial period. By the time that Daoyuan started to use spirit-writing to attract members in the early twentieth century, we do not see any sources suggesting that any of their spirit-writing hands (*fujishou* 扶乩手) were female. In other words, the ritual was completely controlled by trained men. This may have been for the sake of efficacy (*ling* 靈), since women were often viewed as pollutants. Before the ritual began, even male spirit-writing specialists routinely engaged in purification rituals.[19] Consequently, Daoyuan women could only be observers and passive recipients of the resulting sacred messages; it thus restricted their subjective experience of religious agency.

However, the practice of spirit-writing did leave behind some valuable detailed documents on Daoyuan's gender doctrines and charitable teachings for women, which are crucial to our understanding of how women—even those within conservative religious organizations—were able actively to engage with public charitable activities. These instructions were often later compiled and published in Daoyuan's journals, such as *Daode zazhi* 道德雜誌 (Morality magazine) and *Daode yuekan* 道德月刊 (Morality monthly). In other words, most of the social guidelines provided for women by the Daoyuan were actually a result of spirit-writing; that is, direct messages from deities. However, the Daoyuan did try to control the spirit-written messages of individual branches by requiring these to be sent to the highest institutional level for checking and approval. We may assume, therefore, that these published instructions represent the wider vision of the Daoyuan.[20]

When the intended audience was female, these exhortations from a multitude of deities were often written in colloquial language, making them easier for less educated women to understand. This manner of exhorting women directly through deities, rather than through the male leaders of the Daoyuan,

---

19 Smith, *Fortune-Tellers and Philosophers*, 226.
20 Li Guangwei also pointed out that the spirit-written messages which the Daoyuan received, among other things (including the Daoyuan's classics), needed first to be discussed among the members collectively. Only after it had been agreed that these messages were correct and feasible would they be implemented. See Li and Guo, "Minguo Daoyuan fuji huodong."

made their teachings especially authoritative and powerful, thereby increasing the chance of them being followed and executed by devout women in their daily lives. The mysticism involved in the ritual of spirit-writing could create a highly religious, even awe-inspiring atmosphere for those present, unmatchable by any regular means of propaganda. It had the power to vastly increase the appeal of the Daoyuan and facilitate the process of conversion, especially among women seeking spiritual guidance on life's challenges—from domestic strife to disease and death.

1.3   Gender and Religion in Republican China

Historian Xiaofei Kang has noted that the existing scholarship on women and religion in Republican China still contains many gaps compared with the "much more developed and integrated scholarship on women, gender and religion of premodern China, of Taiwan, Hong Kong and overseas Chinese communities, and of post-Mao China."[21] There remains the issue of what she calls "double blindness;" that is, scholars of gender studies tend to neglect the importance of religion, while the field of religious studies fails to pay adequate attention to the gender issue. Among the limited works we have, scholars have studied prominent Chinese religious women's active engagement with the public sphere through Christian schools, hospitals, and social service organizations, such as the Young Women's Christian Association (YWCA) and Women's Christian Temperance Union (WCTU).[22] Others participated in Buddhist schools and organizations, and Daoist groups in urban centers.[23] Clearly, as domestic seclusion was increasingly viewed as a backward social practice, an increasing number of Chinese women engaged with various religious activities beyond the confines of the home, although we still know little about ordinary women's involvement in redemptive societies.[24]

In terms of gender and religious ideology, historians of Chinese religions have noticed that the major Buddhist and Daoist reformers in the Republican period. such as Taixu 太虛 (1890–1947), Yinguang 印光 (1862–1940), Chen Hailiang 陳海亮 (1910–1983), and Chen Yingning 陳攖寧 (1880–1969), reinterpreted

---

21   Kang, "Women, Gender and Religion," 2.
22   For example, see Kwok, *Chinese Women and Christianity*; Littell-Lamb, "Going Public"; and Ma, "Zhonghua Jidujiao funü jiezhi xiehui."
23   For example, see Li, "Fojiao Lianshe yu nüxing zhi shehui canyu"; Liu, "Women and their Daoist Inner Alchemical Practices"; Liu, *Daoist Modern*; and Valussi, "Beheading the Red Dragon."
24   Women's activities in the Wanguo daode hui have been relatively better studied than in other redemptive societies. See Luo, Qiu, and Zhou, *Cong Dongbei dao Taiwan*; and Duara, "Of Authenticity and Woman."

their religious traditions and attempted to incorporate values of gender equality into their discourses in response to the challenges of modernity.[25] However, we still lack an adequate understanding on how redemptive societies adjusted to the new changes of the era regarding this aspect. Prasenjit Duara is the only scholar to examine the personal narratives of "middle class women" in the Worldwide Morality Society, showing how some of them used the very gender ideology that constrained them to empower themselves, carving out a space for their public activities and financial independence. This empowerment was achieved by, according to Duara, "the continued usage of an older language that has come to signify a different, newer meaning" in the women's own interpretations.[26]

This article intends to improve our understanding of the gendered teachings of another leading redemptive society, the Daoyuan, as transmitted through the practice of spirit-writing. It first explicates the sacred texts aimed at women and demonstrates that these spirit-written messages reconstructed the traditional gender norms to accommodate the challenges of modern gender ideologies. In particular, many gender-subjugating contents were removed, while the texts' basic traditionalistic outlook was maintained by essentializing gender difference based on women's supposedly "natural" abilities. This close textual analysis reveals what the current scholarship on these religious organizations fails to address: the assumption that these groups' gender ideologies were basically the same traditional and conservative norms as found in the imperial period, and that only through the women's own interpretations did they acquire room to maneuver.[27] Therefore, what the Daoyuan did with regard to their gender ideology suggests the existence of a far broader reformist social trend in gender issues within the Chinese religious sphere in the early twentieth century than has been previously assumed.

The gods' exhortations to the female members of the Daoyuan represent a view that differed from those of the radical modernizers regarding the Chinese gender traditions in both the past and future. In this view, the Chinese gendered tradition was not an outdated, stagnant obstacle to modernity that could become incompatible with modern scientific principles. The deities, just like some major Buddhist and Daoist reformers of this period, saw the possibility of a continuous vitality and validity in traditional gender doctrines, with some necessary changes that would allow the tradition to evolve in step with the

---

25 Katz, "Chen Hailiang's Vision of Buddhist Family Life"; and Valussi, "Gender as a Useful Category."
26 Duara, "Of Authenticity and Woman," 359.
27 Ibid.

evolution of the women who embodied the tradition. Their basic strategies for reinventing the Chinese gender traditions were compatible with the Daoyuan leaders' other attempts to modernize this religious organization. Both sought to find a respectable position for the Chinese tradition within the emerging global modernity.

Another important issue that historians of modern China have studied is the relationship between gender and "superstition." The intensification of the interactions with the West in the late Qing and early Republican eras allowed progressive intellectuals to introduce two clear-cut categories of "religion" (*zongjiao* 宗教) and "superstition" (*mixin* 迷信) to China via Japan. To avoid being classified as superstitious and thus banned, Chinese Buddhists, Daoists, Confucians, and Muslims attempted, with varying degrees of success, to reorganize their groups following the model of the Christian church, the paradigm of a modern religious organization, but these groups represented, according to historians of Chinese religions Vincent Goossaert and David Palmer, only "the tip of the iceberg of Chinese culture."[28] Many traditional popular cults, practices, and beliefs simply could not be fitted into the new category of "religion". Instead, they were synthesized and institutionalized by their leaders into what historian Prasenjit Duara calls "redemptive societies," in reference to their common project of saving both individuals and the world.[29] Unsurprisingly, many of these redemptive societies, with their large popular following, repeatedly aroused suspicion from both the modernizing state and progressive intellectuals as backward superstitious organizations. To combat this widespread public perception, their leadership made conscious attempts to present a positive image of their organization as both scientific and religious in nature.

Xiaofei Kang has noticed that, since the beginning of the twentieth century, many Chinese elites had regularly attached the label of "superstition" to the trope of "traditional Chinese woman," advocating the necessity and urgency for these women to be educated, saved, and transformed in order to enhance China's modernization process.[30] Elena Valussi argues that, as Chinese religion became secularized and reconceptualized, the dichotomy between religion and superstition became gendered.[31] As we will see in this article, the Daoyuan's spirit-written texts shared many progressive intellectuals' distrustful and condescending views regarding women's unguided spiritual beliefs

---

28   Goossaert and Palmer, *The Religious Question in Modern China*, 91.
29   Duara, "Of Authenticity and Woman," 343.
30   Kang, "Women, Gender and Religion," 15.
31   Valussi, "Men Built Religion," 34–35. I thank the author for sharing the article with me.

and practices. Believing that women were more superstitious than men, the Daoyuan frequently used spirit-writing to exhort their female members in particular to stay away from traditionally popular religious activities such as visiting temples and burning incense.

The strong anti-superstition atmosphere of early twentieth century China, and hence the constant need to distance themselves from superstition, propelled the Daoyuan to use charity as an alternative channel to fulfill their members' pursuit of religious merit for personal salvation. This article shows how the Daoyuan used their spirit-writing to promote the value of charity to women. These spirit-written messages not only applied the traditionally popular concept of "women's benevolence" to empower women, but also used Buddhist theories of rebirth and retribution and the pursuit of religious merit as enticement. This effort correspondingly resulted in charity becoming a major mechanism for Daoyuan women to express their devotion and one of the most important channels for them to engage legitimately with the religious realm beyond the confines of home.

2 The Women's Branches of the Daoyuan

Like their male branches, the women's branches of the Daoyuan had two wings. In the *Nüdaode she* 女道德社 (Women's Morality Society, hereafter the WMS), the female members practiced spiritual self-cultivation; in the Shijie funü hongwanzi hui 世界婦女紅卍字會 (Women's Red Swastika Society, hereafter WRSS), they engaged in charity work, which was regarded as an inseparable part of self-cultivation. Members of the charitable branch had to belong to the religious branch as well. Usually, a religious branch was established first, followed by the charitable branch. Sometimes, in small areas, the religious branch served both functions. Approximately ten big cities, such as Beijing, Shanghai, and Ji'nan, had separately organized charitable branches. In smaller locations, the charitable activities were usually operated in the name of the Women's Morality Society or under the leadership of the local (male) RSS.[32] Essentially, the WMS and the WRSS were united, and the two names were often used interchangeably.

The teachings of the WMS emphasized that the most important goal in life was self-cultivation.[33] The guidelines of the WMS specifically stated its goals as being to "grasp the truth of the *Scripture of the Polar Singularity*, implement the

---

32 Guo, "Ji'nan Daoyuao ji Hongwanzihui," 22.
33 "Cimin pusa lin Shanghai Daoyuan," 21.

true essence of five religions, expound the Great Way, and promote women's virtues" (以參悟太乙真經、貫徹五教真諦、闡明大道、發揚女德為宗旨).[34] Each member had her own religious name (*daoming* 道名), said to be given by the gods through spirit-writing. In addition to studying scripture, the members also spent time studying the techniques of sitting meditation. According to the general regulations of the WMS, each society needed a room for "certifying achievement" (*zhenggong shi* 證功室), where members could obtain certificates reflecting their levels of achievement in self-cultivation, and another room for "reflecting on mistakes" (*xingguo shi* 省過室), where members could regularly go to list the time and frequency of their "mistakes." Illiterate women were allowed to draw one black line under the calendar's date to represent one mistake, rather than writing down the character of "making mistakes" (*fanguo* 犯過), as was the custom among the literate members.[35]

Shandong province had the most women's branches of the Daoyuan, as well as its most active branches. The first women's branch of the Daoyuan was probably established in Ji'nan in 1922, only a year after the establishment of the first men's branch in the same city. It is said that the original motivation was to commemorate the wives and mothers of several major Daoyuan leaders. Around 1924, within Shandong, eight other branches were established. Regarding its charity wing, the WRSS, the first branch was probably established around 1926 in Beijing, where its male branch also originated.[36] The Ji'nan WMS went on to become the national "mother society" in 1931. The WMS in Ji'nan and Qingdao (established around 1930) were especially active and left behind the most source material.

The WMS's expansion usually began at the city level and then at the provincial level, probably through merchants' social and business networks. The Daoyuan generally required that there be over 30 women members in order to open a new branch. By the end of 1924, about 43 women's branches had opened nationwide. By 1927, the overall number of women's branches had increased to 51. After the Nationalists took control, the women's branches seemed to have developed more quickly and steadily, despite the official hostility; by the end of 1935, there were 148 branches nationwide.[37] In 1935, the WMS held a twelve-year anniversary national conference in Ji'nan. The records of this conference are

---

34 "Nüdaode she shegang yu banshi xize." The Scripture of the Polar Singularity was transmitted by the Daoyuan through spirit-writing in the winter of 1921. On this see, DuBois, "The Salvation of Religion?"
35 "Nüdaode she shegang yu banshi xize."
36 Li and Guo, "Minguo Nüdaode she."
37 "Shilüe," 1–13.

among the society's few sources that remain extant today. Few materials remain from the post-1935 development of the women's branches of the Daoyuan.

The general atmosphere in which the women's branches of the Daoyuan originated and throve was a conservative one. Shandong Province was known to be far more conservative than many other Chinese areas in the early twentieth century.[38] Domestic-oriented women seemed to be the major constituency of the women's branches of the Daoyuan in Shandong. Most of these women seemed to be the relatives of male members of the Daoyuan. This was sometimes the case for members of the YWCA and Young Men's Christian Association (YMCA) as well, such as James Yen (1893–1990) and his wife Alice Hui,[39] but it appears to have happened less frequently than in the case of the Daoyuan and was seldom singled out for emphasis. The family connection was especially obvious for the leaders of the WMS, whose relationships with the male members were emphasized in Daoyuan records as an important part of the women's identities. For example, the catalogue of leaders and staff of the Qingdao WMS lists the titles for various positions, the date when individual women became members, and the date they assumed a given position, with a final category noting whose wives (*qi* 妻), concubines (*qie* 妾), and daughters (*nü* 女) they were. However, there are no data indicating the respective percentage of wives, concubines, and daughters that made up the female membership of the Daoyuan in the different regions.[40]

Middle-aged and older women (by contemporary Chinese standards) composed most of the membership of the WMS in Shandong province, although the official regulations state that it would accept any member who was truly devoted to the *Dao* 道—regardless of race, nationality, religion, or social class.[41] For example, the name list for the Qingdao WRSS includes 59 members in 1934, of whom only 18% were under 30 years old; over 62% of the members were aged 30–39 years; and 20% were aged 50–69 years. Similarly, the Ji'nan WRSS had about 37 female staff in 1930, of whom only 3% were under 30 years old; over 59% were aged 30–49 years; 38% were aged 50–69 years.[42] These ages

---

38   For example, the foreign secretaries of local YWCAs in the late 1920s often pointed out the conservativeness of Shandong, as evidenced by the large number of women with bound feet and many young married women remaining at home. See *"Green Year" Supplement* 14, January 4, 1928, 17.
39   On the YWCA in China, see Littell-Lamb, "Going Public." On the YMCA in China, see Keller, "Making Model Citizens."
40   "Qingdao Nüdaode she zhixiu gefang renzhi nianxian."
41   Considering the early marriage age and shorter life expectancy of Chinese women back then, a woman above the age of 30 was often regarded as middle aged.
42   "Ji'nan Funü Hongwanzi hui zhiyuanbiao."

suggest that the majority of Daoyuan women were already mothers or grandmothers and had not received a modern education, if any. Beyond Shandong province, few records remain to show the membership's composition in other regions.[43]

Regardless of regional variations related to membership, the encouragement of male family members probably played a key role in encouraging women from diverse locations to become members. Daoyuan teachings assert that involving female family members in practicing self-cultivation, together with their men, fulfills the classic Chinese principles of *yin* (female) and *yang* (male), complementing each other and producing mutually reinforcing and ameliorative effects. According to one spirit-writing instruction from the Lotus Sage (Liantaisheng 蓮台聖), the highest deity of the WMS: "One *yin* and one *yang* is the Way, if [there is] only male but without female, then *yin* and *yang* will not be balanced, and the truth of the Great Way will be lost. Then how can we even speak of expanding [the society]?" (一陰一陽為之道，若有男無女，則陰陽有偏，以失大道之真，又何以言擴展乎).[44] Thus, women's participation was believed to be beneficial for the self-cultivation of their male family members (and *vice versa*, although this seems to have been less emphasized). In contrast to the YWCA and YMCA, the family rather than the individual was regarded within the Daoyuan as the more crucial unit for religious and charitable practices. Beyond the common practice of praying for blessings for family members, each individual's personal religious practice was believed capable of strengthening the other family members' cultivation—reaching back to previous generations. Consequently, women's engagement with the Daoyuan was not only allowed but highly encouraged by their male relatives. Because the family unit commonly participated together, going to the Daoyuan did not require that women to engage independently with the public sphere, a fact that could both facilitate and limit women's public life.

The women's wing of the Daoyuan was never officially registered with the government as an independent organization under the name of either the WMS

---

43   I was able to locate only a staff list for the Department of Temporary Relief and Service (*linshi jiuji fuwu bu* 臨時救濟服務部) of the Shanghai Women's branches of the Red Swastika Society. It was staffed with modern-educated women as secretaries. The backgrounds of the staff of the Shanghai women's branch were probably quite exceptional and did not represent the majority of the women's branches nationwide. Shanghai was, after all, the most cosmopolitan city in Republican China. More importantly, the coincidental connections through one member's personal social networks that shaped the membership components of the Shanghai branch of WRSS could not be easily replicated elsewhere.

44   "Si yue ba ri Liansheng xun."

or the WRSS. It remained permanently affiliated to the Daoyuan, which contrasted with the independent nature of certain contemporary women's organizations, such as the YWCA (from the YMCA) in China. The 1931 guidelines for the RSS explained that, if both the men's and women's branches registered using the name "Red Swastika", there would then be two separate organizations, which was "inappropriate" and "against propriety (*li* 禮)." In addition, they stated: "Our [Chinese] society is currently facing the tide of reform; applying for separate registrations would be too eye-catching" (況值此維新潮流正盛之際，特予提出立案殊嫌觸目).[45] These concerns, on the one hand, indicate the organization's conservative nature and possibly its fear of attracting too much unnecessary public attention, since it already operated under cover as a charitable organization during the Nationalist regime. On the other hand, this decision may have also been due to its leaders' adherence to the traditional theoretical principle of gender relations: *yin*'s subordinate position to *yang*. This implied that the women's wing should be subordinate to that of the men and should focus mainly on the inner rather than the outer sphere.[46] Official registration would require that female members to engage in direct interactions with the government and the public in general, in contradiction with these ideals. The organizational dependence of the women's branches limited the scope of women's engagement with the public world while offering a convenient way for the male members to supervise women's public activities.

The highest deity of the Daoyuan was Laozu 老祖 (the Great Progenitor), and his approval was to be sought regarding life's most important matters. He presided over the Five Teachers (Confucius, Laozi, the Buddha, Jesus, and Muhammad). On the surface, Laozu represented the five major religions, but appeared, in fact, to have been mainly a Confucian deity. As Laozu himself allegedly said, "By *Dao*, I mean the *Dao* of Confucius and Mencius" (吾之所謂道者, 亦即孔孟之道也).[47] The WMS had its own hierarchical system of deities, each charged with a specific duty. Of the most popular deities, most were of Buddhist origin, except for Meng Mu 孟母 (Mencius' Mother), a typical Confucian deity. This parallels Duara's observation that many women in the Wanguo daode hui, another leading redemptive society of the time, were devout Buddhists who joined the society because they found its teachings compatible with their Buddhist faith.[48]

---

45 "Zhonghua zonghui tichu Hongwanzihui zhangcheng."
46 *Daoci wenda*.
47 Lü, *Daoci gaiyao*, 32.
48 Duara, "Of Authenticity and Woman," 353.

As mentioned above, the highest deity in charge of the WMS was a Buddhist deity named the Lotus Sage (Liantaisheng) but we have little information about her. Our limited sources suggest that she often descended to the altar from major famous Buddhist mountains, such as Mount Putuo 普陀 and Luojia 落伽. Moreover, around 1933, the Wuhan branch of the WMS received a spirit-written message which instructed them to send a photographer to Hongshan 洪山 to take her picture. It was said that the received image was "extremely clear" (極為清晰). Afterwards, the WMS branches nationwide were instructed via spirit-writing to make copies of her image to worship at their local branches.[49] However, I have not seen her spirit photograph in our sources. Below the Lotus Sage, at least ten other deities took charge of different spheres; three were variations of the Bodhisattva of Compassion (Cimin pusa 慈憫菩薩) and had the word *ci* 慈 (compassion or charity) in their titles, such as the Bodhisattva of Spreading Compassion (Hongci pusa 弘慈菩薩), and the Bodhisattva of the Light of Compassion (Ciguang pusa 慈光菩薩). In addition to the major deities, local areas sometimes worshipped regionally-specific deities. The regulations of the WMS required that every society displayed statues of Laozu, the Five Teachers, the Lotus Sage, and the ten Bodhisattvas. Overall, the Chinese religious tradition that the Daoyuan represented is a synthesis of Confucianism, Buddhism, and Daoism, without clear lines of demarcation.

Apart from the deities mentioned above, other popular deities, such as Weituo 韋陀, Jifo 濟佛, and Nanhai Dashi 南海大士, also sometimes offered Daoyuan women exhortations through spirit-writing.[50] However, our sources on the WMS rarely mention how these deities descended. The majority of the records on the WMS focus on the content of the spirit-writing, rather than the practice itself. We know only that, during the "Sand Opening" (*kaisha* 開沙) ceremony to acquire the gods' instructions, both men and women would visit

---

49   "Liantaisheng Hongshan xianxiang." The practice of taking a picture of a deity at that time was often referred to as *linghun zhaoxiang* 靈魂照相/靈魂照像 (spirit-photography). In addition to being another way of communicating with the divine, the produced image often served as material proof of the existence of spirits and deities to believers and attracted more followers. Spirit-photography played a prominent role within redemptive societies and suggests the growing importance of new technologies in the Chinese religious sphere during the early twentieth century. For more, see Schumann, "Science and Spirit-Writing," 149–54.

50   Weituo 韋陀 (Skanda in Sanskrit) is a Mahayana bodhisattva regarded as a devoted guardian of Buddhist monasteries who protects the teachings of Buddhism. Jifo 濟佛 (Monk Ji) is also called Jigong 濟公. According to Meir Shahar, Jigong first appeared in spirit-writing as a popular deity around 1900, at a Boxer spirit-writing séance. For more on Jigong, see Shahar, *Crazy Ji*. Nanhai Dashi 南海大士 is another name for Guanyin 觀音, for it is commonly believed that Guanyin resides in the South Sea.

the local male branch of the Daoyuan but stand on separate sides, since there were no "sand trays" (*shapan* 沙盤, the instrumental medium for spirit-writing) in the women's branches.[51]

Spiritually, the way for women to cultivate themselves was to study the society's general guidelines (*dagang* 大綱). Once women knew its detailed rules (*xize* 細則) and "instructions from the altar" (*tanxun* 壇訓), they were able to assume important responsibilities.[52] Because few of the women members were literate, a representative from the Yingshang branch of Anhui province proposed, at the 1935 National Conference held in Ji'nan, that the Daoyuan should select leaders who were eloquent and knowledgeable to visit local the branches, deliver speeches, and explain the gods' exhortations—thereby helping the members with their self-cultivation.[53] The National Conference approved this proposal, announcing that lecturers would be sent to the local branches on a monthly basis. This was similar to the duty upheld by women lecturers in the Wanguo daode hui, although it is unknown whether or not this plan had the same broad scale as the latter's lecture system.

Although members were generally expected to follow the deities' instructions in all of their activities, the Lotus Sage herself showed flexibility regarding this precept: "Rules are made by human and deity together, and thus should be obeyed by both. If a human fails to adhere to the rules, he should be reported to the higher level to be stopped. If a deity's orders do not follow the rules, it is because of unclear spirit-writing, and thus local societies should report the matter to the mother society to acquire new decrees." (綱則為人、神所共定，亦當神、人所共遵也。人若不合綱則，當呈判以止其進行，而神判如有不合綱則者，乃屬纂靈不清，可仍由各社呈報母社，以便改判也。)[54] This suggests that the Daoyuan's leaders made conscious efforts to regulate and control the spirit-writing messages, which corroborates the argument of Chen Minghua 陳明華 that the Daoyuan's leaders were aware that spirit-writing did not always deliver the most appropriate messages, depending on the professional expertise of those in charge of the ritual, in addition to the Daoyuan's occasional internal power politics.[55]

---

51 This is according to my interviewee Cong Zhaohuan 叢兆桓's recollection. His paternal grandfather's family members were all members of the Qingdao Daoyuan. As a child, he witnessed some of the spirit-writing ceremonies himself. My interviews with Cong were conducted on September 30 and October 27, 2011 and June 26, 2014, at his home in Beijing.
52 "Jiu yue chusi sheke Liansheng xun." However, we know little about how these instructions were transmitted from the altar.
53 "Nüshe yingyou Daoyuan gongtui chidejuzui shenming daozhi."
54 "Nüdaode she shegang yu banshi xize."
55 On the Daoyuan's systematic efforts to train qualified practitioners who would not manipulate the process of spirit-writing, see Chen, "Fuji de zhiduhua."

3 Reconfiguring Traditional Gender Doctrines

An examination of the Daoyuan's gender teachings suggests that the organization reinterpreted the fundamental, traditional gender concepts to make them compatible with modern gender ideologies. These traditional gender concepts include a set of social norms that were broadly shared across Chinese society and popularized by morality books, ledgers of merit and demerit, and other texts, over a long historical period.[56] The Daoyuan's new teachings for women included a redefinition of key gender concepts such as the "inner and outer" (*neiwai* 內外), "talent and virtue" (*cai yu de* 才與德), and the "three followings and four virtues" (*sancong side* 三從四德). Significantly, while maintaining a traditional gendered theoretical framework, this redefinition helped to remove many of the gender-subjugating elements that were out of line with the new era. Additionally, the Daoyuan made connections with Western science, particularly biology, in order to appear modern, as I will show below.

First, with regard to the old rule that "men manage external affairs and women internal affairs" (男主外，女主內), the proclamation of the WMS states that this fits "the modern theory of the division of labor" (現代職業分工之說):

> Since the influence of Europe spread to the east, the doctrine of women's rights has become prevalent in society, and voices on emancipation and reform can be heard without end. Is it known that actually the Sage's decree [on *nei* and *wai*] thoroughly fits with the modern theory of the division of labor, and thus does not mean gender inequality. … [I]t is merely because, with regard to family matters, men and women are different, but in terms of benevolence and charity, there is no difference between China and foreign countries! For this reason, we established the women's wing of the RSS. …
>
> 自歐風東漸，女權之說盛行于世，解放改造不絕於耳。抑知男主外女主內，聖人微旨，蓋深合於現代職業分工之說，非有所輕重於期間也。… 蓋家庭之事，男女有別，社會慈業，中外無分，懿歟休哉！是即我同人創設女界紅卍字會之微意也欤 …[57]

As seen above, the WMS leaders were acutely aware of the ongoing feminist and women's rights movements taking shape around the world, and probably

---

56 On morality books, see Clart and Scott, *Religious Publishing and Print Culture*. On ledgers of merit and demerit, see Brokaw, *The Ledgers of Merit and Demerit*.

57 "Shijie Funü Hongwanzihui xuanyan."

also of the sharp attacks mounted by progressive intellectuals against the traditional Chinese gender norms. In response, they offered fresh justifications to defend women's role in the family: the historic separation of the male and female spheres was interpreted as having nothing to do with gender inequality and everything to do with gender difference.

To be sure, historians of imperial China have pointed out that *nei* 內 (inner quarters) and *wai* 外 (the outer world) were two spheres that were complementary to each other rather than clearly separated, for Confucian teachings, also maintained that the ethical and behavioral training ground for public life was clearly located within the family household,[58] not to mention that, in reality, boundary-crossing women existed throughout Chinese history. These were not merely members of the lower class, who were compelled to work, but also included elite women who justified their travels and other temporary boundary transgressions in the name of fulfilling their family duties.[59] In the early twentieth century, Chinese reformers started to attack women's domestic seclusion as backward, arguing that the family could be seen as the symbolic center of an oppressive "feudal" tradition. Consequently, the domestic realm was blamed, as Gail Hershatter points out, for being "the source of public ills" and of China's weakness in the world rather than the foundation of public order.[60] The public sphere, on the other hand, became the celebrated arena of higher good and virtue, where individual citizens should not hesitate to make personal sacrifices, particularly during times of national crisis. In this way, at least rhetorically, the divide between public and domestic deepened.

However, the Daoyuan chose to justify and maintain the traditional division of labor between the two spheres by emphasizing gender differences based on modern biology. The Lotus Sage further elaborated on this point to the female members of Jinghai Daoyuan (Shandong) in 1923: the difference between the sexes lies in human "nature" (*xing* 性). Men's nature is *qian* 乾 and thus strong, while women's *kun* 坤 and thus soft. These are different "natural endowments" (*bingfu* 稟賦) which are determined by "biology" (*shengli* 生理), and cannot be forcibly changed. Hence, sages in ancient times laid down the rule that women took charge of the domestic sphere and men the public sphere. This was only in order to follow nature rather than because the sages had any personal preferences. Unfortunately, later generations did not fully understand the sages' intention and, consequently, the two sexes were unable to coexist

---

58 Ebrey, *The Inner Quarters*; Ko, *Teachers of the Inner Chambers*; and Mann, *Precious Records*.
59 For examples on women's boundary-crossing activities, see Goodman and Larson, *Gender in Motion*.
60 Hershatter, "Making the Visible Invisible," 310.

in harmony. That explains why today's theory of "women's liberation" (*jiefang* 解放) and "equal rights" (*pingquan* 平權) is flourishing. Although this theory might be fashionable now, it cannot apply forever. Why? Because it neglects the fundamentally different natures of men and women.[61] It should be noted that the Daoyuan's emphasis on gender difference did not always function as restrictively as one might expect, even if it envisioned a fundamentally domestic role for women. This is particularly true if we put it in the context of other configured gender doctrines that the Daoyuan put forward, as I will examine below.

Many social reformers of the early twentieth century advocated similar ideals as an alternative vision of gendered modernity. Some women were even able to use this conservative ideology to justify their public engagement, such as female missionaries and the YWCA women who applied the concept of "social housekeeping" to their social work. During this period, the "social housekeeping" ideas promoted by the YWCA and other Christian groups proved compatible with Chinese understandings of the relationship between the family and society, thereby further facilitating women's adaptation to public life. Around the turn of the century, a new image of women as "social housekeepers" was imported from the United States, which significantly influenced female Chinese Christians.[62] The WCTU strongly advocated this argument. Based on a strain of biological essentialism, it advocated that, as the mothers of the human race, women were destined to be the custodians of the social mores internationally just as they were at home, and that they should work to promote temperance, religion, social justice, relief, and peace.[63] In other words, this expanded vision of women required them to consider themselves as the keepers not merely of the home but also of society. The nation was seen as a macrocosm of the home, needing women's special abilities to straighten out its problems.[64] Many female American missionaries embraced the discourse of social housekeeping and popularized the idea in China. The susceptibility to this idea in China was probably the result of the Confucian idea that described society as composed of many individual families, and family life as a training ground for public life. In addition, many Chinese women believed that females were innately loving and compassionate and thus better suited to social service, preferring social work and charity to the independent careers pursued by men. This Western conception of womanhood thereby offered Chinese women a

---

61 "Liantaisheng lin Jinghai Daoyuan," 23.
62 Kwok, *Chinese Women and Christianity*, 108.
63 Rosenberg, "Missions to the World," 244–45.
64 Kwok, *Chinese Women and Christianity*, 108.

familiar yet modern ideal that could help them to re-conceptualize women's domestic roles in a way that justified their entrance into the public realm.

The Daoyuan developed still further this strategy of recasting the Chinese tradition by justifying women's public education without invoking the Western concept of natural rights. The following exhortation, from the Lotus Sage, replaced the old belief that "ignorance is a virtue in a woman (女子無才便是德)" with a reconsideration of the relationship between "talent" and "virtue":[65]

> From past to present, few women in history had both talent and virtue. For those with virtue but no talent, the worst that can happen is just to be known as narrow and limited. However, if a woman has talent but no virtue, she will take actions that violate the rules. Once that happens, she will exhibit a variety of debauched, extravagant, idle, evil and arrogant behaviors. As a woman, if she acts like this, how can she fulfill her natural duty? Even though she has talent, she is just going to use it to do evil deeds. Therefore, ancient people have the saying that "ignorance is a virtue in a woman." However, what is wrong with women having talent? Only if she merely has talent but no virtue, should we worry that evil deeds will be carried out through talent, and in that case talent is not worth having.

> 不過自古至今，婦女界才德兼全的，實在不可多得。但是有德無才，究竟也不過落個拘于自守的名號。要是有才無德，那就要有軌外的行動了。一有軌外的行動，凡那蕩檢逾閑的種種，以及放僻邪侈、驕縱自恣的舉動，勢必要現于一身。身為婦女的，如果有了這樣的舉動，那還能盡其天職？縱然有才，也不過借才以濟其惡罷了。所以古人有這樣的經過，才說了一句女子無才便是德的話。可是有才智怎麼就不好呢？但是有才無德，那就恐怕依才濟惡，就不如無才的好了。[66]

In other words, the new teaching suggested that it was fine for women to be educated, so long as they remembered to cultivate their virtues. By re-analyzing an ancient saying and concluding that there was nothing wrong with women having talent, the new doctrine cleared away the theoretical obstacles to the education of women. Before proceeding, however, the Lotus Sage added that women's "true learning" and "true *gongfu* 功夫" (usually any skill achieved

---

65 This doctrine was only discovered/invented toward the end of the Ming Dynasty. It is noteworthy that some salient points about the oppressive doctrines of Confucianism were mostly created from the tenth century onward by Neo-Confucian scholars, under the influence of Buddhism.
66 "Jiu yue chushi ri tesheke hufa."

through hard work and practice) were invariably located within the home, which underlines, at least theoretically, the conservative idea that women's primary sphere was the domestic one. The Sage continued to highlight the significance of the domestic sphere, elaborating that if a woman could properly attend to her domestic responsibilities, then the relationships among the family members would be truly virtuous. Such a family would become a model for the world.[67] In other words, women are supposed to be the anchor of family relationships. This directly echoes the traditional focus on women being responsible for harmony within the family. In this way, the teachings of the Daoyuan supported women's education, thereby appearing modern, while simultaneously ensuring that the female members did not neglect their primary duties to their families and become the type of individualistic "new women" promoted by May Fourth intellectuals.

In addition to the traditional theoretical concepts of "inner and outer" and "talent and virtue," the new teachings by the deities also reinterpreted the well-known gender norm of "three followings and four virtues," viewed by many intellectuals during the early twentieth century reformist era as one of the most oppressive elements of the traditional gendered code of conduct that subjugated women to men. Originally, "three followings" meant that a woman should obey her father before marriage, her husband upon marriage, and her son upon her husband's death. However, the newly-interpreted "three followings" became: "[With regard] to the older generation, be filial to parents, and respect parents-in-law; within the same generation, be at peace with sisters-in-law and other relatives through marriage; please [your] husband; down to the lower generation, be benevolent to sons, and loving to daughters" (上孝父母,敬翁姑。中和妯娌,睦戚黨,順丈夫。下慈子愛女).[68] It seems that the new emphasis is no longer on women's submission to male authority but rather on women's important role in harmonizing domestic relationships.

The fundamental goal of the "three followings," the deity Jifo 濟佛 explained to members of the WMS, was to "assist" (*fuzhu* 輔助) their husbands to administer the family and the country. This, however, did not mean that women held less power (*quanli* 權力) than men and should be subordinate to them.[69] This differs from Philip Clart's study of a morality book, *Precious Admonitions for the Instruction of Women*, written by a spirit-writing cult in Western Yunnan 雲南 province in 1921, which still treated the husband-wife relationship

---

67 "Ba yue chuba ri sheke Liansheng xun."
68 Xie, *Daode jinghualu xubian*, 8.
69 "Jifo lin Ji'nan Nüdaode she xun."

in terms of subordination.[70] The exhortation from Jifo added that improving family relationships was the key reason for reforming the family, which was a woman's most important duty. As we can see, this reinterpretation essentially shifted away from a single-sided emphasis on obedience to men toward a greater focus on the significance of cultivating good relationships between the male and female members of the family, while simultaneously signaling the deities' teachings' basic consistency with Confucian values regarding family life.

The new version of the "four virtues" also cast aside that notion's previous emphasis on gender inferiority and hierarchy, instead focusing more on women's harmonizing roles. During the Han dynasty, the well-known female historian Ban Zhao (45–116 CE) summarized the four virtues in the *Nü jie* 女誡 (Lessons for women) as follows: womanly virtue (*fude* 婦德), womanly speech (*fuyan* 婦言), womanly countenance (*furong* 婦容), and womanly conduct (*fugong* 婦功). Womanly virtue, according to Ban Zhao's interpretation, meant that a woman should "not distinguish herself in talent and intelligence" (不必才明绝異)[71] but, in Daoyuan's texts, this was changed to being "chaste, still, with personal integrity" (*zhenjing chaoshou* 貞靜操守). Womanly speech, which previously meant that a woman should "not sharpen her language and speech" (不必辯口利辭), now referred to a woman who "speaks modestly and in a friendly way" (*yanqian yuhe* 言謙語和). Womanly countenance, which used to mean that women should not seek to be "outwardly beautiful or ornamented" (不必顔色美麗), now meant "to be solemn and respectful (*zhuangsu duanjing* 莊素端靜)." Finally, womanly conduct was changed from initially insisting that women should "not outperform others in skill and cleverness" (不必技巧過人) to a new emphasis on "managing the home frugally, and being diligent in cooking and sewing" (勤儉持家、烹饪縫織是也).[72]

These new interpretations of women's virtues may not appear, on the surface, to signal a radical departure from the past. However, they contained subtle but important changes. In particular, most of the rules requiring women to be self-effacing were deleted, thus removing the obstacles to them becoming more active in both family and society. The revised "three followings and four virtues" doctrine now emphasized women's obligation to nurture the family relationships and manage their domestic duties, rather than strictly adhering to a domestic hierarchy. These changes gave women room to maneuver. Never-

---

70　Clart, "Chinese Tradition and Taiwanese Modernity."
71　Zhou, *Zhongguo jiaoyu shigang*, 416. Translation from Lee, *Education in Traditional China*, 470.
72　Xie, *Daode jinghualu xubian*, 8.

theless, despite the elimination of certain egregious phrasing, given the shifts within the acceptable gender norms, the new emphasis still relied on gender difference for its justification. The Daoyuan did not directly address the question of gender inequalities. In fact, some aspects of the organization betrayed a clear, continuing assumption that females were the inferior sex, from the dependent status of the women's wing to a portion of its religious teachings.

We should note that the Daoyuan was not the only redemptive society that redefined the gender norms during this period. The Wanguo daode hui and its leader Wang Fengyi 王鳳儀 (1864–1937) also responded to the challenges posed by the modern ideologies, although not in writing. In 1930, Wang was invited to meet Zhang Shouyi 張壽懿 (1898–1966), the fifth concubine of the warlord Zhang Zuolin 張作霖 (1875–1928, who had been assassinated by the Japanese two years previously). She informed Wang that she had read nearly all of his books and agreed with most of his teachings. However, she thought that the notion of the "three followings" was "not compatible with the current time" (buhe shidai 不合時代) and so should be deleted. Wang replied, "I have already broken the rule of the old three followings. The three followings that I am teaching now are: nature follows the principles of heaven, the heart follows the principles of the *Dao*, and the body follows the principles of the emotions. These are the three true followings!" (我早就打破舊三從了，我所講的三從是性從天理、心從道理、身從情理。這才是真三從呢!)[73] It seems that Wang's three new followings were no longer related to gender and applied equally to both men and women.

While attempting to redefine the traditional gender doctrines, the Daoyuan's leaders perceived that the fundamental problems for Chinese families lay in the interpersonal relationships among the family members. This differed from the diagnosis of the Chinese family offered by the proponents of the New Culture Movement, such as Hu Shi 胡適 (1891–1962), who saw the authority of the family as clashing with individual freedom, and thus strongly urged women to seek personal independence and freedom by walking out of the feudal and oppressive family.[74] It also differed from the issues that YWCA women, such as

---

73 Wang and Zheng, *Wang Fengyi yanxing lu*, 283.
74 The movement's leader, Hu Shi, actively promoted Norwegian dramatist Henrik Ibsen's *A Doll's House* in the pages of *New Youth*. Consequently, the play's protagonist, Nora, who walks out on her husband and children in pursuit of freedom, symbolized to the Chinese audience the struggle of the individual in society to escape the confines of the traditional family and confront the hypocrisy of the law and religion. The publicity given to the play and its heroine in the May Fourth discourse was such that a new term was coined as a synonym for female emancipation: Nora-ism (*nuola zhuyi* 娜拉主義).

Hu Binxia 胡彬夏 (1888–1931), identified as requiring reform—matters of poor hygiene and ignorance of scientific management, which could be fixed only by women becoming modern-educated housewives.[75] The Daoyuan's proposed solution was less radical and technical than it was moral, centering on cultivating better personal virtues. If people, mostly women, treated the other family members better, the number of grievances would be reduced and the degree of harmony would increase. In this sense, Hu Binxia and Daoyuan leaders both highlighted the crucial role that women should play in reforming the Chinese domestic realm, encouraging them to be more active in the new era.

Because the core of the WMS's revised gender doctrines still held that women's true calling lay in the home, it is unsurprising that the WMS's teachings evinced disapproval of the New Culturalist gender ideology that "abetted" women in walking out of their homes in the pursuit of individual freedom and liberation. From the perspective of the WMS, individual liberty too often came at a high cost: the loss of morality and virtue for women. The WMS was not alone in upholding this morality-centered standard. As historian Zhao Yancai 趙炎才 has pointed out, the idea of moral regeneration pervaded every corner of the political discourse in early twentieth-century China.[76] Many Chinese elites believed that political and social crises were born of moral decay—a belief with historical precedents. The late Ming and High Qing were the two most recent historical periods when similar moral concerns were prevalent, particularly at moments when commercialization produced status anxieties among the elites.[77] Unsurprisingly, by the late Qing and early Republican periods, when the social and political crises were acute once again, this way of thinking resurfaced.

4 The Living Reality of Daoyuan Families

The Daoyuan's leaders believed that strained interpersonal relationships caused fundamental problems within the Chinese home for a host of reasons. To begin with, Confucianism had always emphasized the importance of the five

---

75 There were other intellectuals and reformers who promoted home economics and shared Hu Binxia's view on women's important role as modern professional household managers. See Schneider, *Keeping the Nation's House*.
76 Zhao, "Qingmo Minchu daode jiushi sichao."
77 For the late Ming, see Dennerline, *The Chia-Ting Loyalists*; For the High Qing period, see Mann, *Precious Records*.

basic ethical relationships, three of which are intra-familial.[78] In this sense, the focus on harmonizing domestic relationships can be seen as a shift in emphasis within Confucian gender ideology, from hierarchy to harmony, rather than the adoption of an entirely new doctrine. Secondly, the leaders and members of the Daoyuan tended to live within traditional family structures—with wives, concubines, and members of the older and younger generations living together. This not only means that the Daoyuan's members tended to be well to do (with the ample resources necessary to contribute to charity), but also that they were familiar with the daily tensions and strife resulting from many people living under the same roof. Stories about strained relationships between mothers-in-law and daughters-in-law, or among daughters-in-law, had long been common within society. In suggesting that Daoyuan women should focus on cultivating more harmonious domestic relationships, the Daoyuan's leaders were probably motivated by practical concerns related to their own daily lives.

The relationship between a main wife and concubines had always been delicate, tricky, and even violent in some cases. Anthropologist Maria Jaschok points out that, within the household, women often faced other women as rivals "for emotional hold over 'key' males," and notes the important role that the women's different backgrounds played in causing conflict. Clashes between the values and attitudes of, for instance, an ex-prostitute concubine and an upper-class wife added a further dimension to their conflicts over emotional and material resources.[79] We also gain a sense of the prevalence of domestic conflicts through the exhortations to female members of the WMS by the Lotus Sage, which frequently mention women's supposed shortcoming of "being suspicious and jealous." The Sage counseled women to learn how to love every family member,[80] and not think always of "taking advantage of others" (*zhan pianyi* 占便宜), a habit which could "put themselves at a disadvantage" (*chikui* 吃虧) in the long run.[81]

Duara's study of the women in Wanguo daode hui in Manchukuo, a puppet state of the Empire of Japan in Northeast China and Inner Mongolia from 1932 until 1945, also suggests that domestic relationship issues were a major motivation for many women who joined redemptive societies. He notes that many "women with much grief" in their domestic lives belonged to the society.

---

78   These five basic ethical relationships, defined by Confucianism, were (1) ruler and subject; (2) father and son; (3) elder brother and younger brother; (4) husband and wife; and (5) friend and friend.
79   Jaschok, *Concubines and Bondservants*, 25, 27–28, 32.
80   "Liantaisheng lin Ji'nan Nüdaode she xun."
81   "Liantaisheng lin Jingzhao Daoyuan," 25.

These women "either had children that died young, or were 'locked in loveless marriages,' or were seeking solace because a concubine had been brought in to replace them; or if they were the concubines, they were bullied by older wives and in-laws."[82] Duara believes that these societies offered "a rationalization or justification of their fate, a means of coping with their difficult lives, and, often, spiritual solace."[83]

Following the Western models, the Republican legal code of 1930 refused to recognize the legal existence of concubines but, in practice, as Lisa Tran points out, the Nationalist Party's placement of concubinage under the adultery laws, with all of their loopholes, left the custom largely intact.[84] Since adultery is not the same as bigamy, it tended to be regarded as a morality issue. Although a wife could demand a divorce on the grounds of her husband's adultery, she would probably end up losing more than she gained. Without being legally punished, the husband could simply proceed to marry the new concubine and turn her into his main wife, if he desired. In any case, the law was implemented only in some major cities and a widespread discrepancy existed between the code and practice in different regions. In conservative areas, such as Shandong province and northeastern China, where the redemptive societies were most popular, concubinage remained a prevalent custom. It is said that, when Wang Fengyi, founder and spiritual leader of the Wanguo daode hui, was preaching in Shenyang in 1930, the aforementioned fifth concubine of Zhang Zuolin invited him over and asked: "Now it is the era of gender equality, and thus a husband cannot have more than one wife. Why is Old Master (referring to Wang) still teaching about the proper rule between wife and concubines" (現在男女平等，一夫不能多妻。老先生為什麼還講嫡庶道呢)? Wang replied: "I originally did not want to talk about this doctrine, however, for many families, the most painful thing is the disharmony between the main wife and the concubines, and thus they are extremely distressed. If I do not make them understand the proper rule between wife and concubine, I cannot save them from suffering and help them achieve happiness!" (我本不願講這個道，無奈太多的人家，最痛苦的是嫡庶不和，苦惱萬分，不講明白嫡庶道，就不能救她們出苦得樂啊！)[85]

The focus on conflict between wives and concubines in early twentieth century texts (including those of the Daoyuan) might also be due in part to the decline of households in which multiple married brothers lived together (espe-

---

82 Duara, "Of Authenticity and Woman," 353.
83 Ibid.
84 Tran, *Concubines in Court*.
85 Wang, *Wang Fengyi yanxing lu*, 283–84.

cially in cities). As a result, tension between sisters-in-law became less of a concern, while wife/concubine tensions remained. Although more concrete evidence is needed, I suspect that the shift might also have resulted from the rise in the actual domestic status of some concubines in this changing historical period, in which the old rules governing status hierarchies were being broken down, and newly-introduced rules such as monogamy were not yet completely established, leaving room for concubines who gained the favor of husbands to maneuver and upset the status quo.

There is also evidence suggesting that, at times, concubines were far more active Daoyuan members than main wives. For example, my interview with a descendant of the Cong family of Qingdao, Cong Zhaohuan 叢兆桓 (1931–), reveals that, although both the wife (Cong Jingshu 叢靜淑) and the concubine (Cong Wanying 叢婉英) of his grandfather, Cong Liangbi 叢良弼 (1868–1945), were leaders of the Qingdao WMS, as the Vice President, Wanying was far more actively involved in the society's affairs than was the President, Liangbi's main wife, who was illiterate and significantly older.[86] At the 1935 National Conference of the WMS held in Ji'nan, the Lotus Sage even singled out Wanying along with several other active female members for praise as "resolute and devout" (*jiancheng* 堅誠) members "with foresight" (*xianjue* 先覺), thus giving the deity's official approval regarding concubines' activism within the WMS.[87]

5   Motivating Women to Engage in Charity

In addition to reinterpreting the traditional gender doctrines, the Daoyuan's spirit-written texts consistently emphasized charity as a core aspect of women's "outer cultivation." Some of the most elaborate instructions for Daoyuan women engaging in charity come from the texts produced through spirit-writing during the First National Conference of the Women's Morality Society held in Ji'nan in 1935. The leaders deliberately chose the time of the traditional Chongyang 重陽 Festival, usually observed on the ninth day of the ninth month in the Chinese lunar calendar (October 6 of that year). According to the oldest

---

86   This is according to my interviewee Cong Zhaohuan's recollection. The Cong family was an illustrious merchant family who were very active in Qingdao Daoyuan in the early twentieth century. His grandfather, Cong Liangbi, was a major founder of Shandong's match industry in the 1920s and also served as President of the Qingdao RSS for almost twenty years; My interviews with Cong were conducted on September 30 and October 27, 2011 and June 26, 2014 at his home in Beijing.

87   "Jiu yue chushi ri tesheke hufa."

Chinese classical divination text, the *Book of Changes,* nine is a *yang* number; the Daoyuan's leaders selected this date because it was double *yang*. The conference was the biggest-ever congregational event held by this society, as far as we can tell, and it left valuable information regarding the organization's beliefs and activities.

One of the central goals of this conference was to encourage more women to step out of their inner quarters, broaden their horizons, and promote both the "Way" (*dao*) and "charity" (*ci*). The Lotus Sage issued a statement explaining that, in the past, the local WMS branches all relied on the Daoyuan, which is understandable since it was the initial period. However, in the future, if that were to continue, these women's societies would inevitably develop the habit of dependency. Once women have this habit, even though the affairs of the societies were established a long time ago, it would become difficult to develop further.[88] The Lotus Sage also took advantage of the opportunity that this meeting represented to opine that it was time for women to learn to take responsibility and carry out tasks on their own and no longer exclusively rely on the male Daoyuan. She added that, if women could competently play more active leading roles, Laozu could well issue instructions to change the name of the women's "society" (*she* 社) to the women's "Daoyuan," thereby raising the women's wing to an equal level to the men's. If this change occurred, the society would finally be in a position to avoid further criticism for favoring the *yang* force over the *yin* (*yinyang youpian* 陰陽有偏).[89] The statements suggest that these Daoyuan deities once considered the possibility of gradually equalizing the status of its female and the male branches, in much the same way as the YWCA and YMCA operated, although the source of this criticism remains unknown.

The spirit-written texts of the WMS promoted charity as a cause with which it was particularly suitable for women to engage. In this respect, they resembled the teachings of the women's branch of the Wanguo daode hui, although Duara's study did not explain how they justified its new valorization. In the case of the Daoyuan, its spirit-written messages often used the traditionally popular concept of "women's benevolence" to encourage women to engage in charity, arguing that benevolence was part of females' nature and that they should thus be especially good at it. Similarly, in response to the popular opinion that many women were "confined, illiterate and not intelligent enough" to take on the important responsibility of promoting the *Dao* and engaging in charity, the

---

88 "Jiu yue chusi sheke Liansheng xun."
89 Ibid.

Lotus Sage pointed out that women's "natural aptitude" for "benevolence" and "compassion" gave them a unique advantage:

> In terms of charitable relief, neither men nor women can do without the word "benevolence". For women, however, the word "benevolence" just stands for their "natural knowledge and natural aptitude". "Women's benevolence" is a phrase that everyone knows about. With this benevolence, [women] possess the true foundation for applying benevolence and doing charity.
>
> 凡世間不論男女，一言慈救，總離不開一個仁字。可是這個仁字，就是婦女們良知良能罷了。婦女之仁，這一句話，無論何人都是知道的。既有此仁，就有行慈作善的真正根本。

Thus, the Lotus Sage exhorted, instead of sitting at home, considering themselves useless, women should take advantage of the fact that they were especially suited to engage in charitable work. "The true meaning of cultivating the *Dao*" is merely to "uncover and recover (*huifu* 恢復) women's 'natural knowledge and aptitude' (*liangzhi liangneng* 良知良能) from mundane affairs (*chensu* 塵俗)."[90] The Lotus Sage's encouragement of women to engage in charity stemmed mostly from seeing women's involvement in it as an extension and manifestation of their inner benevolence, rather than regarding charity as a separate public realm which women should enter. The outer world was viewed as essentially secondary and supplementary to the inner; at most, an expansion of the inner field, rather than as a parallel sphere of equal importance. Nevertheless, it did help women to think and act beyond the confines of their domestic worlds.

In addition to the age-old concept of "women's benevolence," the Lotus Sage used the theory of Buddhist rebirth (*lunhui* 輪迴) to persuade women to care less about money and donate generously to charity. She explained that money was often the source of evil, and that donating money could help to reduce old sins and grudges. Moreover, if a woman donated, she might be able to transform from a female into a male in her next life—a good outcome, as it involved transforming from *yin* to *yang*. Turning from a man into a woman was a bad outcome, representing heavenly retribution (*yinguo* 因果) for misdeeds. There were reasons why women were female during their current lives, and if they did not engage in self-cultivation and widespread charity, they might have the

---

90 "Jiu yue chusi ri Liantaisheng xun."

misfortune to be female again in their next lives.[91] In this area, the two sexes were not regarded by the Lotus Sage as being of equal status; on the contrary, one was superior to the other.

Apart from avoiding the debacle of being reborn as the inferior sex again in the next life, another attractive reward offered to benevolent women was the promise beyond themselves—that religious merit could be transferred to their relatives and ancestors. At the 1935 conference, the Lotus Sage appealed to the female members, asking them to donate or help raise funds to renovate the building of the mother society in Ji'nan. The incentives were listed in detail: those who raised 500 *yuan* would earn their ancestral spirits a promotion one level higher than their previous merit rank (*guowei* 果位); those who donated 1000 *yuan*, two levels; for over 2000 *yuan*, the ancestral spirits (*xianling* 先靈) of both a woman's natal family (*niangmen* 娘門) and her marital family (*benmen* 本門) could be raised (*chaosheng* 超升) three levels higher. Once the money was received, donors would write down the names of several generations of ancestors (and ranks if they had any), send the names in, and await decisions on their new ranks, which would then be inscribed on new tablets to be enshrined at the Room of the Bodhisattva (*pusa shi* 菩薩室) at the Daoyuan. This resembles an ancient feature of Chinese Buddhism—the idea that a person can be filial as a Buddhist by transferring merit to his/her ancestors—that continued to make Buddhism more appealing in a Chinese context. The Lotus Sage repeatedly emphasized that money can be a source of evil but that, when used for good, it could benefit women's self-cultivation and foster later blessings. If used inappropriately, it can create evil, causing people to fall into a bad rebirth.[92]

Furthermore, Laozu, the highest deity of the Daoyuan, designed a reward system of Buddhist hierarchical ranks in the afterlife for ancestral spirits to attain salvation—thereby providing a means of publicly quantifying their members' good works. The ranks ranged from the lower levels, such as Upāsaka (masculine) or Upāsikā (feminine) (*youpoyisai* 優婆夷塞 in Chinese),[93] to higher ones, such as Arhat Buddha (*Aluohan pusa* 阿羅漢菩薩).[94] It was believed that, the higher the rank the ancestral spirits achieved, the greater

---

91　"Jiu yue chushi ri tesheke hufa."
92　Ibid.
93　They come from the Sanskrit and Pāli words for "attendant." In modern times, they have a connotation of dedicated piety that is best suggested by terms such as "lay devotee" or "devout lay follower."
94　There are four progressive stages of enlightenment in Buddhism, from Sotapanna, Sakadagami, Anagami to Arahat, the last indicating full enlightenment.

the power they could wield to protect their descendants. This reward system of religious merit was used not only for fundraising, but also for other kinds of encouragement. For instance, to encourage more women to attend and participate in the 1935 national conference, the Lotus Sage encouraged their male relatives to accompany them on the journey to Ji'nan. The men and women who attended the Conference were promised that their ancestral spirits would be rewarded with a higher rank on both sides of their families.[95]

The meticulously-quantified Buddhist merit reward system reminds us of the legacy of the ledgers of merit and demerit (*gongguo ge* 功過格) used by elites in the Ming and Qing dynasties to record people's good and bad deeds in order to regulate the local communities to maintain social order, as Cynthia Brokaw has shown.[96] Considering the waves of anti-superstition campaigns that had washed over the country since the late Qing, the Daoyuan's merit reward system could redirect women's "superstitious" tendencies toward productive engagement in charitable outreach activities, serving as a source from which they could derive agency, and further demonstrating the significance of charity as a primary channel for Daoyuan women to display their devotion.

In reality, the female members of the Daoyuan did engage in a variety of charitable activities. A central focus had been disaster relief. My interviewee recalls that the Qingdao WRSS members usually visited the society four times a month—on the first, eighth, fifteenth, and twenty-third day. On each occasion, they donned clean clothes and recited sutras, engaged in sitting meditation, and discussed matters relating to poverty and disaster relief. For example, in 1932, after a disastrous flood hit the southern provinces, the RSS called on their members to raise funds for relief. Qingdao WRSS members decided that they could not simply "watch indifferently" (*moran shizhi* 漠然視之) but instead "should hurry to catch up with [the male members] and not fall behind" (應急起直追不落人後). They set up a "Women's Frugality Relief Committee" (*jiejian chouzhen hui* 節儉籌賑會), proposing that every member should save money by reducing the amount spent on entertaining guests, clothes, food, and so on. After three months, they would send their collected savings to afflicted areas through the Daoyuan. Their proclamation claimed that such frugal and charitable activity was virtuous, "of the greatest merit" (*gongde* 功德), and beneficial to self-cultivation.[97] In addition to donating money, making cotton-padded

---

95 "Jiu yue chushi ri tesheke hufa."
96 Brokaw, *The Ledgers of Merit and Demerit*.
97 "Chuangli jiejian chouzhenhui."

clothes was a common way for Daoyuan women to offer their help in winter, whereas giving porridge to the poor was their regular summer charitable activity. The women's branches nationwide participated in most of the organized relief activities of the RSS, as demonstrated by the many RSS testimonials (*zhengxinlu* 徵信錄) in local Chinese archives which list women's names and donation amounts.[98]

Apart from disaster relief, the WRSS chose to make widows and pregnant women a central concern. The Qingdao Branch set up the Affiliated Institute for Poor Widows and Pregnant Women (Chipin lichan jiujisuo 赤贫嫠产救济所) within the WRSS. From the institute's founding in April 1930, to October 1932, it distributed flour to these women from the first to the fifteenth day of every month. Each person was given 20 *jin* and they distributed thirty bags of flour in monthly increments. The annual budget was 1000 *yuan*,[99] which indicates a small scale of relief.

The WRSS realized that donations alone could not fundamentally address the issue of poverty. Women needed to learn skills that would enable them to make a living on their own. A 1935 conference representative from Jiangsu province proposed establishing a professional school for unemployed women to teach basic Chinese characters and sewing. WMS members could serve as the teachers, and the classes could therefore be offered for free. The proposal was passed unanimously, although we do not know if it was ever implemented.[100]

Establishing elementary schools for girls was another type of charity for the WRSS. The Ji'nan WRSS established an elementary girls' school inside its WMS in February 1927. Initially, there was only one class of 40 students at the beginner's level but, by 1930, there were five classes with a total of 144 students. From 1932 onward, it merged with another elementary school established by the Ji'nan Daoyuan, but the boys and girls remained in separate classes. Over the years, its student numbers fluctuated due to wars and other disasters. By 1939, there were 275 boys and 101 girls.[101] It is possible that the WRSS recruited its student membership through these elementary schools, much like the YWCA. The WRSS' general regulations stipulated that the membership should include students. However, the RSS schools probably did not offer exclusive religious education, as the Nationalist government opposed the requirement of religious courses.

---

98 For an example of women members' donation list, see "Quanzhu shuizai zhenkuan an."
99 "Shijie Funü Hongwanzihui Qingdao fenhui banli ciye."
100 "Qingqiu tongxing gedi nüshe sheli zhiye xueshu."
101 Sung, "Minguo chunian Zhongguo zongjiao tuanti," 266.

According to some former students, the RSS schools performed certain rituals to impart a religious consciousness, such as worshipping Laozu every Monday morning.[102]

6   Admonitions against Superstition

Although the Daoyuan were accused of being, and indeed once classified as, a "superstitious" organization by the Nationalist government and progressive intellectuals, its leaders shared with intellectuals like Liang Qichao 梁啟超 (1873–1929) the idea that religion could be stripped of harmful superstition. In her study of the "invention" of religion in modern China, Rebecca Nedostup argues that this common understanding "formed the key to the cultural reform" of the twentieth century.[103] What the Daoyuan's leaders and progressive intellectuals *dis*agreed about was whether certain specific rituals, such as spirit-writing, should be classified as "religious" or "superstitious." Apart from that, the Daoyuan's leaders seem generally to have internalized the anti-superstition discourse. Like many other organizations seeking to gain legitimacy as religious groups in the Republican Era, the Daoyuan completely omitted texts about liturgical services that had long been regarded as vital religious services but were now labeled as "superstition." As for the controversial practice of spirit-writing, the Daoyuan's repeated insistence on its "scientific" dimension indicates an uneasy attempt to distance it from superstition.

We can also see how the Daoyuan carefully distinguished their religion from superstition in the spirit-writing text quoted below, attributed to the Song-dynasty Buddhist Monk Ji (Jigong) and published in 1922 in their *Daode zazhi*:

> [Jigong]: Sit down and listen. What you refer to as superstition is not those beliefs and practices to which we devote ourselves. … Those people whom our elders refer to as superstitious include both ignorant men and women who engage in idolatry as well as those who claim to believe in gods and buddhas but fail to live by their teachings. … Today, we adhere to the true principle of the sages, immortals, and buddhas. We incorporate the Five Teachings [Buddhism, Daoism, Catholicism, Protestantism, and Islam] as one Great Way, practicing internal and external cultivation, sav-

---

102   Gao, *Hongwanzihui jiqi shehui jiuzhu shiye yanjiu*, 122.
103   Ibid., 8.

ing ourselves while also providing salvation for others. As such, we hardly compare to those who blindly engage in various practices. What do you have to say to that?

坐，吾語汝。汝子所謂迷信者，非吾所奔走者也 … 夫子所謂迷信者，乃愚夫愚婦拜偶像外，信神佛而實不行神佛之事，徒佞神佛為託神佛之保佑。… 今吾乃信神聖仙佛之真理，得五教統歸之大道，內外雙修，度己渡人，非盲從者之可比也。子尚有何說？[104]

In this text, the deity Monk Ji emphasized that Daoyuan's goal lies in the broad category of self-cultivation rather than specific practices to seek immediate benefits, which factor was believed to distinguish their organization from other, superstitious ones.

The Lotus Sage further stressed this point to the women members through spirit-writing:

All of you devotees know that there are some who become a member and seek self-cultivation thinking that this will bring them benefits. However, the benefits you are talking about are different from those that I am referring to. You talk about becoming a member and seeking self-cultivation so as to get protection from the deities, so that they make you rich, or get relief from suffering. In fact, these are not what I meant. What I meant is that since you are willing to pursue self-cultivation, you should start from consciously listening with your hearts. You should often listen to all the altar instructions, and others' reasonable words and remember them in your hearts. As you do this frequently, you will understand and no longer feel confused. Then your mind will be able to think clearly, which will be a major benefit. It is most difficult for women to be in a calm state of mind (*xinping qihe*). Now if you remember these four words in your mind, and no matter what you do, always focus on your mind, then you will do well everywhere.

各方全知道入社求修是想有好處的。但是各方所說的好處跟吾所說的不一樣。你們所說的是入社求修以後神就可以保護了，可以令吾們發財了，不致於再受罪了。其實不是這樣的說法。吾的意思是你們既然願意求修，就要先從存心上著意就好了。常聽壇訓所講的話跟他人所講有道理的話，全記在心裡。如此常了就明白了，不致於再糊塗了。

---

[104] "Lunshuo," 48; Translation quoted from Katz, *Religion in China and Its Modern Fate*, 34.

各方心裡亦自然能想的開了。這裡的好處就大了。心平氣和是女人們最難做到的。你們現在先將這四個字記在心頭，然後無論做什麼事，再將心字提在前頭，那就處處得好了。[105]

It seems that the deity was fully aware that many women did join the organization to seek immediate blessings and thus felt the need to clarify what should be their proper goals, i.e. self-cultivation.

Believing that women were more superstitious than men, the Daoyuan made use of spirit-writing to exhort their female members in particular to refrain from certain activities that the organization defined as superstitious. Women were told that harmonizing domestic relationships could be more beneficial to self-cultivation than indulging in superstitious activities, such as idol worship, burning incense in temples, "practicing alchemy, and exercising *qi*" (*shaodan lianqi* 燒丹練氣).[106] In another spirit-written text, the Lotus Sage warned the female members against blindly following the "popular practices" (*su* 俗) that she regarded as "superstitious" without inquiring into their "origins" (*laiyuan* 來源). Since these practices were groundless, she explained, they represented a kind of "blind cultivation" (*mangxiu xialian* 盲修瞎練) that contributed nothing to society or the family and could not even be relied upon to protect them from life's catastrophes.[107] These instructions resonated with the contemporary, common understandings of what constituted superstitious activities. According to this teaching, rather than visit temples to pray for their sons or blessings for their families, as did many women during the imperial period, Daoyuan women were expected to achieve these goals through engaging in charitable activities (which was believed to be of the "greatest merit") and self-cultivation. The frequent use of the pejorative neologism *mixin* in the deities' teachings served a purpose: by labeling and discrediting spiritual practices that the deities deemed undesirable, irrational, and suspicious, the Daoyuan simultaneously claimed legitimacy for their own organization.

Historian Thomas DuBois has pointed out that the reorientation of redemptive societies around social charity and away from previous "sideline" positions was due to the rapid growth of the "charitable sphere" in Republican China, which outpaced even that of religion and changed the direction that new religions would take.[108] I would add that this reorientation toward charity was also closely linked with these religious groups' pursuit of alternative ways of

---

105 "Liantaisheng lin Jinghai Daoyuan," 24–25.
106 Xie, *Daode jinghualu xubian*, 104.
107 "Liantaisheng lin Ji'nan Daoyuan," 23.
108 DuBois, "The Salvation of Religion?" 90–91.

accumulating religious merit and practicing self-cultivation without conspicuously engaging in what were officially labeled "superstitious" activities. As the Nationalist government grew increasingly suspicious of spiritual activities, charity became one of the few sanctioned fields in which redemptive societies might engage, a field that had also been long regarded as most conducive to religious merit accumulation.[109] Consequently, what we find in the Daoyuan's religious texts is an omission of superstitious-looking liturgical services and frequent warnings, especially issued to women, against visiting temples and burning incense, along with a meticulous quantification of the hierarchical ranks of religious merit associated with charity, suggesting a significant shift in the means to achieve the same end: spiritual salvation.

What did this reorientation mean for the female members of the Daoyuan? It probably had a more direct impact on the lives of the women members than the men, since most of the "superstitious" activities that the Daoyuan criticized were precisely those that had provided women with opportunities to go out, such as visiting temples, burning incense, and worshipping idols. Historian Zhao Shiyu 趙世瑜 has demonstrated that, during the Ming and Qing periods, women frequently used the pretext of participating in exactly these kinds of religious activities to satisfy their desire to go out for entertainment. The fact that the government officials issued so many orders banning these activities but could not stop them is our best evidence of their popularity and importance. Zhao also notes that a total ban on these activities always failed because the women took upon themselves an important part of the religious work for the whole family, including expiating the sins of their husbands and other male kin.[110] During the Republican period, Daoyuan women continued their religious work on behalf of their family. However, with many superstitious activities under increasing scrutiny and nationwide temple destruction campaigns,[111] charity became one of the few remaining legitimate channels for them to accumulate religious merit and engage with the outside world, through their weekly visits to the Daoyuan branches, gathering at administrative meetings, discussing disaster relief, or helping the poor and unfortunate widows in their local communities. In the relatively limited world of the Daoyuan women, charity gradually emerged as a major mechanism for them to express their devotion.

---

109 For a detailed discussion of the belief on charity's important role in accumulating religious merit since the Song Dynasty, see Sung, "Cishan yu gongde," 21–26.
110 Zhao, *Kuanghuan yu richang*, 270–71; for how late imperial officialdom specifically tried to ban women's temple visiting, see Goossaert, "Irrepressible Female Piety."
111 On temple destruction campaigns, see Katz, "'Superstition' and its Discontents."

7   Conclusion

As we have seen, the Daoyuan's use of spirit-writing was not merely to seek deities' protection and blessings in order to avoid personal calamities, which had been a common pursuit of many secret societies and sectarian religious groups in Chinese history. Instead, it had the broad, systematic goal of edifying society, with a particular focus on the female populace, regarding the importance of moral self-cultivation. A sense of moral and social crisis permeated its spirit-writing texts, as revealed by various deities' frequent use of terms like the "turbid world" (*hunzhuo shijie* 混濁世界), "decadent atmosphere" (*tuifei zhifeng* 頹廢之風) to refer to the age in which the Daoyuan members were living.[112] In this sense, the Daoyuan's goal was to save the world from crisis through morality (*daode jiushi* 道德救世), an effort and solution in which they were not alone in believing.

The three arenas (gender doctrines, the value of charity, and admonitions against superstition) of Daoyuan's spirit-writing texts exclusively addressing the women members best showcase the Daoyuan's efforts to reconstruct the Chinese traditions in order to meet the challenges posed by modernity. In the gender realm, despite its overall conservative nature, the Daoyuan realized the urgent need to "reform the women's world" (*gailiang nüjie* 改良女界), along with many contemporary reformers.[113] However, the Daoyuan's gendered teachings disapproved of radical ideas, such as women's liberation, equal rights and freedom, due to these ideas' individualistic and potentially immoral consequences. Fundamentally, their spirit-written texts advocated that changes be based on the traditional gender doctrines while selectively incorporating those elements of the "new culture" (*xin wenhua* 新文化) that suited China's current conditions.[114] In terms of charity, it now became a much-preferred alternative way to accumulate religious merit than other types of superstitious activities that the progressive intellectuals heavily criticized but with which women tended to engage. Overall, as we have seen, spirit-writing clearly played a central role in Daoyuan's transmission of their gender ideology to its female members. It was used as an authoritative, powerful medium that enabled the Daoyuan's leadership to appeal to, guide, and discipline its female constituency through reconstructing the gendered morality in a period of flux and instability.

---

112   For example, see "Jifo lun xingci yaoyi," 16.
113   "Liantaisheng lin Ji'nan daoyuan," 24.
114   "Nanhai dashi lin Jiangning Daoyuan," 21.

Bibliography

Abbreviations
QMA   Qingdao Municipal Archives 青島市檔案館

Primary Sources

"Ba yue chuba ri sheke Liansheng xun 八月初八日社科蓮聖訓." In *Nüdaode she diyijie gonghui yishilu*, QMA.

"Chuangli Jiejian Chouzhen hui huanxing nü tongbao 創立節儉籌賑會喚醒女同胞." In *Qingdao Nüwanzi hui chouzhen* 青島女卍會籌賑. QMA, 63–1–10–2.

"Cimin pusa lin Shanghai Daoyuan xun nüshe xiufang 慈憫菩薩臨上海道院訓女社休方." *Daode zazhi* 道德雜誌 3, no. 2 (1923).

"Jifo lin Ji'nan Nüdaode she xun 濟佛臨濟南女道德學社訓." *Daode zazhi* 道德雜誌 3, no. 11 (1924).

"Jifo lun xingci yaoyi 濟佛論慈濟要義." *Daode zazhi* 道德雜誌 4, no. 4 (1924).

"Jiu yue chushi ri tesheke hufa Weituo xian qudao, fengming chuanxun 九月初十日特社科護法韋陀先驅到，奉命傳訓." In *Nüdaode she diyijie gonghui yishilu*. QMA.

"Jiu yue chusi sheke Liansheng xun 九月初四社科莲聖訓." In *Nüdaode she diyijie gonghui yishilu*. QMA.

"Jiu yue chusi ri Liantaisheng xun 九月初四日蓮台聖訓." In *Nüdaode she diyijie gonghui yishilu*. QMA.

"Liantaisheng Hongshan xianxiang kefou you geshe fenling gongfeng qing gongjue an 蓮台聖洪山現像可否由各社分領供奉請公決案." In *Nüdaode she diyijie gonghui yishilu*. QMA.

"Liantaisheng lin Ji'nan Daoyuan xun nüshe xiufang 蓮台聖臨濟南道院訓女社修方." *Daode zazhi* 道德雜誌 3, no. 9 (1924).

"Liantaisheng lin Ji'nan Nüdaode she xun 蓮台聖臨濟南女道德社訓." *Daode zazhi* 道德雜誌 4, no. 4 (1924).

"Liantaisheng lin Jinghai Daoyuan xun nüshe xiufang 蓮台聖臨靜海道院訓女社修方." *Daode zazhi* 道德雜誌 3, no. 4 (1923).

"Liantaisheng lin Jingzhao Daoyuan xun nüshe xiufang 蓮台聖臨京兆道院訓女社修方." *Daode zazhi* 道德雜誌 3, no. 1 (1923).

"Lunshuo: Jizu pochu mixin bian 論說：濟祖破除迷信辯." *Daode zazhi* 道德雜誌 2, no. 8 (1922).

"Nanhai dashi lin Jiangning Daoyuan xun nüshe xiufang 南海大士臨江寧道院訓女社修方." *Daode zazhi* 道德雜誌 2, no. 8 (1922).

"Nüdaode she shegang yu banshi xize 女道德社社綱與辦事細則." QMA, no page numbers or archival numbers.

"Nüshe yingyou Daoyuan gongtui chidejuzui shenming daozhi shouling anqi qianwang yanjiang bing yanshu xunwen yiqi jinzhan an 女社應由道院公推齒德俱尊深明道旨首領按期前往講演並演述訓文以期展進案." In *Nüdaode she diyijie gonghui yishilu*. QMA.

"Qingdao Nüdaode she zhixiu gefang renzhi nianxian ji gongxing chengji diaochabiao 青島女道德社職修各方任職各方任職年限及功行成績調查表." June 7, 1932, QMA, 63-1-333.

"Qingqiu tongxing gedi nüshe sheli zhiye xueshu bujiu shiye funü zimou shenghuo an 請求通行各地女社設立職業學塾補救失業婦女自謀生活案." In *Nüdaode she diyijie gonghui yishilu*. QMA.

"Shijie Funü Hongwanzi hui Qingdao fenhui banli ciye chengji gaikuang ji tongjibiao 世界婦女紅卍字會青島分會辦理慈業成績概況暨統計表." October, 1932, QMA, vol. 333, catalogue 1, and category B63.

"Shijie Funü Hongwanzi hui xuanyan 世界婦女紅卍字會宣言." In *Shijie Funü Hongwanzi hui jianzhang* 世界婦女紅卍字會簡章. QMA, no archival number.

"Shilüe 事略." In *Ji'nan Nüdaode she shi'er zhou baogao* 濟南女道德社十二周報告. Ji'nan: Ji'nan mushe, 1935. QMA.

"Si yue ba ri Liansheng xun 四月八日蓮聖訓." In *Nüdaode she diyijie gonghui yishilu*. QMA.

"Daoci wenda 道慈問答." QMA, folder 247, catalogue 1, and vol. B63.

"Ji'nan Funü Hongwanzi hui zhiyuanbiao 濟南婦女紅卍字會職員表." Shandong Provincial Archive 山東省檔案館, J162-01-15-3.

Lü, Liangjian 呂梁建. *Daoci gaiyao* 道慈概要, vol. 1. Longkou: Longkou Daoyuan, 1938.

Nüdaode she diyijie gonghui yishilu 女道德社第一屆公會議事錄. Ji'nan: Ji'nan mushe 1935, QMA

"Quanzhu shuizai zhenkuan an 勸助水災賑款案." Proposed by the Mother Society 母社提出. In *Nüdaode she diyijie gonghui yishilu*. QMA.

The "Green Year" Supplement, 1928, The YWCA of the U.S.A. Records, Sophia Smith Collection, Smith College.

Wang Fengyi 王鳳儀, and Zheng Zidong 鄭子東. *Wang Fengyi yanxing lu* 王鳳儀言行錄. Beijing: Zhongguo Huaqiao chubanshe, 2010.

Xie Guanneng 謝冠能. *Daode jinghualu xubian*, 道德精華錄續編, vol. 7. Taibei: Taiwan Daoyuan, 1960.

"Zhonghua zonghui tichu Wanhui zhangcheng zhong ni jiaru Funü Hongwanzi hui ziyang yimian nühui zaixing xiang zhengfu zhuce'an 中華總會提出卍會章程中擬加入婦女紅卍字會字樣以免女會再行向政府注冊案," *Ershi nian ba yue sanshi ri Wanzi hui huiyi yimu* 二十年八月三十日卍字會議議目, QMA, 63-1-10-2.

Secondary Sources

Boltz, Judith Magee. "On the Legacy of Zigu and a Manual on Spirit Writing in Her Name." In *The People and the Dao: New Studies in Chinese Religions in Honour of*

Daniel L. Overmyer, edited by Philip Clart and Paul Crowe, 349–88. Sankt Augustin: Inst. Monumenta Serica, 2009.

Brokaw, Cynthia. *The Ledgers of Merit and Demerit: Social Change and Moral Order in Late Imperial China*. Princeton, N.J.: Princeton University, 1991.

Chen Minghua 陳明華. "Fuji de zhiduhua yu Minguo xinxing zongjiao de chengzhang—Yi Shijie Hongwanzi hui Daoyuan weili (1921–1932) 扶乩的制度化與民國新興宗教的成長—以世界紅卍字會道院為例 (1921–1932)." *Lishi Yanjiu* 歷史研究, no. 6 (2009): 63–78.

Chen Minghua 陳明華. "Minguo xin zongjiao de zhiduhua chengzhang: Yi Shijie Hongwanzi hui Daoyuan wei zhongxin de kaocha (1921–37) 民國新宗教的制度化成長—以世界紅卍字會道院為重心的考察 (1921–1937)." PhD diss., Fudan University, 2010.

Clart, Philip. "Chinese Tradition and Taiwanese Modernity: Morality Books as Social Commentary and Critique." In *Religion in Modern Taiwan: Tradition and Innovation in a Changing Society*, edited by Philip Clart and Charles B. Jones, 84–97. Honolulu: University of Hawai'i Press, 2003.

Clart, Philip, and Gregory Adam Scott, *Religious Publishing and Print Culture in Modern China: 1800–2012*. Berlin, Germany: De Gruyter, 2015.

Dennerline, Jerry. *The Chia-Ting Loyalists: Confucian Leadership and Social Change in Seventeenth-Century China*. New Haven: Yale University Press, 1981.

Duara, Prasenjit. "Of Authenticity and Woman: Personal Narratives of Middle-Class Women in Modern China." In *Becoming Chinese: Passages to Modernity and Beyond*, edited by Wen-Hsin Yeh, 342–64. Berkeley: University of California Press, 2000.

DuBois, Thomas. "The Salvation of Religion? Public Charity and the New Religions of the Early Republic." *Minsu quyi* 民俗曲藝, no. 172 (2011): 73–126.

Ebrey, Patricia. *The Inner Quarters: Marriage and the Lives of Chinese Women in the Sung Period*. Berkeley: University of California Press, 1993.

Gao Pengcheng 高鵬程. *Hongwanzi hui jiqi shehui jiuzhu shiye yanjiu (1922–1949)* 紅卍字會及其社會救助事業研究. Hefei: Hefei gongye daxue chubanshe, 2011.

Goodman, Bryna, and Wendy Larson, ed. *Gender in Motion: Divisions of Labor and Cultural Change in Late Imperial and Modern China*. Lanham: Rowman & Littlefield Publishers, 2005.

Goossaert, Vincent, and David Palmer. *The Religious Question in Modern China*. Chicago: The University of Chicago Press, 2012.

Goossaert, Vincent. "Irrepressible Female Piety: Late Imperial Bans on Women Visiting Temples." *Nan Nü* 10, no. 2 (2008): 212–41.

Guo Dasong 郭大松. "*Ji'nan Daoyuao ji Hongwanzi hui zhi diaocha* bianzheng 《濟南道院暨紅卍字會之調查》辯證." *Qingdao daxue shifan xueyuan xuebao* 青島大學師範學院學報 22, no. 3 (2005): 22.

Hershatter, Gail. "Making the Visible Invisible: The Fate of 'the Private' in Revolutionary

China." In *Going Public: Feminism and the Shifting Boundaries of the Private Sphere*, edited by Joan Scott and Debra Keates, 309–29. Urbana, Ill: University of Illinois Press, 2005.

Jaschok, Maria. *Concubines and Bondservants: A Social History*. London: Zed Books, 1988.

Jordan, David, and Daniel L. Overmyer. *The Flying Phoenix: Aspects of Chinese Sectarianism in Taiwan*. Princeton: Princeton University Press, 2014.

Kang, Xiaofei. "Women, Gender and Religion in Modern China, 1900s–1950s: An Introduction." *Nan Nü* 19, (2017): 1–27.

Katz, Paul. "'Superstition' and its Discontents—On the Impact of Temple Destruction Campaigns in China, 1898–1948." In *Disijie guoji hanxue huiyi lunwenji—Xinyang, shijian yu wenhua tiaoshi* 第四屆國際漢學會議論文集—信仰、實踐與文化調適, 605–82. Taibei, zhongyang yanjiuyuan: Jinglian chuban gongsi, 2013.

Katz, Paul. *Religion in China and Its Modern Fate*. Waltham, MA: Brandeis University Press, 2014.

Katz, Paul. "Chen Hailiang's Vision of Buddhist Family Life: A Preliminary Study." *Journal of Chinese Religions* 47, no. 1 (2019): 33–60.

Keller, Charles. "Making Model Citizens: The Chinese YMCA, Social Activism, and Internationalism in Republican China, 1919–1937." PhD diss., University of Kansas, 1996.

Ko, Dorothy. *Teachers of the Inner Chambers: Women and Culture in Seventeenth-Century China*. Stanford, Calif.: Stanford University Press, 1994.

Kwok, Pui-lan. *Chinese Women and Christianity, 1860–1927*. Atlanta, Ga: Scholars Press, 1992.

Lee, Thomas. *Education in Traditional China, A History*. Leiden: Brill, 2000.

Li Guangwei 李光偉. "Minguo Daoyuan ji Shijie Hongwanzi hui de yuanqi yu fazhan shulun 民國道院暨世界紅卍字會的緣起與發展述論." *Lilun xuekan* 理論學刊 no. 1 (2010): 106–10.

Li Guangwei 李光偉. *Shijie Hongwanzi hui jiqi cishan shiye yanjiu* 世界紅卍字會及其慈善事業研究. Hefei: Hefei gongye daxue chubanshe, 2017.

Li Guangwei 李光偉 and Guo Dasong 郭大松. "Minguo Nüdaode she ji Shijie Funü Hongwanzi hui shishikao 民國女道德社暨世界婦女紅卍字會史事考." *Minguo dang'an* 民國檔案 no. 2 (2009): 74–75.

Li Guangwei 李光偉 and Guo Dasong 郭大松. "Minguo Daoyuan fuji huodong bianzheng 民國道院扶乩活動辨正." *Anhui shixue* 安徽史學, no. 4 (2009): 42–54.

Li Yuzhen 李玉珍. "Fojiao Lianshe yu nüxing zhi shehui canyu—1930 niandai Shanghai Lianshe yu 1960 niandai Taiwan Lianshe zhi bijao 佛教蓮社與女性之社會參與—1930 年代上海蓮社與 1960 年代台灣蓮社之比較." In *Gong yu si: Jindai Zhongguo geti yu qunti zhi chongjian* 公與私：近代中國個體與群體之重建, edited by Huang Ko-wu 黃克武 and Chang Che-chia 張哲嘉, 255–312. Taipei: Academia Sinica, Institute of Modern History, 2000.

Liu, Xun. *Daoist Modern: Innovation, Lay Practice and the Community of Inner Alchemy in Republican Shanghai*. Cambridge, MA: Harvard University Asia Center, Harvard University Press, 2009.

Liu, Xun. "Women and their Daoist Inner Alchemical Practices Seen in two Early Republican Era Journals." Paper presented at the Religion and Gender in Twentieth Century China Symposium, Rutgers University, October 9–10, 2015.

Luo Jiurong 羅九蓉, Huijun Qiu 丘慧君, and Weipeng Zhou 周維朋. *Cong Dongbei dao Taiwan: Wanguo daode hui xiangguan renwu fangwen jilu* 從東北到台灣：萬國禱的會相關人物訪問紀錄. Taibei: Zhongyang yanjiuyuan jindai shi yanjiusuo, 2006.

Littell-Lamb, Elizabeth A. "Going Public: the YWCA, 'New' Women, and Social Feminism in Republican China." PhD diss., Carnegie Mellon University, 2002.

Ma Yanyan 馬琰琰. "Zhonghua Jidujiao funü jiezhi xiehui shiye yanjiu 中華基督教婦女節制協會事業研究." M.A. thesis, Shandong University, 2012.

Mann, Susan. *Precious Records: Women in China's Long Eighteenth Century*. Stanford, Calif.: Stanford University Press, 1997.

Overmyer, Daniel L. "Values in Chinese Sectarian Literature: Ming and Ch'ing Pao-chuan." In *Popular Culture in Late Imperial China*, edited by David Johnson, Andrew J. Nathan, Evelyn Sakakida Rawski, and Judith A. Berling, 219–54. Berkeley: University of California Press, 1987.

Rosenberg, Emily. "Missions to the World: Philanthropy Abroad." In *Charity, Philanthropy, and Civility in American History*, edited by Lawrence Friedman, and Mark McGarvie, 241–59. Cambridge, UK: Cambridge University Press, 2003.

Schneider, Helen. *Keeping the Nation's House: Domestic Management and the Making of Modern China*. Vancouver: University of British Columbia Press, 2011.

Schumann, Matthias. "Science and Spirit-Writing: The Shanghai Lingxuehui 靈學會 and the Changing Fate of Spiritualism in Republican China." In *Text and Context in the Modern History of Chinese Religions: Redemptive Societies and Their Sacred Texts*, edited by Philip Clart, David Ownby, and Chien-chuan Wang, 126–72. Leiden: Brill, 2020.

Shahar, Meir. *Crazy Ji: Chinese Religion and Popular Literature*. Cambridge, Mass: Harvard University, Asia Center, 1998.

Smith, Richard. *Fortune-Tellers and Philosophers: Divination in Traditional Chinese Society*. Boulder: Westview, 1994.

Sung Kwang-yu 宋光宇. "Minguo chunian Zhongguo zongjiao tuanti de shehui cishan shiye—Yi 'Shijie Hongwanzi hui' wei li 民國初年中國宗教團體的社會慈善事業——以「世界紅卍字會」為例." *Guoli Taiwan daxue wenshi zhexue bao* 國立台灣大學文史哲學報 no. 46 (1997): 243–94.

Sung Kwang-yu 宋光宇. "Shishen shangren yu cishan: Minguo chunian yige cishanxing zongjiao tuanti: 'Shijie Hongwanzi hui' 士紳、商人與慈善——民國初年一個慈

善性宗教團體「世界紅卍字會」." *Furen lishi xuebao* 輔仁歷史學報 no. 9 (1998): 141–79.

Sung Kwang-yu 宋光宇. "Cishan yu gongde—Yi Shijie Hongwanzi hui de 'Ganzhen gongzuo' wei li 慈善與功德：以世界紅卍字會的「贛賑工作」為例." *Kaogu renlei xuekan* 考古人類學刊, no. 57 (2001): 1–33.

Tran, Lisa. *Concubines in Court: Marriage and Monogamy in Twentieth-Century China*. Lanham: Rowman & Littlefield Publishers, 2015.

Valussi, Elena. "Beheading the Red Dragon: A History of Female Alchemy in China." PhD diss., London, SOAS University of London, 2003.

Valussi, Elena. "Gender as a Useful Category of Analysis in Chinese Religions—With Two Case Studies from the Republican Period." *Key Concepts in Practice*, no. 5 (2019): 133–78.

Valussi, Elena. "Men Built Religion, and Women Made it Superstitious: Gender and Superstition in Republican China." *Journal of Chinese Religions* 48, no. 1 (May 2020): 1–38.

Zhao Shiyu 趙世瑜. *Kuanghuan yu richang: Ming-Qing yilai de miaohui yu minjian shehui* 狂歡與日常：明清以來的廟會與民間社會. Beijing: Sanlian shudian, 2002.

Zhao Yancai 趙炎才. "Qingmo Minchu daode jiushi sichao de lishi kaocha 清末民初道德救世思潮的歷史考察." *Zhejiang luntan* 浙江論壇, no. 1 (2016): 79–83.

Zhou Yuwen 周愚文. *Zhongguo jiaoyu shigang* 中國教育史綱. Taibei: Zhengzhong shuju gufen youxian gongsi, 2001.

CHAPTER 12

The Phoenix Perches in the Land of the Kami: Spirit-Writing from Yiguandao to Tendō

Nikolas Broy

1   Introduction

This chapter explores the nature, forms, and meanings of spirit-writing in the Chinese popular sect Yiguandao 一貫道 (the Way of Pervading Unity, or simply the Unity Sect). By examining its development from late nineteenth-century Yiguandao to its adaptation by the related group, Tendō 天道 (the Way of Heaven), that emerged in Japan after WWII, this contribution seeks to examine the practices and religious significance of spirit-writing in the Chinese sectarian tradition. Having emerged from the fertile Xiantiandao 先天道 (the Way of Former Heaven) sectarian network during the second half of the nineteenth century, Yiguandao remained a marginal and extremely localized religious group in 1920s Shandong 山東 province. It was not until the 1930s and thanks to the charismatic leadership of the eighteenth patriarch, Zhang Tianran 張天然 (1889–1947), that it developed into a mass phenomenon that was soon to transcend national borders and, since the 1970s, evolved into a religious movement of global significance. As early as the late 1940s, Japan was among the first non-domestic destinations for Yiguandao activists and, in 1949, Japanese Tendō was established by Taiwanese missionaries belonging to Tiandao 天道 (the Way of Heaven), i.e., a smaller faction that rejects the claims to legitimacy of "mainstream" Yiguandao.

Since the mid-nineteenth century some sectarian groups are documented to have employed spirit-writing. But it was not until the Republican period that the practice of spirit-writing in the so-called "redemptive societies"—a term coined by Prasenjit Duara and developed further by David Palmer and others to refer to modern sectarian organizations—attracted the attention of various scholars.[1] Already, contemporaneous observers such as the famous German

---

1   Chao, "The Origin and Growth of the Fu Chi," 11; Sakai, *Kingendai Chūgoku ni okeru shūkyō kessha*, 343–74; Shiga, *Chūgoku no kokkurisan*, 169–75. On the concept of "redemptive societies," see Palmer, "Chinese Redemptive Societies"; Broy, "Syncretic Sects and Redemptive Societies."

missionary and translator of Chinese classics, Richard Wilhelm (1873–1930), describe "occult séances" among the Daoyuan 道院 (the School of the Way) practitioners in considerable detail in his memoirs, published in 1925.[2] Given the prominence of the practice within the sectarian context, it is surprising that there exist few studies about spirit-writing in Yiguandao,[3] even though the practice is well-attested in the sources and fieldwork research. Hence, this chapter aims to contribute to the understanding of spirit-writing in the cosmology and practice of Yiguandao and related groups. The first part considers how spirit-writing was used but also contested in early to present-day Yiguandao. The second part then explores how this strongly Chinese religious practice was transculturated into a non-Chinese context and plays a vital role in an otherwise entirely Japanese Yiguandao-related community. This enables us to probe into the evolution of this specific form of spirit-writing beyond the confines of a Chinese cultural-religious context.

Section one introduces the early history of spirit-writing in Yiguandao and its predecessor Xiantiandao. It argues that from the 1840s onward, spirit-writing was a key instrument in legitimizing the organizational and institutional innovations within this tradition and was continued by early Yiguandao. In section two, I demonstrate the vividness of spirit-writing during the patriarchy of paramount leader, Zhang Tianran, in the 1930s and 1940s. Besides analyzing the practice itself, I also explore its forms, meanings, and functions within Zhang's community until the dawn of the PRC. Section three examines briefly how spirit-writing continued to be a vital aspect of Yiguandao's religious life in Taiwan after 1949, but also a major source of interaction and competition, through local spirit-writing cults. In particular, and despite other claims, I argue that spirit-writing continues to play a vital role in Yiguandao communities even today. Before delving into an analysis of spirit-writing in Japanese Tendō in section five, section four briefly introduces this group to the reader. Finally, the conclusion sums up the analysis and discusses the evolution of spirit-writing specifically against the background of the transculturation of religious practices, amongst which the adaptation of Chinese spirit-writing in a Japanese religious setting presents a fascinating case study.

---

2 Wilhelm, *Die Seele Chinas*, 310–13.
3 For instance, Shiga Ichiko's monograph devotes only two pages to Yiguandao, see Shiga, *Chūgoku no kokkurisan*, 197–98.

2 From Xiantiandao to Yiguandao: Spirit-Writing and Chinese Sectarianism

Scholars such as Takeuchi Fusaji have found that, in 1840s Sichuan 四川 province, the milieu of spirit-writing groups and sectarian traditions began to merge into a new spirit-writing movement—a heterogeneous set of independent networks that focused on particular deities.[4] Among the first sectarian groups to adopt spirit-writing as a regular practice was Xiantiandao, a community that soon began to evolve into a relatively complex network of branches and split-offs, that is sometimes described as the "Xiantiandao matrix." This tradition is important not only because it was the first to integrate *fuji* 扶乩, or spirit-writing, into sectarian practices that usually centered on individual moral self-cultivation and eschatological belief in the Eternal Venerable Mother (Wusheng Laomu 無生老母), but also because it is also the progenitor of Yiguandao.

In particular, government files related to a purge of the movement in 1845 Sichuan that, in the sources, appears under the name "Blue Lotus Sect" (Qinglianjiao 青蓮教) demonstrate the extent to which spirit-writing was integrated into the sect's practices.[5] Confessions by apprehended sect members reveal that the sect's chief deity, Wusheng Laomu[6]—a figure widely venerated by countless sects in late imperial China—, was asked for advice in the case of organizational and religious questions, including the naming of temples and the distribution of religious authority.[7] For instance, the headquarters was named "cloud city" (*yuncheng* 雲城)—a common sectarian symbol for Laomu's paradise that was also adopted by the early Yiguandao.[8] Further-

---

[4] Takeuchi, "Shinmatsu Shisen no shūkyō undō"; Clart, "The Ritual Context of Morality Books," 21–56; Shiga, *Chūgoku no kokkurisan*, 114–16, 151–59; Shiga, "Difang Daojiao zhi xingcheng;" Wang, "Spirit Writing Groups."

[5] On Xiantiandao in this period, see Asai, *Min-Shin jidai minkan shūkyō kessha*, 381–438; Ngai, *Shumin de yongheng*, 97–318.

[6] Throughout this chapter, I shall use the designations Wusheng Laomu, Laomu, and Eternal Mother interchangeably to refer to this supreme divinity. While the first is her traditional name and the last its English translation, Laomu is most frequently used by contemporary Yiguandao practitioners to refer to her in everyday conversation. At least from the 1930s onward, we find yet another appellation in Yiguandao discourses, i.e., the Brightest God on High (Mingming Shangdi 明明上帝), which developed into the sect's primary official naming of Laomu as it is represented on shrines and altars, and in ritual texts.

[7] Memorial to the throne, Daoguang 25/8/28, *Chuanfei zoubing*, 92–93; Memorial to the throne, Daoguang 25/4/5, *Chuanfei zoubing*, 14.

[8] Memorial to the throne, Daoguang 25/8/28, *Chuanfei zoubing*, 98.

more, spirit-writing—called *jibi* 乩筆 in government documents—also laid out prophecies regarding the approaching apocalypse that was predicted to occur between 1845 and 1847. The final catastrophe would be averted only if one joined the sect, followed a vegetarian diet, swore an oath to Laomu, and accepted a set of rules and regulations.[9] Other members of the Xiantiandao network used spirit-writing to claim the descent of the savior Buddha Maitreya, as incarnated in a particular family, who was willing to emerge around the turn from 1847 to 1848.[10] The transcripts of the messages, decrees, and ordinances transmitted by Laomu in 1843 were later published as *Yuncheng baolu* 雲城寶籙 (Precious records from the cloud city), which served as one of Xiantiandao's key books, as it described the organizational and religious outlook of the group.[11] The document shows that, besides the Eternal Mother, other deities also revealed themselves to the sectarians, including Guangong 關公, Zhenwu 真武, and Lü Dongbin 呂洞賓.[12] Apparently, the disputes over religious authority that began to emerge in the insecure decade of the 1840s, which was marked by fierce government repression, led to the establishment of spirit-writing as a means of solving power struggles through Laomu's revelations.[13] Yet, it is ironic that precisely this innovation appears to have been a chief motor of the further bifurcation of the Xiantiandao network into various branches and sects, including Guigendao 歸根道 (the Way of Returning to the Origin), Tongshan she 同善社 (the Fellowship of Goodness), and Yiguandao. The practice of spirit-writing was continued by many Xiantiandao branches and split-offs, including Tongshan she and Yiguandao.[14]

Even though some scholars claim that Yiguandao's factual founder and fifteenth patriarch, Wang Jueyi 王覺一 (1822?–1884?), abolished spirit-writing and it was only the eighteenth patriarch Zhang Tianran who reintegrated the practice,[15] both the archival sources and Wang's own publications attest otherwise.[16] For instance, the probably early 1880s *Linian yili* 歷年易理 (The changes and truths of past years) contains instructions by Laomu regarding how the congregation should be managed and developed further by Wang. The

9   Ibid.
10   Memorial to the throne, Daoguang 25/4/6, by Bao Xing 寶興, *Chuanfei zoubing*, 20.
11   Ngai, *Shumin de yongheng*, 158–59.
12   Ibid., 159–68.
13   Wang, "Xiantiandao qianqishi chutan," 104.
14   On Xiantiandao and Tongshan she, see Shiga, *Chūgoku no kokkurisan*, 173–75; Shiga, "Difang Daojiao zhi xingcheng," 19–20.
15   Lu, *The Transformation of Yiguan Dao*, 35.
16   Zhou, "Yiguandao qianqi lishi chutan," 77, 85.

text begins by explaining that the late twelfth patriarch, Yuan Zhiqian 袁志謙 (1760–1835), conferred the rulership (*daopan* 道盤, lit. "plate of the Dao") upon him through a mediumistic incarnation,[17] a procedure that was applied since the 1840s to decide on questions of religious leadership in the Xiantiandao. In addition, and probably to counter rival claims, the text further explains that Laomu descended to the altar in 1877 to bestow her "heavenly mandate" (*tianming* 天命) to Wang, who could thus claim legitimacy as the rightful heir to Xiantiandao teachings.[18] Another note, dated 1878, states that he established a spirit-writing facility (*jipan* 乩盤)—literally a "divination plate," i.e., the *shapan* 沙盤 or "sand table" used for spirit-writing—at his Dongzhen tang 東震堂 headquarters in Shandong.[19] Finally, the text is supplemented by eleven revelations dated 1886 and transmitted by Wang on the spirit-writing altar.[20] While it is obvious that Wang himself and his followers were keen to apply spirit-writing, it is also true that his attitude toward spirit-writing was far from unambiguous—probably because he was well aware of its ambiguity in regard to alternative claims to authority. For instance, in another note, Wang concedes that, as a child, he did not fully believe in spirit-written revelations, but only accepted the absolute cosmic "principle" (*li* 理) as his sole guide.[21] Furthermore, a set of forty-eight instructions, ascribed to Wang, warns of its fallacies, arguing that not only are there right and wrong messages (鸞筆之事, 有正有邪), but in fact most of them are erroneous. Hence, practitioners are requested to empty their mind, seek instructions from an enlightened master, and recognize the truth rather than solely relying on spirit revelations.[22] This statement must apparently be understood as a strategy for countering an uncritical belief in the power of these messages. Yet, Wang also concedes that, despite his skepticism, he does not dare to disbelieve spirit-writing (*jibi zhi shi* 乩筆之事) altogether.[23]

---

17 *Linian yili*, YGDJJ, vol. 1, 5. The revelations and notes are dated from 1877 to 1884. At the end, the text is supplemented by ten further revelations by Wang, the first of which is dated 1886. Hence, the earliest version of this collection may have been circulated in 1886.

18 *Linian yili*, YGDJJ, vol. 1, 6–7.

19 *Linian yili*, YGDJJ, vol. 1, 14.

20 *Linian yili*, YGDJJ, vol. 1, 49–68. There is still no consensus in the academic world about Wang Jueyi's date of death, as some sources claim that he had hidden from the government and managed to live until the late 1910s, cf. Wang, "Xiantiandao qianqishi chutan," 114. Yet, because there are virtually no traces of him left in the sources after 1884, it is likely that he passed away around 1884, cf. Zhong, *Qingmo Minchu minjian Rujiao*, 36.

21 *Linian yili*, YGDJJ, vol. 1, 37.

22 *Zushi sishiba xun* 祖師四十八訓, in Lin, *Beihai Laoren quanshu*, 25–26.

23 Ibid., 63–65.

While we know very little about spirit-writing between Wang and Zhang Tianran's patriarchy, at least two spirit-written texts from the term of the seventeenth patriarch Lu Zhongyi 路中一 (1848/1853–1925) are extant; namely, *Jiaxiang xinshu* 家鄉信書 (The letter from home, prefaced 1919) and *Wuji shengmu qinyan xueshu* 無極聖母親演血書 (Blood book personally bestowed by the Holy Mother of the Non-Ultimate), revealed in Hubei 湖北 in 1924.[24] While the far more substantial *Jiaxiang xinshu* does not make its revealed nature explicit, a later preface to this text corroborates its origin in a spirit-writing séance.[25] A further book that was produced by spirit-writing and may have been compiled at least partially by 1924 is *Yiguan juelu* 一貫覺路 (The one thread to recognize the way), a collection of revelations by various deceased humans and deities, including Lü Dongbin.[26] One year after Lu passed away and still four years before Zhang officially obtained the patriarchy, a medium channeled Lu's spirit and transmitted a series of important revelations that became highly influential within Yiguandao teachings and practices: first, the *Hunyuan budai zhenjing* 混元布袋真經 (The true scripture of Maitreya Buddha of the primordial origin), a very short apocalyptic text that narrates the annihilations in the final period of our world and the salvation of the sect's pious adherents in the "cloud city;"[27] second, the equally brief *Mile jiuku zhenjing* 彌勒救苦真經 (The true scripture of Maitreya rescuing [sentient beings] from bitterness), which revolves around the same topic but provides less insight into the final catastrophe;[28] and, third, the relatively voluminous *Jin'gong miaodian* 金公妙典 (The marvelous compendium of the Golden Lord), which was revealed in four parts and contains many prophecies about the future of both the sect and China.[29] According to a later preface, that was added in Taiwan in 1989, the text was transmitted not via traditional spirit-writing, but by "borrowing one's aperture"

---

24   *Wuji shengmu qinyan xueshu*, 151. Cf. Pettit, "The Many Faces," 65–68.
25   See Zhou Zhaochang's 周兆昌 (1931–1989) 1955 preface to Tendō's Japanese translation: *Raumu shinsho*, Zhou Zhaochang's preface, no pagination. Zhou was among three missionaries dispatched by Tiandao's Taiwanese headquarters in Kaohsiung to Japan in 1949 and he lived and preached there ever since. This history will be elaborated further in section five of this chapter.
26   *Yiguan juelu*, MDSX, vol. 3, *juan* 1, and MDSX, vol. 6, *juan*. 2. The very first part is dated *jiazi*/11/6, i.e., December 2, 1924, but most of the revelations do not provide similar data (except for that dated 1936). I was also able to locate one message in another collection, where it is dated 1934. Hence, the entire compilation seems to have been edited over a considerable period of time and is thus not representative of the period under discussion.
27   *Hunyuan budai zhenjing*, 35–39.
28   *Mile jiuku zhenjing*, 10–11.
29   *Jin'gong miaodian*, 12–34.

(*jieqiao* 借竅)[30]—an Yiguandao term referring to the mediumistic channeling of a deity's words through one's own mouth (see below).

While the revelations received prior to Zhang Tianran's patriarchy in 1930 are small in number compared to the bulk of texts produced up until Zhang's death in 1947, the three scriptures mentioned above continued to be transmitted, read, and recited in the movement—probably because they were integrated into a mystical narrative of salvation that centered on the "three crows of the metal rooster" (*jinji sanchang* 金雞三唱)—a series of revelations by patriarch Lu, marking the final dissemination of Yiguandao's salvationism, and which are related to a concept that already flourished in Xiantiandao circles by the 1830s.[31] Today, in particular, the *Mile jiuku zhenjing* is comparable to the Buddhist *Heart Sūtra* in terms of how it is perceived to capture the sect's teachings and recited collectively before certain rituals and training classes.[32]

3 Spirit-Writing in the Late Republican Yiguandao

3.1 *The Pantheon and Spirit-Written Messages*

The year 1930 and the beginning of Zhang's patriarchy mark a tremendous increase in the production of spirit-written texts. The compilation *Yiguandaozang* 一貫道藏 (Canon of the Yiguandao) by the Taiwanese Yiguandao historian Lin Rongze 林榮澤 lists close to one-hundred revelations in this period, ranging from prefaces and short pieces of some hundred characters to fully-fledged scriptures obtained from a series of séances.[33] Reviewing the 130 Yiguandao texts collected by the late Li Shiyu 李世瑜 (1922–2010) during his fieldwork in the 1940s, sixty-one, and thus almost half of them, were produced by spirit-writing.[34] Judging from this material, in the 1930s, the majority of the revelations were received from patriarch Lu and Zhang Tianran's divine personas—particularly Jigong Huofo 濟公活佛.[35] Even though we can observe

---

30 See the preface in the online edition: http://www.taolibrary.com/category/category9/c9026/02.htm (accessed January 16, 2020).
31 The concept is mentioned in many Yiguandao writings; see, for instance, the 1937 catechism *Yiguandao yiwen jieda*, 207–8.
32 Fieldwork by the author in South African Buddha halls belonging to Fayi Lingyin 發一靈隱 and Fayi Chongde 發一崇德, November 2017.
33 YGDZ-SDZB, vols. 1–2. See also Lin, *Yiguandao fazhan shi*, 489–97.
34 Li, "Yiguandao diaocha baogao." See also Lin, *Yiguandao lishi*, 342–46 for a detailed list of these sixty-one titles.
35 On Zhang Tianran as Jigong's avatar, see Shahar, *Crazy Ji*, 198–208.

a greater variety of deities revealing themselves through the planchette since the early 1940s, most messages were still transmitted by Yiguandao patriarchs and their divine personas, including the fourteenth patriarch, Yao Hetian 姚鶴天 (d. 1874, one message), Lu Zhongyi, and Zhang Tianran. Zhang's co-leader, Sun Suzhen 孫素真's (1895–1975) divine persona, Yuehui Pusa 月慧菩薩, began to transmit messages only in 1948 and thus at a time when the dispute over the leadership after Zhang's passing had already boiled over and two chief factions had emerged (see section four). Compared to nineteenth-century Xiantiandao, the Eternal Mother seldom reveals herself personally, appearing to prefer to speak through her emissaries. Thus, up until 1951, only five revelations by the Eternal Mother—using her Yiguandao pseudonym, Mingming Shangdi 明明上帝—were received during spirit-writing séances, yet two of them gained particular prominence in the movement and continue to be read and discussed today: the *Huangmu shisan tan* 皇母十三嘆 (Thirteen lamentations of the August Mother) received in 1936 and the 1941 *Huangmu xunzi shijie* 皇母訓子十誡 (Ten precepts of the August Mother for instructing her children). Both narrate the moral degeneration of humankind, its blind attachment to materialism, and the approaching apocalypse that will wipe out this world of ruins, but they also encourage humans to engage in moral and religious cultivation in order to be among those saved by Laomu. They paint the end in vivid colors, prophesizing that the blood of those killed will fill the rivers, their skeletons will form a pile as high as mountains, and only those joining the sect will survive the great annihilation.[36]

It is striking that the phrase "ten precepts" used in the title of the second book is the usual Chinese translation of the Christian term "ten commandments." The impact of Christian and other religious traditions is equally present in certain revelations of this period. For instance, in addition to the Chinese pantheon, Jesus Christ and Mohammad began to reveal themselves through the planchette from December 1938 onward, albeit in a fairly restricted manner and far later than in other Republican "redemptive societies," such as the Daoyuan.[37] Lin's list notes three messages from Jesus Christ (1938, 1940, and 1950) and only one from Muhammad (1938).[38] Yet, it must be kept in mind that not only is this list not exhaustive, but also that these are not the only occurrences of these figures as they often transmit small sections at the beginning of larger texts.[39] Still, these messages are important in various respects, as they

---

36   *Huangmu shisan tan*, 230; *Huangmu xunzi shijie*, 36–37.
37   Clart, "Jesus in Chinese Popular Sects," 1316–20.
38   On Jesus in early Yiguandao revelations, see ibid., 1320–24.
39   See, for instance, *Huangmu xunzi shijie*, 9–10.

demonstrate Yiguandao's drive to become a universal teaching that is valuable to people of various faiths. For instance, Jesus' revelations explore the insufficiencies of the traditional Christian faith and argue that only by receiving the great Dao will Christians be saved.[40]

Besides receiving moral messages from deities and deceased patriarchs, at least since the 1930s, spirit-writing also served as a means of communicating with deceased relatives, minor gods, and also figures from Chinese history and religion. These revelations are called *jieyuan xunwen* 結緣訓文 (revelations that create bonds of karmic affinity). Judging from the 236 revelations that Yiguandao practitioners brought from the mainland to Taiwan up to the early 1950s, only twenty pieces belong to this type.[41] Besides the deceased relatives of the followers, there were also a few historical figures who addressed the sectarians and admonished them in the early 1940s, such as the second Tang emperor, Li Shimin 李世民 (599–649), the Shunzhi 順治皇帝 (1638–1661) and Kangxi 康熙皇帝 (1654–1722) emperors of the Qing, and the poet, Qu Yuan 屈原 (ca. 340–278 BCE).[42] Even though the context of these revelations is unclear, the particular date and nature of the revealing figures as representatives of the Chinese tradition and national pride may lead us to speculate whether their messages aimed to foster patriotic sentiments during the period of Japanese occupation of many regions in northern and eastern China during WWII.

Likewise, from the late 1930s onward, the founders or important representatives of various religious traditions also revealed themselves to Yiguandao practitioners. Besides Confucius, Mencius, Laozi, and Śākyamuni (as well as Jesus and Muhammad, as mentioned above)—all of whom transmitted many messages at an early stage—these were (in chronological order):[43]

(1) 1939: Dong Sihai 董四海 (1619–1650), the founder of Tiandimen 天地門 (Heaven and Earth Sect) alias Yizhuxiangjiao 一炷香教 (the One Stick of Incense Sect).

---

40 Clart, "Jesus in Chinese Popular Sects," 1322.
41 Lin, *Yiguandaoxue yanjiu: shoujuan*, 622.
42 YGDZ-SDZB, vol. 1, 401–3 (Li Shimin); YGDZ-SDZB, vol. 2, 27–30 (Shunzhi and Kangxi emperors, Minguo 31/4/4); 53–55 (Qu Yuan, Minguo 31/5/5).
43 YGDZ-SDZB, vol. 1, 353–54 (Dong Sihai, Minguo 28/2/12); 363–69 (Wang Fengyi, Minguo 28/3/2); 392–400 (Li Tingyu, two revelations, Minguo 29); 415–18 (Zhao Wanzhi, Minguo 29/4/14) and 425–26 (Zhao Wanzhi, Minguo 29/10/3); 427–29 (Shengzong Gufo, Minguo 29/11/13); YGDZ-SDZB, vol. 2, 56–60 (Yinguang, Minguo 31/5/23); 66–73 (Li Tingyu, two revelations, both dated Minguo 31/11/27); 265–70 (Xiao Changming, Minguo 37/8/26). The message related to the members of Tongshan she is collected in Lin, *Yiguandao fazhan shi*, 663–65. Most of these revelations are also collected in the volume *Baiyang jingzang*.

(2) 1939: Wang Fengyi 王鳳儀 (1864–1937), the illiterate farmer from Manchuria who evolved into a popular healer and important leader of the 1930s Wanguo daode hui 萬國道德會 (the International Morality Association).
(3) 1939: Randeng Gufo 燃燈古佛 reveals himself as requested by members of the Tongshan she.
(4) 1940: Fuyang Dijun 復陽帝君 alias Fuyang Daxian 復陽大仙, i.e., Zhao Wanzhi 趙萬秩 (fl. mid-seventeenth-century), venerated as the founder of Guiyidao 皈一道 (the Sect of the Returning to the One).
(5) 1940: Shengzong Gufo 聖宗古佛, the mythical founding figure in the genealogy of Zailijiao 在理教 (the Cosmic Principle Sect).
(6) 1942: The Great Dharma master Yinguang 印光大師 (1861–1940), an outstanding Buddhist figure of the Republican era.
(7) 1943: Li Tingyu 李廷玉 is venerated by many sects, including Guiyidao but also the late Qing Baguajiao 八卦教 (the Eight Trigrams Sect) networks. (The séance was held on the twenty-seventh day of the eleventh lunar month on Minguo 31, or January 3, 1943).
(8) 1948: Xiao Changming 蕭昌明 (1893–1943), the founder of Tiande shengjiao 天德聖教 (Sacred Teaching of Heavenly Virtue).

In particular, the smaller and more traditional sectarian groups—such as Tiandijiao, Guiyidao, Zailijiao, and Baguajiao—had their strongholds in eastern or northeastern China, and thus in the same region as Yiguandao.[44] Clearly, these messages served to elevate Yiguandao in regard to rival groups, as it proclaimed to represent the supreme unity of all teachings. As early as 1942, a small booklet containing some of these revelations had been published as *Wanzu guizhen* 萬祖歸真 (The ten thousand patriarchs reverting to the truth) and obviously served to advertise this self-understanding, probably *vis-à-vis* other religious groups.[45] Grootaers reports a similar booklet entitled *Xuntu guizheng* 訓徒歸正 (Admonish the followers to revert to the truth), that collects three messages ascribed to Li Tingyu.[46] This demonstrates the extent to which the sectarian

---

44 On the sectarian leaders and their groups, see DuBois, *The Sacred Village*, 161–85; Ownby, "Redemptive Societies," 695–97; Sakai, *Kingendai Chūgoku ni okeru shūkyō kessha*, 133–51; Welch and Yü, "The Tradition of Innovation"; Kong, "Lun Baguajiao lishi shenhua"; Li, "Guiyidao diaocha baogao."

45 I was only able to locate an html file of the text, posted on a Taiwanese website documenting tracts and morality books from a variety of religious traditions, including Yiguandao: http://www.taolibrary.com/category/category9/c9023.htm (accessed January 23, 2020). The preface is dated 1942, but there is an apparently newer appendix dated 1948. The text is mentioned neither by Li Shiyu, nor by Grootaers, so its publishing history remains unclear.

46 Grootaers, "Société Secrète Moderne," 341–42.

groups and traditions were not isolated from each other but, in fact, that there was a great deal of interaction and competition among them. Yinguang's spirit revelation produced great publicity for the sect, as it was fiercely attacked in Buddhist circles and journals.[47]

Finally, besides historical figures, minor gods—i.e., deified humans who are not part of Laomu's paradise—also used the planchette to request their initiation into the sect, a procedure that was called "converting the great saints" (*du daxian* 渡大仙). An early example was a revelation by Wong Tai Sin (Huang Daxian 黃大仙) in 1949—a deity particularly popular in Guangdong 廣東 and Hong Kong, but also Zhejiang 浙江.[48] This practice was continued in Taiwan, where local gods (Tudigong 土地公) and even Mazu are said to have "sought the Dao" (*qiudao* 求道), i.e., they were initiated into the sect.[49] In conclusion, the messages received by various deities, historical figures, and religious leaders in the 1930s and 40s highlight Yiguandao's drive and mission to represent the supreme, universal teaching that embraces all other faiths.

3.2 *The Structure of a Séance and the Training of Mediums*

Given this abundance of material, it is unsurprising that the important 1937 catechism, *Yiguandao yiwen jiedao* 一貫道疑問解答 (Answers to doubts about the Unity Sect), takes some time to describe the significance of spirit-writing. According to this text, God (Shangdi 上帝, i.e., the Eternal Mother) dispatched various gods and Buddhas as her emissaries to help humankind to attain final salvation. In order to communicate with them, one needs to erect a phoenix altar (*luantan* 鸞壇), where the spirits of the deities (仙佛之性靈) will borrow the physical body of a person and unite with it (*shenren heyi* 神人合一). The deity will transmit messages to proclaim the ultimate truth of the Dao in order to awaken the world. This is called "transformation through the flying phoenix" (*feiluan xuanhua* 飛鸞宣化).[50] While this phrase is a relatively sophisticated appellation, the practice is also colloquially referred to as *kaisha* 開沙 or *kaitan* 開壇, but terms such as *fuji* are also used. Another related practice is the above-mentioned "borrowing one's aperture" (*jieqiao*), i.e., revealing a deity's words by speaking. While its origins remain somewhat obscure due to the lack of primary sources, it appears to have been in vogue in Yiguandao congregations as early as the 1920s. Thus, the "three crows of the rooster"—the first of which took place in 1926 with the revelation of the texts *Hunyuan budai zhenjing, Mile*

---

47 Discussed at length in ibid., 348–49. Cf. also Li, "Yiguandao diaocha baogao," 116.
48 Dated Minguo 39/4/26, cited in Lin, *Yiguandao fazhan shi*, 882–84.
49 *Meizhou Sima qiudao ji; Xinwei Tudigong*.
50 *Yiguandao yiwen jieda*, YGDJJ, vol. 1, 200–1.

jiuku zhenjing and *Jin'gong miaodian*—are generally believed by sectarians to have been conducted by *jieqiao*. Other texts of the 1930s and 40s also refer to it as a way in which deities utilize humans' abilities to propagate the truth and thus set it on a par with *fuji* divination.[51] It is still practiced today in many Yiguandao branches in Taiwan and overseas, but is discontinued in others.[52] Observed by Sébastien Billioud during his fieldwork in Hong Kong and Paris, he describes *jieqiao* as usually involving a medium speaking in vernacular Chinese (*baihua* 白話).[53] As far as I can discern from the eyewitness accounts of Yiguandao members—as I was unable to attend a *jieqiao* séance in person— the practice also, at times, involves the medium dressing up as the deity and altering its demeanor accordingly.[54] In the 1920s, similar practices appear to have been popular in other sectarian groups also, as Richard Wilhelm notes in his memoirs about his experience of Daoyuan.[55]

Unfortunately, there exist few ethnographic descriptions of Yiguandao spirit-writing séances—probably due to the fact that, in most cases, recording or taking pictures is forbidden. The standard account that is referred to by the majority of later authors is by the ethnographer Li Shiyu, who conducted fieldwork among popular sects in northern China between 1942 and 1948.[56] From a technical point of view, the representation of a séance in the 1952 propaganda movie *Yiguan hairen dao* 一貫害人道 is also relatively accurate, which demonstrates that the makers of the movie—it was produced and released by the Central Film Bureau and thus must have represented an important contribution in the eyes of the Communist Party—must have counted former Yiguandao adherents among their advisors.[57]

According to Li's research, at least since the late 1930s, Yiguandao distinguished between *xiantianji* 先天乩 (former heaven spirit-writing) and *houtianji* 後天乩 (later heaven spirit-writing), the latter of which is understood as spirit-writing conducted by other religious groups—as Yiguandao claims to be able to channel the deities of Laomu's paradise rather than only the minor gods

---

51 *Jin'gong Zushi chandao pian*, 8; *Huangmu xunzi shijie*, 22.
52 Shinohara, *Taiwan ni okeru Ikkandō*, 391–402.
53 Billioud, *Reclaiming the Wilderness*, 78–80.
54 See a talk given by Los Angeles Fayi Chongde member, Bill Krause, in 2015, about his conversion to Yiguandao, entitled: "中西文化與信仰英文 (Tao experience in my life) 英文 演講 正和書院 02 33 01 美國講師 Bill Krause 講座," https://youtu.be/76ELYX17WW4 (accessed April 9, 2018), ca. 57:35.
55 Wilhelm, *Die Seele Chinas*, 313.
56 Li, "Yiguandao diaocha baogao," 106–7. Referred to by Kubo, "Ikkandō ni tsuite," 218–22; Lu, *Yiguandao neimu*, 131–34.
57 Hung, "The Anti-Unity Sect Campaign," 411.

of the ephemeral world.[58] The specialists in charge of the ritual are called the "three talents" (sancai 三才), emulating the cosmological unity of heaven, earth, and humans. The "heavenly talent" (tiancai 天才) is the actual medium who channels the spirits and their words. The one who clears the sand and calls out the characters written by the medium is called rencai 人才 (human talent) as, according to a common saying, heaven and earth do not speak, but only humans do.[59] Finally, the one who records the text is called dicai 地才 (earthly talent). While the first two specialists stand at the actual "sand table," the recorder usually stands at another.[60] The ji 乩 itself is a wooden ring with a longer stick attached, which is used to write the characters in the sand.[61]

The séance itself starts with a report to Laomu, followed by various kowtowing before the altar, first by the leading master—usually a high-ranking specialist of the rank of initiator (dianchuanshi 點傳師)—and then by the mediums. Before ascending to the altar space, the tiancai must also meditate for a while. The possession of the "heavenly talent" is not indicated by sudden movements, as in other forms of Chinese spirit mediumship, but the tiancai begins his task by drawing circles in the sand. After this moment of inception, the actual writing begins. The end of a section or an entire message is indicated by "haha 哈哈." While some of the existing literature takes this "haha" to represent Jigong's characteristic laughter,[62] the phrase is actually used by various deities. The end of a message is also indicated by "haha" or "hahazhi 哈哈止," followed by "tui 退," which refers to the deity returning to its place of origin. The messages are usually composed in literary Chinese and use the traditional meter of four, five, or seven syllables.

According to Li Shiyu, most mediums were boys and, while their training was supposed to take forty-nine days, it often took far longer than this in reality. The daily routine consisted chiefly of meditation, reading, memorizing existing revelations, and, of course, practicing spirit-writing.[63] This is very similar to what Philip Clart and Shiga Ichiko found during their fieldwork among spirit-writing cults in Taiwan and Hong Kong during the 1990s,[64] except Li does not

---

58   Li, "Yiguandao diaocha baogao," 106.
59   *Yiguandao yiwen jieda*, YGDJJ, vol. 1, 202.
60   This practice still appears to be standard in Taiwanese Yiguandao congregations. See the photograph in Ding, "The Construction of Fundamentalism," 153.
61   Some aspects of Yiguandao's spirit-writing are also already documented in the 1937 catechism, *Yiguandao yiwen jieda*, 202–3.
62   Shahar, *Crazy Ji*, 204; Billioud, "Yiguandao's Patriarch Zhang Tianran," 236.
63   Li, "Yǐguandao diaocha baogao," 107.
64   Clart, "The Ritual Context of Morality Books," 254–55; Shiga, *Chūgoku no kokkurisan*, 28–30.

mention the vegetarian regimen of the mediums. Other sources contemporaneous with Li indicate that Yiguandao mediums were also expected to abstain from the consumption of meat and alcohol. Memoirs and confessions by sect members, probably recorded in mainland China after the 1950s, provide further insights into the spirit-writing practices of late Republican Yiguandao. Many of them were published within so-called "literary and historical materials" (*wenshi ziliao* 文史資料), collections of first-hand retrospective accounts of life prior to "liberation," i.e., the founding of the PRC in 1949.[65] While these essays often employ derogatory language in regard to the so-called reactionary sects and secret societies—collectively labeled *huidaomen* 會道門—there is an impressive amount of material on the religious life of sects in late Republican China.

In these accounts, spirit-writing is portrayed as an important aspect of Yiguandao practices. According to the confessions, séances were held not only in religious centers but also in private shrines (*jiating fotang* 家庭佛堂).[66] The rituals usually entailed offering fruit, tea, and incense, plus various kowtowing by the ritual leader and the mediums. Finally, the *dianchuanshi* recites the *Qingtanjing* 請壇經 (Scripture on requesting [the spirits to descend to the] altar), which serves to invite the deities to the altar, only after which will the mediums begin their séances. The *tiancai*'s eyes are closed throughout the entire process, even though many accounts claim that, in fact, the mediums never closed them totally.[67] According to the recollections of Wang Xiaofeng 王效峰 (b. 1919), a Yiguandao follower from 1938 to 1953, who also became a *dianchuanshi* and *tiancai*, and others, the training of the mediums was relatively challenging and took between six months and one year.[68] Following these narratives, there were no restrictions on gender, and children aged between seven and fourteen years were accepted, but only with their parents' agreement. The training regimen was called *lian xue bei bian* 練學背編, thus referring to the four aspects of practicing, studying, memorizing, and composing. The *lian* part refers to learning how to write characters on the sand table and, in particular, how to write them at a 90° angle. *Tiancai* neophytes were also commanded to study not only the sectarian tracts and existing revelations, but also the Confucian *Four Books* (*sishu* 四書, i.e., the *Great Learning*, *Doctrine of the*

---

65   For the nature and academic value of these sources, see Fromm, "Producing History," 37–58.
66   Wei, "Wo suo liaojie de Yiguandao neimu," 185.
67   Ibid., 186.
68   *Yiguandao neimu*, 83–85. Note: this book is not to be confused with Lu Zhongwei's 1998 monograph of the same title that also provides some information from a confession

Mean, the *Analects*, and the *Mencius*). One account mentions that this training was monitored by a private Confucian teacher (*sishu xiansheng* 私塾先生) who instructed the neophytes about phrases and short texts from the *Four Books* and taught them how to write good poems and verses.[69] Besides practicing the technical aspects of writing and composing texts, neophytes were also required to practice meditation (*jingzuo* 靜坐), which basically consisted of keeping one's eyes exactly thirty percent open while focusing on their "mysterious gate" (*xuanguan* 玄關)—a secret spot on one's forehead, which is pointed to and opened during the initiation ritual by the initiator. During contemplation, mediums should breathe naturally and recite the secret mantra (*koujue* 口訣), which is also obtained by every *daoqin* during initiation, silently in their mind. In order to enhance the quality of the writings, sometimes, two classes of *tiancai* neophytes were encouraged to watch and comment on each other's performances. Before engaging in learning the craft of spirit-writing, however, the neophytes had to swear oaths before the altar, including the "clean mouth oath" (*qingkouyuan* 清口愿) to become a vegetarian and refrain from using bad language. Finally, some memoirs claim that the neophytes were not allowed to discuss what they had learned with outsiders, even fellow sect members.[70] While possibly true—as most religious groups that distinguish between insiders and outsiders tend to confine the dissemination of specialist knowledge to the initiated—, this may also have been a later interpolation by the author of this account, guided by the Party's view of *huidaomen* as representing secret, underground, and thus potentially dangerous, antisocial elements that need to be eradicated—a view that persists within the Chinese scholarship on sectarian groups to this day.

While it is usually claimed by Yiguandao followers that the planchette was to be used for sophisticated matters only, the confessions attest that many ordinary practitioners often requested healing and divine cures for diseases from the deities. They, in turn, not only instructed the petitioners about medical treatment, but also encouraged them to print religious books or propagate the Dao themselves in order to reduce their karmic debts and thus recover from illnesses through moral behavior.[71] Many former followers even claimed that, often, the sand of the *shapan* was mixed with water and drunk by the sick

---

recorded shortly after 1949, see Lu, *Yiguandao neimu*, 135. See also: Zan, "Yiguandao de zui'e neimu," 700–1.
69 Zan, "Yiguandao de zui'e neimu," 701.
70 Wei, "Wo suo liaojie de Yiguandao neimu," 186–88.
71 Xu, "Ji'nan 'Yiguandao' de zui'e huodong," 282–83; *Yiguandao neimu*, 86–87; Wei, "Wo suo liaojie de Yiguandao neimu," 192; Zan, "Yiguandao de zui'e neimu," 708–9.

persons.[72] This mirrors the experiences of other Republican-era spirit-writing groups, whose leaders aimed to counter members inquiring about issues, such as individual health and prosperity, including the scientific Shanghai Lingxue hui 靈學會 (Spiritualist Society) studied by Matthias Schumann in another contribution.[73]

3.3 Prophecies and Apocalypses

The revelations received between the 1920s and the 40s not only explain how to restore one's inherent, original nature by engaging in religious and moral cultivation, many texts also paint vivid pictures of the pending apocalypse and the last days of humankind. Particularly against the background of the devastation of the Japanese invasion, civil war, poverty, and famine, many people appeared to have been receptive to these descriptions that were to usher urgency into the sect's messages. Since the end of the 1940s, the looming triumph of the Communist Party's apocalyptic visions became even more prominent, many of which were related to the party and their political cause.[74] Some of them were received during spirit-writing séances and depicted the CCP or Mao Zedong as a demon king (*mowang* 魔王).[75] In his study of Cang county 滄縣 (Hebei 河北 province), Thomas DuBois also uncovered spirit-written prophecies from a neighboring county about an imminent world war that would leave Beijing and Tianjin annihilated by thunder and Manchuria devastated by an atomic bomb.[76] Most of these messages do not reveal their anticommunist content at first glance, but the prophecies are often hidden in the text and need to be deciphered by careful readers. Some of them use homophonic characters to conceal their true intent, such as one message discussed by Lu Zhongwei. In his example, the characters "pig" (*zhu* 豬) and "cat" (*mao* 貓) in the sentence *xiaoxiao Mao Zhu wu neng wei* 小小豬貓無能為 are thought to refer to CCP Chairman Mao and PLA General Zhu De 朱德 (1886–1976) because of their homophony with both individuals' surnames. Hence, the true meaning of the phrase should be "the little Zhu and Mao lack all capabilities."[77]

Other anti-communist revelations work similarly to a crossword puzzle. This method of finding secret "revelations within the revelation"—as they are

---

72 Xu, "Ji'nan 'Yiguandao' de zui'e huodong," 283.
73 Schumann, "Science and Spirit-Writing," 147, 159–60.
74 For a general overview of certain rumors and prophecies allegedly disseminated by Yiguandao in the early PRC, see Zhou, "Gongheguo chuqi Yiguandao."
75 Zan, "Yiguandao de zui'e neimu," 711.
76 DuBois, *The Sacred Village*, 147.
77 Lu, *Yiguandao neimu*, 162–63.

referred to as *xunzhongxun* 訓中訓 by Yiguandao practitioners—is still practiced today and serves as a quality marker for a good spirit revelation.[78] One text of this type by Jigong Huofo, dated 1947, was introduced to me by the owner of an Yiguandao bookshop during my fieldwork in Taipei in early 2017. The woman stressed to me how some intersecting sentences and phrases revealed the true meaning of the text, i.e., that Mao Zedong and the Soviet Army are the enemies, but that Chiang Kai-shek and America would save China.[79] In order to unveil this meaning, the reader needs to fuse several characters first. For instance, the otherwise obscure phrase, 四水高幸日含木, is a reference to the personal name of Chairman Mao: if one takes the phrase 四水高幸 as meaning to place a water radical on the left side and a "four" on top of the character *xing*, the character *ze* 澤 emerges. The same is true for 日含木—literally, the "sun" contains "wood" within—, which makes up the character *dong* 東. Finally, both characters form Mao's personal name, Zedong. While the practice of *xunzhongxun* remains popular in Yiguandao, I am unaware of any revelations today that adopt such a strong political stance, as informants usually told me that, in the temple, people do not discuss politics at all. Hence, these examples should be viewed in light of their historical circumstances and the rampant anti-Communist fears.

4   Post-1949 Developments

This section examines how Yiguandao spirit-writing developed after the founding of the People's Republic, when many leaders and practitioners fled the large-scaled persecution on the mainland to find a new home in Taiwan.[80] It draws on existing scholarship, but also includes ethnographic data collected by the author.

In a diligent effort of compilation, Yiguandao historian Lin Rongze collected 7.401 spirit messages produced between 1920 and 2008.[81] This is an impressive amount that still fails to do justice to the large quantity of spirit-writings—as a number of early texts are missing and it is also unlikely that Lin was able to collect every piece that has been written so far, particularly because Yiguandao

---

78   Cf. Lin, *Yiguandaoxue yanjiu: shou juan*, 379–89; Ding, "The Construction of Fundamentalism," 149.
79   Revelation dated Minguo 36/6/3, by Nanji Fengseng Jidian Heshang 南屏瘋僧濟顛和尚, i.e. Jigong Huofo, MDSX, vol. 3, 75–86, also collected in YGDZ-SDZB, vol. 2, 187–91.
80   On the persecution of Yiguandao, cf. Hung, "The Anti-Unity Sect Campaign."
81   Lin, *Yiguandaoxue yanjiu: juan er*, 121.

in Taiwan has developed into a heterogeneous, complex movement with more than twenty autonomous divisions and branches.[82] Nevertheless, his compilation is instructive about the apparent popularity of this practice to date. While the method of spirit-writing itself seems to follow the format established during the Republican period, today it appears that teenage girls are more likely to become mediums than boys.[83] According to the data collected by Lin, about seventy-five percent of all of the texts that he collected (of which almost ninety-three percent belong to Yiguandao) follow the traditional style, i.e., they are composed of poems written in literary Chinese that employ the traditional meter of four, five, or seven syllables. Yet, sixteen percent of the data includes vernacular language (*baihua* 白話).[84] Lin found that the earliest documented *baihua* revelation dates to 1950 and was transmitted by Jesus Christ.[85] Particularly since the 1980s, this form became more widespread, especially in terms of *jieqao*—probably also in response to the rise of modern telecommunication tools that have improved the recording and documentation of spoken words.

This abundance of material collected by Lin somewhat counters the claim made by Lu Yunfeng in his 2008 monograph that spirit-writing is no longer in vogue in contemporary Yiguandao congregations. According to his research, in the 1980s a dispute about the authenticity and credibility of certain revelations among followers of the Fayi Chongde 發一崇德 branch evolved into a full-blown scandal that soon spread to other divisions and branches. In the end, Lu claims, spirit-writing was discarded by most, if not all, branches.[86] Following fieldwork by Sébastien Billioud and myself in Taiwan and among overseas Yiguandao congregations, Lu's claim cannot be generalized.[87] For instance, I found that, while spirit-writing remains tremendously important in Fayi Chongde, it is only occasionally practiced by Andong 安東 branch and has been abandoned since the 1990s in Jichu Zhongshu 基礎忠恕. In the case of Fayi Chongde, for instance, spirit-writing continues to be an important means for deceased elders to interfere in sectarian activities and organizational matters.[88]

82　On Yiguandao's development in Taiwan, see Lu, *The Transformation of Yiguan Dao*, 47–70.
83　Lin, *Yiguandaoxue yanjiu: shou juan*, 439–40.
84　Cf. Lin, *Yiguandaoxue yanjiu: juan er*, 121. Many examples have been compiled in YGDZ-SDZB, vols. 5, 8, 12, 16, 21, 22, 28, 31, 37, and 41.
85　Lin, *Yiguandaoxue yanjiu: shou juan*, 441.
86　Lu, *The Transformation of Yiguan Dao*, 100–1.
87　Cf. Billioud, *Reclaiming the Wilderness*, 76–78, 112–18, 122–28.
88　Billioud, *Reclaiming the Wilderness*, 122–35.

Besides the production and usage of entirely novel texts, spirit-writing is also used to comment on or even rectify Chinese classics. In a recent project, Lin Rongze published a series of revelations received from Jigong Huofo between 1985 and 1987 as the *Baiyang Yijing* 白陽易經 (*Yijing* for the period of the white yang).[89] Unlike the traditional *Book of Changes*, this novel version is not intended to be used for divination, but instead transmits moral guidelines for everyday life. It has already become a scripture that is discussed and expounded in some Yiguandao training classes.[90] Other examples include the use of spirit-written comments on preexisting texts that originated in other religious contexts. For instance, the *Baixiaojing* 百孝經 (Scripture on the five-hundred expressions of filial duty), which, in its original form, dates back to a revelation by the International Morality Association in Republican China, and was later commented and elaborated on during Yiguandao séances. Officially founded in 1921, the International Morality Association (Wanguo daode hui 萬國道德會)—like Yiguandao—possessed an explicit Confucian orientation and sought to reestablish China's moral foundations through the dissemination of moral tractates, novel commentaries to the Confucian classics, and spirit-writing.[91] The *Baixiaojing* has now become a crucial text for some branches—particularly those belonging to Fayi division—, where it is displayed in Buddha halls and recited at the beginning of training classes.[92] In addition, a slightly abbreviated version of the text has become a major asset in Yiguandao's dealing with the PRC government, as it was published on the mainland in a slightly altered version with government sanctioning since the end of 2009.[93]

In addition, the spirit-written texts produced by other religious traditions and groups also circulate among Yiguandao congregations. One such case is the famous *Taoyuan mingsheng jing* 桃園明聖經 (Peach garden scripture on illuminating saintliness), revealed by Guangong probably in the early 1800s and widely popular in Taiwan,[94] as it is said to have helped Fayi Division Elder Senior Han Yulin 韓雨霖 (1903–1995) to recover from illness after he published and circulated it.[95] Nowadays, the text is often displayed in and circulated by

---

89   See Yiguandao yili bianjiyuan, *Baiyang Yijing*.
90   Fieldwork in an evening training class of Fayi Lingyin 發一靈隱 branch in Xindian district, Taipei, 25 April 2017.
91   Cf. Ownby, "Redemptive Societies," 695–96.
92   Fieldwork in Buddha halls belonging to Fayi Chongde and Fayi Lingyin, Johannesburg and Cape Town, South Africa, November to December 2017.
93   Cf. Ding, "The Construction of Fundamentalism"; on the significance of the *Baixiaojing* and an analysis of the two versions, see Billioud, *Reclaiming the Wilderness*, 189–94.
94   Cf. Goossaert, "The Textual Canonization," 515–16.
95   Ding, "The Construction of Fundamentalism," 149.

Fayi Buddha halls. Another instructive example are the spirit-written commentaries to the *Great Learning* and *Doctrine of the Mean* that were originally produced by the Jiushi xinjiao 救世新教 (New Teachings to Save the World) in the early 1920s and which now serve as training class textbooks for certain Yiguandao congregations.[96]

Spirit-writing was also an important aspect of the interaction and competition with non-sectarian spirit-writing cults and their "phoenix halls" (*luantang* 鸞堂).[97] In his case study of central Taiwan, Philip Clart argues that, on the one hand Yiguandao activists employed spirit-writing largely to attract the followers of these cults. On the other hand, he observes that phoenix hall congregations themselves integrated some of Yiguandao's symbols and eschatology, but not its soteriology.[98] In my fieldwork conducted in Taiwan in 2016 and 2017, I also stumbled across a similar example: a spirit-writing cult located at the Ciling yuan 慈靈院 in Kaohsiung, which appears to call itself Hunyuan Dadao 混元大道 (Great Sect of the Primordial Origin). Besides having adopted specific Yiguandao symbols, such as the Eternal Mother—whom they call Yaochi Laomu 瑤池老母, like the Cihui tang tradition 慈惠堂—, with the character for "mother" (*mu* 母) written at 90° (a specific Yiguandao trait), the cult has also integrated Yiguandao's seventeenth and eighteenth patriarchs, Lu Zhongyi and Zhang Tianran. Both delivered messages via spirit-writing—as do Yuehui Pusa (alias Sun Suzhen) and Santian Zhukao 三天主考 (Chief Examiner of the Three Heavens), i.e., Zhang Maotian 張茂田,[99] the son of Zhang Tianran and his second wife Liu Shuaizhen 劉率真 (1896–1953), who is said to have died young but was promoted to a superior rank in Laomu's heavenly bureaucracy. Patriarch Zhang himself is credited as being the "universal religious leader" (*wanguo jiaozhu* 萬國教主)—also a common title in Yiguandao writings—and is the focus of a 422-page volume of revelations by himself and various other deities, including Laomu.[100]

Besides its symbols, beliefs, and practices being diffused across the wider religious landscape and absorbed by various other religious groups, Yiguandao itself is also a highly heterogeneous movement, that ranges from "mainstream" organizations to "renegade" groups, such as Mile dadao 彌勒大道 (the

---

96 See the study by ibid. On the origin of both texts, see Zhong, *Qingmo minchu minjian Rujiao*, 187–232. See also Matthias Schumann's chapter in this volume, which discusses both works at length.
97 Clart, "The Phoenix and the Mother."
98 Ibid., 24–25.
99 *Hunyuan dadao puchuan*, 25–27, 72–76. On Zhang Maotian and his celestial career, see Billioud, "Yiguandao's Patriarch Zhang Tianran," 214; Li, "Yiguandao diaocha baogao," 102.
100 *Hunyuan dadao Ruzong puchuan*.

Great Way of Maitreya) and Haizidao 亥子道 (the Way of *hai* and *zi*), both of which branched off from Yiguandao in the early 1980s.[101] One of the earliest schisms of which we are aware, which shaped the future development of late Republican-period Yiguandao, transpired after the passing of the paramount leader, Zhang Tianran, in 1947, when two primary factions emerged, both with their own claims to represent the sole, legitimate Yiguandao orthodoxy. On the one hand, there is what I call the "mainstream" Yiguandao—as they are, quantitatively speaking, the larger faction—who evolved from the groups that accepted Sun Suzhen as sharing the eighteenth patriarchy with Zhang—hence, they are sometimes called *shimupai* 師母派 (the "Senior Mistress Faction"). The other group that denied this claim was led by Zhang's wife, Liu Shuaizhen, and their son, Zhang Yingyu 張英譽 (1916–1953), which is why they are sometimes called the "patriarch's son faction" (*shixiongpai* 師兄派).[102] Quantitatively speaking, this group is smaller but has still established a presence both throughout Taiwan and internationally. Probably because the "mainstream" faction claims the brand name "Yiguandao," they prefer the appellation "Way of Heaven" (Tiandao 天道), such as in the official name of their national organization (*Zhonghua minguo Tiandao zonghui* 中華民國天道總會), established in 1990. According to internal documents,[103] Tiandao missionaries arrived in Taiwan in March 1946 when the first temple was established in Jilong 基隆. After Zhang Tianran's death and the ensuing dispute, they began to develop into an autonomous group with its own claims to legitimacy. The Tianhao zongtan 天浩總壇 headquarters was established in Kaohsiung in 1949, but the site of the national association is located in Taipei's Wenshan district 文山區.

Unlike some of the Yiguandao divisions and branches, spirit-writing is practiced regularly in Tiandao even today. Besides providing moral guidance and building affinitive ties with deceased relatives, séances remain an important means of transmitting Laomu's approval of important organizational and institutional matters, including the appointment of elders (*qianren* 前人), initiators, and even preachers (*jiangshi* 講師). Likewise, the names of temples are also

---

101   Lu, *The Transformation of Yiguan Dao*, 101.
102   Cf. Jordan, "The Recent History of the Celestial Way," 447–48. For a highly controversial account of the schism that is based on Zhang Yingyu's confessions and which attributes the reasons to Sun's alleged hunger for power, see Lu, *Yiguandao neimu*, 51–68.
103   During my fieldwork among Tiandao members from March to May 2017, I was shown an untitled historiographic document that was presented to the government as part of an application process to be recognized as a religion. Since 2010, Tiandao is represented in the yearbooks of the Ministry of Interior as a religious group. See the document "Ge zongjiao jiaowu gaikuang."

conferred by spirit-writing.[104] This important information is transmitted by Tianran Gufo 天然古佛 on behalf of Laomu. According to my informant, there are annually ten to 20 séances, most of which take place on important ritual or festive occasions, such as the founding of temples or rituals to save deceased relatives from rebirth and deliver them to Laomu's paradise, entitled *chaoba fahui* 超拔法會.

During my fieldwork I was fortunate to observe a séance held to mark the twentieth anniversary of a temple's founding in late April 2017 in Yilan. The festive program designated the ritual as "the saints and Buddhas approaching the altar" (*xianfo lintan* 仙佛臨壇) and was scheduled to take place at 2–4:40 pm, following a series of other events in the morning—including initiation rituals, a brief lecture, and lunch. The Tiandao elder, Wang Yingyu 王盈裕, was present and took charge of initiating the ritual by presenting incense and reciting the *Qingtanjing*, but only after the "Mother lamp" (*mudeng* 母燈 or "Buddha lamp," *fodeng* 佛燈) had been ignited. The *rencai* was the only male member of the group, and it was striking that those present were not as young as stated in the early history of Yiguandao, but adults aged around forty to fifty years. The *tiancai* medium's eyes were closed throughout the entire writing process. Before the séance started, the senior leader informed everyone that it was forbidden to take pictures or record anything. At the beginning, the medium stood still for about 20 seconds, then began to draw circles in the black sand, after which the writing commenced. Except for the names of individuals and places—that may be two or three characters-long—the *tiancai* usually wrote four characters at the same time in the sand, all at 90°. Every time a deity or dignitary was mentioned, and also at the end of each section, the bystanders would bow once in honor of the messengers. After a long series of various deities and deceased dignitaries had revealed themselves—including well-known Bodhisattvas and Daoist deities, but also specific Tiandao individuals, such as former elders and notable initiators—the main part of the entire séance was transmitted by Tianran Gufo. Before addressing some attendees who had been initiated just a couple of hours earlier with brief advice in terms of commitment and moral behavior, he started his revelation by outlining the cosmology of the Dao. Astonishingly, I was also mentioned—by both my German and Chinese names—and encouraged to seek the utmost truth of the Dao in my research. After the séance finished, elder Wang addressed the attendees and formally closed the session.

---

104 Interview with a Tiandao *dianchuanshi*, Tiandao zonghui, April 21, 2017; informal conversations at a Tiandao event, Yilan, April 30, 2017.

5 Yiguandao Becomes Tendō

Japan is one of the first destinations outside mainland China where Yiguandao activists have brought their faith. While still a marginal religious tradition compared to Japanese "new religions," multiple Yiguandao-related groups are active in Japan, the earliest of which existed by the early 1940s.[105] By adding the suffix "related," I wish to highlight that many of these groups are not part of the "mainstream" Yiguandao movement that I referred to earlier, yet these groups grew out of Yiguandao or Tiandao congregations and even, despite some theological, ritual, and organizational modifications, still share a close resemblance and affinity in terms of their cosmology, practice, and soteriology. Sociologically speaking, they are split-offs that consider themselves the sole orthodox transmission of the Dao. According to 2019 data from the Japanese Ministry of the Interior, there are six Yiguandao and related groups registered with the government.[106] While two of these belong to the mainstream Yiguandao tradition and are related to two Taiwanese divisions, the other four are local Japanese adaptations, two of which I encountered during my fieldwork from April to June 2018: Dōtoku kaikan 道徳会館 (Morality Association) and Tendō. The remaining two sections of this chapter shall focus on the spirit-writing activities of the Way of Heaven in Japan. Except for two very brief introductory essays,[107] the group has not yet been the object of considerable research.

Japanese Tendō was established in 1949 and is genealogically related to Tiandao, described in the previous section. According to the group's historiography as well as data from my own fieldwork among Tiandao practitioners in Taiwan,[108] its first Buddha hall in Japan was established in Kobe 神戸 by missionaries dispatched by the headquarters in Taiwan in 1949. As an important trading port, with close ties to China, Kobe already had an established Chinese community that formed Tendō's main following in the early decades. The first temple was soon to become the Tendō sōtendan 天道総天壇 (Tendō headquarters of the Temple of Heaven) and the organization was registered with the government in 1958. From the 1960s onward, Tendō experienced a gradual shift toward Japanese membership until, finally, in 1983, a major faction disengaged itself from the Taiwanese headquarters to establish an autonomous religious group, based in Japan. This move was instigated by the already powerful *tendenshi* 点伝師 (Ch. *dianchuanshi*), Jo Kinsen 徐錦泉 (Ch. Xu Jinquan,

---

105 Broy, "Zhonghua Yiguandao," 3–4.
106 Bunkachō, *Shūkyō nenkan*.
107 Lai, "Guanyu Yiguandao zai Riben," 342–43; Mu, *Yiguandao gaiyao*, 137–38.
108 "Yuitsu seitō tenmei keishō no nenpu," 5–8. Cf. Lai, "Guanyu Yiguandao zai Riben," 342.

1921–2018), a Taiwanese born Hakka from Xinzhu 新竹, who moved to Japan shortly before the war, but led a secular life before joining the group in 1963.[109] According to Tendō materials, Jo was an extraordinarily talented, committed follower, whose zeal was to change the fortunes of Tendō. By the early 1980s, he is said to have developed a considerable following of up to 300,000 people and, in 1983, a dispute about the organization brought about the rupture.[110] Jo wished to establish a greater degree of local autonomy by introducing an executive council, a move that was rejected by the Taiwanese leaders. According to Tendō narratives, the dispute turned ugly and ended in the police arriving at the temple and trying to mediate between the rival factions. Finally, Jo left with most of his followers and, in 1985, established a new headquarters in the rural, picturesque outskirts of Sanda City 三田市 in Hyōgo Prefecture 兵庫県, about forty kilometers north of downtown Kobe. Initially entitled Tendōsan 天道山, its name was changed to Gyokkōzan Mirokutera 玉皇山弥勒寺 in 2002. Like other large religious sites in Japan, the temple complex is located in the foothills of a small mountain and houses various small shrines and temples devoted not only to Yiguandao practice but also other Chinese and Japanese deities as well.

According to a pamphlet published ca. 1992, the group claimed 800,000 overall followers, amongst whom there were 30.000 regular practitioners.[111] Today, the group operates nine larger branch temples nationwide, which are called *sei'in* 聖院, and more than seven-hundred smaller temples and shrines (called *dan* 壇, Ch. *tan*), most of which are located in private residences. When asked about its following, my informants estimated that there were between 1,300 and 30,000 regular participants belonging to Mirokutera alone—a rather vague calculation based on the number of participants in the annual spring ritual and the number of New Year greeting cards sent out, respectively.[112] Since the ritual festivals and meetings that I attended during my fieldwork at the temple and at an Osaka 大阪 center attracted ca. 20–40 participants at Mirokutera (Sunday events) and there were only five women at a Tuesday afternoon class in Osaka, I assume that the lower estimate might be more accurate in terms of regular practitioners—which, however, does not mean that none of the others practice at all, let alone donate money to the group and its activities.

---

109 I shall use the Japanese terms, translations, and pronunciations of Yiguandao terminology, as they are used by the group. In order to facilitate understanding and comparability, I shall also give the Chinese terms and pronunciations.

110 Tendō sōtendan, *Tendō dōtō soshi den*, 42–47; "Yuitsu seitō tenmei keishō no nenpu."

111 The pamphlet is simply entitled *Tendō* 天道 and was obviously intended to serve as a brochure advertising the group to outsiders. The quantitative data given in the text are dated to 1992.

112 Interview with two informants at Mirokutera, May 20, 2018.

6   Chinese Spirit-Writing in a Japanese Context

The practice of conversing with spirits and deities was not unknown to Japan, and even Western spiritualism—which came into being in 1840s New York—found its way to the country in the second half of the nineteenth century. For instance, a practice partially derived from Western table-turning, called *kokkurisan* こっくりさん (also written 狐狗狸, thus using the Chinese characters for entities often associated with supernatural activities: foxes, *tengu* 天狗, and badgers), gained considerable popularity during the 1880s, to the extent that some observers claimed that the game was played in virtually every household in the late nineteenth century.[113] Quantitative research conducted in the early 1990s found that it was still popular at that time. Thus, close to 100 percent of the younger generation of respondents (the 20–40 year-olds, overall 1,636 individuals) stated that they knew of *kokkurisan* and two-thirds of the 20–30 year-old respondents claimed to have experience of it.[114] Given this apparent popularity, it is surprising that *kokkurisan* is never referred to by Tendō in either publications or personal communications. For instance, in one of his earlier publications, Jo Kinsen only employs general terms to give his readers a sense of the nature of Tendō spirit-writing—such as *reibai* 霊媒 (mediumship) or *kamigakari* 神憑り (spirit possession)—but the term *kokkurisan* is never used.[115]

In general, Tendō follows the Yiguandao and Tiandao style and understanding of spirit-writing. In Tendō publications and on their websites, spirit-writing is usually referred to by its sophisticated Chinese term, "transformation through the flying phoenix" (J. *hiran senka* 飛鸞宣化; Ch. *feiluan xuanhua*). Other terms—such as *furan* 扶鸞 (Ch. *fuluan*)—are rarely used. Following the Xiantiandao understanding, discussed in section two, Laomu—who is called Raumu ラウム / 老母 by the group, a phonetic translation of her Chinese name Laomu—ordered, in 1843, that Tendō should be the sole legitimate way to communicate with the superior deities of her paradise.[116] According to information retrieved from Tendō publications and my own fieldwork data,[117] this practice is strongly aligned with Yiguandao procedures: three individuals take charge of a séance, called the "three talents" (*sansai* 三才). Possessed by the deity, with

---

113 Foster, "Strange Games," 251; cf. Hardacre, "Asano Wasaburō."
114 Imaizumi, "'Kokkurisan,'" 33–34.
115 Jo, *Tamashii ga sukuwareru hon*, 172.
116 See the pamphlet entitled *Tendō*, mentioned above.
117 Besides this pamphlet, see also the webpage "Hiran senka," and Jo, *Tamashii ga sukuwareru hon*, 171–73. I also draw on data from a formal Skype interview with one *tensai* medium, on January 10, 2020. In order to protect his privacy, I use the pseudonym *Yamashita.

eyes closed, the *tensai* 天才 paints circles with a wooden ring before writing the characters that she or he receives from the deities at 90° on the "sand board" (J. *saban* 沙盤, Ch. *shapan*) that is covered with black sand. The *jinsai* 人才 reads aloud the characters written by the former, after which the *chisai* 地才 writes them down. The mediums are usually young individuals who need to be vegetarian and practice contemplation by focusing on their mysterious gate (*shukan meisō* 守関瞑想). According to my informant,[118] there are currently only two *tensai*, both male, who are responsible for all revelations. My informant joined Tendō as an undergraduate more than 20 years ago and quickly became one of the two *tensai* mediums. His training took approximately six months and entailed daily instructions and exercises every morning, noon, and evening.

The messages received are called *go-seikun* 御聖訓 (sacred instructions)—with the addition of the honorific prefix *go* 御 to the Yiguandao term *shengxun* 聖訓. In Tendō, spirit-writing is practiced on a regular basis.[119] Every year, séances—called *go-seikunshiki* 御聖訓式 in Japanese—are staged on various occasions, all of which follow the traditional lunar calendar and thus Yiguandao tradition—unlike Japanese religious and cultural events, most of which were modified according to the general adoption of the Gregorian calendar in 1876. The five most important séances are held to mark the "great rituals of the four seasons" (*shiki taiten* 四季大典, Ch. *siji dadian*), i.e., on the fifteenth day of the third, sixth, ninth, and eleventh lunar months—a set of four great rituals already prescribed in Zhang's community in the late 1930s.[120] The fifth séance is held on New Year's Day and is the only session that follows the Gregorian calendar. These five sessions are particularly important for the group, because they are the occasions when Raumu reveals herself. Accordingly, they are staged at Mirokutera. Another important event is the mid-autumn festival (*chūshūsetsu* 中秋節, Ch. *Zhongqiujie*), on the fifteenth day of the eighth lunar month, as this marks the anniversary of Zhang Tianran's death. It is on this particular day that the senior patriarch—in the group called *onshi* 恩師 ("venerable master," Ch. *enshi*) or Tennen Kobutsu 天然古佛 (Ch. Tianran Gufo)—reveals himself to his followers. Besides these six major events, other, less important séances are held to mark the establishment of new temples or other anniversaries. These are usually held in the respective locations. An undated pamphlet, available on the Tendō website, claims that there have been more than 2,500 spirit mes-

---

118 Interview *Yamashita, January 10, 2020.
119 *Tendō*, undated pamphlet; interview *Yamashita, January 10, 2020.
120 *Zhanding fogui*, 289–90.

sages since the inception of spirit-writing in Japan in 1950.[121] While in the early years the messages were received in Chinese and then translated into Japanese, from ca. 1963 onward, Japanese spirit mediums started to take over and receive messages in their native language.[122] Unlike Yiguandao, I am unaware of any *jieqiao* being practiced in Tendō.

The séances follow a strict sequence that is prescribed in ritual manuals, similar to the procedure described in 1940s Yiguandao and present day Tiandao.[123] While not reported explicitly in the aforementioned accounts, the very first step for all Yiguandao and related groups is to "ignite the lamp" (*tentō* 点灯, Ch. *diandeng*): Yiguandao calls this the "Mother lamp" and in Tendō the "heavenly lamp" (*tsūtentō* 通天灯 or simply *tentō* 天灯); this important ritual artefact is placed on every altar to represent the unfathomably infinite brightness of Raumu. It is also lit for rituals or classes, to invite Raumu to attend the event. While I was unable to attend a séance during my fieldwork, a very brief outsider account was published in a Japanese magazine in 1992.[124] The article describes a séance that lasted for about 45-minutes, held in the Osaka temple in the evening. The attendees were all dressed in black Chinese-style garments. The sand table was covered with iron sand (*satetsu* 砂鉄), which explains its dark color because of the heavy concentration of iron. The medium was 29 years-old and wrote in the sand with his eyes closed.

Writing is considered a way to touch those who are not yet part of the movement or not strongly committed practitioners, yet it is believed to be a mere "expedient means" (J. *hōben* 方便)—a concept originally created in Buddhist thinking as a strategy of guidance toward liberation (Skt. *upāya*)—, as the chief way to understand the intent of the deities is to meditate and channel these through one's mysterious gate (J. *genkan* 玄関, Ch. *xuanguan*).[125] Spirit revelations are of the utmost importance to the community, however, particularly in regard to its development in terms of its organization, ritual, and religious practices.

Luckily, Tendō operates an open-access website that contains a large number of *go-seikun*.[126] It documents important revelations received by Raumu since 1998 as well as those received by Tennen Kobutsu since 1983,[127] but there

---

121 "Tendō ni tsuite."
122 Interview *Yamashita, January 10, 2020.
123 On the ritual sequence, see Tendō sōtendan, *Kenkōrei oyobi tokudō gishiki*, 77–78.
124 "Hakke chāchisuto," 50.
125 Tendō sōtendan, *Tendō tekisuto*, 29–30.
126 See the website "Tengoku (furusato) ni kaeru michi."
127 See the subpages http://seikunn.web.fc2.com/mukunn.html and http://seikunn.web.fc2.com/onnsi.html (accessed May 19, 2019).

are many others as well, albeit not presented in chronological order. While the website fails to attract a huge number of hits—a total of 5,272 as of 27 January 2020 (and 5,373 as of 30 April 2020)[128]—, the spirit messages are disseminated among the group in various ways: besides published collections entitled *Seikunshū* 聖訓集 that are sold at all major chapters, both contemporary and earlier revelations are reprinted and commented on regularly in Tendō's weekly magazine, *Tentsū Shimbun* 天通新聞 (Newspaper for communication with heaven). In addition, spirit messages are also the topic of classes and lectures. While most of them were received at Japanese sites, a few messages were also produced in the overseas branches, such as Taiwan and Mongolia. As far as I can tell from the revelations that I have seen, all of them were obtained by Japanese mediums who seem to travel intensively.[129]

The form of the revelations and style of writing are remarkably similar to the Chinese *xunwen*, which is what makes them difficult to understand for ordinary Japanese people. Accordingly, many technical terms and names of deities are supplemented with *furigana* 振り仮名, a Japanese reading aid attached to Chinese characters. For instance, when calling out its name, a deity will introduce itself by starting with the phrase 吾乃 (I am), which is the usual expression used in Chinese-language *xunwen*. While the meaning of both characters might be intelligible to ordinary Japanese readers—*ware* 吾 means "I" and *sunawachi* 乃ち indicates "i.e." or "that is"—, these readings would not constitute a proper phrase. Hence, the editors chose to render the reading as "*ware wa*," which is the standard expression of "I am" (but which, in standard Japanese, would be written 吾は).[130] As in the Chinese *xunwen*, the end of a particular section is signified by using 哈哈止 (J. *hahha todomu*) and, at the end of an entire revelation before the deity returns to Laomu's paradise, the medium adds the phrase 哈哈退 (*hahha tai*, Ch. *haha tui*).[131] The character 哈 is very rare in Japanese and does not indicate laughter.

Before the chief deity descends, a number of subordinate figures will reveal themselves first in order to transmit short poems and hail the arrival of the main messenger. Most of them are ordinary Yiguandao figures—such as Getsue Bosatsu 月慧菩薩 (Ch. Yuehui Pusa, i.e., Sun Suzhen) and Miroku Kobutsu

---

128 While these numbers again suggest that the overall number of regular practitioners must be quite low, the Tendō website itself also contains a private area for registered members, which provides much more material. As this internal site does not display the number of hits, it is impossible to estimate how many people regularly use it.
129 See, for instance, one revelation by Tennen Kobutsu produced by a Japanese medium in Mongolia on May 24, 2018, see *Tentsū shimbun*, no. 348, June 1, 2018, 2.
130 See, for instance, Tendō sōtendan, *Seikunshū* (5), 1 and *passim*.
131 Ibid.

弥勒古佛 (Ch. Mile Gufo, i.e., Lu Zhongyi), while Zhang Tianran's sons Maotian 茂田 (i.e., Santen Shukō 三天主考, Ch. Santian Zhukao) and Maomeng 茂猛 also often appear—, but there are also a number of dignitaries specific to Tendō: for instance, Jikō Shinkun 慈弘真君 (Ch. Cihong Zhenjun), i.e., Chen Gengjin 陳庚金 (dates unknown), the first Tiandao missionary in Japan. While Laomu's revelations usually entail admonitions regarding moral conduct, Tennen Kobutsu's messages that are received annually at the mid-autumn festival also issue institutional or organizational instructions. Building on the material available, we may distinguish six functions of spirit-writing in Tendō. Due to space limitations, I shall present only a few examples to illustrate this typology.

(1) Moral instruction. For instance, in 1984, Tennen Kōbutsu transmitted ten "prayers" (*ganmon* 願文) that addressed the religious regimen of his followers and admonished them to deepen their attitude of love and care, engage in inner cultivation, and exert the highest moral quality by abiding by the values of *gojō hattoku* 五常八德 (five constants and eight virtues, Ch. *wuchang bade*),[132] i.e., a set of Confucian values that was popularized particularly by nineteenth-century Chinese spirit-writing cults and is, therefore, also popular among Yiguandao.[133]

(2) Legitimacy: As early as 1984 and thus shortly after the rupture with the Taiwan-based Tiandao, Jo Kinsen's group was attested the "orthodox mandate" (*seitō shimei* 正統師命) by Tennen Kobutsu[134]—and this is reiterated regularly during séances. Twenty years later, Jo Kinsen was appointed the 64th overall and nineteenth patriarch in the modern "genealogy of the Dao" (*dōtō* 道統, Ch. *daotong*)[135]—i.e., the only legitimate line of succession of enlightened masters from the dawn of humankind to the present—which, in both Yiguandao and Tiandao's understanding, is impossible, since it is agreed that, after Zhang Tianran, there will be no more patriarchs.

(3) Organization: Since its inception in 1983,[136] Tennen Kobutsu appoints the members of the executive council on behalf of Laomu, which since 2006 consists of 11 members, one chair, and one leader, installed every three years.[137] While the leading posts were filled by the Taiwanese-born Jo Kin-

---

132 "Shimei no ganmon."
133 Cf. Wang, "Spirit Writing Groups," 661–63.
134 "Shimei no ganmon."
135 "Kōshin-sai shinnensetsu go-seikun."
136 "Yuitsu seitō tenmei keishō no nenpu," 6.
137 I was only able to trace the appointments back to 2006 in the data available to me, see "Heijutsu-sai kaki taiten go-seikun 丙戌歲夏季大典御聖訓." The internal website

sen (chair) and his younger brother Jo Arō 徐阿楼 (Ch. Xu Alou, d. 2017) until 2009—and with a Japanese representative thereafter—the other members are entirely Japanese, without Chinese or Taiwanese familial background. Once the deity has made an appointment, the chair or leader usually takes the opportunity to address the attendees and thank Laomu for her trust.

(4) Institutions: At the end of 1997, Tennen Kobutsu transmitted Laomu's order to introduce the new era name, *hakuyō* 白陽 (Ch. *baiyang*), to begin in 1998[138]—a term that, in Yiguandao's cosmology, refers to the third and final period of our universe. Henceforth, all official documents and revelations of the group are dated according to this calendar. To confer "era names" (J. *nengō* 年号) was a characteristic trait of political entities in premodern East Asia, amongst which Japan is the only place where it remains in use. Hence, it is unsurprising that Tendō soon adopted the image of being a "country" on its own. In 2004, Laomu decreed that the Mirokutera would henceforth represent the "divine country *senju*" (*senju shinkoku* 泉珠神国)—with *senju* 泉珠 being a ubiquitous term in Tendō, referring to the highest rank in heaven. They would also develop their own flag and national anthem.[139] In addition, Jo Kinsen is respectfully addressed as the "father of the state" (*kokufu* 国父).

(5) Religious innovations: As early as 1986, Tennen Kobutsu described how *goma* 護摩 rituals may serve as an "expedient means" (*hōben*) to spread the faith, as the benefits and miracles (*kiseki* 奇跡) produced by them would attract followers and convince them.[140] This logic is intrinsically related to the concept of "innerwordly benefits" (*genze riyaku* 現世利益) that, according to Ian Reader and George Watanabe's famous study, constitutes a central aspect in the structure and framework of Japanese religion in general.[141] Following their argument, people in Japan engage in religion particularly because they seek practical benefits—ranging from

---

provides access to earlier messages, according to which the earliest executive council was appointed in 1984 and consisted of seven members plus one chair and one leader, the majority of whom appeared to have a Taiwanese background. See "Kasshi-nen shinnensetsu go-seikun 甲子年新年節御聖訓."

138 "Tendōreki, shinkyū kōtai, hakuyō gannen no sengen." See also a subsequent revelation by Raumu on the Japanese New Year 1998: "Bo'in-sai shinnensetsu go seikun."

139 "Kimi-sai tōki taiten go-seikun." On the use of a flag and anthem, see fieldwork diary, Mirokutera, May 20, 2018.

140 "Jinzai hakkutsu no kokoroe 人材発掘の心得," Shōwa 61/9/18, http://seikunn.web.fc2.com/tyuusyuu86029.html (accessed May 30, 2019).

141 Reader and Tanabe, *Practically Religious*, 16–23.

material or physical ones (such as health, safety, or success in examinations) to intangible assets (such as moral qualities or spiritual insights). Hence, it is unsurprising that Tendō attempted to incorporate such practices in order to address the purported need of prospective Japanese followers. While the pursuit of practical benefits may be found in religions in various historic, cultural, and regional contexts, it is nevertheless significant to note the stark contrast to Yiguandao in this regard. Even though everyday concerns are surely at work there as well, they have not been institutionalized and ritualized in a way comparable to Tendō. The *goma* ritual itself is related to the ancient Vedic practice of *homa*—i.e., votive offerings presented to a deity, usually related to fire—and spread throughout Asia in tandem with Esoteric Buddhist traditions.[142] It is very popular in contemporary Japan and practiced not only by the esoteric Shingon school 真言宗, but other religious traditions as well, such as Shugendō 修験道. It usually entails the ritual burning of wooden planks (called *gomagi* 護摩木) with prayers written by clients, which is typically accompanied by recitations of religious scriptures. While Yiguandao has no relationship with this practice whatsoever, Mirokutera holds regular *goma* rituals, some of which attract hundreds of visitors and constitute a major source of income for the temple. Similar to countless other Japanese religious sites, Mirokutera serves also as a provider of religious services that also sells various sorts of talismans.[143] Even though many of them are highly specific and employ terminology as well as symbols that are not usually seen in regular Japanese temples, as far as I can see from my material, those charms were not produced during spirit-writing séances.

(6) Japanization: In a message received in May 1993, the semi-legendary regent and purported supporter of Buddhism in Japan's early history, Shōtoku Taishi 聖徳太子 (574–622), reports that, after his death, he served as a protector of the country. While it was always his aim to construct a "spiritual nation" (*shinkei kokka* 神系国家), he lamented the intrusion of "foreign enemies" (*gaiteki* 外敵) in the course of Japan's modernization and demons who tried to tear the nation apart after WWII but, thanks to Tendō, he was able to consolidate this "largest spiritual country" (最大の霊系国家).[144] In a similar account, the supreme sun goddess and purported ancestor of Japan's emperors, Amaterasu Ōmikami 天照大神, addressed the attendees in 2013, lamenting that the people of Japan had

---

142 Payne and Orzech, "Homa."
143 Reader and Tanabe, *Practically Religious*, 182–88.
144 Tendōsan Mirokutera, *Shinkai kara no shōgen*, 15–17.

forgotten their kami but noting that Tendō fosters the "rejuvenation of the divine country" (*shinkoku fukkō* 神国復興) and the restoration of its unique "Japanese soul" (*wakon* 和魂).[145] Thus, similar to how the greatness of Chinese civilization is epitomized in Yiguandao teachings, Japan and its purported spiritual culture play a vital role in Tendō's theology.

7 Conclusion

This chapter has explored the forms, meanings, and functions of spirit-writing from late nineteenth-century Chinese Yiguandao to present-day Japanese Tendō. In sum, we may conclude that spirit-writing in Yiguandao, Tiandao, and Tendō is similar in nature and content, and serves similar purposes. For all three traditions, spirit-writing is not only a source of divine inspiration and moral guidance, but it also enacts and legitimizes the institutional, organizational, and religious decisions and innovations. In the eyes of many practitioners, its significance is particularly observable in the fact that the texts produced by spirit-writing constitute Yiguandao's unique textual tradition, as many critics claim that the sect merely capitalizes on the sacred scriptures of other religious traditions. Hence, it is unsurprising that spirit-writing continues to play a vital role in the practice and self-understanding of these three groups.

Despite the abundant similarities, several differences also exist that, however, derive from adaptations to specific temporal and regional needs and circumstances. Apparently, spirit-writing constitutes a relatively flexible practice, that easily serves the needs of a given community. In the period of war, famine, and Communist endangerment in late 1940s/early 1950s mainland China, séances were a major source of apocalyptic prophecies regarding the perils of the CCP and the imminent end of the world, to strengthen the commitment and solidarity of Yiguandao's followers. In post-WWII Taiwan, it continued to represent a powerful tool for domesticating the existing spirit-writing groups and integrating them into Yiguandao. During the past few decades, in particular, the practice has also proved fruitful in producing novel commentaries on Confucian and other Chinese classics and thus representing a vital aspect of Yiguandao practice. In Japan, following the shift toward non-Chinese membership since the 1960s, spirit-writing evolved into a Japanese practice by using indigenous script and incorporating Japanese elements into it. Other Yiguandao-related groups in Japan, such as the aforementioned Dōtoku kaikan,

---

145 "Kishi-sai shinnensetsu go-seikun."

also practice spirit-writing on a regular basis. According to my informants at Dōtoku kaikan,[146] the revealed texts are of great importance to the group, as they are written in colloquial Japanese—and thus are slightly less formal than the writing style used in Tendō—and deliver messages suitable for people living in contemporary Japanese society. Here, the messengers are often figures from Japanese history to whom most people can relate, such as the famous samurai and advocate of Japanese tradition, Saigō Takamori 西郷隆盛 (1828–1877)—who is honored with a statue in Tokyo's Ueno Park—and the intellectual, Fukuzawa Yukichi 福沢諭吉 (1835–1901), who is generally regarded as one of the most important figures in the creation of modern Japan and whose image is printed on the 10.000 Yen banknote.[147]

To my knowledge, Japanese Yiguandao-related groups are among the very few instances where Chinese sectarian groups have adopted a non-Chinese language for spirit-writing. While the Vietnamese Caodai (Đạo Cao Đài 道高臺, Way of the High Terrace) represents a similar example as its spirit-writing practices were adapted from the Sino-Vietnamese sectarian tradition of Minh Sư 明師 (Enlightened Master),[148] it differs due to the fact that Caodai was a Vietnamese religious group from the very beginning, while Tendō and Dōtoku kaikan were Chinese sects—in terms of both membership and language—and only gradually experienced Japanization. In this respect, the experience of these Japanese Yiguandao-related groups is probably more akin to the evolution of the Minh Sư tradition, that itself dates back to Chinese Xiantiandao practitioners who migrated from Guangdong Province in the second half of the nineteenth century and settled particularly in the southern part of the country.[149] According to Lin Rongze's 43-volume compilation of spirit-writings, which entails a great number of *xunwen* revealed in temples outside Taiwan since the mid-1970s,[150] Chinese remains the *lingua franca*. While local languages are sometimes involved, this is usually limited to important terms and short phrases—some of them hidden in *xunzhongxun*.[151] Only a few spirit messages have been revealed entirely in a language other than Chinese, and these are chiefly in Japanese—primarily by Fayi Chongde, the most successful Tai-

---

146 Fieldwork in two Buddha halls, Osaka and Ōtsu 大津, May to June 2018.
147 I have obtained copies of both revelations.
148 Jammes, *Les oracles du Cao Đài*, 58–68; "Divination and Politics."
149 Ngai, *Shumin de yongheng*, 507–16.
150 A collection of revelations from overseas Yiguandao temples—chiefly in Southeast Asia but also Japan and America—dated 1976–1995, see YGDZ-SDZB, vols. 10, 15, 18, 23, 29, 30, 39, and 42. For a statistical overview of the collections, see YGDZ-SDZB, vol. 10, 16–17.
151 See Lin, *Yiguandaoxue yanjiu, shou juan*, 379–89, for some examples in non-Chinese languages.

wanese branch in Japan—plus a few revelations in Thai.[152] Yet, Tendō and Dōtoku kaikan are the only Yiguandao-related groups to practice spirit-writing solely in Japanese. This might be due to its capacity easily to adapt to specific Chinese terminology, as both languages use Chinese characters. In Korea, there also developed highly indigenized forms of Yiguandao, and the Korean language is equally influenced by Chinese, yet spirit messages do not appear to have been transmitted in Korean at all. While some groups stopped using *fuji* at all, others continued to employ written Chinese during séances.[153] Hence, the example of Tendō provides a rare window into the processes of transculturation of Chinese popular sects and their practices in non-Chinese cultural settings. It remains to be seen if other Yiguandao and related groups in other countries also adapt in similar ways to their growing non-Chinese following.[154]

References

Abbreviations

MDSX　　An untitled six-volume collection of spirit revelations and other Yiguandao texts (primarily from the Republican Period) published by Yiguandao followers in 2016 and disseminated for free by the Taipei Yiguandao bookstore Mingde xinling shufang 明德心靈書坊—hence my abbreviation to MingDe ShengXun 明德聖訓.

YGDJJ　　Wang Chien-chuan 王見川, ed. *Minzhong jingdian: Yiguandao jingjuan, Liu Bowen jinrang yu qita* 民眾經典：一貫道經卷、劉伯溫錦囊與其他. 5 vols. Boyang wenhua: Taipei, 2011.

YGDZ-SDZB　　Lin Rongze 林榮澤, ed. *Yiguandao zang: Shengdian zhi bu* 一貫道藏：聖典之部. 43 vols. Lantai chubanshe: Taipei, 2009–2015.

Primary Sources

Baiyang jingzang: zhufo pusa cixun (2) 白陽經藏：諸佛菩薩慈訓 (2). Taipei: Mingde chubanshe, 2012.

152　For a large collection of Japanese *xunwen* revealed from 1976 to 1985, see YGDZ-SDZB, vol. 10, 7–326, 372–475, 509–31, 539–53; vol. 15, 1–85, 99–143, 157–80, 185–202, 256–303, 419–22; for Thai language messages, see YGDZ-SDZB, vol. 34, 1–174.
153　Lee, "Hanguo Yiguandao," 151–53, 159.
154　Cf. Jammes and Palmer, "Occulting the Dao;" "The Bible of the Great Cycle," who precisely studied how Xiantiandao teachings were "occulted" in a tripartite process by Cao Đài practitioners in the early twentieth century in order to conceal the true meaning of these teachings from the non-initiates, and from Westerners.

"Bo'in-sai shinnensetsu go seikun 戊寅歲新年節御聖訓." Heisei 10/1/28, http://seikunn.web.fc2.com/mukunn98005.html (accessed May 20, 2019).

Bunkachō 文化庁 (Agency of Cultural Affairs), ed. *Shūkyō nenkan* (*Reiwa gannenban*) 宗教年間（令和元年版）. Available at https://www.bunka.go.jp/tokei_hakusho_shuppan/hakusho_nenjihokokusho/shukyo_nenkan/index.html (accessed January 15, 2020).

Chuanfei zouping 川匪奏稟. Series of government reports related to the Qinglianjiao case. Microfilm copy held at Fu Sinian Library 傅斯年圖書館 at Academia Sinica, Taipei.

"Hakke chāchisuto 八卦チャーチスト." *AERA* アエラ, April 28, 1992, 50.

"Heijutsu-sai kaki taiten go-seikun 丙戌歲夏季大典御聖訓." Heisei 18/7/10, http://seikunn.web.fc2.com/mukunn06012.html (accessed May 20, 2019).

"Hiran senka 飛鸞宣化." http://seikunn.web.fc2.com/hirannsennka.html (accessed January 7, 2020).

Huangmu shisan tan 皇母十三嘆. Revealed in 1936. YGDZ-SDZB, vol. 1, 193–232.

Huangmu xunzi shijie 皇母訓子十誡. Revealed in 1941. N.p. Fayi Chongde congshu, 1991.

Hunyuan budai zhenjing 混元布袋真經. Revealed in 1925. MDSX, vol. 2, 35–39.

Hunyuan dadao puchuan: Mile zhongzhou zuozhen 混元大道普傳. 彌勒中洲坐鎮. Kaohsiung: Wuji zhixia luanhua Cilingyuan, 2016.

Hunyuan Dadao Ruzong puchuan (*Tianran Gufo*) 混元大道儒宗普傳(天然古佛). Published September 1, 2015 on http://celingyuan.weebly.com/22825263602354224235.html (accessed January 15, 2020).

Jin'gong miaodian 金公妙典. Revealed in 1925. YGDZ-SDZB, vol. 1, 12–34.

Jin'gong Zushi chandao pian 金公祖師闡道篇. Prefaces dated 1936. Tian'entang, no year.

"Jinzai hakkutsu no kokoroe 人材発掘の心得." Shōwa 61/9/18, http://seikunn.web.fc2.com/tyuusyuu86029.html (accessed May 30, 2019).

Jo Kinsen 徐錦泉. *Tamashii ga sukuwareru hon: Raumu no ai wo ishiki suru koto ga hakuyō chijō tengoku e no michi* 魂が救われる本. 老母の愛を意識することが白陽地上天国への道. Tōkyō: Gendai shorin, 1996.

"Kasshi-nen shinnensetsu go-seikun 甲子年新年節御聖訓." Shōwa 59/2/2, https://tendo.net/advanced/goseikun/index.php?code=84001 (accessed August 11, 2020).

"Kimi-sai tōki taiten go-seikun 癸未歲冬季大典御聖訓." Heisei 15/12/8, http://seikunn.web.fc2.com/MUKUNN03025.html (accessed May 21, 2019).

"Kishi-sai shinnensetsu go-seikun 癸巳歲新年節御聖訓." Heisei 25/2/10, http://seikunn.web.fc2.com/mukunn13001.html (accessed May 20, 2019).

"Kōshin-sai shinnensetsu go-seikun 甲申歲新年節御聖訓." Heisei 16/1/22, by Raumu, http://seikunn.web.fc2.com/MUKUNN04002.html (accessed May 19, 2019).

Lin Liren 林立仁, ed. *Beihai Laoren quanshu* 北海老人全書. Banqiao: Zhengyi shanshu chubanshe, 2008.

Linian yili 歷年易理. Shanghai: Chonghuatang, 1941 edition. YGDJJ, vol. 1, 1–70.

Meizhou Sima qiudao ji / Yide Xiangu jieyuan xun 湄州四媽求道記 / 懿德仙姑結緣訓. N.p., 2011.

Mile jiuku zhenjing 彌勒救苦真經. Revealed 1925. YGDZ-SDZB, vol. 1, 10–11.

Raumu shinsho, Kakyō shinsho 老母真書、家郷新書. [Kōbe]: Tendō Nihon sōtendan, 1981.

"Shimei no ganmon 師命の願文, Shōwa gojūkyū-nen chūshūsetsu go-seikun 昭和五十九年中秋節御聖訓." Shōwa 59/9/10, http://seikunn.web.fc2.com/tyuusyuu84019.html (accessed May 19, 2019).

Tendō 天道. Undated pamphlet [ca. 1992].

Tendō ni tsuite 天道について. Undated pamphlet, available online via https://tendo.net/download/about_tendo.PDF (accessed December 17, 2019).

Tendō sōtendan 天道総天壇, ed. *Tendō tekisuto* 天道テキスト. Tentsū shimbunsha 天通新聞社, 2005.

Tendō sōtendan 天道総天壇, ed. *Tendō dōtō soshi den* 天道道統祖師伝. Hakuyō shimbunsha 白陽新聞社, 2006.

Tendō sōtendan 天道総天壇, ed. *Seikunshū* 聖訓集 (5) (*May 7, 1995–July 31, 1996*). Hakuyō shimbunsha, 2009.

Tendō sōtendan 天道総天壇, ed. *Kenkōrei oyobi tokudō gishiki nado reisetsu gaidobukku* 献香礼及び得道儀式等礼節ガイドブック. 2015.

"Tendōreki, shinkyū kōtai, hakuyō gannen no sengen 天道暦、新旧交替、白陽元年の宣言." Heisei 9/12/10, http://seikunn.web.fc2.com/onnsi97073.html (accessed May 30, 2019).

Tendōsan Mirokutera 天道山みろく寺, ed. *Shinkai kara no shōgen: Shōtoku Taishi, Kōbō Daishi nado ga kataru reikai no shinjitsu* 神界からの証言。聖徳太子・弘法大師等が語る霊界の真実. No bibliographical information [ca. 1993].

"Tengoku (furusato) ni kaeru michi 天国（故郷）に帰る道." http://seikunn.web.fc2.com/ (accessed June 6, 2018).

Wanzu guizhen 萬祖歸真. Preface dated 1942. Available at http://www.taolibrary.com/category/category9/c9023.htm (accessed January 23, 2020).

Wei Qingbo 魏清波. "Wo suo liaojie de Yiguandao neimu 我所了解的一貫道內幕." In *Guiyang wenshi ziliao xuanji* 貴陽文史資料選輯, vol. 12, 180–94. Guiyang: Guiyang wenshi ziliao yanjiu weiyuanhui, 1984,

Wuji shengmu qinyan xueshu 無極聖母親演血書. Revealed in 1924. YGDJJ, vol. 2, 151–184.

Xinwei Tudigong, Tudipo qiudao jishi 新威土地公土地婆求道紀實. No bibliographical data.

Xu Zhigang 徐志剛. "Ji'nan 'Yiguandao' de zui'e huodong ji qudi gaikuang" 濟南"一貫道"的罪惡活動及取締概況. In *Shandong wenshi ziliao xuanji* 山東文史資料選輯, vol. 32, 278–91. Ji'nan: Shandong renmin chubanshe, 1992.

Yiguandao neimu 一貫道內幕. Hubei wenshi ziliao 湖北文史資料 45. Hubeisheng, 1995.

Yiguandao yili bianjiyuan 一貫道義理編輯苑, ed. *Baiyang Yijing* 白陽易經. Taipei: Yiguandaoxue yanjiuyuan wenxiangguan, 2016.

Yiguandao yiwen jieda 一貫道疑問解答. Preface dated 1937. YGDJJ, vol. 1, 167–272.

Yiguan juelu 一貫覺路. Revealed 1924 or 1934. MDSX, vol. 3, 1–47 and 6, 59–103.

"Yuitsu seitō tenmei keishō no nenpu 唯一正統天命継承の年譜." *Noah ノア Tendō kikanshi* 天道季刊誌 6 (2006): 3–8.

Zan Daotu 咎道徒. "Yiguandao de zui'e neimu 一貫道的罪惡內幕." In *Jiu Zhongguo de shehui minqing* 舊中國的社會民情, vol. 10, 699–711. Hefei: Anhui renmin chubanshe, 2000.

Zhanding fogui 暫訂佛規. Preface dated 1939. YGDJJ, vol. 1, 273–98.

Secondary Literature

Asai Motoi 浅井紀. *Min-Shin jidai minkan shūkyō kessha no kenkyū* 明清時代民間宗教結社の研究. Tokyo: Kenbun shuppan, 1990.

Billioud, Sébastien. *Reclaiming the Wilderness: Contemporary Dynamics of the Yiguandao*. Oxford: Oxford University Press, 2020.

Billioud, Sébastien. "Yiguandao's Patriarch Zhang Tianran (1889–1947): Hagiography, Deification and Production of Charisma in a Modern Religious Organization." In *The Making of Saints in Modern and Contemporary China: Profiles in Religious Leadership*, edited by Vincent Goossaert, David Ownby, and Ji Zhe, 208–40. Oxford: Oxford University Press, 2017.

Broy, Nikolas. "Syncretic Sects and Redemptive Societies: Toward a New Understanding of 'Sectarianism' in the Study of Chinese Religions." *Review of Religion and Chinese Society* 2, no. 2 (2015): 145–85.

Broy, Nikolas. "Zhonghua Yiguandao biancheng Riben Tiandao: Guanyu 'Xiantian dadao xitong' zongjiao tuanti Ribenhua de yixie sikao 中華一貫道變成日本天道：關於「先天大道系統」宗教團體日本化的一些思考." In *Cong Taiwan dao shijie: Ershiyi shiji Yiguandao de quanqiuhua guoji xueshu yantaohui lunwenji* 從台灣到世界：二十一世紀一貫道的全球化國際學術研討會論文集. Conference proceedings, 2019.

Chao, Wei-pang. "The Origin and Growth of the Fu Chi." *Folklore Studies* 1 (1942): 9–27.

Clart, Philip. "The Ritual Context of Morality Books: A Case-Study of a Taiwanese Spirit-Writing Cult." PhD diss., University of British Columbia, 1996.

Clart, Philip. "The Phoenix and the Mother: The Interaction of Spirit-Writing Cults and Popular Sects in Taiwan." *Journal of Chinese Religions* 25 (1997): 1–32.

Clart, Philip. "Jesus in Chinese Popular Sects." In *The Chinese Face of Jesus Christ*, edited by R. Malek, 1315–33. Nettetal: Steyler, 2007.

Ding, Renjie. "The Construction of Fundamentalism in I-Kuan Tao." In *Religion in Taiwan and China: Locality and Transmission*, edited by Chang Hsun and Benjamin Penny, 135–68. Taipei: Academia Sinica, Institute of Ethnology, 2017.

DuBois, Thomas David. *The Sacred Village: Social Change and Religious Life in Rural North China*. Honolulu: University of Hawai'i Press, 2005.

Foster, Michael Dylan. "Strange Games and Enchanted Science: The Mystery of Kokkuri." *The Journal of Asian Studies* 65, no. 2 (2006): 251–275.

Fromm, Martin. "Producing History through 'Wenshi Ziliao': Personal Memory, Post-Mao Ideology, and Migration to Manchuria." PhD diss., Columbia University, 2010.

"Ge zongjiao jiaowu gaikuang 各宗教教務概況." Download via https://religion.moi.gov.tw/Home/ContentDetail?cid=Report&ci=1 (accessed January 24, 2020).

Goossaert, Vincent. "The Textual Canonization of Guandi." In *Rooted in Hope. In der Hoffnung verwurzelt: Festschrift in Honor of / Festschrift für Roman Malek S.V.D. on the Occasion of His 65th Birthday*, edited by Barbara Hoster, Dirk Kuhlmann, and Zbigniew Wesolowski, 509–26. Abingdon: Routledge, 2017.

Goossaert, Vincent, Jan Kiely, and John Lagerwey, eds. *Modern Chinese Religion*, Part II: *1850–2015*. Leiden: Brill, 2015.

Grootaers, Willem A. "Une Société Secrète Moderne: 一貫道 I-Koan-Tao Bibliographie annotée." *Folklore Studies* 5 (1946): 316–52.

Hardacre, Helen. "Asano Wasaburō and Japanese Spiritualism in Early Twentieth-Century Japan." In *Japan's Competing Modernities: Issues in Culture and Democracy, 1900–1930*, edited by Sharon Minichiello, 133–53. Honolulu: University of Hawai'i Press, 1998.

Hung Chang-tai. "The Anti-Unity Sect Campaign and Mass Mobilization in the Early People's Republic of China." *The China Quarterly*, no. 202 (2010): 400–20.

Imaizumi Toshiaki 今泉寿明. "'Kokkurisan' ni kan suru shakai shinrigaku-teki chōsa: 1930-nendai kara 1992-nen made no ryūkōshi 「こっくりさん」に関する社会心理学的調査 1930 年代から 1992 年までの流行史." *Shūkyō to shakai* 宗教と社会 6, no. 1 (1995): 29–48.

Jammes, Jérémy. "Divination and Politics in Southern Vietnam: Roots of Caodaism." *Social Compass* 57, no. 3 (2010): 357–71.

Jammes, Jérémy. *Les oracles du Cao Đài: Étude d'un mouvement religieux vietnamien et ses réseaux*. Paris: Les Indes savantes, 2014.

Jammes, Jeremy, and David A. Palmer. "Occulting the Dao: Daoist Inner Alchemy, French Spiritism, and Vietnamese Colonial Modernity in Caodai Translingual Practice." *The Journal of Asian Studies* 77, no. 2 (2018): 405–28.

Jammes, Jérémy, and David A. Palmer. "The Bible of the Great Cycle of Esotericism: From the Xiantiandao Tradition to a Cao Đài Scripture in Colonial Vietnam." In *Text and Context in the Modern History of Chinese Religions: Redemptive Societies and Their Sacred Texts*, edited by Philip Clart, David Ownby, and Chien-chuan Wang, 258–308. Leiden: Brill, 2020.

Jordan, David K. "The Recent History of the Celestial Way: A Chinese Pietistic Association." *Modern China* 8, no. 4 (1982): 435–62.

Kong Simeng 孔思孟. "Lun Baguajiao lishi shenhua: Li Tingyu gushi 論八卦教歷史神話：李廷玉故事." *Minjian zongjiao* 民間宗教 3 (1997): 201–25.

Kubo Noritada 窪德忠. "Ikkandō ni tsuite 一貫道について." *Tōyō bunka kenkyūjo kiyō* 東洋文化研究所紀要, no. 4 (1953): 173–249.

Lai Lianjin 賴連金. "Guanyu Yiguandao zai Riben fazhan de guocheng 關於一貫道在日本發展的過程." *Minjian zongjiao* 民間宗教 3 (1997): 341–50.

Lee Gyungwon 李京源. "Hanguo Yiguandao fazhan gaishu 韓國一貫道發展概述." *Huaren zongjiao yanjiu* 華人宗教研究, no. 4 (2014): 147–66.

Li Shiyu 李世瑜. "Guiyidao diaocha baogao (1945–1948) 皈一道調查報告." In Li, *Xianzai Huabei mimi zongjiao*, 215–71.

Li Shiyu 李世瑜. "Yiguandao diaocha baogao (1940–1948) 一貫道調查報告." In *Xianzai Huabei mimi zongjiao*, 45–213.

Li Shiyu 李世瑜, ed. *Xianzai Huabei mimi zongjiao: Zengdingban* 現在華北秘密宗教. 增訂版. Taipei: Lantai, 2007.

Lin Rongze 林榮澤. *Yiguandao lishi: Dalu zhi bu* 一貫道歷史 大陸之部. Taipei: Mingde chubanshe, 2007.

Lin Rongze 林榮澤. *Yiguandao fazhan shi* 一貫道發展史. Taipei: Lantai, 2010.

Lin Rongze 林榮澤. *Yiguandaoxue yanjiu. Shoujuan: lishi yu jingdian quanshi* 一貫道學研究. 首卷：歷史與經典詮釋. Taipei: Yiguan yili bianji yuan, 2013.

Lin Rongze 林榮澤. *Yiguandaoxue yanjiu: juan er: wenxian yanjiu yu zhuanti* 一貫道學研究. 卷二：文獻研究與專題. Taipei: Yiguan yili bianji yuan, 2014.

Lu, Yunfeng. *The Transformation of Yiguan Dao in Taiwan: Adapting to a Changing Religious Economy*. Lanham, MD: Lexington Books, 2008.

Lu Zhongwei 陸仲偉. *Yiguandao neimu* 一貫道內幕. Nanjing: Jiangsu renmin chubanshe, 1998.

Mu Yu 慕禹. *Yiguandao gaiyao* 一貫道概要. Tainan: Tianju shuju, 2002.

Ownby, David. "Redemptive Societies in the Twentieth Century." In Goossaert, Kiely, and Lagerwey, *Modern Chinese Religion*, Part II, 685–727.

Palmer, David A. "Chinese Redemptive Societies and Salvationist Religion: Historical Phenomenon or Sociological Category?" *Minsu quyi* 民俗曲藝, no. 172 (2011): 21–72.

Payne, Richard K., and Charles D. Orzech. "Homa." In *Esoteric Buddhism and the Tantras in East Asia*, edited by Charles D. Orzech, H. Hjort Sørensen, and Richard K. Payne, 133–40. Leiden: Brill, 2011.

Pettit, Jonathan E.E. "The Many Faces of the Golden Sire: Books and Readers in the Early Yiguan Dao." *Journal of Chinese Religions* 44, no. 1 (2016): 35–72.

Reader, Ian, and G.J. Tanabe. *Practically Religious: Worldly Benefits and the Common Religion of Japan*. Honolulu: University of Hawai'i Press, 1998.

Sakai Tadao 酒井忠夫. *Kingendai Chūgoku ni okeru shūkyō kessha no kenkyū* 近・現代中国における宗教結社の研究. Tokyo: Kokusho kankōkai, 2002.

Schumann, Matthias. "Science and Spirit-Writing: The Shanghai Lingxuehui 靈學會

and the Changing Fate of Spiritualism in Republican China." In *Text and Context in the Modern History of Chinese Religions: Redemptive Societies and Their Sacred Texts*, edited by Philip Clart, David Ownby, and Chien-chuan Wang, 126–72. Leiden: Brill, 2020.

Shahar, Meir. *Crazy Ji: Chinese Religion and Popular Literature*. Cambridge, MA: Harvard University Asia Center, 1998.

Shiga Ichiko 志賀市子. *Chūgoku no kokkurisan: furan shinkō to chūka shakai* 中国のこっくりさん 扶鸞信仰と中華社会. Tōkyō: Daishūkan, 2003.

Shiga Ichiko 志賀市子. "Difang Daojiao zhi xingcheng: Guangdong diqu fuluan jieshe yundong zhi xingqi yu yanbian (1838–1953) 地方道教之形成：廣東地區扶鸞結社運動之興起與演變（1838–1953）." *Daojiao yanjiu xuebao: zongjiao, lishi yu shehui* 道教研究學報：宗教、歷史與社會 / *Daoism: Religion, History and Society*, no. 2 (2010): 231–67.

Shinohara Hisao 篠原壽雄. *Taiwan ni okeru Ikkandō no shisō to girei* 台湾における一貫道の思想と儀礼. Tokyo: Hirakawa shuppansha, 1993.

Takeuchi Fusaji 武内房司. "Shinmatsu Shisen no shūkyō undō—furan, senkōkei shūkyō kessha no tanjō 清末四川の宗教運動—扶鸞・宣講型宗教結社の誕生." *Gakushūin daigaku bungakubu kenkyū nenpō* 学習院大学文学部研究年報 37 (1990): 59–93.

Wang, Chien-ch'uan [Wang Chien-chuan]. "Spirit Writing Groups in Modern China (1840–1937): Textual Production, Public Teachings, and Charity." In Goossaert, Kiely, and Lagerwey, *Modern Chinese Religion*, Part II, 651–84.

Wang Chien-chuan 王見川. "Xiantiandao qianqishi chutan: Jian lun qi yu Yiguandao de guanxi 先天道前期史初探: 兼論其與一貫道的關係." In *Taiwan de Zhaijiao yu luantang* 台灣的齋教與鸞堂, edited by Wang Chien-chuan 王見川, 75–114. Taipei: Nantian shuju, 1996.

Ngai Ting-Ming 危丁明. *Shumin de yongheng: Xiantiandao ji qi zai Gang Ao ji Dongnanya diqu de fazhan* 庶民的永恆: 先天道及其在港澳及東南亞地區的發展. Taipei: Boyang wenhua, 2015.

Welch, Holmes, and Chün-fang Yü. "The Tradition of Innovation: A Chinese New Religion." *Numen* 27, no. 2 (1980): 222–46.

Wilhelm, Richard. *Die Seele Chinas*. Wiesbaden: Marixverlag, 2009.

Chung Yun-ying 鍾雲鶯. *Qingmo Minchu minjian Rujiao dui zhuliu Ruxue de xishou yu zhuanhua* 清末民初民間儒教對主流儒學的吸收與轉化. Taipei: Taiwan daxue chubanshe, 2008.

Zhou Jingwei 周經緯. "Gongheguo chuqi Yiguandao yaoyan fenxi 共和國初期一貫道謠言分析." *Lantai shijie* 兰台世界 5 (2016).

Zhou Yumin 周育民. "Yiguandao qianqi lishi chutan: Jian lun Yiguandao yu Yihetuan de guanxi 一貫道前期歷史初探—兼談一貫道與義和團的關係." *Jindaishi yanjiu* 近代史研究, no. 3 (1991): 75–87.

PART 5

*Local Communities
and Transregional Networks*

CHAPTER 13

The Nineteenth-Century Spirit-Writing Movement and the Transformation of Local Religion in Western Guangdong

Ichiko Shiga

1   **Introduction**

Over the past few decades, a number of studies have been conducted on spirit-writing movements in different regions and periods. In particular, spirit-writing groups during the Qing Dynasty, when spirit-writing movements arose throughout China and reached a peak, have attracted considerable attention in the scholarship on Chinese religion. Among them, several studies on spirit-written revelations, scriptures, and their collections, produced by elite literati communities, such as the *Lüzu quanshu* 呂祖全書 (Complete writings of Patriarch Lü) and *Daozang jiyao* 道藏輯要 (Essentials of the Daoist canon), have produced prominent results in this field.[1]

However, there is a need for further discussion about the non-elite, more popular spirit-writing movements in the nineteenth century. This is especially true of the spirit-writing movement that arose after the *gengzi* 庚子 year of the Daoguang 道光 period (1840), when a number of historic spirit-writing séances were conducted in Longnü Temple (Longnü si 龍女寺) by the local Confucian elites of Dingyuan County 定遠縣, Sichuan 四川. The spirit-written revelations in Longnü Temple indicated that a new salvation movement, led by Lord Guan (Guandi 關帝) and other saints (typically Wenchang 文昌, Patriarch Lü, Guanyin 觀音, and other deities), was set to begin in 1840. The post-1840 spirit-written eschatological scriptures, which resulted from this movement and are known as *jiujie jing* 救劫經 (scriptures to save humanity from the apocalypse), usually included the following typical motif: due to people's immoral, sinful deeds, the Jade Emperor (Yudi 玉帝) was so angered that he sent down great catastrophes (*jie* 劫) to exterminate immoral people. Lord Guan and other saints were deeply saddened to see such misery, so they pleaded with the Jade

---

1   See Mori, "Dōzō Shūyō to Shō Yobo no Lyoso fukei shinkou"; Esposito, "The Invention of a Quanzhen Canon"; Lai, "Qingdai sizhong *Lüzu quanshu*."

Emperor for mercy and permission to awaken immoral people through their teachings, which were delivered via spirit-writing. The most typical combination of saviors includes these three gods: Lord Guan, Wenchang, and Patriarch Lü, who are also known as the Three Saints (*san sheng* 三聖) or Three Ministers (*san xiang* 三相).[2]

This eschatological discourse rapidly disseminated throughout China, and became a common idea shared among the local spirit-writing groups across the region.[3] Although there have been a few prominent studies on this new trend within the nineteenth century spirit-writing movements since 1840, little attention has been paid to the question of how local spirit-writing groups incorporated the eschatological idea into their own religious beliefs and practices.[4]

To date, my research has focused on local spirit-writing groups in the Lingnan region 嶺南地區, which stretches across both Guangdong 廣東 and Guangxi 廣西 provinces. What became apparent through my ethnographical and historical research was that successive waves of eschatological ideas, disseminated through the distribution of eschatological scriptures, reached local societies in Lingnan, and took root there, from the late Qing Dynasty onward. Syncretized with local religious beliefs and practices, they influenced and transformed the local religion, and *vice versa*.

I discussed this theme in a previous study on the Chaoshan region 潮汕地區, which is located in eastern Guangdong. In this region, the spirit-writing movement took root at the end of the nineteenth century, during an outbreak of plague. In 1898, one of the most popular deities in Chaoshan, Master Song Dafeng 宋大峰祖師, descended to a spirit-writing altar in a temple of Sanshan Guowang 三山國王廟 (Temple of the Three Mountain Kings) in Haimen 海門, Chaoyang 潮陽 county, for the first time. Song Dafeng warned that "the third period of universal salvation" (*sanqi pudu* 三期普度)[5] was approaching. Master Dafeng encouraged people to organize *xiugu* 修骷 ritu-

---

2 This eschatological discourse is also known as *sanxiang daitian xuanhua* 三相代天宣化 (The Three Ministers proclaiming moral transformation on behalf of Heaven); see Wang, "Spirit Writing Groups in Modern China," 656.
3 Fan, *Qingmo minjian cishan shiye*, 114–23.
4 For a detailed argument, see Goossaert, "Modern Daoist Eschatology"; Wang, "Spirit Writing Groups in Modern China," 654–64.
5 *Sanqi pudu* is a term derived from the eschatological discourse of *sanqi sanfo* 三期三佛 (Three stages of salvation by three Buddhas) that often appeared on precious scrolls (*baojuan* 寶卷) and in eschatological scriptures (*jiujiejing*). It was based on the belief that three savior deities would appear and save human beings from great catastrophes at the end of each set of three periods.

als; that is, the exhumation and burial of unidentified bones and bodies. In the Chaoshan area, Master Dafeng was a local deity, who was traditionally worshiped during *xiugu* rituals that were organized by local charitable associations. At that time, Master Dafeng manifested himself as a savior god who had been sent by the Jade Emperor, and *xiugu* rituals were considered an effective method for averting the great catastrophes (*jie*) resulting from human immorality, eventually leading to the saving of the whole world. In this manner, the local charitable associations began to assume the characteristics of salvationism.[6]

Chen Jinguo 陳進國 pointed out that salvation from apocalypse was effected not only by one supreme god, but as a mission assigned to gods of lower status. Therefore, the tales of salvation from the apocalypse contained great diversity and the possibility of continuing development. In other words, there is great flexibility regarding who inherits heaven's will, or which messengers, saints or Daoist masters are sent on a mission of salvation on behalf of heaven. This is left up to the fertile folk imagination of each local society.[7]

In this article, I will discuss the rise and development of the spirit-writing movements in a local society from the late Qing period to the present day, focusing on the localization of salvationist religion. According to David A. Palmer, the term "salvationist" was first applied to Chinese religious groups by Myron L. Cohen, who held that their focus on individual salvation was a distinguishing feature of the so-called sectarian groups, in contrast to the "popular orthodoxy" of communal religion.[8] Palmer approves of Cohen's view, and summarizes the features of salvationist religion as follows: "a foundational charismatic figure and/or direct divine revelations; a millenarian eschatology; an embodied experience through healing and/or body cultivation; and an outward, expansive orientation through good deeds, evangelism, or philanthropy."[9]

Palmer also pointed out that the teachings and practices of salvationist groups can often engender varying degrees of tension within the surrounding sociocultural environment. However, after exploring the historical transformation of Chinese religion, he concludes that most of salvationist groups' practices and teachings have gradually been blended into the local religious culture.[10]

---

6   Shiga, *Kami to Ki no aida*, 215–29; Shiga, "What Kind of Innovations Did Spirit Writing Bring about for a Popular Saint's Cult?," 172–179.
7   Chen, *Jiujie*, 58.
8   Palmer, "Chinese Redemptive Societies," 43.
9   Ibid., 44.
10 Ibid., 59.

The local religious tradition, which we observed during our field research, can be viewed as a stratified structure. On the base layer of indigenous religion, emigrants and travelers have imported and spread different religious cultures, including the teachings and practices of the salvationist groups, at different times. Various aspects of religious culture from outside penetrated or accumulated in this base layer, forming a number of new layers. Some of the religious beliefs and practices used by different actors interacted with one another to create new dynamics, while others engendered tension with the sociocultural environment, leading to friction or their elimination. Against the continuous political and social changes, some beliefs were forgotten or became buried in the lower layers. In some cases, a belief that had become hidden in an older layer, through being taken up by spiritual mediums or women's spiritual circles, resurfaced.

The field that I will investigate here is western Guangdong (Yuexi 粵西), particularly Wuchuan 吳川, Gaozhou 高州, and Xinyi 信宜, all of which were prominent commercial cities and market towns situated alongside the Jianjiang River 鑒江. The Jianjiang River originates in a mountain in Xinyi, flows through major cities such as Gaozhou, Huazhou 化州, Maoming 茂名, and Dianbai 電白, finally reaches Shajiaoxuan 沙角旋 in Wuchuan, and empties into the South China Sea. In the past, many ships sailed frequently between the cities, towns and villages situated along the river. Therefore, the area along the Jianjiang River formed a cultural region, with common religious beliefs and customs.

The urban area of Gaozhou, where the prefectural capital was located during the imperial era, was the political, economic, and cultural center of the region, called *xia sifu* 下四府 (lower four prefectures), which included Gaozhou, Leizhou 雷州, Lianzhou 廉州, and Qiongzhou 瓊州. Gaozhou prefecture comprised the six counties of Maoming, Xinyi, Huazhou, Dianbai, Shicheng 石城, and Wuchuan, and was called Gaoliang 高涼 in ancient times. The Gaoliang region was an important hub for road and river traffic, linked with Yunnan 雲南, Guizhou 貴州, Guangxi, and even Vietnam. Among the religious worship observed in this region, a leader of the local tribes, Lady Xian 洗夫人, and an ancient Daoist immortal, Pan Maoming 潘茂名, are well known. However, no previous studies have ever attempted to examine spirit-writing groups.

According to my recent research, a large number of spirit-writing halls, which match Palmer's definition of "salvationist religion," were established by local literati and merchants in this region during the Guangxu 光緒 era (1875–1908) or even earlier. This article aims to provide an outline of the spirit-writing groups in western Guangdong, focusing on their savior deities and eschatological scriptures. Employing both historical materials and anthropological data obtained from my field research, I will investigate how the spirit-writing movement that arose after 1840 has transformed the local religious beliefs and practices, up to the present day.

In the first part of this article, I will explore how the nineteenth-century spirit-writing movement was transmitted to western Guangdong and took root among local people, focusing on the propagation route of eschatological scriptures and the actors involved in this movement. Then, I will consider the rise and development of the spirit-writing movement at the end of the nineteenth century, during the outbreak of plague in this region. In the second part of this article, I will consider the localization of the new eschatological idea within the local religion, by following the historical transformation of the local religion since the early twentieth century up until the present day. I will examine two case studies in different socio-religious contexts, based on my field research.

2   The Spread of the Nineteenth-Century Spirit-Writing Movement to Western Guangdong

After 1840, in Sichuan and Yunnan, due to the great impact of the revelations that occurred at the Longnü Temple, a significant number of spirit-writing groups arose and began to reveal similar eschatological messages. Also, some salvationist groups, such as the Xiantiandao 先天道 (The Way of Former Heaven)[11] incorporated the new eschatological discourses into their own eschatological traditions. In this context, new eschatological scriptures appeared, that had a significant influence thereafter, such as the *Jiushengchuan* 救生船 (The boat to save lives), the *Fanxingtu* 返性圖 (A roadmap to return to one's nature) and the *Zhilu baofa* 指路寶筏 (A precious raft to show the way).[12] These texts were based on a vast number of divine messages that were spirit-written at several hundred spirit-writing altars in Sichuan and Yunnan.[13]

---

11   The Xiantiandao emerged as one of several salvationist societies that split from the Qinglianjiao 青蓮教 (Blue Lotus Teachings), founded in Jiangxi 江西 during the Yongzheng 雍正 period (1722–1736). For further details about the Qinglianjiao and the Xiantiandao, see Asai, *Minshin jidai minkan shūkyō kessha no kenkyū*, 387–437.

12   On the religious idea of the *Zhilu baofa*, see Takeuchi, "Shinmatu Shisen no shūkyō undō," 70–86.

13   For recent works on spirit-writing in Sichuan and the surrounding areas, see Wang, "Spirit Writing Groups in Modern China," 658–64. For more details regarding the production and transmission of spirit-written scriptures in Sichuan and Yunnan during the Qing period, see Hu, "*Wendi quanshu* yanjiu," who discusses the transmission of spirit-written scrip-

In Sichuan, not only did spirit-writing groups derive from Longnü Temple, but other spirit-writing groups also produced similar eschatological scriptures, where the Jade Emperor, Lord Guan and other saints engaged in salvation from the apocalypse. Akiko Tsuzuki 都築晶子 introduced a number of these eschatological scriptures that were included in a collection of Daoist scriptures in the *Zunde tang ban Daojiao congdian* 尊德堂板道教叢典 (The Hall of Respectable Virtue's wood block printed collection of Daoist scriptures), published in Chongqing Prefectural City in the Late Qing and Early Republican periods. The majority of the scriptures were produced in Chongqing Prefecture 重慶府, in places such as Jingbei ting 江北廳, Hezhou 合州, Qijiang 綦江, and Jiajiang 夾江, during the period from 1813 to 1894. One of these scriptures, the *Wusheng dijun xuexinwen* 武聖帝君血心文 (The Warrior Lord's devotional messages), is Guandi's spirit-written teaching to save people from an apocalypse due to occur in the *gengshen* year of the Xianfeng 咸豐 reign (1860) as a punishment by the Jade Emperor.[14]

In the second half of the nineteenth-century, such spirit-written scriptures that originated in Sichuan and Yunnan rapidly spread to the coastal areas, including Guangdong. The widespread circulation of these scriptures was largely due to the expanding movement of people between southwestern China and Lingnan, the growing publishing business, and the rise of various religious organizations in Guangdong.

During the late Qing period, due to the increasing amount of commercial activity, migration between Yunnan and Lingnan greatly increased. During the Qianlong 乾隆 period (1735–1796), a new waterway, running via Baise 百色 and Nanning 南寧 in Guangxi along the West River, was developed to transport the copper produced in Yunnan. This West River route was divided into two routes at Cangwu 蒼梧 county near Wuzhou 梧州, with the northern route heading to Hunan 湖南 and the southern to Guangdong. The latter route promoted not only the transportation of copper, but also trade in salt, rice, and a variety of other goods that were produced in Guangxi and Guangdong. As a result, the number of traveling merchants from Lingnan rapidly increased along this route.[15]

In the 1830s, Yunnan opium also began to be transported along the West River route and was widely traded in Guangxi and Guangdong. During the

---

tures relating to the cult of Wenchang between Sichuan and Guizhou; Wang, "Popular Groups Promoting 'The Religion of Confucius'"; Valussi, "The Transmission of the Cult of Lü Dongbin."

14 Tsuzuki, "Ryūkoku Daigaku Ōmiya toshokan," 244–45.
15 Nishikawa, *Unnan Chūkasekai no bōchō*, 137–44.

period 1850–1860, large sections of the West River became impassable due to military blockades and the suppression of rebellions. Traders were forced to use alternative transport routes, one of which ran from southeastern Yunnan through Tonkin then Beihai 北海 to Leizhou Peninsula, including Zhanjiang 湛江 and Wuchuan. The intensified human movement from Yunnan to this western Lingnan region was responsible for the interregional spread of the bubonic plague in later years.[16] This triggered the creation of several new eschatological scriptures in this region, as the plague raged from 1890 to 1892.[17]

The fact that Cantonese merchants nurtured trans-border businesses and networks also promoted the distribution of scriptures from southwestern China to Lingnan. One of the most popular scriptures, the *Guansheng dijun mingsheng jing* 關聖帝君明聖經 (The scripture of the Imperial Lord Guan on illuminating saintliness; hereinafter referred to as the *Mingsheng jing*), is a good example.[18] Its various editions were mostly published by private donations made by devotees, notably Cantonese merchants traveling between Lingnan and Southwest China.[19] As ter Haar discusses, the devotees of the *Mingsheng jing* shared one thing in common, which was that they often lived far from their hometown, without any territorial divine protection.[20] That is why the reputation of the *Mingsheng jing* spread through the networks of Cantonese merchants who were engaged in long, dangerous journeys, and it became increasingly popular through word of mouth.

Moreover, the growing publishing business in Guangdong promoted the popularization and spread of the scriptures. Several cities in Guangdong, including Guangzhou 廣州 and Foshan 佛山, were major publishing centers, where a number of print shops and bookstores operated during the late Qing period. There were also a number of morality bookstores (*shanshu ju* 善書局) or morality book distribution centers (*shanshu liutong chu* 善書流通處) in Guangzhou and other cities. Furthermore, charitable organizations, Daoist and

---

16   Benedict, *Bubonic Plague*, 57–71.
17   At least four new eschatological scriptures were produced in western Guangdong during the period 1891–1892. For further details, see Shiga, "Qingmo Lingnan diqu de shuyi liuxing," 344–52.
18   Regarding the distribution of the *Guandi mingsheng jing* during the late Qing period, see Wang, "Morality Book Publishing," 235–38.
19   For example, "Lingyan ji 靈驗記" (The record of true miracle stories), contained in the *Guandi mingsheng jing quanji* 關帝明聖經全集 (The complete collection of the Imperial Lord Guan on illuminating saintliness), recounts several Cantonese merchants' miraculous experiences.
20   Ter Haar, *Guanyu*, 233.

Buddhist organizations, sectarian groups, such as the Xiantiandao, and small spirit-writing halls, also functioned as morality book presses.[21]

It should be noted that the spirit-writing halls in western Guangdong also made a significant contribution to the widespread circulation of eschatological scriptures. The Congshan tang 從善堂 (Hall of Following Virtue), known as the first morality book center in Hong Kong, originated in Meilu town 梅菉鎮, Wuchuan. The scriptures published by the Congshan tang have been widely circulated not only in Hong Kong, but also in Guangdong, Taiwan and other areas.

Yau Chi-on wrote that the Congshan tang was co-founded by people from Meilu and members of the Wufu tang 五福堂 (Hall of Five Blessings), a native-place association of Bao'an county 寶安縣 in 1898. The Congshan tang reprinted and published several morality books and scriptures, most of which were spirit-written, at the end of the nineteenth century in western and other parts of Guangdong.[22] Undoubtedly, most of the scriptures published by the Congshan tang of Hong Kong are identical to the scriptures and their transcriptions that are being circulated in present-day western Guangdong. As I will discuss later, the Congshan tang descended from a morality book center established in Meilu town in 1887, which may indicate why they possessed several wood blocks of scriptures and morality books.

More importantly, the members of the Congshan tang shared the typical eschatological discourse of the new salvation movement that began in 1840. A manuscript entitled *Nanzhen Congshan zhengtang chuangli sishi zhounian jinian gaishu* 南鎮從善正堂剙立四十週年紀念概述 (The essay on the fortieth anniversary of the foundation of the Nanzhen Congshan zhengtang), written by Huang Guangpan 黃廣攀 (no dates), a disciple of the Congshan tang, in 1935, reads:

> In the Daoguang *gengzi* year, *sanqi pudu* (the third period of universal salvation) had started only 100 years before. ... All of the gods in the heavens assisted in civilizing human beings by encouraging them to carry out good deeds in order to save them from the apocalypse. ... [T]his *sanqi pudu* was really a special movement for universal salvation, which was a deed of great mercy. Originally, it began in Sichuan, Meilu in Guangdong, and elsewhere. Using a spirit-writing pen made from a peach tree branch and a board filled with sand, they demonstrated the principles of karmic

---

21 Yau, "The Xiantiandao and Publishing," 188–201.
22 Yau, "Jiujie jishi," 368–75.

retribution based on *yin-yang* and good and evil in a pertinent, comprehensive manner. Sometimes, they wrote scriptures and moral teachings for preaching by using spirit-writing. ... Our Congshan tang was founded fifty-six years later in the twenty-second year of the Guangxu [period] (1896). Initially, the gentlemen from Meilu went to Hong Kong to preach the Dao. ...

爰於前道光庚子特開三期普度，時限百年。諸天真宰咸予翊贊，以勸善化民，救劫濟世為主旨。... 蓋此"三期普度"乃一"特別普及救濟運動"，其優容之道可謂極矣。原其推行，始於四川及粵之梅菉等處，藉桃筆沙箋，闡示陰陽果報、善惡禍福之理，剀切周詳。或著為經訓，用資宣化。... 我從善堂後首堂五十六載而興，剏立於光緒廿二年。初由梅菉善士宣道至港。...²³

Significantly, the above essay claims that the *sanqi pudu* began in Sichuan as well as in Meilu in Guangdong and elsewhere, almost simultaneously. This implies that spirit-writing groups in Guangdong came to share in the eschatological discourse originating from Sichuan at almost the same time, due to the fast distribution of eschatological scriptures from Sichuan to Meilu.

The following two scriptures, both originating in Sichuan, provide an insight into this process of distribution. The first is the *Yuhuang zhenjing* 玉皇真經 (True scripture of the Jade Emperor), which is one of the most popular scriptures circulating in the form of a transcription or copy in present-day western Guangdong (see Figure 13.1). According to an inscription, it was printed during the twenty-third year of the Guangxu reign (1897) (hereafter referred to as the 1897 edition of the *Yuhuang zhenjing*). It was republished by the Congshan tang of Hong Kong in 1898 as a scripture entitled *Yuhuang shangdi yingyan jiujie zhenjing* 玉皇上帝應驗救劫真經 (True scripture of the responses and proofs of the Jade Emperor saving humanity from the apocalypse; hereafter referred to as the 1898 edition of the *Yuhuang zhenjing*).²⁴ The inscriptions to both the 1897 and 1898 versions contain the same sentence: "*Baochan san pin* 寶懺三品 (Three sutras of precious penance; that is, the *Yuhuang zhenjing*), given by the Jade Emperor to this secular world, first transmitted to Sichuan, and then to Guangxi. ..." (寶懺三品, 玉帝發下凡世, 先傳西蜀, 次傳廣西 ...).

---

23 Yau, *Shan yu ren tong*, 281–85.
24 My own edition was printed using recut blocks in Hong Kong in 1934, sponsored by disciples of the Congshan tang.

A clue to the origin of the *Yuhuang zhenjing* may be found in a scripture entitled the *Yuhuang Wangmu jiujie zhenjing* 玉皇王母救劫真經 (True scriptures of the Jade Emperor and Queen Mother to save humanity from the apocalypse),[25] a bound volume of the *Yuhuang jiujie zhenjing* 玉皇救劫真經 and the *Wangmu xiaojie jiushi zhenjing* 王母消劫救世真経 (True scripture of the Queen Mother to prevent catastrophe and save humanity from the apocalypse). The first is identical to the *Yuhuang zhenjing* circulating in Guangdong and Hong Kong, except for a few different characters. The *Yuhuang Wangmu jiujie zhenjing* contains a preface that was spirit-written by Lord Guan, who descended to a study room in Yanmen 雁門 in the fourth year of the Xianfeng reign (1854):

> Guansheng dijun prefaced: ... Even the creators of all beings have to take the trouble to manifest and save humanity by spirit-writing. ... So, opening my eyes of wisdom and looking around, I saw a *xiantan* (celestial altar) located at the intersection between the eastern and northern part of Sichuan, where these two scriptures were finally transmitted. Both scriptures were originally an expression of the Jade Emperor and Queen Mother's benevolent feelings about saving humanity. They were published in Linshui last year, and then published in Guang'an. Apart from these two places, there have not been any reprinted editions. Fortunately, Mr. Jiang, Mr. Tao and other gentlemen have now made up their minds to reprint them. What a noble deed this is! ...[26]

> 關聖帝君敘：... 則雖萬靈真宰，亦不辭勞瘁，而飛鸞顯化，借乩沙以救生靈矣。... 爰開南天慧眼四觀，見川東川北交界之所有一仙壇，遂降而為此二經之。二經者，固玉皇王母救世之婆心，所釀而成者也。自去年刊於鄰水，繼又刊於廣安，外此遂無人翻板。今幸有姜陶文生等，發心重刻，誠美舉也。...

This passage shows that the *Yuhuang Wangmu jiujie zhenjing* was produced via spirit-writing at a *xiantan* 仙壇 (celestial altar) in Sichuan before 1854 and that the preface by Guandi was added at a later date. The scripture had been reprinted in Linshui 鄰水, Guang'an 廣安 and other places in Sichuan since 1853. Additionally, it began to be diffused throughout southwestern China. Although it is uncertain where the *xiantan* was located, it must have stood in an

---

25 The *Yuhuang Wangmu jiujie zhenjing* that I referred to is an edition reprinted in 1906; blocks stored at the Tongshan tang in Jinwo 晉沃 (Shanxi 山西), included in volume 9 of *Zhongguo yuyan jiujieshu huibian*.

26 *Yuhuang Wangmu jiujie zhenjing*, 320–22.

area fairly close to the eastern part of the Sichuan Basin including Linshui and Guang'an,[27] and also not far from Dingyuan County, where the Longnü Temple was located.

Thereafter, the *Yuhuang jiujie zhenjing* and the *Wangmu xiaojie jiushi zhenjing* began to be widely distributed, both jointly and separately, in southwestern China and other regions. The *Wangmu xiaojie jiushi zhenjing* was published in Kaijun 開郡, Yunnan, as a new edition entitled *Wushang Yaochi Wangmu xiaojie jiushi baochan* 無上瑤池王母消劫救世寶懺 (Precious Repentance of the Queen Mother of the Jasper Pool to prevent catastrophe and save humanity from the apocalypse), with a preface that was spirit-written in 1860.[28] In 1896, it was reprinted with a preface that was spirit-written by Fuyou dijun 孚佑帝君 (Lü Dongbin), who descended to the Baoyuan gong 保元宮 (Palace of Preserving Elements) in Longzhou 龍州, Guangxi.[29] The *Yuhuang jiujie zhenjing* was published by a spirit-writing hall called the Mudao xianguan 慕道仙館 (Celestial Hall for People Worshipping the Dao) in Shantou 汕頭 in eastern Guangdong in 1896. Although there is no other evidence that the *Yuhuang zhenjing* was published in Guangxi apart from the inscription, it was possibly passed on to Wuchuan through Guangxi at the beginning of the Guangxu reign.[30]

27　Guang'an was the location for the Shancheng tang 善成堂 headquarters, which was a publishing house established by Fu Jinduo 傅金鐸 in Chongqing in 1750–1751. The Shancheng tang published many spirit-written scriptures compiled by Fu Jinquan 傅金銓 (active 1800–1842), an alchemist, religious leader, and publisher, after he moved to Eastern Sichuan in 1817; see Valussi, "Printing and Religion," 13.

28　The digital library of the Museum of World Religions contains several editions of the *Wangmu xiaojie jiushi zhenjing*, including a bound volume of the *Wushang Yaochi Wangmu xiaojie jiushi baochan* 無上瑤池王母消劫救世寶懺. The following title was printed on the front page: "Xiaojie baochan transmitted in Kaijun, Yunnan, in the summer of 1860. Reprinted in 1927 by the Henan mingxing tang 河南明星堂, Guangzhou." (消劫寶懺：咸豐十年歲在庚申夏六月降於雲南開郡，民國丁卯 (1927) 仲春重刊，廣州河南明星堂藏板。) See http://ehdwlgalll.idv.tw/gbs/964 (accessed May 11, 2016). The same edition, *Yaochi Wangmu xiaojiejiushi baochan quanbu* 瑤池王母消劫救世寶懺全部 (R. 1976 · NLVNPF-0147), was passed on to Vietnam and owned by the Yushan ci 玉山祠 in Hanoi 河內. See http://lib.nomfoundation.org/collection/1/volume/192/ (accessed December 9, 2019).

29　The digital version is listed in *Shanshu tushuguan* 善書圖書館 (Digital library of morality books); see http://taolibrary.com/category/category67/c67021.htm (accessed December 9, 2019). Chen Jinguo referred to the same edition in his article, which he found in a Daoist temple in Minxi 閩西. He pointed out that the Baoyuan gong was located in the Longyun dong 龍雲洞 in Xiaolian cheng 小連城, Longzhou county 龍州. Guangxi. Marshal Su Yuanchun 蘇元春 (1844–1908), the military commander of Guangxi, who defeated the French Army at the Sino-Vietnamese border, established the command center in the Baoyuan gong; see Chen, "Wairu neifo." 278.

30　A transcription of the *Yuhuang zhenjing*, which I found in the Gonghuang miao 宮皇

The second example is the *Mingsheng jing*, which is also quite popular in western Guangdong. Most of the *Mingsheng jing* texts chanted by the followers of spirit-writing halls in present-day Gaozhou and Wuchuan are transcriptions that have been handwritten by local people after 1990. Their original text is a wood block printed scripture, which I found in the Sansheng gong 三聖宮 (Palace of the Three Saints), a spirit-writing hall in Shigu town 石鼓鎮, Gaozhou. However, it is severely damaged and lacks several pages, including the front cover. Therefore, its year of completion is unknown. Fortunately, I found almost the same text in the form of a tattered wood block scripture in a temple in Gaozhou city. This was a booklet entitled the *Wenwudi shengjing tongbian* 文武帝聖經統編 (Bound volume of sacred scriptures by the Martial God and the Civil God), which was recently reprinted by a word-processor,[31] based on a recut-block edition by Fuwen lou 富文樓 (Building of Rich Texts), a print shop in Gaozhou prefecture, in 1892.[32] It is fairly certain that the *Wuwendi shengjing tongbian* originated from the old wood block scripture that I found in the Sansheng gong, although some stories of the miraculous events which occurred in Maoming in 1889 were added.

What is notable is that the *Mingsheng jing* circulating in Gaozhou is the same version as that in the afore-mentioned *Zunde tang ban Daojiao congdian* which was published in Chongqing. The Zunde tang's edition of the *Mingsheng jing*, formally entitled the *Gufo yingyan Mingsheng jing dingben sanjuan* 古佛應驗明聖經定本三卷 (Three volumes of the standard text for the *Scripture of Responses and Proofs of the Ancient Buddha on Illuminating Saintliness*), was published in Sichuan in 1847. It differs from other editions of the *Mingsheng jing* found in other collections, mainly regarding Guandi's title, which is described as *Tongming shouxiang* 通明首相 (The Minister of Brightness).[33] The *Wenwudi shengjing tongbian* adopts the same title.

One preface, that was spirit-written by a deity named Fenglaizi 蓬萊子 in the *Wenwudi shengjing tongbian*, reads:

廟 (Temple of the Jade Princess) of Maopo 茂坡 in Gaozhou suggests that the *Yuhuang zhenjing* was published at the beginning of the Guangxu period, as its afterword, written in 1896, reads: "The *Yuhuang jing* was printed and distributed by the Meishan tang 梅善堂 (Hall of Plum and Goodness) of Wuchuan in 1879 (玉皇經一編由梅善堂於光緒五年所刻分送)."

31   The booklet was made by the Xinshan tang 信善堂 (Hall of Faith and Virtue) of Dianbai in 2002.

32   According to the frontispiece, the printing of this recut-block edition was sponsored by Xie Pengling 謝彭齡 (n.d.) and Xie Yiling 謝頤齡 (n.d.), who were students (*tongsheng* 童生) within the lower level of the civil examination system.

33   Tsuzuki, "Ryukoku Daigaku Ōmiya toshokan," 270.

THE NINETEENTH-CENTURY SPIRIT-WRITING MOVEMENT

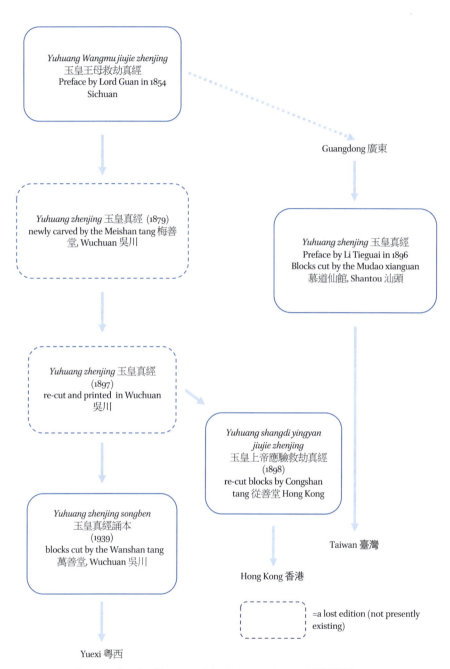

FIGURE 13.1 The spread and publication of the *Yuhuang zhenjing* 玉皇真經

Since the *Mingsheng jing* was produced in Yuquan, a number of literal mistakes have been made. ... Fortunately, two men from Yucheng town (Chongqing) in eastern Sichuan received a spirit-written instruction from the Lord.[34] This is extremely fortunate. For that reason, the two men were delighted. The revised edition is already widespread in Sichuan. The further [the *Mingsheng jing*] spread from Sichuan, the more difficult its circulation might become or, if in the future [the message of the] *Mingsheng jing* will be hidden again, more mistakes will arise. Needless to say, our spirit-writing hall, that often publishes and reprints scriptures, should take far greater care. Don't frustrate our Lord anymore. Today, I (Fenglaizi) descended to our spirit-writing altar because of this [issue]. I hope that you gentlemen embody a compassionate heart and will widely engrave, print and disseminate [this text], in order to circulate it among everybody. ...[35]

夫明聖一經，起自玉泉，迨其後錯亂甚矣。... 幸渝城二子，蒙帝木筆書明。蓋亦幸中這甚幸者也。故二子喜不勝喜。亦已付刊於省中矣。省與各州遙遙相隔，恐勢阻難通。將來明聖復隱，差錯又甚矣。況本堂乩書，屢屢催刻，使於此而猶不用心。不使帝於一憂中，還深一傷者乎。我今來壇蓋為此也。願諸君子體此婆心，廣鐫印送，使彼此流通。...[36]

The afterword reads: "In the middle of the summer of the third year of the Guangxu reign (1877), because a spirit-written message was sent down to the city of Guhuai Pingjie 古懷平傑 in Guangxi, we published a new book. I, Chen Yong, a pupil from Huazhou, am writing this at the beginning of the winter of the *gengyin* year (1890)" (光緒三年歲在丁丑孟夏中浣乩降於西粵古懷平傑市翻改新本 當歲庚寅季冬上浣化州後學陳鏞敬書).[37] The prefaces and afterword suggest that this revised edition was created in Chongqing in 1843, then taken to Guangxi and published as a new edition by the spirit-writing hall in 1890. Although the location of this hall is unknown, it must have been relatively close to Huazhou.

---

34 The two scholars in Yucheng received the spirit-written instruction from Lord Guan on June 15, 1843, which was the deity's birthday, (癸卯六月望旬恭逢關聖帝君聖誕之辰), according to another preface entitled "Fan'gai *Mingsheng jing* xu 翻改明聖經序" (Preface of the revised *Scripture on Illuminating Saintliness*).
35 *Wenwudi shengjing tongbian*, 2–3.
36 I have added the punctuation to this quotation.
37 The afterword, in *Wenwudi shengjing tongbian*.

As the transmission routes of the two above scriptures that originated in Sichuan indicate, they were distributed in western Guangdong via Guangxi and had been reprinted there by the beginning of the Guangxu period. It can be assumed that they were transported by Cantonese merchants. As I mention later, the earliest spirit-writing halls arose in western Guangdong between the Daoguang (1820–1850) and Tongzhi 同治 periods (1861–1875). Given this, the claim by Huang Guangpan, a Congshan tang disciple, that the movement for universal salvation began in Sichuan and Meilu almost simultaneously appears feasible. It is likely that the eschatological discourses originating in Sichuan spread to western Guangdong and began to take root among the local people from the mid-nineteenth century.

3   The Rise of the Spirit-Writing Movement in Western Guangdong

In this section, I will explore how the spirit-writing movement arose and developed in western Guangdong. Firstly, let us examine a local gazetteer, entitled the *Meilu fuzhi* 梅菉賦志 (Records of the ode to Meilu), which was edited in 1896. It includes the following statement:

> Educating people and cultivating moral customs by preaching the Sacred Edict: … The public preaching began at the Wumiao (Warrior Temple)[38] in the thirteenth year of the Guangxu [reign] (1887).
>
> 講聖諭化民成俗：… 光緒十三年後設在武廟。[39]
>
> Establishing a morality book center and serving as a good model for the world: a number of people donated books before. In the thirteenth year of the Guangxu [period] (1887), officials, gentlemen, and merchants donated money and established a morality book center in the Warrior Temple, where scripture chanters were employed to chant the *Mingsheng jing*. In the sixteenth year of the Guangxu [period] (1890), it was moved to Lanxi village and was rebuilt as the Sansheng gong (The Palace of the Three Saints).

---

38   The Wu miao 武廟 (Warrior temple) indicates the temple which worships Lord Guan 關帝 as the main deity.
39   *Meilu fuzhi bufenjuan*, 574.

置善書扶世垂型：前送善書者良多。光緒十三年，官紳商民捐賣置善書設局在武廟,並延經生誦明聖經。十六年移設藍溪鄉三聖宮。⁴⁰

The palace was called "The Three Saints". It was established in Lanxi village in the seventeenth year of the Guangxu [period] (1891). The Palace of the Three Saints enshrined Wendi, Wudi and Lüdi, and set up the memorial tablets [of the members related] to the morality book center.

宮稱三聖：藍溪鄉光緒十七年新建。文帝、武帝、呂帝宮，並設善書局祿位。⁴¹

The above passages indicate that a morality book center was established in the Warrior Temple in Meilu in 1887. Later, this was moved to Lanxi village 藍溪鄉 in Changqi town 長歧鎮, on the outskirts of Meilu, and rebuilt as the Palace of the Three Saints in 1891, enshrining Lord Guan, Wenchang, and Patriarch Lü. According to other descriptions in the *Meilu fuzhi*, it appears that several preachers from the Tongwen yixue 同文義學, a public free school in Meilu town, used to deliver public lectures at the morality book center. Judging from the deities and scriptures, it is possible that they were influenced by the post-1840 spirit-writing movement.

Several questions now arise. First, what was the exact nature of the morality book center? It was founded in the Warrior Temple, one of the major temples in Meilu town, which was reconstructed in 1877. A community of merchants from Guangzhou formed around the Warrior Temple, because there were a Yangcheng huiguan 羊城會館 (a guildhall for the people of Guangzhou) and a Guanghuo hang 廣貨行 (company trading in Cantonese goods) situated close to the temple. Therefore, the merchants from Guangzhou held political power regarding the organization of the Warrior Temple.⁴² It is also possible that a number of merchants from Guangzhou supported and participated in the morality book center's activities. Judging from the descriptions in *Meilu fuzhi*, such as that it was founded through donations by various strata in Meilu, and that public lectures on the Sacred Edict were delivered by preachers from the public school, it seems reasonable to assume that the morality book center possessed some of the characteristics of a public sector organization. In addition, several small printing houses and stationery stores were located on a street

---

40   Ibid.
41   Ibid., 546.
42   Wu, "Qingdai Guangdong Meilu zhen," 38.

called Kangqi lou 康歧樓, close to the Warrior Temple.[43] The morality book center was in a convenient location for printing books.

The second question is why the morality book center, with such a public nature, was established in Meilu town. Meilu's location was important for transportation, because three rivers, the Jianjiang, the Xiaodongjiang and the Meihuajiang, converged there. Although only a *xu* 墟 (market town), Meilu flourished as a collection and distribution center of commodities from Yunnan, Guilin 桂林, Southern Guangdong and overseas. By the late Qing period, it had developed into a leading commercial city in the area, where a large number of merchants gathered from other cities. That is why Meilu came to be called *xiao Foshan* 小佛山 (Little Foshan).[44] In other words, Meilu was a hub for people, goods, money, and ideas, in which the Cantonese merchants' transregional networks played an important role.

The third question is whether the Congshan tang of Hong Kong was a successor to the Palace of the Three Saints. It is difficult to claim a direct relationship between them, although it is possible that the members of the Congshan tang were in some way linked to the Palace of the Three Saints. The pantheon of the Congshan tang, even today, consists of seven deities; namely, the Jade Emperor, the Jade Princess (Yuhuang gongzhu 玉皇宮主), the Jade Prince (Yuhuang taizi 玉皇太子), Lord Guan, Wenchang dijun, Fuyou dijun (Lü Dongbin), and Cangqiong dijun 蒼穹帝君. The same pantheon features in the introduction to the 1898 edition of the *Yuhuang zhenjing* which was published by the Congshan tang. The *Meilu fuzhi* fails to mention which deities were enshrined in the Palace of the Three Saints, except for the Jade Emperor and the Three Saints. However, as we will discuss in detail below, active salvationist groups worshipped the Jade Princess in Wuchuan and Gaozhou during the Republican period. According to the *Wuchuan xianzhi* (2001) 吳川縣志 (Gazetteer of Wuchuan County), they originated in Changqi town, where the Palace of the Three Saints was located.[45] No territorial temples enshrined the Jade Princess apart from the Palace of the Three Saints in Changqi town. Therefore, it seems reasonable to suppose that the pantheon consisting of the seven deities, includ-

---

43 This is an oral account by my informant who lives in Meilu. This is supported by an afterword in *Wangmu huasheng zhenjing* 王母化生真經 (True scripture of the Queen Mother's manifestation), which I found in a scripture hall in Gaozhou. It was printed from blocks cut by a print house called Yongjixiang 永吉祥 located in Kangqilou Street.

44 Wu, "Qingdai Guangdong Meilu zhen," 27. *Xiao Foshan* was a nickname given to towns resembling Foshan, which was one of the most flourishing commercial cities in late Qing period Guangdong.

45 Wuchuan shi difangzhi bangongshi, *Wuchuan xianzhi*, 970.

ing the Jade Princess, was created in the Palace of the Three Saints, and later adopted by the Congshan tang.

The combination of gods, Lord Guan, Wenchang and Patriarch Lü, enshrined in the Palace of the Three Saints, suggests that the worship of the Three Saints took root in this area by at least 1891. However, it is possible that it spread earlier than the Guangxu period, since there exists a spirit-writing hall in Gaozhou, also called the Sansheng gong 三聖宮, which enshrines the Three Saints, which was founded in the second year of the Tongzhi period (1863). Its founder was Zhang Meichu 張梅初 (no dates), who was not only a teacher in the private primary school in the village, but also a geomancer.

In the seventeenth year of the Guangxu period (1891), when the Palace of the Three Saints was founded in Lanxi village, an epoch-making event occurred in Xinyi, as the bubonic plague broke out in western Guangdong in this year, and the first compiled eschatological scripture was created there. The new eschatological scripture was entitled the *Wenwu jiujie baosheng yongming jing* 文武救劫葆生永命經 (Scripture of Wen[chang] and Guandi to save humanity from the apocalypse and to protect human life, hereinafter referred to as the *Wenwu baosheng yongming jing*), and its main motif was salvation by the Three Saints.

The creation of the *Wenwu baosheng yongming jing* was directly triggered by the outbreak of the plague, which prevailed in Xinyi, Gaozhou, Shicheng, and Wuchuan from October 1890 to July 1891. In the city of Xinyi and its suburbs, about a thousand people died between February and March 1891. In Meilu town, more than three thousand people had died by April of that year.[46] During this time, not only in Xinyi but also elsewhere in western Guangdong, new eschatological scriptures were produced.[47]

The *Wenwu baosheng yongming jing* was a bound volume of the *Wenchang dijun jiujie baosheng jing* 文昌帝君救劫葆生經 (Scripture of Wenchang to save humanity from the apocalypse and to protect human life) and the *Wudi jiujie yongming jing* 武帝救劫永命經 (Scripture of the Warrior Lord to save humanity from the apocalypse and to grant eternal life). Both of them were produced

---

46 *Gaozhou fuzhi, juanmo* 卷末, appendix: 34.
47 For example, two eschatological scriptures, the *Yuhuang Shangdi yingyan jiushi zhenjing* 玉皇上帝應驗救世真經 (True scripture of the responses and proofs of the Jade Emperor to save the world) and the *Tianhou yuanjun jiuku jiunan zhenjing* 天后元君救苦救難真經 (True scripture of Tianhou for the relief of afflicted and suffering humans), were produced at a spirit-writing altar in the Guangzhou guildhall (*huiguan* 會館) in Chikan port 赤坎埠 in Zhanjiang, on the Leizhou Peninsula, in spring 1892, when the plague had not completely abated. Both scriptures referred to the plague pandemic, mentioning that "a strange disease" (*yizheng* 異症) was prevailing.

in the sixth lunar month of 1891 at the Wenwu erdi gong 文武二帝宮 (Palace of the Two Lords, Wenchang and Lord Guan) in Zhenlong 鎮隆鎮, the capital town of Xinyi county.[48]

The *Wenchang dijun jiujie baosheng jing* was inspired by the tradition of the Wenchang eschatological scriptures, that can be traced back to the Song period.[49] However, it was also influenced by the new spirit-writing movement that began in 1840. The following is an extract:

> The earth was full of the wickedness of humankind. Foul air and dirty water were everywhere. Even by using up the water from the Eastern Sea, one could not drown out the filth. Even by using all the bamboo slips for writing gained from Western mountain, it would still be difficult to create a complete list of the crimes of humankind. Looking at the unbearable situation, the Jade Emperor felt outraged. Deities and monsters inspected the world and prepared a detailed record. ... The catastrophe had just occurred ... the flames of war raged far and wide, gunfire licked the heavens, with the bones of the dead piled up like mountains. Disease and epidemics spread. ... At this time, I (Wenchang dijun) grieved for humankind and pled persistently with the Jade Emperor on their behalf that they should not be destroyed completely. To bring salvation to humankind, I accompanied Guandi and Lüdi (referring to Patriarch Lü) as they knelt and reported to the Jade Emperor for seven days and seven nights. Touched by our honest compassion, the Jade Emperor finally agreed to [our] pleas. Regardless of hardship, we will continue to encourage and teach them. ... Finally, we hope that they will exit the mystifying paths. By rowing the precious raft, we hope to attain the shore of enlightenment together with them.[50]

---

48   In this article, I refer to *Wenwudi jiujie baosheng yongmingjing*, reprinted by the Tongyou shantang 同友善堂 of Guangzhou in 1898, owned by Tôyô bunka kenkyûjo, Tokyo University.

49   Several passages and words in the *Wenchang dijun jiujie baosheng jing* were clearly borrowed from the *Wenchang dijun jiujiejing* 文昌帝君救劫經 (Scripture of Lord Wenchang to save humanity from the apocalypse), which was also called *Yuanhuang dadao zhenjun jiujie baojing* 元皇大道真君救劫寶經 (Precious scripture of the True Lord of the Great Way of the Original Sovereign on saving humans from the apocalypse) in *Zangwai daoshu* (3:905–908), and *Yuanshi tianzun Zitong dijun benyuanjing* 元始天尊梓童帝君本願經 (Scripture on the original vow of Lord Zitong, expounded by the Heavenly Worthy of Primordial Beginning) in *Daozang* (DZ 29); see Shiga, "Formation of a New Daoist Community," 114–15.

50   *Wenwu jiujie baosheng yongming jing*, 9–10.

罪孽滔天，腥熏滿地，水雖盡乎東海，莫灌其污，竹縱罄乎西山，難紀其惡。…，玉皇震怒，群省生嗔，鬱結薄空，妖魔巡世，校察圖籙 … 劫將一轉 … 兵戈迭起，骸骨成山，疫癘頻仍，腦肝塗地。… 吾目民艱。關心世乱。深憫蚩蚩黎庶。苦求赫赫玉皇。大開方便之門。廣予再生之路。偕同關呂二帝跪奏。通明七天。懇竭斯誠。准如所請。不辭勞瘁，疊為提撕。… 望彼輩早出迷津。寶筏仍撐。願斯民同登覺岸。…

In addition, the *Wudi jiujie yongming jing* contained the following sentences: "In the *gengzi* year (1840), I (Guandi) accompanied Wenchang and Lüdi 呂帝 as they knelt and reported [to the Jade Emperor] for seven days and seven nights. Touched by our honest compassion, [the Jade Emperor] allowed us broadly to bestow his great blessing by enlightening [humankind] through spirit-writing everywhere. … Since then, the movement has continued for several decades and spread everywhere." (歲在庚子初時。吾偕文呂二帝跪奏。通明七日。尽竭精誠。哀求恩准群真。宏施大澤。隨處飛鸞開化。… 領旨迄今。數十年來未息。普天之下。)[51] Clearly therefore, the followers believed that the *Wenwu baosheng yongming jing* was created as a part of the salvation movement that began in 1840.

The *Wenwu baosheng yongming jing* was published in fall 1891 by the spirit-writing hall called the Fushan tang 復善堂 (Hall of Revitalizing Goodness),[52] appending Patriarch Lü's preface that had been spirit-written at the Doucheng jingtang 竇城經堂 (Scripture Hall of Dou city[53]) in Xinyi. The scripture also referred to several spirit-writing halls in this region, including the morality book center in Meilu. This indicates that several spirit-writing halls had arisen in this region by the 1890s. The followers of these spirit-writing halls interacted with each other and gradually began to share common ideas. In other words, they developed a community with the ability to produce a coherent scripture with a strong eschatological idea.

Shortly afterward, the *Wenwu baosheng yongming jing* began to spread outside the prefecture. The *Erdijing lingyan ji* 二帝經靈驗記 (Scripture of the miraculous legend of Wendi and Wudi), attached at the end of the scripture, suggests how it spread. For instance, a merchant from Nanhai county, who

---

51 Ibid., 30–31.
52 The name of the Xinyi Fushan tang and its *duilian* (couplets), which were spirit-written by Lord Guan, are printed on the back of the front page of *Wenwu jiujie baosheng jing Wudi jiujie youmingjing hebian*, which was reprinted by the Baojing ge of Yangcheng (Guangzhou) in 1909.
53 Dou zhou 竇州 is an old name for Xinyi.

visited Xinyi on business, was asked to take more than twenty copies of the scripture to Guangzhou. The scriptures were so heavy that he was going to hire laborers to carry them. Miraculously, the scriptures suddenly became light. When he arrived at Yangjiang River 陽江, he encountered a storm, and it was impossible to cross the flooded river yet, as soon as his ship set sail, the rain stopped, and the sky cleared. As a result, he was able to carry the scriptures easily.

After the plague broke out in western Guangdong, it quickly spread to Guangzhou and Hong Kong in 1894, and then to the Chaoshan region in 1898. The plague facilitated the spirit-writing movement in each affected region.[54] The *Wenwu baosheng yongming jing* was the first eschatological scripture that was compiled in response to the first epidemic in Guangdong. Therefore, the distribution of the scripture had a considerable influence on the later spirit-writing movements both in Guangdong and outside the province.

In Shantou, in 1896, a new edition of the *Wenwu baosheng yongming jing* was published along with Guanyin's preface that was spirit-written at the Mudao Xianguan 慕道仙館 and circulated in Hong Kong and Taiwan. In the twentieth century, the first edition was taken to Vietnam and reprinted at the spirit-writing altar in Hai Duong province, in northern Vietnam, in 1909.[55]

From the above, it follows that the spirit-writing movement arose and developed in western Guangdong during the second half of the nineteenth century. Simultaneously, the worship of the Three Saints and the eschatological discourse gradually became shared by the local spirit-writing halls and took root in this region. In 1887, the Morality Book Center was established in the Warrior Temple in Meilu. Its successor, the Palace of the Three Saints, which was established in 1891, created its own pantheon, including the Three Saints, the Jade Princess and the Jade Prince, which was passed onto the Congshan tang of Hong Kong, which was established in 1896.

Furthermore, directly triggered by the outbreak of the plague in 1891, the community of the local spirit-writing halls eventually produced the first compiled eschatological scripture, the *Wenwu jiujie baosheng yongming jing*, the main motif of which was the new salvation movement of the Three Saints. This scripture had a strong influence on the later spirit-writing movements not only in Western Guangdong but also outside the region.

---

54 See Shiga, "Qingmo Lingnan diqu de shuyi liuxing."
55 The Vietnamese edition of the *Baosheng yongming jing* was reprinted by the Zhishan tan 止善壇 (Altar of Endless Moral Pursuit of Perfection) in Renli 仁里 village, Nam Sách 南策 (present Hai Duong province).

4 Spirit-Writing Halls in Present Day Gaozhou

After the spirit-writing movement arose during the second half of the nineteenth century in western Guangdong, what effect did it have on the local religion? And how were its eschatological ideas localized and transformed through time up to the present day? As further discussion, I will outline the historical transformations and current conditions of several spirit-writing halls, focusing on their savior deities and liturgies, by employing both oral and written materials obtained from my field research conducted in this region during 2017–2019.[56] Although my data and observation are still at a preliminary stage, I will examine two case studies from different socio-religious contexts.

The first concerns spirit-writing halls in the northern Gaozhou area, where the main communal temples in the villages usually have groups for chanting sutras, called *jingtang* 經堂 (literally, a "scripture hall"). A *jingtang* is organized by lay people in the village who are called *jingsheng* 經生 (literally, "student of scriptures"). While this activity was restricted to men before 1950, nowadays women too can become *jingsheng*. They assemble in the temple and chant scriptures, such as the *Mingsheng jing* or *Yuhuang zhenjing*, on the first and fifteenth lunar day of every month. They sometimes hold a spirit-writing séance on the birthdays of gods or other festive occasions. *Jingtang*s are usually centered on rituals related to worshipping Lord Guan. The villagers informed me, "It can't be called a *jingtang* without enshrining Guandi." *Jingtang*s also provide ritual services, like scripture chanting troupes (*songjing tuan* 誦經團), to their communities.[57] The members of *jingtang*s are sometimes invited to conduct rituals to make celebrations held by a family or other temples. They rarely engage in funeral rituals.

The following two *jingtang*s from the northern Gaozhou area may serve as an example:

4.1 The Jingxiu jingtang 敬修經堂 (Scripture Hall of Respect and Cultivation)

This was the oldest *jingtang* in the area. It is found in the back hall of Zhouxiang Community Temple (Zhouxiang shemiao 周享社廟), which is located in

---

56 My field research in Gaozhou lasted approximately two weeks. I was almost always accompanied by Chen Dongqing 陳冬青, the director of the Gaozhou City Museum. I also referred to his book, *Gaozhou shehui lishi diaocha*, to choose the research sites. All field research was supported by JSPS KAKENHI (Grants-in-Aid for Scientific Research (C)), Grant Number JP. 18K00079.

57 On scripture chanting, see also the chapter by Paul Katz in this volume.

Caojiang Town 曹江. The plaque inscription, which reads Chengru zhai 承儒齋 (Hall for Supporting Confucianism), on the front wall of the main hall, indicates that the Jingxiu jingtang espouses Confucianism. It enshrines Lord Guan and his liegemen, Guanping 關平 and Zhoucang 周倉, on the main altar, and also Lady Xian, on another altar. In addition, a spiritual tablet of Wang Tianjun 王天君 (Heavenly Marshal Wang) is enshrined in the corner. Three characters are engraved at the top of the tablet, Puling xuan 普齡軒, which indicate one of the house names for each branch of the Jingxiu tang.[58]

According to the inscription on the wall, the Jingxiu jingtang was founded in 1891 (the seventeenth year of the Guangxu period), when the god descended and manifested himself in this village for the first time. The god gave his adherents spirit-written messages. As mentioned above, 1891 was the year when the bubonic plague was raging in this area. Lord Guan descended not only to the Wenwu erdi gong in Xinyi, but also to other temples at that time. The founder of this hall was a man called Zhou Tianjian 周天健 (b. 1848) from a landowning family in Caojiang town.[59] When he went to Guangzhou to sit a civil service examination, he became acquainted with members of the Zhenling xuan Jingxiu tang in Guangzhou, who taught him how to chant scriptures.[60] During the period 1896–1897, when several other epidemics broke out, the god issued medical prescriptions to cure disease. After the Republican period, the main hall was built in 1924.

During the Republican period, Zhou Tianjian's son, Dao Xuan 道煊 (b. 1879), who was ordained a member of the Caojiang town committee, became head of the temple.[61] Managed by such local elites, the Jingxiu jingtang seemed to have maintained a good relationship with the government at that time. In the 1930s, an inspection group consisting of government officials visited this hall. It included Chen Jitang 陳濟棠 (1890–1954), a powerful military leader who governed Guangdong Province, Lin Guopei 林國佩 (no dates), the

---

58 According to my interview with the members, there were three Jinxiu tang in Guangdong during the Qing period. The Jingxiu tang in Guangzhou was called Zhenling xuan 鎮齡軒, that in Huizhou 惠州 was called Huiling xuan 惠齡軒 and that in Gaozhou was called Puling xuan. The location and activities of the other halls of the Jingxiu tang are unknown.

59 *Mingwan Zhoushi zupu* 明灣周氏族譜 (Lineage genealogy of the Zhou surname in Mingwan), shown to me by Zhou Shanli 周善禮 (n.d.), a core member of the Jingxiu jingtang, reads: "[Tianjian] was born in 1848. He studied at the Guozijian 国子監 (Imperial Academy) and had detailed knowledge of the six classics and dynastic histories. He came top in many exams, but was unable to pass the Imperial Examination" (道光戊申年生國學生淹貫六經縱橫諸史屢試高等不能取一第).

60 Interview with Zhou Shanli, August 15, 2019.

61 According to the *Mingwan Zhoushi zupu*, Dao Xuan was born in 1879.

president of the provincial congress, and Teng Yunshan 滕雲山 (no dates), a scholar of Chinese classics.[62]

However, after 1949, due to the repression of religious organizations, the activities of the Jingxiu jingtang were banned. Finally, all the temple buildings and statues were demolished during the Cultural Revolution. After the Reform Era, the members gradually resumed their activities, and consequently decided to rebuild the temple. The work was finally completed in 1988.[63]

The Jingxiu jingtang owns a variety of scriptures and morality books, including the *Guandi jiujie baochan* 關帝救劫寶懺 (The precious penance of Guangdi to save humanity from the apocalypse), the *Mingsheng jing* and the *Yuhuang zhenjing*. Noteworthy among their books are several liturgical manuals, which seem to have been edited during the late Qing and Republican periods. There are at least seven volumes, containing the rules for rituals for various purposes, ritual documents to be submitted to deities, such as *biaowen* 表文 (petition), *shuwen* 疏文 (memorial), *bangwen* 榜文 (announcement), and talismans to be used in the rituals. Although all of the books are titled "Confucian," the style and pantheon are similar to those of the Daoist liturgy. It is clear that some ritual specialists who had knowledge of Daoist liturgy were involved in the production of these manuals. My informant said that all of them were based on the divine messages that had been spirit-written there and had not been brought back from the Zhenling xuan in Guangzhou.[64] To discuss them as a whole is beyond the scope of this paper, but I would like to point out several key words and phrases related to the eschatological discourse in the following three books.

The first is the *Xinke Rujiao keji, juan er* 新刻儒教科集卷二 (The new series of Confucian rituals, volume 2), which is a wood block printed book that was printed during the Guangxu period. The front cover states: "Edited by the Maobei Jingxiutang, where the Deities of Three Teachings descended" (三教群真降茂北敬修堂編輯). The first part of the book contains "regulations" (*zhangcheng* 章程), which consist of several rules about rituals: setting up ritual sites, layout of the deities, the ritual implements and their colors, the ritual documents, and the scriptures to be chanted. The layout of the deities suggests a hierarchy among them: the Jade Emperor, Laozi, and Confucius were ranked top, followed by the Three Kings, Lord Guan, Wenchang, and Patriarch Lü.

---

62 This is based on the inscription entitled "Chongjian Maobei Jingxiu jingtang jianjie 重建茂北敬修經堂簡介" (Brief introduction to rebuilding Maobei Jingxiu jingtang), of unknown date, on the wall of the Jingxiu jingtang.
63 Ibid.
64 See footnote 58.

The second is the *Rujiao biaoshu keji* 儒教表疏科集 (Collection of Confucian ritual documents), which is a hand-written transcription. The cover page contains the following descriptions, "spirit-written in 1898" and "recorded by the Maobei Jingxiu jingtang" (茂北敬修經堂). The content starts with the titles of the deities addressed on the envelopes used in the rituals, followed by documents in several formats designed for a variety of rituals, such as the birthdays of deities, *zhai* 齋 services for the dead, and *jiao* 醮 celebrations. In the majority of the ritual documents, the sender identifies himself as "a disciple of the Jingxiu jingtang taught by the Lord of Xietian" (協天教授敬修經堂弟子) and addresses "Your highness, the Sovereign Lord Sage Guan, the Emperor of Zhonghuang" (中皇大帝関聖帝君殿下). In addition, several descriptions often appear in the ritual documents, such as "the Emperor of Zhonghuang espouses Confucianism" (中皇大帝承儒教主), "to accumulate *jiao* merits by relying on Confucianism" (仗儒修建醮功), and "Confucian ritual" (*Ruchang* 儒場), which indicate that Lord Guan celebrates the rituals by relying on Confucian power.

The *Rujiao yuebiao ke* 儒教月表科 (The forms of monthly documents for Confucian rituals) also contains various ritual documents, in which the Three Kings occupy an important role. A form of *biaowen* for praying for safety reads: "The Sovereign Lord Sage Guan, the Sovereign Lord of Zitong and the Sovereign Lord of Fuyou, who control three worlds, and oversee the ten directions, can descend anywhere through spirit-writing. How can you still fear that you are riding on an ocean of suffering without a paddle?" (關聖帝君、梓橦帝君、孚佑帝君殿下，職司三界，鑒臨十方，到處飛鸞，何患苦海無楫?) This passage shows that the liturgy of the Jingxiu jingtang is based on spirit-writing and the eschatological discourse centered on Lord Guan.

Several aspects of the liturgy of the Jingxiu jingtang suggest that it was influenced, albeit possibly indirectly, by the Confucian altars, based on spirit-writing and rituals centered on Lord Guan, which spread across southwestern China during the late Qing period.[65] Furthermore, the fact that the title Zhonghuang dadi 中皇大帝 (Emperor of Central Eminence) is often used to refer to Lord Guan in the ritual documents also suggests the possibility that the Jingxiu jingtang accepted the story that Lord Guan succeeded the Jade Emperor on his position and was given the title Zhonghuang 中皇 (Central Eminence), which

---

65 See Wang, "Popular Groups Promoting 'The Religion of Confucius.'" It is also possible that the liturgy of Zhenling xuan in Guangzhou, where the founder Zhou Tianjian learned how to chant scriptures, was influenced by the Confucian altars in southwestern China. Unfortunately, I lack definite information about either Zhenling xuan or the members in charge of producing the Jingxiu jingtang's liturgy. Future research is needed to explore the background of the liturgical tradition.

was spread by several spirit-writing groups in southwestern China, and quickly transmitted to Hunan, Hubei 湖北, Guangdong, Zhejiang 浙江, Shanghai 上海, and Taiwan 台灣.[66]

In the 1990s, a core member of the Jingxiu jingtang, who was also a ritual specialist, often instructed other *jingtangs*' members on how to conduct rituals and chant scriptures. However, recently, his advanced age has prevented his participation in any events. Nowadays, large-scale rituals are rarely conducted, except for chanting scriptures on special occasions.

4.2 *Shanqing jingtang* 善慶經堂 (*Scripture Hall of Goodness and Happiness*)

This hall is in the Warrior Temple located in Dong'an Town 東岸鎮 in the northern part of Gaozhou, close to Zhenlong Town in Xinyi. Its main altar enshrines Lord Guan. The altar to the left of this enshrines the Eight Immortals, while the one to the right enshrines Guanyin.

According to the inscription on the wall dating to 2009 and my interviews with a core member,[67] the history of the Shanqing jingtang is as follows: during an epidemic in 1919, Lord Guan descended to the human world and gave medical prescriptions at a Warrior Temple in Sanya tang 三丫塘 of Xinyi. At that time, three men of Dong'an town, He Taiwen 何泰文 (no dates), a merchant, Chen Jianzhi 陳鑒之 (no dates), a teacher, and Wu Shouyi 吳壽頤 (no dates), a doctor of Chinese medicine, went to Sanya tang to request prescriptions to cure the disease. Afterward, they obtained Lord Guan's incense ash from Sanya tang, and later enshrined it in their new temple, that was established in 1921.[68]

---

66   See Wang, "Taiwan 'Guandi dang Yuhuang' chuanshuo," 413–20; Wang, "Daoyan," 11–13; Zhu, "Qingmo yilai Guandi shengge yundong," 209–28. In present day Gaozhou, the title Zhonghuang dadi is still used in several ritual documents written by ritual specialists. However, the villagers only know that Zhonghuang dadi is one of Lord Guan's other titles. They neither understand why Lord Guan was called this, nor know that he was given this position by the Jade Emperor.

67   An interview with Pang Boguang 龐伯光, the former head of the cultural center of Dong'an town, conducted on August 16, 2019. He is in charge of the Shanqing jingtang.

68   This custom is generally called *fenxiang* 分香 (dividing incense) in Chinese popular religion. When establishing a new temple, people usually adopt *fenxiang*, which means that they invite their patron god's incense ash from an older or powerful temple and enshrine it in their new temple. In many cases, the newly-established temple regards the original temple as its "mother temple" or "ancestor temple." In some cases, the temple's members make a pilgrimage to the mother temple annually or every few years in order to rejuvenate the spiritual power by refreshing the incense ash.

The Warrior Temple at Sanya tang, located in Beijie town 北界鎮 in Xinyi, about thirty kilometers north-west of Dong'an town, was established during the Daoguang period. It also has a scripture hall centered on the worship of Lord Guan. Another scripture hall in Dong'an town was also established by inviting the incense ash from this temple during the Republican period. Therefore, it seems that the Warrior Temple in Sanya tang served as a kind of center for the neighboring scripture halls.[69]

Wu became a spirit-writing medium, called *gongsang* 降生 in the local dialect, and prescribed medicine. In 1941, the temple was transferred to its present site, and it was renamed the Warrior Temple. In those days, an increasing number of followers were visiting the temple for worship. Due to the change in administration in 1949, the circumstances of the temple changed significantly. All of the temple buildings and statues were demolished in 1957, and the reconstruction of the temple did not begin until 1993. In 2008, the *jiao* celebration, a completion ceremony, was held by Daoist masters invited from Guangxi. At present, spirit-writing séances are rare. The only activities in which the members engage are chanting scriptures on the first and the fifteenth lunar day of every month and Lord Guan's birthday.

The Shanqing jingtang also owns several hand-written transcriptions of scriptures, including the *Mingsheng jing*, *Guansheng dijun jiujie zhenjing* 關聖帝君救劫真經 (True scripture of Lord Guan to save humanity from the apocalypse), *Bada xianshen zhenjing* 八大仙神真經 (True scriptures of the Eight Immortals), and *Baosheng yongming jing songben* 葆生永命經誦本 (Recitation book of the scripture to protect human life and grant eternal life). The latter is a hand-written transcription of the original, produced in the Wenwu erdi gong in Xinyi in 1891. There are no liturgical manuals. My informant stated that all the scriptures owned by the Shanqing jingtang were transcriptions of the scriptures owned by the Warrior Temple in Sanya tang of Xinyi.

To sum up, it is clear that the spirit-writing movement and its eschatological discourse took root in the local religion and created the new pantheon and liturgies of the scripture halls established inside the local communal temples, which persist as important aspects of local religious life even today, despite successive governments' attempts to suppress them.

---

69 This is based on my field research on the Warrior Temple in Sanya tang, conducted on December 20, 2019. This temple also has a scripture hall centered on the worship of Lord Guan. Its members informed me that people from Dong'an town would have often visited the temple in the distant past.

After the 1990s, several scripture halls were reorganized, and their religious activities were revived. Spirit-written scriptures were also restored through reverent followers' careful transcriptions and are still chanted today. However, recently, their activities have declined due to aging and the decreasing size of the local community. Due to the absence of specialists with an ability to interpret the written teachings for lay followers, the apocalyptic tone of the eschatological words and passages in the scriptures and ritual documents has gradually been weakened, and these have simply become a part of the sutra chanted during routine rituals. The story of the salvation movement by the Three Saints is virtually forgotten among local people.

5   The Transformation of Local Religion in Wuchuan after the Twentieth Century

The second case study concerns the successors of the Palace of the Three Saints in Lanxi village, Wuchuan, which differs from the first case study in terms of both social and religious factors, such as religiosity, organization, social class, and gender.

Today, in Lanxi village, stands a Daoist temple called the Shengxian gong 聖賢宮 (Palace of Sages), registered as a "venue for religious activity" (*zongjiao huodong changsuo* 宗教活動場所) by the local government's Administration for Religious Affairs (Zongjiao ju 宗教局). The Shengxian gong also hosts the Wuchuan branch office of the Daoist Association of Zhanjiang city (Zhanjiang shi Daojiao xiehui Wuchuan banshi chu 湛江市道教協會吳川辦事處).

The Shengxian gong's two-story building enshrines the San Qing 三清 (Three Pure Ones) in its middle section, Wenchang, Guandi, Confucius, and Beidi 北帝 (Emperor of the North) stand on the left side, and Yue Fei 岳飛 (1103–1142), Kanghuang 康皇 (Emperor Kang), Huaguang dadi 華光大帝 (Emperor of Huaguang), and other gods on the right side on the first floor. On the second floor, the Jade Princess is enshrined in the middle section, with the three mothers (*san mu* 三母)—Dimu 地母 (Mother of Earth), Yaochi jinmu 瑤池金母 (Golden Mother of the Jasper Pool), and Guanyin 觀音 to the left, and the Eight Immortals (Ba daxian 八大仙) to the right.

There are two written records regarding the history of the Shengxian gong: the first is a brief introduction that is printed in the Shengxian gong's booklet. The second is an inscription entitled "Preface [written on the occasion] of the Restoration of the Old Temple of the Three Saints" (復建三聖古廟序), which was engraved in 1995. According to these two records, the Shengxian gong is clearly the successor to the Palace of the Three Saints that was established in

Lanxi village in 1891. The Palace of the Three Saints was demolished under the political oppression of religion surrounding the Xinhai Revolution 辛亥革命 in 1911.[70] At that time, one of the god's statues floated down a river and was retrieved by local people. They built a new temple to enshrine it near a wharf called Shuikoudu 水口渡 in Meilu. Shortly afterwards, they established a charitable society called Tongshan tang 同善堂 (The Hall of Goodness) in the new temple, where they continued to conduct public preaching and other charitable activities. After 1949, being regarded as "feudal superstition," the Tongshan tang was forced to suspend their activities. After the Reform Era, the Tongshan tang building was supposed to be torn down to make way for a new bridge in Shuikoudu. Therefore, the followers began to search for a new site on which to reconstruct their temple.

One day, in 1994, a goddess possessed an illiterate boy in Shajiaoxuan, Wuyang town 吳陽鎮, and issued spirit-written instructions that a new temple should be constructed on the original site in Lanxi village, Changqi town.[71] Shortly afterwards, the followers held a spirit-writing séance in the Tongshan tang. The Jade Princess descended again and left the following spirit-written message: "Lanxi has been a flourishing place for a thousand years, where two streams combine. If you believe and reconstruct your temple there, whatever you wish will be granted regarding the building of the Jade transcendent." (藍溪之地旺千秋，旺向雙溪水合流，諸君信時移廟建，有求皆應玉仙樓。) After much consultation with local people and the government, the present Shengxian gong temple was eventually reconstructed, sponsored by private donations. Registered as Daoist, the new temple enshrines the San Qing.

The afore-mentioned Tongshan tang appears identical to the Tongshan tang, which was banned as one of the secret societies or so-called *fandong huidaomen* 反動會道門 (reactionary sects and secret societies) of the 1950s. According to an article in the *Wuchuan xianzhi*, there were several small religious

---

70 A Congshan tang disciple, Huang Guangpan mentioned in his essay, *Nanzhen Congshan zhengtang chuangli sishi zhounian jinian gaishu* (see note 21): "After the Xinhai Revolution, due to the drastic change in the domestic situation, religion rapidly declined, the ancestor hall in Meilu was abolished and its chair died a martyr" (曩者辛亥鼎革，國內潮流激變，神教凌替，梅菉母堂阤遭解散，主事者以身殉). See Yau, *Shan yu ren tong*, 283.

71 The brief introduction in the Shengxian gong's booklet fails to specify which goddess possessed the boy, but the Jade Princess is a likely candidate. As mentioned above, two branch halls of the Tongshan tang used to exist in Shajiaoxuan, both of which enshrined the Jade Princess as their main deity. My interview with female villagers Shajiaoxuan, conducted on August 20, 2019, revealed that worshipping the Jade Princess has been quite popular in this area, and that she would often possess spirit mediums and leave oral massages.

organizations that belonged to redemptive societies,[72] such as the Tongshan she 同善社 (Fellowship of Goodness), Xiantiandao, and Guigendao 歸根道 (The Way of Returning to the Root) in Wuchuan at that time. The Tongshan tang was among these. It was also known as the Gonghuang miao 宮皇廟 (Temple of the Jade Princess) or Taihe dong 太和洞 (Cave of Supreme Harmony), and was managed by local elites, such as bureaucrats and the gentry. During the 1930s–1940s, this organization spread from Changqi town to Shuikoudu in Meilu and neighboring counties, eventually attracting more than 3,000 members. Even the two branch halls in Shajiaoxuan had 223 members. They often held spirit-writing séances and provided spiritual medicine and water to cure disease.[73]

Although the Tongshan tang was described as a heterodox, criminal group in the above article, in fact it was a typical redemptive society of the Republican period. The present Shengxian gong maintains an inscription entitled "The Regulations of the Tongshan tang in the Old Temple of Three Saints" (三聖古廟同善堂堂規) (unknown date), which is divided into seven points. Points one to three include ethical and moral principles relating to general daily life, such as "honesty and unselfishness" (zhengzhi wusi 正直無私), "respect for seniority" (zhangyou youxu 長幼有序), "help others and benefit everybody" (jiren liwu 濟人利物), "respect scrap paper bearing written or printed characters and five kinds of grain" (jingxi zizhi wugu 敬惜字紙五穀),[74] and "abstain from killing and release life" (jiesha fangsheng 戒殺放生). The fifth point presents the names of Three Saints (Confucius, Lord Guan and Yue Fei). The seventh point mainly describes moral teachings for women; namely, "the three forms of obedience and the four virtues" (sancong side 三從四德). These points show that the Tongshan tang was a charitable society that preached the three teachings and basic Confucian morality.

The description of how "the Tongshan tang spread from Changqi town to Shuikoudu" in the Wuchuan xianzhi supports the idea that it was the succes-

---

72   The term "redemptive societies" was coined by Prasenjit Duara, referring to the new religious movements of the first half of the twentieth century; see Duara, "The Discourse of Civilization," 117. David Ownby defines this term perfectly in his review article, where he states: "redemptive societies offered … a form of spirituality based on traditional beliefs in morality and healing power that is combined in a package straddling the traditional and the modern and grounded in emotional claims to what might be called 'Chineseness.'"; see Ownby, "Redemptive Societies," 687.

73   Wuchuan shi difangzhi bangongshi, Wuchuan xianzhi, 970.

74   Jingxi zizhi is a folk custom based on the Confucian practice of paying respect to written characters and the papers containing them. Burning and sending them to heaven is considered a good deed for accumulating merit.

sor of the Palace of the Three Saints. It seems probably that the Palace of the Three Saints, the Tongshan tang, and the Shengxian gong were connected historically.

However, we notice immediately the difference between the pantheons of these three organizations. The original pantheon of the Palace of the Three Saints, where the Three Saints (Lord Guan, Wenchang and Patriarch Lü) occupied an important position, was superseded by Confucius, Lord Guan and Yue Fei at the time of the Tongshan tang.[75] Due to the construction of the Shengxian gong, the deities enshrined became further diversified. In addition, the Jade Princess, who is an unfamiliar deity to people outside the area, played the most important role, as it was her spirit-written instruction that promoted the reconstruction of the Shengxian gong.

6   Who Is the Jade Princess?

According to the adherents of the Shengxian gong, the Jade Princess, the Jade Emperor's third daughter, is the most popular goddess in this area. Her statue shows a beautiful young lady riding on a phoenix, a sword in her right hand, and a ritual implement with a diagram of *taiji* 太極[76] and eight trigrams (*bagua* 八卦) in her left. She descends and manifests herself in the human world through spirit-writing on the fifteenth day of the fourth and seventh lunar months, respectively, every year.

I have never observed a spirit-writing séance at the Shengxian gong, but the abbot demonstrated the procedure for me. The spirit-writing altar of the Shengxian gong looks like a coat-hanger, with a board below and a pole above it. A spirit-writing pen hangs from the pole by a red string. A medium holds the pen in his two index fingers and places it on the board, which is covered with millet. Once a god descends, the pen will move and write a divine message on the board.

What is the origin of the Jade Princess? The story of the Jade Princess is reminiscent of folk legends about a fairy descending from heaven to the human world, such as Zhi Nü 織女 (Weaver Maid) or the Seven Fairies (Qi Xiannü 七仙女). However, according to my anthropological research and historical doc-

---

75   Yue Fei was probably added to the Three Saints in the Tongshan tang due to the influence of the *Shenci cunfeizhi biaozhun* 神祠存廢標準 (Standards for the preservation or eradication of gods), which was promulgated in 1928 by the Nanjing National Government; see Sakai, *Kingendai Chūgoku ni okeru shūkyō kessha no kenkyū*, 435.

76   *Taiji* is a Chinese cosmological idea, meaning the heart of all existence.

uments like local gazetteers, no communal temples have enshrined the Jade Princess in this area and there exist no folk tales about her. Therefore, it is hard to regard the worship of the Jade Princess as part of the folk tradition and indigenous to the local society.[77]

The Jade Princess might have joined the pantheon of the Palace of the Three Saints after 1891, when the temple was established in Lanxi village. In the 1898 edition of the *Yuhuang zhenjing*, she was ranked highly, next to the Jade Emperor, and also given a special title "Xigong yuque dangling zhangguan yuhuang gongzhu pudu tianzun 西宮玉闕當令掌管玉皇宮主普渡天尊" (The Jade Princess, the Celestial Worthy of Universal Salvation, who Governs the West Court of the Heavenly Palace).

She may have been enshrined in the Palace of the Three Saints with her brother, as a relative of the Jade Emperor. Originally, she was just one of the many deities who were enshrined beside the Jade Emperor. However, she was soon promoted to the high rank of standing next to the Jade Emperor in the court of heaven. This was possible through her manifestations and revelations transmitted through spirit writing by her.

Whether the worship of the Jade Princess belonged to a native folk tradition or not, the main point is that it evolved, spread, and survived even after the Palace of the Three Saints was demolished in the early twentieth century. This was possible mainly due to the efforts of several salvationist groups as the successor of the Palace of the Three Saints. One is the above mentioned Tongshan tang. It was one of the centers of the Jade Princess cult, as its common name Gonghuang miao (Temple of the Jade Princess) indicates.

Another center of the cult is a territorial temple, also called Gonghuang miao, located in Maopo in Xiangshan Town 祥山鎮, Gaozhou. Part of the inscription hung on the wall in the temple reads: "its original name was the Qingshan si 青山寺 (Temple of the Green Hill), also known as the Gonghuang lou 宮皇樓 (Tower of the Jade Princess), the Jingtan 經壇 (Scripture Altar), and Cunshan kuntang 存善坤堂 (Hall for Females doing Good Deeds). It was built in 1800 and then restored twice, in 1863, 1926." (原名青山寺，又名宮皇樓，經壇，存善坤堂。始建於嘉慶庚申年 (1800)，清朝同治癸亥年 (1863) 和民國丙寅年 (1926) 兩次重修。) A total of seventy-four gods' statues are

---

[77] Recently I stated that the Jade Princess was originally a folk fairy called *Gongzhu* 宮主 (a court lady), who was linked to the tradition of the goddess 紫姑 *Zigu*. Gongzhu appeared in the *Xiantai zhenjing* 冼太真經 (The True Scripture of Lady Xian), which was edited from the spirit written teachings of Lady Xian, *Gongzhu* and other folk fairies, when they descended at the altar of a scripture hall in Gaozhou, in 1876. See Shiga, "Qingmo yilai feiluan jiujie yundong de bentuhua yu difang zongjiao," 94–97.

enshrined there, including Lord Guan, the Eight Immortals, the Queen Mother, and Guanyin. The main deity is the Jade Princess.

According to several interviews with villagers and a document written by the village committee of Southern Maopo 南茂坡 (hereinafter referred as to the Southern Maopo village document), the Gonghuang miao was established by a merchant from Guangxi. He donated a large sum of money that he had obtained by selling cows so that the temple might be constructed. Afterward, the followers invited and enshrined the Jade Princess from Meilu. It cannot be proven that the Gonghuang miao was managed by a specific salvationist group, but it appears to have assumed the characteristics of salvationist religion.

Chen Dongqing 陳冬青 quoted the following passage from the *Luojiang liuyun* 羅江流韻 (The idyllic life on Luojiang River), which was written by Liang Rui 梁瑞 (no dates), chief of the Cultural Affairs Bureau of Huazhou: "During the heyday of the Gonghuang miao, several nuns, Daoists, and even foreign missionaries stayed there, providing free medical care as the main religious activity" (鼎盛時期尼姑道人雲集，西洋傳教士也一度入廟勾留，以施醫為名進行宗教活動).[78] My informants recalled that a few nuns had lived in the temple prior to 1949.

The Gonghuang miao owns various hand-written scriptures, including the *Yuhuang zhenjing, Wangmu zhenjing* 王母真經 (The True scripture of the Queen Mother) and *Qixian gongnü zhenjing* 七仙宮女真經 (The true scripture of the Seven Immortal Court Ladies). One of them, entitled *Gonghuang sanshiliu shou jishi* 宮皇三十六首乩詩 (Thirty-six spirit-written poems by the Jade Princess), contains a poem that begins: "I took power by imperial order of the Jade Emperor, my father, who governs the Highest Heaven. I descended to the human world by order of the Jade Emperor and ruled over immortals living in all mountains. Several years have passed since I descended to the secular world. Now, I begin the general salvation from the apocalypse through spirit-writing." (玉旨批行我掌權父皇，統管大羅天，承命臨凡當度主，廣度三山五嶽仙。皇命金枝下凡塵數載，飛鸞到於今，大開普度。)[79]

In addition, my informants showed me two notebooks, one of which records several revelations that were spirit-written by the Jade Princess and the deity Li Daxian 李大仙 between February and May, 1941. The notebook also contains

---

78 Chen, *Gaozhou wenwu diaocha*, 37.
79 *Gonghuang sanshiliu shou jishi* (hand-written manuscript, unknown date and author, n. page.) The instructions that were spirit-written by the Jade Princess in the notebooks do not specifically address women.

the thirty-six poems that were spirit-written by the Jade Princess, mentioned above. The nineteenth poem describes the general salvation (*pudu* 普度) as follows:

> When the general salvation begins, I will continue to descend to the spirit-writing altar all day and night. I worry about the world and my people. I must hurry to save them from suffering, but they do not easily enter the gate of a benevolent society. The third period of general salvation is now beginning, and all men and women should be aware of that.

> 為著普度大開期，晝夜飛鸞不時離，憂世憂民馳驅苦，難人深入善門基。三期普度在此時，凡間男女要當知。

The other notebook contains the oath for the initiation (*ruhudao shiwen* 入護道誓文) and the Jade Princess's twelve rules for initiates (*Yuhuang gongzhu zhenyan ruhudao guilü shi'ertiao* 玉皇宮主真言入護道規律十二條), both of which suggest that the Gonghuang miao was an organization with a membership system. My informants stated that the Gonghuang miao was originally a *kuntang* 坤堂 (hall for females). A *qiantang* 乾堂 (hall for males) was also established nearby, which enshrined the Jade Prince.[80] The above suggests that it is possible that the Gonghuang miao was managed by members who were influenced by some kind of salvationist religion, which was popular among women like the Xiantiandao.[81] The Jade Princess's representation as a savior goddess was possibly shaped by precious scrolls and scriptures, like the *Yulu jinpan* 玉露金盤 (Golden needle for ordering the world), which related the story of a fairy descending to the human world, produced by the Xiantiandao.

It should further be noted that the Jade Princess has become the most popular goddess in present-day Wuchuan, and that her worship surpasses that of Lady Xian or Tianhou 天后. In Shuikoudu, where the Tongshan tang was originally located, stand two temples that enshrine the Jade Princess today. One is

---

80   As a reference, the introduction to *Yuhuang ciyu zhenjing* 玉皇賜雨真經 (Scripture of the Jade Emperor), published by the Congshan tang of Hong Kong in 1898, was spirit-written by the Jade Prince, who descended to the altar in the Xieshan qiantang 協善乾堂 (Hall for males assisting goodness) of the Lingshan dong 靈山洞 (Cave of Spiritual Mountain) in 1894. The locations of the Xieshan qiantang and Lingshan dong are unknown. I am grateful to Prof. Yau Chi-on for sharing the scripture.
81   Fu Daoxiang's 傅道祥 (n.d.) branch of the Xiantiandao had an influence around the area called *xia sifu* 下四府 (lower four prefectures), including Gaozhou, Leizhou, Lianzhou, and Qiongzhou; see Yau, *Shanshu yu Zhongguo zongjiao*, 316.

called the Sansheng Gonghuang miao 三聖宮皇廟 (Temple of the Three Saints and the Jade Princess), which was established in the 1990s. The other is called the Gantang Gonghuang miao Tongshan tang 甘棠宮皇廟同善堂 (Hall of Goodness in the Gantang Temple of the Jade Princess), also known as the Taihe dong Gantang Tongshan tang 太和洞甘棠同善堂 (Gantang Hall of Goodness, in the Cave of Supreme Harmony), established in 2002. Both temples claim to be the successor to the old Tongshan tang. During my visit in August 2019, each temple held a *jiao* celebration on the fifteenth day of the seventh lunar month, which attracted many followers living nearby.

The two branch halls of the Tongshan tang in Shajiaoxuan, Wuyang 吳陽 town, were also revived after the 2000s. One of them, the Shenghe tang 聖赫堂 (Hall of Holiness and Brightness), was originally established in 1943 and reconstructed in 2012. In this hall, the statue of the Jade Princess is in a higher position than all of the many other deities enshrined.

During this same visit in August 2019, a few female villagers chanted scriptures, including the *Tianjing zhenjing* 天經真經 (True scripture of celestial immortals), also known as the *Siqi pudu jiujie zhenjing* 四期普度救劫真經 (True scripture of the fourth period of general salvation from the apocalypse). In this scripture, the Jade Princess is given a special title: "Kaitian juedi dinggai qiankun siqi zhuwan Yuhuang gongzhu jiujie tianzun 開天闢地頂蓋乾坤四期助挽玉皇宮主救劫天尊" (Yuhuang Gongzhu, Heavenly Worthy Who Saves Humanity from the Apocalypse, Who Opens Heaven and Earth, Being the Top of All Humanity during the Fourth Period of General Salvation). According to my informants, it was spirit-written by a medium from this village more than twenty years ago.[82] The role and status of the Jade Princess as a savior from then apocalypse continues to be updated and intensified through spirit-writing mediums' oral and written revelations, using eschatological words and phrases.

To sum up, the cult of the Jade Princess is sustained to the present day by devout believers, mainly ordinary female villagers. What sustained the cult of the Jade Princess with such vitality? A few possible reasons I can offer are as follows: one is people's adherence to the healing power of the medicine prescribed by the Jade Princess. In the villages, where the public medical services remain insufficient, folk therapies like spirit-written prescriptions and talismans still play an important role in the healthcare system. Especially for women, who often take an active role in their family's healthcare, spirit-written medical pre-

---

82 The female villagers told me that the (male) spirit medium was often invited to the Shengxian gong to hold spirit-writing séances at that time and wrote several scriptures. He had no formal schooling, but had been educated by his parents, who were teachers before 1949. He had recently passed away, at the age of eighty-six.

scriptions form part of the more familiar and reliable medical interventions.[83] Of course, it is also important to note that shamanistic practices are inseparable from such folk therapies, and that both spirit-writing and spirit possession remain active in the villages.

Another likely reason is that the cult of the Jade Princess provides a spiritual community for women, who are usually excluded from the core ritual worship of high-ranking male gods like Kanghuang and Beidi, held as part of the Nianli 年禮 (literally, an "annual routine"), a large-scale regional festival, which is the most significant and important annual event in this region.[84]

7   Conclusion

In the region, situated as it is along the Jianjiang River in western Guangdong, several spirit-writing groups, called *jingtang* (scripture halls), arose between the Tongzhi (or even earlier) and Guangxu periods, influenced by the growing spirit-writing movements of the late Qing period. They engaged in various charitable activities, such as public preaching, the chanting of scriptures, and burning discarded paper, similarly to other spirit-writing groups in other regions of Guangdong.

At the same time, several eschatological scriptures that originated in southwestern China, such as the *Mingsheng jing* and *Yuhuang zhenjing*, began to be transmitted to Guangdong by the growing number of migrants who were traveling between southwestern China and Lingnan, especially Cantonese merchants. As such, the scriptures spread regionally, and the typical eschatological discourse—the punishment of the Jade Emperor and the salvation movement by the Three Saints (Lord Guan, Wenchang and Patriarch Lü)—also began to take root within the local religion. In 1887, the local elites established the morality book center in the Warrior Temple in Meilu, Wuchuan, where they preached and chanted the *Mingsheng jing*.

In 1891–92, the outbreak of plague in this region enhanced the apocalyptic visions within the local society. People believed that the Jade Emperor was truly sending down a great catastrophe to exterminate bad people. They held

---

83 According to the limited research available, the family members who have most frequent contact with "Danki," a Fujianese spirit medium in Taiwan and Singapore, are mothers and grandmothers, who tend to oversee the whole family's healthcare; see Wang, *Taiwan shāmanizumu no minzoku yiryō mekanizumu*, 92–95; Fukuura, *Toshi no Jibyō*, 171–99.

84 For further details of the Nianli, see Zheng, "Religious Diversity and Patrimonialization," 21–31.

spirit-writing séances, praying for divine protection in the Wenwu erdi gong in Xinyi in the sixth lunar month of 1891, Lord Guan's birthday. These séances eventually produced a new eschatological scripture, the *Wenwu baosheng yongmingjing*, the main theme of which was the post-1840 salvation movement by the Three Saints. Undoubtedly, the discourse and pantheon of the eschatological salvation had a great impact on the local religion at the end of the nineteenth century.

Finally, I discussed how the new eschatological idea has been localized, by following the historical transformation of the local religion from the early twentieth century up until the present day. I summarized the main points arising from the two case studies—the scripture halls in northern Gaozhou, and the successors of the Palace of the Three Saints in Wuchuan—as well as referring to other scholars' studies.

What is common to both cases is that the eschatological discourse and salvation pantheon were promptly merged into the new scriptures and liturgies produced by the local spirit-writing groups by the end of the nineteenth century. In the early twentieth century, despite the continuing political oppression against popular religion, most groups survived. By the 1940s, new groups and branches derived from the older ones, sharing common beliefs and practices, and spread widely throughout the region.

During the Republican period, both in the scripture halls and in the successors of the Palace of the Three Saints, activities persisted as important aspects of local religious life. These locations provided various religious services for the local community, such as spirit-writing séances, folk medicine, and ritual services, including the chanting of scriptures on gods' birthdays or other festival occasions. In particular, the groups espousing Confucianism, like the Jingxiu jingtang and Tongshan tang, gained active support from the government.

The scripture halls in northern Gaozhou were typical of the literati spirit-writing groups, if we follow Goossaert and Palmer's categorization of redemptive societies in the early twentieth century into three strands, based on their forms of religiosity.[85] The scripture halls were religious communities centered on spirit-writing, the worship of Lord Guan, and the liturgy espousing Confucianism, which were managed by the local elites, mainly consisting of male followers.

---

85 They categorized the following three groups: (1) modern Confucian associations, (2) literati spirit-writing groups, and (3) lay salvationist groups which practiced, in varying combinations, meditation and inner alchemy, sutra recitation, vegetarianism, and millenarian proselytism; see Goossaert and Palmer, *The Religious Question in Modern China*, 94.

On the other hand, the successors of the Palace of the Three Saints in Wuchuan conformed to two types of religiosity: one was a literati spirit-writing group, the other a lay salvationist group. The former is embodied in the Tongshan tang, which focused on charitable activities and public preaching, and was managed by elite male followers. The latter is embodied in the Gonghuang miao of Maopo. Although many questions remain regarding the past conditions of the Gonghuang miao, it seems to have been a type of religious organization with a membership system, that also provided accommodation for celibate specialists and practitioners. Judging from the revelations and poems that were spirit-written prior to 1949, it is likely that it was managed by members who were influenced by some kind of salvationist religion.

It should be noted that, regardless of the Tongshan tang or Gonghuang miao, the female followers' focus was the worship of the Jade Princess, who was believed to have been sent to the human world on a mission to offer general salvation from the apocalypse on the order of her father, the Jade Emperor. Although her origin remains unclear, it is possible that the Jade Princess' representation as a savior goddess was shaped by the eschatological discourses within the scriptures produced by salvationist religion.

The scripture halls in western Guangdong are somewhat similar to the "village sectarians" that Thomas DuBois discussed in his field study of rural North China. He characterized two sects, the Teaching of the Most Supreme (Taishang men 太上門) and Heaven and Earth Teaching (Tiandi men 天地門) in rural Cang County 滄縣, as village sectarians. These two sects took deep root within the local society and have remained active through the twentieth century, in contrast to monastic Buddhism, the Li Sect (Lijiao 理教) and the Way of Penetrating Unity (Yiguandao 一貫道), characterized by a highly specialized theological, liturgical tradition and an apocalyptic vision, which rapidly collapsed or lost their presence by the 1960s. Analyzing the reason for this tenacity, DuBois pointed out that "both sects perform ceremonials of public and private religious life: the calendar of annual festivals, occasional ceremonies ... as well as blessing, exorcisms, funerals. ... [S]pecialists of these two sects also serve as an important source of knowledge about the sacred and are often portrayed as moral exemplars."[86] Outside funeral rituals, those functions also apply to the scripture halls in western Guangdong.

Naturally, there exist several differences between the scripture halls and the sectarian groups in rural Cang County. From my perspective, one of the most important differences is the networks of followers and the training systems

---

86 Dubois, *The Sacred Village*, 152–53.

for religious specialists, including spirit-writing mediums. Unlike the sectarian groups in rural Cang County, the scripture halls in western Guangdong evolved and spread through the distribution network of new scriptures and the loose networks of followers, rather than through external and institutional networks of members belonging to specific salvationist groups. They originally had neither a training system for specialists nor a master-disciple relationship to transmit the teachings, which is common to sectarians.

In nineteenth-century western Guangdong, the spirit-writing hall community received abundant human resources from literati and religious specialists, familiar with the written religious traditions. They had the ability to create new scriptures and liturgies, by incorporating eschatological ideas into their existing religious knowledge. However, the second generation started to face a limited supply of specialists under the growing modernization and secularization that has been occurring since the twentieth century. Due to the shortage of religious specialists and intellectuals who had the ability to interpret written texts, the original meaning of the eschatological discourse almost vanished.

After the 1990s, when the scripture halls were revived one after another, the shortage of specialists became more serious. Some old specialists, who had been involved in the activities of the scripture halls before 1949, helped to revive the neighboring scripture halls or used their religious knowledge to instruct lay followers. However, after the 2000s, due to the old specialists' passing or advanced age, the activity of the scripture halls rapidly declined.

On the other hand, we should also note the remarkable prosperity of the Jade Princess cult. It was localized and survived to become one of the most popular cults in this region during the twentieth century. Particularly after the 1990s, the Jade Princess cult served as the driving force for the revival of local religious groups, as shown in the case of the Shengxian gong in Lanxi Village, which was reconstructed as a consequence of spirit-written messages by the Jade Princess. A possible reason for this sustainability and flexibility is that the Jade Princess cult is deeply-rooted in the shamanism that is widely practiced in local communities, which has not only mainly been maintained by female followers in the oral tradition but is also capable of providing access to written traditions via male spirit-writing mediums.

We may assume that gender and shamanism are important factors for understanding the historical transformation of local spirit-writing groups. A promising direction for future research on local spirit-writing movements would be to focus on the indigenous folk culture that lies hidden behind the lower layers of the local religious tradition.

Bibliography

Abbreviations

DZ *Daozang* 道藏, numbers following Kristofer Schipper and Franciscus Verellen, eds. *The Taoist Canon: A Historical Companion to the Daozang (Daozang Tongkao* 道藏通考). Chicago: University of Chicago Press, 2004, 3 vols.

Primary Sources

Gaozhou fuzhi, wushisi juan moyi juan 高州府志五十四卷末一卷. 1889. In *Zhongguo fangzhi congshu, Huanan difang Guangdong sheng 68* 中國方志叢書華南地方廣東省 68. Taipei: Chengwen chubanshe, 1967.

Gonghuang sanshiliu shou jishi 宮皇三十六首乩詩. Handwritten manuscript, n.p., n.d.

Guandi mingsheng jing quanji 關帝明聖經全集. In *Zangwai daoshu*, vol. 4.

Guandi mingsheng zhenjing 關帝明聖真經. Reprinted in 1874 from wood block print, blocks stored at the Sanyuan tang, Dadi street, Foshan town.

Gufo yingyan Mingsheng jing dingben sanjuan 古佛應驗明聖經定本三卷. In *Zunde tang ban Daojiao congdian* 尊德堂板道教叢典. Sichuan, n.d.

Meilu fuzhi bufenjuan 梅菉賦志不分卷. Manuscript. Edited by Huang Lu 黃爐. In *Guangdong shengli Zhongshan tushu guancang xijian fangzhi congkan* 廣東省立中山圖書館藏稀見方志叢刊, edited by Ni Junming 倪俊明, vol. 27, 459–629. Peking: Guojia tushuguan chubanshe, 2011.

Qixian gongnü zhenjing 七仙宮女真經. Handwritten manuscript, n.p., n.d.

Rujiao biaoshu keji 儒教表疏科集. Handwritten manuscript. Maobei Jingxiu jingtang, Gaozhou, Guangdong, 1898.

Rujiao yuebiao ke 儒教月表科. Handwritten manuscript, n.p., n.d.

Tianjing zhenjing 天經真經; or, *Siqi pudu jiujie zhenjing* 四期普度救劫真經. Handwritten manuscript, n.d.

Tianhou yuanjun jiuku jiunan zhenjing 天后元君救苦救難真經. Reprint, Hong Kong, 1948.

Wangmu huasheng zhenjing 王母化生真經. Handwritten manuscript, n.p., n.d. Originally wood block print, blocks cut by the Yongji xiang, Kangqilou, Wuchuan.

Wangmu xiaojie jiushi zhenjing 王母消劫救世真經. Longzhou, Guangxi: Baoyuan gong, 1896. http://taolibrary.com/category/category67/c67021.htm (accessed December 9, 2019).

Wendi jiujie baosheng jing Wudi jiujie youmingjing hebian 文帝救劫葆生經武帝救劫永命經合編. Reprint, Baojing ge, Guangzhou, 1909.

Wendi jiujie baosheng jing Wudi jiujie youmingjing hebian 文帝救劫葆生經武帝救劫永命經合編. Reprint, Zhishan tang, Renli, Nam Sác, Vietnam, 1909.

Wenwu erdi baosheng yongming jing 文武二帝葆生永命經. In *Jindai Guandi, Yuhuang jingjuan yu xuanmen zhenzhong wenxian* 近代關帝、玉皇經卷與玄門真宗文獻,

edited by Wang Chien-chuan 王見川, vol. 6, 407–84. Taipei: Boyang wenhua, 2012. Originally published at the Mudao xianguan, Shantou, Guangdong, 1896.

Wenwu jiujie baosheng jing yongmingjing hebian 文武救劫葆生經永命經合編. Reprint, Tongyou shantang, Guangzhou, 1898.

Wenwudi shengjing tongbian 文武帝聖經統編. Booklet retyped by a word-processor. Made by the Xinshan tang, Dianbai, Guangdong, 2002.

Wuchuan shi difangzhi bangongshi 吳川市地方志辦公室, eds. *Wuchuan xianzhi* 吳川縣志. Zhengzhou: Xinxi gongchengsuo, 2001.

Wushang Yaochi Wangmu xiaojie jiushi baochan 無上瑤池王母消劫救世寶懺. Kaijun, Yunnan, 1860. Reprinted from wood blocks stored at the Henan Mingxing tang, Guangzhou. http://ehdwlgalll.idv.tw/gbs/964 (accessed May 11, 2016).

Xinke Rujiao keji, juan er 新刻儒教科集卷二. Edited by the Maobei Jingxiu tang. Wood block print. n.d.

Yaochi Wangmu xiaojie jiushi baochan quanbu 瑤池王母消劫救世寶懺全部 (R. 1976・NLVNPF-0147). Kaijun, Yunnan, 1860. Reprinted from wood blocks stored at the Yushan Wenwu erdi dian in Hanoi. http://lib.nomfoundation.org/collection/1/volume/192/ (accessed December 9, 2019).

Yuanshi tianzun Zitong dijun benyuanjing 元始天尊梓童帝君本願經. DZ 29.

Yuhuang ciyu zhenjing 玉皇賜雨真經. Congshan tang, Hong Kong, 1898.

Yuhuang Shangdi yingyan jiujie zhenjing 玉皇上帝應驗救劫真經. Congshan tang, Hong Kong, 1898. Reprinted from recut blocks in Hong Kong, 1934.

Yuhuang Shangdi yingyan jiushi zhenjing 玉皇上帝應驗救世真經. Zhanjiang, Guangdong, 1892. Reprint, Hong Kong, 1974.

Yuhuang Wangmu jiujie zhenjing 玉皇王母救劫真經. In *Zhongguo yuyan jiujieshu huibian* 中國預言救劫書彙編. Edited by Wang Chien-chuan 王見川, Song Jun 宋軍, and Fan Chun-wu 范純武, vol. 9, 313–75. Taipei: Xinwenfeng, 2010.

Yuhuang zhenjing 玉皇真經. Handwritten manuscript, n.d. Originally published by the Meishan tang, Wuchuan, 1879. Reprinted from recut blocks in Wuchuan, Guangdong, 1897.

Yuhuang zhenjing 玉皇真經. In *Minjian sicang Taiwan zongjiiao ziliao huibian: minjian xinyang. Minjian wenhua (di'er ji)* 民間私藏臺灣宗教資料彙編：民間信仰.民間文化（第二輯）, edited by Wang Chien-chuan 王見川, Li Shiwei 李世偉, Fan Chun-wu 范純武, Gao Zhihua 高致華, and Kan Zhengzong 闞正宗, vol. 14, 11–47. Taipei: Boyang wenhua, 2010.

Yuhuang zhenjing songben 玉皇真經誦本. Photocopied booklet, n.d. Originally published in 1939, blocks cut by the Wanshan tang, Wuchuan.

Wangmu zhenjing 王母真經. Handwritten manuscript, n.d.

Yulu jinpan 玉露金盤. Reprint, 1904. Blocks stored at Henan, Yuedong. Originally wood block printed at the Danchengtai, 1880.

Secondary Sources

Asai Motoi 淺井紀. *Minshin jidai minkan shūkyō kessha no kenkyū* 明清時代民間宗教結社研究. Tokyō: Kenbun shuppan, 1990.

Benedict, Carol. *Bubonic Plague in Nineteenth-century China*. Stanford, California: Stanford University Press, 1996.

Chen Dongqing 陳冬青. *Gaozhou shehui lishi diaocha* 高州社會歷史調查. Hong Kong: Xianggang keji daxue chuban jishu zhongxin, 2011.

Chen Dongqing 陳冬青. *Gaozhou wenwu diaocha yu kaoshu* 高州文物調查與考述. Guangzhou: Guangdong lüyou chubanshe, 2018.

Chen Jinguo 陳進國. "Wairu neifo: Xinfaxian de Guigendao (Rumen) jingjuan ji jiujie quanshanshu gaishu 外儒內佛：新發現的歸根道(儒門)經卷及救劫勸善書概述." *Yuanguang foxue xuebao* 圓光佛學學報 10 (2006): 233–89.

Chen Jinguo 陳進國. *Jiujie: Dangdai jidu zongjiao de tianye yanjiu* 救劫：當代濟度宗教的田野研究. Beijing: Shehui kexue wenxian chubanshe, 2017.

Duara, Prasenjit. "The Discourse of Civilization and Pan-Asianism." *Journal of World History* 12, no. 1 (2001): 9–130.

Dubois, Thomas David. *The Sacred Village: Social Change and Religious Life in Rural North China*. Honolulu: University of Hawai'i Press, 2005.

Esposito, Monica. "The Invention of a Quanzhen Canon: The Wondrous Fate of the *Daozang Jiyao*." In *Quanzhen Daoists in Modern Chinese History and Society*, edited by Xun Liu and Vincent Goossaert, 44–77. Berkley: Institute of East Asian Studies, 2014.

Fan Chun-wu 范純武. *Qingmo minjian cishan shiye yu luantang yundong* 清末民間慈善事業與鸞堂運動. Taipei: Boyang wenhua shiye youxiangongsi, 2015.

Fukuura Atsuko 福浦厚子. *Toshi no Jibyō: Singapore niokeru shinsei kūkan no jinruigaku* 都市の寺廟：シンガポールにおける神聖空間の人類学. Yokohama: Shunpūsha, 2018.

Goossaert, Vincent. "Modern Daoist Eschatology: Spirit-Writing and Elite Soteriology in Late Imperial China." *Daoism: Religion, History and Society* / 道教研究學報：宗教、歷史與社會, no. 6 (2014): 219–46.

Goossaert, Vincent, and David A. Palmer. *The Religious Question in Modern China*. Chicago & London: The University of Chicago Press, 2011.

Hu Jiechen 胡劼辰. "*Wendi quanshu* yanjiu: Qingdai Wenchang dijun xinyang de wenxian shi 文帝全書研究：清代文昌帝君信仰的文獻史." PhD diss., Chinese University of Hong Kong, 2017.

Lai Chi Tim 黎志添. "Qingdai sizhong *Lüzu quanshu* yu Lüzu fuji daotan de guanxi 清代四種《呂祖全書》與呂祖扶乩道壇的關係." *Zhongguo wenzhe yanjiu jikan* 中國文哲研究集刊, no. 42 (2013): 183–230.

Mori Yuria 森由利亜. "Dōzō Shūyō to Shō Yobo no Lyoso fukei shinkou 道蔵輯要と蒋予蒲の呂祖扶乩信仰." *Tōhō Shūkyō* 東方宗教 98 (2001): 33–52.

Nishikawa Kazutaka 西川和孝. *Unnan Chūkasekai no bōchō: Pūarucha to kōzan kaihatu nimiru ijyūsenryaku* 雲南中華世界の膨張：プーアル茶と鉱山開発にみる移住戦略. Tokyo: Keiyū sha, 2015.

Ownby, David. "Redemptive Societies." In *Modern Chinese Religion*, Part II: *1850–2015*, edited by Vincent Goossaert, Jan Kiely, and John Lagerwey, vol. 2, 685–727. Leiden: Brill, 2015.

Palmer, David A. "Chinese Redemptive Societies and Salvationist Religion: Historical Phenomenon or Sociological Category?" *Minsu quyi* 民俗曲藝, no. 172 (2011): 21–72.

Sakai Tadao 酒井忠夫. *Kingendai Chūgoku ni okeru shūkyō kessha no kenkyū* 近・現代中国における宗教結社の研究. Tokyo: Kokusho Kankōkai, 2002.

Shiga Ichiko 志賀市子. *Kami to Ki no aida: Chūgoku Tōnanbu niokeru Muenshisha no Maisō to Saishi*〈神〉と〈鬼〉の間: 中国東南部における無縁死者の埋葬と祭祀. Tokyo: Fūkyōsha, 2012.

Shiga Ichiko 志賀市子. "Qingmo Lingnan diqu de shuyi liuxing yu jiujiejing zhi puji 清末嶺南地區的鼠疫流行與救劫經之普及." In *1894–1920 niandai lishi jubian zhong de Xianggang* 1894–1920 年代歷史鉅變中的香港, edited by Siu Kwok Kin 蕭國健 and Yau Chi-on 游子安, 341–61. Hong Kong: Sik Sik Yuen and Center for Hong Kong History and Culture studies, Chuhai College of Higher Education, 2016.

Shiga, Ichiko. "Formation of a New Daoist Community in the 19th Century Lingnan Area: Sacred Places, Networks and Eschatology." In *Dōkyō no seichi to chihōshin* 道教の聖地と地方神, edited by Masaaki Tsuchiya 土屋昌明 and Vincent Goossaert, 93–129. Tokyo: Tohō Shoten, 2016.

Shiga, Ichiko, "What Kind of Innovations Did Spirit Writing Bring about for a Popular Saint's Cult? A Case of the Song Dafeng Cult in 19th Century Chaozhou." In Lieux saints et pèlerinages: La tradition taoïstes vimante (Holy Sites and Pilgrimages: The Daoist Living Tradition), edited by Vincent Goossaert and Masaaki Tsuchiya 土屋昌明, 151–184. Turnhout: Brepols, 2022.

Shiga Ichiko. "Qingmo yilai feiluan jiujie yundong de bentuhua yu difang zongjiao: Yi Yuexi Jianjiang liuyu de nüxian xinyang weizhu 清末以來飛鸞救劫運動的本土化與地方宗教:以粵西鑒江流域的女仙信仰為主."*Shanshu, jingjuan yu wenxian* 善書、經卷與文獻 7 (2023), edited by Fan Chun-wu 范純武, 75–128. Taipei: Boyang wenhua.

Takeuchi Fusaji 武內房司. "Shinmatu Shisen no shūkyō undō: Fulan・Senkōgata shūkyō kessha no tanjō 清末四川の宗教運動：扶鸞・宣講型宗教結社の誕生." *Gakushūin Daigaku bungakubu kenkyū nenpō* 學習院大學文學部研究年報 37 (1990): 59–93.

Ter Haar, Barend J. *Guan Yu: The Religious Afterlife of a Failed Hero*. Oxford: Oxford University Press, 2017.

Tsuzuki Akiko 都築晶子. "Ryukoku Daigaku Ōmiya toshokan zou *Sontokudōban Dōkyō sōten* kaisetsu: Shinmatsu Minkokusho no Jyūkeifu niokeru minkan shūkyō kyōkan

龍谷大学大宮図書館蔵『尊徳堂板道教叢典』解説：清末民国初の重慶府における民間宗教経巻." *Ryukoku Daigaku ronshū* 龍谷大學論集 461 (2003): 238–300.

Wang Chien-chuan 王見川. "Taiwan 'Guandi dang Yuhuang' chuanshuo de youlai 臺灣「關帝當玉皇」傳說的由來." In *Hanren zongjiao, minjian xinyang yu yuyanshu de tansuo* 漢人宗教、民間信仰與預言書的探索, edited by Wang Chien-chuan, 411–30. Taipei: Boyang wenhua, 2008.

Wang Chien-chuan 王見川. "Daoyan 導言," in *Jindai Guandi, Yuhuang jingjuan yu xuanmen zhenzhong wenxian* 近代關帝、玉皇經卷與玄門真宗文獻第一冊, edited by Wang Chien-chuan, vol. 1, 1–22. Taipei: Boyang wenhua, 2012.

Wang, Chien-Chuan. "Morality Book Publishing and Popular Religion in Modern China: A Discussion Centered on Morality Book Publishers in Shanghai." Translated by G.A. Scott. In *Religious Publishing and Print Culture in Modern China, 1800–2012*, edited by Philip Clart and G.A. Scott, 233–64. Boston: De Gruyter, 2015.

Wang, Chien-ch'uan [Wang Chien-chuan]. "Spirit Writing Groups in Modern China (1840–1937): Textual Production, Public Teachings, and Charity." In *Modern Chinese Religion*, Part II: *1850–2015*, edited by Vincent Goossaert, Jan Kiely, and John Lagerwey, vol. 2, 651–84. Leiden: Brill, 2015.

Wang, Chien-Chuan. "Popular Groups Promoting 'The Religion of Confucius' in the Chinese Southwest and Their Activities since the Nineteenth Century (1840–2013): An Observation Centered on Yunnan's Eryuan County and Environs." Translated by Stacy Mosher. In *The Varieties of Confucian Experience: Documenting a Grassroots Revival of Tradition*, edited by Sébastien Billioud, 90–121. Leiden and Boston: Brill, 2018.

Wang Zhenyue 王貞月. *Taiwan shāmanizumu no minzoku iryō mekanizumu* 台灣シャーマニズムの民俗医療メカニズム. Fukuoka: Chūgoku shoten, 2011.

Wu Tao 吳滔. "Qingdai Guangdong Meilu zhen de kongjian jiegou yu shehui zuzhi 清代廣東梅菉鎮的空間結構與社會組織." *Qingshi yanjiu* 清史研究, no. 2 (May 2013): 26–43.

Yau Chi-on 游子安. "Jiujie jishi: Xianggang Congshan tang zhi jingshu yu shanye, 1896–1936 救劫濟世：香港從善堂之經書與善業 1896–1936." In *1894–1920 niandai lishi jubian zhong de Xianggang* 1894–1920 年代歷史巨變中的香港, edited by Siu Kwok Kin 蕭國健 and Yau Chi-on 游子安, 362–78. Hong Kong: Sik Sik Yuen and Center for Hong Kong History and Culture studies, Chuhai College of Higher Education, 2016.

Yau Chi-on 游子安. *Shan yu ren tong: Ming-Qing yilai de cishan yu jiaohua* 善與人同：明清以來的慈善與教化. Beijing: Zhonghua shuju, 2005.

Yau Chi-on 游子安. *Shanshu yu Zhongguo zongjiao* 善書與中國宗教. Taipei: Boyang wenhua, 2012.

Yau, Chi-on. "The Xiantiandao and Publishing in the Guangzhou-Hong Kong Area from the Late Qing to the 1930s: The Case of the Morality Book Publisher Wenzaizi." Translated by Philip Clart. In *Religious Publishing and Print Culture in Modern China, 1800–2012*, edited by Philip Clart and Gregory A. Scott, 187–231. Boston: De Gruyter, 2015.

Valussi, Elena. "Printing and Religion in the Life of Fu Jinquan." *Daoism: Religion, History and Society* / 道教研究學報：宗教、歷史與社會, no. 4 (2012): 1–52.

Valussi, Elena. "The Transmission of the Cult of Lü Dongbin to Sichuan in the Nineteenth Century, and the Transformation of the Local Religious Milieu." *Daoism: Religion, History, and Society* / 道教研究學報：宗教、歷史與社會, no. 7 (2015): 117–169.

Zangwai daoshu 藏外道書. Edited by Hu Daojing 胡道靜 et al. 36 vols. Chengdu: Bashu shushe, 1992–94.

Zheng, Shanshan. "Religious Diversity and Patrimonialization: A Case Study of the Nianli Festival in Leizhou Peninsura, China." *Approaching Religion* 7, no. 1 (2014): 21–31.

Zhu Mingchuan 朱明川. "Qingmo yilai Guandi shengge yundong: Jiantan Daojiao Jingmingpai zai jindai 清末以來關帝升格運動：兼談道教淨明派在近代." In *Lishi, yishu yu Taiwan renwen luncong 14* 歷史、藝術與台灣人文論叢 14, edited by Li Shyh-wei 李世偉, 209–28. Taipei: Boyang wenhua, 2017.

CHAPTER 14

The Rise of Spirit-Writing Cults in Chaozhou: Reassessing the Role of Charitable Halls

Li Guoping 李國平

1   Introduction

Over the past few decades, the history of spirit-writing cults (*fuluan jieshe* 扶鸞結社) from the nineteenth century to the present has been the subject of many studies.[1] Most early studies focus on spirit-writing cults in Taiwan 台灣 and Hong Kong 香港 but, during the last ten years, scholars have gradually begun to pay more attention to other regions, such as Guangdong 廣東 and Shanghai 上海.[2] However, the history of spirit-writing cults in places other than Taiwan and Hong Kong is still lacking in thorough studies, the Chaozhou 潮州 region being an example.

The purpose of this paper is to reassess one significant type of spirit-writing organization, the charitable hall (*shantang* 善堂 or *shanshe* 善社), in Chaozhou, and offer an overview of the varied forms of local spirit-writing cults. It aims to correct two misleading tendencies in previous studies; namely, to view all charitable halls as belonging to a single type, and to examine spirit-writing by focusing solely on charitable halls. As my research shows, charitable halls were established by a variety of actors through differing activities, while not all spirit-writing groups evolved into charitable halls. Furthermore, this study provides a glimpse into how the nineteenth century spirit-writing movement flourished in Chaozhou.

By the end of the Qing dynasty, spirit-writing was playing a novel role in the changing society, and spirit-writing cults became an energetic, widespread religious trend. As Clart points out, the second half of the nineteenth century witnessed the emergence of a new type of spirit-writing cult that was influenced by Daoist cults; its novelty was manifest in several significant aspects—the new

---

1   There were several pioneering works: Clart, "The Ritual Context of Morality Books"; Fan, *Qing mo minjian cishan shiye yu luantang yundong*; Wang, *Taiwan de zhaijiao yu luantang*; Wang, *Taiwan de Enzhugong xinyang*; and Shiga, *Xianggang Daojiao yu fuji xinyang*.
2   See Shiga, "Difang Daojiao zhi xingcheng"; and Wang, "Spirit Writing Groups in Modern China."

cults were driven by a millenarian sense of mission, regarded moral exhortation as their very purpose of being, and were one institutional product of the nineteenth-century movement of religious synthesis.[3] Wang Chien-chuan argues that "from the 1840s a distinctive new development emerged whereby spirit writing produced increasingly eschatological texts on saving humanity from the turning of the *kalpa* 救劫."[4] In the first half of the twentieth century, this new spirit-writing movement spread throughout China.[5]

Based on its regional traits, scholars use various terms to describe this movement in different regions; for example, Shiga Ichiko uses "Daoist hall movement" (*daotang/daotan yundong* 道堂/道壇運動) to describe the movement of religious and philanthropic cults that arose in Guangdong at the end of the Qing dynasty and came down in a continuous line to the modern Hong Kong Daoist halls.[6] As she points out: "Cantonese spirit-writing cults are more Daoist in character: the word '*daotan*' literally means 'Daoist shrine,' many cults worship Lüzu as the main deity, and some identify themselves as descendants of the Quanzhen school."[7] She also contends that three kinds of organization played a prominent role in the spirit-writing cult movement of Guangdong province: Daoist halls devoted to Patriarch Lü, the Xiantiandao 先天道 (Way of Former Heaven), and charitable halls in Chaoshan 潮汕. Moreover, she mentions that the spirit-writing cults in Chaoshan were usually known as charitable halls.[8] Therefore, understanding charitable halls is critical to the study of the spirit-writing movement in Chaozhou. This local movement played an important role in the new spirit-writing movement. For example, in the first half of the twentieth century, huge numbers of spirit-writing groups emerged in Chaozhou; Dejiao 德教 (Virtuous Teaching) originated there and became a well-known, influential sect in Southeast Asia.[9]

The Chaozhou region is located in the southeastern part of Guangdong province and today roughly covers three prefecture-level cities—Shantou 汕

---

3 Clart, "The Ritual Context of Morality Books," 15–17. The link between Daoism and eschatology is an important aspect of spirit-writing cults. Cf. Goossaert, "Modern Daoist Eschatology"; and Lai, "The Cult of Spirit-Writing in the Qing." For spirit-writing cults in Guangdong, cf. Shiga Ichiko's works mentioned in this article.
4 Wang, "Spirit Writing Groups in Modern China," 655.
5 On the spread and local adaptation of this movement, see also the contribution by Shiga Ichiko to this volume.
6 Shiga, *Xianggang Daojiao yu fuji xinyang*, 145–51.
7 Shiga, "Manifestations of Lüzu," 189.
8 Shiga, "Difang Daojiao zhi xingcheng," 233–35, 244.
9 Cf. Formoso, *De Jiao*; Chen, "Haiwai Huaren zongjiao wenshu"; Li, "Nanyang Dejiao zonghui yanjiu."

頭, Chaozhou 潮州, and Jieyang 揭陽.[10] Even though from the Tang dynasty to the present Chaozhou was usually affiliated with Guangdong, the distinctions between Chaozhou culture and Canton culture are obvious, partly due to the wide distance between the two cities and the fact that they are separated by the Lotus Mountains (Lianhua shanmai 蓮花山脈); for example, in Chaozhou, the local dialect is *Chaozhou hua* 潮州話, a sub-dialect of the Southern Min (*Minnan* 閩南).[11]

This article consists of three sections. The first briefly discusses the various definitions of the charitable halls in Chaozhou proposed by previous studies and describes the primary activities of charitable halls. The second describes the development of four different types of charitable hall from 1860 to 1949 and focuses on charitable halls that practiced spirit-writing. This section also discusses the distinctions between these four types of charitable hall and explores the role of spirit-writing within them. The third provides an overview of spirit-writing groups from the end of the Qing dynasty to the Republic, and describes various spirit-writing cults in the town of Xiashan 峽山, where I recently conducted fieldwork. This fieldwork data demonstrates the complexity of the spirit-writing cults in terms of the pantheon and organizational forms of such charitable halls and temples. The conclusion summarizes my findings and discusses the relationship between the charitable halls and spirit-writing cults in Chaozhou. The primary sources used in this article can be divided into three types: (1) spirit-writing books created by local cults, (2) other literature created by local cults; for example, inscriptions and the history of the hall (*tangshi* 堂史), and (3) local gazetteers (*fangzhi* 方志), newspapers, and reports. Most of these sources date back to the period between the Qing dynasty and the Republic.

---

10 Several scholars use "Chaoshan" to refer to this area. Below I use simply 'Chaozhou,' except in citations. Chaozhou has a strong local culture; for example, *Chaozhou cai* 潮州菜 (cuisine), *Chaozhou yinyue* 潮州音樂 (music), and *Chaozhou xi* 潮州戲 (opera). In the present study, Chaozhou refers to a cultural region, and its scope was roughly identical to Chaozhou prefectural (*fu* 府) in the late Qing, including nine counties and one sub-prefecture (*ting* 廳): Haiyang 海陽, Chaoyang 潮陽, Jieyang 揭陽, Raoping 饒平, Huilai 惠來, Dabu 大埔, Chenghai 澄海, Puning 普寧, Fengshun 豐順, and Nan'ao ting 南澳廳. Chaozhou city refers to the prefecture-level city, i.e., Chaozhoufu 潮州府.

11 The Southern Min dialects emerged from at least the fourth century, centered around southern Fujian 福建 (mainly Quanzhou 泉州 and Zhangzhou 漳州). Today, these dialects are spoken in Fujian, Taiwan, eastern Guangdong, Hainan 海南, and southern Zhejiang 浙江. The history of the Southern Min dialects in Chaozhou dates back to as early as the twelfth century.

2   The Various Definitions and Primary Activities of Charitable Halls

Non-governmental charitable organizations came into existence in the Jiangnan 江南 area at the end of the Ming dynasty, from whence they spread throughout China. Fuma Susumu 夫馬進 defines charitable societies (*shanhui* 善會) as free associations in which individuals voluntarily participate with the aim of performing good deeds, and charitable halls (*shantang*) as the former's administrative offices and facilities that implement charitable activities.[12] These charitable halls became organizations that allowed the gentry to establish a good reputation and participate in public affairs. Among them were comprehensive charitable halls (*zonghexing shantang* 綜合性善堂)[13] and specialized charitable associations, such as those that provided coffins and assisted with burials (*shiguan zhuzang shanhui* 施棺助葬善會) in the Jiang-Zhe 江浙 area. These organizations began to grow in popularity at the beginning of the Jiaqing 嘉慶 reign (1796–1820).[14] Since, during the period following the Taiping wars (1851–1864), social disintegration escalated to a national scale, the charitable organizations found themselves in very different social surroundings, and experienced vast changes.[15] By the second half of the nineteenth century, two distinct aspects began to converge: the eschatological discourse and charitable activism. Many spirit-writing cults had begun to adopt the eschatological discourse, mentioned above, and saw charity as one way to redeem the world. As a result, an increasing number of charity-oriented spirit-writing halls emerged. For example, the Shiquan hui 十全會 (Ten Completions Society) in Sichuan 四川 province was established in 1866 by a spirit-writing cult devoted to Emperor Guan (Guandi 關帝).[16]

Most scholars apply a narrow definition to Chaozhou charitable halls and emphasize their regional distinction.[17] Lin Juncong 林俊聰 argues that the

---

12   Fuma, *Zhongguo shanhui*, 1.
13   These halls became involved in a variety of charitable activities; for instance, providing coffins, burying corpses, offering medicine, and "cherishing [written] characters" (*xizi* 惜字).
14   Leung, *Shishan yu jiaohua*, 278–306.
15   Crucial changes pertain to four aspects: first, the managers tended to be from local merchant groups; second, the scope of charitable activities was expanding quickly; third, the charitable agenda was departing from the old tradition and embracing new issues; and fourth, modern new philanthropists sometimes became involved in the construction of the infrastructure. See Leung, "Charity, Medicine, and Religion," 580.
16   Wang, "Spirit Writing Groups in Modern China," 664–79. See also Yamada, "'Shan' yu geming," 71–78.
17   Cf. Ma and Ji, *Chaoshan shantang daguan*; Yang, "Chaoshan diqu de shantang"; Shi, "Xiang-

Chaoshan charitable halls are a kind of non-governmental organization that oversees charity and relief, and are devoted to ancient saints or immortals, such as Patriarch Great Peak (Dafeng zushi 大峰祖師), the God of Northern Heaven (Xuantian shangdi 玄天上帝), and Immortal He Yeyun 何野雲.[18] Xu Yuan 徐苑 focuses on how the network of charitable halls came into being, emphasizing that these organizations have used *shantang* or *shanshe* as autonyms in order to claim membership of a particular category—the Chaoshan charitable halls—since the escalating anti-superstition campaigns of the late 1920s.[19] Tan Chee-Beng argues that the *shantang* in Chaoshan and Southeast Asia are saint-based, charitable temples, organized around the worship of one or more saint or deity; he finds it more appropriate to treat these *shantang* as distinct religious organizations rather than focus on them solely as the spirit-writing centers known as phoenix halls (*luantang* 鸞堂).[20] Based on the strong local flavor of charitable halls in Chaozhou, these scholars are inclined to keep charitable halls separate from other religious organizations, such as Buddhist temples and village temples (*cunmiao* 村廟). These halls were established by different groups, however, with diverse backgrounds and aims, so viewing all *shantang* as one unique, distinctive type is to oversimplify these halls and underestimates their inner distinctions. Instead of stressing the regional nature of *shantang*, much may be gained from examining the religious (or secular) identity of these charitable halls. As the following will show, they clearly differed in terms of their pantheon and transregional integration, depending on whether they were secular, sectarian, or engaged in spirit-writing.

Shiga Ichiko studies these charitable halls in the context of the new spirit-writing movement. She contends that: the locations where spirit-writing was practiced in Chaoshan are usually known as *shantang*; most charitable halls are devoted to Patriarch Great Peak, Patriarch Song Chaoyue 宋超月, and other monks; and the rituals performed by these halls have a strong Buddhist flavor, with a few halls calling themselves "Buddhist halls" (*fotang* 佛堂).[21] Her view

cun zhili shiye xia de xiandai Chaoshan shantang yanjiu"; Liu, "Wanqing shiqi Chaoshan diqu cishan jiuji shiye."
18 Lin, *Chaoshan miao tang*, 539–40.
19 Xu, "Dafeng zushi," 4.
20 Tan, "Shantang," 76, 97–98. "A phoenix hall is a voluntary religious association of congregational character centering upon communication with the gods by means of [spirit-writing]." See Clart, "The Ritual Context of Morality Books," 1.
21 Shiga, "Difang Daojiao zhi xingcheng," 244. Shiga Ichiko also argues that these charitable halls belong to the Daoist hall movement, since they were influenced by the nineteenth-century spirit-writing movement and share similarities with Daoist halls in Guangdong and Hong Kong, and phoenix halls in Taiwan. In addition, she points out that a few chari-

that the spirit-writing cults in Chaoshan are usually known as *shantang* may be misleading. To my understanding, many charitable halls were established by spirit-writing groups, but these spirit-writing charitable halls were only part of the spirit-writing movement in Chaozhou. As I will show below, many spirit-writing cults did not describe their organizations as *shantang* or *shanshe* and rarely participated in charitable activities.

The above views are partly based on the situation of charitable halls which have been revived in recent years and are centered around deities. As Tan Chee-Beng points out: "It is precisely their religious nature that accounts for their resilience."[22] However, these views fail to reflect the complexity of the category of the charitable hall in history. Moreover, no matter how differently scholars define charitable halls in Chaozhou, their studies always focus on organizations that clearly name themselves *shantang* or *shanshe*. In other words, these organizations possess a self-identity as a charitable hall. From the nineteenth to the twentieth centuries, many new cults enthusiastically participated in charitable activities, repeatedly emphasized the significance of goodness, and widely used the Chinese character *shan* 善.[23] Although these organizations bore similar titles, they were established by various groups and had different backgrounds. Moreover, many organizations may be considered charitable halls even though the character *shan* did not feature in their titles.

One reason why the charitable halls in Chaozhou have been grouped together in the previous research is that, if we examine their charitable work, they were all comprehensive charitable halls, engaged in comparable activities. The earliest hall now known in Chaozhou is the Ciji huitang 慈濟會堂 (Hall of the Benevolent Association), which was established by the local gentry in 1719. This hall, centered around the provision of free coffins (*shiguan* 施棺) and burial of corpses (*yanku* 掩骷), built a shrine devoted to restless ghosts.[24] The gentry may have operated the hall for only a few decades, since later local gazetteers no longer recorded it. Since the 1860s, several organizations have been established which had a similarly comprehensive approach but named themselves *shan*-

---

table halls began to refer to themselves as "Daoist organizations" (*Daojiao tuanti* 道教團體) after moving to Hong Kong. She, therefore, uses the term "Daoist hall movement" to include all new spirit-writing cults throughout Guangdong province. See Shiga, "Chūgoku Koanton-shō Shiosen chiiki no zendō," 41; Shiga, "Difang Daojiao zhi xingcheng," 234–35.

22   Tan, "*Shantang*," 98.
23   *Shan* is a common character used in building/organization titles of spirit-writing cults; for example, Tongshan she 同善社, Yushan tang 育善堂, and Baode shantang 報德善堂. Yau Chi-on 游子安 points out that many Hong Kong Daoist Halls use *shan* in their name. See Yau, *Shanshu yu Zhongguo zongjiao*, 187.
24   *Jieyang xianzhi, juan* 8, *miaoyu* 廟宇, 7a–8a; rpd. 576–77.

tang/shanshe. After the 1890s, the development of charitable halls ushered in an era of popularization that lasted nearly sixty years. Based on an appendix in Xu Yuan's thesis, there were 295 charitable halls: eight were established before 1861, 19 between 1861 and 1890, 57 between 1891 and 1920, 82 between 1920 and 1949, and 23 after 1949; in the city of Chaozhou, 38 came into being between 1860 and 1949, and 68 were of unknown date.[25] Most of the undated halls were established before 1949, and the majority of these halls were not revived after 1978. These figures imply that *shantang* had become a popular kind of organization in Chaozhou since the 1890s. These halls engaged in similar charitable activities; for example, providing free coffins, burying bones, offering free medicine, transmitting morality books, and hosting celebrations. They also enthusiastically supported and participated in the construction of the infrastructure and public services, such as building hospitals, constructing schools, building and maintaining roads and bridges, erecting public tombs, and organizing fire brigades. These charitable halls played a significant role in maintaining the social order and promoting social management, and shared similarities with contemporary charitable organizations in other areas of China.

From the aspect of charitable activities, these halls are indistinguishable but their backgrounds, aims, and religious practices highlight the existence of important differences between them, even though they were all called *shantang* or *shanshe*. For a more accurate understanding of Chaozhou's charitable halls in history, it is important to determine whether these halls were centered around deities; if so, whether they were spirit-writing groups; and, if so, whether they were sectarian groups.[26] In this way, charitable halls can be divided into four groups. Several halls were not centered around deities and distanced themselves from Buddhism and Daoism. This type of charitable hall claimed a new "secular" identity and was deeply enmeshed in the changing, early twentieth century religious discourses. A second type of charitable hall was operated by spirit-writing cults and embedded in the nineteenth-century

---

25 Xu, "Dafeng zushi," 119–57. The number of charitable halls varies in other studies; for example, according to a thesis by Lin Guixian, no halls was established in the 1840s, three in the 1850s, five in the 1860s, 17 in the 1870s, nine in the 1880s, nine in the 1890s, and 18 in the 1900s. See Liu, "Wan Qing shiqi Chaoshan diqu cishan jiuji shiye yanjiu," 30.

26 I use the term "sect" to denote "voluntary religious communities that come into being and are maintained outside official recognized and/or state-sanctioned religious organizations and usually create a novel but officially contested synthesis of religious symbols, belief, and practices." See Broy, "Syncretic Sects and Redemptive Societies," 168. Compared to a cult, a sect possesses a well-developed, non-localized membership structure, and usually has many institutions in different places; for example, Xiantiandao and Yiguandao 一貫道 (Way of Pervading Unity).

spirit-writing movement. Consequently, they placed great emphasis on self-cultivation and moral reform resulting from eschatological discourses. A third type was run by sectarian groups and should be discussed in terms of their sectarian beliefs and practices. Importantly, sectarian halls were integrated into networks that transcended the Chaoshan region. Lastly, there were other religious cults that were linked to individual halls. Below, I describe these types separately.

3   Four Types of Charitable Hall

3.1   *Charitable Organizations*

These halls were not centered around deities and were more inclined to be "secular" charitable organizations, although some of their activities involved religion; for example, they circulated morality books and held public lectures to transmit the principle of retribution (*yinguo baoying* 因果報應). These organizations were frequently located in the urban areas and supported by the gentry and merchants. A few local officials also assisted with the construction of these halls. These organizations were mainly concerned about local interests, aiming to reform local society and improve local welfare through various charitable activities. Only a minority of charitable halls in Chaozhou belong to this type of "charitable organization," with possibly one or two per city. These charitable organizations possessed rich economic and political resources and played an important role in the construction and administration of modern cities.

The earliest organization labeled *shantang* that belongs to this category in Jieyang city is the Jieyang shantang 揭陽善堂. A retired senior official, Ding Richang 丁日昌 (1823–1882), initiated its construction. From his writings, we learn that he and the local gentry proposed to build a charitable hall to transmit morality books and exhort people to do good deeds at the beginning of the Guangxu reign (1871–1908), but this proposal was opposed by some local elites. In 1880, Ding renewed the proposal and received support from other gentry and local officials, so the Jieyang shantang was established to preach the *Shengyu* 聖諭 (Sacred edict),[27] seek help for those suffering due to cold and hunger, pro-

---

27   In 1670, Emperor Kangxi 康熙 issued the *Sacred Edict* (Sixteen items). In 1724, Emperor Yongzheng 雍正 added an amplified instruction to each item and named the new book *Shengyu guangxun* 聖諭廣訓 (Amplified instructions on the sacred edict). This book became one of the most prevalent and influential books during the Qing dynasty. After 1670, lecturing on the *Sacred Edict* (*jiang shengyu* 講聖諭) gradually became a regular

vide for widows, widowers and orphans, offer free medicine, help people to stop taking opium, and publicize the teaching of good and bad karma.[28] This hall was mainly concerned with local welfare and relief work; for instance, in 1882, it cooperated with the local gentry and officials to raise funds for flood relief in Fengshun 豐順 county.[29] Through this hall, Ding Richang inquired about local people's exemplary deeds of chastity and filial piety, whom the hall then helped to apply for and build honorary archways (*paifang* 牌坊) as official recognition.[30]

The Furen shantang 輔仁善堂 (Charitable Hall for Supporting Benevolence) in Chaozhou city was established by the gentry on the order of the Chaozhou prefect (*zhifu* 知府) Li Shibin 李士彬 (1835–1913).[31] This hall was located at No. 43, Kaiyuan Street 開元, and the tablet above its door was inscribed by Li Shibin in 1896.[32] Many participants were merchants, and this hall also became a temporary meeting place for merchants; for example, in 1906, the gentry and merchants invited people from commercial and educational circles to assemble there to discuss the management of the Yue Han 粵漢 railway. After this meeting, a chamber of commerce was established, which the local officials viewed as the basis for local autonomy.[33]

In the first half of the twentieth century, charitable halls became the backbone of firefighting in Chaozhou city.[34] In 1909, several fires broke out in Chaozhou city, and members of the charitable halls served as firefighters, protecting local people's safety and property.[35] The Haiyang Self-Government Bureau (Haiyang zizhi ju 海陽自治局) conferred with the directors of charitable halls and the business gentry regarding firefighting, inoculation, and

---

activity for local officials, eventually being carried out by private initiators from the countryside to the cities. Cf. Wang, "Qingting *Shengyu guangxun* zhi banxing," 255–76.
28 Ding Richang, "Shantang xu 善堂序," in *Jieyang xian xu zhi, juan* 4, 65a–67b.
29 *Fengshun xianzhi, juan* 2, 25a–26b.
30 *Fengshun xianzhi, juan* 6, *jiexiao* 節孝: 21ab; 26a; 27a; 29ab; 30b; 37b; 39a; 40a. The government used archways to commend people for their extraordinary feats, such as success in civil examinations and loyal behavior.
31 "Chaojun Furen shantang zhi gailiang."
32 Weng and Xu, "Gaishu jiefang qian Chaozhoucheng de cishan tuanti," 137–38.
33 "Chaozhou dai zhao Yue Han lu gu zhi huiyi"; "Xiang ji Chaojun huiyi dai zhao Yue Han lu gu qingxing." By the end of the Qing dynasty, various associations with local autonomy, related to education, public hygiene, roads, commerce, and charity, had been established by the local elite. Cf. Sun, "Qingmo difang zizhi yanjiu"; Zhang, "Qingmo Guangdong difang zizhi yanjiu."
34 Zhong, "Jiefang qian de xiaofang shanju," 54–55.
35 "Jun zhong dieci huojing"; "Zhu juan Baode shantang jiuhuo zhi yongyue."

public hygiene,[36] after which a firefighting association was established.[37] During the Republican period, twenty charitable halls in Chaozhou city had fire brigades.[38]

Public lectures, initially on morality books, were regularly held in Furen shantang. In 1905, morality books were replaced by reports of social reforms (*xingli chubi* 興利除弊, literally, to promote what is beneficial and remove what is harmful) in newspapers.[39] In 1909, the Second Public Lecturing Office (Di er xuangjiang suo 第二宣講所)[40] was established in Furen shantang, and the public lectures were mainly about current affairs and Western knowledge. This office formed part of local self-government.[41]

In 1882, Fang Yao 方耀 (1834–1891), a well-known senior officer, led merchants of the Chaoshu liuyi huiguan 潮屬六邑會館 (Guild of Six Counties Affiliated to Chao[zhou]) in the establishment of the Tongji shantang 同濟善堂 (Charitable Hall of Communal Relief). This hall imitated the regulation of Guangzhou's charitable halls,[42] and was the earliest charitable hall in Shantou. Initially, it was operated by six primary managers (*zongli* 總理) and 24 managers on duty (*zhili* 值理), but this management model changed over time. The hall established many affiliated organizations, such as the Tongji yiyuan 同濟醫院 (Hospital of Communal Relief) and the Tongji zhongxuexiao 同濟中學校 (Middle School of Communal Relief).[43] From the end of the Qing dynasty, Tongji shantang had a profound impact on the local economy, politics, and society; for example, the managers of Tongji shantang mediated inter-village conflicts in Raoping 饒平 county and was commended by the local magistrate

---

36   "Haiyang zizhiju jiyi xiaofang"; "Ji jun weisheng shi."
37   "Jun shang xiaofanghui yi ju bin"; "Jun shang xiaofanghui binwen"; "Xunjingju duiyu jun shang qing she xiaofang zhi pici."
38   Wen and Xu, "Gaishu jiefang qian Chaozhoucheng de cishan tuanti," 143–44.
39   "Chaojun Furen shantang zhi gailiang."
40   In 1906, the Qing government issued the *Xuebu zouding gesheng quanxuesuo zhangcheng* 學部奏定各省勸學章程 (Regulation on promoting education presented by the provinces and approved by the Ministry of Education). This *Regulation* required local educational associations (*jiaoyu hui* 教育會) to establish public lecturing agencies in order to publicize policies and educate people. Cf. Su and Zhang, "Qingmo xuanjiangsuo tanxi," 201–16. The Di yi xuanjiang suo 第一宣講所 (First Public Lecturing Office) in Chaozhou city was set up by the Chaozhou prefect Chen Zhaotang 陳兆棠 in 1909.
41   "Ji jun Di'er xuanjiangsuo shi"; "Chaojun Di er xuanjiangsuo kaimu zhi jisheng."
42   In Guangzhou, the first post-Taiping charitable organization was the Aiyu shantang 愛育善堂 (Charity Hall of Love and Nurturing), instigated by the provincial General Restoration Bureau in 1871. For more on charitable halls in Guangzhou, see Leung, "Charity, Medicine, and Religion."
43   Xian, "Shantou shi cishantuan shilüe," 21–22; "Shantou shi cishan tuanti yilanbiao."

in 1904,[44] and also submitted a joint petition to the authorities of Chenghai 澄海 county regarding banning the export of oxen.[45] In 1903, Tongji shantang issued a public announcement that this hall focused on local charitable activities and was not allowed to associate with Buddhist monks and Daoist priests.[46] Tongji shantang consciously maintained its distance from both Buddhism and Daoism. In other words, from the perspective of Tongji shantang, the question of whether a charitable hall is associated with Buddhism and Daoism is significant in terms of distinguishing one hall from another. Thereby, they tried to set themselves apart from the many halls that were associated with Patriarch Great Peak and other Buddhist or Daoist deities.

The above descriptions on Furen shantang and Tongji shantang are primarily based on the *Lingdong ribao* 嶺東日報 (*Lingdong Daily News*), a newspaper established by the new elite who advocated reform and actively spread Western knowledge. The editors of *Lingdong ribao* displayed a bias against local religion and harshly criticized the local cults. With regard to charitable halls like the Furen and Tongji, the editors appreciated their contributions to the local society but also noticed distinctions between the different charitable halls. One report, "Etang chuxian 惡堂出現" (Emergence of evil halls), states that, during the recent plagues, people who performed spirit-writing or were spirit-mediums (*fuluan jiangji* 扶鸞降乩) had established charitable halls everywhere. This report reflects how the editors discriminated against charitable halls that were centered around the practice of spirit-writing or spirit-mediumship, and labeled them "evil halls," even though these halls performed good deeds.[47] In other words, whether a charitable hall was centered around deities, relied on spirit mediums (*tongji* 童乩), and focused on spirit-writing were important distinctions for the contemporary elite. This should be viewed in light of the changing role of religion in Chinese society at that time. At the turn of the century, the elite's views on religion changed greatly, due to a "transition from pre-1898 Confucian fundamentalism and anticlericalism to early twentieth-century anti-superstition."[48] How to deal with religion became a core question for the reform movements. Whether or not a charitable hall was

---

44   "Raoping xiedou zhi tiaoting"; "Jiangxu tiaohe xiedou."
45   "Qing jin gengniu chukou." In the first half of the twentieth century, oxen had become the focus of an emerging animal protection movement, since many oxen were slaughtered, and their meat was mainly shipped to Japan. Cf. Poon, "Buddhist Activism and Animal Protection," 103–7.
46   "Tongji shantang gaobao."
47   "Etang chuxian."
48   Goossaert, "1898," 328.

involved in religious worship was a focus of the elite. In his study of the temple destruction campaigns from 1898 to 1948, Paul Katz points out, "The relationship between religion and the state in China underwent a major shift in the modern era. The attacks on temples and their rituals [were] being undertaken more vigorously during some periods of time than others."[49] While charitable activities were usually welcomed, newspapers such as *Lingdong Daily* began to criticize harshly the religious practices of many *shantang*.[50] Some energetic spirit-writing cults or *tongji* cults were occasionally harassed and disrupted by the government.[51] The friction with the government intensified after 1928, when the Guomindang assumed power (see below).

3.2 *Spirit-Writing Cults*

Influenced by the spirit-writing movement, new spirit-writing cults sprang up in Chaozhou from the end of the nineteenth century. From this point onward, charitable halls became favored locations in which these cults could conduct regular activities. As a result, hundreds of charitable halls were established during the first half of the twentieth century that centered around spirit-writing séances and differed from the above "secular" charitable organizations. Doing good deeds was a way for the cult members to accumulate merits and cultivate themselves. Their essential ambition was "to proclaim moral transformation on behalf of Heaven" (*daitian xuanhua* 代天宣化) through spirit-writing. Spirit-writing altars were crucial to these charitable halls, and instructions from deities played a key role in the development of these halls. One reason why they called themselves *shantang* or *shanshe* was to attract support and gain legality. However, in addition these autonyms, they also called themselves phoenix halls (*luantang*), Buddhist halls (*fotang*), and Daoist halls (*daotang* 道堂).[52]

The emergence of spirit-writing charitable halls in Chaozhou was linked to the occurrence of disasters and the worship of Patriarch Great Peak. At

---

49　Katz, "'Superstition' and Its Discontents," 609–10.
50　For instance, under instructions from Patriarch Great Peak, the Mian'an shantang cast a bell to pray for blessings and protection against the plague, a practice ridiculed by the editors of *Lingdong ribao*. See "Xuan zhong zhiyi zhi kexiao." This practice was, however, accepted by the Chaoyang magistrate. See "Zhaozao liuzong 肇造留蹤" (Foundation trace) (1913). This stele still stands today at the front of Mian'an shantang.
51　"Feng shentan chong xuefei"; "Yaoyan huozhong zhi Wu Kun bei na."
52　These spirit-writing cults were the products of religious synthesis. In the local spirit-written books, they would use various terms to describe their institutions. The term *daotang* can also be interpreted as a cultivation hall, a place where the cult members cultivate themselves.

the end of the nineteenth century, a plague of rats wrought havoc on the area, and Chaoyang county suffered severely, which led to a new era of spirit-writing charitable halls. Mian'an shantang nianfo she 棉安善堂念佛社 (Society for Reciting Buddha's Name of the Mian'an Charitable Hall) was a typical example. This hall was located in the Yanwu 演武 pavilion of Chaoyang city (a.k.a. Miancheng 棉城) and devoted to Patriarch Great Peak.[53] When Miancheng inhabitants experienced a plague of rats in 1898, the local gentry brought the incense fire (xianghuo 香火)[54] of Patriarch Great Peak to Miancheng and established a new altar. Centered around this altar, the members of a pre-existing Nianfo she 念佛社 (Society for Reciting Buddha's Name) actively participated in the relief work by performing spirit-writing, offering medicine, and burying corpses. They claimed that numinous charms (lingfu 靈符) and elixir water (danshui 丹水) from Patriarch Great Peak saved innumerable lives. The following year, one Xiao Mingqin 蕭鳴琴 (1875–1908) raised funds to build a new hall named Mian'an shantang 棉安善堂,[55] which occupied an important position among charitable halls devoted to Patriarch Great Peak. In the first half of the twentieth century, a large proportion of charitable halls were devoted to Patriarch Great Peak, but it is unknown whether earlier charitable halls already worshipped him. Once most charitable halls had been established, a legend emerged that, at the turn of the Ming and Qing dynasties, the villagers dreamed that Patriarch Great Peak instructed them to perform good deeds, such as burying unclaimed corpses and offering free medicine.[56]

This particular combination of charity and Patriarch Great Peak worship quickly spread in Chaozhou. In 1899, under instructions from Patriarch Great Peak through spirit-writing, members of Nianfo she brought the incense fire to Shantou port and performed charitable deeds there. They first worshipped Patriarch Great Peak in Tongji waiju 同濟外局, and this altar was subsequently transferred to a temple devoted to Immortal Hua Tuo 華佗, a Chinese physician

---

53 According to historical sources, Patriarch Great Peak was originally a monk who performed countless good deeds and spared no effort to build a bridge in Chaoyang county during the Shaoxing 紹興 reign of the Song dynasty (1131–1162). He died of exhaustion before the bridge was completed, and the gentry built the Hall for Rewarding Benevolence (Baode tang 報德堂) worship Patriarch Great Peak. See Xu Lai 徐來, "Baode tang ji 報德堂記 (1351)," in Chaoyang xianzhi, juan 15, 14b–15b.

54 This process is usually known as qing xianghuo 請香火. Worshippers take a statue and incense ash from a temple or altar to a new place through a series of rituals, then worshippers establish a new altar.

55 "Zhaozao liuzong."

56 Lin, Taiguo Dafeng zushi chongbai, 26–28.

who lived during the Eastern Han dynasty. In 1901, local merchant groups and other Patriarch Great Peak cults supported the construction of a new hall. In 1903, the hall was completed, which Patriarch Great Peak named Cunxin shantang Nianfo she 存心善堂念佛社 (Society for Reciting Buddha's Name, Charitable Hall for Keeping Kindheartedness) through the planchette.[57] In 1901, the magistrate of Chenghai county supported the construction, and erected a sign stating that it had been erected by Cunxin shantang 存心善堂. The inscription also mentions that Patriarch Great Peak takes pity on the degenerating human mind and prevalence of natural disasters and so expounds moral teachings by means of spirit-writing (*feiluan chanhua* 飛鸞闡化), thereby saving humans everywhere.[58]

Charitable halls became popular locations for many new spirit-writing cults, especially Patriarch Great Peak cults. In a spirit-written book named *Song Dafeng Fozu jiujie zhenjing* 宋大峰佛祖救劫真經 (Song Buddhist Patriarch Great Peak's true scripture for saving from the apocalypse), Patriarch Great Peak describes how he built charitable halls under orders of the Jade Emperor:

> I observe and learn that the morals of the world have become abnormal, and that the human mind has become careless. When Heaven sends down calamities, good and evil [people] will not be distinguished in the world. I take the risk to present a memorial [to the Jade Emperor] and am granted the authority to establish charitable halls and compose the *True Scripture* to save living people universally.
>
> 本道觀知世道反常，人心不苟，天降劫難之期，四方善惡不明之分。余冒奏准旨，建立善堂，著出《真經》普渡世人。[59]

Charitable halls were viewed as places that distinguished benefactors from the rest of the world. Patriarch Great Peak also became a presiding deity who composed morality books to awaken the world. The composition of such books also constitutes a difference between the charitable halls that engaged in spirit-writing and those that did not. Patriarch Great Peak also asked other deities to compose books; for example, he asked Immortal White Cloud (Baiyun xiangu 白雲仙姑) to compose the *Yushu puhua xinbian* 玉書普化新編 (New collection of jade books for universal transformation).[60]

---

57   "Cunxin shantang chengli ji gechu yizhong bei." Cai, *Cunxin tangwu*, 26.
58   "Chenghai xian zhengtang wei Cunxin shantang zhi chushi xiaoyu shi bei."
59   *Song Dafeng Fozu jiujie zhenjing*, 1a. This book is in the possession of Mr. Ma Qingxian 馬慶賢. I thank him for sharing it with me.
60   *Yushu puhua xinbian*, 8b.

Among charitable activities, composing morality books and "refining restless bones" (*xiuku* 修骷)[61] were regarded as two great meritorious acts and frequently became a new hall's contribution in order to gain a foothold in the local society. Many spirit-writing charitable halls participated in "refining restless bones" and built public tombs. For example, an official investigation of 1936 shows that, in Chaoyang county, 97 public graveyards were built from 1902 to 1935, almost all of which were owned by a total of more than thirty charitable halls.[62] "Refining restless bones" entailed collecting and burying bones in public tombs, during which process deities instructed the participants on how to perform a variety of rituals and continuously encouraged them through the planchette to persist in this great good deed. Ghosts were summoned to spirit-writing altars by deities to disclose their own evil sins as warnings to the living. This provided not only an opportunity for disciples to cultivate themselves, but also a lively religious lesson. The spirit-writing instructions that were produced during this practice were compiled as morality books (see below), a common theme of which was saving beings in both this world and the underworld (*yinyang liangdu* 陰陽兩度 or *yinyang tongdu* 陰陽同渡).[63] This idea was supportive of the practice of refining restless bones.

The deities and activities associated with charitable halls operated by spirit-writing groups came under increasing pressure from the Nationalist government in 1928. With the "Standards to Determine Temples to be Destroyed and Maintained" (*Shenci cunfei biaozhun* 神祠存廢標準), enacted by the Ministry of the Interior in November, 1928, the campaign entered its most rigid decade, and many forms of Chinese religious life were subjected to immense pressure.[64] In the twelfth lunar month of the seventeenth year of the Republic (January 11–February 2 1929), an order to destroy illegitimate temples was carried out in Chaoshan, and the Pochu mixin weiyuanhui 破除迷信委員會 (Committee for Destroying Superstitions) in Shantou put Patriarch Great Peak cults on their list, which sparked a process of negotiation. The Cunxin shantang

---

61 *Xiuku*, a.k.a. *xiukulou* 修骷髏, *xiushan* 修山, *xiubaixing* 修百姓, can be initiated by a charitable hall or village. The ritual includes inviting deities through spirit-writing (sometimes a spirit medium), collecting and laying bones in urns (*jindou* 金斗), the appointment of tomb kings by deities, burying all urns, performing a Buddhist ritual to save ghosts, and offering regular sacrifices. For more information about *xiuku*, see Xu, "Dafeng zushi," 86–109; Shiga, "Shen yu gui zhijian," 39–64; Li et al., "Yuedong yanhai diqu," 10–15; Formoso, "Hsiu-Kou-Ku," 217–34; Formoso, "From Bone to Ashes," 192–216.
62 "Chaoyang xian gongmu yizhong diaocha tongji biao," 21–35.
63 Cf. *Jueshi xinpian*; *Chaosheng cihang*. Both books are in the possession of Mr. Ma Qingxian.
64 Katz, "'Superstition' and Its Discontents," 611–12.

in Shantou immediately responded to this decision and selected Zhan Tianyan 詹天眼 (1899–after 1974), the hall's director and primary manager of Mian'an shantang, to deal with this issue. Five days later, the hall called a conference, which representatives of more than 100 shantang attended. These representatives elected Zhan as chair and decided to submit a joint petition for protecting the Patriarch, in which they emphasized that the Patriarch was a monk who had performed charitable deeds and belonged to the type of former sages (xianzhe 先哲), a category of deities who were deemed suitable for worship by the government. The charitable halls, they argued, had inherited the spirit of the Patriarch to perform good deeds. If the committee banned the Patriarch, the members' devotion to their charitable work would falter. If a plague or other crisis occurred, the members would be fearful and so the social stability would be affected.[65] About a month later, the Public Security Office in Shantou agreed that the Patriarch belonged to the category of former sages and so should be protected. The Ministry of the Interior later also agreed with this conclusion.[66] The temple destruction campaign thus forced some shantang, in particular those devoted to Patriarch Great Peak, to unite and fight for legal recognition. During the Republic, the campaign restrained the religious activities of the shantang, especially those located in the urban areas, but did not produce serious destruction. The number of shantang continued to grow, and they were viewed as, or transformed into, modern charitable societies. This was certainly also because the activities of these new organizations compensated for the deficiencies of the city and village administrations, which secured them public support.

During the Republic, spirit-writing cults helped the charitable halls to flourish, and almost all halls contained the terms shantang or shanshe in their titles. Some halls or societies added the term shan to their original title; for example, Baode tang 報德堂 (Hall for Rewarding Benevolence) became Baode shantang (Charitable Hall for Rewarding Benevolence), Chengjing she 誠敬社 (Society for Sincerity and Reverence) became Chengjing shanshe, and Leshan she 樂善社 (Society for Enjoying Good Deeds) became Leshan shanshe. This change may have been due to the temple destruction campaigns, discussed above but also implies, however, that the concept of shantang/shanshe was gradually being accepted by local society.

---

65   See the "Baocun Dafeng zushi jinian bei 保存大峰祖師紀念碑" (Memorial to Protecting Patriarch Great Peak) (1929), which currently stands before Mian'an shantang.
66   Ibid.

3.3 Sectarian Charitable Halls

A few charitable halls were established by sectarian groups, most of which were centered around deities and performed spirit-writing. These were similar to the aforementioned spirit-writing charitable halls apart from the fact that the sectarian charitable halls had more systematically developed religious teachings, were widely connected with other groups of the same sect and maintained a strict hierarchy among the members. It is, therefore, more appropriate to study these charitable halls in the context of their sectarian background and institutions. In addition to *shantang*, they frequently called themselves *daotan* 道壇, *daotang* 道堂, and *daochang* 道場.

The most influential sect in Chaozhou was the Xiantiandao.[67] From the 1880s, Liao Shenxiu 廖慎修 (fl. 1884–1894) began to preach in Huilai 惠來 county and converted the local people, such as a lay Buddhist named Zhu Guoyuan 朱果緣 (1832–after 1912).[68] Liao Shenxiu founded Yuchao tang 育潮堂 (Hall for Cultivating Chao[zhou]) and regarded converting Chaozhou people as his duty. Although unable to speak the Chaozhou dialect and requiring the services of Zhu Cunyuan 朱存元 (1878–1918), Guoyuan's nephew, as an interpreter, Liao Shenxiu frequently and enthusiastically preached in Chaozhou. Through his persistent efforts, dozens of halls were established and thousands of local people were converted.[69] From the 1890s onward, Zhu Guoyuan and Zhu Cunyuan actively transmitted the Way, especially in Puning 普寧 county.[70] The latter established many halls, which frequently used *shan* in their title, like Jueshan tang 覺善堂 (Hall for Awakening Goodness), Xishan tang 習善堂 (Hall for Learning Goodness), Jishan tang 集善堂 (Hall for Gathering Goodness), Dashan tang 達善堂 (Hall for Achieving Goodness), Mingshan tang 明善堂 (Hall for Illuminating Goodness), and Xueshan tang 學善堂 (Hall for Studying Goodness).[71] These halls were also involved in charitable work[72] and were easily confused with charitable halls. Other Xiantiandao groups also named their halls *shantang*; for example, Chongxin shantang 崇心善堂 (Charitable Hall for Believing in the Mind) in 1926, and Guangzheng shantang 廣正善堂 (Charita-

---

67   The Sect of Former Heaven, established in the early eighteenth century, was the most influential and enduring redemptive society. This tradition combined the lay Daoist practices of inner alchemy with the cult of the Unborn Mother. See Goossaert and Palmer, *The Religious Question in Modern China*, 98–99.
68   Zhu, *Zhu xianshi yuanyou ji baojuan*, 9–14.
69   Ngai, "Zhongguo minjian zongjiao de nan chuan Taiguo," 24–26.
70   Zhu, *Zhu xianshi yuanyou ji baojuan*, esp. 35–67.
71   Ibid., 61, 66. The Jueshan tang was set up in 1901, and others followed in 1902.
72   Newspapers report, for example, that Jueshan tang buried corpses in 1909. See "Lu bi shi."

ble Hall of Wideness and Uprightness) in 1931 in Chenghai.[73] The members of these charitable halls followed a strict hierarchy and were expected to abide by a variety of regulations of Xiantiandao, such as the *Shiliu tiaogui* 十六條規 (Sixteen regulations).

A typical case of a Xiantiandao charitable hall is Lian'an shantang 練安善堂 (Charitable Hall of Peaceful Lian) in the town of Haimen 海門. It was established by the Huashan she 化善社 (Society of Transformation and Goodness), and their spirit-written texts from 1926 to 1935 were compiled as *Xinbian jiujie baoxun* 新編救劫寶訓 (New collection of precious instructions on saving from the Kalpa). The data below are drawn from this book. In 1926, disciples congregated in the Sanshan shengwang miao 三山聖王廟 (Temple of Holy Kings of Three Mountains)[74] to "invite the carriage" (*qingluan* 請鑾),[75] and then revelations from Patriarch Great Peak ordered them to perform the *xiuku* ritual. Following spirit-written instructions, the disciples repaired abandoned tombs and buried bones from Keshibu 壳石埔. Meanwhile, a spirit-writing (*fuluan* 扶鑾 or *feiluan* 飛鑾) altar was established there. At this temporary altar,[76] a statue of Patriarch Great Peak was erected, and Bodhisattvas were invited to attend the ritual altar, which was a sacred site that only a few people could access. The whole process of *xiuku* was centered around spirit-writing instructions. Chanting sutras was the daily routine of disciples. Common scriptures included the *Shigao lingwen* 十誥靈文 (Numinous essay of ten admonitions), *Jin'gangjing* 金剛經 (Diamond sutra), *Mituojing* 彌陀經 (Amitābha sutra), *Jiukujing* 救苦經 (Sutra for relieving suffering), *Yuhuang jing* 玉皇經 (Scripture of the Jade Emperor), and a series of *Chaoyouwen* 超幽文 (Essays to save ghosts). Once the tombs had been repaired and the bones buried, Patriarch Great Peak presided over a large-scale ritual (*jiao* 醮) to save ghosts universally. Between 1926 and 1935, *xiuku* was the core work of Lian'an shantang, and its scope covered the whole of Haimen town. More than 30,000 graves were repaired. In 1926, disciples requested instructions on how to establish a charitable society (*shanshe* 善社). The following year, Patriarch Great Peak formally

---

73   *Chenghai xianzhi*, 586.
74   Sanshan shengwang refer to the Kings of Three Mountains (Sanshan guowang 三山國王), Chaozhou's most popular deities.
75   *Qingluan* refers to spirit-writing. *Luan* 鑾 may be an alternative character for *luan* 鸞. The character 鑾 is also used in terms relating to gods, such as "divine carriage" (*luanjia* 鑾駕) and "divine chair" (*luanzuo* 鑾座).
76   The primary work of *xiuku* was to collect and bury bones in a public tomb. Once the tomb's location had been decided, a temporary altar would be built, which was then dismantled once the tomb was completed.

named the society Lian'an huashan she 練安化善社. Yao Zhichu 姚智初 (no dates), a local merchant, became the society's leader (*shezhang* 社長). After this, disciples reconstructed a local temple named Baode tang 報德堂 (Hall for Rewarding Benevolence)[77] and renamed it Lian'an shantang. In addition, Lian'an shantang also performed other charitable work, such as offering free medicine and collecting papers containing written characters (*shizizhi* 拾字紙),[78] although this hall emphasized that refining restless bones was its primary task. After several early leaders passed away, confidence in spirit-writing waned and the development of Lian'an shantang slowed in the 1930s. The members began to doubt the reliability of revelations through spirit-writing and the spirit-writers were forced to cease their practice.[79]

The case of Lian'an shantang indicates that spirit-writing was an integral part of charitable activities. This can be traced back to the end of the Qing dynasty, when spirit-writing became interwoven with charitable work, and served to motivate philanthropy.[80] Accordingly, Clart argues that "a close functional connection existed in the nineteenth century between spirit-writing and public lecturing, and between spirit-writing cults and charitable societies."[81]

3.4   *Other Cults*

A few charitable halls were centered around deities (e.g., Dafeng zushi, Xuantian shangdi, and Dasheng fozu 大聖佛祖), but had not been established by spirit-writing or sectarian groups. They relied on other methods, such as spirit-mediums (*tongji* 童乩), spirit blocks (*beijiao* 杯筊), and spirit slips, to communicate with deities. A distinctive feature of these halls is that they did not view the composition of morality books as an effective way to cultivate themselves and save the world but, rather, focused on local charitable work and mutual aid for their members. These organizations were similar to local temples that engaged in charitable work, and many had Daoist links.

The *Guangdong nianjian* 廣東年鑒 (Guangdong yearbook) of the Republican period mentions that, besides the Daoist temples (*daoguan* 道觀), charitable associations (*shanshe* 善社) became another kind of Daoist organization in

---

77   This hall was devoted to Dafeng zushi and originally established in 1898.
78   *Shizizhi* or *xizi* was a popular good deed that commonly featured in the "ledgers of merit and demerit" (*gongguo ge* 功過格). In general, it entailed collecting paper containing writing and burning it in certain places, such as pagodas for showing respect to written characters (*jingzi ta* 敬字塔).
79   *Xinbian jiujie baoxun, juanshang* 卷上, 1a, 2a–3a, 4a, 24a–b, 29a; *juanxia* 卷下, 44b, 50b, 52ab.
80   Fan, *Qing mo minjian cishan shiye yu luantang yundong*, 1–20.
81   Clart, "The Ritual Context of Morality Books," 41.

Guangdong. These associations used established religious organizational forms to assemble and demonstrate the aim of salvation through performing charitable deeds. They were usually centered around deities such as Taishang laojun 太上老君, Patriarch Lü, Guan Yu 關羽, and Sun Wukong 孫悟空. Most of the members of these charitable associations, of both genders, were from the middle social stratum, such as well-to-do merchants.[82]

Chengjing shanshe 誠敬善社 was one of five grand charitable halls (*wuda shantang* 五大善堂) in Shantou city that originated from a pilgrimage to visit Xuantian shangdi in Shantou. From roughly 1912 onward, this group undertook an annual pilgrimage to Mt. Xuanwu 玄武 in Lufeng 陸豐 county. On around their third annual pilgrimage, they decided to bring the incense of Xuantian shangdi to Shantou and establish Chengjing she. This society gradually turned its focus to charitable work and was renamed Chengjing shanshe. In 1945, Chengjing shanshe had 877 members, many of whom were merchants and only four of whom were female. The first item of "regulations for members" (*sheyuan guize* 社員規則) was that the purpose of Chengjing shanshe was to worship Xuantian shangdi piously and sincerely, save the world, and serve society, while the fifth item pertained to mutual assistance regarding festivities, funerals as well as other social and community-based services.[83]

A few charitable halls relied on spirit mediums to communicate with deities and attract worshippers; for example, Tongnian shantang 同念善堂 (Charitable Hall of Common Thought) in Helong 鶴隴 village, Chaoan 潮安. This hall originated from a Shengmu niangniang 聖母娘娘 cult. In 1934, several rich villagers brought the incense of Shengmu to Helong from nearby Anxin shantang 安心善堂 (Charitable Hall of Peaceful Mind) and established a spirit altar in a local temple devoted to Sanshan guowang 三山國王. Then, a spirit medium of Shengmu began to lead and encourage worshippers to do good deeds, such as offering clothing, providing coffins, and refining restless bones. When the statue of Shengmu was moved to a new shrine (*shengdian* 升殿) in 1938, the spirit-medium performed the "running the fire road" (*zouhuolu* 走火路) ritual[84] to demonstrate the divine authority of Shengmu. In 1946, a new temple was established, named Tongnian shantang.[85] The late Qing newspaper, *Lingdong*

---

82 *Guangdong nianjian* 廣東年鑑 (1942), cited from Yau, *Shanshu yu Zhongguo zongjiao*, 190.
83 Cf. Xian, "Shantou shi cishantuan shilüe," 16–17; *Shantou Chengjing shanshe sheyuan guize*, 1a, 4a–12b; Lin, *Chengjing shanshe*, 159.
84 This practice aims to demonstrate a spirit medium's divine power, who must run barefoot along a road of charcoal fire of at least ten meters.
85 Su, *Tongnian shantang zhi*, 6–19.

Daily, also states that many charitable halls relied on spirit-mediums to communicate with deities (see above). According to an investigation by Xu Yuan, more than half of charitable halls were not involved in spirit-writing.[86]

4   An Overview of the Spirit-Writing Cults and Their Relation to Charitable Halls

As shown above, although most charitable halls were established by spirit-writing groups, it would be misguided to equate charitable halls with spirit-writing cults. Moreover, charitable halls were just one of the institutional forms of the spirit-writing cults. The view that the spirit-writing cults in Chaoshan are usually known as *shantang* is inaccurate and misleading.[87] In addition to charitable halls, spirit-writing groups also established temples (*miao* 廟), nunneries (*an* 庵), palaces (*gong* 宮), pavilions (*ge* 閣), and immortal abodes (*xianguan* 仙館). These organizations are rarely considered in the previous studies, where the concept of charitable halls fails to cover fully the complexity of the spirit-writing cults.

From the end of the nineteenth century onward, many sects were active in Chaozhou, and spirit-writing was a common practice among them. During the campaign to ban "reactionary sects and secret societies" (*fandong huidaomen* 反動會道門)[88] from 1950 to 1953, organizations like Yiguandao 一貫道 (Way of Pervading Unity), Tongshan she 同善社 (Fellowship of Goodness), Xiantiandao, and Tian'endao 天恩道 (Way of Heavenly Blessing) were destroyed. Local gazetteers provide the official data on the organizations that were destroyed and on the believers who were arrested or transformed (see TABLE 14.1).[89]

This table offers a rough impression of the various sects operating in Chaozhou. The number of Xiantiandao disciples may be incorrect or imply that most disciples escaped the campaign. As discussed above, Xiantiandao was the most influential sect in the area.

By the twentieth century, spirit-writing cults had become widespread in Chaozhou. Most of the cults were small-scale and established spirit-writing altars in private houses. These new cults were centered around certain deities and rapidly spread between villages. While the focus has been on large-scale spirit-writing organizations like charitable halls and temples, it should be noted

---

86   Xu, "Dafeng zushi," 119–57.
87   Shiga, "Difang Daojiao zhi xingcheng," 244.
88   More about this campaign, see Palmer, "Heretical Doctrines," 123–26.
89   *Shantou shi zhi*, 917–18.

TABLE 14.1 Number of organizations destroyed and members arrested

Name	Number of Daotan/Daotang	Number of Leaders	Number of Disciples
Yiguandao	245	17,812 (merged)	
Tongshanshe	14	93	3,795
Xiantiandao	302	296	2,874
Tian'endao	47	140	1,096

that these widespread, small cults formed the basis of the nineteenth-century spirit-writing movement; for example, many spirit-writing altars devoted to Immortal Li Bai 李白 emerged in Chenghai county very quickly, frequently based in small shops.[90]

Local disasters triggered a few new cults. In 1902, when Chaoyang was suffering a prolonged drought, many villagers set up spirit-writing altars to pray for rain.[91] That same year, dozens of city inhabitants formed the Xixin she 洗心社 (Society for Cleaning the Mind) when a plague ravished Jieyang. Initially, this society paid particular attention to public hygiene and worshipped spirit-writing deities on the street. The following year, the deity Zhang Fei 張飛 and the City God instructed the members through the planchette to establish a primary school. Consequently, the Yuxue gongshu 餘學公塾 (Public School of Inherited Teachings) was established to teach the five cardinal relationships (wulun 五倫); namely, ruler-subject (junchen 君臣), father-son (fuzi 父子), husband-wife (fuqi 夫婦), between brothers (xiongdi 兄弟), and between friends (pengyou 朋友).[92] This society also reprinted the scriptures, such as the Xietian dadi mingsheng jing 協天大帝明聖經 (Scripture for illuminating Sageliness by the Great Emperor who assists Heaven).

The reprinting and composition of morality books were the primary activities of the spirit-writing cults, and a few new cults began republishing and reciting the scriptures. In 1896, the Mudao Xianguan 慕道仙館 (Immortal Abode for Seeking the Way) in Shantou republished the Yuhuang zhenjing 玉皇真經 (Perfected scripture of the Jade Emperor), Wendi jiujie baosheng jing 文帝救劫葆生經 (Scripture for protecting life by Wendi to save [humanity] from the apoc-

---

90 "Li Qinglian er wei ren mouli zhi ju hu."
91 "Nongjia shuyao."
92 "Zun shen she jiao."

alypse), and *Wudi jiujie yongming jing* 武帝救劫永命經 (Scripture of longevity by Wudi to save [humanity] from the apocalypse).[93] Each contained a preface that had revealed been by the deity Li Tieguai 李鐵拐 and Bodhisattva Guanyin, respectively, in the Immortal Abode. Then, the first half of the twentieth century witnessed the production of a host of local, spirit-written books. Among the 22 books I have gathered, two were created in the 1900s, three in the 1910s, six in the 1920s, nine in the 1930s, and five in the 1940s.[94] Six were created from 1900 to 1924 and sixteen from 1925 to 1949. Another five books that I cannot currently access were published after 1933, with four in the 1940s. Only ten were created by groups calling themselves *shantang* or *shanshe*.

The current investigative data can supplement these fragmented descriptions based on historical literature. During my fieldwork in Xiashan town,[95] I visited 54 villages and currently creating a detailed record of the local temples. In general, each village has at least one temple. Twenty-four spirit-writing altars and seven *shantang* were discovered (see the appendix), and more than a half of these cults still engage in regular spirit-writing activities. At these altars, the spirit-writing deities differ from those found in Taiwan's phoenix halls, where the divinities are Guansheng dijun 關聖帝君, Fuyou dijun 孚佑帝君, Siming zhenjun 司命真君, Yue Wumuwang 岳武穆王, Xuantian shangdi, Wenchang dijun 文昌帝君, Huoluo lingguan 豁落靈官, and so on.[96] Among the 31 temples in Xiashan, the common deities are Patriarch Lü (8), Li Bai (8), Patriarch Great Peak (7), He Yeyun (4), and Taishang laojun (4). Among the seven *shantang*, six are devoted to Patriarch Great Peak. As shown above, the spirit-writing charitable halls are closely related to the worship of Patriarch Dafeng. In her studies on the spirit-writing movement in Guangdong province, Shiga Ichiko argues that Daoist halls devoted to Patriarch Lü, mainly located in the Pearl River Delta, constituted one of three kinds of organization, but she neglects the important role of the Patriarch Lü cults in Chaozhou. Based on my fieldwork, Patriarch Lü and Li Bai are the most common deities. Further research on the spirit-writing movement in Chaozhou should pay more attention to these cults instead of focusing solely on *shantang*. Nineteen altars/halls have a clear record of their foundation, and nine were established in the 1930s and 40s. Combined with the

---

93 On these scriptures, see also the chapter by Shiga Ichiko in this volume.
94 Three books are counted twice: *Jiujie jindeng* (Golden lamp for saving from the apocalypse, 1903–1904, 1910), *Shanzong baojuan* (Precious scroll for revering goodness, 1919–1920), *Xinbian jiujie baoxun* (1926–1935).
95 Xiashan was located in the east of Chaoyang county. Currently, it is affiliated to Chaonan district 潮南區 and is a new district seat.
96 Wang, *Taiwan de Enzhugong xinyang*, 49–51.

evidence that more local spirit-written books were created from 1925 to 1949, it appears that the zenith of the spirit-writing movement in Chaozhou occurred between 1930 and 1949.

5   Conclusion

Since the 1860s, many spirit-writing cults, especially Patriarch Great Peak cults, established *shantang*, and the first half of the twentieth century witnessed the flourishing of *shantang* in Chaozhou. The popularization of *shantang* was a direct outcome of this new religious movement, and a concrete demonstration of the religious idea that doing good deeds can avert calamities. The link between spirit-writing and *shantang* explains Shiga Ichiko's claim that spirit-writing cults in Chaozhou are usually known by this name. However, *shantang* is merely one type of spirit-writing organization in Chaozhou. Certain cults may be affiliated with specific terms indicating buildings or organizations, but there is no fixed pattern. Even if *shantang* is defined in a broad sense, most spirit-writing organizations cannot be regarded as *shantang*. Also, the composition of organizations called *shantang* exceeded the scope of the spirit-writing cults.

The above instead showed that the charitable halls in Chaozhou were internally diverse and engaged in different religious practices, if any. They can be divided into the four types investigated above: (1) Charitable organizations, which did not originate from spirit-writing cults and were more akin to "secular" organizations that focused on local interests, aimed to reform the local society and improve local welfare through various traditional charitable activities; (2) New spirit-writing cults that were embedded in the local culture, which combined goodness (*shan*) and spirit-writing, and not only contributed to local charitable work but also practised self-cultivation and aimed to save human beings through moral teachings received from deities; (3) Organizations established by sects such as Xiantiandao and Yiguandao, that were very similar to the second type but had their own sectarian thoughts and regulations and were closely associated with other groups in the same sect, forming a network; and (4) Other religious cults that were influenced by the new religious movements and were more similar to local temples.

It should be remembered that these are ideal types and that actual empirical cases may cross these divisions; for example, when a spirit-writing cult begins to shift its attention to charity and eventually changes into a charitable hall, when a charitable hall adds so many more religious functions that its focus of activity shifts, or when a cult replaces spirit mediums (*tongji*) with spirit-writing and introduces more eschatology. These four types also illustrate the historical development and different phases that charitable halls in Chaozhou passed through over time.

The above typology not only indicates the internal diversity of the category of *shantang* but also highlights the blurred boundaries of that category itself. Tan Chee-Beng suggests treating Chaoshan *shantang* as distinct religious organizations. For him, *shantang* refers to a specific combination of charity and religion while the reference to Chaoshan emphasizes the regional character. This approach allows scholars to draw a clear line between *shantang* and other types of associations and so effectively focus on a neatly-defined research subject— namely, organizations that are titled *shantang/shanshe*. However, many religious organizations, such as Buddhist temples, also regularly engage in charitable work. How can we distinguish *shantang* from religious organizations that are involved in charity? This is a key question that must be answered by future studies through considering both their internal and external differences regarding other religious organizations. Moreover, the combination of the charitable hall and phoenix hall was a national trend since the late Qing.[97] While we should emphasize the distinctive features of *shantang* in Chaozhou, it is also important to explore how the national religious trend facilitated the formation of a new "type" of local religious organization.

In conclusion, from the perspective of the nineteenth-century spirit-writing movement, it is misguided to lump Chaozhou's spirit-writing cults together under the shared label of "*shantang*." Instead, it is necessary to distinguish between the names and basic functions of any given organization, which also serves as a reminder to be mindful of the distinction between autonyms and analytical terminology.

Acknowledgements

I wish to thank Prof. Philip Clart for several insightful comments on a previous version of this article, and Elena Valussi and Matthias Schumann, who organized the conference and gave valuable comments.

---

[97] Fan, *Qing mo minjian cishan shiye yu luantang yundong*, 105–12.

Appendix

TABLE 14.2 Spirit-writing Altars and *shantang* in Xiashan Town

Name	Time	Main Deities	Other Deities	Location
Leshan shanshe 樂善善社	1942/1984	Dou Chengyang zushi 竇成陽祖師	Dafeng zushi 大峰祖師, Gushengye 孤聖爺, Zhufo pusa 諸佛菩薩, Xuanzun laozu 玄尊老祖, Mingyue daoren 明月道人, Yunyue zhenren 雲月真人	Xiashan jiedao 峽山街道
Chisong Huang xian ci 赤松黃仙祠	1940s/1997	Huang daxian zushi 黃大仙祖師	Zhang Yu xianshi 張禹仙師, Wang Zhang xianshi 王章仙師	Xiashan jiedao
Yuchan baotan 玉禪寶壇	1962/1999	Baxian 八仙, Jiutian xuannü 九天玄女	Dasheng fozu 大聖佛祖, Daoist deities	Xiashan zhenju 峽山鎮區
Hongji shantang 宏濟善堂	1875/1999	Dafeng zushi	Guhun guizi 孤魂鬼子	Taxiayang 塔下洋
Hede shantang 和德善堂	?/1984	Dafeng zushi	Shengmu niangniang 聖母娘娘, Li Bai xianshi 李白仙師, He Yeyun 何野雲, Guhun guizi, Zhufo pusa	Goutou xiang 溝頭鄉
Xianshi gumiao 仙師古廟	?/2002	Han Zhongli 漢鍾離, Li Tieguai 李鐵拐, Lü Dongbin 呂洞賓	Nanchen beidou 南辰北斗	Xigou xiang 西溝鄉
Xianshi miao 仙師廟		Lilao xianshi 李老仙師		Shangxigou 上西溝
Tianhui xingjun gong 天會星君宮	?/2009	Tianhui xingjun 天會星君	Dafeng zushi	Dongshan xiang 東山鄉
Qinxin tan 勤心壇	?/1984	Li Bai xianshi		Shaxi xiang 沙溪鄉
Lühua ge 呂花閣	1934/1980	Li Chunyang zushi 李純陽祖師, Lü Chunyang zushi 呂純陽祖師	Baxian 八仙, Nanchen beidou	Taoxi xiang 桃溪鄉
Zunhua gong 尊化宮	1940/1993	Li Chunyang zushi, Lü Chunyang zushi	Baxian, Nanchen beidou	Taoxi xiang 桃溪鄉
Dade shantang 大德善堂	?/1989	Dafeng zushi	Gushengye 孤聖爺, Zhufo pusa	Shangdongpu xiang 上東浦鄉
Yuanqiao gong 圓喬宮	?/1995	Tianyi xingjun 天乙星君	Yang Junsong xianshi 楊筠松仙師	Chenhepo xiang 陳禾陂鄉
Chunhua gong 純化宮	?/2013	Lü Chunyang zushi	Li Bai xianshi	Liantang xiang 蓮塘鄉
Zhende shantang 振德善堂	1949/1985	Dafeng zushi	Guhun guizi	Yingdabu xiang 英大埔鄉

TABLE 14.2 Spirit-writing Altars and *shantang* in Xiashan Town (*cont.*)

Name	Time	Main Deities	Other Deities	Location
Shande tang 善德堂	?/2001	Dafeng zushi	Jiutian xuannü 九天玄女, Guanyin niangniang 觀音娘娘	Dazhai xiang 大宅鄉
Xianshi gong 仙師宮	1938/1994	Li Chunyang zushi, Lü Chunyang zushi	Taibai jinxing 太白金星, Wangmu niangniang 王母娘娘	Dazhai xiang
Lezhen gong 樂真宮	1946/1996	Lü Chunyang zushi		Nantian xiang 南田鄉
Nantian tan 南天壇	1940s/1979	Taishang laojun 太上老君		Nantian xiang
Nantian tan 南天壇	1990s	Taishang laojun		Nantian xiang
Qitai tang 齊泰堂	1930s/2005	Qitian dasheng 齊天大聖	Taishang laojun, Guanyin niangniang	Nantian xiang
zhaimen 寨門		Lü Chunyang zushi	Guansheng dijun 關聖帝君	Shanglong xiang 上隴鄉
Qingshan tang 慶善堂	1738/1987	Shengmu niangniang	Guhun guizi, Zhufo pusa, Dadi laoye 大帝老爺	Longmei xiang 隴美鄉
Tianli xianshi 天李仙師	1996	Li Bai xianshi, Yang Tian xianshi 楊天仙師	Baosheng dadi 保生大帝	Yangnei xiang 洋內鄉
Shengmu gumiao 聖母古廟	?/1990	Shengmu niangniang	Li Bai xianshi	Yangnei xiang
Li Bai tang 李白堂	1983	Li Bai xianshi	Xuantian shangdi 玄天上帝	Yangnei xiang
San'guan ge 三觀閣	1996	Yang Junsong xianshi, He Yeyun xianshi, Li Bai xianshi		Renjiatou 人家頭
Zunhua gong 尊化宮	1983	Li Chunyang zushi, Lü Chunyang zushi		Dachao xiang 大潮鄉
Shicheng ge 世誠閣	?/1993	Li Bai xianshi	Damo zushi 達摩祖師, Li Daoming zushi 李道明祖師, Huang Daxian zushi	Dongzhai xiang 東宅鄉
Huanrong tan 歡容壇	?/1993	Yang Zhaowei xianshi 楊兆為仙師	He Yeyun xianshi, Li Chunyang xianshi, Li ningyang xianshi 李凝陽仙師	Sishui xiang 泗水鄉
Penglai xian'ge 蓬萊僊閣	?/1990	Yang Junsong xianshi	Liu Chunfang 柳春芳仙師, He Yeyun xianshi	Sidong xiang 泗東鄉

Bibliography

Broy, Nikolas. "Syncretic Sects and Redemptive Societies: Toward a New Understanding of 'Sectarianism' in the study of Chinese Religions." *Review of Religion and Chinese Society* 2 (2015): 145–85.

Cai Mutong 蔡木通. *Cunxin tangwu (1899–2014)* 存心堂務. Shantou: Cunxin cishanhui 存心慈善會, 2014.

"Chaojun Di er xuanjiangsuo kaimu zhi jisheng 潮郡第二宣講所開幕之紀盛." *Lingdong ribao* 嶺東日報, May 18, 1909.

"Chaojun Furen shantang zhi gailiang 潮郡輔仁善堂之改良." *Lingdong ribao* 嶺東日報, December 4, 1905.

Chaosheng cihang 超生慈航. Shantou: Dongya yinwuju 東亞印務局, 1934.

"Chaoyang xian gongmu yizhong diaocha tongji biao 潮陽縣公墓義塚調查統計表." *Chaoyang xianzheng gongbao* 潮陽縣政公報, no. 5 (1936): 21–35.

Chaoyang xianzhi 潮陽縣志 (*Longqing* 隆慶). Shanghai: Shanghai guji shudian 上海古籍書店, 1963.

"Chaozhou dai zhao Yue Han lu gu zhi huiyi 潮州代招粵漢路股之會議." *Lingdong ribao* 嶺東日報, March 28, 1906.

Chen Jingxi 陳景熙. "Haiwai Huaren zongjiao wenshu yu wenhua chuancheng: Xin Ma Dejiao zixi wenxian (1947–1966) yanjiu 海外華人宗教文書與文化傳承：新馬德教紫系文獻（1947–1966）研究." PhD diss., Zhongshan daxue, 2010.

"Chenghai xian zhengtang wei Cunxin shantang zhi chushi xiaoyu shi bei 澄海縣正堂為存心善堂址出示曉諭事碑." *Shengping wenshi* 昇平文史, no. 1 (1996): 109.

Chenghai xianzhi 澄海縣志. Guangzhou: Guangdong renmin chubanshe, 1992.

Clart, Philip. "The Ritual Context of Morality Books: A Case-Study of a Taiwanese Spirit-Writing Cult." PhD diss., University of British Columbia, 1996.

"Cunxin shantang chengli ji gechu yizhong bei 存心善堂成立及各處義冢碑." *Shengping wenshi* 昇平文史, no. 1 (1996): 110.

"Etang chuxian 惡堂出現." *Lingdong ribao* 嶺東日報, October 7, 1903.

Fan Chun-wu 范純武. *Qing mo minjian cishan shiye yu luantang yundong* 清末民間慈善事業與鸞堂運動. Taipei: Boyang wenhua, 2015.

"Feng shentan chong xuefei 封神壇充學費." *Lingdong ribao* 嶺東日報, December 12, 1904.

Fengshun xianzhi 豐順縣志 (*Guangxu* 光緒). Taipei: Chengwen chubanshe, 1967.

Formoso, Bernard. *De Jiao: A Religious Movement in Contemporary China and Overseas.* Singapore: NUS Press, 2010.

Formoso, Bernard. "From Bone to Ashes: The Teochiu Management of Bad Death in China and Overseas." In *Buddhist Funeral Cultures of Southeast Asia and China*, edited by Paul Williams and Patrice Ladwig, 192–216. Cambridge: Cambridge University Press, 2012.

Formoso, Bernard. "*Hsiu-Kou-Ku*: The Ritual Refining of Restless Ghosts among the Chinese of Thailand." *Journal of the Royal Anthropological Institute*, no. 2 (1996): 217–34.

Fuma Susumu 夫馬進. *Zhongguo shanhui, shantang shi yanjiu* 中國善會善堂史研究. Translated by Wu Yue 伍躍, Yang Wenxin 楊文信 and Zhang Xuefeng 張學鋒. Beijing: Shangwu yinshuguan, 2005.

Goossaert, Vincent. "1898: The Beginning of the End for Chinese Religion." *The Journal of Asian Studies* 65, no. 2 (2006): 307–36.

Goossaert, Vincent. "Modern Daoist Eschatology: Spirit-Writing and Elite Soteriology in Late Imperial China." *Daoism: Religion, History and Society* 道教研究學報：宗教、歷史與社會, no. 6 (2014): 219–46.

Goossaert, Vincent, and Palmer, David A. *The Religious Question in Modern China*. Chicago: University of Chicago Press, 2011.

"Haiyang zizhiju jiyi xiaofang 海阳自治局集议消防." *Lingdong ribao* 嶺東日報, April 30, 1909.

"Ji jun Di er xuanjiangsuo shi 記郡第二宣講所事." *Lingdong ribao* 嶺東日報, May 1, 1909.

"Ji jun weisheng shi 記郡衛生事." *Lingdong ribao* 嶺東日報, May 10, 1909.

"Jiangxu tiaohe xiedou 獎許調和械鬥." *Lingdong ribao* 嶺東日報, July 27, 1904.

Jieyang xian xu zhi 揭陽縣續志 (*Guangxu* 光緒). Taipei: Chengwen chubanshe, 1967.

Jieyang xianzhi 揭陽縣志 (*Yongzheng* 雍正). Beijing: Shumu wenxian chubanshe, 1991.

Jueshi xinpian 覺世新篇. Shanghai: Sida yinshuasuo, 1931.

"Jun shang xiaofanghui binwen 郡商消防會稟文." *Lingdong ribao* 嶺東日報, May 6, 1909.

"Jun shang xiaofanghui yi ju bin 郡商消防會已具稟." *Lingdong ribao* 嶺東日報, May 5, 1909.

"Jun zhong dieci huojing 郡中迭次火警." *Lingdong ribao* 嶺東日報, 28.04.1909.

Katz, Paul R. "'Superstition' and its Discontents: On the Impact of Temple Destruction Campaigns in China, 1898–1948." In *Disi jie guoji Hanxue huiyi lunwenji: xinyang, shijian yu wenhua tiaoshi* 第四屆國際漢學會議論文集：信仰、實踐與文化調適, edited by Kang Bao 康豹 (Paul R. Katz) and Liu Shu-fen 劉淑芬, vol. 2, 605–82. Taipei: Academia Sinica, 2013.

Leung Ki Che 梁其姿. *Shishan yu jiaohua: Ming Qing de cishan zuzhi* 施善與教化：明清的慈善組織. Shijiazhuang: Hebei jiaoyu chubanshe, 2001.

Leung, Angela Ki Che 梁其姿. "Charity, Medicine, and Religion: The Quest for Modernity in Canton (ca. 1870–1937)." In *Modern Chinese Religion*, Pt. II: *1850–2015*, edited by Vincent Goossaert, Jan Kiely, and John Lagerwey, vol. 2, 579–612. Leiden: Brill, 2016.

Lai, Chi-Tim. "The Cult of Spirit-Writing in the Qing: The Daoist Dimension." *Journal of Daoist Studies*, no. 8 (2015): 112–33.

Li Guoping 李國平, Tang Xiaokang 唐曉康, Wu Rongxing 吳榕青, and Yan Jianzhen

顏堅真. "Yuedong yanhai diqu de 'baixinggongma' xinyang yu minsu: yi Huilai xian wei zhongxin 粵東沿海地區的'百姓公媽'信仰與民俗：以惠來縣為中心." *Hanshan shifan xueyuan xuebao* 韓山師範學院學報 35, no. 2 (2014): 10–15.

"Li Qinglian er wei ren mouli zhi ju hu 李青蓮而為人謀利之具乎." *Lingdong ribao* 嶺東日報, December 10, 1904.

Li Qunfeng 李群峰. "Nanyang Dejiao zonghui yanjiu (1956–1995) 南洋德教總會研究（1956–1995）." MA thesis, Ji'nan daxue, 2013.

Lin Juncong 林俊聰. *Chaoshan miao tang* 潮汕廟堂. Guangzhou: Guangdong gaodeng jiaoyu chubanshe, 1998.

Lin Wushu 林悟殊. *Taiguo Dafeng zushi chongbai yu Huaqiao baode shantang yanjiu* 泰國大峰祖師崇拜與華僑報德善堂研究. Taipei: Shuxin chubanshe, 1996.

Lin Xiangxiong 林湘雄 ed. *Chengjing shanshe: Chuangli bainian jinian tekan* 誠敬善社：創立百年紀念特刊. Shantou: Chengjing shanshe fulihui, 2015.

Liu Guixian 劉桂仙. "Wanqing shiqi Chaoshan diqu cishan jiuji shiye 晚清時期潮汕地區慈善救濟事業." MA thesis, Hunan shifan daxue, 2017.

"Lu bi shi 路斃屍." *Lingdong ribao* 嶺東日報, May 13, 1909.

Ma Ximin 馬希民 and Ji Yun 際雲. *Chaoshan shantang daguan* 潮汕善堂大觀. Shantou: Shantou daxue chubanshe, 2001.

"Nongjia shuyao 農家述要." *Lingdong ribao* 嶺東日報, 27.09.1902.

Palmer, David A. "Heretical Doctrines, Reactionary Secret Societies, Evil Cults: Labeling Heterodoxy in Twentieth-Century China." In *Chinese Religiosities: Afflictions of Modernity and State Formation*, edited by Mayfair Mei-hui Yang, 113–34. Berkeley: University of California Press, 2008.

Poon, Shuk-wah. "Buddhist Activism and Animal Protection in Republican China." In *Concepts and Methods for the Study of Chinese Religions III: Key Concepts in Practice*, edited by Paul Katz and Stefania Travagnin, 91–112. Berlin: de Gruyter, 2019.

"Qing jin gengniu chukou 請禁耕牛出口." *Lingdong ribao* 嶺東日報, March 19, 1904.

"Raoping xiedou zhi tiaoting 饒平械鬥之調停." *Lingdong ribao* 嶺東日報, July 18, 1904.

Shantou Chengjing shanshe sheyuan guize 汕頭誠敬善社社員規則. Shantou: *Qichang yinwuju*, 1945.

"Shantou shi cishan tuanti yilanbiao 汕頭市慈善團體一覽表." *Shehui jikan* 社會季刊, no. 1 (1941): 46.

Shantou shi zhi 汕頭市志. Vol. 1. Beijing: Xinhua chubanshe, 1999.

Shi Enyu 石恩宇. "Xiangcun zhili shiye xia de xiandai Chaoshan shantang yanjiu 鄉村治理視野下的現代潮汕善堂研究." MA thesis, Huanan nongye daxue, 2016.

Shiga Ichiko 志賀市子. "Manifestations of Lüzu in Modern Guangdong and Hong Kong: The Rise and Growth of Spirit-writing Cults." In *Daoist Identity: History, Lineage, and Ritual*, edited by Livia Kohn and Harold D. Roth, 185–210. Honolulu: University of Hawai'i Press, 2002.

Shiga Ichiko 志賀市子. "Chūgoku Koanton-shō Tyousuwa chiiki no zendō: zenkyo to kukōron o chūshin ni 中国広東省潮汕地域の善堂——善挙と救劫論を中心に." *Ibaraki Kirisuto-kyō daigaku·kiyō* 茨城キリスト教大学紀要, no. 42 (2008): 41–60.

Shiga Ichiko 志賀市子. "Difang Daojiao zhi xingcheng: Guangdong diqu fuluan jieshe yundong zhi xingqi yu yanbian (1838–1953) 地方道教之形成：廣東地區扶鸞結社運動之興起與演變." *Daoism: Religion, History and Society* 道教研究學報：宗教、歷史與社會, no. 2 (2010): 231–67.

Shiga Ichiko 志賀市子. "Shen yu gui zhijian: Yuedong Hailufeng diqu de yizhong xinyang yu qi yanbian 神與鬼之間：粵東海陸豐地區的義塚信仰與其演變." *Lishi renleixue xuekan* 歷史人類學學刊, no. 2 (2011): 39–64.

Shiga Ichiko 志賀市子. *Xianggang Daojiao yu fuji xinyang: lishi yu rentong* 香港道教與扶乩信仰：歷史與認同. Translated by Song Jun 宋軍. Hong Kong: Chinese University Press, 2013.

Song Dafeng Fozu jiujie zhenjing 宋大峰佛祖救劫真經. Shantou: Shangwu yinshuguan, 1933.

Su Quanyou 蘇全有 and Zhang Chao 張超. "Qingmo xuanjiangsuo tanxi 清末宣講所探析." *Henan ligong daxue xuebao* 河南理工大學學報 15, no. 2 (2014): 201–16.

Su Shaoqin 蘇紹欽. *Tongnian shantang zhi* 同念善堂誌. Chao'an: Tongnian shantang, 2012.

Sun Ting 孫婷. "Qingmo difang zizhi yanjiu 清末地方自治研究." MA thesis, Shandong daxue, 2010.

Tan, Chee-Beng. "*Shantang*: Charitable Temples in China, Singapore, and Malaysia." *Asian Ethnology* 71, no. 1 (2012): 75–107.

"Tongji shantang gaobao 同濟善堂告白." *Lingdong ribao* 嶺東日報, September 12, 1903.

Wang Ermin 王爾敏. "Qingting *Shengyu guangxun* zhi banxing ji minjian zhi xuanjiang shiyi 清廷《聖諭廣訓》之頒行及民間之宣講拾遺." *Jindaishi yanjiusuo jikan* 近代史研究所集刊, no. 22 (1993): 255–76.

Wang Chien-chuan 王見川. *Taiwan de zhaijiao yu luantang* 台灣的齋教與鸞堂. Taipei: Nantian shuju, 1996.

Wang, Chien-chuan 王見川. "Spirit Writing Groups in Modern China (1840–1937): Textual Production, Public Teachings, Charity." In *Modern Chinese Religion*, Pt. II: *1850–2015*, edited by Vincent Goossaert, Jan Kiely, and John Lagerwey, vol. 2, 651–84. Leiden: Brill, 2016.

Wang Zhiyu 王志宇. *Taiwan de Enzhugong xinyang* 台灣的恩主公信仰. Taipei: Wenjin chubanshe, 1997.

Wei Dingming 危丁明. "Zhongguo minjian zongjiao de nan chuan Taiguo: Xiantiandao de anli 中國民間宗教的南傳泰國：先天道的案例." In *Taiguo Huaren zongjiao yanjiu* 泰國華人宗教研究, edited by Chen Jingxi, 20–79. Bangkok: Taiguo Dejiaohui Zizhen'ge.

Weng Zhaorong 翁兆榮 and Xu Zhensheng 許振聲. "Gaishu jiefang qian Chaozhoucheng de cishan tuanti: shantang 概述解放前潮州城的慈善團體：善堂." *Chaozhou wenshi ziliao* 潮州文史資料, no. 8 (1989): 137–52.

Xian Zhenming 冼振明. "Shantou shi cishantuan shilüe 汕頭市慈善團史略." *Shehui jikan* 社會季刊, no. 1 (1941): 14–22.

"Xiang ji Chaojun huiyi dai zhao Yue Han lu gu qingxing 詳紀潮郡會議代招粵漢路股情形." *Lingdong ribao* 嶺東日報, April 2, 1906.

Xinbian jiujie baoxun 新編救劫寶訓. Shantou: Minglixuan, 1936.

Xu Yuan 徐苑. "Dafeng zushi, shantang ji qi yishi: zuowei Chaoshan diqu wenhua tixi de Chaoshan shantang zongshu 大峰祖師、善堂及其儀式：作為潮汕地區文化體系的潮汕善堂綜述." MA thesis, Xiamen daxue, 2006.

"Xuan zhong zhiyi zhi kexiao 懸鐘治疫之可笑." *Lingdong ribao* 嶺東日報, May 18, 1905.

"Xunjingju duiyu jun shang qing she xiaofang zhi pici 巡警局對于郡商請設消防之批詞." *Lingdong ribao* 嶺東日報, May 10, 1909.

Yamada Masaru 山田賢. "'Shan' yu geming: Qingmo minchu de Sichuan difang shehui '善'與革命：清末民初的四川地方社會." Translated by Gu Changjiang 顧長江. *Xinshixue* 新史學, no. 10 (2019): 71–88.

Yang Zhengjun 楊正軍. "Chaoshan diqu de shantang: xiandaihua beijing xia zongjiao fuxing de shetuan yinsu yanjiu 潮汕地區的善堂：現代化背景下宗教復興的社團因素研究." Ph.D. diss., Zhongshan daxue, 2010.

"Yaoyan huozhong zhi Wu Kun bei na 妖言惑眾之吳坤被拿." *Lingdong ribao* 嶺東日報, May 22, 1905.

Yau Chi-on 游子安. *Shanshu yu Zhongguo zongjiao* 善書與中國宗教. Taipei: Boyang wenhua, 2012.

Yushu puhua xinbian 玉書普化新編. Vol. 1. Tangkeng: Wenguang yinwuju, 1944.

Zhang Zubao 張祖寶. "Qingmo Guangdong difang zizhi yanjiu 清末廣東地方自治研究." MA thesis, Ji'nan daxue, 2008.

Zhong Hao 锺浩. "Jiefang qian de xiaofang shanju 解放前的消防善舉." *Shengping wenshi* 昇平文史, no. 1 (1996): 54–55.

Zhu Cunyuan 朱存元. *Zhu xianshi yuanyou ji baojuan* 朱先師緣遊記寶卷. Bang Bua Thong: Tongxuan shantang, 1964.

"Zhu juan Baode shantang jiuhuo zhi yongyue 助捐報德善堂救火之踴躍." *Lingdong ribao* 嶺東日報, April 28, 1909.

"Zun shen she jiao 遵神設教." *Lingdong ribao* 嶺東日報, March 5, 1903.

CHAPTER 15

Spirit-Writing Altars in Contemporary Hong Kong: A Case Study of Fei Ngan Tung Buddhism and Daoism Society

Luo Dan 羅丹

1   Introductory Remarks

The Daoist spirit-writing altar (*fuji daotan* 扶乩道壇)[1] is a crucial feature of Daoism in Hong Kong. Most of these altars moved to Hong Kong from Guangdong 廣東 province during the period from the late Qing Dynasty to the Republican Era for various reasons, such as the chaos caused by war and economic recession.[2] In fact, religious societies focusing on spirit-writing had been playing an active role in Chinese religion at least since the Qing Dynasty, and spirit-writing is still in use in certain societies in Taiwan, Hong Kong, and even Southeast Asia nowadays.[3] These spirit-writing societies (*fuji tuanti* 扶乩團體) are a specific phenomenon of modern and even contemporary Chinese religion and occupy an important place in its development. Anthropologists and historians have already conducted a great deal of research on the history of Chinese religion. Some have also devoted themselves to studying the history of Daoist spirit-writing altars. However, they have paid insufficient attention to how this type of religious society evolved in the contemporary era. The goal of this paper is to reveal the place and pattern of spirit-writing within religious societies, particularly the development of such societies in urban areas, based on the case of the Fei Ngan-tung Daoism and Buddhism Society 飛雁洞佛道社 (hereinafter referred to as FNT) in Hong Kong.

---

1   In Hong Kong, Daoist societies worshipping Lü Chunyang zhenjun 呂純陽真君 (Lüzu) are called *daoguan* 道觀, *daotang* 道堂, *xianguan* 仙觀/館, *daotan* 道壇, or *xianyuan* 仙院. The differences between these terms mainly lie in the scale of organization and housing of these Daoist altars. A Daoist altar (*daotan* 道壇) mainly refers to Daoist altars which are small scale and focus on spirit-writing. Although, in Hong Kong, certain Daoist altars have already grown into large-scale Daoist temples, most of the *daotang* believing in Lüzu remain small-scale halls. To ensure a unified style, in this article, I will use the folk term "Daoist altar" (*daotan*) to refer to these Daoist societies.
2   Lai, Yau, and Wu, *Xianggang Daojiao*, 2–3.
3   Shiga, *Xianggang Daojiao yu fuji xinyang*, 11; Fan, "Qingmo minjian cishan shiye," 8.

Religious societies that practiced spirit-writing (*fuji* 扶乩, *fuji* 扶箕, *fuluan* 扶鸞, *feiluan* 飛鸞) have different designations according to their self-identity and local traditions in different regions. These designations include, for example, *jitan* 乩壇, *luantan* 鸞壇, *daotan*, *shantan* 善壇, *shantang* 善堂,[4] and *luantang* 鸞堂. In fact, since the Republican era, many of these societies have launched various enterprises and changed their identity to gain approval and legitimacy as orthodox religions. They also reveal different development patterns in different regions. There have been many ground-breaking research projects on the development of these societies since the Qing Dynasty.[5] Specific to the case of the Pearl River Delta is the fact that, when "the spirit-writing movement" (*luantang yundong* 鸞堂運動) emerged in the late Qing, spirit-writing based on Lüzu beliefs played a major role in this movement, appearing successively in Guangdong province. While researching the history of Daoist Lüzu altars (*Lüzu daotang* 呂祖道堂) in Guangdong from the late nineteenth to the early twentieth centuries, Shiga Ichiko discovered that, from 1848 to 1947, Lüzu was the main god worshipped at 22 of the 29 Daoist altars in the Pearl River Delta region.[6] The Daoist Lüzu altars, that gained high popularity among believers during the latter half of the nineteenth century in the Pearl River Delta, should be regarded as the integration of a spirit-writing cult with a belief in Lü Dongbin. The formation of these altars can be considered an independent phenomenon, which exemplifies how modern Daoism developed in Guangdong.[7]

From the late nineteenth century to date, Daoist Lüzu altars use spirit-writing to clarify divine messages, to promote the publication of morality books, and to assist with philanthropy. Apart from their individual moral obligations, the members of these Daoist Lüzu altars adopt the same approach as the members of charity halls (*shantang*).[8] Charity halls reached a peak during an outbreak of the plague in 1894. Following the panic caused by the plague, several spirit-writing altars started to play an active role in Hong Kong and

---

4   On *shantang* and their link to spirit-writing, see the contribution by Li Guoping to this volume.
5   See, for example, Jordan and Overmyer, *Flying Phoenix*, and its later Chinese translation, Jiao and Ou, *Feiluan*. See also Shahar, *Crazy Ji*; Clart, "The Ritual Context of Morality Books"; Clart, "Chinese Tradition and Taiwanese Modernity," 84–97; Wang, "Qingmo Minchu Zhongguo de Jigong xinyang yu fuji tuanti," 139–69; Katz, "Spirit-writing Halls and the Development of Local Communities," 103–84.
6   Shiga, *Xianggang Daojiao yu fuji xinyang*, 146–48.
7   Lai, *Guangdong difang Daojiao yanjiu*, 114–19.
8   Ibid., 118. For a detailed distinction between spirit-writing halls and *shantangs*, see Li Guoping in this volume.

Guangdong and began to organize philanthropic activities following instructions obtained through spirit-writing. After the plague abated, in the early twentieth century, these spirit-writing altars gradually expanded their membership, organized regular activities, and finally established Daoist altars.[9] Among these spirit-writing altars, the history of the Sing Kung Cho Tong 省躬草堂,[10] the Puji Altar 普濟壇,[11] and the Yushan tang 與善堂[12] have been described in detail. This developmental pattern, progressing from a spirit-writing society to a charitable organization to a Daoist society, is typical of many Daoist groups which established altars in Hong Kong.

From the late Qing Dynasty to the early Republican Era, following the trend of "appropriating temple property to establish schools" (*miaochan xingxue* 廟產興學) and eradicating superstition, the government of the Republic of China in Nanjing 南京 began to implement policies that strengthened the governance and banned superstition and popular religion. In 1928, the Ministry of Internal Affairs promulgated "Measures for Eliminating Divination and Astrology" (*feichu zhanshi xingxiang wuxi kanyu banfa* 廢除占筮星象巫覡堪輿辦法) and "Standards for the Preservation and Abolition of Shrines" (*shenci cunfei biaozhun* 神祠存廢標準), and organized nationwide campaigns to eradicate superstition. The Nationalist Government of Guangzhou took a leading role in this trend. In July 1929, the Guangzhou Government founded a Guangzhou Customs Reform Committee (Guangzhou shi fengsu gaige weiyuanhui 廣州市風俗改革委員會) that was solely responsible for eradicating superstitious activities.[13]

During this period, many Daoist altars in Guangdong were banned by the government and found it difficult to maintain their normal operations. For this reason, they moved to Hong Kong or established branch altars in Hong Kong.[14] Following the regime change in China in 1949, even more Daoist altars moved

---

9   Shiga, "Yibajiusi nian suigang diqu de shuyi," 1–3.
10 For an analysis of the management strategies of Hong Kong Daoist altars, see Shiga, "Jindai Guangzhou de daotang," 307–33. For more details on the early historical stage of the Sing Kung Cho Tong, see Leung, "Daotang hu? Shantang hu?" 394–434.
11 Shiga, *Xianggang Daojiao yu fuji xinyang*, 211–12.
12 Lai, *Guangdong difang Daojiao yanjiu*, 118–19.
13 On this society and the situation at the time in Guangzhou in general, see Poon, *Negotiating Religion in Modern China*.
14 Several Daoist altars moved to Hong Kong between 1910 and the 1930s; e.g., Wong Tai Sin Temple 黃大仙祠 (later, Sik Sik Yuen 嗇色園 became its managing institution), Po Tho Tong 抱道堂, Fung Ying Seen Koon 蓬瀛仙館, Yuhu xiandong 玉壺仙洞, Tung Sin Tan 通善壇, Fok Hing Tong, the Hong Kong Society for the Promotion of Virtue 道德會福慶堂, etc. See Yau, *Daofeng bainian*; Liang, *Liwu jishi*; Lai, Yau, and Wu, *Xianggang Daojiao*.

to Hong Kong. As representatives of these Daoist altars, both Sik Sik Yuen 嗇色園 and Po Tho Tong 抱道堂 were founded in 1921, Fung Ying Seen Koon 蓬瀛仙館 in 1929, Tung Sin Tan 通善壇 in 1938, Wun Chuen Sin Kwoon 云泉仙觀 in 1944, Ching Chung Koon 青松觀 in 1950, and the Yuen Yuen Institute 圓玄學院 in 1953. Those Daoist Lüzu altars, that had moved to Hong Kong from their ancestral halls in Guangdong, later became the pillars of Hong Kong Daoism. The special political environment in Hong Kong, and the implementation of the separation of church and state and freedom of religion by the British Colonial Government, enabled these Daoist spirit-writing altars to maintain their original religious form.[15]

At an early stage, the majority of the Daoist Lüzu altars in Hong Kong were "managed through spirit-writing" (*yi ji zhi tan* 以乩治壇). Spirit-writing was the major activity of these Daoist altars and guided their development, with all major administrative decisions being taken through spirit-writing.[16] Initially, most of the Daoist altars belonged to small religious societies and were neither open to the public nor practiced Daoist rituals. According to research by historians of Daoism in Hong Kong, prior to the 1950s, Daoist altars in Hong Kong engaged in spirit-writing as their major activity and would only practice public rituals (*fashi* 法事) on the birthdays of gods and during liturgical services (*fahui* 法會) (such as the Qingming Festival 清明法會 on the fourth day of the forth month and the Zhongyuan Festival 中元法會 on the fifteen of the seventh month). Most of their rituals, however, were Buddhist in form and adopted the vocal chanting style of Buddhism (*Shijia* 釋家). Except in a very few cases, most of the Daoist altars had not yet developed nor practiced Daoist rituals.[17]

This situation continued until the Ching Chung Koon appeared in the 1950s. As recorded in *Baosong baohe ji* 寶松抱鶴記 (The history of the Precious Pine and Crane Temple),[18] He Qizhong 何啟忠 (1916–1968), the founder of Ching Chung Koon, learned spirit-writing at a young age. In 1941, he founded a spirit-writing altar named Zhibao tai 至寶台 in Guangzhou, and later became a disciple of a Daoist of the 23rd generation master of the Longmen 龍門 Lineage of Quanzhen 全真, receiving an official certificate (*dudie* 度牒) for Daoists,

---

15 Lai, Yau, and Wu, *Xianggang Daojiao*, 19 and 24.
16 Ibid., 26.
17 Tung Sin Tan, a Daoist society in Hong Kong, which originated from the Chashan qingyun dong 茶山慶雲洞 in Nanhai of Guangdong, inherited the Daoist rituals of its ancestral altar in Chashan when it was founded in 1938, but these Daoist rituals were not handed down to later generations, because the Daoist altar kept them secret from the outside world. On Daoist altars in Hong Kong practicing Buddhist rituals, see Lai, Yau, and Wu, *Xianggang Daojiao*, 124; Lai, Yau, and Wu, *Xianggang daotang keyi*, 40–42.
18 Yi, *Baosong baohe ji*.

issued by the Yingyuan gong 應元宮 in 1944.[19] That same year, he founded the Zhibao lineage 至寶派, a new lineage of Quanzhen Daoism, with new generation names,[20] following divine instructions from Lüzu. Through spirit-writing, He Qizhong claimed that this lineage was one and the same with the Longmen school.[21]

That same year also, Hou Baoyuan 侯寶垣 (1914–1999), the abbot of Ching Chung Koon, later joined the Zhibao tai, and received his ordination name by following the Bao 寶 generation of Zhibao lineage, as indicated by divine messages. We can speculate that the orthodox Daoist concepts advocated by Zhibao tai and its identification with the Quanzhen School had a significant influence on Hou Baoyuan. When he later took charge of the Daoist rituals at Ching Chung Koon, he insisted on adopting Quanzhen Daoist rituals (Quanzhen Daojiao keyi 全真道教科儀), to distinguish Ching Chung Koon from other Daoist altars in Hong Kong, which primarily practiced Buddhist rituals. In the 1950s, Hou Baoyuan visited Daoist temples in various regions in order to search for scripture texts, gathered new disciples by holding training sessions every year and also invited famous ritual masters (*gaogong fashi* 高功法師) in Hong Kong to teach the disciples Daoist rituals and nurture scripture-reciters.[22] At that time, Ching Chung Koon was not the only Daoist altar that claimed a Quanzhen School origin. Some of the Daoist altars that were founded before the 1950s also emphasized that they had an identity and origin associated with Quanzhen; for instance, Foon Ying Seen Koon[23] and Yuk Wu Sin Tung

---

19   As for the official certificate for Daoists that He Qizhong received in the Yingyuan gong, in Shiga Ichiko's opinion, according to the situation at that time, it is hard to imagine that Yingyuan gong could have established a consecration ritual to grant an official certificate to Daoists. For this reason, Shiga Ichiko is suspicious about how He Qizhong received his official certificate. See Shiga, *Xianggang Daojiao yu fuji xinyang*, 253–54.

20   The lineage poem for the Zhibao lineage at that time was: *zhi bao tai qian fa dao gen* 至寶台前發道根, *shan yuan guang jie jiu fan ren* 善緣廣結救凡人, *jiu mei zun xun shi zu xun* 九美遵循師祖訓, *gong cheng xing man ke chao shen* 功成行滿可超身. See Yi, *Baosong baohe ji*, 159–160.

21   Ibid.

22   On the history of Daoist rituals in Hong Kong, see Lai, Yau, and Wu, *Xianggang daotang keyi*.

23   Founded in 1929 in Fanling, Foon Ying Seen Koon was jointly founded by He Jinyu 何近愚, Chen Luankai 陳鸞楷 (who were Daoists of the Longmen lineage), and Mai Xingjie 麥星階, Abbot of Sanyuan gong 三元宮 in Guangzhou, for the purpose of establishing a genuine, tranquil venue for practicing the Longmen lineage. Initially, Daoists could practice by themselves in Foon Ying Seen Koon. Since the founding of this Daoist temple to date, disciples in Foon Ying Seen Koon have always declared themselves to be the inheritors of Longmen. Currently, no documents have been found that confirm that Mai Xingjie, Abbot of Sanyuan gong in Guangzhou, used to teach Daoist rituals in Hong Kong, nor that Mai

玉壺仙洞.[24] However, these Daoist altars did not place emphasis on Daoist rituals, instead chanting the scriptures and holding dharma assemblies according to Buddhist rituals. It was only after Ching Chung Koon appeared in the early 1950s that the concept of "Quanzhen Daoist rituals" arose among Daoist altars. The founding of Ching Chung Koon and the development of its Daoist rituals had an undeniable influence on the Hong Kong Daoist altars and their ability to practice "Quanzhen Daoist rituals."

From the late 1960s to the 1970s, the Daoist altars in Hong Kong adjusted their pattern of religious services to satisfy the demands of the urban residents and began to conduct funeral services.[25] In this context, Daoist rituals became more widely employed. As the Quanzhen Daoist rituals achieved maturity, many Daoist altars were faced with the task of transforming their management patterns. Moreover, it was difficult to find a spirit-writing practitioner (*jishou* 乩手) who could receive instructions from the gods competently, which resulted in a decline in the practice of spirit-writing in Hong Kong.[26] Spirit-writing, as the cornerstone of many Daoist altars, gradually declined and its importance decreased. Many Daoist altars even ceased the practice of spirit-writing altogether.[27] It appears that the development of the Daoist rituals enabled many Daoist societies in Hong Kong to complete the transition from spirit-writing altars to Daoist altars (*daotan*).

The object of this paper, Fei Ngan Tung, is a spirit-writing altar that was founded against this historical background. In the following pages, I will pres-

---

Xingjie and the other founders took scripture books from the Sanyuan gong to Hong Kong but, according to some records, Sanyuan gong kept several scripture books at Foon Ying Seen Koon during World War II, the nature of which remains unknown.

24 Yuk Wu Sin Tung was founded in 1932. Its ancestral hall is the Leshan tang 樂善堂 in Shunde. Before the 1950s, this Daoist hall merely focused on spirit-writing, but it emphasized that it also belongs to the Longmen branch of the Quanzhen School.

25 According to Shiga's analysis, when Daoist societies began to conduct funeral and merit rituals, they realized the dominant position of *Nanmolao* 喃嘸佬 (the Zhengyi at-home Daoist ritual specialists in the Pearl River Delta region) in this field. To clarify that they did not belong to the same category as *Nanmolao*, Daoist societies have taken several measures, including training scripture-reciters, placing emphasis on their amateur nature, and using specific concepts and labels, e.g., "civil merits singing" (*wenchang gongde* 文唱功德) vs. "military merits singing" (*wuchang gongde* 武唱功德) and the "Quanzhen School" vs the "Zhengyi School," to demonstrate their orthodoxy. See Shiga, *Xianggang Daojiao yu fuji* xinyang, 293.

26 In 1988, Zhongli 鍾離 transmitted a divine text at the Yuqing bieguan 玉清別館: "It is difficult to look for *luansheng*" (鸞生難求); see *Xuanyin hekan*, 515.

27 No specific statistics are available regarding the exact number of Daoist altars that suspended spirit-writing, but it appears that Fung Ying Seen Koon, Wong Tai Sin Temple, the Yuen Yuen Institute, and Xinggong caotang did so in the 1970s.

ent the most important events in FNT's history which reveal the significance of spirit-writing in this society, including the founding of the society, the introduction of Daoist rituals to the altar and the confirmation of its Daoist origin through a field visit to Sichuan 四川. After reviewing the main history of FNT, I will describe the spirit-writing ritual, how it is practiced today, and the role it plays for believers. I intend to focus on this case study in order to reveal the main factors that have shaped the development of this contemporary spirit-writing society.

2   The Birth of a Spirit-Writing Altar

Daoist Lüzu altars not only successfully transplanted their original form of organization in the Pearl River Delta to Hong Kong, but also developed into Daoist groups with unique Hong Kong characteristics.[28] In the late 1970s, the Hong Kong economy began to thrive and all trades flourished, as the city transformed into an international metropolis. As the process of urbanization accelerated, the Daoist altars in Hong Kong began to adjust their religious services to suit the needs of the citizens. They developed in parallel with the evolution into a modern society, and it was against such a background that FNT came into being.

After the end of the Vietnam War in 1975, a large number of Vietnamese refugees fled their homeland. In May 1975, Hong Kong accepted the first batch of Vietnamese refugees, comprising 3,743 people in total, and established transit centers to assist these refugees to settle abroad. However, from the late 1970s, the refugee flow became a more serious problem so, in July 1979, the British Hong Kong government signed an international convention on refugees in Geneva. This convention stipulated that certain Southeast Asian countries and regions, including Hong Kong, would be listed as "First-Tier Asylums," that should accept Vietnamese refugees unconditionally for the time being.[29] For this reason, refugees who escaped from Vietnam would be accepted by the Hong Kong government first, after which the refugees' status would be screened by Western countries in order to determine their resettlement destination. Between 1975 and 1978, more than 100,000 Vietnamese refugees, mainly from South Vietnam, arrived in Hong Kong.[30] They were intellectuals and Chinese people residing in Vietnam, with a high economic status.

---

28   Lai, Yau, and Wu, *Xianggang Daojiao*, 32–45.
29   Yang, Ye, and Zhu, *Yuenan chuanmin zai Xianggang*, 1.
30   Ibid., 2.

Our story begins in 1979, in a refugee camp on Argyle Street 亞皆老街, where police officers from correctional institutions and nurses would often amuse themselves by studying divination and fortune-telling in their spare time. An ethnically Chinese refugee from Vietnam (who called himself Master Ming 明道長) lived in the refugee camp. One day, he saw police officers practicing divination, and informed them that he could invite his patriarch to tell their fortune. The police officers were skeptical about this and tested him by asking him a few questions. To their surprise, Master Ming correctly answered them all. At that time, Master Ming was around twenty-one or twenty-two years of age. He told the police officers that he had adopted Lüzu (Lü Dongbin) as his patriarch while still in Vietnam and could communicate with the gods. Lüzu once told him that he must remain single throughout his life, and that this would make it easier for him to receive their messages. Later, about thirty Hong Kong people began to flock around Master Ming. They would gather in the refugee camp every Sunday and ask Master Ming to seek solutions to their problems, and some even asked Master Ming to heal their illnesses.

A police officer who often participated in these meetings told his relative, Liu Songfei 劉松飛 (1930–2021), the wondrous story of Master Ming. Liu was working for *The Kung Sheung Daily News* 工商日報 at that time. He had become a disciple of Daoism at a Daoist altar in mainland China at a young age and took a great interest in Daoism and prophecy. One Sunday, accompanied by one of his relatives, Liu visited the refugee camp to meet Master Ming, and asked him a few questions at their first meeting. After welcoming the gods (*qingshen* 請神), Master Ming answered each of Liu's questions, and each of his answers proved correct. Since then, Liu Songfei began visiting the refugee camp every Sunday to see Master Ming. As Liu recalled later, when Master Ming welcomed the gods, he did not need to face the statues of the gods, but merely recited their names silently. When the gods descended, Master Ming would lose consciousness, and "the gods would give answers to people's questions via Master Ming's tongue" (仙佛藉著其口舌). It was thus a form of spirit-possession.

In December 1979, as an increasing number of local people began to have faith in Master Ming, he suddenly declared that Lüzu had some oracles for them. He invited them to visit a villa in Sai Kung Nam Wai 西貢南圍 at 8 p.m. on the 16th day of the first lunar month of 1980 and required them to fast and perform their ablutions beforehand. On that day, around 30 Hong Kong people visited Master Ming in the villa and waited for Lüzu to descend. At 8 p.m., Master Ming suddenly declared that Lüzu had descended to the altar, and he spoke out loud: "I will establish Fei Ngan Tung in Hong Kong for worshipping the Three Gods of Cizun" (香港要創辦飛雁洞，用以供奉慈尊三帝).[31] Then he asked the people on the spot, "Who's Liu Songfei?" (誰是劉松飛？)[32] Liu stood up and said, "I am," (我是) but he did not know why Master Ming had inquired about him. Master Ming, pointing at Liu, declared, "You're designated by Master Lüzu as the abbot of FNT." (呂祖仙師指定你擔任飛雁洞的主持。) Liu was astounded, being completely unprepared for this appointment. Seeing Liu's hesitation, Master Ming allowed him to consider the matter for 15 minutes. After mulling it over for a while, Liu finally agreed to become the abbot of FNT.

Afterwards, Master Ming, on the instruction of Lüzu, appointed a Mr. Zheng, the owner of a local enterprise, as the deputy abbot. Mr. Zheng joined the meeting, those present testified, at the same moment as Lüzu announced the arrival of the future deputy abbot.

While Liu Songfei remained confused about how to run a Daoist altar, Master Ming's refugee status was confirmed by the government, meaning that he would soon emigrate to Canada. This was undoubtedly a great shock to Liu, but Master Ming told him that, before arriving in Hong Kong, he had already promised Lüzu that he would establish FNT in Hong Kong and had now fulfilled his task. Master Ming gave Liu a couple of divining blocks (*bubei* 卜杯) on behalf of Lüzu, and told him that if there was anything that he could not understand, he would seek the advice of Lüzu through these, or practice spirit-writing. Liu tried out the divining blocks and, in response, Lüzu told him that he did not understand how to run a Daoist altar, and that he could seek advice from Ching Chung Koon concerning religious affairs, and from the gods regarding the internal affairs within the organization.

Later, following Lüzu's advice, Liu selected 18 people from Master Ming's 30-odd followers to form a Board of Directors for FNT. They rented a 400 square foot room on Fu Yan Street 輔仁街 in Kwun Tong 觀塘[33] in which to worship the Three Gods of Cizun. During the early days of FNT, these 18 people would each pay a 60 HKD per month membership fee to cover the room rent and other

---

31 As introduced by FNT, the Three Gods of Cizun are Guansheng dijun 關聖帝君, Fuyou dijun 孚佑帝君, and Wenchang dijun 文昌帝君. The Three Gods of Cizun are also worshipped in the Qingyun nanyuan of Ho Chi Minh, where they accompany the god Cihang daoren 慈航道人 in the main hall. See Wang, "Yuenan fangdao yanjiu."

32 As recalled by Liu Songfei, Master Ming did know Liu Songfei's name.

33 Being an industrial zone of Hong Kong, religious activities in Kwun Tong attracted the attention of scholars, who began to conduct investigations in this region in the 1980s to learn more about the traditional Chinese religious customs there. These investigations, however, did not cover the institutional religious groups, such as the Buddhist and Daoist groups. See Mai, "Chengshi gongye huanjing," 252–65.

petty expenses. In fact, all the fees paid by the board members were kept by the property owner in a donation box on the altar, because he had been cured of asthma by Master Ming through a "talisman throwing spell."[34]

After the establishment of FNT, Liu Songfei invited Master Yi 易道長 from Ching Chung Koon, to be the main spirit writing practitioner (*jishou*) of FNT. At that time, Master Yi was 91 years old, but appeared well, both physically and mentally. He would arrive at the altar every Sunday to practice spirit-writing and answer the disciples' questions.[35] In FNT's initial stage, its key activity was spirit-writing.[36]

After Master Yi started working for FNT, at the end of 1980, he received a divine message from Lüzu, instructing FNT on the directions and principles for conducting religious activities in the future: "If you gather strength, the treasure cave will last forever. If you want to promote and enhance the religious message, first incite and push public interest. The most important thing is coming together; it is here that strength lies." (團結力量，寶洞永存，若要弘揚法顯，推崇眾意為先，團結者為貴，力量在斯。)[37]

Another divine message also indicated that the scale of FNT must be expanded and that further branches should be established.[38] Such divine messages made Liu Songfei and other disciples feel more confident about running the Daoist altar, and they determined to strengthen the position of spirit-writing within it. From 1980 onward, Liu and the FNT disciples began to determine the nature of the routine activities at FNT. Spirit-writing would be practiced every other day and disciples and followers were eligible to seek advice and receive spiritual healing for free from FNT.

Spirit-writing activities were carried out smoothly at FNT, but the Board of Directors suffered from internal divisions. After a year, 16 board members left FNT in quick succession, leaving only Liu Songfei and Mr. Zheng. Liu speculated that those members had left due to dissatisfaction with the divine mes-

---

34　According to Liu Songfei, "throwing a talisman" (*feifu* 飛符) means using the healer's own spiritual power to transmit the talisman to a remote place or person for the purpose of healing his/her disease or rescuing him/her from suffering without the need to draw talismans face-to-face.
35　Master Yi's full name was Yi Daoling 易道陵. Liu Songfei and the others in FNT knew little about Master Yi, apart from the fact that he was elderly when he passed away, several years later.
36　Informant: Mr. Zheng, date: 4/08/2011, venue: FNT.
37　This divine message was provided by FNT.
38　Informant: Liu Songfei, date: 15/12/2010, venue: FNT. I could not find this divine message during my fieldwork at FNT.

sages that had appointed him and Mr. Zheng as abbot and deputy abbot.[39] At that point, FNT was merely a loose organization, being a spirit-writing group supported by Liu Songfei and a few disciples, who used to seek advice from Master Ming. For this reason, whenever there was a festival, FNT members would contribute money and dine together, maintaining their friendly relationship.

However, as the efficacy of FNT's spirit-writing messages became more widely known, and because FNT did not charge for its services, an increasing number of people visited FNT to obtain instructions from the gods and seek medical treatment. Still, some disciples suspected that FNT was poorly managed and questioned the whereabouts of the donations. Some people even suspected that FNT was a fraudulent organization. For this reason, Liu Songfei became determined to provide FNT with legal status. Thus, FNT, as a newly-established Daoist altar, was registered under the Companies Ordinance of Hong Kong and, on June 11, 1982, "Fei Ngan Tung Buddhism and Daoism Society" was founded.[40] Meanwhile, based on the instructions contained in the divine messages, Liu declared FNT to be an altar that practiced both Daoism and Buddhism.[41] However, I was unable to find the divine message, which indicated that disciples should practice both Daoism and Buddhism, in FNT's internal publications of the early 1980s.

---

39 Informant: Liu Songfei, date: 28/03/2011, venue: Fei Ngan Tung.
40 Initially, Chinese religious venues (*Huaren zongjiao changsuo* 華人宗教場所) had to be registered with the Chinese Affairs Office of the Hong Kong government and keep records in accordance with the "1928 Regulations for Chinese Temples" (*Huaren miaoyu tiaoli* 華人廟宇條例). See "Huaren miaoyu tiaoli." For example, in the 1920s and 1930s, Wong Tai Sin Temple closed its doors and refused to allow believers in to worship the gods to evade this regulation. Since the 1950s, several Daoist temples in Hong Kong began to apply to the government authorities to be registered as a legal entity and obtain the title of "limited company." Later, several Daoist altars in succession were registered as limited companies. Several Daoist altars even successfully registered themselves as non-profit, charitable organizations and received a tax exemption qualification; for example, Yuen Yuen Institute registered as a limited company in 1956; Wong Tai Sin Temple became a legal entity in 1965; and Fung Ying Seen Koon registered as a limited company in 1972. Today, religious altars in Hong Kong can register in accordance with the Companies Ordinance (Gongsi fa 公司法) of Hong Kong and operate and develop in accordance with the law. See Lai, Yau, and Wu, *Xianggang Daojiao*, 161; Ngai, Zhong, and Yau, *Xiangjiang xianji*; Ngai, "Xianggang de chuantong zongjiao guanli," 35–44; Lang and Ragvald, "Upward Mobility of a Refugee God," 54–87.
41 Informant: Liu Songfei, date: 15/12/2010. Identical information was provided by Mr. Zheng.

3   From a New Spirit-Writing Altar to a New Daoist Altar

FNT was registered as the "Fei Ngan Tung Buddhism and Daoism Society" under the leadership of Liu Songfei, and a Board of Directors was also established to manage this newly established Daoist society.[42] These measures reassured the members who had previously doubted the legality of FNT. After that, because of its spirit-writing ritual, which also built its religious reputation, FNT attracted more supporters. Some of them firmly believed in the efficacious power of Lüzu and wanted to become disciples of FNT. Then, in the mid-1980s, FNT welcomed its first batch of disciples. According to the divine messages from Lüzu, ordination names (*daohao* 道號) were given to these disciples, based on their generational status in FNT. In total, six generations were represented by six names: "Dao 道," "De 德," "Wen 文," "Zhang 章," "Chong 崇," and "Gao 高," and each of them was conferred to 100 disciples. The 18 people who established the FNT Board of Directors belonged to the "Dao" generation.[43] The first batch of disciples belonged to the "De" generation, and they received Daoist monastic names based on the Chinese characters transmitted through divine messages. By 2012, the disciples of FNT had been ranked down to the "Gao" generation, but very few disciples of the "De" generation remained, apart from three to four core members, who would still often handle the routine affairs of the Daoist society.

In the mid-1980s, Master Yi, advanced in age, left his job as the *jishou* of FNT, and Master Peng 彭道長, a Daoist who originally worked for Tung Sin Tan, was invited to assume the post. At that time, FNT received a divine message from Lüzu, requiring them to start the recitation of litanies (*baichan* 拜懺). There was no scripture-reciter (*jingsheng* 經生) in FNT, however, who could practice Daoist rituals. Uncertain on how to proceed, Liu Songfei recalled the instructions of Lüzu when FNT was founded, "to seek advice from Ching Chung Koon if there was anything that he could not understand" (道堂不懂的地方可以去請教青松觀). Liu used to visit Ching Chung Koon himself, attending Daoist rituals, and had become acquainted with the Daoists there. Therefore, he phoned Hou Baoyuan, the abbot of Ching Chung Koon, and asked whether it was possible for him to learn Daoist rituals from Ching Chung Koon, and whether Hou could give him some scriptures. Hou agreed, and Liu sent two disciples to Ching Chung Koon to fetch the scriptures. His disciples returned with a sheet of paper,

---

42   In Hong Kong, more than 100 religious societies registered as members of the Hong Kong Taoist Association, with four of them being named a "Daoism and Buddhism Society," including FNT.

43   Today, Mr. Zheng, the deputy abbot, is the only disciple of the "Dao" generation remaining at FNT.

however, with very few scriptures printed on it, which left Liu feeling disappointed and frustrated, since he had expected to receive a box full of scriptures from Ching Chung Koon.

Fortunately for FNT, Ching Chung Koon sent a ritual master Lu 盧 to assist FNT. In 1985, after receiving donations from disciples and believers, FNT purchased real-estate on Fu Yan Street 輔仁街, which became FNT's head-quarters. That same year, following spirit-written instructions, FNT began to invite Master Lu to recite litanies at the altar on the first and fifteenth day of each month. Whenever Master Lu recited litanies, some of the disciples of FNT, mostly women, would kneel outside the altar and kowtow. The recitation of litanies has been practiced at the altar ever since. In 1987, Master Lu, who was well-acquainted with some of the women disciples of the "De 德" generation, asked them, "Since you've knelt down and kowtowed, why don't you learn how to practice Daoist rituals by yourselves?" (既然跟著跪拜，為什麼不學習經識呢？) They agreed and thought that if they could master the procedures of Daoist rituals, they would not require the help of others. They informed Liu Songfei of their wish, and Liu offered them support. Soon after, they began to learn the Daoist rituals from Master Lu.

Among these disciples, a female named De Quan 德全 later became a right-hand assistant to Liu Songfei, and a master of Daoist rituals. Now all of the disciples in the society call De Quan their master leader (*da shixiong* 大師兄). De Quan is responsible for training the disciples in Daoist rituals and providing ritual services for believers. De Quan's original name is Jian Xiaojuan 簡小娟 (a pseudonym). In the 1980s, she was a weaver in a sweater factory in Hong Kong. In 1986, a significant change happened in her life, which made her feel depressed, so "she needed a harbor to shelter her emotions" (心情上需要一個避風港).[44] Introduced by a friend, she went to FNT, hoping to find solutions to her problems via spirit-writing, and obtained several divine messages from Lüzu. After reading them, she felt relieved, and her mood improved. After that, she often visited FNT and asked to become a disciple. After asking Lüzu via divining blocks, Liu Songfei granted her request. Jian Xiaojuan and a few other female disciples joined FNT, and she was given the ordination name De Quan. At that time, she was 30-years old. After participating in FNT for more than two decades, in 2012, De Quan explained that she had remained at FNT because "she is unwilling to move around" (她不願意到處走). This was just like in the past, when she worked in the sweater factory and remained there until it went out of business. If we review her experiences at FNT, however, we discover that she

---

44   Informant: De Quan, date: 14/10/2012, venue: FNT.

did not leave FNT like other disciples did, not only because of her attachment to this Daoist society, but also because of the vital role that she had played in developing Daoist rituals for FNT.

In the 1980s, when De Quan and a few other female disciples decided to study Daoist rituals, due to the growth of the economy in Hong Kong, an increasing number of citizens began to invite ritual experts to conduct ritual services for merit (*gongde fashi* 功德法事) for the deceased, or rituals for the deliverance (*chaodu yishi* 超度儀式) of ancestors. Since many of the Daoist altars in Hong Kong began to conduct rituals for ordinary people in the 1970s, their income also increased, as the general public's demand for these services soared. Hence, the income generated by the Daoist ritual services occupied an increasingly higher proportion among the sources of funds of the Daoist altars. From the example of Tung Sin Tan provided by Shiga Ichiko, it appears that sixty percent of Tung Sin Tan's income in 1987 came from *gongde fashi*, the celebration of the birthdays of gods, and ancestor tablets (*zuxian paiwei* 祖先牌位). As for Daoist altars that conducted more *gongde fashi*, such as Ching Chung Koon, Fung Ying Seen Koon 蓬瀛仙館 and the Yuen Yuen Institute, their income from this activity accounted for an even higher proportion.[45] Before establishing FNT, Liu Songfei used to worship gods at the Song Yin Yuan Buddhism and Daoism Society 松蔭園佛道社, and Ching Chung Koon, and participated in Daoist rituals there, so he had some knowledge of the *gongde fashi* held by Daoist societies in Hong Kong, but the income of FNT prior to that had relied solely on donations by believers and disciples, and was relatively unstable. Liu had clearly realized that obtaining a stable income by providing requiem services for believers was extremely important to the operation and development of FNT. This was certainly one of the reasons why he supported De Quan's plan to study Daoist rituals.

Another reason why FNT incorporated Daoist rituals was their ambition to be perceived as a legitimate religious organization. In Hong Kong at that time, the practices of Maoshan Daofa 茅山道法 and Liuren shengong 六壬神功, which were said to be passed down from Maoshan and based on a belief in the Liuren xianshi 六壬仙師 (the transcendent masters of the six *ren*), were very popular. They were also referred to as "spirit boxing" (*shenda* 神打) and "divine skills" (*shengong* 神功).[46] However, it was common to see people being "pos-

---

45   See Shiga, *Xianggang Daojiao yu fuji xinyang*, 124–25.
46   These two practices are widespread in Hong Kong and usually thought to have originated from Qingzhujiao 青竹教 (The Teaching of Green Bamboo) on Mount Mao or Liurenjiao 六壬教 (The Teaching of Six *ren*) and Youminjiao 遊民教 (The Teaching of Yau Man). Qingzhujiao was founded by Hu Rong 胡容 (no dates), a Hakka person whose ancestors

sessed by demons" (走火如魔) and experiencing life-threatening experiences after practicing "spirit boxing." For this reason, religious practices like "spirit boxing" were not recognized as orthodox, but considered superstitious and heretical in nature. The Hong Kong media often investigated these activities and warned the citizens to be prudent when participating in them.[47] Against this background, FNT increasingly felt the need to gain a more orthodox image. It was located in an old and shabby tenement building in an industrial area, so it was difficult for people to see what was happening inside. Although FNT was named the "Buddhism and Daoism Society," it only practiced spirit-writing in its early years and did not practice the Daoist or Buddhist rituals with which most people were familiar. For this reason, people could easily regard FNT as a suspicious religious group, which hindered FNT from building up a positive public image. To be regarded as an "orthodox religious group" and acquire a stable status, FNT needed to develop Daoist rituals and become a "Daoist society."

While disciples like De Quan had mastered certain rituals, other disciples within the altar, encouraged by Liu Songfei, also began to learn scripture recitation and tried to learn the rituals. In 1987, there were fewer than ten scripture-reciters in the society but more than 20 by the early 1990s. Initially, Master Lu

---

came from Huiyang 惠陽 in Guangdong province, and who came to Hong Kong in the 1940s. Youminjiao was founded by You Zhenfei 遊振飛 (no dates) during the late Qing to fight against the Qing government in Jiangxi 江西 province. It is said that the efficacy of these practices originated from the psychic power (*nianli* 念力) of the master. Practitioners imagined the real face of the patriarch while casting spells. The talisman was then burnt, thrown into some water which became "talisman water." The disciples drank the water from their hands and, later, shouted loudly, "Taishang laojun, please give me support with your mighty power" (太上老君扶持弟子，大顯威靈), requesting the patriarch or a god to descend to their bodies and protect them. Afterwards, they believed their body to be so strong that it could never again be harmed by knives or bullets, and that the divine power would protect them. See Chen, *Xianggang dalingyi*, 215–18.

47 In the early 1980s and 1990s, several Hong Kong newspapers reported that an increasing number of primary school students in Wong Tai Sin District were practicing spirit boxing. *Kengqiang ji* 鏗鏘集 (The Common Sense), a programme on Hong Kong Radio, undertook an undercover investigation into several primary and secondary school students from across the city who were practicing spirit boxing. All of them believed that they were possessed by ghosts and needed to protect themselves or help their friends by learning spirit boxing. *The Common Sense* interviewed teachers and psychologists for this special, 25-minute edition, and asked them to analyze why the students were engaging in spirit boxing. The experts were worried about "the superstitious behavior" of the teenagers and thought that engaging in spirit boxing might harm their physical and psychological health. See *Kengqiang ji*, "Buwen cangtian wen guishen." To date, many Hong Kong citizens, mainly adults, still practice spirit boxing. See further the report "Qinzi huodong di shenda" in the *Pingguo ribao* 蘋果日報 (Apple Daily).

taught the disciples to recite the "Yaotan zan 瑤壇讚" (Hymn of the Altar of the Immortals) and instructed them in the practice of rituals like Zan xing 讚星 (Hymn to all stars).[48] Moreover, FNT inherited several rituals from Ching Chung Koon, such as "chanting" (*qiang kou* 腔口) and kowtowing, as well as receiving the texts of several scriptures about frequently-practiced rituals. In 1990, FNT began to learn how to recite litanies, and practiced the "Lüzu chan 呂祖懺" (Confession to Lüzu), a litany with rich Hong Kong features. In 1991, Liu Songfei invited Master Ling Shizheng 凌十正[49] from Tung Sin Tan to teach disciples a ritual for the Saving and Sublimating of the Souls of the Deceased in Darkness, namely the Sanchu tou 三齣頭. After learning this, De Quan and other female disciples mastered the procedures for practicing Sanchu tou and started to perform ritual services. Finally, FNT declared the establishment of a new department, the Daoist Ritual Department (Jingchan bu 經懺部), of which De Quan was appointed the director, while the spirit-writing activities were allocated to the Spirit-Writing Department (Jitan bu 乩壇部).

As scripture-reciters gradually began to master the methods of the Daoist rituals, Liu Songfei designed uniforms with FNT badges for the disciples, in addition to a formal suit and sportswear to wear while handling routine affairs at the altar. He required all the disciples to wear these uniforms when they attended rituals and events. Apart from these uniforms, he also ordered the scripture-reciters, who performed the Daoist rituals, to wear long blue gowns, Zhuangzi scarves, white socks and black canvas shoes. He also ordered ritual master cassocks for disciples who were eligible to become ritual masters. The disciples paid for these uniforms at their own expense.

4   A Journey in Search of Orthodoxy: The Daoist Origins of FNT

In 1984, the Chinese government signed the "Sino-British Joint Declaration" with the British government. Despite the fact that the religious circles in Hong

---

48   "*Zan xing*" means praising all stars for fortune.
49   Master Ling Shizheng (1925–) is a native of Shenjing Village 深井村 in Panyu 番禺, Guangdong province. Originally named Huifang 惠芳, Master Ling is the current Director of the Daoist Ritual Department of Tung Sin Tan in Hong Kong. She learned Daoist rituals from Hou Baoyuan in the 1960s and began to hold training sessions for scripture-reciters in Tung Sin Tan in 1978. She has had numerous students and used to teach Daoist rituals at several Daoist altars in Hong Kong, e.g., the Shanji Buddhism and Daoism Society (Shanji Fo-Dao she 善濟佛道社), Tung Sin Tan, the Fei Ngan Tung Buddhism and Daoism Society, the Tung Sin Buddhism and Daoism Society 同善佛道社 and Yiwan sheng tan 一灣聖壇. See Lai, Yau, and Wu, *Xianggang daotang keyi*, 79–82.

Kong had been dubious and even terrified about Hong Kong's return to China, the transfer of sovereignty to China was inevitable, and they were considering strategies to cope with this issue. Both the Catholic and Protestant Churches in Hong Kong strongly urged the government to protect their legal religious rights, but the Daoist groups sought to avoid adopting an antagonistic attitude towards the Beijing government. They adopted policies of conciliation instead, such as strengthening the personnel exchanges between Hong Kong and the mainland and offering financial assistance to Daoist temples on the mainland.[50]

By the early 1990s, most of the Daoist altars in Hong Kong had adopted a positive attitude towards the Daoist groups on the mainland. Their primary tasks involved finding a place of origin on the mainland and providing financial assistance to their ancestral Daoist temples there.[51] In this phase, the NFT, after expanding for more than a decade, continued to attract more disciples, increasing the numbers of the "De 德" and the "Wen 文" generation. The Daoist altar was developing steadily, and the new disciples provided regular donations.[52] However, lacking a Daoist origin on the mainland,[53] FNT needed to consider the legitimacy of its claim to a Daoist identity. Meanwhile, many of the Daoist temples in Hong Kong had begun to build relationships with Daoist temples on the mainland. The question of how FNT itself could open up new room for expansion and establish a relationship with the Daoist circles on the mainland became an important issue that this new Daoist altar had to face.

The year 1993 marked an important turning point in the history of FNT. On April 8, 1993, FNT disciples received the following divine message from Lüzu:

> Geese from the North flying south, with head but no tail. Pursuing a dragon, a thousand miles away, [before] finally returning to earth. First [venturing] to Qingcheng Mountain, then [returning] back here. [I], the

---

50 Shiga, *Xianggang Daojiao yu fuji* xinyang, 284.
51 For example, Wun Chuen Seen Koon helped its ancestral temple Wun Chuen Seen Koon on Mount Xiqiao 西樵山 in Nanhai 南海 to renovate its old buildings; Tung Sin Tan donated funds to its ancestral temple Qingyun Dong 慶雲洞 on Mount Cha 茶山 in Nanhai to cover renovations.
52 These are called "Dade 大德" disciples.
53 As for the origin of the Daoist altars in Hong Kong, see Yau, *Daofeng bainian*, 20–23, where a table lists the origins of the Daoist altars in Hong Kong and Macau from the late Qing Dynasty to the 1970s. According to the statistics I have calculated, based on this table, of the 43 Daoist altars in Hong Kong, 37 can trace their origins back to the mainland. Of the remaining six Daoist altars, some were built by Daoists from the mainland, and others by Daoist disciples who were practicing Daoism in Hong Kong.

SPIRIT-WRITING ALTARS IN CONTEMPORARY HONG KONG 581

Patriarch], bestow my favor and let my numinous light appear. [You] must bring three treasures to transform the *qi* and complete perfection. The southern melon is better than the northern one, a section of arrowroot being cut off, but the fiber remains attached. It is not until we have traced our roots and pursued the dragon that we can speak of success.

南飛北雁，有頭無尾；千里尋龍，終須歸地。先到青城，再到本地；祖師恩賜，靈光顯現；需帶三寶，化氣成真；南瓜勝北，絲斷藕蓮；莫謂無功，尋根究龍。54

This divine text advised FNT, which had been established 13 years previously, to search for its roots in Sichuan province. This was an important task for this young Daoist altar, which lacked a place of Daoist origin. Lüzu sent another divine message that same day, which seemed to predict the disciples' encounters on their travel to find their roots: "The Patriarch has come to the altar for an inspection. Everything is prepared, and powerful numinosity has been manifested. There are many rocks on the road, and the path is rugged. When the years pass and bodies grow old, [however], the numinous light [of the deities] will provide support." (祖師臨壇，翻究本地。萬事俱成，威靈顯現。石頭路上，道路崎嶇。年老體邁，靈光扶持。) After receiving these two divine messages, Liu Songfei immediately called a meeting with his disciples to discuss them, but they had no idea about the exact location mentioned in the divine texts. The only location they could confirm was Mount Qingcheng 青城山, in Sichuan. Liu thus decided to organize a delegation to visit Chengdu 成都, the province's capital, to look for clues.55

Liu Songfei summoned 18 of the disciples and formed a delegation that was tasked with finding the Daoist roots of FNT. This delegation consisted of Liu Songfei himself, 17 disciples, and Master Peng 彭道長, the *jishou* of FNT at that time. Arranged by the China Travel Service, a travel agency in Hong Kong, the 19-member FNT delegation set out on their journey to Chengdu on April 19.

While travelling to Chengdu, the *jishou* received instructions from Lüzu, indicating that "the cranes are chirping throughout the Ninth Heaven, [predicting] that [you] will soon arrive in Sichuan province. There is a [special] object in Sichuan. Once it manifests, then [you will be able] to see it. I have verified its

---

54 All of the divine messages in this section were provided by De Hong 德宏, the *jishou* of FNT at present.
55 See the "Heming shan" report in the *Fubao* 福報 newspaper.

form and revealed its essence, based on its form. As soon as the trip is arranged, there [should] really be no other pursuit." (鶴鳴九天，快到四川。川中有物，物現即見。我本參相，借相現真。行程安頓，實無他求。)

On April 20, the delegation departed from Chengdu for Mount Qingcheng, according to the instructions set out in the divine messages. The religious activities of Daoism on Mount Qingcheng had been gradually restored since 1979. A Mount Qingcheng Daoist Association was founded in December of that year, and Fu Yuantian 傅圓天 (1925–1997)[56] was appointed its president. Since 1984, most of the Daoist temples on Mount Qingcheng have been managed by the Mount Qingcheng Daoist Association, which also began to provide Daoist services to people in locations where the conditions permitted it, and became the Daoist association with the highest revenue on the mainland.[57] In 1993, Daoist temples were developing well on Mount Qingcheng, making this location second only to the Baiyun Temple (Baiyun guan 白雲觀) in Beijing and Tianshi fu 天師府 on Mount Longhu 龍虎山 in terms of Daoist renown.

This, however, was initially of little comfort to the delegation. Despite the repeated divine messages from Lüzu, the FNT disciples failed to find any clues. In the evening of the third day following their arrival in Sichuan, when they were dining in a restaurant in Chengdu, they encountered a Mr. Wu 吳, Vice President of the Zongjiao shiwu weiyuanhui 宗教事務委員會 (Religious Affairs Commission) of Sichuan province. Hearing that Mount Heming 鶴鳴山 had been included on the delegation's travel itinerary, Mr. Wu informed the disciples that Mount Heming was an undeveloped tourist destination, and that both the Religious Affairs Commission and the Bureau of Tourism hoped to develop tourism on this mountain, so he was willing to accompany the delegation on their visit there. Prior to 1993, Mount Heming was still an impoverished place. Although the Daoist temples on the mountain were opened to the public in 1987, by 1992, only Ziyang Hall 紫陽殿 and the Immortals Temple 神仙祠 had been renovated. There were only nine Daoists in the temple, and it was not a well-known tourist spot.[58] Compared with the wealthy Mount Qingcheng, Mount Heming, as the place where Daoism originated, was shabby, and neither the FNT disciples nor the tour guide were familiar with this place. For this reason, the FNT delegation was delighted when Chief Wu offered to accompany them on their visit.

---

56 Fu Yuantian, a famous Quanzhen Daoist, was Vice President of the Zhongguo Daojiao xiehui 中國道教協會 (Taoist Association of China) from 1992 to 1997.
57 Zhang, "Gaige shinian," 1–5.
58 Wei, "Dayi Heming shan daoguan," 14–16.

On April 24, Chief Wu accompanied the FNT delegation on their visit to Mount Heming in Dayi County 大邑縣. In Yingxian ge 迎仙閣 on Mount Heming, Mr. Wu introduced Master Sha Mingming 沙明明, who had arrived there 20 days previously and was preparing to practice Daoism. The disciples expressed their hope to Master Sha Mingming that they would find their Daoist roots in Sichuan, and Master Sha told the disciples that the *feiyan dong* 飛雁洞 (Fei Ngan Tung in Cantonese)[59] that they might be looking for was a cave on this mountain. When Heavenly Master Zhang Daoling 張道陵[60] was instructing two of his disciples, he told them that they would become immortals after jumping into the valley from the cave. He then jumped into the valley himself, and was caught by a passing crane in flight, which carried him up to heaven where he became an immortal.

The FNT disciples were excited after hearing his remarks. They set foot on Mount Heming with Mr. Wu and Master Sha to look for the cave among the old buildings on the mountain. They arrived at a hill which was surrounded by walls and iron doors. Master Sha said that *feiyan dong* was located here, but that the hill was currently listed as a military conservation area, and no one was allowed to enter. After inquiring, the delegation discovered that they could arrive at *feiyan dong* via a shabby cave nearby. After ascending a narrow mountain path, they arrived at the foot of the mountain where *feiyan dong* was located, as described by Sha Mingming. The FNT disciples began to pay homage to Heavenly Master Zhang on a flat ground below the cave. At this moment, Sha Mingming claimed that he had received a message from Master Lüzu.[61] This divine message allowed all of the disciples to make a wish, respectively, to reward them for finding this place. The disciples of FNT felt cheered by hearing from Master Sha, believing that they had completed the task set by Lüzu. On their way down the hill, Sha, pointing at a tree, declared to Liu Songfei that "Master Lüzu has given instructions to build a Lüzu Temple here" (呂祖恩師賜示在此興建呂祖廟). He told Liu Songfei that, two days earlier, he had received instructions from the gods in a dream, saying that many people would arrive at Mount Heming to build a temple there.

---

59   The Chinese characters *fei yan dong* means the cave of the flying crane.
60   Zhang Daoling was the ancient founder of Zhengyi dao 正一道 (Orthodox Unity Daoism), to whom Laozi 老子 manifested himself in 142 CE. Zhang Daoling is considered the first generation of Heavenly Masters 天師.
61   According to interviews with the FNT disciples, Sha Mingming was a medium who could receive message from the gods.

That evening, the disciples worshipped Lüzu and respectfully asked him for divine instructions:

> As far as today's journey is concerned, if heaven and man enjoy it together, if everyone [involved] is meritorious and virtuous, all of these efforts will not have been made for nothing. In the coming days, [however,] the ritual affairs must still be executed. These are fundamental!
>
> 至於今日行程，天人共賞，諸位功德，當不唐捐。日後法務，還要執行，此是家鄉。

Lüzu expressed his appreciation of this journey by the FNT disciples and confirmed that Mount Heming was the place where FNT originated. After reading the divine messages from Lüzu, Liu Songfei assumed that he had fulfilled his task of finding the roots of FNT. In addition, he asked Lüzu whether he should build a temple on Mount Heming, and Lüzu stated: "Of course, you should accumulate more merits by building a temple. It will take three years to build this temple. It will be located in the East and face West." (建洞功德，當然要行。為期三年，坐東向西。)

After receiving an affirmative answer, Liu Songfei asked Lüzu again whether they should build a temple in Hong Kong. This time, Lüzu's response was less positive. He merely advised them to await a suitable opportunity: "As to the merit of building a temple, the more, the better. A just cause will enjoy abundant support, both through manpower and material resources. [However,] when there is an appropriate time to protect the [Daoist] doctrine, it will reveal itself through an auspicious omen. For the time being, there is no need to worry [about it]." (建廟功德，並不怕多。人力物力，得道多助。屆時護法，自會顯現。顯現有兆，暫不擔心。) After returning to Hong Kong, FNT was praised by Lüzu again. So far, Liu Songfei and his disciples had successfully completed their trip, that lasted six days, and confirmed that Mount Heming was the exact place where FNT originated. Later, so the account goes, they learned that Mount Heming was a sacred place of the Zhengyi School 正一道 of Daoism, and received divine messages from Lüzu, demanding that they convert to Heavenly Master Zhang and become disciples of the Zhengyi School.

This root-finding journey helped FNT to find the place of their Daoist origin on the mainland and establish a relationship with the Daoist circles in mainland China. This place of origin not only legitimized their founding but, more importantly, because Mount Heming holds a lofty position in Daoism, other Daoist temples in Guangdong province, which served as the origin of many

Daoist altars in Hong Kong, could hardly compete with Mount Heming. The link to the mountain, however, proved vital also in other respects. Since the Heavenly Master Zhang had left numerous legends on Mount Heming, the FNT disciples thought that they should not only practice the way of Quanzhen, but also needed a Zhengyi identity.

Once FNT had confirmed Mount Heming in Sichuan as its place of Daoist origin in 1993, they began to shift their focus of development gradually to the mainland, according to the spirit-written instructions and decisions taken by Liu Songfei, and made a series of donations to Daoist temples on the mainland for renovation and reconstruction projects.[62] Although Liu Songfei declared that he had acted according to the instructions received through spirit-writing, sometimes the tasks to which the divine texts referred, particularly the direction of the development of the Daoist altar, were questioned by other members of the altar. The bigger a Daoist altar's development goal is, the larger its scope of activity, and the more questions it will be asked. In the late 1990s, several disciples and believers left FNT, because they were dissatisfied with certain approaches of FNT.[63]

The journey to find their origin could be said to have been an important chapter in the entire developmental history of FNT. They confirmed that their Daoist origin was on Mount Heming, which was where Daoism originated. Compared with Guangdong, Mount Heming was doubtlessly more convincing to disciples, and enjoys a high status in the Daoist world.

Furthermore, this journey also provided FNT with an opportunity to participate in philanthropic activities in Daoist circles on the mainland. After engaging in philanthropy since the 1990s, they applied successfully to become a non-profit charitable society (*fei mouli cishan jigou* 非牟利慈善機構) in Hong Kong in 1998.

5 Spirit-Writing in Practice

For any spirit-writing society, it is difficult to maintain the unity of the members and ensure that everyone in the organization is pursuing the same objective. FNT was founded as a religious organization by spirit-writing in the begin-

---

62 For the renovation and reconstruction project in which FNT participated from 1993–2013, please see Luo, "Dangdai fuluan tuanti," 189–207.

63 Informant: Wen Jun 文君, date: 24/07/2014, venue: Hongcheng xianguan 泓澄仙館, Quarry Bay, Hong Kong.

ning of 1980s. And it believed that it had a sacred mission to popularize the information that it received via divine messages. Any decision made by this altar would influence its position in the believers' minds and influence the cohesion within the organization. If a believer were dissatisfied with a decision made by the altar, he or she would complain about it, and might even choose to leave the altar. In FNT, spirit-writing was the core of the communication with the gods. "Any measure and decision in the altar would be obtained from divine messages and implemented later" (洞內任何的舉措以及決定都從乩文中得知，並將之貫徹執行).[64] But not all of the disciples or believers were interested in the affairs of the Daoist altar, such as the journey to find its roots and the need to establish branch altars. What they cared about was the religious services that FNT provided to believers, particularly spirit-writing, disease healing, and solving the problems of believers through the efficacy of the deities.

Although many of the Daoist altars in Hong Kong gradually stopped offering spirit-writing services to believers due to the changing management methods and the difficulty of finding spirit-writing practitioners, there remained sufficient market demand for this way of conveying the instructions of the gods. Those who were curious about spirit-writing or believed in its power, when unable to find a spirit-writing service at the larger Daoist altars, would visit altars like FNT, which could satisfy their needs. Under most circumstances, what these believers cared about was the accuracy of the spirit-writing instructions and the divine power shown by FNT. Therefore, upholding the instructions contained in the divine messages was vital to this Daoist altar, as was maintaining the faith of believers and the attraction of the Daoist altar.

In the above, I have described the central position of spirit-writing in FNT from the perspective of the development process of this Daoist altar. I will now discuss how this ritual practice is used in the actual ritual space within the Daoist altar. When a God descends to the altar, the *jishou* uses a phoenix brush (*jibi* 乩筆) to write characters on a tray of sand. These characters are recorded by an assistant and become the oracles from the gods.[65] In the next part, I will discuss the spirit-writing rituals that FNT conducted at its head altar in Kwun Tong on March 20, 2011, to offer a clearer picture of the features of spirit-writing in FNT.

---

64   This information was provided by Liu Songfei.
65   See the lecture given by Yau, "Fuji zai Xianggang."

5.1 Categories of Spirit-Writing Rituals and the Members of the Spirit-Writing Department (*Jitan bu* 乩壇部)

The spirit-writing rituals in FNT can be divided into two categories. The first category is instructions at the altar (*tanxun* 壇訓): the *jishou* receives information from a god regarding the internal affairs of the Daoist altar, or provides predictions on a certain social trend or global situation. The second category is receiving divine texts for believers or disciples who request guidance or medicine through spirit-writing (*wenshi* 問事). In general, FNT opens the altar to welcome the gods and conduct spirit-writing rituals every Sunday after they have completed the Daoist rituals.

FNT adopted the form of "single person spirit-writing" (*danren ji* 單人乩) for its spirit-writing rituals, which means that there is only one *jishou*. There is a copyist (*bilusheng* 筆錄生) to assist him/her, and a service man (*tangwusheng* 堂務生) who is responsible for delivering divine messages. The *jishou* cannot be replaced by anyone else, at random, due to his/her uniqueness, but the other assistants may be replaced. However, copying divine messages during the process of spirit-writing requires experience and a certain level of education. For this reason, the copyist is a relatively fixed position. Occasionally, the copyist may also be replaced by other senior disciples but, when I examined the divine texts that they had copied, I saw that, unlike when the experienced *jishou* was in charge, several changes had been made to the divine texts, and the layout was confused and untidy. On the day I observed the spirit-writing ritual of FNT in Kwun Tong, the main *jishou* was De Hong 德宏, who had recently been appointed the *jishou* of FNT, during the 2011 Spring Festival. Zhangchi 章池[66] and A-Guan 阿關, both disciples of FNT, held the post of copyist and service man, respectively.

5.2 The Spirit-Writing Séance (tanxun)

As a routine, the FNT conducts Daoist rituals every Sunday morning, and the disciples eat a vegetarian lunch at the Daoist altar at noon. Later in the afternoon, most of the scripture-reciters and disciples leave the Daoist altar, while those required to assist with spirit-writing affairs remain at the altar and await the beginning of the spirit-writing ritual. On that day in Kwun Tong, I saw approximately 36 disciples and eight believers participating in the Daoist rituals in the morning. When the spirit-writing ritual began in the afternoon, 16 disciples and around 26 believers remained present.

---

66 Zhangchi is a disciple who receives payment from FNT. She works as a full-time scripture-reciter in the Daoist Rituals Department and assists the director of the Department, De Quan, to handle issues related to Daoist rituals.

At 2.30 p.m., Liu Songfei and two scripture-reciters from the god-welcoming team (*yingsheng zu* 迎聖組), dressed in Daoist robes, entered the altar to offer incense to the gods. After burning the incense, Liu Songfei held some talisman water in his hands and purified the altar. De Hong, who held the position of *jishou*, entered the altar at that point. She offered incense to the gods and held her hands in the air above the incense burner for a while. Liu Songfei sprinkled some talisman water over her hands for the purpose of purification. De Hong then knelt at the altar, awaiting the gods' instructions. When a certain god descends to the altar, the *jishou* resonates with the god, and notifies Liu Songfei of its presence. On that day, the first god to descend to the altar was Lüzu. Liu Songfei, facing the Sanqing baodian 三清寶殿, a shrine dedicated to Lüzu, cried out, "[We] respectfully welcome Master Lüzu of Pure Yang to descend to the altar" (恭迎純陽呂祖仙師臨壇). Two scripture-reciters of the gods-welcoming team struck the chime stones (*qing* 磬) and wooden fish (*muyu* 木魚), and cried out: "Kowtow three times and recite the 'Precious Admonitions of Patriarch Lü' (Lüzu xianshi baogao 呂祖仙師寶誥) three times," at which point everyone at the altar knelt down and began to recite these admonitions.

The disciples recited the "Precious Admonitions of Patriarch Lü" three times, then read the word "Heaven-Honored One" (*tianzun* 天尊) in the last sentence in the style of vocal chanting. While the disciples were reciting the scriptures, the *jishou* kowtowed three times to Lüzu at the altar.

After the disciples finished reciting the admonitions, the *jishou* entered the spirit-writing altar. The copyist sat at the copying desk, ready to write down the divine texts. The service man stood beside the spirit-writing tray, which is shaped like a traditional sand tray. A T-shaped wooden phoenix brush was placed in the sand tray. After entering the spirit-writing altar, the *jishou* bowed to the phoenix brush. After concentrating attentively for a moment, she raised the phoenix brush and began to draw circles in the sand tray. Believers outside the spirit-writing altar could clearly hear the rustling sound of the phoenix brush as it moved through the sand. Unlike many other spirit-writing altars, at FNT, the phoenix brush does not write characters in the sand tray, but draws circles, during which the *jishou* receives instructions from the gods in her mind, and begins to read aloud the divine texts, which are written down by the copyist. This is what was received on that day:

> The Lotus appears in the sea of suffering, [but] all disciples make a united effort. Only if the Great Dao is pursued through non-action will the light of the [Daoist] doctrine appear.
>
> A streak of light shows, a [lump] of coal delivered in the midst of snow. Numerous nations join in to help, and we should help even more.

Enlightenment appears in the dharma-sea, a small boat of compassion within the sea of suffering. The one boat of the Buddha's teachings of the swan,[67] [manifesting] the support of the power of its vow.

For those cultivating themselves at home, the power [generated by] recitation is also equal. Every merit is recorded and accomplishes auspicious results.

Please remember what I said. You will realize the truth one day.

苦海蓮花現，眾子一力心，大道行無為，才有法光現。
光明露曙光，雪中有送炭，眾國合力援，援手應多伸。
菩提法海現，苦海一慈航，雁門一佛舟，願力一援手。
在家修行者，唸力亦同樣，百日功德記，如意是吉祥。
不忘有記著，他日知箇中。[68]

As the *jishou* finished reading aloud the divine message, the circles drawn by the phoenix brush began to diminish in size, until the brush became motionless in the middle of the sand tray. At that time, the *jishou* placed the phoenix brush down and bowed. The service man or the *jishou* herself swept the sand flat with a small wooden stick. After the copyist finished copying the divine texts, the service man delivered them to Liu Songfei, who read them silently initially and then aloud to the disciples and believers.

Afterwards, the *jishou* notified everyone at the altar of the descent of a second god, and informed Liu Songfei that Heavenly Master Zhang had descended to the altar. Liu Songfei and two scripture-reciters bowed in front of the Xuanfa xuanmen dian 玄法玄門殿, a shrine dedicated to Heavenly Master Zhang, and cried out: "[We] respectfully welcome Celestial Ritual Heavenly Master Zhang to descend to the altar" (恭迎玄法張天師臨壇). Two scripture-reciters of the gods-welcoming team struck the chime stones and wooden fish and cried out: "Kowtow three times and recite the 'Precious Admonitions of Heavenly Master Zhang' three times." (三叩首，念《張天師寶誥》三遍。) At that, everyone at the altar knelt down and began to recite the "Precious Admonitions of the Celestial One Essential Heavenly Master Zhang" (Zhengyi yuanshi datianzun Zhang tianshi baogao 正一元始大天尊張天師寶誥) three times. The final word in the last sentence was also recited in the style of vocal chanting.

---

67 A metaphor for the teachings of Buddhism.
68 All of the divine messages in this section were provided to me by FNT.

The *jishou* entered the altar, raised the phoenix brush, and began to draw several circles in the sand tray, after which she started to read aloud the message that had been received:

> I bestow the talisman today; the abbot having asked for it and it being granted through the divination blocks. The [Daoist] doctrine can hardly fill the whole world, which is why you disciples must practice it even more. Rectify your hearts and never forget the favor of the great Dao. We also must make preparations for the ritual on the birthday of the deity, and everything has to be carried out in an appropriate manner, carefully, one step after another. [I] ask my fellow students to arrange this. There is no time to waste. Time flies, and the person responsible must arrange it quickly.

> 我符今日賜，主持來叩問，卜杯亦可以。法難滿塵寰，眾子多修持，願是真心行，無忘大道恩。寶誕法會期，安排亦準備，妥善來行之，一步一慎行。同學請安排，不可再蹉跎，時光已流逝，舵手速安排。

During the process of spirit-writing, the *jishou* gazed steadily at the sand tray. As she read out the divine messages, from time to time, she monitored the copyist's movements. The *jishou* reminded the copyist to pay attention to certain words in the divine messages that are easy to confuse. For example, when the *jishou* read out *yuan bao shi ping'an* 願保是平安 (We wish [the gods] to protect our safety), she told the copyist immediately: "The *shi* 是 in this sentence is the same as *shi* in *shifei* (right or wrong)" (是，是非的是). If she found mistakes in the copyist's writing, she would draw the copyist's attention to them.

Jigong 濟公 was the third god to descend to the altar that day. After she finished receiving the divine messages from Jigong, the *jishou* swept the sand flat with a small wooden stick.

Finally, the *jishou* signaled to everyone in the altar that the gods would leave and ascend to heaven. Liu Songfei saluted the main hall and read aloud: "[We] respectfully escort Master Lüzu, Heavenly Master Xuanfa and Master Jigong back to the palace" (恭送呂祖仙師、玄法天師、濟佛仙師回宮). The believers knelt, kowtowed three times, and recited "Golden Carriage Heaven-Honored One, Great Heaven-Honored One" (Luanyu fanjia tianzun, da tianzun 鑾輿返架天尊，大天尊) to escort the gods.

5.3 *Requesting Guidance through Spirit-Writing* (wenshi)

After escorting the gods back to heaven, De Hong briefly rested in her office,[69] before returning to the spirit-writing altar to offer guidance through spirit-writing and give medicine to the believers and disciples. Every Sunday afternoon, believers wishing to request guidance or seeking herbal medicine would first sign in at the reception desk, take a number, and queue up according to the sequence of registration. There is a divine message decoding office at FNT; here, senior disciples of FN explain the meaning of the divine messages to believers free of charge. Believers receive an explanation of the divine texts or clarify the meaning of the divine texts by themselves. For people who request guidance through spirit-writing, the god who descends to the altar is usually Lüzu, while for people who require medicine, Jigong tends to descend. The paper containing the divine message that FNT gives believers usually follows a uniform layout. The divine texts usually begin with words such as: "Instructions from Master Lüzu" (*Lüzu enshi cishi* 呂祖恩師賜示).

In general, the enquiries made through spirit-writing can be divided into two categories at the Daoist altars of Hong Kong: one approach is "oral spirit-writing" (*kaikou ji* 開口乩), where the inquirer informs the *jishou* of the question. This approach is common at spirit-writing altars such as Tong Sin Tan and Shengshan zhentang 省善真堂; the other is "silent spirit-writing" (*moji* 默乩), where the inquirer mulls over the question silently, and does not have to tell the *jishou*. When the *jishou* receives the instructions for the inquirer from the gods, he/she writes them down and hands them over. Only a small number of spirit-writing altars use this method, and FNT is one of them.

On this particular day, after the *jishou* and the copyist were ready for the spirit-writing, a disciple responsible for "protecting the altar" (*hutan* 護壇) called out the number of the first believer, and guided the believer to inquire by spirit-writing. A believer offered incense to the gods first, then knelt before the incense desk on the main altar, pondering a question silently. The service man delivered the believer's number to the spirit-writing altar to inform the *jishou* and copyist about the believer's number and how many questions he/she had asked. Some believers asked one question, but some asked two. The *jishou* bowed to the phoenix brush and began to practice spirit-writing, similarly to *tanxun*. The copyist delivered the divine messages that she had copied to the service man. After receiving the divine texts, the service man walked toward

---

69   De Hong has a desk in the office. She usually handles affairs for the Daoist altars in this office.

the guardrail of the altar and delivered the divine messages to the believer, after which the disciple guided the next believer forward to receive spirit-writing.

The questions that the believers posed covered an extremely wide range of topics, but most of the believers visited FNT in the hope of obtaining solutions to their problems from the gods. Some believers visit FNT for spirit-writing on someone else's behalf. On that day, I asked four believers why they had come to FNT to request this service. Their responses were as follows:

> Ms. A, a 38-year-old office worker: she had begun to request guidance through spirit-writing at FNT several months previously and had found the divine messages to be efficacious. On that day, she came to FNT to inquire about a work-related matter. The divine texts told her that she could have hope only by "making more effort" (*nuli jia nuli* 努力加努力).
>
> Ms. B, a 70-year-old pensioner: she had heard about the efficacy of the spirit-writing at FNT, and she had come to FNT for the first time that day to inquire about her daughter's marriage.
>
> Mr. C, a 28-year-old student: this was his first visit to FNT, and he had come to inquire about his father's physical condition. He received the following divine texts: "You still do not have it in your hands. You could only get hold of things today. People and events are still immature. It's better to wait for a lucky chance" (手中仍未有，把握在今天，人事仍未熟，等待結合緣), but he was confused about what this message meant.
>
> Ms. D, 70-years-old: she had come to FNT seeking medicine. She used to have problems with her legs which forced her to use a wheelchair. Later, she heard that FNT was capable of healing diseases, and visited the altar for help. She had obtained medicine from FNT for many years, and had recovered, because Liu Songfei healed her leg problem. She said, "Abbot Liu has obtained medicine for me from a warehouse in heaven" (劉主持爲我請到了天上倉庫的藥).

5.4 *Seeking Healing and Asking for Medicine* (wenbing qiuyao 問病求藥)

The session during which the believers could request guidance through spirit-writing lasted for about two hours. Once the spirit-writing was complete, the *jishou* returned to her office to rest. After they received their divine messages, most of the believers left, but a few remained at the altar, waiting for Liu Songfei to give instructions.

At 5 p.m., the Daoist altar began to provide healing and medicine service to believers. They did not need to take a number, but just register at the reception desk and wait for their name to be called. The procedures for healing and seeking medicine differ from that for requesting guidance through spirit-writing. Not all believers receive a prescription. Liu Songfei first used divining blocks to ask Jigong whether the believer needed healing through a spirit-writing prescription. If the result of the inquiring divining block was a *sheng* divining block (*shengbei* 勝杯),[70] this meant that Jigong was willing to heal the believer, so the believer waited for the *jishou* to reveal the divine texts; if the believer received a *bao* divining block (*baobei* 寶杯),[71] this meant that Jigong refused to heal him/her, and he/she could only drink talisman water for healing.

A service man declared the start of the ritual. The believers and disciples wishing to seek healing stood in a queue outside the altar. At the altar, Liu Songfei held a talisman in his hand and pointed a sword at it to enhance its efficacy. Later, he ignited the talisman and placed it into a huge gourd that was standing beside the sacred altar. This gourd was made after FNT moved to its new address in 2008. It is 80 centimeters high and can hold more than ten liters of water. After finishing this ritual, Liu Songfei explained, "This big gourd contains talisman water. What I did just now was not burning the talisman but asking the gods to send sacred talismans down to the sacred water. This water could heal all diseases, exorcise epidemics, and dispel evil spirits." (這個大葫蘆里裝的都是法水。我剛才那不是燒符，而是請仙佛降神符到這神水中，能治百病，驅瘟辟邪。)[72]

After melting the talisman in the sacred water in the gourd, Liu Songfei performed the *sanding li* 三鼎禮 (three kowtows and nine salutes), and placed the divining block above the burning incense and rotated it three times to purify it. At that moment, the service man outside the altar told the believer at the head of the queue to kneel, and to notify Liu Songfei of his name. Liu Songfei called out the name of this believer to the gods and threw the divining block to the ground. The result of the inquiry was the *bao* divining block. The service man told this believer to stand up and notified him that, because his request for healing had been rejected by Jigong, he should take some talisman water home with him to drink, and that he could try again next time. Then, the service man told the second believer to kneel for the divining block. On that day,

---

70 A diving block is a kind of Chinese traditional divination, made of two wooden, crescent-shaped blocks. In Guangdong, the diving block has both a positive and a negative side, called *shengbei*.
71 A diving block with negative sides is called *baobei*.
72 Informant: Liu Songfei, date: 20/03/2011, venue: FNT.

the first three believers who requested a divining block received a *bao* divining block, but the fourth believer received a *sheng* divining block. The service man told this believer to stand aside and wait to receive a spirit-written prescription.

That afternoon, 13 people visited FNT to seek medicine. Eight of them received a *sheng* divine block, and five a *bao* divining block.

Later, those eight believers who had received *sheng* divining blocks knelt before the altar, waiting for the *jishou* to give them a spirit-written prescription (*jifang* 乩方). The *jishou* entered the altar and began to give out the prescriptions, one by one. The procedure was the same as that of providing guidance through spirit-writing to believers. Each person was given a different prescription, but most of them consisted of talisman water with the addition of flower tea. As each prescription was handed out, the service man would prepare "medicinal materials" according to the instructions within the divine texts. Before the *jishou* entered the altar, the service men had already made the flower tea and put it aside to prepare the prescriptions. One believer, who had received a *sheng* divining block, showed me the prescription and medicine that she had received. The prescription stated that she was suffering from excessive internal heat (*shanghuo* 上火), and needed to drink talisman water with added Pu'er 普洱, chrysanthemum and rose.

De Hong informed me that all the prescriptions issued by FNT in the 1990s were composed of Chinese herbal medicine, rather than the flower tea that the altar uses now, because it was difficult for people with other religious beliefs to accept the herbal medicine prescribed by FNT through spirit-writing. For this reason, in 2000, considering the needs of these people, FNT asked the gods whether they could replace the traditional Chinese herbal medicine with flower tea of a mild nature, and the gods agreed. Since then, all the prescriptions issued by FNT are composed of flower tea.

A 78-year-old lady, who had received a *sheng* divining block, also showed me the prescription that she had received. It stated that she needed to drink talisman water with flower tea. In addition, Jigong had agreed to let Liu Songfei heal her illness through his divine power. Due to illness, she had used a wheelchair for several years. After receiving the divine texts, Liu Songfei told the service man to push the old lady's wheelchair beside the altar, then stood at the altar to heal the old lady's illness by conjuring the talisman power. He made a "preaching mudra" (*shuofa yin* 說法印, *dharmacakra-mudrā*) with his left hand, placed his hand on his stomach, made a gesture like a sword with his right hand, drew more than ten circles above the old lady's head while muttering incantations, pointed his right hand heavily several times on both sides of the old lady's head and completed the conjuring of the power.

By 8 p.m., after receiving their prescriptions and divine texts from FNT to solve their problems, the believers left the Daoist altar one by one, and FNT's activities for that Sunday ended.

6 Concluding Remarks

It is undeniable that the history of FNT is exceptional. It was founded by a young Vietnamese refugee who received oracles from the gods and, subsequently, appointed Liu Songfei as abbot of this Daoist altar. Although FNT advocated spirit-writing activities and followed a policy of "managing the altar through spirit-writing" (*yi ji zhi tan*), two aspects, seeking an orthodox religious image and obtaining funds, led Liu Songfei to devote himself to developing the Daoist rituals in the mid- and late-1980s, which FNT inherited from Hong Kong Daoist altars. The FNT made the transition from being a Daoist altar merely engaged in spirit-writing activities, to become a Daoist altar that also incorporated Daoist rituals. In this way, they completed the first step in the transformation from a spirit-writing altar to a Daoist altar.

After the FNT had acquired a stable source of funds, the legitimacy and orthodox identity of this Daoist altar became the most urgent problem that FNT faced. Meanwhile, against the background of Hong Kong's return to the mainland, like other Daoist altars in Hong Kong, FNT also needed to establish appropriate strategies for handling the new political situation. Therefore, in the mid- and late-1990s, FNT embarked on a journey to the mainland and found their Daoist origin on Mount Heming, a sacred Daoist site in mainland China. Thereafter, they began to conduct philanthropic activities on the mainland, and the journey to Mount Heming became a line of demarcation for the development of this Daoist altar.

From the perspective of religious concepts and practice, as already mentioned in the introduction to this article, the spirit-writing altars in Hong Kong developed according to the framework of Daoism. They began to develop in the form of spirit-writing altars since the late Qing Dynasty and early Republican Era, and later established Daoist altars after introducing the rituals and system of Daoism. In the 1970s, some of the Daoist altars in Hong Kong, which had originally been spirit-writing altars, abandoned spirit-writing and concentrated their efforts instead on developing into orthodox Daoist altars. In the contemporary era, such a framework for developing from a spirit-writing altar into a Daoist altar has been retained, so FNT might be said to be a typical case of such an extension.

When we reflect on the past and present of FNT, spirit-writing still plays an important role in its religious activities, especially for those believers with

FIGURE 15.1   Spirit-writing ritual in FNT, March 2011
PHOTO BY AUTHOR

specific needs. However, the direction in which this religious society has developed, all of the major changes, whether the inclusion of Daoist rituals or search for their Daoist roots on Mount Heming, were initiated for the purpose of gaining legitimacy and orthodoxy. In other words, FNT was seeking to draw closer to traditional Daoism. We may therefore assume that gaining a Daoist identity and image was more important to FNT than their identity as a spirit-writing altar.

The next question that arises is: if FNT continues to proceed along the historical trajectory of the Daoist spirit-writing altars in Hong Kong, during this process of transformation, will FNT suspend spirit-writing like other Daoist altars, such as Foon Ying Seen Koon and Wong Tai Sin Temple, and practice Daoist rituals only?[73] I cannot answer this question here but, based on the case of FNT, we can gain some clues as to why some of the Daoist spirit-writing altars in Hong Kong have suspended spirit-writing and changed their management patterns.

---

73   For the development of spirit-writing altars which have suspended spirit-writing, see Ting, "You 'Ao-fatang' dao 'tianxian jinlongtang'," 1–66; Liao, "Dang luantang buzai fuluan," 116–30.

Bibliography

Chen Yun 陳雲. *Xianggang dalingyi (chuji): Shenyi chuanshuo ji minjian xinyang* 香港大靈異（初集）：神異傳說及民間信仰. Hong Kong: Huaqianshu chuban gongsi, 2010.

Clart, Philip A. "The Ritual Context of Morality Books: A Case-study of a Taiwanese Spirit-writing Cult." PhD diss., University of British Columbia, 1996.

Clart, Philip A. "Chinese Tradition and Taiwanese Modernity: Morality Books as Social Commentary and Critique." In *Religion in Modern Taiwan: Tradition and Innovation in a Changing Society*, edited by Philip A. Clart and Charles B. Jones, 84–97. Honolulu: University of Hawai'i Press, 2003.

Fan Chun-wu 范純武. "Qingmo minjian cishan shiye yu luantang yundong 清末民間慈善事業與鸞堂運動." MA thesis, National Chung Cheng University, 1996.

"Heming shan sansheng gong sannian luocheng, wushi duoming dizi canjia kaiguang dadian 鶴鳴山三聖宮三年落成，五十多名弟子參加開光大典." *Fubao* 福報 3, May 20, 1997.

"Huaren miaoyu tiaoli 華人廟宇條例." *Hong Kong Government Gazette* 74 (1928): 154.

Jiao Dawei 焦大衛 [David K. Jordan] and Ou Danian 歐大年 [Daniel L. Overmyer]. *Feiluan* 飛鸞. Translated by Zhou Yumin 周育民. Hong Kong: Zhongwen daxue chubanshe, 2005.

Jordan, David K., and Daniel L. Overmyer. *The Flying Phoenix: Aspects of Chinese Sectarianism in Taiwan*. Princeton: Princeton University Press, 1986.

Katz, Paul R. "Spirit-writing Halls and the Development of Local Communities: A Case Study of Puli (Nantou County)." *Minsu quyi* 民俗曲藝, no. 174 (December 2011): 103–84.

Kengqiang ji 鏗鏘集. "Buwen cangtian wen guishen 不問蒼天問鬼神." Produced by Hong Kong Radio Station. Aired August 2, 1990.

Lai Chi-tim 黎志添. *Guangdong difang Daojiao yanjiu: Daoguan, daoshi ji keyi* 廣東地方道教研究：道觀、道士及科儀. Hong Kong: Zhongwen daxue chubanshe, 2007.

Lai Chi-tim 黎志添, Yau Chi-on 游子安, and Wu Zhen 吳真. *Xianggang daotang keyi lishi yu chuancheng* 香港道堂科儀歷史與傳承. Hong Kong: Zhonghua shuju, 2007.

Lai Chi-tim 黎志添, Yau Chi-on 游子安, and Wu Zhen 吳真. *Xianggang Daojiao: Lishi yuanliu jiqi xiandai zhuanxing* 香港道教：歷史源流及其現代轉型. Hong Kong: Zhonghua shuju, 2010.

Lang, Graeme, and Lars Ragvald. "Upward Mobility of a Refugee God: Hong Kong's Huang Daxian." *Stockholm Journal of East Asian Studies*, no. 1 (1988): 54–87.

Leung Ki-che 梁其姿. "Daotang hu? Shantang hu? Qingmo Minchu Guangzhou chengnei Xinggong caotang de dute moshi 道堂乎？善堂乎？清末民初廣州城內省躬草堂的獨特模式." In *Ming-Qing diguo jiqi jinxiandai zhuanxing* 明清帝國及其近現代轉型, edited by Chen Yongfa 陳永發, 394–434. Taipei: Yunchen wenhua shiye youxian gongsi, 2011.

Liang Dehua 梁德華, ed. *Liwu jishi: Xianggang Daojiao cishan shiye zonglan* 利物濟世：香港慈善事業總覽. Hong Kong: Xianggao daojiao lianhehui, 2011.

Liao Hsiao-ching 廖小菁. "Dang luantang buzai fuluan: Xianggang dapu xinggong caotang de kaocha 當鸞堂不再扶鸞：香港大埔省躬草堂的考察." In *Zongjiao renleixue, di wu ji* 宗教人類學第五輯, edited by Chen Jinguo 陳進國 and Jin Ze 金澤, 116–30. Beijing: Shehui kexue wenxian chubanshe, 2014.

Luo Dan 羅丹. "Dangdai fuluan tuanti de banshan shijian: Yi Xianggang Feiyandong Fo-Daoshe weili 當代扶鸞團體的辦善實踐：以香港飛雁洞佛道社為例." In *Zongjiao renleixue, di wu ji* 宗教人類學第五輯, edited by Chen Jinguo 陳進國 and Jin Ze 金澤, 189–207. Beijing: Shehui kexue wenxian chubanshe, 2014.

Mai Yesi 邁耶斯 [John Myers]. "Chengshi gongye huanjing zhong de Zhongguo chuantong zongjiao xisu: Yi guantang weili 城市工業環境中的中國傳統宗教習俗：以觀塘為例." In *Zhushen jianianhua: Xianggang zongjiao yanjiu* 諸神嘉年華：香港宗教研究, edited by Chan Shun-hing 陳慎慶, 252–65. Oxford: Oxford University Press, 2002.

Ngai Ting-ming 危丁明. "Xianggang de chuantong zongjiao guanli chutan: Cong 'Wenwumiao tiaoli' dao 'Huaren miaoyu tiaoli' 香港的傳統宗教管理初探：從《文武廟條例》到《華人廟宇條例》." *Tianye yu wenxian* 田野與文獻, no. 49 (2007): 35–44.

Ngai Ting-ming 危丁明, Zhong Jiexiong 鍾潔雄, and Yau Chi-on 游子安. *Xiangjiang xianji: Seseyuan lishi yu huangdaxian xinyang* 香江顯跡：嗇色園歷史與黃大仙信仰. Hong Kong: Seseyuan, 2006.

Poon, Shuk-wah. *Negotiating Religion in Modern China: State and Common People in Guangzhou, 1900–1937*. Hong Kong: Chinese University of Hong Kong Press, 2011.

"Qinzi huodong di shenda, sansui nü kan daopi jing, zhuanjia ze jiaohuai xilu 親子活動睇神打，三歲女看刀劈頸，專家責教壞細路." *Pingguo ribao* 蘋果日報, February 10, 2012.

Shahar, Meir. *Crazy Ji: Chinese Religion and Popular Literature*. Cambridge, MA: Harvard University Press, 1998.

Shiga Ichiko 志賀市子. "Jindai Guangzhou de daotang: Xinggong caotang de yiyao shiye jiqi shiying zhanlue 近代廣州的道堂：省躬草堂的醫藥事業以及其適應戰略." In *Xianggang ji Huanan Daojiao yanjiu* 香港及華南道教研究, edited by Lai Chi-tim 黎志添, 307–33. Hong Kong: Zhonghua shuju, 2005.

Shiga Ichiko 志賀市子. "Yibajiusi nian suigang diqu de shuyi liuxing yu fuluan de jishi 一八九四年穗港地區的鼠疫流行與扶鸞的乩示." *Daojiao wenhua yanjiu zhongxin tongxun* 道教文化研究中心通訊, no. 4 (October 2006): 1–3.

Shiga Ichiko 志賀市子. *Xianggang Daojiao yu fuji xinyang: Lishi yu rentong* 香港道教與扶乩信仰：歷史與認同. Translated by Song Jun 宋軍. Hong Kong: Zhongwen daxue chubanshe, 2013.

Ting Jen-chieh 丁仁傑. "You 'Ao-fatang' dao 'Tianxian jinlongtang': Hanren minjian shequ zhong de fuluan yu zongjiao shijian, chongfang *Feiluan* 由「奧法堂」到「天

仙金龍堂」：漢人民間社區中的扶鸞與宗教實踐，重訪《飛鸞》." *Taiwan renlei xuekan* 臺灣人類學刊 8, no. 3 (2010): 1–66.

Wang Chien-chuan 王見川. "Qingmo Minchu Zhongguo de Jigong xinyang yu fuji tuanti: Jiantan Zhongguo jishenghui de youlai 清末民初中國的濟公信仰與扶乩團體：兼談中國濟生會的由來." *Minsu quyi* 民俗曲藝, no. 162 (Dec. 2008): 139–69.

Wang Ka 王卡. "Yuenan fangdao yanjiu baogao 越南訪道研究報告." *Zhongguo Daojiao* 中國道教, no. 2 (1998): 38–46.

Wei Fuhua 衛復華. "Dayi Heming shan daoguan yange chutan 大邑鶴鳴山道觀沿革初探." *Zongjiao xue yanjiu* 宗教學研究, no. 3–4 (1992): 14–16.

Xuanyin hekan 玄音合刊. Hong Kong: Daojiao mingshan xueyuan, 2001.

Yang Peishan 楊佩珊, Ye Jianmin 葉健民, and Zhu Jialing 朱笳綾. *Yuenan chuanmin zai Xianggang* 越南船民在香港. Hong Kong: Xianggang minzhu tongmeng, 1991.

Yau Chi-on 游子安, ed. *Daofeng bainian: Xianggang Daojiao yu daoguan* 道風百年：香港道教與道觀. Hong Kong: Pengying xianguan daojian wenhua shujuku, Liwen chubanshe, 2002.

Yau Chi-on 游子安. "Fuji zai Xianggang: 1920–1970s 扶乩在香港：1920 年至 1970年代." Lecture, the Hong Kong Institute of Education, January 14, 2011.

Yi Jueci 易覺慈, ed. *Baosong baohe ji* 寶松抱鶴記. Hong Kong: Yunhe shanfang, 1962.

Zhang Ming 章明. "Gaige shinian zhong de Daojiao 改革十年中的道教." *Zongjiao xue yanjiu* 宗教學研究, nos. 1–2 (1989): 1–5.

CHAPTER 16

A Motley Phoenix? On the Diversity of Spirit-Writing Temples and Their Practices in Puli, Taiwan

Paul R. Katz

1 Introductory Remarks

This paper draws on both secondary scholarship as well as my own historical and ethnographic research to assess the impact of Taiwanese spirit-writing temples on communal life, based on a case study of phoenix halls located in the town of Puli 埔里 (Nantou 南投 County, central Taiwan). While spirit-writing rites (usually referred to as *fuji* 扶乩, *fuluan* 扶鸞, or *feiluan* 飛鸞) can be performed at some local temples (often using small deity palanquins known as *nianjiaozai* 輦轎仔) as well as by redemptive societies (*jiushi tuanti* 救世團體) such as the Yiguandao 一貫道 (Way of Pervading Unity), this paper focuses on sacred sites called "phoenix halls" (*luantang* 鸞堂). The core theme of this study is that of diversity, including: 1) Discrepancies among phoenix hall membership, especially in terms of gender; 2) Variations in members' activities, which include not only spirit-writing but also philanthropy, publishing, and a variety of other rituals; 3) Differences in practice by time period and geographic area. The paper's structure is as follows: I begin with a review of previous scholarship on Taiwanese phoenix halls and their activities. Next is the case study of Puli phoenix halls, followed by the paper's conclusion.

An extensive body of research has been done on the social history of temple cult communities in late imperial and modern Taiwan, with results including Donald deGlopper's book on Lukang 鹿港, Stephan Feuchtwang's classic examination of Taipei City's leading sacred sites, Steven Sangren's work on religion and society in Ta-hsi 大溪, Kristofer M. Schipper's seminal study on how temples could structure urban life in Tainan 台南, etc.[1] Regrettably, however, less emphasis has been placed on the social historical development of Taiwanese spirit-writing temples. Of the research on these sacred sites undertaken during

---

[1] DeGlopper, *Lukang*; Feuchtwang, "City Temples"; Sangren, *Magical Power*; Schipper, "Neighborhood Cult Associations."

the past few decades, most has stressed their histories, the activities undertaken by their leadership, and the so-called "Confucian" (Rujia 儒家, Rujiao 儒教) values expressed in the morality books (*shanshu* 善書) they publish, including those composed during spirit-writing (generally referred to as *luanshu* 鸞書).[2] One notable exception is David Jordan and Daniel Overmyer's jointly-authored *The Flying Phoenix*, which vividly portrays the tensions and schisms which have pock-marked the histories of numerous phoenix halls and other spirit-writing groups.[3]

One way to more effectively consider the communal facets of phoenix halls is to do so in light of Vincent Goossaert and David Palmer's thoughtful distinction between ascriptive communities and voluntary congregations. The former, which feature compulsory membership, are generally comprised of temple cults, lineages, and corporations, all of which can play important roles in various public affairs. The latter, characterized by individual participation in different forms of self-cultivation, encompass a wide range of groups, including those practicing pilgrimage and spirit-writing.[4] The data presented in the pages below indicate that while Taiwanese phoenix halls tend to be voluntary in nature, some have become active in public affairs in ways we would normally expect for ascriptive groups. Thus, it seems particularly noteworthy that many of Taipei City's most renowned temples, including the Zhinan gong 指南宮 and Xingtian gong 行天宮, started out as sacred sites for spirit-writing rites staged by voluntary associations, a point made as early as the 1970s in the work of Stephan Feuchtwang.[5] Moreover, the case study of Puli phoenix halls presented below reveals that such groups could mold communal life by engaging in various philanthropic activities, organizing communal rituals, etc.

Paying closer attention to the social aspects of phoenix halls also allows us to better appreciate their inherent diversity. Throughout Taiwan, such sacred sites are home to highly variegated communities of men and women committed to the pursuit of vastly different activities, including self-cultivation, publishing, ritual, moral edification, and community activism. Their initiated members (literally "disciples of the phoenix" or *luansheng* 鸞生) tend to sub-divide into many different groups, and people belonging to one group may not necessarily choose to participate in another group's activities. In general, about a dozen or even fewer male initiates are in charge of a hall's spirit-writing rituals. Those

---

2 See the review of previous scholarship presented below, as well as my state of the field article. Katz, "Bridging the Gaps."
3 Jordan and Overmyer, *Flying Phoenix*.
4 Palmer and Goossaert, *The Religious Question in Modern China*, 24–27.
5 Feuchtwang, "City Temples," 293–300. See also Kang, "Taiwan de Lü Dongbin xinyang."

who actually transcribe poetic and prose messages from the gods are recognized with titles like Chief Wielder (*zheng luansheng* 正鸞生; *zhengji* 正乩) and Assistant Wielder (*fu luansheng* 副鸞生; *fuji* 副乩), while their assistants are referred to as Sand Sweeper (*saosha sheng* 掃砂生), Scribe (*bilu sheng* 筆錄生), etc. While much previous scholarship has investigated these individuals, it is essential to note that many initiates do not directly participate in spirit-writing rituals, especially women. Some devote themselves to performing rites for worshipping a hall's deities, especially scripture chanting (*songjing* 誦經) and the liturgies for reciting divine injunctions (*qing'gao* 請誥) held prior to each spirit-writing session. Others manage the hall's finances and communal activities, including philanthropy, pilgrimages, and participation in festivals. There are also worshippers listed as "believers" (*xintu* 信徒) (especially on forms submitted to the government), who have the right to attend temple committee meetings but may not necessarily be initiated members of the group. Finally, large numbers of men and women who are not formal members at all visit the hall only a few times a year in order to make offerings or pose questions to the gods. To these individuals, a phoenix hall seems little different from any other communal temple. Accordingly, phoenix halls might best be conceived of as voluntary associations of religious self-cultivation for initiated members that are open to non-members, while also playing active roles in the social and religious activities of the communities where they are located.

The phenomena described in this paper hardly existed in isolation; on the contrary, they represent a form of continuity between modern China and Taiwan. Spirit-writing thrived in China during the late Qing and Republican eras, helping to shape the development of many different religious movements and groups. Overlap between Buddhism and spirit-writing was widespread during the late imperial era,[6] and persisted well into modern times as well.[7] For example, spirit-writing exerted a profound influence on the Buddhist practices of one of Shanghai's most famous elites, Wang Yiting 王一亭 (1867–1938), with one of the first religious groups he is mentioned as joining in 1916 (and later leading) being the Zhongguo jisheng hui 中國濟生會 (China Rescuing Life Association). A number of sources claim that Wang joined this group after being converted by Jigong 濟公, an eccentric Buddhist monk worshipped as a popular deity, taking the dharma name Jueqi 覺器 during a spirit-writing ritual. Even monastic leaders like Yinguang 印光 (1861–1940) and Taixu 太虛 (1887–1947) were not

---

6 Yau, *Shan yu ren tong*, 153–55.

7 For an overview of these phenomena, see Katz, "Elite Religious Life," 275–350; Wang, "Spirit-writing Groups." See also the contributions by Fan Chun-wu and Matthias Schumann in this volume.

unsympathetic to spirit-writing, providing that such rites were used by lay worshippers to further the cause of philanthropy, not serve as an aid to Buddhist self-cultivation.[8]

Moreover, as we will see in the case study of Puli below, spirit-writing and Daoist practices often overlapped. Spirit-writing was an integral component of many lay Daoist organizations that tended to be organized around altars (*tan* 壇) or halls (*tang* 堂) dedicated to the worship of Lü Dongbin 呂洞賓 yet also featured the inclusion of Buddhist deities like Jigong. Devout believers could be formally accepted as disciples during spirit-writing rituals, practicing "cultivating life" (*yangsheng* 養生) and internal alchemy (*neidan* 內丹) while preserving records of spirit-writing rituals in massive canons usually referred to as *quanshu* 全書.[9] Spirit-writing associations featuring Daoist beliefs and practices proved to be extremely popular throughout much of China,[10] one of the best known having originated at the Gu meihua guan 古梅花觀 (Venerable Plum Flower Temple; also known as the Chunyang gong 純陽宮 or Hall of Purified Yang), located on Mount Jin'gai (Jin'gaishan 金蓋山) in Huzhou 湖州. Under the leadership of Min Yide 閔一得 (1758–1836; one of the most renowned figures of the Longmen 龍門 branch of Quanzhen 全真 Daoism) as well as his disciples, branch altars and their spirit-writing practices spread to cover much of the Jiangnan 江南 region.[11]

Spirit-writing also played a significant role in shaping the growth of modern China's redemptive societies, including the Tongshan she 同善社 (Fellowship of Goodness), the Daoyuan 道院 (Society of the Way, as well as its better-known philanthropic branch, the Shijie hongwanzi hui 世界紅卍字會 or World Red Swastika Society), the Wanguo daode hui 萬國道德會 (Universal Morality Society), the Zailijiao 在理教 (Teachings of the Abiding Principle), and the Yiguandao. During the flux and instability that marked the late Qing and Republican eras, redemptive societies gained notoriety not only for their emphasis on proper moral conduct and engagement in philanthropic activities, but also for their practice of spirit-writing rituals.[12] One recent study by

---

8   Studies of these phenomena include Wang, "Qingmo Minchu Zhongguo de Jigong xinyang"; Fan, "Jinxiandai Zhongguo Fojiao yu fuji"; Katz, *Religion in China*, 143–46.
9   Goossaert, "Rise of Divine Saviors"; Liu, *Daoist Modern*; Fan, "Feiluan, xiuzhen yu banshan"; Lai, "Zheng Guanying 'xiandao' yu 'jiushi' de sixiang yu shijian."
10 Overviews may be found in Goossaert, *The Daoists of Peking*, 308–19; Shiga, "The Manifestations of Lüzu"; Yuria, "Identity and Lineage"; Lai, "Hong Kong Daoism"; Wu, *Jiangnan Quanzhen Daojiao*; Lai, Yau, and Wu, *Xianggang Daojiao*, 7–48, 87–118.
11 Esposito, "*Daozang jiyao*"; Chen, "Shanghai Daojiaoshi"; Gao, "Jin'gaishan wangluo"; Wang, *Huzhou Jin'gaishan Gu Meihuaguan zhi*; Wang, "Wuxing Quanzhendao shiliao."
12 See Ownby, "Redemptive Societies"; DuBois, *The Sacred Village*, 107–20; Duara, *Sovereignty*

Yau Chi On 游子安 reveals that, in contrast to the general decline of communal temples, sacred sites belonging to voluntary religious groups found ways to survive and even flourish during these trying times, developing in new settings such as large cities and overseas.[13] Some redemptive societies and their spirit-writing rites continue to thrive throughout Taiwan and other parts of the world today, most notably the Yiguandao.[14]

In addition, spirit-writing could impact the lives of individual elites who did not necessarily choose to join a religious group. One example of modern Chinese elite religiosity that also sheds light on the convoluted interaction between Buddhist and spirit-writing involves the renowned boxing instructor Chen Weiming 陳微明 (1881–1958), who relied on spirit-writing to communicate with his son on a regular basis following his tragic passing at age 26. Records of spirit-writing messages exchanged between father and son appeared in print for many months before the journal publishing these texts decided to cease doing so due to objections by some of its readers.[15] In another instance, the Shanghai literatus Gao Chuiwan 高吹萬 (1879–1958) attempted to use spirit-writing to contact the soul of his teenage daughter following her tragic death just prior to her marriage.[16] Other elites who did not practice spirit-writing also evinced an interest in such practices.[17]

2 Review of Previous Scholarship

As noted above, the vast majority of research on spirit-writing in modern Taiwan has focused on the history of sacred sites, the lives of the elites who helped found and lead them, and the beliefs and practices described in the texts that they produced. Based on Wang Chien-chuan 王見川's 1996 state of the field article,[18] we can see that early scholarship on phoenix halls examined records of their activities dating to the Japanese colonial era (1895–1945),

---

  and Authenticity, 103–22, 139–40, 154–62; Billioud and Thoraval, *The Sage and the People*; Chiang, "1930 niandai Tianjin Duliu zhen shangren"; Sun, *Kindai Chūgoku no kakumei*; Sakai, *Kingendai Chūgoku ni okeru shūkyō kessha no kenkyū*.

13 Yau, "Dadao nanxing."

14 Sung, *Tiandao chuandeng*; Lin, *Yiguandao fazhanshi*; Chung, *Wang Jueyi*; Lu, *The Transformation of Yiguandao*.

15 A detailed account of these events may be found in Katz, *Religion in China*, 114–16.

16 Zhou, "Minguo shiqi yige wentan juzi jibixia de lingjie."

17 One such elite, Xu Dishan 許地山 (1893–1941), composed a detailed study of spirit-writing's historical development; see Xu, *Fuji mixin di yanjiu*.

18 Wang, "Taiwan luantang yanjiu." See also Cheng, *Taiwan fuji yu luanshu*.

especially suppression campaigns resulting from the ability of leading halls to cure members of opium addiction, thereby posing a threat to the colonial monopoly.[19] Research conducted from the 1980s to early 1990s treated the growth of renowned sacred sites and their texts, as well as the ways in which the contents of these works helped shed light on social changes that marked the modern era. One of the leading figures of that era was the late Sung Kuang-yu 宋光宇 (1949–2016), whose pioneering research on works like the *Diyu youji* 地獄遊記 (A journey to earth prison) plus the groups that produced them (such as the Shengxian tang 聖賢堂 (Hall of Worthies) in Taichung 台中, which also published the magazine *Luanyou zazhi* 鸞友雜誌) called attention to the significance of phoenix halls in modern-day Taiwan.[20]

The 1990s were marked by an increasing number of studies that blended historical research and fieldwork, many of which traced the transmission patterns of phoenix hall beliefs and practices. Wang Chien-chuan and Li Shih-wei 李世偉 have been (and remain) two of Taiwan's most productive scholars in this field, combining combined historical research and fieldwork to collect vast amounts of new data, especially scriptures, biographical accounts of religious leaders, and newspaper accounts of religious activities, while presenting clear and thorough descriptions of phoenix hall development. Wang Chien-chuan's research has relied on a wealth of primary sources, including phoenix halls' own records, to trace their networks of transmission and affiliation,[21] including links to local elite families,[22] while Li Shih-wei has focused on forms of "Confucian religion" (Rujiao 儒教) promoted by local elites (sometimes referred to by Li as "Confucians" or *rushi* 儒士) via socio-religious organizations that include not only phoenix halls but also related groups such as poetry societies (*shishe* 詩社), literary societies (*wenshe* 文社), and charitable societies (*shanshe* 善社).[23] Wang and Li have also collected a significant amount of information on Hakka spirit-writing halls, which has helped spark a wave of new research on this topic by the next generation of scholars.[24] In addition, Wang Chih-yu 王志宇 and Philip Clart have traced the growth of spirit-writing groups in parts of central Taiwan, while also delineating the impact of their textual traditions as well as their interaction with other voluntary religious associations like the

---

19 See the classic study by Wang, "Riju chuqi Taiwan zhi jiangbi hui."
20 Sung, "Cong *Diyu youji*"; Sung, "Jiedu Qingmo zai Taiwan zhuanzuo de shanshu." Sung has also called our attention to the importance of spirit-painting. See Sung, *Zhengzong shenji*.
21 Wang, "Qingmo Riju chuqi Taiwan de luantang."
22 Wang, "Lüelun Chen Zhonghe jiazu."
23 Li, *Riju shidai Taiwan de Rujiao*; Li, "Binhai fu shengdao."
24 Li, "Miaoli Kejia diqu de luantang diaocha"; Wang, "Guangfu qian Taiwan Kejia diqu luantang chutan."

Yiguandao.[25] Other scholars have studied phoenix halls and spirit-writing rites in the contexts of colonial-era resistance[26] and the importance of religious specialists known as ritualists (*lisheng* 禮生).[27]

One of Wang Chien-chuan's most important contributions is a study of stories about Guandi 關帝's being promoted to the position of Jade Emperor (usually referred to as *Guandi dang Yudi* 關帝當玉帝 or *Guangong zuo tiangong* 關作坐天公). Wang's research convincingly demonstrates that accounts of Guandi's "promotion" appear to have arisen in the course of spirit-writing rituals in southwest China during the early twentieth century, and were linked to the Xiantiandao 先天道 (Way of Former Heaven). These beliefs then spread throughout China during the 1920s and 1930s and apparently traveled to Taiwan with mainlander sectarians after 1945, where they were actively promoted by the Shengxian tang, a large-scale spirit-writing temple in Taichung. Wang also provides a stimulating account of the reception accorded to this new belief, which appears to have been mixed at best, especially among non-sectarian temples.[28]

Philip Clart's work has provided key perspectives for the field, including his analysis of one phoenix hall scripture *Guanyin miaodao lianhua jing* 觀音妙道蓮華經 (Guanyin's *Lotus Sutra* of the marvelous Dao), which reveals a strikingly sophisticated layering of Guanyin devotionalism around a core devoted to a cosmology of the universal Dao, in which the popular and more accessible worship of Guanyin is used as an entry point into the more esoteric points of the "marvellous Dao" (*miaodao* 妙道) of phoenix hall doctrine. Clart's analysis is a potential key for understanding the articulation of syncretism in spirit-writing texts, and his ethnographic approach to textual production, while impossible to replicate for the study of early twentieth century groups, provides important insights into how spirit writing may have influenced their inner dynamics.[29]

The twenty-first century has witnessed a growing number of MA and Ph.D. theses by younger scholars, many of whom were trained by the individuals mentioned above. For example, Chen Chien-hung 陳建宏's study of the Puji tang 普濟堂 in Ta-hsi 大溪 traced its development from a minor phoenix hall

---

25   Wang, *Taiwan de Enzhugong xinyang*; Clart, "The Phoenix and the Mother"; Clart, "Chinese Tradition and Taiwanese Modernity"; Wang, "Zhanhou Taiwan xinxing luantang," 351–84.
26   See for example Katz, *When Valleys Turned Blood Red*, 59, 65–66, 81, 93–96, 101–2, 157, 175, 199, 251.
27   Lee, "Lisheng yu daoshi."
28   Wang, "Taiwan 'Guandi dang Yudi' chuanshuo de youlai." See also ter Haar, *Guan Yu*, 239–43.
29   Clart, "Anchoring Guanyin."

into a mammoth public temple (*difang gongmiao* 地方公廟) that played a leading role in not only local charitable activities but also organizing the town's annual procession for Guandi.[30] In addition, MA theses by Chang Yu-chih 張有志 and Cheng Pao-chen 鄭寶珍 presented a wealth of new findings on the Daiquan tang 代勸堂, a prominent phoenix hall situated atop Flying Phoenix Mountain (Feifeng shan 飛鳳山) in Jiuqionglin 九芎林 (Hsinchu 新竹) which played a vital role in the spread of spirit-writing to other halls in Taiwan, including some in Puli (see below).[31] Chou Yi-jan 周怡然 has examined similar processes in the context of literati networks that centered on these sacred sites, some of which also functioned as academies (*shuyuan* 書院) or other establishments that promoted classical education.[32] There has also been a growth in research on phoenix halls located in southern Taiwan, including Chang Er-wen 張二文's pioneering doctoral dissertation on Hakka sites in Liudui 六堆,[33] Chiu Yen-chou 邱延州's study of the networks such sites established in Fengshan 鳳山 (Kaohsiung),[34] and Chung An 鍾安's research on the Guang-shan tang 廣善堂 in Meinong 美濃.[35] In addition, Chiang Chao-chan 江趙展 has completed an MA thesis on one of northern Taiwan's most important phoenix halls, the Xingzhong tang 行忠堂, founded in Tamsui 淡水 by the Li 李 family in 1899, which explores the development of this site in terms of its dissemination of beliefs and practices as well as its ability to adapt to changing times.[36]

Some of the above-mentioned scholars presented their newest findings at an international conference held in Yilan 宜蘭 in May 2018. Chiang Chao-chan explored a number of changes the Xingzhong tang experienced during the postwar era,[37] including the advent of verbal communications for spirit-writing rituals, a decline in healing practices (also common among Puli phoenix halls; see below), the addition of new deities like the Three Pure Ones (Sanqing 三清) and Maitreya Buddha (Mile Fo 彌勒佛), the creation of a special room for dream divination (*qimengshi* 祈夢室; also used by the Zhinan gong to great effect during the colonial era), and choosing to stage Dipper Bushel Cere-

---

30   Chen, "Gongmiao yu difang shehui."
31   Chang, "Rizhi shiqi Gaoxiong diqu luantang"; Cheng, "Taiwan Liudui Kejia diqu luantang."
32   Chou, "Zhongzhan qian Miaoli Kejia diqu luantang."
33   Chang, "Liudui Kejia diqu luanshu."
34   Chiu, "Fengshan diqu luantang xinyang."
35   Chung, "Luantang yu difang shehui."
36   Chiang, "Jiazu yu luantang."
37   Overviews of religious change in the context of postwar Taiwan's development include: Jordan, "Popular Practice of Religion"; Clart and Jones, *Religion in Modern Taiwan*; Madsen, *Democracy's Dharma*.

monies (*lidou fahui* 禮斗法會) plus Daoist Offering Ceremonies (*jianjiao fahui* 建醮法會) featuring scripture chanting troupes (*songjing tuan* 誦經團), all of which constituted a new type of religious ecology. Thus, the history of the Xingzhong tang reveals the gradual disappearance of older types of phoenix hall beliefs and practices followed by the adoption of new ones. There were also papers by Chiu Yen-chou on the interactions between different phoenix halls in Fengshan plus their links to local temples (both of which were tied into local elite networks), as well as Chang Er-wen on how the members of Liudui phoenix halls took care of local charitable cemeteries (*yizhong* 義塚) as a form of philanthropy.[38]

Another innovative facet of recent research involves gender issues, particularly women's pursuit of self-cultivation. Huang Pingying 黃萍瑛's study of female disciples (*nüluan* 女鸞) at one Puli phoenix hall provides a thoughtful account of their motivations for becoming members, their age at initiation, the struggles they encounter during their training, and the joys they experience from successfully completing self-cultivation. Huang raises an important point about the "invisibility" of female disciples in research on this topic, noting that their main form of ritual practice, namely scripture recitation, has been largely ignored by scholars researching phoenix halls. However, inasmuch as female disciples represent a sizeable proportion of a hall's membership, and the scripture recitation rituals they perform can provide a major source of prestige (not to mention income), the roles these female disciples play clearly merits far more attention in the future.[39]

3   Case Study: Phoenix Halls in Puli

The data presented below were collected during a research project undertaken from 2008 to 2010,[40] the goal of which was to investigate the social history and

---

[38] Chiang, "Zhanhou Xingzhong tang de bianqian"; Chiu, "Fengshan diqu luantang shehui wangluo"; Chang, "Liudui Kejia diqu luanshu." All three papers were presented at The Culture of Flying Phoenix and Popular Religions International Conference, Lanyang Museum and Fo Guang University, May 28–29, 2018.

[39] Huang, "Dangdai Puli luansheng." See also the contributions by Elena Valussi and Xia Shi in this volume.

[40] This project was funded by a two-year National Science Council (國科會) research grant (NSC 97-2410-H-001-112-MY2). I would like to thank Chiu Cheng-lueh 邱正略, Huang Pingying and Yeh Yu-lun 葉育倫 for their invaluable assistance. Published works include: Katz, "Spirit-writing and Hakka Migration"; Katz, "Spirit-writing Halls"; Katz, "Taiwan de difang shequn."

current communal activities of phoenix halls in the town of Puli (see Table 16.1). During the project, my assistants and I traced the geographic distribution of Puli's spirit-writing halls (many are concentrated in the town itself, but others lie on its outskirts or foothills), studied their historical growth, explored the roles played by local elites, delineated their internal organization as well as networks of connections, and analyzed the significance of their rituals and festivals. The historical and ethnographic materials that we obtained reveal that phoenix halls continue to impact Puli's religious life today through their engagement with local networks of power, while their ritual, educational, and philanthropic activities have helped shape communal life. One might even be so bold as to say that some of these sites have developed along the lines of patterns similar to those of major public temples.

Gary Seaman's path-breaking work on the importance of phoenix halls in Puli's modern history has proved invaluable for my own research, especially his detailed and stimulating study of one such site that developed out of a household spirit-writing altar, the Xingjue tang 醒覺堂. This hall's founder, Gu Tianquan 辜添泉 (fl. 1936–1937), brought a statue of the immortal Lü Dongbin (also known as Benevolent Lord Lü or Lü Enzhu 呂恩主) back with him from Taipei following the Pacific War, which became the focus of a new spirit-writing cult that arose in 1946. After many years marked by complex patterns of religious development, including the adoption of spirit-medium practices centering on the Monkey deity Sun Wukong 孫悟空 (Qitian dasheng 齊天大聖) as well as a schism among the group's members, the Xingjue tang eventually grew into a thriving phoenix hall by the 1950s. Seaman's study reveals the importance of Puli's phoenix halls in local political life after the collapse of the colonial era's *hokō* 保甲 system, as well as the ways in which local elites strive to use these sacred sites in order to increase their symbolic capital and manipulate local networks of power.[41]

3.1 *Hakka Migration*

The role phoenix halls played in shaping Puli's patterns of migration and ethnic interaction may be seen in the historical development of one of central Taiwan's most prominent Hakka phoenix halls, the Canzan tang 參贊堂.[42] Located in Yongxing 永興 (Yixin 一新) Village, this temple was founded in 1902, and appears to have been linked by division of incense (*fenxiang* 分香) to Puli's oldest spirit-writing temple, the Huaishan tang 懷善堂.[43] At the same time, the

---

41 Seaman, *Temple Organization*. See also Chen, *Xuanping gong Xingjue tang zhi*, 60–61.
42 For more on this temple's history, see Katz, "Spirit-writing and Hakka Migration."
43 Division of incense refers to the act of taking incense ashes from the burner of an existing

Canzan tang also appears to have had ties to northern Taiwan Hakka phoenix halls, especially the Daiquan tang, with spirit-writing practices being brought to Puli by Hakka migrants by Hakka migrants from Hsinchu who journeyed there to work in the local camphor industry. Therefore, the growth of the Canzan tang constitutes one example of the key role of Hakka migration and ritual networks, which have been studied by Li Shih-wei, Chang Yu-chih, and Chou Yi-ran (see above).[44] This hall's history is also inseparable from the renowned Hakka cult of the Heroes (Yiminye 義民爺), which spread to Puli via division of incense from its home temple in Xinpu 新埔 (Hsinchu County),[45] as well as Hakka ritual associations (changhui 嘗會) founded by local elites at the Canzan tang to support their worship.[46]

Despite the paucity of source material about the Canzan tang's early history, the relationship between this hall and the Daiquan tang was clearly a close one. This can be seen in the case of two poems composed by Yang Fulai 楊福來 (1874–1948), the renowned Chief Wielder of the Daiquan tang. From 1915 to 1939 Yang spent considerable time visiting phoenix halls in central and southern Taiwan, training local wielders, participating in spirit-writing rites, and assisting in the production of morality books. Yang's travels included the Canzan tang, which he visited sometime during the 1920s. Yang was so attracted by this hall that at one point he considered abandoning his post at the Daiquan tang and becoming Chief Wielder at the Canzan tang, only to be dissuaded by the Maitreya Buddha during a spirit-writing ritual.[47]

Other evidence for the profound influence of northern Taiwan Hakka on Puli's spirit-writing cults may be found in the history of the Yuhua tang 育化堂, whose first Chief Wielder, Liu Wangjin 劉旺進 (1886–1969) trained in spirit-writing at the Longtian gong Xuanhua tang 龍天宮宣化堂 (dedicated to Shennong 神農) in Dahu 大湖 (Miaoli 苗栗 County).[48] The presence of devoted Hakka spirit-writers is even noted in historical accounts about

---

temple cult and mixing them into the ashes of a new cult's burner. See Schipper, "Cult of Pao-sheng ta-ti."

44 Li, "Miaoli Kejia diqu de luantang diaocha"; Chang, "Rizhi shiqi Gaoxiong diqu luantang"; Chou, "Zhongzhan qian Miaoli Kejia diqu luantang."

45 Detailed studies of the history of this cult include: Chuang, "Xinzhu Fangliao Yimin Miao"; Lai, *Yiminye xinyang*; Lin, *Jiazu yu simiao*.

46 For more on Hakka ritual associations, see Cohen, "Minong 美濃's Corporations"; Lin, "Kejia diyu shehui zuzhi de bianqian." See also Cohen, *Kinship, Contract, Community, and State*.

47 Cheng, "Taiwan Liudui Kejia diqu luantang," 19–26. See also Wang, "Guangfu qian Taiwan Kejia diqu luantang chutan."

48 *Zhaoping gong Yuhua tang jianshi*, 23.

Puli's venerable Presbyterian church located in Ailan 愛蘭 (Wuniulan 烏牛欄), one of which describes white-clothed Hakka circumambulating Nantou's scenic Sun Moon Lake (Riyue Tan 日月潭) in September 1916, preaching the word of the Three Benevolent Ones (San enzhu 三恩主; namely Lü Dongbin, Guandi, and Wenchang 文昌) and encouraging people to adopt a vegetarian diet.[49]

3.2 Local Elites and Networks of Power

The materials collected during our research indicate that the rapid growth of Puli's phoenix halls has in large part resulted from the efforts of local elites, including those who manage these sacred sites and those who perform as Chief Wielders and Assistant Wielders during their rites. These elites consisted of not only gentry and highly educated literati but also less educated men (and some women) with the power to influence communal affairs.[50] It is essential to note that many of the elites described below actively patronized local religious activities not only as a means of augmenting their symbolic capital and tapping into local networks of power, but also as acts of individual devotion.[51] In terms of occupation, a sizeable percentage of these elites were rice merchants, including Xu Qinghe 許清和 (1896–1982) and Luo Yinhan 羅銀漢 (1895–1975; father of late Academia Sinica Vice-President Luo Tongbi 羅銅壁 (1927–2019)),[52] but others made a living in professions linked to phoenix hall activities, particularly healing and publishing (prominent examples include Chen Shilian 陳石鍊 (1900–1974), Shi Baichuan 施百川 (1876–1919), Lin Wenxiong 林文雄 (1924–2006), Chen Nanyao 陳南要 (1916–1988), and Qiu Shitou 邱石頭 (1916–1992)). There were also quite a few scholars and poets, most notably Wang Zisheng 王梓聖 (1914–1997), the Chief Wielder of the Yuhua tang. In addition, phoenix hall leaders have featured a number of prominent politicians (including former mayor Bai Jinzhang 白金章 (b. 1924) and numerous other elected representatives). It is thus hardly a coincidence that these sites are also key nodes in electoral politics, with three candidates running for elected office in 1997 (Peng Baixian 彭百顯 (b. 1949), Zhang Hongming 張鴻銘 (b. 1955) (b. 1965), and Ma Wenjun 馬文君) worshipping at phoenix halls and asking the gods about their campaigns' prospects.

---

49 Lai, *Taiwan tulong chuanqi*, 42–43, 50–51.
50 For more on this definition of the term "elite", see Esherick and Rankin, "Introduction," 10–13; Chen, "Qingdai bei Taoyuan."
51 These issues are discussed in Kang, "Zhongguo dizhi wanqi yijiang simiao yishi"; Katz, "Local Elites and Sacred Sites." See also Goossaert, "Diversity and Elite Religiosity."
52 *Xuanping gong Yuhua tang jianshi*, 19–21.

Puli elites also played active roles in the Yuhua tang, with the list of this hall's leadership reading like a veritable Puli "Who's Who", including Zheng Jinshui 鄭錦水 (1907–1928), Su Shumu 蘇樹木 (1902–1979), Xu Qinghe, Chen Nanyao, Chen Shilian, and Luo Yinhan. Many of these men were involved in more than one phoenix hall and even some public temples as well, while others not only managed temples but helped perform spirit-writing rituals. A few were even related by marriage, with one of Xu Qinghe's daughters marrying one of Luo Yinhan's sons.

One important Hakka elite was Cai Kunxiang 蔡堃祥 (1862–1931), a Xinpu native who migrated to Puli during the 1880s and 1890s and devoted himself to a wide range of charitable activities, including the construction and management of sacred sites like the Canzan tang.[53] Another leading elite patron of the Canzan tang was You Chao'an 游朝安 (1843–1909), a Hakka whose ancestors came to Taiwan from Zhao'an 詔安. The You and Cai families appear to have been particularly close, so much so that when the Three Benevolent Ones declared that Cai Kunxiang's son Cai Jinchuan 蔡錦川 (b. 1920) needed an adoptive father (yifu 義父) in order to be cured of an illness,[54] the man chosen for this role was none other than You Chao'an. Plains Aborigine elites also patronized the Canzan tang, including Zhang Shichang 張世昌 (1862–1927) and members of the Zhang Dasheng 張大陸 settlement group (kenhu 墾戶). This indicates the importance of interaction between Plains Aborigines and Hakka in Taiwanese history, which seem similar to the links between the Hakka and *She* 畬 ethnic groups in south China.[55] On an even broader level, such phenomena point to the potential of voluntary religious associations like phoenix halls to bridge ethnic and sub-ethnic boundaries.

Networking is also a central component of phoenix hall development. While some practitioners choose to identify themselves using the autonym ("Divine Teachings of the Confucian Religion" or Ruzong shenjiao 儒宗神教), which suggests the presence of an organized religion, most halls do not belong to a centralized organization.[56] Inasmuch as the average phoenix hall boasts only a small number of initiated members who regularly participate in its ritual calendar, it is essential that different halls support each other's activities. In other words, for a phoenix hall to survive it must generate and maintain networks of mutual assistance, which is particularly important for activities such

---

53 Cai, *Jiyang tang*, 207.
54 Interview with Cai Jinchuan (October 25, 2007).
55 Such patterns of interaction are discussed in Shepherd, *Statecraft and Political Economy*. See also Yang, "Jingjiu bushuai de 'lunsiquan'."
56 Clart, "Confucius and the Mediums."

as training new wielders and producing morality books. Such phenomena are readily apparent in the case of Puli's phoenix halls, the leaders of which devoted considerable effort to establishing and maintaining ties to other halls. For example, the mutual assistance they provided could be critical when it came time to train new mediums. During the revival of spirit-writing practices that took place following the Japanese colonial era, the Huaishan tang's Chief Wielder Lin Zaitian 林再添 (1913–1987) provided vital support when the Yuhua tang used spirit-writing to compose morality books such as the *Yinwu xian* 引悟線 (String leading to enlightenment) and *Pomi zhen* 破迷針 (Needle to pierce superstition).[57] The Yuhua tang later returned the favor when Huaishan tang members were using spirit-writing to produce the *Dachi bian* 打痴鞭 (Whip for thrashing the ignorant).[58] Similar patterns are discussed in Chiu Yen-chou's study of spirit-writing halls in Fengshan, some of which were founded by local practitioners who had learned these ritual techniques elsewhere.[59]

Elite activism and networks of connections were especially apparent in the ways that phoenix halls worked to organize Puli's Daoist offering festivals (*jiao* 醮) during the early decades of the postwar era, including performing spirit-writing to determine the dates these communal ceremonies were to be held. Many Puli phoenix hall elites took the lead in staging these mammoth ritual events, particularly during the years 1948, 1952, 1972, and 1975, with just over 50% of the organizers serving as phoenix hall managers (28 out of 51 individuals). Such trends were most pronounced in 1948 (57%), 1952 (100%, but limited source base) and 1972 (70%). It also seems extremely significant that spirit-writing rituals for coordinating the planning phases of these offering rites were usually performed by Puli's leading phoenix hall, the Yuhua tang, but on a few occasions were also held at the Hengji gong 恒吉宮, Puli's most venerable public temple dedicated to the goddess Mazu 媽祖. Spirit-writing rites at the Yuhua tang were presided over solely by that hall's wielders, but on occasions when they were performed at the Hengji gong all of Puli's wielders would gather there, with the chief and assistant wielders being chosen by means of a divining block ritual. Once the wielders had been selected, the gods would provide detailed instructions on how the offering festival was to be carried out. The significance of spirit-writing in planning these rites declined rapidly by the 1980s however, due to the election of a new chairman of the board at the

---

57 Katz, "Spirit-writing Halls."
58 *Zhaoping gong Yuhua tang jianshi*, 31.
59 Chiu, "Fengshan diqu luantang shehui wangluo." For more on spirit-writing networks, see the contributions by Zhu Mingchuan 朱明川 and Luo Dan 羅丹 in this volume.

Hengji gong who apparently was not on good terms with the Yuhua tang's leadership and had a dim view of spirit-writing rituals. Valuable comparable data may be found in Chen Chien-hung's study of Ta-hsi's Puji tang, which proved active in local ritual life to the point of organizing one of the town's largest festivals.[60] In addition, Chiu Yen-chou's MA thesis reveals that Fengshan elites were active in both phoenix halls and temples, with both types of sacred sites serving as public spaces where people could worship, visit, stage weddings, etc.[61]

3.3   *Daoist Influence*

The history of Puli's phoenix halls was also marked by mutually beneficial interaction between Daoism and spirit-writing traditions, with Daoism contributing to the development of some of these sacred sites.[62] For example, the Xingling si 醒靈寺 engaged in extensive cooperation with Daoist leaders as early as 1962, when it invited the 63rd Heavenly Master Zhang En'pu 張恩溥 (1894–1969) to perform rituals in celebration of Laozi 老子's birthday (Taishang laojun shengdan 太上老君聖誕). As a result, the hall rescheduled its annual Bushel Lantern Festival (*Lidou qi'an fahui* 禮斗祈安法會) from the ninth lunar month to the second lunar month, a practice that persists to the present day. Just over twenty years later (from 1983 to 1985), the hall's leadership invited a leading Daoist master from Qingshui 清水 (Taichung) named Cai Maoxiong 蔡茂雄 (fl. 1962–1985) to instruct its members in Daoist liturgy, including the *fabiao* 發表, *wugong* 午供, and *fendeng* 分燈 rites; Cai had accompanied the Heavenly Master on his visit to the Xingling si in 1962, and also served an instructor at the China Daoism Institute (Zhonghua Daojiao xueyuan 中華道教學院), located at another leading sacred site that had started out as a phoenix hall yet also had close links to Daoism, the Zhinan gong. Some of the Xingling si's leading male worshippers chose to study with Cai, but many women did so as well. The temple's current group of Daoist ritualists, the Xuanmen Troupe (Xuanmen zu 玄門組), is composed almost entirely of married women, and only the women perform Daoist rites. Other spirit-writing groups in Taiwan have interacted extensively with Daoism, as can be seen in Wang Chien-chuan's stimulating discussion of the links between Cihui tang 慈惠堂 groups and the Daoist Heavenly Master Zhang (Zhang Tianshi 張天師) beginning in the 1960s.[63] More recently, Chiang

---

60   Chen, "Gongmiao yu difang shehui."
61   Chiu, "Fengshan diqu luantang shehui wangluo."
62   For more information on the connection between spirit-writing altars and Daoism, see also the contributions by Luo Dan and Li Guoping in this volume.
63   Wang, "Cihui tang yu Zhang Tianshi."

Chao-chan's research has shown that such interaction also marked the history of Danshui's Xingzhong tang.[64]

At the same time, however, other members of the Xingling si have maintained membership in Buddhist and lay Buddhist groups, the Shamen Troupe (Shamen zu 沙門組) and the Longhua Troupe (Longhua zu 龍華組). The Longhua Troupe, most of whose members are women, is the temple's oldest group of ritualists, having been founded by senior members during the early years of the postwar era. The Shamen Troupe was formed during the 1960s, with temple members learning Buddhist rites under the tutelage of a Buddhist monk from Fengyuan 豐原 (Taichung County). While control over the performance of longevity (tianshou 添壽) rites on behalf of worshippers has shifted from the Shamen Troupe to the Xuanmen Troupe, all three groups take part in the temple's annual Bushel Lantern Festival. All this indicates the need to recognize the importance of Daoism to the Xingling si's historical development, while also avoiding the tendency to label this sacred site and its membership using the adjective "Daoist".

Puli's phoenix halls also play highly visible roles in contributing to communal welfare. Most phoenix halls engage in at least one or two forms of philanthropy, including offering scholarships to students in need, feeding the poor, healing the sick, providing emergency relief, caring for the elderly, etc. The most active phoenix halls include the Yuhua tang and the Xingling si, while the Xingjue tang has established its own foundation to promote these efforts (the Xingjue wenjiao jijinhui 醒覺文教基金會).

3.4 *Members and Their Practices*

When we turn our attention to membership and practices, it soon becomes clear that while Puli's sacred sites are referred to as "phoenix halls", spirit-writing rituals represent only one facet of their religious life, and, depending on whom one interviews/observes, may not even constitute a hall's most important activity. Our observations suggest that only a few dozen initiated members (*luansheng*) regularly take part in organizing and undertaking a given hall's activities, with even fewer participating in spirit-writing sessions. Initiation represents a venerable rite of passage for spirit-writing and many other voluntary associations and marks a key difference between such groups and ascriptive ones. In order to earn the right to be initiated (*ruluan* 入鸞), one must offer long-term service at the temple under the watchful eyes of overseers

---

64   Chiang, "Zhanhou Xingzhong tang de bianqian."

(*jianluan* 監鸞) chosen by the hall's deities. Once a worshipper is considered ready for initiation, final approval must be given at a special meeting of all initiated members.

In light of the fact that relatively little research has been done on women members of phoenix halls,[65] my research assistants and I made every effort to interview female *luansheng* (*nüluan* 女鸞; of the 151 *luansheng* we interviewed, 51 were women). Female *luansheng* tend to undergo initiation relatively late in their lives. Among male members for whom we have data, 47% were initiated after age 41; for female members, the figure is 66%. One factor underlying this discrepancy may well be the fact that most women have little choice but to wait for their children to grow up enough so that they have the time to commit themselves fully to a phoenix hall's activities.[66] Other women hinted that, in the interests of ritual purity, they felt more comfortable joining after reaching menopause. I would also note that more women than men become initiated members because of an interest in practicing scripture chanting (21% vs. only 12%). Regardless of whether they are menopausal, initiated women rarely take part in spirit-writing sessions, except for occasions when they wish to pose questions to the temple's deities (see below). Be that as it may, while such questions generally center on family well-being, most of the initiated women at phoenix halls prefer to devote their efforts to other ritual activities related to their mission of self-cultivation, such as reading or chanting scriptures. This suggests a contrast with women who are active in temples that do not practice spirit-writing, including those who join such temples' scripture chanting troupes: the initiated women who participate in a phoenix hall's ritual life tend to be especially concerned with their own self-cultivation.

At Puli's phoenix halls, spirit-writing rituals are but the acme of an evening-long liturgical program that usually begins with scripture chanting. Some of the most frequently used texts derive from Daoist or spirit-writing ritual traditions, including the *Nandou zhenjing* 南斗真經 (True scripture of the Southern Dipper), *Beidou zhenjing* 北斗真經 (True scripture of the Northern Dipper), *Sanguan dadi zhenjing* 三官大帝真經 (True scripture of the Great Emperors of the Three Offices), *Taoyuan mingsheng jing* 桃園明聖經 (Scripture of illuminating sageliness of the Peach Grove), *Dadong zhenjing* 大洞真經 (True scripture

---

65   For more on this topic, see Huang, "Dangdai Puli luansheng." Decades earlier, David Jordan and Daniel Overmyer had started to pay attention to women members of phoenix halls; see Jordan and Overmyer, *Flying Phoenix*, 158–65, 174–80, 184–212.

66   This seems similar to phenomena that Kang Xiaofei observed; see Kang "Rural Women," 42–52. For an overview of these issues, see Kang, "Women and the Religious Question." See also Jia, Kang, and Yao, *Gendering Chinese Religion*.

of the Great Cavern), and *Zaowang zhenjing* 灶王真經 (True Scripture of the Lord of the Stove). This is followed by the recitation of spells for inviting deities (*qingshen zhou* 請神咒) and moralistic exhortations from the gods (*qing'gao* 請誥; also referred to as "precious injunctions" or *baogao* 寶誥). Once these rites have been completed, the wielders and other initiated members who specialize in spirit-writing start making offerings of incense to the hall's deities, following which they perform an "inviting the gods" (*qingshen* 請神) ritual, generally using a text entitled *Shenzhou heben* 神咒合本 (Compendium of divine spells). The deities who wish to attend that night's spirit-writing session are supposed to arrive by the time the last spell is recited, at which point the planchette (*jibi* 乩筆) should start to move. With the exception of the Canzan tang, where these rites are performed in Hakka, all other halls use Southern Min.

3.5 Healing and Other Services

It is essential to recognize that the spirit-writing rituals performed at phoenix halls involve far more than the presentation of moral exhortations from the gods; they also address worshippers' more mundane concerns. While most previous scholarship on spirit-writing rituals has focused on their importance in the production of morality books, such rites actually consist of two key components: 1) The production of poems and prose statements from the gods, and 2) Deities answering questions posed by worshippers (*wenshi* 問事; *jishi* 濟世). At most phoenix halls, approximately half or even more of each session is devoted to the gods responding to worshippers' questions. Men and women with concerns that they wish to pose to the deities need to complete a "petition slip" (*bingdan* 禀單), which usually consists of the supplicant's name and address, as well as a brief description of the problem requiring divine assistance (in some cases age and gender are indicated as well). At some phoenix halls, the scribes recite the contents of the petition; at others, they are simply placed on the altar for the gods' consideration. Petitions can be filed on the day of the rites or even a few days beforehand and can be picked up a few days after their completion. In today's Internet Age, some phoenix halls (most notably the Xingjue tang) allow worshippers to pose questions via the hall's website (http://www.spk.org.tw/), with divine responses e-mailed to worshippers after the rites have concluded.[67]

The vast majority of requests center on issues of health and career, as well as choosing an auspicious date for a special event. Of the 101 petitions we recorded

---

[67] Philip Clart's project to construct a database of these materials from one phoenix hall in central Taiwan promises to shed even more light on this issue. Details may be found in the PowerPoint presentation he gave at the conference on "Spirit-Writing in Chinese History" in June 2019.

while witnessing 18 spirit-writing rituals at the seven halls we studied from July 2009 to July 2010, a total of 40 (39%) were related to health issues (*jiankang* 健康). An additional 19 (19%) concerned worshippers' fate (including career choices; *yuntu* 運途), while 12 more (12%) centered on issues of public interest (mainly temple construction projects; *gongshibing* 公事稟). In cases where information for gender was available, there was an even split between male and female worshippers, while in terms of location approximately 86% of the supplicants were from Puli. Another clear example of the importance of this phenomenon may be found in records of 8,140 questions worshippers posed to the deities of the Daohua tang 導化堂. Of these, a total of 3,691 (45.3%) concerned health issues, with 1,233 (15.2%) involving choosing an auspicious date (*ze jiri* 擇吉日) and 659 (8.1%) centering on questions of fate (*yuntu* 運途). An additional 620 questions (7.6%) treated issues of public interest (*gongshibing* 公事稟).[68] Healing proves especially vital in attracting worshippers who choose to be initiated.[69] One key example involves Chen Shilian (a physician), who became a member of the Yanhua tang 衍化堂 after its deities proved efficacious in healing his wife's illness.[70] All in all, the emphasis on healing (both physical and psychological) seems little different from what goes on at temples and household altars all over Taiwan, where spirit-mediums (*jitong* 乩童; *tangki* 童乩 in Southern Min) are possessed by the gods.[71]

Many of Puli's phoenix halls once relied on spirit-writing rites for the composition of prescriptions (*yaofang* 藥方) as well as medicinal divination slips (*yaoqian* 藥籤) for adults and children, but these are not widely used today for fear of violating public health regulations.[72] In the case of the Daohua tang, for example, its deities proclaimed in 1985 that such practices were to cease ("talismans may be granted in the future, but prescriptions are forbidden" 來日賜符可，施方不准). Worshippers endeavored to revive the issuing of prescriptions in 1987 and even as late as 1996, all to no avail. Some members from the Yanhua tang complained that the cessation of these practices has contributed to a decline in the number of worshippers making offerings at this phoenix hall. A number of halls (including the Daohua tang and the Yanhua tang) have shifted to issuing "celestial prescriptions" (*tianfang* 天方), namely talismans (*fu* 符) adorned with spirit-writing that are usually burned,

---

68   These practices are discussed in Katz, "Spirit-writing Halls," 127–28.
69   For more on this phenomenon, see Jordan and Overmyer, *Flying Phoenix*, xvii–xviii.
70   *Yanhua tang zhi*, 15–17.
71   Chao, "*Danggi* [童乩] Temple"; Lin, *Materializing Magic Power*.
72   A few halls retain Chinese medicine pharmacies on their premises, but in theory the prescriptions they fill should not have been written by the gods during spirit-writing sessions.

with the ashes being infused in water or tea.[73] Some phoenix halls also prepare "cinnabar water" (*danshui* 丹水) that is stored in jars housed in the hall and is believed to have potent healing properties. Not all phoenix halls are following the government's lead, however, as the Xingling si retains the use of medicinal divination sticks while housing on its premises a pharmacy for traditional Chinese medicines where the required herbs can be acquired.

Apart from healing, phoenix halls provide other services for their members as well. At the Daohua tang and Yanhua tang, for example, the gods issue celebratory rhymed couples to celebrate members' marriages, and messages of condolence when a worshipper passes away. Other poems are issued to praise hall members for the diligence of their participation and contributions to the hall's development.[74] There have also been occasions when the gods stage underworld trials of deceased scoundrels as a means of moral edification.[75] Some of the most striking records involve the appearance of deceased hall members who claim to have become deities, for, as Clart has noted, "Salvation, in the conception of Taiwanese phoenix halls, basically means deification".[76] In Puli, deification occurred for elites like You Chao'an and Shi Baichuan, who told worshippers through spirit-written messages they had been appointed City Gods (Chenghuang 城隍) in Chia-yi 嘉義 and Shaanxi 陝西 respectively.[77] However, deification is hardly restricted to local elites; there is also the moving story of the poor but devout tenant farmer Pan Adun 潘阿敦, who after diligent service to the Yanhua Tang and its surrounding community is now said to have taken his rightful place among the gods.[78] Regardless of the service provided, the needs of individual worshippers are granted high priority, with spirit-writing allowing expressions of individual testimony. In this sense, then, phoenix halls clearly conform to the criteria for congregational groups in stressing various forms of self-cultivation intended to achieve individual salvation, yet also have the potential to perform a wide range of communal functions.

---

73 Some worshippers claim that celestial prescriptions are five-colored pills that appear in the hall's incense burner following lengthy scripture-chanting rituals.
74 Examples of these texts may be found on pages 59–73 of the *Yanhua tang zhi*.
75 See Katz, "Spirit-writing Halls," 128–29. For more on ideas of divine justice in Chinese religion, see Katz, *Divine Justice*.
76 Clart, "Confucius and the Mediums," 8, see also 9, 36.
77 You Chao'an's account may be found in the *Xinghua jinpian*, 243–45 (the Xinghua tang 醒化堂 was originally located in Rinan 日南 (Taizhong), but later moved to Puli and was reconstructed as the Xingling si). For the account of Shi Baichuan, see the *Pomi zhen*, 360–61.
78 *Yanhua tang zhi*, 73–75.

4   Concluding Remarks

The findings presented in this paper reveal that phoenix halls in modern Taiwan could develop into vibrant organizations with the potential to shape communal life by means of their charitable deeds, educational activities, publication projects, leadership roles in communal rites, etc. In addition, their membership tends to be highly diverse, attracting a wide range of men and women interested in not only spirit-writing but also healing, scripture recitation, philanthropy, etc. The social facets of these halls have important implications for the distinction between ascriptive and voluntary groups discussed in the paper's Introduction. The one theme that appears to bind various phoenix hall practices together seems to be individual self-cultivation, which suggests a clear difference between ascriptive public temples and voluntary phoenix halls: namely that many phoenix halls provide additional levels of religious activism and emphasis on morality that are less prominent in temple cults. In short, phoenix halls can assume a public mantle while also continuing to stress the significance of individual self-cultivation. The above perspective can in turn help us better differentiate between levels of religiosity in communal life, with phoenix halls contributing to the establishment of communities for spiritual training that emphasize education, morality, philanthropy, and other forms of social activism, as well as proselytizing and public transmission of these values and practices. Phoenix halls also provide opportunities for women not only to perform acts of worship but also play leading roles in practices like scripture-chanting.

I would like to conclude by pointing to issues that might merit further research in the future. The first involves the history of Cross-Strait ties between Taiwanese phoenix halls and their counterparts in China. During the Japanese colonial era, despite the fact that members of some Taiwanese spirit-writing groups, including renowned leaders like Yang Mingji 楊明機 (1899–1985), reprinted religious works that had been transmitted to Taiwan from China (especially morality books), direct contact seems to have been minimal. The reasons for this have yet to be fully determined, but may be because many Taiwanese groups arose during the 1890s and 1900s, when Cross-Strait religious ties were at a low ebb, while similar associations in China tended to be highly active in the Jiangnan region (where fewer Taiwanese practitioners journeyed than Fujian 福建). There are occasional instances of Cross-Strait interaction, however. For example, some Taiwanese religious elites journeyed to Longhu shan 龍虎山 to print their morality books or have them validated by the Heavenly Master, including members of the Bixia gong 碧霞宮 (a phoenix hall located in Yilan), who in 1907 took a spirit-writing text there for inspection and approval (*jianding* 鑑定) by the 62nd Heavenly Master Zhang Yuanxu 張元旭 (1862–1925) before bringing it to Amoy for publication.[79] In addition, Wen Degui 溫德貴 (fl. 1899–1901) and other members of the venerable Daiquan tang brought spirit-writing texts to Quanzhou 泉州 for publication in 1901. Spirit-writing texts could also be spread via distribution outlets utilized by bookstores, with Quanzhou's Shanshu liutongchu 善書流通處 proving especially significant in the religious history of modern Taiwan. This was the case for the Lanji Bookstore (Lanji shuju 蘭記書局), established in 1925 by Huang Maosheng 黃茂盛 (1901–1978). Huang was deeply committed to both preserving traditional Chinese culture and transmitting moral values, making regular journeys to religious publishing centers in China to collect religious works and periodicals to be distributed in Taiwan free of charge. Huang's efforts attracted the support of Chinese religious elites, including Wang Yiting. Huang met Wang during his trips to China, and became a member of one charitable-religious organization that Wang had helped found (the Zhongguo liangxin chongshan hui 中國良心崇善會). One result of this friendship was Wang's composing a preface for a morality book entitled *Jingshen Lu* 精神錄 (Records of the essence and spirit) compiled by the renowned Donggang 東港 physician and philanthropist Chen Jiangshan 陳江山 (1899–1976), which was published by the Lanji Bookstore in 1929. This work, which contains a preface by Huang and a calligraphic couplet by Wang, subsequently spread back across the Taiwan Strait, with five editions totaling 6,700 copies being produced in both Taiwan and China prior to the outbreak of the Second World War.[80]

Another promising topic is how phoenix halls have attempted to utilize the mass media to propagate their beliefs and practices. In recent years, Fan Chunwu 范純武, Wang Chien-chuan, and Yau Chi On, have begun to assess the role of the mass media in the development of spirit-writing groups and other sectarian movements. On the one hand, redemptive societies and spirit-writing associations in China, Taiwan, and overseas Chinese communities utilized modern printing techniques to publicize the morality books they produced. On the other hand, these groups also made use of newspapers and periodicals to publicize their religious ideals and philanthropic deeds.[81] In Taiwan, spirit-writing

---

79   For more on Zhang's life and career, see Goossaert, "Zhang Yuanxu."
80   Katz, "An Unbreakable Thread?" See also Katz, *Religion in China*, 105–7. The transmission of spirit-writing and other religious texts from China to Taiwan also marked the history of the *Daozang jinghua* 道藏精華 (Essence of the Daoist Canon), a major anthology compiled by Xiao Tianshi 蕭天石 (1909–1986) and published in Taipei between 1953 and 1983. See Elena, "Transmission of Daoist Scriptures."
81   Yau, *Shan yu ren tong*; Fan, "Bade"; Wang, "Morality Book Publishing." See also Katz, "Illuminating Goodness."

organizations like the Shengxian tang have followed in the footsteps of their Republican-era forebears by publishing religious books and periodicals, sometimes even with the help of full-time staff.[82] However, religious websites have yet to fully utilize the communicative potential of the Internet to stimulate new forms of religious action, in part due to traditional notions of authentic religious experience plus the tendency to quantify merit based on the numbers of printed books that one sponsors.[83] Exceptions include the case of Puli's Xingjue tang mentioned above, which has a website where worshippers can post questions for use in that hall's spirit-writing rituals. The extent to which such trends may become more prevalent among other phoenix halls remains to be seen.

Acknowledgements

This study is dedicated to the late Daniel L. Overmyer (1935–2021), whose commitment to excellence and caring mentorship contributed to the growth of our field and served as inspiration to us all.

---

[82] Clart, "Merit beyond Measure"; Clart, "Taiwanese Spirit-Writing Cults."
[83] Clart, "Mediums and the New Media." For thought-provoking comparative perspectives, see Clart, "New Technologies"; Tarocco, *The Cultural Practices*; Tarocco, "Technologies of Salvation"; Billioud, *The Varieties of Confucian Experience*.

Appendix:

TABLE 16.1 Puli's Phoenix Halls

Name	Alternate name	Location	Village	Founding date	Main deities	Morality books and other texts (dates)	Dates of spirit-writing rituals
Huaishan tang 懷善堂	City God Temple (Chenghuang miao 城隍廟)	Downtown	Nanmenli 南門里	1900	Three Benevolent Ones (San Enzhu 三恩主) City God (Chenghuang zunshen 城隍尊神)	*Dachi bian* 打痴鞭 (1950) *Huaishan* 懷善 (1972)	Ceased in 2003
Zhenyuan gong Canzan tang 真元宮 參贊堂	Tainiu keng Dijun miao 牛坑帝君廟	Tainiu keng	Yixinli 一新里	1902	Three Benevolent Ones	*Canzan cujinji* 參贊萃錦集 (1971) *Canzan cujinji xuji* 參贊萃錦集續集 (1984) *Canzan cujinji disanji* 參贊萃錦集第三集 (2002)	1st, 11th and 21st of each lunar month
Yuheng gong Tongtian tang 玉衡宮 通天堂		Downtown	Pachengli 杷城里	1909	Three Benevolent Ones	*Dengguang liushinian* 鐙光六十年 (1979)	Ceased in 1998
Zhaoping gong Yuhua tang 昭平宮 育化堂	Confucius Temple (Kongzi miao 孔子廟)	Downtown	Qingxinli 清新里	1911	Guan Yu (Guansheng dijun 關聖帝君) Confucius (Kongzi 孔子)	*Pomi zhen* 破迷針 (1947) *Yinwu xian* 引悟線 (1949) *Canghai yizhu* 滄海遺珠 (3 volumes; 1968, 1996, 1997) *Songchun xiancao* 頌春仙藻 (2006)	7th, 17th and 27th of each lunar month

TABLE 16.1 Puli's Phoenix Halls (cont.)

Name	Alternate name	Location	Village	Founding date	Main deities	Morality books and other texts (dates)	Dates of spirit-writing rituals
Xuanping gong Xingjue tang 宣平宮醒覺堂		Zhuzai shan 珠仔山	Zhugeli 珠格里	1946	Three Benevolent Ones	*Xuanping gong Xingjue tangzhi* 宣平宮醒覺堂誌 (2004, 2009) *Juexing luansheng* 覺醒鸞聲 (2006)	2nd, 12th and 22nd of each lunar month
Qilin ge Daohua tang 麒麟閣導化堂		Maizai jiao 梅仔腳	Beihaili 北梅里	1946	Bodhisattva Guanyin (Guanshiyin pusa 觀世音菩薩) Three Benevolent Ones	*Qilin ge Daohua tang jianshi* 麒麟閣導化堂簡史 (2006)	1st, 11th and 21st of each lunar month
Xingling si 醒靈寺		Damalin 大瑪璘	Ailanli 愛蘭里	1949	Three Benevolent Ones	*Xinghua jinpian* 醒化金篇 (ca. 1947) *Xingling jijin* 醒靈集錦 (1978, 2009) *Lühu zhi qiu* 綠湖之秋 (1980)	3rd, 13th and 23rd of each lunar month
Baohu gong Tiandi tang 寶湖宮天地堂	Earth Mother Temple (Dimu miao 地母廟)	Baohujue 寶湖崛	Pipali 枇杷里	1950	Earth Mother (Dimu 地母)	*Baohu qiongzhang* 寶湖瓊章 (2004)	Ceased in 1995
Hengshan gong Yanhua tang 恆山宮衍化堂		Niumian shan 牛眠山	Niumianli 牛眠里	1950	Three Benevolent Ones	*Luanji duanxunji* 鸞乩鍛訓記 (1998) *Yanhua tangzhi* 衍化堂誌 (2000)	3rd, 13th and 23rd of each lunar month
Zhaode tang 昭德堂		Shigang 史港	Shigangli 史港里	1951	Three Benevolent Ones	*Puli Zhaode tang bingxunian duanlian xinji zhuanji* 埔里昭德堂丙戌年煅練新乩尊輯 (2007)	3rd, 13th and 23rd of each lunar month

A MOTLEY PHOENIX? 625

TABLE 16.1 Puli's Phoenix Halls (cont.)

Name	Alternate name	Location	Village	Founding date	Main deities	Morality books and other texts (dates)	Dates of spirit-writing rituals
Shouzhen gong 受鎮宮		Xiaopu she 小埔社	Guangchengli 廣成里	1959	Great Emperor of the Dark Heavens (Xuantian shangdi 玄天上帝)	*Wuche shizhen* 悟徹世針 (1978)	1st, 5th, 11th, 15th, 21st and 25th of each lunar month
Yuqing gong Liangxian tang 玉清宮 良顯堂		Qixia 崎下	Dachengli 大城里	1974	Great Emperors of the Five Manifestations (Wuxian dadi 五顯大帝)	N/A	1st, 6th, 11th, 16th, 21st and 26th of each lunar month

Bibliography

Billioud, Sébastien, ed. *The Varieties of Confucian Experience: Documenting a Grassroots Revival of Tradition*. Leiden: Brill, 2018.

Billioud, Sébastien, and Joël Thoraval. *The Sage and the People. The Confucian Revival in China*. Oxford, New York: Oxford University Press, 2015.

Chang Er-wen 張二文. "Taiwan Liudui Kejia diqu luantang yu minjian wenhua shanyang zhi yanjiu 臺灣六堆客家地區鸞堂與民間文化闡揚之研究." PhD diss., National Dong Hwa University, Department of Chinese Language and Literature, 2014.

Chang Er-wen 張二文. "Liudui Kejia diqu luanshu zhong de youming xiangxiang yu shijian 六堆客家地區鸞書中的幽冥想像與實踐." Paper presented at The Culture of Flying Phoenix and Popular Religions International Conference. Lanyang Museum and Fo Guang University, May 28–29, 2018.

Chang Yu-chih 張有志. "Rizhi shiqi Gaoxiong diqu luantang zhi yanjiu 日治時期高雄地區鸞堂之研究." MA thesis, National Tainan University, Graduate Institute of Taiwan Culture, 2007.

Chao Shin-yi. "A *Danggi* [童乩] Temple in Taipei: Spirit-Mediums in Modern Urban Taiwan." *Asia Major*, 3rd ser., 15, no. 2 (2002): 129–56.

Chen Chien-hung 陳建宏. "Gongmiao yu difang shehui—Yi Daxi zhen Puji Tang wei li (1902–2001) 公廟與地方社會—以大溪鎮普濟堂為例（1902–2001）." MA thesis, National Central University, Graduate Institute of History, 2004.

Chen Shih-jung 陳世榮. "Qingdai bei Taoyuan de difang jingying ji 'gonggong lingyu' 清代北桃園的地方菁英及「公共領域」." *Guoli zhengzhi daxue Lishi xuebao* 國立政治大學歷史學報 (*The Journal of History, NCCU*) 18 (2001): 203–42.

Chen Yaoting 陳耀庭. "Shanghai Daojiaoshi 上海道教史." In *Shanghai zongjiaoshi* 上海宗教史, edited by Ruan Renze 阮仁澤 and Gao Zhennong 高振農, 353–438. Shanghai: Shanghai renmin chubanshe, 1992.

Cheng Chih-ming 鄭志明. *Taiwan fuji yu luanshu xianxiang—Shanshu yanjiu de huigu* 臺灣扶乩與鸞書現象—善書研究的回顧. Chiayi: Nanhua University College of Management, 1998.

Cheng Pao-chen 鄭寶珍. "Rizhi shiqi Kejia diqu luantang fazhan: Yi Xinzhu Jiuqionglin Feifeng Shan Daiquan Tang wei li 日治時期客家地區鸞堂發展：以新竹九芎林飛鳳山代勸堂為例." MA thesis, National Central University, Graduate Institute of Hakka Society and Culture, 2008.

Chiang Chao-chan 江趙展. "Jiazu yu luantang: Yi Danshui Xingzhong tang wei taolun zhongxin 家族與鸞堂：以淡水行忠堂為討論中心." MA thesis, National Taiwan Normal University, Graduate Institute of History, 2018.

Chiang Chao-chan 江趙展. "Zhanhou Xingzhong tang de bianqian ji qi xianghuo quanwei zhi xin xingtai 戰後行忠堂的變遷及其香火權威之新型態." Paper presented at The Culture of Flying Phoenix and Popular Religions International Conference. Lanyang Museum and Fo Guang University, May 28–29, 2018.

Chiang Chu-shan 蔣竹山. "1930 niandai Tianjin Duliu zhen shangren de zongjiao yu shehui huodong: Yi Tianli jiao weili 1930 年代天津獨流鎮商人的宗教與社會活動—以「天理教」為例." In *Ming-Qing yilai minjian zongjiao de tansuo: jinian Dai Xuanzhi jiaoshou lunwen ji* 明清以來民間宗教的探索：紀念戴玄之教授論文集, edited by Wang Chien-chuan 王見川 and Chiang Chu-shan 蔣竹山, 266–91. Taipei: Shangding wenhua, 1996.

Chiu Yen-chou 邱延洲. "Fengshan diqu luantang xinyang ji qi shehui wangluo zhi yanjiu: Yi Fengyi shiyi luantang wei zhongxin 鳳山地區鸞堂信仰及其社會網絡之研究：以鳳邑十一鸞堂為中心." MA thesis, National Kaohsiung Normal University, Graduate Institute of Taiwan History, Culture and Languages, 2014.

Chiu Yen-chou 邱延洲. "Fengshan diqu luantang shehui wangluo de jianli yu wending jizhi 鳳山地區鸞堂社會網絡的建立與穩定機制." Paper presented at The Culture of Flying Phoenix and Popular Religions International Conference. Lanyang Museum and Fo Guang University, May 28–29, 2018.

Chou Yi-jan 周怡然. "Zhongzhan qian Miaoli Kejia diqu luantang zhi yanjiu 終戰前苗栗客家地區鸞堂之研究." MA thesis, National Central University, Graduate Institute of Hakka Society and Culture, 2008.

Chuang Ying-chang 莊英章. "Xinzhu Fangliao Yimin Miao de jianli ji qi shehui wenhua yiyi 新竹枋寮義民廟的建立及其社會文化意義." *Di'erjie guoji Hanxue huiyi lunwenji* 第二屆國際漢學會議論文集, 223–39. Nankang: Academia Sinica, 1989.

Chung An 鍾安. "Luantang yu difang shehui: Yi nan Taiwan Meinong Guangshan tang wei li 鸞堂與地方社會：以南臺灣美濃廣善堂為例". MA thesis, National Taiwan Normal University, Graduate Institute of History, 2021.

Chung Yun-ying 鍾雲鶯. *Wang Jueyi shengping ji qi* Lishu hejie *litian zhi yanjiu* 王覺一生平及其《理數合解》理天之研究. New Taipei City: Hua Mulan Publishing, 2011.

Clart, Philip A. "The Phoenix and the Mother: The Interaction of Spirit-Writing Cults and Popular Sects in Taiwan." *Journal of Chinese Religions* 25 (1997): 1–32.

Clart, Philip A. "Chinese Tradition and Taiwanese Modernity: Morality Books as Social Commentary and Critique." In *Religion in Modern Taiwan: Tradition and Innovation in a Changing Society*, edited by Philip A. Clart and Charles B. Jones, 84–97. Honolulu: University of Hawai'i Press, 2003.

Clart, Philip A. "Confucius and the Mediums: Is there a 'Popular Confucianism'?" *T'oung Pao* 89, fasc. 1/3 (2003): 1–38.

Clart, Philip A. "Merit beyond Measure: Notes on the Moral (and Real) Economy of Religious Publishing in Taiwan." In *The People and the Dao: New Studies of Chinese Religions in Honour of Prof. Daniel L. Overmyer*, edited by Philip Clart and Paul Crowe, 127–42. Sankt Augustin: Institut Monumenta Serica, 2009.

Clart, Philip A. "Anchoring Guanyin: Appropriative Strategies in a New Phoenix Hall Scripture." *Minsu quyi* 民俗曲藝 173 (2011): 101–28.

Clart, Philip A. "Mediums and the New Media: The Impact of Electronic Publishing on

Temple and Moral Economies in Taiwanese Popular Religion." *Journal of Sinological Studies* 3, no. 1 (2012): 127–41.

Clart, Philip A. "New Technologies and the Production of Religious Texts in China, 19th–21st Century." In *Modern Chinese Religion*, Part II: *1850–2015*, edited by Vincent Goossaert, Jan Kiely, and John Lagerwey, vol. 1, 560–78. Leiden: Brill, 2015.

Clart, Philip A. "Competition, Entrepreneurship, and Network Formation among Taiwanese Spirit-Writing Cults." In *Jindai Huaren zongjiao huodong yu minjian wenhua—Sung Kuang-yu jiaoshou jinian wenji* 近代華人宗教活動與民間文化—宋光宇教授紀念文集, edited by Li Shih-wei 李世偉, 107–63. Taipei: Boyang wenhua, 2019.

Clart, Philip A., and Charles B. Jones, eds. *Religion in Modern Taiwan: Tradition and Innovation in a Changing Society*. Honolulu: University of Hawai'i Press, 2003.

Cohen, Myron L. "Minong 美濃's Corporations: Religion, Economy and Local Culture in 18th and 19th Century Taiwan." In *Renleixue zai Taiwan de fazhan: Jingyan yanjiu pian* 人類學在台灣的發展：經驗研究篇, edited by Hsu Cheng-kuang 徐正光 and Lin Mei-rong 林美容, 223–89. Taipei: Institute of Ethnology, Academia Sinica, 1999.

Cohen, Myron L. *Kinship, Contract, Community, and State: Anthropological Perspectives on China*. Stanford: Stanford University Press, 2005.

DeGlopper, Donald R. *Lukang: Commerce and Society in a Chinese City* Albany: State University of New York Press, 1995.

DuBois, Thomas David. *The Sacred Village: Social Change and Religious Life in Rural North China*. Honolulu: University of Hawai'i Press, 2005.

Duara, Prasenjit. *Sovereignty and Authenticity. Manchukuo and the East Asian Modern*. Lanham: Rowman & Littlefield, 2003.

Esherick, Joseph W., and Mary Backus Rankin. "Introduction". In *Chinese Local Elites and Patterns of Dominance*, edited by Esherick and Rankin, 1–25. Berkeley: University of California Press, 1990.

Esposito, Monica. "The Discovery of Jiang Yuanting's *Daozang jiyao* in Jiangnan: A Presentation of the Daoist Canon of the Qing Dynasty." In *Kōnan dōkyō no kenkyū* 江南道教の研究, edited by Esposito, 79–110. Kyoto: Jinbun Kagaku Kenkyūjo, 2007.

Fan Chun-wu 范純武. "Jinxiandai Zhongguo Fojiao yu fuji 近現代中國佛教與扶乩." *Yuanguang Foxue xuebao* 圓光佛學學報, 3 (1999): 261–92.

Fan Chun-wu 范純武. "Feiluan, xiuzhen yu banshan—Zheng Guanying yu Shanghai zongjiao shijie 飛鸞、修真與辦善—鄭觀應與上海的宗教世界." In *Cong chengshi kan Zhongguo de xiandaixing* 從城市看中國的現代性, edited by Wu Jen-shu 巫仁恕, Lin May-li 林美莉, and Kang Bao 康豹 [Paul R. Katz], 247–74. Nankang: Institute of Modern History, Academia Sinica, 2010.

Fan Chun-wu 范純武. "Bade: Jindai Zhongguo jiushi tuanti de daode leimu yu shijian 八德: 近代中國救世團體的道德類目與實踐." In *Gaibian Zhongguo zongjiao de wushinian, 1898–1948* 改變中國宗教的五十年，1898–1948, edited by Kang Bao 康

豹 [Paul R. Katz] and Gao Wansang 高萬桑 [Vincent Goossaert], 225–59. Nankang: Academia Sinica, Institute of Modern History, 2015.

Feuchtwang, Stephan. "City Temples in Taipei Under Three Regimes." In *The Chinese City Between Two Worlds*, edited by Mark Elvin and G. William Skinner, 263–301. Stanford: Stanford University Press, 1974.

Gao Wansang 高萬桑 [Vincent Goossaert]. "Jin'gaishan wangluo: Jinxiandai Jiangnan de Quanzhen jushi zuzhi 金蓋山網絡：近現代江南的全真居士組織." In *Quanzhendao yanjiu* 全真道研究, edited by Zhao Weidong 趙衛東, vol. 1, 319–39. Jinan: Qilu shushe, 2011.

Goossaert, Vincent. *The Daoists of Peking, 1800–1949. A Social History of Urban Clerics*. Cambridge, MA: Harvard University Press. 2007.

Goossaert, Vincent. "Spirit Writing, Canonization, and the Rise of Divine Saviors: Wenchang, Lüzu, and Guandi, 1700–1858." *Late Imperial China* 36, no. 2 (2015): 82–125.

Goossaert, Vincent. "Diversity and Elite Religiosity in Modern China: A Model." *Approaching Religion* 7, no. 1 (2017): 10–20.

Goossaert, Vincent. "Zhang Yuanxu: The Making and Unmaking of a Daoist Saint." In *Making Saints in Modern China*, edited by David Ownby, Vincent Goossaert and Ji Zhe, 78–98. New York: Oxford University Press, 2017.

Goossaert, Vincent, and David Palmer. *The Religious Question in Modern China*. Chicago: Chicago University Press, 2011.

Huang Pingying 黃萍瑛. "Dangdai Puli luansheng de zongjiao shenghuo: Yi Yuhua Tang nüluan wei kaocha 當代埔里鸞生的宗教生活：以育化堂女鸞為考察." *Minsu quyi* 民俗曲藝 184 (2014): 279–334.

Jiyang tang Caishi dazupu 濟陽堂蔡氏大族譜, edited by Cai Jinchuan 蔡錦川. Unpublished manuscript, 1972.

Jia, Jinhua, Xiaofei Kang, and Ping Yao, eds. *Gendering Chinese Religion: Subject, Identity, and Body*. Albany, NY: State University of New York Press, 2014.

Jordan, David K. "Changes in Postwar Taiwan and their Impact on the Popular Practice of Religion." In *Cultural Change in Postwar Taiwan*, edited by Stevan A. Harrell and Huang Chün-chieh, 137–60. Boulder, CO: Westview Press, 1994.

Jordan, David K., and Daniel L. Overmyer. *The Flying Phoenix. Aspects of Chinese Sectarianism in Taiwan*. Princeton: Princeton University Press, 1986.

Kang Bao 康豹 [Paul R. Katz]. "Taiwan de Lü Dongbin xinyang—Yi Zhinan gong wei li 台灣的呂洞賓信仰－以指南宮為例." *Xinshixue* 新史學 6, no. 4 (1995): 21–43.

Kang Bao 康豹 [Paul R. Katz]. "Zhongguo dizhi wanqi yijiang simiao yishi zai difang shehui de gongneng 中國帝制晚期以降寺廟儀式在地方社會的功能." In *Zhongguoshi xinlun: Zongjiao fence* 中國史新論·宗教分冊, edited by Lin Fu-shih 林富士, 439–76. Taipei: Academia Sinica and Linking Publishing, 2011.

Kang, Xiaofei. "Rural Women, Old Age, and Temple Work: A Case from Northwestern Sichuan." *China Perspectives* 4 (2009): 42–53.

Kang, Xiaofei. "Women and the Religious Question in Modern China." In *Modern Chinese Religion, Part II: 1850–2015*, edited by Vincent Goossaert, Jan Kiely and John Lagerwey, vol. 1, 491–559. Leiden: Brill, 2015.

Katz, Paul R. "Local Elites and Sacred Sites in Hsin-chuang—The Growth of the Titsang An during the Japanese Occupation." In *Xinyang, yishi yu shehui: Disanjie guoji Hanxue huiyi lunwenji* 信仰、儀式與社會：第三屆國際漢學會議論文集, edited by Lin Mei-rong 林美容, 179–227. Nankang: Institute of Ethnology, Academia Sinica, 2003.

Katz, Paul R. *When Valleys Turned Blood Red: The Ta-pa-ni Incident in Colonial Taiwan.* Honolulu: University of Hawai'i Press, 2005.

Katz, Paul R. *Divine Justice: Religion and the Development of Chinese Legal Culture.* London: Routledge, 2009.

Katz, Paul R. "Spirit-writing and Hakka Migration in Taiwan—A Case Study of the Canzan Tang 參贊堂 in Puli 埔里, Nantou 南投 County." In *Zhongguo difang zongjiao yishi lunji* 中國地方宗教儀式論集, edited by Tam Wai Lun 譚偉倫, 469–514. Hong Kong: Chinese University of Hong Kong Press, 2011.

Katz, Paul R. "Spirit-writing Halls and the Development of Local Communities—A Case Study of Puli 埔里 (Nantou 南投 County)." *Minsu quyi* 民俗曲藝 174 (2011): 103–84.

Katz, Paul R. "An Unbreakable Thread? Preliminary Observations on the Interaction between Chinese and Taiwanese Religious Traditions under Japanese Colonial Rule." *Taiwan zongjiao yanjiu* 臺灣宗教研究 11, no. 2 (2012): 39–70.

Katz, Paul R. "Luantang yu jindai Taiwan de difang shequn—Puli de ge'an yanjiu 鸞堂與近代臺灣的地方社群—埔里的個案研究." In *Shijiu shiji yilai Zhongguo difang Daojiao de bianqian* 十九世紀以來中國地方道教的變遷, edited by Lai Chi Tim 黎志添, 1–70. Hong Kong: Joint Publishing HK, 2013.

Katz, Paul R. *Religion in China and its Modern Fate.* Waltham, MA: Brandeis University Press, 2014.

Katz, Paul R. "Illuminating Goodness—Some Preliminary Considerations of Religious Publishing in Modern China." In *Religious Publishing and Print Culture in Modern China, 1800–2012*, edited by Philip Clart and Gregory Adam Scott, 265–94. Boston and Berlin: De Gruyter, 2014.

Katz, Paul R. "Spirit-writing and the Dynamics of Elite Religious Life in Republican era Shanghai." In *Jindai Zhongguo de zongjiao fazhan lunwenji* 近代中國的宗教發展論文集, edited by Ting Jen-chieh 丁仁傑, et al., 275–350. Taipei: Academia Historica, 2015.

Katz, Paul R. "Bridging the Gaps: Methodological Challenges in the Study of Taiwanese Popular Religion." *International Journal of Taiwan Studies* 1 (2018): 33–63.

Lai Chi Tim 黎志添. "Zheng Guanying 'xiandao' yu 'jiushi' de sixiang yu shijian: jian ping qi dui Qingmo Minchu Daojiao fazhan de yingxian ji yiyi 鄭觀應「仙道」與「救

世」的思想和實踐:兼評其對清末民初道教發展的影響及意義." *Zhongguo wenhua yanjiusuo xuebao* 中國文化研究所學報, 67 (2018): 151–202.

Lai Chi Tim 黎志添, Yau Chi On 游子安, and Wu Zhen 吳真. *Xianggang Daojiao* 香港道教. Hong Kong: Zhonghua shuju, 2010.

Lai, Chi-tim. "Hong Kong Daoism: A Study of Daoist Altars and Lü Dongbin Cults." *Social Compass*, 50, no. 4 (2003): 459–70.

Lai Kuan-yi 賴貫一. *Taiwan tulong chuanqi* 台灣土龍傳奇. Nantou: Shanshui caise yinshua gufen youxian gongsi, 2003.

Lai Yu-ling 賴玉玲. *Baozhong ting Yiminye xinyang yu difang shehui fazhan: Yi Yangmei Zhuang wei li* 褒忠亭義民爺信仰與地方社會發展:以楊梅聯庄為例. Zhubei: Xinzhu County Cultural Affairs Bureau, 2005.

Lee Fong-mao 李豐楙. "Lisheng yu daoshi: Taiwan minjian shehui zhong liyi shijian de liangge mianxiang 禮生與道士:臺灣民間社會中禮儀實踐的兩個面向." In *Shehui, minzu yu wenhua zhanyan guoji yantaohui lunwenji* 社會、民族與文化展演國際研討會論文集, edited by Wang Chiu-kuei 王秋桂, et. al, 331–64. Taipei: Center for Chinese Studies, 2001.

Li Shih-wei 李世偉. "Miaoli Kejia diqu de luantang diaocha 苗栗客家地區的鸞堂調查." *Minjian zongjiao* 民間宗教 3 (1997): 315–26.

Li Shih-wei 李世偉. *Riju shidai Taiwan de Rujiao jieshe yu huodong* 日據時代臺灣的儒教結社與活動. Taipei: Wenchin Publishing Company, 1999.

Li Shih-wei 李世偉. "Binhai fu shengdao: Zhanhou Taiwan minjian Rujiao jieshe yu huodong (1945–1970) 濱海扶聖道:戰後臺灣民間儒教結社與活動(1945–1970)." *Minsu quyi* 民俗曲藝 172 (2010): 205–30.

Lin Kuei-ling 林桂玲. *Jiazu yu simiao: Yi Zhubei Linjia yu Fangliao Yimin Miao wei li (1749–1895)* 家族與寺廟:以竹北林家與枋寮義民廟為例(1749–1895). Zhubei: Xinzhu County Cultural Affairs Bureau, 2005.

Lin Kuei-ling 林桂玲. "Kejia diyu shehui zuzhi de bianqian: Yi bei Taiwan 'changhui' wei zhongxin de taolun 客家地域社會組織的變遷:以北臺灣「嘗會」為中心的討論." PhD diss., Graduate Institute of History, National Tsing Hua University, 2013.

Lin Rong-ze 林榮澤. *Yiguandao fazhanshi* 一貫道發展史. Taipei: Lantian Publishing, 2010.

Lin, Wei-Ping. *Materializing Magic Power: Chinese Popular Religion in Villages and Cities*. Cambridge, MA and London: Harvard University Press, 2015.

Liu, Xun. *Daoist Modern: Innovation, Lay Practice, and the Community of Inner Alchemy in Republican Shanghai*. Cambridge: Harvard University Asia Center, 2009.

Lu, Yunfeng. *The Transformation of Yiguandao in Taiwan: Adapting to a Changing Religious Economy*. Lanham: Rowman and Littlefield, 2008.

Madsen, Richard. *Democracy's Dharma: Religious Renaissance and Political Development in Taiwan*. Berkeley and Los Angeles: University of California Press, 2007.

Ownby, David. "Redemptive Societies in the Twentieth Century." In *Modern Chinese*

Religion, Part II: 1850–2015, edited by Vincent Goossaert, Jan Kiely and John Lagerwey, vol. 2, 685–727. Leiden: Brill, 2015.

Pomi zhen 破迷針. Puli: Yuhua tang, 1947.

Sakai Tadao 酒井忠夫. *Kingendai Chūgoku ni okeru shūkyō kessha no kenkyū* 近、現代中國における宗教結社の研究. Tokyo: Tokyo kabushiki kaishi kokusho kankōkai, 2002.

Sangren, P. Steven. *History and Magical Power in a Chinese Community*. Stanford, CA: Stanford University Press, 1987.

Schipper, Kristofer M. "Neighborhood Cult Associations in Traditional Tainan." In *The City in Late Imperial China*, edited by G. William Skinner, 651–76. Stanford: Stanford University Press, 1977.

Schipper, Kristofer M. "The Cult of Pao-sheng ta-ti and its Spreading to Taiwan—A Case Study of *fen-hsiang*." In *Development and Decline of Fukien Province in the 17th and 18th Centuries*, edited by E.B. Vermeer, 397–416. Leiden: E.J. Brill, 1990.

Seaman, Gary W. *Temple Organization in a Chinese Village*. Taipei: The Orient Cultural Service, 1978.

Shepherd, John R. *Statecraft and Political Economy on the Taiwan Frontier, 1600–1800*. Stanford, CA: Stanford University Press, 1993.

Shiga Ichiko. "The Manifestations of Lüzu in Modern Guangdong and Hong Kong: The Rise of Spirit-writing Cults." In *Daoist Identity: History, Lineage, and Ritual*, edited by Livia Kohn and Harold Roth, 185–209. Honolulu: University of Hawai'i Press, 2002.

Sun Jiang 孫江. *Kindai Chūgoku no kakumei to himitsu kessha: Chūgoku kakumei no shakaishi kenkyū (1895–1955)* 近代中國の革命と秘密結社：中國革命の社會史的研究 (一八九五——一九五五). Tokyo: Kyūko sho-in, 2007.

Sung Kuang-yu 宋光宇. "Cong *Diyu youji* kan dangqian Taiwan shehui wenti 從地獄遊記看當前台灣社會問題." In *Minjian xinyang yu shehui yantaohui* 民間信仰與社會研討會, edited by Taiwan Provincial Government Department of Civil Affairs and Tung-hai University Department of Sociology, 116–36. Taichung: Taiwan Provincial Government, 1982.

Sung Kuang-yu 宋光宇. "Jiedu Qingmo zai Taiwan zhuanzuo de shanshu *Juewu xuanxin* 解讀清末在臺灣撰作的善書《覺悟選新》." *Bulletin of the Institute of History & Philology, Academia Sinica* 65, no. 3 (1994): 673–723.

Sung Kuang-yu 宋光宇, ed. *Zhengzong shenji shuhuace* 正宗神乩書畫冊. Taipei: Zhengzong shuhuashe, 1995.

Sung Kuang-yu 宋光宇. *Tiandao chuandeng: Yiguandao yu xiandai shehui* 天道傳燈：一貫道與現代社會. Banqiao: Sanyang Publishing, 1996.

Tarocco, Francesca. *The Cultural Practices of Modern Chinese Buddhism: Attuning the Dharma*. New York: Routledge, 2007.

Tarocco, Francesca. "Technologies of Salvation: (Re)locating Chinese Buddhism in the Digital Age." *Journal of Global Buddhism* 18 (2017): 155–75.

ter Haar, Barend. *Guan Yu: The Religious Afterlife of a Failed Hero*. Oxford: Oxford University Press, 2017.

Valussi, Elena. "War, Nationalism and Xiao Tianshi's Transmission of Daoist Scriptures from China to Taiwan." *Asia Major* 30, no. 1 (2015): 143–89.

Wang Chien-chuan 王見川. "Qingmo Riju chuqi Taiwan de luantang—Jianlun 'Ruzong shenjiao' de xingcheng 清末日據初期臺灣的鸞堂——兼論「儒宗神教」的形成." *Taibei wenxian* 臺北文獻 112 (1995): 49–83.

Wang Chien-chuan 王見川. "Taiwan luantang yanjiu de huigu yu zhanwang 臺灣鸞堂研究的回顧與前瞻." *Taiwan shiliao yanjiu* 臺灣史料研究 6 (1995): 199–222.

Wang Chien-chuan 王見川. "Guangfu qian Taiwan Kejia diqu luantang chutan 光復前臺灣客家地區鸞堂初探." *Taibei wenxian* 臺北文獻 124 (1998): 81–101.

Wang Chien-chuan 王見川. "Lüelun Chen Zhonghe jiazu de zongjiao xinyang yu quanshan huodong 略論陳中和家族的宗教信仰與勸善活動." In *Taiwan de minjian zongjiao yu xinyang* 臺灣的民間宗教與信仰, edited by Wang Chien-chuan 王見川 and Li Shih-wei 李世偉, 123–46. Luzhou: Boyang wenhua, 2000.

Wang Chien-chuan 王見川. "Taiwan 'Guandi dang Yudi' chuanshuo de youlai 台灣「關帝當玉帝」傳說的由來." In *Taiwan de minjian zongjiao yu Xinyang* 臺灣的民間宗教與信仰, edited by Wang Chien-chuan 王見川 and Li Shih-wei 李世偉, 213–40. Luzhou: Boyang wenhua, 2000.

Wang Chien-chuan 王見川. "Cihui Tang yu Zhang Tianshi 慈惠堂與張天師." In *Taiwan de minjian zongjiao yu Xinyang* 臺灣的民間宗教與信仰, edited by Wang Chien-ch'uan 王見川 and Li Shih-wei 李世偉, 261–72. Luzhou: Boyang wenhua, 2000.

Wang Chien-chuan 王見川. "Qingmo Minchu Zhongguo de Jigong xinyang yu fuji tuanti: Jian tan Zhongguo Jisheng hui de youlai 清末民初中國的濟公信仰與扶乩團體：兼談中國濟生會的由來." *Minsu quyi* 民俗曲藝 162 (2008): 139–69.

Wang, Chien-Chuan. "Morality Book Publishing and Popular Religion in Modern China: A Discussion Centered on Morality Book Publishers in Shanghai." Translated by Gregory Adam Scott. In *Religious Publishing and Print Culture in Modern China, 1800–2012*, edited by Philip A. Clart and Gregory Adam Scott, 233–64. Boston and Berlin: De Gruyter, 2014.

Wang, Chien-ch'uan [Wang Chien-chuan]. "Spirit-writing Groups in Modern China (1840–1937): Textual Production, Public Teachings, and Charity." Translated by Vincent Goossaert. In *Modern Chinese Religion*, Part II: *1850–2015*, edited by Vincent Goossaert, Jan Kiely and John Lagerwey, vol. 2, 651–84. Leiden: Brill, 2015.

Wang Chih-yu 王志宇. *Taiwan de Enzhugong xinyang: Ruzong shenjiao yu feiluan quanhua* 臺灣的恩主公信仰：儒宗神教與飛鸞勸化. Taipei: Wenchin Publishing Company, 1997.

Wang Chih-yu 王志宇. "Zhanhou Taiwan xinxing luantang Fengyuan Baode dadaoyuan zhi yanjiu: Jiaoyi yu zongjiao huodong mianxiang de guancha 戰後臺灣新興鸞堂豐原寶德大道院之研究：教義與宗教活動面向的觀察." *Taiwan wenxian* 臺灣文獻 62, no. 3 (2011): 351–84.

Wang Shih-ching 王世慶. "Riju chuqi Taiwan zhi jiangbi hui yu jieyan yundong 日據初期台灣之降筆會與戒煙運動." *Taiwan wenxian* 台灣文獻 34, no. 4 (1986): 111–51.

Wang Zongyao 王宗耀. *Huzhou Jin'gaishan Gu Meihuaguan zhi* 湖州金蓋山古梅花觀志. Huzhou: Huzhou Daojiao xilie neibu congshu, 2003.

Wang Zongyu 王宗昱. "Wuxing Quanzhendao shiliao 吳興全真道史料." In *Scriptures, Schools and Forms of Practice in Daoism: A Berlin Symposium*, edited by Poul Andersen and Florian Reiter, 215–32. Wiesbaden: Harrassowitz, 2005.

Wu Yakui 吳亞魁. *Jiangnan Quanzhen Daojiao* 江南全真道教. Hong Kong: Zhonghua shuju, 2006.

Xinghua jinpian 醒化金篇. Nantou: Xinghua tang, 1947.

Xu Dishan 許地山. *Fuji mixin di yanjiu* 扶箕迷信底研究. Changsha: Shangwu yinshuguan, 1941.

Xuanping gong Xingjue tang zhi 宣平宮醒覺堂誌, edited by Chen Sung-ming 陳松明. Nantou: Xuanping Gong Xingjue Tang weiyuanhui 2004.

Yanhua tang zhi 衍化堂誌. Nantou: Yanhua Tang, 1998.

Yang Yanjie 楊彥杰. "Jingjiu bushuai de 'lunsiquan': Minxi shanqu de yizhong shenming chongbai moshi 經久不衰的「輪祀圈」：閩西山區的一種神明崇拜模式." *Minsu quyi* 民俗曲藝 206 (2019): 81–114.

Yau Chi On 游子安. *Shan yu ren tong: Ming-Qing yilai de cishan yu jiaohua* 善與人同：明清以來的慈善與教化. Beijing: Zhonghua shuju, 2005.

Yau Chi On 游子安. "Dadao nanxing: 1920 zhi 1930 niandai Gang, Xing Tianqing caotang yu Daoyuan zhi daomai yinyuan 大道南行：1920 至 1930 年代港、星天清草堂與道院之道脈因緣." In *Gaibian Zhongguo zongjiao de wushinian, 1898–1948* 改變中國宗教的五十年，1898–1948, edited by Kang Bao 康豹 [Paul R. Katz] and Gao Wansang 高萬桑 [Vincent Goossaert], 141–67. Nankang: Academia Sinica, Institute of Modern History, 2015.

Yuria, Mori. "Identity and Lineage: The *Taiyi jinhua zongzhi* and the Spirit-writing Cult to Patriarch Lü in Qing China." In *Daoist Identity: History, Lineage, and Ritual*, edited by Livia Kohn and Harold Roth, 165–84. Honolulu: University of Hawai'i Press, 2002.

Zhaoping gong Yuhua tang jianshi 昭平宮育化堂簡史. Nantou: Yuhua Tang, 2001.

Zhou Yumin 周育民. "Minguo shiqi yige wentan juzi jibixia de lingjie 民國時期一個文壇巨子乩筆下的靈界." *Minjian zongjiao* 民間宗教 1 (1995): 37–55.

Index

academies (*shuyuan* 書院)　124, 181, 259, 277, 314, 355, 607
Ailan 愛蘭 (Wuniulan 烏牛欄)　611
ancestors　2, 39, 42, 103, 255*n*3, 430, 474, 512*n*68, 515*n*70, 577
　　ancestor tablets (*zuxian paiwei* 祖先牌位)　577
Anxin shantang 安心善堂 (Charitable Hall of Peaceful Mind)　551
aphorisms (*ge yan* 格言)　104, 275
apocalypse　11, 19*n*64, 27, 71, 77–78, 86, 103, 109, 150, 447, 449, 451, 459–60, 475, 487, 489, 492, 494–97, 504–5, 510, 513–14, 519, 521–22, 524, 545, 554. See also *jie* 劫, and kalpa
Apostle John　13
Aristotle (384–322 BC)　13
ascriptive communities　601, 615, 620
ash-table (*huitan* 灰壇)　49–50
automatic writing　7, 13, 216, 226, 235

bade 八德 (eight virtues)　126, 472
bagu wen 八股文 (eight-legged essays)　9, 187, 188
Baguajiao 八卦教 (the Eight Trigrams Sect)　453
Bai Yuchan 白玉蟾 (1134/1194–1229)　81, 113, 326–27
Baiyun Temple (Baiyun guan 白雲觀)　360*n*23, 582
ban/prohibitions on spirit-writing　21–22, 80, 83, 94, 113–21, 125, 181, 186, 240, 241, 280, 295, 344, 391, 404, 409, 436, 510, 515, 547, 552, 566. See also criticism of spirit-writing
　　Daming huidian 大明會典 (Collected statutes of the Great Ming)　186
　　Daming lü 大明律 (Code of the Great Ming)　114
　　Daqing lüli 大清律例 (Codes and cases of the Great Qing)　186
　　licentious shrines (*yinci* 淫祠)　94
　　Tongzhi tiaoge 通制條格 (Articles from the comprehensive regulations)　113
Baode tang 報德堂 (Hall for Rewarding Benevolence)　547

baogao 寶誥 (precious invocation)　329, 588–89, 617
baojuan 寶卷 (precious scrolls)　152, 158–59, 366, 405, 520
Baosong baohe ji 寶松抱鶴記 (The history of the Precious Pine and Crane Temple)　567
baoying 報應 (divine responses, retribution)　27, 41, 48–51, 61, 66, 68, 72, 220, 378–79, 378*n*114, 383, 388, 388*n*150, 410, 495, 539
baxian 八仙 (Eight Transcendents)　118, 124, 557
Beijing 北京　21, 117, 151, 210, 220, 264, 311, 315, 317, 318–19, 320, 335*n*48, 357, 359–60, 359*n*19, 360*n*23, 410, 411, 416*n*51, 459, 580, 582
Beiyang 北洋 period (1916–1927)　16, 22, 356, 358, 360, 362, 364, 385, 388
benevolence (*ren* 仁)　277, 370, 372, 383*n*129, 387, 390*n*154, 410, 428–30, 540
biji xiaoshuo 筆記小說 (brush notes and small talks)　172
biji 筆記 (brush notes)　40, 60, 91*n*5, 92, 172, 292–94, 304
bilu 筆籙 (brush register)　9, 43, 52, 174, 187–89, 587, 602
bilusheng 筆錄生 (copyist)　587–91
Bing she 冰社 (Ice Club)　318
Bixia gong 碧霞宮　620
Bixia yuanjun 碧霞元君　151, 162
British Society for Psychical Research　225–26
bu 卜　185, 298. See also divination
Buddha　39, 42, 74, 103, 110, 122, 217, 219, 227, 247, 307, 375, 377*n*104, 402, 414, 430, 433, 447, 449, 454, 462–63, 465–66, 488*n*5, 498, 544–45, 589, 607, 610. See also Dasheng fozu 大聖佛祖
Buddhism　19–20, 23, 24, 44–45, 69, 83, 92, 102, 103, 122, 126, 144, 145, 147, 197, 199, 218, 243, 255*n*3, 256, 263, 268, 313, 335, 336*n*51, 356*n*8, 359*n*20, 362, 366*n*53, 387*n*145, 402, 407, 408, 409, 414–15, 420*n*65, 429–31, 433, 454, 465, 470, 474,

INDEX

Buddhism (cont.)   494, 524, 538, 542, 546n61, 564, 567, 568–69, 572n33, 574, 577–79, 602, 603, 604
  Buddhist clerics   19–20, 336n51, 453, 542, 615
  Buddhist temples   95, 97, 536, 556
  Buddhist values   19
  Chan 禪   256n3, 280, 386n140
  lay Buddhist   19, 124, 242, 548, 615
  Pure Land   243, 245, 256n3
  tantric   41, 44–45, 62, 239
Bushel Lantern Festival (*Lidou qi'an fahui* 禮斗祈安法會)   614–15

calligraphy   58, 233, 303–4, 621
canonization   14, 57, 272, 302, 367
Canzan tang 參贊堂   609–10, 612, 617, 623
Caodai/ Đạo Cao Đài 道高臺 (Way of the High Terrace)   476
celebratory rhymed couples   619
Changzhou 長洲   148, 264, 268, 269, 284, 361n28
chanting   9, 10, 17, 193, 197, 214, 239, 549, 567, 579, 588
  scripture chanting   329, 508, 512–13, 522–23, 569, 602, 608, 616, 620
Chaoan 潮安   551
Chaozhou 潮州   12, 27, 180n31, 532–56
charitable hall. *See shantang* 善堂
charity   3, 9–10, 9–10, 17, 19, 23, 26, 27, 86, 171, 281, 347, 358, 360, 362, 383, 391, 393, 403–4, 406, 410–11, 413–15, 417, 419, 425, 427–33, 435–37, 489, 493, 515–16, 524, 533, 550, 532–56, 565–66, 565–66, 574n40, 585, 595, 600–3, 605, 607–8, 608–9, 612, 620–21
  emergency relief (*jizhen* 急賑)   360, 615
  food for the indigent   3
  philanthropic society (*shanshe* 善社)   359, 532, 536–38, 543, 547, 549–51, 554, 556, 605. *See also shantang* 善堂, and *shanhui* 善會
  relief work   356, 360, 403–4, 432, 540, 544
  support for widows   3, 432, 436, 540
  The Affiliated Institute for Poor Widows and Pregnant Women (Chipin lichan jiujisuo 赤贫嫠产救济所)   432

Chen Chien-hung 陳建宏   606, 614
Chen Danran 陳澹然 (1859–1930)   343
Chen Huanzhang 陳煥章 (1880–1933)   355
Chen Jiangshan 陳江山 (1899–1976)   621
Chen Jinggu 陳靖姑   325
Chen Jitang 陳濟棠 (1890–1954)   391, 509
Chen Lanyun 陳蘭雲 (no dates)   147
Chen Weiming 陳微明 (1881–1958)   604
Chen Wenshu 陳文述 (1774–1845)   146, 147
Chen Yingning 陳攖寧 (1880–1969)   407
Chen Yongbin 陳用賓 (1550–1617)   104
Chen Zhong 陳伀 (fl. 1236)   62, 64, 70, 71, 74, 77, 78n97
Cheng Hao 程顥 (1032–1085)   320, 367
Cheng Minzheng 程敏 (1446–1499)   115
Cheng Yi 程頤 (1033–1107)   25, 257, 259, 261n20, 262, 270, 271, 284, 320, 367, 368n64
Chengdu 成都   11, 63, 162, 581–82
Chengjing she 誠敬社 (Society of Sincerity and Reverence)   547, 551
Cheng-Zhu Learning   257–60, 258n10, 262–63, 267–68, 271, 280–81
Chiang Chao-chan 江趙展   607, 615
Chiang Kai-shek 蔣介石 (1887–1975)   239, 240, 391, 392, 460
China Daoism Institute (Zhonghua Daojiao xueyuan 中華道教學院)   614
Ching Chung Koon 青松觀   567–69, 572–73, 575–77, 579
Chiu Yen-chou 邱廷州   607, 608, 613, 614
Chongyang 重陽 Festival   427
chopsticks   25, 92–93, 136, 138, 178–79
Chosŏn   13. *See also* Korea
Christianity   20, 256, 299–300, 355–56, 356n8, 362, 387n146, 402–3, 402n3, 407, 409, 412, 419, 451–52
Cihui tang 慈惠堂   463, 614
Ciji huitang 慈濟會堂 (Hall of the Benevolent Association)   537
City gods   71, 553, 619, 623
Clart, Philip   5, 8, 365n50
classical learning (*jingxue* 經學)   355, 358, 360, 364, 389, 393, 395
communal welfare   539–40, 555, 615
community activism   16–17, 28, 393, 535, 601, 620

INDEX

Confucianism   26, 103, 126, 126n150, 199, 255–57, 260, 281, 344, 355–56, 355n4, 356n8, 358, 362–63, 367, 369–70, 371n79, 377, 380, 384–95, 387n146, 389n152, 402, 415, 424–25, 425n78, 509, 511, 523, 523n85
   Confucian classics   23, 26, 126, 257–58, 266, 276, 298, 355–95, 462
   Confucius   78, 258–59, 269–70, 274, 280, 282, 295, 301, 357–58, 363–67, 363n35, 369–71, 373–78, 375n99, 376n101, 376n103, 376n104, 380, 382, 385, 389n153, 391, 393–94, 402, 414, 452, 510, 514, 516–17, 623
   popular Confucianism   281, 356, 356n12, 394
   Rujiao 儒教 (Confucian religion)   282, 343, 355, 356, 510–11, 601, 605
Cong Liangbi 叢良弼 (1868–1945)   427, 427n86
Cong Wanying 叢婉英   427
Cong Zhaohuan 叢兆桓 (1931–)   416n51, 427
Congshan tang 從善堂 (Hall of Following Virtue)   494–95
criticism of spirit-writing   21, 45, 59, 72, 80–83, 113, 139, 210, 227, 238–39, 279, 294, 386, 391, 542–43. See also ban/prohibitions on spirit-writing
cultivating life (yangsheng 養生)   603
Cunxin shantang 存心善堂   545, 546–47

Dafeng zushi 大峰祖師   488–89, 536, 542–47, 544n53, 549, 550, 554–55, 557
Dahei tianshen 大黑天神 (Great God of the Black Heaven)   101
Dahu 大湖   610
Daiquan tang 代勸堂   607, 610, 621
danshui 丹水 (elixir water/cinnabar water)   544, 619
Dao   71, 82, 155, 364, 366–76, 378, 380, 382–84, 390, 412, 414, 428, 452, 454, 458, 465
Daode xueshe 道德學社 (Morality Society)   356n9, 357n14
Daode yuekan 道德月刊 (Morality monthly)   406
Daode zazhi 道德雜誌 (Morality magazine)   406, 433

637

daohao 道號 (ordination names)   568, 576. See also faming 法名 (initiation names)
Daohua tang 導化堂   618–19, 624
Daoism   2, 45, 65, 71, 81–82, 92, 101–2, 113–25, 145, 147, 197–99, 207, 255n3, 256, 313, 356n8, 361n30, 362, 373n87, 402, 415, 433, 533n3, 538, 542, 564–96, 614–15. See also Zhengyi School
   daofa 道法 (Daoist ritual). See ritual
   daoguan 道觀 (Daoist monastery/temple)   3, 10, 19, 24, 63, 95, 97, 125, 180n31, 208, 497n29, 514, 550, 564n1, 568, 574n40, 580, 582, 584–85
   Daoist Offering Ceremonies (jianjiao fahui 建醮法會)   48, 608, 613
   Daoist priests   2, 8, 18, 24–25, 45, 47–48, 51, 54, 60–61, 71, 79, 86, 98, 102, 272–73, 326, 542
   daotan 道壇 (Daoist altar)   9, 533, 548, 553, 564–65, 564–81, 585–87, 591, 593, 595–96
   daotang 道堂 (Daoist hall)   9, 533, 536–37, 543, 548, 553, 554, 564–65, 569n24
   fu 符. See talisman
Daoist Canon (Daozang 道藏)   23, 41, 48, 50, 55, 62, 69, 79–80, 82, 82n109, 105, 139, 175, 180, 182, 360n23
   Daozang jinghua 道藏精華 (Essence of the Daoist canon)   621
   Daozang xubian 道藏續編 (Sequel to the Daoist canon)   148n45
   Zhengtong Daozang 正統道藏 (Daoist canon of the Zhengtong reign)   111
Daomen dingzhi 道門定制 (Fixed institutions for Daoism)   80, 113. See also criticism of spirit-writing
daotong 道統 (genealogy of the way)   264, 271–72, 280, 357, 366–72, 366n53, 376–77, 393, 472
Daoxue 道學. See Neo-Confucianism
Daoyuan 道院 (School of the Way)   13n44, 26, 158, 243n82, 346, 357, 359, 361–62, 361n31, 376, 391, 393, 402–37, 445, 451, 455, 603. See also redemptive societies
Daozang jiyao 道藏輯要 (Essentials of the Daoist canon)   3–4, 154, 195, 487, 621n80

Chongkan Daozang jiyao 重刊道藏輯要 (Reprint of the Essentials of the Daoist canon)   11
Dasheng fozu 大聖佛祖   550, 557. *See also* Buddha
Daxue 大學 (Great learning)   258, 358, 365, 367, 370–71, 370n73, 370n75, 376, 378, 383–87, 457, 463
Daxue zhengshi 大學證釋 (*The Great Learning*, verified and explicated)   365, 368–70, 374–75, 384–87, 389–90, 394, 394n168
deGlopper, Donald   600
Dejiao 德教 (Virtuous Teaching)   533. *See also* redemptive societies
demons   45, 67, 77–78, 81, 94, 105, 113, 144, 162, 192, 195, 240, 292–94, 339–40, 459, 474, 578
Deng Bingquan 鄧秉佺 (1924–1999)   329, 331, 332
Deng tianjun xuanling bamen baoying neizhi 鄧天君玄靈八門報應內旨 (Inner instructions on obtaining a divine response through the eight gates of the dark spirits, [revealed by] Heavenly Lord Deng)   51
Deng tianjun xuanling bamen baoying neizhi 鄧天君玄靈八門報應內旨 (Inner instructions on obtaining a divine response through the eight gates of the dark spirits, [revealed by] Heavenly Lord Deng)   72
Deng Zhenwen 鄧貞文 (born 1961)   329
dianchuanshi 點傳師 (Yiguandao initiator)   456–57, 466
Dianshizhai huabao 點石齋畫報 (Illustrated news of the lithographic studio)   140
diexian 碟仙 (Transcendent of the Plate)   25, 206–48
Ding Fubao 丁福保 (1874–1952)   19, 225
Ding Richang 丁日昌 (1823–1882)   539, 540
Dingyuan 定遠   11
Dipper Bushel Ceremonies (*lidou fahui* 禮斗法會)   608
disciples (*dizi* 弟子)   16, 46, 49, 57–59, 67–70, 73, 78, 81, 84–85, 121, 144, 195, 258–59, 261, 261n19, 265, 269–70, 274, 279–80, 319, 327, 339, 359, 366, 369, 402, 494, 501, 511, 515n70, 525, 546, 549–50, 552–53, 567–68, 571, 573–93, 601, 603, 608
divination   7n20, 9–10, 40, 42, 44, 47n8, 48, 53, 52–55, 59–60, 71–72, 79, 81, 82n108, 92, 96, 113, 116, 136, 140, 173–75, 177, 179–80, 182–89, 192–93, 198, 206, 226, 248, 258, 296, 301, 303, 304, 306–7, 313, 329, 331, 334–35, 339, 347, 404–5, 428, 455, 462, 467, 571, 590, 593n70, 607, 618–19. *See also* prediction
   bazi 八字 (eight characters)   230, 296, 297
   dissecting of characters (*cezi* 測字)   304
   fortune telling   238, 247, 292, 571
   jibu 箕卜 (sieve divination)   138, 189
   mantic arts (*shushu* 術數)   26, 291–92, 294–95, 297, 302–8, 311
   divining blocks (*bubei* 卜杯)   572, 576, 593–94, 613
Diyu youji 地獄遊記 (A journey to earth prison)   605
dizi 弟子. *See* disciples
Dong Suhuang 董素皇   97–98
Dong zhenjun jiangbi shilu 董真君降筆實錄 (Authentic records of the Transcendent Master Dong descending into the brush)   98, 98n32. *See also Jiangbi shilu* 降筆實錄, and *Xuandi shilu* 玄帝實錄
Donggang 東港   621
Donglin Academy   265. *See also* academies
Dongling xiaozhi 洞靈小志 (Anecdotes of observing anomalies)   313
Dōtoku kaikan 道徳会館 (Morality Association)   466, 475–77
Doumu 斗母   3, 147, 159, 261, 261n20, 272n47, 282
Doutang 斗堂 (Dipper Shrine)   325–26, 328
dreams   47n8, 47–50, 55, 58, 63–64, 66, 69, 93, 124, 146, 155, 177, 236, 292, 544, 583, 607
du mojie 度末劫 (to escape the coming apocalypse)   71
Du Qiaolin 杜喬林 (1571–1638)   261n20, 262, 270
Duan Qirui 段祺瑞 (1865–1936)   360, 377, 383n131, 384–86, 387, 387n143, 387n145, 388n150, 390n153
Duan Zhengyuan 段正元 (1864–1940)   357

INDEX

Duara, Prasenjit 5*n*14, 356, 402, 408, 409, 414, 425, 426, 428, 444, 516*n*72
Duke of Zhou 周公 369
Dushu Pei xianren 督署裴真人 (Immortal Pei the Governor) 336

Earth gods 71, 219
education 3, 26, 73, 134, 209, 234, 324, 346, 387*n*146, 390, 404, 413, 420–21, 432, 540, 540*n*33, 587, 607, 609, 620
emperors 15, 24, 43, 54, 83, 314, 474
　Ming Chengzu 成祖, Emperor Zhu Di 朱棣 112, 343
　Ming Emperor Chongzhen 崇禎 145, 305
　Ming Emperor Jianwen 建文, Zhu Yunwen 朱允炆 343
　Ming Shizong 世宗, Emperor Jiajing 嘉靖 14, 105*n*61, 117–21, 126, 270, 320*n*19
　Ming Taizu 太祖, Emperor Zhu Yuanzhang 朱元璋 21*n*71, 76, 104, 105*n*60, 114
　Ming Xianzong 憲宗, Emperor Chenghua 成化 116–18, 126
　Ming Xiaozong 孝宗, Emperor Hongzhi 弘治 115
　Qing Emperor Puyi 溥儀 318, 335*n*48
　Qing Gaozong 高宗, Emperor Qianlong 乾隆 273, 280, 292, 492
　Qing Renzong 仁宗, Emperor Jiaqing 嘉慶 134, 161, 302*n*20, 535
　Qing Shengzu 聖祖, Emperor Kangxi 康熙 119, 258–59, 263, 302, 452, 539*n*27
　Qing Shizong 世宗, Emperor Yongzheng 雍正 295–96, 539*n*27
　Qing Shizu 世祖, Emperor Shunzhi 順治 258, 452
　Song Duzong 度宗 110
　Song Guangzong 光宗 95
　Song Huizong 徽宗 94
　Song Lizong 理宗 105–6
　Song Renzong 仁宗 93
　Song Shenzong 神宗 93
　Tang Taizong 太宗, Emperor Li Shimin 李世民 452
　Yuan Mingzong 明宗 270
　Yuan Shizu 世祖, Emperor Kublai 102*n*46
end of the world 3, 150, 475

Erxiang she 二香社 (Double Incense Club) 327
eschatology 3, 11, 13–14, 27, 43, 68, 76–77, 84–86, 143, 150, 153, 195, 302, 312, 359, 384, 393, 446, 463, 487–95, 501, 504–8, 510–11, 513–14, 521–25, 533, 535, 539, 556. See also apocalypse
examinations 2, 9, 11, 43, 59–60, 108, 115, 138–41, 149–50, 178, 187–90, 209, 227, 230, 256, 258, 260, 261–64, 268, 281, 291, 302, 308, 313–14, 337, 355–56, 367, 393, 474, 498*n*32, 509, 540*n*30
exorcism 24, 41, 45, 47, 50, 52, 59, 62–64, 66, 70–73, 78–79, 84, 160, 198*n*75, 256, 302, 325, 339, 524, 593. See also fashi 法師

faming 法名 (initiation names) 326, 327, 333, 339, 359, 360, 364. See also daohao 道號
fandong huidaomen 反動會道門 (reactionary sects and secret societies) 23, 457, 515, 552
fangshi 方士 (master of techniques) 60, 119
fangzhi 方志. See local gazetteers
fashi 法師 24, 41, 44–46, 48, 50, 56–57, 70–72, 84–85, 85*n*115, 134, 160. See also ritual, and exorcism
fashu 法術 (ritual techniques) 40–41, 44–45, 49–51, 55, 60–61, 80, 86, 256, 339, 613
fazhi 法職 (ordination grade) 326
Fei Ngan Tung Daoism and Buddhism Society 飛雁洞佛道社 564–96
Feifeng shan 飛鳳山 607
feiluan xuanhua 飛鸞宣化 (transformation through the flying phoenix) 111, 454, 468
female alchemy 158, 159–62, 188, 406. See also inner alchemy
female disciples 576–77, 579, 608
female immortals 53, 93, 140, 144–46, 148–49, 155–56, 158–62, 196–97, 406
Fengshan 鳳山 607, 608, 613, 614
fenxiang 分香 (division of incense) 97, 97*n*31, 512*n*68, 609–10, 609*n*43
Feuchtwang, Stephan 600, 601
five teachings (*wujiao* 五教) 256, 402, 414–15, 433
flying phoenix. See spirit-writing
fotang (Buddhist hall) 457, 462, 536, 543

Four Books (*sishu* 四書)   257, 258, 276, 367, 370, 386, 457
Fu she 復社 (Revival Society)   197
Fu Yuantian 傅圓天 (1925–1997)   582, 582n56
fuji daotan 扶乩道壇. *See* spirit-writing
Fuji mixin di yanjiu 扶乩迷信底研究 (An investigation of the superstition of spirit-writing)   22, 173, 176
fuji tuanti 扶乩團體 (spirit-writing groups). *See* spirit-writing
Fujian 福建   79, 97, 122, 143, 210n9, 262, 263, 320, 322n26, 336, 522n83, 534n11, 620
Fuma Susumu 夫馬進   535
Fung Ying Seen Koon 蓬瀛仙館   566–69, 574n40, 577, 596
Furen shantang 輔仁善堂 (Charitable Hall for Supporting Benevolence)   540, 541, 542
futi 附體/ *fushen* 附身. *See* spirit-possession
Fuxi 伏羲   369
Fuyou Dijun 孚佑帝君   359, 365n49, 497, 503, 554, 572n31. *See also* Lü Dongbin 呂洞賓/ Lüzu 呂祖
Fuzhou 福州   9, 26, 79, 112, 43–45, 361n28

Gao Chuiwan 高吹萬 (1879–1958)   241, 242, 243, 247, 604
Gao Panlong 高攀龍 (1562–1626)   259, 280
Gaoshang dadong Wenchang silu ziyang baolu 高上大洞文昌司祿紫陽寶籙 (Precious purple *yang* register of the Wenchang Office for Official Careers, of the Most High Great Cavern)   65, 70, 111
gender   14, 17, 25–26, 133–62, 179, 404–10, 414, 417–27, 437, 457, 489–90, 514, 525, 551, 600, 608, 617–18
  concubines   117, 135, 143, 147, 150, 176, 188, 404, 412, 423, 425–27
Gengsi bian 庚巳編 (A compilation from the year *gengsi*)   115, 123
ghost   53, 103, 178, 189–90, 194, 196–97, 207, 214, 226–28, 236–37, 241, 244–45, 247, 275–76, 292–94, 296, 298–302, 306, 308, 537, 546, 549, 578n47
Goddess of the Privy. *See* Zigu 紫姑
god-welcoming team (*yingsheng zu* 迎聖組)   588

Gonghuang miao 宮皇廟 (Temple of the Jade Princess)   497–98, 497n30, 516, 518–21
Gonghuang sanshiliu shou jishi 宮皇三十六首乩詩 (Thirty-six spirit-written poems by the Jade Princess)   519
gongsang 降生 (spirit medium)   513
gongzhu 宮主 (court lady)   503, 518n77, 520–21
Goossaert, Vincent   1n1, 2, 2n4, 5, 14, 17, 18, 24, 133, 134, 139, 150, 160, 161, 174, 174n16, 175, 190, 199, 255, 283, 299, 327, 376n101, 409, 523, 601
great unity (*datong* 大同)   362, 391
Gu meihua guan 古梅花觀 (Venerable Plum Flower Temple)   603
Gu Xiancheng 顧憲誠 (1550–1612)   259
Guandi 關帝 (Lord Guan)   3, 5, 11, 13–14, 121–22, 126, 134, 141, 153, 161, 256n5, 447, 462, 487, 492–93, 496, 498, 500n34, 501n38, 504–6, 508–17, 513n69, 519, 522–23, 535, 551, 572n31, 606–7, 611, 623
Guangdong 廣東   3, 6, 12, 16, 27, 95, 212, 237, 391, 454, 476, 487–525, 532–56, 565–67, 567, 578n46, 579n49, 584, 585, 593n70
Guangshan tan 廣善壇 (Altar for Spreading Goodness)   359
Guansheng dijun jiujie zhenjing 關聖帝君救劫真經 (True scripture of Lord Guan to save humanity from the apocalypse)   513
Guansheng dijun mingsheng jing 關聖帝君明聖經 (The scripture of the Imperial Lord Guan on illuminating saintliness)   493, 498–501, 508, 510, 513, 522
Guanyin miaodao lianhua jing 觀音妙道蓮華經 (Guanyin's *Lotus Sutra* of the marvelous Dao)   606
Guanyin 觀音   19, 151–52, 161–62, 415n50, 487, 507, 512, 514, 519, 554, 558, 606, 624
Guigendao 歸根道 (The Way of Returning to the Origin)   447, 516. *See also* redemptive societies
Guigong 桂宮 (The Osmanthus Palace)   325
Guizhou 貴州   11, 65, 159, 490, 492n13
Guo Baicang 郭柏蒼 (1815–1890)   314
Guo Baiyin 郭柏蔭 (1807–1884)   314
Guo Fuzhong 郭輔衷 (1872–)   315
Guo Jiesan 郭階三 (1778–1856)   314
Guo Zebi 郭則泌 (1880–?)   317

INDEX

Guo Zengxin 郭曾炘 (1855–1928)　311, 313, 314, 315, 317, 318, 319, 320, 321, 322, 327, 332, 334n48, 337, 347
Guo Zeshou 郭則壽 (1883–1943)　311, 317, 334, 340, 341
Guo Zesu 郭則涑 (1886–?)　317
Guo Zeyun 郭則澐 (1882–1947)　313, 314, 315, 317, 318, 319, 334n48, 335, 337, 346
guocui 國粹. *See* national essence
Guomindang 國民黨　22, 239, 242, 391, 543. *See also* Nationalist Party
Gyokkōzan Mirokutera 玉皇山弥勒寺　467, 469, 473–74

Haimen 海門　231, 488, 549
Hakka　28, 150, 467, 577n46, 605, 607, 609–12, 617
　Hakka cult of the Heroes (Yiminye 義民爺)　610
　Hakka ritual associations (*changhui* 嘗會)　610
Han Yu 韓愈 (768–824)　261n20, 366n53, 369
Han Zhongli 漢鍾離　557
Hangzhou 杭州　56, 61, 83, 147, 148, 178, 238, 239
Hanlin Academy (Hanlin yuan 翰林院)　181, 314
Hanxue 漢學 (Han Learning)　368
Hanyi kexue dagang 漢譯科學大綱 (Chinese translation of *The Outline of Science*)　225
He Hongren 何弘仁 (no dates)　322, 322n25
He Longxiang 賀龍驤 (ca. 1900)　162
He Qizhong 何啟忠 (1916–1968)　567, 568, 568n19
He Xiangu xunnei wen 何仙姑訓內文 (He Xiangu instructs the inner chambers)　157
He Xiangu 何仙姑　154–55, 154–55, 157, 159
He Ziyun 何紫雲　148
healing　1, 9–10, 50, 61, 66, 71, 71n79, 79, 134, 458, 489, 516n72, 521, 573, 586, 592–95, 607, 611, 615, 617–20. *See also* medicine
Heavenly Master Daoism. *See* Tianshidao 天師道
Heavenly Master Zhang (Zhang Tianshi 張天師)　56, 81, 113, 118, 583–85, 589–90, 614, 621

Hebei 河北　291, 402, 459
Helong 鶴矓　551
Henan 河南　182, 259, 359, 497n28
Hengji gong 恒吉宮　613–14
heterodoxy　21, 82, 118, 277, 296, 341, 346, 366, 394, 516
Hong Kong　3, 6, 12, 20, 27, 171, 172, 179, 180, 193, 213, 214, 293n4, 311n2, 312n5, 323, 324, 324n29, 325, 326, 332, 333, 335, 335n49, 348, 407, 454, 455, 456, 494–96, 495n24, 503, 507, 520n80, 532, 533, 536n21, 537n23, 564–96
Hongjiao zhenjun 宏教真君 (Perfected Ruler Hongjiao)　329
Hongwanzi hui 紅卍字會 (Red Swastika Society)　23n84, 402–3, 410, 414, 417, 427n86, 431–33. *See also* redemptive societies
Hongyi 弘一 (1880–1942)　336n51
Hou Baoyuan 侯寶垣 (1914–1999)　568, 575, 579n49
Hsieh Tsung-hui 謝聰輝　52, 60, 64, 65, 108, 109, 139, 173, 181–82, 208
Hsinchu 新竹　607, 610
Hu Binxia 胡彬夏 (1888–1931)　424, 424n75
Hu She 護社 (The Protection Society)　334
Hu Shi 胡適 (1891–1962)　240, 423n74
Huaishan tang 懷善堂　609, 613, 623
Huang Daozhou 黃道周 (1585–1646)　197, 198, 261n20, 262–63, 268, 270, 273–80, 285, 344
Huang Maosheng 黃茂盛 (1901–1978)　621
Huanglian shengmu 黃蓮聖母　150
Huashan she 化善社 (Society of Transformation and Goodness)　549
huashu 化書 (Book of transformations)　70, 78, 180. *See also Wenchang huashu* 文昌化書, *and Zitong dijun huashu* 梓潼帝君化書
Huaxia zheyi chanwei she 華夏哲義闡微社 (Chinese Society for Occult Philosophy)　212
Hubei 湖北　10, 24, 85, 182, 211n19, 314, 337, 449, 512
huiguan 會館 (guildhalls)　3, 502, 504n47, 541
human nature (*xing* 性)　367, 371, 370–75, 383–84, 418

Hunan 湖南 153, 182, 212, 245, 314, 337, 492, 512
Huoluo lingguan 豁落靈官 554
hypnosis (*cuimianshu* 催眠術) 225–27. *See also* mesmerism (*chuanqishu* 傳氣術)

Immortal He Yeyun 何野雲 536, 554, 557–58
Immortal Master Pei (Pei Xianshi 裴仙師) 328, 336–37
Immortal White Cloud (Baiyun xiangu 白雲仙姑) 545
incantations 43–44, 49, 60n48, 63, 95–96, 95n21, 123, 174, 207, 209, 212, 216–17, 219, 238, 245, 296, 594. *See also* ritual
initiation 41, 46, 61, 68, 458, 520, 608, 616
inner alchemy (*neidan* 內丹) 11, 15n50, 17n56, 67, 75, 76, 135, 141, 149, 153–54, 153–62, 188, 263, 405–6, 435, 497n27, 523n85, 548n67, 603
Inoue Enryō 井上圓了 (1858–1919) 216
Islam 20, 256, 356n8, 362, 433

Jade Emperor (Yudi 玉帝) 48, 52, 59, 65, 71, 77, 85, 102, 105, 152, 197, 262, 269, 487, 489, 492, 495–96, 503–6, 510–12, 517–19, 522, 524, 545, 606
Japan 210n9, 225, 238, 239, 240, 245, 266, 314, 323, 360, 364, 391, 403, 405, 409, 423, 425, 444–45, 449n25, 452, 459, 466–77, 476n150, 542n45, 604, 613, 620
Jesus 13, 363n35, 375n99, 376, 377n104, 402, 414, 451, 452, 461
Ji Rongshu 紀容舒 (1685–1764) 291
Ji Yun 紀昀 (1724–1805, Ji Xiaolan 紀曉嵐) 14n47, 15, 25, 194, 199, 291–308
Jiang Chaozong 江朝宗 (1861–1943) 360, 361n31, 364, 365, 379, 383, 388n150, 392
Jiang Zonglu 蔣宗魯 (1521–1588) 104
jiangbi 降筆 (causing gods to descend into a brush) 8, 50–52, 56, 58, 61, 64, 66, 69, 70–71, 72, 73, 76, 92, 97–105, 107, 114, 181n37
Jiangbi shilu 降筆實錄 (Authentic records [obtained through the practice of] descending into the brush) 64, 98, 98n32. *See also Xuandi shilu* 玄帝實錄, and *Dong zhenjun jiangbi shilu* 董真君降筆實錄
jiangji 降乩 (descending into the stylus) 5, 122–25, 126, 378, 542
jiangluan 降鸞 (descent of the phoenix) 172
Jiangnan 江南 11, 19n65, 76, 85, 101, 135, 141, 148, 149, 150, 196, 307, 603, 620
Jiangxi 江西 54, 60, 66, 85, 117, 121n127, 491n11, 578n46
Jiangxi lu 講習錄 (Record of discussion and study) 258, 274, 278, 280, 282
jiangxue 講學 (learning-through-discussion) 271n46, 273, 278
Jianjiang River 鑒江 490, 503, 522
jiao 醮 (offerings) 55, 59, 113, 113n96, 238, 511, 549, 613. *See also* offerings
jibi 乩筆 (stylus-brush) 447–48, 586, 617. *See also luanbi* 鸞筆
jibi 箕筆 (sieve-brush) 51, 54–55, 79, 210
jie 劫 27, 71, 78, 102–3, 105, 127, 150, 321, 325, 487, 495–97, 504–6, 510, 513, 521, 533, 545, 549, 553. *See also* apocalypse, and kalpa
Jieyang 揭陽 534, 534n10, 539, 553
Jieyang shantang 揭陽善堂 539–40
jifang 乩方 (spirit-written prescription) 93, 329, 334n48, 521, 593, 594. *See also* medicine
Jigong 濟公 19, 415n50, 433, 450, 456, 460, 462, 590–91, 593–94, 602–3
Ji'nan 濟南 12, 361n28, 393, 402, 410, 411, 412, 416, 427, 430, 431, 432
Jin Shengtan 金聖嘆 (1608–1661) 144, 145
Jingming zhongxiao fa 淨明忠孝法 (Pure and bright, loyal and filial liturgy) 66, 67–69, 73, 86, 318
Jingshen lu 精神錄 (Records of the essence and spirit) 621
jingsheng 經生 (scripture-reciter) 508, 569n25, 575, 579, 579n49, 587–89
jingtang 經堂 (scripture hall) 506, 508–13, 522–23
Jingxiu jingtang 敬修經堂 508–12
jingxue 經學. *See* classical learning
jingzuo 靜坐. *See* meditation

INDEX

Jinsi lu 近思錄 (Reflections on things at hand) 265
jiujie jing 救劫經 (scriptures to save humanity from the apocalypse) 27, 487, 488, 488*n*5, 491–97, 493*n*17, 504*n*47, 505, 505*n*49, 507, 513, 521, 522–23, 545
Jiuqionglin 九芎林 607
Jiushi xinjiao 救世新教 (New Religion to Save the World) 26, 256, 357, 365, 463. *See also* New Religion to Save the World
Jiushisi huashu 九十四化書 (The book of 94 transformations) 106
jixian 箕/乩仙 (transcendents of the stylus) 97, 121, 124, 319
Jo Kinsen 徐錦泉 (Ch. Xu Jinquan 1921–2018), 466–67, 468, 472–73, 473
Jordan, David K. 28*n*86, 601, 616*n*65
Jueshan tang 覺善堂 (Hall for Awakening Goodness) 548, 548*n*72

kaifa 開筊 (sailing the raft) 9, 325, 332
Kaifeng 開封 21*n*71, 83, 93, 94, 125, 126
kaisha 開沙 (opening the sand) 9, 415
Kālacakra Dharma Society (Shilun jingang fahui 時輪金剛法會) 238–39
kalpa 77, 102–3, 105, 127, 150, 267, 325, 366, 533, 549. *See also* apocalypse, and *jie* 劫
Kamlan Koon 金蘭觀 180
Kang Youwei 康有為 (1858–1927) 282, 355, 367, 370*n*75, 376, 387*n*146
Kaohsiung 449*n*25, 463, 464, 607
kaozheng xue 考證學 (evidential learning) 281
Karl Marx 13
kexue lingji 科學靈乩 (Scientific Numinous Stylus) 25, 210–11, 212–14, 214–22, 231, 236, 233–41, 244, 247–48
King Wen 文王 368
King Wu 武王 368
kokkurisan (狐狗狸さん or コックリさん) 216, 468
Kongjiao hui 孔教會 (Confucian Religion Association) 355. *See also* Confucianism
Korea 13, 43, 477. *See also* Chosŏn
Koxinga (Zheng Chenggong 鄭成功 1624–1662), 322, 322*n*26, 323

Kuai yuan 獪園 (Garden of mischief) 121, 124
Kuang Fu 匡阜 326–27
Kunning miaojing 坤寧妙經 (Wondrous scripture on Kun's peace) 157, 159, 188
Kwun Tong 觀塘 572, 572*n*33, 586–87

Lady Xian 洗夫人 490, 509, 518*n*77, 520
Lai Chi-tim 黎志添 4*n*8, 18, 142
Lan Daoxing 藍道行 (no dates) 117, 118–21
Lanji Bookstore 蘭記書局 621
Laozi 老子 262, 363*n*35, 371, 377*n*104, 402, 414, 452, 510, 583*n*60, 614
Laozi 老子 371*n*79
Laozu 老祖 (Venerable Patriarch) 243*n*82, 362*n*31, 414–15, 428, 430, 433, 557
latrine 135–36, 173, 176–77, 405. *See also* Zigu 紫姑
law 22, 20–24, 42, 45, 94, 103, 104, 114, 113–14, 116, 120, 126, 184, 186, 209, 211*n*19, 280, 296, 324, 331, 344, 391, 423*n*74, 426, 543, 547, 574*n*40, 575, 580. *See also* ban/prohibitions on spirit-writing
lay communities 2–4, 10, 18, 134–35, 197
Le'an Dashi 泐庵大師 144–46
Lei Shizhong 雷時中 (Mo'an 默庵 1221–1295), 57–58
leifa 雷法. *See* ritual
Leshan she 樂善社 (Society for Enjoying Good Deeds) 547, 557
Li Bai 李白 (701–762) 101*n*44, 197, 261*n*20, 553, 554, 557, 558
Li Shibin 李士彬 (1835–1913) 540
Li Tieguai 李鐵拐 554, 557
Li Yuhong 李玉鋐 (1661–?) 187, 197
Li Zisheng 李孜省 (?–1487) 117, 118, 126
Lian'an shantang 練安善堂 549
Liang Qichao 梁啟超 (1873–1929) 433
Liang Shuming 梁漱溟 (1893–1988) 390*n*154
Lianhua shanmai 蓮花山脈 (Lotus Mountains) 534
Liantaisheng 蓮台聖 (Lotus Sage) 413, 415–16, 418, 420, 425, 427–31, 434–35
Liao Shenxiu 廖慎修 (fl. 1884–1894) 548
Liaozhai zhiyi 聊齋誌異 (Strange tales from the Liaozhai studio) 292
Libu youshilang 禮部右侍郎 (Ministry of Rites) 314

Lidou 禮斗 (Worshipping Dipper)   326
Liji 禮記 (Book of rites)   258, 386n140
Lin Chunxiu 林淳修 (no dates)   159
Ling hui 靈薈 (Numinous collection)   124
ling 靈 (efficacy)   5, 26, 46, 60, 75, 94, 100, 162, 194, 210n12, 219, 224–25, 228, 234, 236, 244, 303, 304, 334, 339, 374, 406, 574–75, 578n46, 586, 592–93. See also numinous
Lingdong ribao 嶺東日報 (Lingdong daily news)   542–43, 543n50, 552
Lingxue hui 靈學會 (Spiritualist Society)   7n22, 21n67, 210, 212n21, 225–27, 248, 347, 459. See also redemptive societies, and spiritualism
Lingxue yaozhi 靈學要誌 (Spiritualist magazine)   225, 227, 378n114
Lingying Dadi huashu shishi 靈應大帝化書事實 (Circumstances of the book of transformations of the Great Emperor of Numinous Response)   110, 181
Lingying guan 靈應觀 (Monastery of the Numinous Response)   102
literary societies   318, 324, 605
literati   2, 11–12, 14, 16, 18, 24–26, 41, 43, 53–54, 60–61, 73, 80, 93, 101n46, 116, 124–26, 137–41, 143–49, 160, 173, 178–79, 179n27, 186, 194–95, 197, 199, 207, 209, 213, 247, 260, 263, 295, 304, 311–48, 386, 405, 487, 490, 523–25, 523n85, 607, 611. See also Confucianism
Liu Ansheng 劉安勝 (late twelfth century)   57, 71n79, 106, 181
Liu Danming 劉瞻明 (no dates)   241, 242–47
Liu Qiao 劉樵 (fl. 1727–1749)   188, 268
Liu Shouyuan 柳守元   330, 330n40
Liu Songfei 劉松飛 (1930–2021)   571–79, 581, 583–85, 588, 589, 590, 592–94, 595
Liudui 六堆   607, 608
Liu-han Altar 了閑壇   26, 311–48
lixue 理學 (Learning of the principle)   266–67, 271, 279n80
local gazetteers   59, 140, 153, 261n16, 274, 322, 501, 503, 518, 534, 537
Lodge, Sir Oliver (1851–1940)   226
Longhu shan 龍虎山   81, 113, 582, 620
Longhua Troupe (Longhua zu 龍華組)   615

Longmen Lineage 龍門派   147, 567–69, 603
Longnü si 龍女寺 (Temple of the Dragon Maiden)   11, 14, 487, 491–92, 497
Longtian gong Xuanhua tang 龍天宮宣化堂   610
Lord Xin 辛天君   57–58, 69–70, 76, 78, 82
Lord Xu 許真君 (Xu Xun 許遜)   39, 62, 66–68, 70, 71, 74, 84–85, 178
Lou Dexian 婁德先   320–22, 323, 325, 331–32, 340, 342, 345, 347n70
Loushi gong 婁師宮 (Master Lou Palace)   334, 347
Lu Can 陸粲 (1494–1552)   115
Lü Dongbin 呂洞賓 / Lüzu 呂祖   3–5, 14, 20, 27, 75, 121–22, 124, 124n142, 126, 134, 141, 147, 152–55, 159n77, 160–61, 171n1, 180n31, 191, 193, 195, 197, 219, 261n20, 268, 302, 302n20, 326–32, 358–66, 363n39, 370–72, 370n74, 377n106, 386n140, 393–94, 447, 449, 487–88, 497, 502–6, 510, 517, 522, 533, 551, 554, 557–58, 564n1, 565, 567–68, 570–76, 579–84, 588, 590–91, 603, 609, 611. See also Fuyou dijun
Lu Jiuyuan 陸九淵 (Xiangshan 象山   1139–1193), 259, 271, 284, 369n73
Lu Longqi 陸隴其 (1630–1692)   271, 279
Lu Xun 魯迅 (1881–1936)   238
Lu You 陸遊 (1125–1209)   138, 180, 189, 190, 197
Lü Yuansu 呂元素 (no dates)   59, 80–81, 82, 113
Lu Zongyu 陸宗輿 (1876–1941)   360, 364, 365n47, 368, 388n150
luanbi 鸞筆 (phoenix brush)   8, 51, 113, 175, 186, 586, 588–91
luanshou 鸞手 (phoenix hand)   98, 190n58
luantan 鸞壇 (phoenix altar)   9, 111, 182, 454, 565
luantang 鸞堂 (phoenix hall)   346, 463, 536, 536n20, 543, 554, 556, 565, 600–2, 604–22
Lufei Kui 陸費逵 (1886–1941)   225, 227
Lufeng 陸豐   551
Lüjing ting yezuo 綠靜亭夜座 (Night in the bright green pavilion)   315
Lunyu 論語 (The analects)   256n5, 258, 266, 274, 295, 367

INDEX

Jinsi lu 近思錄 (Reflections on things at hand) 265
jiujie jing 救劫經 (scriptures to save humanity from the apocalypse) 27, 487, 488, 488*n*5, 491–97, 493*n*17, 504*n*47, 505, 505*n*49, 507, 513, 521, 522–23, 545
Jiuqionglin 九芎林 607
Jiushi xinjiao 救世新教 (New Religion to Save the World) 26, 256, 357, 365, 463. *See also* New Religion to Save the World
Jiushisi huashu 九十四化書 (The book of 94 transformations) 106
jixian 箕/乩仙 (transcendents of the stylus) 97, 121, 124, 319
Jo Kinsen 徐錦泉 (Ch. Xu Jinquan 1921–2018), 466–67, 468, 472–73, 473
Jordan, David K. 28*n*86, 601, 616*n*65
Jueshan tang 覺善堂 (Hall for Awakening Goodness) 548, 548*n*72

kaifa 開筏 (sailing the raft) 9, 325, 332
Kaifeng 開封 21*n*71, 83, 93, 94, 125, 126
kaisha 開沙 (opening the sand) 9, 415
Kālacakra Dharma Society (Shilun jingang fahui 時輪金剛法會) 238–39
kalpa 77, 102–3, 105, 127, 150, 267, 325, 366, 533, 549. *See also* apocalypse, and *jie* 劫
Kamlan Koon 金蘭觀 180
Kang Youwei 康有為 (1858–1927) 282, 355, 367, 370*n*75, 376, 387*n*146
Kaohsiung 449*n*25, 463, 464, 607
kaozheng xue 考證學 (evidential learning) 281
Karl Marx 13
kexue lingji 科學靈乩 (Scientific Numinous Stylus) 25, 210–11, 212–14, 214–22, 231, 236, 233–41, 244, 247–48
King Wen 文王 368
King Wu 武王 368
kokkurisan (狐狗狸さん or コックリさん) 216, 468
Kongjiao hui 孔教會 (Confucian Religion Association) 355. *See also* Confucianism
Korea 13, 43, 477. *See also* Chosŏn
Koxinga (Zheng Chenggong 鄭成功 1624–1662), 322, 322*n*26, 323

Kuai yuan 獪園 (Garden of mischief) 121, 124
Kuang Fu 匡阜 326–27
Kunning miaojing 坤寧妙經 (Wondrous scripture on Kun's peace) 157, 159, 188
Kwun Tong 觀塘 572, 572*n*33, 586–87

Lady Xian 洗夫人 490, 509, 518*n*77, 520
Lai Chi-tim 黎志添 4*n*8, 18, 142
Lan Daoxing 藍道行 (no dates) 117, 118–21
Lanji Bookstore 蘭記書局 621
Laozi 老子 262, 363*n*35, 371, 377*n*104, 402, 414, 452, 510, 583*n*60, 614
Laozi 老子 371*n*79
Laozu 老祖 (Venerable Patriarch) 243*n*82, 362*n*31, 414–15, 428, 430, 433, 557
latrine 135–36, 173, 176–77, 405. *See also* Zigu 紫姑
law 22, 20–24, 42, 45, 94, 103, 104, 114, 113–14, 116, 120, 126, 184, 186, 209, 211*n*19, 280, 296, 324, 331, 344, 391, 423*n*74, 426, 543, 547, 574*n*40, 575, 580. *See also* ban/prohibitions on spirit-writing
lay communities 2–4, 10, 18, 134–35, 197
Le'an Dashi 泐庵大師 144–46
Lei Shizhong 雷時中 (Mo'an 默庵 1221–1295), 57–58
leifa 雷法. *See* ritual
Leshan she 樂善社 (Society for Enjoying Good Deeds) 547, 557
Li Bai 李白 (701–762) 101*n*44, 197, 261*n*20, 553, 554, 557, 558
Li Shibin 李士彬 (1835–1913) 540
Li Tieguai 李鐵拐 554, 557
Li Yuhong 李玉鋐 (1661–?) 187, 197
Li Zisheng 李孜省 (?–1487) 117, 118, 126
Lian'an shantang 練安善堂 549
Liang Qichao 梁啟超 (1873–1929) 433
Liang Shuming 梁漱溟 (1893–1988) 390*n*154
Lianhua shanmai 蓮花山脈 (Lotus Mountains) 534
Liantaisheng 蓮台聖 (Lotus Sage) 413, 415–16, 418, 420, 425, 427–31, 434–35
Liao Shenxiu 廖慎修 (fl. 1884–1894) 548
Liaozhai zhiyi 聊齋誌異 (Strange tales from the Liaozhai studio) 292
Libu youshilang 禮部右侍郎 (Ministry of Rites) 314

INDEX

Lidou 禮斗 (Worshipping Dipper)　326
Liji 禮記 (Book of rites)　258, 386*n*140
Lin Chunxiu 林淳修 (no dates)　159
Ling hui 靈薈 (Numinous collection)　124
ling 靈 (efficacy)　5, 26, 46, 60, 75, 94, 100, 162, 194, 210*n*12, 219, 224–25, 228, 234, 236, 244, 303, 304, 334, 339, 374, 406, 574–75, 578*n*46, 586, 592–93. *See also* numinous
Lingdong ribao 嶺東日報 (Lingdong daily news)　542–43, 543*n*50, 552
Lingxue hui 靈學會 (Spiritualist Society)　7*n*22, 21*n*67, 210, 212*n*21, 225–27, 248, 347, 459. *See also* redemptive societies, and spiritualism
Lingxue yaozhi 靈學要誌 (Spiritualist magazine)　225, 227, 378*n*114
Lingying Dadi huashu shishi 靈應大帝化書事實 (Circumstances of the book of transformations of the Great Emperor of Numinous Response)　110, 181
Lingying guan 靈應觀 (Monastery of the Numinous Response)　102
literary societies　318, 324, 605
literati　2, 11–12, 14, 16, 18, 24–26, 41, 43, 53–54, 60–61, 73, 80, 93, 101*n*46, 116, 124–26, 137–41, 143–49, 160, 173, 178–79, 179*n*27, 186, 194–95, 197, 199, 207, 209, 213, 247, 260, 263, 295, 304, 311–48, 386, 405, 487, 490, 523–25, 523*n*85, 607, 611. *See also* Confucianism
Liu Ansheng 劉安勝 (late twelfth century)　57, 71*n*79, 106, 181
Liu Danming 劉瞻明 (no dates)　241, 242–47
Liu Qiao 劉樵 (fl. 1727–1749)　188, 268
Liu Shouyuan 柳守元　330, 330*n*40
Liu Songfei 劉松飛 (1930–2021)　571–79, 581, 583–85, 588, 589, 590, 592–94, 595
Liudui 六堆　607, 608
Liu-han Altar 了閑壇　26, 311–48
lixue 理學 (Learning of the principle)　266–67, 271, 279*n*80
local gazetteers　59, 140, 153, 261*n*16, 274, 322, 501, 503, 518, 534, 537
Lodge, Sir Oliver (1851–1940)　226
Longhu shan 龍虎山　81, 113, 582, 620
Longhua Troupe (Longhua zu 龍華組)　615

Longmen Lineage 龍門派　147, 567–69, 603
Longnü si 龍女寺 (Temple of the Dragon Maiden)　11, 14, 487, 491–92, 497
Longtian gong Xuanhua tang 龍天宮宣化堂　610
Lord Xin 辛天君　57–58, 69–70, 76, 78, 82
Lord Xu 許真君 (Xu Xun 許遜)　39, 62, 66–68, 70, 71, 74, 84–85, 178
Lou Dexian 婁德先　320–22, 323, 325, 331–32, 340, 342, 345, 347*n*70
Loushi gong 婁師宮 (Master Lou Palace)　334, 347
Lu Can 陸粲 (1494–1552)　115
Lü Dongbin 呂洞賓 / Lüzu 呂祖　3–5, 14, 20, 27, 75, 121–22, 124, 124*n*142, 126, 134, 141, 147, 152–55, 159*n*77, 160–61, 171*n*1, 180*n*31, 191, 193, 195, 197, 219, 261*n*20, 268, 302, 302*n*20, 326–32, 358–66, 363*n*39, 370–72, 370*n*74, 377*n*106, 386*n*140, 393–94, 447, 449, 487–88, 497, 502–6, 510, 517, 522, 533, 551, 554, 557–58, 564*n*1, 565, 567–68, 570–76, 579–84, 588, 590–91, 603, 609, 611. *See also* Fuyou dijun
Lu Jiuyuan 陸九淵 (Xiangshan 象山)　1139–1193), 259, 271, 284, 369*n*73
Lu Longqi 陸隴其 (1630–1692)　271, 279
Lu Xun 魯迅 (1881–1936)　238
Lu You 陸遊 (1125–1209)　138, 180, 189, 190, 197
Lü Yuansu 呂元素 (no dates)　59, 80–81, 82, 113
Lu Zongyu 陸宗輿 (1876–1941)　360, 364, 365*n*47, 368, 388*n*150
luanbi 鸞筆 (phoenix brush)　8, 51, 113, 175, 186, 586, 588–91
luanshou 鸞手 (phoenix hand)　98, 190*n*58
luantan 鸞壇 (phoenix altar)　9, 111, 182, 454, 565
luantang 鸞堂 (phoenix hall)　346, 463, 536, 536*n*20, 543, 554, 556, 565, 600–2, 604–22
Lufei Kui 陸費逵 (1886–1941)　225, 227
Lufeng 陸豐　551
Lüjing ting yezuo 綠靜亭夜座 (Night in the bright green pavilion)　315
Lunyu 論語 (The analects)　256*n*5, 258, 266, 274, 295, 367

INDEX

Luo Hongxian 羅洪先 (1504–1564)   261n20, 262, 266, 284
Lüshan 閭山   325
Lüzu qingwei sanpin zhenjing 呂祖清微三品真經 (Lüzu's Qingwei veritable scripture in three chapters)   327
Lüzu quanshu 呂祖全書 (Complete collection of Patriarch Lü)   4, 121n131, 153–55, 153–55, 153n63, 191–93, 487
Lüzu xianshi baogao 呂祖仙師寶誥 (Precious admonitions of Patriarch Lü)   588

magic pendulum (*mobai* 魔擺)   231–32
magnetism   224–25
Magu 麻姑   147, 159
Mahākāla. *See* Dahei tianshen 大黑天神
Maitreya Buddha (Mile Fo 彌勒佛)   19, 447, 449, 464, 607, 610
Manchukuo   238, 425
Marshal Temple 元帥廟   328
Marshal Tian 田公元帥   326–28
Master Bao 包宗師   326, 327
Master Lou (Lou zhenren 婁真人)   311–17, 319–22, 324–48
May Fourth   210, 231, 240, 248, 364, 385, 395, 421, 423n74
Mazu 媽祖   161, 454, 613
medicine   93, 144, 155, 209, 320, 329, 331, 334–35, 347, 458, 512–13, 516, 519, 521–23, 535n13, 538, 540, 544, 550, 574, 587, 591–95, 618–19. *See also* healing
  medical divination slips   334, 618
  prescriptions   40, 108, 112, 329, 339, 370, 509, 521, 618
  spirit-written prescription. *See jifang* 乩方
meditation   4, 9–10, 20, 43, 73, 383, 402–3, 411, 431, 456, 458, 523n85
mediumism   7, 21, 60, 71, 126, 190n58, 448, 450, 521n82. *See also* spirit-possession
Meinong 美濃   607
Mengxi bitan 夢溪筆談 (Brush talks from the dream brook)   93, 177
Mengzi 孟子 (372?–289? bce)   256n3, 258, 271, 280, 358, 366–69, 394, 414, 452
Mengzi 孟子 (also *Mencius*)   258, 275n66, 279, 367, 458

merchants   16, 41, 326, 346, 403–4, 411, 427n86, 490, 492–93, 501–3, 506, 519, 539–40, 550–51, 611
mesmerism (*chuanqishu* 傳氣術)   225. *See also* hypnosis (*cuimianshu* 催眠術)
messages of condolence   619
messianic cosmology   76, 366
Mian'an shantang 棉安善堂 (Mian'an Charitable Hall)   543n50, 544, 547
Miaoli 苗栗   610
Miaoshan 妙善   152, 156. *See also* Guanyin 觀音
millenarianism   11, 489, 533
Min Yide 閔一得 (1758–1836)   147, 148n45, 603
Mingming Shangdi 明明上帝 (The Brightest God on High)   446n6, 451
Ministry of the Interior   364, 466, 547
Mohammed   13, 376, 377n104
moral conduct   305, 472, 603
moral edification   601, 619
moral exhortations from the gods   376, 617
moral sermons (*xuanhua* 宣化, *xuanjiang* 宣講)   9, 126, 267, 454, 468, 543
moral transformation (*hua* 化)   66, 105–9, 112, 387, 387n146, 488n2
morality books (*shanshu* 善書)   4, 27, 47, 78, 86, 103–4, 157–58, 161, 209, 233, 282, 302, 305, 379, 383, 417, 421, 453n45, 493–94, 501–3, 506–7, 510, 538–39, 541, 545–46, 550, 553, 565, 601, 610, 613, 617, 620–22
Mount Baoping 寶屏   107, 108
Mount Fenghuang 鳳凰   105, 106, 109, 113
Mount Heming 鶴鳴山   582–85, 595, 596
Mount Jin'gai 金蓋   17n56, 603
Mount Xuanwu 玄武   551
Mudao xianguan 慕道仙館 (Celestial Hall for People Worshipping the Dao)   497, 507, 553

Nancun chuogeng lu 南村輟耕錄 (Nancun's records from resting from ploughing)   96, 101, 186
Nanhai Dashi 南海大士   415. *See also* Guanyin 觀音
Nanjing 南京   56, 68, 73, 239, 240, 343, 361n28, 517n75, 566

Nanmolao 喃嘸佬   569*n*25
Nantou 南投   600, 611
Nanyan 南岩   99
national essence (*guocui* 國粹)   355, 358, 369*n*71, 389
national learning (*guoxue* 國學)   355, 357, 357*n*13, 369, 389–90, 389*n*152, 390*n*153, 395
Nationalist Party   6, 22, 239, 359, 426. *See also* Guomindang 國民黨
neidan 內丹. *See* inner alchemy
Neo-Confucianism   25, 126, 197, 320, 367, 369*n*71, 374, 420*n*65
networks   3, 5, 8, 10–13, 16–20, 27–28, 64, 231, 333, 411, 413*n*43, 444, 446–47, 453, 493, 503, 524, 536, 539, 555, 605, 607–14
networks of mutual assistance   551, 612–13
New Culture Movement   356, 395, 424, 437
New Life Movement (Xin shenghuo yundong 新生活運動)   240, 391–92
New Religion to Save the World   264, 355–95. *See also* Jiushi xinjiao 救世新教, and redemptive societies
newspapers   7*n*20, 211–12, 235–36, 238, 241, 313, 471, 534, 541, 543, 548*n*72, 551, 578*n*47, 605, 621. *See also* periodicals
Nianfo she 念佛社 (Society for Reciting Buddha's Name)   544–45
North China Famine   238, 360, 459, 475
Nü jie 女誡 (Lessons for women)   422
Nüdan hebian 女丹合編 (Collection of female alchemy)   162
Nüdan shiji houbian 女丹詩集後編 (Collection of poems on female alchemy, second section)   155
Nüdan shiji qianbian 女丹詩集前編 (Collection of poems on female alchemy, first section)   155
nüdan 女丹. *See* female alchemy
Nüdaode she 女道德社 (Women's Morality Society)   410–16, 417–18, 421, 424, 425, 427, 428, 432
Nüjindan fayao 女金丹法要 (Essential methods for the female golden elixir)   155, 159
nüluan 女鸞 (female disciples)   608, 616. *See also* disciples
numinous   5, 102, 124, 210*n*12, 236, 544, 581. *See also* ling 靈

oath   46, 261–63, 271, 447, 458, 520
offerings   8, 46, 56, 59, 61, 71–72, 79, 113*n*96, 243, 336, 414, 457, 474, 535*n*13, 538, 544, 546*n*61, 550–51, 580, 586, 602, 615, 617–18. *See also jiao* 醮
officials   2, 13–16, 20–21, 41, 53–54, 58, 60–61, 65, 67, 73, 76–77, 83–84, 93, 107, 112–21, 151, 178, 181–82, 196–97, 211*n*18, 242, 258–59, 262, 269, 272–73, 277, 280, 292, 295–96, 298, 305–6, 311–22, 324, 329–33, 336–37, 340*n*60, 341, 343–47, 360, 364, 403, 436, 501, 509, 539–40
oracles (*lingqian* 靈籤)   55, 207, 209, 302–3, 314, 405*n*15, 571, 586, 595
oral spirit-writing (*kaikou ji* 開口乩)   591
ordination   49, 52, 56, 58–60, 65–66, 70, 73, 81, 326, 329, 422, 568, 576
orthodoxy   14, 15*n*52, 25, 28, 59, 151, 222, 243, 256–58, 264, 269–71, 273, 275, 277, 281, 295, 344, 357, 367, 370, 377, 382*n*127, 394, 464, 466, 472, 489, 565, 568, 569*n*25, 578–85, 595–96
Ouija board   13, 25, 211, 216, 216*n*25. *See also* spiritualism
Overmyer, Daniel L. (1935–2021)   28*n*86, 139, 405, 601, 616*n*65, 622

Palmer, David A.   12, 409, 444, 489, 490, 523
Panchen Lama   238, 239
Patriarch Great Peak. *See* Dafeng zushi 大峰祖師
Patriarch Song Chaoyue 宋超月   536
Peixian Palace 裴仙宮   328
Peng Dingqiu 彭定求 (1645–1719)   255–83, 344, 377, 382*n*127, 406
Peng Long 彭瓏 (1613–1689)   264, 268
Peng Shaosheng 彭紹升 (1740–1796)   19*n*65, 256*n*3, 257*n*7, 258–59, 268, 276, 281, 282
Peng Sunyu 彭孫遹 (1631–1700)   261*n*18, 263, 264, 271
Pengxi 蓬溪   108–9
periodicals   211, 227, 273, 621–22. *See also* newspapers
petitions (*zhang* 章)   2, 49, 59, 458, 510, 542, 547
petition slip (*bingdan* 稟單)   617

INDEX

shangzhang 上章 (send up petitions) 196
philanthropy. *See* charity
philosophy   212, 222, 230, 234, 258*n*10, 295*n*12, 311, 335, 336*n*51, 363*n*35, 369*n*71, 389*n*152, 389*n*153
phoenix halls. *See luantang* 鸞堂
phoenix-stylus. *See luanbi* 鸞筆, and *jibi* 乩筆
pijiang 批降 (obtaining a god-written response on a document submitted to him)   8, 49, 51–52, 64, 71–72
pilgrimage   66, 512*n*68, 551, 601–2
planchette   7, 172, 216, 275, 277, 405, 451, 454, 458, 545–46, 553, 617
poetry   4, 14, 52*n*21, 53–54, 59–60, 62, 64, 75–77, 79–80, 93, 95–97, 101*n*44, 114, 116, 123, 138, 143, 145–49, 154–55, 156*n*68, 159, 161, 178, 180, 183, 188–90, 191, 195–97, 209, 213, 255, 259, 260*n*16, 261*n*20, 267, 267*n*71, 276, 292, 302–8, 313, 315–24, 315*n*12, 326–27, 333, 343, 452, 458, 461, 471, 519, 524, 568*n*20, 602, 610–11, 617, 619
  poetry societies (*shishe* 詩社)   605
  responsive poems (*changhe* 唱和)   125, 318, 335
politics   116–21, 387–88, 416, 460, 541, 611
popular culture   291, 312, 325
popular religion   15, 18–19, 83, 103, 114, 127, 143, 149, 153, 198–99, 312, 324–48, 402, 410, 512*n*68, 523, 566
precious injunctions. *See baogao* 寶誥
prediction   14, 26, 43, 56, 68, 95–96, 101, 116, 124, 179, 237, 291, 297, 298, 302–3, 301–3, 306, 447, 581. *See also* divination
prophecy   42, 66, 76–77, 125, 260, 302, 447, 449, 451, 459–60, 475, 571. *See also* divination
proselytizing   523*n*85, 620
psyche   207
psychic power (*xinling nengli* 心靈能力)   206, 578*n*46
psychical research (*xinlingxue* 心靈學)   225, 231–33, 248, 405
psychology   199, 212, 226–28, 231–33, 241, 578*n*47, 618
  behaviourist psychology   233
  experimental psychology   226, 233

Pu Songling 蒲松齡 (1640–1715)   292
publishers   27, 209–10, 212*n*20, 214, 230, 233–35, 248, 265*n*28, 497*n*27
Puji Altar 普濟壇   566
Puji tang 普濟堂   606, 614
Puli 埔里   16, 28, 600–625
Purple Maiden. *See* Zigu 紫姑

Qi Xun 戚勳 (?–1644)   322, 322*n*24, 332
Qian Nengxun 錢能訓 (1869–1924)   360, 361*n*31, 375, 377
Qian Qianyi 錢謙益 (1582–1664)   144–45
Qian Xi 錢希 (1872–1930)   148
qiang kou 腔口. *See* chanting
qie 妾. *See* concubines
Qinghe neizhuan 清河內傳 (Esoteric biography of Qinghe)   65, 107
Qingxian jifa 請仙箕法 (Methods for requesting transcendent [messages] through the sieve)   209
Qingyun tan 青雲壇   151
Qiqu 七曲   106, 109–12, 113
Quanzhen Daojiao keyi 全真道教科儀 (Quanzhen Daoist rituals)   568
Quanzhen 全真   533, 567–69, 569*n*25, 582*n*56, 585, 603
Qunzhen shijue 群真詩決 (Poetic formulae by all the perfected)   155

Raumu ラウム/老母   468–71. *See also* Wusheng Laomu 無生老母
recitation of litanies (*baichan* 拜懺)   575–76
reciting divine injunctions (*qing'gao* 請誥)   602, 617
recorded sayings. *See yulu* 語錄
redemptive societies (*jiushi tuanti* 救世團體)   3, 5–6, 9, 12–13, 17–18, 21, 23, 26–27, 194, 243*n*82, 248, 255, 346, 356–57, 361, 362, 376–77, 383, 385, 388, 391, 393, 402–3, 402*n*1, 405, 407–9, 414, 415*n*49, 423, 425–26, 436, 444, 451, 516, 516*n*72, 548*n*67, 600, 603–4, 621. *See also* Daoyuan, Dejiao, Guigendao, Hongwanzi hui, Jiushi xinjiao, Lingxue hui, New Religion to Save the World, Shijie funü hongwanzi hui, Tiande shengjiao, Tongshan she, Wanguo

648   INDEX

daode hui, Wushan she, Yiguandao, Zailijiao, and Zhongguo jisheng hui
religion (*zongjiao* 宗教)   361n30, 362n32, 377, 387–88, 387n146, 409, 464n103, 514, 574n40, 582
   religious affiliation   9, 17–20
   religious cults   5, 555
   religious merit   403, 410, 430–31, 436–37
   religious universalism   13, 391–92
   religious websites   622
revelation   2, 14, 19n64, 27, 39–48, 51–86, 67n70, 85n115, 101, 148, 173, 174n16, 182, 194–95, 197–98, 219, 327, 332–33, 335n48, 340, 447–65, 469–72, 473n138, 476n150, 477, 487, 489, 518–19, 521, 524, 550
righteousness (*yi* 義)   277, 319, 324, 372
ritual
   Daoist ritual (*daofa* 道法)   2, 8, 15n50, 18, 20, 24, 28, 41, 44–51, 53, 56–59, 62, 66, 70–72, 74, 79, 80–82, 84, 117, 119, 133, 139–41, 160, 175, 190, 199, 256–61, 269, 272, 326, 567–70, 567n17, 575–79, 587, 595–96, 614
   Daoist thunder rites (*leifa* 雷法)   117, 195
   liturgy   17, 45, 47, 49, 66–67, 69, 71–73, 80–81, 183, 199, 258, 267–73, 282, 355, 510–11, 523, 614
   ritual masters   134, 139, 160, 181–82, 192–93, 195, 568, 576, 579. *See also fashi* 法師
   ritual techniques. *See fashu* 法術
Rujiao biaoshu keji 儒教表疏科集 (Collection of Confucian ritual documents)   511
Rujiao yuebiao ke 儒教月表科 (The forms of monthly documents for Confucian rituals)   511
Rumen fa yu 儒門法語 (Model words of the Confucian school)   260, 264–67, 265n28, 271, 272, 273, 275, 277n74, 279, 282, 284
Rutan 儒壇 (Confucian altar)   9, 18, 255–56, 255n2, 257, 263, 511
Ruzong shenjiao 儒宗神教 (Divine Teachings of the Confucian Religion)   612

Śākyamuni   375n99, 377n104, 452
salvation   41–42, 49, 57, 71, 85–86, 134, 152–53, 156, 226, 239, 248, 267, 296, 403, 410, 430, 434, 436, 449–50, 454, 487–92, 494, 501, 503–4, 506–7, 514, 518–25, 551, 619
San Qing 三清. *See* Three Pure Ones
Sanchu tou 三齣頭   579
sancong side 三從四德 (three followings and four virtues)   158, 417, 422, 516
Sangren, Steven   152, 600
sanqi pudu 三期普度 (third period of universal salvation)   488, 488n5, 494–95
Sanshan Guowang miao 三山國王廟 (Temple of the Three Mountain Kings)   488, 549
Sanshan guowang 三山國王 (The Kings of the Three Mountains)   549n74, 551
Sansheng gong 三聖宮 (Palace of the Three Saints)   498, 501, 504
Schipper, Kristofer M.   198, 600
science   21–22, 25, 206m, 210–16, 210n12, 220, 222–41, 243–44, 247–48, 390, 405, 408–9, 417, 424, 433, 459
scripture chanting. *See* chanting
scripture/textual production   2–6, 11, 13, 39, 41, 64, 74, 79, 85n115, 108, 116, 140, 149, 153, 171–72, 190–93, 199, 213, 255, 267, 275, 280, 302, 319, 365, 368, 450, 462, 554, 606, 610, 617. *See also* revelation
Seaman, Gary   609
self-cultivation   5, 11, 14, 28, 42, 47, 67, 70, 75–76, 85, 135, 144, 148, 150, 153–57, 159, 161–62, 263, 302n20, 358, 360, 365n49, 370, 373–74, 383, 386–88, 394, 403–4, 410–11, 413, 416, 429–31, 434–37, 446, 555, 601–3, 608, 616, 619–20
self-divinization   1, 20, 56–59, 65, 134
Sha Mingming 沙明明 (no dates)   583, 583n61
Shaanxi 陝西   203n7
Shamen Troupe (Shamen zu 沙門組)   615
Shandong 山東   402, 404, 411–13, 412n38, 418, 426, 427n86
Shanghai 上海   7n22, 22n76, 150, 210, 211, 212, 213, 214, 221, 225, 226–27, 231, 233–41, 242, 245, 248, 347, 361n28, 405, 410, 413n43, 459, 512, 532, 602, 604
Shanghai Jinwen tang 上海錦文堂   212, 212n20, 230–31, 233–34

INDEX

Shangqing 上清 (Upper Clarity) 2n3, 7, 43, 56, 65, 174n16. *See also* Daoism
shanhui 善會 (charitable societies) 535, 547, 550
Shanqing jingtang 善慶經堂 (Scripture Hall of Goodness and Happiness) 512–14
shanshe 善社 (charitable society/association) 359, 365n50, 532, 538, 549–54. *See also* charity
shanshu ju 善書局 (morality bookstores) 493
shanshu 善書. *See* morality books
shantan 善壇 (charitable altar) 9, 359, 565, 567
shantang 善堂 (charitable hall) 9, 27, 346, 505n48, 532, 535–56, 565
Shao Yong 邵雍 (1011–1077) 280
shapan 沙盤 (sand trays) 1, 49, 95, 111, 172, 191–93, 231, 245, 246, 416, 448, 458, 456–59, 465, 469, 470, 494, 586, 588–90
Shen Kuo 沈括 (1031–1095) 93, 177
Shen Yixiu 沈宜修 (no dates) 145
Shenbao 申報 211, 212n20, 214, 215, 234, 236, 237–38, 243
shendao 神道 (the divine way) 375n99, 377–84. *See also* teachings based on the divine way
Shengde tan 盛德壇 (Shengde Altar) 226, 347–48
Shengmu niangniang 聖母娘娘 551, 557–58
Shengxian gong 聖賢宮 (Palace of Sages) 514–15, 515n71, 516, 517, 525
Shengxian tang 聖賢堂 (Hall of Worthies) 605–6, 622
Shennong 神農 369, 610
Shi Kefa 史可法 (1602–1645) 320, 320n21
Shiga Ichiko 志賀市子 173, 179, 190, 216, 445n3, 456, 533, 536, 554, 555, 565, 568n19, 569n25, 577
shiguan 施棺 (free coffins) 535, 537, 538
Shiji 史記 (Records of the Grand Historian) 272
Shijia 釋家. *See* Buddhism
Shijie funü hongwanzi hui 世界婦女紅卍字會 (Women's Red Swastika Society) 410–14, 413n43, 431–33. *See also* redemptive societies

Shijie Hongwanzi hui 世界紅卍字會. *See* Hongwanzi hui 紅卍字會
shiluan 侍鸞 (to serve the Phoenix) 180
Shiquan hui 十全會 (Ten Completions Society) 256n5, 535
shizhang 誓章. *See* oath
shouyin daxian 守印大仙 (immortal guardians of the official seals) 336
Shun 舜 368, 376n102
Shuowen jiezi 說文解字 (Explaining single-component graphs and analysing compound characters) 184, 185
Sichuan 四川 255n2, 487, 491–92, 494–97, 497n27, 498, 500, 501, 535, 570, 581–85
sieve-writing 94, 123
Siku quanshu 四庫全書 (Complete books from the four treasuries) 25, 265n28, 292, 294, 302
silent spirit-writing (*moji* 默乩) 591
Siming zhenjun 司命真君 554
single person spirit-writing (*danren ji* 單人乩) 65, 209, 587
sishu 四書. *See* Four Books
Six Classics 367, 509n59
sizi 伺 (嗣子) (servant-desciples) 327–29, 331
social activism. *See* community activism
songjing 誦經. *See* chanting
Southeast Asia 3, 13, 476n150, 533
spells for inviting deities 617
spirit-mediums 41, 44–45, 92, 94, 113, 116, 123, 126, 191, 193, 207–8, 214–33, 247, 296, 542, 552, 609, 618
spirit-possession 43, 45, 43–46, 50, 53, 56, 59–60, 62, 71, 74, 76, 81–82, 80–86, 92, 123, 125, 140, 174n16, 193, 196, 208, 228, 239, 468, 522, 571. *See also* mediumism
  jiang tong 降童 92
  tongji 童乩 / *jitong* 乩童 125, 542–43, 550, 555
spirits 7, 43–46, 51, 53–54, 61–62, 72, 79, 81–82, 84, 113, 113n93, 115, 119, 174, 206–7, 213, 216–17, 226–29, 241, 248, 257, 263, 275–76, 278, 292, 298–301, 303–8, 318, 336–43, 346, 376n103, 379, 382n127, 383, 415n49, 430–31, 454, 456–57, 468, 593
spiritualism 6–7, 13, 22n76, 25, 142, 210–

11, 219*n*27, 225–27, 231–32, 248, 348, 378*n*114, 405, 468. See also Lingxue hui 靈學會
spirit-writing
  broom 174, 178
  feiluan 飛鸞 (flying phoenix) 8, 51–53, 65, 85, 106, 111, 139, 174, 180–83, 190, 206, 208, 213, 245, 256, 256*n*5, 375, 377, 454, 468, 545, 549, 565, 600, 601
  fuhe 扶鶴 (supporting the crane) 8, 206
  fuji 扶乩 (supporting the stylus) 8–9, 52, 86, 91–92, 122–25, 171–74, 179, 184–87, 206, 210*n*12, 304–6, 308, 325, 357, 404, 446, 454–55, 477, 564–65, 600
  fuji 扶箕 (supporting the sieve) 8, 51, 77, 91, 140, 172–74, 176, 180, 206, 565
  fuji tuanti 扶乩團體 (spirit-writing groups) 9*n*30, 11, 16, 21, 56, 65, 69, 85, 153, 172, 256, 312, 319, 327, 346–47, 356, 446, 459, 475, 488, 490, 492, 495, 512, 522–25, 532–33, 537–38, 552, 564, 566, 574, 585, 601, 605, 614, 620–21
  fuluan 扶鸞 (supporting the phoenix) 8, 51–52, 81, 83, 91–92, 97, 111, 115, 125, 172–75, 179–84, 206, 468, 532, 565, 600
  jijia 乩架 (stylet) 172
  jishou 乩手 (spirit-writing hands) 190*n*58, 406. See also *luanshou* 鸞手
  spirit-writing altars 7, 9–10, 12, 15, 16*n*54, 19–20, 21*n*76, 25–26, 57, 70–71, 98, 99, 107–8, 111, 126, 134, 147–48, 150, 153, 161, 180*n*31, 196, 226, 255–57, 265, 281, 311–48, 357, 359, 361, 370, 376, 406, 448, 488, 491, 500, 504*n*47, 517, 543, 546, 552–54, 557, 564–96, 609
  spirit-writing books (*luanshu* 鸞書) 4, 209, 534, 601
  spirit-writing cults (*fuluan jieshe* 扶鸞結社) 12, 60, 64, 79, 302*n*20, 312, 421, 445, 463, 472, 532–56, 565, 610
  spirit-writing movement (*fuluan yundong* 扶鸞運動) 27, 359, 377, 393, 446, 487–525, 532–33, 536*n*21, 537, 539, 543, 553–56, 565
  spirit-writing rites 315, 330–31, 335*n*49, 600–601, 604, 606, 610, 613, 618
  spirit-writing temples 112, 346–47, 600, 606, 609
  stylus. See spirit-writing

Su Shi 蘇軾 (Dongpo 東坡 1037–1101) 53, 93, 115, 137, 138, 179, 261*n*20
subconscious 206, 211, 232, 241
Sun Bu'er 孫不二 154, 155, 159, 160
Sun Wukong 孫悟空 551, 609
Sung Kuang-yu 宋光宇 (1949–2016) 605
supernatural 42, 80, 227, 293–94, 300–2, 308, 313, 340, 468
superstition (*mixin* 迷信) 6, 10, 21–23, 171, 173, 199, 210, 213–14, 220, 222, 227–29, 236–37, 239–40, 247–48, 291, 294, 391, 393, 403–4, 409–10, 431, 433–37, 515, 536, 542, 546, 566, 578, 613
sutra 20, 74–75, 103, 239, 431, 495, 508, 514, 523*n*85, 549, 606
Suzhou 蘇州 12, 144–49, 188, 256, 260, 264, 268, 269, 273, 274
symbolic capital 609, 611
syncretism 402, 488, 606

Ta-hsi 大溪 600, 606, 614
Taichung 台中 605, 606, 614, 615
Taishang laojun 太上老君 63, 551, 554, 558, 578*n*46, 614
Taishang wuji zongzhen Wenchang dadong xianjing 太上無極總真文昌大洞仙經 (Great cavern immortal scripture, by Wenchang, [head of] all transcendents, of the supreme Ultimate) 64, 75
Taiwan 台灣 3, 6, 8, 12, 16, 17, 17*n*58, 18, 19, 22–23, 27, 28, 171, 172, 175, 179, 242, 312, 322*n*26, 335*n*49, 346, 356*n*12, 394, 407, 444, 445, 449, 450, 452, 453*n*45, 454, 455, 456, 456*n*60, 460–65, 466–67, 471, 472–73, 475, 476, 494, 507, 512, 532, 534*n*11, 536*n*21, 554, 564, 600–622
Taixu 太虛 (1887–1947) 407, 602
talismans (*fu* 符) 43–45, 50, 61, 72–73, 79, 83, 95*n*21, 96, 111, 114, 123–24, 145, 174, 186, 191–96, 197, 209, 219, 329, 334*n*48, 339–41, 474, 510, 521, 573, 573*n*34, 578*n*46, 588, 590, 593–94, 618
  talismanic water 117, 124
Tamsui 淡水 607
Tang Junyi 唐君毅 (1909–1978) 311
Tang 湯 368
Tanyangzi 曇陽子 (1557–1580) 143–44, 196, 196*n*72

INDEX 651

Tao Zongyi 陶宗儀 (c. 1329–c. 1412) 96, 101, 186
Taoyuan mingsheng jing 桃園明聖經 (Peach garden scripture on illuminating saintliness) 462, 616
teachings (*jiao* 教) 16, 19–20, 39, 41, 46–47, 57, 68, 70, 73, 75, 77–78, 81, 85, 94, 103–4, 106, 147, 197–99, 255*n*3, 256–59, 265, 266*n*31, 273, 278–79, 294–95, 299, 321, 331, 362–63, 367, 370–72, 375, 377–78, 381, 385–90, 392, 402–4, 406–8, 410, 413–15, 417–18, 420–24, 426, 428, 433, 435, 437, 448–50, 452–54, 475, 477*n*154, 488–92, 495, 514, 516, 518*n*77, 524–25, 540, 545, 548, 555, 589
teachings based on the divine way (*shendao shejiao* 神道設教) 362, 388. *See also shendao* 神道
temple cults 28, 600–601, 610*n*43, 620
tendenshi 点伝師 466. *See dianchuanshi* 點傳師
Tendō 天道 (the Way of Heaven) 444–45, 449*n*25, 466–77
Three Benevolent Ones (San enzhu 三恩主) 611, 612, 623
Three Gods of Cizun (Cizun sandi 慈尊三帝) 572
Three Ministers (*san xiang* 三相) 488
Three Pure Ones (San Qing 三清) 269, 514, 515, 588, 607
three saints (*sansheng* 三聖) 152, 488, 498, 501–4, 507, 514–18, 521–24
three teachings (*sanjiao* 三教) 20, 103, 197–99, 255*n*3, 256–57, 363, 510
thunder gods 51, 54, 58, 76, 82, 84, 139
Tian'endao 天恩道 (Way of Heavenly Blessing) 552–53
Tiandao 天道 (Way of Heaven) 449*n*25, 464–66, 468, 472, 475
Tiande shengjiao 天德聖教 (Sacred Teaching of Heavenly Virtue) 453. *See also* redemptive societies
Tianfei gong 天妃宮 (Place of the Celestial Concubine) 145
Tianhuang zhidao taiqing yuce 天皇至道太清玉冊 (Jade slips of great clarity on the supreme path of the Celestial Sovereigns) 190–91

Tianjin 天津 12, 311, 318–19, 358, 361*n*28, 364–65, 364*n*41, 365*n*49, 382, 390*n*156, 459
Tianjing zhenjing 天經真經 (True scripture of celestial immortals) 521
Tianran Gufo 天然古佛/Tennen Kobutsu 465, 469, 470, 471*n*129, 472–73
Tianshi fu 天師府 582
Tianshidao 天師道 45, 102*n*48. *See also* Heavenly Master Daoism
Tiantai Le fashi lingyi ji 天台泐法師靈異記 (Record of the strange and mysterious [story] about Master Le from Tiantai) 144, 145
Tianxin zhengfa 天心正法 62, 73
Tongji shantang 同濟善堂 (Charitable Hall of Communal Relief) 541–42
Tongming shouxiang 通明首相 (The Minister of Brightness). 498
Tongnian shantang 同念善堂 (Charitable Hall of Common Thought) 551
Tongshan she 同善社 (Fellowship United in Goodness) 357*n*13, 357*n*14, 391, 402–3, 447, 452*n*43, 453, 516, 537*n*23, 552, 553, 603. *See also* redemptive societies
Tongyuan tan 通元壇 340
transcendent 25, 47, 53, 55–57, 59, 62, 64, 66–69, 75, 92–99, 112, 114–26, 120*n*122, 124*n*142, 140, 178, 184, 186–88, 194–97, 208–12, 217–19, 222, 226–27, 229–30, 233–41, 242–48, 375, 515
Tung Sin Tan 通善壇 566*n*14, 567, 567*n*17, 575, 577, 579, 580*n*51

under-world trials 619
unity of the three teachings (*sanjiao heyi* 三教合一) 20, 363. *See also* three teachings

vegetarianism 19, 103, 183, 447, 457–58, 469, 523*n*85, 587, 611
vegetarian halls (*zhaitang* 齋堂) 9
Vietnam 12, 12*n*41, 43, 266*n*32, 476, 490, 497*n*28, 507, 507*n*55, 570–71, 595
visualization 43–46, 49–51, 56, 68–69, 72, 86
voluntary congregations 536*n*20, 538*n*26, 601–2, 604–5, 612, 615, 620

Wanfa guizong 萬法歸宗 (Ten thousand methods to return to the origin)   194–95, 197, 199

Wang Biqing 王弼卿 (1895–1968)   311–12, 312n5, 323, 332, 333, 343

Wang Chien-chuan 王見川   10, 19, 24, 65, 173, 181, 186, 206, 208, 357n13, 376n103, 533, 604, 605, 606, 614, 621

Wang Chih-yu 王志宇   605

Wang Chong 王充 (27–ca. 97)   301, 304n23

Wang Duan 汪端 (1793–1839)   147–48, 148

Wang Fengyi 王鳳儀 (1864–1937)   423, 426, 453

Wang Ji 王畿 (1498–1583)   259, 277, 279

Wang Shizhen 王世貞 (1526–1590)   123, 144, 196n72

Wang Shouren 王守仁 (Yangming 陽明 1472–1529), 256n3, 258, 259, 271, 271n46, 273, 274, 277, 278–80, 284, 367, 369n73

Wang Yishu 汪以恕 (no dates)   212–13, 215–16, 216–20, 228–29, 241, 242

Wang Yiting 王一亭 (1867–1938)   19, 602, 621

Wanguo daode hui 萬國道德會 (Worldwide Morality Society)   402n3, 403, 407n24, 414, 416, 423, 425–26, 428, 453, 462, 603. *See also* redemptive societies

Wei Zhongxian 魏忠賢 (1568–1627)   320

Weituo 韋陀 (Skanda)   415n50

Wen Degui 溫德貴 (fl. 1899–1901)   621

Wenchang dijun qishisan hua shu 文昌帝君七十三化書 (The book of the 73 transformations of the Divine Lord Wenchang)   106–7

Wenchang huashu 文昌化書 (Wenchang's book of transformations)   107–11, 182

Wenchang 文昌   3, 5, 8, 10–11, 14, 40, 52, 55, 57, 60, 64–66, 66n65, 69–71, 74–75, 77–78, 84–85, 99, 99n35, 105–12, 107n72, 108n73, 139, 141, 153, 159, 173–74, 180–83, 188, 190–91, 195, 197, 258, 260–63, 260n16, 266n32, 267–70, 272–74, 281–82, 302, 302n20, 325, 347n70, 376, 487–88, 492n13, 502–6, 510, 514, 517, 522, 554, 572n31, 611. *See also* Zitong 梓潼

Wendi quanshu 文帝全書 (Complete collection of Thearch Wen)   4, 159, 188, 193, 268, 269

wenshi ziliao 文史資料 (literary and historical materials)   457

wenshi 問事 (requesting guidance through spirit-writing)   587, 591–92, 593, 617

Wenwu jiujie baosheng yongming jing 文武救劫葆生永命經 (Scripture of Wen[chang] and Guandi to save humanity from the apocalypse and to protect human life)   504

White Deer Grotto Academy (Bailudong shuyuan 白鹿洞書院)   277

winnowing sieve   92, 206, 208

Women's Christian Temperance Union   407, 419

Women's Morality Society. *See* Nüdaode she

Wong Tai Sin (Huang Daxian 黃大仙)   454, 557, 558, 566n14, 569n27, 574n40, 578n47, 596

Wu Peifu 吳佩孚 (1874–1939)   360, 392

Wuchuan 吳川   490

Wudang Mountains 武當山   10, 19, 24, 76, 97–105, 101n42, 107, 113

Wudang shan Xuandi chuixun 武當山玄帝垂訓 (Instructions handed down by the Dark Emperor on Mount Wudang)   19, 102, 103–5

Wudang shan Xuantian shangdi chuixunwen 武當山玄天上帝垂訓文 (Instructions revealed by Supreme Emperor of the Dark Heavens from Wudang Mountains)   78

Wuji shengmu qinyan xueshu 無極聖母親演血書 (Blood book personally bestowed by the Holy Mother of the Non-Ultimate)   449

wujing 五經 (five classics)   257, 258, 276. *See also* Confucianism

wuleifa 五雷法 (five thunder magic)   339

Wulong monastery 五龍宮   97

Wumen tang ji 午夢堂集 (Collection from the Noon Dream Hall)   146

Wushan she 悟善社 (Society for Awakening to Goodness)   210, 227, 346, 357–64, 361n28, 364n41, 378n114, 385, 388, 390–91. *See also* redemptive societies

Wusheng Laomu 無生老母   151–52, 159,

INDEX

161–62, 243*n*82, 366, 446–48, 446*n*6, 451, 454–56, 471–73
Wutong 五通 59*n*43

Xiafu Lü da zongshi 霞府呂大宗師 (Great Lineage Master Lü of Xiafu) 329
Xiafu shoushu Huang poguan 霞府收疏黃婆官 (Secretary of the Purple Cloud Palace) 331
Xiafu wu zongshi 霞府五宗師 (Five Lineage Masters of the Purple Cloud Palace) 326
Xiafu zhifa Deng shizhe 霞府執法鄧使者 (Deng Law Enforcement Official of the Purple Cloud Palace) 331
Xiafu 霞府 325–43, 345–46
Xiamen 廈門 312, 322, 323, 335, 335*n*49, 336*n*51, 347*n*70
Xiangyang 襄陽 64, 97, 98, 99, 100, 107
xianshi 仙師 (immortal/transcendent masters) 67, 68, 98, 327–29, 337–41, 577. *See also* transcendent
Xiantiandao 先天道 (the Way of Former Heaven) 444–51, 468, 476, 477*n*154, 491, 491*n*11, 494, 516, 520, 533, 538*n*26, 548–49, 548*n*67, 552–53, 555, 606
Xiashan 峽山 534, 554, 554*n*95, 557–58
Xietian dadi mingsheng jing 協天大帝明聖經 (Scripture for illuminating Sageliness by the Great Emperor who assists Heaven). 553
Xiguan Lüzu Palace 西關呂祖宮 328, 330*n*41, 331
Xiling guiyong 西泠閨詠 (Poems from within the inner chambers at West Lake) 146, 147
Xin qingnian 新青年 (New youth) 21, 227, 423*n*74
Xin shenghuo yundong 新生活運動. *See* New Life Movement
Xingjue tang 醒覺堂 609, 615, 617, 622, 624
Xingling si 醒靈寺 614–15, 619, 624
Xingtian gong 行天宮 601
Xingzhong tang 行忠堂 607–8, 615
Xinjiang 308
Xinke Rujiao keji, juan er 新刻儒教科集卷二 (The new series of Confucian rituals, volume 2) 510

Xinling tonggan lu 心靈感通錄 (Records of spiritual communication) 241–47
Xinpu 新埔 610, 612
Xinyi 信宜 490, 504–5, 506, 506*n*52, 506*n*53, 507, 509, 512–13, 523
Xishan tang 習善堂 (Hall for Learning Goodness) 548
xiujiu 休咎 (good and bad fortune) 306, 307
xiuxing 修行. *See* self-cultivation
Xiwangmu nüxiu zhengtu shize 西王母女修正途十則 (Xiwangmu's ten precepts on the proper female path) 148, 160
Xiwangmu 西王母 154, 159, 162
Xixin she 洗心社 (Society for Cleaning the Mind) 553
Xiyou ji 西遊記 (Journey to the West) 104, 246
xizi 惜字 (cherishing [written] characters) 3, 535*n*13, 550, 550*n*78
Xu Brothers (Xu Zhizheng 徐知證 and Xu Zhi'e 徐知諤) 55, 79, 112
Xu Dishan 許地山 (1893–1941) 22, 53, 60, 92*n*6, 95*n*21, 143, 173, 175, 176, 179, 199, 206–7, 207, 208, 209, 211, 336, 343, 604*n*17
Xu xian hanzao 徐仙翰藻 (Literary writings of the Xu transcendents) 112
Xuandi shilu 玄帝實錄 (Authentic records of the Dark Emperor.) 97–100, 98*n*32. *See also Jiangbi shilu* 降筆實錄, and *Dong zhenjun jiangbi shilu* 董真君降筆實錄
Xuandi 玄帝 (Dark Emperor) 97–100, 102–5, 116
xuanguan 玄關 (mysterious pass) 458, 470
xuanluan 懸鸞 (suspended phoenix) 8, 208
Xuantian Shangdi qisheng lu 玄天上帝啟聖錄 (Record of epiphanies by the Supreme Emperor of the Dark Heaven) 63, 98*n*32, 99
Xuantian Shangdi 玄天上帝 (God of Northern Heaven) 62, 98*n*32, 536, 551, 554, 558. *See also* Zhenwu
Xue Xuan 薛瑄 (1389–1464) 261*n*20, 262, 266, 284
Xueshan tang 學善堂 (Hall for Studying Goodness) 548

xunwen 訓文 (admonitions) 78, 452, 471, 476, 477*n*152. *See also* revelation
Xunzi 荀子 (third century BCE) 368, 369*n*71

Yan Hui 顏回 (*zi* Ziyuan 子淵 521–481) 78, 78*n*97, 270, 274*n*62, 280, 376, 376*n*100
Yan Song 嚴嵩 (1480–1567) 119–20, 320*n*19
Yang Fulai 楊福來 (1874–1948) 610
Yang Jisheng 楊繼盛 (1516–1555) 320, 320*n*19
Yang Lian 楊漣 (1572–1625) 320
Yang Mingji 楊明機 (1899–1985) 620
Yang Xi 楊羲 (330–c. 386) 56, 207
Yangming Learning 259, 271, 273, 278*n*80, 279, 280
Yanhua tang 衍化堂 618–19, 624
yanku 掩骼 (burial of corpse) 537
Yao 堯 368
Yaochi Laomu 瑤池老母 159, 463, 514
yaoqian 藥籤. *See* medicine
Yau Chi On 游子安 537*n*23, 621
Ye Shaoyuan 葉紹袁 (1589–1648) 144, 145–46, 147, 148, 196*n*73
Ye Xiaoluan 葉小鸞 (1617–1632) 145–47, 196, 196*n*73
Ye Xiaowan 葉小紈 (no dates) 145
Yellow Emperor 黃帝 369
Yiguandao 一貫道 (Way of Pervading Unity) 13, 17*n*57, 22, 27, 366, 384, 394–95, 444–77, 524, 538*n*26, 552, 555, 600, 603, 606. *See also* redemptive societies
Yiguan-daozang 一貫道藏 (Canon of the Yiguandao) 450
Yijian zhi 夷堅志 (Records of the listener) 59, 94
Yijing 易經 (Book of changes) 266, 303, 365*n*49, 369, 462
Yili 伊犁 308
Yinguang 印光 (1862–1940) 20, 242, 243, 244, 407, 453, 454, 602
yinsi 淫祀 (lascivious cults) 344
Yisheng baode zhuan 翊聖保德傳 (Hagiography of [the Transcendent Lord] Who Assists the Saint and Protects Virtue) 47, 55, 68, 76, 77

Yiyuan 異苑 (A garden of marvels) 136, 136*n*7, 138, 176
you siluan 右司鸞 (Chief Spirit-writing Medium) 312, 323
You Tong 尤侗 (1618–1704) 144, 145, 147, 148, 197, 261*n*18, 263, 264
Young Women's Christian Association 407, 412, 412*n*38, 413, 414, 419, 428, 432
Yu the Great 大禹 368
Yuanshi tianzun shuo Zitong benyuan jing 元始天尊說梓潼本願經 (Scripture on the original vow of Zitong as expounded by the Heavenly Worthy of Original Commencement) 105, 111
Yuanshi tianzun shuo Zitong Dijun yingyan jing 元始天尊說梓潼帝君應驗經 (Scripture on the responses and proofs of the Divine Lord of Zitong as expounded by the Heavenly Worthy of Original Commencement) 105
Yuanshi tianzun 元始天尊 106
Yuanying 圓瑛 (1878–1953) 336*n*51
Yuchao tang 育潮堂 (Hall for Cultivating Chao[zhou]) 548
Yue Fei 岳飛 (1103–1142) 83, 178, 514, 516, 517, 517*n*75
Yue Ke 岳珂 (1183–1243) 83, 186
Yue Wumuwang 岳武穆王 554
Yuen Yuen Institute 圓玄學院 567, 569*n*27, 574*n*40, 577
Yuewei caotang biji 閱微草堂筆記 (Brush notes from the Thatched Hut of Subtle Views) 291–310, 297*n*14
Yuhua tang 育化堂 610–15, 623
Yuhuang 玉皇 65, 173. *See also* Jade Emperor
Yuhuang gongzhu 玉皇宮主 (Jade Princess) 161, 503, 507, 518, 520, 521, 514–22, 524–25
Yuhuang jing 玉皇經 (Scripture of the Jade Emperor) 65, 75, 109, 498*n*30
Yuhuang shangdi yingyan jiujie zhenjing 玉皇上帝應驗救劫真經 (True scripture of the responses and proofs of the Jade Emperor saving humanity from the apocalypse) 495, 499, 503, 518
Yuhuang Wangmu jiujie zhenjing 玉皇王母救劫真經 (True scriptures of the

INDEX

Jade Emperor and Queen Mother to save humanity from the apocalypse) 496, 499
Yuju xinchan 268–70
Yuju xinchan 玉局心懺 (Jade bureau heart penance liturgy) 258, 267, 272–74, 282
yulu 語錄 (recorded sayings) 47, 68, 261n20
Yunnan 雲南 11, 16, 104, 157, 246, 291, 365n50, 376n100, 376n103, 490, 491–93, 497, 497n28, 503
Yushan Lüzu Temple 于山呂祖廟 328
Yushan tang 與善堂 566
Yutang dafa 玉堂大法 (Great Rites of the Jade Hall) 73

Zailijiao 在理教 (Teaching of the Abiding Principle) 403, 453, 603. *See also* redemptive societies
zhaitang 齋堂. *See* vegetarianism
Zhang Binglin 章炳麟 (1869–1936) 355, 369n71, 389, 389n153
Zhang Duanyi 張端義 (fl. late twelfth to mid-thirteenth centuries) 100–1
Zhang Ezi 張惡子. *See* Wenchang 文昌
Zhang Fei 張飛 553
Zhang Guo 張果 124
Zhang Mingdao 張明道 (no dates) 64, 97, 98
Zhang Sanfeng quanji 張三丰全集 (Complete collection of Zhang Sanfeng) 4, 154
Zhang Shouyi 張壽懿 (1898–1966) 423
Zhang Tianran 463–64
Zhang Tianran 張天然 (1889–1947) 445, 447, 449, 450–51, 469, 472
Zhang Yuchu 張宇初 (1361–1410) 81, 82
Zhang Zuolin 張作霖 (1875–1928) 423, 426
Zhao'an 詔安 612
zhaoxian 召仙 (inviting immortals) 8, 51, 123
Zhen'gao 真誥 (Declarations of the perfected) 2n3, 174n16, 207
Zhengyi 正一 School 270, 569n25, 583n60, 584, 585. *See also* Daoism
zhenren 真人 (Perfected) 2n3, 57, 59, 99, 105, 155, 272, 315, 332, 341, 368n64, 557
Zhenwu 真武 10, 19, 54–55, 62–65, 69–71, 74, 76–78, 80, 82, 84–86, 98–101, 100n37, 103–4, 139, 141, 261n20, 447

Zhibao lineage 至寶派 568
Zhibao tai 至寶台 567
zhiguai 志怪 (accounts of the strange) 172, 293, 313
Zhinan gong 指南宮 601, 607, 614
Zhishen lu 質神錄 (Record of soliciting confirmation from the spirits) 268, 282
Zhong Shiming 鍾世銘 (1879–1965) 360, 364, 364n41, 365, 389–90
Zhongguo jisheng hui 中國濟生會 (China Life Saving Society) 357, 602. *See also* redemptive societies
Zhongguo liangxin congshan hui 中國良心崇善會 621
Zhonghuang dadi 中皇大帝 (Emperor of Central Eminence) 511, 512n66
Zhongyong 中庸 (Doctrine of the mean) 258, 275–76, 358, 365–66, 365n50, 367, 370–74, 370n75, 376, 377, 378, 380, 382n128, 383–84
Zhongyong zhengshi 中庸證釋 (*The Doctrine of the Mean*, verified and explicated) 365, 368, 370, 373–74, 384, 394
Zhou Dunyi 周敦頤 (1017–1073) 25, 197, 259, 261n20, 262, 270, 271, 284, 320, 367
Zhou Mi 周密 (1232–1298) 60, 96
Zhou Qifeng 周岐鳳 (no dates) 114
Zhou Xingnan 周醒南 (1885–1963) 322, 323
zhou 咒. *See* incantations
Zhouyi 周易 (Zhou changes) 335. *See also* *Yijing* 易經
Zhu Cunyuan 朱存元 (1878–1918) 548
Zhu Gui 朱珪 (1731–1807) 302, 304
Zhu Guoyuan 朱果緣 (1832–after 1912) 548
Zhu Xi 朱熹 (1130–1200) 257–58, 265, 266–67, 271, 272, 275n65, 276, 277, 280, 280n86, 284, 367–70, 368n62, 370n75, 372, 374, 376, 378, 380–81, 386, 386n140, 389n153, 394
Zhuangzi 莊子 272, 371n79
zibeishi 字輩詩 (generation poems) 326, 333n45
Zigu 紫姑 (Purple Maiden) 2, 8, 16–17, 40, 51, 53–54, 72, 93–95, 123–24, 124n142, 134–41, 140n20, 145, 153, 160, 173–74, 336, 405, 405n15, 518n77
Zitong dijun huashu 梓潼帝君化書 (Book

of transformations of the Imperial Lord of Zitong)   58, 65, 85, 107–8, 108*n*72, 111

Zitong 梓潼   10, 58, 64–65, 77, 85, 99, 105–12, 108*n*73, 140, 505*n*49, 511. *See also* Wenchang 文昌

Zixia dujie zhimi jiubu zhenjing 紫霞度劫指迷九部真經 (True scripture in nine chapters for crossing over the turning of the kalpa and pointing out the way in the Purple Cloud Palace)   325, 327–28

Zixia neixiang leiyin puhua zhenren 紫霞內相雷音溥化真人 (Thunder Master and Prime Minister in the Purple Cloud Palace)   315

Zixia neixiang 紫霞內相 (Prime Minister in the Purple Cloud Palace)   325, 339

Zixu altar 紫虛壇   64, 69, 97–99

Zunde tang ban Daojiao congdian 尊德堂板道教叢典 (The Hall of Respectable Virtue's wood block printed collection of Daoist scriptures)   492, 498

Printed in the United States
by Baker & Taylor Publisher Services